EUROPEAN THEORIES
OF THE DRAMA

European Theories of The Drama

WITH A SUPPLEMENT ON THE

AMERICAN DRAMA

AN ANTHOLOGY OF DRAMATIC THEORY
AND CRITICISM FROM ARISTOTLE TO THE
PRESENT DAY, IN A SERIES OF SELECTED
TEXTS, WITH COMMENTARIES, BIOGRA-
PHIES, AND BIBLIOGRAPHIES

BY

Barrett H. Clark

CROWN PUBLISHERS   NEW YORK

TO
MY WIFE
A COLLABORATOR WHO INSPIRED
AND MADE POSSIBLE
THIS WORK

INTRODUCTION

European Theories of the Drama in its present form is a new book: the addition of a substantial body of new material from the United States not included in the earlier editions justifies that statement. It is also an old book, including the entire text as it appeared in the latest revised edition of 1929.

In its earliest form *European Theories of the Drama* was publishd in 1918; it was revised to a greater or less extent three times during the following few years. In the Introduction to the 1929 edition I wrote that the "early years of the 20th Century are still too close to us, and any attempt to select the most important theories promulgated since 1900 would prove unwise because we cannot yet determine exactly how important any new theory is going to be." I added that even though I had included certain theories written since 1900, the authors of them were "products of the 19th Century."

I had hoped that by 1947 it would be possible to bring the entire book up to date by printing a representative, if not a fairly complete collection of dramatic theories from among the many pronouncements that have reflected or influenced the work of playwrights in Europe since 1900, particularly in Russia, France, England, Italy, Spain and Germany. It is possible that if war had not intervened I might have been able to carry out such a plan; I even attempted it, but after two years I gave up. I consulted scholars and other specialists in this country; I corresponded with playwrights and critics, directors and managers abroad, but I found that even a preliminary investigation of texts covering many important dramatic movements in certain countries could not be undertaken. It would, of course, be possible to bring this section or that up to date, but I felt that such a course would be unsatisfactory and offer only a distorted picture without balance or truth, and I therefore decided to leave the European part of the book as it was.

However, it seemed to me that the phenomenal growth of a native drama in the United States since 1900, and particularly since 1920, should somehow be allowed to reflect itself in a book, or shall we say, be added to a book which in 1918 could be accurately described only as *European Theories of the Drama*. And so this new volume, still designated by the same title, carries a supplement. The work could more accurately be described as *European and American* (or shall we say *United States?*) *Theories of the Drama,* but I am allowing the old title to stand, because in its original form with its first title the book seems to have fixed itself firmly in the minds of those who have already used it.

It will be noticed that I have not followed the somewhat elaborate scheme of bibliographical and editorial classification adopted in the older part of the volume. To do this would give an air of finality to my selections which I have not intended. The amount of dramatic theorizing which has found its way into print in the United

States is staggering. Aside from the periodical writing of critics in the newspapers and magazines, and counting only prefaces, books, and essays in books, I have read over twenty-five hundred items in order to choose the twelve pieces that go into my Supplement, and I print these with the reservation that they are still more or less tentative exhibits chosen from among many others, some of which are of equal importance.

In my original Introduction to *European Theories of the Drama* I wrote that it was "an attempt to set before the reader the development of the theory of dramatic technique in Europe from Aristotle to the present time. It has been my purpose to select such texts and parts of texts as have been influential in shaping the form of plays." I now add that the aims and implications of the book are somewhat wider, and that the texts included in it are likewise a reflection of the ideas and ideals on playwriting which their authors often attempt to set before the drama's practitioners.

I had imagined, when the book first appeared, that it would prove useful only, or chiefly, to students curious about the hows and whys of playwriting. I did not think it could be of much practical use to playwrights. But I have been surprised to learn from several writers who were "required" to read the book in college that it somehow furnished hints that helped them, and in one case a well-known and successful playwright told me that the book had actually made him decide to become a playwright. The late Thomas Wolfe told me ruefully that he too had been made to use the book as a college text, and if he had not turned to novel writing he might have tried more seriously to become the playwright I think he could have been. I have similar evidence from several other playwrights, but I will name no names, and I leave the drawing of conclusions to others. If *European Theories of the Drama* proves useful in any way to any playwright, I shall be happy. That is more than I ever hoped for.

Before listing my formal acknowledgments of help and encouragement, I should like to thank the many college and university instructors and special non-academic lecturers who have used the book as a text; not so much for using it as for telling me how they have used it and how it has proved helpful to them and their students; I cannot mention here the names of all who have urged me to revise the book or (during the difficult war years) simply to keep it in print. But I must mention in particular John Mason Brown and Arthur Edwin Krows, both of whom are now embodied in my new text as integral parts of the work. Playwrights who have made similar requests are nearly as numerous.

Many who helped me nearly thirty years ago are now dead; my gratitude to them is deep and abiding. Among them are the late Sir Arthur Pinero, Henry Arthur Jones, J. E. Spingarn, Brander Matthews, George Pierce Baker, Montrose J. Moses, and Clayton Hamilton. Aside from the standard histories of literature and cyclopedias, the books to which I am most indebted are George Saintsbury's *History of Criticism* and J. E. Spingarn's *A History of Literary Criticism in the Renaissance.*

Special thanks are due to several persons in advising me on points affecting the selection and preparation of the texts in the Supplement. The following have given help and advice, both by letter and in person: Arthur Edwin Krows, Ludwig

Lewisohn, George Jean Nathan, Joseph Wood Krutch, Eugene O'Neill, John Howard Lawson, Maxwell Anderson, John Mason Brown, and John Gassner. This book was originally dedicated to my wife, Cecile S. Clark. It is now re-dedicated to her, twenty-nine years later. And with reason. I am under the greatest obligation to her for doing a vast amount of stale, if not unprofitable reading; for transcribing texts, collating MS, and for the immense labor of preparing a large part of the index.

The text.—In almost every case I have been able to get the best published translation of standard and classic works originally written in a foreign language, but when this was out of the question, I have had to use the next best, and I have not scrupled to modify these after referring to the original and, in a few exceptional cases, to make use—with proper permission—of a phrase or note from the unobtainable standard translation. For convenience' sake I have modernized the spelling throughout, and to a certain extent standardized such matters as punctuation, paragraphing and capitalization.

BARRETT H. CLARK
1947.

CONTENTS

CONTENTS xiii

CONTENTS

SUPPLEMENT ON THE UNITED STATES

xvi

CONTENTS

ANCIENT GREECE

EUROPEAN THEORIES OF THE DRAMA

GREEK DRAMATIC CRITICISM

With the exception of the more or less fragmentary *Poetics* of Aristotle there is very little in Greek literature touching upon the subject of dramatic theory. What we possess are (1) quotations from Greek writers like Theophrastus (in the *Ars Grammatica* of Diomedes), and from Greek dramatists (in *The Deipnosophists* of Athenæus); (2) passages from Aristophanes; and (3) works or fragments of a more general character, of such writers as Plato and Dionysius of Halicarnassus; and (4) the Scholia, or commentaries on the dramatists.

Of dramatic criticism proper there is nothing either in Plato or Aristophanes; Plato's *Republic, Phædrus, Ion, Laws,* and other dialogues contain a good deal on the subject of poetry, and much on dramatic poetry, but, as might be expected, the philosopher is concerned rather with the moral and philosophic than the purely literary and dramatic aspects. Aristophanes' *Frogs* in particular is full of dramatic criticism of an indirect kind, but it is neither so objective nor so organized as to entitle it to serious consideration as a distinct theory of the drama. It is only by inference that the student may form any definite idea of Aristophanes' esthetic ideals. In M. Egger's indispensable *Histoire de la Critique chez les Grecs* there is quoted a passage attributed to Antiphanes on tragedy and comedy. Another short passage, attributed to Simylus, practically completes the list.

It was not likely that any considerable body of dramatic theory should be formulated before the close of the great dramatic epoch ushered in by Æschylus, so that the absence of any such work as the *Poetics* during that period is not surprising. Aristotle had before him the masterpieces of his country and was able to set forth a complete body of doctrine. While it has been pointed out that he was at a decided disadvantage in not knowing the literature of at least one other nation besides his own, it is doubly fortunate that so well-balanced a philosopher should have happened at the right time to sum up the dramatic theory of the age which immediately preceded him.

Of the rhetoricians and grammarians who followed Aristotle, of the great mass of Scholia on the tragedians and Aristophanes, there is very little to be said. Most of the commentators were concerned almost altogether with questions of philology, grammar, and the more formal aspects of the drama. Much later, Plutarch—in his *Comparison of Aristophanes and Menander* and elsewhere—turns to the drama, but his remarks are applicable mainly to the moral and stylistic side. Athenæus (in the third century A. D.) did no more than collect passages from earlier writers, some few of which are concerned with the drama.

General works on Greek literature, criticism and critics:

Paul Masqueray, *Bibliographie pratique de la Litterature grecque, des origines à la fin de la période romaine* (Paris, 1914).

W. Christ, *Geschichte der griechischen Literatur* (in Müller's *Handbuch der klassischen Altertumswissenschaft*. Bd. VII, München, 1890).

Emile Egger, *Essai sur l'histoire de la Critique chez les Grecs* (Paris, 3rd ed., 1887).

Gilbert Murray, *A History of Ancient Greek Literature* (New York, new ed., 1900).

L. D. Barnett, *Greek Drama*, (London, 1900).

Lewis Campbell, *A Guide to Greek Tragedy*, etc. (London, 1891).

A. et M. Croiset, *Histoire de la Littéra-*

ture grecque. (Abridged ed., Paris, 1900. Translated as *An Abridged History of Greek Literature,* by George F. Heffelbower, (New York, 1904).

A. E. Haigh, *The Attic Theater* (Oxford, 1898). *The Tragic Drama of the Greeks* (Oxford, 1896).

C.-A.-N. Maignien, *Du Théâtre tragique des Grecs,* etc. (Lyon, 1839).

R. G. Moulton, *The Ancient Classical Drama* (Oxford, 1898).

Patin, *Etudes sur les tragiques grecs,* 4 vols. (Paris, 1841).

L. M. Watt, *Attic and Elizabethan Tragedy* (London, 1908).

H. Weil, *Etudes sur le drame antique* (Paris, 1897).

F. C. Welcker, *Die grieschischen Tragödien,* 3 vols. (Bonn, 1839.)

Artaud, *Fragments pour servir à l'histoire de la comédie attique* (Paris, 1863).

William Wilson Baker, *De Comicis græcis litterarum judicibus* (*Harvard Studies in Class. Phil.,* vol. 15, pp. 121–240. Cambridge, 1904).

Faustin Colin, *Clef de l'Histoire de la Comédie grecque* (Paris, 1856).

F. M. Cornford, *The Origin of Attic Comedy* (London, 1914).

Demetrius Detscheff, *De Tragœdiarum Græcarum conformatione scænica ac dramatica* (Göttingen, 1904).

M.-G. Guizot, *Ménandre; étude historique et littéraire sur la comédie et la société grecque* (Paris, 1855).

José Hillebrand, *Esthetica Litteraria Antiqua Classica,* etc. (Maguntiae, 1828).

A. Théry, *Histoire des opinions littéraires* (2nd ed., Paris, 1849).

Ernst Howald, *Die Anfänge der literarischen Kritik bei den Grieschen* (Kirchhain, 1910).

Abbé Jacquet, *Parallèle des tragiques grecs et françois* (Lille et Lyon, 1760).

Ph. E. Legrand, *Pour l'Histoire de la Comédie nouvelle* (*Rev. des Etudes grecques,* vol. XV, Paris, 1902).

E. du Méril, *Histoire de la Comédie ancienne,* 2 vols. (Paris, 1864–69).

E. Müller, *Geschichte der Theorie der Kunst bei den Alten,* 2 vols. (Breslau, 1834–37).

J.-J. Rousseau, *De l'Imitation théâtrale, essai tiré des Dialogues de Platon* (Amsterdam, 1764).

George Saintsbury, *A History of Criticism,* vol. 1 (2nd ed., New York, 1902).

Ad. Trendelemburg, *Grammaticorum Græcorum de arte tragica judiciorum reliquiæ* (Bonn, 1867).

Leslie Morton Turner, *Du Conflit tragique chez les Grecs et dans Shakespeare* (Paris, 1913).

ARISTOTLE

Aristotle was born at Stagira in the year 384 B. C. The most trustworthy biographical account of his life is by Dionysius of Halicarnassus, in his *Epistle on Demosthenes and Aristotle*: "Aristotle was the son of Nichomachus, who traced back his descent and his art to Machaon, son of Esculapius; his mother being Phæstis, a descendant of one of those who carried the colony from Chalcis to Stagira. He was born in the 99th Olympiad in the archonship at Athens of Diotrephes (384–383), three years before Demosthenes. In the archonship of Polyzelus (367–366), after the death of his father, in his eighteenth year, he came to Athens, and having joined Plato, spent twenty years with him. On the death of Plato (May 347), in the archonship of Theophilus (348–347) he departed to Hermias, tyrant of Atarneus and, after three years' stay, during the archonship of Eubulus (345–344) he moved to Mitylene, whence he went to Philip of Macedon in the archonship of Pythodotus (343–342), and spent eight years with him as tutor of Alexander. After the death of Philip (336), in the archonship of Euænetus (335–334), he returned to Athens and kept a school in the Lyceum for twelve years. In the thirteenth, after the death of Alexander (June 323), in the archonship of Cephisodorus (323–322 having departed to Chalcis, he died of disease (322), after a life of three-and-sixty years."

The Poetics (or, *The Poetic,* according to the translation of the present version) of Aristotle is the earliest critical treatise extant dealing with dramatic practice and theory. Besides being a summing-up of the first great age of dramatic activity, it has exercised incalculable influence over the dramatists of all European and many other nations. There are few if any important contributions to dramatic theory and criticism which fail to take account of the work, but owing to its obviously incomplete form, the many corrupt portions of the text, its compact and elliptical style, it has been constantly misinterpreted, misquoted, and misunderstood. The famous Unities, the terms "Imitation" and "Purgation," have in particular proved troublesome to the Italian critics of the Renaissance and to their followers in France. Of late years, however, a number of valuable annotated editions, with copious notes and explanatory matter, have gone far to clear up the misunderstanding. Among the recent English editions, the most significant is S. H. Butcher's *Aristotle's Theory of Poetry and Fine Art,* containing the original text, a translation, and a commentary.

While Aristotle based his treatise upon the Greek poets with whose work he was acquainted, his general premises and his conclusions are in the main applicable to drama in general. Although there was an abridged version of the *Poetics* extant in the late Middle Ages, it cannot properly be maintained to have made its appearance until 1498, when Giorgio Valla published at Venice a Latin translation of it. This was followed by the Greek text, in the Aldine *Rhetores Græci* (1508).

From that time forward, the text was translated into the vernacular, commented upon, and criticized; its influence was soon to become of the greatest importance, not only in Italy, but in France, Germany, and England.

Editions:

Among the many hundred editions of Aristotle, it is necessary to mention only a few. Practically all the emendations, commentary, and theory of earlier editions are to be found in I. Bywater's *Aristotle on the Art of Poetry,* (text, translation, and notes, Oxford, 1909), and in S. H. Butcher's *Aristotle's Theory of Poetry and Fine Art* (with text of the *Poetics,* translation, bibliography, and commentary, 4th edition, revised, London, 1911). Briefer editions — translation and notes only — are *Aristotle's Treatise on Rhetoric and Poetic,* translated, with analysis and examination questions, by Theodore Buckley (Bohn ed., London, 1914); A. O. Prickard, *Aristotle on the Art of Poetry* (London, 1891); and Lane Cooper, *Aristotle on the Art of Poetry* (Boston, 1913).

On Aristotle and his works:

Notes, etc. in above editions.

André Dacier, *La Poétique traduite en François, avec des remarques critiques* (Paris, 1692).

Charles Batteux, *Les Quatre Poétiques d'Aristote, d'Horace, de Vida, de Despréaux, avec les traductions et des remarques* (Paris, 1771).

George Saintsbury, *A History of Criticism,* vol. 1 (New York, 1900).

J. E. Spingarn, *A History of Literary Criticism in the Renaissance* (2nd ed., New York, 1908).

Moise Schwab, *Bibliographie d'Aristote* (Paris, 1896).

THE POETIC [1]

[360–322 B. C.]

CHAP. I

Let us speak concerning poetry itself, and its [different] species; what power each possesses, and how fables must be

composed, in order that poetry may be such as is fitting: further still, [let us show] of how many and what kind of

[1] The present translation, by Theodore Buckley, is reprinted from the Bohn edition (London and New York, late ed., 1914). The foot-notes, unless otherwise designated and signed "Ed." are from that edition. Those parts of the text enclosed in brackets (by the

parts it consists; and in like manner [let us treat] concerning such other things as pertain to this method, beginning, conformably to nature, first from such things as are first.

The epic, therefore, and tragic poetry, and moreover comedy, and dithyrambic poetry, and the greatest part of the art pertaining to the flute and the lyre,[2] are all entirely imitations. They differ, however, in three things; for [they differ] either by imitating through means different in kind, or by imitating different objects, or in a different, and not after the same manner. For as certain persons assimilating, imitate many things by colors and figures, some indeed through art, but others through custom, [and others through voice]; thus also in the aforementioned arts, all of them indeed produce imitation in rhythm, words, and harmony; and in these, either distinctly, or mingled together, as, for instance, the arts of the flute and the lyre alone employ harmony and rhythm; and this will also be the case with any other arts which possess a power of this kind, such as the art of playing on reed-pipes. But the arts pertaining to dancing imitate by rhythm, without harmony; for dancers, through figured rhythms, imitate manners, and passions, and actions. But the epic alone imitates by mere words[3] or meters, and by these either mingling them with each other, or employing one certain kind of meters, which method has been adopted up to the present time. For otherwise we should have no common name by which we could denominate the Mimes of Sophron and Xenarchus, and the dialogues of Socrates; or those who imitate by trimeters, or elegies, or certain other things of this kind; except that men joining with meter the verb *to make*,[4] call some of these *makers of elegies*, but others epic *makers*, not as poets according to imitation, but denominating them in common according to measure. For they are accustomed thus to denominate them, if they write anything medical or musical in verse. There is, however, nothing common to Homer and Empedocles except the measure; on which account, it is right indeed to call the former a poet; but the latter a physiologist rather than a poet. In like manner, though some one mingling all the measures, should produce imitation, as Chæremon has done in his *Centaur*, a mixed rhapsody of all the meters, yet he must not be called a poet. Let it then be thus laid down concerning these particulars. But there are some kinds of poetry which employ all the before-mentioned means, I mean, rhythm, melody and measure, such as dithyrambic poetry and the Nomes,[5] and also tragedy and comedy. But these differ, because some of them use all these at once, but others partially. I speak, therefore, of these differences of the arts in respect to the means by which they produce imitation.

CHAP. II

ON IMITATION AND ITS USUAL OBJECTS

But since imitators imitate those who do something, and it is necessary that these should either be worthy or depraved persons (for manners nearly al-

---

editor of the Bohn edition) are considered either by him or by some other editor either as of doubtful authenticity or else are merely aids to render the sense clearer. Sections XX, XXI, and XXII are omitted. They deal with diction, language, grammar, and the like. Section XX is, according to Butcher "probably interpolated"; also a passage in section XXI. Section XXII is for the most part authentic, but is concerned with minor points of language. Section XXV is also omitted, as it deals mainly with objections, or "Problems."— Ed.

2 Cithern-playing was one of the favorite accomplishments of the Athenian youth.

3 There is much difficulty about this definition of ἐποποιία, as λόγοις ψιλοῖς is supposed by some to mean *prose* (see Robortello, p. 14), by others, *verse without music*. The sense is, therefore, "by prose or by meter, but unaccompanied by song."

4 It may be necessary to observe, that the Greek word (ποιητης — *poiétes*) whence *poeta*, and *poet*, is, literally, *maker*; and maker, it is well known, was once the current term for *poet* in our language; and to write verses, was, to *make*. Sir Philip Sidney, speaking of the Greek word, says, "wherein, I know not whether by luck or wisdom, we Englishmen have *met* with the Greeks, in calling him *maker*." *Defense of Poesy.*— Twining.

5 In dithyrambic or *Bacchic* hymns, and in the *Nomes*, which were also a species of hymns to Apollo and other deities, *all* the means of imitation were employed *together*, and *throughout*: in tragedy and comedy, *separately*; some of them in one part of the drama, and some in another. In the *choral* part, however, at least, if nowhere else, *all*, melody, rhythm, and words, must probably have been used *at once*, as in the hymns.— Twining.

ways depend on these alone, since all men differ in their manners by vice and virtue); it is necessary either [to imitate] those who are better than we are, or those who are worse, or such as are like ourselves,[6] in the same manner as painters do. For Polygnotus, indeed, painted men more beautiful than they are, but Pauson less so, and Dionysius painted them as they are.[7] But it is evident that each of the before-mentioned imitations will have these differences; and imitation is different, by imitating different things after this manner. For there may be differences of this kind in dancing, in playing on the flute, on the lyre, and also in orations and mere measure. Thus Homer imitates better men [8] [than exist], but Cleophon men as they are; and Hegemon the Thasian, who first made parodies, and Nicochares, who wrote the *Deliad,* imitate worse characters. In like manner in dithyrambics and the Nomi, [as Timotheus and Philoxenus have imitated the Persians and the Cyclops,] one may imitate. By this very same difference, also, tragedy differs from comedy. For the one seeks to imitate worse, but the other better men than are.

CHAP. III

THE THIRD DIFFERENCE OF POETRY ACCORDING TO THE MANNER OF IMITATING

There is also a third difference of these, consisting in the manner in which one may imitate each of them. For by the same instruments the same things may be imitated, the poet sometimes himself narrating, and sometimes assuming another person [as Homer does [9]]; or speaking as the same person without any change; or as all imitate [who do so] by deed and action. But imitation con-

sists in these three differences, as we said in the beginning; viz. in the means, the objects, or the manner. Hence, Sophocles will in one respect be the same imitator as Homer, for both of them imitate elevated characters; and in another the same as Aristophanes, for both of them imitate persons engaged in acting; [10 whence also it is said that certain persons call their works *dramas,* because they imitate those who are engaged in *doing* something. On this account the Dorians lay claim to the invention of tragedy and comedy; of comedy indeed the Megarians, as well those who are natives of Greece, as being invented by them at the time when their government was a democracy, as those of Sicily. For thence was the poet Epicharmus, who was much prior to Chonides and Magnes. But some of those Dorians who inhabit Peloponnesus lay claim to tragedy, making names an evidence. For they allege that they call their villages *komai,* but the Athenians *demoi;* as if comedians were not so denominated from *komazein,* [i. e. *to revel*] but from their wandering through villages, being ignominiously expelled from the cities. The verb *poiein* also, or *to make,* is by the Dorians denominated *dran,* but by the Athenians *prattein.*] And thus much concerning the differences of imitation, as to their number and quality.

CHAP. IV

THE CAUSES AND PROGRESS OF POETRY

Two causes, however, and these physical, appear to have produced poetry in general. For to imitate is congenial to men from childhood. And in this they differ from other animals, that they are most imitative, and acquire the first disciplines through imitation; and that all men delight in imitations. But an evidence of this is that which happens in the works [of artists]. For we are delighted on surveying very accurate images, the realities of which are painful to the view; such as the forms of the most contemptible animals, and dead bodies. The cause, however, of this is that learning is not only most delightful

---

6 Or, " those who are commonly found."

7 Polygnotus and Dionysius lived about Ol. 80; Pauson about Ol. 90.

8 Superior, that is, in courage, strength, wisdom, prudence, etc.— in *any* laudable, useful, or admirable quality, whether such as we denominate *moral,* or not. If superiority of *moral* character only were meant, the assertion would be false.— It is necessary to remember here, the *wide* sense in which the ancients used the terms *virtue, vice — good, bad,* etc.— Twining.

9 But this assertion is not correct, and Ritter shows that the words are spurious.

10 The learned note of Ritter seems to condemn the whole of this passage as spurious.

to philosophers, but in like manner to other persons, though they partake of it but in a small degree. For on this account, men are delighted on surveying images, because it happens that by surveying they learn and infer what each particular is; as, that *this* is an image of *that man;* since, unless one happen to have seen [the reality], it is not the imitation that pleases, but [it is through] either the workmanship, or the color, or some other cause of the like kind. But imitation, harmony, and rhythm being natural to us, (for it is evident that measures or meters are parts of rhythms [11]), the earliest among mankind, making a gradual progress in these things from the beginning, produced poetry from extemporaneous efforts. But poetry was divided according to appropriate manners. For men of a more venerable character imitated beautiful actions, and the actions of such men; but the more ignoble imitated the actions of depraved characters, first composing vituperative verses, in the same manner as the others composed hymns and encomiums. Of the authors, therefore, before Homer, we cannot mention any poem of this kind; though it is probable that there were many such writers. But if we begin from Homer, there are such for instance as his *Margites,* and some others, in which, as being suited, the measure is Iambic. Hence, also, the Iambic verse is now called, because in this meter they used to *Iambize* (i. e. defame) each other. Of ancient poets, likewise, some composed heroic poems, and others Iambic. But as Homer was the greatest of poets on serious subjects, (and this not only because he alone imitated well, but also because he made dramatic imitations), thus too he first demonstrated the figures of comedy, not

dramatically exhibiting invective, but ridicule. For the *Margites* bears the same analogy to comedy, as the *Iliad* and *Odyssey* to tragedy. But when tragedy and comedy had appeared, those poets who were naturally impelled to each kind of poetry, some, instead of writing Iambics, became comic poets, but others, instead of [writing] epic poems, became the authors of tragedies, because these forms [of poetry] are greater and more esteemed than those. To consider, therefore, whether tragedy is now perfect in its species or not, regarded as well with reference to itself as to the theaters, is the business of another treatise. Both tragedy and comedy, therefore, at first originated from extemporaneous efforts. And tragedy, indeed, originated from those who led the dithyramb, but comedy from those who sung the Phallic verses, which even now in many cities remain in use; and it gradually increased as obvious improvements became known. And tragedy, having experienced many changes, rested when it had arrived at its proper nature. Æschylus, also, first increased the number of players from one to two, abridged the functions of the chorus, and made one of the players act the chief part. But Sophocles introduced three players into the scene, and added scenic painting. Further still, the magnitude [of tragedy increased] from small fables and ridiculous diction, in consequence of having been changed from satyric [12] composition, it was late before it acquired dignity. The meter also of tragedy, from tetrameter, became Iambic (for at first they used tetrameter in tragedy, because poetry was then satyrical, and more adapted to the dance, but dialogue being adopted, nature herself discovered a suitable meter; for the Iambic measure is most of all adapted to conversation. And as an evidence of this, we most frequently speak in Iambics in familiar discourse with each

11 " RHYTHM differs from METER, inasmuch as RHYTHM is *proportion, applied to any motion whatever;* METER *is proportion, applied to the motion of* WORDS SPOKEN. Thus, in the drumming of a march, or the dancing of a hornpipe, there is *rhythm,* though *no meter;* in Dryden's celebrated *Ode* there is METER as well as RHYTHM, because the poet with the *rhythm* has associated certain *words.* And hence it follows, that, though ALL RHYTHM IS RHYTHM, yet ALL RHYTHM IS NOT METER." Harris's *Philol. Inquiries.* p. 67,— where it is also observed, very truly, that " no English word expresses *rhythmus* better than the word *time.*" P. 69, note.— Twining.

12 *Satyric,* from the share which those fantastic beings called *Satyrs,* the companions and *play-fellows* of *Bacchus,* had in the earliest Tragedy, of which they formed the chorus. *Joking* and *dancing* were essential attributes of these rustic semi-deities. Hence the " *ludicrous language* " and the " *dancing genius* " of the old Tragedy, to which the TROCHAIC or *running* meter here spoken of was peculiarly adapted.— Twining.

other; but we seldom speak in hexameters, and then only when we depart from that harmony which is adapted to conversation). Again, tragedy is said to have been further adorned, with a multitude of episodes, and other particulars. Let, therefore, thus much said suffice concerning these things; for it would perhaps be a great toil to discuss every particular.

CHAP. V

ON COMEDY AND ITS ORIGIN — DIFFERENCE OF EPIC AND TRAGEDY

But comedy is, as we have said, an imitation indeed of bad characters, yet it does not imitate them according to every vice, [but the ridiculous only]; since the ridiculous is a portion of turpitude. For *the ridiculous is a certain error, and turpitude unattended with pain, and not destructive.* Thus, for instance, a ridiculous face is something deformed and distorted without pain. The transitions, therefore, of tragedy, and the causes through which they are produced, are not unknown; but [those of] comedy have escaped our knowledge, because it was not at first an object of attention. For it was late before the magistrate gave a chorus to comedians [13]; but prior to that period, the choruses were voluntary. Comedy, however, at length having obtained a certain form, those who are said to have been poets therein are commemorated. But it is unknown who it was that introduced masks or prologues, or a multitude of players, and such like particulars. But Epicharmus and Phormis [were the first] to compose fables; which, therefore, originated from Sicily. But among the Athenians, Crates, rejecting the Iambic form, first began generally to compose speeches and fables. The epic, therefore, is an attendant on tragedy, [with the exception of the long meter,] since through this it is an imitation of worthy characters and actions. But it differs from tragedy in that it has a simple meter, and is a narration. It also [differs from it] in length. For tragedy is especially limited by one period of the sun, or admits but a small variation

from this period; but the epic is not defined within a certain time, and in this it differs; though at first they observed the same conduct with tragedy, no less than epic poetry. With respect to the parts, however, [of the epic and tragedy,] some are the same in both, but others are peculiar to tragedy. Hence he who knows what is a good or bad tragedy, knows the same in respect to epic poetry. For those things which the epic possesses are to be found in tragedy; but everything which tragedy contains is not in the epic.

CHAP. VI

ON THE FORM AND END OF TRAGEDY, AND ON ITS SIX PARTS, ESPECIALLY THE PLOT

Concerning, therefore, imitative poetry in hexameters, and comedy, we shall speak hereafter. Let us now, however, speak concerning tragedy, assuming the definition of its essence as arising from what has been already said.[14] *Tragedy, therefore, is an imitation of a worthy or illustrious and perfect action, possessing magnitude, in pleasing language, using separately the several species of imitation in its parts, by men acting, and not through narration, through pity and fear effecting a purification from such like passions.* But by *pleasing language,* I mean language possessing rhythm, harmony, and melody. And it *uses separately the several species [of imitation],* because some parts of the tragedy are alone perfected through meters, and others again through melody. But since they produce imitation by acting, in the first place the ornament of the spectacle [15] will be a certain part of the trag-

13 This was almost equivalent to the modern "licensing" of plays, but was probably conducted with more taste and less absurdity.

14 This much discussed definition of tragedy is thus rendered by Butcher: "Tragedy, then, is an imitation of an action that is serious, complete, and of a certain magnitude; in language embellished with each kind of artistic ornament, the several kinds being found in separate parts of the play; in the form of action, not of narrative; through pity and fear effecting the proper purgation of these emotions."— Ed.

15 "*Decoration* — literally, the decoration of the *spectacle,* or *sight.* In other places it is called the *spectacle,* or *sight* only — ὄψις· It comprehends *scenery, dresses* — the whole visible apparatus of the theater. I do not know any single English word that answers fully to the Greek word."— Twining.

edy, and in the next place the *melopœia* [16] and the diction. For by these they produce imitation. But I call diction, indeed, the composition of the meters; and *melopœia* that, the whole power of which is apparent. Since, however, [tragedy] is an imitation of action, and action is effected by certain agents, who must needs be persons of a certain description both as to their manners and their sentiments, (for from these we say that actions derive their quality), hence there are naturally two causes of actions, sentiments and moral habit, and through these actions all men obtain or fail of the object of their wishes. But a fable, indeed, is an imitation of action; for I mean by a *fable* here, the composition of incidents. By *manners*, I mean those things according to which we say that agents are persons of a certain character; and by *sentiment*, that through which those who speak demonstrate any thing, or explain their meaning. It is necessary, therefore, that the parts of every tragedy should be six, from which the tragedy derives its quality. But these are, fable and manners, diction and sentiment, spectacle and *melopœia*. Of these parts, however, two pertain to the means by which they imitate; one, to the manner; and three, to the objects. And besides these, there are no other. [Not a few [tragic poets], therefore, as I may say, use all these parts.] For every tragedy has scenic apparatus, manners, and a fable, and melody, and, in a similar manner, sentiment. But the greatest of these is the combination of the incidents. For tragedy is an imitation not of men, but of actions, [of life, and of felicity. For infelicity consists in action, and the end is a certain action, and not a quality]. Men, however, are persons of a certain character, according to their manners; but according to their actions, they are happy, or the contrary. The end of tragedy, therefore, does not consist in imitating manners, but it embraces

manners on account of actions; so that the action and the fable are the end of tragedy. But the end is the greatest of all things. Moreover, without action, tragedy cannot exist; but it may exist without manners. For most modern tragedies are without manners; and in short, many poets are such as among painters Zeuxis is when compared with Polygnotus. For Polygnotus, indeed, painted the manners of the good; but the pictures of Zeuxis are without manners. Further still, if any one place in a continued series moral speeches, sayings, and sentiments well framed, he will not produce that which is the work of tragedy; but that will be much more a tragedy which uses these things as subordinate, and which contains a fable and combination of incidents. Add to this, that the greatest parts by which fable allures the soul, are the *revolutions* and *discoveries*. Again, it is likewise an evidence of this, that those who attempt to write tragedies acquire the power of expressing a thing in tragic diction and manners accurately, before they can compose a fable, as was the case with nearly all the first poets. The fable, therefore, is the principal part, and as it were the soul of tragedy; but the manners are next in rank. [Just as in painting, if any one were to spread the most beautiful pigments on promiscuously, he would not please the view so much as by outlining an image with white color only. Tragedy also is an imitation of action, and on this account, especially, [an imitation] of agents. But the sentiments rank third. And by them [I mean] *the power of explaining what is inherent in the subject, and adapted to it*, which is the peculiar province of politics [17] and rhetoric. For the ancient poets represent those whom they introduce as speaking politically; but those of the present day, rhetorically. But the manners are whatever shows what the deliberate choice is. Hence those speeches are without manners, in which there is altogether nothing that the speaker may

16 *Melopœia* — literally, the *making*, or the *composition*, of the *Music*; as we use *Epopœia*, or according to the French termination, which we have naturalized. *Epopee*, to signify epic *poetry*, or *epic-making*, in general.— I might have rendered it, at once, the MUSIC: but that it would have appeared ridiculous to observe, of a word so familiar to us, even that "*its meaning is obvious*."— Twining.

17 The reader here must not think of our modern *politics*.— The *political*, or *civil art*, or *science*, was, in Aristotle's view, of wide extent and high importance. It comprehended *ethics* and *eloquence*, or the art of public speaking; everything, in short, that concerned the well-being of a *state*.— Twining.

choose or avoid. But *sentiment is that through which they show that a certain thing is, or is not, or by which they universally enunciate something.* And the fourth part of tragedy is diction. But I say, as was before observed, that *diction is interpretation by the means of words, and which also has the same power in verse and prose.* But of the remaining five, the *melopœia* is the greatest of the embellishments. But the scenic decoration is alluring indeed; yet it is most inartificial, and is in the smallest degree akin to poetry. For the power of tragedy remains, even when unaccompanied with scenic apparatus and players. And further still, the art of the mechanic possesses more power in constructing the scenic apparatus than that of the poet.]

CHAP. VII

ON THE REQUISITES AND LENGTH OF TRAGIC ACTION

These things being defined, let us in the next place show what the combination of the incidents ought to be, since this is the first and greatest part of tragedy. But it is granted to us that tragedy is the imitation of a perfect and whole action, and of one which possesses a certain magnitude; for there may be a whole which has no magnitude. But a whole is that which has a beginning, middle, and end. And the beginning is that which necessarily is not itself posterior to another thing; but another thing is naturally expected to follow it. On the contrary, the end is that which is itself naturally adapted to be posterior to another thing, either from necessity, or for the most part; but after this there is nothing else. But the middle is that which is itself after another thing, and after which there is something else. Hence, it is necessary that those who compose fables properly, should neither begin them casually, nor end them casually, but should employ the above-mentioned forms [of beginning, middle, and end]. Further still, since that which is beautiful, whether it be an animal, or any thing else which is composed from certain parts, ought not only to have these parts arranged, but a magnitude also which is not casual. For the beau-

tiful consists in magnitude and order. Hence, neither can any very small animal be beautiful; for the survey of it is confused, since it is effected in a time nearly insensible. Nor yet a very large animal; for it is not surveyed at once, but its subsistence as one and a whole escapes the view of the spectators; such as if, for instance, it should be an animal of ten thousand stadia in length. Hence, as in bodies and in animals it is necessary there should be magnitude; but such as can easily be seen; thus also in fables, there should be length, but this such as can easily be remembered.[18] The definition, however, of the length with reference to contests [19] and the senses, does not fall under the consideration of art. For if it were requisite to perform a hundred tragedies, [as is said to have been the case more than once], the performance ought to be regulated by a clepsydra. But the definition [of the length of the fable] according to the nature of the thing, is this, that the fable is always more beautiful the greater it is, if at the same time it is perspicuous. Simply defining the thing, however, we may say, [that a fable has an appropriate magnitude], when the time of its duration is such as to render it probable that there can be a transition from prosperous to adverse, or from adverse to prosperous fortune, according to the necessary or probable order of things as they take place. This is a sufficient definition of magnitude.

CHAP. VIII

ON UNITY OF THE FABLE

The fable, however, is one, not as some suppose, if one person is the subject of it; for many things which are infinite in kind happen [to one man] from a certain number of which no one event arises. Thus, also, there are many actions of

18 The unity here spoken of, it must be remembered, is not *absolute* and *simple*, but *relative* and *compound*, unity; a unity consisting of different *parts*, the relation of which to each other and to the whole, is easily perceived at one view. On this depends the perception of beauty in *form*.— In objects too extended, you may be said to have *parts*, but no *whole*: in very minute objects the *whole*, but no *parts*.— Twining.

19 i. e. to its representation at the dramatic contests.

one man, from which no one action is produced. Hence all those poets appear to have erred who have written the *Heracleid,* and *Theseid,* and such like poems. For they suppose that because Hercules was one person, it was fit that the fable should be one. Homer, however, as he excelled in other things, appears likewise to have seen this clearly, whether from art, or from nature. For in composing the *Odyssey,* he has not related every thing which happened to Ulysses; such as the being wounded in Parnassus,[20] and pretending to be insane[21] at the muster of the Greeks; one of which taking place, it was not necessary or probable that the other should happen; but he composed the *Odyssey,* as also his *Iliad,* upon one action. It is requisite, therefore, that as in other imitative arts one imitation is the imitation of one thing, thus, also, [in tragedy], the fable, since it is an imitation of action, should be the imitation of one action, and of the whole of this, and that the parts of the transactions should be so arranged, that any one of them being transposed, or taken away, the whole would become different and changed. For that which when present or not present produces no sensible [difference], is not a part of the fable.

CHAP. IX

ON THE DIFFERENCE BETWEEN HISTORY AND POETRY, AND HOW HISTORICAL MATTER SHOULD BE USED IN POETRY

But it is evident from what has been said, that it is not the province of a poet to relate things which have happened, but such as might have happened, and such things as are possible according to probability, or which would necessarily have happened. For an historian and a poet do not differ from each other

because the one writes in verse and the other in prose; for the history of Herodotus might be written in verse, and yet it would be no less a history with meter than without meter. But they differ in this, that the one speaks of things which have happened, and the other of such as might have happened. Hence, poetry is more philosophic, and more deserving of attention, than history. For poetry speaks more of universals, but history of particulars. But *universal* indeed in relating or performing certain things which happen to a man of a certain description, either probably or necessarily, [to which the aim of poetry is directed in giving names[22]]; but *particular* consists in narrating what, [for example], Alcibiades did, or what he suffered. In comedy, therefore, this is now become evident. For [comic poets] having composed a fable through things of a probable nature, they thus give whatever names they please[23] to their characters, and do not, like Iambic poets, write poems about particular persons. But in tragedy they cling to real names. The cause, however, of this is that the possible is credible. Things, therefore, which have not yet been done, we do not yet believe to be possible; but it is evident that things which have been done are possible; for they would not have been done if they were impossible. Not, indeed, but that in some tragedies there are one or two of known names, and the rest are feigned; as, for instance, in *The Flower* of Agatho. For in this tragedy, the things and the names are alike feigned, and yet it delights no less. Hence, one must not seek to adhere entirely to traditional fables, which are the subjects of tragedy. For it is ridiculous to make this the object of search, because even known subjects are known but to a few, though at the same time they delight all men. From these things, therefore, it is evident that a poet ought rather to be the author of fables than of

---

20 *This* incident is, however, related, and at considerable length, in the xixth book of the *Odyssey* (v. 563 of Pope's translation), but digressively, and incidentally; it made no essential part of his *general plan.*— Twining.

21 A ridiculous story.—" To avoid going to the Trojan war, Ulysses pretended to be mad; and, to prove his insanity, went to plow with an *ox* and a *horse;* but Palamedes, in order to detect him, laid his infant son, Telemachus, in the way of the plow; upon which Ulysses immediately stopped, and thereby proved himself to be in his right senses."— Twining.

22 Ritter well observes that the perspicuity of this otherwise clear passage is destroyed by this absurd interpolation.

23 Thus nearly all the names in the comedies of Terence and Plautus, thus Dromo and Sosia are applied to slaves, Pamphilus to a lover, Glycerium or Philumena to a lady, Pyrgopolinices or Thraso to soldiers.

meters, inasmuch as he is a poet from imitation, and he imitates actions. Hence, though it should happen that he relates things which have happened, he is no less a poet. For nothing hinders but that some actions which have happened are such as might both probably [24] and possibly have happened, and by [the narration of] such he is a poet.

But of simple plots and actions, the episodic are the worst. But I call the plot episodic, in which it is neither probable nor necessary that the episodes follow each other. Such plots, however, are composed by bad poets indeed, through their own want of ability; but by good poets, on account of the players. For, introducing [dramatic] contests, and extending the plot beyond its capabilities, they are frequently compelled to distort the connexion of the parts. But, since tragedy is not only an imitation of a perfect action, but also of actions which are terrible and piteous, and actions principally become such, [and in a greater degree, when they happen contrary to opinion], on account of each other. . . . For thus they will possess more of the marvelous, than if they happened from chance and fortune; since, also, of things which are from fortune, those appear to be most admirable, which seem to happen as it were by design. Thus the statue of Mityus at Argos killed him who was the cause of the death of Mityus

24 It may appear to the reader to be a strange observation, that "*some true* events MAY be *probable.*" But he will recollect what sort of *events*, and what sort of *probability*, Aristotle here speaks of: i.e. of *extraordinary events*, such as Poetry requires, and of that more *strict* and *perfect probability*, that closer connection and *visible* dependence of circumstances, which are always required from the *poet*, though in *such* events, not often to be found in *fact*, and real life, and therefore not expected from the *historian*.

This general, and, if I may call it so, *possible* sort of *probability*, may be termed, *the probability of romance;* and these lines of Agatho furnish a good apological motto for the novel writer. It might be prefixed, perhaps, without impropriety, even to the best productions of the kind — to a CLARISSA or a CECILIA. Nothing is so commonly complained of in such works, as their *improbability*: and often, no doubt, the complaint is well-founded: often, however, the criticism means nothing more than that the events are *uncommon*, and proves nothing more than the want of fancy, and an extended view of human life in the reader. If the events were *not* uncommon, where would the book find readers ? — Twining.

by falling as he was surveying it. For such events as these seem not to take place casually. Hence it is necessary that fables of this kind should be more beautiful.

CHAP. X

FABLES, EITHER SIMPLE OR COMPOUND

Of fables, however, some are simple, and others complex; for so also are the actions of which fables are the imitations. But I call the action *simple,* from which taking place, as it has been defined, with continuity and unity, there is a transition without either revolution or *discovery;* but complex, from which there is a transition, together with discovery, or revolution, or both. It is necessary, however, that these should be effected from the composition itself of the fable, so that from what has formerly happened it may come to pass that the same things take place either necessarily or probably. For it makes a great difference whether these things are effected on account of these, or after these.

CHAP. XI

Now, revolution is a mutation, as has been stated, of actions into a contrary condition; and this, as we say, according to the probable, or the necessary. Thus in the *Œdipus* the messenger who comes with an intention of delighting Œdipus and liberating him from his fear respecting his mother, when he makes himself known, produces a contrary effect. Thus, too, in the *Lynceus,* he indeed is introduced as one who is to die, and Danaus follows with an intention of killing him; but it happens from the course of incidents, that Lynceus is saved, and Danaus is slain. And discovery is, as the name signifies, a change from ignorance to knowledge, or into the friendship or hatred of those who are destined to prosperous or adverse fortune. The discovery, however, is most beautiful, when at the same time there are, as in the *Œdipus,* revolutions. There are, therefore, other discoveries also. For sometimes it happens, as has been before observed, that there are discoveries of things inanimate and casual; or if some one has performed, or has not performed, a thing, there is a recognition of it; but the discovery which especially pertains to the fable and the action is that before mentioned. For a discovery and revolution of this kind will excite either pity or fear; and tragedy is supposed to be an imitation of such actions [as excite fear and pity]. Again, it will happen that infelicity and felicity will be in such like discoveries. But since discovery is a discovery of certain persons, some [discoveries] are of one person only with reference to another, when it is evident who the other person is, but sometimes it is necessary to discover both persons. Thus Iphigenia was recognized by Orestes through the sending of an epistle; but another discovery was requisite to his being known by Iphigenia. [Two parts of the fable, therefore, viz. revolution and discovery, are conversant with these things; but the third part is pathos. And of these, revolution and discovery have been already discussed. Pathos, however, is an action destructive, or lamentable; such as death when it is obvious, grievous pains, wounds, and such like particulars.]

CHAP. XII

ON THE PARTS OF TRAGEDY

[But we have before spoken of the parts of tragedy which are requisite to constitute its quality. The parts of tragedy, however, according to quantity, and into which it is separately divided, are as follows: prologue,[25] episode,[26] exode,[27] and chorus, of the parts of which one is the *parados*,[28] but the other is the *stasimon*.[29] These [five] parts, therefore,

25 *Prologue* — This may be compared to our first *act*. — Twining.

26 *Episode* — i. e. *a part introduced, inserted*, etc. as all the *dialogue* was, originally, between the choral odes. — Twining.

27 *Exode* — i. e. *the going out*, or *exit*; the concluding *act*, as we should term it. The Greek tragedies never *finished* with a choral ode. — Twining.

28 *Parode* — i. e. *entry* of the chorus upon the stage; and hence the term was applied to *what they first sung*, upon their entry. — Twining.

29 *Stasimon* — i. e. *stable*; because, as it is explained, these odes were sung by the choral troop when fixed on the stage, and at rest: whereas the *parode* is said to have been sung *as they came on*. Hence, the *trochaic* and *anapæstic* measures, being lively and full of

are common to all [tragedies]; but the peculiar parts are [the songs] from the scene and the *kommoi*. And the prologue, indeed, is the whole part of the tragedy, prior to the entrance of the chorus. The episode is the whole part of the tragedy between two complete odes of the chorus. The exode is the whole part of the tragedy, after which there is no further melody of the chorus. And of the chorus, the parados, indeed, is the first speech of the whole chorus; but the stasimon is the melody of the chorus, without anapæst and trochee: and the commos [30] is the common lamentation of the chorus and from the scene. But we have before shown what the parts of tragedy are which must necessarily be used; but the parts of it according to quantity, and into which it is separately divided, are these.[31]]

CHAP. XIII

THE ESSENTIALS FOR A TRAGIC PLOT

In the next place we must show, as consequent to what has been said, what those who compose fables ought to aim at, and beware of, and whence the purpose of tragedy is effected. Since, therefore, it is necessary that the composition of the most beautiful tragedy should not be simple, but complex, and that it should be imitative of fearful and piteous actions — (for this is the peculiarity of such imitation) — in the first place it is evident that it is not proper that worthy men should be represented as changed from prosperity to adversity, (for this is neither a subject of terror nor commiseration, but is impious,) nor should depraved characters [be represented as changed] from adversity to prosperity; for this is the most foreign from tragedy of all things, since it possesses nothing which is proper; for it neither appeals to moral sense, nor is piteous, nor fearful. Nor, again, must a very depraved man be represented as having fallen from prosperity into adversity. For such a composition will indeed possess moral

motion, were adapted to the *parode*, but not to the *stasimon*. — Twining.

30 From a verb signifying to *beat* or *strike*; alluding to the gestures of violent grief.

31 Ritter, who has illustrated this whole chapter with great learning and taste, allows

tendency, but not pity or fear. For the one is conversant with a character which does not deserve to be unfortunate; but the other, with a character similar [to one's own]. [And pity, indeed, is excited for one who does not deserve to be unfortunate; but fear, for one who resembles oneself]; so that the event will neither appear to be commiserable, nor terrible. There remains therefore the character between these. But a character of this kind is one who neither excels in virtue and justice, nor is changed through vice and depravity, into misfortune, from a state of great renown and prosperity, but has experienced this change through some [human] error; such as Œdipus and Thyestes, and other illustrious men of this kind. Hence it is necessary that a plot which is well constructed, should be rather single [32] than twofold, (though some say it should be the latter,) and that the change should not be into prosperity from adversity, but on the contrary into adversity from prosperity, not through depravity, but through some great error, either of such a character [as we have mentioned], or better rather than worse. But the proof of this is what has taken place. For of old the poets adopted any casual fables; but now the most beautiful tragedies are composed about a few families; as for instance, about Alcmæon, Œdipus, Orestes, Meleager, Thyestes, and Telephus, and such other persons as happen either to have suffered or done things of a dreadful nature. The tragedy, therefore, which is most beautiful according to art, is of this construction. Hence they erroneously blame Euripides, who accuse him of having done this in his tragedies, and for making many of them terminate in misfortune. For this method, as we have said, is right; of which this is the greatest evidence, that in the scenes, and contests of the players, simple fables which terminate unhappily appear to be most tragical, if they are properly acted.

And Euripides, though he does not manage other things well, yet appears to be the most tragic of poets.[33] The fable, however, ranks in the second place, though by some it is said to be the first composition, which has a twofold construction, such as the *Odyssey,* and which terminates in a contrary fortune, both to the better and worse characters. It appears, however, to rank in the first place, through the imbecility of the spectators.[34] For the poets, in composing their plots, accommodate themselves to the wish of the spectators. This pleasure, however, is not [properly] derived from tragedy, but is rather suited to comedy. For there, though the greatest enemies be introduced, as Orestes and Ægisthus, yet in the end they depart friends, and no one falls by the hand of the other.

CHAP. XIV

OF TERROR AND PITY

Terror and pity, therefore, may be produced from the sight. But they may also arise from the combination of the incidents, which is preferable, and the province of a better poet. For it is necessary that the fable should be so composed that he who hears the things which are transacted, may be seized with horror, and feel pity, from the events, without the assistance of the sight; and in this manner any one who hears the fable of Œdipus is affected. But to effect this through spectacle is more inartificial, and requires great expense. But they who produce not the terrible, but the monstrous alone, through scenic representation, have nothing in common with tragedy. For it is not proper to expect every kind of pleasure from tragedy, but that which is appropriate. Since, how-

its utility, but doubts that it is the work of Aristotle.

32 What is here meant by a *single* fable, will appear presently from the account of its opposite — the *double* fable. It must not be confounded with the *simple* fable, though in the original both are expressed by the same word. The *simple* fable is only a fable *without revolution, or discovery.*—Twining.

33 But below, xv. 5. Euripides is justly charged with the improper introduction of comic characters and language. The praise applies only to the catastrophe.

34 That weakness which cannot bear strong emotions, even from fictitious distress. To some minds, everything that is not *cheerful* is *shocking.*— But, might not the preference here attributed to *weakness,* be attributed to better causes — the gratification of philanthropy, the love of justice, order, etc.! — the same causes which, just before, induced Aristotle himself to condemn as *shocking* and *disgusting,* those fables which involve the virtuous in calamity. Twining.

ever, it is necessary that the poet should procure pleasure from pity and fear through imitation, it is evident that this must be effected by the circumstances. Let us, then, ascertain what kind of events appear to be dreadful or lamentable. But it is necessary that actions of this kind should either be those of friends towards each other, or of enemies, or of neither. If, therefore, an enemy kills an enemy, he does not show any thing which is an object of pity, neither while he does the deed, nor when he is about to do it, except what arises from the deed itself. And this will be the case when one of those who are neither friends nor enemies do the same. But when these things happen in friendships, as when a brother kills a brother, or a son his father, or a mother her son, or a son his mother, or intends to do it, or does any thing else of the like kind — such subjects are to be sought for. One must not, therefore, [completely] alter the received fables. I mean, for instance, such as the fable of Clytemnestra being slain by Orestes, and of Eriphyle by Alcmæon. But it is necessary that the poet should invent the plot, and use in a becoming manner those fables which are handed down. What, however, we mean by [using fables] in a becoming manner, let us explain more clearly. Now, the action may take place in such a way as the ancients have represented it, viz. knowingly with intent; as Euripides represents Medea killing her children. Men may also do an action, who are ignorant of, and afterwards discover their connexion [with, the injured party,] as in the *Œdipus* of Sophocles. This, therefore, is extraneous to the drama,[35] but is in the tragedy itself; as in the *Alcmæon* of Astydamas, or Telegonus in the *Ulysses Wounded*.[36] Further still,

besides these there is a third mode, when some one is about to perpetrate, through ignorance, an atrocious deed, but makes the discovery before he does it. And besides these there is no other mode. For it is necessary to act, or not; and that knowing, or not knowing. But of these, to intend to perpetrate the deed knowingly, and not to perpetrate it, is the worst; for it is wicked and not tragical; because it is void of pathos. [Hence, no poet introduces a character of this kind except rarely; as in the *Antigone,* in which Hæmon [endeavors to kill his father] Creon, [but does not effect his purpose.] [37]] For the action here ranks in the second place. But it is better to perpetrate the deed ignorantly, and having perpetrated to discover; for then it is not attended with wickedness, and the discovery excites horror. The last mode, however, is the best; I mean, as in the *Cresphontes,* in which Merope is about to kill her son, but does not, in consequence of discovering that he was her son. Thus, too, in the *Iphigenia in Tauris,* in which the sister is going to kill the brother, [but recognizes him]; and in the *Helle,* the son is about to betray his mother, but is prevented by recognizing her. Hence, as has been formerly observed, tragedies are not conversant with many families; for poets were enabled to discover incident of this kind in fables, not from art, but from fortune.[38] They were compelled, therefore, to direct their attention to those families in which calamities of this kind happened.

And thus we have spoken sufficiently concerning the combination of the incidents, and have shown what kind of fables ought to be employed.

CHAP. XV

With respect to manners, however, there are four things to which one ought to direct attention: one, indeed, and the first, that they be good. But the tragedy will indeed possess manners, if, as was said, the words or the action render any deliberate intention apparent; containing good manners, if the deliberate intention

---

[35] The murder of Laius by Œdipus, his son, is supposed to have happened a considerable time before the beginning of the action.— Twining.

[36] Of these two dramas nothing more is known than the little that Aristotle here tells us. In the first, the poet adhered so far to history, as to make Alcmæon *kill* his mother Eriphyle, but with the improvement (according to Aristotle's idea), of making him do it *ignorantly.* The story of Telegonus is, that he was a son of Ulysses by Circe; was sent by her in quest of his father, whom he wounded, without knowing him, in a skirmish relative

to some sheep, that he attempted to carry off from the island of Ithaca.— Twining.

[37] Ritter condemns this passage.

[38] i. e. to history or tradition.

is good. But manners are to be found **in each** genus; for both a woman and a slave may be good; though perhaps of these, the one is less good, and the other is wholly bad.[39] In the second place, the manners must be adapted to the persons. For there are manners which are characterized by fortitude, but it is not suited to a woman to be either brave or terrible. In the third place, the manners must be similar. For this, as was before observed, differs from making the manners to be good and adapted. In the fourth place, they must be uniform; for if he is anomalous who exhibits the imitation, and expresses such like manners, at the same time it is necessary that he should be uniformly unequal. The example, however, of depraved manners is indeed not necessary; such, for instance, as that of Menelaus in the *Orestes,* but an example of unbecoming and unappropriate manners is, the lamentation of Ulysses in the tragedy of *Scylla,*[40] and the speech of Menalippe; and the example of anomalous manners in the *Iphigenia in Aulis.* For Iphigenia supplicating does not at all resemble the Iphigenia in the latter part of the tragedy. It is requisite, however, in the manners as well as in the combination of the incidents, always to investigate, either the necessary or the probable; so that such a person should say or do such things, either necessarily or probably; and that it be necessary or probable that this thing should be done after that. It is evident, therefore, that the solutions of fables ought to happen from the fable itself, and not as in the *Medea,*[41] from the machinery, and in the tragedy called the *Iliad,* from the particulars respecting the sailing away

[from Troy]. But we must employ machinery in things which are external to the drama, which either happened before, and which it is not possible for men to know, or which happened afterwards, and require to be previously foretold and announced. For we ascribe to the gods the power of seeing all things, but we do not admit the introduction of anything absurd in the incidents,[42] but if it is introduced it must be external to the tragedy; as in the *Œdipus* of Sophocles. Since, however, tragedy is an imitation of better things, it is necessary that we should imitate good painters. For these, in giving an appropriate form to the image, depict the similitude, but increase the beauty.[43] Thus, also, it is requisite that the poet, in imitating the wrathful and the indolent, and those who are similarly affected in their manners, should form an example of equity, as asperity; such as Agatho and Homer have represented Achilles. These things, indeed, it is necessary to observe; and besides these, such perceptions of the senses as are attendant upon poetry, besides the necessary ones.[44] For in these, errors are frequently committed. But concerning these things enough has been said in the treatises already published.

CHAP. XVI

[45 What discovery, however, is, has been before stated. But with respect to the species of recognition, the first indeed is the most inartificial, and that which most poets use through being at a loss, and is effected through signs. But of

---

39 This is observed, to show the consistence of this *first* precept with the next. The manners must be drawn *as* good as may be, consistently with the observance of *propriety,* with respect to the *general* character of different sexes, ages, conditions, etc. It might have been objected — "You say the character must be *good.* But suppose the poet has to represent, for instance, a slave? — the character of slaves in general is notoriously *bad.*" — The answer is — *anything* may be good *in its kind.* — Twining.

40 Of the *Scylla* nothing is known. — Some fragments remain of *Menalippe the Wise* (for this was the title), a tragedy of Euripides, the subject of which is a curiosity.

41 Of Euripides. Medea is carried off, at the end of the tragedy, in a chariot drawn by flying dragons. — Twining.

42 By *incidents of the fable,* Aristotle here plainly means all those actions or events which are *essential parts* of the *subject* or *story,* whether previous to the action, and necessary to be known, or included in it, and actually represented *in* the drama.

43 This seems intended to explain his *third* precept, of *resemblance* in the manners; to reconcile it with his *first,* and to show what *sort* of likeness the nature of tragic imitation requires. — Twining.

44 i. e. to the *sight,* and the *hearing;* in other words, to actual *representation.*

45 The reader, who recollects the conclusion of Sect. 14, where the author took a formal leave of the "*fable and its requisites,*" and proceeded to the *second* essential part of tragedy, the *manners,* will hardly be of Dacier's opinion, who contends that this section is rightly placed. His reasons are perfectly unsatisfactory. — Twining.

these, some are natural, such as the "lance with which the earth-born [46] race are marked," or the stars [on the bodies of the sons] in the *Thyestes* of Carcinus. Others are adventitious, and of these some are in the body, as scars; but others are external, such as necklaces; and such as [the discovery] through a small boat, in the *Tyro*.[47] These signs also may be used in a better or worse manner. Thus Ulysses, through his scar, is in one way known by his nurse, and in another by the swineherds. For the discoveries which are for the sake of credibility, are more inartificial, and all of them are of this kind; but those which are from revolution, as in the "Washing of Ulysses,"[48] are better. And those recognitions rank in the second place, which are invented by the poet, on which account they are inartificial. Thus Orestes in the *Iphigenia* discovers that he is Orestes.[49] For she indeed recognizes her brother through a letter, but Orestes himself speaks what the poet designs, but not what the fable requires; on which account it is near to the above-mentioned error; since he might have introduced some [of the real things as signs]. Thus, too, in the *Tereus* of Sophocles, the "voice of the shuttle [produced a recognition]." But the third mode of discovery is through memory, from the sensible perception of something by sight, as in the *Cyprii* of Dicæogenes; for on seeing the picture a certain person weeps. And in the *Tale of Alcinous;* for Ulysses, on hearing the lyrist, and recollecting the story, weeps; whence also [all these] were recognized. The fourth mode of discovery is derived from syllogism,[50] as in the *Choephoræ* — a person like me is arrived — there is no person like me but Orestes. — Orestes, therefore, is arrived. Thus too in the *Iphigenia* [51] of Polyides the sophist. For it was probable that Orestes would syllogistically conclude that because his sister had been immolated, it would likewise happen to him to be sacrificed. Thus also in the *Tydeus* [52] of Theodectes, a certain person comes to discover his son, and himself perishes.[53] Another example also is in the *Phinidæ*. For the women, on seeing the place, inferred what their fate would be, viz. that they must needs perish in this place; for they were exposed in it from their infancy. There is also a certain compound [discovery], which is produced from the false inference of the spectator, as in the *Ulysses the False Messenger*. For he says he should know the bow, which he had not seen; but the [audience], as if he must be known through this, on this account infer falsely. The best recognition, however, of all, is that which arises from the things themselves, astonishment being excited through the probable circumstances; as in the *Œdipus* of Sophocles and the *Iphigenia;* (for it is probable that she would be willing to send letters); since such things alone are without fictitious signs and necklaces.[54] But the recognitions which rank in the second place, are those which are derived from syllogism.]

<hr>

[46] The descendants of the original Thebans, who, according to the fabulous history, sprung from the earth when Cadmus sowed the dragon's teeth, etc.— This *noble race* are said to have been distinguished by the natural mark of a lance upon their bodies.

[47] Sophocles wrote two tragedies of this name, neither of them preserved.— The story of Tyro leads us to suppose, that Aristotle means the little boat, trough, or, as some render it, *cradle*, in which Tyro had exposed her children, on, or near, the river: the particular manner of the discovery it would be in vain to guess.

[48] The ancients distinguished the different parts of Homer's poems by different titles accommodated to the different subjects, or episodes; and, in referring to him, they made use of these, not of the division into *books*. Thus, the part of the sixth book of the *Odyssey* above referred to, was called *The Washing*. The *Tale of Alcinous* was another title, which will presently be mentioned.— Twining.

[49] I follow Ritter, who supplies "to Iphigenia." The older editors interpolated the passage.

[50] *Occasioned* by reasoning; — i. e. by reasoning (or rather, *inference*, or *conclusion*), *in the person discovered.*

[51] The subject appears to have been the same as that of the *Iphigenia in Tauris* of Euripides. We are to suppose, that *Orestes* was discovered to his sister by this natural exclamation, at the moment when he was led to the altar of Diana to be sacrificed.— Twining.

[52] Of this and the preceding tragedy, we know nothing but what we learn here: i. e. that in the one, *a father*, and in the other, the *daughters* of Phineus, were discovered, and, probably, saved, by those exclamations.— Twining.

[53] Nothing of this play is known.

[54] All this passage is hopelessly corrupt.

CHAP. XVII

It is necessary, however, that the poet should form the plots, and elaborate his diction, in such a manner that he may as much as possible place the thing before his own eyes.[55] For thus the poet perceiving most acutely, as if present with the transactions themselves, will discover what is becoming, and whatever is repugnant will be least concealed from his view. An evidence of this is the fault with which Carcinus is reproached. For Amphiaraus had left the temple, which was concealed from the spectator, who did not perceive it, and the piece was driven from the stage in consequence of the indignation of the spectators. For the poet as much as possible should cooperate with the gestures [of the actor]; since those are naturally most adapted to persuade who are themselves under the influence of passion. Hence, also, he agitates others who is himself agitated, and he excites others to anger who is himself most truly enraged. Hence, poetry is the province either of one who is naturally clever, or of one who is insane. For these characters, the one is easily fashioned, but the other is prone to ecstasy. It is likewise necessary that the poet should in a general way lay down the fables composed by others, and those which he composes himself, and afterwards introduce episodes and lengthen out [the play]. But I say that he should give a general sketch after this manner. Thus, for instance, in the *Iphigenia*, a certain virgin on the point of being sacrificed, and vanishing from the view of those who were to sacrifice her, and being brought to another country in which it was a law to sacrifice strangers to a certain goddess, she is appointed the priestess of these rites. Some time after, it happened that the brother of the priestess came to this place; [but on what account? Because some god had ordered him, for a certain reason which does not pertain to the general view of the tragedy,] to come thither, [but why he did so is foreign to the fable]. The brother, therefore, coming, and being made captive, discovered [his sister], when he is going to be sacrificed; wheth-

er, as Euripides says, [by an epistle,] or, as Polyides feigns, speaking according to probability, because he said, it was not only requisite that the sister, but that he also should be sacrificed: — and hence safety arises. After these things, the poet having given names to the persons, should insert the episodes; and he must be careful that the episodes be appropriate; as that of the insanity through which Orestes was taken captive, and his being saved through expiation. In dramas, therefore, the episodes are short, but by these the epopee is lengthened. For the fable of the *Odyssey* is short, viz. a certain man wandering for many years, and persecuted by Neptune, and left alone. And besides this, his domestic affairs being so circumstanced, that his wealth is consumed by suitors, and stratagems are plotted against his son. But driven by a tempest, he returns, and making himself known to certain persons, he attacks the suitors, and is himself saved, but destroys his enemies. This, therefore, is the peculiarity of the fable, but the rest is episode.

CHAP. XVIII

[In every tragedy, however, there is a complication and development.[56] And external circumstances indeed, and some of those that are internal, frequently form the complication; but the rest the development. I call, however, the complication, the whole of that which extends from the beginning to the last part, from which there is a transition to good fortune; but I call the development that part which extends from the beginning of the transition to the end. Thus in the *Lynceus* of Theodectes, the past transactions, and the capture of the son, are the complication; but the part which extends from the charge of murder to the end, is the development. But of tragedy there are four species; for so many parts of it have also been enumerated. And one species is the complicated, of which the

56 Literally, the *tying* and *untying*. With the French, *Nœud* and *Dénouement* are convenient and established terms. I hope I shall be pardoned for avoiding our awkward expressions of the *intrigue* and *unraveling* of a plot, etc. I could find no terms less exceptionable than those I have used.— Twining.

whole is revolution and discovery; another, the pathetic, such as the tragedies of *Ajax* and *Ixion;* another, the moral,[57] such as the *Phthiotides* and the *Peleus;* but the fourth is another such as the *Phorcides* [58] and the *Prometheus,* and tragedies which represent what passes in Hades. It is especially necessary, therefore, that the poet should endeavor to have all these species; or at least that he should have the greatest and most of them, especially since men of the present age calumniate the poets. For as there have been good poets in each part of tragedy, they now expect one poet to excel in all the parts. But it is right to call tragedy different and the same, though not perhaps with any reference to the fable; but this [may be the case with those] of which there is the same plot and solution. But many poets complicate well, and develop badly.[59] But both these should always be applauded.[60] But it is necessary to recollect, as has been often observed, that we must not make tragedy an epic system. Now, I call that tragedy an epic system, which consists of many fables; as if some one should compose a tragedy from the whole fable of the *Iliad.* For in the *Iliad,* on account of its length, the parts receive an appropriate magnitude. But in dramas, the effect produced would be very contrary to expectation. The truth

of this is indicated by such as have represented [in one tragedy] the whole destruction of Troy, and not some part of it, as the *Niobe* or *Medea* of Euripides, and who have not acted like Æschylus; for these have either been condemned, or contend without success; since Agatho also failed in this alone. But in revolutions, and in simple actions, those poets admirably effect their aim. For this is tragical, and has a moral tendency. This, however, takes place when a wise but a depraved man, such as Sisyphus, is deceived; and a brave but unjust man is vanquished. But this is probable, as Agatho says. For it is probable that many things may take place contrary to probability. It is necessary likewise to conceive the chorus to be one of the players and a part of the whole, and that it coöperates with the players, not as in Euripides,[61] but as in Sophocles. But with other tragedians, the choral songs do not more belong to that fable, than to any other tragedy; on which account the chorus sing detached pieces, inserted at pleasure,[62] of which Agatho was the inventor. What difference, however, does it make, to sing inserted pieces, or to adapt the diction of one drama to another, or the whole episode?

CHAP. XIX

Of the other parts of tragedy enough has now been said. But it remains that we should speak concerning the diction and the sentiments. The particulars,

[57] i. e. in which the delineation of *manners* or *character* is predominant. Our language, I think, wants a word to express *this* sense of the Greek ἠθικὸν, and the Latin, *moratum.* *Mannered* has. I believe, sometimes been used in this sense; but so seldom, as to sound awkwardly. We know nothing of the subjects here given as examples.— Twining.

[58] Æschylus wrote a tragedy so named. It is difficult to imagine what he could make of these three curious personages, who were *born old women,* lived underground, and had but one eye among them, which they used by turns; carrying it. I suppose, in a case, like a pair of spectacles. Such is the tale! — Twining.

[59] No fault so common. It was with the Greek tragedians, probably, as with Shakspeare.— "In many of his plays the latter part is evidently neglected. When he found himself near the end of his work, and in view of his reward, he shortened the labor, to snatch the profit. He therefore remits his efforts where he should most vigorously exert them, and his catastrophe is improbably produced, or imperfectly represented." Johnson's Pref. to Shakspeare.— Twining.

[60] This passage is contradictory and unintelligible. Ritter condemns the whole as spurious.

[61] This expression does not, I think, necessarily imply any stronger censure of Euripides, than that the choral odes of his tragedies were, in general, more loosely connected with the subject than those of Sophocles; which, on examination, would, I believe, be found true. For that *this* is the fault here meant, not the improper " choice of the persons who compose *the chorus,*" as the ingenious translator of Euripides understands, is, I think, plain from what immediately follows; the connection being this: —" Sophocles is, in this respect, *most* perfect; Euripides *less* so; as to the *others, their* choral songs are *totally foreign* to the subject of their tragedies."

[62] It is curious to trace the gradual extinction of the chorus. At first, it was *all;* then, relieved by the intermixture of dialogue, but still *principal;* then, *subordinate* to the dialogue; then, digressive, and *ill connected* with the piece; then, borrowed from *other pieces* at pleasure — and so on, to the fiddles and the act-tunes. The performers in the *orchestra* of a modern theater are little, I believe, aware,

therefore, respecting the sentiments, are unfolded in the treatise on *Rhetoric,* to which it more properly belongs. But those things pertain to the sentiments, which it is requisite to procure by a reasoning process. And the parts of these are, to demonstrate, to refute, and to excite the passions; such as pity, or fear, or anger, and such like; and besides these, to amplify and extenuate. It is evident, however, that in things, also, it is requisite to derive what is useful from the same forms, when it is necessary to procure objects of pity, or things that are dreadful, or great, or probable. Except that there is this difference, that things in tragedy ought to be rendered apparent without teaching, but in an oration they are to be shown by the speaker, and in consequence of the speech. For what employment would there be for the orator, if the things should appear [of themselves] pleasing, and not through the speech? But of things pertaining to diction, there is one species of theory respecting the forms of speech, which it is the province of the actor to know, and of him who is a master artist in this profession. Thus, for instance, [it is requisite he should know,] what a mandate is, what a prayer, narration, threats, interrogation and answer are, and whatever else there may be of this kind. For from the knowledge or ignorance of these, the poetic art incurs no blame of any moment. For who would think that Homer errs in what he is reproved for by Protagoras? viz. that while he fancies he prays, he commands, when he says, "The wrath, O goddess, sing." For, says he, to order a thing to be done, or not to be done, is a mandate. Hence, this must be omitted as a theorem pertaining to another art, and not to poetry.

.   .   .   .   .

CHAP. XXIII

ON THE EPIC POEM

Concerning the poetry, however, which is narrative and imitative in meter, it is evident that it ought to have dramatic

that they occupy the *place,* and may consider themselves as the lineal descendants, of the ancient *chorus.* *Orchestra* was the name of that part of the ancient theater which was appropriated to the chorus.

fables, in the same manner as tragedy, and should be conversant with one whole and perfect action, which has a beginning, middle, and end, in order that, like one whole animal, it may produce its appropriate pleasure; [63] and that it may not be like the custom of histories, in which it is not necessary to treat of one action, but of one time, viz. of such things as have happened in that time, respecting one or more persons, the relation of each of which things to the other is just as it may happen. For as the sea-fight at Salamis, and the battle with the Carthaginians in Sicily, though they happened at the same time, tend nothing to the same end; thus also in successive times, one thing may sometimes be connected with another, from which no one end is produced. But nearly all poets do this. Hence, as we have before observed, in this respect also Homer will appear to be divine, when compared with other poets, because he did not attempt to sing of the whole of the Trojan war, though it had a beginning and an end. For if he had, it would have been very great, and not sufficiently conspicuous; or if it had been of a moderate size, it would have been intricate through the variety of incidents.[64] But now, having selected one part of the war, he has made use of many episodes; such as the catalogue of the ships, and other episodes, with which he has adorned his poem. Other poets, however, have composed a fable about one man, and one time, and one action, consisting of many parts; as the authors of the *Cyprias,* and the *Lesser Iliad.* [With respect to the *Iliad* and *Odyssey,* therefore, one or two tragedies only could be made from each. But many might be made from the *Cypriacs;* and from the *Lesser Iliad* more than eight; such as the *Judgment of the Arms, Philoctetes, Neoptolemus, Eurypylus, The Begging* [of *Ulysses*], the *Lacænæ,* the

63 i. e. opposed (as appears from what follows) to that which *history* gives. *Unity of interest* is essential to the pleasure we expect from the epic poem; and this cannot exist, at least in the degree required, without *unity of action.*— Twining.
64 Because "*the length of the whole would*" then "*not admit of a proper magnitude in the parts*"; and thus an *epic poem* constructed upon an *historical plan,* would be exactly in the same case with a *tragedy* "constructed on an *epic plan.*"— Twining.

Destruction of Troy, the *Return of the Greeks, Sinon,* and the *Troades.*

CHAP. XXIV

ON THE SPECIES, PARTS, ETC. OF EPIC POETRY

Again, it is requisite that the epic should have the same species as tragedy. [For it is necessary that it should be either simple, or complex, or ethical, or pathetic.] The parts also are the same, except the music and the scenery. For it requires revolutions, discoveries, and disasters; and besides these, the sentiments and the diction should be well formed; all which were first used by Homer, and are used by him fitly. For of his two poems, the *Iliad* indeed contains the simple and pathetic; but the *Odyssey,* the complex; for through the whole of it there is discovery [65] and moral. And besides these things, he excelled all poets in diction and sentiment. The epic, however, differs from tragedy in the length of the composition, and in the meter. But the proper boundary of its length has been before described; for it should be such that the beginning and the end may be seen at one view. [And this will be effected if the compositions are shorter than those of the ancient poets, and brought to the same length with the multitude of tragedies that are recited at one hearing.[66]] But it is the peculiarity of the epic to possess abundantly the power of extending its magnitude; for tragedy is not capable of imitating many actions that are performed at the same time, but that part only which is represented in the scene, and acted by the players. But in the epic, in consequence of its being a narration, many events may be introduced which have happened at the same time, which are properly connected with the subject, and from which the bulk of the poem is increased. Hence, this con-

tributes to its magnificence, transports the hearer to different places, and adorns the poem with dissimilar episodes. For similitude of events rapidly produces satiety, and causes tragedies to fail. But heroic meter is established by experience as adapted to the epic. For if any one should attempt narrative imitation in any other meter, or in many meters mingled together, the unfitness of it would be apparent. For heroic meter is of all others the most stable and ample. [Hence it especially receives foreign words and metaphors. For narrative imitation excels all others.] But Iambics and tetrameters have more motion; the one being adapted to dancing, but the other to acting. It would, however, be still more absurd, to mingle them together, as Chæremon did. Hence, no one has composed a long poem in any other measure than the heroic; but, as we have said, Nature herself teaches us to distinguish the measure best suited. Homer, indeed, deserves to be praised for many other things, and also because he is the only poet who was not ignorant what he ought to do himself. For it is requisite that the poet should speak in his own person as little as possible; for so far as he does so he is not an imitator. Other poets, therefore, take an active part through the whole poem, and they only imitate a few things, and seldom. But Homer, after a short preface, immediately introduces a man or a woman, or something else that has manners; for there is nothing in his poem unattended with manners. It is necessary, therefore, in tragedies to produce the wonderful; but that which is contrary to reason (whence the wonderful is best produced) is best suited to the epopee, from the agent not being seen. In the next place, the particulars respecting the pursuit of Hector would appear ridiculous in the scene; the Greeks indeed standing still, and not pursuing, and Achilles making signs to them, by the motion of his head, not to engage.[67] But in the epic this is concealed. Now, the wonderful pleases; of which this is an indica-

---

[65] See Pope's translation, xvi. 206, etc., where Ulysses discovers himself to Telemachus — xxi. 212, to the shepherds — xxiii. 211, to Penelope — xxiv. 375, to his father — ix. 17, to Alcinous — iv. 150, etc., Telemachus is discovered to Menelaus by his tears — v. 189, to Helen, by his resemblance to his father — xix. 545, Ulysses is discovered to the old nurse, by the scar.— Twining.

[66] This is quite contrary to Aristotle's own opinion.

[67] Pope's *Iliad,* xxii. 267.— Perhaps the idea of stopping a whole army by a nod, or shake of the head (a circumstance distinctly mentioned by Homer, but sunk in Mr. Pope's version), was the absurdity here *principally* meant. If this whole Homeric scene were represented

tion, that all men, when they wish to gratify their hearers, add something to what they relate. Homer also in the highest degree taught others how to feign in a proper manner. But this is a paralogism. For men fancy that when the consequent followers or results from the antecedent, the consequent may be converted, and that the antecedent will follow from the consequent. This, however, is false. [But why, if the antecedent be false, so long as this other be otherwise, should the consequent necessarily follow? For through knowing the consequent to be true, our soul paralogizes, and concludes that the antecedent also is true. And there is an example of this in *The Washing*.] Again, one should prefer things which are impossible but probable, to such as are possible but improbable. Fables also should not be composed from irrational parts, [but as much as possible, indeed, they should have nothing irrational in them: if, however, this is impossible, care should be taken that the irrational circumstance does not pertain to the fable, as in the case of Œdipus not knowing how Laius died. For it must not be brought into the drama, like the narration of the Pythian games in the *Electra*, or him who, in the tragedy of the Mysians, comes from Tegea to Mysia without speaking.] It is ridiculous, therefore, to say, that otherwise the fable would be destroyed; for such fables should not at first be composed. But if they are composed, and it appears more reasonable that they should be, the absurdity also must be admitted; since the irrational circumstances in the *Odyssey*, such as Ulysses being left [on the shore of Ithaca by the Phœacians], would evidently have been intolerable, if they had been fabricated by a bad poet. But now the poet conceals the absurdity, and renders it pleasing by the addition of other beauties. The diction, likewise, should be labored in the sluggish parts of the poem, and which exhibit neither manners nor sentiment. For a very splendid diction conceals the manners and the reasoning.

on our stage, in the best manner possible, there can be no doubt that the effect would justify Aristotle's observation. It would certainly set the audience in a roar.— Twining.

CHAP. XXVI

One may, however, question whether epic or tragic imitation is the more excellent. For if that imitation is the better which is less troublesome to the spectator, and such an imitation pertains to better spectators, that which imitates every thing is evidently attended with molestation. For, as if the spectators will not perceive what is acted without the addition of much movement, they make great gesticulations; just as bad players on the flute turn themselves round, when it is requisite to imitate the action of the discus, or when they sing of Scylla, draw to themselves the coryphæus, or leader of the band. Such, then, is tragedy, as the modern actors are in the estimation of their predecessors. Hence, Myniscus called Callipides an ape, in consequence of carrying his imitation to a great excess. And there was also a similar opinion respecting Pindar [the player]. But as these latter actors are to the former, so is the whole art of tragedy to the epopee. They say, therefore, that the epopee is calculated for hearers of the better sort, on which account it does not require scenery; but that tragedy is calculated for the vulgar. Hence, tragic imitation, which is troublesome to the spectator, will evidently be inferior to epic imitation.

In the first place, however, this accusation does not pertain to the poet, but the actor; since it is possible in reciting epic poetry to overdo action, as Sosistratus did, and singing likewise, as Mnastheus of Opus did. In the next place, neither is all motion to be despised, since neither is every kind of dancing, but only that which is bad; and hence Callipedes was blamed, as others now are for imitating light women. Further still, tragedy, in the same manner as the epopee, may fulfil its purpose without gesture; for by reading, it is manifest what kind of thing it is. If, therefore, it is in other respects better, it is not necessary that it should be accompanied [by motion and gesture]. In the next place, tragedy has every thing which the epic possesses. For it may use meter, and it has also music and scenery, as no small parts, through which the pleasure it produces **is** most apparent. To which may be added, that it possesses perspicuity, both when it is read, and when it is acted. The end, too, of its imitation is confined in less extended limits. For being crowded into a narrower compass, it becomes more pleasing than if it were diffused through a long period of time. Thus, for instance, if one were to put the *Œdipus* of Sophocles into as many verses as the *Iliad,* [it would be less pleasing]. Again, the imitation of the epic has less unity [than tragic imitation]; of which this is an indication, that from any kind of [epic] imitation, many tragedies may be produced. Hence, if he who writes an epic poem should choose a fable perfectly one, the poem would necessarily either appear short, as if curtailed, or if it should be accompanied with length of meter, it would seem to be languid. But if he should compose one fable from many fables, I mean, if the poem should consist of many actions, it would not possess unity. Thus, the *Iliad* and *Odyssey* contain many such parts, which of themselves possess magnitude, though these poems are composed, as much as possible, in the most excellent manner, and are most eminently the imitation of one action. If, therefore, tragedy excels in all these particulars, and besides this, in the work of art, (for neither tragic nor epic imitation ought to produce a casual pleasure, but that which has been stated), it is evident that it will be more excellent than the epopee, in consequence of attaining its end in a greater degree. And thus much concerning tragedy, and the epic, as to themselves, their species, and their parts, their number, and their difference, what the causes are of their being good or bad, and also concerning the objections which may be made to them, and the solutions of the objections.

ANCIENT ROME

LATIN DRAMATIC CRITICISM

Latin literature yields little more material in dramatic criticism and theory than Greek. As is pointed out in another place, there is but one complete treatise extant — the *Ars Poetica* of Horace — and that is far from satisfactory as a unified and clear statement of the aims or achievements of the Latin drama. From the beginnings of Latin literary criticism with Cicero, to the time of Horace, there is practically nothing relating to the subject. Cicero himself, in his *Letters, Orations,* and various treatises, evolves interesting ideas on the drama, but nowhere sums up any sort of complete theory of body of doctrine. If the works of Varro and Lucilius had been preserved, it is doubtful whether Horace would have occupied his present position of solitary grandeur and importance, but in the absence of anything but fragments from these authors and from the numerous other critics of his time and anterior to him, we must assign to him a place of the first magnitude. Mention ought perhaps be made of a few paragraphs on the rise of comedy in Livy's history, *Ab urbe condita Libri* (vii, ii, iv, and following), written about the time of Christ. Not until Quintilian is there anything approaching a systematic study of dramatists, while Quintilian himself—in the *Institutiones Oratoriae,* Books VI and X — adopts an historical rather than theoretical method, and passes brief judgments on Greek and Latin authors. The *Noctes Atticae* of Aulus Gellius is the last of the Latin writings with any pretension to originality concerned with our subject.

A careful study of Henry Nettleship's second series of *Lectures and Essays* — chapter on *Latin Criticism* —, and of Saintsbury's *History of Criticism* — first volume — will enlighten the student as to the details of the subject, but he will find little other than fragments and titles of lost works if he goes to original sources.

References on Latin Criticism and Latin Literature in General:

E. Hübner, *Bibliographie der klassischen Altertumwissenschaft; Grundriss zu Vorlesungen über die Geschichte und Encyklopädie der klassischen Philologie* (Berlin, 2nd ed., 1889).

J. C. F. Baehr, *Geschichte der römischen Literatur,* 4 vols. (Karlsruhe, 2d ed., 1868–72).

G. Bernhardy, *Grundriss der römischen Literatur* (Braunschweig, 5th ed., 1872).

R. W. Browne, *A History of Roman Classical Literature* (London 1853).

M. S. Dimsdale, *A History of Latin Literature* (London & New York, 1915).

J. Wight Duff, *A Literary History of Rome* (New York, 1909).

H. Joachim, *Geschichte der römischen Literatur* (Leipzig, 1896).

J. W. Mackail, *Latin Literature* (New York, 1895).

Henry Nettleship, *Lectures and Essays* (Oxford, 1885).

Henry Nettleship, *Lectures and Essays* (2d series, Oxford, 1895).

George Saintsbury, *A History of Criticism,* vol. 1, (New York, 1900).

J. E. Sandys, *A History of Classical Scholarship,* 3 vols. (Cambridge, 1903).

M. Schanz, *Geschichte der römischen Literature,* 3 parts (München, 1890–1901).

W. S. Teuffel, *Geschichte der römischen Literatur,* 3 parts (München, 1890– Eng. tr. from revised and enlarged ed. by L. Schwabe by G. C. W. Warr, 2 vols., London, 1891–92).

Gaston Boissier, *Le Poète Attius. Etude sur la Tragédie latine pendant la République* (Paris, 1857).

Philippe Fabia, *Les Théâtres de Rome au*

temps de Plaute et de Térence (*Rev. de Phil.*, XXI, Paris, 1897).

J. F. D'Alton, *Horace and His Age* (London, 1917. See especially chapter on Literary Criticism).

G. Michaut, *Sur les Tréteaux latins* (Paris, 1912).

W. R. Hardie, *Literary Criticism at Rome* (*In Lectures on Classical Subjects*, London, 1903).

HORACE

Quintus Horatius Flaccus, known in English as Horace, was born at Venusia, near the border of Apulia, in 65 B. C. His father, a former slave who had freed himself before the birth of his son, sent him to school in Rome. As a young man Horace went to Athens and studied philosophy at the famous schools. When the Civil War broke out he enlisted in the army of Brutus, served at Philippi, and came back to Rome not long after. Deprived of his property as a result of the proscriptions, he began life anew at the age of twenty-four as clerk in a public office. Not long after, he attracted the attention of Mæcenas, and soon became acquainted with Varius and Vergil, henceforth devoting himself to literary pursuits. His first work, the first book of *Satires*, was published 35 B. C. About a year later, Mæcenas presented him with the celebrated Sabine Farm, and Horace was at liberty to the end of his life to do as he liked. Before he died he was famous: the Emperor Augustus commissioned him to write the fourth book of *Odes*. He died eight years before the birth of Christ.

The *Epistle to the Pisos,* or *Art of Poetry,* has been assigned by various authorities to the period between 24 and 7 B. C. Professor Nettleship (in his *Lectures and Essays*) believes it to have been written between 24 and 20 B. C. Its interest and value are considerably enhanced in view of the fact that it is, in Professor Saintsbury's words, " the only complete example of literary criticism that we have from any Roman." It is significant that the greater part of its subject-matter is concerned with the drama. While it has been clearly substantiated that Horace drew upon a non-extant treatise by Neoptolemus of Parium, an Alexandrian critic of uncertain date, the

fact that Horace made use of and molded the ideas of his predecessor is important. The *Art of Poetry* is on the whole a somewhat arbitrary manual; the greatest importance is there attached to the purely formal side of writing; the dramatist must adhere closely to the five acts, the chorus, and so on; proportion, good sense, decorum, cannot be neglected. Of the practical value of the work before the Renaissance, it is impossible to know; of its influence since that time, it can only be said that it was as widespread as that of Aristotle. Horace's doctrine of " pleasure and profit " was to be repeated innumerable times, and is still a criterion of criticism. Mr. Spingarn's statement that " critical activity in nearly all the countries of western Europe seems to have been ushered in by the translation of Horace's *Ars Poetica* into the vernacular tongues " is but another proof of the popularity of the work.

Editions:

Of the numerous Latin texts of Horace, that of Bentley is on the whole the best, though there are numerous others. This was reëdited by Zangemeister in 1869. Among modern commentaries are that of J. C. Orelli (4th ed. revised by O. Hirschfelder and J. Mewes, 1886–90), and of A. Kiessling (revised by R. Heinze, 1898–1908). The standard English commentary is the two-volume edition of E. C. Wickham (1874–96).

English translations abound. Among the early versions is *The Works of Horace,* translated by several hands [Dryden, Congreve, etc.] 2 vols., London, 1757–59. See also *The Works of Horace,* translated by C. Smart, revised by T. A. Buckley (late Bohn editions, n. d. ; *The Works of Horace,* translated by I. Lonsdale and S. Lee (London, 1873); and

A Poetical Translation of the Works of
Horace, by P. Francis, 2 vols. (ed. Lon-
don, 1831).

On Horace and His Works:

H. H. Milman, The Works of Horace,
with English Notes critical and ex-
planatory, by C. Anthon. (New edi-
tion, with Life of Horace, by H. H.
Milman, New York, 1875.)

Rev. W. Tuckwell, Horace (London,
1905).

Gaston Boissier, L'Art poétique d'Hor-
ace et la Tragédie romaine (Rev., de
Philol., Vol. XXII, Paris, 1898).

Albert S. Cook, The Art of Poetry. The
Poetical Treatises of Horace, Vida,
and Boileau, with the Translations by
Howes, Pitt, and Soame, (with notes
and intro., Boston, 1892).

George Converse Fiske, Lucilius, The Ars
Poetica of Horace, and Persius (Har-

vard Studies in Class. Philol., Vol.
XXIV, Cambridge, 1913).

Paul Lejay, La Date et le but de l'Art
poétique d'Horce (Rev. de l'instruc-
tion pub. en Belgique, vols. XLV and
XLVI, Bruxelles, 1902-3).

Henry Nettleship, Lectures and Essays
(Oxford, 1885).

E. Norden, Die Komposition und Litera-
turgattung der horäzischen Epistola ad
Pisones (Hermes, vol. 40, Berlin, 1905).

Alois Patin, Der Aufbau der Ars poetica
des Horaz (Studien zur Geschichte und
Kultur des Altertums, Bd. 4, Heft 1,
Paderborn, 1910).

George Saintsbury, A History of Criti-
cism, vol. 1 (New York, 1900).

Johann Vahlen, Ueber Horatius' Brieq
an die Pisonen (Kön.-preuss. Akad.
d. Wissensch. Sitzungsb., p. 589, Ber-
lin, 1906).

THE ART OF POETRY [1]
[EPISTOLA AD PISONES]
(24-20 B. C.?)

If a painter should wish to unite a
horse's neck to a human head, and spread
a variety of plumage over limbs [of
different animals] taken from every part
[of nature], so that what is a beautiful
woman in the upper part terminates un-
sightly in an ugly fish below — could you,
my friends, refrain from laughter, were
you admitted to such a sight? Believe,
ye Pisos, the book will be perfectly like
such a picture, the ideas of which, like
a sick man's dreams, are all vain and
fictitious: so that neither head nor foot
can correspond to any one form. "Poets
and painters [you will say] have ever
had equal authority for attempting any
thing." We are conscious of this, and
this privilege we demand and allow in
turn: but not to such a degree that the
tame should associate with the savage;
nor that serpents should be coupled with
birds, lambs with tigers.

[1] Translated, complete, by C. Smart, from
The Works of Horace literally translated into
English Prose (New York, n. d.). Unsigned
footnotes are by the translator. The brackets
enclose words or phrases by the translator in-
tended to complete the sense of the original.
—Ed.

In pompous introductions, and such as
promise a great deal, it generally hap-
pens that one or two verses of purple
patch-work, that may make a great show,
are tagged on; as when the grove and
the altar of Diana and the meandering
of a current hastening through pleasant
fields, or the river Rhine, or the rainbow,
is described. But here there was no
room for these [fine things]: perhaps,
too, you know how to draw a cypress:
but what is that to the purpose, if he
who is painted for the given price, is
[to be represented as] swimming hope-
less out of a shipwreck? A large vase
at first was designed: why, as the wheel
revolves, turns out a little pitcher? In
a word, be your subject what it will, let
it be merely simple and uniform.

The great majority of us poets — fa-
ther, and youths worthy such a father —
are misled by the appearance of right.
I labor to be concise, I become obscure:
nerves and spirit fail him that aims at
the easy: one, that pretends to be sub-
lime, proves bombastical: he who is too
cautious and fearful of the storm, crawls
along the ground: he who wants to vary

his subject in a marvelous manner, paints the dolphin in the woods, the boar in the sea. The avoiding of an error leads to a fault, if it lack skill.

A statuary about the Æmilian school shall of himself, with singular skill, both express the nails, and imitate in brass the flexible hair; unhappy yet in the main, because he knows not how to finish a complete piece. I would no more choose to be such a one as this, had I a mind to compose any thing, than to live with a distorted nose, [though] remarkable for black eyes and jetty hair.

Ye who write, make choice of a subject suitable to your abilities; and revolve in your thoughts a considerable time what your strength declines, and what it is able to support. Neither elegance of style nor a perspicuous disposition, shall desert the man by whom the subject matter is chosen judiciously.

This, or I am mistaken, will constitute the merit and beauty of arrangement, that the poet just now say what ought just now to be said, put off most of his thoughts, and waive them for the present.

In the choice of his words, too, the author of the projected poem must be delicate and cautious, he must embrace one and reject another: you will express yourself eminently well, if a dexterous combination should give an air of novelty to a well-known word. If it happen to be necessary to explain some abstruse subjects by new-invented terms, it will follow that you must frame words never heard of by the old-fashioned Cethegi: and the license will be granted, if modestly used: and new and lately-formed words will have authority, if they descend from a Greek source, with a slight deviation. But why should the Romans grant to Plautus and Cæcilius a privilege denied to Vergil and Varius? Why should I be envied, if I have it in my power to acquire a few words, when the language of Cato and Ennius has enriched our native tongue, and produced new names of things? It has been, and ever will be, allowable to coin a word marked with the stamp in present request. As leaves in the woods are changed with the fleeting years; the earliest fall off first: in this manner words perish with old age, and those

lately invented flourish and thrive, like men in the time of youth. We and our works are doomed to death: whether Neptune, admitted into the continent, defends our fleet from the north winds, a kingly work; or the lake, for a long time unfertile and fit for oars, now maintains its neighboring cities and feels the heavy plow; or the river, taught to run in a more convenient channel, has changed its course which was so destructive to the fruits. Mortal works must perish: much less can the honor and elegance of language be long-lived. Many words shall revive, which now have fallen off; and many words are now in esteem shall fall off, if it be the will of custom, in whose power is the decision and right and standard of language.

Homer has instructed us in what measure the achievements of kings, and chiefs, and direful war might be written.

Plaintive strains originally were appropriated to the unequal numbers [of the elegiac]: afterwards [love and] successful desires were included. Yet what author first published humble elegies, the critics dispute, and the controversy still waits the determination of the judge.

Rage armed Archilochus with the iambic of his own invention. The sock and the majestic buskin assumed this measure as adapted for dialogue, and to silence the noise of the populace, and calculated for action.

To celebrate gods, and the sons of gods, and the victorious wrestler, and the steed foremost in the race, and the inclination of youths, and the free joys of wine, the muse has allotted to the lyre.

If I am incapable and unskillful to observe the distinction described, and the complexions of works [of genius], why am I accosted by the name of "Poet"? Why, out of false modesty, do I prefer being ignorant to being learned?

A comic subject will not be handled in tragic verse: in like manner the banquet of Thyestes will not bear to be held in familiar verses, and such as almost suit the sock. Let each peculiar species [of writing] fill with decorum its proper place. Nevertheless sometimes even comedy exalts her voice, and passionate Chremes rails in a tumid strain: and a tragic writer generally expresses grief in a prosaic style. Telephus and Peleus, when they are both in poverty and exile, throw aside their rants and gigantic expressions if they have a mind to move the heart of the spectator with their complaint.

It is not enough, that poems be beautiful; let them be tender and affecting, and bear away the soul of the auditor whithersoever they please. As the human countenance smiles on those that smile, so does it sympathize with those that weep. If you would have me weep you must first express the passion of grief yourself; then, Telephus or Peleus, your misfortunes hurt me: if you pronounce the parts assigned you ill, I shall either fall asleep or laugh.

Pathetic accents suit a melancholy countenance; words full of menace, an angry one; wanton expressions, a sportive look; and serious matter, an austere one. For nature forms us first within to every modification of circumstances; she delights or impels us to anger, or depresses us to the earth and afflicts us with heavy sorrow: then expresses those emotions of the mind by the tongue, its interpreter. If the words be discordant to the station of the speaker, the Roman knights and plebeians will raise an immoderate laugh. It will make a wide difference, whether it be Davus that speaks, or a hero; a man well-stricken in years, or a hot young fellow in his bloom; and a matron of distinction, or an officious nurse; a roaming merchant, or the cultivator of a verdant little farm; a Colchian, or an Assyrian; one educated at Thebes, or one at Argos.

You that write, either follow tradition, or invent such fables as are congruous to themselves. If as a poet you have to represent the renowned Achilles; let him be indefatigable, wrathful, inexorable, courageous, let him deny that laws were made for him, let him arrogate everything to force of arms. Let Medea be fierce and untractable, Ino an object of pity, Ixion perfidious, Io wandering, Orestes in distress.

If you offer to the stage anything unattempted, and venture to form a new character, let it be preserved to the last such as it set out at the beginning, and be consistent with itself. It is difficult to write with propriety on subjects to which all writers have a common claim; and you with more prudence will reduce the *Iliad* into acts, than if you first introduce arguments unknown and never treated of before. A public story will become your own property, if you do not dwell upon the whole circle of events, which is paltry and open to every one; nor must you be so faithful a translator, as to take the pains of rendering [the original] word for word; nor by imitating throw yourself into straits, whence either shame or the rules of your work may forbid you to retreat.

Nor must you make such an exordium, as the Cyclic writer of old: "I will sing the fate of Priam, and the noble war." What will this boaster produce worthy of all this gaping? The mountains are in labor, a ridiculous mouse will be brought forth. How much more to the purpose he, who attempts nothing improperly? "Sing for me, my muse, the man who, after the time of the destruction of Troy, surveyed the manners and cities of many men." He meditates not [to produce] smoke from a flash, but out of smoke to elicit fire, that he may thence bring forth his instances of the marvelous with beauty, [such as] Antiphates, Scylla, the Cyclops, and Charybdis. Nor does he date Diomed's return from Meleager's death, nor trace the rise of the Trojan war from [Leda's] eggs: he always hastens on to the event: and hurries away his reader into the midst of interesting circumstances, no otherwise than as if they were [already] known; and what he despairs of, as to receiving a polish from his touch, he omits; and in such a manner forms his fictions, so intermingles the false with the true, that the middle is not inconsistent with the beginning, nor the end with the middle.

Do you attend to what I, and the public in my opinion, expect from you [as a dramatic writer]. If you are desirous of an applauding spectator, who will wait for [the falling of] the curtain, and till the chorus calls out "your plaudits"; the manners of every age must be marked by you, and a proper decorum assigned to men's varying dispositions and years. The boy, who is just able to pronounce his words, and prints the ground with a firm tread, delights to play with his fellows, and contracts and lays aside anger without reason, and is subject to change every hour. The beardless youth, his guardian being at length discharged, joys in horses, and dogs, and the verdure of the sunny Campus Martius; pliable as wax to the bent of vice, rough to advisers, a slow provider of useful things, prodigal of his money, high-spirited, and amorous, and hasty in deserting the objects of his passion. [After this,] our inclinations being changed, the age and spirit of manhood seeks after wealth, and [high] connections, is subservient to points of honor; and is cautious of committing any action which he would subsequently be industrious to correct. Many inconveniences encompass a man in years; either because he seeks [eagerly] for gain, and abstains from what he has gotten and is afraid to make use of it: or because he transacts every thing in a timorous and dispassionate manner, dilatory, slow in hope, remiss, and greedy of futurity. Peevish, querulous, a panegyrist of former times when he was a boy, and chastiser and censurer of his juniors. Our advancing years bring many advantages along with them. Many our declining ones take away. That the parts [therefore] belonging to age may not be given to a youth, and those of a man to a boy, we must dwell upon those qualities which are joined and adapted to each person's age.

An action is either represented on the stage, or, being done elsewhere, is there related. The things which enter by the ear affect the mind more languidly, than such as are submitted to the faithful eyes, and what a spectator presents to himself. You must not, however, bring upon the stage things fit only to be acted behind the scenes: and you must take away from view many actions, which elegant description may soon after deliver in presence [of the spectators]. Let not Medea murder her sons before the people; nor the execrable Atreus openly dress human entrails; nor let Progne be metamorphosed into a bird, Cadmus into a serpent. Whatever you show to me in this manner, not able to give credit to, I detest.

Let a play which would be inquired after, and though seen, represented anew, be neither shorter nor longer than the fifth act. Neither let a god interfere, unless a difficulty worthy a god's unraveling should happen; nor let a fourth person be officious to speak.[2]

Let the chorus[3] sustain the part and manly character of an actor: nor let them sing anything between the acts which is not conducive to, and fitly coherent with, the main design. Let them both patronize the good,[4] and give them friendly advice, and regulate the passionate, and love to appease those who swell [with rage]: let them praise the repast of a short meal, the salutary effects of justice, laws, and peace with her open gates: let them conceal what is told to them in confidence, and supplicate and implore the gods that prosperity may return to the wretched, and abandon the haughty. The flute (not as now, begirt with brass and emulous of the trumpet, but), slender and of simple form, with few stops, was of service to accompany and assist the chorus, and with its tone was sufficient to fill the rows that were not as yet too crowded, where an audience, easily numbered, as being small and sober, chaste and modest, met together. But when the victorious Romans began to extend their territories, and an ampler wall encompassed the city, and their genius was indulged on festivals by drinking wine in the day-time without censure; a greater freedom arose both to the numbers [of poetry], and the measure [of music]. For what taste could an unlettered clown and one just dismissed from labors have, when in company with the

---

[2] The poet does not forbid a fourth person to speak, but would have him say very little, as the Scholiast understands the precept. Indeed, a conversation of three people is most agreeable, because it is less confused and less divides the attention of an audience.— Rodell.

[3] The chorus was not introduced between the acts, merely to relieve the audience, but had a part in the play, and concurred with the other actors to carry on the plot, and support the probability of it. The Choriphæus, or first person of the chorus, entered in the acts, and spoke for all those of whom the chorus was composed; "officiumque virile defendat." The chorus filled up the intervals of the acts with their songs, which were composed of reflections upon what was past, or their apprehensions of what might happen.— Francis.

[4] The chorus, says the poet, is to take the side of the good and virtuous; i. e. is always to sustain a moral character.

polite; the base, with the man of honor? Thus the musician added new movements and a luxuriance to the ancient art, and strutting backward and forward, drew a length of train over the stage: thus likewise new notes were added to the severity of the lyre, and precipitate eloquence produced an unusual language [in the theater]: and the sentiments [of the chorus, then] expert in teaching useful things and prescient of futurity, differ hardly from the oracular Delphi.

The poet who first tried his skill in tragic verse for the paltry [prize of a] goat, soon after exposed to view wild satyrs naked, and attempted raillery with severity, still preserving the gravity [of tragedy]: because the spectator on festivals, when heated with wine and disorderly, was to be amused with captivating shows and agreeable novelty. But it will be expedient so to recommend the bantering, so the rallying satyrs, so to turn earnest into jest; that none who shall be exhibited as a god, none who is introduced as a hero lately conspicuous in regal purple and gold, may deviate into the low style of obscure, mechanical shops; or, [on the contrary] while he avoids the ground, affect cloudy mist and empty jargon. Tragedy, disdaining to prate forth trivial verses, like a matron commanded to dance on festival days, will assume an air of modesty, even in the midst of wanton satyrs. As a writer of satire, ye Pisos, I shall never be fond of unornamented and reigning terms: nor shall I labor to differ so widely from the complexion of tragedy, as to make no distinction, whether Davus be the speaker. And the bold Pythias, who gained a talent by gulling Simo; or Silenus, the guardian and attendant of his pupil-god [Bacchus]. I would so execute a fiction taken from a well-known story, that anybody might entertain hopes of doing the same thing; but, on trial, should sweat and labor in vain. Such power has a just arrangement and connection of the parts: such grace may be added to subjects merely common. In my judgment, the Fauns, that are brought out of the woods, should not be too gamesome with their tender strains, as if they were educated in the city, and almost at the bar; nor, on the other hand, should blunder out their obscene and scandalous speeches. For [at such stuff] all are offended, who have a horse, a father, or an estate: nor will they receive with approbation, nor give the laurel crown, as the purchasers of parched peas and nuts are delighted with.

A long syllable put after a short one is termed an iambus, a lively measure, whence also it commanded the name of trimeters to be added to iambics, though it yielded six beats of time, being similar to itself from first to last. Not long ago, that it might come somewhat slower and with more majesty to the ear, it obligingly and contentedly admitted into its paternal heritage the steadfast spondees; agreeing, however, by social league, that it was not to depart from the second [5] and fourth place. But this [kind of measure] rarely makes its appearance in the notable [6] trimeters of Accius, and brands the verse of Ennius brought upon the stage with a clumsy weight of spondees, with the imputation of being too precipitate and careless, or disgracefully accuses him of ignorance in his art.

It is not every judge that discerns inharmonious verses, and an undeserved indulgence is [in this case] granted to the Roman poets. But shall I on this account run riot and write licentiously? Or should not I rather suppose, that all the world are to see my faults; secure, and cautious [never to err] but with hope of being pardoned? Though, perhaps, I have merited no praise, I have escaped censure.

Ye [who are desirous to excel], turn over the Grecian models by night, turn them by day. But our ancestors commended both the numbers of Plautus, and his strokes of pleasantry; too tamely, I will not say foolishly, admiring each of them; if you and I but know how to distinguish a coarse joke from a smart repartee, and understand the proper cadence, by [using] our fingers and ears.

5 The iambic yields only the odd places to the spondee, the first, third, and fifth, but preserves the second, fourth, and sixth for itself. This mixture renders the verse more noble, and it may be still *trimeter*, the second foot being iambic. The comic poets, better to disguise their verse, and make it appear more like common conversation, inverted the tragic order, and put spondees in the even places.—Dacier.

6 Ironically spoken.

Thespis [7] is said to have invented a new kind of tragedy, and to have carried his pieces about in carts, which [certain strollers] who had their faces besmeared with lees of wine, sang and acted. After him Æschylus, the inventor of the vizard mask and decent robe, laid the stage over with boards of a tolerable size, and taught to speak in lofty tone, and strut in the buskin. To these succeeded the old comedy, not without considerable praise: but its personal freedom degenerated into excess and violence, worthy to be regarded by law; a law was made accordingly, and the chorus, the right of abusing being taken away, disgracefully became silent.

Our poets have left no species of the art unattempted; nor have those of them merited the least honor, who dared to forsake the footsteps of the Greeks, and celebrate domestic facts; whether they have instructed us in tragedy, or in comedy. Nor would Italy be raised higher by valor and feats of arms, than by its language, did not the fatigue and tediousness of using the file disgust every one of our poets. Do you, the descendants of Pompilius, reject that poem, which many days and many a blot have not ten times subdued to the most perfect accuracy. Because Democritus believes that genius is more successful than wretched art, and excludes from Helicon all poets who are in their senses, a great number do not care to part with their nails or beard, frequent places of solitude, shun the baths. For he will acquire, [he thinks,] the esteem and title of a poet, if he neither submits his head, which is not to be cured by even three Anticyras, to Licinius the barber. What an unlucky fellow am I, who am purged for the bile in spring-time! Else nobody would compose better poems; but the purchase is not worth the expense. Therefore I will serve instead of a whetstone, which though not able of itself to cut, can make steel sharp: so I, who can write no poetry myself, will teach the duty and business [of an author]; whence he may be stocked with rich materials; what nourishes and forms the poet; what gives grace, what not; what is the tendency of excellence, what that of error.

To have good sense, is the first principle and fountain of writing well. The Socratic papers will direct you in the choice of your subjects; and words will spontaneously accompany the subject, when it is well conceived. He who has learned what he owes to his country, and what to his friends; with what affection a parent, a brother, and a stranger, are to be loved; what is the duty of a senator, what of a judge; what the duties of a general sent out to war; he, [I say,] certainly knows how to give suitable attributes to every character. I should direct the learned imitator to have a regard to the mode of nature and manners, and thence draw his expressions to the life.[8] Sometimes a play, that is showy with common-places, and where the manners are well marked, though of no elegance, without force or art, gives the people much higher delight and more effectually commands their attention, than verse void of matter, and tuneful trifles.

To the Greeks, covetous of nothing but praise, the muse gave genius; to the Greeks the power of expressing themselves in round periods. The Roman youth learn by long computation to subdivide a pound into an hundred parts. Let the son of Albinus tell me, if from five ounces one be subtracted, what remains? He would have said the third of a pound.— Bravely done! you will be able to take care of your own affairs. An ounce is added: what will that be? Half a pound. When this sordid rust and hankering after wealth has once tainted their minds, can we expect that such verses should be made as are worthy of being anointed with the oil of cedar, and kept in the well-polished cypress? [9]

---

[7] *Thespis.* A native of Icarius, a village in Attica, to whom the invention of the drama has been ascribed. Before his time there were no performers except the chorus. He led the way to the formation of a dramatic plot and language, by directing a pause in the performance of the chorus, during which he came forward and recited with gesticulation a very theological story. — Wheeler.

[8] Truth, in poetry, means such an expression, as conforms to the general nature of things; falsehood, that which, however suitable to the particular instance in view, doth yet not correspond to such general nature.— Tr.

[9] To preserve their books, the ancients rubbed them with oil of cedar, and kept them

Poets wish either to profit or to delight; or to deliver at once both the pleasures and the necessaries of life. Whatever precepts you give, be concise, that docile minds may soon comprehend what is said, and faithfully retain it. All superfluous instructions flow from the too full memory. Let whatever is imagined for the sake of entertainment, have as much likeness to truth as possible; let not your play demand belief for whatever [absurdities] it is inclinable [to exhibit]: nor take out of a witch's belly a living child, that she had dined upon. The tribes of the seniors rail against everything that is void of edification: the exalted knights disregard poems which are austere. He who joins the instructive with the agreeable, carries off every vote,[10] by delighting and at the same time admonishing the reader. This book gains money for the Sosii; this crosses the sea, and continues to its renowned author a lasting duration.

Yet there are faults, which we should be ready to pardon: for neither does the string [always] form the sound which the hand and conception [of the performer] intends, but very often returns a sharp note when he demands a flat; nor will the bow always hit whatever mark it threatens. But when there is a great majority of beauties in a poem, I will not be offended with a few blemishes, which either inattention has dropped, or human nature has not sufficiently provided against. What therefore [is to be determined in this matter]? As a transcriber, if he still commits the same fault though he has been reproved, is without excuse; and the harper who always blunders on the same string, is sure to be laughed at; so he who is excessively deficient becomes another Chœrilus; whom, when I find him tolerable in two or three places, I wonder at with laughter; and at the same time am I grieved whenever honest Homer grows drowsy? But it is allowable, that sleep should steal upon [the progress of] a long work.

As is painting, so is poetry: some pieces will strike you more if you stand near, and some if you are at a greater distance: one loves the dark; another, which is not afraid of the critic's subtile judgment, chooses to be seen in the light; the one has pleased once; the other will give pleasure if ten times repeated.

O you elder of the youths, though you are framed to a right judgment by your father's instructions, and are wise in yourself, yet take this truth along with you, [and] remember it; that in certain things a medium and tolerable degree of eminence may be admitted: a counselor and pleader at the bar of the middle rate is far removed from the merit of eloquent Messala, nor has so much knowledge of the law as Cassellius Aulus, but yet he is in request; [but] a mediocrity in poets neither gods, nor men, nor [even] the booksellers' shops have endured. As at an agreeable entertainment discordant music, and muddy perfume, and poppies mixed with Sardinian[11] honey give offense, because the supper might have passed without them; so poetry, created and invented for the delight of our souls, if it comes short ever so little of the summit, sinks to the bottom.

He who does not understand the game, abstains from the weapons of the Campus Martius: and the unskillful in the tennis ball, the quoit, and the troques, keeps himself quiet; lest the crowded ring should raise a laugh at his expense: notwithstanding this, he who knows nothing of verses presumes to compose. Why not! He is free-born, of a good family; above all, he is registered at an equestrian sum of monies, and clear from every vice. You, [I am persuaded,] will neither say nor do anything in opposition to Minerva: such is your judgment, such your disposition. But if ever you shall write anything, let it be submitted to the ears of Metius [Tarpa], who is a judge, and your father's, and mine; and let it be suppressed till the ninth year, your papers being laid up within your own custody. You will have it in your power to blot out what you have not made public: a word once sent abroad can never return.

---

in cases of cypress, because these kinds of wood were not liable to corruption.

10 *Omne tulit punctum.* Alluding to the manner of voting at the comitia by putting a point over the name of a candidate.— Tr.

11 Sardinia was full of bitter herbs, from whence the honey was bitter. White poppy seed, roasted, was mingled with honey by the ancients.

Orpheus, the priest and interpreter of the gods, deterred the savage race of men from slaughters and inhuman diet; hence said to tame tigers and furious lions. Amphion, too, the builder of the Theban wall, was said to give the stones motion with the sound of his lyre, and to lead them whithersoever he would, by engaging persuasion. This was deemed wisdom of yore, to distinguish the public from private weal; things sacred from things profane; to prohibit a promiscuous commerce between the sexes; to give laws to married people; to plan out cities; to engrave laws on [tables of] wood. This honor accrued to divine poets, and their songs. After these, excellent Homer and Tyrtæus animated the manly mind to martial achievements with their verses. Oracles were delivered in poetry, and the economy of life pointed out, and the favor of sovereign princes was solicited by Pierian strains, games were instituted, and a [cheerful] period put to the tedious labors of the day; [this I remind you of,] lest haply you should be ashamed of the lyric muse, and Apollo the god of song.

It has been made a question, whether good poetry be derived from nature or from art. For my part, I can neither conceive what study can do without a rich natural vein, nor what rude genius can avail of itself: so much does the one require the assistance of the other, and so amicably do they conspire [to produce the same effect]. He who is industrious to reach the wished-for goal, has done and suffered much when a boy; he has sweated, and shivered with cold; he has abstained from love and wine; he who sings the Pythian strains, was first a learner, and in awe of a master. But [in poetry] it is now enough for a man to say to himself: "I make admirable verses: a murrain seize the hindmost: it is scandalous for me to be outstripped, and fairly to acknowledge that I am ignorant of that which I never learned."

As a crier who collects the crowd together to buy his goods, so a poet rich in land, rich in money put out at interest, invites flatterers to come [and praise his works] for a reward. But if he be one who is well able to set out an elegant table, and give security for a poor

man, and relieve him when entangled in gloomy lawsuits; I shall wonder if with his wealth he can distinguish a true friend from a false one. You, whether you have made, or intend to make, a present to any one, do not bring him full of joy directly to your finished verses: for then he will cry out: "Charming, excellent, judicious"; he will turn pale; at some parts he will even distill the dew from his friendly eyes; he will jump about; he will beat the ground [with ecstasy]. As those who mourn friends at funerals for pay, do and say more than those that are afflicted from their hearts; so the sham admirer is more moved than he that praises with sincerity. Certain kings are said to ply with frequent bumpers, and by wine make trial of a man whom they are sedulous to know, whether he be worthy of their friendship or not. Thus, if you compose verses, let not the fox's concealed intentions impose upon you.

If you had recited anything to Quintilius, he would say, "Alter, I pray, this and this": if you replied, you could do it no better, having made the experiment twice or thrice in vain; he would order you to blot out, and once more apply to the anvil your ill-formed verses: if you choose rather to defend than correct a fault, he spent not a word more nor fruitless labor, but you alone might be fond of yourself and your own works, without a rival. A good and sensible man will censure spiritless verses, he will condemn the rugged, on the incorrect he will draw across a black stroke with his pen; he will lop off ambitious [and redundant] ornaments; he will make him throw light on the parts that are not perspicuous; he will arraign what is expressed ambiguously; he will mark what should be altered; [in short,] he will be an Aristarchus:[12] he will not say, "Why should I give my friend offense about mere trifles?" These trifles will lead into mischiefs of serious consequence, when once made an object of ridicule, and used in a sinister manner.

12 Aristarchus was a critic, who wrote above four score volumes of comments on the Greek poets. His criticisms on Homer were so much esteemed that no line was thought genuine until he had acknowledged it. He was surnamed the prophet or diviner, for his sagacity.— Francis.

Like one whom an odious plague or jaundice, fanatic phrensy or lunacy, distresses; those who are wise avoid a mad poet, and are afraid to touch him: the boys jostle him, and the incautious pursue him. If, like a fowler intent upon his game, he should fall into a well or a ditch while he belches out his fustian verses and roams about, though he should cry out for a long time, "Come to my assistance, O my country-men"; not one would give himself the trouble of taking him up. Were any one to take pains to give him aid, and let down a rope; "How do you know, but he threw himself in hither on purpose?" I shall say: and will relate the death of the Sicilian poet. Empedocles, while he was ambitious of being esteemed an immortal god, in cold blood leaped into burning Ætna. Let poets have the privilege and license to die [as they please]. He who saves a man against his will, does the same with him who kills him [against his will]. Neither is it the first time that he has behaved in this manner; nor, were he to be forced from his purposes, would he now become a man, and lay aside his desire of such a famous death. Neither does it appear sufficiently, why he makes verses: whether he has defiled his father's ashes, or sacrilegiously removed the sad enclosure of the vindictive thunder: it is evident that he is mad, and like a bear that has burst through the gates closing his den, this unmerciful rehearser chases the learned and unlearned. And whomsoever he seizes, he fastens on and assassinates with recitation: a leech that will not quit the skin, till satiated with blood.

THE MIDDLE AGES

DRAMATIC CRITICISM OF THE MIDDLE AGES

The absence of any body of dramatic work, and the unsettled conditions of Europe between the disintegration of the Roman Empire and the earliest dawn of the Renaissance, easily account for the dearth of dramatic criticism during the Middle Ages. Such doctrine as exists is in the form of more or less cut-and-dried commentary, most of it based on other work of a similar nature. Or else we have the altogether moral—chiefly non-literary—treatises of Tertullian (*De Spectaculis*) and of St. Cyprian on the same subject, dating respectively from the second and third centuries. The greater part of these treatises and fragments are little more than repetitions of the ideas of Aristotle and Horace or of other early Greek and Latin writers. The chief interest of the fragmentary tractates of Donatus, Evanthius, and Diomedes, is due to their preserving stray sentences from Cicero and Theophrastus. Donatus quotes Cicero's famous saying on comedy—that it is "imitatio vitae, speculum consuetudinis, imago veritatis"—Diomedes, Theophrastus' definitions of comedy and tragedy. Donatus (together with Evanthius—the commentaries *De Comœdia et Tragœdia* are often printed together) acquired no small degree of fame for his *Commentary* on Terence, which appeared for many years in nearly every edition of the Latin dramatist. Diomedes, another fourth century grammarian, devotes sections of the Third Book of his *Ars Grammatica* to a summary treatment of dramatic principles. This is based upon the non-extant *De Poetis* of Suetonius. The early Church Fathers—St. Ambrose, Lactantius, Chrysostom, Prudentius and even Augustine—had written on the drama, but their attitude, needless to say, was almost exclusively a moral one. The Seventh century scholar, Isidore of Seville, in his encyclopedic *Origines*—or *Etymologiae*—gives two small sections to drama, but these yield nothing new. They merely help bridge the gap from Horace to the Renaissance. The Moorish philosopher Averroës made an abridged version of Aristotle's *Poetics* in the Twelfth century, and added his commentary. Mr. Spingarn mentions Johannes Januensis de Balbis, who in the year 1286, distinguishes tragedy and comedy in his *Catholicon*. Horace who, as has been pointed out, was the chief inspiration of these sporadic treatises, is at least referred to by John of Salisbury (Twelfth century), in his *Policraticus*. The *Magnae Derivationes* of Uguccione da Pisa has been pointed out as a source of Dante's definitions of comedy and tragedy. Dante himself, in the fourteenth century, on the threshold of the Renaissance, still adheres to the Horatian theory. The brevity, the tone of final authority, the dependence on classical precedent in Dante's *Epistle* may well serve to illustrate the state of mind of mediæval scholars so far as they were concerned with dramatic theory.

General references on the literature of the Middle Ages:

J. E. Sandys, *A History of Classical Scholarship from the Sixth Century B. C. to the end of the Middle Ages* (Cambridge, 1903).
George Saintsbury, *A History of Criticism*, vol. I (New York, 1900).

J. E. Spingarn, *A History of Literary Criticism in the Renaissance* (2nd ed., New York, 1908). For additional matter, fuller bibl. and notes, see Fusco's translation, as *La Critica Letteraria nel Rinascimento*, with a preface by Croce (Bari, 1905).
W. P. Ker, *The Dark Ages* (New York, 1904).

A. Ebert, *Allgemeine Geschichte der Literatur des Mittelalters im Abendlande*, 3 vols. (Leipzig, 1874–87).

Max Manitius, *Geschichte der lateinischen Literatur des Mittelalters*. Teil I. (From Justinian to the middle of the 10th century.) (München, 1911.)

F. J. Snell, *The Fourteenth Century* (New York, 1899).

A. H. L. Heeren, *Geschichte der klassischen Literatur im Mittelalter*, 2 vols. (330–1400 A. D.) (Göttingen, 1822).

Amable Jourdain, *Recherches critiques sur l'age et l'origine des traductions latines d'Aristote, et sur les commentaires grecs ou arabes employés par les docteurs scolastiques* (2nd ed., Paris, 1843).

G. Gregory Smith, *The Transition Period* (New York, 1900).

Henry Hallam, *Introduction to the Literature of Europe, in the Fifteenth, Sixteenth, and Sevententh Centuries* (new ed., London, 1872).

Karl Borinski, *Die Antike in Poetik und Kunsttheorie. I. Mittelalter, Renaissance, Barock* (Leipzig, 1914).

Léon Clédat, *Le Théâtre au moyen-age* (Paris, 1897).

ÆLIUS DONATUS

The only facts known about Donatus are that he flourished in the middle of the fourth century, A. D., and that he was the teacher of St. Jerome. His best known works are the various grammatical and rhetorical treatises recently gathered together under the title of *Ars Grammatica;* the *Enarrationes* and scholia on the plays of Terence, and the fragment *De Comœdia et Tragœdia.* The *Grammar* was used for centuries and the word *Donat* became a common noun designating an elementary grammar. The *Commentaries* and fragment on *Comedy and Tragedy* were included in all the early printed editions of Terence. The influence exerted by these works extended throughout the Middle Ages into the seventeenth century, until the *Poetics* of Aristotle was known and accepted throughout the greater part of civilized Europe. Giraldi Cintio in Italy, and Lope de Vega in Spain, owe not a little to the *Commentaries* and the *De Comœdia et Tragœdia.*

The fragment here printed contains little that is new and original; the references and quotations from Horace are sufficient indication of the source of most of his ideas. His importance lies rather in the fact that he is the last of the Latins to formulate any theory, even a derived one, of the drama. He belongs to the Middle Ages in spirit; his scholastic mind and temper were evidently what appealed to his followers. He is the connecting link between Horace and Dante: Donatus is the last of the Romans: Dante, though his meager reference to drama is of the spirit of the Middle Ages is chronologically the immediate precursor of the early Renaissance critics.

Editions:

P. Wessner, *Aeli Donati quod tertur Comentum Terenti,* 2 vols. (Leipzig, 1902–05).

Donati Fragmentum de Comœdia et Tragœdia (in Gronovius' *Thesaurus Graecarum Antiquitatum*), vol. VIII (Venetiis, 1735).[1]

The first printed edition of the Commentaries on Terence was published at Cologne, 1470–72, and was followed by three others in the same century.—Most of these contained the *De Comœdia et Tragœdia.*

References: (On late Latin and Middle Ages literature, see references under Latin Dramatic Criticism.)

On Donatus and his works:

Encyclopedia Britannica, 11th ed., vol. 8 (Cambridge, 1910).

Nouvelle Biographie générale, vol. 14 (Paris, 1855).

---

[1] Together with this fragment is another, entitled *Eranthii et Donati de Tragœdia et Comœdia.*— Ed.

Biographie universelle, vol. 11 (Paris, 1852).

Ludwig Schopen, *De Terentio et Donato eius interprete* (Bonn, 1821).

Minton Warren, *On Five New Manuscripts of the Commentary of Donatus to Terence* (in *Harvard Studies in Classical Philology*, vol. XVII, Cambridge, U. S. A., 1906).

J. E. Sandys, *A History of Classical Scholarship*, vol. I (Cambridge, 1903).

G. Saintsbury, *A History of Criticism*, vol. 2 (New York, 1902).

J. E. Spingarn, *A History of Literary Criticism in the Renaissance* (New York, 1908).

Gustave Lanson, *L'Idée de la tragédie avant Jodelle* (in *Revue d'histoire littéraire de la France*, Paris, 1904).

Wilhelm Cloetta, *Beiträge zur Litteraturgeschichte des Mittelalters und der Renaissance* (Halle, 1890–92).

H. T. Karsten, *De comm. Don. ad Terenti fabulas origine et compositione* (Leiden, 1907).

ON COMEDY AND TRAGEDY [1]
[De Comœdia et Tragœdia]
(4th Century A. D.)

Comedy is a story treating of various habits and customs of public and private affairs, from which one may learn what is of use in life, on the one hand, and what must be avoided, on the other. The Greeks defined it as follows: κωμωδία ἐστὶν ἰδιωτικῶν καὶ πολιτικῶν πραγμάτων ἀκίνδυνος περιοχή. Cicero says that comedy is "a copy of life, a mirror of custom, a reflection of truth." Comedies, moreover, are so named from early custom; since in country towns compositions of this sort were originally played among the Greeks; as in Italy the people used to be held at crossroads by games where a measure of speech was introduced while the acts were being changed. Or ἀπὸ των κωμῶν; this is, from the acts of the lives of men who inhabit country towns because of the mediocrity of the happy; not in kingly halls, like tragic characters. Comedy, indeed, comprises action and speech, since it is verse based upon a representation of life and an imitation of customs. It is uncertain which of the Greeks first invented comedy; of the Latins there is no doubt. Livius Andronicus first invented comedy and the national drama; he said, "Comedy is the mirror of everyday life," nor was this without reason. For as we gaze into a mirror we easily perceive the features of the truth in the reflection; and so, in reading a comedy do we easily observe the reflection of life and of cus-

tom. The plan of its origin moreover comes all the way from foreign states and customs, for the Athenians, preserving the culture of Attica, when they wished to observe people living evil lives, used to come from every quarter with joy and alacrity to the country towns and there used to make known the life of individuals using their names; hence the name is made, as it is called in a comedy. These compositions, moreover, were first acted in pleasant meadows. Nor were rewards lacking whereby the talents of learned men might be incited to the art of writing; prizes were offered to the actors as well, that they might practice the pleasing modulations of speech for the pleasure of praise. Also a goat was given to them, because this animal was considered a charm against mistakes; hence the name of tragedy. Some, however, preferred that tragedy should be spoken of and called from the lees, or dregs of oil, which is a watery fluid. When these plays were first acted by artists for the glory of Father Liber, the actual authors of the comedies and tragedies began to worship and adore the divinity of this god as to a paternal deity. A probable explanation of this exists; for these unfinished verses were so produced that it was best for his glory and wondrous deeds to be thereby honored and proclaimed; then, little by little the renown of this art spread. Thespis, however, first brought these writings to the notice of every one. Afterwards, Æschylus, following the ex-

---

[1] Translated, complete, for the present collection by Mildred Rogers. It has not before appeared in English.— Ed.

ample, made some public. Of these Horace speaks thus in his *De Arte Poetica:*

Ignotum tragicae genus invenisse Camaenae dicitur, et plaustris vexisse Poemata Thespis, quae canerent, agerentque peruncti faecibus ora post hunc personae, pallaeque repertor honestae Æschylus, et modicis instravit pulpita tignis: Et docuit magnumque loqui, nitique cothurno. Successit vetus hic Comoedia non sine multa laude: sed in vitium libertas excidit, et vim Dignam lege regi: lex est accepta: chorusque turpiter obticuit sublato jure nocendi. Nil intentatum nostri liquere Poetae: nec minimum meruere decus, vestigia Graeca ausi deserere, et celebrare domestica facta, vel qui praetextas, vel qui docuere togatas.

[see p. 33]

Story [*fabula*] is the generic term, and its two chief divisions are comedy and tragedy. If the plot be Latin it is called *Praetexta;* comedy has, moreover, many subdivisions. For it may be in Greek dress; in Roman, it may be a comedy of the booths — Atellanian — or farcical — *Rhintonica* — or the *bare-foot* — *Planipedia.* This term of *Bare-foot* is applied because of the low order of the plot or the poorness of the players, who wear no sock or buskin on the stage or platform, but go bare-footed; or it may be because these comedies are not concerned with the affairs of people in towers or attics but of the inhabitants of low humble places. Cincius and Faliscus are said to have been the first actors who played comedy; Minutius and Prothonius the first who played tragedy.

All comedies are subdivided into four classes: the title-rôle, the scene of action, the situation, and the outcome. Here follow certain examples: of the title rôle, are the *Phormio*, the *Hecyra*, the *Curculio*, the *Epidicus.* Of the scene are the *Andria*, the *Leucadia*, and the *Brundisina.* Of the situation are the *Eunuchus*, the *Asinaria*, and the *Captivi.* Of the outcome are the *Commorientes*, the *Adelphi*, and the *Heautontimorumenos.* There are three kinds of comedy: the *Palliata*, in which the actors wear Greek costumes; by some this is called the *Tabernaria.* Secondly, the *To-*

gata, in which the actors wish to wear togas. Thirdly, the *Atellana;* this sort of comedy is full of witticisms and jokes; this is a time-honored form. Every comedy is divided into four parts: the prologue, the *Protasis*, the *Epitasis*, and the *Catastrophe.* The prologue is the first speech, called πρόλογος by the Greeks; that is, an address preceding the actual structure of the story. There are four kinds of prologues: Συσατικὸς, a laudatory passage wherein the author or the story is praised; Αναποριϰὸς, one in which an opponent is cursed or the audience thanked; Ὑποθετιϰὸς, one telling the plot of the play; and one, Μιϰτὸς, a composite which contains all of the above elements. There were some who wished this to be between a prologue and a preface, inasmuch as a prologue is to a certain extent the introduction of the story wherein something more is told than in the plot, to the audience; either from the poet or from needs of the drama itself or the actor. The preface is where an account of the plot is given. The first part, or *Protasis*, is the beginning of the action of the drama, wherein part of the play is developed, and part withheld in order to create suspense. The second part, or *Epitasis* marked the ascent and further development of difficulties or, as I have said, the knot of the entire coil. The last part, or *Catastrophe,* is the solution, pleasing to the audience, and made clear to every one by an explanation of what has passed.

In a great many stories the titles themselves stand before the authors' names; in some, the authors precede the titles. Antiquity explains this variety of usage, for when certain narratives were first given out their titles were mentioned before their authors, so that no unpopularity could harm them because of the author. When, however, after the publication of many works the author had gained some renown, their names stood first, so that through the attraction of their names their works were successful.

It is obvious that acts were written for various games. For there are four kinds of games which the Curule Ædiles provided for the public. There are the *Megalenses* games, sacred to the great gods; these are called μεγαλεσίοs by the Greeks. There are the funeral games instituted to keep back the populace while the funeral rites decreed for a Patrician were being carried out. There are the plebeian games given for the benefit of the plebs. There are the Apollonian games sacred to Apollo. On the stage there were always two altars; one to the right for Liber, one to the left for the god in whose honor the festival was held. Hence Terence's Andrian says, *Ex ara hac sume verbenas.* [Take some foliage from the altar.]

They always bring on Ulysses in Greek costume either because he finally pretended madness when he wanted to be ruler so that he should not be forced ignorantly to go to war, or because of his unusual wisdom under the cover of which he was of such great help to his comrades. For his nature was always that of a deceitful person. Some say that the inhabitants of Ithaca, like the Locrians, always wore *pallas.* The actors impersonating Achilles and Neoptolemus wear diadems, though never royal scepters. The reason of this convention is held to be that they never entered the rites of conspiracy with the other Greek youths to carry on the war with Troy, nor were they ever under the command of Agamemnon.

The old men in comedies wear white costumes, because they are held to be the oldest sort. Young men wear a variety of colors. The slaves in comedy wear thick shawls, either as a mark of their former poverty, or in order that they may run the faster. Parasites wear twisted *pallas.* Those who are happy wear white robes; the unhappy wear soiled robes; the rich wear royal purple, paupers wear reddish-purple; the soldier carries a purple *chlamys;* a girl wears a foreign robe; a procurer, a robe of many colors; yellow, to designate greed, is given to the courtesan. These garments are called *syrmata* — attired in trains because they are dragged. This custom originated from the luxuriant extravagances of the stage. The same garments worn by mourning characters denote neglect through carelessness.

Woven curtains are spread on the stage as ornament; they are painted in many colors, and were used in Rome after the custom of the Attalian kingdom; in place of these, Liparian hangings were used at a later period. There is also a curtain used for farces; this is hung before the audience while the sets of the production are being changed.

The actors speak the dialogue. The songs are arranged in measures, not by the author, but by some one skilled in music of this sort. For all the songs are not sung throughout in the same measures, but in different ones, in order to mark which group of three are singing the reciprocal measures of the song. The people who used to make this sort of measures placed their name at the front, above the title and the author and the cast.

Songs of this sort were arranged for flutes so that when these had been heard, many of the people could learn what play was going to be acted before the title was announced to the audience. They were, moreover, played on "equal" or "unequal" flutes, and right- or left-handed. The right-handed, or Lydian, ones proclaimed the production of a comedy of serious and solemn character; the left-handed, or Serranian, ones announced humor in the comedy in the lightness of its catastrophe. In cases, though, where a "right" and "left" ceremony was required, it meant that the play combined seriousness and gayety combined.

DANTE ALIGHIERI

Dante Alighieri was born at Florence in May, 1265. His family was of noble extraction, though they had been for some time in reduced circumstances. Little is known of the poet's early years except what is told in the *Vita Nuova:* his love for Beatrice, whom he first saw when he was nine years old. His second meeting, nine years later, resulted in the writing of his first known work, a sonnet.

This sonnet, copies of which he sent to various poets, brought him friends, chief among whom was Guido Cavalcanti. Beatrice died in 1290, and the young Dante devoted himself heart and soul to the study of philosophy and literature. At the same time, however, he engaged in business and political enterprises. In 1289 he fought with the Florentine Guelfs in the Battle of Campaldino. In the *Divina Commedia* he relates that he was engaged in other battles. Not later than 1298 Dante married. Of his married life little is known, except that when he settled at Ravenna in later years his wife was not with him. They had four children, all of whom were born in Florence before 1304. In 1295, or the year after, he enrolled in the Guild of Physicians and Apothecaries, and began an active political career, which was to end in disaster. In the year 1300 he went as ambassador to San Gimignano on a special mission. Soon after, in the same year, he was elected one of the six Priors, who stood highest in the government of Florence. It was not long before one of the numerous political feuds — between the Blacks and the Whites — broke out. The leaders of both factions were banished, and Dante was sent on a mission to Rome. In his absence from home, in 1301, Charles of Valois entered Florence and sowed seeds of discord. The next year Dante learned that he had been fined on a false charge of corrupt dealings. He disregarded the fine and was condemned to exile on pain of death. He never saw Florence again. For nearly twenty years he lived in poverty, wandering from city to city. Very little is known of these last years. He went first to Siena, where he joined other conspirators in an attempt to return, but in 1304 he left the conspirators, and went to Verona and later Padua. He was in Paris, and perhaps in England during the following years, but was again in Italy in 1310 and 1311. The letters he wrote to the Florentines at that time, full of imprecations and threats, resulted in his exclusion from the number of exiles who were finally allowed to return in 1311. After further wanderings, he went to Verona again, where he was the guest of Can Grande della Scala, to whom he wrote his famous *Epistle.* In 1317 or 1318 he went to Ravenna, where he lived with his children and finished the *Divina Commedia,* on which he had been working for many years. Toward the end of his life he visited Mantua and Piacenza. In 1321 he was sent as ambassador to Venice to settle a dispute, but the Venetians, refusing to allow the ambassadors to return by sea, forced them to pursue a difficult and unhealthy route; Dante was taken ill in consequence, and in September, 1321, died at Ravenna.

The *Epistle to Can Grande* was written not later than 1318, and was first printed, in very corrupt form, by G. Baruffaldi (Venice, 1700). It contains a full explanation of the scope and purpose of the *Divina Commedia.* Dante's remarks on comedy, which are here re-printed, are incidental. They are interesting rather as a link in the dramatic tradition extending from Donatus to the early Renaissance critics, than as an intrinsically valuable document. Dante reiterates the usual philological statement as to the etymology of the word "Comedy" and quotes Horace in support of his use of the word in connection with his poem.

Editions:

Among the standard texts of Dante containing the *Epistolæ* is *Tutte le opere di Dante Alighieri; nuovamente rivedute nel testo dal Dr. E. Moore,* etd., with dictionary, indexes, etc., by Paget Toynbee (3rd ed., Oxford, 1904), and Karl Witte's *Dantis Alighieri Epistolae quae extant, cum notis* (Patavii, 1827). Besides the translation here used, are: P. H. Wicksteed, *Translation of the Latin Works of Dante* (London, 1904), and Katharine Hilliard's translation of the *Convito* (London, 1889).

On Dante and his works:
Edward Moore, *Studies in Dante,* 4 series (Oxford, 1896–1917).
Charles Allen Dinsmore, *Aids to the Study of Dante* (Boston, 1903).
C. H. Grandgent, *Dante* (New York, 1916).
J. R. Smith, *The Earliest Lives of Dante* (New York, 1901).
Paget Toynbee, *Dante Alighieri, His Life and his Works* (4th ed., New York, 1910).

Paget Toynbee, *Dante Studies and Researches* (London, 1902).

G. A. Scartazzini, *Enciclopedia Dantesca*, 2 vols. (Milano, 1905).

George Saintsbury, *A History of Criticism*, vol. 1 (New York, 1902).

Vittorio Imbriani, *Studi Danteschi* (Firenze, 1891).

Karl Witte, *Dante-Forschungen*, 1st and 2nd series (Halle, 1869, Heilbronn, 1876. Translated by C. Mabel Lawrence and Philip H. Wicksteed as *Essays on Dante*, Boston, 1898).

Cesare Balbo, *Vita di Dante* (augmented ed., Firenze, 1853).

F. J. Snell, *Handbook to the Works of Dante* (London, 1909).

Special references on the *Epistle to Can Grande*:

C. S. Latham, *A Translation of Dante's Eleven Epistles* (Boston, 1892).

Francesco d'Ovidio, *L'Epistola a Cangrande* (In *Revista d'Italia*, anno 2, v. 3, Roma, 1899).

Francesco Torraca, *L'Epistola a Cangrande* (In *Revista d'Italia*, anno 2, pp. 601–636, Roma, 1899).

C. H. Herford, *Dante's Theory of Poetry* (In *Quarterly Review*, v. 213, London, 1910).

EPISTLE TO CAN GRANDE [1]

[Epistola XI]

(Written about 1318)

Section 10.— The title of the book is: "Here beginneth the Comedy of Dante Alighieri, a Florentine by birth, but not by character." And for the comprehension of this it must be understood that the word "Comedy" is derived from κώμη, village, and ᾠδή, which meaneth song; hence comedy is, as it were, a *village song*. Comedy is in truth a certain kind of poetical narrative that differeth from all others. It differeth from tragedy in its subject-matter,— in this way, that Tragedy in its beginning is admirable and quiet, in its ending or catastrophe foul and horrible; and because of this the word "Tragedy" is derived from τράγος, which meaneth *goat*, and ᾠδή. Tragedy is, then, as it were, a *goatish song;* that is, foul like a goat, as doth appear in the tragedies of Seneca. Comedy, indeed, beginneth with some adverse circumstances, but its theme hath a happy termination, as doth appear in the comedies of Terence. And hence certain writers were accustomed to say in their salutations in place of a greeting, "a tragic beginning and a comic ending." Likewise they differ in their style of language, for Tragedy is lofty and sublime, Comedy mild and humble,— as Horace says in his *Poetica*, where he concedeth that sometimes comedians speak like tragedians and conversely:

Interdum tamen et vocem comoedia tollit,
Iratusque Chremes tumido delitigat ore;
Et tragicus plerumque dolet sermone pedestri.

From which it is evident why the present work is called a comedy. For if we consider the theme, in its beginning it is horrible and foul, because it is Hell; in its ending, fortunate, desirable, and joyful, because it is Paradise; and if we consider the style of language, the style is careless and humble, because it is the vulgar tongue in which even housewives hold converse. . . .

[1] Extract from *A Translation of Dante's Eleven Letters*, by C. S. Latham (Boston, 1892).

ITALY — I

THE RENAISSANCE

ITALIAN DRAMATIC CRITICISM OF THE RENAISSANCE

The Italian Renaissance, bringing with it as it did a re-birth of interest in the art and literature of antiquity, is the starting point of modern literary criticism. After the discovery of the ancient texts, commentators, translators, editors were not wanting, and it was not long before they began to expound theories of their own. It has already been shown (p. 28) how the *Ars Poetica* of Horace had been the basis of what was written on the subject of the drama between the Augustan period and the early Renaissance. Donatus and Diomedes both quote largely from it, and most of their ideas were based upon it. Aristotle, on the other hand, was practically unknown; his influence in classical antiquity was, according to Spingarn, "so far as it is possible to judge, very slight." The manuscript of the *Poetics* was preserved in the East. The first Oriental version was translated from the Syriac into Arabic (about 935 A. D.) by Abu-Baschar. In the twelfth century Averroës made an abridged version; this in turn was translated into Latin in the thirteenth century by a German of the name of Hermann, and by Mantinus of Tortosa in Spain in the fourteenth. One of the extremely rare references to Aristotle is found in Roger Bacon; Petrarch just mentions him.

Giorgio Valla published his Latin translation of the *Poetics* at Venice in 1498. This was followed by the Aldine edition of the original Greek text in 1508. In 1536 Allessandro de' Pazzi published the Greek original together with a revised Latin text, and in 1548 Robortello published the first commentary (with a Latin translation). Bernardo Segni, in 1549, was the first to publish an Italian translation.

Among the earliest treatises on the art of poetry was that of Vida, whose *De Arte Poetica* appeared in 1527; contrary to practically every other work of similar title, this influential poem contains no reference to the drama. Two years later, however, Trissino published the first four books of his *Poetica*, but not until 1563, when two books were added, did he consider the drama. Dolce's translation of Horace in 1535 was followed the next year by the vernacular *Poetica* of Daniello, whose few references to tragedy and comedy, based upon Horace and Aristotle, are the first of their kind to appear in the Italian language. The same year saw Pazzi's edition and Trincaveli's Greek text. From this time on, the influence of Aristotle as an arbiter in the art of poetry was to spread. Robortello's *In Librum Aristotelis de Arte Poetica Explicationes* (1548) is the first complete commentary on the *Poetics*. Segni's translation was published the next year. In 1550 appeared Maggi's *Explicationes* (written with Lombardi), similar to the commentary of Robortello. Both are diffuse, detailed, and pedantic, and rarely depart from what the authors understood, or misunderstood, in Aristotle. Muzio [Mutio] published an *Arte Poetica* in 1551. Varchi in his *Lezzioni* (1553) upheld the Aristotelian ideals of tragedy. The *Discorso sulle Comedie e sulle Tragedie* of the famous novelist Giraldi Cintio, which was written in 1543, but not published until 1554, carried on the Aristotelian tradition begun by Daniello. This was to continue in one form or another throughout the Renaissance and be taken up later in France. Minturno's two treatises, *De Poeta* (1559) and *Arte Poetica* (1564), the first in Latin, the second in Italian, were the fullest discussions of the theory of poetry and drama yet written. The influence of Aristotle and Horace is everywhere evident, but, as will be seen from the extracts here printed, the Italian critic has expounded and amplified after his own manner. The *Commentarii* of Vettori [Victorius], printed in 1560, was another Latin treatise explaining the *Poetics*. The following year Julius Cæsar Scaliger, one of the most influential theorists since antiquity, published his Latin work, *Poetices Libri Septem*. As Scaliger had lived in France for some years (his book was published at Lyons) and was acquainted with many contemporary writers, his influence was widespread, though not so much so during the sixteenth as the seventeenth century. The *Poetics* of Scaliger, which was an "attempt to reconcile Aristotle's *Poetics*, not only with the precepts of Horace and the definitions of the Latin grammarians, but with the whole practice of Latin tragedy, comedy, and epic poetry," is a long, erudite and dogmatic treatise in which the canons of Aristotle are narrowed and confined to rules of the strictest sort. In 1563 the last two parts of Trissino's *Poetica* appeared. Castelvetro was the next to enter the field of criticism. His *Poetica* (a commentary on and translation of Aristotle's *Poetics*) was published in 1570. This work was of prime importance, for one reason because it contained the first formulation of the unity of place, supposed to have been derived from Aristotle. The immediate effect of this, as will be seen later, was to start the endless discussion in France of the famous "three Unities." Jean de la Taille, in 1572, was the first to insist on them in that country. Castelvetro was likewise the first to consider a play as limited and directly affected by stage representation. The Italian critics from the time of Castelvetro to the end of the century, carried on discussions of varying degrees of importance, though none of them exerted an influence equal to that of Scaliger, Castelvetro or Minturno. Piccolomini's edition of the *Poetics* was published in 1575, Viperano's *De Arte Poetica* in 1579. Patrizzi's *Della Poetica* (1586), Tasso's *Discorsi dell' Arte Poetica* (1587), Denores' *Poetica* (1588), Buonamici's *Discorsi Poetici* (1597), Ingegneri's *Poesia Rappresenta-*

tiva (1598), and Summo's *Discorsi Poetici* (1600), testify to the prodigious activity of the period.

Such are the outstanding works which treat in greater or less degree the theory of the drama. If we add the prefaces and prologues to the plays of Cecchi, Giraldi Cintio, Gelli, Aretino, and Il Lasca (the *Gelosia*, *Strega*, and *L'Arzigoglio* in particular) and the references in the works of Speroni,[1] Luisino,[2] Partenio,[3] Fracastoro,[4] Capriano,[5] Michele,[6] Beni,[7] and Zinano[8] are included, the list of writers on the subject of the drama is nearly exhausted.

The Renaissance critics had discovered Aristotle; the study of the *Poetics*, and that of the *Ars Poetica* of Horace, was the basis of their commentaries. Much of the great mass of this material is textual comment, more or less intelligent and illuminating; much is repetition, classification, philological analysis; but out of it all there emerges the true spirit of enlightened criticism. The beginning of the sixteenth century was a period of darkness; the end found Italy the fountain-head of Europe. France, Spain; and England, followed in her wake, adopting with modifications what she had been the first to discover and discuss.

[1] A letter, written in 1565, on the interpretation of the word *katharsis*. (Sperone Speroni, vol. V, *Opere*, Venezia, 1740.) Also *Giuditio sopra la tragedia de Canace*, etc. (1550).

[2] F. Luisino, *In Librum Q. Horatii Flacci de Arte Poetica Commentarius* (1554).

[3] B. Partenio, *Della Imitatione Poetica* (1560).

[4] G. Fracastoro, *Naugerius, sive de Poetica Dialogus* (1555).

[5] G. P. Capriano, *Della Vera Poetica* (1555).

[6] Agostino Michele, *Discorso in cui si dimostra come si possono scrivere le Commedie e le Tragedie in Prosa* (1592).

[7] Paolo Beni, *Disputatio in qua ostenditur præstare Comœdiam atque Tragœdiam metrorum vinculis solvere* (1600).

[8] Zinano, *Discorso della Tragedia* (Reggio, 1590).

References on Italian literature in general:

G. Tiraboschi, *Storia della letteratura italiana*, 9 vols. (Firenze, 1805–1813).

F. De Sanctis, *Storia della letteratura italiana*, 2 vols. (6th ed. Napoli, 1893).

A. Bartoli, *Storia della letteratura italiana*, 7 vols. (Firenze, 1878–89).

F. Flamini, *Studi di storia letteraria italiana e straniera* (Livorno, 1895).

G. Koerting, *Geschichte der Literatur Italiens im Zeitalter der Renaissance*, 3 vols. (Leipzig, 1878–84).

A. Gaspary, *Geschichte der italienischen Literatur,* 2 vols. (Strassburg, 1885–88).

A. Ebert, *Allgemeine Geschichte der Literatur des Mittelalters im Abendland,* 3 vols. (Leipzig, 1874-87).

Nicola Zingarelli, *Storia letteraria d'Italia* (Milano, 1903).

A. D'Ancona e O. Bacci, *Manuale della letteratura italiana,* 5 vols. (Torino, 1897–1900).

G. Mazzoni, *Avviamento allo studio critico delle lettere italiane* (Firenze, 1907).

J. A. Symonds, *Renaissance in Italy,* 7 vols. (New York, 1888).

V. Canello, *Storia della letteratura italiana nel secolo XVI* (Milano, 1880).

B. Croce, *La Critica letteraria* (2nd ed., Roma, 1896).

——, *Estetica come scienza dell' espressione e linguistica generale* (2nd ed., Milano, 1904).

——, *Per la storia della critica e storiografia letteraria* (Napoli, 1903).

——, *Saggi sulla letteratura italiana del seicento* (Bari, 1910).

Francis Henry Cliffe, *A Manual of Italian Literature* (London, 1896).

Richard Garnett, *A History of Italian Literature* (New York, 1898).

W. Cloetta, *Beiträge zur Litteraturgeschichte des Mittelalters und der Renaissance,* 2 vols. (Halle, 1890–92).

Kritischer Jahresbericht über die Fortschritte der Romanischen Philologie (München, Leipzig, Erlangen, etc., 1890 to date), is always useful.

Robert F. Arnold, *Kultur der Renaissance* (Leipzig, 1905).

References on Italian drama:

A. d'Ancona, *Origini del teatro italiano,* 2 vols. (2nd ed., Torino, 1891).

Des Boulmiers, *Histoire anécdotique et raisonnée du théâtre italien,* etc., 7 vols. (Paris, 1769).

G. Apollinaire, *Le Théâtre italien* (Paris, 1910).

P. Bettoli, *Storia del teatro drammatico italiano dalla fine del secolo XV alla fine del secolo XIX* (Bergamo, 1901).

P. Emiliani-Giudici, *Storia del teatro in Italia* (Milano, 1860).

J. L. Klein, *Geschichte des italienischen Dramas* (Leipzig, 1868).

E. Masi, *Studi sulla storia del teatro italiano* (Firenze, 1891).

F. et C. Parfaict, *Histoire de l'ancien théâtre italien,* etc. (Paris, 1767).

L. Riccoboni, *Histoire du théâtre italien,* etc. (Paris, 1730).

——, *Dell' Arte Rappresentativa, Capitoli sei* (London, 1728).

E. Bertana, *La Tragedia* (In the *Storie dei generi letterati italiani,* Milano, 1906).

F. Neri, *La tragedia italiana del cinquecento* (Roma, 1904).

G. B. Pellizzaro, *La commedia del secolo XVI* (Vicenza, 1901).

D'Origny, *Annales du Théâtre italien depuis son origine jusqu'à nos jours,* 3 vols. (Paris, 1788).

A. Biancale, *La Tragedia italiana del 500* (Roma, 1901).

Luigi Tonelli, *Il Teatro italiano* (Milano, 1924).

References on the literature of the Italian Renaissance, especially on dramatic criticism:

J. E. Spingarn, *A History of Literary Criticism in the Renaissance* (2d ed., New York, 1908. Italian translation, *La Critica letteraria nel Rinascimento,* by Antonio Fusco, Bari, 1905, contains additional material and full bibliography).

George Saintsbury, *A History of Criticism,* vol. 2 (New York, 1902).

J. E. Sandys, *A History of Classical Scholarship,* vol. 2 (Cambridge, 1903).

Alfredo Rolla, *Storia delle idee estitiche in Italia* (Torino, 1905).

I. G. Isola, *Critica del Rinascimento,* 2 vols. (Livorno, 1907).

T. Klette, *Beiträge zur Geschichte und Litteratur der italienischen Gelehrtenrenaissance,* 3 parts (Greifswald, 1888–90).

K. Vossler, *Poetische Theorien in der italienischen Frührenaissance* (Berlin, 1900).

F. Foffano, *Ricerche letterarie* (Livorno, 1897).

Max J. Wolff, *Die Theorie der italienischen Tragödie im 16. Jahrhundert* (In *Archiv für der neueren Sprachen und Literaturen,* Bd. 128, n. serie, bd. 28, Braunschweig, 1912).

K. Borinski, *Die Poetik der Renaissance, und die Anfänge der litterarischen*

Kritik in Deutschland (Berlin, 1886).
——, *Die Antike in Poetik und Kunst-theorie. I, Mittelalter, Renaissance, Barock* (Leipzig, 1914).
H. Breitinger, *Les Unités d'Aristote avant le Cid de Corneille* (2nd ed., Genève, 1895).
J. Ebner, *Beitrag zu einer Geschichte der dramatischen Einheiten in Italien* (Erlangen, 1898).
A. Graf, *Attraverso il Cinquecento* (Torino, 1888).
A. Benoist, *Les Théories dramatiques avant les Discours de Corneille* (In *Annales de la Faculté des Lettres de Bordeaux,* 1891).
Aug. Théry, *Histoire des opinions littéraires chez les anciens et chez les modernes,* 2 vols. (new ed., Paris, 1849).
L. Ceci, *Un' occhiata allo svolgimento storico della critica letteraria e politica del seicento* (Firenze, 1878).
Dannheisser, *Zur Geschichte der Einheiten* (In *Zeitschrift für französische Sprache und Litteratur,* v. XIV (1892).

BERNARDINO DANIELLO

Nothing is known of the life of Bernardino Daniello except that he was a native of Lucca and that he died at Padua in 1565. He was a scholar, he made translations from and commentaries on classical works, and wrote on Dante. His *Poetica* was his most famous work.

Daniello's *Poetica* (1536) is without doubt the first work of its sort since antiquity, and the few passages relating to the drama are of great historical importance. Daniello's ideas are of course derived from the ancients, but they are clearly stated, and must have exercised a profound influence over his contemporaries and successors. Saintsbury says: "The first author of one [a theory of poetry] is generally taken to be Daniello ... it has such good claims to be among the very earliest vernacular disputations of a general character on poetry in Italy." There is a mixture of Aristotle and Horace in the work. According to

Spingarn, "In the *Poetica* of Daniello (1536) occurs the first allusion in modern literary criticism to the Aristotelian notion of ideal imitation." The idea that it is the function of the poet to teach and to delight is decidedly Horatian, as are indeed the critic's rules for tragedy and comedy.

Edition:

The only edition of Daniello's *Poetic* is that printed at Venice in 1536: *La Poetica di Bernardino Daniello Lucchese.*

On Daniello and his works:

Colle, *Storia scientifica-letteraria dello studio in Padua* (Padova, 1824–25).
J. E. Spingarn, *A History of Literary Criticism in the Renaissance* (New York, 1908).
George Saintsbury, *A History of Criticism,* vol. 2 (New York, 1902).

POETICS [1]
[*La Poetica*]
(1536)

... And the materials and subjects may be many and varied, for to some, as to the writers of comedy, they may be of more common stuff: every-day occurrences, not to say lowly and common-

place, while the tragic poets treat of deaths of high kings and the ruin of great empires. ...   [p. 34.]

... Similarly, one must be careful that the plot of tragedies be clearly put together, and as tragedy is an imitation of

[1] Translated selections by Lander MacClintock.—Ed.

the most terrible and pitiful things, it does not seem to me permissible to introduce into it just and virtuous men changed into unjust and wicked ones through the adversity of fortune — a thing rather shocking than pitiful or fearful. On the contrary, one must show the wicked and the evil changed by fortune into good and just men. Nor does one deny the right to the tragic poet to lower himself when he wishes, to humble speech, in order to weep and lament. For it does not seem right for a man who is banished from his country, however great and noble his lineage, to use pompous and proud words to other people. Nor is the writer of comedy to be prevented from using some of the grandiloquence of the tragic poet, on occasion. As for instance, an angry father to his son in order to have more power and influence over him. And since some things are done on the stage and some only referred to, it behoves us to see what can be acted, and what cannot. The things which cannot be done are the cruel deeds, the impossible, and the unseemly. As if Medea, in full view of the gaping multitude should kill her own children and then tear the murdered ones

limb from limb. And as if Progne with her husband and sister and sons should, in full view of the spectators, grow wings and become birds; and in comedies there should be lascivious kisses, embraces, and the like. Comedy should not exceed the limit of five acts, nor comprise less; four characters must not speak at once, but only two or three at most, while the others stand to one side quietly listening. Nor must any deity be brought in, except in cases where man is unable by his own efforts to unravel some tangle without divine aid and intercession. Let the chorus in tragedy (since they are no longer employed in comedy, but in their stead, and between the acts music and songs and *Moresche* and jesters, in order that the stage may not remain empty)— let the chorus in tragedy, I say, take the part of the just and the good, wrongfully oppressed, and favor these. Let them advise friends, favor those who hate sin, laud sobriety, justice, law, and peace, and pray the gods that, disdaining fortune, lofty palaces and proud towers with their summits menacing heaven, they descend to console the miserable and the afflicted.　　[p. 38.]

.　　.　　.　　.　　.

ANTONIO SEBASTIANO (MINTURNO)

Antonio Sebastiano, better known under the name of Minturno, was born at Trajetto. Very little is known of his life, which was spent in the church. He was Bishop of Ugento, and assisted at the Council of Trent. In 1565 he was transferred to Crotone in Calabria, where he died in 1574. Besides his *Poetica* and *De Poeta,* he wrote a number of religious works and some *Rime.* In his day, he was considered a man of great learning.

To the contributions to the Renaissance theory of poetry Minturno has added the Horatian element of " delight," as well as instruction. Minturno's interpretation of Aristotle is on the whole intelligent and illuminating. The first of Minturno's two treatises was the *De Poeta,* written in Latin and published in 1559. It is a long and thoroughgoing Art of Poetry, based upon Lat-

in literature; the *Arte Poetica,* in Italian, published in 1563, takes its examples to a certain extent from Italian literature, though of necessity most of the plays discussed are Greek and Latin. While both works are similar in character, there is, on the whole, very little repetition in the *Poetica,* which is a much clearer and more interesting treatment of the subject than the *De Poeta.* Minturno's treatises soon became known abroad, and his influence was felt in Spain, France, and England, at a comparatively early date.

Editions:

The *De Poeta Libri Sex* was published at Venice in 1559, the *Arte Poetica,* also at Venice, in 1563. Neither has been translated. In H. B. Charlton's *Castelvetro's Theory of Poetry* (Manchester, 1913), there are many quotations from both works.

On Minturno and his works:

Nouvelle Biographie générale, vol. 38 (Paris, 1861).

Nuova Enciclopedia italiano, vol. 14 (Torino, 1882).

Crescimbeni, Istoria della vulgar poesia Lib. II (Roma, 1698, and later).

René Rapin, Avertissement (In Réflexions touchant la Poétique, Paris, 1674.

His critical Works, translated, appeared in London in 1706).

Ughelli, Italia Sacra, vol. IX (ed. 1721).

H. Breitinger, Les Unités d'Aristote avant le Cid de Corneille (Genève, 1895).

J. E. Spingarn, A History of Literary Criticism in the Renaissance (2nd ed., New York, 1908).

George Saintsbury, A History of Criticism, vol. 2 (New York, 1902).

THE ART OF POETRY [1]

[Arte Poetica]

(1563)

. . . . .

Ang. What is dramatic poetry?

Min. Imitations of things — to be presented in the theater — complete and perfect in form and circumscribed as to length. Its form is not that of narration; it introduces several persons who act and converse. Their speech is suave and pleasing, and they may dance or sing, since dramatic poetry employs the three mediums of expression, using them individually or conjointly. Nor should there be lacking a proper stage equipment for the pleasure and profit of the onlooker.

Ang. How many kinds of subjects are treated in the theater?

Min. Three in all. One class records serious and grave happenings and concerns those of high rank — the great and the illustrious. This is the field of the tragic poet. A second recognizes the middle strata of society — common folk of the city or the country: the farmer, the common soldier, the petty merchant, and similar persons. These afford matter for comedy. The third division has to do with humble persons, mean and ludicrous, with all those in fact who seem most fitted to provoke merriment, thus supplying subject matter for satirical poetry.

Ang. So, then, dramatic poetry is divided into three parts?

Min. It has in truth three divisions.

The first of these is called tragedy, the second comedy, and the third by the ancients was termed satyric drama.

Ang. A little later I will question you in detail concerning the nature of each of these forms. But now I should like to have you elucidate further the general definition of dramatic poetry.

Min. You will understand it clearly if you remember that during our conversation of yesterday I said that the dramatic poet differs in technique from the lyric or the epic poet. The lyric poet simply narrates, without laying aside his own personality; the epic poet sometimes retains his personality and sometimes abandons it, speaking at times for himself, and as often introducing other persons who speak. But the dramatic poet, of whom we are now speaking, from first to last speaks through the lips of others. This may be observed not only in the tragedies of Sophocles and of Euripides but also in some of our own — notably the work of Dolce and of Alemanni, two of the brightest ornaments of our literature — as well as in the comedies of Terence and Plautus.

. . . . .

Min. The common purpose of all poets is, as Horace teaches, that of providing pleasure and profit. But the manner in which each poet may delight and instruct will be demonstrated when we discuss the different forms of poetry. And although stage apparatus is a necessary complement of dramatic poetry, however, since dramatic poetry has three divisions, we

---

[1] Extracts here translated — by Ida Treat O'Neil — for the first time in English. The treatise is in dialogue form.— Ed.

can better understand what each division demands in the way of apparatus when discussing each of the three forms separately. So that, reserving the discussion of these two topics to a fitting place and time, there now remains for me to answer your question concerning the length of the dramatic form.

Ang. That, indeed, remains for discussion.

Min. How long a time should be given to the actual performance of the dramatic poem is not for the poet to determine. For even if there were a hundred tragedies or a hundred comedies to be presented, each would demand a certain definite period of time. Just as when there are many speakers and lawyers concerned in a single case, each must be given an opportunity for expression. But in so far as the nature of the subject is concerned, the action should be prolonged until there ensues some change of fortune — from good to ill, or from grievous to gay. One who carefully studies the works of the greatest among the ancients will discover that the action of the dramatic poem transpires in a day, or is never prolonged beyond two, just as it is said that the action of the longest epic poem should transpire in a year.

Ang. How much time shall we give to the performance of these poems, since their action takes place in less than two days?

Min. Not less than three hours nor more than four; lest neither too great brevity rob the work of its beauty and leave the desire of the hearers unsatisfied, nor excessive length deprive the poem of its proportion, spoil its charm, and render it boresome to the beholders. And indeed the wise poet should so measure the time with the matter to be presented that those who hear the work should rather deplore its brevity than regret having remained too long to listen.

Ang. I now understand perfectly the definition of dramatic poetry. Now will you tell me how many divisions there are to the dramatic poem, that I may better understand its composition?

Min. I shall answer you as I answered Signor Vespasiano yesterday when he questioned me concerning the parts of the epic poem, that the divisions are not of the same nature, since some concern the quality and some the quantity — that is, the body — of the work. And since the quality of the poem is due partly to the very essence of the work and partly to chance, there are six essential parts of such a poem: the plot, the manners or customs, the sentiments expressed, the words, the singing, and the apparatus of the stage. I shall not attempt to define four of these divisions, for they are characteristic of every form of poetry, and I have already spoken sufficiently concerning them during the discussion of epic poetry yesterday. I shall refer to them when it is necessary during the explanation of the individual poems. If you have no objection I shall postpone until that time the discussion of the singing and of the stage apparatus

Ang. And why not?

Min. It is a most reasonable arrangement, for dramatic poetry is either tragedy, or comedy, or satyric drama; that is to say, the genus is found in each of its species, nor can it be separated from them, as you may easily understand. Just as the animal is to be found in man, in the horse, in the lion, and in every other sort of animal, so it cannot exist independently, separated from them, except in the mind, or according to Plato, where mortal eye may not see.

Ang. I shall not ask you how the accidental quality of the poem may be divided, for I remember well that yesterday you informed Signor Vespasiano that such divisions are the episodes. These, like the plot, are imitations of the deeds and the sayings of others; they are garnished with the same ornaments as the plot, adorned with like colors, and tending toward the same end. And since the action of the poem must transpire in one or two days, and must arrive speedily at its conclusion in order to satisfy the impatience of the onlookers who cannot remain indefinitely in the theater, these episodes should be neither so frequent nor so long as in epic poetry, which may include the happenings of a year as well as many other incidents brought from without to render the poem longer and more varied. The episodes in a dramatic poem should be few and brief. But I should like to inquire how many and of what nature are the parts into which the body of the poem may be divided?

Min. We may say that there are four of them, since that was the opinion of Aristotle, and we shall name them as he did: Prologues, Discourses, Choruses, and Exits. I will reserve the explanation of each of these until I come to treat the different forms of dramatic poetry, since each of them has its prologues, its discourses, its choruses, and its exits.

.   .   .   .   .

Min. Tragedy is concerned with the imitation of serious and weighty happenings, embodied in a complete and perfect form, circumscribed as to length. The language of tragedy is suave. The divisions of the poem are so organized that each has its place. It does not simply narrate, but introduces persons who act and speak, arousing feelings of pity and terror, and tending to purge the mind of the beholder of similar passions, to his delight and profit.

Ang. Will you elucidate all the parts of the definition?

Min. In yesterday's discussion I spoke at length of the meaning of "imitation," which may be regarded as the basis of all poetry, as well as of painting and sculpture. In the same discourse I explained in full how the form, in every sort of poetry, must be unified, complete, and perfect, and of a given length. Today I have said enough concerning the length. But since every complete action has a beginning, a middle, and an end, as I demonstrated yesterday, we should consider not only how long the action should be prolonged and where it should finish, but also where it should begin. And truly, he who would make a good beginning in narrating an incident, should begin where it is fitting, neither commencing his narration with the most recent details, nor going back to those most remote and faraway.

.   .   .   .   .

Min. You are doubtless aware already that what distinguishes tragedy from comedy and satyric drama is the imitation of grave and weighty happenings, together with the ennobling influence upon manners. Thus, since these grave and weighty happenings furnish the matter for tragedy, the ennobling or purifi-cation of manners is the end toward which all effort is directed.

Ang. I should like you to speak at greater length concerning the matter and the purpose, particularly the purpose.

Min. Then, you will understand the purpose of tragic poetry when you have learned the mission of the tragic poet. His mission is no other than that of employing verses so instructive, so pleasing, and so moving, that they tend to purge of passion the mind of the hearer. All dramatic poets whose plays are presented in the theater declare that their mission is to instruct, but the tragic poet creates before our eyes an image of life, showing us the behavior of those who, remarkable among men for their rank, their position, and for the favors of fortune, have fallen into extreme misery through human error. From this we learn not to place too great trust in worldly prosperity, that nothing here below is so durable and stable that it may not fall and perish, no happiness but may change to misery, nothing so high but that it may become base and infamous. And seeing others endure such changes of fortune, we learn to guard against unexpected evil, and if misfortune does come, we may learn to endure it patiently. The tragic poet aside from the suavity of his verse and the elegance of his speech, affords much pleasure to the onlooker by the use of singing and dancing. In fact, he presents nothing that does not please us, nor does he move us without charm; but with the force of his words and the weight of his thoughts, he can stir up passions in the mind, producing wonder, fear, and pity. What is more tragic than to move others? What is so moving as the terrible unexpected, such as the cruel death of Hippolytus, the wild and piteous madness of Hercules, the unhappy exile of Œdipus? And all this terror and pity frees us most pleasantly from similar passions, for nothing else so curbs the indomitable frenzy of our minds. No one is so completely the victim of unbridled appetites, that, being moved by fear and pity at the unhappiness of others, he is not impelled to throw off the habits that have been the cause of such unhappiness. And the memory of the grave misfortunes of others not only renders us more ready and willing o support our own; it makes us more wary in avoiding like ills. The physician who with a powerful drug extinguishes the poisonous spark of the malady that afflicts the body, is no more powerful than the tragic poet who purges the mind of its troubles through the emotions aroused by his charming verses.

. . . . .

Min. Before I define comedy, I shall speak briefly of its three general divisions and how and when they came into being. During the feasts of Bacchus, or of the pastoral Apollo, the young men warmed with food and wine used to jest among themselves, speaking often of the defects of the great men of those days when the Republic was in the hands of the people, who listened eagerly to slander of the nobles and of the prominent citizens. It was this that gave the idea of comedy to the poets, already given to attacking the evil customs of the age. So it was that these poets, possessing a certain erudition and charm of style, following the custom of the young men at the feasts of their gods, began to write little plays and present them publicly.

. . . . .

Ang. But before you define comedy, tell me what is the mission of the comic poet?

Min. What else but that of teaching and pleasing? According to Plato, the gods took pity on the tedious life of mortals, wearied with never-ending tasks and labors, and that they might not lack recreations and that they might take heart again, the gods established festivals, banquets, and games, favored by Bacchus, Apollo, and the Muses. Then mankind, celebrating these holidays with poetry and with music, discovered comedy. And comedy not only delighted the hearer with imitations of pleasant things and with the charm of words, but since in those days poetry afforded a certain way in which to educate children to a proper manner of living — it even bet-

tered their lives, affording as it did an image of their customs and everyday existence. It pleased them greatly to see the happenings of their own lives enacted by other persons. I shall not speak of the suavity of the language which is always one of the delights of comedy. The comic poet moves his hearers, though he does not stir them as deeply as the tragic poet. The comic poet awakes in the souls of those who listen pleasant and humane feelings.

. . . . . .

Ang. Will you define comedy for us?

Min. Though Cicero may define comedy as an imitation of life, a mirror of manners, an image of truth, nevertheless according to the opinion of Aristotle, we might say that it is no other than an imitation of pleasing and amusing happenings, whether public or private. It must be presented in a complete and perfect form, and is circumscribed as to length. It does not consist of simple narration, but introduces persons of humble or mediocre fortune, who act and converse just as do the others. Its language is suave and pleasing, and it lacks neither singing nor dancing. . . . Its construction is even, and each part has its proper place.

Ang. Explain to me the divisions of the definition.

Min. I shall not speak of its presentation — in verses, with dancing and singing, sometimes with all three forms and sometimes with only part — nor concerning the subject matter or the form (that it should be unified and perfect and of a given length). I have already said enough concerning these things. Nor will I lose time in explaining that the incidents adapted to comedy are amusing and ludicrous, and that the persons are of humble station and equal rank; for this is the very nature of comedy, and is what distinguishes it from tragedy.

. . . . . .

JULIUS CÆSAR SCALIGER

Julius Cæsar Scaliger, as he called himself, was born probably at Padua in 1484. He was the son of Benedetto Bordoni, a miniature painter. His own version of his noble parentage and life's adventures has been discredited and it has been established that he studied at the University of Padua, was graduated with a degree of M.D., and left home to seek his fortune. He went to Verona, where he made many acquaintances. In 1525 the Bishop of Agen induced him to come to Agen, where he continued his practice. In France, where he spent the last part of his life, he fell in love with a young woman, and in 1528 became a naturalized Frenchman and married her. He pursued literary and scientific studies, which occupied him to the end of his life. Among his first literary efforts are his tracts attacking Erasmus; but the great scholar refused to reply. He then attacked Cardan, who died shortly after. During his long residence at Agen he gradually became known not only in France, but throughout Europe. One of the few facts in his life of which any record exists is a charge of heresy in 1538, but Scaliger was acquitted. He died at Agen in 1558, one of the most celebrated men of his time.

Besides the *Poetices,* Scaliger's literary works include a number of rather crude poems, several letters, dissertations and commentaries on Hippocrates, Aristotle, and Theophrastus, various fragments of treatises on botany, and a tractate on comic meters, *De comicis dimensionibus.* Few similar works have enjoyed such universal renown as the *Poetices Libri Septem,* first published at Lyons in 1561. The work, written in Latin, is long, rambling, sketchy, violent in tone, dogmatic, scholastic, and pedantic, but with all its imperfections it was the first work to attempt a standardization of literary form and content. Aristotle was not only Scaliger's guiding light; he was so twisted and misinterpreted as to become the most rigorous of taskmasters.

Editions:

The *Poetices Libri Septem* was first published at Lyons in 1561. Often reprinted during the sixteenth and seventeenth centuries. The only English translation is a slim volume of selections: *Select Translations from Scaliger's Poetics,* by F. M. Padelford (New York, 1905).

On Scaliger and his works:

Biographie universelle, vol. 38 (Paris, 1861).

Joseph Justus Scaliger, *De Vetustate et splendore gentis Scaligeræ et Julii Cæseris Scaligeri* (Leyden, 1594).

Magen, *Documents sur Julius Cæsar Scaliger et sa famille* (Agen, 1873).

Bourrousse de Laffore, *Etude sur Jules César de Lescale* (Agen, 1860).

J. E. Spingarn, *A History of Literary Criticism in the Renaissance* (New York, 1908).

George Saintsbury, *A History of Criticism,* vol. 2 (New York, 1902).

Victor Beranek, *Martin Optiz in seinem Verhältnis zu Scaliger und Ronsard* (Wien, 1883).

Jakob Bernays, *Zwei Abhandlungen über die aristotelische Theorie des Dramas* (Berlin, 1880).

E. Lintilhac, *De J.-C. Scaligeri Poetica* (Paris, 1887).

Scaligeriana, 2 series (complete ed., Amsterdam, 1740).

Eduard Brinkschulte, *Julius Cæsar Scaligers kunsttheoretische Anschauungen* (Bonn, 1913).

Charles Nisard, *Les Gladiateurs de la République des lettres au XVᵉ, XVIᵉ, et XVIIᵉ siècles,* 2 vols. (Paris, 1860).

H. Breitinger, *Les Unités d'Aristote avant le Cid de Corneille* (2nd ed., Genève, 1895).

Antoine Benoist, *Les Théories dramatiques avant les Discours de Corneille* (In *Annales des Facultés des lettres de Bordeaux,* 1892).

POETICS [1]

[Poetices Libri Septem]

(1561)

Tragedy, like comedy, is patterned after real life, but it differs from comedy in the rank of the characters, in the nature of the action, and in the outcome. These differences demand, in turn, differences in style. Comedy employs characters from rustic, or low city life, such as Chremes, Davus, and Thais. The beginning of a comedy presents a confused state of affairs, and this confusion is happily cleared up at the end. The language is that of everyday life. Tragedy, on the other hand, employs kings and princes, whose affairs are those of the city, the fortress, and the camp. A tragedy opens more tranquilly than a comedy, but the outcome is horrifying. The language is grave, polished, removed from the colloquial. All things wear a troubled look; there is a pervading sense of doom, there are exiles and deaths. Tradition has it that the Macedonian king Archelaus, the intimate friend and patron of Euripides, asked the poet to make him the hero of a tragedy, but that Euripides replied: "Indeed, I cannot do it; your life presents no adequate misfortune."

. . . . .

The definition of tragedy given by Aristotle is as follows: "Tragedy is an imitation of an action that is illustrious, complete, and of a certain magnitude, in embellished language, the different kinds of embellishments being variously employed in the different parts, and not in the form of narration, but through pity and fear effecting the purgation of suchlike passions." I do not wish to attack this definition other than by adding my own: A tragedy is the imitation of the adversity of a distinguished man; it employs the form of action, presents a disastrous dénouement, and is expressed in impressive metrical language. Though Aristotle adds harmony and song, they are not, as the philosophers say, of the essence of tragedy; its one and only essential is acting. Then the phrase "of

a certain magnitude" is put in to differentiate the tragedy from the epic, which is sometimes prolix. It is not always so, however, as the work of Musæus illustrates. Further, the mention of purgation is too restrictive, for not every subject produces this effect. "A certain magnitude," to return to the phrase, means not too long and not too short, for a few verses would not satisfy the expectant public, who are prepared to atone for the disgusting prosiness of many a day by the enjoyment of a few hours. Prolixity, however, is just as bad, when you must say with Plautus: "My legs ache with sitting, and my eyes with looking." (I, 6.)

. . . . .

Although tragedy resembles this epic poetry, it differs in rarely introducing persons of the lower classes, such as messengers, merchants, sailors, and the like. Comedies, on the other hand, never admit kings, save in such a rare instance as the *Amphitryon* of Plautus. I would limit this generalization, of course, to those plays which employ Greek characters and the Greek dress, for the Romans have admitted at will the dignified toga and *trabea.* . . . Tragedy and comedy are alike in mode of representation, but differ in subject-matter and treatment. The matters of tragedy are great and terrible, as commands of kings, slaughters, despair, suicides, exiles, bereavements, parricides, incests, conflagrations, battles, the putting out of eyes, weeping, wailing, bewailing, eulogies, and dirges. In comedy we have jests, revelling, weddings with drunken carousals, tricks played by slaves, drunkenness, old men deceived and cheated of their money. . . .

Now, a tragedy, provided it is a genuine tragedy, is altogether serious, but there have been some satyrical plays which differed little from comedies. Save in the gravity of some of the characters. We have an illustration in the *Cyclops* of Euripides, where all is wine and jesting, and where the outcome is so happy that all the companions of Ulysses are released, and the Cyclops

[1] Re-printed from *Select Translations from Scaliger's Poetics*, by F. M. Padelford (Yale University Press, New Haven, 1905). — Ed.

alone suffers in the loss of his eye. The conclusion of this play was not unlike that of a mime, for the stage was wholly deserted on the exit of Ulysses, the giant with the rock alone remaining.

There are, on the other hand, many comedies which end unhappily for some of the characters. . . . Hence it is by no means true, as has hitherto been taught, that an unhappy issue is essential to tragedy. It is enough that the play contain horrible events.

When authors take their plots from history, they must be careful not to depart too widely from the records. In the early writers such care was by no means taken. Thus Æschylus followed Greek history in binding Prometheus to the rock, but he invented the fiction of his undoing by the thunderbolt, for tragic effect. There should be no dire event at the end, but only at the beginning, where he is bound to Caucasus. However, some have it that the eagle was driven away by Hercules; others that he killed it with his arrows; and still others that Prometheus was set free by Jupiter himself, because he warned the god not to cohabit with Thetis, lest she should bear him a son more illustrious than the father. Euripides invented stories about Helen which were utterly contrary to well-known history. The same author has been censured for bringing wicked and impure women into his plays. What is viler, the critic says, than Phædra, Jocasta, Canace, and Pasiphae, by whose infamy society is corrupted? But we reply that these women were not creatures of his imagination, but were taken from life. Forsooth, if we are to hear of no wickedness, history must be done away with. So those comedies should be prized which make us condemn the vices which they bring to our ears, especially when the life of impure women ends in an unhappy death.

.   .   .   .   .

The events themselves should be made to have such sequence and arrangement as to approach as near as possible to truth, for the play is not acted solely to strike the spectator with admiration or consternation — a fault of which, according to the critics, Æschylus was often guilty — but should also teach, move, and please. We are pleased either with jests, as in comedy, or with things serious, if rightly ordered. Disregard of truth is hateful to almost every man. Therefore neither those battles or sieges at Thebes which are fought through in two hours please me, nor do I take it to be the part of a discreet poet to pass from Delphi to Athens, or from Athens to Thebes, in a moment of time. Thus Æschylus has Agamemnon killed and buried so suddenly that the actor has scarcely time to breathe. Nor is the casting of Lichas into the sea by Hercules to be approved, for it cannot be represented without doing violence to truth.

The content of a play should be as concise as possible, yet also as varied and manifold as possible; for example, Hecuba in Thrace, Achilles forbidding her return, Polydorus already killed, the murder of Polyxena, and the blinding of Polymnestor. Since dead persons cannot be introduced, their apparitions, or ghosts, or specters, are substituted. Thus, as noted above, Æschylus introduces the apparitions of Polydorus and Darius, and in Ovid, Ceÿx appears to Alcyone. If a tragedy is to be composed from this last story, it should not begin with the departure of Ceÿx, for as the whole time for stage-representation is only six or eight hours, it is not true to life to have a storm arise, and the ship founder, in a part of the sea from which no land is visible. Let the first act be a passionate lamentation, the chorus to follow with execrations of sea-life; the second act, a priest with votive offerings conversing with Alcyone and her nurse, altars, fire, pious sentiments, the chorus following with approbation of the vows; the third act, a messenger announcing the rising of a storm, together with rumors as to the ship, the chorus to follow with mention of shipwrecks, and much apostrophizing of Neptune; the fourth act tumultuous, the report found true, the shipwrecks described by sailors and merchants, the chorus bewailing the event as though all were lost; the fifth act, Alcyone peering anxiously over the sea and sighting far off a corpse, followed by the resolution, when she was about to take her own life. This sample outline can be expanded by the introduction of other characters. (III, 97.)

LODOVICO CASTELVETRO

Lodovico Castelvetro was born at Modena in 1505 of an old and noble family. His education was thorough and varied. He attended the universities of Bologna, Ferrara, Padua, and Siena. He studied law and took a degree at Siena in that profession out of deference to his father's wishes. After making a trip to Rome, he returned to Siena, where he applied himself to the studies for which he felt himself best suited. His relinquishment of the law displeased his parents, and he returned, in bad health, to Modena. There he engaged in literary pursuits, in spite of his poor health. He was a conspicuous figure in Modena in what practically amounted to an academy. In 1553 he began the bitter literary quarrel with Caro which resulted eventually in his exile. It began with a criticism of a poem of Caro's, and soon both parties resorted to intrigue and even violence. Caro is said to have started the inquiry which led to the arrest of several members of the " academy " on the suspicion of heresy. While Castelvetro himself was not arrested, he decided to go to Rome and defend himself, but seeing that he was not likely to make out a good case he escaped and went to Chiavenna on the Swiss-Italian frontier. In 1561 he was excommunicated. He then appealed to the Council of Trent and was advised to return to Rome. He determined, however, to leave the country, and went to Lyons, but the war of the Catholics and Protestants, then in progress, soon forced him to leave. He went to Geneva, and thence to Chiavenna, where he lectured. Not long after, Castelvetro's brother, who was in the good graces of Maximilian II, urged Lodovico to come to Vienna. In that city he published his *Poetica,* dedicating it to Maximilian. On the outbreak of the plague he returned to Chiavenna, where he died in 1571.

Castelvetro's translation of Aristotle's *Poetics* and his lengthy commentary are, like the work of Scaliger, a landmark in modern dramatic criticism. Like Scaliger's treatise, Castelvetro's is crude, pedantic, and inaccurate, but to the schol-

ars of the time it was infinitely suggestive. Castelvetro not only interpreted Aristotle too freely, he frequently mistranslated him in order to establish a point. Castelvetro's formulation of the three Unities was the beginning of innumerable disputes throughout Europe.

Editions:

The *Poetica d'Aristotele vulgarizzata e esposta* was first published at Vienna in 1570. But the second edition (Basle, 1576) contains important additions. The *Opera Varie Critiche,* with Muratori's Life of Castelvetro, appeared in Milan in 1727. The only English translation of the *Poetica* consists in the important passages, quoted in H. B. Charlton's *Castelvetro's Theory of Poetry* (Manchester, 1913).

On Castelvetro and his work:

L. Muratori, *Vita dell' autore* (in the *Opere Varie Critiche,* Milano, 1727).

Nouvelle Biographie générale, vol. 9 (Paris, 1854).

A. Caro, *Apologia degli Academici di Bianchi di Roma contra M. Lodovico Castelvetro* (Parma, 1588).

Cavazzuti, *Lodovico Castelvetro* (Modena, 1903).

A. Plonchar, *Della Vita e delle opere di L. Castelvetro* (Conegliano, 1878).

Bayle, *Dictionary* (2nd ed., London, 1735).

H. B. Charlton, *Castelvetro's Theory of Poetry* (Manchester Univ. Press, 1913).

A. Fusco, *La Poetica di Lodovico Castelvetro* (Napoli, 1904).

George Saintsbury, *A History of Criticism,* vol. 2 (New York, 1902).

J. E. Spingarn, *A History of Literary Criticism in the Renaissance* (2nd ed., New York, 1908).

H. Breitinger, *Les Unités d'Aristote avant le Cid de Corneille* (Genève, 1895).

A. Benoist, *Les Théories dramatiques avant les Discours de Corneille* (in *Annales de la Faculté des lettres de Bordeaux,* 1891).

POETICS [1]

[Poetica d'Aristotele vulgarizzata e esposta]

(1570)

MISCELLANEOUS CRITICAL WORKS

[Opere Varie Critiche] [1]

(printed 1727)

Tragedy cannot effect its proper function with a reading, without staging and acting.

In poetry there are possible two modes of representing action, viz., either by words and things, or by words alone; one of these modes is more similar to the thing represented, the other less; words and things together are the more similar mode, words alone the less; for in the former, words are represented by words and things by things, whilst in the latter both words and things are represented by words alone.

The time of the representation and that of the action represented must be exactly coincident . . . and the scene of the action must be constant, being not merely restricted to one city or house, but indeed to that one place alone which could be visible to one person.

Tragedy ought to have for subject an action which happened in a very limited extent of place and in a very limited extent of time, that is, in that place and in that time, in which and for which the actors representing the action remain occupied in acting; and in no other place and in no other time. . . .

The time of action ought not to exceed the limit of twelve hours.

There is no possibility of making the spectators believe that many days and nights have passed, when they themselves obviously know that only a few hours have actually elapsed; they refuse to be so deceived.

It is more marvelous when a great

mutation of a hero's fortune is made, in a very limited time and a very limited place, than when it is made in a longer time and in varied and larger places.

It was Aristotle's opinion that the plot of tragedy and comedy ought to comprise one action only, or two whose interdependence makes them one, and ought rather to concern one person than a race of people. But he ought to have justified this, not by the fact that a plot is incapable of comprising more actions, but by the fact that the extreme temporal limit of twelve hours and the restriction of the place for the performance, do not permit a multitude of actions nor the action of a whole race, nor indeed do they permit the whole of one complete action, if it is of any length: and this is the principal reason and the necessary one for the unity of action, that is, for the limitation of the plot to but one action of one person, or two actions, which by their interdependence can be counted one.

No drama can be praiseworthy which has not two actions, that is, two plots, though one is principal and the other accessory.

There is no doubt that there is more pleasure in listening to a plot containing many and diverse actions than in listening to that which contains but one.

Singleness of plot is not in the least introduced on account of its necessity, but on account of the poet's eagerness for glory, and to demonstrate the excellence and the singularity of his genius . . . for the judgment and the industry of the poet is demonstrated when with a plot comprising but a single action of

[1] Re-printed from *Castelvetro's Theory of Poetry,* by H. B. Charlton (Manchester, 1913). — Ed.

a single person, that is, with a plot apparently without any promise of success in it, he nevertheless furnishes the spectators with as much delight as other poets can scarcely do with plots comprising many persons. . . . The plot of drama should necessarily comprise one action of one person, or two, interdependent on each other. . . .

Tragedy is an imitation of an action, magnificent, complete, which has magnitude, and comprises each of those species, which represent with speech made delightful separately in its parts, and not by narration, and, moreover, induces through pity and fear, the purgation of such passions.

Tragedy can have either a happy or a sorrowful ending, as can comedy; but the joy or the sorrow of the tragic ending is different from the joy or the sorrow of the comic ending. The joyful dénouement of tragedy is formed by the cessation to the hero or to one dear to him, of impending death or sorrowful life or threatened loss of kingship; and the sorrowful dénouement is formed by the occurrence of these things. The happy dénouement of comedy is formed by the removal of insult from the hero or from one dear to him, or by the cessation of a longstanding shame, or by the recovery of an esteemed person or possession which was lost, or by the fulfillment of his love; and the sorrowful dénouement of comedy is formed by the occurrence of the opposite of these things.

Tragedy without a sad ending cannot excite and does not excite, as experience shows, either fear or pity.

The solution of the plot ought to be brought about by the plot itself, i.e., the striking of the danger and the ceasing of the difficulty should themselves be constituents of the plot, following the nature of the danger and of the difference by verisimilitude.

. . . Tragedy is not imitation of men, but of actions.

The plot is the constitution of the things, i.e., the invention of the things or the subject: which invention or subject comprises the invention of the visible things and the invention of the invisible things.

In most actions, men do not hide their character, but exhibit them.

Poets who make tragedies without character and thought, do not really imitate human action; for in the operation of human action, character and thought are always revealed, though sometimes more, sometimes less.

I fail to see how there could be a good tragedy without character.

If the plot is the end of tragedy and of all poetry, if it is not a thing accessory to character, but on the contrary, character is necessary to the plot, then many authors of great fame, ancient and modern, including Julius Cæsar Scaliger, have gravely erred in their opinion that it was the intention of good poets like Homer and Vergil to depict and demonstrate to the world, let us say, an indignant captain as excellently as possible, a valiant soldier, a wise man, and their moral natures; with much more of the same twaddle: for if this were true, then character would not be, as Aristotle says, secondary to action, but action would be secondary to character. Moreover, such a subject could not be really poetic: it is much rather philosophic.

Character comes in because persons come in in action; but persons are not introduced in action because a display of character is required.

Though character is not a part of the action, yet it accompanies it inseparably, being revealed together with the action: hence character ought not to be considered as part separate from the action, for without it the action would not be performed.

In questions constituting the species of poetry, no account at all should be taken of goodness or badness, extreme or moderate: these things should be considered only in so far as the aim is to arouse pity and fear in the minds of the audience.

•   •   •   •   •

If poetry has been fashioned primarily for delight, and not for utility, why in one species of poetry, i.e., tragedy, is utility chiefly sought? Why is not delight sought primarily ir this species, without regard to utility?

•   •   •   •   •

According to Aristotle, there are four kinds of pleasure. The first is the pleasure arising from the sad state of a person, good or moderately good, who falls from happiness to misery: this pleasure we have called oblique, and shown that it is caused obliquely. The second is the pleasure arising from the happy fate of a person, good or moderately good, and from the sad state of the wicked; this pleasure we have called direct, and shown that it arises directly. The third is the pleasure of the happy fate common to persons of all kinds, friends and enemies: this pleasure can be called direct popular pleasure. The fourth is the pleasure caused by a fearful and monstrous spectacle; this can be called artificial spectacular pleasure. Now, Aristotle accepts in tragedy the first and second kinds of pleasure, and commends them, the first, however, more than the second; but he will not have them in comedy: the third and the fourth, as far as tragedy is concerned, he dismisses with blame.

•   •   •   •   •

[In the same work Castelvetro states in tabular form the various functions and parts of comedy.]

•   •   •   •   •

The function of comedy is the being moved by pleasing things appealing to the sentiments or the imagination. Comedy has to do with human turpitude, either of mind or of body; but if of the mind, arising from folly, not from vice; if of the body, a turpitude neither painful nor harmful.

•   •   •   •   •

The greatest source of the comic is deception, either through folly, drunkenness, a dream, or delirium; or through ignorance of the arts, the sciences, and one's own powers; or through the novelty of the good being turned in a wrong direction or of the engineer hoist with his own petard; or through deceits fashioned by man or by fortune.

•   •   •   •   •

Its plot comprises only actions possible to happen, those which have actually happened having no place in it at all.[2]

[From the *Opere Varie Critiche,* p. 81]

The private action of a private citizen is the subject of comedy, as the actions of kings are the subject of tragedy.

[2] By way of comparison with the theoretical treatises above-printed, a few lines are here included from the *Prologue* to Gianmaria Cecchi's play, *La Romanesca* (1574): "The *Farsa* is a new third species between tragedy and comedy. It enjoys the liberties of both, and shuns their limitations; for it receives into its ample boundaries great lords and princes, which comedy does not, and, like a hospital or inn, welcomes the vilest and most plebeian of the people, to whom Dame Tragedy has never stooped. It is not restricted to certain motives; for it accepts all subjects — grave and gay, profane and sacred, urbane and crude, sad and pleasant. It does not care for time or place. The scene may be laid in a church, or a public square, or where you will; and if one day is not long enough, two or three may be employed. What, indeed, does it matter to the *Farsa?* In a word, this modern mistress of the stage is the most amusing, most convenient, the sweetest, prettiest country lass that can be found upon our earth." (From J. A. Symonds' *Renaissance in Italy,* vol. 2. New York, n. d.).— Ed.

FRANCE — I

FRENCH DRAMATIC CRITICISM OF THE RENAISSANCE

While many of the ideas incorporated into the dramatic treatises of the later Renaissance in France were derived from Minturno, Scaliger, Castelvetro, and other Italian theorists, the beginnings in France hark back to the Middle Ages and antiquity. The commentaries and fragments of Donatus and Diomedes were first published toward the end of the fifteenth century. Horace was also known to the grammarians and scholars, while the architectural treatises of Vitruvius and Alberti, containing chapters on the theater, were freely drawn upon. As in Italy, Aristotle's *Poetics* was seldom referred to; not until the middle of the sixteenth century does he become a force to be reckoned with. Among the earliest French writings on the drama was the introductory matter — *Praenotamenta* — to Jodocus Badius' edition of Terence (1504). This is practically a summing-up of the doctrines of the Middle Ages. Badius' edition of Seneca (1514), in which he was aided by others, contains commentaries, and the usual excerpts from Donatus and Diomedes. These preliminary and running commentaries constituted a veritable "practical dramaturgy." Meantime, foreign influences were at work: Polydorus Vergil's *De rerum inventoribus* (1513), with its section on comedy, was known, and later (1544) translated into French; Erasmus' *Adages, Colloquies,* and *Letters,* however meager in their references to Aristotle, helped to disseminate the ideas of preceding ages. Lazare de Baïf, one of the first translators of Greek plays, composed a *Diffinition de la tragédie* which he prefixed to his version of the *Electra* (1537). His conception in this note, as in the *Dedication* to his *Hecuba* (1544), was purely classical. In Buchanan's *Dedication* to his Latin translation of the *Alcestis* (printed 1554), there is a new note: the poet urges the tragic writer to turn aside from the conventional themes of murder, parricide, etc. Meanwhile, the numerous editions of Terence (1529, 1542, and 1552) were reprinted with the commentaries of Donatus, Diomedes, and quotations from Horace. In Jean Bouchet's *Epistre responsive au Roy de la Basoche de Bordeaux* (written in 1526, and published in 1545) the usual classification of drama into the two categories of Comedy and Tragedy is modified to include the *Satyre.*

The very earliest Rhetorics and Arts of Poetry are of little importance as regards dramatic theory. The first of these is Eustache Deschamps' *Art de dictier* (finished in 1392). Together with the numerous treatises on versification, they may be ignored. Pierre Fabri's manual, *Le Grand et vray art de pleine Rhetorique,* was published in 1521; this was followed in 1539 by Gracian du Pont's *L'Art poétique,* which contains little that is not found in Fabri's work. Both Arts belong in spirit to the late Middle Ages. The *Art poétique* of Thomas Sebillet, published in 1548, is interesting chiefly because of the parallel made between the old French "moralité" and the tragedies of antiquity. The work likewise contains probably the first trace of the influence of Aristotle's *Poetics* in France. Sebillet, whose work appeared only a year before Du Bellay's *Deffense,* foreshadows, in spirit at least, some of the reforms advocated by the spokesman of the *Pléïade.* Joachim Du Bellay's *Deffense et illustration de la langue françoise* (1549) heralded the opening of a new era and announced the close of the old. Of vast importance in the realm of French literature, it contains nothing but a single brief reference to drama — in which he urges dramatists to write plays after the manner of the ancients. This manifesto was answered in 1550 by the *Quintil Horatian sur la Deffense et illustration de la langue françoise,* the author of which was recently proved to be Barthélemy Aneau, instead

69

of Charles Fontaine, to whom it had been ascribed as late as 1898. Among the early distinct references to Aristotle's theory is the three-line sentence [1] from a speech in Jodelle's *Cléopâtre,* the first French tragedy (1552); it states the famous Unity of Time, derived and developed from a passage in the *Poetics.* Another *Art Poétique,* that of Jacques Peletier du Mans (1555), though based to a great extent so far as drama is concerned, upon Horace, Donatus, and Diomedes, incorporates many of the theories of the *Pléiade.* It was up to that date the fullest exposition of dramatic theory in France. One of the few independent-minded dramatists of the period was Jacques Grévin who, in his prefatory *Bref Discours pour l'intelligence de ce théâtre,* printed with his tragedy, *La Mort de César* (1562), maintained that he was justified in using the soldiers in his play as a chorus, that he should not be blamed for refusing to follow the example of the ancients, because "different nations demand different ways of doing things." While he mentions Aristotle, he is hopelessly ignorant of the meaning and significance of the *Poetics.* Pierre Ronsard, the chief of the *Pléiade,* makes a few references to drama in his three short treatises on poetry: *Abrégé de l'Art poétique françois* (1565), and the first and second *Préfaces* to the *Franciade* (1572 and 1587, respectively). But by all odds the most significant treatise of the period was Jean de la Taille's *Art de la Tragédie,* prefixed to his play *Saül le furieux* (1572). By this time Aristotle was an authority, and his Italian commentators well known in France. As has already been pointed out, Taille was influenced by Castelvetro, from whom he received and stated the theory of the three unities, which were for the first time in France distinctly formulated in his short preface. Two important works, the *Arts poétiques* of Pierre de Laudun d'Aigaliers (1598), and of Vauquelin de la Fresnaye (published 1605), are among the last works of their kind of the French Renaissance. Laudun was "probably the first European critic to argue formally against" [2] the twenty-four rule supposed to have been laid down by Aristotle. Vauquelin practically translates the whole of Horace's *Ars Poetica* in his treatise, while the rest of his work is based on Aristotle and his Italian commentators.

It is impossible to mention every writer of this period who in a preface, an Art of Poetry, or letter, refers to the drama. There are, however, a number of dramatists and a few others whose casual references are of value and interest. To the two books on architecture already mentioned as containing sections on the theater may be added Serlio's work on perspective, which was translated into French in 1545 by Jehan Martin. The prefaces, dedications, etc., of many printed plays of Alexandre Hardy and Robert Garnier may be consulted; likewise the prefaces to the following plays: *Les Abuzez* (1543), by Charles Étienne; *Abraham sacrifiant* (1550) by Théodore de Bèze; *Les Corrivaux* (1562) by Jean de la Taille; *Aman,* by André de Rivaudeau; *Les Jaloux, Les Esprits,* and *Dedication* to *Monsieur d'Ambroise* (all of 1579) by Pierre de Larivey, also the same author's *Prologue* to *La Constance,* printed in 1611; *Régulus* (1582) by Jean de Beaubreuil; *Les Néapolitaines* (1584) by François d'Amboise; and *Esther* (1585) by P. Mathieu.

[1] *Avant que ce soleil, qui vient ores de naître,*
   Ayant tracé son jour chez sa tante se plonge,
   Cléopâtre mourra!

[2] J. E. Spingarn, *A History of Literary Criticism in the Renaissance* (1908).

General References on French literature:

L. Petit de Julleville (editor), *Histoire de la langue et de la littérature française des origines à 1900,* 8 vols. (Paris, 1896–99).

Ferdinand Brunetière, *Histoire de la littérature française classique,* 3 vols. (Paris, 1905–12).

——, *Manuel de l'histoire de la littérature française* (Paris, 1897).

Gustave Lanson, *Histoire de la littérature française* (12th ed., Paris, 1912).

Emile Faguet, *Histoire de la littérature française*, 2 vols. (Paris, 1900).

René Doumic, *Histoire de la littérature française* (Paris, 1900).

J. Demogeot, *Histoire de la littérature française* (24th ed., Paris, 1892).

H. P. Junker, *Grundriss der Geschichte der französischen Literatur*, (2nd ed., Münster, 1894).

Edward Dowden, *A History of French Literature* (New York, 1897).

C. H. Conrad Wright, *A History of French Literature* (Oxford, 1912).

Nicéron, *Mémoires pour servir à l'histoire des hommes illustres dans la république des lettres*, 43 vols. (Paris, 1729-45).

[La Vallière] *Bibliothèque du Théâtre François*, 3 vols. (Dresde, 1768).

De Léris, *Dictionnaire portatif historique et littéraire des théâtres* (2nd ed., Paris, 1763).

P.-L. Jacob (ed.), *Bibliothèque dramatique de Monsieur de Soleinne* (catalog), 5 vols. (Paris, 1843-44).

Gustave Lanson, *Manuel bibliographique de la littérature française moderne, (1500-1900)*, 5 vols. (Paris, 1909-14).

L.-P. Betz, *La littérature comparée* (2nd ed., Strasbourg, 1904).

Charles Gidel, *Histoire de la littérature française, depuis son origine jusqu'à la Renaissance*, (Paris, 1875).

——, The same: . . . *depuis la Renaissance jusqu'à la fin du XVIIe siècle* (Paris, 1877).

F. Godefroy, *Histoire de la littérature française depuis le XVIe siècle jusqu'à nos jours*, 10 vols. (2nd ed., Paris, 1878-79).

General References on French Drama:

François et Claude Parfaict, *Histoire du Théâtre François depuis son origine jusqu'à présent* (Paris, 1754-55).

S. Chappuzeau, *Le Théâtre français* (ed., Paris, 1876).

Beauchamps, *Recherches sur les Théâtres de France* (Paris, 1735).

J. Baudrais, *Essais historiques sur l'origine et les progrès de l'art dramatique en France* 3 vols. (Paris, 1791).

Germain Bapst, *Essai sur l'histoire du théâtre* (Paris, 1893).

W. Creizenach, *Geschichte des neueren Dramas*, 3 vols. (Halle, 1893-1909).

J. L. Klein, *Geschichte des Dramas*, 13 vols. (Leipzig, 1865-76).

L. Petit de Jullevile, *Le Théâtre en France* (7th ed., Paris, 1908).

C. Barthélemy, *Histoire de la Comédie en France* (Paris, 1886).

A. Royer, *Histoire universelle du théâtre*, 6 vols. (Paris, 1869-70).

Ferdinand Brunetière, *Les Epoques du Théâtre français (1636-1850)*. (Paris, 1892.)

——, *L'Evolution d'un genre: la Tragédie (In Etudes critiques sur l'histoire de la littérature française*, 7 ème série, Paris, 1905).

Fontenelle, *Histoire du Théâtre françois* (In vol. III, *Œuvres*, Paris, 1790).

J.-L. Geoffroy, *Cours de littérature dramatique*, 6 vols. (Paris, 1819-20).

Julien Le Rousseau, *Le Progrès de la littérature dramatique* (Paris, 1865).

Léon Levrault, *Drame et Tragédie* (Paris, n. d.).

——, *La Comédie* (Paris, n. d.).

Eugène Lintilhac, *Histoire générale du théâtre en France*, 5 vols. (Paris, 1904-11).

H.-J.-J. Lucas, *Histoire philosophique et littéraire du théâtre français depuis son origine jusqu'à nos jours*, 3 vols. (2nd ed., Bruxelles, 1862-63).

Frederick Hawkins, *Annals of the French Stage*, 2 vols. (London, 1884).

Chevalier de Mouhy, *Abrégé de l'histoire du théâtre françois*, 3 vols. (Paris, 1780).

Karl Mantzius, *A History of Theatrical Art*, trans. by Louise von Cossel, 6 vols. (London, 1903-09).

D. Germano, *Evolution historique du théâtre français* (Caltanissetta, 1902).

Paul de Saint-Victor, *Les Deux Masques*, 3 vols. (Paris, 1880-84).

References on early French literature and Criticism:

Paul Albert, *La Littérature française des origines à la fin du XVIe siècle* (Paris, 1894).

E. Langlois, *De Artibus Rhetoricæ Rhythmicæ* (Paris, 1890).

Heinrich Morf, *Geschichte der französischen Literatur im Zeitalter der Renaissance* (2nd ed., Strassburg, 1914).

Emile Egger, *L'Hellénisme en France*, 2 vols. (Paris, 1869).

Emile Faguet, *Le Seizième siècle* (Paris, 1893).

———, *La Tragédie française au XVI* siècle* (2nd ed., Paris, 1912).

———, *Les Manifestes dramatiques avant Corneille* (In *Revue des cours et conférences*, IX, No. 6, Paris, 1900).

Emile Chasles, *La Comédie en France au XVI* siècle* (Paris, 1862).

C.-A. Sainte-Beuve, *Tableau historique et critique de la Poésie française et du théâtre français au XVI* siècle* (Revised and augmented eds., Paris, 1842 and after).

Ferdinand Brunetière, *L'Evolution des genres dans l'histoire de la littérature. Introduction: L'Evolution de la critique depuis la Renaissance jusqu'à nos jours* (6th ed., Paris, 1914).

Henri Carton, *Histoire de la critique littéraire en France* (Paris, 1886).

Léon Levrault, *La Critique littéraire* (Paris, n. d.).

Eugène Lintilhac, *La Théorie du théâtre en France de Scaliger à Victor Hugo* (In *Nouvelle Revue*, N. S., IX, Paris, 1901).

J. Marsan, *La Pastorale dramatique en France à la fin du XVI* siècle et au commencement du XVII* siècle* (Paris, 1905).

E. J. B. Rathery, *Influence de l'Italie sur les lettres françaises depuis le XIII* siècle jusqu'au règne de Louis XIV* (Paris, 1853).

Eugène Rigal, *De Jodelle à Molière* (Paris, 1911).

———, *Le Théâtre français avant la période classique* (Paris, 1901).

———, *Alexandre Hardy et le théâtre français à la fin du XVI* siècle et au commencement du XVII* siècle* (Paris, 1889).

A. Rosenbauer, *Die poetischen Theorien der Plejade nach Ronsard und Dubellay* (Erlangen, 1895).

Emile Roy, *Etude sur le Théâtre français du XIV* et XV* siècles* (Paris, 1901).

T. Rucktäschel, *Einige Arts poétiques aus der Zeit Ronsard's und Malherbe's* (Leipzig, 1889).

G. Gregory Smith, *The Transition Period* (New York, 1900).

J. E. Spingarn, *A History of Literary Criticism in the Renaissance* (2nd ed., New York, 1908).

George Saintsbury, *A History of Criticism*, vol. 2 (New York, 1902).

Joseph Texte, *L'Influence italienne dans la Renaissance française* (In *Etudes de littérature européene*, Paris, 1898).

Arthur Tilley, *From Montaigne to Molière* (London, 1908).

———, *The Literature of the French Renaissance*, 2 vols. (Cambridge, 1904).

Henri Tivier, *Histoire de la littérature dramatique en France depuis ses origines jusqu'au Cid* (Paris, 1873).

Pierre Toldo, *La Comédie française de la Renaissance* (In *Revue d'histoire littéraire de la France*, Paris, 1897–98–99, 1900).

P. Villey, *Les Sources d'idées au XVI* siècle. Textes choisis et commentés* (Paris, 1912).

Ernest Martineche, *La Comédie espagnole en France* (Paris, 1900).

J. W. Cunliffe, *Early French Tragedy in the Light of Recent Scholarship* (*Journal of Comparative Literature*, I, 1903).

Jules Guillemot, *L'Evolution de l'idée dramatique* etc. (Paris, 1910).

A. Benoist, *Les Théories dramatiques avant les Discours de Corneille* (In *Annales de la Faculté des Lettres de Bordeaux*, 1891).

H. Breitinger, *Les Unités d'Aristote avant le Cid de Corneille* (2nd ed., Genève, 1895).

M.-A.-A. Chassang, *Des essais dramatiques imités de l'antiquité au XIV* et XV* siècles* (Paris, 1852).

E. Cougny, *Des Représentations dramatiques et particulièrement de la comédie politique dans les collèges au seizième siècle* (Paris, 1868).

Jules Haraszti, *La Comédie française de la Renaissance et la scène* (In *Revue d'histoire littéraire de la France*, Paris, 1905).

H. C. Lancaster, *A Neglected Passage on the Three Unities of the French Classical Drama* (In *Modern Language Ass'n Publications*, vol. XXIII, Cambridge, Mass., 1908).

———, *The French Tragi-comedy: its Origin and Development from 1552 to 1628* (Baltimore, 1907).

Gustave Lanson, *Le Théâtre français au temps d'Alexandre Hardy* (In *Hommes et Livres*, Paris, 1895).

———, *Les Origines de la tragédie clas-*

sique en France (In *Revue d'histoire littéraire de la France,* Paris, 1903).

——, *L'Idée de la tragédie avant Jodelle* (In *Revue d'histoire littéraire de la France,* Paris, 1904).

——, *La Substitution de la tragédie aux mystères et aux moralités* (*Revue d'histoire littéraire de la France,* Paris, 1903).

——, *La Tragédie en France avant Corneille* (In *Bulletin de l'Association des Elèves de Sèvres,* 1906).

Georges Péllissier, *Les Arts Poétiques antérieurs à Vauquelin* (In *L'Art Poétique de Vauquelin de la Fresnaye,* Paris, 1885).

Charles Arnaud, *Les Théories dramatiques au XVIIe siècle. Etude sur la vie et les œuvres de l'Abbé d'Aubignac* (Paris, 1888).

Adolf Ebert, *Entwicklungsgeschichte der französische Tragödie, vornehmlich im XVI. Jahrhundert.* (Gotha, 1858).

Hecq et Paris, *La. Poétique française au Moyen-âge et à la Renaissance* (Bruxelles, 1896).

Marcel Hervier, *Les Ecrivains français jugés par leurs contemporains. I. VIe et XVIIe siècles* (Paris, 1911).

Alfred Michiels, *Histoire des idées littéraires en France,* 2 vols. (Bruxelles, 3rd ed., 1848).

Philarète Chasles, *Etudes sur le seizième siècle en France* (Paris, 1848).

A. Darmsteter et A. Hatzfeld, *Le Seizième siècle en France* (Paris, 1878).

B. Pifteau and J. Goujon, *Histoire du théâtre en France des origines au Cid (1398–1630)* (Paris, 1879).

René Bray, *La Tragédie cornélienne devant la critique classique* (Paris, 1927).

THOMAS SEBILLET

Thomas Sebillet — or Sibilet, as it is often spelled — was born in 1512, probably at Paris. The little that is known of his life has been gleaned from his writings. He studied for the law and was an "avocat" in the Parlement de Paris, but he soon turned to literary pursuits. He went to Italy in 1549. He was the friend of some of the most prominent literary men of his day, among them Du Bellay, Pasquier, and L'Estoile. He was imprisoned for political reasons. A speech of his, made in Parlement in 1589, gives evidence of his more or less reactionary attitude toward the political movements of his day. He died at Paris the same year.

Sebillet's *Art Poétique* is a distinct departure from the Rhetorics and Poetics which preceded it. Sebillet, as the friend of Du Bellay, must have been influenced by many of the ideas which were about to be promulgated by the members of the *Pléiade.* It is highly significant that his book, which precedes Du Bellay's *Deffense* by one year, advocates some of the reforms suggested in that epoch-making manifesto. Spingarn says that Sebillet's passage about the French Morality "exhibits perhaps the earliest trace of the

influence of Italian ideas on French criticism." He also remarks that it exhibits in all probability the "first trace of Aristotelianism in French critical literature." Sebillet's work may, therefore, stand as a sort of dramatic manifesto of the *Pléiade,* for as has been said, Du Bellay scarcely touches upon the drama.

Editions:

The *Art Poétique François pour l'instruction des jeunes studieus et encor peu avancez en la poésie françoise* was first published at Paris in 1548. It went through seven editions in a little over twenty-five years. It has been re-printed by the *Société des Textes français modernes,* and edited by Félix Gaiffe, Paris, 1910.

Among Sebillet's other works are political tracts, various translations (1581 and 1584), and a translation of Euripides *Iphigenia* (Paris, 1549).

On Sebillet and his work:

Félix Gaiffe, Introduction to re-print of the *Art Poétique* (Paris, 1910).

Erich Lüken, *Du Bellay's Deffence et illustration de la largue françoyse in ihrem Verhältnis zu Sebillets Art Poétique* (Oldenburg, 1913).

Nouvelle Biographie générale, vol. 43 (Paris, 1867).

Biographie universelle, vol. 39.

Ferdinand Brunetière, *Histoire de la Lit-* *térature française classique,* vol. 1 (Paris, 1905).

J. E. Spingarn, *A History of Literary Criticism in the Renaissance* (2nd ed., New York, 1908).

George Saintsbury, *A History of Criticism,* vol. 2 (New York, 1902).

ART OF POETRY [1]

[Art poétique]

(1548)

(Book 2. Chapter VIII)

Dialogue and its Kinds. The Eclogue, the Morality, and the Farce

A common and successful sort of poem is that written in the " prosomilitical " or conversational style, which, by proso-popœia employs personalities speaking in their own persons. This sort of poem is called by the Greeks a Dialogue.

Dialogue.— The Dialogue includes a number of sub-divisions, which we shall consider in due order. But you must notice that each of these kinds has a common and particular name by which it is known: as, for instance, *Eclogue, Morality,* and *Farce.* But, exclusive of these particular terms, the poem in which characters are introduced, speaking to each other, goes under the generic term of Dialogue. What, I ask, is Marot's *Le Jugement de Minos?* And what are many other such poems which you will find in reading the French poets? Indeed, you will find the Dialogue utilized even in epigrams, as in the second book of Marot's *Epigrammes,* the one beginning:

MAROT

Muse, dy moy, pourquoy à ma maitresse *Tu n'as sceu dire Adieu à son depart?*

SA MUSE

Pource que lors je mouru de déstresse, *Et que d'un mort un mot jamais ne part.*

MAROT

Muse, dy moy, comment donques Dieu- *gard* *Tu luy peus dire ainsi de mort ravie?*

SA MUSE

Va pauvre sot, son céleste regard *La revoyant m'a redonné la vie.*

And Saint-Gelays' *Epitaphe de feu Monsieur Budé,* which is as follows:

A. Qui est ce corps que si grand peuple suyt?

B. Las c'est Budé au cercœil estendu.

A. Que ne font donc lés cloches plus grand bruit.

B. Son bruit sans cloche est asséz entendu.

A. Que n'a lon plus en torches despendu,
  Selon la mode acoustumée et saint?

B. A fin qu'il soit par l'obscur entendu
  Que dés François la lumiére est esteinte.

The Eclogue.— The Eclogue is Greek by invention, Latin by usurpation, and French by imitation. For Theocritus the Greek poet is the one whom Vergil used as a model in his *Eclogues,* and these works of Vergil were the models of Marot and other French poets. All three sorts [that is, Greek, Latin, and French] must be your example. Notice now that this poem, which they called *Eclogue,* is more often than not in dialogue form, in which shepherds and the like are introduced, in pastoral settings, conversing of deaths of princes, the calamities of the times, the overthrow of republics, the happy outcomes and events of fortune, poetic praises, or the like, in the form of very obvious allegory, so obvious that the names of the characters, the people themselves and the rightful application of the pastoral dialogue will stand revealed like painting under a glass

[1] Here translated, with omissions, for the first time into English, by the editor.— Ed.

— as in the *Tityre* of M. de Vergile and in the *Eclogue* he wrote on the death of Madame Loyse [de Savoye] mother of the late King François, first of his name and of glorious memory; and in that which he wrote at the request of the late King, the characters in which went under the names of Pan and Robin. . . .

The Morality.— Greek or Latin Tragedy.— The French Morality in some way represents Greek and Latin tragedy, principally in that it treats of grave and important subjects. If the French had managed to make the ending of the Morality invariably sad and dolorous, the Morality would now be a tragedy.

The Temper of the French.— But in this, as in everything else, we have followed our temperament, which is to take from what is foreign not everything we see, but only what we judge will be to our advantage. For in the Morality, as the Greeks and Latins did in their tragedies, we show illustrious deeds, magnificent and virtuous, true, or at least true to life; and otherwise as regards what is useful for information on our customs and life, not binding ourselves to any sadness or pleasure of the issue. . . .

The Second Kind of Morality.— There is another sort of Morality, besides the one I have already spoken about, in which we follow the allegory, or moral sense (hence the name Morality), which treats either a moral proposition, in which some character, neither man nor woman, represents some attributed abstraction, or else some other allegory intended for our instruction, or guidance in our manners.

The Virtue of the Morality.— In spite of everything, I believe that the first virtue of the Morality, and of every other sort of Dialogue, is the expression of the moral sense of the piece, or allegory. . . . In spite of the fact that, as Horace says in his *Ars Poetica* the poet mingles the delightful with the profitable and earns the applause and approbation of every one, we to-day do not write pure Moralities nor pure and simple farces, desiring rather to mix the two, and derive pleasure and profit, by employing consecutive and alternate rhyme, short and long lines, and making of our plays a hotch-potch.

Farce. Latin Comedy.— Our farce has little of the Latin Comedy in it. And, to tell the truth, the acts and scenes of Latin comedy would result only in a tiresome polixity. For the true subject of the French Farce or *Sottie* is a trifling, broad piece, inciting pleasure and laughter.

The subjects of Greek and Latin comedy were far different, for in them there was more morality than laughter, and often as much of truth as of fable. Our Moralities stand midway between comedy and tragedy and our Farces are in reality what the Latins called *Mimes,* or *Priapees,* the purpose and end of which was unrestrained laughter, for every licence was permitted, as is nowadays the case with our own farces.

JEAN DE LA TAILLE

Jean de la Taille was born at Bondaroy about 1540. His noble birth and good education enabled him to make a name for himself, which he did, both as soldier and man of letters. He studied at first under Muret, then entered the law department of the University of Orléans. But his interest in literature led him to abandon his profession. It is sure that he was influenced by Ronsard and Du Bellay. Regarding his military exploits, we know that he was in camp near Blois in 1563, in the battle of Dreux, at Arnay-le-Duc with the Prince of Navarre, and at Loudun in 1568. After Arnay-le-Duc he entered the service of the Prince. He took cold after the battle of Coutras, and died.

Taille was not merely a theorist, like Sebillet, but a practising dramatist as well. Although he disagreed with Sebillet and maintained that the old French farce and morality were *amères épiceries,* and that the true drama had scarcely begun in France, he was none the less an innovator. Perhaps his chief importance consists in his having formulated the third Unity, that of *place*. It is probable that this was derived from Castelvetro's *Poetica*, which had just appeared (1570). In common with other theorists, he upheld the dignity of tragedy, and forbade the dramatist's introducing violence and bloodshed on the stage. His references to Aristotle mark the final acceptance in France of the *Poetics*.

On the drama:

Preface to *Les Corrivaux* (1562). *Art de la Tragédie*, in *Saül le furieux* (1572).

Editions:

With the exception of the very rare first edition of Taille's *Saül le furieux* (1572) which contains the *Art de la Tragédie*, there is only one edition, the reprint of the *Art* by itself in Hugo Schlensog's dissertation on the *Lucelles* of Louis le Jars and Jacques Duhamel (Freiburg i. Br., 1906). Taille's comedy *Les Corrivaux* (1562) with prefatory matter touching upon the drama, is reprinted in the *Œuvres* (see below). Taille's works, including two plays besides those already mentioned, but excluding *Saül* and the *Art de la Tragédie*, and with a *Notice* on the author, are reprinted: *Œuvres*, 4 vols., edited by René de Maulde (Paris, 1878).

On Taille and his works:

Prefaces to the editions cited.
A. Werner, *Jean de la Taille und sein' Saül le furieux* (Leipzig, 1908).
G. Baguenault de Puchesse, *Jean et Jacques de la Taille* (in *Lectures et Mémoires de Sainte-Croix*, vol., VI, Orléans, 1889).
Biographie universelle, vol. 40 (Paris).
J. E. Spingarn, *A History of Literary Criticism in the Renaissance* (2nd ed., New York, 1908).

THE ART OF TRAGEDY [1]
[*Art de la tragédie* (in) *Saül le furieux*]
(1572)

Madame, the pitiable disasters falling to the lot of France during your Civil Wars, and the death of King Henry, and the King his son, and the King of Navarre your uncle, and the deaths of so many other princes, lords, knights and gentlemen, are all so great and sorrowful that one needs no other material with which to make tragedies. Although such things are the proper material for tragedy, they would only remind us of past and present sorrows, and I shall willingly leave them aside, preferring rather to describe the unhappiness of others than our own. . . . I now wish to dedicate to you a tragedy about the most miserable prince who ever wore crown, the first whom God chose to rule over His people. This is the first play I have ever written. I wish here, in making this dedication, to reveal to all one of the most marvelous secrets of the whole Bible, one of the greatest mysteries of that great Lord of the World, and one of His most terrible providences. In order that you may enjoy the pleasure I desire for you without further delay, it has occurred to me to give you a sort of overture, and some foretaste of the tragedy, by clarifying the principal points, merely in touching upon them.

Tragedy is by no means a vulgar kind of poetry; it is rather the most elegant, beautiful, and excellent of all. Its true province is the depiction of the pitiful ruin of lords, the inconstancy of fortune, banishments, wars, pests, famines, captivity, and the execrable cruelties of tyrants; in short, tears and extreme misery. It does not treat of those things which happen every day and for clear reasons — such as a natural death, or the death of a man by the hand of his enemy, or an execution according to law, — the result of one's just deserts. Such occurrences do not easily move us,

[1] Translated for the first time, with slight abridgments, by the editor.— Ed.

JEAN DE LA TAILLE

would scarcely bring a tear to the eye. This is because the true and only end of tragedy is to move and arouse keenly the passions of each of us; and to this end the subject must be pitiful and poignant in itself, and able at once to arouse in us some passion. Such a subject is the story of him who was made to eat his own sons, the father, though unwittingly, being the sepulchre of his children; or of him who could find no executioner to end his days and his sorrows, and was forced to perform the terrible deed with his own hand. Nor must the story treat of very bad lords, who deserve punishment for their horrible crimes; nor, for the same reason, must it treat of the wholly good, men of pure and upright lives, like Socrates — even though he was unjustly poisoned. This is why subjects of the sort will always be cold, and unworthy the name of tragedy. This is why the story of Abraham, in which God merely tries Abraham and pretends to make him sacrifice Isaac, is not a fit subject, because there is no misfortune at the end. Likewise with the story of Goliath, the enemy of Israel and of our religion; when Goliath is killed by his enemy David, we are so far from feeling compassion that we are rather delighted and relieved. The story, or play, must always be presented as occurring on the same day, in the same time, and in the same place. One must also be careful to do nothing on the stage but what can easily and decently be performed; no murders or other forms of death, pretended or otherwise, for the audience will invariably detect the trick. It was not art when some one, with too little reverence, performed the crucifixion of our great Savior on the stage. As to those who declare that a tragedy must always be joyous at the first and sad at the end, and a comedy (which is like a tragedy as regards the art and general form, but not the subject) be just the reverse, let me tell them that this is not always the case, among the great diversity of subjects and manner of treating them in both kinds. The principal point in tragedy is to know how to dispose and construct it well, so that the story may change, rise and fall, turning the minds of the spectators hither and thither, allowing them to see joy suddenly turned to sorrow, and sorrow to joy, as happens in actual life. The story must be well combined, interlaced, broken up, and begun again, and most especially, conducted at the end to the resolution and point which the author originally designed. Nor must there be anything in it useless, superfluous, or out of place. If the subject be taken from the divine writings, avoid long discourses on theology, for these are what detract from the plot; they belong rather to a sermon. And for the same reason, do not introduce that sort of character which is called *Faincte* [*Invented*] which never existed, like Death, Truth, Avarice, the World, and suchlike, for it would be necessary to have people "invented" in the same way to take pleasure in them. So much for the subject. As for the art necessary to treat it and write it down, it must be divided into five acts, at end of each of which the stage is free of actors, and the sense perfectly clear. There must be a chorus, that is, a company of men or women who, at the end of the act, hold discourse upon what has been said during it, and, above all, to keep silent and yet express without words what is happening off-stage. The tragedy must not start with the very beginning of the story or subject, but toward the middle, or the end (and this is one of the principal secrets of the art I am speaking of), after the manner of the best ancient poets and their great heroical works, in order that the audience may not listen coldly, but with the attention, born of the knowledge of the beginning, and being in sight of the end afterward. But it would take me too long to outline in detail that which the great Aristotle in his *Poetics*, and Horace after him (though not so adroitly) has written at greater length than I, who am attempting only to make clear this matter to you; my discourse is not intended for the ears of the very serious and learned. I shall treat only of the tragedies, comedies, farces, and moralities (wherein there is often neither sense nor reason, but only ridiculous discourses and nonsense), and other sorts of plays which are not constructed with true art, as were the plays of Sophocles, Euripides, and Seneca, and are consequently ignorant, ill-made, and insignificant things, good merely as pastimes for the lower classes, the common people, and frivolous-minded. I wish that all such trivial nonsense which spoils the purity of our language, could be banished from France, and that we had adopted and naturalized true tragedy and comedy, which have scarcely become known to us, and which would indeed in French form possess what grace they now have in Latin and Greek. I would to heaven that our kings and great ones knew what pleasure there is in hearing recited and seeing acted a real tragedy or comedy on a stage such as I could devise, and which was formerly held in such high esteem as a pleasure for the Greeks and Romans. And I venture to assert that such plays, simply acted by intelligent actors who, with the propriety of their acting and recitation, in a language not smacking of Latin, by a direct and fearless pronunciation not reminiscent of the student nor the pedant, and with none of the nonsense of farce, would serve as the most pleasant pastime to the great — when they come for rest to the city, after exercising, hunting and hawking. Besides, I do not care (in thus writing) about the bitter malice and brutal contempt of those who, because they are fighters, look down upon men of letters, as if knowledge and virtue, which reside only in the spirit, enfeebled the body, the heart, and the arms; and nobility were dishonored by another sort of nobility, to wit, knowledge.

. . . . .

Now, as France has not yet a true tragedy, unless it be a translation, I publish this one, under your protecting favor, Madame, as you are one of the few of our time who protect the arts and sciences, and in order to make your name known to posterity, your kindness, your knowledge and courtesy, and that future generations may know that you sometimes took notice of those who had something to say besides the usual vulgarities and barbarities of the ignorant.[2] . . .

[2] It may be well to record the words of at least one critic, probably the first in Europe, who vigorously protested against the Unity of Time. In the *Art poétique* (1598) of Pierre de Laudun d'Aigaliers, the author says: " In the first place, this law, if it is observed by any of the ancients, need not force us to restrict our tragedies in any way, since we are not bound by their manner of writing or by the measure of feet and syllables with which they compose their verses. In the second place, if we were forced to observe this rigorous law, we should fall into one of the greatest of absurdities, by being obliged to introduce impossible and incredible things in order to enhance the beauty of our tragedies, or else they would lack all grace; for besides being deprived of matter, we could not embellish our poems with long discourses and various interesting events. In the third place, the action of the *Troades*, an excellent tragedy by Seneca, could not have occurred in one day, nor could even some of the plays of Euripides or Sophocles. In the fourth place, according to the definition already given [on the authority of Aristotle], tragedy is the recital of the lives of heroes, the fortune and grandeur of kings, princes, and others; and all this could not be accomplished in one day. Besides, a tragedy must contain five acts, of which the first is joyous, and the succeeding ones exhibit a gradual change as I have already indicated above; and this change a single day would not suffice to bring about. In the fifth and last place, the tragedies in which this rule is observed are not any better than the tragedies in which it is not observed; and the tragic poets, Greek and Latin, or even French, do not and need not and cannot observe it, since very often in a tragedy the whole life of a prince, king, emperor, noble, or other person is represented; — besides a thousand other reasons which I could advance if time permitted, but which must be left for a second edition." Translated by J. E. Spingarn, in his *History of Literary Criticism in the Renaissance*.

Ronsard's brief plea on behalf of the Unity of Time (in the *Première Préface* to *La Franciade*, 1572) runs as follows: " Tragedy and comedy are circumscribed and limited to a short space of time, that is, to one whole day. The most excellent masters of this craft commence their works from one midnight to another, and not from sunrise to sunset, in order to have greater compass and length of time." (Translated by Spingarn, in the book cited above.) — Ed.

SPAIN

SPANISH DRAMATIC CRITICISM OF THE GOLDEN AGE

Spanish literature as a whole has been rather freer from outside influence than that of other nations. The drama of the great age — the late sixteenth and early seventeenth centuries — was decidedly unclassic. The masterpieces of Lope de Vega and Calderon are, compared with the masterpieces of Corneille and Racine, shapeless and crude; they resemble rather the plays of the Elizabethans. The earliest Spanish criticism touching upon the theory of the drama are: the *Arte de Trobar* (written 1423, and later known as the *Arte cisoria*) of Enrique, Marquis (?) de Villena; the *Preface* to *The Proverbs* (1437) the *Letter* to the Constable of Portugal, of the Marquis de Santillana; and the *Arte* of Juan del Encina. The first of these was finished in 1434, the next two about the same time, while the last was published in 1496. Agore de Molina wrote a treatise on poetics which he prefixed to his *Conde Lucanor* (1575). But Spanish criticism proper did not begin until toward the close of the sixteenth century. Juan Diaz (or Alfonso) Rengifo's *Arte Poética Española* (1592), was a standard treatise on rhetoric, and was derived for the most part from Italian Renaissance critics.[1] Alfonso Lopéz [*El Pinciano*] published in 1596 his *Filosofia Antigua Poética*, in effect a protest against the prevailing "irregular" drama; Juan de la Cueva finished the writing of his *Egemplar poético* about 1606 (published in 1774); Carvallo published his *Cisne de Apolo* in 1602; Luis Carrillo his *Libro de Erudicion Poética* in 1611; while Cascales' *Tablas poéticas* did not appear until 1616. All these works are unmistakably Italian in origin, and such elements of classicism as are found in them are derived through Minturno, Scaliger, Robortello, and their contemporaries

Juan de Mariana's *Tratado contra los Juegos Públicos* (1609) may be mentioned among the attacks on these of the day. (An earlier attack, *De Rege*, appeared ten years before.) In 1609 Lope de Vega published his famous manifesto, the *Arte nuevo de hazer comedias en este tiempo*, which was a protest against the rules, especially the Unities. Cervantes' attack on Lope's practice appeared in the 48th chapter of *Don Quixote*, part I, which was published in 1605. Lope had already won his case, however, and a number of "defenders" of the form in which he had succeeded, published their justifications of his dramatic methods. The most interesting of these defenses is found in the *Cigarrales de Toledo* of the dramatist Tirso de Molina, which was published in 1624. Before this defense appeared, however, Lope had been defended by Francisco de la Barreda (in his *Invectiva y Apologia*, 1622), Julius Columbarius (in his *Expostulatio Spongiae*—1618), Alfonso Sanchez; and by Carlos Boil and "Ricardo de Turia" (Pedro Juan de Rejanle y Toledo). Boil's *Romance a un licenciado que desebea hacer comedias*, and Turia's *Apologético de las comedias españolas* both appeared in the *Norte de la Poesía española* (1616). In the Dedication to his play *Pompeyo* (1618) Cristóbal de Mesa protests against the licence of Lope's dramas. There is another in Cristóbal Suarez de Figueroa's *El Pasagero* (1618). Among the later manifestos may be mentioned Diego de Colmenares' *Censura de Lope de Vega Carpio, o discurso de la nueva poesia, con una respuesta* (1630), Gonzales de Salas' *Nueva Idea de la Tragedia Antigua*, etc. (1633), and Juan Perez de Montalban's *Prologue* to the first volume of his *Comedias* (1638), his *Para Todos* (1632), José Pellicer de Salas y Tovar's *Idea de la Comedia de Castilla* (1639). Calderon, the dominating figure of the mid-seventeenth century, is said to have

[1] A curious and valuable document of the time, though not dealing with dramatic technique, is *El viage entrenido* (1603–04) of Agustin de Rojas Villandrando.— Ed.

written on the drama, but his *Defensa de la comedia* has not yet been published. The various *Prefaces* contain very little dramatic theory. One of the most important critics of the period was the celebrated Balthazar Gracián, whose *Agudeza y certe de ingenio* was published in 1648. In 1650 appeared Diego Vich's *Breve discurso de las Comedias y de su representacion*. With the decline of the drama came a corresponding decline of dramatic criticism and theory. Not until the advent of Luzan was there any outstanding Art of Poetry, criticism, or preface.

THE EIGHTEENTH CENTURY

The eighteenth century in Spain marks the decline of the Golden Age of Spanish drama, and the ascendancy of foreign, chiefly French, influence. The outstanding figure is Luzan, whose *Poética* was published in 1737. It was the author's purpose to make Spanish poetry conform to "rules prevailing among the cultured nations." He drew largely upon Boileau, Aristotle and the contemporary Italian critics: Muratori, Gravina, etc. His ideas were opposed in the *Diario de los Literatos de España,* founded in 1737 by Francisco Manuel de Huerta y Vega and Juan Martinez Salafranca, and Leopoldo Geronimo Puig. He was likewise defended, in the same paper, by José Gerardo de Hervás y Cobo de la Torre, who in 1742 wrote a *Sátira contra los malos escritores de su tiempo.* Feyjoo's magazine, in imitation of the *Spectator,* the *Teatro Critico universal,* first appeared in 1726, and continued until 1739. His *Cartas eruditas y curiosas* (1740–60) went far to disseminate European ideas of literature into Spain. Martin Sarmiento is the author of a posthumous *Memorias para la historia de la poesia, y poetas espanoles* (1745). In 1749 Blas de Nasarre wrote a preface (*Dissertacion o prólogo*) to two of Cervantes' plays, and attempted to discredit the old plays of Spain. José Carrillo then attacked Nasarre the following year in his *Sinrazon impugnada,* and Zabaleta in his *Discurso crítico* (1750) defended Lope and his school. In the same year, Tomas de Iriarte published a translation of Horace's *Ars Poetica.* Mon-

tiano y Luyando furthered the work of gallicizing Spanish literature in his defense of the French rules as used in his plays; his *Discurso sobre las Tragedias* appeared in 1750; one of comedies being published the same year, and a third in 1753. Among the more pedantic writings was the *Retórica* (1757) of Gregorio Mayans y Siscar, chiefly derived from the Latins. Luis Joseph Velazquez published his *Origines de la Poesia Castellana* three years before. Nicolás Fernandez de Moratin, a dramatist of unequal power, wrote a number of tractates and prefaces, some of which defended his own plays, while others attacked the old *autos,* which were at the time prohibited. In 1762 he pleaded for the French rules in the preface of his unsuccessful play, *La Petimetra.* The same year he published three discourses, chief among which was the *Desengaño al Teatro Español.* In 1770 he published the preface to his play *Hormesinda,* which was written, however, by Bernascone. It was attacked by Juan Pelaez in the *Reparos sobre la Tragedia intitulada Hormesinda.* The quarrel continued, and in 1773 Sebastian y Latre issued a defense of the Unities in his *Ensayo sobre el Teatro Español.* The publication, in 1785–86, of Vicente Garcia de la Huerta's selection of old plays in his *Teatro Español,* and the prefaces, especially the *Escena Española defendida* (1786), called down upon him the wrath of a number of writers, who blamed him for omitting such dramatists as Lope de Vega, Tirso, and Alarcón. The tracts and pamphlets of the time were numerous, though few of them are of any value. Among Huerta's antagonists may be mentioned Forner, Samaniego, Iriarte and Jovellanos. The popular dramatist, Ramon de la Cruz, especially in his preface to the *Teatro* (1786–91), did much to free the drama from formal restrictions. He was also the first to introduce Shakespeare to his country. His version of *Hamlet* is dated 1772. Leandro Fernandez de Moratin, one of the best dramatists of the late eighteenth century, was an ardent admirer of Shakespeare (he made a version of *Hamlet* in 1798), and of Molière. His early plays were written according to the French "rules," but in his prefaces and pamphlets he soon declared his independence. His plays *Derrota de los Pedantes* (1789), and *Comedia Nueva* (1792) are attacks on dramatists and outworn rules. In the *Prólogo* of the first part of the second volume of his Works, he further discusses his theories. The Duke of Almodóvar went still further in destroying the old Spanish tradition; his *Década Epistolar sobre el Estado de las Letras en Francia* appeared in 1781.

NINETEENTH AND TWENTIETH CENTURIES

The modern epoch in Spain produced many dramatists: from the very beginnings to the present time Spain's dramatic output has been uninterrupted. The nineteenth and twentieth centuries, however, have contributed little beyond the plays themselves, and recently, a mass of historical erudition. The Romantic impetus from France was felt early in Spain, with the dramatist Martinez de la Rosa, who was followed by the Duke de Révas, and Antonio Garcia Gutierrez (author of *El Trovador*), Hartzenbusch, Zorilla, and Tamayo y Baus, all representatives, save only Tamayo, of the first half of the century.

More recent drama—with José Echegaray, Benito Pérez-Galdós and Jacinto Benavente—has held its own with that of modern nations, and the twentieth century boasts at least a dozen younger dramatists. Chief among the critics and historians is Marcelino Menéndez y Peláyo, whose *Historia de las Ideas estéticas en España* belongs to the eighties.

General references on Spanish Literature:

George Ticknor, *History of Spanish Literature*, 3 vols. (6th ed., Boston, 1888. Spanish translation, with additions and corrections, by Gayangos and Vedia, 4 vols., Madrid, 1851–56).

J. C. L. S. de Sismondi, *De la Littérature du midi de l'Europe* (3rd ed., 4 vols., Paris, 1829. Translated as *Historical View of the Literature of the South of Europe*, 2 vols. Bohn ed., London, 1853).

James Fitzmaurice-Kelly, *History of Spanish Literature* (London, 1898).

——, *Bibliographie de l'histoire de la littérature espagnole* (Paris, 1913).

Heinrich Morf, *Die romanishen Literaturen und Sprachen* (Berlin, 1909).

F. Wolf, *Studien zur Geschichte der spanischen und portugiesischen Nationalliteratur* (Berlin, 1859).

H. B. Clarke, *Spanish Literature: an Elementary Handbook* (2nd ed., London, 1909).

Rudolf Beer, *Spanische Literaturgeschichte*, 2 vols. (Leipzig, 1903).

Angel Salcedo y Ruiz, *La Literatura Española*, 3 vols. (2nd ed., Madrid, 1915–16).

Ernest Mérimée, *Précis d'histoire de la littérature espagnole* (Paris, 1908).

Julio Cejador y Frauca, *Historia de la lengua y literatura castellana*, 5 vols. to date (Madrid, 1915–16).

Hispanic Society of America (pub.) *Bibliographie hispanique* (New York, annual nos. 1905 to date).

F. Bouterwek, *History of Spanish Literature* (Trans. by T. Ross, London, 1847).

P. A. Becker, *Geschichte der spanishen Literatur* (Strassburg, 1904).

Spanish Literature [a bibliography] (in *Pratt Institute Lectures*, nos. 30–31, Brooklyn, 1894–95).

William Hanssler, *A Handy Bibliographical Guide to the Study of the Spanish Language and Literature, etc.* (St. Louis, 1915).

A. Puibusque, *Histoire comparée des littératures espagnole et française*, 2 vols. (Paris, 1843).

B. de los Rios de Lampérez, *Del siglo d'oro* (*Estudios literarios*) (Madrid, 1910).

M. Menéndez y Pelayo, *Estudios de crítica literaria*, 5 vols. (Madrid, 1893–1908).

Boris de Tannenberg, *L'Espagne littéraire, portraits d'hier et d'aujourd'hui* (Paris, 1903).

A. Morel-Fatio, *L'Espagne au XVIe et au XVIIe siècle* (Heilbronn, 1878).

——, *Etudes sur l'Espagne*, 2 vols. (2nd ed., Paris, 1895–1906).

P. F. B. García, *La Literatura española en el siglo XIX* (Madrid, 1891).

José Manuel Aicardo, *De literaturia contemporánea* (2d ed., Madrid, 1905).

General references on Spanish drama:

Casiano Pellicer, *Tratado historico sobre el Origen y progresos de la Comedia y del histrionismo en España* (Madrid, 1804).

A. F. von Schack, *Geschichte des dramatischen Literatur und Kunst in Spanien*, 2 vols. (Berlin, 1845–46).

——, *Nachträge*, etc. (Frankfurt a/M., 1854).

Adolf Schaeffer, *Geschichte des spanischen Nationaldramas*, 2 vols. (Leipzig, 1890).

Franz Grillparzer, *Studien zum spanischen Theater* (in vol. 17, Cotta ed. *Grillparzers sämtliche Werke*).

Louis de Viel-Castel, *Essai sur le Théâtre espagnol*, 2 vols. (Paris, 1882).

José Yxart, *El arte escénico en España* (Madrid, 1894–96).

C. A. de la Barrera y Leirado, *Catálogo bibliográfico del teatro antiguo Español desde sus orígenes hasta mediados del siglo XVIII* (Madrid, 1860).

John Chorley, *Notes on the National Drama in Spain* (*Fraser's Magazine*, London, July, 1859).

Cotarelo y Mori, *Bibliografia de las controversias sobre la Licitud del Teatro en España* (Madrid, 1904).

M. Damas-Hinard, *Discours sur l'histoire et l'esprit du théâtre espagnol* (Paris, 1847).

J. Ebner, *Zur Geschichte des klassischen Dramas in Spanien* (Passau, 1908).

Juan Nicolás Böhl von Faber, *Teatro Español anterior á Lope de Vega* (Hamburgo, 1832).

Alfred Gassier, *Le Théâtre espagnol* (Paris, 1898).

Antonio Cánovas del Castillo, *El Teatro español* (Barcelona, 1906).

M. A. Fée, *Etudes sur l'ancien théâtre espagnol* (Paris, 1873).

Manuel Cañete, *Teatro Español del siglo XVI* (Madrid, 1885).

G. H. Lewes, *The Spanish Drama* (London, 1845).

H. Lucas, *Le Théâtre espagnol* (Paris, 1851).

A. Morel-Fatio and L. Rouanet, *Le Théâtre espagnol* (Paris, 1900).

José Francos Rodréguez, *El Teatro en España* (Madrid, 1908).

J. Sánchez Arjona, *Noticias referentes á los anales del teatro en Sevilla desde Lope de Rueda hasta fines del siglo XVII* (Sevilla, 1898).

A. Ludwig Stiefel, *Spanisches Drama bis 1800* (in *Kritischer Jahresbericht über die Fortschritte der romanischen Philologie*, vol. 7, 1905).

Tomas de Erauso y Zavaleta, *Discurso Crítico sobre . . . las Comedias de España* (Madrid, 1750).

C. Pérez Pastor, *Nuevos Datos acerca del Histrionismo español en los siglos XVI–XVII* (Madrid, 1901).

Henri Mérimée, *L'Art dramatique à Valencia, depuis les origines jusqu' au commencement du XVIIe siècle* (Toulouse, 1913).

The. G. Ahrens, *Zur Charakteristik des spanischen Dramas im Anfang des XVII. Jahrhunderts* (Halle, 1911).

M. Damis-Hinard, *Le Théâtre espagnol au siècle d'or* (Paris, 1853).

David Hannay, *The Later Renaissance* (New York, 1898).

A. Morel-Fatio, *La Comedia espagnole du XVIIe siècle* (Paris, 1885).

——, *Les défenseurs de la Comedia* (in the *Bulletin hispanique* Bordeaux, 1902).

H. A. Rennert, *The Spanish Stage in the Time of Lope de Vega* (New York, 1909).

A. Anaya, *An Essay on Spanish Literature . . . followed by a History of the Spanish Drama* (London, 1818).

L. Viardot, *Etudes sur l'histoire des institutions de la littérature, du théâtre, et des beaux-arts en Espagne* (Paris, 1835).

J.-J.-A. Bertrand, *L. Tieck et le théâtre espagnol* (Paris, 1914).

Henry Lyonnet, *Le Théâtre en Espagne* (Paris, 1897).

Manuel Bueno, *Teatro Español contemporáneo* (Madrid, 1909).

A. J. Bastinos, *Arte dramático español contemporáneo* (Barcelona, 1914).

F. W. Chandler, *Aspects of Modern Drama* (New York, 1914).

Barrett H. Clark, *The Continental Drama of Today* (2nd ed., New York, 1914).

Barrett H. Clark, *A Study of the Modern Drama* (Revised ed., New York, 1928).

J. P. W. Crawford, *Spanish Drama Before Lope de Vega* (Philadelphia, 1922).

References on Spanish criticism:

Marcelino Menéndez y Pelayo, *Historia de las Ideas estéticas en España*, 9 vols. (2nd ed., Madrid, 1890, and following).

F. Fernandez y Gonzalez, *Historia de la*

Crítica literaria en España, etc. (Madrid, 1870).

J. E. Spingarn, *A History of Literary Criticism in the Renaissance* (2nd ed., New York, 1908).

George Saintsbury, *A History of Criticism*, vol. 2 (New York, 1902).

H. Breitinger, *Les Unités d'Aristote avant le Cid de Corneille* (Genève, 1895).

H. J. Chaytor, *Dramatic Theory in Spain* (Cambridge, 1925).

MIGUEL DE CERVANTES SAAVEDRA

Miguel de Cervantes Saavedra was born at Alcalá de Henares in 1547. In all probability Miguel was with his father and the rest of the family in their various residences, in Valladolid, Madrid, Seville, and again, in 1556, Madrid. It was in this city that he first met Lope de Rueda, one of the early Spanish dramatists. In 1569 Cervantes' first work — six small poems — appeared in a large collection edited by Cervantes' supposed schoolmaster, Juan Lopez de Hoyos. Toward the end of the same year, Cervantes was in Rome with Cardinal Acquaviva. It is probable that in 1570 he enlisted in the regular army, that the following year he was on board the *Marquesa* during the Battle of Lepanto, and that he was wounded. He returned to Messina and recuperated, and was, in 1572, transferred to another regiment. He spent the greater part of the ensuing three years in Palermo and Naples. In 1575 he was granted leave to return to Spain, but the ship in which he and his brother embarked was captured by pirates, the passengers carried into slavery and placed under guard at Algiers. During the next two years he made two or three unsuccessful attempts to escape, and in 1577 was bought by the Viceroy. Several attempts on the part of Cervantes and his family to free him, proved fruitless, until in 1580 a ransom was raised and he went to Constantinople; thence he returned to Spain. During the next few years he wrote a number of plays. In 1584 he married and the following year published his novel, *Galatea*. In 1587 Cervantes went to Seville to assist in the provis-

ioning of the Armada, for he found it impossible to make a living by writing. He was employed in the commissary department until 1590, when he applied to the king for a position in the American colonies, but was refused. Two years later he was imprisoned for an unknown reason, but was soon released. He was continually getting into financial difficulties with the government, and was finally dismissed. Between the publication of the *Galatea* and *Don Quixote*, in 1605, Cervantes had written only a few occasional poems. *Don Quixote* was immediately successful, though the author received little compensation. During the next few years he wrote very little. In 1612 he became reconciled with Lope de Vega, whom he had criticized in *Don Quixote*. The next year he published his *Novelas exemplares*, in 1614 the *Viaje del Parnaso*. In 1615 he published a volume of plays and *entremeses*, with an interesting preface. Meanwhile a second part of the *Don Quixote* had made its appearance in 1614, in which the author, who called himself Alonso Fernandez de Avellaneda, tried to cover the subjects which Cervantes had announced in the first part. In all probability this imposture set Cervantes to work, for in 1615 the true second part appeared. While he was engaged in publishing his *Persiles y Sigismunda* he died, in 1616.

Cervantes' importance as a critic of the drama lies in his having set himself against the national type of play. There may have been some personal animus in his attack, as Lope de Vega had referred slightingly to him a short time before the publication of *Don Quixote*, and Lope was the chief representative of the popular drama. It is rather odd, too, that many of Cervantes' own plays were written more or less in the manner of Lope. The famous passage on the drama (Chapter 48 of the first part) contains, as has been pointed out, a curious parallel to Sidney's strictures on English drama, particularly where he speaks of the absurdity of the violation of the Unity of Time.

On the drama:
Don Quixote, part 1, chapter 48 (1605).
Viaje del Parnaso (1614).
Preface to *Ocho comedias y ocho entremeses nuevos* (1615).
[The play] *El Rufián Dichoso* (1615).

Editions:
The first part of *Don Quixote* was published at Madrid in 1605. There are innumerable editions, among the best of which is that in the Hartzenbusch edition of the *Obras completas*, 12 vols. (Madrid, 1863–64). The *Complete Works* are in course of publication, under the editorship of James Fitzmaurice-Kelly, 8 vols. (Glasgow, 1901–06). Among the editions of *Don Quixote* may be mentioned those of Clemencin, 6 vols. (Madrid, 1833–39), and Fitzmaurice-Kelley and Ormsby,

2 vols. (London, 1899–1900). English translations by Shelton, Motteux, Smollett and Ormsby (numerous modern editions). There is a French translation of some of Cervantes' plays, together with the *Preface* referred to: *Théâtre de Michel Cervantes*, translated by Alphonse Royer (Paris, n. d.). The *Viaje del Parnaso*, with an interesting appendix, is translated by James Y. Gibson (London, 1883).

On Cervantes and his works:
Leopold Rius, *Biblografía crítica de las obras de Miguel de Cervantes Saavedra*, 3 vols. (Madrid, 1895–1905).
Martin Fernandez de Navarrete, *Vida de Miguel de Cervantes Saavedra* (Madrid, 1819).
James Fitzmaurice-Kelly, *Miguel de Cervantes Saavedra, a Memoir* (Oxford, 1913).
M. A. Buchanan, *Cervantes as a Dramatist* (in *Modern Language Notes*, vol. 33, 1908).
N. Díaz de Escovar, *Apuntes escénicos cervantinos*, etc. (Madrid, 1905).
Marcel Dieulafoy, *Le Théâtre édifiant* (Paris, 1907).
S. Salas Garrido, *Exposición de las ideas estéticas de Miguel de Cervantes Saavedra* (Malaga, 1905).

DON QUIXOTE [1]
[*Don Quixote*]
(1605)

" . . . . I was discouraged, too, whenever I reflected on the present state of the drama, and the absurdity and incoherence of most of our modern comedies, whether fictitious or historical; for the actor and author both say that they must please the people, and not produce compositions which can only be appreciated by half a score of men of sense; and that they would rather gain subsistence by the many than reputation by the few. What other fate, then, could I expect but that, after racking my brains to produce a reasonable work, I should get

nothing but my labor for my pains? I have occasionally endeavored to persuade theatrical managers that they would not only gain more credit, but eventually find it much more advantageous to produce better dramas; but they will not listen to reason. Conversing one day with a fellow of this kind, I said, ' Do you not remember that, a few years since, three tragedies were produced which were universally admired; that delighted both the ignorant and the wise, and the vulgar as well as the cultivated; and that by those three pieces the players gained more than by thirty of the best which have since been represented?' 'I suppose you mean the *Isabella*, *Phyllis*, and

1 Re-printed extracts from the anonymous translation of *Don Quixote* (New York, n. d.). — Ed.

Alexandra,' he replied. 'The same,' said I; 'And pray recollect, that although they were written in strict conformity to the rules of art, they were successful: the whole blame, therefore, is not to be ascribed to the taste of the vulgar. There is nothing absurd, for instance, in the play of *Ingratitude Revenged,* nor in the *Numantia,* nor in the *Merchant Lover,* much less in the *Favorable Enemy,* or in some others composed by ingenious poets, to their own renown and the profit of those who acted them.' To these I added other arguments, which I thought in some degree perplexed him, but were not so convincing as to make him reform his erroneous practice."

"Signor Canon," said the priest, "you have touched upon a subject which has revived in me an old grudge I have borne against our modern plays, scarcely less than I feel towards books of chivalry; for though the drama, according to Cicero, ought to be the mirror of human life, an exemplar of manners and an image of truth, those which are now produced are mirrors of inconsistency, patterns of folly, and images of licentiousness. What, for instance, can be more absurd than the introduction in the first scene of the first act of a child in swaddling clothes, that in the second makes his appearance as a bearded man? Or to represent an old man valiant, a young man cowardly, a footman rhetorician, a page a privy councillor, a king a water carrier, and a princess a scullion? Nor are they more observant of place than of time. I have seen a comedy, the first act of which was laid in Europe, the second in Asia, and the third in Africa; and had there been four acts, the fourth would doubtless have been in America. If truth of imitation be an important requisite in dramatic writing, how can anyone with a decent share of understanding bear to see an action which passed in the reign of King Pepin or Charlemagne ascribed to the Emperor Heraclius, who is introduced carrying the cross into Jerusalem, or receiving the holy sepulchre, like Godfrey of Boulogne, though numberless years had elapsed between these actions? and, when the piece is founded on fiction, to see historical events mingled with facts relating to different persons and times? — and, all this

without any appearance of probability, but, on the contrary, full of the grossest absurdity? And yet there are people who think all this perfection, and call everything else mere pedantry. The sacred dramas, too — how they are made to abound with faults and incomprehensible events, frequently confounding the miracles of one saint with those of another; indeed, they are often introduced in plays on profane subjects, merely to please the people. Thus is our natural taste degraded in the opinion of cultivated nations, who, judging by the extravagance and absurdity of our productions, conceive us to be in a state of ignorance and barbarism. It is not a sufficient excuse to say that the object in permitting theatrical exhibitions being chiefly to provide innocent recreation for the people, it is unnecessary to limit and restrain the dramatic author within strict rules of composition; for I affirm that the same object is, beyond all comparison, more effectually attained by legitimate work. The spectator of a good drama is amused, admonished, and improved by what is diverting, affecting and moral in the representation; he is cautioned against deceit, corrected by example, incensed against vice, stimulated to the love of virtue. Such are the effects produced by dramatic excellence; but they are not to be expected on our present stage, although we have many authors perfectly aware of the prevailing defects, but who justify themselves by saying that, in order to make their works saleable, they must write what the theater will purchase. We have a proof of this even in the happiest genius of our country, who has written an infinite number of dramatic works with such vivacity and elegance of style, such loftiness of sentiment, and richness of elocution, that his fame has spread over the world; nevertheless, in conforming occasionally to the bad taste of the present day, his productions are not all equally excellent. Besides the errors of taste, some authors have indulged in public and private scandal, insomuch that the actors have been obliged to abscond. These and every other inconvenience would be obviated if some intelligent and judicious person of the court were appointed to examine all plays before they are acted, and without whose approbation none should be performed. Thus guarded, the comedian might act without personal risk, and the author would write with more circumspection; and by such a regulation, works of merit might be more frequent, to the benefit and honor of the country. And, in truth, were the same or some other person appointed to examine all future books of chivalry, we might hope to see some more perfect productions of this kind to enrich our language, and which, superseding the old romances, would afford rational amusement, not only to the idle alone, but to the active; for the bow cannot remain always bent, and relaxion both of body and mind, is indispensable to all."

(I, 48).

FELIX LOPE DE VEGA CARPIO

Lope Felix de Vega Carpio — better known simply as Lope de Vega — was born at Madrid in 1562. According to all accounts, he was very precocious; he himself claims to have written a four-act play at the age of twelve. Very little is known of his youth except that he became a page in the service of the Bishop of Carthagena, and that he went to the University at Alcalá de Henares. When he left the University — probably in 1581 — he worked under Gerónimo Velazquez, a theater manager in Madrid. In 1583 he became a member of the Expedition to the Azores. On his return, he had begun to acquire a reputation as a poet and dramatist. In 1588 he was banished temporarily for writing libels. He went to Valencia, but shortly after returned to Madrid, and carried off and married the daughter of a former regidor of the city. They went to Lisbon, whence Lope embarked in the Armada, on the *San Juan.* During the stormy voyage and in the midst of the combat Lope was writing with the utmost assiduity. When he returned to Spain he settled at Valencia, where he continued to write. In 1590 he left and went to Alba de Tórmes, where he became secretary to the Duke of Alba. After the death of his wife, probably in 1595, Lope left Alba de Tórmes and went to Madrid, where he married again in 1598, the same year in which he published his novel, the *Arcadia.* He continued to publish poems, novels and epics. About the year 1609 Lope seems to have turned his thoughts toward religion, and in that year he describes himself as a Familiar of the Inquisition. The following year he entered a monastery and in 1614 was admitted to the order, after the death of his son and wife. But, as ever, he found time to make love, write poems and plays, and participate in state functions. Toward the end of his life, he seems to have been overcome by remorse, after the death of one of his favorite mistresses and the drowning of another son. He died in 1635. Throughout his long career he wrote plays, the number of which ranges somewhere between twelve and twenty-five hundred.

Lope is primarily important as a dramatist, though in his prefaces, dedications, and verses, and above all in his *Arte nuevo de hacer comedias en este tiempo* (probably 1609), he showed clear vision and common sense as a critic of his own work. His *Arte nuevo* is a document of the utmost importance, because it voices the sentiments of the greater part of the dramatists and public of the time. It is an explanation and justification of the free and unclassic romantic drama of the Golden Age of Spain.

On the drama:

Prefaces and dedications to the various *Comedias,* especially in *Partes* IX (1618), XIII (1620), XVII (1622), XIX (1627), and XXIII (1638). These are reprinted in *Obras* ed. by Menéndez y Pelayo for the Real Academia Española, 13 vols. (Madrid, 1890-1902). The *Arte nuevo de hacer comedias en este tiempo* originally appeared in the *Rimas* (Madrid, 1609). The *Rimas* are published in facsimile by the Hispanic Society of America (New York, 1903). The *Arte* by Morel-Fatio, with notes, in the *Bulletin hispanique* (Paris, Oct.-Dec., 1904). Also in H. J. Chaytor's *Dramatic Theory in Spain* (Cambridge, 1925). It is translated as *The New Art of Making Plays in This Age*, by William T. Brewster, with an introduction by Brander Matthews (Dramatic Museum of Columbia University, New York, 1914).

On Lope de Vega and his works:

Pérez de Montalban, *Fama Póstuma* (Madrid, 1636).
——, *Para todos* (Madrid, 1632).
Henry Richard, Lord Holland, *Some Account of the Lives and Writings of Lope Felix de Vega Carpio and Guillen de Castro* (London, 1817).
Cayetano Alberto de la Barrera, *Nueva Biografía de Lope de Vega* (Madrid, 1890).
Alfred Morel-Fatio, *Les Origines de*

Lope de Vega (In the *Bulletin hispanique*, VII, p. 38, Paris, 1905).
Cristóbal Pérez Pastor, *Datos desconocidos para la Vida de Lope de Vega* (In *Homenaje á Menéndez y Pelayo*. Madrid, 1900. New ed., in Tomillo's *Proceso de Lope de Vega*, etc., Madrid, 1901).
Hugo Albert Rennert, *The Life of Lope de Vega* (London, 1904).
——, *The Spanish Stage in the Time of Lope de Vega* (New York, 1909).
James Fitzmaurice Kelly, *Lope de Vega and the Spanish Drama* (London, 1902).
Camille Le Senne and Guillot de Saix, *Lope de Vega, L'Etoile de Séville. Etude et version française intégrale. Préface par Henry Roujon* (Paris, 1912).
Brander Matthews, *Introduction to The New Art of Writing Plays*, etc. (New York, 1914).
Camille Pitollet, *La Poétique de Lope* (In *Le Siècle, Paris*, Nov., 1905).
Rudolph Schevill, *The Dramatic Art of Lope de Vega* (Berkeley, Cal., 1918).

THE NEW ART OF WRITING PLAYS IN THIS AGE[1]
[*Arte nuevo de hacer comedias en este tiempo*]
(1609)

1. You command me, noble spirits, flower of Spain,— who in this congress and renowned academy will in short space of time surpass not only the assemblies of Italy which Cicero, envious of Greece, made famous with his own name, hard by the Lake of Avernus, but also Athens, where in the Lyceum of Plato was seen high conclave of philosophers,— to write you an art of the play which is to-day acceptable to the taste of the crowd.

2. Easy seems this subject, and easy it would be for any one of you who had written very few comedies, and who knows more about the writing of them and of all these things; for what condemns me in this task is that I have written them without art.

3. Not because I was ignorant of the precepts; thank God, even while I was a

tyro in grammar, I went through the books which treated the subject, before I had seen the sun run its course ten times from the Ram to the Fishes;

4. But because, in fine, I found that comedies were not at that time, in Spain, as their first devisers in the world thought that they should be written; but rather as many rude fellows managed them, who confirmed the crowd in its crudeness; and so they were introduced in such wise that he who now writes them artistically dies without fame and guerdon; for custom can do more among those who lack light of art than reason and force.

5. True it is that I have sometimes written in accordance with the art which few know; but, no sooner do I see coming from some other source the monstrosities full of painted scenes where the crowd congregates and the women who canonize this sad business, than I return to that same barbarous habit, and when I have to write a comedy I lock in

---

[1] Translated by William T. Brewster in the *Papers on Play-Making I*, with an introduction by Brander Matthews (Dramatic Museum of Columbia University, New York. 1914).

the precepts with six keys, I banish Terence and Plautus from my study, that they may not cry out at me; for truth, even in dumb books, is wont to call aloud; and I write in accordance with that art which they devised who aspired to the applause of the crowd; for, since the crowd pays for the comedies, it is fitting to talk foolishly to it to satisfy its taste.

6. Yet the comedy has its end established like every kind of poem or poetic art, and that has always been to imitate the actions of men and to paint the customs of their age. Furthermore, all poetic imitation whatsoever is composed of three things, which are discourse, agreeable verse, harmony, that is to say music, which so far was common also to tragedy; comedy being different from tragedy in that it treats of lowly and plebeian actions, and tragedy of royal and great ones. Look whether there be in our comedies few failings.

7. *Auto* was the name given to them, for they imitate the actions and the doings of the crowd. Lope de Rueda was an example in Spain of these principles, and to-day are to be seen in print prose comedies of his so lowly that he introduces into them the doings of mechanics and the love of the daughter of a smith; whence there has remained the custom of calling the old comedies *entremeses,* where the art persists in all its force, there being one action and that between plebeian people; for an *entremes* with a king has never been seen. And thus it is shown how the art, for very lowness of style, came to be held in great disrepute, and the king in the comedy to be introduced for the ignorant.

8. Aristotle depicts in his *Poetics,*—although obscurely,— the beginning of comedy; the strife between Athens and Megara as to which of them was the first inventor; they of Megara say that it was Epicarmus, while Athens would have it that Maynetes was the man. Ælius Donatus says it had its origin in ancient sacrifices. He names Thespis as the author of tragedy,— following Horace, who affirms the same,— as of comedies, Aristophanes. Homer composed the *Odyssey* in imitation of comedy, but the *Iliad* was a famous example of tragedy, in imitation of what I called

my *Jerusalem* an epic, and added the term *tragic;* and in the same manner all people commonly term the *Inferno,* the *Purgatorio,* and the *Paradiso* of the celebrated poet, Dante Alighieri, a comedy, and this Manetti recognizes in his prologue.

9. Now, everybody knows that comedy, as if under suspicion, was silenced for a certain time, and that hence also satire was born, which being more cruel, more quickly came to an end, and gave place to the New Comedy. The choruses were the first things; then the fixed number of the characters was introduced; but Menander, whom Terence followed, held the choruses in despite, as offensive. Terence was more circumspect as to the principles; since he never elevated the style of comedy to the greatness of tragedy, which many have condemned as vicious in Plautus; for in this respect Terence was more wary.

10. Tragedy has as its argument history, and comedy fiction; for this reason it was called flat-footed, of humble argument, since the actor performed without buskin or stage. There were comedies with the *pallium,* mimes, comedies with the toga, *fabulae atellanae,* and comedies of the tavern, which were also, as now, of various sorts.

11. With Attic elegance the men of Athens chided vice and evil custom in their comedies, and they gave their prizes both to the writers of verse and to the devisers of action. For this Tully called comedies "the mirror of custom and a living image of the truth,"— a very high tribute, in that comedy ran even with history. Look whether it be worthy of this crown and glory!

12. But now I perceive that you are saying that this is merely translating books and wearying with painting this mixed-up affair. Believe me, there has been a reason why you should be reminded of some of these things; for you see that you ask me to describe the art of writing plays in Spain, where whatever is written is in defiance of art; and to tell how they are now written contrary to the ancient rule and to what is founded on reason, is to ask me to draw on my experience, not on art, for art speaks truth which the ignorant crowd gainsays.

13. If, then, you desire art, I beseech you, men of genius, to read the very learned Robortello of Udine and you will see in what he says concerning Aristotle and especially in what he writes about comedy, as much as is scattered among many books; for everything of to-day is in a state of confusion.

14. If you wish to have my opinion of the comedies which now have the upper hand and to know why it is necessary that the crowd with its laws should maintain the vile chimera of this comic monster, I will tell you what I hold, and do you pardon me, since I must obey whoever has power to command me,— that, gilding the error of the crowd, I desire to tell you of what sort I would have them; for there is no recourse but to follow art, observing a mean between the two extremes.

15. Let the subject be chosen and do not be amused,— may you excuse these precepts!— if it happens to deal with kings; though, for that matter, I understand that Philip the Prudent, King of Spain and our lord, was offended at seeing a king in them; either because the matter was hostile to art or because the royal authority ought not to be represented among the lowly and the vulgar.

16. This is merely turning back to the Old Comedy, where we see that Plautus introduced gods, as in his *Amphitryon* he represents Jupiter. God knows that I have difficulty in giving this my approbation, since Plutarch, speaking of Menander, does not highly esteem Old Comedy. But since we are so far away from art and in Spain do it a thousand wrongs, let the learned this once close their lips.

17. Tragedy mixed with comedy and Terence with Seneca, though it be like another minotaur of Pasiphae, will render one part grave, the other ridiculous; for this variety causes much delight. Nature gives us good example, for through such variety it is beautiful.

18. Bear in mind that this subject should contain one action only, seeing to it that the story in no manner be episodic; I mean the introduction of other things which are beside the main purpose; nor that any member be omitted which might ruin the whole of the context. There is no use in advising that it should take place in the period of one sun, though this is the view of Aristotle; but we lose our respect for him when we mingle tragic style with the humbleness of mean comedy. Let it take place in as little time as possible, except when the poet is writing history in which some years have to pass; these he can relegate to the space between the acts, wherein, if necessary, he can have a character go on some journey; a thing that greatly offends whoever perceives it. But let not him who is offended go to see them.

19. Oh! how lost in admiration are many at this very time at seeing that years are passed in an affair to which an artificial day sets a limit; though for this they would not allow the mathematical day! But, considering that the wrath of a seated Spaniard is immoderate, when in two hours there is not presented to him everything from Genesis to the Last Judgment, I deem it most fitting if it be for us here to please him, for us to adjust everything so that it succeeds.

20. The subject once chosen, write in prose, and divide the matter into three acts of time, seeing to it, if possible, that in each one the space of the day be not broken. Captain Virués, a worthy wit. divided comedy into three acts, which before had gone on all fours, as on baby's feet, for comedies were then infants. I wrote them myself, when eleven or twelve years of age, of four acts and of four sheets of paper, for a sheet contained each act; and then it was the fashion that for the three intermissions were made three little *entremeses,* but to-day scarce one, and then a dance, for the dancing is so important in comedy that Aristotle approves of it, and Athenæus, Plato and Xenophon treat of it, though this last disapproves of indecorous dancing; and for this reason he is vexed at Callipides, wherein he pretends to ape the ancient chorus. The matter divided into two parts, see to the connection from the beginning until the action runs down; but do not permit the untying of the plot until reaching the last scene; for the crowd, knowing what the end is, will turn its face to the door and its shoulder to what it has awaited three hours face to face; for in what appears, nothing more is to be known.

21. Very seldom should the stage remain without some one speaking, because the crowd becomes restless in these intervals and the story spins itself out at great length; for, besides its being a great defect, the avoidance of it increases grace and artifice.

22. Begin then, and, with simple language, do not spend sententious thoughts and witty sayings on family trifles, which is all that the familiar talk of two or three people is representing. But when the character who is introduced persuades, counsels or dissuades, then there should be gravity and wit; for then doubtless is truth observed, since a man speaks in a different style from what is common when he gives counsel, or persuades, or argues against anything. Aristides, the rhetorician, gave us warrant for this; for he wishes the language of comedy to be pure, clear, and flexible, and he adds also that it should be taken from the usage of the people, this being different from that of polite society; for in the latter case the diction will be elegant, sonorous, and adorned. Do not drag in quotations, nor let your language offend because of exquisite words; for, if one is to imitate those who speak, it should not be by the language of Panchaia, of the Metaurus, of hippogriffs, demi-gods and centaurs.

23. If the king should speak, imitate as much as possible the gravity of a king; if the sage speak, observe a sententious modesty; describe lovers with those passions which greatly move whomever listens to them; manage soliloquies in such a manner that the recitant is quite transformed, and in changing himself, changes the listener. Let him ask questions and reply to himself, and if he shall make plaints, let him observe the respect due to women. Let not ladies disregard their character, and if they change costumes, let it be in such wise that it may be excused; for male disguise usually is very pleasing. Let him be on his guard against impossible things, for it is of the chiefest importance that only the likeness of truth should be represented. The lackey should not discourse of lofty affairs, not express the conceits which we have seen in certain foreign plays; and in no wise let the character contradict himself in what he has said; I mean to

say, forget,— as in Sophocles one blames Œdipus for not remembering that he has killed Laius with his own hand. Let the scenes end with epigram, with wit, and with elegant verse, in such wise that, at his exit, he who spouts leave not the audience disgusted. In the first act set for the case. In the second weave together the events, in such wise that until the middle of the third act one may hardly guess the outcome. Always trick expectancy; and hence it may come to pass that something quite far from what is promised may be left to the understanding. Tactfully suit your verse to the subjects being treated. *Décimas* are good for complainings; the sonnet is good for those who are waiting in expectation; recitals of events ask for *romances*, though they shine brilliantly in *octavas*. *Tercets* are for grave affairs and *redondillas* for affairs of love. Let rhetorical figure be brought in, as repetition or anadiplosis, and in the beginning of these same verses the various forms of anaphora; and also irony, questions, apostrophes, and exclamations.

24. To deceive the audience with the truth is a thing that has seemed well, as Miguel Sánchez, worthy of this memorial for the invention, was wont to do in all his comedies. Equivoke and the uncertainty arising from ambiguity have always held a large place among the crowd, for it thinks that it alone understands what the other one is saying. Better still are the subjects in which honor has a part, since they deeply stir everybody; along wth them go virtuous deeds, for virtue is everywhere loved; hence we see, if an actor chance to represent a traitor, he is so hateful to every one that what he wishes to buy is not sold him, and the crowd flees when it meets him; but if he is loyal, they lend to him and invite him, and even the chief men honor him, love him, seek him out, entertain him, and acclaim him.

25. Let each act have but four sheets, for twelve are well suited to the time and the patience of him who is listening. In satirical parts, be not clear or open, since it is known that for this very reason comedies were forbidden by law in Greece and Italy; wound without hate, for if, perchance, slander be done, expect not applause, nor aspire to fame.

26. These things you may regard as aphorisms which you get not from the ancient art, which the present occasion allows no further space for treating; since whatever has to do with the three kinds of stage properties which Vitruvius speaks of, concerns the impresario; just as Valerius Maximus, Petrus Crinitus, Horace in his *Epistles,* and others describe these properties, with their drops, trees, cabins, houses, and simulated marbles.

27. Of costume Julius Pollux would tell us if it were necessary, for in Spain it is the case that the comedy of to-day is replete with barbarous things: a Turk wearing the neck-gear of a Christian, and a Roman in tight breeches.

28. But of all, nobody can I call more barbarous than myself, since in defiance of art I dare to lay down precepts, and I allow myself to be borne along in the vulgar current, wherefore Italy and France call me ignorant. But what can I do if I have written four hundred and eighty-three comedies, along with one which I have finished this week? For all of these, except six, gravely sin against art. Yet, in fine, I defend what I have written, and I know that, though they might have been better in another manner, they would not have had the vogue which they have had; for sometimes that which is contrary to what is just, for that very reason, pleases the taste.

How Comedy reflects this life of man,
  How true her portraiture of young and old;
How subtle wit, polished in narrow span,
  And purest speech, and more too you behold;
What grave consideration mixed with smiles,
  What seriousness, along with pleasant jest;
Deceit of slaves; how woman oft beguiles
  How full of slyness is her treacherous breast;
How silly, awkward swains to sadness run,
  How rare success, though all seems well begun.

Let one hear with attention, and dispute not of the art; for in comedy everything will be found of such a sort that in listening to it everything becomes evident.

TIRSO DE MOLINA

Gabriel Tellez, known as Tirso de Molina, was born at Madrid probably in 1570. He was graduated from the University of Alcalá, and in 1613 he took orders. Very little is known of his life, though it is likely that he traveled a great deal and was a soldier. Toward the end of his life he became prior of the Monastery at Soria. He was a prolific playwright, whose chief claim lies in his having created the character of Don Juan. He died at Soria in 1648.

Tirso was one of the defenders of the free romantic *comedia,* and his few references to the drama are in defense of Lope de Vega, the greatest of the writers of that sort of play. In his *Cigarrales de Toledo* (1624), he includes a play, *El Vergonzoso en Palacio,* and after it introduces a fictitious discussion in dialogue-form. One person attacks Tirso for violating the Unities. Another, Tirso himself, speaking through him, assails the critic and defends the free form. Tirso's criticism is rather a reflection of the spirit of the time than a true defense of a form which very few writers adhered to or wished for.

On the drama:

Tirso's only remarks on dramatic theory are found in the *Cigarrales de Toledo* (1624).

Editions:

The various editions of the plays contain biographies, and in some cases extracts from the *Cigarrales de Toledo.* The passages on the drama are quoted fully in Menéndez y Peláyo's *Historia de las ideas estéticas en España* (2nd ed., Madrid 1890, ff.). Reprinted in H. J. Chaytor's *Dramatic Theory in Spain* (Cambridge, 1925). The plays are found in the *Comedias escogidas,* 2 vols. (Madrid, 1850), and in the *Comedias de Tirso de Molina,* 2 vols. (Madrid, 1906–07).

On Tirso de Molina and his works:

M. Menéndez y Pelayo, *Estudios de*

crítica literaria, 5 vols. (2nd series, Madrid, 1893–1908).

P. Muñoz Peña, *El teatro del Maestro Tirso de Molina* (Madrid, 1889).

B. de los Ríos de Lampérez, *Tirso de Molina* (Madrid, 1906).

Artículos biográficos y críticos de varios autores acerca de . . . Tellez y sus obras (In the *Biblioteca de autores españoles,* vol. 5, pp. xi–xxxv, Madrid, 1850).

THE ORCHARDS OF TOLEDO [1]

[*Cigarrales de Toledo*]

(1624)

". . . Among the many blemishes (pardon my presumption!) what tries my patience is to see how ruthlessly the poet disregards in this play the limits and laws with which the first inventors of drama [*comedia*] so carefully defined its cardinal principle, namely, that a play must concern itself with an action whose beginning, middle, and end occupy at the most twenty-four hours, and one and the same place. He has cunningly given us a spectacle of the conquest of love covering a period of at least a month and a half. And yet, even in that time, it seems to us impossible (with the preservation of any decency) that so illustrious and discreet a lady should bring herself so blindly to pursue a shepherd, make him her secretary, declare her purpose through riddles, and finally risk her reputation to the bold ruthlessness of a man of such humble origin." The ill-natured disputant was continuing when Don Alejo, interrupting him, answered: " Your point is not well taken, since the play under discussion has observed the laws which are now recognized; and it seems to me that the position merited by our modern Spanish plays, which are comparable to those of antiquity, marks a distinct step in advance, however they fail to take into account the cardinal principle of the Masters. What if these Masters did maintain that a play must represent an action which could logically take place within twenty-four hours? What greater inconvenience can there be than that within that short time a dis-

creet gallant should fall in love with a prudent lady, court her, make love to her, woo her — all within a single day, if you please, and after claiming her for the morrow, must needs marry her that very night? What opportunity is there to arouse jealousy, engender despair, bring hope to the lover, and depict all the other uncertainties and accidents without which love is a matter of no importance? Or how can a lover boast that he is constant and loyal, if there be not allowed several days to elapse,— months, even years,— in which he may prove his constancy? These inconveniences are greater in the judgment of any one of moderate intelligence, than that which would ensue were the audience allowed to witness everything without leaving their seats, in order to follow the happenings of many days. Just as he who reads a story in a few pages covering the events of a protracted period and occuring in many places, so the spectator at a play — which is an image and representation of the story's action — can see it interpret and shadow forth the ortunes of the lovers, depicting to the life what happens to them. Now, since these things cannot happen in the space of a single day, the dramatist must assume that everything happens as he shows it, in order that the action may be perfect. Not in vain is poetry called a living picture, imitating the passive picture which, in the small space of a yard and a half of plane surface shows perspective and distance in manner to bestow upon the beholder an illusion of reality. It is not just that the license granted to the

---

[1] Especially translated sections for this collection by Winifred Ayres Hope.— Ed.

pencil be withheld from the pen. And if you argue by way of reply that we of the same craft owe it to the initiators to guard their principles intact, I answer that although veneration is due the masters for having set out in difficulty — which hampers all things in their beginning — yet it is undeniable that, adding perfection to *their* invention (a thing necessary, but at the same time easy), it is Genius which, when the fundamental laws fail to help, knows how to change the accidental, improving it by experience. There is this difference between Nature and Art: that what the former began, cannot be changed; thus the pear-tree will bear pears to eternity, and the oak the uncouth acorn, and notwithstanding the difference of soil and the varying influences of the atmosphere and climate to which they are subject, she produces them over and over again. Amid other changes, species is constant. Does it matter how much the Drama may modify the laws of its ancestors, ingeniously mixing tragedy with comedy and producing a pleasant type of play of the two — and partaking of the character of each — introducing serious characters from the one, and waggish and absurd characters from the other? I claim that if the preeminence in Greece of Æschylus and Euripides (as among the Latins of Seneca and Terence) suffices to establish the laws of these Masters who are now so vigorously upheld, the excellence of our Spanish Lope de Vega makes his improvements in both styles of play so conspicuous that the authority he brings to this improvement is sufficient to reform the old laws. And since the Drama is so highly esteemed for subtlety and perfection, that fact makes it a school in itself, and gives us, who are proud to be followers, the right to be proud of such a Master, and gladly to defend his doctrine against whosoever shall violently impugn it. As to the fact that in many passages of his writings he says that he does not observe the ancient art, in order that he may make his own acceptable to the people, that is only the result of his innate modesty; it is said so that malicious ignorance may not attribute to arrogance what is as a matter of fact well-bred perfection. As for us, it is right that we should look to him as the reformer of the New Drama; and such we esteem him.

ENGLAND — I

ELIZABETHAN PERIOD

ELIZABETHAN DRAMATIC CRITICISM

English literary criticism is derived partly from the ancients, and partly from the Italian scholars. Recent research has revealed many Italian sources drawn upon by Sidney and Jonson. The earliest formal treatise touching upon literature in England is Leonard Coxe's *Arte or Crafte of Rhetoryke*, written about 1524; this was derived in part from Melanchthon. Thomas Wilson's *Arte of Rhetorike* followed in 1553. More important still is Roger Ascham's *Scholemaster* (1570) which contains the first reference in English to Aristotle's *Poetics*. George Whetstone's *Dedication* to *Promos and Cassandra* (1578) is a curious criticism of the drama of other nations and an attempt to reconcile Platonism and the drama. The English stage was at several times the subject of controversies between the dramatists and their adherents, and the Puritanical element. The first of these controversies called forth a number of interesting attacks and defenses, among them three or four of some value as criticism of the drama. In 1577 John Northbrooke published his *Treatise wherein Dicing, Dauncing, vaine Playes or Enterluds, with other idle Pastimes, &c., commonly used on the Sabaoth Day, and reproued by the Authoritie of the Word of God and auntient Writers.* Then followed Stephen Gosson's *The Schoole of Abuse* (1579), another attack. Thomas Lodge replied in his *Defence of Poetry, Music, and Stage Plays* (1579). Later in the same year Gosson published his *A Short Apologie of the Schoole of Abuse*, etc. Henry Denham's *A Second and Third Blast of Retreat from Plays and Theatres* appeared in 1580. Gosson's *Playes confuted in five Actions*, etc., was published about 1582. About this time Sir Philip Sidney wrote his *Defence of Poesy*, or *Apologie for Poetry* (published 1595), a reply to the Puritan attacks on the stage. Three further attacks may be mentioned: Philip Stubbes' *The Anat-*omie of Abuses* (1583), George Whetstone's *A Touchstone for the Time* (1584), and William Rankins' *A Mirrour of Monsters* (1587). William Webbe's *A Discourse of English Poetrie* (1586) is a more ambitious formal treatise on writing, while Puttenham's *Arte of English Poesie* (1589) furthered the work of classification and introducing foreign — chiefly Italian — meters and forms. Sir John Harington's *Apologie of Poetry* (1591) was, like Sidney's similar work, a defense against the Puritan attacks. When Sidney's *Defence* was published in 1595, it was already fairly well known, as it had circulated in manuscript for some years. It is rigidly classical in its sections on the drama, and follows the Italian Renaissance scholars in requiring greater verisimilitude, and an adherence to the Unities. It is curious to note the absence of any such declaration of independence as Lope de Vega's *New Art* among the Elizabethan dramatists, most of whom were opposed in practice to all formulas. The greatest critical treatises of the period were classic in tendency, and the two most important — Sidney's and Jonson's — are directed against current practices in playwriting. Bacon's remarks on the drama — in the *Essays*, the *Advancement of Learning*, and the *De Augmentis* — could be condensed into one or two pages. The dramatists themselves had comparatively little to say of their art; a dozen Dedications and a few Prologues of Jonson,[1] Chapman,[2] Fletcher,[3] Marston,[4] Middleton,[5] Hey-

[1] Prologue to *Every Man in His Humour* (printed 1616). *To the Readers* in *Sejanus* (printed 1605); Dedication to *Volpone* (printed 1607); *Prologue to Epicœne* (printed 1609?).
[2] *Dedication* to *The Revenge of Bussy d'Ambois* (printed 1613).
[3] *Preface* to *The Faithful Shepherdess* (printed 1609).
[4] *To the General Reader*, in *Sophronisba* (printed 1606).
[5] *Preface* to *The Roaring Girl* (printed 1611).

99

wood,[6] Webster,[7] and Field,[8] are practically all that have direct bearing upon the subject. Ben Jonson's *Discoveries* closes the period. This work (published in 1641) is of prime importance, though unfortunately it is, as has been said, not a representative apology or explanation of the current practice, but an attack upon it.[9]

NOTE. If only to prove the scantiness of dramatic theory among the dramatists of the Elizabethan period, I have below re-printed a few brief extracts from the most important prefaces to plays:

John Webster, *To the Reader* (in *The White Devil*, 1612): ". . . If it be objected this is no true dramatic poem, I shall easily confess it; *non potes in nugas dicere plura meas, ipse ego quam dixi.* Willingly, and not ignorantly, in this kind have I faulted; for should a man present to such an auditory the most sententious tragedy that ever was written, observing all the critical laws, as height of style and gravity of person, enrich it with the sententious chorus, and, as it were, liven death in the passionate and weighty Nuntius; yet, after all this divine rapture, *O dura messorum ilia,* the breath that comes from the uncapable multitude is able to poison it; and, ere it be acted, let the author resolve to fix to every scene this of Horace, *Haec porcis hodie comedenda relinques. . . .*"

John Fletcher, *To the Reader* (in *The Faithful Shepherdess*, 1609): "If you be not reasonably assured of your knowledge in this kind of poem, lay down the book, or read this, which I would wish had been the prologue. It is a pastoral tragicomedy, which the people seeing when it was played, having ever had a singular gift in defining, concluded to be a play of country hired shepherds in gray cloaks, with curtailed dogs in strings, sometimes laughing together, and sometimes killing one another; and, missing Whitsun-ales, cream, wassail, and morris-dances, began to be angry. In their error I would not have you fall, lest you incur their cen-

6 Dedication to *The Iron Age* (printed 1632).
7 *To the Reader*, in *The White Devil* (printed 1612).
9 *To the Reader* in *Woman is a Weathercock.* (1612).

sure. Understand, therefore, a pastoral to be a representation of shepherds and shepherdesses with their actions and passions, which must be such as may agree with their natures, at least not exceeding former fictions and vulgar traditions; they are not to be adorned with any art, but such improper ones as nature is said to bestow, as singing and poetry; or such as experience may teach them as the virtues of herbs and fountains, the ordinary course of the sun, moon, and stars, and such like. But you are ever to remember shepherds to be such as all the ancient poets, and modern, of understanding, have received them; that is, the owners of flocks, and not hirelings. A tragicomedy is not so called in respect of mirth and killing, but in respect it wants death, which is enough to make it no tragedy, yet it brings some near it, which is enough to make it no comedy, which must be a representation of familiar people, with such kind of trouble as no life be questioned; so that a god is as lawful in this as in a tragedy, and mean people as in a comedy. Thus much I hope will serve to justify my poem, and make you understand it; to teach you more for nothing, I do not know that I am in conscience bound."

Thomas Middleton, *To the Comic Playreaders, Venery and Laughter* (in *The Roaring Girl*, 1611): "The fashion of play-making I can properly compare to nothing so naturally as the alteration of apparel; for in the time of the great crop-doublet, your huge bombastic plays, quilted with mighty words to lean purpose, was only then in fashion: and as the doublet fell, neater inventions began to set up. Now, in the time of spruceness, our plays follow the niceness of our garments, single plots, quaint conceits, lecherous jests, dressed up in hanging sleeves; and those are fit for the times and termers. Such a kind of light-color stuff, mingled with divers colors, you shall find this published comedy; good to keep you in an afternoon from dice at home in your chambers; and for venery, you shall find enough for sixpence, but well couched an you mark it. . . ."

General references on English literature:

A. W. Ward and A. R. Waller, editors, *The Cambridge History of English Literature*, 14 vols. (Cambridge and New York, 1907-17).

Henry Morley, *English Writers*, 11 vols. (London, 1887-95).

Andrew Lang, *History of English Literature* (London, 1912).

R. P. Halleck, *History of English Literature* (New York, 1900).

Richard Garnett and Edmund Gosse, *English Literature*, 4 vols. (New York, 1908).

Stopford A. Brooke, *English Literature* (Ed., New York, 1907).

M. L. Mézières, *Histoire critique de la littérature anglaise*, 3 vols. (Paris, 1834).

William Vaughn Moody and R. M. Lovett, *A History of English Literature* (New York, 1911).

W. R. Nicoll and T. Seccombe, *A History of English Literature*, 3 vols. (New York, 1907).

H. S. Pancoast, *An Introduction to English Literature* (New York, 1894. See 3rd ed.).

George Saintsbury, *A Short History of English Literature* (New York, 1898).

G. Körting, *Grundriss der Geschichte der englischen Literatur* (3rd ed., Münster, 1899).

Leslie Stephen and Sidney Lee, *Dictionary of National Biography*, 66 vols. (London, 1885-1901).

E. Engel, *A History of English Literature* (London, 1902).

General references on English drama:

R. W. Lowe, *Bibliographical Account of English Theatrical Literature* (London, 1888).

K. L. Bates and L. B. Godfrey, *English Drama, a Working Basis* (Wellesley, 1896).

David Erskine Baker, *Biographia Dramatica*, etc., 3 vols. (Continuation, London, 1811).

——, *The Companion to the Playhouse*, 2 vols. (London, 1764).

W. R. Chetwood, *The British Theatre* (Dublin, 1750).

J. L. Klein, *Geschichte des Dramas*, vols. 12 and 13 (Leipzig, 1865-76).

Benjamin Brawley, *A Short History of the English Drama* (New York, 1921).

W. Creizenach, *Geschichte des neueren Dramas* (Halle, 1893-1909; vol. iv translated by Cécile Hugon as *The English Drama in the Age of Shakespeare*, London, 1916).

John Doran, *Annals of the English Stage*, 2 vols. (London, 1864).

A. W. Reed, *Early Tudor Drama* (London, 1926).

Percy Fitzgerald, *New History of the English Stage* (London, 1882).

Agnes M. Mackenzie, *The Playgoer's Handbook to the English Renaissance Drama* (London, n. d.).

F. G. Fleay, *A Biographical Chronicle of the English Drama* (London, 1891).

John Genest, *Some Account of the English Stage*, 10 vols. (Bath, 1832).

E. Malone, *Historical Account of the Rise and Progress of the English Stage* (in 3rd vol., ed. of Shakespeare, London, 1821).

A. S. Rappoport, *The English Drama* (London, n. d.).

R. F. Sharp, *A Short History of the English Stage* (London, 1909).

A. W. Ward, *History of English Dramatic Literature to the Death of Queen Anne*, 3 vols. (New York, 1899).

Arnold Wynne, *The Growth of English Drama* (Oxford, 1914).

Felix E. Schelling, *English Drama* (New York, 1914).

T. Hawkins, *The Origin of the English Drama*, 3 vols. (Oxford, 1773).

E. K. Chambers, *The Mediæval Stage*, 2 vols. (Oxford, 1903).

Charles Dibdin, *A Complete History of the Stage*, 5 vols. (London, 1800).

John Downes, *Roscius Anglicanus, or an historical view of the Stage*, etc. (new ed., London, 1789).

S. A. Dunham, *Lives of British Dramatists*, 2 vols. (London, 1847).

Thomas Gilliland, *The Dramatic Mirror: containing the History of the Stage, from the earliest period to the present time*, etc., 2 vols. (London, 1808).

L. N. Chase, *The English Heroic Play* (New York, 1903).

Jeanette Marks, *English Pastoral Drama* (London, 1908).

F. H. Ristine, *English Tragicomedy* (New York, 1910).

Felix E. Schelling, *The English Chronicle Play* (New York, 1902).

A. H. Thorndike, *Tragedy* (Boston, 1908).

Allardyce Nicoll, *British Drama* (New York, 1925).

Donald Clive Stuart, *The Development of Dramatic Art* (New York, 1928).

Watson Nicholson, *The Struggle for a Free Stage in London* (Boston, 1906).

References on Elizabethan drama:

Felix E. Schelling, *Elizabethan Drama*, 2 vols. (Boston, 1908).

——, *Elizabethan Playwrights* (New York, 1925).

J. P. Collier, *The History of English Dramatic Poetry to the Time of Shakespeare and Annals of the Stage to the Restoration*, 3 vols. (new ed., London, 1879).

J. M. Robertson, *Elizabethan Literature* (New York, 1914).

Felix E. Schelling, *English Literature During the Lifetime of Shakespeare* (New York, 1910).

T. Seccombe and J. W. Allen, *The Age of Shakespeare*, 2 vols. (London, 1903).

F. Guizot, *Shakespeare and His Times* (trans., New York, 1855).

William Hazlitt, *Lectures on the Dramatic Literature of the Age of Queen Elizabeth* (London, 1821).

A. Mézières, *Prédécesseurs et contemporains de Shakespeare* (Paris, 1881).

——, *Contemporains et successeurs de Shakespeare* (Paris, 1881).

George Saintsbury, *History of Elizabethan Literature* (ed., London, 1906).

M. A. Scott, *The Elizabethan Drama, especially in its Relations to the Italians of the Renaissance* (New Haven, 1894).

A. C. Swinburne, *The Age of Shakespeare* (London, 1908).

J. A. Symonds, *Shakespeare's Predecessors in the English Drama* (London, 1881).

Barrett Wendell, *The Temper of the Seventeenth Century in English Literature* (New York, 1904).

E. P. Whipple, *Literature of the Age of Elizabeth* (Boston, 1869).

F. S. Boas, *Shakespeare and his Predecessors* (ed., New York, 1904).

J. W. Cunliffe, *The Influence of Italian on Early Elizabethan Drama* (in *Modern Philology*, 4, 1906).

——, *The Influence of Seneca on Elizabethan Tragedy* (London, 1893).

N. Drake, *Shakespeare and His Times* (London, 1817).

Harriet Ely Fansler, *The Evolution of Technique in Elizabethan Tragedy* (Chicago, 1914).

W. J. Courthope, *History of English Poetry*, vols. I–III (London, 1895–1903).

F. G. Fleay, *A Chronicle History of the London Stage* (1559–1642) (London, 1890).

J.-J. Jusserand, *Le Théâtre en Angleterre jusqu' aux prédecesseurs immédiats de Shakespeare* (2nd ed., Paris, 1881).

[W. C. Hazlitt. ed.] *The English Drama and Stage Under the Tudor and Stuart Princes—1543–1664—Illustrated by a Series of Documents, Treatises, and Poems*, etc. (London, 1869).

J. A. Lester, *Connections Between the Drama of France and Great Britain, particularly in the Elizabethan Period* (Cambridge. Mass., 1902).

L. Einstein, *The Italian Renaissance in England* (New York, 1902).

J. P. Collier, ed., *The Alleyn Papers* (London, 1843).

W. K. Chambers, *The Elizabethan Stage*, 4 vols. (New York, 1923).

References on English criticism, Elizabethan in particular:

George Saintsbury, *A History of English Criticism* (New York, 1911).

H. S. Symmes, *Les Débuts de la critique dramatique en Angleterre jusqu' à la mort de Shakespeare* (Paris, 1903).

J. E. Spingarn, *A History of Literary Criticism in the Renaissance* (2nd ed., New York, 1908).

Felix E. Schelling, *Poetic and Verse Criticism of the Reign of Elizabeth* (Philadelphia, 1891).

L. S. Friedland, *Dramatic Unities in England* (in *Journal of English and Germanic Philology*, vol. 10, no. 1, 1911).

David Klein, *Literary Criticism from the Elizabethan Dramatists* (New York, 1910).

Laura J. Wylie, *Studies in the Evolution of English Criticism* (Boston, 1894).

P. Hamelius, *Die Kritik in der englischen Litteratur der 17. und 18. Jahrhunderts* (Leipzig, 1897).

C. W. Moulton, *The Library of Literary Criticism of English and American Authors*, 8 vols. (Buffalo, 1901–05).

F. Gregory Smith, *Elizabethan Critical Essays*, 2 vols. (Oxford, 1904).

SIR PHILIP SIDNEY

Philip Sidney was born at Penshurst in 1554. He came of a noble and well-known family, his father being Deputy of Ireland. He attended school at Shrewsbury and later went to Oxford, which he left in 1571 without taking his degree, and went to stay with his father at Ludlow. The next year he went to Paris with a commission to negotiate for the marriage of the Queen with the Duke d'Alençon. He remained there in the King's service and was a witness of the Massacre of St. Bartholomew, and escaped with his life only by taking refuge in the English Embassy. From Paris the young Philip escaped to Germany, visiting Strassburg, Heidelberg, and Frankfurt. Together with his friend Languet, he traveled for the next three years, through Austria, Hungary, and Italy; he returned through Bohemia and Germany, and was again at Ludlow in 1575. His uncle Leicester readily took the young man under his protection, and Sidney became a courtier. In 1577 he was sent to confer with Rudolf II and the Elector Palatine in Germany on political business, and returned home by way of the Netherlands, where he met William of Orange. His diplomatic missions were highly successful, and before long he found himself in the Queen's confidence. He was later involved in trouble incident to attacks made upon his father's administration in Ireland. In 1579 the Queen was again considering an alliance with the former Duke d'Alençon, now the Duke d'Anjou. His opposition to the match brought him into disfavor, and in 1580 he retired from Court, and began work on his *Arcadia*. Soon, however, the disgraced Leicester induced his nephew to return to Court. In 1583 he was knighted, and the same year his marriage to a daughter of Walsingham caused him to relinquish certain claims he had in America. But two years after, he was planning an expedition to the New World, and would have gone had not Drake informed the Queen that he was about to sail — contrary to her wishes. Two months later Sidney went to the

Low Countries, and the following year engaged in war. He died from a wound received at Zutphen.

Sidney's only work concerned with the drama was the *Apologie for Poetry* — or *Defence of Poesie*. This was begun in all probability in 1581, as a reply to Gosson's *The Schoole of Abuse* (1579), a Puritan attack on plays and poetry. Sidney's *Defence* is more than a reply, it is a glorification of art and its influence on the mind and conduct of human beings. He touches, incidentally, as it were, on the various forms of literature, and his remarks on the drama reveal an extensive knowledge of the classics and the Italian commentators on Aristotle. Aristotle first became an influence in English literature through the *Apologie*, and the first mention of the Unities is likewise found in this work. It must be borne in mind that the *Apologie* was written before the great period of activity in the field of Elizabethan drama, and that the plays upon which Sidney might base his judgments or make strictures, were the indigenous interludes, moralities, farces, and classical tragedies written prior to 1580.

Editions:

Two editions appeared at London in 1595: *The Defence of Poesie,* and *An Apologie for Poetrie*. The latter is generally regarded as the better text of the two. It is re-printed in Arber's *English Reprints* and in the first volume of G. Gregory Smith's *Elizabethan Critical Essays, 2* vols. (Oxford, 1904).

On Sidney and his works:

Collins, *Sidney Papers, 2* vols. (London, 1745).
Fulke Greville, *Life of Sidney* (London, 1652).
Fox Bourne, *Memoir of Sir Philip Sidney* (London, 1862).
Julius Lloyd, *Life of Sir Philip Sidney* (London, 1862).
Prefaces to the Arber, Grosart, and Smith eds. of Sidney's works.

J. A. Symonds, *Sir Philip Sidney* (*English Men of Letters Series*, late ed., London, 1906).
J. E. Spingarn, *A History of Literary*

Criticism in the Renaissance (2nd ed., New York, 1908).
George Saintsbury, *A History of Criticism*, vol. 2 (New York, 1902).

AN APOLOGIE FOR POETRY[1]

(or *A Defence of Poesie*)

(1595)

. . . .

No, perchance it is the Comic, whom naughty play-makers and stage-keepers have justly made odious. To the argument of abuse, I will answer after. Only thus much now is to be said, that the comedy is an imitation of the common errors of our life, which he representeth in the most ridiculous and scornful sort that may be; so as it is impossible that any beholder can be content to be such a one.

Now, as in Geometry the oblique must be known as well as the right, and in Arithmetic the odd as well as the even, so in the actions of our life, who seeth not the filthiness of evil wanteth a great foil to perceive the beauty of virtue. This doth the comedy handle so in our private and domestical matters, as with hearing it we get as it were an experience, what is to be looked for of a niggardly Demea, of a crafty Davus, of a flattering Gnato, of a vainglorious Thraso, and not only to know what effects are to be expected, but to know who be such, by the signifying badge given them by the comedian. And little reason hath any man to say that men learn by seeing it so set out, sith, as I said before, there is no man living but, by the force truth hath in nature, no sooner seeth these men play their parts, but wisheth them in Pistrinum; although perchance the sack of his own faults lie so behind his back that he seeth not himself dance the same measure; whereto yet nothing can more open his eyes than to find his own actions contemptibly set forth. So that the right use of comedy (I think) by nobody be blamed, and much less of the high and excellent tragedy, that openeth the greatest wounds,

and showeth forth the ulcers that are covered with tissue; that maketh kings fear to be tyrants, and tyrants manifest their tyrannical humors; that with stirring the effects of admiration and commiseration, teacheth the uncertainty of this world, and upon how weak foundations guilden roofs are builded; that maketh us know

Qui sceptra saevus duro imperio regit,
Timet timentes, metus in auctorem redit.

But how much it can move, Plutarch yieldeth a notable testimony of the abominable tyrant Alexander Pheræns, from whose eyes a tragedy well made and represented, drew abundance of tears, who, without all pity, had murdered infinite numbers, and some of his own blood. So as he, that was not ashamed to make matters for tragedies, yet could not resist the sweet violence of a tragedy. And if it wrought no further good in him, it was that he, in despite of himself, withdrew himself from hearkening to that which might mollify his hardened heart.

. . . .

Our Tragedies, and Comedies (not without cause cried out against), observing rules neither of honest civility nor of skillful poetry, excepting *Gorboduc* (again, I say, of those that I have seen), which notwithstanding, as it is full of stately speeches and well sounding phrases, climbing to the height of Seneca's style, and as full of notable morality, which it doth most delightfully teach, and so obtain the very end of poesy; yet in truth it is very defectious in the circumstances: which grieveth me, because it might not remain as an exact model of all tragedies. For it is faulty both in place and time, the two necessary companions of all corporal actions. For

[1] Re-printed, with omissions, from Smith's *Elizabethan Critical Essays* (Oxford, 1904).—Ed.

where the stage should always represent but one place, and the uttermost time presupposed in it should be, both by Aristotle's precept and common reason, but one day: there is both many days, and many places, inartificially imagined. But if it be so in *Gorboduc,* how much more in all the rest? Where you shall have Asia of the one side, and Afric of the other, and so many other under-kingdoms, that the player, when he cometh in, must ever begin with telling where he is, or else the tale will not be conceived. Now ye shall have three ladies walk to gather flowers, and then we must believe the stage to be a garden. By and by we hear news of shipwreck in the same place, and then we are to blame, if we accept it not for a rock. Upon the back of that, comes out a hideous monster, with fire and smoke, and then the miserable beholders are bound to take it for a cave. While in the meantime, two armies fly in, represented with four swords and bucklers, and then what hard heart will not receive it for a pitched field?

Now, of time they are much more liberal. For ordinary it is that two young princes fall in love: after many traverses, she is got with child, delivered of a fair boy; he is lost, groweth a man, falls in love, and is ready to get another child, and all this in two hours' space: which how absurd it is in sense, even sense may imagine, and art hath taught, and all ancient examples justified: and at this day, the ordinary players in Italy will not err in. Yet will some bring in an example of *Eunuchus* in Terence, that containeth matter of two days, yet far short of twenty years. True it is, and so was it to be played in two days, and so fitted to the time it set forth. And though Plautus hath in one place done amiss, let us hit with him, and not miss with him.

But they will say, how then shall we set forth a story, which containeth both many places, and many times? And do they not know that a tragedy is tied to the laws of poesy, and not of history? not bound to follow the story, but having liberty either to feign a quite new matter, or to frame the history to the most tragical conveniency? Again, many things may be told which cannot be shewed, if they know the difference be-

twixt reporting and representing. As for example, I may speak (though I am here) of Peru, and in speech digress from that to the description of Calcutta: but in action, I cannot represent it without Pacolet's horse: and so was the manner the ancients took, by some *Nuncius* to recount things done in former time, or other place.

Lastly, if they will represent an history, they must not (as Horace saith) begin *Ab ovo:* but they must come to the principal point of that one action, which they will represent. By example this will be best expressed. I have a story of young Polydorus delivered for safety's sake, with great riches, by his father Priam to Polymnestor, king of Thrace, in the Trojan War time. He, after some years, hearing the overthrow of Priam, for to make the treasure his own, murdereth the child: the body of the child is taken up by Hecuba; she the same day findeth a sleight to be revenged most cruelly of the tyrant. Where now would one of our tragedy-writers begin but with the delivery of the child? Then should he sail over into Thrace, and so spend I know not how many years, and travel numbers of places. But where doth Euripides? Even with the finding of the body, leaving the rest to be told by the spirit of Polydorus. This need no further to be enlarged, the dullest wit may conceive it.

But besides these gross absurdities, how all their plays be neither right tragedies, nor right comedies: mingling kings and clowns, not because the matter so carrieth it: but thrust in clowns by head and shoulders, to play a part in majestical matters, with neither decency nor discretion. So as neither the admiration and commiseration, nor the right sportfulness, is by their mongrel Tragi-comedy obtained. I know Apuleius did somewhat so, but that is a thing recounted with space of time, not represented in one moment: and I know, the ancients have one or two examples of Tragi-comedies, as Plautus hath *Amphitryo.* But if we mark them well, we shall find that they never, or very daintily, match hornpipes and funerals. So falleth it out, that, having indeed no right comedy, in that comical part of our tragedy we have nothing but scurrility, unworthy of any chaste ears: or some extreme shew of doltishness indeed fit to lift up a loud laughter and nothing else: where the whole tract of a comedy should be full of delight, as the tragedy should be still maintained in a well-raised admiration.

But our comedians think there is no delight without laughter: which is very wrong, for though laughter may come with delight, yet cometh it not of delight, as though delight should be the cause of laughter. But well may one thing breed both together. Nay, rather in themselves they have as it were a kind of contrariety: for delight we scarcely do, but in things that have a conveniency to ourselves or to the general nature: laughter almost ever cometh of things most disproportioned to ourselves and nature. Delight hath a joy in it, either permanent or present. Laughter hath only a scornful tickling. For example, we are ravished with delight to see a fair woman, and yet are far from being moved to laughter. We laugh at deformed creatures, wherein certainly we cannot delight. We delight in good chances, we laugh at mischances; we delight to hear the happiness of our friends or country, at which he were worthy to be laughed at that would laugh; we shall contrarily laugh sometimes to find a matter quite mistaken and go down the hill against the bias, in the mouth of some such men, as for the respect of them, one shall be heartily sorry, yet he cannot choose but laugh; and so is rather pained, than delighted with laughter. Yet I deny not, but that they may go well together; for as in Alexander's picture well set out, we delight without laughter, and in twenty mad antics we laugh without delight: so in Hercules, painted with his great beard and furious countenance, in woman's attire, spinning at Omphale's commandment, it breedeth both delight and laughter.

But I speak to this purpose, that all the end of the comical part be not upon such scornful matters as stirreth laughter only: but, mixt with it, that delightful teaching which is the end of poesy. And the great fault even in that point of laughter, and forbidden plainly by Aristotle, is, that they stir laughter in sinful things, which are rather execrable than ridiculous; or in miserable, which are rather to be pitied than scorned. For what is it to make folks gape at a wretched beggar, or a beggarly clown; or, against law of hospitality, to jest at strangers because they speak not English so well as we do? What do we learn? Sith it is certain

Nil habet infelix paupertas durius in se,
Quam quod ridiculos homines facit.

But rather a busy loving courtier, a heartless threatening Thraso; a self-wise-seeming schoolmaster; an awry-transformed traveler: these if we saw walk in stage names, which we play naturally, therein were delightful laughter, and teaching delightfulness: as in the other, the tragedies of Buchanan do justly bring forth a divine admiration. But I have lavished out too many words of this play matter. I do it because, as they are excelling parts of poesy, so is there none so much used in England, and none can be more pitifully abused. Which like an unmannerly daughter, shewing a bad education, causeth her mother Poesy's honesty to be called into question.

*   *   *   *   *   *

BEN JONSON

Ben Jonson was born at Westminster in 1573. His first education was received at a school near his home, and continued at the Westminster School, where he received a thorough training. It has sometimes been said that he went to Cambridge, but this has never been proved. It is likely that he applied himself to a trade, probably bricklaying—his stepfather's trade. Either a few years before or after 1592 he was a soldier in the Low Countries. He was married no later than that year. About five years after, he had become an actor, and in 1597 was engaged to revise plays. The next year he produced *Every Man in his Humour*, in which Shakespeare acted. *The Case is Altered* also belongs to the same year. At this time he was in prison as the result of a duel in which he had killed his adversary. He was released by benefit of clergy — having turned Catholic meanwhile — and again set to work for the stage. In *Cynthia's Revels* (1600) he gave offense to two of his fellow-dramatists, Dekker and Marston, and forestalled their attack by writing *The Poetaster* (1601). Dekker replied with his *Histriomastrix* (1602). Jonson next turned his attention to tragedy, and produced *Sejanus* in 1603. He then turned his hand to masques for the court of King James, recently called to the throne, and was associated for years with Inigo Jones. By 1604 he had become reconciled with Dekker and Marston and collaborated with them in the writing of the comedy *Eastward Ho* (1604). Together with his collaborators, Jonson was again sent to prison for some offense caused by the play, and the next year he and Chapman were imprisoned for the same reason, but were soon after freed. The next few years saw the production of Jonson's best works: *Volpone, or the Fox* (1605), *Epicœne* (1609), *The Alchemist* (1610), *Bartholomew Fair* (1614), and a number of his finest masques. In 1616 Jonson determined to write no more for the stage, except to compose occasional masques. In 1618 he went to Scotland, remaining there a year and a half and making the acquaintance of Drummond of Hawthorndon, who has preserved the famous *Conversations* with Jonson. His return to England was marked by several visits to his noble friends and patrons, for he had become a well-known figure. After the accession of Charles I, Jonson turned once more to the stage, and produced his later comedies. He died in 1637.

Jonson's attitude toward poetry and drama was largely influenced by Sidney's *Defence*. In the Introduction to his *Seventeenth Century Essays*, Mr. Spingarn quotes parallel passages from the two poets. Jonson's critical utterances, in his *Prologues, Prefaces*, his *Conversations* with Drummond, and, throughout the *Discoveries*, were to a great extent the result of definite literary influences. He was a classic, no doubt, and sought support in the doctrines of Aristotle, Horace, and their modern imitators. The influence exerted on him by Heinsius has been pointed out. Jonson had himself translated Horace's *Ars Poetica*. Mr. Spingarn regards Jonson as "perhaps the first Englishman with the critical temper." Jonson's criticism is to be found in many places, but its crystallization is in the *Discoveries*, published in 1641. But it was left to Dryden to develop a well-defined system of criticism.

On the drama:

Jonson's critical utterances are scattered through the prologues and in the dialogue of *Every Man in his Humour*, *Every Man Out of his Humour*, and *The Poetaster*.

The more important criticisms are:

To the Readers, in *Sejanus* (printed 1605).
To the Most Noble and Most Equal Sisters, the two Famous Universities, etc., in *Volpone, or the Fox* (printed 1607).
Prologue to *Epicœne* (printed 1609?).
Timber; or, Discoveries made upon Men and Matter (1641).
Ben Jonson's Conversations with William Drummond of Hawthornden (published London, 1842).

Editions:

The first and second folios of Jonson' works appeared respectively in 1616 and 1640. The first modern edition is that of Gifford, 9 vols., London, 1816. This is re-printed in 3 vols. (London, 1870). There are numerous other editions, among them a 2-volume selection of the plays (Mermaid Series, London and New York, 1893–94).
The *Discoveries* have been often re-printed: by Felix E. Schelling (Boston, 1892); by J. E. Spingarn, *Critical Essays of the Seventeenth Century*, vol. 1 (Oxford, 1908); Maurice Castelain (Paris, 1907); and H. Morley (London, 1892).

On Jonson and his works:

Prefatory material to editions cited.
A. C. Swinburne, *A Study of Ben Jonson* (London, 1889).

J. A. Symonds, *Ben Jonson* (London, 1886).

C. H. Herford, *Ben Jonson* (in *Dictionary of National Biography*, vol. 30, London, 1892).

W. H. T. Baudissin, *Ben Jonson und seine Schule*, 2 vols. (Leipzig, 1836).

M. Castelain, *Ben Jonson, l'homme et l'œuvre* (Paris, 1907).

P. Aronstein, *Ben Jonson's Theorie des Lustspiels* (in *Anglia*, vol. 17, Halle, 1894).

H. Grossmann, *Ben Jonson als Kritiker* (Berlin, 1898).

H. Reinsch, *Jonson's Poetik und seine Beziehungen zu Horaz* (Naumburg, 1898).

Felix E. Schelling, *Jonson and the Classical School* (*Modern Language Association Publications*, Baltimore, 1898).

P. Simpson, *"Tanquam Explorator": Jonson's Method in the Discoveries* (*Modern Language Review*, vol. 2, 1907).

R. A. Small. *The Stage-quarrel Between Ben Jonson and the so-called Poetasters* (in *Forschungen zu englische Sprache und Literatur*, Breslau, 1899).

J. E. Spingarn, *Sources of Jonson's "Discoveries"* (in *Modern Philology*, vol. 2, 1905).

G. Gregory Smith, *Ben Jonson* (London, 1919).

TIMBER; OR DISCOVERIES MADE UPON MEN AND MATTER [1]
(1641)

. . . . . .

The parts of a comedy and tragedy.— The parts of a comedy are the same with a tragedy, and the end is partly the same, for they both delight and teach; the comics are called δıδάσκαλοι of the Greeks no less than the tragics.

Aristotle.— Plato. — Homer. — Nor is the moving of laughter always the end of comedy; that is rather a fowling for the people's delight, or their fooling. For, as Aristotle says rightly, the moving of laughter is a fault in comedy, a kind of turpitude that depraves some part of a man's nature without a disease. As a wry face without pain moves laughter, or a deformed vizard, or a rude clown dressed in a lady's habit and using her actions; we dislike and scorn such representations which made the ancient philosophers ever think laughter unfitting in a wise man. And this induced Plato to esteem of Homer as a sacrilegious person, because he presented the gods sometimes laughing. As also it is divinely said of Aristotle, that to seem ridiculous is a part of dishonesty, and foolish.

The wit of the old comedy.— So that what either in the words or sense of an author, or in the language or actions of men, is awry or depraved does strangely stir mean affections, and provoke for the most part to laughter. And therefore it

was clear that all insolent and obscene speeches, jests upon the best men, injuries to particular persons, perverse and sinister sayings (and the rather unexpected) in the old comedy did move laughter, especially where it did imitate any dishonesty, and scurrility came forth in the place of wit, which, who understands the nature and genius of laughter cannot but perfectly know.

Aristophanes. — Plautus. — Of which Aristophanes affords an ample harvest, having not only outgone Plautus or any other in that kind, but expressed all the moods and figures of what is ridiculous oddly. In short, as vinegar is not accounted good until the wine be corrupted, so jests that are true and natural seldom raise laughter with the beast, the multitude. They love nothing that is right and proper. The farther it runs from reason or possibility with them the better it is.

Socrates.— Theatrical wit.— What could have made them laugh, like to see Socrates presented, that example of all good life, honesty, and virtue, to have him hoisted up with a pulley, and there play the philosopher in a basket; measure how many foot a flea could skip geometrically, by a just scale, and edify the people from the engine. This was theatrical wit, right stage jesting, and relishing a playhouse, invented for scorn and laughter; whereas, if it had savored of equity, truth, perspicuity, and candor, to have tasten a wise

1 Re-printed, with omissions, from Schelling's edition of the *Discoveries* (Boston, 1892).— Ed.

or a learned palate,— spit it out presently! this is bitter and profitable: this instructs and would inform us: what need we know anything, that are nobly born, more than a horse-race, or a hunting-match, our day to break with citizens, and such innate mysteries?

The cart.— This is truly leaping from the stage to the tumbril again, reducing all wit to the original dung-cart.

Of the magnitude and compass of any fable, epic or dramatic.

What the measure of a fable is.— The fable or plot of a poem defined.— The epic fable, differing from the dramatic.— To the resolving of this question we must first agree in the definition of the fable. The fable is called the imitation of one entire and perfect action, whose parts are so joined and knit together, as nothing in the structure can be changed, or taken away, without impairing or troubling the whole, of which there is a proportionable magnitude in the members. As for example: if a man would build a house, he would first appoint a place to build it in, which he would define within certain bounds; so in the constitution of a poem, the action is aimed at by the poet, which answers place in a building, and that action hath his largeness, compass, and proportion. But as a court or king's palace requires other dimensions than a private house, so the epic asks a magnitude from other poems, since what is place in the one is action in the other; the difference is in space. So that by this definition we conclude the fable to be the imitation of one perfect and entire action, as one perfect and entire place is required to a building. By perfect, we understand that to which nothing is wanting, as place to the building that is raised, and action to the fable that is formed. It is perfect, perhaps not for a court or king's palace, which requires a greater ground, but for the structure he would raise; so that space of the action may not prove large enough for the epic fable, yet be perfect for the dramatic, and whole.

What we understand by whole.— Whole we call that, and perfect, which hath a beginning, a midst, and an end. So the place of any building may be whole and entire for that work, though too little for a palace. As to a tragedy or a comedy, the action may be convenient and perfect that would not fit an epic poem in magnitude. So a lion is a perfect creature in himself, though it be less than that of a buffalo or a rhinocerote. They differ but in specie: either in the kind is absolute; both have their parts, and either the whole. Therefore, as in every body so in every action, which is the subject of a just work, there is required a certain proportionable greatness, neither too vast nor too minute. For that which happens to the eyes when we behold a body, the same happens to the memory when we contemplate an action. I look upon a monstrous giant, as Tityus, whose body covered nine acres of land, and mine eye sticks upon every part; the whole that consists of those parts will never be taken in at one entire view. So in a fable, if the action be too great, we can never comprehend the whole together in our imagination. Again, if it be too little, there ariseth no pleasure out of the object; it affords the view no stay; it is beheld, and vanisheth at once. As if we should look upon an ant or pismire, the parts fly the sight, and the whole considered is almost nothing. The same happens in action, which is the object of memory, as the body is of sight. Too vast oppresseth the eyes, and exceeds the memory; too little scarce admits either.

What is the utmost bounds of a fable.— Now, in every action it behooves the poet to know which is his utmost bound, how far with fitness and a necessary proportion he may produce and determine it; that is, till either good fortune change into the worse, or the worse into the better. For as a body without proportion cannot be goodly, no more can the action, either in comedy or tragedy, without his fit bounds: and every bound, for the nature of the subject, is esteemed the best that is largest, till it can increase no more; so it behooves the action in tragedy or comedy to be let grow till the necessity ask a conclusion; wherein two things are to be considered: first, that it exceed not the compass of one day; next, that there be place left for digression and art. For the episodes and digressions in a fable are the same that household stuff and furniture are in a house. And so far from the measure and extent of a fable dramatic.

What by one and entire.— Now that it should be one and entire. One is considerable two ways; either as it is only separate, and by itself, or as being composed of many parts, it begins to be one as those parts grow or are wrought together. That it should be one the first away alone, and by itself, no man that hath tasted letters ever would say, especially having required before a just magnitude and equal proportion of the parts in themselves. Neither of which can possibly be, if the action be single and separate, not composed of parts, which laid together in themselves, with an equal and fitting proportion, tend to the same end; which thing out of antiquity itself hath deceived many, and more this day it doth deceive.

Hercules. — *Theseus.* — *Achilles.* — *Ulysses.*— *Homer and Vergil.*— *Æneas.*— *Venus.*— So many there be of old that have thought the action of one man to be one, as of Hercules, Theseus, Achilles, Ulysses, and other heroes; which is both foolish and false, since by one and the same person many things may be severally done which cannot fitly be referred or joined to the same end: which not only the excellent tragic poets, but the best masters of the epic, Homer and Vergil, saw. For though the argument of an epic poem be far more diffused and poured out than that of tragedy, yet Vergil, writing of Æneas, hath pretermitted many things. He neither tells how he was born, how brought up, how he fought with Achilles, how he was snatched out of the battle by Venus; but that one thing, how he came into Italy, he prosecutes in twelve books. The rest of his journey, his error by sea, the sack of Troy, are put not as the argument of the work, but episodes of the argument. So Homer laid by many things of Ulysses, and handled no more than he saw tended to one and the same end.

Theseus. — *Hercules.* — *Juvenal.* — *Codrus.*— *Sophocles.*— *Ajax.*— *Ulysses.*— Contrary to which, and foolishly, those poets did, whom the philosopher taxeth, of whom one gathered all the actions of Theseus, another put all the labors of Hercules in one work. So did he whom Juvenal mentions in the beginning, "hoarse Codrus," that recited a volume compiled, which he called his *Theseide,* not yet finished, to the great trouble both of his hearers and himself; amongst which there were many parts had no coherence nor kindred one with another, so far they were from being one action, one fable. For as a house, consisting of divers materials, becomes one structure and one dwelling, so an action, composed of divers parts, may become one fable, epic or dramatic. For example, in a tragedy, look upon Sophocles his *Ajax:* Ajax, deprived of Achilles' armor, which he hoped from the suffrage of the Greeks, disdains; and, growing impatient of the injury, rageth, and runs mad. In that humor he doth many senseless things, and at last falls upon the Grecian flock and kills a great ram for Ulysses: returning to his senses, he grows ashamed of the scorn, and kills himself; and is by the chiefs of the Greeks forbidden burial. These things agree and hang together, not as they were done, but as seeming to be done, which made the action whole, entire, and absolute.

The conclusion concerning the whole, and the parts.— *Which are episodes.*— *Ajax and Hector.*— *Homer.*— For the whole, as it consisteth of parts, so without all the parts it is not the whole; and to make it absolute is required not only the parts, but such parts as are true. For a part of the whole was true; which, if you take away, you either change the whole or it is not the whole. For if it be such a part, as, being present or absent, nothing concerns the whole, it cannot be called a part of the whole; and such are the episodes, of which hereafter. For the present here is one example: the single combat of Ajax and Hector, as it is at large described in Homer, nothing belongs to this Ajax of Sophocles.

You admire no poems but such as run like a brewer's cart upon the stones, hobbling:

Et, quae per salebras, altaque saxa cadunt,
   Accius et quidquid Pacuviusque vomunt
Attonitusque legis terrai, frugiferai.

TO THE READERS[2]

(Dedication of *Sejanus: His Fall*)

(1605)

. . . First, if it be objected that what I publish is no true poem in the strict laws of time, I confess it: as also in the want of a proper chorus; whose habit and moods are such and so different, as not any, whom I have seen since the ancients, no, not they who have most presently affected laws, have yet come in the way of. Nor is it needful, or almost possible in these our times, and to such auditors as commonly things are presented, to observe the old state and splendor or dramatic poems, with preservation of any popular delight. But of this I shall take more seasonable cause to speak, in my observations upon Horace his *Art of Poetry*, which, with the text translated, I intend shortly to publish. In the meantime, if in truth of argument, dignity of persons, gravity and height of elocution, fullness and frequency of sentence, I have discharged the other offices of a tragedy writer, let not the absence of these forms be imputed to me, wherein I shall give you occasion hereafter, and without my boast, to think I could better prescribe, than omit the due use for want of convenient knowledge. . . .

2 Re-printed, with omissions, from the Gifford-Cunningham edition of Jonson's *Works.—* Ed.

DEDICATION TO VOLPONE, OR THE FOX[3]

[*To the Most Noble and Most Equal Sisters,*
The Two Famous Universities,
For Their Love and Acceptance Shown to His Poem in the Presentation,
Ben Jonson,
The Grateful Acknowledger,
Dedicates both it and Himself]
(1607)

. . . I have labored for their instruction and amendment, to reduce not only the ancient forms, but manners of the scene, the easiness, the propriety, the innocence, and last, the doctrine, which is the principal end of poesy, to inform men in the best reason of living. And though my catastrophe may, in the strict rigor of comic law, meet with censure, as turning back to my promise; I desire the learned and charitable critic to have so much faith in me, to think it was done of industry: for, with what ease I could have varied it nearer his scale (but that I fear to boast my own faculty) I could here insert. But my special aim being to put the snaffle in their mouths that cry out, We never punish vice in our interludes, &c., I took the more liberty; though not without some lines of example, drawn even in the ancients themselves, the goings out of whose comedies are not always joyful, but oft-times the bawds, the servants, the rivals, yea, and the masters are mulcted; and fitly, it being the office of a comic poet to imitate justice, and instruct to life, as well as purity of language, or stir up gentle affections: to which I shall take the occasion elsewhere to speak. . . .

3 Re-printed, with omissions, from the Gifford-Cunningham edition of the *Works.—* Ed.

FRANCE — II

CLASSICAL PERIOD

FRENCH DRAMATIC CRITICISM OF THE SEVENTEENTH CENTURY

While no very distinct line of demarcation can be drawn between the end of the sixteenth and beginning of the seventeenth centuries in French literary criticism, it is at least convenient to consider the sixteenth as marking the end of a stage in the development from the traditions of the Middle Ages and an important connecting link with the century in which the classic ideal received its final impetus in the *Art Poétique* of Boileau (1674). The main current was in favor of classicism, i. e., an adherence to the precepts, however misunderstood, of Aristotle and Horace; but from time to time there arose a voice in protest; Grévin and Laudun d'Aigaliers, among others, objected to the rigid Rules, and declared in favor of greater liberty. The same sort of protest was heard occasionally in the following century, from Ogier, in his *Préface* to Schélandre's *Tyr et Sidon* (1628), from Hardy, rather by his practice, however, than in his prefaces; from Durval in his preface to *Agarite* (1636), from Molière later in the century; and from numerous others. But in spite of these more or less sporadic manifestos, the main current was rigidly classic. The earlier prefaces, like that of Pierre Troterel to his play *Les Corrivaux* (1612), of Maréschal to *La Généreuse Allemande* (1621), Isnard's preface to Pichou's *La Filis de Scire* (1631), Gombauld's to *Amaranthe* (1631), Jean de Mairet's veritable Poetic prefixed to his *Silvanire* (1631), the occasional prefaces to Du Ryer's, Claveret's, and Desmarets de Saint-Sorlin's plays — all helped to pave the way for Jean Chapelain's many and oft-repeated pleas for the Unities, and the famous *Cid* Controversy. This controversy, which will be treated at greater length in connection with Chapelain, called forth a large number of pamphlets, for and against the young Corneille, whose " irregular " *Cid*, produced in 1636,

was one of the most successful plays of the century. Georges de Scudéry's *Observations sur le Cid* (published in 1637, when nearly all the controversial tracts appeared) was followed in quick succession by Faret's (?) *Deffense du Cid*, further attacks and defenses by Corneille himself, Mairet, Scudéry again, Sorel, the anonymous *Discours à Cliton*, and finally by the *Sentimens de l'Académie françoise sur la tragi-comédie du Cid* (1638), written principally and edited by Chapelain. Corneille's *Préfaces*, *Avertissements*, and the like, begun in 1632 in *Clitandre* — were appearing meanwhile, but his most important critical and theoretical contributions, the *Discours* and *Examens*, were not printed until the edition of 1660. Other indications of the general trend of ideas on the drama may be found in works of less importance from the viewpoint of actual influence on contemporaries; in the *Lettres* of Chapelain and of Jean-Louis Guez de Balzac, many of which are concerned with the question of the Rules and the *Cid* Controversy, while a single letter of Racan (to Ménage, 1654) registers another protest against the strict regulations of classicism. Following immediately upon the *Cid* controversy came Sarasin's *Discours sur la Tragédie* (1639), a formal treatise founded upon Aristotelian principles, and, the next year, La Mesnardière's *Art Poétique*, a pedantic and voluminous ultra-classic work. Another pedantic work, but of vaster importance and fame, appeared in 1657, the *Pratique du théâtre*, of François Hédelin, Abbé d'Aubignac. This was the first work attempting to treat of the actual writing of plays, though the author more often than not strays from his professed purpose and theorizes at great length. Corneille, who had long struggled to reconcile his practice with his theory, and his theory with his practice, replied to d'Aubignac and his other critics in his famous *Discours* and *Examens* (1660). Molière, on the other hand, whose first critical words appeared in 1659, nowhere attempts to "justify" himself in like manner, but roundly declares that to please is the great and only rule. Racine, whose *Préface* to *La Thébaïde* was first printed in 1664, is in his own way a follower of Aristotle. Rapin's *Réflexions sur la Poétique* (1674), translated into English by Rymer almost immediately after its publication in French, is a rather heavy and scholastic piece of work. But the same year (1674) saw the publication of the celebrated *Art Poétique* of Boileau, which contains in concise form all the more or less consistent attempts to formulate a definite classic standard. Boileau stands for order, "good sense," and reason. Among the earliest French "essays" are the handful of short writings of Saint-Evremond, composed between 1666 and 1677, on Racine and Corneille, on ancient, French, English, and Italian drama. Toward the end of the century there appeared a number of larger treatises, dealing with aspects of the drama, none of which, however, was of great importance. Baillet's *Jugement des savants* (1687), and Bayle's celebrated *Dictionnaire historique et critique* (1697), and the welter of pamphlets and books occasioned by the *Ancients and Moderns Quarrel*, are not primarily concerned with the drama, though they may be consulted on particular points.

General references on Seventeenth Century French literature: .

Paul Albert, *La Littérature française au XVIIe siècle* (Paris, 1895).

A. Dupuy, *Histoire de la littérature française au XVIIe siècle* (Paris, 1892).

Emile Faguet, *Le Dix-septième siècle* (Paris, 1890).

L.-H. Follioley, *Histoire de la littérature française au XVIIe siècle*, 3 vols. (Tours, 1885).

F. Lotheissen, *Geschichte der französischen Literatur im 17. Jahrhundert*, 4 vols. (Wien, 1874–84).

Georges Longhaye, *Histoire de la littérature française au XVIIe siècle*, 5 parts (Paris, 1895–98).

F. Guizot, *Corneille et son temps* (new ed., Paris, 1852. Translated as *Corneille and his Times*, New York, 1871).

Paul Lacroix, *XVIIe Siècle: Lettres, Sciences, et arts* (Paris, 1882).

Voltaire, *Le Siècle de Louis XIV* (Paris, 1751).

Demogeot, *Tableau de la Littérature française au XVIIe siècle avant Corneille et Descartes* (Paris, 1859).

On the drama of the seventeenth century:

Jules Bonnassies, *Les Auteurs dramatiques et la Comédie française à Paris aux XVIIe et XVIIIe siècles* (Paris, 1874).

F. Delavigne, *La Tragédie chrétienne au XVIIe siècle. Etudes littéraires* (Toulouse, 1847).

Eugène Despois, *Le Théâtre français sous Louis XIV* (Paris, 1874).

G. Fagniez, *L'Art dramatique et le goût public dans la première moitié du XVIIe siècle* (in the *Correspondant*, N. S., vol. 216, Paris, 1913).

Victor Fournel, *La Littérature indépendante et les écrivains oubliés au XVIIe siècle* (Paris, 1862).

Eleanor Jourdain, *An Introduction to the French Classical Drama* (Oxford, 1912).

Jules Lemaître, *La Comedie après Molière et le Théâtre de Dancourt* (Paris, 1882).

Eugène Lintilhac, *La Comédie: XVIIe siècle* (Paris, 1908).

Eugène Rigal, *Le Théâtre français avant la période classique* (Paris, 1901).

On French criticism in the seventeenth century:

Francisque Vial et Louis Denise, *Idées et doctrines du XVIIe siècle* (Paris, 1906).

Auguste Bourgoin, *Les Maîtres de la critique au XVIIe siècle* (Paris, 1889).

Charles Arnaud, *Les Théories dramatiques au XVIIe siècle. Etude sur la vie et les œuvres de l'Abbé d'Aubignac* (Paris, 1888).

Charles Livet, *Précieux et ridicules* (2nd ed., Paris, 1870).

M. Wilmotte, *La Critique littéraire au XVII siècle* (in *Etudes critiques sur la tradition littéraire en France*, Paris, 1909).

George Saintsbury, *A History of Criticism*, vol. 2 (New York, 1902).

F. Delfour, *Les Ennemis de Racine au XVIIe siècle* (Paris, 1859).

General references on the *Académie française*:

Pellisson et d'Olivet, *Histoire de l'Académie françoise* (new ed., 2 vols., Paris, 1858).

Paul Mesnard, *Histoire de l'Académie française* (Paris, 1857).

A. Fabre, *Chapelain et nos deux premières Académies* (Paris, 1890).

L. Petit de Julleville, *Histoire de la langue et de la Littérature française*, vol. 4 (Paris, 1897).

G. Boissier, *L'Académie française sous l'Ancien Régime* (Paris, 1909).

Charles Marty-Laveaux, *Les Régistres de l'Académie française*, 3 vols. (Paris, 1893).

C.-A. Sainte-Beuve, *L'Académie française* (in *Nouveaux Lundis*, vol. 12, Paris, 1863-70).

Leon Vincent, *The French Academy* (Boston, 1901).

FRANÇOIS OGIER

François Ogier (who signs himself in one place as a "native of Paris") was born early in the seventeenth century. Nothing is known of him except through his various writings. He entered the church at an early age and became "prédicateur du roi." He manifested an early liking for letters, and began his literary career with an attack on Garasse's *Doctrine curieuse* (1623). The argument was continued, and resulted in Ogier's *Jugement et Censure* of the *Doctrine*. After a good deal of controversy the opponents were reconciled. J.-L. G. de Balzac took part in the quarrel and sided with Ogier, who later defended Balzac in the *Apologie*, in 1627. In 1628 he published the *Préface* to Jean de Schélandre's play, *Tyr et Sidon*, originally published in 1608. In 1648 Ogier went to Munster and was present at the signing of the Treaty of Westphalia. The next year he returned to Paris, preached for some time, and finally retired, devoting his efforts entirely to writing and the publishing of his works. He died at Paris in 1670.

With the exception of the *Préface* to Schélandre's play, Ogier's works consist of poems, sermons, and various criticisms of literature. Ogier was not a man of the theater, though his interest in the drama is manifest in the *Préface*. He was, indeed, little more than an amateur, but perhaps as such he was better able to realize the futility of subjecting poets and dramatists to rules. It was he, rather than Chapelain and Boileau, who applied the standard of reason and commonsense to works of art. But, as has been pointed out, the current of the time was against him, and it did not turn until the early years of the nineteenth century.

Editions:

The second edition of Schélandre's *Tyr et Sidon,* which contains Ogier's preface, was published at Paris in 1628. Its exact title is *Préface au Lecteur, par F.O.P.* [François Ogier, Parisien]. The *Préface* and play are re-printed in the eighth volume of Viollet-le-duc's *Ancien Théâtre françois* (Paris, 1856).

On Ogier and his work:

Bayle, *Dictionnaire* (English ed., London, 1735).

Nouvelle Biographie générale, vol. 38 (Paris, 1861).

George Saintsbury, *A History of Criticism,* vol. 2 (New York, 1902).

Aulard, article in *Bulletin de la Faculté des lettres de Poitiers* (Avril, 1883).

PREFACE TO TYRE AND SIDON [1]

[*Préface au Lecteur* (to) *Tyr et Sidon*]

(1628)

. . . Those who favor the ancient poets will find something to criticize in our author's invention, and those who follow the moderns will find some little fault with his style. These former, who are the erudite, for whose criticism we have the highest regard, say that our tragi-comedy is not composed according to the rules that the ancients have pre-scribed for the stage, on which they were willing to perform nothing but events which can take place in the course of one day. And yet, in the first as well as in the second part of our play, there are found things which cannot be in-cluded in a single day, but which re-quire an interval of several days to be put into execution.

But then, too, the ancients, in order to avoid this inconvenience of connect-ing in a few hours events far removed in time, have fallen into two errors as important as those that they wished to avoid: the one, in the fact that, fore-seeing very well that a variety of events is necessary to render the performance pleasing, they cause a number of inci-dents and encounters to take place in one and the same day, which probably cannot have happened in such a short space of time. That offends the judi-cious spectator who desires a real or imaginary interval between those events, in order that in his mind he may not discover anything too unnatural in them, and that it may not seem that the char-acters are assigned to appear at a given moment, like *Dei ex Machinâ*, which were also used very often out of season. This fault is noticeable in nearly all the plays of the ancients, and especially in those in which there occurs some recog-nition of a child formerly abandoned; for directly, in order to strengthen some conjecture founded on age, features, or on some ring or other clew, the person who was employed to lose it, the shep-herd who has reared it, the old woman who has nursed it, etc., all meet and suddenly appear on the stage, as if by magic, although it is probable that all these people can be assembled only after the expenditure of much time and pains. All the tragedies and comedies of the an-cients are full of examples of this kind.

Sophocles himself, the most regular of all, in his *Œdipus Rex*, which is offered to us by the experts as the model of a perfect tragedy, has fallen into this error: for, at the very moment when Creon has returned from the Delphian oracle, when great difficulty is being experienced in attempting to discover the author of Laïus' death, at the mo-ment when they have sent for a former servant who may have some information concerning it, and who is to arrive forth-with, suddenly the poet brings upon the scene the old man who had formerly carried off the child Œdipus, and who had received him from the hands of this old servant whom they are expecting. So that the entire affair is revealed in a moment, for fear that the action of the tragedy may exceed in length the time of one day. Who does not see at this point that the unexpected arrival of the old man from Corinth has been prepared beforehand and is too farfetched, and that it is not at all likely that a man who was not called in for this purpose, should arrive and converse with Œdipus just in the short interval of time which elapses since Laïus' old servant has been sent for? Is not this to bring these two characters together in spite of them-selves, and to discover at one moment the secret of the death of this unfortu-nate prince?

Because of this consideration for put-ting off nothing to an imaginary mor-row, it happens, too, that the poets cause certain actions to follow one other immediately, although of necessity they require an appreciable interval between them in order to be appropriately car-ried out. As when Æschylus brings in Agamemnon with funeral ceremony, ac-companied by a long train of mourners and by libations, at the very moment when he has just been killed. Whereas

1 Translated, with minor omissions, for the first time in English, by August Odebrecht.— Ed.

this murder must have thrown the entire royal house and the whole city into disorder, when the body is to be concealed or abandoned by the murderers, and when the whole stage should be filled with violent outbursts of compassion and of vengeance, they march in great solemnity and in good order in the funeral procession of this unhappy prince, whose blood is still warm and who, so to speak, is only half dead.

The second disadvantage that the ancient poets have incurred because they wish to confine the events of a tragedy within one day, is their being compelled continually to introduce messengers in order to relate the events which have occurred on the preceding days, and the purpose of the events which are taking place on the stage at the moment. So that, in nearly all the acts, these gentlemen entertain the audience with a lengthy enumeration of tiresome intrigues which make the spectator lose patience, however well disposed he may be to listen. Indeed it is a tedious thing, that one and the same person should occupy the stage all the time, and it is more suitable for a good inn than becoming to an excellent tragedy to see messengers continually arriving there. Here it is necessary to avoid as much as possible those tiresome speakers who relate the adventures of others, and to put the persons themselves into action, leaving these long narrations to the historians or to those who have taken charge of composing the plots and the subjects of the plays that are being performed. What difference is there, pray, between The Persians of Æschylus and a simple narrative of what occurred between Xerxes and the Greeks? Is there anything so dull or so uninteresting? And the disgust of the reader, whence comes it if not from the fact that a messenger plays in it the part of all the characters, and that the poet has refused to violate that law that we are wrongfully accused of having violated? But I am in no mood to criticize further the works of a poet who had the courage to fight valiantly for the liberty of his country, during those famous days of Marathon, of Salamis and of Platæa. Let us leave him to hold forth in such a way as may please him concerning the

flight of the Persians, since he had such a good share in their defeat, and let us pass on.

Poetry, and especially that which is written for the theater, is composed only for pleasure and amusement, and this pleasure can arise only from the variety of the events which are represented on the stage, which events, not being able to occur easily in the course of one day, the poets have been constrained to abandon gradually the practice of their predecessors who confined themselves within too narrow limits; and this change is not so recent that we have no examples of it from antiquity. Whoever will carefully consider the *Antigone* of Sophocles will find that a night intervenes between the first and the second burial of Polynices; otherwise, how could Antigone have deceived the guards of the body of this unfortunate prince the first time, and avoid being seen by so many people, except in the darkness of the night? For on the second occasion she comes to the body aided by a heavy rain which causes all the guards to retire, while she, in the midst of the storm, buries her brother and pays her last respects to him. Whence it happens that the tragedy of *Antigone* represents the events of two days at least; since the pretended crime of that princess presupposes Creon's law which is proclaimed publicly and in broad daylight, on the stage and in the presence of the elders of Thebes. Here then is the order of this tragedy: the law or the interdiction of Creon, made and proclaimed during the day; the first burial of Polynices, that I maintain took place at night; the second during a great storm in broad daylight; that is the second day.

But we have a much more famous example of a comedy by Menander (for our critics demand that we observe the same rule in comedies as in tragedies in relation to the difficulty that we are considering) entitled Ἑαυτοντιμορυμένος, translated by Terence, in which, without any doubt, the poet includes the events of two days, and introduces the actors who bear witness to the fact in very plain terms. In act one, scene two, Chremes warns his son not to stray too far from the house, in view of the fact that it is already very late. In act two, scene four, Clitipho and his band enter the house to sup with the old man, and the night is spent there in pleasant occupations. The next day Chremes rises early to inform Menedemus of the return of his son, and he goes out of the house rubbing his eyes and uttering these words: *Luces cit hoc iam,* etc., *the day is beginning to dawn,* etc. For if there is any one bold enough to say that Menander and Terence have erred in this passage, and that they have forgotten themselves in respect to the proprieties that must be preserved in the theater, let him beware lest he offend as well the leading men among the Romans, Scipio and Lælius, whom Cornelius Nepos considers to be the real authors of this comedy, rather than Terence.

It can be seen, then, by this, that the ancients and the most excellent masters of the profession have not always observed that rule which our critics desire to make us so religiously preserve at the present time. For if, however, they have nearly always observed it, it is not because they believed themselves absolutely compelled to do so in order to satisfy the spectator's imagination, to which they had done just as much violence in the two ways that I have pointed out, but it was their custom to dare to deviate only very slightly from the path that had been marked out for them by their predecessors. Which appears in the fact that the least innovations in the theater are cited by the ancients as very important and very remarkable changes in the state. Sophocles invented the buskin and added three actors to the choruses that before his time consisted only of twelve. This change is of very little importance and concerns only the stature of the actor and the size of the choruses, which are always unpleasant of whatever size or quality they appear.

Now, in my opinion, there are two reasons why the ancient writers of tragedy have not dared to deviate, unless it be very little and by degrees, from their first models. The first is that their tragedies formed a part of the worship of the gods and of the ceremonies of religion, in which, innovations being always offensive and changes hard to appreciate, unless they take place of

their own accord and, as it were, imperceptibly, it happened that the poets dared undertake nothing that was not in keeping with the usual custom. And perhaps that is also the reason why, although they represent atrocious deeds, accompanied and followed by murders and other kinds of cruelty, on the other hand, they never shed blood in the presence of the audience, and all those bloody executions are understood to take place behind the scenes, and that, for fear that the solemnity of the occasion may be desecrated by the sight of some homicide; for, if one consider well, the Ajax of Sophocles does not kill himself on the stage, but in a neighboring thicket, from which his voice and his last sighs can be easily heard.

The second reason why ancient tragedies are nearly all alike and are, nearly all of them, full of choruses and of messengers, arises from the fact that the poets, wishing to carry off the prize destined to the one who composed the best work, forced themselves to write according to the desire and taste of the people and of the judges, who, without doubt, would have refused to admit among the number of contestants any one who had not followed the rules of composition observed before his time on such occasions. The subject matter itself, on which the poets were to work that year, was prescribed and suggested. From which it can be seen that nearly all ancient tragedies have the same subject, and that the same plots are treated by Æschylus, Sophocles, and Euripides, tragic authors of whom alone a few complete works have come down to us. From this it has also happened that these subjects and plots have been taken from a small number of Greek tales or stories well known to the people, who would not have been contented to being entertained by other exhibitions than those based upon events that had occurred at Thebes and at Troy. Add to this that the Athenians who had received the tragedies of Æschylus with extraordinary applause, desired as a special favor that they might still be performed in public after the death of their author. A fact which gave them such a reputation that the tragic poets who followed concluded that they must not deviate from a model that was held in such high repute, and that it was necessary to conform to public opinion since it was that of the master.

Since then, the Latins, who had submitted themselves to the inventions of the Greeks, as holding the arts and the sciences from them, did not dare to disturb the limits that had been prescribed, for them, and especially in regard to the subject of which we are speaking. For the Romans, who had imitated the Greeks in other kinds of poetry, and who had even competed with them for the prize in epic and lyric poetry, confined themselves, or very nearly so, to mere translation of their tragedies, and they have treated no subject which had not been exhibited several times on the stages of Greece.

I will not mention Accius, Nævius, Pacuvius, and a few others, of whose works we possess many fragments classed by the grammarians under the title of Greek tales; the only Latin tragedies which were composed in a better age, and that remain to us, are nearly all Greek, as well in subject matter as in form, except the *Thebaïd*, in the fact that it does not introduce any choruses, and the *Octavia*, because its subject is a roman story; but the latter is the work of an amateur, if we are to believe Justus Lipsius, and scarcely deserves to be taken into consideration.

After the Latins, the drama, as well as the other forms of more polite literature having been abandoned, barbarism succeeded this long interregnum of the humanities, that resumed their authority only within the memory of our fathers. In this restoration, however, several errors were committed, but it is not my purpose to speak of that in this place, and I cannot undertake it without making a volume out of a preface, and saying many good things that are not to the point. Only, I should wish that Francis Bacon, the public critic of human knowledge, had made some mention of it in his books, for it seems that his subject obliged him to do so.

I confine myself here to poetry alone, and say that the too intense eagerness of wishing to imitate the ancients has caused our best poets to fail to attain either the reputation or the excellence of the ancients. They did not consider that the taste of nations is different, as well in matters pertaining to the mind as in those of the body, and that, just as the Moors, and without going so far, the Spaniards, imagine and prefer a type of beauty quite different from that which we prize in France, and just as they desire their sweethearts to have a different figure, and features other than those that we desire to see in ours, to such a degree that there are some men who will form an idea of their beauty from the same features that we should consider homely, just so, it must not be doubted that the minds of nations have preferences quite different from one another, and altogether dissimilar feelings for the beauty of intellectual things, such as poetry; but philosophy, nevertheless, has no part in this matter: for it expects, to be sure, that the minds of all men, under whatever sky they may be born, shall agree in one and the same opinion concerning the things necessary for the sovereign good, and it strives as far as possible to unite them in the search after truth, because there can be but one truth; but as for matters that are merely amusing and unimportant, such as this of which we are speaking, it allows our opinions to take whatever direction they please, and does not extend its jurisdiction over this matter.

This truth granted, it opens a gentle and pleasing way to settle the quarrels that arise daily between those who attack and those who defend the works of the ancient poets; for, as I cannot refrain from censuring two or three scribblers who call Pindar stupid and extravagant, Homer a dreamer, etc., etc., and those who have imitated them in these latter days, so too, I think it remarkable that they should be proposed to us as perfect models, from which we are not permitted to deviate ever so little. To this we must reply, that the Greeks worked for Greece, and were successful in the judgment of the cultured people of their day, and that we shall imitate them much better if we grant something to the genius of our own country and to the preferences of our own language, than if we compel ourselves to follow step by step their plan and their style as a few of our writers have done. Here it is that the judgment must be brought into play as in everything else, choosing from the ancients that which can adapt itself to our own times and to the temperament of our nation, without, however, finding fault with the works that, during so many centuries, have met with public approval. They were considered in their day from a point of view different from that of the present time, and people perceived a certain charm in them which is concealed from us and to discover which it would be necessary to have breathed the air of Attica at birth and to have been reared in the midst of those excellent men of ancient Greece.

Surely, just as our stomachs refuse some meats and fruits which are considered delicacies in foreign countries, in the same manner our minds fail to enjoy a certain passage or a certain composition by a Greek or by a Latin which, in former times, has been held in high admiration. The Athenians must certainly have found other beauties in the verses of Pindar than those which our minds of the present day discover in them, since they rewarded a single word with which this poet favored their city, more generously than would the princes of to-day recompense an *Iliad* composed in their honor.

We must not then be so infatuated with the theories that the ancients have held, nor with the art which they have set up, allowing ourselves to be led like the blind; but we must examine and consider these theories themselves by the circumstances of time, place, and the persons for whom they were composed, adding to them and taking away in order to adapt them to our use, a method that Aristotle would have sanctioned: for this philosopher, who demands that supreme reason be obeyed on all occasions, and who concedes nothing to popular opinion, does not refrain from admitting at this point that poets should grant something to the convenience of the actors, in order to facilitate their acting, and should make many allowances for the stupidity and the mood of the spectators. Surely he would have conceded much more to the preference and to the judgment of a whole nation, and if he had laid down rules for a play which

was to have been performed before people as impatient and fond of change and novelty as we are, he would have been very careful not to weary us with those narrations of the messengers, so frequent and so tiresome, nor would he have made a chorus recite almost a hundred and fifty lines at a stretch, as does Euripides in his *Iphigenia in Aulis.*

Hence, the ancients themselves, recognizing the faults of their drama, and that the little variety observed in their plays depressed the spectators, were compelled to introduce satyrs as a form of interlude, which, by virtue of an unrestrained license to slander and abuse persons of the highest rank, held the attention of the people, who delight ordinarily to hear ill spoken of others.

This plan of ordering and arranging, which they used, is our reason for not hesitating to justify the invention of tragi-comedies, introduced by the Italians, in view of the fact that it is much more reasonable, in the course of the same conversation, to mingle grave matters with the least serious, and to bring them together in a single plot for a play or for a story, than to mingle extraneously satyrs with tragedies that have no connection with one another, and that confuse and disturb the sight and the understanding of the audience; for, to say that it is improper to show in a single play the same persons speaking now of serious, important, and tragic matters, and immediately after of commonplace, vain, and humorous things, is to be unacquainted with the nature of human life, whose days and hours are very often interrupted by laughter and by tears, by joy and by sorrow, according as they are filled with happiness or troubled by misfortune. Some one of the gods endeavored formerly to mingle joy with sorrow in order to make of them a single compound; he was unable to accomplish this, but then he joined them behind one another. That is why they ordinarily follow so closely after one another, and nature herself has shown us that there is scarcely any difference between them, since artists note that the movements of muscles and nerves that give an expression of laughter to the countenance, are the same that serve to make us weep and to assume the expression of sorrow by which we manifest extreme grief. And then, after all, those who demand no variation or change in the inventions of the ancients, are arguing here merely about the word and not about the thing itself: for, what is the *Cyclops* of Euripides but a tragi-comedy full of jests and wine, of satyrs and Silenus, on the one hand; of blood and rage and baffled Polyphemus on the other?

The question, then, is an old one, although it goes by a new name; it merely remains to treat it as is fitting, to make each character speak in a manner that is becoming to the subject, and to know how to step down appropriately from the cothurnus of tragedy (for it is permissible in this discussion to make use of these terms) to the slipper of comedy, as our author has done.

Everybody knows how different should be the style that is used in such different matters: the one lofty, elevated, superb; the other, mediocre and less serious. That is why Pliny the Younger rather humorously nicknamed two of his country homes *Tragedy* and *Comedy,* because one was situated on a mountain, and the other below on the sea-shore. . . .

JEAN CHAPELAIN

Jean Chapelain, the son of a notary and an ambitious mother, was born at Paris in 1595. From the first, Jean was destined by his parents for a literary career. He studied early under the famous Nicolas Bourbon. As a young man, his knowledge and his ability as a conversationalist afforded him a place in many of the literary salons of the day. His *Préface* to the *Adone* of Marini increased his already growing reputation. He was the friend and counsellor of the Précieux, and a welcome guest at the Hôtel de Rambouillet. Among his friends and admirers were Balzac, Malherbe, Corneille, Richelieu, while the Duc de Longueville pensioned him in order that he might devote all his time to writing. The work upon which he most prided himself was the famous *La Pucelle,* upon which he worked for twenty-five years. The first twelve cantos were published in 1656, and proved a disastrous failure. The criticisms and attacks on the poem did much to destroy Chapelain's reputation as the greatest poet of his time, though he was still considered an important critic. He died at Paris in 1674.

Ever since Boileau's venomous attacks, Chapelain has presented a rather ridiculous figure in French literature. But that he was a man of great importance — and even paved the way for much of Boileau's own work — is unquestioned. His work in connection with the foundation of the *Académie française,* his formulation of various critical dogmas and the rôle he played in the *Cid* Controversy, entitle him to a position of the utmost importance in seventeenth century French criticism.

The Cid Controversy [1]

The enormous success of Corneille's *Le Cid,* first produced in 1636, occasioned considerable jealousy among the so-called "arbiters of taste." Georges de Scudéry, a rival of the author's, published early in 1637 his *Observations sur le Cid,* in which he set out to prove that the subject of the play was worthless, that it violated the chief rules of the drama, that the handling of the subject was not good, that it contained many bad lines, and that its chief beauties were stolen. Corneille answered this onslaught in his *Lettre apologétique,* which was rather a counter-attack in Scudéry's manner, than a dignified response. Several others took up the quarrel, some championing Corneille and some his opponent. Of less importance were the *Deffense du Cid,* considered by some to have been written by Faret; *Le Souhait du Cid,* possibly from the hand of Sir-

[1] For a history of the Quarrel and re-print of the principal pamphlets, see Armand Gasté, *La Querelle du Cid* (Paris, 1898).

mond; then Scudéry's own *La Preuve des passages alléguez dans les Observations sur le Cid,* and Sorel's (?) *Le Jugement du Cid.* Of considerable interest is the anonymous *Discours à Cliton* — which has been attributed in turn to the Comte de Belin, Claveret, and Mairet — containing the *Traicté de la disposition du Poème Dramatique, et de la prétendue Règle de vingt-quatre heures.* Mairet's *Epistre familière au Sieur Corneille sur la Tragi-comédie du Cid* was answered by Corneille, or a friend of his, in the *Advertissement au Besançonnois Mairet.* Then came the famous *Les Sentimens de l'Académie française sur la Tragi-comédie du Cid,* published at the end of the year 1637. Among the many comments on this document the most interesting are letters of Balzac to Scudéry (1638), Scudéry's reply, and Scudéry's *Lettre de Monsieur de Scudéri à Messieurs de l'Académie française;* and, finally, Chapelain's twenty-six *Lettres* (re-printed in the Thamizey de Larroque edition, cited below) written in 1637, all touching upon the Quarrel.

After Corneille's first reply to Scudéry, the latter suggested referring the matter to the recently-founded Academy, and Corneille at least made no protest. The Academy accepted the task, and Chapelain wrote out a first draft of what was afterwards to become the *Sentimens.* The committee appointed to collaborate with Chapelain seems to have done nothing, and Chapelain presented his draft to Richelieu, to whose advantage it was to bring discredit upon Corneille's play. The Cardinal was pleased with the work in general, but suggested changes and asked Chapelain to make it more "worthy of the Academy." For some time the Academy deliberated and finally passed the MS, which was sent to press; but Richelieu, finding it too "flowery," stopped the printing, revised certain sections, and at last allowed the whole to be published in December, 1637.

That the *Sentimens* is essentially the work of Chapelain seems sure; he was a man of integrity, and he himself declares that the "whole idea" and "all the reasoning" are his. Possibly some allowance must be made for Chapelain's "absolute deference" and "blind obedience" to the Cardinal's wishes; Richelieu undoubtedly saw in Corneille a dangerous rival, and not only requested but commanded that the Academy bring an adverse criticism against *Le Cid.* Still, Chapelain's conscience forced him to acknowledge the many beauties of the "irregular" play.

In this work, as well as in the *Lettres,* prefaces, dissertations, and other miscellaneous work, he went far to establish that set of absolute rules which guided — and cramped — French drama and literature for many years. In the words of Lanson, Chapelain "practically founded dogmatic criticism." He was the disciple of Good-Sense and Reason, the cornerstones of Neo-classicism.

On the drama:

The *Lettres* belong to two different periods, and are full of literary discussions, criticism, and ideas. The first group includes the correspondence with Balzac, and belongs to the years 1632–40. The second, written to many European scholars, including Gronovius, Huet, Heinsius, and Vossius, belong to the period 1659–73. The principal edition is the selection of *Lettres,* 2 vols. (edited by Ph. Tamizey de Larroque, Paris, 1880–83). Selections from the *Lettres* and miscellaneous material are found in Camusat's *Mélanges de Littérature, tirez des Lettres manuscrites de M. Chapelain* (Paris, 1726). The last section of this book, on the men of letters of the day, is re-printed in Collas' *Chapelain,* cited below.

A great many letters and other MSS. of Chapelain have never been printed. There are three of interest, however, re-printed in the appendix of Charles Arnaud's *Les Théories dramatiques au XVIIe siècle* (Paris, 1887). The first of these, *Trois Dissertations inédites de Chapelain,* is a *Démonstration de la Règle des Vingt-quatre heures et Réfutation des Objections,* dated 1630; the second, a *Sommaire d'une Poétique dramatique;* and the third (undated, like the preceding) a *Variante du Sommaire précédent.* This last is translated in the present volume.

Editions:

Les Sentimens de l'Académie françoise sur la Tragi-comédie du Cid was first published in 1637, though the title-page bears the date of 1638. It was re-printed in 1678, probably in 1693, and in 1701; also in the Marty-Laveaux edition of *Les Œuvres de Pierre Corneille*, vol. 12 (Paris, 1862), in Gasté's *La Querelle du Cid* (Paris, 1898), in Georges Collas' *Jean Chapelain* (Paris, 1911), and in Colbert Searles' *Les Sentiments de L'Académie française sur la Tragi-comédie du Cid* (Univ. of Minnesota, Minneapolis, 1916). This edition contains in parallel columns Chapelain's original MS., the corrections, and the printed version.

On Chapelain and his works:

Introductions to the Thamizey de Larroque, Camusat, and Searles editions above cited.

Georges Collas, *Jean Chapelain* (Paris, 1911).

Pierre Brun, *Jean Chapelain* (in *Revue d'histoire littéraire de la France*, Paris, 1902).

Alois Mühlan, *Jean Chapelain als litterarischer Kritiker* (Leipzig, 1884).

Biographie universelle, vol. 7 (Paris, 1844).

La Grande Encyclopédie, vol. 10 (Paris).

Nouvelle Biographie générale, vol. 9 (Paris, 1854).

Segrais, *Segraisiana*, 2 vols. (Paris, 1721; Amsterdam, 1723).

J.-E. Fidao-Justiniani, *L'Esprit classique et la Préciosité au XVII⁰ siècle* (Paris, 1914).

Adrien Baillet, *Jugement des savants*, 8 vols. (Paris, 1722-30).

Goujet, *Bibliothèque françoise*, 18 vols. (Paris, 1701-26. See vol. 17).

F. Guizot, *Corneille et son Temps*, translated as *Corneille and his Times*, New York, 1871 (chap. on *Chapelain*).

Abbé Fabre, *Les Ennemis de Chapelain* (Paris, 1888).

E. Hunger, *Der Cidstreit in chronologischen Ordnung* (Leipzig, 1891).

René Kerviter, *La Bretagne à l'Académie française au XVII⁰ siècle* (Paris, 1879).

Charles Arnaud, *Les Théories dramatiques au XVII⁰ siècle. Etude sur la vie et les œuvres de l'Abbé d'Aubignac* (Paris, 1887).

H. Moulin, *Chapelain, Huet, Ménage* (Caën, 1882).

A. Bourgoin, *Les Maîtres de la critique au XVII⁰ siècle* (Paris, 1889).

OPINIONS OF THE FRENCH ACADEMY ON THE TRAGI-COMEDY "THE CID" [2]

(*Les Sentimens de l'Académie françoise sur la Tragi-comédie du Cid*)

(1637)

. . . Nature and Truth have put a certain value to things, which cannot be altered by that which chance or opinion set up; to attempt to judge them by what they seem, and not what they are, is to condemn oneself at the outset. It is true enough that the great Masters are not themselves in very close agreement on this point. Some, too much inclined, it seems, toward pleasure, hold that delight is the true purpose of dramatic poetry; others, more sparing of men's time and holding it too dear to be given over to amusements which yield only pleasure and no profit, maintain that its

2 Here translated for the first time, by the editor.— Ed.

real end is to instruct. Though each expresses himself in such different terms, it will on closer examination be seen that both are in agreement; and if we judge them with what favor we should, we shall see that those who claim pleasure as the sole end are too reasonable to exclude anything that is not conformable to reason. We must believe — if we would do them justice — that by pleasure they mean the pleasure which is not the enemy but the instrument of virtue, and which purges men, insensibly and without disgust, of their vicious practices, and which is useful because it is good, and which can never leave regret in the mind for having surprised it, nor in the soul for having corrupted it. And so they only seem to disagree with the others, for it is true that if the pleasure they demand be not profit itself, it is at least the source whence of necessity it flows; and that wherever there is pleasure there is profit, and that both are produced from the same sources.

Hence, they are at one, and we agree with them both, and we can all of us together say that a play is good when it produces a feeling of reasonable content. But, as in music and painting, we should not consider every concert and every picture good if it please the people but fail in the observance of the rules of their respective arts, and if the experts, who are the sole judges, did not by their approval confirm that of the multitude. Hence we must not say with the crowd that a poem is good merely because it pleases, unless the learned and the expert are also pleased. Indeed, it is impossible that there can be pleasure contrary to reason, unless it be to a depraved taste — as, for instance, a liking for the bitter and the acid. We are not here concerned with satisfying the libertine and the vicious man, who only laughs at adulteries and incests, and who does not object to violations of the laws of nature, provided he is amused. Nor have we to do with pleasing those who are ignorant and untutored, who would be no more moved at seeing the sufferings of Penelope than of Clytemnestra. Evil examples are contagious, even in the theater; the representations even of feigned acts produce only too many real crimes; and there is great danger in diverting the people with pleasures which may some day result in public catastrophes. We must be careful to guard their eyes and ears against things of which they should not know, and keep them from learning of cruelty or perfidy, unless at the same time examples are accompanied with the just retribution, so that they may take home with them after the performance at least some fear mixed with their pleasure. But, for that matter, it is impossible to please any one with disorder and confusion, and if it happens that irregular plays sometimes please, it is only by reason of what is regular in them, because of certain unquestioned and extraordinary beauties

which transport the soul so far that for a long time after, it is incapable of detecting the deformities which accompany them, and which serve, imperceptibly, to bring out the faults, while the understanding is yet dazzled by the brilliancy of the good. And on the other hand, if certain regularly-constructed plays give little pleasure, it must not be thought that this is the fault of the rules, but of the author, whose sterile wit was unable to exercize his art upon sufficently rich material. . . .

. . . Now, the natural, rather than the true is, according to Aristotle, the province of epic and dramatic poetry, which, having for its purpose the pleasure and profit of the auditor or the spectator, the epic or dramatic poet can the more surely encompass by making use of the natural, or verisimilar, rather than what is simply true, or matter of fact, because it convinces men the more easily as it finds no resistance in them, which it would if the poet adhered to mere facts, and which might well be so strange and incredible that they would think them false and refuse to be persuaded of them. But since several things are required to make a story natural — that is, observation of time, of place, of the condition, age, manners and customs, and passions,— the principal point of all is that each personage must behave according to his character as set forth early in the poem. For instance, an evil man must not do good deeds. And the reason why this exact observation is required is that there is no other way of producing the Marvelous, which delights the mind with astonishment and pleasure, and is the perfect means adopted by poetry to arrive at the end of profit. It is indeed a great undertaking to try to create the rare effect of the Marvelous from so common a thing as the natural. And so, we believe with the Masters that herein lies the greatest merit for him who knows well how to do it; and as the difficulty is great, there are few who can succeed. And that is why so many, despairing of success, resort to that false Marvelous which results in the unnatural, what is not true to life, and which may be called the Monstrous, and try to pass off on the crowd as the true Marvelous that which deserves only the name of Miraculous.

SUMMARY OF A POETIC OF THE DRAMA [1]

(*Sommaire d'une Poétique dramatique*)

(Posthumous)

The object of representative as well as of narrative poetry is the imitation of human action; their necessary condition is truth to life [*le vraysemblable*]; in its perfection it strives for the marvelous.

From the judicious union of the verisimilar and the marvelous springs the excellence of works of this sort. Both these elements belong to invention.

In Tragedy, which is the noblest form of drama, the poet imitates the actions of the great; in Comedy, those of people in middle or low condition. The ending of Comedy is happy.

Tragi-comedy was known to the Ancients only as tragedy with a happy ending. Witness the *Iphigenia in Tauris*. The modern French have made the form very popular, and as a result of the characters and the action have put it into a class nearer to tragedy than to comedy.

The Pastoral was invented and introduced by the Italians less than a hundred years after the Eclogue; it is a sort of Tragi-comedy, imitating the actions of shepherds, but in a more elevated manner and with higher sentiments than can be employed in the Eclogue.

In plays, poets depict, besides action, the various manners, customs, and passions of human beings.

They take particular care to make each personage speak according to his condition, age, and sex; and by propriety they mean not only that which is decent, but what is fitting and appropriate to the characters — be they good or evil — as they are at first set forth in the play.

In their tragedies and comedies a good plot never had more than one principal action, to which the others are related. This is what is termed Unity of Action.

They have allowed to the development of the action of a play the space of a single natural day. This is what is termed the Twenty-four-hour rule.

1 Translated complete, for the first time, by the editor.— Ed.

They have set the physical limit of their action to a single place. This is what is termed the Unity of Place.

All this is a necessary corollary to the verisimilar, without which the mind is neither moved nor persuaded.

The action of the play consists in exposition of the story, its complication [*embrouillement*] and its development.

The most worthy and agreeable effect that can be produced by a play, is that as a result of the artful conduct of the story the spectator is left suspended and puzzled to know the outcome, and cannot decide what the end of the adventure will be.

The Latins divided plays into five acts, while the Greeks divided them only into scenes.

Each act has several scenes. It will seem too short if it have only four, and too long if more than seven.

In the first act the principal points of the story are made clear; in the second, complications arise; in the third, the trouble deepens; in the fourth, matters look desperate; in the fifth, the knot is loosed — in a natural way, however, but in an unforeseen manner — and from this results the Marvelous.

There are some who insist that no more than three characters should appear on the stage at the same time in the same scene, in order to avoid confusion. I approve of this, except when it applies to the last scenes of the last act, where everything ought to point toward the end and where confusion only renders the unraveling more noble and more beautiful.

Others insist that each scene be intimately bound to the other. This, it is true, produces a more agreeable effect; but the practice of the Ancients proves how unnecessary it is.

What seems most necessary to me is that no character should enter or leave without apparent reason.

FRANÇOIS HÉDELIN, ABBÉ D'AUBIGNAC

François Hédelin, better known as the Abbé d'Aubignac, was born at Paris in 1604. His father was an "avocat" in the Parlement and his mother a daughter of the famous Ambroise Paré. In 1610 the family moved to Nemours. At an early age François took part in the conversations of the Précieux and literary people with whom his father, a man of some literary taste and accomplishments, was acquainted. His own education, which was partly a study of modern and ancient languages, was, according to him, of his own making; his precocity was the wonder and delight of his parents and their friends. In his twenty-third year he was made an "avocat au Parlement"; the same year, 1627, he published his first work, a study, *Des Satyres, brutes, monstres et démons.* For a time he practiced law at Nemours, with some success, but before long went to Paris and entered the Church. Just after his ordination as a priest, he was appointed private tutor to the Duc de Fronsac, a nephew of Cardinal Richelieu, and son of the Marshal de Brézé. This was a turning-point in his life, for in the house of the Duke he became acquainted with the great men of his time, chief among them the Cardinal himself, who did much toward the shaping of his career. He was given the Abbey of Aubignac in recognition of his services, but in the meantime he had spent his patrimony on the education of the Duke. He experienced considerable difficulty in securing the pension to which he was entitled. His political opinions seemed sufficient reason to Condé for a refusal. As a result, d'Aubignac says (in 1663) that for seventeen years he had not been to court. He preached, wrote plays, pamphlets, a novel, dissertations of various kinds, and his celebrated *Pratique du théâtre.* He founded an *Académie des belles lettres,* probably in 1654. His last years were filled with disappointments. He died in 1676.

D'Aubignac touched the life of his time at many diverse points. A recognized arbiter of taste, a scholar, an author, a Précieux, a man of the world

and an abbé, he was for many years regarded as one of the foremost men of his age. Even after his death his opinions were respected by such men as Corneille and Racine. His principal title to fame rests on the famous *Pratique du théâtre* (1657), which was studied by many practicing dramatists. Racine's copy of the book is still in existence and his annotations are re-printed in M. Arnaud's life of d'Aubignac. (See below.) The curious mixture of pedantry and absurdity which goes hand in hand with much that is wise and sane, has done great harm to the author's reputation, while possibly Condé's mot, "I am obliged to Monsieur d'Aubignac for having so exactly followed Aristotle's rules, but I will never forgive the rules of Aristotle for having put Monsieur d'Aubignac upon writing so bad a tragedy," has served to call attention to the great disparity between the author's theory and his practice. The *Pratique* was intended, and to a certain extent is, a practical manual, the first of its kind. Its importance lies in the author's having insisted that a play is intended to be performed, and not merely read. This is by no means a new idea; Aristotle himself had laid down the principle, though he had not developed it, while Castelvetro was the first in modern times to insist on the close relation between the dramatist and the performance of a play in a theater before an audience.

On the drama:

D'Aubignac's dramatic writings are not confined to the *Pratique du théâtre,* though this is his most important contribution to the subject. He carried on a long and rather absurd discussion with Ménage on the duration of the action in the *Heautontimorumenos* of Terence. The first published work of d'Aubignac on the subject was the *Discours sur la troisième comédie de Térence, intitulée: "Héautontimorumenos,"* published at Paris anonymously in 1640. The next was the *Térence justifié,* published in 1656.

Both were re-printed under the title of *Térence justifié* in the Amsterdam 2-volume edition of the *Pratique*, in 1715. In 1663 came the *Deux Dissertations en forme de remarques sur deux tragédies de M. Corneille* (Paris, 1663), and, later in the same year, the *Troisième et Quatrième Dissertations* on further plays of Corneille. These are vitriolic attacks on Corneille. The *Dissertation sur la condamnation des Théâtres* was published in 1666. He is likewise the author of two plays, *Cyminde* (1642), and *Zénobie* (1647).

Editions:

La Pratique du théâtre was first published at Paris in 1657, and re-printed there in 1669. The same work, together with the *Discours* on Terence, and one of Ménage, was re-printed in 2 vols. (Amsterdam, 1715). It was translated, anonymously, as *The Whole Art of the Stage, now made English* (London, 1684). Several passages of the original French are quoted in Arnaud's life of d'Aubignac.

On the Abbé d'Aubignac and his works:

Charles Arnaud, *Les Théories dramatiques au XVIIᵉ siècle. Etude sur la vie et les œuvres de l'Abbé d'Aubignac* (Paris, 1887).

Charles Livet, *Précieux et ridicules* (2nd ed., Paris, 1870).

Adrien Baillet, *Jugement des savants* (new ed., Paris, 1722-30).

Saint-Marc Girardin, *J.-J. Rosseau* (in vol. 2, Paris, 1870).

George Saintsbury, *A History of Criticism*, vol. 2 (New York, 1902).

THE WHOLE ART OF THE STAGE [1]
[*La Pratique du théâtre*]
(1657)

OF THE RULES OF THE ANCIENTS
CHAPTER IV

. . . Therefore, here are five objections which have been ordinarily made to me against the rules of the Ancients:

First, that we are not to make laws to ourselves from custom and example, but from reason; which ought to prevail over any authority.

Secondly, that the Ancients themselves have often violated their own rules.

Thirdly, that divers poems of the Ancients had been translated and acted upon our stage with very ill success.

Fourthly, that divers of our modern plays, though quite contrary to these rules, have been acted with great applause.

And last of all, that if these rigorous maxims should be followed, we should very often lose the greatest beauty of all true stories, their incidents having most commonly happened at different times and in different places.

As to the first objection, I answer that

[1] Re-printed from the anonymous translation, *The Whole Art of the Stage* (London, 1684).

the rules of the stage are not founded upon authority, but upon reason; they are not so much settled by example as by the natural judgment of mankind, and if we call them the rules and the art of the Ancients 'tis only because they have practiced them with great regularity and much to their glory; having first made many observations upon the nature of moral actions and upon the probability of human accidents in this life and thereby drawing the pictures after the truth of the original and observing all due circumstances, they reduce to an art this kind of poem whose progress was very slow, though it were much in use among them and much admired all the world over. But, however, I am very sparing of citing their poems and when I do it it is only to show with what agreeable artifice they kept to these rules, and not to buoy up my opinion by their authority.

As for the second objection, it seems not considerable; for reason, being alike all the world over, does equally require everybody's submission to it, and if our modern authors cannot without offense be dispensed from the rules of the stage, no more could the Ancients; and where they have failed I do not pretend to excuse them. My observations upon Plautus show very well that I do propose the Ancients for models only in such things as they appear to have followed reason; and their example will always be an ill pretext for faults, for there is no excuse against reason. In things which are founded only in custom, as in grammar, or in the art of making a verse with long or short syllables, the learned may often use a license against the received practice and be imitated in it by others, because custom may often have countenanced a thing not well of itself. But in all that depends upon commonsense and reason, such as are the rules of the stage, there to take a license is a crime; because it offends not custom but natural light, which ought never to suffer an eclipse.

I must not omit, for the glory of the Ancients, that if they have sometimes violated the art of dramatic poems, they have done it for some more powerful and inducing reason than all the interest of the play could amount to. As for example, Euripides in *The Suppliants* has preferred the glory of his country to that of his art, of which I have spoken elsewhere.

The third objection has no force but in the ignorance of those that allege it. For if some poems of the Ancients, and even those which were most in esteem with them, have not succeeded upon our stage, the subject and not the want of art, has been the cause of it; and sometimes likewise the changes made by the translators, which destroyed all the graces of the original; they have added improbable scenes between princes and have showed out of time that which the Ancients had carefully concealed with art; and very often changed a fine relation into an impertinent, ridiculous spectacle. But that which is more worthy our consideration is that there were certain stories, fitted for the stage of Athens with great ornaments, which would be an abomination upon ours. For example, the story of Thyestes, so that we may say that either the moderns have corrupted the Ancients, by changing their whole economy, or the imperfection of the matter stifled the excellency of the art.

To destroy the fourth objection, we need only to remember that those plays of ours which took with the people and with the Court, were not liked in all their parts, but only in those things which were reasonable and in which they were conformable to the rules. When there were any passionate scenes they were praised; and when there was any great appearance or noble spectacle, it was esteemed; and if some notable event was well managed, there was great satisfaction shown; but if in the rest of the play or even in these beauties of it, any irregularities were discovered or any fault against probability and decency, either in the persons, time, or place, or as to the state of the things represented, they were condemned as faults. And all the favor that was shown the poet was that out of the desire of preserving what was fine, the spectators were somewhat more indulgent to what was amiss.

There, that success so much bragged on is so far from contradicting the rules of the stage that, quite contrary, it established their authority. For these rules being nothing but an art, to cause the finest incidents to please with decency and probability, it sufficiently appears how necessary they are since by common consent all that comes up to them is approved of and all that varies from them is in some measure condemned. Examples would extremely illustrate this truth if I were not afraid to anger some of our poets by instructing the others at their cost.

The fifth objection is absolutely ridiculous. For the rules of the stage do not at all reject the most notable incidents of any story, but they furnish us with inventions, how so to adjust the circumstances of the action, time, and place as not to go against all probable appearance, and yet not to represent them always as they are in story, but such as they ought to be, to have nothing but what's agreeable in them. 'Tis that, then, that we are to seek, and of which in the following Discourse I shall communicate my thoughts.

OF THE SUBJECT OF DRAMATIC POEMS
(Book 2, Chapter 1)

Supposing here what the poet ought to know of that part of a drama which the Ancients called the Fable, we, the Story or Romance, and I in this place the Subject — I will only say that for subjects merely invented and of which one may as well make a tragedy as a comedy, if they do not take, 'tis perfectly the poet's fault, and a fault without excuse or pretext, which he can never clear himself of; for, being master as well of the matter as of the form, the miscarriage of the play can be attributed to nothing but to his want of conduct in the thing and to the errors of his own imagination. But, as for subjects drawn from story or from the fables of the Ancients, he is more excusable if he misses of success in the representation of them, for he may be many ways constrained; as if a great man command him to preserve certain circumstances, not 'so fit for the stage, or that he does it himself out of some consideration more important to him than the glory of being a good poet would be. But if he be free of his choice, he may be sure that he shall be blamed if his play does not take, it being certain that art out of an ill story may make an excellent drama; as for example, if there be no plot, the poet must make one; if it be too intricate, he must make it looser and easier, if too open and weak, he must strengthen it by invention, and so for the rest. On the other side, there is no story so rich in itself but an ill poet may so spoil the beauty of it that it will be hardly known to be the same story.

Besides, one is not to think that all fine stories are fit to appear with success upon the stage, for very often the beautifullest part of them depends upon some circumstance which the theater cannot suffer; and it was for this that I advised one who had a mind to undertake the loves of Antiochus and Stratonica to let it alone; for the most considerable incident in it being the cunning of the physician in discovering the prince's passion by causing all the ladies in the court to pass one by one before the prince's bed that so by the emotion of his pulse he might judge which of them it was that caused his disease. I thought it would be very odd to make a play where the hero of it should always be abed, and that it would be hard to change the circumstance so as to preserve the beauty of it, and that besides, the time and place of the scene would 'be difficult to bring together; for if Antiochus be supposed sick abed in the morning, 'twould be improbable to lay much action upon him all the rest of that day; and to place the scene in a sick man's chamber or at his door would be as unlikely.

'Twas for the same reason that the Théodore of Corneille had not all the approbation it deserved; 'tis in itself a most ingenious play, the plot being well carried and full of variety, where all the hints of the true story are made use of to advantage, the changes and turns very judicious and the passions and verse worthy the name of so great a man. But because the whole business turns upon the prostitution of Theodora to the public stews, it would never please; not but that the poet, in that too, has taken care to expose things with great modesty and nicety, but still one is forced to have the idea of that ugly adventure so often in one's imagination, particularly in the narrations of the fourth act, that the spectators cannot but have some disgust at it.

There are a hundred stories like these, and harder yet to manage for the stage; and likewise, on the contrary, there are lucky ones which seem to have happened on purpose, as that of Sophonisba, who is a widow, and married again, loses her kingdom and recovers it, all in one day.

The way, therefore, of choosing a subject is to consider whether it be founded upon one of these three things; either upon noble passions, as *Mariamne* and the *Cid;* or upon an intricate and pleasing plot, as *Cleomedon or The Disguis'd Prince;* or upon some extraordinary spectacle and show, as *Cyminda or The Two Victims;* and if the story will bear more circumstances of this nature or that the poet's imagination can fitly supply the play with them, it will be still the better, provided he observe a just moderation, for though a poem ought not to be without a plot nor without passions or noble spectacles, yet to load a subject with any of them, is a thing to be avoided. Violent passions too often repeated do, as it were, numb the soul and its sympathy:

the multitude of incidents and intrigues distract the mind and confound the memory, and much show takes up more time than can be allowed it, and is hard to bring on well. 'Tis for this reason that some of our poets who had contrived in every act a memorable incident and a moving passion did not find that the success answered their expectation.

I am asked what is the measure of employing those things? I shall answer, 'tis every one's natural judgment; and it may happen that a drama may be so luckily contrived that the preparation of the incidents and the variety of the passions shall correct the defect of the abundance of them, and that the art of the machines shall be so well understood that they may easily be made use of in every act, as I formerly propounded to Cardinal Richelieu, but hitherto they are little in use in our ordinary theaters.

'Tis besides most commonly asked here how far the poet may venture in the alterations of a true story, in order to the fitting of it for the stage. Upon which we find different opinions among both the ancient and modern critics; but my opinion is that he may do it not only in the circumstances but in the principal action itself, provided he make a very good play of it; for as the dramatic poet does not much mind the time, because he is no chronologist, no more does he nor the epic poet much mind the true story, because they are no historians. They take out of the story so much as serves their turn and change the rest, not expecting that anybody should be so ridiculous as to come to the theater to be instructed in the truth of history.

The stage, therefore, does not present things as they have been, but as they ought to be, for the poet must in the subject he takes reform everything that is not accommodated to the rules of his art; as a painter does when he works upon an imperfect model.

'Twas for this reason that the death of Camilla by the hands of her brother Horatius was never liked of upon the stage, though it be a true adventure; and I for my part gave my opinion that to save in some measure the truth of the story and yet not to offend against the decency of the stage, it would have been better that that unfortunate maid, seeing her brother come towards her with his sword drawn, had run upon it of herself, for by that means she would still have died by the hand of Horatius, and yet he might have deserved some compassion, as unfortunate but innocent, and so the story and the stage would have agreed.

In a word, the historian ought to recite matter of fact, and if he judges of it he does more than he ought to do; the epic poet is to magnify all events by great fictions where truth is, as it were, sunk and lost; and the dramatic poet ought to show all things in a state of decency, probability, and pleasingness. 'Tis true that if story is capable of all the ornaments of dramatic poetry, the poet ought to preserve all the true events; but if not, he is well grounded to make any part of it yield to the rules of his art and to the design he has to please.

Many against this do allege the authority of Horace, who says that " he ought in story to follow the common received opinion, or at least to invent things that may be as conformable to it as possible." But I answer that Horace in that place does not treat of the subject of the play, but of the customs and morals that ought to be given the actors [characters], who ought not to be represented different from what they were believed; as it would be to make Cæsar a coward, or Messalina chaste. And this Vossius has well observed in his *Poetic Art,* and I wonder that people should be abused by citations applied quite contrary to the sense of the author; and yet I am not of opinion that a known story yet fresh in the minds of the people can suffer to be considerably changed without great caution; but in such a case I should advise the poet rather to abandon such a subject than to make an ill play of it out of a humor of following truth; or at least to manage it so as not to check directly the received opinion among the vulgar. If we examine well the sense of Aristotle, I believe he will be found to be of this opinion; and as for the Ancient poets, they have always taken that liberty, the same story having hardly ever been treated the same way by different poets. As for example, the adventures of Polydorus are very different in Euripides and Vergil. Sophocles kills Hemon and Antigone, but Euripides, who has made the same story in two plays, marries them together in one, contrary to what he himself had done before in the other called *The Phœnician Ladies*. The same Sophocles in *Œdipus* makes Jocasta strangle herself, and Euripides makes her live till the combat of her sons Eteocles and Polynices, and then kill herself upon their dead bodies. *Orestes* and *Electra* are very different in many circumstances, though both works of the same poet. In a word, the four [three] tragic poets of the Greeks whose works we have, are all different in the disposition of the same stories, and I believe that they were the cause of that grand disorder and confusion there is in story and chronology in those old times, because that they having changed both the times and events for their own ends, have influenced some historians who thought to pick out of them the truth of story, and so made all things uncertain. Anybody that will read the *Electra* of Euripides, that of Sophocles, and the *Choephoræ* of Æschylus, will easily see that they made no difficulty of contradicting one another and themselves.

As for the different kinds of subjects, letting alone those ordinary divisions of Aristotle and his commentators, I here propose three sorts of subjects.

The first consists of incidents, intrigues, and new events, when almost from act to act there is some sudden change upon the stage which alters all the face of affairs, when almost all the actors have different designs; and the means they take to make them succeed come to cross one another and produce new and unforeseen accidents, all which gives a marvelous satisfaction to the spectators, it being a continual diversion, accompanied with an agreeable expectation of what the event will be.

The second sort of subjects are of those raised out of passions; when out of a small fund the poet does ingeniously draw great sentiments and noble passions to entertain the auditory; and when out of incidents that seem natural to his subject, he takes occasion to transport his actors into extraordinary and violent sentiments, by which the spectators are ravished and their soul continually moved with some new impression.

The last sort of subjects are the mixed or compound of incidents and passions, when by unexpected events, but noble ones, the actors break out into different passions; and that infinitely delights the auditory, to see at the same time surprising accidents and noble and moving sentiments, to which they cannot but yield with pleasure.

Now, 'tis certain that in all these three sorts of subjects the poet may succeed, provided the disposition of his play be ingenious; but yet I have observed some difference, according to which they take more or less.

Subjects full of plot and intrigue are extreme agreeable at first, but being once known, they do not the second time please us so well, because they want the graces of novelty, which made them charm us at first, all our delight consisting in being surprised, which we cannot be twice.

The subjects full of passions last longer and affect us more, because the soul which received the impression of them does not keep them so long nor so strongly as our memory does the events of things; nay, it often happens that they please us more at second seeing, because that the first time we are employed about the event and disposition of the play, and by consequent do less enter into the sentiments of the actors; but having once no need of applying our thoughts to the story, we busy them about the things that are said, and so receive more impressions of grief or fear.

But it is out of doubt that the mixed or compound are the most excellent sort, for in them the incidents grow more pleasing by the passions which do as it were uphold them, and th passions seem to be renewed and spris afresh, by the variety of the unthough-of ucidents; so that they are both l se their graces, a great time to make here (and I think

We are not to f vations that I have it one of the bes ect) that if the subject is not nable to the customs and mann ell as opinions of the spectators himself take, what pains soever all he employs to set his soeve according dramatic poems must play they are to the people be-b e often represented; and proceeds that the success is different though the play be still the same. Thus the Athenians delighted to see upon their theater the cruelties of kings and the misfortunes befalling them, the calamities of illustrious and noble families, and the rebellion of the whole nation for an ill action of the prince, because the state in which they lived being popular, they loved to be persuaded that monarchy was always tyrannical, hoping thereby to discourage the noble men of their own commonwealth from the attempt of seizing the sovereignty, out of fear of being exposed to the fury of a commonalty who would think it just to murder them. Whereas, quite contrary among us, the respect and love which we have for our princes cannot endure that we should entertain the public with such spectacles of horror. We are not willing to believe that kings are wicked, nor that their subjects, though with some appearance of ill-usage, ought to rebel against their power, or touch their persons, no, not in effigy. And I do not believe that upon our stage a poet could cause a tyrant to be murdered, with any applause, except he had very cautiously laid the thing. As for example, that the tyrant were an usurper and the right heir should appear and be owned by the people, who should take that occasion to revenge the injuries they had suffered from the tyrant. But usurpation alone against the will of the people, would not justify without horror the death of the sovereign by the hands of his rebellious subjects. We have seen the trial of it in a play called *Timoleon*, whom no consideration of state or common good, no love nor generosity towards his country, could hinder from being considered as the murderer of his brother and his prince; and for my part, I esteem that author who avoided to have been killed upon the stage after the v..... The crime he had offered to Lucretia. The horror into of Alboin inspired horror into of Alboin inspired Court, though others whole French full of noble incid were a tragedy gauage, and lofty language.

We have had upon of Mr. Du Ryer, a..... the *Esther* events, fortified with st..ith great composed in the whole m..ions, and but the success was..t art; Paris than at Rouen; and er at .....lay-

ers at their return to Paris told us the good fortune they had had at Rouen, everybody wondered at it without being able to guess the cause; but for my part I think that Rouen, being a town of great trade, is full of a great number of Jews, some known and some concealed, and that by that reason they making up a good part of the audience, took more delight in a piece which seemed entirely Jewish, by the conformity it had to their manners and customs.

We may say the same thing of comedies, for the Greeks and Romans, with whom the debauches of young people with courtesans was but a laughing matter, took pleasure to see their intrigues represented, and to hear the discourses of those public women, with the tricks of those ministers of their pleasures countenanced by the laws. They were also delighted to see old covetous men overreached and cheated of their money by the circumvention of their slaves in favor of their young masters. They were sensible to all these things because they were subject to them one time or another. But amongst us all this would be ill received, for as Christian modesty does not permit persons of quality to approve of those examples of vice, so neither do the rules by which we govern our families all of those flights of our servants, nor do we need to defend ourselves against them. 'Tis for the same reason that we see in the French Court tragedies take a great deal better than comedies, and that on the contrary, the people are more affected with the latter and particularly with the farces and buffooneries of the stage; for in this Kingdom the persons of good quality and education have generous thoughts and designs, to which they are carried either by the motives of virtue or ambition, so that their life has a great conformity with the characters of tragedy, but the people, meanly born and dirtily bred, have low sentiments and are thereby disposed to approve of the meanness and filthiness represented in farces, as being the image of those things which they both use to say and do; and this ought to be taken notice of, not only in the principal part of the poem, but in all its parts and particularly in passions, as we shall say more amply in a chapter about them; for, if there be any act or scene that has not that conformity of manners to the spectators, you will suddenly see the applause cease and in its place a discontent succeed, though they themselves do not know the cause of it. For the stage and eloquence are alike in this, that when even it triumphs and overcomes, it is in abomination with the audience who thereupon are apt to conclude with themselves, *That 'tis better to embrace virtue through the hazard of persecution, than to follow vice even with hopes of impunity.*

'Tis. thus principally that the stage ought to be instructive to the public by the knowledge of things represented; and I have always observed that it is not agreeable to the audience that a man who swerves from the way of virtue should be set right, and repent, by the strength of precepts and sentences: we rather desire it should be by some adventure that presses him, and forces him to take up reasonable and virtuous sentiments. We should hardly endure that Herod should recall his sentence against Mariamne upon a remonstrance of one of the seven wise men of Greece: but we are pleased to see that after the death of the Queen, his love becomes his tormentor; and, having opened his eyes, drives him into so sincere a repentance, that he is ready to sacrifice his life to the regret he has for his crime.

As for the other way of teaching morality, it depends much on the ingeniousness of the poet, when he strengthens his theatrical action with divers pithy and bold truths, which being imperceptibly worked into his play, are as it were the nerves and strength of it. For, in a word, that which I condemn in common didactics, is their style and manner of expression, not the things themselves, since those great truths which are as it were the foundation of the conduct of human actions, I am so far from banishing them off the stage, that quite contrary, I think them very necessary and ornamental, which to attain, I give these following observations.

First, these general maxims must be so fastened to the subject, and linked by many circumstances with the persons acting, that the actor may seem to think more of that concern of his he is about, than of saying fine things; that is, to speak in terms of rhetoric, he must reduce the thesis to the hypothesis, and of universal propositions make particular applications; for by this means the poet avoids the suspicion of aiming to instruct pedantically, since his actors do not leave their business which they are about. For example, I would not have an actor spend many words to prove that Virtue is always persecuted; but he may say to the party concerned:

Do you think to have better measure than virtue has always had, and can you expect to be privileged from persecution more than Socrates or Cato?

And so continue a little speaking still to the party present, and upon the subject in hand, by which means these discourses seem a little to keep off from being too general precepts, and so disgust the less.

Secondly, in all these occasions the poet must use figurative speech, either by interrogation, irony, or others that his fancy shall suggest; for these figures, by not circumstancing minutely the general propositions, make them more florid, and so by ornaments free them from the didactic character. As, for example, if there be a design of advising a young woman to obey her parents: instead of preaching downright obedience to her, I think an irony would do better. As thus:

That's a fine way indeed, for a virtuous young lady to attain the reputation of a good daughter, to be carried away by her own passions, and neglect not only the censure of the best sort of people, but break through the fences of duty and honor!

My third observation is, that when any of these great maxims are to be proposed bluntly and in plain words, it be done in as few words as may be; by that means they do not cool the stage, but add something to the variety of it; but there must be care taken that this do not happen in the midst of a violent passion; for besides that in those cases men do not naturally speak sentences, the actor cannot then appear with that moderation which those reflections require. Seneca is very guilty of this fault in all his tragedies, where most commonly in the heat of passion all his fine commonplaces are bestowed upon the audience.

We have nevertheless some examples

of didactic propositions made in direct terms and at length not without some success in Corneille, which to attain as well as he, requires the same ingenuity and art. The expressions must be strong, and seem to have been said only for that particular subject to which they are applied, and that requires a particular genius and much study to accomplish.

I have observed besides, that common truths, though in a didactic style, yet do very well upon the stage in the mouth of a rogue or a cheat, when his character is known; for the spectator is delighted to see him cunningly use all the maxims and discourses of a good man to intents and purposes quite contrary, so that by that means 'tis all figurative, and moves the attention of the audience.

One may likewise successfully enough burlesque all these common truths, but that can be performed nowhere but in comedy, where by that means they forsake their natural state, and are disguised under a new appearance, which causes both variety and ornament. But tragedy in its own nature is too grave to admit of anything so low and buffoon as this would be; neither do I remember to have met with anything of that kind in any serious tragedy; I say serious tragedy, because that in satirical tragedy there was admitted a mixture of heroic actions and low buffooneries; and therefore this disguising of serious precepts might have room among the rest in them.

PIERRE CORNEILLE

Pierre Corneille was born at Rouen in 1606. He came of a middle-class family of lawyers and petty officials. He attended the Jesuit College at Rouen, where he received a sound training in the classics; he later studied law and received a degree in 1624, and practiced at least part of the time, both as lawyer and in an official capacity in the department of waters and forests and the marine. During his early years he was a student of literature, and at the age of twenty-three he wrote his first play, *Mélite.* This was successfully produced by Mondory in Paris. It was followed in quick succession by five comedies, a tragicomedy, and a tragedy, all of which appeared and were produced between 1629 and 1636. Although he went to Paris occasionally, Corneille resided in Rouen until 1662. In 1636, or early in 1637, he produced *Le Cid,* which marked not only the beginning of the poet's success, but the veritable beginning of modern French tragedy. Aside from its incalculable influence on the drama of the time and of succeeding times, it precipitated the famous *Cid* Controversy. The success of the play and the honors heaped upon Corneille brought the poet into disfavor with Richelieu, who sought to discredit

the author of the "irregular" *Cid.* But the public would be influenced by no Academic attacks, and the poet's future was assured. And yet Corneille was troubled and discouraged by the many attacks on his work, and we find him years afterward attempting to justify himself and reconcile his theory with his practice. In his next play, *Horace* (1640), he replied to his critics by writing a "regular" play, which is little below *Le Cid* in power. Then followed *Cinna* (1640), *Polyeucte* (1642 or 1643), and *La Mort de Pompée* (1643–44). After this play, there is a noticeable diminution in the poet's power, followed by discouragement and what practically amounted to poverty, together with a certain measure of neglect. His last play, *Suréna,* was produced in 1674. His later years were once more troubled with a quarrel, this time over his *Sophinisbe* (1663), in which the Abbé d'Aubignac and Donneau de Visé were his adversaries. In 1647 Corneille, after two unsuccessful attempts to secure election, was admitted to the Academy. He died at Paris in 1684.

The theoretical works of Molière and Racine are only relatively important; those of Corneille would entitle him to fame had he written no plays. Corneille's various prefaces, his *Examens,* and three *Discours,* are indicative of the trend of classicism in the literature of the seventeenth century. Together with the similar writings of Chapelain, Boileau, and d'Aubignac, they established the pseudo-Aristotelian and Horatian precepts in France. That these commentators on and idolators of Aristotle understood the *Poetics* imperfectly, makes little difference. Jules Lemaître, in his *Corneille et la Poétique d'Aristote* says, "Corneille's critical work taken as a whole is nothing but an ingenious, and in turn triumphant and despairing commentary on Aristotle's *Poetics;* or, rather a lengthy duel with Aristotle." Lemaître very wisely goes on to say that Corneille boasts in places of having dared do what no one before him had done, and elsewhere prides himself on having observed the Rules more rigorously than any one else. But out of the great mass of Corneille's controversial writing there emerges the basic ideal of the century: to please, but please according to the Rules.

Corneille was influenced by the Italian Renaissance critics — Robortello, Minturno, Castelvetro, and Scaliger — and by the Dutch scholar, Daniel Heinsius, whose *De Tragœdiae Constitutione,* an Aristotelian treatise, appeared in 1611 at Leyden. Heinsius, together with his fellow-countryman Vossius [or Voss], who published a *De Arte Poetica* in 1609, exercised considerable influence throughout Europe.

Of the various prefaces, notices, dedications, exclusive of the *Examens,* the following may be consulted on the subject of the drama:

Préface to *Clitandre* (1632).
Au Lecteur in *La Veuve* (1634).
A Monsieur XXX in *La Suivante* (1637).
A Monsieur P. T. N. G. in *Médée* (1635).
Mariana (Avertissement) in *Le Cid* (1648 ed.).
Epître in *Le Menteur* (1644).
Au Lecteur in *La Mort de Pompée* (1644).
Epître in *La Suite du Menteur* (1645).
Appian Alexandrin (Avertissement) in *Rodogune* (1647).

Au Lecteur in *Héraclius* (1647).
A Monsieur de Zuylichem in *Don Sanche d'Aragon* (1650).
Au Lecteur in *Nicomède* (1651).
Au Lecteur in *Œdipe* (1659).
Au Lecteur in *Sertorius* (1662).
Au Lecteur in *Sophonisbe* (1663).
Au Lecteur in *Othon* (1665).
Au Lecteur in *Agésilas* (1666).
Au Lecteur in *Attila* (1668).

Editions:

Corneille's earlier works were published separately and in small collections prior to 1660 (when the *Théâtre de Corneille* was published at Paris, in three volumes). Each of these contained one of the *Discours;* the *Examens* also appeared in this edition for the first time. Voltaire's edition, with his full commentaries, appeared at Geneva, as the *Théâtre de Pierre Corneille,* in 12 vols. The standard modern edition of the complete works (with biography, an album, notes, etc.) is in the *Grands Ecrivains* series: *Œuvres de P. Corneille,* edited by Ch. Marty-Laveaux, 12 vols. (Paris, 1862–68). The edition of 1660 contains the three *Discours — De l'Utilité et des parties du poème dramatique; De la Tragédie, et des moyens de la traiter selon le vraisemblable et le nécessaire;* and *Des Trois Unités, d'Action, de Jour, et de Lieu.* Each is printed in a volume, prefatory to the plays. All the early plays are each accompanied with an *Examen;* the plays from *Sertorius* to *Suréna* are without them. Among the *Œuvres diverses* in the Marty-Laveaux edition are a few letters and verses touching upon the drama. The most interesting of these is the already cited *Lettre apologétique* to Scudéry; there is another, *To Zuylichem* (no. 14, dated 1650) that is also curious. The editions of 1644 (first part), 1648 (second part), and 1663, of Corneille's plays, each contains an *Au Lecteur.* The prefaces, etc., are almost invariably printed in any edition of Corneille, the *Discours* occasionally. Outside the Marty-Laveaux edition, they are to be found in the *Œuvres des deux Corneille* (Pierre and Thomas), in two volumes, edited by Charles Louandre

(Paris, 1889), and in the Calmann-Lévy re-print.

On Corneille and his works:

See introductions to Voltaire, Louandre, and Marty-Laveaux eds. above referred to.

See references to the *Cid* Quarrel under *Chapelain*.

E. Picot, *Bibliographie cornélienne* (Paris, 1876).

P. Le Verdier et Ed. Pelay, *Additions à la Bibliographie cornélienne* (Paris, 1908).

Abbé Granet, *Recueils de dissertations sur plusieurs tragédies de Corneille et de Racine*, 2 vols. (Paris, 1740).

J.-L. G. de Balzac, *Dissertations sur la gloire*, and *Sur le Romain* (in *Œuvres*, 2 vols., Paris, 1665).

Fontenelle, *Vie de Corneille* (in *Œuvres*, vol. 3, 1790 ed.).

——, *Parallèle de Corneille et de Racine* (in *Œuvres*, vol. 3, 1790 ed.).

F. Guizot, *Corneille et son Temps* (2nd ed., Paris, 1852. Translated as *Corneille and his Times*, New York, 1871).

C.-A. Sainte-Beuve, *Portraits littéraires*, vol. 1 (Paris, 1862).

——, *Nouveaux Lundis*, vol. 7 (Paris, 1863–70).

——, *Port-Royal* (3rd ed., 7 vols., 1869–71).

St. René Taillandier, *Corneille et ses contemporains* (Paris, 1864).

M. J. Taschereau, *Histoire de la vie et des ouvrages de P. Corneille* (Paris, 1855).

Charles Arnaud, *Les Théories dramatiques au XVIIᵉ siècle. Etude sur la vie et les œuvres de l'Abbé d'Aubignac* (Paris, 1887).

F. Bouquet, *Points obscurs et nouveaux de la vie de Corneille* (Paris, 1888).

Ferdinand Brunetière, *Corneille* (in *Etudes critiques sur l'histoire de la littérature française*, vol. 6, 3rd ed., Paris, 1911).

Emile Deschanel, *Le Romantisme des classiques Iᵉʳᵉ série, Corneille, Rotrou,*

Molière, les don Juan de toutes les littératures (Paris, 1882).

René Doumic, *Corneille* (in *Etudes sur la littérature française*, vol. 5, Paris, 1906).

Jules Lemaître, *Corneille et la Poétique d'Aristote* (Paris, 1888).

Eugène Rambert, *Corneille, Racine, et Molière, deux cours sur la poésie dramatique française au XVIIᵉ siècle* (Paris, 1862).

Henry M. Trollope, *Corneille and Racine* (Philadelphia, 1881).

Gustave Lanson, *Corneille* (4th ed., Paris, 1913).

——, *Sur les Discours de Corneille* (in the *Revue des Cours et Conférences*, Paris, 1900–01).

Francisque Sarcey, *Quarante ans de théâtre*, vol. 2 (Paris, 1900).

Emile Faguet, *Propos de théâtre*, vols. 1 & 2 (Paris, 1903–08).

——, *En Lisant Corneille* (Paris, 1913).

——, *Drame ancien, drame moderne* (Paris, 1898).

——, *XVIIᵉ Siècle* (Paris, 1890).

Hippolyte Parigot, *Le Génie et le métier de Corneille* (in *Génie et métier*, Paris, 1894).

Prosser Hall Frye, *Corneille: the Neoclassic Tragedy and the Greek* (in *Literary Reviews and Criticisms*, New York, 1908).

Guillaume Huszar, *Corneille et le théâtre espagnol* (Paris, 1903).

J. B. Segall, *Corneille and the Spanish Drama* (New York, 1902).

R. Le Brun, *Corneille devant trois siècles* (Paris, 1906).

Leon H. Vincent, *Corneille* (Boston, 1901).

Saegert, *Essai sur les théories dramatiques de Corneille, d'après ses discours et ses examens* (Colberg, 1860).

J.-A. Lisle, *Essai sur les théories dramatiques de Corneille d'après des discours et ses examens* (Paris, 1852).

Dr. Kewitsch, *Sur les théories dramatiques de Corneille, d'après ses Discours et ses examens* (Paris, 1852).

J. Boehm, *Die dramatischen Theorien P. Corneille's* (Berlin, 1901).

FIRST DISCOURSE[1]

ON THE USES AND ELEMENTS OF DRAMATIC POETRY

[Premier Discours. De l'Utilité et des Parties du Poème dramatique]

(1660)

Although, according to Aristotle, the sole end of dramatic poetry is to please the audience, and although the majority of these poems have pleased, nonetheless I maintain that many of them have failed to achieve their end. " It must not be claimed," says this philosopher, " that dramatic poetry gives us every sort of pleasure, but only that which is fitting," and continues to say that in order to find that pleasure which it fitting to the audience, the poet must follow the precepts of the art and give that pleasure according to them. It is evident that there are precepts because there is an art, but it is not evident just what the precepts are. We agree on the name but not on the thing; on the words but not on their meaning. The poet must observe unity of action, time and place. No one denies this, but it is a matter of no small difficulty to determine what unity of action is and to realize the extent and limit of the allotted unity of time and place. The poet must treat his subject according to " the probable " and " the necessary." This is what Aristotle says, and all his commentators repeat the words which appear to them so clear and intelligible that not one of them has deigned any more than Aristotle himself to tell us what the " probable " and the " necessary " are. And many of them have so neglected the latter requisite, which in all cases save one,— in connection with the discussion on comedy,— is always mentioned in company with the former, that a false maxim has been established. " The subject of a tragedy must be probable "; thus applying only half of the philosopher's precept to the matter of subject and the manner in which it is to be treated. A subject of tragedy must not be merely probable. Aristotle himself cites as an example *The Flower* of Agatho wherein the names of people and things were purely fictitious, as in comedy. The great sub-

jects which appeal to our emotions and in which our inclinations are set in conflict with the laws of duty and humanity, ought always to extend beyond the limits of the probable.

Such plays would indeed find no audience capable of believing, unless they were aided by the authority of history, which is empirically persuasive, or by common knowledge, which supplies an audience of those whose attitudes are already formed. It is not " probable " that Medea should kill her children; that Clytemnestra should murder her husband; or Orestes stab his mother, but historical legend states these facts, and the representation of these great crimes excites no incredulity in the minds of the audience. It is neither true nor " probable " that Andromeda, at the mercy of a sea-monster, was rescued from her perilous situation by a flying knight with wings on his feet; but this is a story which has been handed down, and which was accepted by the ancients; and, since it has been transmitted even to us, no one would think of taking offense when he sees the story represented on the stage. In giving these instances I do not mean to imply that the poet may invent at haphazard: that which truth or common belief takes for granted would be rejected were there no other basis for a play than mere versimilitude or public opinion. That is why our wise man says " Subjects come from fortune, or chance,"— which causes things to happen,—" and not from art," which imagines them. She is the mistress of happenings, and the choice she allows us to make among those happenings which she presents to us contains a mystic warning not to take advantage of her, nor to utilize for dramatic purposes any happenings which are not to her liking. And so " the ancient tragedies are concerned with the stories of very few families, because very few families were fit subjects for tragedies." Succeeding generations have, however, afforded us a suffi-

[1] Translated, with occasional omissions, especially for this collection by Beatrice Stewart MacClintock. Never before translated.— Ed.

cient number of other family tragedies to enable us to go beyond the limits of ancient times and not follow in the footsteps of the Greeks, but this does not mean that we should overstep their precepts. We should, if possible, accommodate ourselves to them and make them applicable to our practice. We have in our plays left out the chorus, and this has forced us to substitute more episodes than the Greeks used. This is an instance of going beyond the precepts. We should never go against them, even though in practice we do go beyond.

We should know what these precepts are, but unfortunately, Aristotle, and Horace after him, wrote in so obscure a fashion that they needed interpreters; but also, unfortunately, those who have endeavored to act in that capacity have, for the most part, considered the text from a philosophical and dramatic view point. Since these men were better versed in scholarship and metaphysics than in a knowledge of the theater, their commentaries are likely rather to render us more learned but not one jot more enlightened as to the actual meaning. With fifty years of practical experience of the theater I shall make bold to set forth in a straightforward manner some of my ideas on the subject without attempting any definite evidence and with no intention of trying to persuade any one to reject his theories for mine.

At the opening of this *Discourse,* when I said that "the sole end of the drama is to please the audience," I did not mean to enforce this maxim arbitrarily upon those who strive to ennoble dramatic art by considering it as a means to supply moral purpose as well as pleasure. A dispute on this question would be useless because it is impossible to please according to the rules without at the same time supplying a moral purpose, ["utilité"] of some sort. It is a fact that from one end to the other of Aristotle's *Poetics* not once does he make use of the word; on the contrary, he says that the end of drama is the pleasure we experience in observing the actions of men imitated. He prefers that part of the drama which has to do with the subject rather than with the "manners" portrayed, because the former contained what was most pleasing, like the "agnitions" and the

"peripeties." Also, in his definition of tragedy, he includes the elements of pleasure in the subject which is at the bottom of it. And, finally, he preferred tragedy to the epic because it included material decoration and music,— both powerful agents of pleasure — because it was the shortest and least diffuse of literary forms, and the pleasure he derived made it therefore the more perfect. But let us remember that we learned from Horace that we cannot please the greatest number unless we include in our work a moral purpose. Grave and serious people, old men and lovers of virtue, will be bored if they find nothing of profit for them. *Centuriae seniorum,* etc. Thus, if the moral purpose does not enter into it unless it is decked out in pleasant style, it is none the less needful and much wiser, as I have already said, to endeavor to find just what place it should assume, than to start a useless dispute regarding the value of plays of this kind. It appears that there are four kinds of plays in which there is some sort of moral intent.

The first sort of play is that which contains maxims and moral instructions, scattered throughout. These should be sparingly used and only on the rarest occasions inserted in general discourses, and then in small doses, especially when they are put into the mouth of an impassioned character, or into the mouth of another with whom he is speaking, for, under the circumstances, he would not have the patience to listen or peace of mind to conceive and speak them. Instinct counsels, for instance, where a man of importance who is trained and sure of himself, is being consulted by a king, and then speeches of this sort may be found more frequently and be of greater extent, but it is always well to reduce them from the general to the specific. I vastly prefer having my character say, "Love gives you great cause for uneasiness," than "Love gives those who are in its power great cause for uneasiness." Be it understood, I do not wish to do away entirely with this latter method of pronouncing moral and political maxims. Every one of my poems would present a sorry appearance if I eliminated that which I mixed into it; but again one must not accentuate them too much without applying the general to the particular, otherwise it is an ordinary situation which never fails to tire the listener, because it slackens the action. However well this exhibition of morality succeeds, we must always suspect it of being one of the vain ornaments which Horace orders us to curtail.

The second use of dramatic poetry is in the simple description of the vices and virtues, which never misses its effect if well conceived, and if the marks of it are so clear that one cannot confuse the two nor take vice for virtue.

The one, though unhappy, is loved, and the other is hated, though triumphant. The ancients were often satisfied with this description without troubling to have good actions rewarded and bad ones punished. Clytemnestra and her lover kill Agamemnon with impunity. Medea does the same with her own children and Atreus with those of her brother, Thyestes, which are served to him to eat.

It is true that, on carefully considering these actions which they chose for the climax of their tragedies, they who were punished were criminals in crimes greater than their own. Thyestes had abused the wife of his brother, but the vengeance which he exacts has something more horrible in it than the first crime. Jason was a traitor to abandon Medea, to whom he owed all; but for her to kill his children under his eyes is too strong a punishment. Clytemnestra complained of the concubines which Agamemnon brought from Troy, but he had not attempted to take her life as she attempts to take his; and these masters of art have found the crime of his son, Orestes, who kills her to avenge his father, still greater than the first, since they gave him avenging Furies to torment him and gave none to his mother who peaceably enjoys with her Ægisthus the kingdom of the husband whom she assassinated.

Our theater rarely allows such subjects. The *Thyestes* of Seneca did not have great success. *Medea* was more popular at the same time. To understand it rightly, the perfidy of Jason and the violence of the king of Corinth, makes her appear so unjustly oppressed that the listener takes her side very easily and considers her vengeance as a just act which she commits herself against those who oppress her. It is this interest which one has in the virtuous which forces one to come to this other manner of ending the dramatic poem, by the punishment of wicked actions and the reward of good ones which is not an art precept but a custom which we have adopted, which one can abandon only at one's own risk. It has existed since the time of Aristotle, and it may be that it did not please this philosopher to excess, since he says,—" It has had a vogue only by the imbecility of the judgment of the spectators, and those who practice it are gratifying the tastes of the populace and write according to the desires of their audience. Truly it is certain that we could not see an honest man in our theater without wishing him prosperity and regretting his misfortune. That is why when he (the honest man) remains overcome by them, we leave with sorrow and carry away a kind of indignation against the author and the actor, but when the plot fills our expectations and virtue is rewarded, we leave with complete joy, and carry with us entire satisfaction, both of the work and those who represent it. The success of virtue against misfortunes and perils excites us to embrace it, and the fatal success of crime or injustice is capable of enlarging the natural of it, through the fear of like misfortune." It is in this that the third use of the theater consists, just as the fourth consists in the purgation of the passions through the means of pity and fear. But since this use is peculiar to tragedy I shall explain myself on that subject in the second volume, where I shall treat of tragedy in particular, and proceed now to the examination of the parts which Aristotle attributes to the dramatic poem.

I say the dramatic poem in general, as in treating this material, he speaks only of tragedy, since all that he says of it is applicable to comedy also, and that the difference in these two kinds of poetry consists only in the dignity of the characters and in the actions which they imitate and not in the manner of the imitation nor in the things which serve in this imitation. The poem is composed of two kinds of parts.

The first are called parts of quantity or

extension, and Aristotle names four of them,— the prologue, the episode, the exodus and the chorus. The others can be called integral parts; they meet each other in each of these first to form the whole. This philosopher finds six of them,— the subject, the manners, the sentiments, the diction, the music and the stage decoration. Of these six only the technique of the subjects depends rightly on the art of poetry. The others need subsidiary arts. The manners on moral, the sentiments on rhetoric, the diction on grammar, and the two other parts have each their art of which the poet need not be instructed because he can have it supplied by others. That is why Aristotle does not treat of them. But since it is necessary that he execute everything concerning the first four himself, the knowledge of the arts on which they depend is absolutely necessary unless he has received from nature sufficiently strong and deep judgment to supply that lack. The requirements of the subject are different for tragedy and comedy. I shall speak only on that which concerns the latter, which Aristotle defines simply an imitation of low and knavish persons. I cannot refrain from saying that this definition does not satisfy me, and since many scholars hold that his treatise on Poetry has not come to us in its entirety I want to believe that in that which time has stolen of it there was a more complete one. Dramatic Poetry, according to him, is an imitation of actions, and he stops here at the condition of the person, without saying what must be the actions. However, this definition is in agreement with the custom of his time when only people of very mediocre condition were made to speak in comedy. But it (the definition) is not entirely just for our time, in which even kings may come into comedy when their actions are not above it. When one puts on the scene a simple love intrigue between kings, and when they run no risk either of their life or of their State, I do not think that even though the characters are illustrious the action is sufficiently important to aspire to the dignity of tragedy. The dignity of tragedy needs some great State interest or passion nobler and more virile than love, such as ambition or vengeance,

which leads us to expect greater misfortune than the loss of a mistress. It is fit to mix love in it because it always has much attraction and can serve as a basis to those other interests and other passions of which I speak. But it must content itself with second rank in the poem and leave the first to the other.

This maxim will at first seem new. It is, however, a practice of the ancients, with whom we see no tragedy in which there is only a love-interest to unravel. Quite the contrary: they often banished it completely from their poems, and those who wish to consider mine will acknowledge that, following their example, I have never let it take the first place, and that in *Le Cid*, which is without doubt the play most full of love which I have made, the duty of birth and the care of honor assume a more important place than the two lovers inspire.

I shall go further, even though there are big State interests, and a royal character stills his passion through the care he must have of his glory, as in *Don Sanche*, if one does not meet the risk of death, loss of States, or banishments, I do not think that it has a right to a higher name than comedy, but to answer at all to the dignity of which it (comedy) represents the actions, I have thought to call it heroic to distinguish it from ordinary comedies. This is without example amongst the ancients, but is it also without example amongst them that put kings on the stage without one of those great hazards. We must not bind ourselves slavishly to the imitation of them so that we dare not try something of our own when this does not go contrary to the rules of art, were it only to deserve that praise Horace gave the poets of his time: *Nec minimum meruere decus,* etc., and not to come under the shameful judgment: *O imitatores, servum pecus!* "What will serve now as an example," says Tacitus, "has been once without example, and what we do without example may serve as such one day."

Comedy, then, differs from tragedy in that the latter requires an illustrious, extraordinary, serious subject, while the former stops at a common, playful subject. The latter demands great dangers for its hero; the former contents itself with the worry and displeasures of those to whom it gives the first rank amongst the actors. Both have this in common, that the action must be complete and finished, that is, in the event which finishes it the spectator must be so clearly informed of the feelings of all who have had a part in it that he leaves with his mind quiet and doubting of nothing. Cinna conspires against Augustus. His conspiracy is discovered. Augustus has him arrested. If the poem stopped there the action would be incomplete, because the listener would leave in the uncertainty of what this Emperor would have commanded of the ungrateful favorite. Ptolemy fears that Cæsar, who comes to Egypt, will favor his sister, with whom he is in love, and forces him to give her her part of the kingdom which her father left her in his will. To attract favor on his side by great sacrifice, he slays Pompey. This is not enough. We must see how Cæsar receives this great sacrifice. He arrives, becomes angry and threatens Ptolemy, and wants to force him to slay the inciters of this attack and illustrious death. The latter, surprised at the unexpected welcome, resolves to anticipate Cæsar, and conspires against him to avoid, by his loss, the misfortune with which he sees himself threatened. That is still not enough. We must know what will result from this conspiracy. Cæsar is warned and Ptolemy, dying in a combat with his ministers, leaves Cleopatra in peaceful possession of the kingdom of which she demanded half. Cæsar is out of danger. The listener has nothing more to ask, and leaves satisfied because the action is complete. For comedy, Aristotle demands as the only precept that it may have as ending, the enemies becoming friends. Which must be understood in a more general sense than what the words seem to carry and to extend it to a reconciliation, as when one sees his son returning into the good favor of a father who has been angry with him for his debauchery, which was the usual end to ancient comedies; or two lovers separated by some trick done them, or by some controlling power, are reunited by the unraveling of that trick or by the consent of those who placed the obstacle there, as nearly always happens in our comedy, which very rarely has other endings than marriages. We must be careful, however, that this agreement does not come by a simple change of will but by an event which furnishes the occasion for it. Otherwise there would be no great art to the "dénouement" of a play, if, after having upheld it during two acts, on the authority of a father who does not approve the love of his son or daughter, he should suddenly consent to it in the fifth for the sole reason that it is the fifth and that the author would not dare to make six. It needs a considerable motive which forces him to it as say, his daughter's lover saved his life in some meeting or when, on the point of being assassinated by his enemies or that by some un-hoped for incident he should be recognized as being of high rank and greater fortune than he appeared.

Since it is necessary that the action be complete, one must also not add anything further, since when the effect has been attained, the listener desires nothing more and is bored by all the rest. So it is that the expressions of joy which two lovers show on being reunited after many obstacles, must be very short. I know not what beauty the arguments between Menelaus and Teucer on the burial of Ajax, whom Sophocles has pass away in the fourth act, could have had for the Athenians, but I do know that in our time the quarrel between Ajax and Ulysses for the weapons of Achilles after the latter's death wearied many ears, although it (the subject) came from a good hand. I have not been able to see how one can bear the fifth act of *Mélite* and of *La Veuve*. One only sees the first actors reunited and they have no place there but to be made acquainted with the authors of the treachery and the violence which has separated them. Nevertheless, they could have been informed of them already, had I wished it, and they seemed to be on the stage only to serve as witnesses to those of secondary importance, which makes all this end slackened in which they have no part. I dare not attribute the success of these two comedies to ignorance of the rules — which was very general at that time — inasmuch as those rules, well or poorly observed, must make their good or bad effect on those who, even without knowing them, abandon themselves to the current of natural feeling. But I can only acknowledge that that old habit which was observed at the time, of not seeing anything better ordered, was the cause of the lack of indignation against these defects and the newness of an agreeable kind of comedy which up to that time had not appeared on the scene, has caused the admiration, all the parts of the whole pleasing at sight even though it did not have all the just proportions.

Comedy and tragedy resemble each other again in that their subjects "must have the requisite size, that is, that it must not be so little that it escapes from sight at an atom, nor so vast that it confuses the memory of the listener and bewilders his imagination." In such manner does Aristotle explain the conditions of a poem, and he adds that "to be of the proper size it must have a beginning, a middle, and an end." These terms are so general that they seem to signify nothing, but, to understand them well, they exclude the momentary actions which have not these three parts. A poem must have, then, to be of the right size, a beginning, a middle and an end. Cinna conspires against Augustus and tells of his conspiracy to Emilia. This is the beginning. Maximus warns Augustus of it. This is the middle. Augustus forgives him. This is the end. Therefore, in the comedies of this first volume I have nearly always had two lovers on good terms, then I had them quarrel as a result of some treachery. I reunited them by the unraveling of this treachery which had separated them. . . . Enough on the subject of comedy and the requirements necessary to it. Truth to nature is one of which I shall speak later. Besides, the developments of it must always be happy — which is not a requirement of tragedy, where we have the choice of making a change from happiness to unhappiness, and *vice versa*. This needs no remark. I come to the second part of the poem, which is *Manners*. Aristotle prescribes four conditions: that they be good, suitable, similar, and equal. These are terms which he says so little about that he leaves great occasion to doubt his meaning.

I cannot imagine how one can conceive "good" to mean "virtuous." Most poems, ancient as well as modern, would remain in a pitiful state if one cut out all in the way of bad or vicious character, or characters stained by some weakness which does not comport with virtue. Horace took great care generally to describe the "manners" of every age, and attributes to them more faults than virtues, and when he advises us to describe Medea as proud and indomitable, Ixion as treacherous, Achilles carried away by anger to the point of holding that laws are not made for him and declaring that he takes right by might, Horace allows us very few virtues. One must therefore find a goodness compatible with this kind of manners; and if I may express my conjectures on what Aristotle requires by that, I believe it is the brilliant and elevated character of a criminal or virtuous habit. Just as much as is proper and suitable to the person that one presents. Cleopatra in *Rodogune* is very wicked. There is no parasite which repels her so long as she can be kept on her throne, which she prefers to everything, so great is her attachment to power; but all her crimes are accompanied by a loftiness of soul which has something so high in it that, while one despises her actions, one admires the source from which they spring. I dare say the same of *Le Menteur*. Lying is doubtless a vicious habit, but the chief character in this play utters his lies with such presence of mind and quickness that this imperfection acquires grace and makes the listeners acknowledge that to lie in such a manner is a vice of which imbeciles are incapable. As a third example, those who wish to consider the way in which Horace describes the anger of Achilles will not be far from my idea. It has for foundation a passage of Aristotle's which follows closely enough the one I am trying to explain. "Poetry," says he, "is an imitation of people better than in actual life, and, as painters often make flattering portraits which are more beautiful than the original and still keep the resemblance, in such a manner the poets representing choleric or slovenly men must idealize these qualities which they give them, so that from them a beautiful example of equity and stoicism can be drawn. It is thus that Homer made Achilles good." These last words should be noticed to show that Homer gave to Achilles' transports of anger that goodness necessary to manners which I think consists in that loftiness of character, of which Robortello speaks in the following manner,—" *Unum quodque genus per se supremos quosdam habet decoris gradus, et absolutissimam recipit formam, non tamen degenerans a sua natura, et effigie pristina.*" This text of Aristotle's which I mentioned may present some difficulty in that it says that the manners of choleric or slovenly men must be depicted with such a degree of excellence that one sees in them a high example of equity and austerity. There is a likeness between austerity and anger, and that is what Horace attributes to Achilles in this verse: *Iracundus inexorabilis acer.* But there is no likeness between equity and slovenliness. I cannot see what it has to do in his character. It is that which causes me to doubt if the Greek word ῥαθυμά has been given the meaning of Aristotle's by the Latin interpreter which I have followed. Pacius says, *Desides;* Victorius, *Inertes;* Heinsius, *Segnes;* and the word *Fainéants* of which I have made use to put it into our language, answers these three versions well enough, but Castelvetro expresses it in his by *mansueti,* or *debonnair,* or *full of mildness;* and not only does this word mean the opposite of anger, but also it would agree better with what Aristotle calls ἐπιείκεια, of which he requires a good example from us. These three interpreters translate the Greek word by that of *equity* or *integrity,* which would agree better with the *soave [mild]* of the Italian, than with their *segnes, desides, inertes,* provided one understands by that only a natural kindness which slowly angers, but I would still prefer that of *good humor,* of which the other makes use to express it in his language, and I think that to keep its value in our language one could change it to *compliance,* or *equitable facility —* to approve, to excuse and to support everything that happens. It is not that I wish to be judged among such great men, but I cannot deny the Italian version of this passage seems to me to have something more correct than any of the three Latin versions. Among this diversity of interpretations everyone is free to choose, since one has the right even to put them all aside, when a new one appears. Another idea comes to me concerning what Aristotle means by this goodness that he imposes on them as a first condition. That is, that they must be as virtuous as possible, so that we do not exhibit the vicious and criminal on the stage if the subject which we are treating does not require them. He himself expresses this thought when wishing to mark an example of mistake against this rule, he uses that of Menelaus in Euripedes' *Orestes,* whose fault is not in being unjust but in being unjust without necessity.

. . . . . .

In the second place, morals must be suitable. This requirement is easier to understand than the first. The poet must consider the age, dignity, birth, occupation and country of those whom he paints; he must know what one owes to one's country, to one's parents, to one's friends, to one's king; what the office of a magistrate or an army general, so that he may verify and then show what he wants his public to love, and eliminate those whom he wants it to hate, because it is an infallible maxim that to achieve success one must get the audience on the side of the important characters. It is well to remark also that what Horace says of the morals of each age is not a rule that one can dispose of without scruple. He makes young men prodigal and old men avaricious. The contrary often happens each day without causing surprise, but one must not act like the other even though he sometimes has passions and habits which would be more suitable to him. It is only natural for a young man to be in love; not so, an old man. This does not prevent an old man from falling in love. We have enough proof before us, but he would be considered insane if he wanted to court like a youth, and if he tried to win by his personal charm. He may hope that he will be listened to, but this hope must be founded on his wealth or his qualities, but not on his person, and his pretentions cannot be reasonable if he does not think to have to do with the soul interested sufficiently to put aside everything for the attraction of riches or the ambition of rank. The quality of "equalness" which Aristotle asks of morals refers particularly to the people which history or fable teach us to know and which we must always depict such as we find them. That is what Horace means by this verse, *Sit Medea,* etc. He who should depict Ulysses as a great warrior or Achilles as a great orator or Medea as a mild and humble woman would commit himself to public ridicule. Therefore, these two qualities between which some interpreters have great pains in finding the difference, but which Aristotle finds without pointing it out, will agree easily as long as one separates them and uses the word "seemly" to designate persons who have never existed except in the soul of the poet, reserving the other who are known through history or through fable as I have just said. There remains to speak of equality, which forces us to keep in our character the manners which we gave them in the beginning: *Servetur,* etc. Inequality can enter into it all the same, not only when we bring persons of a light and uncertain spirit, but also when in keeping the equality inside, we show inequality on the exterior, according to the occasion. Such is Chimène in the matter of her love. She still strongly loves Rodrigue in her heart, but this love acts differently in the presence of the King and differently in the presence of Rodrigue, and that is what Aristotle calls "manners," unequally equal. One difficulty presents itself which must be cleared up as to what Aristotle means when he says, "that tragedy can be made without morals and that most of those of the moderns of his time have none." The meaning of this passage is quite difficult to understand, seeing that, according to him, it is by morals that a man is a wicked man or a good man, witty or stupid, timid or bold, constant or irresolute, good or bad politically, and that it is impossible to put any on the stage who is not good or wicked and that he have not any of those other qualities. To make these two sentiments agree which seem so opposed to each other, I notice that this philosopher goes on to say that "if a poet has done some

fine moral narrations and very sententious discourses, he has not by that done anything yet which concerns tragedy." This has made me consider that "manners" are not only the foundation of action, but also of reasoning. A man of condition thinks and acts as such; a wicked man acts and thinks as such, and both the one and the other depict divers moral maxims according to his habit. It is, therefore, these maxims of conduct that tragedy can do without, not the conduct itself, since it is the essence of action, and that action is the soul of tragedy, where one must speak only in and for the action of the tragedy. Therefore, to explain this passage of Aristotle's by the other, we can say that when he speaks of a tragedy without "manners" he means a tragedy in which the actors simply announce their feelings or base them only on reasonings drawn from fact as Cleopatra in the second act of *Rodogune,* and not on maxims of morality or politics, as Rodogune in the first act. I must repeat again: to create a theatrical poem in which none of the actors are either good or bad, prudent or imprudent, is entirely impossible. After "manners" come sentiments, by which the actor makes known what he wishes or does not wish, and in which he can content himself with a simple acknowledgment of what he proposes to do, without strengthening it with moral reasoning, as I have just said. This part requires rhetoric to depict the passions and troubles of the soul, to consult, deliberate, exaggerate or extenuate; but there is this difference, between the dramatic poet and the orator, that the latter can exhibit his art and make it extraordinary with full freedom, and the other must hide with care, because it is never he who speaks, and those whom he has speak are not orators. To complete this *Discourse* I need only speak of the parts, of quantity, which are,— the prologue, the episode, the exodus and the chorus. The prologue is that which is recited before the first song of the chorus. The episode is that which is recited between the songs of the chorus and the exodus, that which is recited after the last song of the chorus. That is all Aristotle tells us of it; he gives us an idea of the posi-

PIERRE CORNEILLE

tion of the parts and their order, in representation, rather than the part of the action which they contain. Therefore, to apply them to our use, the prologue is our first act, the episode constitutes the three following, and the exodus the last. I reduce this prologue to our first act following the intention of Aristotle and to supplement in part what he has not told us or what the years have robbed from his books. I say that it must contain the seed of all that is going to happen, as much for the principal action as for the episode, so that no actors come into the following act who are not known by this first, or at least named by someone who shall have been brought into it. This maxim is new and rather strict; I have not always kept it, but I judge that it helps a great deal to create a veritable unity of action by the binding of all those which come in the poem. The ancients often have left it particularly in the *Agnitions,* for which they nearly always use people who appeared by chance in the fifth act, and would have appeared in the tenth if the piece had had ten acts. Such is that old man of Corinth in the *Œdipus* of Sophocles and Seneca where he seems to fall from a cloud by a miracle, at a time when the actors would not know what to do next nor what pose to take if he came an hour later. I have brought him in only in the fifth, just as they did, but I have prepared his coming from the first in making Œdipus say that he expects him. In like manner in *La Veuve,* though Célidan does not appear until the third act, he is brought in by Alcidon, who is of the first. It is not the same with the Moors in *Le Cid,* for which there is no preparation whatsoever in the first act. The litigant of Poitiers in *Le Menteur* had the same fault, but I found the means of correcting it in this edition where the dénouement is prepared by Philiste and not by the litigant. I desire, then, that the first act contain the basis of all the acts and shut the door to all other extraneous matter. Though this first act often does not give all the necessary information for the entire understanding of the subject and all the actors do not appear in it it is sufficient if they are spoken of, which they must be in this act. That which I say must only be understood of the characters who act in the piece through some important personal interest or carry important news to produce a notable effect. A servant who acts only by his master's order, a father who shows himself only to consent to or prevent a marriage of his children, a wife who consoles or advises her husband; in a word, all those people without action do not have to be introduced in the first act. This first act was called the prologue in Aristotle's time and ordinarily one made it the opening of the subject, to instruct the listener in all that happened before the beginning of the action, and in all that he would have to know in order to understand what he was going to see. The method of giving this instruction has changed with the times. Euripides used it quite boldly in bringing in now a god in a machine through whom the listeners received this knowledge, now one of the principal characters who instructed them himself, as in *Iphigenia* and *Helena,* where his two heroines first tell all their history to the listener without having any actor to whom to address her speech. I do not mean to say that when an actor speaks he cannot inform the listener about many things, but he must do so through the passion which moves him, and not through a simple narration. The monologue of Emilia which opens the play of *Cinna* acquaints the public with the fact that Augustus killed her father, and that to avenge his death she forces her lover to plot against him; but it is by the unrest and fear which the danger to which he exposes Cinna arouses in her mind that we have the knowledge of it. The poet especially must remember that when an actor is alone in the theater it is taken for granted that he is thinking to himself, and speaks but to let the listener know what he thinks. Therefore it would be an unforgivable error if another actor should by this means learn his secret. One excuses that in a passion which is so violent that it is forced to burst out. even though one has no one to listen to; I should not want to condemn it in another, but I would have difficulty in bearing it myself. Our century has also invented a sort of prologue for plays of the *Deus ex Machinâ* type, but they do not bear upon the subject and are only a clever eulogy of the prince before whom these plays are to be enacted. In *Andromède*, Melpomene borrows rays from the sun in order to light up her theater for the king for whom she has prepared a magnificent pageant. The prologue of *La Toison d'or* referring to His Majesty's wedding and the peace with Spain has something still more brilliant. These prologues must be full of invention and I believe to do them justice only imaginary gods of antiquity may play a part in them. These, however, also talk about matters relating to our time in poetic fiction, which is a great help to our theater. The episodes according to Aristotle at this point are three middle acts, but as he applies this name elsewhere to actions which have nothing to do with the principal one and which are ornaments of no value whatsoever, I shall say that, although these three acts are called episodes, it does not mean that they are only made up of episodes. Augustus' consultation in the second act of *Cinna,* the remorse of this ungrateful one, that which he tells Emilia, Maximus' effort to persuade the object of his hidden love to flee with him, are only episodes, but Maximus' advice to the emperor through Euphorbus, the prince's uncertainties and Livia's advice belong to the principal action, and in *Héraclius* those three acts have more principal action than episode. These episodes are of two kinds and can be made up of the principal actors' special acts. These acts, however, are not needed in the principal action, or else they are made up of the secondary lovers' interests. These people are commonly called episodic characters. Both of these must start in the first act and be part of the principal action, that is, be of some use, and especially the episodic characters

must be so closely intermingled with the principal ones that but one intrigue embroils them all. Aristotle condemns detached episodes and says, "that poor poets write them through ignorance and good ones in favor of the actors to furnish them with work." The Infante of *Le Cid* belongs to this number and she can be condemned or exonerated by Aristotle's words according to the rank that I shall be given among our moderns. I shall not mention the exodus, which is nothing more than our fifth act. I think I have explained the principal use of it when I say that the action of the Dramatic Poem must be complete. I shall only add this word, that one must if one can, reserve all the climax and even defer it until the end. The more one defers it the more the mind will remain in expectancy and the desire to know to which side it will turn, creates the impatience which causes it to be received with more pleasure. This does not happen when it begins with this act. The listeners who know too much have no more curiosity, and their attention wanes during all the rest, which tells nothing new. The opposite is seen in *Mariamne* whose death, though coming in the interval which separates the fourth act from the fifth, has not prevented the displeasure of Herod which occupies all the latter to please extraordinarily, but I would not advise every one to depend on this example. Miracles do not occur every day, and though the author has well deserved the great success on account of the great mental effort he made to depict the despair of the monarch, perhaps the excellency of the author which upheld this character contributed much to this. That is what came to me in thinking of the uses and elements of the Dramatic Poem.

JEAN-BAPTISTE POQUELIN MOLIÈRE

Jean-Baptiste Poquelin, known as Molière, was born in Paris in 1622. He came of a good middle-class family, his father being an upholsterer, and one of

the king's *valets de chambre tapissiers.* About 1636 the boy was sent to the best "college" of the time, the Collège de Clermont, where his first instruction was received from the Jesuits. After a four years' course he went to Orléans to study law, and there he may have received a degree. His movements are little known, though it is fairly certain that for a while he worked in his father's shop in Paris, while there is evidence of his having definitely given up in 1643 what intention he may have had of pursuing his father's calling. In that year he joined ten actors and actresses and helped to found a company called *L'Illustre Théâtre*. Not long after, he took the stage name of Molière. The strolling players were not very successful in their attempts to win the public, and after three years, what was left of the original troupe decided to leave Paris and tour the provinces. The twelve years which the young actor spent in this way were full of valuable experiences. When he returned to Paris he was the head of a company of highly trained actors, an artist himself, and a good man of business. The first of his plays, with the exception of a few purely imitative attempts, was *L'Etourdi*, which was produced at Lyon in 1653. The second play, *Le Dépit amoureux*, was produced at Béziers in 1656. Two years later, after having secured the protection of the Duc d'Anjou, Molière brought his troupe to Paris and presented Corneille's *Nicomède* before the King and Queen in the Louvre. A little interlude of Molière's, now lost, followed the tragedy; this so pleased the King that he allowed the company to remain in Paris and play on alternate nights in the Théâtre du Petit-Bourbon. From this time on, Molière was firmly established in the favor of the King and the Court, and put forth his dramatic masterpieces in quick succession. In the year 1673, during a production of *Le Malade imaginaire*, in which he was himself playing, he was stricken and taken home, where he died soon after.

Compared with his work as a practicing playwright, Molière's critical contributions are not of prime importance. In his neglect of the Rules, and in his principle that to please is the best criterion of success, he seems distinctly modern. He has no creed but this, and in the few places (in his plays and prefaces) where he states it, he never tries to impose his theories, or want of them, upon others. His practice came first, and the theory after.

On the drama:

Préface to *Les Précieuses ridicules* (1660).
Avertissement to *Les Fâcheux* (1662).
Préface to *L'Ecole des femmes* (1663).
La Critique de l'Ecole des femmes (1663).
L'Impromptu de Versailles (produced 1663, printed 1682).
Préface (1st ed., 1669) and *Placets au Roi* (2nd ed., 1669), in *Tartufe*.
Au Lecteur in *L'Amour médecin* (1676).

Editions:

The first complete edition of the works of Molière is *Les Œuvres de Monsieur de Molière*, 8 vols. (Paris, 1682). Among the numerous modern editions, see that edited by Despois and Mesnard in the *Grands Ecrivains* series: *Œuvres de Molière*, 13 vols. (Paris, 1873–1900). See also, Henri Van Laun's *The Dramatic Works of J. B. Poquelin Molière*, 6 vols. (Edinburgh, 1878), and Katharine Prescott Wormeley's translation of seventeen plays: *Molière*, 6 vols. (Boston, 1894).

On Molière and his works:

Charles Varlet de La Grange, *Régistre* (1658–1685).
J.-L. Le G. Grimarest, *La Vie de M. de Molière* (Paris, 1705).
Louis Riccoboni, *Observations sur la Comédie et sur le génie de Molière* (Paris, 1736).
J.-F. Cailhava, *Etudes sur Molière*, etc. (Paris, 1802).
C.-A. Sainte-Beuve, *Port-Royal*, 6 vols. (6th ed., Paris, 1901).
——, *Causeries du Lundi*, 13 vols. (Paris, 1851–57).
Jules Claretie, *Molière, sa vie et ses œuvres* (Paris, 1873).
Edouard Fournier, *Etudes sur la vie et les œuvres de Molière* (Paris, 1885).
Gustave Larroumet, *La Comédie de Molière* (Paris, 1886).
Jules Loiseleur, *Les Points obscurs dans la vie de Molière* (Paris, 1877).

A. P. Malassis, *Molière jugé pas ses con-temporains* (Paris, 1877).

E. Martineche, *Molière et le Théâtre espagnol* (Paris, 1905).

Paul Mesnard, *Notice biographique sur Molière* (in vol. X of the *Grands Ecri-cains* series, Paris, 1889).

Louis Moland, *Vie de J.-B. P. Molière* (Paris, 1892).

——, *Molière et la comédie italienne* (Paris, 2nd ed., 1867).

Jules-Antoine Taschereau, *Histoire de la vie et des ouvrages de Molière* (Paris, 1825).

Henri Davignon, *Molière et la vie* (Paris, 1904).

Brander Matthews, *Molière, his Life and his Works* (New York, 1910).

H. C. Chatfield-Taylor, *Molière, a Biog-raphy* (New York, 1906).

Leon H. Vincent, *Molière* (Boston, 1902).

Eud. Soulié, *Recherches sur Molière et sur sa famille* (Paris, 1863).

Henry M. Trollope, *The Life of Molière* (New York, 1905).

Emile Faguet, *En Lisant Molière* (Paris, 1914).

Sir F. T. Marzials, *Molière* (London, 1906).

Special bibliographies and reprints of documents may be found in Lacroix's *Collection Molièresque* (Paris, 1867-75); Lacroix and Monval's *Nouvelle Collection Molièresque* (Paris, 1879-90); Monval's *Le Molièriste,* 10 vols. (Paris, 1879-89); Lacroix's *Bibliog-raphie Molièresque* (Paris, 1875); Ar-thur Desfeuilles' *Notice bibliographique* in vol. 9 in the Mesnard-Despois *Mo-lière;* the *Catalogue of the Molière Collection* in Harvard College Library; and the Bibliography in Chatfield-Taylor's *Molière.*

SCHOOL FOR WIVES CRITICIZED[1]
[*La Critique de l'Ecole des femmes*]
(1663)

(Scene vi.)

Dorante.— You are, then, Marquis, one of those grand gentlemen who will not allow the pit to have common sense, and who would be vexed to join in their laugh, though it were at the best thing conceivable? . . . Speaking generally, I would place considerable reliance on the applause of the pit, because, amongst those who go there, many are capable of judging the piece according to rule, whilst others judge it as they ought, al-lowing themselves to be guided by cir-cumstances, having neither a blind prej-udice, nor an affected complaisance, nor a ridiculous refinement. . . .

(Scene vii.)

Uranie.— . . . Let us not apply to ourselves the points of general censure; let us profit by the lesson, if possible, without assuming that we are spoken

[1] Re-printed extracts from Henri Van Laun's *Dramatic Works of J. B. Poquelin Molière,* 6 vols. (Edinburgh, 1878).— Ed.

against. All the ridiculous delineations which are drawn on the stage should be looked on by every one without annoy-ance. They are public mirrors, in which we must never pretend to see ourselves. To bruit it about that we are offended at being hit, is to state openly that we are at fault. . . .

Dorante.— . . . Indeed, I think that it is much easier to soar with grand sen-timents, to brave fortune in verse, to arraign destiny and reproach the Gods, than to broach ridicule in a fit manner, and to make the faults of all mankind seem pleasant on the stage. When you paint heroes you can do as you like. These are fancy portraits, in which we do not look for a resemblance; you have only to follow your soaring imagination, which often neglects the true in order to attain the marvelous. But when you paint men, you must paint after nature. We expect resemblance in these por-traits; you have done nothing, if you do not make us recognize the people of your day. In a word, in serious pieces, it suffices to escape blame, to speak good sense, and to write well. But this is not enough in comedy. You must be merry; and it is a difficult undertaking to make gentlefolk laugh. . . .

Lysidas.— Those who are versed in Horace and Aristotle, Madame, see at once that this comedy sins against all the rules of Art.

Uranie.— I confess that I am not familiar with those gentlemen, and that I do not know the rules of Art.

Dorante.— You are a most amusing set with your rules of Art, with which you embarrass the ignorant, and deafen us perpetually. To hear you talk, one would suppose that those rules of Art were the greatest mysteries in the world; and yet they are but a few simple observations which good sense has made upon that which may impair the pleasure taken in that kind of poems; and the same good sense which in former days made these observations, makes them every day easily, without resorting to Horace and Aristotle. I should like to know whether the great rule of all rules is not to please; and whether a play which attains this has not followed a good method? Can the whole public be mistaken in these matters, and cannot every one judge what pleases him? . . . in short, if pieces according to rule do not please, and those do please which are not according to rule, then the rules must, if necessary, have been badly made. So let us laugh at the sophistry with which they would trammel public taste, and let us judge a comedy only by the effect which it produces upon ourselves. Let us give ourselves up honestly to whatever stirs us deeply, and never hunt for arguments to mar our pleasure.

Uranie.— For my part, when I see a play, I look only whether the points strike me; and when I am well entertained, I do not ask whether I have been wrong, or whether the rules of Aristotle would forbid me to laugh.

Dorante.— It is just as if a man were to taste a capital sauce, and wished to know whether it were good according to the recipe in a cookery-book.

Uranie.— Very true; and I wonder at the critical refinements of certain people about things in which we should think for ourselves.

Dorante.— You are right, Madame, in thinking all these mysterious critical refinements very odd. For really, if they are to subsist, we are reduced to discrediting ourselves. Our very senses must be slaves in everything; and, even in eating and drinking, we must no longer dare find anything good, without permission from the committee of taste.

Lysidas.— So, Monsieur, your only reason is that *The School for Wives* [*L'Ecole des femmes*] has pleased you; you care not whether it be according to rule, provided—

Dorante.— Gently, Monsieur Lysidas; I do not grant you that. I certainly say that the great art is to please; and that, as this comedy has pleased those for whom it was written, I think that is enough, and that we need not care about anything else. But at the same time, I maintain that it does not sin against any of the rules to which you allude. I have read them, thank Heaven! as well as other men, and I could easily prove that perhaps we have not on the stage a more regular play than this. . . .

Lysidas.— What, sir! when the protasis, the epitasis, the peripetia—

Dorante.— Nay, Monsieur Lysidas, you overwhelm us with your fine words. Pray, do not seem so learned. Humanize your discourse a little, and speak intelligibly. Do you fancy a Greek word gives more weight to your arguments? And do you not think that it would look as well to say, "the exposition of the subject," as the "protasis"; "the progress of the plot," as the "epitasis"; "the crowning incident," as the "peripetia"?

Lysidas.— These are terms of art that we are allowed to make use of. But as these words offend your ears, I shall explain myself in another way; and I ask you to give me a plain answer to three or four things which I have to say. Can a piece be endured which sins against the very description of a play? For, after all, the name of a dramatic poem comes from a Greek word which signifies to act, in order to show that the nature of the form consists in action. But, in this comedy, there are no actions. . . .

PREFACE TO TARTUFE [2]
[*Préface* (to) *Tartufe*]
(1669)

... I am well aware that, in reply, those gentlemen have endeavored to insinuate that the stage is not fit for the discussion of these subjects; but, by their leave, I ask them upon what they base this beautiful axiom. It is a theory which they only advance, and which they do not prove by any means; and it would doubtless not be difficult to show them that with the ancients, comedy derived its origin from religion, and was a part of their mysteries; that the Spaniards, our neighbors, never celebrate a feast in which a comedy is not mixed up; and that, even amongst us it owes its birth to the cares of a brotherhood to which the Hôtel de Bourgogne still belongs; that it was a place given to them to represent in it the most important mysteries of our faith; that comedies printed in Gothic characters, under the name of a doctor of the Sor-

bonne, may still be seen there; and, without carrying the matter so far, that, in our days, sacred pieces of M. de Corneille have been performed, which were the admiration of the whole of France. If it be the aim of comedy to correct man's vices, then I do not see for what reason there should be a privileged class. Such a one is, in the State, decidedly more dangerous in its consequences than any other, and we have seen that the stage possesses a great virtue as a corrective medium. The most beautiful passages in a serious moral are most frequently less powerful than those of a satire; and nothing admonishes the majority of people better than the portrayal of their faults. To expose vices to the ridicule of all the world is a severe blow to them. Reprehensions are easily suffered, but not so ridicule. People do not mind being wicked; but they object to being made ridiculous. ...

[2] Re-printed extracts from Van Laun's translation (see " On Molière," ante).— Ed.

JEAN RACINE

Jean Racine was born at Ferté-Milon, Le Valois, in 1639, of middle-class parents, both of whom died within three years of his birth. The child was brought up by his grandparents. The grandfather dying when the boy was ten years old, he was left alone with his grandmother, whom he regarded thenceforth as his mother. His preliminary education was received at the College de Beauvais, where he spent the years between 1650 or 1651 and 1655, and then entered the famous school of Port-Royal, where he remained for three years. In all probability he was a good student, and when he left he possessed a wide acquaintance with and love for the Greek and Latin authors, especially the Greek tragedians. On leaving Port-Royal, he went to the College d'Harcourt

to study philosophy and logic. Not finding these to his taste, he left the College and became a sort of secretary to the Duc de Luynes. One of his earliest works, an ode written on the occasion of the marriage of Louis XIV in 1660, was highly praised by the venerable Chapelain. Racine wished to write — he had also written two plays besides the ode — but his friends at Port-Royal feared that his interest in literature would prove an evil influence upon him, and persuaded him to go south and put himself under the care of his uncle, a canon. During the year or more which he spent at Uzes, he applied himself to the study of theology, although his notes on Pindar and Homer prove that his interest in his beloved authors was not dead. In fact, his first play, *La Thé-*

baïde, was written at this period. Even though he did more or less formally enter the Church, his subsequent actions show that he soon ceased active work in connection with it. *La Thébaïde* was accepted by Molière and produced at the *Palais-Royal* in 1664. He left Uzes in 1662 and returned to Paris. Here he made the acquaintance of Boileau, and produced his plays. After the production of *Phèdre* in 1677, for reasons which are somewhat obscure, he abandoned playwriting, and lived on the various pensions and salaries of which he was the recipient, married, and produced no work until he was commissioned by Madame de Maintenon to write a play for the girls of Saint-Cyr. He produced *Esther*, in 1689, and followed it in 1691, by *Athalie*, which was performed at Saint-Cyr and Versailles. He died in 1699.

Racine, like Molière, is important rather as a practicing dramatist than as a critic. His remarks on his own plays are full of interest, however, as they explain how and why he wrote as he did; they are, like Molière's prefaces, the theory after the performance. Racine was from first to last a classical writer; his passion was for clearness and compactness, and it is little wonder that his critical theories are founded on Aristotle and Horace. His very first manifesto, the *Préface to La Thébaïde* (1664), contains a protest against the double plot. The *Première Préface to Alexandre le grand* (1666) is a defense of his "natural" treatment of character; likewise the *Première Préface to Andromaque* (1668). The various prefaces to *Britannicus* (1670), *Bajazet* (1672), *Mithridate* (1673), *Phèdre* (1677), and two or three others, are, taken as a whole, pleas for regularity, order, and reason.

On the drama:

Préface to La Thébaïde (1664).
Première Préface (1666), to *Alexandre le grand*, and *Seconde Préface* (1676).
Première Préface (1668) to *Andromaque; Seconde Préface* (1676).
Au Lecteur to Les Plaideurs (1669).
Première Préface (1670) to *Britannicus,* and *Seconde Préface* (1676).

Préface to Bérénice (1674).
Première Préface (1672) to *Bajazet; Seconde Préface* (1676).
Préface to Mithridate (1673).
Préface to Iphigénie (1675).
Préface to Phèdre (1677).
Préface to Esther (1689).
Préface to Athalie (1691).

The *Lettres* in volumes VI and VII of the Mesnard edition are interesting, but contain little on the drama. The *Fragments de la Poétique d'Aristote* are to be found in vol. V of the same edition.

Editions:

The standard edition of the complete works is the *Œuvres de J. Racine,* edited by Paul Mesnard, in the *Grands Ecrivains* series, 8 vols. (Paris, 1865–73).

On Racine and his works:

Louis Racine, *Mémoires sur la vie de Jean Racine,* 2 vols. (Lausanne and Genève, 1747. Reprinted in vol. I of the Mesnard ed.).
Fontenelle, *Parallèle de Corneille et de Racine* (Paris, 1693).
Stendhal, *Racine et Shakespeare* (Paris, 1823).
C.-A. Sainte-Beuve, *Portraits littéraires,* vol. I (Paris, 1830).
——, *Port-Royal,* vol. 6 (Paris, 1860).
——, *Nouveaux Lundis,* vols. 3 and 10 (Paris, 1862 ff).
F. Deltour, *Les Ennemis de Racine au XVIIe siècle* (Paris, 1859).
H. Taine, *Nouveaux essais de critique et d'histoire* (Paris, 1865).
Ferdinand Brunetière, *Racine* (in *Etudes critiques sur l'histoire de la littérature française,* vol. 1, 7th ed., Paris, 1911).
Paul Mesnard, Introduction to *Grands Ecrivains* ed. of *Œuvres* (cited above. Also Bibliography in vol. 7).
E. Deschanel, *Le Romantisme des classiques. Racine* (Paris, 1883).
P. Stapfer, *Racine et Victor Hugo* (Paris, 1887).
Francisque Sarcey, *Quarante Ans de théâtre,* vol. 2 (Paris, 1900).
Emile Faguet, *Propos de théâtre,* vol. 1 (Paris, 1903).
Jules Lemaître, *Impressions de théâtre,* vols. 1, 2, and 4 (Paris, 1888–90).

Jules Lemaître, *Jean Racine* (Paris, 1908).

P. Robert, *La Poétique de Racine* (Paris, 1890).

P. Monceaux, *Racine* (Paris, 1892).

Gustave Larroumet, *Racine* (4th ed., Paris, 1911).

PREFACE TO LA THÉBAÏDE [1]

[*Préface* (to) *La Thébaïde*]

(1664)

The reader will surely be a little more indulgent toward this play than toward those that follow, because I was very young when I wrote it. Certain verses I had previously written happened to fall into the hands of some people of culture, who urged me to write a tragedy, and proposed the subject of *La Thébaïde.* This subject had already been treated by Rotrou, in his *Antigone;* but he killed off the two brothers at the beginning of the third act. The remainder of the drama was in a way the beginning of another tragedy, introducing entirely new interests. It combined within itself two distinct plots, one of which was the plot of Euripides' *Phœnician Women,* the other that of Sophocles' *Antigone.* I saw that the double plot tended to spoil his [Rotrou's] play, which was, however, full of beautiful things. I constructed my play on practically the same plot as the *Phœnician Women* of Euripides. As to the *Thebaid* which is found among Seneca's works, I am inclined to agree with Heinsius and maintain not only that it was not written by Seneca, but that it is

[1] Translated, for the first time into English by the editor.— Ed.

the work of some rhetorical declaimer who had no idea what a tragedy was.

The catastrophe of my play is possibly a little too sanguinary; indeed, there is scarcely a character who is not killed off at the end. But then, this is the story of the Thebaid, the most tragic of antiquity.

Love which, ordinarily, assumed so important a rôle in tragedy, I have practically neglected; I doubt whether I should give it a more important place were I to re-write the play. It would be necessary to have one of the brothers in love, or else both; but what chance had I to give them any other interest but that famous hatred, which consumed them both? If I could not have either of the brothers in love, there remained for me only to place the love-interest in characters of secondary importance; and this is what I have done. But even then, the passion of love seems strangely out of place and ineffective. In short, I am of the opinion that lovers' tenderness and jealousies can have no legitimate place amid all the incest, parricide, and other horrors which go to make up the story of Œdipus and his fated family.

FIRST PREFACE TO ANDROMAQUE [2]

[*Première Préface* (to) *Andromaque*]

(1668)

... However that may be, the public has treated me so well that I am not bothered by the disappointment of two or three individuals who would have us re-cast all the heroes of antiquity and make them paragons of perfection. I think their intention of putting only such impeccable examples of humanity on the stage admirable, but I beg them to re-

[2] Extracts, here translated for the first time into English, by the editor.— Ed.

member that it is not for me to change the laws of the drama. Horace tells us to describe Achilles as ferocious, inexorable, violent — as he actually was. And Aristotle, far from asking us to portray perfect heroes, demands on the contrary that tragic characters — whose misfortunes bring about the tragic catastrophe — should be neither wholly good nor wholly bad. He does not want them to be extremely good, because the unishment of a good man would excite ndignation rather than pity in the audience; nor that they be excessively bad, because there can exist no pity for a scoundrel. They must therefore stand midway between the two extremes, be virtuous and yet capable of folly, and fall into misfortune through some fault which allows us to pity without detesting them.

FIRST PREFACE TO BRITANNICUS [3]

[*Première Préface* (to) *Britannicus*]

(1670)

... Personally, I have always believed that since tragedy was the imitation of a complete action — wherein several persons participate — that action is not complete until the audience knows in what situation the characters are finally left. Sophocles always informs us of this: in the *Antigone* he writes as many lines to show Hæmon's fury and Creon's punishment after the death of the princess, as I have written in Agrippina's imprecations, the retreat of Junia, the punishment of Narcissa and the despair of Nero, after the death of Britannicus.

How could these difficult judges be pleased? It would be an easy task, had I wished to violate commonsense a little. I should have but to abandon the natural for the extraordinary. Instead of a simple plot, with very little material — as befits an action supposed to take place within the compass of a single day and which, proceeding by degrees toward the end, is sustained solely by the interest, sentiments, and passions of the characters — I could just as well have crowded the very same story with a number of incidents which could not actually have happened within a whole month, with any number of stage-tricks, as astonishing as they would be false to nature, with a number of declamatory passages wherein the actors would utter the exact opposite of what they ought to utter. I might, for instance, have represented some hero as drunk, wishing to make his mistress hate him, out of sheer caprice; or a mouthing Lacedæmonian, a conqueror scattering maxims upon love; a woman giving lessons in pride to a warrior — in any of these ways I might have satisfied the gentle-

men. But what would that small group of intelligent people whom I must please, have said? How would I have dared appear, so to speak, before those great men of antiquity whom I have taken for my models? Because, when I make use of their thoughts, I think of them actually as spectators. When we take our inspiration from them we should always ask ourselves, "What would Homer and Vergil say, if they were to read these lines? What would Sophocles say if he saw this scene?" However all this may be, I have never tried to prevent any one's criticizing my works adversely; that would be impossible: *Quid de te alii loquantur ipsi vident*, says Cicero, *sed loquentur tamen:* "Others must be careful how they speak of you; but be sure that they will speak of you, in some way or other."

I only beg the reader's forgiveness for this little preface, which I wrote merely to explain and justify my tragedy. What more natural than to defend oneself when one believes oneself unjustly attacked? I think that Terence wrote his prologue solely to justify and defend himself against the critics who spoke in disparagement of the old poet of evil intentions, *malevoli veteris poetae,* and who came to raise their voices against him, up to the very moment his comedies were performed.

... *occœpta est agi:*
Exclamat, etc.
Hardly has the curtain risen, but there he is, crying out, etc. (Prologue to the "*Eunuchus*" of Terence.)

There is one objection which might have, but has not, been urged against me. Still, what escaped the spectators may become evident to the reader: I make

---

[3] Extracts, here translated, by the editor, for the first time into English.— Ed.

Junia join the Vestals. Now, according to Aulus Gellius the Vestals received no one under six years of age, nor over ten. But here the people take Junia under their protection, and I thought that in consideration of her rank, her virtue, and her misfortune, an exception might be made regarding her age as other exceptions had been made in the cases of so many men who deserved to be made consuls.

PREFACE TO BÉRÉNICE [4]

[*Préface* (to) *Bérénice*]

(1674)

. . . I have for some time cherished the desire to try whether I could write a tragedy with the extremely simple plot so much admired by the ancients, for simplicity is one of the first precepts which they have left us. " Whatever you write," says Horace, " it must be simple, and it must be one." The ancients admired the *Ajax* of Sophocles, which is concerned wholly with the story of Ajax killing himself with sorrow over the refusal to give him Achilles' arms. They admired the *Philoctetes,* the subject of which is merely the coming of Ulysses for the arrows of Hercules. The *Œdipus* itself, though full of incidents, is less crowded than the simplest tragedy of our times. And finally, we see those who favored Terence justly placing him above all other comic poets, for the elegance of his style and his careful observation of the manners of his day, but confessing none the less that Plautus had a distinct advantage over him, namely, in the simplicity of the majority of his plots. It was doubtless this marvelous simplicity that caused the ancients to praise him so highly. How much simpler must Menander have been, since Terence was obliged to take two of that poet's comedies to make one of his own!

Nor must one assume that this rule was based entirely upon caprice; no, nothing but what is true to life can appeal to us in tragedy. But what sort of truth to life is there when within the space of one day a multitude of things happen that would in actual life occupy many weeks? There are some who believe that this simplicity is a confession of the author's poverty of invention. They are not aware that on the contrary,

4 Extracts, here translated, by the editor, for the first time into English.— Ed.

an author's invention is most severely put to the test in making something out of nothing, and that the introduction of a host of incidents has always been the refuge of poets who felt their own want of genius, and power to interest their auditors through five acts of simple plot, sustained by the force of passion, beauty of ideas, and elegance of expression. I am far from believing that my play contains all these elements, but on the other hand, I do not think that the audience blamed me too much for having written a tragedy so honored with their tears, the thirtieth performance of which was as well attended as the first.

Not that certain people have not censured me for that very simplicity I strove so diligently to attain: they believed that a tragedy so denuded of intrigue could not be according to the rules of dramatic art. I wished to know whether the tragedy had bored them, and learned that they all admitted that it had not, but had moved them, and that they would willingly witness it again. What more could they demand? I beg them to think well enough of themselves not to believe that a play which stirs them and gives them pleasure, *can* be absolutely at variance with the rules. The principal rule is to please and to stir; all others are simply means to arrive at that end. The rules are long and complicated, and I advise those who criticize the play on the grounds just mentioned not to bother about them: they have more important business to attend to. Let them leave to us the trouble of interpreting Aristotle's theory of poetry, and reserve for themselves the pleasure of weeping and being moved, and allow me to tell them what a musician said to King Philip of Macedon, when the latter maintained that a certain song was not written according to the rules: "Heaven keep you, Sire, from being so unfortunate as to know such things better than I do!"

PREFACE TO PHÉDRE [5]
[*Préface* (to) *Phèdre*]
(1677)

... What I can say is that in no other of my plays have I given virtue so exalted a place as in this: the slightest evil is severely punished; the very thought of crime is made as horrible as the commission of it; the weaknesses of love itself are treated as veritable shortcomings; the passions are exhibited with the purpose of showing the disorder into which they lead us; vice is introduced in such wise as to make us detest it in all its horrible deformity. This should properly be the chief purpose of those who work for the public; this is what the ancients kept constantly in mind. Their plays were a veritable school where virtue was of no less importance than with the philosophers. Hence it was that Aristotle laid down the rules of dramatic poetry, and Socrates, the wisest of the philosophers, did not disdain to speak of the tragedies of Euripides. We should like our works to be as solid and full of useful instruction as were those of antiquity. This might be a means to reconcile tragedy to a number of celebrated persons who either because of their piety or their beliefs, have of late condemned it, and who would undoubtedly cast a more favorable eye upon it if the dramatists endeavored to instruct as well as please their auditors, and so came nearer to the true end of all tragedy.

5 Extracts, here translated by the editor, for the first time into English.— Ed.

NICOLAS BOILEAU-DESPRÉAUX

Nicolas Boileau-Despréaux, the son of Gilles Boileau, was born at Paris in 1636. His mother died when he was two years old, and the lad seems to have been somewhat neglected. From his early youth he is said to have had but one passion, "the hatred of dull books." He was educated at the College de Beauvais, and later went to study theology at the Sorbonne. Giving this up, he studied law and was admitted to the bar in 1656, but the law disgusted him and the next year, on the death of his father who left him a comfortable income, he directed his attention exclusively to study and writing. Among his earliest works are a few indifferent poems. The first of his *Satires,* in which his true genious found expression, dates from 1660. Though it was "imitated" from Juvenal, it is distinctly of the poet's own time and spirit. This was followed by others, of which twelve ultimately appeared. In these he attacked many authors of the preceding generations—among them Chapelain, Scudéry, and Quinault—and went far toward destroying the earlier traditions. He was, on the other hand, friendly toward Racine and Molière. Another of his effective attacks contributed to the downfall of the elaborate romance of the Mlle. de Scudéry type, and was called *Dialogue des héros de roman.* Though it was written in 1664, it was not published until 1713. The *Satires* appeared in the first authorized edition in 1666, and the *Epîtres* from 1669 on. These attracted considerable attention and brought him into Court favor. Louis XIV granted him a generous pension and in 1677 made him Historiographer to the King. In the 1674 edition of his *Œuvres diverses* he published for the first time his celebrated poems, *L'Art poétique* and mock-heroic poem *Le Lutrin*. In the same year he also published his translation of Longinus *On the Sublime*, the *Réflexions* on which appeared in 1693. He was admitted to the Academy in 1684. His last years were spent partly at Auteuil and partly at Paris. They were not very productive. He died in 1711.

The *Art poétique* was primarily the poet's justification of his attacks in the *Satires*. In it he tried to bring to the bar of reason the various "bad" poems which he had ridiculed. Though at first he had ridiculed, he was now to criticize. His Rules, his precepts, his generalities are but obiter dicta, conclusions rather than statements. But the work as a whole exercised incalculable influence until the so-called Romantic revolt in the early years of the nineteenth century.

On the drama:

The *Art poétique* (1674), is practically Boileau's only drama criticism, though he incidentally touches upon the subject in a few of his *Epîtres* and *Satires*.

Editions:

The *Art poétique* first appeared in the *Œuvres diverses* in 1674. Of the "original" editions the best are in the *Œuvres* published in 1674, 1694, 1701, and 1713. Among the annotated *Œuvres*, see the 4-volume ed. by Berriat Saint-Prix, 1830; the 4-volume Gidel ed., 1873, and the Pauly 2-volume ed., 1891. The best ed. of the *Art poétique* is in the single volume, with notes and introduction by Brunetière (7th ed.,

Paris, 1911). The *Works of Monsieur Boileau* were translated "by several hands" and with a Life by Des Maizéaux in 2 vols., London, 1712. *The Art of Poetry* was translated by Sir William Soames, "revised by Dryden," London, 1683. This is reprinted in Albert S. Cook's *The Art of Poetry*, together with the similar treatises of Horace and Vida, Boston, 1892.

On Boileau and his work:

P. Desmaizéaux, *La Vie de Monsieur Boileau-Despréaux* (Paris, 1712).

Bolæana (Paris, 1713).

D'Alembert, *Eloge de Despréaux* (Paris, 1779).

C.-A. Sainte-Beuve, *Port-Royal*, vol. 6 (latest ed., Paris, 1901).

——, *Portraits littéraires*, vol. 1 (Paris, 1862).

——, *Causeries du Lundi*, vol. 6 (Paris, 1857–62).

Ferdinand Brunetière, Article on *Boileau* in *La Grande Encyclopédie*, vol. 7 (Paris).

——, Introduction to *L'Art Poétique* (7th ed., Paris, 1911).

——, *L'Esthétique de Boileau* (in *Etudes critiques sur l'histoire de la littérature française*, vol. 6, Paris, 3rd ed., 1911).

D. Nisard, *Examen des Poétiques d'Aristote, d'Horace, et de Boileau* (St. Cloud, 1845).

George Saintsbury, *A History of Criticism*, vol. 2 (New York, 1902).

Charles Dejob, *Lessing et Boileau* (in the *Revue des Cours et Conférences*, Paris, 1897).

A. Bourgoin, *Les Maîtres de la critique au XVIIᵉ siècle* (Paris, 1889).

THE ART OF POETRY [1]
[*Art poétique*]
(1674)

There's not a monster bred beneath the sky,
But, well-disposed by art, may please the eye;
A curious workman, by his skill divine,

From an ill object makes a good design.
Thus, to delight us, Tragedy, in tears
For Œdipus, provokes our hopes and fears;
For parricide Orestes asks relief,
And to increase our pleasure, causes grief.

[1] Re-printed from Sir William Soames' edition of Boileau's *Art of Poetry* (London, 1683).— With omissions.— Ed.

You then that in this noble art would
rise,
Come and in lofty verse dispute the
prize.
Would you upon the stage acquire re-
nown,
And for your judges summon all the
town?
Would you your works forever should
remain,
And after ages past be sought again?
In all you write observe with care and
art
To move the passions and incline the
heart.
If in a labored act, the pleasing rage
Cannot our hopes and fears by turns en-
gage,
Nor in our mind a feeling pity raise,
In vain with learned scenes you fill your
plays;
Your cold discourse can never move the
mind
Or a stern critic, naturally unkind,
Who, justly tired with your pedantic
flight,
Or falls asleep or censures all you write.
The secret is, attention first to gain,
To move our minds and then to enter-
tain,
That, from the very opening of the
scenes,
The first may show us what the author
means.

I'm tired to see an actor on the stage
That knows not whether he's to laugh or
rage;
Who, an intrigue unraveling in vain,
Instead of pleasing keeps my mind in
pain.
I'd rather much the nauseous dunce
should say
Downright, "My name is Hector in the
play,"
Than with a mass of miracles, ill-
joined,
Confound my ears, and not instruct my
mind.
The subject's never soon enough ex-
pressed.

Your place of action must be fixed, and
rest.
A Spanish poet may with good event
In one day's space whole ages repre-
sent;

There oft the hero of the wandering
stage
Begins a child, and ends the play of
age.
But we, that are by reason's rule con-
fined,
Will that with art the poem be designed,
That unity of action, time, and place,
Keep the stage full, and all our labors
grace.

Write not what cannot be with ease
conceived;
Some truths may be too strong to be be-
lieved.
A foolish wonder cannot entertain;
My mind's not moved if your discourse
be vain.
You may relate what would offend the
eye;
Seeing indeed would better satisfy,
But there are objects which a curious
art
Hides from the eyes, yet offers to the
heart.

The mind is most agreeably surprised,
When a well-woven subject, long dis-
guised,
You on a sudden artfully unfold,
And give the whole another face and
mold.

At first the Tragedy was void of art,
A song, where each man danced and
sung his part,
And of god Bacchus roaring out the
praise,
Sought a good vintage for their jolly
days;
Then wine and joy were seen in each
man's eyes,
And a fat goat was the best singer's
prize.
Thespis was first, who, all besmeared
with lee,
Began this pleasure for posterity,
And with his carted actors and a song
Amused the people as he passed along.
Next Æschylus the different persons
placed,
And with a better mask his players
graced,
Upon a theater his verse expressed,
And showed his hero with a buskin
dressed.
Then Sophocles, the genius of his age,

Increased the pomp and beauty of the
  stage,
Engaged the Chorus song in every part,
And polished rugged verse by rules of
  art;
He in the Greek did those perfections
  gain
Which the weak Latin never could at-
  tain.

Our pious fathers, in their priest-rid
  age,
As impious and profane abhorred the
  stage.
A troop of silly pilgrims, as 'tis said,
Foolishly zealous, scandalously played,
Instead of heroes and of love's com-
  plaints,
The angels, God, the Virgin, and the
  saints.
At last right reason did his laws reveal,
And showed the folly of their ill-placed
  zeal,
Silenced those nonconformists of the age,
And raised the lawful heroes of the
  stage;
Only the Athenian mask was laid aside,
And Chorus by the music was supplied.

Ingenious love, inventive in new arts,
Mingled in plays, and quickly touched
  our hearts;
This passion never could resistance find,
But knows the shortest passage to the
  mind.
Paint, then, I'm pleased my hero be in
  love,
But let him not like a tame shepherd
  move;
Let not Achilles be like Thyrsis seen,
Or for a Cyrus show an Artamene;
That, struggling oft, his passions we
  may find
The frailty, not the virtue of his mind.

Of romance heroes shun the low de-
  sign,
Yet to great hearts some human frailties
  join.
Achilles must with Homer's heart en-
  gage —
For an affront I'm pleased to see him
  rage;
Those little failings in your hero's heart
Show that of man and nature he has
  part.

To leave known rules you cannot be al
  lowed;
Make Agamemnon covetous and proud,
Æneas in religious rites austere;
Keep to each man his proper character
Of countries and of times the humors
  know,
From different climates different cus-
  toms grow;
And strive to shun their fault, who
  vainly dress
An antique hero like a modern ass,
Who make old Romans like our English
  move,
Show Cato sparkish, or make Brutus
  love.[2]

In a romance those errors are excused;
There 'tis enough that, reading, we're
  amused,
Rules too severe would there be useless
  found;
But the strict scene must have a juster
  bound,
Exact decorum we must always find.

If then you form some hero in your
  mind,
Be sure your image with itself agree,
For what he first appears he still must
  be.

Affected wits will naturally incline
To paint their figures by their own de-
  sign;
Your bully poets bully heroes write;
Chapman in Bussy D'Ambois took de-
  light,
And thought perfection was to huff and
  fight.[3]

Wise nature by variety does please;
Clothe differing passions in a differing
  dress;
Bold anger in rough haughty words ap-
  pears;
Sorrow is humble and dissolves in tears.

Make not your Hecuba with fury rage,
And show a ranting grief upon the stage,

[2] The original runs:
*Gardez donc de donner, ainsi que dans Clélie,
L'air, ni l'esprit françois à l'antique Italie.*
— Ed.

[3] The original reads:
*Tout à l'humeur gasconne en un auteur
Calprenède et Juba parlent du même ton.*

Or tell in vain how "the rough Tanaïs
bore
His sevenfold waters to the Euxine
shore."
These swollen expressions, this affected
noise,
Shows like some pedant that declaims
to boys.
In sorrow you must softer methods keep,
And, to excite our tears, yourself must
weep.
Those noisy words with which ill plays
abound
Come not from hearts that are in sad-
ness drowned.

The theater for a young poet's rimes
Is a bold venture in our knowing times.
An author cannot easily purchase fame;
Critics are always apt to hiss and blame;
You may be judged by every ass in
town —
The privilege is bought for half-a-crown.
To please, you must a hundred chances
try,
Sometimes be humble, then must soar on
high,
In noble thoughts must everywhere
abound,
Be easy, pleasant, solid, and profound;
To these you must surprising touches
join,
And show us a new wonder in each line;
That all, in a just method well-designed
May leave a strong impression in the
mind.
These are the arts that tragedy main-
tain.

.   .   .   .   .

The great success which tragic writers
found
In Athens first the comedy renowned.
The abusive Grecian there, by pleasing
ways,
Dispersed his natural malice in his plays;
Wisdom and virtue, honor, wit, and
sense,
Were subject to buffooning insolence;
Poets were publicly approved and
sought,
That vice extolled and virtue set at
naught;
A Socrates himself, in that loose age,
Was made the pastime of a scoffing
stage.
At last the public took in hand the cause,

And cured this madness by the power of
laws,
Forbade, at any time or any place
To name the persons or describe the face.
The stage its ancient fury thus let fall,
And comedy diverted without gall,
By mild reproofs recovered minds dis-
eased,
And, sparing persons, innocently pleased.[4]

Each one was nicely shown in this new
glass,
And smiled to think he was not meant
the ass.
A miser oft would laugh at first, to find
A faithful draught of his own sordid
mind;
And fops were with such care and cun-
ning writ,
They liked the piece for which themselves
did sit.

You, then, that would the comic laur-
els wear,
To study nature be your only care.
Whoe'er knows man, and by a curious art
Discerns the hidden secrets of the heart;
He who observes, and naturally can paint
The jealous fool, the fawning sycophant,
A sober wit, an enterprising ass,
A humorous Otter, or a Hudibras,—
May safely in those noble lists engage,
And make them act and speak upon the
stage.
Strive to be natural in all you write,
And paint with colors that may please
the sight.
Nature in various figures does abound,
And in each mind are different humors
found;
A glance, a touch, discovers to the wise,
But every man has not discerning eyes.

All-changing time does also change the
mind,
And different ages different pleasures
find.
Youth, hot and furious, cannot brook de-
lay,
By flattering vice is easily led astray;
Vain in discourse, inconstant in desire,
In censure rash, in pleasures all on fire.
The manly age does steadier thoughts
enjoy;

4 Original:
. . . *Et plut innocemment dans les vers de*
Ménandre.   — Ed.

Power and ambition do his soul emply;
Against the turns of fate he sets his
    mind,
And by the past the future hopes to find.
Decrepit age, still adding to his stores,
For others heaps the treasure he adores,
In all his actions keeps a frozen pace,
Past time extols, the present to debase;
Incapable of pleasures youth abuse,
In others blames what age does him re-
    fuse.
Your actors must by reason be con-
    trolled;
Let young men speak like young, old men
    like old.

  Observe the town and study well the
    court,
For thither various characters resort.
Thus 'twas great Jonson purchased his
    renown,
And in his art had borne away the
    crown,
If, less desirous of the people's praise,
He had not with low farce debased his
    plays,
Mixing dull buffoonry with wit refined,
And Harlequin with noble Terence
    joined.
When in *The Fox* I see the tortoise
    hissed,
I lose the author of *The Alchemist*.[5]

  The comic wit, born with a smiling air,
Must tragic grief and pompous verse
    forbear;
Yet may he not, as on a market-place,

[5] In the above passage — beginning with
"Thus 'twas," it is necessary to restore
"Molière" for "Jonson"; "Tabarin" for
"Harlequin"; "ridiculous sack in which
Scapin is rolled," for "When in *The Fox* I
see the tortoise hissed"; and "*Le Mis-
anthrope*" for "*The Alchemist*."— Ed.

With bawdy jests amuse the populace.
With well-bred conversation you must
    please,
And your intrigue unravelled be with
    ease;
Your action still should reason's rules
    obey,
Nor in an empty scene may lose its way.
Your humble style must sometimes gently
    rise,
And your discourse sententious be and
    wise,
The passions must to nature be confined,
And scenes to scenes with artful weaving
    joined.
Your wit must not unseasonably play,
But follow business, never lead the way.
Observe how Terence does this evil shun:
A careful father chides his amorous son;
Then see that son whom no advice can
    move,
Forget those orders, and pursue his love!
'Tis not a well-drawn picture we dis-
    cover,
'Tis a true son, a father, and a lover.

  I like an author that reforms the age,
And keeps the right decorum of the
    stage,
That always pleases by just reason's
    rule;
But for a tedious droll, a quibbling fool,
Who with low nauseous bawdry fills his
    plays,
Let him begone, and on two trestles raise
Some Smithfield stage, where he may act
    his pranks,
And make Jack-Puddings speak to
    mountebanks.[6]

               (Book III.)

[6] Original: "Amusing the *Pont-Neuf* with
his stale nonsense, and playing his pranks to
the assembled lackeys."— Ed.

SAINT-EVREMOND

  Charles de Marguetel de Saint-Denis,
sieur de Saint-Evremond, was born of an
old and noble family at the Château de
Saint-Denis-le-Guast (near Coutances),
in 1610. He was destined to a career in
the magistrature and was sent to Paris
to study in 1619. His education was
continued, with special emphasis on phi-
losophy, at Paris and at Caën. He began
his law study in 1628, but gave it up at
the end of a year and entered the army.
He participated in many campaigns.
After twenty years of service he was
made *maréchal de camp*, after losing his

lieutenancy as the result of an ill-advised joke on his former friend Condé. During his military career he read and studied and wrote. The *Comédie des académiciens* (written 1642–43) and *Maximes* (1647), belong to this period. In 1659 he wrote a letter to Créqui criticizing the Treaty of the Pyrenees, and as a result he was forced to leave France. He went at first to Holland, then (1661) to England, where he spent the remainder of his life. His existence in England was evidently a not unhappy exile, for he was in particular favor with Charles II and his two successors; and when in 1688, he was permitted to return to his native country, he did not take advantage of the offer. He died at London in 1703, and was buried in Westminster Abbey.

Saint-Evremond is important in the history of dramatic criticism both relatively and intrinsically. His knowledge, both of books and life, and his comparative freedom from prejudice, gave him peculiar advantages over such contemporaries as Boileau. It seems that his stay in England, besides affording him the incalculable advantage of knowing another nation and its literature, gave him a vantage point from which he was able to judge and discriminate wisely in the questions which were being debated in his own country. His impartiality in the Ancients and Moderns Quarrel is an example of this detachment. He was one of the few Frenchmen of his time who was able, or cared, to adopt what is now known as the comparative system of criticism. His championship of Corneille is sane, invigorating, and interesting. The score of writings in which he discussed the drama are probably the earliest specimens of the modern essay.

On the drama:

Dissertation sur la tragédie de Racine intitulée: Alexandre le Grand (1666).
Résponse de M. de Saint-Evremond à M. de Corneille (1668).
De la Tragédie ancienne et moderne (1672).
Sur les Caractères des tragédies (1672).
A un auteur qui me demandait mon sentiment d'une pièce où l'héroïne ne faisait que se lamenter (1672).

Sur les tragédies (1677).
Sur nos comédies, excepté celles de Molière, où l'on trouve le vrai esprit de la comédie, et sur la comédie espagnole (1677).
De la comédie italienne (1677).
De la comédie anglaise (1677).
Sur les opéras (1677).
Défense de quelques pièces de théâtre de M. Corneille (1677).[1]

(All the above are in the English translation cited.)

Editions:

With the exception of the works already mentioned, very little of Saint-Evremond was published during his lifetime. The first authorized edition, which is not, however, complete, was the *Œuvres meslées,* 3 vols., London, 1705. This was followed by the 7-vol. ed. of 1708, the Amsterdam ed. in 1727, and Paris ed. in 1740. Among the modern editions, see the *Œuvres mêlées,* edited in 3 vols. by Giraud (Paris, 1865), and Ch. Gidel's single-volume ed. of the *Œuvres choisis* (Garnier, Paris, after 1866). The *Œuvres* were translated as *The Works of Monsieur de St. Evremond,* 3 vols. (London, 1714. This contains a *Life* by P. Des Maizéeaux).

On Saint-Evremond and his works:

Introductions to the various editions cited.
G. Merlet, *Saint-Evremond* (Paris, 1869).
F. Pastrello, *Etude sur Saint-Evremond et son influence* (Trieste, 1875).
A. Bourgoin, *Les Maîtres de la critique au XVIIe siècle* (Paris, 1889).
C.-A. Sainte-Beuve, *Causeries du Lundi,* vol. 4 (Paris, 1857–62).
Gilbert et Gidel, *Eloges de Saint-Evremond* (Paris, 1866).
La Grande Encyclopédie, vol. 29 (Paris).
George Saintsbury, *A History of Criticism,* vol. 2 (New York, 1902).
W. Melville Daniels, *Saint-Evremond en Angleterre* (Versailles, 1907).

[1] The dates in each case refer to writing. All these essays were first published in 1705.—Ed.

OF ANCIENT AND MODERN TRAGEDY [2]
[*De la Tragédie ancienne et moderne*]
(Written 1672)

There were never so many rules to write a good tragedy by, and yet so few good ones are now made that the players are obliged to revive and act all the old ones. I remember that the Abbé d'Aubignac wrote one according to the laws he had so imperiously prescribed for the stage. This piece had no success, notwithstanding which he boasted in all companies that he was the first French writer that had exactly followed the precepts of Aristotle; whereupon the Prince of Condé said wittily: " I am obliged to Monsieur d'Aubignac for having so exactly followed Aristotle's rules, but I will never forgive the rules of Aristotle for having put Monsieur d'Aubignac upon writing so bad a tragedy."

It must be acknowledged that Aristotle's *Art of Poetry* is an excellent piece of work; but, however, there's nothing so perfect in it as to be the standing rules of all nations and all ages. Descartes and Gassendi have found out truths that were unknown to Aristotle. Corneille has discovered beauties for the stage of which Aristotle was ignorant; and as our philosophers have observed errors in his *Physics,* our poets have spied out faults in his *Poetics,* at least with respect to us, considering what great change all things have undergone since his time. The gods and goddesses amongst the Ancients brought events that were great and extreme upon the theater, either by their hatred or their friendship, by their revenge or their protection; and among so many supernatural things, nothing appeared fabulous to the people, who believed there passed a familiar correspondence between gods and men. Their gods, generally speaking, acted by human passions; their men undertook nothing without the counsel of the gods, and executed nothing without their assistance. Thus in this mixture of the divinity and humanity, there was nothing which was not credible.

But all this profusion of miracles is downright romance to us at this time of day. The gods are wanting to us, and we are wanting to the gods; and if, in imitation of the Ancients, an author would introduce his angels and saints upon our stage, the bigots and puritans would be offended at it, and the libertines would certainly think him weak. Our preachers would by no means suffer a confusion of the pulpit and the theater, or that the people should go and learn those matters from the mouth of comedians which themselves deliver in their churches, with such authority to the whole people.

Besides this, it would give too great an advantage to the libertines, who might ridicule in a comedy those very things which they receive at church with a seeming submission, either out of respect to the place or to the character of the person that utters them.

But let us put the case that our doctors should freely leave all holy matters to the liberty of the stage; let us likewise take it for granted that men of the least devotion would hear them with as great an inclination to be edified as persons of the profoundest resignation; yet certain it is that the soundest doctrines, the most Christian actions, and the most useful truths, would produce a kind of tragedy that would please us the least of anything in the world.

The spirit of our religion is directly opposite to that of tragedy. The humility and patience of our saints carry too direct an opposition to those heroical virtues that are so necessary for the theater. What zeal, what force is there which Heaven does not bestow upon Nearchus and Polyeucte? And what is there wanting on the part of these new Christians to answer fully the end of these happy gifts? The passion and charms of a lovely young bride make not the least impression upon the mind of Polyeucte. The politic considerations of Felix, as they less affect us, so they make a less impression. Insensible both of prayers and menaces, Polyeucte has a greater desire to die for God than other men have to live for themselves. Never-

---

[2] Re-printed from the anonymous translation of the *Works* (London, 1714).— Ed.

theless, this very subject, which would make one of the finest sermons in the world, would have made a wretched tragedy, if the conversation of Pauline and Sévère, heightened with other sentiments and other passions, had not preserved that reputation to the author which the Christian virtues of our martyrs had made him lose.

The theater loses all its agreeableness when it pretends to represent sacred things; and sacred things lose a great deal of the religious opinion that is due to them by being represented upon the theater.

To say the truth, the histories of the Old Testament are infinitely better suited to our stage. Moses, Samson, and Joshua would meet much better success than Polyeucte and Nearchus, for the wonders they would work there would be a fitter subject for the theater. But I am apt to believe that the priests would not fail to exclaim against the profanation of these sacred histories, with which they fill their conversations, their books, and their sermons; and to speak soberly upon the point, the miraculous passage through the Red Sea, the sun stopped in his career by the prayer of Joshua, and whole armies defeated by Samson with the jawbone of an ass — all these miracles, I say, would not be credited in a play, because we believe them in the Bible; but we should be rather apt to question them in the Bible, because we should believe nothing of them in the play.

If what I have delivered is founded on good and solid reasons, we ought to content ourselves with things purely natural, but at the same time, such as are extraordinary; and in our heroes to choose the principal actions which we may believe possible as human, and which may cause admiration in us, as being rare and of an elevated character. In a word, we should have nothing but what is great, yet still let it be human. In the human, we must carefully avoid mediocrity; and fable in that which is great.

I am by no means willing to compare the *Pharsalia* to the *Æneid;* I know the just difference of their value; but as for what purely regards elevation, Pompey, Cæsar, Cato, Curio, and Labienus, have done more for Lucan than Jupiter, Mercury, Juno, Venus, and all the train of the other gods and goddesses have done for Vergil.

The ideas which Lucan gives us of these great men are truly greater, and affect us more sensibly, than those which Vergil gives us of his deities. The latter has clothed his gods with human infirmities to adapt them to the capacity of men; the other has raised his heroes so as to bring them into competition with the gods themselves.

Victrix causa diis placuit, sed victa Catoni.

In Vergil, the gods are not so valuable as the heroes; in Lucan, the heroes equal the gods. To give you my opinion freely, I believe that the tragedy of the Ancients might have suffered a happy loss in the banishment of their gods, their oracles and their soothsayers.

For it proceeded from these gods, these oracles, and these diviners, that the stage was swayed by a spirit of superstition and terror, capable of infecting mankind with a thousand errors, and overwhelming them with numerous mischiefs. And if we consider the usual impressions which tragedy made at Athens in the minds of the spectators, we may safely affirm that Plato was more in the right, who prohibited the use of them, than Aristotle, who recommended them; for as their tragedies wholly consisted in excessive motions of fear and pity, was not this the direct way to make the theater a school of terror and of compassion, where people only learnt to be affrighted at all dangers, and to abandon themselves to despair upon every misfortune?

It will be a hard matter to persuade me that a soul accustomed to be terrified for what regards another, has strength enough to support misfortunes that concern itself. This perhaps was the reason why the Athenians became so susceptible of the impressions of fear, and that this spirit of terror which the theater inspired into them with so much art became at last but too natural to their armies.

At Sparta and Rome, where only examples of valor and constancy were publicly shown, the people were no less brave and resolute in battle than they were unshaken and constant in the calamities of the Republic. Ever since this art of fearing and lamenting was set up at

Athens, all those disorderly passions which they had, as it were, imbibed at their public representations, got footing in their camps and attended them in their wars.

Thus a spirit of superstition occasioned the defeat of their armies, and a spirit of lamentation made them sit down contented with bewailing their great misfortunes, when they ought to have found out proper remedies for them. For how was it possible for them not to learn despair in this pitiful school of commiseration? The persons they usually represented upon it were examples of the greatest misery and subjects but of ordinary virtues.

So great was their desire to lament that they represented fewer virtues than misfortunes, lest a soul raised to the admiration of heroes should be less inclined to pity the distressed; and in order to imprint these sentiments of affliction the deeper in their spectators, they had always upon their theater a chorus of virgins or of old men, who furnished them upon every event, either with their terrors or with their tears.

Aristotle was sensible enough what prejudice this might do the Athenians, but he thought he sufficiently prevented it by establishing a certain *Purgation,* which no one hitherto has understood, and which in my opinion he himself never fully comprehended. For can anything be so ridiculous as to form a science which will infallibly discompose our minds, only to set up another, which does not certainly pretend to cure us? Or to raise a perturbation in our souls for no other end than to endeavor afterwards to calm it, by obliging it to reflect upon the dejected condition it has been in?

Among a thousand persons that are present at the theater, perhaps there may be six philosophers that are capable of recovering their former tranquillity by the assistance of these prudent and useful meditations; but the multitude will scarce make any such judicious reflections, and we may be almost assured that what we see constantly represented on the theater, will not fail, at long run, to produce in us a habit of these unhappy motions.

Our theatrical representations are not subject to the same circumstances as those of the Ancients were, since our fear never goes so far as to raise this superstitious terror, which produced such ill effects upon valor. Our fear, generally speaking, is nothing else but an agreeable uneasiness, which consists in the suspension of our minds; 'tis a dear concern which our soul has for those objects that draw its affection to them.

We may almost say the same of pity as 'tis used on our stage. We divest it of all its weakness, and leave it all that we call charitable and human. I love to see the misfortune of some great unhappy person lamented; I am content with all my heart that he should attract our compassion; nay, sometimes, command our tears; but then I would have these tender and generous tears paid to his misfortunes and virtues together, and that this melancholy sentiment of pity be accompanied with vigorous admiration, which shall stir up in our souls a sort of an amorous desire to imitate him.

We were obliged to mingle somewhat of love in the new tragedy, the better to remove those black ideas which the ancient tragedy caused in us by superstition and terror. And in truth there is no passion that more excites us to everything that is noble and generous than a virtuous love. A man who may cowardly suffer himself to be insulted by a contemptible enemy will yet defend what he loves, though to the apparent hazard of his life, against the attacks of the most valiant. The weakest and most fearful creatures — those creatures that are naturally inclined to fear and to run away — will fiercely encounter what they dread most, to preserve the object of their love. Love has a certain heat which supplies the defect of courage in those that want it most. But to confess the truth, our authors have made as ill an use of this noble passion as the Ancients did of their fear and pity; for if we except eight or ten plays where its impulses have been managed to great advantage, we have no tragedies in which both lovers and love are not equally injured.

We have an affected tenderness where we ought to place the noblest sentiments. We bestow a softness on what ought to be most moving; and sometimes when we mean plainly to express the graces of nature, we fall into a vicious and mean simplicity.

We imagine we make kings and emperors perfect lovers, but in tragedy we make ridiculous princes of them; and by the complaints and sighs which we bestow upon them where they ought neither to complain nor sigh, we represent them weak, both as lovers and as princes.

Our great heroes upon the theater generally make love like shepherds; and thus the innocence of a sort of rural passion supplies with them the place of glory and valor.

If an actress has the art to weep and bemoan herself after a moving lively manner, we give her our tears, at certain places which demand gravity; and because she pleases best when she seems to be affected, she shall put on grief all along, indifferently.

Sometimes we must have a plain, unartificial, sometimes a tender and sometimes a melancholy whining love, without regarding where that simplicity, tenderness, or grief is requisite; and the reason of it is plain: for as we must needs have love everywhere, we look for diversity in the manners, and seldom or never place it in the passions.

I am in good hopes we shall one day find out the true use of this passion, which is now become too common. That which ought to sweeten cruel or calamitous accidents, that which ought to affect our very souls, to animate our courage and raise our spirits, will not certainly be always made the subject of a little affected tenderness or of a weak simplicity. Whenever this happens, we need not envy the Ancients; and without paying too great a respect to Antiquity, or being too much prejudiced against the present age, we shall not set up the tragedies of Sophocles and Euripides as the only models for the dramatic compositions of our times.

However, I don't say that these tragedies wanted anything that was necessary to recommend them to the palate of the Athenians; but should a man translate the Œdipus, the best performance of all Antiquity, into French, with the same spirit and force as we see it in the original, I dare be bold to affirm that nothing in the world would appear to us more cruel and more opposite to the

true sentiments which mankind ought to have.

Our age has at least this advantage over theirs, that we are allowed the liberty to hate vice and love virtue. As the gods occasioned the greatest crimes on the theater of the Ancients, these crimes captivated the respect of the spectators, and the people durst not find fault with those things which were really abominable. When they saw Agamemnon sacrifice his own daughter, and a daughter too that was so tenderly loved by him, to appease the indignation of the gods, they only considered this barbarous sacrifice as a pious obedience, and the highest proof of a religious submission.

Now, in that superstitious age, if a man still preserved the common sentiments of humanity, he could not avoid murmuring at the cruelty of the gods; he must needs be cruel and barbarous to his own fellow-creatures; he must, like Agamemnon, offer the greatest violence both to nature and to his own affection.

Tantum relligio potuit suadere malorum, says Lucretius, upon the account of this barbarous sacrifice.

Nowadays we see men represented upon the theater without the interposition of the gods; and this conduct is infinitely more useful both to the public and to private persons, for in our tragedies we neither introduce any villain who is not detested, nor any hero who does not cause himself to be admired. With us, few crimes escape unpunished and few virtues go off unrewarded. In short, by the good examples we publicly represent on the theater, by the agreeable sentiments of love and admiration that are discreetly interwoven with a rectified fear and pity, we are in a capacity of arriving to that perfection which Horace desires:

Omne tulit punctum, qui miscuit utile dulci, which can never be effected by the rules of ancient tragedy.

I shall conclude with a new and daring thought of my own, and that is this: we ought, in tragedy, before all things whatever, to look after a greatness of soul well expressed, which excites in us a tender admiration. By this sort of admiration our minds are sensibly ravished, our courages elevated, and our souls deeply affected.

ENGLAND — II

FROM THE RESTORATION TO THE NINETEENTH CENTURY

Between the publication of Jonson's *Discoveries* (1641) and that of Dryden's *Essay of Dramatick Poesie* (1668), there is no outstanding piece of dramatic criticism in English. However, Davenant's efforts to create the opera, his *Preface to Gondibert* and Hobbes' reply, in 1650, together with the former's *Dedication* and *To the Reader* prefixed to his *Siege of Rhodes* (printed 1663), deserve passing notice as connecting links. Sir Robert Howard's *Preface* to *Four New Playes* (1665), which called forth Dryden's reply, and Howard's further *Preface*—to *The Great Favourite* (1668)—Richard Flecknoe's *A Short Discourse of the English Stage* (1664), and the various prefaces, dedications, and prologues, especially of Shadwell's *The Sullen Lovers* (1668) and of *The Humourists* (1671), are further indications of interest in dramatic controversies. Thomas Rymer entered the field a few years after Dryden. His *Preface* to his translation of Rapin's *Réflexions sur la poétique* (1674) attacked all stragglers from the narrow path prescribed by the rigid neo-classicists; he followed this with a severe criticism of the Elizabethans, in *The Tragedies of the Last Age Consider'd*, etc. (1678), and in 1693 he published his *Short View of Tragedy*, etc., containing the famous onslaught on *Othello*. Milton published his short dissertation on tragedy with his *Samson Agonistes* (1671) as a sort of apology. It is based almost entirely upon the Italian Renaissance critics' conception of Aristotle's remarks on tragedy. Other contemporaries of Dryden, who dominated the last years of the century are, among others of less importance: the Duke of Buckingham, whose *Essay upon Poetry* was published in 1682; Ravenscroft's preface to the play *Dame Dobson* (1684); Sedley, whose *Bellamira* (1687) had a short *Preface;* Sir Thomas Pope Blount, whose exten-

sive treatise — *De Re Poetica* — with numerous excerpts from ancient and modern poets, appeared in 1694; and the dramatists, Blackmore — *Prefaces to Prince Arthur* (1695) and *King Arthur* (1697) — and Dilke — *Preface* to *The City Lady* (1697). Of Dryden's thirty odd prefaces, essays, etc., on the drama, the first, the *Epistle Dedicatory* to his play *The Rival Ladies,* was published in 1664. This was followed by the *Essay of Dramatick Poesie* (1668), and the *Defence,* the same year. Nearly every one of his plays carries a preface, dedication, or separate essay defending his dramatic practice, setting forth some theory, or attacking the practice or theory of others. His last word on the drama is found in the *Discourse on Epick Poetry,* prefixed to his translation of the *Æneid* in 1697, three years before his death. Dryden was a great critic, one of the greatest of all time. " He established (let us hope for all time)," says Saintsbury, "the English fashion of criticizing, as Shakespeare did the English fashion of dramatizing,— the fashion of aiming at delight, at truth, at justice, at nature, at poetry, and letting the rules take care of themselves." The controversy between the Puritans and the stage assumed its most violent form in the famous Collier dispute. In 1696 Jeremy Collier, a Nonjuring clergyman, published his *Short View of the Profaneness and Immorality of the English Stage.* This pamphlet was aimed primarily against the dramatists who " profaned " the stage with immoral characters and situations, and who attacked the clergy. While his purpose was primarily a moral one, there is a good deal of literary criticism in his work. There is no doubt that he was a most important factor in changing the tone of the plays of his generation, and stultifying the comedies of the next. The *Short View* called forth many replies, some of which were anonymous. Congreve replied with his *Amendments upon Mr. Collier's False and Imperfect Citations*, etc., the same year. Collier at once riposted with his *Defence of the Short View*, etc. Farquhar is the probable author of *The Adventures of Covent Garden*, in which he answered Collier by suggesting that the "best way of answering Mr. Collier was not to have replied at all." Vanbrugh, who together with Congreve and Dryden, was specifically attacked, replied in his *Vindication of the Relapse*, etc. (1699). John Dennis, a critic of no mean ability, defended the stage in a lengthy treatise on *The Usefulness of the Stage to the Happiness of Mankind, to Government, and to Religion*, etc. (1698). When, in 1705, Collier published his *Dissuasive from the Play House*, Dennis again answered with *A Person of Quality's Answer to Mr. Collier's Letter*. Before the Collier controversy started, Dennis had written his first criticism, the *Impartial Critick* (1693), in reply to Rymer's *Short View of Tragedy*. Among his subsequent dramatic criticisms may be mentioned: *An Essay on the Operas* (1706), *An Essay on the Genius and Writings of Shakespeare* (1712), *Remarks upon Cato, A Tragedy* (1713), *A Defence of Sir Fopling Flutter, a Comedy* (1722), *Remarks on a Play, call'd The Conscious Lovers, a Comedy* (1723), *The Stage Defended from Scripture, Reason and the Common Sense of Mankind for Two Thousand Years* (1726). Drake's *Antient and Modern Stages survey'd* (1699) called forth Collier's *Second Defence of the Short View*, etc. (1700). E. Filmer's *A Defence of Plays*, etc. (1707), found Collier once more ready with an answer, *A Farther Vindication of the Short View*, etc. (1708). *Mr. Collier's Dissuasive from the Play House* (1703), completes the list of the clergyman's attacks on the stage. Among the many defenses of Collier may be mentioned the anonymous *A Representation of the Impiety and Immorality of the English Stage*, etc. (1704). Formal treatises on the art of poetry made their appearance late in the new century. Edward Bysshe's *Art of English Poetry* (probably 1700) is of great historical importance, and sums

up the neo-classic tendencies of the time. This was followed in 1721 by Charles Gildon's *Complete Art of Poetry*. It was probably Gildon who "improved" and continued Gerard Langbaine's *Lives and Characters of the English Dramatic Poets*, etc., which was published in 1699 (?). Addison, great as he was in other fields, is not important as a dramatic critic. In the *Spectator*, however, he touches on drama at several points.[1] In *The Tatler, The Guardian*, and other papers, Richard Steele also occasionally wrote on the drama, and in the dedications and prefaces to his plays (*The Funeral*, 1702, *The Lying Lover*, 1704, *The Conscious Lovers*, 1723). Farquhar, the last of the great Restoration dramatists, made his contributions to dramatic criticism in the *Prologue* to *Sir Harry Wildair* (1701) and in the *Discourse upon English Comedy* (1702). The latter, which is of course much fuller, is a sort of summing-up of the theories of drama held by many dramatists. It contains a vigorous protest against Aristotle and the Rules, and a loose definition of comedy as a moral guide, with the Horatian ingredient of the "useful" and the "pleasing." The Shakespearean Prefaces of the seventeenth century contain interesting critical matter. The most important are collected by D. Nichol Smith in his *Eighteenth Century Essays on Shakespeare*, which contains the following, among others: Nicholas Rowe's *Some Account of the Life . . . of Mr. William Shakespeare* (1707); Pope's *Preface* (1725); essays of Theobald (1733), Hanmer (1744), Warburton (1747), Johnson (1765), and Farmer's *Essay on the Learning of Shakespeare* (1767). Pope's *Essay on Criticism* (1711) may also be consulted for its sections relating to the drama. Many literary critics of the period referred to the drama in the course of their writings on general literature, rhetoric, and poetry. David Hume's *Essay on Tragedy* (1742), Joseph Warton's papers in *The Adventurer* (on *The Tempest*, Nos. 93 and 97, and on *King Lear*, Nos. 113, 116, and 122); Colley Cibber's *Apology* (1740) — deal with various aspects of the drama, while Blair, Hurd, and Kames are more es-

[1] In Nos. 39 to 42, 44, 45, 58 to 63, 258, 290, 296, 419, 446.

pecially concerned with the historical, rhetorical, and esthetic sides. Burke's *Essay on Tragedy*, and *On the Sublime and Beautiful* (1756), are concerned almost wholly with purely esthetic considerations, and Samuel Foote's *Roman and English Comedy Considered and Compared* (1747) is little more than a curious document on contemporary plays and acting. Dr. Johnson's contribution to the criticism of the drama is not great in extent, but is important as an indication of the spirit of the times. His essays in the *Rambler*, the *Idler*, and the *Adventurer*, the casual remarks in the *Lives of the Poets* (1789–91), and the *Preface* to his edition of Shakespeare (1765) are practically his only dramatic criticism.

Goldsmith was not a great critic, but his knowledge of the stage and inborn shrewdness make his observations in *The State of Polite Learning* (1759), the *Preface* to *The Good-Natur'd Man* (1768), and the *Essay on the Theatre* (1772), dramatic manifestos, attractive and interesting. They indicate the reaction against the Sentimental Comedy, which was at that time in its heyday. The century closed with a few treatises on the more formal aspects of dramatic criticism, like Cooke's *Elements of Dramatic Criticism* (1775), J. Penn's *Letters on the Drama* (1796), B. Walwyn's *Essay on Comedy* (1782), and Samuel Wyte's *The Theatre, a Didactic Essay* (1790).

General references Restoration and eighteenth-century literature:

T. S. Perry, *English Literature of the Eighteenth Century* (New York, 1883).

John Dennis, *The Age of Pope* (London, 1899).

Leslie Stephen, *English Literature and Society in the Eighteenth Century* (London, ed., 1910).

——, *History of English Thought in the Eighteenth Century*, 2 vols. (ed. New York, 1877).

Edmund Gosse, *A History of Eighteenth Century Literature* (London, 1889).

——, *Seventeenth Century Studies* (London, 1883).

R. Garnett, *The Age of Dryden* (London, 1903).

A. Beljame, *Le Public et les hommes de lettres en Angleterre au dix-huitième siècle* (2nd ed., Paris, 1897).

George Saintsbury, *The Peace of the Augustans* (London, 1916).

General references on the drama:

Downs, John, *Roscius Anglicanus, or, An Historical Review of the Stage . . . from 1660 to 1706* (London, 1708. "With additions," by Davies, 1789).

G. H. Nettleton, *English Drama of the Restoration and Eighteenth Century* (New York, 1914).

Theophilus Cibber, *Dissertations on the Theatres*, etc. (London, 1756).

Ernest Bernbaum, *The Drama of Sensibility (1696–1780)* (Boston, 1915).

Thomas Betterton (?), *The History of the English Stage, from the Restoration to the Present Time*, etc. (London, 1741).

H. T. E Perry, *The Comic Spirit in Restoration Drama* (New Haven, 1925).

A.-A. de Grisy, *Histoire de la comédie anglaise au dix-septième siècle* (Paris, 1878).

W. Harvey-Jellie, *Les Sources du théâtre anglais à l'époque de la Restauration* (Paris, 1906).

D. H. Miles, *The Influence of Molière on Restoration Comedy* (New York, 1910).

J. Fitzgerald Molloy, *Famous Plays, with a Discourse by way of Prologue on the Playhouses of the Restoration* (London, 1886).

John Palmer, *The Comedy of Manners* (New York, 1913).

——, *Comedy* (New York, n. d.).

Malcolm Elwin, *The Playgoer's Handbook to Restoration Drama* (London, 1928).

O. Waterhouse, *The Development of English Sentimental Comedy in the 18th Century* (in *Anglia*, vol. 30, Halle, 1907).

William Cooke, *Memoirs of Charles Macklin . . . forming an History of the Stage during almost the whole of the last century* (2nd ed., London, 1806).

E. N. S. Thompson, *The Controversy Between the Puritans and the Stage* (New Haven, 1903).

Ernest B. Watson, *Sheridan to Robertson* (Cambridge, Mass., 1926).

Kathleen M. Lynch, *The Social Mode of Restoration Comedy* (New York, 1926).

Percy Fitzgerald, *A New History of the English Stage, from the Restoration*

Joseph Wood Krutch, Comedy and Conscience After the Restoration (New York, 1924).

Alwin Thaler, Shakspere to Sheridan, (Cambridge, Mass., 1922).

Allardyce Nicoll, A History of Restoration Drama (Cambridge, 1923).

——, A History of Early Eighteenth Century Drama (Cambridge, 1925).

——, A History of Late Eighteenth Century Drama (Cambridge, 1927).

Bonamy Dobrée, Restoration Comedy (Oxford, 1924).

Special works on criticism:

P. Hamelius, Die Kritik in der eng-

lischen Literatur der 17. und 18. Jahrhunderts (Leipzig, 1897).

A. Beljame, Le Public et les hommes de lettres en Angleterre au dix-huitième siècle (2nd ed., Paris, 1897).

George Saintsbury, A History of Criticism, vol. 2 (New York, 1902).

——, A History of English Criticism (New York, 1911).

For collections of contemporary essays, see J. E. Spingarn, Critical Essays of the Seventeenth Century, 3 vols. (Oxford, 1908–09); W. H. Durham, Critical Essays of the Eighteenth Century (New Haven, 1915); R. M. Alden, Readings in English Prose of the Eighteenth Century (Boston, 1911).

JOHN DRYDEN

John Dryden was born at Aldwinkle, Northamptonshire, in 1631. He came of a Puritan family, which had been for years very active in the political world. Dryden was sent to school at Westminster. He published some verses at the age of eighteen. In 1650 he entered Trinity College, Cambridge, and took a degree of B.A. four years later, but it is probable that he spent also the next three years at Cambridge. He went to London in 1657. His first important literary effort, Heroic Stanzas to the memory of Cromwell, was published in 1659. This was followed the next year by verses on the return of Charles. In order to add to his slender income, he turned to the stage, and after two unsuccessful attempts he produced his first play, The Wild Gallant, in 1663. This comedy was not well received, and Dryden confesses that his forte was not comedy. The same year he produced The Rival Ladies, and married Lady Elizabeth Howard. The Indian Queen (1664), written in collaboration with Sir Robert Howard, his wife's brother, enjoyed considerable success. Dryden followed this with The Indian Emperor (1665). During the Plague Dryden lived with his father-in-law in Wiltshire, where he wrote his Essay of Dramatick Poesie (1668). Howard's preface to his Four New Playes (1665) called forth a reply from Dryden: A Defence of an Essay of Dramatique Poesie (1668). From the re-opening of the theaters in 1666, to 1681, Dryden wrote little except his

plays. The production of Buckingham's satirical play The Rehearsal in 1671, in which Dryden was the chief personage, called forth the preface Of Heroic Plays and Defence of the Epilogue (1672). All for Love, in all probability the poet's greatest play, was performed in 1678. He continued to produce plays to the end of his career. In 1681 he turned to satire and wrote Absalom and Achitophel, which achieved instant and widespread popularity. This was followed by other satires. In 1687, after his conversion to the Catholic Church, he wrote The Hind and the Panther, a plea for Catholicism. His Catholic leanings lost for him the laureateship and other offices when the Revolution came. During his last ten years he translated many of the Latin classics: Vergil, Ovid, Lucretius, Horace, Theocritus, and others, and modernied Chaucer. He died in 1700, and was buried in Westminster Abbey.

Dryden's contribution to English literature, besides his poems and plays, was the invention of a direct and simple style for literary criticism. He improved upon the prose of the Elizabethan writers in the matter of ridding English of its involved forms, even if through that process he lost some of its gorgeous ornament and rugged strength. Jonson's method in criticism was after all not much more than the note-book method of jotting down stray thoughts and opinions and reactions. Dryden elaborated his ideas, sought the weight

of authority, argued both sides of the
question, and adduced proofs. Dryden
performed an inestimable service to his
countrymen in applying true standards
of criticism to the Elizabethans and in
showing them a genuine and sympa-
thetic if occasionally misguided love for
Shakespeare. Dryden also enjoyed the
advantage of being able to bring his
knowledge of the drama of Spain and
France to bear on his criticism of Eng-
lish dramatists, while it has already been
pointed out what debts he owes to Cor-
neille as a critic.

On the drama:

Epistle Dedicatory, in *The Rival Ladies*
   (1664).
An Essay of Dramatick Poesie, with its
   Epistle Dedicatory (1668).
*A Defence of an Essay of Dramatique
   Poesie* (1668).
Dedication to *The Indian Emperor*
   (1667).
Preface to *Secret Love, or, The Maiden
   Queen* (1668).
Preface to *The Wild Gallant* (1669).
Preface to *The Tempest* (1670).
Preface to *Tyrannick Love* (1670).
Preface to *The Mock Astrologer* (1671).
Of Heroick Plays, in *The Conquest of
   Granada* (1672).
Epilogue, and *Defence of the Epilogue*
   to the second part of *The Conquest of
   Granada* (1672).
Epistle Dedicatory in *Marriage a-la-
   Mode* (1673).
Epistle Dedicatory in *The Assignation*
   (1673).
Preface to *The State of Innocence*
   (1675).
Dedication to *Aurengzebe* (1676).
Preface to *All for Love* (1678).
Dedication of *Limberham* (1678).
Preface to *Œdipus* (1679).
Preface to *Troilus and Cressida* (1679).
Dedication of *The Spanish Fryar* (1681).
The Vindication of the Duke de Guise
   (1683).
Preface to *Albion and Albanius* (1685).
Preface to *Don Sebastian* (1690).
Dedication of *Amphitryon* (1690).
Preface to *Cleomenes* (1692).
*A Discourse on the Origin and Progress
   of Satire* (preface to Dryden's and
   others' translation of *Juvenal,* 1693).

Dedication of *Third Part of Poetical
   Miscellanies* (1693).
Dedication of *Love Triumphant* (1694).
A Parallel of Poetry and Painting (in
   Dryden's translation of Du Fresnoy's
   De Arte Graphica, 1695).
Preface to Dryden's son's *The Husband
   his own Cuckold* (1696).
A Discourse on Epick Poetry (preface
   to Dryden's translation of the *Æneid,*
   1697).

Editions:

*The Comedies, Tragedies and Operas
   written by John Dryden, Esq.,* were
published in 2 vols. (London, 1701).
Congreve edited the *Dramatick Works*
in 6 vols. (London, 1717). The first
collected edition of the *Works* was ed-
ited by Sir Walter Scott, 18 vols.
(1808). This edition, revised and cor-
rected by George Saintsbury (18 vols.,
Edinburgh, 1882-93) is the standard.
Edmund Malone edited the prose
works as *Critical and Miscellaneous
Prose Works,* 4 vols. (London, 1800).
The important essays are edited as
Essays of John Dryden, by W. P. Ker,
2 vols. (Oxford, 1900). *The Best
Plays of John Dryden,* 2 vols., edited
by Saintsbury (New York, n.d.) con-
tain numerous essays. *Dramatic Es-
says of John Dryden,* edited by W. H.
Hudson, are published in *Everyman's
Library* (New York, n.d.). There are
annotated editions of the *Essays of
Dramatick Poesie* by T. Arnold (Ox-
ford, 1903), and Von Schunck (New
York, 1899). *Essays on the Drama,*
edited by W. Strunk (1908).

The *Letters* may be consulted for bio-
graphical data. One (No. IX, Malone
ed.) refers to Rymer and his ideas.
The *Heads of an Answer to Rymer*
(1711); and the *Preface to Notes and
Observations on the Empress of Mo-
rocco* (1674, attributed to Dryden),
may be consulted, as well as the *Notes
and Observations,* etc., 2nd edition, by
Settle (1687).

On Dryden and his works:

Prefaces to works cited.
Samuel Johnson, *John Dryden* (in *Lives*

of the Most Eminent English Poets (ed., London, 1871).

T. B. Macaulay, *Dryden* (in *Critical and Miscellaneous Essays,* in *Complete Works,* London, 1879).

George Saintsbury, *John Dryden* (in *English Men of Letters* series, London, 1881).

James Russell Lowell, *Among My Books* (Boston, 1870).

A. Beljame, *Le Public et les hommes de lettres en Angleterre, 1660–1744* (2nd ed., Paris, 1897).

J. Churton Collins, *Essays and Studies* (London, 1895).

F. Bobertag, *Dryden's Theorie des Dramas* (in *Englische Studien,* vol. 4, Heilbronn, 1881).

William E. Bohn, *The Development of John Dryden's Criticism* (in *Modern Language Association Publications,* vol. 22, Cambridge, U. S. A., 1907).

G. S. Collins, *Dryden's Dramatic Theory and Praxis* (Leipzig, 1892).

P. H. Frye, *Dryden and the Critical Canons of the Eighteenth Century* (in *Literary Reviews and Criticisms,* New York, 1908).

F. Ohlsen, *Dryden as a Dramatist and Critic* (Altona, 1883).

Margaret Sherwood, *Dryden's Dramatic Theory and Practice* (New Haven, 1898).

F. Weselmann, *Dryden als Kritiker* (Göttingen, 1893).

R. Garnett, *The Age of Dryden* (London, 1895).

W. J. Courthope, *History of English Poetry,* vols. 3 and 4 (London, 1903).

N. Delius, *Dryden und Shakespeare* (Berlin, 1869).

P. Hamelius, *Die Kritik in der englischer Litteratur der 17. und 18. Jahrhunderts* (Leipzig, 1897).

AN ESSAY OF DRAMATICK POESIE [1]
(1668)

6. Eugenius [2] was going to continue this discourse, when Lisideius [3] told him that it was necessary, before they proceded further, to take a standing measure of their controversy; for how was it possible to be decided who writ the best plays, before we know what a play should be? But, this once agreed on by both parties, each might have recourse to it, either to prove his own advantages, or to discover the failings of his adversary.

He had no sooner said this, but all desired the favor of him to give the definition of a play; and they were the more importunate, because neither Aristotle, nor Horace, nor any other who had writ of that subject, had ever done it.

Lisideius, after some modest denials, at last confessed he had a rude notion of it; indeed, rather a description than a definition; but which served to guide him in his private thoughts, when he was to make a judgment of what others writ: that he conceived a play ought to be, *A just and lively image of human nature, representing its passions and humors, and the changes of fortune to which it is subject, for the delight and instruction of mankind.*

This definition, though Crites [4] raised a logical objection against it — that it was only *genere et fine,* and so not altogether perfect, was yet well received by the rest, Crites, being desired by the company to begin, spoke on behalf of the ancients, in this manner:

" If confidence presage a victory, Eugenius, in his own opinion, has already triumphed over the ancients: nothing seems more easy to him, than to overcome those whom it is our greatest praise to have imitated well; for we do not only build upon their foundations, but by their models. Dramatic Poesy had time enough, reckoning from Thespis (who first invented it) to Aristophanes, to be

---

[1] Re-printed — with omissions of portions not relating to the drama — from the Everyman's Library edition of *Dramatic Essays by John Dryden* (London and New York, n. d.). — Ed.

[2] Generally thought to be Lord Buckhurst.— Ed.

[3] Generally thought to be Sir Charles Sedley. — Ed.

[4] Generally thought to be Sir Robert Howard.— Ed.

born, to grow up, and to flourish in maturity. It has been observed of arts and sciences, that in one and the same century they have arrived to great perfection; and no wonder, since every age has a kind of universal genius, which inclines those that live in it to some particular studies: the work then, being pushed on by many hands, must of necessity go forward.

"Is it not evident, in these last hundred years, when the study of philosophy has been the business of all the virtuosi in Christendom, that almost a new nature has been revealed to us? That more errors of the school have been detected, more useful experiments in philosophy have been made, more noble secrets in optics, medicine, anatomy, astronomy, discovered, than in all those credulous and doting ages from Aristotle to us? — so true it is, that nothing spreads more fast than science, when rightly and generally cultivated.

"Add to this, the more than common emulation that was in those times of writing well; which though it be found in all ages and all persons that pretend to the same reputation, yet poesy, being then in more esteem than now it is, had greater honors decreed to the professors of it, and consequently the rivalship was more high betwen them; they had judges ordained to decide their merit, and prizes to reward it; and historians have been diligent to record of Æschylus, Euripides, Sophocles, Lycophron, and the rest of them, both who they were that vanquished in these wars of the theater, and how often they were crowned: while the Asian kings and Grecian commonwealths scarce afforded them a nobler subject than the unmanly luxuries of a debauched court, or giddy intrigues of a factious city: — *Alit æmulatio ingenia* (says Paterculus), *et nunc invidia, nunc admiratio incitatio nem accendit:* Emulation is the spur of wit; and sometimes envy, sometimes admiration, quickens our endeavors.

"But now, since the rewards of honor are taken away, that virtuous emulation is turned into direct malice; yet so slothful, that it contents itself to condemn and cry down others, without attempting to do better: it is a reputation too unprofitable to take the necessary pains

for it; yet, wishing they had it, that desire is incitement enough to hinder others from it. And this, in short, Eugenius, is the reason why you have now so few good poets, and so many severe judges. Certainly, to imitate the ancients well, much labor and long study is required; which pains, I have already shown, our poets would want encouragement to take, if yet they had ability to go through the work. Those ancients have been faithful imitators and wise observers of that nature which is so torn and ill represented in our plays; they have handed down to us a perfect resemblance of her; which we, like ill copiers, neglecting to look on, have rendered monstrous, and disfigured. But, that you may know how much you are indebted to those your masters, and be ashamed to have so ill requitted them, I must remember you, that all the rules by which we practice the drama at this day (either such as relate to the justness and symmetry of the plot, or the episodical ornaments, such as descriptions, narrations, and other beauties, which are not essential to the play), were delivered to us from the observations which Aristotle made, of those poets, who either lived before him, or were his contemporaries: we have added nothing of our own, except we have the confidence to say our wit is better; of which, none boast in this our age, but such as understand not theirs. Of that book which Aristotle has left us, περὶ τῆς Ποιητικῆς, [*The Poetics*] Horace his *Art of Poetry* is an excellent comment, and, I believe, restores to us that Second Book of his concerning Comedy, which is wanting in him.

"Out of these two have been extracted the famous Rules, which the French call *Des Trois Unités,* or, The Three Unities, which ought to be observed in every regular play; namely, of Time, Place, and Action.

"The unity of time they comprehend in twenty-four hours, the compass of a natural day, or as near as it can be contrived; and the reason of it is obvious to every one, — that the time of the feigned action, or fable of the play, should be proportioned as near as can be to the duration of that time in which it is represented: since, therefore, all plays are acted on the theater in the space of time much within the compass of twenty-four hours, that play is to be thought the nearest imitation of nature, whose plot or action is confined within that time; and, by the same rule which concludes this general proportion of time, it follows, that all the parts of it are (as near as may be) to the equally subdivided; namely, that one act take not up the supposed time of half a day, which is out of proportion to the rest; since the other four are then to be straitened within the compass of the remaining half: for it is unnatural that one act, which being spoke or written is not longer than the rest, should be supposed longer by the audience; it is therefore the poet's duty to take care that no act should be imagined to exceed the time in which it is represented on the stage; and that the intervals and inequalities of time be supposed to fall out between the acts.

"This rule of time, how well it has been observed by the ancients, most of their plays will witness; you see them in their tragedies (wherein to follow this rule is certainly most difficult), from the very beginning of their plays, falling close into that part of the story which they intend for the action or principal object of it, leaving the former part to be delivered by narration: so that they set the audience, as it were, at the post where the race is to be concluded; and, saving them the tedious expectation of seeing the poet set out and ride the beginning of the course, they suffer you not to behold him till he is in sight of the goal, and just upon you.

"For the second unity, which is that of Place, the ancients meant by it, that the scene ought to be continued through the play, in the same place where it was laid in the beginning: for, the stage on which it is represented being but one and the same place, it is unnatural to conceive it many,— and those far distant from one another. I will not deny but, by the variation of painted scenes, the fancy, which in these cases will contribute to its own deceit, may sometimes imagine it several places, with some appearance of probability; yet it still carries the greater likelihood of truth if those places be supposed so near each other as in the same town or city; which may all be comprehended under the larger denomination of one place; for a greater distance will bear no proportion to the shortness of time which is allotted, in the acting, to pass from one of them to another; for the observation of this, next to the ancients, the French are to be most commended. They tie themselves so strictly to the unity of place that you never see in any of their plays a scene changed in the middle of an act: if the act begins in a garden, a street, or chamber, 'tis ended in the same place; and that you may know it to be the same, the stage is so supplied with persons, that it is never empty all the time: he who enters second, has business with him who was on before; and before the second quits the stage, a third appears who has business with him. This Corneille calls *la liaison des scènes*, the continuity or joining of the scenes; and 'tis a good mark of a well-contrived play, when all the persons are known to each other, and every one of them has some affairs with all the rest.

"As for the third unity, which is that of Action, the ancients meant no other by it than what the logicians do by their *finis*, the end or scope of any action; that which is the first in intention, and last in execution: now the poet is to aim at one great and complete action, to the carrying on of which all things in his play, even the very obstacles, are to be subservient; and the reason of this is as evident as any of the former. For two actions, equally labored and driven on by the writer, would destroy the unity of the poem; it would be no longer one play, but two: not but that there may be many actions in a play, as Ben Jonson has observed in his *Discoveries;* but they must be all subservient to the great one, which our language happily expresses in the name of *under-plots:* such as in Terence's *Eunuch* is the difference and reconcilement of Thais and Phædria, which is not the chief business of the play, but promotes the marriage of Chærea and Chremes's sister, principally intended by the poet. There ought to be but one action, says Corneille, that is, one complete action, which leaves the mind of the audience in a full repose; but this cannot be brought to pass but by many other imperfect actions, which conduce to it, and hold the audience in a delightful suspense of what will be.

"If by these rules (to omit many other drawn from the precepts and practice of the ancients) we should judge our modern plays, 'tis probable that few of them would endure the trial: that which should be the business of a day, takes up in some of them an age; instead of one action, they are the epitomes of a man's life; and for one spot of ground, which the stage should represent, we are sometimes in more countries than the map can show us.

"But if we allow the Ancients to have contrived well, we must acknowledge them to have written better. Questionless we are deprived of a great stock of wit in the loss of Menander among the Greek poets, and of Cæcilius, Afranius, and Varius, among the Romans; we may guess at Menander's excellency by the plays of Terence, who translated some of his; and yet wanted so much of him, that he was called by C. Cæsar the half-Menander; and may judge of Varius, by the testimonies of Horace, Martial, and Velleius Paterculus. 'Tis probable that these, could they be recovered, would decide the controversy; but so long as Aristophanes and Plautus are extant, while the tragedies of Euripides, Sophocles, and Seneca, are in our hands, I can never see one of those plays which are now written but it increases my admiration of the ancients. And yet I must acknowledge further, that to admire them as we ought, we should understand them better than we do. Doubtless many things appear flat to us, the wit of which depended on some custom or story, which never came to our knowledge; or perhaps on some criticism in their language, which being so long dead, and only remaining in their books, 'tis not possible they should make us understand perfectly. To read Macrobius, explaining the propriety and elegancy of many words in Vergil, which I had before passed over without consideration as common things, is enough to assure me that I ought to think the same of Terence; and that in the purity of his style (which Tully so much valued that he ever carried his works about him) there is yet left in him great room

for admiration, if I knew but where to place it. In the meantime I must desire you to take notice that the greatest man of the last age, Ben Jonson, was willing to give place to them in all things: he was not only a professed imitator of Horace, but a learned plagiary of all others; you track him everywhere in their snow: if Horace, Lucan, Petronius Arbiter, Seneca, and Juvenal, had their own from him, there are few serious thoughts which are new in him: you will pardon me, therefore, if I presume he loved their fashion, when he wore their clothes. But since I have otherwise a great veneration for him, and you, Eugenius, prefer him above all other poets, I will use no farther argument to you than his example: I will produce before you Father Ben, dressed in all the ornaments and colors of the ancients; you will need no other guide to our party, if you follow him; and whether you consider the bad plays of our age, or regard the good plays of the last, both the best and worst of the modern poets will equally instruct you to admire the ancients."

Crites had no sooner left speaking, but Eugenius, who had waited with some impatience for it, thus began:

"I have observed in your spech, that the former part of it is convincing as to what the moderns have profited by the rules of the ancients; but in the latter you are careful to conceal how much they have excelled them; we own all the helps we have from them, and want neither veneration nor gratitude, while we acknowledge that, to overcome them, we must make use of the advantages we have received from them: but to these assistances we have joined our own industry; for, had we sat down with a dull imitation of them, we might then have lost somewhat of the old perfection, but never acquired any that was new. We draw not therefore after their lines, but those of nature; and having the life before us, besides the experience of all they knew, it is no wonder if we hit some airs and features which they have missed. I deny not what you urge of arts and sciences, that they have flourished in some ages more than others; but your instance in philosophy makes for me: for if natural causes be more known now than in the time of Aristotle, because more studied, it follows that poesy and other arts may, with the same pains, arrive still nearer to perfection; and, that granted, it will rest for you to prove that they wrought more perfect images of human life than we; which seeing in your discourse you have avoided to make good, it shall now be my task to show you some part of their defects, and some few excellencies of the moderns. And I think there is none among us can imagine I do it enviously, or with purpose to detract from them; for what interest or fame or profit can the living lose by the reputation of the dead? On the other side, it is a great truth which Velleius Paterculus affirms: *Audita visis libentius laudamus; et præsentia invidia præterita admiratione prosequimur; et his nos obrui, illis instrui credimus:* that praise or censure is certainly the most sincere, which unbribed posterity shall give us.

"Be pleased then in the first place to take notice that the Greek poesy, which Crites has affirmed to have arrived to perfection in the reign of the old comedy, was so far from it that the distinction of it into acts was not known to them; or if it were, it is yet so darkly delivered to us that we cannot make it out.

"All we know of it is from the singing of their Chorus; and that too is so uncertain, that in some of their plays we have reason to conjecture they sung more than five times. Aristotle indeed divides the integral parts of a play into four. First, the *Protasis,* or entrance, which gives light only to the characters of the persons, and proceeds very little into any part of the action. Secondly, the *Epitasis,* or working up of the plot; where the play grows warmer, the design or action of it is drawing on, and you see something promising that it will come to pass. Thirdly, the *Cantastasis,* called by the Romans, *Status,* the height and full growth of the play: we may call it properly the counter-turn, which destroys that expectation, imbroils the action in new difficulties, and leaves you far distant from that hope in which it found you; as you may have observed in a violent stream resisted by a narrow passage,— it runs round to an eddy, and carries back the waters with more swift-

ness than it brought them on. Lastly, the *Catastrophe,* which the Grecians called λύσις, the French *le dénouement,* and we the discovery, or unraveling of the plot: there you see all things settling again upon their first foundations; and, the obstacles which hindered the design or action of the play once removed, it ends with that resemblance of truth and nature, that the audience are satisfied with the conduct of it. Thus this great man delivered to us the image of a play; and I must confess it is so lively, that from thence much light has been derived to the forming it more perfectly into acts and scenes: but what poet first limited to five the number of the acts, I know not; only we see it so firmly established in the time of Horace, that he gives it for a rule in comedy,— *Neu brevior quinto, neu sit productior actu.* So that you see the Grecians cannot be said to have consummated this art; writing rather by entrances than by acts, and having rather a general indigested notion of a play, than knowing how and where to bestow the particular graces of it.

"But since the Spaniards at this day allow but three acts, which they call *Jornadas,* to a play, and the Italians in many of theirs follow them, when I condemn the ancients, I declare it is not altogether because they have not five acts to every play, but because they have not confined themselves to one certain number: it is building an house without a model; and when they succeeded in such undertakings, they ought to have sacrificed to Fortune, not to the Muses.

"Next, for the plot, which Aristotle called τό μῦθος, and often τῶν πραγμάτων σύνθεσις, and from him the Romans *Fabula;* it has already been judiciously observed by a late writer, that in their tragedies it was only some tale derived from Thebes or Troy, or at least something that happened in those two ages; which was worn so threadbare by the pens of all the epic poets, and even by tradition, itself of the talkative Greeklings (as Ben Jonson calls them), that before it came upon the stage it was already known to all the audience: and the people, so soon as ever they heard the name of Œdipus, knew as well as the poet, that he had killed his father by a mistake, and committed incest with his mother, before the play; that they were now to hear of a great plague, an oracle, and the ghost of Laïus: so that they sat with a yawning kind of expectation, till he was to come with his eyes pulled out, and speak a hundred or more verses in a tragic tone, in complaint of his misfortunes. But one *Œdipus, Hercules,* or *Medea,* had been tolerable: poor people, they escaped not so good cheap; they had still the *chapon bouillé* set before them, till their appetites were cloyed with the same dish, and, the novelty being gone, the pleasure vanished; so that one main end of Dramatic Poesy in its definition, which was to cause delight, was of consequence destroyed.

" In their comedies, the Romans generally borrowed their plots from the Greek poets; and theirs was commonly a little girl stolen or wandered from her parents, brought back unknown to the city, there [falling into the hands of] some young fellow, who, by the help of his servant, cheats his father; and when her time comes, to cry,— *Juno Lucina, fer opem,*— one or other sees a little box or cabinet which was carried away with her, and so discovers her to her friends, if some god do not prevent it, by coming down in a machine, and taking the thanks of it to himself.

" By the plot you may guess much of the characters of the persons. An old father, who would willingly, before he dies, see his son well married; his debauched son, kind in his nature to his mistress, but miserably in want of money; a servant or slave, who has so much wit to strike in with him, and help to dupe his father; a braggadocio captain, a parasite, and a lady of pleasure.

" As for the poor honest maid, on whom the story is built, and who ought to be one of the principal actors in the play, she is commonly a mute in it: she has the breeding of the old Elizabeth way, which was for maids to be seen and not to be heard; and it is enough you know she is willing to be married, when the fifth act requires it.

" These are plots built after the Italian mode of houses,— you see through them all at once: the characters are indeed the imitation of nature, but so narrow, as if they had imitated only an eye

or an hand, and did not dare to venture on the lines of a face, or the proportion of a body.

" But in how strait a compass soever they have bounded their plots and characters, we will pass it by, if they have regularly pursued them, and perfectly observed those three unities of time, place, and action; the knowledge of which you say is derived to us from them. But in the first place give me leave to tell you, that the unity of place, however it might be practiced by them, was never any of their rules: we neither find it in Aristotle, Horace, or any who have written of it, till in our age the French poets first made it a precept of the stage. The unity of time, even Terence himself, who was the best and most regular of them, has neglected: his *Heautontimorumenos,* or *Self-Punisher,* takes up visibly two days, says Scaliger; the two first acts concluding the first day, the three last the day ensuing; and Euripides, in tying himself to one day, has committed an absurdity never to be forgiven him; for in one of his tragedies he has made Theseus go from Athens to Thebes, which was about forty English miles, under the walls of it to give battle, and appear victorious in the next act; and yet, from the time of his departure to the return of the Nuntius, who gives the relation of his victory, Æthra and the Chorus have but thirty-six verses; which is not for every mile a verse.

" The like error is as evident in Terence his *Eunuch,* when Laches, the old man, enters by mistake into the house of Thais; where, betwixt his exit and the entrance of Pythias, who comes to give ample relation of the disorders he has raised within, Parmeno, who was left upon the stage, has not above five lines to speak. *C'est bien employer un temps si court,* says the French poet, who furnished me with one of the observations: and almost all their tragedies will afford us examples of the like nature.

" It is true, they have kept the continuity, or, as you called it, *liaison des scènes,* somewhat better: two do not perpetually come in together, talk, and go out together; and other two succeed them, and do the same throughout the act, which the English call by the name of single scenes; but the reason is, because they have seldom above two or three scenes, properly so called, in every act; for it is to be accounted a new scene, not only every time the stage is empty; but every person who enters, though to others, makes it so; because he introduces a new business. Now the plots of their plays being narrow, and the persons few, one of their acts was written in a less compass than one of our well-wrought scenes; and yet they are often deficient even in this. To go no further than Terence; you find in the *Eunuch,* Antipho entering single in the midst of the third act, after Chremes and Pythias were gone off; in the same play you have likewise Dorias beginning the fourth act alone; and after she had made a relation of what was done at the Soldiers' entertainment (which by the way was very inartificial, because she was presumed to speak directly to the audience, and to acquaint them with what was necessary to be known, but yet should have been so contrived by the poet as to have been told by persons of the drama to one another, and so by them to have come to the knowledge of the people), she quits the stage, and Phædria enters next, alone likewise: he also gives you an account of himself, and of his returning from the country, in monologue; to which unnatural way of narration Terence is subject in all his plays. In his *Adelphi,* or *Brothers,* Syrus and Demea enter after the scene was broken by the departure of Sostrata, Geta, and Canthara; and indeed you can scarce look unto any of his comedies, where you will not presently discover the same interruption.

"But as they have failed both in laying of their plots, and in the management, swerving from the rules of their own art by misrepresenting nature to us, in which they have ill satisfied one intention of a play, which was delight; so in the instructive part they have erred worse: instead of punishing vice and rewarding virtue, they have often shewn a prosperous wickedness, and an unhappy piety: they have set before us a bloody image of revenge in Medea, and given her dragons to convey her safe from punishment, a Priam and Astyanax murdered, and Cassandra ravished, and the lust and murder ending in the victory of him who acted them: in short, there is no indecorum in any of our modern plays, which if I would excuse, I could not shadow with some authority from the ancients. . . .

"But, to return from whence I have digressed, to the consideration of the ancients' writing, and their wit (of which by this time you will grant us in some measure to be fit judges). Though I see many excellent thoughts in Seneca, yet he of them who had a genius most proper for the stage, was Ovid; he had a way of writing so fit to stir up a pleasing admiration and concernment, which are the objects of a tragedy, and to show the various movements of a soul combating betwixt two different passions, that, had he lived in our age, or in his own could have writ with our advantages, no man but must have yielded to him; and therefore I am confident the *Medea* is none of his: for, though I esteem it for the gravity and sententiousness of it, which he himself concludes to be suitable to a tragedy,— *Omne genus scripti gravitate tragœdia vincit,*— yet it moves not my soul enough to judge that he, who in the epic way wrote things so near the drama as the story of Myrrha, or Caunus and Biblis, and the rest, should stir up no more concernment where he most endeavored it. The masterpiece of Seneca I hold to be that scene in the *Troades* where Ulysses is seeking for Astyanax to kill him: there you see the tenderness of a mother so represented in Andromache, that it raises compassion to a high degree in the reader, and bears the nearest resemblance of anything in the tragedies of the ancients to the excellent scenes of passion in Shakspeare, or in Fletcher: for love-scenes, you will find few among them; their tragic poets dealt not with that soft passion, but with lust, cruelty, revenge, ambition, and those bloody actions they produced; which were more capable of raising horror than compassion in an audience: leaving love untouched, whose gentleness would have tempered them; which is the most frequent of all the passions, and which, being the private concernment of every person, is soothed by viewing its own image in a public entertainment.

"Among their comedies, we find a scene or two of tenderness, and that where you would least expect it, in Plautus; but to speak generally, their lovers say little, when they see each other, but *anima vita mea;* Ζωὴ καὶ ψυχῆ, as the women in Juvenal's time used to cry out in the fury of their kindness. Any sudden gust of passion (as an ecstasy of love in an unexpected meeting) cannot better be expressed than in a word and a sigh, breaking one another. Nature is dumb on such occasions; and to make her speak would be to represent her unlike herself. But there are a thousand other concernments of lovers, as jealousies, complaints, contrivances, and the like, where not to open their minds at large to each other, were to be wanting to their own love, and to the expectation of the audience; who watch the movements of their minds, as much as the changes of their fortunes. For the imaging of the first is properly the work of a poet; the latter he borrows from the historian."

Eugenius was proceeding in that part of his discourse, when Crites interrupted him. "I see," said he, "Eugenius and I are never like to have this question decided betwixt us; for he maintains the moderns have acquired a new perfection in writing; I can only grant they have altered the mode of it. Homer described his heroes men of great appetites, lovers of beef broiled upon the coals, and good fellows; contrary to the practice of the French Romances, whose heroes neither eat, nor drink, nor sleep, for love. Vergil makes Æneas a bold avower of his own virtues:

Sum pius Æneas, fama super æthera notus;

which, in the civility of our poets is the character of a fanfaron or Hector: for with us the knight takes occasion to walk out, or sleep, to avoid the vanity of telling his own story, which the trusty 'squire is ever to perform for him. So in their love-scenes, of which Eugenius spoke last, the ancients were more hearty, were more talkative: they writ love as it was then the mode to make it; and I will grant thus much to Eugenius, that perhaps one of their poets had he lived in our age, *si foret hoc nostrum fato delapsus in ævum* (as Horace says of Lucilius), he had altered many things; not that they were not natural before, but that he might accommodate himself to the age

in which he lived. Yet in the meantime, we are not to conclude anything rashly against those great men, but preserve to them the dignity of masters, and give that honor to their memories, *quos Libitina sacravit,* part of which we expect may be paid to us in future times."

This moderation of Crites, as it was pleasing to all the company, so it put an end to that dispute; which Eugenius, who seemed to have the better of the argument, would urge no farther: but Lisideius, after he had acknowledged himself of Eugenius his opinion concerning the ancient, yet told him, he had forborne, till his discourse were ended, to ask him why he preferred the English plays above those of other nations? and whether we ought not to submit our stage to the exactness of our next neighbors?

"Though," said Eugenius, "I am at all times ready to defend the honor of my country against the French, and to maintain, we are as well able to vanquish them with our pens, as our ancestors have been with their swords; yet, if you please," added he, looking upon Neander,[5] "I will commit this cause to my friend's management; his opinion of our plays is the same with mine, and besides, there is no reason, that Crites and I, who have now left the stage, should reënter so suddenly upon it; which is against the laws of comedy."

"If the question had been stated," replied Lisideius, "who had writ best, the French or English, forty years ago, I should have been of your opinion, and adjudged the honor to our own nation; but since that time" (said he, turning towards Neander), "we have been so long together bad Englishmen that we had not leisure to be good poets. Beaumont, Fletcher, and Jonson (who were only capable of bringing us to that degree of perfection which we have), were just then leaving the world; as if in an age of so much horror, wit, and those milder studies of humanity, had no farther business among us. But the Muses, who ever follow peace, went to plant in another country: it was then that the great Cardinal Richelieu began to take them into his protection; and that, by his

5 Generally thought to be Dryden.— Ed.

encouragement, Corneille, and some other Frenchmen, reformed their theater (which before was as much below ours, as it now surpasses it and the rest of Europe). But because Crites in his discourse for the ancients has prevented me, by observing many rules of the stage which the moderns have borrowed from them, I shall only, in short, demand of you, whether you are not convinced that of all nations the French have best observed them? In the unity of time you find them so scrupulous that it yet remains a dispute among their poets, whether the artificial day of twelve hours, more or less, be not meant by Aristotle, rather than the natural one of twenty-four; and consequently, whether all plays ought not to be reduced into that compass. This I can testify, that in all their dramas writ within these last twenty years and upwards, I have not observed any that have extended the time to thirty hours: in the unity of place they are full as scrupulous; for many of their critics limit it to that very spot of ground where the play is supposed to begin; none of them exceed the compass of the same town or city. The unity of action in all plays is yet more conspicuous; for they do not burden them with under-plots, as the English do: which is the reason why many scenes of our tragi-comedians carry on a design that is nothing of kin to the main plot; and that we see two distinct webs in a play, like those in ill-wrought stuffs; and two actions, that is, two plays, carried on together, to the confounding of the audience; who, before they are warm in their concernments for one part, are diverted to another; and by that means espouse the interest of neither. From hence likewise it arises that the one half of our actors are not known to the other. They keep their distances, as if they were Montagues and Capulets, and seldom begin an acquaintance till the last scene of the fifth act, when they are all to meet upon the stage. There is no theater in the world has anything so absurd as the English tragi-comedy; 'tis a drama of our own invention, and the fashion of it is enough to proclaim it so; here a course of mirth, there another of sadness and passion, and a third of honor and a duel: thus, in two hours and a half, we run through all the fits of Bedlam. The French affords you so much variety on the same day, but they do it not so unseasonably, or *mal à propos,* as we: our poets present you the play and the farce together; and our stages still retain somewhat of the original civility of the Red Bull:

Atque ursum et pugiles media inter carmina poscunt.

The end of tragedies or serious plays, says Aristotle, is to beget admiration, compassion, or concernment; but are not mirth and compassion things incompatible? and is it not evident that the poet must of necessity destroy the former by intermingling of the latter? that is, he must ruin the sole end and object of his tragedy, to introduce somewhat that is forced into it, and is not of the body of it. Would you not think that physician mad, who, having prescribed a purge, should immediately order you take restringents?

" But to leave our plays, and return to theirs. I have noted one great advantage they have had in the plotting of their tragedies; that is, they are always grounded upon some known history: according to that of Horace, *Ex noto fictum carmen sequar;* and in that they have so imitated the ancients that they have surpassed them. For the ancients, as was observed before, took for the foundation of their plays some poetical fiction, such as under that consideration could move but little concernment in the audience, because they already knew the event of it. But the French goes farther:

Atque ita menitur, sic veris falsa remiscet Primo ne medium, medio ne discrepet imum.

He so interweaves truth with probable fiction that he puts a pleasing fallacy upon us; mends the intrigues of fate, and dispenses with the severity of history, to reward that virtue which has been rendered to us there unfortunate. Sometimes the story has left the success so doubtful that the writer is free, by the privilege of a poet, to take that which of two or more relations will best suit with his design: as for example, in the death of Cyrus, whom Justin and some others report to have perished in the Scythian war, but Xenophon affirms to have died in his bed of extreme old age. Nay more, when the event is past dispute, even then we are willing to be deceived, and the poet, if he contrives it with appearance of truth, has all the audience of his party; at least during the time his play is acting: so naturally we are kind to virtue, when our own interest is not in question, that we take it up as the general concernment of mankind. On the other side, if you consider the historical plays of Shakspeare, they are rather so many chronicles of kings, or the business many times of thirty or forty years, cramped into a representation of two hours and a half; which is not to imitate or paint nature, but rather to draw her in miniature, to take her in little; to look upon her through the wrong end of a perspective, and receive her images not only much less, but infinitely more imperfect than the life: this, instead of making a play delightful, renders it ridiculous: —

Quodcunque ostendis mihi sic, incredulus odi.

For the spirit of man cannot be satisfied but with truth, or at least verisimility; and a poem is to contain, if not τὰ ἔτυμα, yet ἐτύμοισιν ὁμοῖα, as one of the Greek poets has expressed it.

"Another thing in which the French differ from us. and from the Spaniards, is that they do not embarrass or cumber themselves with too much plot; they only represent so much of a story as will constitute one whole and great action sufficient for a play; we, who undertake more, do but multiply adventures which, not being produced from one another, as effects from causes, but rarely following, constitute many actions in the drama, and consequently make it many plays.

"But by pursuing closely one argument, which is not cloyed with many turns, the French have gained more liberty for verse, in which they write; they have leisure to dwell on a subject which deserves it; and to represent the passions (which we have acknowledged to be the poet's work), without being hurried from one thing to another, as we are in the plays of Calderon, which we have seen lately upon our theaters under the name of Spanish plots. I have taken notice but of one tragedy of ours whose plot has that uniformity and unity of design in it, which I have commended in the French; and that is *Rollo,* or rather, under the name of Rollo, the Story of Bassianus and Geta in Herodian: there indeed the plot is neither large nor intricate, but just enough to fill the minds of the audience, not to cloy them. Besides, you see it founded upon the truth of history,— only the time of the action is not reducible to the strictness of the rules; and you see in some places a little farce mingled, which is below the dignity of the other parts, and in this all our poets are extremely peccant: even Ben Jonson himself, in *Sejanus* and *Catiline,* has given us this oleo of a play, this unnatural mixture of comedy and tragedy; which to me sounds just as ridiculously as the history of David with the merry humors of Golia's. In *Sejanus* you may take notice of the scene betwixt Livia and the physician which is a pleasant satire upon the artificial helps of beauty: in *Catiline* you may see the parliament of women; the little envies of them to one another; and all that passes betwixt Curio and Fulvia: scenes admirable in their kind, but of an ill mingle with the rest.

"But I return again to the French writers, who, as I have said, do not burden themselves too much with plot, which has been reproached to them by an ingenious person of our nation as a fault; for, he says, they commonly make but one person considerable in a play; they dwell on him, and his concernments, while the rest of the persons are only subservient to set him off. If he intends this by it,— that there is one person in the play who is of greater dignity than the rest, he must tax, not only theirs, but those of the ancients and, which he would be loth to do, the best of ours; for it is impossible but that one person must be more conspicuous in it than any other, and consequently the greatest share in the action must devolve on him. We see it so in the management of all affairs; even in the most equal aristocracy, the balance cannot be so justly poised but some one will be superior to the rest, either in parts, fortune, interest, or the consideration of some glorious exploit; which will reduce the greatest part of business into his hands.

"But, if he would have us to imagine, that in exalting one character the rest of them are neglected, and that all of them have not some share or other in the action of the play, I desire him to produce any of Corneille's tragedies, wherein every person, like so many servants in a well-governed family, has not some employment, and who is not necessary to the carrying on of the plot, or at least to your understanding it.

"There are indeed some protatic persons in the ancients, whom they make use of in their plays, either to hear or give the relation: but the French avoid this with great address, making their narrations only to, or by such, who are some way interested in the main design. And now I am speaking of relations, I cannot take a fitter opportunity to add this in favor of the French, that they often use them with better judgment and more à propos than the English do. Not that I commend narrations in general,— but there are two sorts of them. One, of those things which are antecedent to the play, and are related to make the conduct of it more clear to us. But 'tis a fault to choose such subjects for the stage as will force us on that rock because we see they are seldom listened to by the audience and that is many times the ruin of the play; for, being once let pass without attention, the audience can never recover themselves to understand the plot: and indeed it is somewhat unreasonable that they should be put to so much trouble, as that, to comprehend what passes in their sight, they must have recourse to what was done, perhaps, ten or twenty years ago.

"But there is another sort of relations, that is, of things happening in the action of the play, and supposed to be done behind the scenes; and this is many times both convenient and beautiful; for by it the French avoid the tumult to which we are subject in England, by representing duels, battles, and the like; which renders our stage too like the theaters where they fight prizes. For what is more ridiculous than to represent an army with a drum and five men behind it; all which

the hero of the other side is to drive in before him; or to see a duel fought, and one slain with two or three thrusts of the foils, which we know are so blunted that we might give a man an hour to kill another in good earnest with them.

"I have observed that in all our tragedies, the audience cannot forbear laughing when the actors are to die; it is the most comic part of the whole play. All *passions* may be lively represented on the stage, if to the well-writing of them the actor supplies a good commanded voice, and limbs that move easily, and without stiffness; but there are many *actions* which can never be imitated to a just height: dying especially is a thing which none but a Roman gladiator could naturally perform on the stage, when he did not imitate or represent, but do it; and therefore it is better to omit the representation of it.

"The words of a good writer, which describe it lively, will make a deeper impression of belief in us than all the actor can insinuate into us, when he seems to fall dead before us; as a poet in the description of a beautiful garden, or a meadow, will please our imagination more than the place itself can please our sight. When we see death represented, we are convinced it is but fiction; but when we hear it related, our eyes, the strongest witnesses, are wanting, which might have undeceived us; and we are all willing to favor the sleight, when the poet does not too grossly impose on us. They therefore who imagine these relations would make no concernment in the audience, are deceived, by confounding them with the other, which are of things antecedent to the play: those are made often in cold blood, as I may say, to the audience; but these are warmed with our concernments, which were before awakened in the play. What the philosophers say of motion, that, when it is once begun, it continues of itself, and will do so to eternity, without some stop put to it, is clearly true on this occasion: the soul being already moved with the characters and fortunes of those imaginary persons, continues going of its own accord; and we are no more weary to hear what becomes of them when they are not on the stage, than we are to listen to the news of an absent mistress. But it is objected, that if one part of the play may be related, then why not all? I answer, some parts of the action are more fit to be represented, some to be related. Corneille says judiciously that the poet is not obliged to expose to view all particular actions which conduce to the principal: he ought to select such of them to be seen, which will appear with the greatest beauty, either by the magnificence of the show, or the vehemence of passions which they produce, or some other charm which they have in them; and let the rest arrive to the audience by narration. 'Tis a great mistake in us to believe the French present no part of the action on the stage; every alteration or crossing of a design, every new-sprung passion, and turn of it, is a part of the action, and much the noblest, except we conceive nothing to be action till the players come to blows; as if the painting of the hero's mind were not more properly the poet's work than the strength of his body. Nor does this anything contradict the opinion of Horace, where he tells us,

Segnius irritant animos demissa per aurem,
Quam quæ sunt oculis subjecta fidelibus.

For he says immediately after,

　　　　　Non tamen intus
Digna geri promes in scenam; *multaq;* tolles
Ex oculis, quæ mox narret facundia præsens.

Among which many he recounts some:

Nec pueros coram populo Medea trucidet,
Aut in avem Progne mutetur, Cadmus in anguem, etc.

That is, those actions which by reason of their cruelty will cause aversion in us, or by reason of their impossibility, unbelief, ought either wholly to be avoided by a poet, or only delivered by narration. To which we may have leave to add, such as, to avoid tumult (as was before hinted), or to reduce the plot into a more reasonable compass of time, or for defect of beauty in them, are rather to be related than presented to the eye. Examples of all these kinds are frequent, not only among all the ancients, but in the best received of our English poets. We find Ben Jonson using them in his *Magnetic Lady,* where one comes out from dinner, and relates the quarrels and disorders of it, to save the undecent appearance of them on the stage, and to abbreviate the story; and this in express imitation of Terence, who had done the same before him in his *Eunuch,* where Pythias makes the like relation of what had happened within at the Soldiers' entertainment. The relations likewise of Sejanus's death, and the prodigies before it, are remarkable; the one of which was hid from sight, to avoid the horror and tumult of the representation; the other, to shun the introducing of things impossible to be believed. In that excellent play, *A King and no King,* Fletcher goes yet farther; for the whole unraveling of the plot is done by narration in the fifth act, after the manner of the ancients; and it moves great concernment in the audience, though it be only a relation of what was done many years before the play. I could multiply other instances, but these are sufficient to prove that there is no error in choosing a subject which requires this sort of narrations; in the ill management of them, there may.

"But I find I have been too long in this discourse, since the French have many other excellencies not common to us; as that you never see any of their plays end with a conversion, or simple change of will, which is the ordinary way which our poets use to end theirs. It shows little art in the conclusion of a dramatic poem, when they who have hindered the felicity during the four acts, desist from it in the fifth, without some powerful cause to take them off their design; and though I deny not but such reasons may be found, yet it is a path that is cautiously to be trod, and the poet is to be sure he convinces the audience that the motive is strong enough. As for example, the conversion of the Usurer in *The Scornful Lady* seems to me a little forced; for, being an Usurer, which implies a lover of money to the highest degree of covetousness,— and such the poet has represented him,— the account he gives for the sudden change is, that he has been duped by the wild young fellow; which in reason might render him more wary another time, and make him punish himself with harder fare and coarser clothes, to get up again what he had lost: but that he should look on it as a judgment, and so repent, we may expect to hear in a sermon, but I should never endure it in a play.

" I pass by this; neither will I insist on the care they take that no person after his first entrance shall ever appear, but the business which brings him upon the stage shall be evident; which rule, if observed, must needs render all the events in the play more natural; for there you see the probability of every accident, in the cause that produced it; and that which appears chance in the play, will seem so reasonable to you, that you will there find it almost necessary: so that in the exit of the actor you have a clear account of his purpose and design in the next entrance (though, if the scene be well wrought, the event will commonly deceive you); for there is nothing so absurd, says Corneille, as for an actor to leave the stage only because he has no more to say.

.   .   .   .   .

Lisideius concluded in this manner; and Neander, after a little pause, thus answered him:

" I shall grant Lisideius, without much dispute, a great part of what he has urged against us; for I acknowledge that the French contrive their plots more regularly, and observe the laws of comedy, and decorum of the stage (to speak generally), with more exactness than the English. Farther, I deny not but he has taxed us justly in some irregularities of ours, which he has mentioned; yet, after all, I am of opinion that neither our faults nor their virtues are considerable enough to place them above us.

" For the lively imitation of nature being in the definition of a play, those which best fulfill that law ought to be esteemed superior to the others. 'Tis true, those beauties of the French poesy are such as will raise perfection higher where it is, but are not sufficient to give it where it is not: they are indeed the beauties of a statue, but not of a man, because not animated with the soul of poesy, which is imitation of humor and passions: and this Lisideius himself, or

any other, however biassed to their party, cannot but acknowledge, if he will either compare the humors of our comedies, or the characters of our serious plays, with theirs. He who will look upon theirs which have been written till these last ten years, or thereabouts, will find it a hard matter to pick out two or three passable humors amongst them. Corneille himself, their arch-poet, what has he produced except *The Liar*, and you know how it was cried up in France; but when it came upon the English stage, though well translated, and that part of Dorante acted to so much advantage as I am confident it never received in its own country, the most favorable to it would not put it in competition with many of Fletcher's or Ben Jonson's. In the rest of Corneille's comedies you have little humor; he tells you himself, his way is, first to show two lovers in good intelligence with each other; in the working up of the play to embroil them by some mistake, and in the latter end to clear it, and reconcile them.

" But of late years Molière, the younger Corneille, Quinault, and some others, have been imitating afar off the quick turns and graces of the English stage. They have mixed their serious plays with mirth, like our tragi-comedies, since the death of Cardinal Richelieu; which Lisideius and many others not observing, have commended that in them for a virtue which they themselves no longer practice. Most of their new plays are, like some of ours, derived from the Spanish novels. There is scarce one of them without a veil, and a trusty Diego, who drolls much after the rate of *The Adventures*. But their humors, if I may grace them with that name, are so thin-sown, that never above one of them comes up in any play. I dare take upon me to find more variety of them in some one play of Ben Jonson's than in all theirs together; as he who has seen *The Alchemist, The Silent Woman*, or *Bartholomew Fair*, cannot but acknowledge with me.

" I grant the French have performed what was possible on the ground-work of the Spanish plays; what was pleasant before, they have made regular: but there is not above one good play to be writ on all those plots; they are too much alike to please often; which we need not the experience of our own stage to justify. As for their new way of mingling mirth with serious plot, I do not, with Lisideius, condemn the thing, though I cannot approve their manner of doing it. He tells us, we cannot so speedily recollect ourselves after a scene of great passion and concernment, as to pass to another of mirth and humor, and to enjoy it with any relish: but why should he imagine the soul of man more heavy than his senses? Does not the eye pass from an unpleasant object to a pleasant in a much shorter time than is required to this? and does not the unpleasantness of the first commend the beauty of the latter? The old rule of logic might have convinced him, that contraries, when placed near, set off each other. A continued gravity keeps the spirit too much bent; we must refresh it sometimes, as we bait in a journey that we may go on with greater ease. A scene of mirth, mixed with tragedy, has the same effect upon us which our music has betwixt the acts; which we find a relief to us from the best plots and language of the stage, if the discourses have been long. I must therefore have stronger arguments, ere I am convinced that compassion and mirth in the same subject destroy each other; and in the meantime cannot but conclude, to the honor of our nation, that we have invented, increased, and perfected a more pleasant way of writing for the stage than was ever known to the ancients or moderns of any nation, which is tragi-comedy.

"And this leads me to wonder why Lisideius and many others should cry up the barrenness of the French plots above the variety and copiousness of the English. Their plots are single; they carry on one design, which is pushed forward by all the actors, every scene in the play contributing and moving towards it. Our plays, besides the main design, have under-plots or by-concernments, of less considerable persons and intrigues, which are carried on with the motion of the main plot: as they say the orb of the fixed stars, and those of the planets, though they have motions of their own, are whirled about by the motion of the *primum mobile,* in which they are contained. That similitude expresses much of the English stage; for if contrary motions may be found in nature to agree; if a planet can go east and west at the same time; — one way by virtue of his own motion, the other by the force of the first mover; — it will not be difficult to imagine how the under-plot, which is only different, not contrary to the great design, may naturally be conducted along with it.

"Eugenius has already shown us, from the confession of the French poets, that the unity of action is sufficiently preserved, if all the imperfect actions of the play are conducing to the main design; but when those petty intrigues of a play are so ill ordered, that they have no coherence with the other, I must grant that Lisideius has reason to tax that want of due connection; for coördination in a play is as dangerous and unnatural as in a state. In the meantime he must acknowledge, our variety, if well ordered, will afford a greater pleasure to the audience.

"As for his other argument, that by pursuing one single theme they gain an advantage to express and work up the passions, I wish any example he could bring from them would make it good; for I confess their verses are to me the coldest I have ever read. Neither, indeed, is it possible for them, in the way they take, so to express passion, as that the effects of it should appear in the concernment of an audience, their speeches being so many declamations, which tire us with the length; so that instead of persuading us to grieve for their imaginary heroes, we are concerned for our own trouble, as we are in tedious visits of bad company; we are in pain till they are gone. When the French stage came to be reformed by Cardinal Richelieu, those long harangues were introduced to comply with the gravity of a churchman. Look upon the *Cinna* and the *Pompey;* they are not so properly to be called plays, as long discourses of reason of state; and *Polyeucte* in matters of religion is as solemn as the long stops upon our organs. Since that time it is grown into a custom, and their actors speak by the hour-glass, like our parsons; nay, they account it the grace of their parts, and think themselves disparaged by the poet, if they may not twice or thrice in a play entertain the audience with a speech of an hundred lines. I deny not but this may suit well enough with the French; for as we, who are a more sullen people, come to be diverted at our plays, so they, who are of an airy and gay temper, come thither to make themselves more serious: and this I conceive to be one reason why comedies are more pleasing to us, and tragedies to them. But to speak generally: it cannot be denied that short speeches and replies are more apt to move the passions and beget concernment in us, than the other; for it is unnatural for any one in a gust of passion to speak long together, or for another in the same condition to suffer him, without interruption. Grief and passion are like floods raised in little brooks by a sudden rain; they are quickly up; and if the concernment be poured unexpectedly in upon us, it overflows us: but a long sober shower gives them leisure to run out as they came in, without troubling the ordinary current. As for comedy, repartee is one of its chiefest graces; the greatest pleasure of the audience is a chase of wit, kept up on both sides, and swiftly managed. And this our forefathers, if not we, have had in Fletcher's plays, to a much higher degree of perfection than the French poets can reasonably hope to reach.

"There is another part of Lisideius his discourse, in which he rather excused our neighbors than commended them; that is, for aiming only to make one person considerable in their plays. 'Tis very true what he has urged, that one character in all plays, even without the poet's care, will have advantage of all the others; and that the design of the whole drama will chiefly depend on it. But this hinders not that there may be more shining characters in the play: many persons of a second magnitude, nay, some so very near, so almost equal to the first, that greatness may be opposed to greatness, and all the persons be made considerable, not only by their quality, but their action. 'Tis evident that the more the persons are, the greater will be the variety of the plot. If then the parts are managed so regularly, that the beauty of the whole be kept entire, and that the variety become not a perplexed and confused mass of accidents, you will find it infinitely pleasing to be led in a labyrinth of de-

sign, where you see some of your way before you, yet discern not the end till you arrive at it. And that all this is practicable, I can produce for examples many of our English plays: as *The Maid's Tragedy*, *The Alchemist*, *The Silent Woman*: I was going to have named *The Fox*, but that the unity of design seems not exactly observed in it: for there appear two actions in the play; the first naturally ending with the fourth act; the second forced from it in the fifth; which yet is the less to be condemned in him, because the disguise of Volpone, though it suited not with his character as a crafty or covetous person, agreed well enough with that of a voluptuary; and by it the poet gained the end at which he aimed, the punishment of vice, and the reward of virtue, both which that disguise produced. So that to judge equally of it, it was an excellent fifth act, but not so naturally proceeding from the former.

"But to leave this, and pass to the latter part of Lisideius his discourse, which concerns relations: I must acknowledge with him, that the French have reason to hide that part of the action which would occasion too much tumult on the stage, and to choose rather to have it made known by narration to the audience. Farther, I think it very convenient, for the reasons he has given, that all incredible actions were removed; but whether custom has so insinuated itself into our countrymen, or nature has so formed them to fierceness, I know not; but they will scarcely suffer combats and other objects of horror to be taken from them. And indeed, the indecency of tumults is all which can be objected against fighting: for why may not our imagination as well suffer itself to be deluded with the probability of it, as with any other thing in the play? For my part, I can with as great ease persuade myself that the blows are given in good earnest, as I can that they who strike them are kings or princes, or those persons which they represent. For objects of incredibility,— I would be satisfied from Lisideius, whether we have any so removed from all appearance of truth, as are those of Corneille's *Andromède*; a play which has been frequented the most of any he has writ. If the Perseus, or the son of a heathen god, the Pegasus, and the Monster, were not capable to choke a strong belief, let him blame any representation of ours hereafter. Those indeed were objects of delight; yet the reason is the same as to the probability: for he makes it not a ballet or masque, but a play, which is to resemble truth. But for death, that it ought not to be represented, I have, besides the arguments alleged by Lisideius, the authority of Ben Jonson, who has forborne it in his tragedies; for both the death of Sejanus and Catiline are related: though in the latter I cannot but observe one irregularity of that great poet; he has removed the scene in the same act from Rome to Catiline's army, and from thence again to Rome; and besides, has allowed a very inconsiderable time, after Catiline's speech, for the striking of the battle, and the return of Petreius, who is to relate the event of it to the senate: which I should not animadvert on him, who was otherwise a painful observer of τὸ πρέπον, or the *decorum* of the stage, if he had not used extreme severity in his judgment on the incomparable Shakspeare for the same fault.— To conclude on this subject of relations; if we are to be blamed for showing too much of the action, the French are as faulty for discovering too little of it: a mean betwixt both should be observed by every judicious writer, so as the audience may neither be left unsatisfied by not seeing what is beautiful, or shocked by beholding what is either incredible or undecent.

" I hope I have already proved in this discourse, that though we are not altogether so punctual as the French in observing the laws of comedy, yet our errors are so few, and little, and those things wherein we excel them so considerable, that we ought of right to be preferred before them. But what will Lisideius say, if they themselves acknowledge they are too strictly bounded by those laws, for breaking which he has blamed the English? I will allege Corneille's words, as I find them in the end of his *Discourse of the Three Unities:* ' Il est facile aux spéculatifs d'estre sévères,' etc. 'Tis easy for speculative persons to judge severely; but if they would produce to public view ten or twelve pieces of this nature, they would perhaps give more latitude to the rules than I have done, when by experience they had known how much we are limited and constrained by them, and how many beauties of the stage they banished from it.' To illustrate a little what he has said: By their servile observations of the unities of time and place, and integrity of scenes, they have brought on themselves that dearth of plot, and narrowness of imagination, which may be observed in all their plays. How many beautiful accidents might naturally happen in two or three days, which cannot arrive with any probability in the compass of twenty-four hours? There is time to be allowed also for maturity of design, which, amongst great and prudent persons, such as are often represented in tragedy, cannot, with any likelihood of truth, be brought to pass at so short a warning. Farther; by tying themselves strictly to the unity of place, and unbroken scenes, they are forced many times to omit some beauties which cannot be shown where the act began; but might, if the scene were interrupted, and the stage cleared for the persons to enter in another place; and therefore the French poets are often forced upon absurdities; for if the act begins in a chamber, all the persons in the play must have some business or other to come thither, or else they are not to be shown that act; and sometimes their characters are very unfitting to appear there: as, suppose it were the king's bed-chamber; yet the meanest man in the tragedy must come and dispatch his business there, rather than in the lobby or courtyard (which is fitter for him), for fear the stage should be cleared, and the scenes broken. Many times they fall by it in a greater inconvenience; for they keep their scenes unbroken, and yet change the place; as in one of their newest plays, where the act begins in the street. There a gentleman is to meet his friend; he sees him with his man, coming out from his father's house; they talk together, and the first goes out: the second, who is a lover, has made an appointment with his mistress; she appears at the window, and then we are to imagine the scene lies under it. This gentleman is called away, and leaves his servant with his mistress; presently her father is heard from within; the young lady is afraid the serving-man should be discovered, and thrusts him into a place of safety, which is supposed to be her closet. After this, the father enters to the daughter, and now the scene is in a house; for he is seeking from one room to another for this poor Philipin, or French Diego, who is heard from within, drolling and breaking many a miserable conceit on the subject of his sad condition. In this ridiculous manner the play goes forward, the stage being never empty all the while: so that the street, the window, the houses, and the closet, are made to walk about, and the persons to stand still. Now what, I beseech you, is more easy than to write a regular French play, or more difficult than to write an irregular English one, like those of Fletcher, or of Shakspeare?

" If they content themselves, as Corneille did, with some flat design, which, like an ill riddle, is found out ere it be half proposed, such plots we can make every way regular, as easily as they; but whenever they endeavor to rise to any quick turns and counterturns of plot, as some of them have attempted, since Corneille's plays have been less in vogue, you see they write as irregularly as we, though they cover it more speciously. Hence the reason is perspicuous why no French plays, when translated, have, or ever can succeed on the English stage. For, if you consider the plots, our own are fuller of variety; if the writing, ours are more quick and fuller of spirit; and therefore 'tis a strange mistake in those who decry the way of writing plays in verse, as if the English therein imitated the French. We have borrowed nothing from them; our plots are weaved in English looms: we endeavor therein to follow the variety and greatness of characters which are derived to us from Shakespeare and Fletcher; the copiousness and well-knitting of the intrigues we have from Jonson; and for the verse itself we have English precedents of elder date than any of Corneille's plays. Not to name our old comedies before Shakespeare, which were all writ in verse of six feet, or Alexandrines, such as the French now use,—I can show in Shakespeare many scenes of rhyme together, and the like in Ben Jonson's tragedies: in *Catiline* and *Sejanus* sometimes thirty

or forty lines,— I mean besides the Chorus, or the monologues; which, by the way, showed Ben no enemy to this way of writing, especially if you read his *Sad Shepherd,* which goes sometimes on rhyme, sometimes on blank verse, like an horse who eases himself on trot and amble. You find him likewise commending Fletcher's pastoral of *The Faithful Shepherdess,* which is for the most part rhyme, though not refined to that purity to which it hath since been brought. And these examples are enough to clear us from a servile imitation of the French.

" But to return whence I have digressed: I dare boldly affirm these two things of the English drama;— First, that we have many plays of ours as regular as any of theirs, and which, besides, have more variety of plot and characters; and secondly, that in most of the irregular plays of Shakspeare or Fletcher (for Ben Jonson's are for the most part regular), there is a more masculine fancy and greater spirit in the writing than there is in any of the French. I could produce, even in Shakspeare's and Fletcher's works, some plays which are almost exactly formed; as *The Merry Wives of Windsor,* and *The Scornful Lady:* but because (generally speaking) Shakspeare, who writ first, did not perfectly observe the laws of comedy, and Fletcher, who came nearer to perfection, yet through carelessness made many faults.

" If this comedy and some others of his were translated into French prose (which would now be no wonder to them, since Molière has lately given them plays out of verse, which have not displeased them), I believe the controversy would soon be decided betwixt the two nations, even making them the judges. But we need not call our heroes to our aid. Be it spoken to the honor of the English, our nation can never want in any age such who are able to dispute the empire of wit with any people in the universe. And though the fury of a civil war, and power for twenty years together abandoned to a barbarous race of men, enemies of all good learning, had buried the muses under the ruins of monarchy; yet, with the restoration of our happiness, we see revived poesy lifting up its head, and already shaking off the rubbish which lay so heavy on it. We have seen since his majesty's return, many dramatic poems which yield not to those of any foreign nation, and which deserve all laurels but the English. I will set aside flattery and envy: it cannot be denied but we have had some little blemish either in the plot or writing of all those plays which have been made within these seven years; (and perhaps there is no nation in the world so quick to discern them, or so difficult to pardon them, as ours:) yet if we can persuade ourselves to use the candor of that poet, who, though the most severe of critics, has left us this caution by which to moderate our censures —

> ubi plura nitent in carmine, non
> ego paucis
> Offendar maculis; —

if, in consideration of their many and great beauties, we can wink at some slight and little imperfections, if we, I say, can be thus equal to ourselves, I ask no favor from the French. And if I do not venture upon any particular judgment of our late plays, 'tis out of the consideration which an ancient writer gives me: *vivorum, ut magna admiratio,*

ita censura difficilis: betwixt the extremes of admiration and malice, 'tis hard to judge uprightly of the living. Only I think it may be permitted me to say, that as it is no lessening to us to yield to some plays, and those not many, of our own nation in the last age, so can it be no addition to pronounce of our present poets, that they have far surpassed all the ancients, and the modern writers of other countries. . . . For a play is still an imitation of nature; we know we are to be deceived, and we desire to be so; but no man ever was deceived but with a probability of truth; for who will suffer a gross lie to be fastened on him? Thus we sufficiently understand that the scenes which represent cities and countries to us are not really such, but only painted on boards and canvas; but shall that excuse the ill painture or designment of them? Nay, rather ought they not be labored with so much the more diligence and exactness, to help the imagination? since the mind of man does naturally tend to truth; and therefore the nearer anything comes to the imitation of it, the more it pleases."

.   .   .   .   .

PREFACE TO TROILUS AND CRESSIDA [1]

(1679)

THE GROUNDS OF CRITICISM IN TRAGEDY

Tragedy is thus defined by Aristotle (omitting what I thought unnecessary in his definition). It is an imitation of one entire, great, and probable action; not told, but represented; which, by moving in us fear and pity, is conducive to the purging of those two passions in our minds. More largely thus: Tragedy describes or paints an action, which action must have all the proprieties above named. First, it must be one or single; that is, it must not be a history of one man's life, suppose of Alexander the Great, or Julius Cæsar, but one single action of theirs. This condemns all Shakspeare's historical plays, which are rather chronicles represented, than trag-

[1] Re-printed, complete, from the Everyman's Edition of *Dramatic Essays by John Dryden* (London and New York, n. d.).— Ed.

edies; and all double action of plays. As, to avoid a satire upon others, I will make bold with my own *Marriage a la Mode*, where there are manifestly two actions not depending on one another: but in *Œdipus* there cannot properly be said to be two actions, because the love of Adrastus and Eurydice has a necessary dependence on the principal design into which it is woven. The natural reason of this rule is plain; for two different independent actions distract the attention and concernment of the audience, and consequently destroy the intention of the poet; if his business be to move terror and pity, and one of his actions be comical, the other tragical, the former will divert the people, and utterly make void his greater purpose. Therefore, as in perspective, so in Tragedy, there must be a point of sight in which all the lines terminate; otherwise the eye wanders, and the work is false. This was the practice of the Grecian stage. But Terence made an innovation in the Roman: all his plays have double actions; for it was his custom to translate two Greek comedies, and to weave them into one of his, yet so that both their actions were comical, and one was principal, the other but secondary or subservient. And this has obtained on the English stage, to give us the pleasure of variety.

As the action ought to be one, it ought, as such, to have order in it; that is, to have a natural beginning, a middle, and an end. A natural beginning, says Aristotle, is that which could not necessarily have been placed after another thing; and so of the rest. This consideration will arraign all plays after the new model of Spanish plots, where accident is heaped upon accident, and that which is first might as reasonably be last; an inconvenience not to be remedied, but by making one accident naturally produce another, otherwise it is a farce and not a play. Of this nature is *The Slighted Maid;* where there is no scene in the first act which might not by as good reason be in the fifth. And if the action ought to be one, the tragedy ought likewise to conclude with the action of it. Thus in *Mustapha,* the play should naturally have ended with the death of Zanger, and not have given us the grace-cup after dinner, of Solyman's divorce from Roxolana.

The following properties of the action are so easy that they need not my explaining. It ought to be great, and to consist of great persons, to distinguish it from Comedy, where the action is trivial, and the persons of inferior rank. The last quality of the action is, that it ought to be probable, as well as admirable and great. 'Tis not necessary that there should be historical truth in it; but always necessary that there should be a likeness of truth, something that is more than barely possible; *probable* being that which succeeds, or happens, oftener than it misses. To invent therefore a probability, and to make it wonderful, is the most difficult undertaking in the art of Poetry; for that which is not wonderful is not great; and that which is

not probable will not delight a reasonable audience. This action, thus described, must be represented and not told, to distinguish Dramatic Poetry from Epic: but I hasten to the end or scope of Tragedy, which is, to rectify or purge our passions, fear, and pity.

To instruct delightfully is the general end of all poetry. Philosophy instructs, but it performs its work by precept; which is not delightful, or not so delightful as example. To purge the passions by example is therefore the particular instruction which belongs to Tragedy. Rapin, a judicious critic, has observed from Aristotle, that pride and want of commiseration are the most predominant vices in mankind; therefore, to cure us of these two, the inventors of Tragedy have chosen to work upon two other passions, which are fear and pity. We are wrought to fear by their setting before our eyes some terrible example of misfortune, which happened to persons of the highest quality; for such an action demonstrates to us that no condition is privileged from the turns of fortune; this must of necessity cause terror in us, and consequently abate our pride. But when we see that the most virtuous, as well as the greatest, are not exempt from such misfortunes, that consideration moves pity in us, and insensibly works us to be helpful to, and tender over, the distressed; which is the noblest and most god-like of moral virtues. Here it is observable that it is absolutely necessary to make a man virtuous, if we desire he should be pitied: we lament not, but detest, a wicked man; we are glad when we behold his crimes are punished, and that poetical justice is done upon him. Euripides was censured by the critics of his time for making his chief characters too wicked; for example, Phædra, though she loved her son-in-law with reluctancy, and that it was a curse upon her family for offending Venus, yet was thought too ill a pattern for the stage. Shall we therefore banish all characters of villainy? I confess I am not of that opinion; but it is necessary that the hero of the play be not a villain; that is, the characters, which should move our pity, ought to have virtuous inclinations, and degrees of moral goodness in them. As for a perfect character of virtue, it never was in Nature, and therefore there can be no imitation of it; but there are alloys of frailty to be allowed for the chief persons, yet so that the good which is in them shall outweigh the bad, and consequently leave room for punishment on the one side and pity on the other.

After all, if any one will ask me whether a tragedy cannot be made upon any other grounds than those of exciting pity and terror in us, [Le] Bossu, the best of modern critics, answers thus in general: That all excellent arts, and particularly that of poetry, have been invented and brought to perfection by men of a transcendent genius; and that, therefore, they who practice afterwards the same arts are obliged to tread in their footsteps, and to search in their writings the foundation of them; for it is not just that new rules should destroy the authority of the old. But Rapin writes more particularly thus, that no passions in a story are so proper to move our concernment as fear and pity; and that it is from our concernment we receive our pleasure is undoubted; when the soul becomes agitated with fear for one character, or hope for another, then it is that we are pleased in Tragedy, by the interest which we taken in their adventures.

After the plot, which is the foundation of the play, the next thing to which we ought to apply our judgment is the manners; for now the poet comes to work above ground. The ground-work, indeed, is that which is most necessary, as that upon which depends the firmness of the whole fabric; yet it strikes not the eye so much as the beauties or imperfections of the manners, the thoughts, and the expressions.

The first rule which [Le] Bossu prescribes to the writer of an Heroic Poem, and which holds too by the same reason in all Dramatic Poetry, is to make the moral of the work; that is, to lay down to yourself what that precept of morality shall be which you would insinuate into the people; as, namely, Homer's (which I have copied in my *Conquest of Granada*) was, that union preserves a commonwealth and discord destroys it; Sophocles, in his *Œdipus,* that no man is to be accounted happy before his death. 'Tis the moral that directs the whole action of the play to one center; and that

action or fable is the example built upon the moral, which confirms the truth of it to our experience: when the fable is designed, then, and not before, the persons are to be introduced, with their manners, characters, and passions.

The manners, in a poem, are understood to be those inclinations, whether natural or acquired, which move and carry us to actions, good, bad, or indifferent, in a play; or which incline the persons to such or such actions. I have anticipated part of this discourse already in declaring that a poet ought not to make the manners perfectly good in his best persons; but neither are they to be more wicked in any of his characters than necessity requires. To produce a villain, without other reason than a natural inclination to villainy, is, in Poetry, to produce an effect without a cause; and to make him more a villain than he has just reason to be is to make an effect which is stronger than the cause.

The manners arise from many causes; and are either distinguished by complexion, as choleric and phlegmatic, or by the differences of age or sex, of climates, or quality of the persons, or their present condition. They are likewise to be gathered from the several virtues, vices, or passions, and many other commonplaces, which a poet must be supposed to have learned from Natural Philosophy, Ethics, and History; of all which whosoever is ignorant does not deserve the name of poet.

But as the manners are useful in this art, they may be all comprised under these general heads: first, they must be apparent; that is, in every character of the play some inclinations of the person must appear; and these are shown in the actions and discourse. Secondly, the manners must be suitable, or agreeing to the persons; that is, to the age, sex, dignity, and the other general heads of manners: thus, when a poet has given the dignity of a king to one of his persons, in all his actions and speeches that person must discover majesty, magnanimity, and jealousy of power, because these are suitable to the general manners of a king. The third property of manners is resemblance; and this is founded upon the particular characters of men as we have them delivered to us by relation or history; that is, when a poet has the known character of this or that man before him, he is bound to represent him such, at least not contrary to that which fame has reported him to have been. Thus, it is not a poet's choice to make Ulysses choleric or Achilles patient, because Homer has described 'em quite otherwise. Yet this is a rock on which ignorant writers daily split; and the absurdity is as monstrous as if a painter should draw a coward running from a battle, and tell us it was the picture of Alexander the Great.

The last property of manners is that they be constant and equal, that is, maintained the same through the whole design: thus, when Vergil had once given the name of *pious* to Æneas, he was bound to show him such, in all his words and actions, through the whole poem. All these properties Horace has hinted to a judicious observer: 1. *Notandi sunt tibi mores;* 2. *Aut famam sequere;* 3. *Aut sibi convenientia finge;* 4. *Servetur ad imum, qualis ab incepto processerit, et sibi constet.*

From the manners, the characters of persons are derived; for, indeed, the characters are no other than the inclinations as they appear in the several persons of the poem; a character being thus defined — that which distinguishes one man from another. Not to repeat the same things over again which have been said of the manners, I will only add what is necessary here. A character, or that which distinguishes one man from all others, cannot be supposed to consist of one particular virtue, or vice, or passion only; but 'tis a composition of qualities which are not contrary to one another in the same person; thus, the same man may be liberal and valiant, but not liberal and covetous; so in a comical character, or humor (which is an inclination to this or that particular folly), Falstaff is a liar, and a coward, a glutton, and a buffoon, because all these qualities may agree in the same man; yet it is still to be observed that one virtue, vice, and passion ought to be shown in every man as predominant over all the rest; as covetousness in Crassus, love of his country in Brutus; and the same in characters which are feigned.

The chief character or hero in a trag-

edy, as I have already shown, ought in prudence to be such a man who has so much more of virtue in him than of vice, that he may be left amiable to the audience, which otherwise cannot have any concernment for his sufferings; and it is on this one character that the pity and terror must be principally, if not wholly, founded: a rule which is extremely necessary, and which none of the critics, that I know, have fully enough discovered to us. For terror and compassion work but weakly when they are divided into many persons. If Creon had been the chief character in *Œdipus,* there had neither been terror nor compassion moved, but only detestation of the man and joy for his punishment; if Adrastus and Eurydice had been made more appearing characters, then the pity had been divided and lessened on the part of Œdipus: but making Œdipus the best and bravest person, and even Jocasta but an underpart to him, his virtues, and the punishment of his fatal crime, drew both the pity and the terror to himself.

By what has been said of the manners, it will be easy for a reasonable man to judge whether the characters be truly or falsely drawn in a tragedy; for if there be no manners appearing in the characters, no concernment for the persons can be raised; no pity or horror can be moved but by vice or virtue; therefore, without them, no person can have any business in the play. If the inclinations be obscure, it is a sign the poet is in the dark and knows not what manner of man he presents to you; and consequently you can have no idea, or very imperfect, of that man, nor can judge what resolutions he ought to take or what words or actions are proper for him. Most comedies made up of accidents or adventures are liable to fall into this error; and tragedies with many turns are subject to it; for the manners can never be evident where the surprises of fortune take up all the business of the stage; and where the poet is more in pain to tell you what happened to such a man than what he was. Tis one of the excellencies of Shakespeare that the manners of his persons are generally apparent, and you see their bent and inclinations. Fletcher comes far short of him in this, as indeed he does almost in everything: there are but glimmerings of manners in most of his comedies, which run upon adventures; and in his tragedies, Rollo, Otto the King and no King, Melantius, and many others of his best, are but pictures shown you in the twilight; you know not whether they resemble vice or virtue, and they are either good, bad, or indifferent, as the present scene requires it. But of all poets, this commendation is to be given to Ben Jonson, that the manners even of the most inconsiderable persons in his plays are everywhere apparent.

By considering the second quality of manners, which is, that they be suitable to the age, quality, country, dignity, etc., of the character, we may likewise judge whether a poet has followed nature. In this kind, Sophocles and Euripides have more excelled among the Greeks than Æschylus, and Terence more than Plautus among the Romans. Thus, Sophocles gives to Œdipus the true qualities of a king in both those plays which bear his name; but in the latter, which is the *Œdipus Colonæus,* he lets fall on purpose his tragic style; his hero speaks not in the arbitrary tone, but remembers, in the softness of his complaints, that he is an unfortunate blind old man, that he is banished from his country, and persecuted by his next relations. The present French poets are generally accused that, wheresoever they lay the scene, or in whatsoever age, the manners of their heroes are wholly French. Racine's Bajazet is bred at Constantinople, but his civilities are conveyed to him, by some secret passage, from Versailles into the Seraglio. But our Shakspeare, having ascribed to Henry the Fourth the character of a king and of a father, gives him the perfect manners of each relation, when either he transacts with his son or with his subjects. Fletcher, on the other side, gives neither to Arbaces nor to his king, in the *Maid's Tragedy,* the qualities which are suitable to a monarch; though he may be excused a little in the latter, for the king there is not uppermost in the character; 'tis the lover of Evadne, who is king only in a second consideration; and though he be unjust, and has other faults which shall be nameless, yet he is not the hero of the play. 'Tis true, we find him a lawful prince (though I never heard of any king that was in Rhodes), and therefore Mr. Rymer's criticism stands good, that he should not be shown in so vicious a character. Sophocles has been more judicious in his *Antigone;* for, though he represents in Creon a bloody prince, yet he makes him not a lawful king, but an usurper, and Antigona herself is the heroine of the tragedy: but when Philaster wounds Arethusa and the boy, and Perigot his mistress, in the *Faithful Shepherdess,* both these are contrary to the character of manhood. Nor is *Valentinian* managed much better; for though Fletcher has taken his picture truly, and shown him as he was, an effeminate, voluptuous man, yet he has forgotten that he was an emperor, and has given him none of those royal marks which ought to appear in a lawful successor of the throne. If it be inquired what Fletcher should have done on this occasion — ought he not to have represented Valentinian as he was? — [Le] Bossu shall answer this question for me by an instance of the like nature: Mauritius, the Greek emperor, was a prince far surpassing Valentinian, for he was endued with many kingly virtues; he was religious, merciful, and valiant, but withal he was noted of extreme covetousness, a vice which is contrary to the character of a hero or a prince: therefore, says the critic, that emperor was no fit person to be represented in a tragedy, unless his good qualities were only to be shown and his covetousness (which sullied them all) were slurred over by the artifice of the poet. To return once more to Shakspeare; no man ever drew so many characters, or generally distinguished 'em better from one another, excepting only Jonson. I will instance but in one to show the copiousness of his intention; it is that of Caliban, or the monster, in the *Tempest.* He seems there to have created a person which was not in nature, a boldness which, at first sight, would appear intolerable; for he makes him a species of himself, begotten by an incubus on a witch; but this, as I have elsewhere proved, is not wholly beyond the bounds of credibility, at least the vulgar still believe it. We have the separated notions of a spirit and of a witch (and spirits, according to Plato, are vested with a subtle body; according to some of his followers have different sexes); therefore, as from the distinct apprehensions of a horse and of a man imagination has formed a centaur, so from those of an incubus and a sorceress Shakspeare has produced his monster. Whether or no his generation can be defended I leave to philosophy; but of this I am certain, that the poet has most judiciously furnished him with a person, a language, and a character, which will suit him, both by father's and mother's side: he has all the discontents and malice of a witch and of a devil, besides a convenient proportion of the deadly sins; gluttony, sloth, and lust are manifest; the dejectedness of a slave is likewise given him, and the ignorance of one bred up in a desert island. His person is monstrous, and he is the product of unnatural lust; and his language is as hobgoblin as his person; in all things he is distinguished from other mortals. The characters of Fletcher are poor and narrow in comparison of Shakspeare's; I remember not one which is not borrowed from him, unless you will accept that strange mixture of a man in the *King and no King;* so that in this part Shakspeare is generally worth our imitation, and to imitate Fletcher is but to copy after him who was a copyer.

Under this general head of manners the passions are naturally included as belonging to the characters. I speak not of pity and of terror, which are to be moved in the audience by the plot; but of anger, hatred, love, ambition, jealousy, revenge, etc., as they are shown in this or that person of the play. To describe these naturally, and to move them artfully, is one of the greatest commendations which can be given to a poet: to write pathetically, says Longinus, cannot proceed but from a lofty genius. A poet must be born with this quality: yet, unless he help himself by an acquired knowledge of the passions, what they are in their own nature, and by what springs they are to be moved, he will be subject either to raise them where they ought not to be raised, or not to raise them by the just degrees of nature, or to amplify them beyond the natural bounds, or not to observe the crises and turns of them in their cooling and decay; all which errors proceed from want of judgment in the poet, and from being unskilled in the principles of moral philosophy. Nothing is more frequent in a fanciful writer than to foil himself by not managing his strength; therefore, as in a wrestler, there is first required some measure of force, a well-knit body and active limbs, without which all instruction would be vain; yet, these being granted, if he want the skill which is necessary to a wrestler he shall make but small advantage of his natural robustuousness: so, in a poet, his inborn vehemence and force of spirit will only run him out of breath the sooner if it be not supported by the help of Art. The roar of passion, indeed, may please an audience, three parts of which are ignorant enough to think all is moving which is noise, and it may stretch the lungs of an ambitious actor who will die upon the spot for a thundering clap; but it will move no other passion than indignation and contempt from judicious men. Longinus, whom I have hitherto followed, continues thus: *If the passions be artfully employed, the discourse becomes vehement and lofty: if otherwise, there is nothing more ridiculous than a great passion out of season:* and to this purpose he animadverts severely upon Æschylus, who writ nothing in cold blood, but was always in a rapture and in fury with his audience: the inspiration was still upon him, he was ever tearing it upon the tripos; or (to run off as madly as he does from one similitude to another) he was always at high-flood of passion, even in the dead ebb and lowest water-mark of the scene. He who would raise the passion of a judicious audience, says a learned critic, must be sure to take his hearers along with him; if they be in a calm, 'tis in vain for him to be in a huff: he must move them by degrees, and kindle with 'em; otherwise he will be in danger of setting his own heap of stubble on fire, and of burning out by himself, without warming the company that stand about him. They who would justify the madness of poetry from the authority of Aristotle have mistaken the text and consequently the interpretation: I imagine it to be false read where he says of poetry that it is Εὐφυοῦς ἢ μανικοῦ, that it had always somewhat in it either of a genius or of a madman. 'Tis more probable that the original ran thus, that poetry was Εὐφυοῦς οὐ μανικοῦ, that it belongs to a witty man, but not to a madman. Thus then the passions, as they are considered simply and in themselves, suffer violence when they are perpetually maintained at the same height; for what melody can be made on that instrument, all whose strings are screwed up at first to their utmost stretch and to the same sound? But this is not the worst: for the characters likewise bear a part in the general calamity if you consider the passions as embodied in them; for it follows of necessity that no man can be distinguished from another by his discourse when every man is ranting, swaggering, and exclaiming with the same excess: as if it were the only business of all the characters to contend with each other for the prize at Billingsgate, or that the scene of the tragedy lay in Bet'lem. Suppose the poet should intend this man to be choleric and that man to be patient, yet when they are confounded in the writing you cannot distinguish them from one another: for the man who was called patient and tame is only so before he speaks; but let his clack be set agoing, and he shall tongue it as impetuously, and as loudly, as the errantest hero in the play. By this means the characters are only distinct in name; but, in reality, all the men and women in the play are the same person. No man should pretend to write who cannot temper his fancy with his judgment: nothing is more dangerous to a raw horseman than a hot-mouthed jade without a curb.

It is necessary therefore for a poet, who would concern an audience by describing of a passion, first to prepare it and not to rush upon it all at once. Ovid has judiciously shown the difference of these two ways in the speeches of Ajax and Ulysses: Ajax, from the very beginning, breaks out into his exclamations, and is swearing by his Maker,

— *Agimus, proh Jupiter, inquit.* Ulysses, on the contrary, prepares his audience with all the submissiveness he can practice, and all the calmness of a reasonable man; he found his judges in a tranquillity of spirit, and therefore set out leisurely and softly with 'em, till he had warmed 'em by degrees; and then he began to mend his pace and to draw them along with his own impetuousness: yet so managing his breath that it might not fail him at his need, and reserving his utmost proofs of ability even to the last. The success, you see, was answerable; for the crowd only applauded the speech of Ajax —

Vulgique secutum
Ultima murmur erat:

but the judges awarded the prize, for which they contended, to Ulysses —

Mota manus procerum est; et quid facundia posset
Tum patuit, fortisque viri tulit arma disertus.

The next necessary rule is to put nothing into the discourse which may hinder your moving of the passions. Too many accidents, as I have said, encumber the poet as much as the arms of Saul did David; for the variety of passions which they produce are ever crossing and justling each other out of the way. He who treats of joy and grief together is in a fair way of causing neither of those effects. There is yet another obstacle to be removed, which is pointed wit, and sentences affected out of season; these are nothing of kin to the violence of passion: no man is at leisure to make sentences and similes when his soul is in an agony. I the rather name this fault that it may serve to mind me of my former errors; neither will I spare myself, but give an example of this kind from my *Indian Emperor.* Montezuma, pursued by his enemies and seeking sanctuary, stands parleying without the fort and describing his danger to Cydaria in a simile of six lines —

As on the sands the frighted traveler
Sees the high seas come rolling from afar, etc.

My Indian potentate was well skilled in the sea for an inland prince, and well improved since the first act, when he sent his son to discover it. The image had not been amiss from another man at another time: *sed nunc non erat hisce locus:* he destroyed the concernment which the audience might otherwise have had for him; for they could not think the danger near when he had the leisure to invent a simile.

If Shakspeare be allowed, as I think he must, to have made his characters distinct, it will easily be inferred that he understood the nature of the passions: because it has been proved already that confused passions make undistinguishable characters: yet I cannot deny that he has his failings; but they are not so much in the passions themselves as in his manner of expression: he often obscures his meaning by his words, and sometimes makes it unintelligible. I will not say of so great a poet that he distinguished not the blown puffy style from true sublimity; but I may venture to maintain that the fury of his fancy often transported him beyond the bounds of judgment, either in coining of new words and phrases, or racking words which were in use into the violence of a catachresis. It is not that I would explode the use of metaphors from passion, for Longinus thinks 'em necessary to raise it: but to use 'em at every word, to say nothing without a metaphor, a simile, an image, or description, is, I doubt, to smell a little too strongly of the buskin. I must be forced to give an example of expressing passion figuratively; but that I may do it with respect to Shakspeare, it shall not be taken from anything of his: 'tis an exclamation against fortune, quoted in his *Hamlet* but written by some other poet —

Out, out, thou strumpet, Fortune! all you gods,
In general synod, take away her power;
Break all the spokes and felleys from her wheel,
And bowl the round nave down the hill of Heav'n,
As low as to the fiends.

And immediately after, speaking of Hecuba, when Priam was killed before her eyes —

The mobbled queen
Threatening the flame, ran up and down
With bisson rheum; a clout about that head

Where late the diadem stood; and for a robe,
About her lank and all o'er-teemed loins,
A blanket in th' alarm of fear caught up,
Who this had seen, with tongue in venom steep'd
'Gainst Fortune's state would treason have pronounced;
But if the gods themselves did see her then,
When she saw Pyrrhus make malicious sport
In mincing with his sword her husband's limbs,
The instant burst of clamour that she made
(Unless things mortal move them not at all)
Would have made milch the burning eyes of heaven,
And passion in the gods.

What a pudder is here kept in raising the expression of trifling thoughts! Would not a man have thought that the poet had been bound prentice to a wheelwright for his first rant? and had followed a ragman for the clout and blanket in the second? Fortune is painted on a wheel, and therefore the writer, in a rage, will have poetical justice done upon every member of that engine: after this execution, he bowls the nave down-hill, from Heaven, to the fiends (an unreasonable long mark, a man would think); 'tis well there are no solid orbs to stop it in the way, or no element of fire to consume it: but when it came to the earth it must be monstrous heavy to break ground as low as the center. His making milch the burning eyes of heaven was a pretty tolerable flight too: and I think no man ever drew milk out of eyes before him: yet to make the wonder greater, these eyes were burning. Such a sight indeed were enough to have raised passion in the gods; but to excuse the effects of it, he tells you perhaps they did not see it. Wise men would be glad to find a little sense couched under all these pompous words; for bombast is commonly the delight of that audience which loves poetry but understands it not: and as commonly has been the practice of those writers who, not being able to infuse a natural passion into the mind, have made it their business to ply the ears, and to stun their judges by the noise. But Shakspeare does not often thus; for the passions in his scene between Brutus and Cassius are extremely natural, the thoughts are such as arise from the matter, the expression of 'em not viciously figurative. I cannot leave this subject before I do justice to that divine poet by giving you one of his passionate descriptions: 'tis of Richard the Second when he was deposed and led in triumph through the streets of London by Henry of Bullingbrook: the painting of it is so lively, and the words so moving, that I have scarce read anything comparable to it in any other language. Suppose you have seen already the fortunate usurper passing through the crowd, and followed by the shouts and acclamations of the people; and now behold King Richard entering upon the scene: consider the wretchedness of his condition and his carriage in it; and refrain from pity if you can —

As in a theater, the eyes of men,
After a well-graced actor leaves the
*   stage,*
Are idly bent on him that enters next,
Thinking his prattle to be tedious:
Even so, or with much more contempt,
*   men's eyes*
Did scowl on Richard: no man cried,
*   God save him:*
No joyful tongue gave him his welcome
*   home,*
But dust was thrown upon his sacred
*   head,*
Which with such gentle sorrow he shook
*   off,*
His face still combating with tears and
*   smiles*
(The badges of his grief and patience),
That had not God (for some strong pur-
*   pose) steel'd*
The hearts of men, they must perforce
*   have melted,*
And barbarism itself have pitied him.

To speak justly of this whole matter: 'tis neither height of thought that is discommended, nor pathetic vehemence, nor any nobleness of expression in its proper place; but 'tis a false measure of all these, something which is like them, and is not them; 'tis the Bristol-stone which appears like a diamond; 'tis an extrava-

gant thought instead of a sublime one; 'tis roaring madness instead of vehemence; and a sound of words instead of sense. If Shakspeare were stripped of all the bombasts in his passions, and dressed in the most vulgar words, we should find the beauties of his thoughts remaining; if his embroideries were burnt down, there would still be silver at the bottom of the melting-pot: but I fear (at least let me fear it for myself) that we, who ape his sounding words, have nothing of his thought, but are all outside; there is not so much as a dwarf within our giant's clothes. Therefore, let not Shakspeare suffer for our sakes; 'tis our fault, who succeed him in an age which is more refined, if we imitate him so ill that we copy his failings only and make a virtue of that in our writings which in his was an imperfection.

For what remains, the excellency of that poet was, as I have said, in the more manly passions; Fletcher's in the softer: Shakspeare writ better betwixt man and man; Fletcher betwixt man and woman: consequently, the one described friendship better; the other love: yet Shakspeare taught Fletcher to write love: and Juliet and Desdemona are originals. 'Tis true the scholar had the softer soul; but the master had the kinder. Friendship is both a virtue and a passion essentially; love is a passion only in its nature, and is not a virtue but by accident: good nature makes friendship; but effeminacy love. Shakspeare had an universal mind, which comprehended all characters and passions; Fletcher a more confined and limited: for though he treated love in perfection, yet honor, ambition, revenge, and generally all the stronger passions, he either touched not, or not masterly. To conclude all, he was a limb of Shakspeare.

I had intended to have proceeded to the last property of manners, which is, that they must be constant, and the characters maintained the same from the beginning to the end; and from thence to have proceeded to the thoughts and expressions suitable to a tragedy: but I will first see how this will relish with the age. It is, I confess, but cursorily written; yet the judgment, which is given here, is generally founded upon experience; but because many men are shocked at the name of rules, as if they were a kind of magisterial prescription upon poets, I will conclude with the words of Rapin, in his *Reflections* on Aristotle's work of *Poetry:* " If the rules be well considered, we shall find them to be made only to reduce Nature into method, to trace her step by step, and not to suffer the least mark of her to escape us: 'tis only by these that probability in fiction is maintained, which is the soul of poetry. They are founded upon good sense, and sound reason, rather than on authority; for though Aristotle and Horace are produced, yet no man must argue that what they write is true, because they writ it; but 'tis evident, by the ridiculous mistakes and gross absurdities which have been made by those poets who have taken their fancy only for their guide, that if this fancy be not regulated, it is a mere caprice, and utterly incapable to produce a reasonable and judicious poem."

JOHN MILTON

John Milton was born at London in 1608. His father was an Oxford man, and a musician of note. John received a very careful education both at school and at home. He was graduated from St. Paul's at the age of fifteen. Even before that time he is said to have written verses, in Latin and in English. He attended Christ's College, Cambridge, where he remained for over seven years. Some of his earliest known poems date from his college days, especially the *Ode on the Morning of Christ's Nativity* (1629). The years between 1632 and 1638 Milton spent with his father at Horton. He intended to enter the church, but finding himself unable to subscribe to its tenets, he decided to devote his energies to literature. During his stay in the country he wrote *L'Allegro* and *Il Penseroso, Comus,* which was performed in 1634, and *Lycidas* (1638). From Horton he went to the Continent. Toward the end of the year he was brought home by news of the Civil War. He returned in August of the next year, and became imbroiled in various religious controversies. At the same time he was giving a great deal of thought to projects for an epic or tragedy he hoped to write. In 1643 he was married, but his wife deserted him soon after. This called forth his tract on divorce, *The Doctrine and Discipline of Divorce,* etc. (1643). Two years later he was reconciled with his wife, who returned to him. In 1649 he became a Latin Secretary under Cromwell, and wrote a number of political pamphlets. He became blind in 1652, and his wife died the next year. He married again in 1656. He continued as secretary until the Restoration. At that time he was considered a menace to the government, and was arrested, but soon after released. His second wife died in 1660, and he married for the third time in 1663. *Paradise Lost* was begun in 1658, and finished five years later, but not published until 1667. In 1671, together with *Paradise Found,* he published his drama *Samson Agonistes,* with the preface on tragedy. He died in 1674.

Milton's contribution to the theory of the drama is slight enough, for practically his only reference to the subject is in the preface—*Of that sort of Dramatic Poem which is call'd Tragedy* — to his unactable pseudo-Greek play, *Samson Agonistes.* This is a defense of the form, based not primarily on Greek, but on Italian Renaissance ideas. The play is an exemplification of the theory. Professor Thorndike in his *Tragedy,* says: "Though the play stands by itself, it may be said to represent a tendency to turn to Greek rather than to French models, a tendency boasted of by Dryden and Crowne, and fully manifest in the next century. And it takes its place at the head of the numerous, if sporadic, tragedies on Greek models that extend from the Restoration to the present day."

On the drama:

Of that sort of Dramatic Poem which is call'd Tragedy (1671).

Editions:

The Works of John Milton, etc., 8 vols., ed. by I. Mitford (London, 1851). See See aso *The Poetical Works of John Milton,* edited by John Masson (Globe ed., London, 1877 ff). For special editions of *Samson Agonistes,* see those edited by J. C. Collins (Oxford, 1883), and by A. W. Verity (Cambridge, 1892). The Preface alone is re-printed in the second volume of J. E. Spingarn's *Critical Essays of the Seventeenth Century* (Oxford, 1908).

On Milton and his works:

S. A. Brooke, *Milton* (London, 1879).

R. Garnett, *Life of John Milton* (London, 1890).

D. Masson, *The Life of John Milton,* 6 vols. (Cambridge, 1859–80. Index vol., 1894).

W. A. Raleigh, *Milton* (London, 1890).

A. Schmidt, *Miltons dramatische Dichtungen* (Königsberg, 1864).

W. P. Trent, *John Milton* (New York, 1899).

Matthew Arnold, *Mixed Essays* (London, 1879).

——, Essays in Criticism, 2nd series (London, 1888).

I. Bywater, *Milton and the Aristotelian Definition of Tragedy* (In *Jour. of Phil.,* xxvii, p. 267, 1900).

OF THAT SORT OF DRAMATIC POEM WHICH IS CALLED TRAGEDY [1]

([Preface to] *Samson Agonistes*)

(1671)

Tragedy, as it was anciently composed, hath been ever held the gravest, moralest, and most profitable of all other poems; therefore said by Aristotle to be of power, by raising pity and fear, or terror, to purge the mind of those and such like passions, that is, to temper and reduce them to just measure with a kind of delight, stirred up by reading or seeing those passions well imitated. Nor is Nature wanting in her own effects to make good this assertion; for so in physic, things of melancholic hue and quality are used against melancholy, sour against sour, salt to remove salt humors. Hence philosophers and other gravest writers, as Cicero, Plutarch, and others, frequently cite out of tragic poets, both to adorn and illustrate their discourse. The Apostle Paul himself thought it not unworthy to insert a verse of Euripides into the text of Holy Scripture, *I Cor.* 15. 33; and Paræus, commenting on the Revelation, divides the whole Book, as a tragedy, into acts, distinguished each by a chorus of heavenly harpings and song between. Heretofore men in highest dignity have labored not a little to be thought able to compose a tragedy. Of that honor Dionysius the Elder was no less ambitious than before of his attaining to the Tyranny. Augustus Cæsar also had begun his *Ajax,* but, unable to please his own judgment with what he had begun, left it unfinished. Seneca the philosopher is by some thought the author of those tragedies (at least the best of them) that go under that name. Gregory Nazianzen, a Father of the Church, thought it not unbeseeming the sanctity of his person to write a tragedy, which he entitled *Christ Suffering.* This is mentioned to vindicate tragedy from the small esteem, or rather infamy, which in the account of many it undergoes at this day, with other common interludes; happening through the poets' error of intermixing comic stuff with tragic sadness and gravity, or introducing trivial and vulgar persons; which by all judicious hath been counted absurd and brought in without discretion, corruptly to gratify the people. And though ancient tragedy use no Prologue, yet using sometimes, in case of self-defense or explanation, that which Martial calls an *Epistle,* in behalf of this tragedy, coming forth after the ancient manner, much different from what among us passes for best, thus much beforehand may be Epistled: that Chorus is here introduced after the Greek manner, not ancient only, but modern, and still in use among the Ital-

---

1 Reprinted from the second volume of J. E. Spingarn's *Critical Essays of the Seventeenth Century* (Oxford, 1908).— Ed.

ians. In the modeling therefore of this poem, with good reason, the Ancients and Italians are rather followed, as of much more authority and fame. The measure of verse used in the Chorus is of all sorts, called by the Greeks *Monostrophic,* or rather *Apolelymenon,* without regard had to *Strophe, Antistrophe,* or *Epode,* which were a kind of stanzas framed only for the music, then used with the chorus that sung, not essential to the poem, and therefore not material; or being divided into stanzas or pauses, they may be called *Allæostropha.* Division into act and scene, referring chiefly to the stage (to which this work never was intended) is here omitted.

It suffices if the whole drama be found not produced beyond the fifth act; of the style and uniformity, and that commonly called the plot, whether intricate or explicit — which is nothing indeed but such economy or disposition of the fable as may stand best with verisimilitude and decorum — they only will best judge who are not unacquainted with Æschylus, Sophocles, and Euripides, the three tragic poets unequaled yet by any, and the best rule to all who endeavor to write tragedy. The circumscription of time, wherein the whole drama begins and ends is, according to the ancient rule and best example, within the space of twenty-four hours.

THOMAS RYMER

Thomas Rymer was born, probably at Yafforth Hall, Yorkshire, in 1641. He won distinction at school in his studies, and entered Cambridge in 1658. He did not, however, take his degree. He studied law and in 1673 was admitted to the bar. His first published work was a translation of Cicero's *Prince* (1668). In 1674 he published his translation of René Rapin's *Réflexions sur la poétique,* as the *Reflexions on Aristotle's Treatise of Poesie.* Three years later he published his tragedy of *Edgar,* which failed. It appeared in print the following year, when his *Tragedies of the Last Age Consider'd* was first published. The next few years he put forth a few occasional poems some political works and translations from the Latin. In 1692 he was appointed historiographer royal, and in 1693 published his *Short View of Tragedy,* which called forth considerable comment. The same year he began work on his *Fœdora,* a collection of historical documents relative to England's foreign alliances, which appeared between 1704 and 1713. Rymer died at London in 1713.

Rymer's criticism of Shakespeare has brought him into such disrepute that to this day he is regarded rather as a wild heretic than the sincere though often misguided critic he really was. He was a strict neo-classic, and the carelessness of the Elizabethans aroused all his ire as a follower of Rapin and the extremists from across the Channel. Rymer stood for verisimilitude, good sense, order, and balance; he could not see the greatness of a Shakespeare when that greatness was accompanied by absurdities and shortcomings. A great deal of what he says about the Elizabethans is quite true, and many of his remarks are sane, but he was utterly unable to make necessary allowances. In an age that could see little good in the Elizabethans, it was but natural that Pope should consider Rymer "one of the best critics we ever had," just as it was to be expected that Macaulay should think him "the worst critic that ever lived."

On the drama:

The Preface of the Translator, in Rapin's *Reflexions on Aristotle's Treatise of Poesie* (1674).

The Tragedies of the Last Age Consider'd and Examin'd by the Practice of the Ancients and by the Common Sense of All Ages (1678).

A Short View of Tragedy, Its Original Excellency and Corruption, With Some Reflections on Shakespear and Other Practitioners for the Stage (1693).

Editions:

The *Preface* to Rapin, and excerpts from *The Tragedies of the Last Age* and *A Short View* are reprinted in the second volume of Spingarn's *Critical Essays of the Seventeenth Century* (Oxford, 1908).

On Rymer and his works:

Introduction to the first volume of Spingarn's *Critical Essaus of the Seventeenth Century* (Oxford, 1908).

Samuel Johnson, *Dryden* (in *Lives of the Poets;* ed., Oxford, 1908).

Encyclopedia Britannica, vol. 23 (11th ed., Cambridge, 1910).

Sir T. N. Talfourd, *Critical and Miscellaneous Writings*, 3rd American ed., Boston, 1854).

A. Hofherr, *Thomas Rymer's dramatische Kritik* (Heidelberg, 1908).

George Saintsbury, *A History of Criticism*, vol. 2 (New York, 1902).

A SHORT VIEW OF TRAGEDY, ITS ORIGINAL EXCELLENCY AND CORRUPTION, WITH SOME REFLECTIONS ON SHAKESPEAR AND OTHER PRACTITIONERS FOR THE STAGE [1]

(1693)

CHAP. I

THE CONTENTS

The Chorus keeps the poet to rules. A show to the spectators. Two senses to be pleased. The eye, by the show and the action. Plays acted without words. Words often better out of the way. Instance in Shakespeare. Ben Jonson and Seneca noted. To the ear, pronunciation is all in all. The story of Demosthenes. Mistakes in judging. Two sorts of judges. At Athens a third sort. Judges upon oath. In France judges divided about the "Cid." Cardinal Richelieu against majority. At the "Thomus M-rus," weeping unawares. Horace angry with shows. The French opera inconsistent with nature and good sense. Burlesque verse. At Paris Christ's Passion in burlesque. A tragedy of Æschylus. The defeat of Xerxes. The subject and economy. How imitated for our English stage. King John of France, Francis I prisoners. The Spanish Armada in '88. An imitation recommended to Mr. Dryden.

What reformation may not we expect, now that in France they see the necessity

[1] Re-printed from the extracts in the second volume of J. E. Spingarn's *Critical Essays of the Seventeenth Century* (Oxford, 1908). This chapter is complete.— Ed.

of a chorus to their tragedies? Boyer and Racine, both of the Royal Academy, have led the dance: they have tried the success in the last plays that were presented by them.

The chorus was the root and original, and is certainly almost always the necessary part, of tragedy.

The spectators thereby are secured that their poet shall not juggle, or put upon them in the matter of *place* and *time* other than is just and reasonable for the representation.

And the poet has this benefit: the chorus is a goodly show, so that he need not ramble from his subject, out of his wits for some foreign toy or hobby-horse to humor the multitude.

Aristotle tells us of two senses that must be pleased: our sight and our ears. And it is in vain for a poet, with Bayes in *The Rehearsal*, to complain of injustice and the wrong judgment in his audience, unless these two senses be gratified.

The worst on it is that most people are wholly led by these senses, and follow them upon content, without ever troubling their noodle farther.

How many plays owe all their success to a rare show? Even in the days of Horace, enter on the stage a person in a costly strange habit. Lord, what clapping, what noise and thunder, as heaven and earth were coming together! Yet not one word

Dixit adhuc aliquid? Nil sane: quid placeat ergo
Lana Tarentino violas imitata veneno.

Was there aught said? Troth, no! What then did touch ye? Some Prince of Bantam, or a *Mamamouche*.

It matters not whether there be any plot, any characters, any sense, or a wise word from one end to the other, provided in our play we have the Senate of Rome, the Venetian Senate in their Pontificalibus, or a blackamoor ruffian, or Tom Dove, or other four-legged hero of the Bear-garden.

The eye is a quick sense, will be in with our fancy and prepossess the head strangely. Another means whereby the eye misleads our judgment is the action. We go to see a play acted; in tragedy is represented a memorable action, so the spectators are always pleased to see action, and are not often so ill-natured to pry into and examine whether it be proper, just, natural, in season or out of season. Bayes in *The Rehearsal* well knew this secret. The two Kings are at their Coranto; nay, the moon and the earth dance the Hey; anything in nature or against nature, rather than allow the serious council or other dull business to interrupt or obstruct the action.

This thing of Action finds the blind-side of humankind an hundred ways. We laugh and weep with those that laugh or weep; we gape, stretch, and are very *dotterels* by example.

Action is speaking to the eyes; and all Europe over, plays have been represented with great applause in a tongue unknown and sometimes without any language at all.

Many, peradventure, of the tragical scenes in Shakespeare, cried up for the action, might do yet better without words. Words are a sort of heavy baggage that were better out of the way at the push of action, especially in his bombast circumstance, where the words and action are seldom akin, generally are inconsistent, at cross purposes, embarrass or destroy each other; yet to those who take not the words distinctly, there may be something in the buzz and sound that, like a drone to a bagpipe, may serve to set off the action.

For an instance of the former, would not a rap at the door better express Iago's meaning than

—Call aloud.
IAGO.   Do, with like timorous accent and dire yell
As when, by night and negligence, the fire
Is spied in populous cities?

For what ship? Who is arrived? The answer is:

'Tis one Iago, Ancient to the General.
He has had most favorable and happy speed;
Tempests themselves, high seas, and howling winds,
The guttered rocks and congregated sands,
Traitors ensteeped to clog the guiltless keel.
As having sense of beauty, do omit
Their common natures, letting go safely by
The divine Desdemona.

Is this the language of the Exchange or the Insuring office? Once in a man's life he might be content at Bedlam to hear such a rapture. In a play one should speak like a man of business; his speech must be Πολιτικὸς, which the French render *Agissante*, the Italians *Negotiosa* and *Operativa*; but by this gentleman's talk one may well guess he has nothing to do. And he has many companions that are

—Hey day!
I know not what to do nor what to say.

It was then a strange imagination in Ben Jonson to go stuff out a play with Tully's Orations, and in Seneca, to think his dry morals and a tedious strain of sentences might do feats or have any wonderful operation in the drama.

Some go to *see*, others to *hear*, a play. The poet should please both; but be sure the spectators are satisfied, whatever entertainment he give his audience.

But if neither the show nor the action cheats us, there remains still a notable vehicle to carry off nonsense, which is the pronunciation.

By the loud trumpet which our courage aids,

We learn, that sound as well as sense persuades.

Demosthenes had a good stock of sense, was a great master of words, could turn a period, and draw up his tropes in a line of battle; and fain would he have seen some effect of his Orations: nobody was moved, nobody minded him. He goes to the playhouse, bargains with an actor, and learned of him to speak roundly and gracefully. From that time, Who but Demosthenes? Never such a leading man! Whenever he spake, no division, not a vote to the contrary, the whole House were with him, *Nemine contradicente.* This change observed, a friend went to him for the secret. "Tell me," says he, "Your nostrum, tell me your receipt. What is the main ingredient that makes an orator?" Demosthenes answered: "Pronunciation." —"What then the next thing?"—"Pronunciation."—"Pray then what the third?"— Still was the answer, "Pronunciation."

Now, this was at Athens, where want of wit was never an objection against them. So that it is not in song only that a good voice diverts us from the wit and sense. From the stage, bar, or the pulpit, a good voice will prepossess our ears and, having seized the pass, is in a fair way to surprise our judgment.

Considering then what power the show, the action, and the pronunciation have over us, it is no wonder that wise men often mistake and give an hasty judgment, which upon a review is justly set aside.

Horace divides the judges into *Majores Numero,* and the few of *better sort;* and these for the most part were of different judgments. The like distinction may hold in all nations: only at Athens there was a third sort, who were judges upon oath, Judges in Commission, by the government sworn to do right, and determine the merits of a play without favor or affection.

But amongst the moderns never was a cause canvassed with so much heat between the play-judges as that in France about Corneille's *Tragedy of the Cid.* The majority were so fond of it that with them it became a proverb, *Cela est plus beau que le Cid.* On the other side,

Cardinal Richelieu damned it, and said: "All the pudder about it was only between the ignorant people and the men of judgment."

Yet this Cardinal with so nice a taste had not many years before been several times to see acted the *Tragedy of Sir Thomas More,* and as often wept at the representation. Never were known so many people crowded to death as at that play. Yet was it the manufacture of Jehan de Serre, one about the form of our Flecknoe or Thomas Jordan, the same De Serre that dedicated a *Book of Meditations* to King Charles I and went home with pockets full of medals and reward.

By this instance we see a man the most sharp and of the greatest penetration was imposed upon by these cheating senses, the eyes and the ears, which greedily took in the impression from the show, the action, and from the emphasis and pronunciation, though there was no great matter of fable, no manners, no fine thoughts, no language; that is, nothing of a tragedy, nothing of a poet all the while.

Horace was very angry with these empty shows and vanity, which the gentlemen of his time ran like mad after.

Insanos oculos, et gaudia vana.

What would he have said to the French opera, of late so much in vogue? There it is for you to bewitch your eyes and to charm your ears. There is a cup of enchantment, there is music and machine; Circe and Calypso in conspiracy against nature and good sense. 'Tis a debauch the most insinuating and the most pernicious; none would think an opera and civil reason should be the growth of one and the same climate. But shall we wonder at anything for a sacrifice to the Grand Monarch? Such worship, such idol! All flattery to him is insipid unless it be prodigious. Nothing reasonable or within compass can come near the matter. All must be monstrous, enormous, and outrageous to nature, to be like him, or give any echo on his appetite.

Were Rabelais alive again, he would look on his Gargantua as but a pigmy.

The hero's race excels the poet's

thought. The Academy Royal may pack up their modes and methods, and *pensées ingénieuses;* the Racines and the Corneilles must all now dance to the tune of Baptista. Here is the opera; here is Machine and Baptista, farewell Apollo and the Muses!

Away with your opera from the theater! Better had they become the heathen temples, for the Corybantian priests and (*Semiviros Gallos*) the old capons of Gaul, than a people that pretend from Charlemagne or descend from the undoubted loins of German and Norman conquerors.

In the French, not many years before, was observed the like vicious appetite and immoderate passion for *vers burlesque.*

They were current in Italy an hundred years ere they passed to this side the Alps. But when once they had their turn in France, so right to their humor, they overran all; nothing wise or sober might stand in their way. All were possessed with the spirit of burlesque, from Doll in the dairy to the matrons at Court and maids of honor. Nay, so far went the frenzy, that no bookseller would meddle on any terms without burlesque; insomuch that *Ann.* 1649 was at Paris printed a serious treatise with this title:

— *La Passion de Nostre Seigneur, En Vers Burlesques.*

If we cannot rise to the perfection of intrigue in Sophocles, let us sit down with the honesty and simplicity of the first beginners in tragedy. As for example:

One of the most simple now extant is *The Persians* by Æschylus.

Some ten years after that Darius had been beaten by the Greeks, Xerxes (his father Darius being dead) brought against them such forces by sea and land, the like never known in history; Xerxes went also in person, with all the *Maison de Roy, Satrapie,* and Gendarmerie: all were routed. Some forty years afterwards the poet takes hence his subject for a tragedy.

The Place is by Darius' tomb, in the Metropolis of Persia.

The Time is the night, an hour or two before daybreak.

First, on the stage are seen fifteen persons in robes proper for the Satrapa, or chief Princes in Persia. Suppose they met so early at the tomb, then sacred, and ordinarily resorted to by people troubled in mind, on the accounts of dreams or any thing not boding good. They talk of the state of affairs: of Greece and of the Expedition. After some time take upon them to be the Chorus.

The next on the stage comes Atossa, the Queen Mother of Persia; she could not lie in bed for a dream that troubled her, so in a fit of devotion comes to her husband's tomb, there luckily meets with so many wise men and counselors to ease her mind by interpreting her dream. This, with the Chorus, makes the Second Act.

After this, their disorder, lamentation, and wailing is such that Darius is disturbed in his tomb, so his ghost appears, and belike stays with them till daybreak. Then the Chorus concludes the Act.

In the fourth Act come the Messengers with sad tidings which, with the reflections and troubles thereupon, and the Chorus, fill out this Act.

In the last, Xerxes himself arrives, which gives occasion of condoling, howling and distraction enough to the end of the tragedy.

One may imagine how a Grecian audience that loved their country and gloried in the virtue of their ancestors, would be affected by this representation.

Never appeared on the stage a ghost of greater consequence. The Grand Monarch Darius, who had been so shamefully beaten by those petty provinces of the united Grecians, could not now lie quiet in his grave for them, but must be raised from the dead again, to be witness of his son's disgrace and of their triumph.

Were a tragedy after this model to be drawn for our stage, Greece and Persia are too far from us. The scene must be laid nearer home: as at the Louvre; and instead of Xerxes we might take John King of France, and the Battle of Poitiers. So if the Germans or Spaniards were to compose a play on the Battle of Pavia, and King Francis were there taken prisoner, the scene should not be laid at Vienna or at Madrid, but at the Louvre. For there the tragedy would principally operate, and there all the lines most naturally center.

But perhaps the memorable adventure of the Spaniards in '88 against England may better resemble that of Xerxes. Suppose, then, a tragedy called *The Invincible Armada.*

The place, then, for the action may be at Madrid, by some tomb or solemn place of resort; or, if we prefer a turn in it from good to bad fortune, then some drawing-room in the palace near the King's bed-chamber.

The time to begin, twelve at night.

The scene opening presents fifteen grandees of Spain, with their most solemn beards and accouterments, met there (suppose) after some ball or other public occasion. They talk of the state of affairs, the greatness of their power, the vastness of their dominions, and prospect to be infallibly, ere long, lords of all. With this prosperity and goodly thoughts transported, they at last form themselves into the Chorus, and walk such measures, with music, as may become the gravity of such a Chorus.

Then enter two or three of the Cabinet Council, who now have leave to tell the secret, that the preparations and the Invincible Armada was to conquer England. These, with part of the Chorus, may communicate all the particulars, the provisions, and the strength by sea and land, the certainty of success, the advantages of that accession, and the many tun of tar-barrels for the Heretics. These topics may afford matter enough, with the Chorus, for the Second Act.

In the Third Act, these gentlemen of the Cabinet cannot agree about sharing the preferments of England, and a mighty broil there is amongst them. One will not be content unless he is King of Man; another will be Duke of Lancaster. One, that had seen a coronation in England, will by all means be Duke of Acquitaine, or else Duke of Normandy. (And on this occasion two competitors have a juster occasion to work up and show the muscles of their passion than Shakespeare's Cassius and Brutus.) After — the Chorus.

The Fourth Act may, instead of Atossa, present some old Dames of the Court, used to dream dreams and see sprites, in their night-rails and forehead-clothes, to alarm our gentlemen with new apprehensions, which make distraction and disorders sufficient to furnish out this Act.

In the last Act the King enters, and wisely discourses against dreams and hobgoblins, to quiet their minds. And the more to satisfy them and take off their fright, he lets them to know that St. Loyola had appeared to him and assured him that all is well. This said, comes a Messenger of the ill news; his account is lame, suspected, he sent to prison. A Second Messenger, that came away long after but had a speedier passage; his account is distinct, and all their loss credited. So, in fine, one of the Chorus concludes with that of Euripides: "Thus you see the gods brings things to pass often otherwise than was by man proposed."

In this draft we see the fable, and the characters or manners of the Spaniards, and room for fine thoughts and noble expressions, as much as the poet can afford.

The First Act gives a review or ostentation of their strength in battle array.

In the Second, they are in motion for the attack and we see where the action falls.

In the Third, they quarrel about dividing the spoil.

In the Fourth, they meet with a repulse, are beaten off by a van-guard of dreams, goblins, and terrors of the night.

In the Fifth, they rally under their King in person, and make good their ground, till overpowered by fresh troops of conviction, and mighty Truth prevails.

For the First Act, a painter would draw Spain hovering and ready to strike at the Universe.

In the Second, just taking England in her pounces.

But it must not be forgotten, in the Second Act, that there be some Spanish Friar or Jesuit, as St. Xavier (for he may drop in by miracle anywhere), to ring in their ears the Northern Heresy, like Iago in Shakespeare —" Put money in thy purse, I say, put money in thy purse."— So often may he repeat the Northern Heresy. "Away with your secular advantages, I say, the Northern

Heresy; there is roast meat for the Church; *Voto a Christo,* the Northern Heresy!"

If Mr. Dryden might try his pen on this subject doubtless to an audience that heartily love their country and glory in the virtue of their ancestors, his imitation of Æschylus would have better success, and would pit, box, and gallery, far beyond anything now in possession of the stage, however wrought up by the unimitable Shakespeare.

WILLIAM CONGREVE

William Congreve was born at Bardsey in 1670. His father was sent, soon after the son's birth, to Ireland, where he was in command of a garrison at Youghal. William received his first schooling at Kilkenny, and later attended the University of Dublin, where he made the acquaintance of Swift. He then went to London and entered the Middle Temple as a law student. His first literary work was a novel, *Incognita.* In 1693 he was, however, to give evidence of his genius in *The Old Bachelor,* a brilliant comedy, which was eminently successful. The next year he produced *The Double Dealer,* which was not successful, but which Dryden, who had stood sponsor for the first play, highly praised. *Love for Love* (1695) and *The Mourning Bride* (1697) a tragedy, followed the unsuccessful play. Then came Collier's famous attack on the stage (1698), which called forth Congreve's *Amendments upon Mr. Collier's False and Imperfect Citations,* etc., the same year. Meanwhile he had written his *Letter Concerning Humour in Comedy* in 1696. In 1700 Congreve produced his masterpiece, *The Way of the World.* The play was not a success, and from the year 1700 to his death in 1729 Congreve never wrote another play; a small volume of indifferent verses, a sort of masque, and parts of a play translated from Molière, are the result of his literary efforts during the rest of his life. Congreve was doubtless somewhat discouraged over the Collier controversy; he was piqued over the coolness with which his last, and greatest, comedy was received, he was in poor health — and besides, he did not need money. Congreve's life during the eighteenth century contains little of interest. He spent his time in traveling, in cultivating his friends, in writing occasional verses, and a poor opera; he was a victim of the gout, and became blind by 1710. He was next employed in several minor capacities, which assured him at least a comfortable income, for when he died he left ten thousand pounds to the Duchess of Marlborough.

Congreve is the master of the English comedy of manners. His remarks on the drama possess not only some of the qualities which make his dramatic work effective, they are in addition a valuable comment on the comedies of Congreve's own age. Like Dryden, Congreve uses the comparative method, but maintains truthfully that real humor is indigenously English, and that "it does not seem to have found such increase on any other soil." The *Prefaces* and *Dedications* to the plays, in spite of their brevity, are full of interesting and suggestive remarks. For instance, in the *Epistle Dedicatory to The Double Dealer,* he says: "I designed the moral first, and to that moral I invented the fable, and do not know that I have borrowed one hint of it anywhere. I made the plot as strong as I could, because it was single; and I made it single, because I would avoid confusion, and was resolved to preserve the three unities of the drama." Like many practicing theorists, Congreve's theory and his practice do not always coincide, but his plea for the Unities is more sensible than that of any other theorist of the time. The same *Epistle* contains equally interesting remarks on the soliloquy and characterization. The *Dedication to The Way of the World* also contains sundry references to the art of the dramatist. The *Dedication* to *The*

Mourning Bride contains a few of the cut-and-dried formulas on tragedy and the moral end of that form.

On the drama:

Epistles Dedicatory to *The Double-Dealer* (1694).
Concerning Humour in Comedy (in *Letters upon Several Occasions*, etc., 1696).
Dedication to *The Mourning Bride* (1697).
Amendments upon Mr. Collier's False and Imperfect Citations, etc. (1698).
Dedication to *The Way of the World* (1700).

Editions:

The first edition of Congreve's collected *Works* appeared in 3 vols. (London, 1710). The dramatic works have been often reprinted: *The Dramatic Works of Wycherley, Congreve, Vanbrugh and Farquhar*, by Leigh Hunt (London, 1849); *The Comedies of William Congreve*, edited by W. G. S. Street, 2 vols. (London, 1895); *The Best Plays of William Congreve*, edited by A. C. Ewald (*Mermaid* ed., New York, 1903). A number of Congreve's letters are found in Monck Berkeley's *Literary Relics*. *Concerning Humour in Comedy* is reprinted by J. E. Spingarn in vol. 3, of *Critical Essays of the Seventeenth Century*, Oxford, 1909.

On Congreve and his works:

Prefaces to editions cited.
Samuel Johnson, *Congreve* (in *Lives of the Poets*, eds. cited).
William Hazlitt, *Lectures on the English Comic Writers*, etc. (London, 1818. Reprint in *Everyman's Library*, New York, n.d.).
Charles Lamb, *The Artificial Comedy of the Last Century* (in *Essays of Elia*, E. V. Lucas ed. of the *Works*, London, 1907).
T. B. Macaulay, *Leigh Hunt* (in *Critical and Miscellaneous Essays*, ed. Montague, London, 1903).
Leslie Stephen, *William Congreve* (in *Dictionary of National Biography*, vol. 12, London, 1887).
A. C. Swinburne, *Miscellanies* (London, 1886).
W. M. Thackeray, *The English Humourists of the Eighteenth Century*, etc. (London, 1853. Reprinted in *Everyman's Library*, New York, n.d.; also *Biographical* ed., vol. 7, London, 1897).
Charles Wilson, *Memoirs of the Life, Writings and Amours of W. Congreve, Esq.*, etc. (London, 1730).
C. F. Armstrong, *William Congreve* (in *From Shakespeare to Shaw*, London, 1913).
Edmund Gosse, *Life of William Congreve* (London, new ed., 1924).
A. Bennewitz, *Congreve und Molière* (Leipzig, 1890).
George Meredith, *An Essay on Comedy* (London, 1897).
D. Schmid, *Congreve, sein Leben und seine Lustspiele* (Wien, 1897).

CONCERNING HUMOR IN COMEDY [1]

(1696)

Dear Sir:
You write to me that you have entertained yourself two or three days with reading several comedies of several authors; and your observation is that there is more of humor in our English writers than in any of the other comic poets, ancient or modern. You desire to know my opinion, and at the same time my thought, of that which is in general called *Humor* in comedy.

I agree with you in an impartial preference of our English writers in that particular. But if I tell you my thoughts of humor, I must at the same time confess that which I take for true humor has not been so often written by them as is generally believed; and some who have valued themselves and have been esteemed by others for that kind of writing, have seldom touched upon it. To

[1] Re-printed from the third volume of J. E. Spingarn's *Critical Essays of the Seventeenth Century* (Oxford, 1909).— Ed.

make this appear to the world would require a long and labored discourse, and such as I neither am able nor willing to undertake. But such little remarks as may be within the compass of a letter, and such unpremeditated thoughts as may be communicated between friend and friend without incurring the censure of the world, or setting up for a dictator, you shall have from me, since you have enjoined it.

To define humor perhaps were as difficult as to define wit; for, like that, it is of infinite variety. To enumerate the several humors of men were a work as endless as to sum up their several opinions. And, in my mind, *Quot homines tot sententiae,* might have been more properly interpreted of humor; since there are many men of the same opinion in many things, who are yet quite different in humors. But though we cannot certainly tell what wit is, or what humor is, yet we may go near to show something which is not wit or not humor, and yet often mistaken for both. And since I have mentioned wit and humor together, let me make the first distinction between them, and observe to you that *wit is often mistaken for humor.*

I have observed that when a few things have been wittily and pleasantly spoken by any character in a comedy, it has been very usual for those who make their remarks on a play while it is acting, to say, *Such a thing is very humorously spoken; There is a great deal of humor in that part.* Thus the character of the person speaking, may be, surprisingly and pleasantly is mistaken for a character of humor, which indeed is a character of wit. But there is a great difference between a comedy wherein there are many things *humorously,* as they call it, which is *pleasantly,* spoken, and one where there are several characters of humor, distinguished by the particular and different humors appropriated to the several persons represented, and which naturally arise from the different constitutions, complexions, and dispositions of men. The saying of humorous things does not distinguish characters; for every person in a comedy may be allowed to speak them. From a witty man they are expected; and even a fool may be permitted to stumble on 'em by

chance. Though I make a difference betwixt wit and humor, yet I do think that humorous characters exclude wit: no, but the manner of wit should be adapted to the humor. As, for instance, a character of a splenetic and peevish humor should have a satirical wit. A jolly and sanguine humor should have a facetious wit. The former should speak positively; the latter, carelessly: for the former observes and shows things as they are; the latter rather overlooks nature, and speaks things as he would have them, and wit and humor have both of them less alloy of judgment than the others.

As wit, so its opposite, *folly, is sometimes mistaken for humor.*

When a poet brings a character on the stage committing a thousand absurdities, and talking impertinencies, roaring aloud, and laughing immoderately on every or rather upon no occasion, this is a character of humor.

Is anything more common than to have a pretended comedy stuffed with such grotesques, figures and farce fools? Things that either are not in nature, or, if they are, are monsters and births of mischance, and consequently, as such, should be stifled and huddled out of the way, like *Sooterkins.* That mankind may not be shocked with an appearing possibility of the degeneration of a godlike species. For my part, I am as willing to laugh as anybody, and as easily diverted with an object truly ridiculous; but at the same time, I can never care for seeing things that force me to entertain low thoughts of any nature. I don't know how it is with others, but I confess freely to you, I could never look long upon a monkey without very mortifying reflections, though I never heard anything to the contrary why that creature is not originally of a distinct species. As I don't think humor exclusive of wit, neither do I think it inconsistent with folly; but I think the follies should be only such as men's humors may incline 'em to, and not follies entirely abstracted from both humor and nature.

Sometimes *personal defects are misrepresented for humors.*

I mean, sometimes characters are barbarously exposed on the stage, ridiculing natural deformities, casual defects in the senses, and infirmities of age.

Sure the poet must be very ill-natured himself, and think his audience so, when he proposes by showing a man deformed, or deaf, or blind, to give them an agreeable entertainment, and hopes to raise their mirth by what is truly an object of compassion. But much need not be said upon this head to anybody, especially to you, who, in one of your Letters to me concerning Mr. Jonson's *Fox*, have justly expected against this immortal part of ridicule in Corbaccio's character; and there I must agree with you to blame him whom otherwise I cannot enough admire for his great mastery of true humor in comedy.

External habit of body is often mistaken for humor.

By *external habit* I do not mean the ridiculous dress or clothing of a character, though that goes a good way in some received characters. (But undoubtedly, a man's humor may incline him to dress differently from other people.) But I mean a singularity of manners, speech, and behavior, peculiar to all or most of the same country, trade, profession, or education. I cannot think that a humor which is only a habit or disposition contracted by use or custom; for by a disuse, or compliance with other customs, it may be worn off or diversified.

Affectation is generally mistaken for humor.

These are indeed so much alike that at a distance they may be mistaken one for the other. For what is humor in one may be affectation in another; and nothing is more common than for some to affect particular ways of saying and doing things, peculiar to others whom they admire and would imitate. Humor is the life, affectation the picture. He that draws a character of affectation shows humor at the second hand; he at best but publishes a translation, and his pictures are but copies.

But as these two last distinctions are the nicest, so it may be most proper to explain them by particular instances from some author of reputation. Humor I take either to be born with us, and so of a natural growth, or else to be grafted into us by some accidental change in the constitution, or revolution of the internal habit of body, by which it becomes, if I may so call it, naturalized.

Humor is from nature, habit from custom, and affectation from industry.

Humor shows us as we are.

Habit shows us as we appear under a forcible impression.

Affectation shows what we would be under a voluntary disguise.

Though here I would observe by the way that a continued affectation may in time become a habit.

The character of Morose in *The Silent Woman* I take to be a character of Humor. And I choose to instance this character to you from many others of the same author, because I know it has been condemned by many as unnatural and farce; and you have yourself hinted some dislike of it for the same reason, in a Letter to me concerning some of Jonson's plays.

Let us suppose Morose to be a man naturally splenetic and melancholy; is there anything more offensive to one of such a disposition than noise and clamor? Let any man that has a spleen (and there are enough in England) be judge. We see common examples of this humor, in little, every day. 'Tis ten to one but three parts in four of the company that you dine with are discomposed and startled at the cutting of a fork or scratching a plate with a knife. It is a proportion of the same humor that makes such or any other noise offensive to the person that hears it; for there are others who will not be disturbed at all by it. Well, but Morose, you will say, is so extravagant, he cannot hear any discourse or conversation above a whisper. Why, it is his excess of this humor that makes him become ridiculous, and qualifies his character for comedy. If the poet had given him but a moderate proportion of that humor, 'tis odds but half the audience would have sided with the character and have condemned the author for exposing a humor which was neither remarkable nor ridiculous. Besides, the distance of the stage requires the figure represented to be something larger than the life; and sure a picture may have figures larger in proportion, and yet be very like the original. If this exactness of quantity were to be observed in wit, as some would have it in humor, what would become of those comedies that are designed for men of wit? I believe that if a poet should steal a dialogue of any length from the extempore discourse of the two wittiest men upon earth, he would find the scene but coldly received by the town. But to the purpose.

The character of Sir John Daw in the same play is a character of affectation. He everywhere discovers an affectation of learning, when he is not only conscious to himself, but the audience also plainly perceives that he is ignorant. Of this kind are the characters of Thraso in *The Eunuch* of Terence, and Pyrgopolinices in the *Miles Gloriosus* of Plautus. They affect to be thought valiant, when both themselves and the audience know they are not. Now, such a boasting of valor in men who were really valiant would undoubtedly be a humor; for a fiery disposition might naturally throw a man into the same extravagance, which is only affected in the characters I have mentioned.

The character of Cob in *Every Man in his Humour* and most of the under characters in *Bartholomew Fair,* discover only a singularity of manners, appropriate to the several educations and professions of the persons represented. They are not humors, but habits contracted by custom. Under this head may be ranged all country-clowns, sailors, tradesmen, jockeys, gamesters, and such-like, who make use of *cants* or peculiar dialects in their several arts and vocations. One may almost give a receipt for the composition of such a character: for the poet has nothing to do but to collect a few proper phrases and terms of art, and to make the person apply them by ridiculous metaphors in his conversation with characters of different natures. Some late characters of this kind have been very successful; but in my mind they may be painted without much art or labor, since they require little more than a good memory and superficial observation. But true humor cannot be shown without a dissection of nature, and a narrow search to discover the first seeds from whence it has its root and growth.

If I were to write to the world, I should be obliged to dwell longer upon each of these distinctions and examples, for I know that they would not be plain enough to all readers. But a bare hint is sufficient to inform you of the notions which I have on this subject: and I hope by this time you are of my opinion, that humor is neither wit, nor folly, nor personal defect, nor affectation, nor habit, and yet that each and all of these have been both written and received for humor.

I should be unwilling to venture even on a bare description of humor, much more to make a definition of it, but now my hand is in, I'll tell you what serves one instead of either. I take it to be *A singular and unavoidable manner of doing or saying anything, peculiar and natural to one man only, by which his speech and actions are distinguished from those of other men.*

Our humor has relation to us and to what proceeds from us, as the accidents have to a substance; it is a color, taste, and smell, diffused through all; though our actions are never so many and different in form, they are all splinters of the same wood, and have naturally one complexion, which, though it may be disguised by art, yet cannot be wholly changed: we may paint it with other colors, but we cannot change the grain. So the natural sound of an instrument will be distinguished, though the notes expressed by it are never so various, and the divisions never so many. Dissimulation may by degrees become more easy to our practice; but it can never absolutely transubstantiate us into what we would seem: it will always be in some proportion a violence upon nature.

A man may change his opinion but I believe he will find it a difficulty to part with his humor, and there is nothing more provoking than the being made sensible of that difference. Sometimes one shall meet with those who perhaps innocently enough, but at the same time impertinently, will ask the question, *Why are you not merry? Why are you not gay, pleasant, and cheerful?* then, instead of answering, could I ask such a one, *Why are you not handsome? Why have you not black eyes and a better complexion?* Nature abhors to be forced.

The two famous philosophers of Ephesus and Abdera have their different sects at this day. Some weep and others laugh, at one and the same thing.

I don't doubt but you have observed several men laugh when they are angry, others who are silent, some that are loud; yet I cannot suppose that it is the passion of anger which is in itself different, or more or less in one than in t'other, but that it is in the humor of the man that is predominant, and urges him to expect it in that manner. Demonstrations of pleasure are as various: one man has a humor of retiring from all company, when anything has happened to please him beyond expectation; he hugs himself alone, and thinks it an addition to the pleasure to keep it secret. Another is upon thorns till he has made proclamation of it, and must make other people sensible of his happiness before he can be so himself. So it is in grief and other passions. Demonstrations of love and the effects of that passion upon several humors are infinitely different; but here the ladies who abound in servants are the best judges. Talking of the ladies, methinks something should be observed of the humor of the fair sex, since they are sometimes so kind as to furnish out a character for comedy. But I must confess I have never made any observation of what I apprehend to be true humor in women. Perhaps passions are too powerful in that sex to let humor have its course; or may be by reason of their natural coldness, humor cannot exert itself to that extravagant degree which it often does in the male sex. For if ever anything does appear comical or ridiculous in a woman, I think it is little more than an acquired folly or an affectation. We may call them the weaker sex, but I think the true reason is because our follies are stronger and our faults are more prevailing.

One might think that the diversity of humor, which must be allowed to be diffused throughout mankind, might afford endless matter for the support of comedies. But when we come closely to consider that point, and nicely to distinguish the differences of humors, I believe we shall find the contrary. For though we allow every man something of his own, and a peculiar humor, yet every man has it not in quantity to become remarkable by it; or, if many do become remarkable by their humors, yet all those humors may not be diverting. Nor is it only requisite to distinguish what humor will be diverting, but also how much of it, what part of it to show in light, and what to cast in shades, how to set it off by preparatory scenes, and by opposing other humors to it in the same scene. Through a wrong judgment, sometimes, men's humors may be opposed when there is really no specific difference between them, only a greater proportion of the same in one than in t'other, occasioned by his having more phlegm, or choler, or whatever the constitution is from whence their humors derive their source.

There is infinitely more to be said on this subject, though perhaps I have already said too much; but I have said it to a friend, who I am sure will not expose it, if he does not approve of it. I believe the subject is entirely new, and was never touched upon before; and if I would have anyone to see this private essay, it should be some one who might be provoked by my errors in it to publish a more judicious treatise on the subject. Indeed I wish it were done, that the world, being a little acquainted with the scarcity of true humor and the difficulty of finding and showing it, might look a little more favorably on the labors of them who endeavor to search into nature for it and lay it open to the public view.

I don't say but that very entertaining and useful characters, and proper to comedy, may be drawn from affectation and those other qualities which I have endeavored to distinguish from humor; but I would not have such imposed on the world for humor, nor esteemed with equal value with it. It were perhaps the work of a long life to make one comedy true in all its parts, and to give every character in it a true and distinct humor. Therefore every poet must be beholding to other helps to make out his number of ridiculous characters. But I think such a one deserves to be broke, who makes all false monsters; who does not show one true humor in a comedy, but entertains his audience to the end of the play with everything out of nature.

I will make but one observation to you more, and have done; and that is grounded upon an observation of your own, and which I mentioned at the beginning of my letter, viz., that there is more of humor in our English comic writers than in any others. I do not at all wonder at it, for I look upon humor to be almost of English growth; at least, it does not seem to have found such increase on any other soil. And what appears to me to be the reason of it is the greater freedom, privilege, and liberty which the common people of England enjoy. Any man that has a humor is under no restraint or fear of giving it vent; they have a proverb among them, which, may be, will show the bent and genius of the people as well as a longer discourse: "He that will have a may-pole, shall have a may-pole." This is a maxim with them, and their practice is agreeable to

it. I believe something considerable too may be ascribed to their feeding so much on flesh, and the grossness of their diet in general. But I have done; let the physicians agree that. Thus you have my thoughts of humor, to my power of expressing them in so little time and compass. You will be kind to show me wherein I have erred; and as you are very capable of giving me instruction, so I think I have a very just title to demand it from you, being without reserve,
Your real friend,
and humble servant,
W. CONGREVE.

GEORGE FARQUHAR

George Farquhar was born in Londonderry, Ireland, in 1677 or 1678. Little is known of his early years beyond the fact that he went to school in his native town and entered Trinity College, Dublin, in 1694. He remained there about a year. Not long after he made the acquaintance of the actor Robert Wilks, through whom he obtained a position on the Dublin stage, where he acted many parts during 1696. He accidentally wounded an actor and left the stage, having decided to write plays. He went to London that or the following year. *Love and a Bottle*, his first comedy, was produced at Drury Lane in 1698, and enjoyed a fair degree of popularity. It is interesting to know that soon after his arrival he discovered Nance Oldfield and with Vanbrugh's help, secured her a place with Rich. Farquhar's next play brought him a certain fame. This was *The Constant Couple*, produced in 1699. The next year found him in Holland, probably for his health. *Sir Harry Wildair*, his next play, was produced in 1701. *The Inconstant* and *The Twin Rivals* belong to the year 1702. Later in the same year Farquhar published a little collection of miscellaneous prose and verse, in which he included his *Discourse upon Comedy*. He was married probably the next year. He spent the following three in recruit-

ing for the army, though he collaborated with Motteux in an adaptation from the French, called *The Stage Coach* (1704). Two years later *The Recruiting Officer* was performed at Drury Lane. Though it was successful, Farquhar was harassed with debts and was forced to sell a commission which he held. During an illness in 1707 he wrote *The Beaux' Stratagem*, at the instigation of his friend Wilks. He died a few weeks after the first performance.

Farquhar's importance as a dramatist consists in his having combined many of the elements of the comedy of his time and evolving them into a form which was later developed by Goldsmith and Sheridan. One of the dire results of Collier's attack on the stage was the conversion of Farquhar. *The Twin Rivals* (1702) and its *Preface* constitute Farquhar's reply to Collier; the play, in the author's words, sets out to prove that "an English comedy may answer the strictness of poetical justice." This was precisely the "poetical justice" which Addison attacked in the *Spectator*, the conventional reward of virtue and punishment of vice. The *Discourse* published the same year contains a defense of the drama against Collier and his followers, but in general, it is merely a light essay, anti-classic in its rejection of the Unities.

On the drama:

Preface: To the Reader, in *The Constant Couple* (1700).
Prologue to *Sir Harry Wildair* (1701).
A Discourse Upon Comedy in Reference to the English Stage (1702).
Preface to *The Inconstant* (1703).
Preface to *The Twin-Rivals* (1705).
To All Friends round the Wrekin, in *The Recruiting Officer* (1706).

Editions:

The first collected edition of the plays is *The Comedies of Mr. George Farquhar,* published at London in 1709. The *Discourse* appeared in the *Works,* in 1714. It was first published in 1702, in the volume entitled *Love and Business.* The *Letters* are published in most of the editions after 1728, together with biographical notices. The *Discourse* is reprinted in *A Discourse upon Comedy, The Recruiting Officer, and The Beaux Stratagem,* by Louis A. Strauss (Boston, 1914), and by W. H. Durham, in *Critical Essays of the Eighteenth Century* (New Haven, 1915). The *Dramatic Works,* ·edited by A. C. Ewald in 2 vols., are reprinted (Lon-

don, 1892), and *Four Plays,* edited by William Archer, *Mermaid Series* (New York, 1905); also in Leigh Hunt's *Dramatic Works of Wycherley, Congreve, Vanbrugh, and Farquhar* (London, 1849 ff.).

On Farquhar and his works:

Prefatory matter to editions cited.
Christian Heinrich Schmid, *George Farquhar* (in *Englisches Theater,* erster theil, Introduction, Leipzig, 1772).
Heinrich Döring, *George Farquhar* (in *Encyclopädie der Wissenschaften und Kunste,* Leipzig, 1818).
Otto Hallbauer, *Life and Works of George Farquhar* (Holzminden, 1880).
Leslie Stephen, *George Farquhar* (in *Dictionary of National Biography,* vol. 18, London, 1889).
Edmund Gosse, *Gossip in a Library* (London, 1891).
David Schmid, *George Farquhar; sein Leben, und seine Original-Dramen* (Wien, 1904).
J. G. Robertson, *Lessing and Farquhar* (In *Modern Language Review,* vol. 2, 1907).

A DISCOURSE UPON COMEDY IN REFERENCE TO THE ENGLISH STAGE
In a Letter to a friend [1]
(1702)

But in the first place I must beg you, sir, to lay aside your superstitious veneration for antiquity, and the usual expressions on that score; that the present age is illiterate, or their taste is vitiated; that we live in the decay of time, and the dotage of the world is fallen to our share.—

'Tis a mistake, sir; the world was never more active or youthful, and true downright sense was never more universal than at this very day; 'tis neither confined to one nation in the world, nor to one part of a city; 'tis remarkable in

[1] Re-printed, with omissions, from *A Discourse Upon Comedy, The Recruiting Officer, and The Beaux' Stratagem, by George Farquhar,* edited by Louis A. Strauss (Boston, 1914).— Ed.

England as well as France, and good genuine reason is nourished by the cold of Sweden [Swedeland] as by the warmth of Italy; 'tis neither abdicated the court with the late reigns, nor expelled the city with the play-house bills; you may find it in the Grand Jury at Hick's-Hall, and upon the bench sometimes among the justices: then why should we be hampered so in our opinions, as if all the ruins of antiquity lay so heavily on the bones of us that we could not stir hand nor foot! No, no, sir, *ipse dixit* is removed long ago, and all the rubbish of old philosophy, that in a manner buried the judgment of mankind for many centuries, is now carried off; the vast tomes of Aristotle and his commentators are all taken to pieces, and their infallibility is lost with all persons of a free and unprejudiced reason.

Then above all men living, why should the poets be hoodwinked at this rate, and by what authority should Aristotle's rules of poetry stand so fixt and immutable? Why, by the authority of two thousand years' standing; because thro' this long revolution of time the world has still continued the same.— By the authority of their being received at Athens, a city the very same with London in every particular, their habits the same, their humors alike, their public transactions and private societies *A la mode France;* in short, so very much the same in every circumstance that Aristotle's criticisms may give rules to Drury Lane, the Areopagus give judgment upon a case in the King's Bench, and old Solon shall give laws to the House of Commons.

But to examine this matter a little farther: All arts and professions are compounded of these two parts, a speculative knowledge, and a practical use; and from an excellency in both these, any person is raised to eminence and authority in his calling. The lawyer has his years of student in the speculative part of his business; and when promoted to bar, he falls upon the practice, which is the trial of his ability. Without all dispute, the great Cook has had many a tug at the bar, before he could raise himself to the bench; and had made sufficiently evident his knowledge of the laws in his pleadings, before he was admitted to the authority of giving judgment upon the case.

The physician, to gain credit to his prescriptions, must labor for a reputation in the cure of such and such distempers; and before he sets up for a Galen or Hippocrates, must make many experiments upon his patients. Philosophy itself, which is a science the most abstract from practice, has its public acts and disputations; it is raised gradually, and its professor commences doctor by degrees; he has the labor of maintaining theses, methodizing his arguments, and clearing objections; his memory and understanding is often puzzled by oppositions counciled in fallacies and sophisms, in solving all which he must make himself remarkable, before he pretends to impose his own systems upon

the world. Now, if the case be thus in philosophy, or in any branch thereof, as in ethics, physics, which are called sciences, what must be done in poetry, that is denominated an art, and consequently implies a practice in its perfection?

Is it reasonable that any person that has never writ a distich of verses in his life should set up for a dictator in poetry; and without the least practice in his own performance must give laws and rules to that of others? Upon what foundation is poetry made so very cheap and so easy a task by these gentlemen? An excellent poet is the single production of an age, when we have crowds of philosophers, physicians, lawyers, divines every day, and all of them competently famous in their callings. In the two learned commonwealths of Rome and Athens, there was but one Vergil and one Homer, yet have we above a hundred philosophers in each, and most part of 'em, forsooth, must have a touch at poetry, drawing it into Divisions, Subdivisions, etc., when the wit of 'em all set together would not amount to one of Martial's *Epigrams.*

Of all these I shall mention only Aristotle, the first and great law-giver in this respect, and upon whom all that followed him are only commentators. Among all the vast tracts of this voluminous author we don't find any fragment of an epic poem, or the least scene of a play, to authorize his skill and excellence in that art. Let it not be alleged that for ought we know he was an excellent poet, but his more serious studies would not let him enter upon affairs of this nature; for everybody knows that Aristotle was no cynic, but lived in the splendor and air of the court; that he loved riches as much as others of that station, and being sufficiently acquainted with his pupils' affection to poetry, and his complaint that he wanted an Homer to aggrandize his actions, he would never have slipt such an opportunity of farther ingratiating himself in the king's favor, had he been conscious of any abilities in himself for such an undertaking; and having a more noble and copious theme in the exploits of Alexander than what inspired the blind bard in his hero Achilles. If his epistles to Alexander were always answered with a considerable present, what might he have expected from a work like Homer's upon so great a subject, dedicated to so mighty a prince, whose greatest fault was his vain glory, and that took such pains to be deified among men?

It may be objected that all the works of Aristotle are not recovered; and among those that are lost some essays of this kind might have perished. This supposition is too weakly founded; for altho' the works themselves might have 'scaped us, 'tis more than probable that some hint or other, either in the life of the conqueror, or philosopher, might appear to convince us of such a production. Besides, as 'tis believed he writ philosophy, because we have his books; so I dare swear he writ no poetry, because none is extant, nor any mention made thereof that ever I could hear of.

But stay — without any farther enquiry into the poetry of Aristotle, his ability that way is sufficiently apparent by that excellent piece he has left behind him upon that subject.— By your favor, sir, this is *Petitio Principii*, or, in plain English, give me the sword in my own hand, and I'll fight with you.— Have but a little patience till I make a flourish or two, and then, if you are pleased to demand it, I'll grant you that and everything else.

How easy were it for me to take one of Doctor Tillotson's sermons, and, out of the œconomy of one of these discourses, trump you up a pamphlet and call it *The Art of Preaching!* In the first place I must take a *Text*, and here I must be very learned upon the etymology of this word text; then this text must be divided into such and such *Partitions*, which partitions must have their hard names and derivations; then these must be spun into *Subdivisions*, and these backed by proofs of Scripture, *Ratiocinatio Oratoris, Ornamental Figurarum Rhetoricarum*, and *Authoritas Patrum Ecclesiæ*, with some rules and directions how these ought to be managed and applied. And closing up this difficult pedantry with the *Dimensions of Time* for such an occasion, you will pay me the compliment of an excellent preacher, and affirm that any sermon whatsoever, either by a Presbiter at Geneva, or Jesuit in Spain, that deviates from these rules deserves to be hissed, and the priest kicked out of his pulpit. I must doubt your complaisance in this point, sir; for you know the forms of eloquence are divers, and ought to be suited to the different humor and capacities of an audience. You are sensible, sir, that the fiery, choleric humor of one nation must be entertained and moved by other means than the heavy, flegmatic complexion of another; and I have observed in my little travels, that a sermon of three-quarters of an hour that might please the congregation at St. James's would never satisfy the meeting house in the City, where people expect more for their money; and, having more temptations of roguery, must have a larger portion of instruction.

Be pleased to hear another instance of a different kind, tho' to the same purpose. I go down to Woolwich, and there upon a piece of paper I take the dimensions of the Royal Sovereign, and from hence I frame a model of a man-of-war: I divide the ship into three principal parts, the keel, the hull, and the rigging; I subdivide these into their proper denominations, and by the help of a sailor, give you all the terms belonging to every rope and every office in the whole ship; will you from hence infer that I am an excellent shipwright, and that this model is proper for a trading junck upon the Volga, or a Venetian galley in the Adriatic sea?

But you'll object, perhaps, that this is no parallel case, because that Aristotle's *Ars Poetica* was never drawn from such slight observations, but was the pure effect of his immense reason, thro' a nice inspection into the very bottom and foundation of nature.

To this I answer, that verity is eternal, as that the truth of two and two making four was as certain in the days of Adam as it is now; and that, according to his own position, nature is the same *apud omnes Gentes*. Now, if his rules of poetry were drawn from certain and immutable principles, and fixed on the basis of nature, why should not his *Ars Poetica* be as efficacious now as it was two thousand years ago? And why should not a single plot, with perfect unity of time and place, do as well at Lincoln's-Inn-Fields as at the play-house in Athens? No, no, sir, I am apt to believe that the philosopher took no such pains in poetry as you imagine; the Greek was his mother tongue, and Homer was read with as much veneration among the school-boys as we learn our Cate- chism. Then where was the great busi- ness for a person so expert in mood and figures as Aristotle was to range into some order a parcel of terms of art, drawn from his observations upon the *Iliads,* and these to call the model of an epic poem? Here, sir, you may imagine that I am caught, and have all this while been spinning a thread to strangle my- self. One of my main objections against Aristotle's criticisms is drawn from his non-performance in poetry; and now I affirm that his rules are extracted from the greatest poet that ever lived, which gives the utmost validity to the precept, and that is all we contend for.

.   .   .   .   .

Neither is Aristotle to be allowed any farther knowledge in dramatic than in epic poetry. Euripides, whom he seems to compliment by rules adapted to the model of his plays, was either his con- temporary or lived but a little before him; he was not insensible how much this author was the darling of the city, as appeared by the prodigious expense dis- bursed by the public for the ornament of his plays; and, 'tis probable, he might take this opportunity of improving his interest with the people, indulging their inclination by refining upon the beauty of what they admired. And besides all this, the severity of dramatic rage was so fresh in his memory in the hard usage that his brother soph not long before met with upon the stage, that it was conven- ient to humor the reigning wit, lest a second Aristophanes should take him to task with as little mercy as poor Socra- tes found at the hands of the first.

I have talked so long to lay a founda- tion for these following conclusions: Aristotle was no poet, and consequently not capable of giving instructions in the art of poetry; his *Ars Poetica* are only some observations drawn from the works of Homer and Euripides, which may be mere accidents resulting casually from the composition of the works, and not any of the essential principles on which they are compiled; that without giving himself the trouble of searching into the

nature of poetry, he has only compli- mented the heroes of wit and valor of his age, by joining with them in their appro- bation; with this difference, that their applause was plain, and his more scho- lastic.

But to leave these only as suppositions to be relished by every man at his pleas- ure, I shall without complimenting any author, either ancient or modern, inquire into the first invention of comedy; what were the true designs and honest inten- tions of that art; and from a knowledge of the *end,* seek out the *means,* without one quotation of Aristotle, or authority of Euripides.

In all productions either divine or hu- man, the final cause is the first mover, because the end or intention of any ra- tional action must first be considered be- fore the material or efficient causes are put in execution. Now, to determine the final cause of comedy we must run back beyond the material and formal agents, and take it in its very infancy, or rather in the very first act of its generation, when its primary parent, by proposing such or such an end of his labor, laid down the first sketches or shadows of the piece. Now, as all arts and sciences have their first rise from a final cause, so 'tis certain that they have grown from very small beginnings, and that the cur- rent of time has swelled 'em to such a bulk that nobody can find the fountain by any proportion between the head and the body; this, with the corruption of time, which has debauched things from their primitive innocence to selfish de- signs and purposes, renders it difficult to find the origin of any offspring so very unlike its parent.

This is not only the case of comedy, as it stands at present, but the condition also of the ancient theaters; when great men made shows of this nature a rising step to their ambition, mixing many lewd and lascivious representations to gain the favor of the populace, to whose taste and entertainment the plays were chiefly adopted. We must therefore go higher than either Aristophanes or Menander to discover comedy in its primitive institu- tion, if we would draw any moral design of its invention to warrant and author- ize its continuance.

I have already mentioned the difficulty

of discovering the invention of any art in the different figure it makes by succession of improvements; but there is something in the nature of comedy, even in its present circumstances, that bears so great a resemblance to the philosophical mythology of the ancients, that old Æsop must wear the bays as the first and original author; and whatever alterations or improvements farther application may have subjoined, his *Fables* gave the first rise and occasion.

Comedy is no more at present than *a well-framed tale handsomely told as an agreeable vehicle for counsel or reproof.* This is all we can say for the credit of its institution, and is the stress of its charter for liberty and toleration. Then where should we seek for a foundation but in Æsop's symbolical way of moralizing upon tales and fables? with this difference: that his stories were shorter than ours. He had his tyrant Lyon, his statesman Fox, his beau Magpie, his coward Hare, his bravo Ass, and his buffoon Ape, with all the characters that crowd our stages every day; with this distinction, nevertheless, that Æsop made his beasts speak good Greek, and our heroes sometimes can't talk English.

But whatever difference time has produced in the form, we must in our own defense stick to the end and intention of his fables. *Utile Dulce* was his motto, and must be our business; we have no other defense against the presentment of the grand jury, and, for ought I know, it might prove a good means to mollify the rigor of that persecution, to inform the inquisitors that the great Æsop was the first inventor of these poor comedies that they are prosecuting with so much eagerness and fury; that the first laureate was as just, as prudent, as pious, as reforming, and as ugly as any of themselves; and that the beasts which are lugged upon the stage by the horns are not caught in the city, as they suppose, but brought out of Æsop's own forest. We should inform them, besides, that those very tales and fables which they apprehend as obstacles to reformation were the main instruments and machines used by the wise Æsop for its propagation; and as he would improve men by the policy of beasts, so we endeavor to reform brutes with the examples of men.

Fondlewife and his young spouse are no more than the eagle and cockle; he wanted teeth to break the shell himself, so somebody else run away with the meat. The fox in the play is the same with the fox in the fable, who stufft his guts so full that he could not get out at the same hole he came in; so both Reynards, being delinquents alike, come to be trussed up together. Here are precepts, admonitions, and salutary innuendoes for the ordering of our lives and conversations couched in these allegories and allusions. The wisdom of the ancients was wrapt up in veils and figures; the Ægyptian hierogliphics and the history of the heathen gods are nothing else. But if these pagan authorities give offense to their scrupulous consciences, let them but consult the tales and parables of our Savior in holy Writ, and they may find this way of instruction to be much more Christian than they imagine. Nathan's fable of the poor man's lamb had more influence on the conscience of David than any force of downright admonition. So that by ancient practice and modern example, by the authority of Pagans, Jews, and Christians, the world is furnished with this so sure, so pleasant, and expedient an art of schooling mankind into better manners. Now, here is the primary design of comedy illustrated from its first institution; and the same end is equally alleged for its daily practice and continuance.— Then, without all dispute, whatever means are most proper and expedient for compassing this end and intention, they must be the *just rules of comedy,* and the *true art of the stage.*

We must consider, then, in the first place, that our business lies not with a French or a Spanish audience; that our design is not to hold forth to ancient Greece, nor to moralize upon the vices and defaults of the Roman Commonwealth. No, no; an English play is intended for the use and instruction of an English audience, a people not only separated from the rest of the world by situation, but different also from other nations as well in the complexion and temperament of the natural body as in the constitution of our body politic. As we are a mixture of many nations, so we have the most unaccountable medley of humors among us of any people upon earth; these humors produce variety of follies, some of 'em unknown to former ages; these new distempers must have new remedies, which are nothing but new counsels and instructions.

Now, sir, if our *Utile*, which is the end, be different from the ancients, pray let our *Dulce*, which is the means, be so too; for you know that to different towns there are different ways; or, if you would have it more scholastically, *ad diversos fines non idem conducit medium;* or, mathematically, one and the same line cannot terminate in two centers. But waving this manner of concluding by induction, I shall gain my point a nearer way, and draw it immediately from the first principle I set down: *That we have the most unaccountable medley of humors among us of any nation upon earth;* and this is demonstrable from common experience. We shall find a Wildair in one corner, and a Morose in another; nay, the space of an hour or two shall create such vicissitudes of temper in the same person that he can hardly be taken for the same man. We shall have a fellow bestir his stumps from chocolate to coffee-house with all the joy and gaiety imaginable, tho' he want a shilling to pay for a hack; whilst another, drawn about in a coach and six, is eaten up with the spleen, and shall loll in state with as much melancholy, vexation, and discontent, as if he were making the Tour of Tyburn. Then what sort of a *Dulce,* (which I take for the pleasantry of the tale, or the plot of the play) must a man make use of to engage the attention of so many different humors and inclinations? Will a single plot satisfy everybody? Will the turns and surprises that may result naturally from the ancient limits of time be sufficient to rip open the spleen of some and physic the melancholy of others, screw up the attention of a rover and fix him to the stage in spight of his volatile temper and the temptation of a mask? To make the moral instructive, you must make the story diverting. The splenetic wit, the beau courtier, the heavy citizen, the fine lady, and her fine footman come all to be instructed, and therefore must all be diverted; and he that can do this best, and with most applause, writes the best

comedy, let him do it by what rules he pleases, so they be not offensive to religion and good manners.

But *hic labor, hoc opus:* how must this secret of pleasing so many different tastes be discovered? Not by tumbling over volumes of the ancients, but by studying the humor of the moderns. The rules of English comedy don't lie in the compass of Aristotle or his followers, but in the pit, box, and galleries. And to examine into the humor of an English audience, let us see by what means our own English poets have succeeded in this point. To determine a suit at law we don't look into the archives of Greece or Rome, but inspect the reports of our own lawyers, and the acts and statutes of our Parliaments; and by the same rule we have nothing to do with the models of Menander or Plautus, but must consult Shakespeare, Johnson, Fletcher, and others, who, by methods much different from the ancients, have supported the English stage and made themselves famous to posterity. We shall find that these gentlemen have fairly dispensed with the greatest part of critical formalities; the decorums of time and place, so much cried up of late, had no force of decorum with them; the economy of their plays was *ad libitum,* and the extent of their plots only limited by the convenience of action. I would willingly understand the regularities of *Hamlet, Macbeth, Henry the Fourth,* and of Fletcher's plays: and yet these have long been the darlings of the English audience, and are like to continue with the same applause, in defiance of all the criticisms that ever were published in Greek and Latin.

But are there no rules, no decorums, to be observed in comedy? Must we make the condition of the English stage a state of anarchy? No, sir — for there are extremes in irregularity as dangerous to an author as too scrupulous a deference to criticism; and as I have given you an instance of one, so I shall present you an example of the t'other.

There are a sort of gentlemen that have had the jaunty education of dancing, French, and a fiddle, who, coming to age before they arrive at years of discretion, make a shift to spend a handsome patrimony of two or three thousand pound, by soaking in the tavern all night, lolling a-bed all the morning, and sauntering away all the evening between the two play-houses with their hands in their pockets; you shall have a gentleman of this size, upon his knowledge of Covent-Garden and a knack of witticizing in his cups, set up immediately for a playwright. But besides the gentleman's wit and experience, here is another motive: there are a parcel of saucy, impudent fellows about the play-house called door-keepers, that can't let a gentleman see a play in peace, without jogging and nudging him every minute. *Sir, will you please to pay? — Sir, the act's done, will you please to pay, sir?* I have broke their heads all round two or three times, yet the puppies will still be troublesome. Before gad, I'll be plagued with 'em no longer; I'll e'en write a play myself; by which means my character of wit shall be established, I shall enjoy the freedom of the house, and to pin up the basket, pretty Miss —— shall have the profits of my third night for her maidenhead. Thus we see what a great blessing is a coming girl to a play-house. Here is a poet sprung from the tail of an actress, like Minerva from Jupiter's head. But my spark proceeds: — My own intrigues are sufficient to found the plot, and the devil's in 't if I can make my character talk as wittily as those in the *Trip to the Jubilee.* But stay — What shall I call it, first? Let me see — *The Rival Theatres.—* Very good, by gad, because I reckon the two houses will have a contest about this very play.— Thus having found a name for his play, in the next place he makes a play to his name, and thus he begins.

ACT I. SCENE: *Covent-Garden. Enter* PORTICO, PIAZA, *and* TURNSTILE.

Here you must note that Portico, being a compound of practical rake and speculative gentleman, is ten to one the author's own character, and the leading card in the pack. Piaza is his mistress, who lives in the square, and is daughter to old Pillariso, an odd, out-o'the-way gentleman, something between the character of Alexander the Great and Solon, which must please because it is new.

Turnstile is maid and confident to Piaza, who, for a bribe of ten pieces, lets Portico in at the back-door; so the first act concludes.

In the second, enter Spigotoso, who was butler, perhaps, to the Czar of Muscovy, and Fossetana his wife. After these characters are run dry, he brings you in, at the third act, Whinewell and Charmarillis for a scene of love to please the ladies, and so he goes on without fear or wit till he comes to a marriage or two, and then he writes — *Finis.*

'Tis then whispered among his friends at Will's and Hippolito's, that Mr. Such-a-one has writ a very pretty comedy; and some of 'em, to encourage the young author, equip him presently with prologue and epilogue. Then the play is sent to Mr. Rich or Mr. Betterton in a fair, legible hand, with the recommendation of some gentleman that passes for a man of parts and a critic. In short, the gentleman's interest has the play acted, and the gentleman's interest makes a present to pretty Miss ——; she's made his whore, and the stage his cully, that for the loss of a month in rehearsing, and a hundred pound in dressing a confounded play, must give the liberty of the house to him and his friends for ever after.

Now, such a play may be written with all the exactness imaginable, in respect of unity in time and place; but if you inquire its character of any person, tho' of the meanest understanding of the whole audience, he will tell you 'tis intolerable stuff; and upon your demanding his reasons, his answer is, *I don't like it.* His humor is the only rule that he can judge a comedy by, but you find that mere nature is offended with some irregularities; and tho' he be not so learned in the drama, to give you an inventory of the faults, yet I can tell you that one part of the plot had no dependence upon another, which made this simple man drop his attention, and concern for the event; and so, disengaging his thoughts from the business of the action, he sat there very uneasy, thought the time very tedious, because he had nothing to do. The characters were so uncoherent in themselves, and composed of such variety of absurdities, that in his knowledge of nature he could find no original for such a copy; and being therefore unacquainted with any folly they reproved, or any virtue that they recommended, their business was as flat and tiresome to him as if the actors had talked Arabic.

Now, these are the material irregularities of a play, and these are the faults which downright mother-sense can censure and be offended at, as much as the most learned critic in the pit. And altho' the one cannot give me the reasons of his approbation or dislike, yet I will take his word for the credit or disrepute of a comedy sooner perhaps than the opinion of some virtuosos; for there are some gentlemen that have fortified their spleen so impregnably with criticism, and hold out so stiffly against all attacks of pleasantry, that the most powerful efforts of wit and humor cannot make the least impression. What a misfortune is it to these gentlemen to be natives of such an ignorant, self-willed, impertinent island, where let a critic and a scholar find never so many irregularities in a play, yet five hundred saucy people will give him the lie to his face, and come to see this wicked play forty or fifty times in a year. But this *Vox Populi* is the devil, tho', in a place of more authority than Aristotle, it is called *Vox Dei*. Here is a play with a vengeance, (says a critic,) to bring the transaction of a year's time into the compass of three hours; to carry the whole audience with him from one kingdom to another by the changing of a scene: where's the probability, nay, the possibility of all this? The devil's in the poet, sure; he don't think to put contradictions upon us?

Look'ee, sir, don't be in a passion. The poet does not impose contradictions upon you, because he has told you no lie; for that only is a lie which is related with some fallacious intention that you should believe it for a truth. Now, the poet expects no more that you should believe the plot of his play than old Æsop designed the world should think his eagle and lion talked like you and I; which, I think, was every jot as improbable as what you quarrel with; and yet the fables took, and I'll be hanged if you yourself don't like 'em. But besides, sir, if you are so inveterate against improbabilities, you must never come near the playhouse at all; for there are several improbabilities, nay, impossibilities, that all the

criticisms in nature cannot correct: as, for instance, in the part of Alexander the Great, to be affected with the transactions of the play, we must suppose that we see that great conqueror, after all his triumphs, shunned by the woman he loves, and importuned by her he hates; crossed in his cups and jollity by his own subjects, and at last miserably ending his life in a raging madness. We must suppose that we see the very Alexander, the son of Philip, in all these unhappy circumstances, else we are not touched by the moral, which represents to us the uneasiness of human life in the greatest state, and the instability of fortune in respect of worldly pomp. Yet the whole audience at the same time knows that this is Mr. Betterton who is strutting upon the stage and tearing his lungs for a livelihood. And that the same person should be Mr. Betterton and Alexander the Great at the same time is somewhat like an impossibility, in my mind. Yet you must grant this impossibility in spite of your teeth, if you han't power to raise the old hero from the grave to act his own part.

Now for another impossibility: The less rigid critics allow to a comedy the space of an artificial day, or twenty-four hours; but those of the thorough reformation will confine it to the natural, or solar, day, which is but half the time. Now, admitting this for a decorum absolutely requisite,— this play begins when it is exactly six by your watch, and ends precisely at nine, which is the usual time of the representation. Now, is it feazible in *rerum natura*, that the same space or extent of time can be three hours by your watch and twelve hours upon the stage, admitting the same number of minutes or the same measure of sand to both? I'm afraid, sir, you must allow this for an impossibility, too; and you may with as much reason allow the play the extent of a whole year; and if you grant me a year, you may give me seven, and so to a thousand. For that a thousand years should come within the compass of three hours is no more an impossibility than that two minutes should be contained in one; *Nullum minu continet in se majus* is equally applicable to both.

So much for the decorum of Time: now for the regularity of Place. I might make the one a consequence of t'other, and allege that by allowing me any extent of time, you must grant me any change of place, for the one depends upon t'other; and having five or six years for the action of a play, I may travel from Constantinople to Denmark, so to France, and home to England, and rest long enough in each country besides. But you'll say: How can you carry us with you? Very easily, sir, if you be willing to go. As for example: here is a new play; the house is thronged, the prologue's spoken and the curtain drawn represents you the scene of Grand Cairo. Whereabouts are you now, sir? Were not you the very minute before in the pit in the English play-house talking to a wench, and now, *presto pass*, you are spirited away to the banks of the river Nile. Surely, sir, this is a most intolerable improbability; yet this you must allow me, or else you destroy the very constitution of representation. Then, in the second act, with a flourish of the fiddles, I change the scene to Astrachan. *O, this is intolerable!* Look'ee, sir, 'tis not a jot more intolerable than the other; for you'll find that 'tis much about the same distance between Egypt and Astrachan, as it is between Drury-Lane and Grand Cairo; and if you please to let your fancy take post, it will perform the journey in the same moment of time, without any disturbance in the world to your person. You can follow Quintus Curtius all over Asia in the train of Alexander, and trudge after Hannibal, like a cadet, through all Italy, Spain, and Afric, in the space of four or five hours; yet the devil a one of you will stir a step over the threshold for the best poet in Christendom, tho he make it his business to make heroes more amiable, and to surprise you with more wonderful accidents and events.

I am as little a friend to those rambling plays as anybody, nor have I ever espoused their party by my own practice; yet I could not forbear saying something in vindication of the great Shakespear, whom every little fellow can form an *A[o]ristus primus* will presume to condemn for indecorums and absurdities; sparks that are so spruce upon their Greek and Latin that, like our fops in travel, they can relish nothing but

what is foreign, to let the world know they have been abroad forsooth; but it must be so, because Aristotle said it; now, I say it must be otherwise, because Shakespear said it, and I'm sure that Shakespear was the greater poet of the two. But you'll say that Aristotle was the greater critic.— That's a mistake, sir, for criticism in poetry is no more than judgment in poetry; which you will find in your lexicon. Now, if Shakespear was the better poet, he must have the most judgment in his art; for everybody knows that judgment is an essential part of poetry, and without it no writer is worth a farthing. But to stoop to the authority of either, without consulting the reason of the consequence, is an abuse to a man's understanding; and neither the precept of the philosopher nor example of the poet should go down with me, without exam[in]ing the weight of their assertions. We can expect no more decorum or regularity in any business than the nature of the thing will bear; now, if the stage cannot subsist without the strength of supposition and force of fancy in the audience, why should a poet fetter the business of his plot and starve his action for the nicety of an hour or the change of a scene; since the thought of man can fly over a thousand years with the same ease, and in the same instant of time, that your eye glances from the figure of six to seven on the dial-plate; and can glide from the Cape of Good-Hope to the Bay of St. Nicholas, which is quite across the world, with the same quickness and activity as between Covent-Garden Church and Will's Coffee-House. Then I must beg of these gentlemen to let our old English authors alone.— If they have left vice unpunished, virtue unrewarded, folly unexposed, or prudence unsuccessful, the contrary of which is the *Utile* of comedy, let them be lashed to some purpose; if any part of their plots have been independent of the rest, or any of their characters forced or unnatural, which destroys the *Dulce* of plays, let them be hissed off the stage. But if by a true decorum in these material points, they have writ successfully and answered the end of dramatic poetry in every respect, let them rest in peace, and their memories enjoy the encomiums due to their merit, without any reflection for waving those niceties, which are neither instructive to the world nor diverting to mankind, but are, like all the rest of critical learning, fit only to set people together by the ears in ridiculous controversies, that are not one jot material to the good of the public, whether they be true or false.

And thus you see, sir, I have concluded a very unnecessary piece of work; which is much too long if you don't like it. But let it happen any way, be assured that I intended to please you, which should partly excuse, sir,

Your most humble Servant.

JOSEPH ADDISON

Joseph Addison was born at Milston, Wiltshire, in 1672. He was a student at the Charter House, which he left in 1687, to enter Queen's College, Oxford. After two years he was transferred to Magdalen, where he was graduated in 1693. He distinguished himself while at college for his shyness and his scholarship. In the year of his graduation he published his *Account of the Greatest English Poets*. Through Dryden, to whom he addressed some complimentary verses, he was introduced to Tonson, who set him to work translating Juvenal, Persius, Vergil, and Herodotus. While he was still at Oxford, where he remained on a fellowship after his graduation, he was on the point of taking orders, but a royal pension was obtained for him, and he set forth on his travels on the Continent. He started in 1699, spent a year and a half in France, a year in Italy, and another in Switzerland, Austria, and Germany; and after a stay of some months in Holland, he returned to England toward the end of 1703. He was reduced in circumstances, and had little hope of preferment in politics, so that he was forced to join the writers in Grub Street. But, owing to a change in the tide of affairs, and to Addison's popularity after the publication of his poem, *The Campaign,* he was made Under-Secretary of State. Meantime he was engaged in literary work, and in 1706 he produced an unsuccessful opera, *Rosamond*. Two years later Addison was deprived of his position as Under-Secretary, but was offered a Secretaryship in Ireland under the Lord Lieutenant. In 1711 he lost the post owing to a change

of the Ministry. Steele's *Tatler* papers began to appear in 1709, and Addison's first contribution dates from the same year. In 1711 he and Steele brought out the first number of *The Spectator,* which continued until 1714. In 1713 his tragedy of *Cato* was performed and met with great success because rather of its political timeliness than for any dramatic power inherent in it. An unsuccessful play, *The Drummer,* was produced, anonymously, in 1714. During the winter of 1715–16 Addison was employed by the Whig Party to uphold its interests, and he published *The Freeholder,* a political paper; his reward was in all probability the position of Commissioner for Trade and Colonies. In 1716 he married the Countess of Warwick. In 1717 he was made a Secretary of State. Failing in health, he resigned the position a year later. The next year he engaged in further political controversy, which resulted in a break with Steele. The following year he died.

Of Addison's criticism as a whole it may be said that it represented a commonsense attitude based upon neo-classic ideals. Of his dramatic criticism proper, confined as it was almost wholly to five or six *Spectator* essays, there is not so much to be said. These essays were written before he had evolved the critical standards which add so materially to the value of his later contributions. However, the drama essays briefly sum up the rationalistic tendency of criticism in the early eighteenth century. Addison condemned English tragedy because it was not sufficiently moral, and he proceeded to write a dull tragedy in order to show what beautiful and stately sentiments should go into tragedy. He was rigidly classic in his denunciation of the tragi-comedy. Not until Johnson published his 156th *Rambler* (in 1751) was the classic spell broken.

On the drama:

The Spectator, nos. 39, 40, 41, 42, 44, 45, 58, 59, 60, 61, 62, 63, 258, 290, 296, 419, and 446 (1711-12).

Editions:

The best modern edition of the complete works, is Hurd's *The Works of Joseph Addison*, 6 vols. (Bohn ed., London,

1854–56)). A convenient edition of *The Spectator* is the reprint of the first edition, in Everyman's Library, 4 vols. (London and New York, 1906). See Thomas Arnold's *Selections from Addison's papers contributed to the Spectator* (Oxford, 1866 ff.).

On Addison and his works:

Thomas Tickell, *Life of Joseph Addison* (*Preface* to 1st ed. of Addison's *Works*, London, 1721).
Lucy Aikin, *The Life of Joseph Addison*, 2 vols. (London, 1843).
W. J. Courthope, *Addison* (London, 1884).

THE SPECTATOR [1]
(1711)

No. 39.   Saturday, April 14.

Multa fero, ut placem genus irritabile vatum.
Cum scribo. . . .   HOR.

As a perfect tragedy is the noblest production of human nature, so it is capable of giving the mind one of the most delightful and most improving entertainments. A virtuous man, says Seneca, struggling with misfortunes, is such a spectacle as gods might look upon with pleasure. And such a pleasure it is which one meets with in the representation of a well-written tragedy. Diversions of this kind wear out of our thoughts everything that is mean and little. They cherish and cultivate that humanity which is the ornament of our nature. They soften insolence, soothe affliction, and subdue the mind to the dispensations of Providence.

It is no wonder, therefore, that in all the polite nations of the world, this part of the drama has met with public encouragement.

The modern tragedy excels that of Greece and Rome in the intricacy and disposition of the fable; but, what a Christian writer would be ashamed to

1 Re-printed, with omissions, from vol. 1 of *The Spectator* (Everyman's Library, London and New York, 1906).— Ed.

own, falls infinitely short of it in the moral part of the performance. . . .

.   .   .   .   .   .

No. 40.   Monday, April 16

The English writers of tragedy are possessed with a notion that when they represent a virtuous or innocent person in distress, they ought not to leave him till they have delivered him out of his troubles, or made him triumph over his enemies. This error they have been led into by a ridiculous doctrine in modern criticism, that they are obliged to an equal distribution of rewards and punishments, and an impartial execution of poetical justice. Who were the first that established this rule I know not; but I am sure it has no foundation in nature, in reason, or in the practice of the ancients. We find that good and evil happen alike to all men on this side of the grave; and as the principal design of tragedy is to raise commiseration and terror in the minds of the audience, we shall defeat this great end if we always make virtue and innocence happy and successful. Whatever crosses and disappointments a good man suffers in the body of the tragedy, they will make but small impression on our minds, when we know that in the last act he is to arrive at the end of his wishes and desires.

When we see him engaged in the depth of his afflictions, we are apt to comfort ourselves, because we are sure he will find his way out of them; and that his grief, how great soever it may be at present, will soon terminate in gladness. For this reason the ancient writers of tragedy treated men in their plays as they are dealt with in the world, by making virtue sometimes happy and sometimes miserable, as they found it in the fable which they made choice of, or as it might affect their audience in the most agreeable manner. Aristotle considers tragedies that were written in either of these kinds, and observes that those which ended unhappily, had always pleased the people, and carried away the prize in the public disputes of the stage, from those that ended happily. Terror and commiseration leave a pleasing anguish in the mind, and fix the audience in such a serious composure of thought, as is much more lasting and delightful than any little transient starts of joy and satisfaction. Accordingly, we find that more of our English tragedies have succeeded, in which the favorites of the audience sink under their calamities, than those in which they recover themselves out of them. The best plays of this kind are *The Orphan, Venice Preserved, Alexander the Great, Theodosius, All for Love, Œdipus, Oroonoko, Othello*, etc. *King Lear* is an admirable tragedy of the same kind as Shakespeare wrote it, but as it reformed according to the chimerical notion of poetical justice, in my humble opinion it has lost half its beauty. At the same time I must allow that there are very noble tragedies which have been framed upon the other plan and have ended happily; as indeed most of the good tragedies which have been written since the starting of the above-

mentioned criticism, have taken this turn, as *The Mourning Bride, Tamerlane, Ulysses, Phædra and Hippolytus*, with most of Mr. Dryden's. I must also allow that many of Shakespeare's, and several of the celebrated tragedies of antiquity, are cast in the same form. I do not therefore dispute against this way of writing tragedies, but against the criticism that would establish this as the only method, and by that means would very much cramp the English tragedy, and perhaps give a wrong bent to the genius of our writers.

The tragi-comedy, which is the product of the English theater, is one of the most monstrous inventions that ever entered into a poet's thoughts. An author might as well think of weaving the adventures of Æneas and Hudibras into one poem, as of writing such a motley piece of mirth and sorrow. But the absurdity of these performances is so very visible that I shall not insist upon it.

The same objections which are made to tragi-comedy may in some measure be applied to all tragedies that have a double plot in them; which are likewise more frequent upon the English stage than upon any other. For though the grief of the audience in such performance be not changed into another passion, as in tragi-comedies, it is diverted upon another object, which weakens their concern for the principal action, and breaks the tide of sorrow by throwing it into different channels. This inconvenience, however, may in a great measure be cured, if not wholly removed, by the skillful choice of an under-plot, which may bear such a near relation to the principal design, as to contribute towards the completion of it, and be concluded by the same catastrophe.

.　　.　　.　　.　　.　　.

SAMUEL JOHNSON

Samuel Johnson, the son of a bookseller and magistrate, was born at Lichfield, in 1709. At school he soon distinguished himself as a talented scholar and at the age of eighteen returned home, where he studied and read. The Johnson family was unable to send Samuel to college, but through the generosity of a friend he was sent to Oxford, where he remained only two years, when he reached the end of his meager resources. He spent the next five years near his home, endeavoring to make a living by hack work. In 1735 he married Elizabeth Porter, who brought him a small dowry. After his marriage he tried to secure pupils, but during a year and half only three came to him. One of these was David Garrick. In 1737 he went to London, and after many privations, in the following year was employed to write for the *Gentleman's Magazine*, for which he reported parliamentary proceedings. His first work of any importance was *London* (1738), a satirical poem in imitation of Juvenal. The book was published anonymously, but the author's name soon became known. As a result, Pope tried to get Johnson a position as teacher, but was unable to do so. Johnson again went to work as before. He had made the acquaintance of Savage, and at his death in 1743 he wrote his biography, which was published anonymously. From this time forward, Johnson's reputation grew, so that in 1747 he was employed by a number of booksellers to write the *Dictionary of the English Language*, which was the greatest monument of his life. It appeared in 1755. Meanwhile he sought relaxation in other work, and published *The Vanity of Human Wishes*, after Juvenal, in 1749. The same year Garrick produced his tragedy of *Irene*, part of which was written before Johnson's arrival in London. Although the play was scarcely successful, Johnson reaped considerable profit. In 1750 he began publishing articles and essays after the manner of *The Spectator*, and continued until two years later. *The Rambler* was at first coldly received, but after the essays had been collected into book-form, it was one of the most popular works of the day. Mrs. Johnson died in 1752, and her death left Johnson in a more melancholy mood than usual. The publication of the *Dictionary* did much for his fame, but little for his pocket, and twice in 1755 he was sent to jail for debt. He wrote miscellaneous essays for the *Literary Magazine* and planned his edition of Shakespeare, and in 1758 issued in book-form another collection of essays, *The Idler*. At this time he wrote *Rasselas* in a week, and sold it for a hundred pounds, to defray

the expenses of his mother's funeral. In 1762 George III offered Johnson a pension of three hundred pounds, which the needy author accepted, and which enabled him henceforward to do work of a more congenial nature. But he had a duty to discharge: for nine years he had been planning the edition of Shakespeare and spending the money sent in by subscribers. In 1765 the work appeared. The *Introduction* and *Notes* were very unequal, and Johnson was severely criticized for the slovenliness and inadequacy of his work. His laziness was such that between 1765 and 1775 he produced nothing but three political tracts. But his personal influence was growing, and he reigned over the famous literary coterie of which Goldsmith, Burke, Reynolds, Gibbon, Garrick, and others were members. Boswell was ever present, and it is due to his assiduity that we possess the celebrated *Life of Johnson.* In 1773 Boswell accompanied him on a trip to the Hebrides, which resulted in the publication of his *Journey to the Hebrides,* two years later. In 1777 he undertook to write brief biographical notices for an edition of the English poets which was about to be published. The short notices which he had originally intended to supply grew to considerable size. The first four volumes appeared in 1779, the last six, two years later. His last years were spent in pain and anxiety, and after a long period of ill-health, he died in 1784.

Johnson is the representative orthodox critic of the eighteenth century, and yet his orthodoxy, so far as his opinions on the drama are concerned, was not too exclusive or rigid. While he was continually insisting upon the necessity for a moral in works of art, and judging poetry by the sense rather than by the music, he was not intolerant to the authors who violated accepted rules. In his *Preface to Shakespeare* (1768) he mentions the poet's mingling of the tragic and the comic in a single play, saying that "this is a practice contrary to the rules of criticism will be readily allowed," but he adds what is of great significance: "but there is always an appeal open from criticism to nature." This sentence belongs with the famous one in the 156th *Rambler,* on

Tragi-comedy: " It ought to be the first endeavor of a writer to distinguish nature from custom, or that which is established because it is right from that which is right only because it is established; that he may neither violate essential principles by a desire of novelty, nor debar himself from the attainment of beauties within his view by a needless fear of breaking rules which no literary dictator had authority to enact." Professor Saintsbury declares that " With this utterance, this single utterance, all the ruling doctrines of sixteenth, seventeenth, and eighteenth century criticism receive notice to quit."

On the drama:

Lives of the Poets (especially *Rowe, Congreve, Dryden, Otway, Addison,* and *Gay*); in *The Rambler* (especially Nos. 125, 139, and 156); the *Preface to Shakespeare* (1765).

Editions:

The first collected edition — *The Works of Samuel Johnson,* edited by Arthur Murphy, in 12 vols.,— appeared in London in 1792. The Oxford Edition of the *Works* (11 vols., Oxford, 1825) is a standard. A good modern edition is *The Works of Samuel Johnson,* 16 vols. (Troy, N. Y., 1903). Special editions of the *Lives of the Poets* are edited by Mrs. Alex. Napier, 3 vols. (London, 1890), and by Arthur Waugh, 6 vols. (London, 1896). See also Matthew

Arnold's *Six Chief "Lives of the Poets,"* with a preface (London, 1878). The *Letters of Samuel Johnson,* collected and edited by G. Birkbeck Hill, 2 vols. (Oxford, 1892), and *Johnsonian Miscellanies,* arranged and edited by the same, 2 vols. (Oxford, 1892-97); together with *The Essays of Samuel Johnson,* edited by Stuart J. Reid (London, 1888), should be consulted. Also Raleigh's *Johnson on Shakespeare* (London, 1908).

On Johnson and his works:

See prefatory matter to editions cited above.

Sir John Hawkins, *Life of Samuel Johnson* (London, 1787).

James Boswell, *Life of Samuel Johnson,* 2 vols. (London, 1791). Standard edition by G. Birkbeck Hill, 6 vols., Oxford, 1887).

Leslie Stephen, *Samuel Johnson* (London, 1878).

Lieut.-Col. F. Grant, *Samuel Johnson* (London, 1887).

W. P. Courtney, *A Bibliography of Samuel Johnson* (Oxford, 1905).

T. B. Macaulay, *Samuel Johnson* (in *Works,* London, 1879).

G. Birkbeck Hill, *Johnson; his Friends and Critics* (London, 1878).

Thomas Seccombe, *The Age of Johnson* (London, 1900).

John Dennis, *Dr. Johnson* (London, 1905).

George Saintsbury, *A History of Criticism,* vol. 2 (New York, 1902).

THE RAMBLER [1]

(1751)

No. 125. Tues., May 28, 1751.

Descriptas servare vices, operumque colores,
Cur ego, si nequeo ignoroque, poeta salutor?

Hor. *De Ar. Poet.* 86.

But if, through weakness, or my want of art,
I can't to every different style impart

[1] Re-printed from the *Works of Samuel Johnson,* Troy, N. Y., 1903

The proper strokes and colors it may claim,
Why am I honor'd with a poet's name?
Francis.

It is one of the maxims of the civil law, that *definitions are hazardous.* Things modified by human understandings, subject to varieties of complication, and changeable as experience advances knowledge, or accident influence caprice, are scarcely to be included in any standing form of expression, be cause they are always suffering some alteration of their state. Definition is, indeed, not the province of man; everything is set above or below our faculties. The works and operations of nature are too great in their extent, or too much diffused in their relations, and the performances of art too inconstant and uncertain, to be reduced to any determinate idea. It is impossible to impress upon our minds an adequate and just representation of an object so great that we can never take it into our view, or so mutable that it is always changing under our eye and has already lost its form while we are laboring to conceive it.

Definitions have been no less difficult or uncertain in criticisms than in law. Imagination, a licentious and vagrant faculty, unsusceptible of limitations and impatient of restraint, has always endeavored to baffle the logician, to perplex the confines of distinction, and burst the inclosures of regularity. There is therefore scarcely any species of writing, of which we can tell what is its essence, and what are its constituents; every new genius produces some innovation, when invented and approved, subverts the rules which the practice of foregoing authors had established.

Comedy has been particularly unpropitious to definers; for though perhaps they might properly have contented themselves with declaring it to be *such a dramatic representation of human life, as may excite mirth,* they have embarrassed their definition with the means by which the comic writers obtained their end, without considering that the various methods of exhilarating their audience, not being limited by nature, cannot be comprised in precept. Thus, some make comedy a representation of mean, and others of bad, men; some think that its essence consists in the unimportance, others in the fictitiousness, of the transaction. But any man's reflections will inform him, that every dramatic composition which raises mirth, is comic; and that, to raise mirth, it is by no means universally necessary that the personages should be either mean or corrupt, nor always requisite that the action should be trivial, nor ever that it should be fictitious.

If the two kinds of dramatic poetry had been defined only by their effects upon the mind, some absurdities might have been prevented, with which the compositions of our greatest poets are disgraced, who, for want of some settled ideas and accurate distinctions, have unhappily confounded tragic with comic sentiments. They seem to have thought that as the meanest of personages constituted comedy, their greatness was sufficient to form a tragedy; and that nothing was necessary but that they should crowd the scene with monarchs, and generals, and guards; and to make them talk at certain intervals of the downfall of kingdoms, and the rout of armies. They have not considered that thoughts or accidents, in themselves ridiculous, grow still more grotesque by the solemnity of such characters; that reason and nature are uniform and inflexible: and that what is despicable and absurd, will not, by any association with splendid titles become rational or great; the most important affairs, by an intermixture of an unseasonable levity, may be made contemptible; and the robes of royalty can give no dignity to nonsense or to folly.

"Comedy," says Horace, "sometimes raises her voice"; and tragedy may likewise, on proper occasions, abate her dignity; but as the comic personages can only depart from their familiarity of style, when the more violent passions are put in motion, the heroes and queens of tragedy should never descend to trifle, but in the hours of ease and intermissions of danger. Yet in the tragedy of *Don Sebastian,* when the King of Portugal is in the hands of his enemy, and, having just drawn the lot, by which he is condemned to die, breaks out into a wild boast that his dust shall take possession of Afric, the dialogue proceeds thus between the captive and his conqueror:

Muley Moluch. *What shall I do to conquer thee?*
Seb. *Impossible.*
Souls have no conquerors.
M. Mol. *I'll shew thee for a monster thro' my Afric.*
Seb. *No, thou canst only shew me for a man:*

Afric is stored with monsters; man's a
prodigy
Thy subjects have not seen.
M. Mol. *Thou talk'st as if*
Still at the head of battle.
Seb. *Thou mistak'st,*
For then I would not talk.
Benducar. *Sure he would sleep.*

This conversation, with the sly remark of the Minister [Benducar], can only be found not to be comic because it wants the probability necessary to representations of common life, and degenerates too much towards buffoonery and farce.

The same play affords a smart return of the General to the Emperor, who, enforcing his orders for the death of Sebastian, vents his impatience in this abrupt threat:

> *. . . No more replies,*
> *But see thou dost it, or —*

To which Dorax answers,

Choke in that threat: I can say Or as loud.

A thousand instances of such impropriety might be produced, were not one scene in *Aureng-Zebe* sufficient to exemplify it. Indamora, a captive queen, having Auren-Zebe for her lover, employs Arimant, to whose charge she had been intrusted, and whom she had made sensible of her charms, to carry her message to his rival.

(Arimant, with a letter in his hand; Indamora.)

Arim. *And I the messenger to him from you?*
Your empire you to tyranny pursue:
You lay commands, both cruel and unjust,
To serve my rival, and betray my trust.
Ind. *You first betrayed your trust, in loving me;*
And should not I my own advantage see?
Serving my love, you may my friendship gain;
You know the rest of your pretences vain.
You must, my Arimant, you must be kind:

'Tis in your nature, and your noble mind.
Arim. *I'll to the king, and straight my trust resign.*
Ind. *His trust you may, but you shall never mine.*
Heaven made you love me for no other end,
But to become my confidant and friend:
As such, I keep no secret from your sight,
And therefore make you judge how ill I write:
Read it, and tell me freely then your mind;
If 'tis indited, as I meant it, kind.
Arim. *"I ask not Heaven my freedom to restore.*
(Reading.
But only for your sake —" I'll read no more:
And yet I must —
"Less for my own, than for your sorrows sad —"
(Reading.
Another line, like this, would make me mad —
Heaven! she goes on — yet more — and yet more kind!
(As reading.
Each sentence is a dagger to my mind.
"See me this night —
(Reading.
Thank fortune who did such a friend provide,
For faithful Arimant shall be your guide."
Not only to be made an instrument,
But pre-engaged without my own consent!
Ind. *Unknown to engage you still augments my score,*
And gives you scope of meriting the more.
Arim. *The best of men*
Some interest in their actions must confess:
None merit, but in hope they may possess.
The fatal paper rather let me tear,
Than, like Bellerophon, my own sentence bear.
Ind. *You may; but 'twill not be your best advice:*
'Twill only give me pains of writing twice.
You know you must obey me, soon or late:

Why should you vainly struggle with
your fate?
Arim. *I thank thee, Heaven, thou has*
been wondrous kind!
Why am I thus to slavery designed,
And yet am cheater with a free-born
mind?
Or make thy orders with my reason suit,
Or let me live by sense, a glorious
brute —
(She frowns.
You frown, and I obey with speed, be-
fore
The dreadful sentence comes, See me no
more:

In the same scene every circumstance concurs to turn tragedy to farce. The wild absurdity of the expedient; the contemptible suggestion of the lover; the folly of obliging him to read the letter, only because it ought to have been concealed from him; the frequent interruptions of amorous impatience; the faint expostulations of a voluntary slave; the imperious haughtiness of a tyrant without power; the deep reflection of the yielding rebel upon fate and free-will; and his wise wish to lose his reason as soon as he finds himself about to do what he cannot persuade his reason to approve, are sufficient to awaken the most torpid risibility.

There is scarce a tragedy of the last century which has not debased its most important incidents, and polluted its most serious interlocutions with buffoonery and meanness; but though perhaps it cannot be pretended that the present age has added much to the force and efficacy, it has at least been able to escape many faults, which either ignorance have overlooked or indulgence had licensed. The later tragedies, indeed, have faults of another kind, perhaps more destructive to delight, though less open to censure. That perpetual tumor of phrase with which every thought is now expressed by every personage, the paucity of adventurers which regularly admits, and the unvaried equality of flowing dialogue has taken away from our present writers almost all that dominion over the passions which was the boast of their predecessors. Yet they may at least claim this commendation, that they avoid gross faults, and that if they can-

not often move terror or pity, they are always careful not to provoke laughter.

No. 156. Saturday, September 14, 1751.

Nunquam aliud, natura, aliud sapientia
dicit.
Juv. *SAT. XIV.* 321.
For wisdom ever echoes Nature's voice.

. . . . . .

That many rules have been advanced without consulting nature or reason, we cannot but suspect when we find it peremptorily decreed by the ancient masters, that only three speaking personages should appear at once upon the stage; a law which, as the variety and intricacy of modern plays has made it impossible to be observed, we now violate without scruple, and, as experience proves, without inconvenience.

The original of this precept was merely accidental. Tragedy was a monody, or soliloquy sung in honor of Bacchus, improved afterwards into a dialogue by the addition of another speaker; but the ancients, remembering that the tragedy was at first pronounced only by one, durst not for some time venture beyond two; at last, when custom and impunity had made them daring, they extended their liberty to the admission of three, but restrained themselves by a critical edict from further exorbitance.

By what accident the number of acts was limited to five, I know not that any author has informed us; but certainly it is not determined by any necessity arising either from the nature of action or propriety of exhibition. An act is only the representation of such a part of the business of the play as proceeds in an unbroken tenor, or without any intermediate pause. Nothing is more evident than that of every real, and by consequence of every dramatic action, the intervals may be more or fewer than five; and indeed the rule is upon the English stage every day broken in effect, without any other mischief than that which arises from an absurd endeavor to observe it in appearance. Whenever the scene is shifted the act ceases, since some time is necessarily supposed to elapse while the personages of the drama change their place.

With no greater right to our obedience have the critics confined the dramatic action to a certain number of hours. Probability requires that the time of action should approach somewhat nearly to that of exhibition, and those plays will always be thought most happily conducted which crowd the greatest variety into the least space. But since it will frequently happen that some delusion must be admitted, I know not where the limits of imagination can be fixed. It is rarely observed that minds, not prepossessed by mechanical criticism, feel any offense from the extension of the intervals between the acts; nor can I conceive it absurd or impossible, that he who can multiply three hours into twelve or twenty-four, might imagine, with equal ease, a greater number.

I know not whether he who professes to regard no other laws than those of nature, will not be inclined to receive tragi-comedy to his protection, whom, however generally condemned, her own laurels have hitherto shaded from the fulminations of criticism. For what is there in the mingled drama which impartial reason can condemn? The connection of important with trivial incidents, since it is not only common but perpetual in the world, may surely be allowed on the stage, which pretends only to be the mirror of life. The impropriety of suppressing passions before we have raised them to the intended agitation, and of diverting the expectation from an event which we keep suspended only to raise it, may be speciously urged. But will not experience show this objection to be rather subtle than just? Is it not certain that the tragic and comic affections have been moved alternately with equal force, and that no plays have oftener filled the eye with tears, and the heart with palpitation, than those which are variegated with interludes of mirth?

I do not, however, think it safe to judge of works of genius merely by the event. The resistless vicissitudes of the heart, this alternate prevalence of merriment and solemnity, may sometimes be more properly ascribed to the vigor of the writer than the justness of the design; and, instead of vindicating tragi-comedy by the success of Shakespeare, we ought, perhaps, to pay new honors to that transcendent and unbounded genius that could preside over the passions in sport; who, to actuate the affections, needed not the slow gradation of common means, but could fill the heart with instantaneous jollity or sorrow, and vary our disposition as he changed his scenes. Perhaps the effects even of Shakespeare's poetry might have been yet greater, had he not counteracted himself; and we might even have been more interested in the distresses of his heroes, had we not been so frequently diverted by the jokes of his buffoons.

There are other rules more fixed and obligatory. It is necessary that of every play the chief action should be single; and since a play represents some transaction, through its regular maturation to its final event, two actions equally important must evidently constitute two plays.

As the design of tragedy is to instruct by moving the passions, it must always have a hero, a personage apparently and incontestably superior to the rest, upon whom the attention may be fixed and the anxiety suspended. For though of two persons opposing each other with equal abilities and equal virtue, the auditor will inevitably in time choose his favorite, yet as that choice must be without any cogency of conviction, the hopes or fears which it raises will be faint and languid. Of two heroes acting in confederacy against a common enemy, the virtues or dangers will give little emotion, because each claims our concern with the same right, and the heart lies at rest between equal motives.

It ought to be the first endeavor of a writer to distinguish nature from custom; or that which is established because it is right, from that which is right only because it is established; that he may neither violate essential principles by a desire of novelty, nor debar himself from the attainment of beauties within his view, by a needless fear of breaking rules which no literary dictator had authority to enact.

OLIVER GOLDSMITH

Oliver Goldsmith was born, probably at Smith-Hill House, Elphin, Roscommon, Ireland, in 1728. Soon after his birth his family moved to Kilkenny West, where Oliver first went to school. At the age of nine he left the little school at Kilkenny, and attended several academies. In 1744 he went to Trinity College, Dublin, where he barely managed to make a living. His personal ungainliness and crude manners prevented his making many acquaintances, and his life at college was miserable. He was graduated in 1749, after the death of his father, and went to live with his mother. He cast about him in search of a profession. He was a tutor at one time, but lost his position as the result of a quarrel. He decided later to emigrate to America, but missed his ship. He then determined to study law, and once again set forth to Dublin, where he gambled away the fifty pounds which had been given him. When he was twenty-four he was again endowed and went to Edinburgh to study medicine, where for a year and a half he made some slight pretense at attending lectures, and then went to Leyden, presumably to continue his studies. From Holland he proceeded on a walking tour through Flanders, France, Switzerland, and the north of Italy, earning his board and keep with his flute. In 1756 he returned to England, without a penny in his pocket, although he had, according to his own statement, received a doctor's degree. In London he turned his hand to every sort of work: translation, the writing of superficial histories, children's books, and general articles. One of the works of this period which is still included in the *Works* is the *Enquiry into the State of Polite Learning in Europe.* Through the publication of *The Bee* and the *Life of Beau Nash,* Goldsmith achieved considerable popularity, and his fortunes began to mend. He belonged to the circle of Johnson, Burke, Reynolds, and was one of "The Club." *The Traveller* appeared in 1764, and his reputation as a poet was firmly established. *The Vi-*

car of Wakefield, published two years later, increased his popularity, and when he produced his first play, *The Good-natur'd Man* (1768), though the play was not a success, it was widely read in book-form. In 1770 came *The Deserted Village,* and three years after his dramatic masterpiece, *She Stoops to Conquer,* which was highly successful. Goldsmith was meanwhile busy with a great deal of hack-work — the *Natural History,* the histories of England, Rome, and Greece — which was very remunerative. But Goldsmith's carelessness, his intemperance, and his habit of gambling, soon brought him into debt. Broken in health and mind, he died in 1774.

In one of his earliest works, the *Enquiry into the Present State of Polite Learning* (1759), Goldsmith gave utterance to the thought which was to be his guiding star in the field of the drama. He says: "Does the poet paint the absurdities of the vulgar, then he is *low;* does he exaggerate the features of folly, to render it more ridiculous, he is then very *low.* In short, they have proscribed the comic or satirical muse from every walk but high life, which, though abounding in fools as well as the humblest station, is by no means so fruitful in absurdity." It was Goldsmith's mission to render natural the comedy of his time, and strike a decisive blow at the *genteel* or *sentimental* comedy, which he later termed a "kind of *mulish* production, with all the defects of its opposite parents, and marked with sterility." Goldsmith wrote comparatively little on the drama — the passages in the *Enquiry* already referred to, an occasional paragraph in the *Essays,* the important *Essay on the Theatre,* and the brief *Preface* to *The Good-natur'd Man* — are practically all he had to say on the subject.

On the drama:

An Enquiry into the Present State of Polite Learning in Europe (London, 1759). (The *Citizen of the World* and *The Bee* may also be consulted for occasional references to the drama.)

Preface to *The Good-natur'd Man* (1768).
An Essay on the Theatre; or, a Comparison Between Laughing and Sentimental Comedy (1772).

Editions:

The first general edition of Goldsmith is the *Miscellaneous Works* (London, 1775). The best modern edition is the *Works*, edited by J. W. M. Gibbs, 5 vols. (London, 1884–86). A good annotated edition of the plays, with a bibliography and reprint of the *Essay on the Theatre*, is *The Good-natur'd Man* and *She Stoops to Conquer*, with an introduction by Austin Dobson (Boston, 1911).

On Goldsmith and his works:

Sir James Prior, *The Life of Oliver Goldsmith*, 2 vols. (London, 1837).
John Forster, *The Life and Adventures of Oliver Goldsmith*, 2 vols. (2nd ed., London, 1854).
Washington Irving, *The Life of Oliver Goldsmith*, 2 vols. (New York, 1844 ff.).
W. M. Thackeray, *The English Humourists of the Eighteenth Century* (modern reprint in Everyman's Library, n.d.).
William Black, *Goldsmith* (London, 1878).
Austin Dobson, *Life of Oliver Goldsmith* (revised ed., New York, 1899).
F. F. Moore, *The Life of Oliver Goldsmith* (latest ed., New York, 1911).

AN ESSAY ON THE THEATRE; OR, A COMPARISON BETWEEN LAUGHING AND SENTIMENTAL COMEDY [1]

(1772)

The theater, like all other amusements, has its fashions and its prejudices: and when satiated with its excellence mankind begin to mistake change for improvement. For some years tragedy was the reigning entertainment; but of late it has entirely given way to comedy, and our best efforts are now exerted in these lighter kinds of composition. The pompous train, the swelling phrase, and the unnatural rant, are displaced for that natural portrait of human folly and frailty, of which all are judges, because all have sat for the picture.

But as in describing nature it is presented with a double face, either of mirth or sadness, our modern writers find themselves at a loss which chiefly to copy from; and it is now debated, whether the exhibition of human distress is likely to afford the mind more entertainment than that of human absurdity?

Comedy is defined by Aristotle to be a picture of the frailties of the lower part of mankind, to distinguish it from tragedy, which is an exhibition of the misfortunes of the great. When comedy, therefore, ascends to produce the characters of princes or generals upon the stage, it is out of its walks, since low life and middle life are entirely its object. The principal question, therefore, is, whether, in describing low or middle life, an exhibition of its follies be not preferable to a detail of its calamities? Or, in other words, which deserves the preference,— the weeping sentimental comedy so much in fashion at present, or the laughing, and even low comedy, which seems to have been last exhibited by Vanbrugh and Cibber?

If we apply to authorities, all the great masters in the dramatic art have but one opinion. Their rule is, that as tragedy displays the calamities of the great, so comedy should excite our laughter by ridiculously exhibiting the follies of the lower part of mankind. Boileau, one of the best modern critics, asserts that comedy will not admit of tragic distress:—

Le comique, ennemi des soupirs et des pleurs,
N'admet point dans ses vers de tragiques douleurs.

Nor is this rule without the strongest foundation in nature, as the distresses of the mean by no means affect us so

---

[1] Re-printed from *The Good-Natur'd Man and She Stoops to Conquer*, by Oliver Goldsmith,, with an Introduction by Austin Dobson (Boston, 1911).— Ed.

strongly as the calamities of the great. When tragedy exhibits to us some great man fallen from his height, and struggling with want and adversity, we feel his situation in the same manner as we suppose he himself must feel, and our pity is increased in proportion to the height from which he fell. On the contrary, we do not so strongly sympathize with one born in humbler circumstances, and encountering accidental distress: so that while we melt for Belisarius, we scarcely give halfpence to the beggar who accosts us in the street. The one has our pity, the other our contempt. Distress, therefore, is the proper object of tragedy, since the great excite our pity by their fall; but not equally so of comedy, since the actors employed in it are originally so mean, that they sink but little by their fall.

Since the first origin of the stage, tragedy and comedy have run in distinct channels, and never till of late encroached upon the provinces of each other. Terence, who seems to have made the nearest approaches, always judiciously stops short before he comes to the downright pathetic; and yet he is even reproached by Cæsar for wanting the *vis comica*. All the other comic writers of antiquity aim only at rendering folly or vice ridiculous, but never exalt their characters into buskined pomp, or make what Voltaire humorously calls *a tradesman's tragedy*.

Yet notwithstanding this weight of authority, and the universal practice of former ages, a new species of dramatic composition has been introduced, under the name of *sentimental* comedy, in which the virtues of private life are exhibited, rather than the vices exposed; and the distresses rather than the faults of mankind make our interest in the piece. These comedies have had of late great success, perhaps from their novelty, and also from their flattering every man in his favorite foible. In these plays almost all the characters are good, and exceedingly generous; they are lavish enough of their *tin* money on the stage; and though they want humor, have abundance of sentiment and feeling. If they happen to have faults or foibles, the spectator is taught, not only to pardon, but to applaud them, in con-

sideration of the goodness of their hearts; so that folly, instead of being ridiculed, is commended, and the comedy aims at touching our passions without the power of being truly pathetic. In this manner we are likely to lose one great source of entertainment on the stage; for while the comic poet is invading the province of the tragic muse, he leaves her lovely sister quite neglected. Of this, however, he is no way solicitous, as he measures his fame by his profits.

But it will be said, that the theater is formed to amuse mankind, and that it matters little, if this end be answered, by what means it is obtained. If mankind find delight in weeping at comedy, it would be cruel to abridge them in that or any other innocent pleasure. If those pieces are denied the name of comedies, yet call them by any other name and, if they are delightful, they are good. Their success, it will be said, is a mark of their merit, and it is only abridging our happiness to deny us an inlet to amusement.

These objections, however, are rather specious than solid. It is true that amusement is a great object of the theater, and it will be allowed that these sentimental pieces do often amuse us; but the question is, whether the true comedy would not amuse us more? The question is, whether a character supported throughout a piece, with its ridicule still attending, would not give us more delight than this species of bastard tragedy, which only is applauded because it is new?

A friend of mine, who was sitting unmoved at one of these sentimental pieces, was asked how he could be so indifferent? "Why, truly," says he, "as the hero is but a tradesman, it is indifferent to me whether he be turned out of his counting-house on Fish Street Hill, since he will still have enough left to open shop in St. Giles's."

The other objection is as ill-grounded; for though we should give these pieces another name, it will not mend their efficacy. It will continue a kind of *mulish* production, with all the defects of its opposite parents, and marked with sterility. If we are permitted to make comedy weep, we have an equal right to make tragedy laugh, and to set down in blank verse the jests and repartees of all the attendants in a funeral procession.

But there is one argument in favor of sentimental comedy, which will keep it on the stage, in spite of all that can be said against it. It is, of all others, the most easily written. Those abilities that can hammer out a novel are fully sufficient for the production of a sentimental comedy. It is only sufficient to raise the characters a little; to deck out the hero with a riband, or give the heroine a title; then to put an insipid dialogue, without character or humor, into their mouths, give them mighty good hearts, very fine clothes, furnish a new set of scenes, make a pathetic scene or two, with a sprinkling of tender melancholy conversation through the whole, and there is no doubt but all the ladies will cry and all the gentlemen applaud.

Humor at present seems to be departing from the stage, and it will soon happen that our comic players will have nothing left for it but a fine coat and a song. It depends upon the audience whether they will actually drive those poor merry creatures from the stage, or sit at a play as gloomy as at the Tabernacle. It is not easy to recover an art when once lost; and it will be but a just punishment, that when, by our being too fastidious, we have banished humor from the stage, we should ourselves be deprived of the art of laughing.

ITALY — II

FROM THE RENAISSANCE TO THE PRESENT DAY

ITALIAN DRAMATIC CRITICISM OF THE SEVENTEENTH CENTURY

For at least a century the great Renaissance critics overshadowed their successors in Italy, and the record of seventeenth century criticism is largely one of more or less pedantic compilation, classification, and repetition. The lack of a new interest in antiquity, such as served Daniello, Trissino, Scaliger and Castelvetro, and the scanty offerings of native dramatic products, are sufficient to account for the lack of outstanding contributions to dramatic theory. Beni's *Disputatio* (1600) was among the last works mentioned under Italian Renaissance Criticism. Close upon it, in 1601, came Giovanni Bernardo Brandi's *Trattato dell' Arte Poetica*. In 1613 appeared Chiodino da Monte Melone's rhetorical treatise, and in 1618 Pellegrino's *Discorso della Poetica*, and soon after, the similar works of Udeno Nisieli and Giovanni Colle Bellunese. A curious work of the time is P. M. Cecchini's *Frutti delle moderne commedie etavisi a chi le recita* (1628). An ambitious effort was Celso Zani's *Poetica ecclesiastica e civile . . . nella quale si' pone in chiaro la Diffinizione della Poesia commune alla Trayedia e all' Epopeja* (1643). The list is practically complete with the minor works on poetics by Flavio Querengo and Benedetto Menzini. In 1699 A. Perrucci published his *Dell' arte rappresentativa premeditata e all' improvviso.*

ITALIAN DRAMATIC CRITICISM OF THE EIGHTEENTH CENTURY

Four critics of varying importance opened the new century with works which exerted considerable influence: Crescimbeni, Gravina, Muratori, and Quadrio, contributed historical and critical works many of which were effective in restoring Italy to a position of honor in the critical world. Giovanni Maria Crescimbeni published *La Bellezza della volgar Poesia* in 1700, but enlarged it for the edition of 1730. For the most part his work was one of compilation. Another work, a sort of historical survey, was Gianvincenzo Gravina's *Della Ragion poetica* (1704), though of course his *Della Tragedia* is of greater interest and importance as a dramatic tract. A man of greater insight and learning was Ludovico Antonio Muratori, whose *Della perfetta Poesia italiana* (1706) exerted greater influence than the works of any of his group. Scipione Maffei and F. Palesi wrote minor works on literature and the drama, while Luigi Riccoboni wrote his treatises on the theaters in Italy and elsewhere in Europe, besides a theoretical work, *Dell' arte rappresentativa* (1725). Francesco Xavier Quadrio opened the way for the comparative study and criticism of literature, and his *Della Storia della Ragione d'ogni Poesia* (1739–52) is an ambitious attempt to cover the entire field of poetry. Francesco Maria Zanotti wrote a *Poetica* in 1768, and Girolamo Tiraboschi continued, though with greater knowledge and insight, the work of Crescimbeni, in his *Storia della Letteratura italiana* (1772–82). Meantime the dramatists themselves began to explain their theories. The eighteenth century marks the dawn of a truly national Italian drama. Scipione Maffei's *Merope* was produced in 1714, and not long after Apostolo Zeno, considered the father of modern opera, came into prominence. With the advent of Carlo Goldoni, an innovator of the greatest importance, the *Commedia dell' Arte (Comedy of Masks, or Improvised Comedy)*, was attacked. The *Commedia dell' Arte,* in which a scenario served as the basis of a series of improvised dialogues by a number of well-recognized type characters, had been the most practised of Italian dramatic products. Goldoni, whose aim it was to imitate Molière and introduce a sort of realistic comedy into Italy, felt it necessary to do away with the *Commedia dell' Arte,* and in his numerous prefaces, and particularly in his *Mémoires* (1787) he argued against the old form. His principal antagonist was the dramatist Carlo Gozzi, whose *fiabi,* or dramatized fairy tales, were an attempt to resuscitate the art of the old *Commedia dell' Arte.* In his *Prefaces,* or *Ragionamenti* and in his *Memorie* (1797) [1] he maintains

his theories against Goldoni's. Meanwhile Zeno's successor, Pietro Metastasio, carried on his work, and his operas were popular throughout the world until the nineteenth century. His chief critical contribution to the theory of the drama was a commentary on Aristotle, *Estratto dell' Arte Poetica d'Aristotile* (1782). Vittorio Alfieri, one of the greatest dramatists of Italy, touched upon dramatic matters in his autobiography (*Vita di Vittorio Alfieri scritta da esso,* 1804), and in his various *Lettere* and essays on tragedy, but his revolutionary spirit was manifest rather in his plays than in his references to the theory behind them.

Almost contemporary with Alfieri were the three great Revolutionary poets and dramatists: Manzoni, Foscolo, and Monti, each of whom contributed to the Romantic triumph in Italy. Manzoni, in particular, was an important figure; his *Preface* to the play *Carmagnola* (1820) and his *Letter on the Unities* (1823), are landmarks of dramatic theory.

[1] A brief extract from Carlo Gozzi's *Memoirs* (1797), translated by J. A. Symonds (London, 1890):

"You cannot fabricate a drama worthy to impress the public mind for any length of time by heaping up absurdities, marvels, scurrilities, prolixities, puerilities, insipidities, and nonsense. The neglect into which the imitations of my manner speedily fell proves this. Much the same may be said about those other species — romantic or domestic, intended to move tears or laughter — those cultured and realistic kinds of drama, as people call them, though they were generally devoid of culture and of realism, and were invariably as like each other as two peas, which occupied our stage for thirty years at least. All the good

and bad that has been written and printed about my fables; the fact that they still hold the stage in Italy and other countries where they are translated in spite of their comparative antiquity; the stupid criticisms which are still being vented against them by starving journalists and envious bores, who join the cry and follow these blind leaders of the blind — criticisms only based upon the titles and arguments I chose to draw from old wives' tales and stories of the nursery — all this proves that there is real stuff in the fabulous, poetical allegorical genre which I created. I say this without any presumptuous partiality for the children of my fancy; nor do I resent the attacks which have been made upon them, for I am human enough to pity the hungry and the passion-blinded."— Ed.

ITALIAN DRAMATIC CRITICISM OF THE NINETEENTH AND TWENTIETH CENTURIES

The Italian drama of the nineteenth century — or all but the closing years — was based upon the traditions of the past. There is very little of note in the field of dramatic criticism proper, though at least two great literary critics and estheticians ought to be named: Francesco de Sanctis and Benedetto Croce.

Each of these writers has contributed valuable material to esthetics and criticism, but comparatively little to dramatic theory.

The modern dramatists have likewise had little to say, though Giuseppe Giacosa has lectured widely on the subject of his own art.

General references on Italian literature from the Renaissance to the present day:

A. d'Ancona e O. Bacci, *Manuale della letteratura italiana*, 6 vols. (Firenze, 1904–08).

Vernon Lee, *Studies of the Eighteenth Century in Italy* (2nd ed., Chicago, 1908).

M. Mignon, *Etudes de littérature italienne* (Paris, 1912).

Richard Garnett, *A History of Italian Literature* (New York, 1909).

L. Collison-Morley, *Modern Italian Literature* (Boston, 1912).

V. Rossi, *Storia della letteratura italiana per uso dei licei*, 3 vols. (Milano, 1907).

Tullio Concari, *Il Settecento* (in series *Storia letteraria*, etc., Milano, 1898–1900).

M. Landau, *Geschichte der italienischen Literatur im 18. Jahrhundert* (Berlin, 1899).

Amédée Roux, *Histoire de la littérature contemporaine en Italie*, etc. (1859–74) (Paris, 1896).

L. Étienne, *Histoire de la littérature italienne* (Paris, 1884).

H. Hauvette, *La Littérature italienne* (Paris, 1906).

G. Mazzoni, *L'Ottocento* (in series *Storia letteraria*, etc., Milano, 1898–1913).

References on Italian drama from the Renaissance to the present day:

E. Masi, *Studi sulla Storia del teatro italiano* (Firenze, 1891).

Giuseppe Guerzoni, *Il Teatro italiano nel secolo XVIII* (Milano, 1876).

Philippe Monnier, *Venise au XVIIIe siècle* (Lausanne, 1907. Translated anonymously, Boston, 1910).

Eugenio Camerini, *I Precursori del Goldoni* (Milano, 1872).

G. G. de Rossi, *Del Moderno teatro italiano* (Bassano, 1794).

P. F. Biancolelli, *Nouveau Théâtre italien* (Anvers, 1713).

L. Stoppate, *La Commedia popolare in Italia* (Padova, 1887).

Michele Scherillo, *La Commedia dell' Arte in Italia* (Torino, 1880).

O. Marchini-Capasso, *Goldoni e la Commedia dell' Arte* (Napoli, 1912).

L. Riccoboni, *Histoire du Théâtre italien* (Paris, 1731).

Winifred Smith, *The Commedia dell' Arte* (New York, 1912).

Anonymous, *An Essay upon the Present State of the Theatre in France, England, and Italy* (London, 1760).

J. C. Walker, *Historical and Critical Essay on the Revival of the Drama in Italy* (Edinburgh, 1805).

——, *Historical Memoir on Italian Tragedy*, etc. (London, 1799).

Charles Rabany, *Carlo Goldoni. Le Théâtre et la vie en Italie au XVIIIe siècle* (Paris, 1896).

Carlo Goldoni, *Mémoires* (Paris, 1787. Reprinted with preface and notes by Guido Mazzoni in two volumes as *Memorie di Carlo Goldoni*, Firenze, 1907. Translated by John Black as *Memoirs of Carlo Goldoni*, 2 vols., London, 1814. Abridged ed., edited by W. D. Howells, Boston, 1877).

——, *Lettere* (Modern edition, Bologna, 1907).

H. C. Chatfield-Taylor, *Goldoni, a Biography* (New York, 1913).

E. M. Leopardi, *Il Melodramma del Metastasio e la sua fortuna nel secolo XVIII* (Napoli, 1909).

Charles Burney, *Memoirs of the Life and Writings of the Abate Metastasio*, etc., 3 vols. (London, 1796).

Nathan Haskell Dole, *A Teacher of Dante*, etc. (New York, 1908).

Carlo Gozzi, *Memorie inutili*, etc., 3 vols. (Venezia, 1797. Translated, with an introduction, by J. A. Symonds, as *Memoirs of Carlo Gozzi*, 2 vols., London, 1890).

Giovanni Battista Magrini, *I Tempi, la Vita e gli Scritti di Carlo Gozzi* (Benevento, 1883).

G. Costetti, *Il Teatro italiano nel 1800* (Rocca di S. Cassiano, 1901).

Gaetano Zocchi, *Il Teatro italiano a' tempi nostri* (Prato, 1885).

Addison McLeod, *Plays and Players of Modern Italy* (London, 1912).

Henry Lyonnet, *Le Théâtre en Italie* (Paris, 1900).

——, *Pulcinella et Cie* (Paris, 1901).

Jean Dornis, *Le Théâtre italien contemporain* (Paris, 1898).

A. Lalia-Paternostro, *Studi drammatici* (Napoli, 1903).

Barrett H. Clark, *A Study of the Modern Drama* (2nd ed., New York, 1928).

G. M. Scalinger, *Teatro sociologico* (Napoli, 1902).

F. Martini, *Al teatro* (Firenze, 1908).

Cesare Levi, *Letteratura drammatica* (Milano, 1900).

References on Italian dramatic criticism and theory from the Renaissance to the present day:

G. Trezza, *La critica moderna* (2nd ed., Bologna, 1880).

Lander MacClintock, *The Contemporary Drama of Italy* (Boston, 1920).

L. Morandi, *Antologia della nostra critica letteraria moderna* (4th ed., Città di Castello, 1889).

P. Ferrieri, *Francesco de Sanctis e la critica letteraria* (Milano, 1888).

George Saintsbury, *A History of Criticism*, vols. 2 and 3 (New York, 1902–04).

A. Galletti, *Le Teorie drammatiche e la tragedia in Italia nel secolo XVIII* (Cremona, 1901).

CARLO GOLDONI

Carlo Goldoni was born at Venice in 1707. From his earliest years he appears to have been interested in the theater: his toys were puppets and his books, plays. It is said that at the age of eight he attempted to write a play. The boy's father placed him under the care of the philosopher Caldini at Rimini but the youth soon ran away with a company of strolling players and came to Venice. There he began to study law; he continued his studies at Pavia, though he relates in his *Memoirs* that a considerable part of his time was spent in reading Greek and Latin comedies. He had already begun writing at this time, and, as the result of a libel in which he ridiculed certain families of Pavia, he was forced to leave the city. He continued his law studies at Udine, and eventually took his degree at Modena. He was employed as law clerk at Chioggia and Feltre, after which he returned to his native city and began practicing. But his true vocation was the theater, and he made his bow with a tragedy, *Amalasunta,* produced at Milan, but this was a failure. His next play, *Belisario,* written in 1734, succeeded. He wrote other tragedies for a time, but he was not long in discovering that his bent was for comedy. He had come to realize that the Italian stage needed reforming, and adopting Molière as his model, he went to work in earnest, and in 1738 produced his first real comedy, *L'Uomo di mondo.* During his many wanderings and adventures in Italy, he was constantly at work, and when, at

Leghorn, he became acquainted with the manager Medebac, he determined to pursue the profession of playwriting in order to make a living. He was employed by Medebac to write plays for his theater in Venice. He worked for other managers, and produced during his stay in that city some of his most characteristic works. In 1761 he went to Paris, where he continued to write. Among the plays which he wrote in French, the most successful was *Le Bourru bienfaisant,* produced on the occasion of the marriage of Louis XVI and Marie Antoinette in 1771. He enjoyed considerable popularity in France, and when he retired to Versailles the King gave him a pension. But when the Revolution broke out, he was deprived of it. The day after his death, however, the Convention voted to restore the pension. He died in 1793.

Goldoni was the great reformer of Italian comedy. His importance, which consisted rather in giving good examples than precepts, lay in his having regularized the drama of his country, and freed it from the conventionality of the *Commedia dell' Arte,* or improvised comedy. He rightly maintained that Italian life and manners were susceptible of artistic treatment such as had not before been given them. Although Goldoni admired Molière and often tried to emulate if not imitate him, his plays are gentler and more optimistic in tone. He relates at considerable length in his *Memoirs* the state of Italian comedy when he began writing, and his works are a lasting monument to the changes which he brought about. Goldoni's plays are themselves the justification of his theory, and need no explanation, but his theories are interesting and valuable. These he set forth in his *Memoirs*, his prefaces, and in many places throughout the play *Il Teatro comico*.

On the drama:

Outside the many prefaces to the various editions, Goldoni's principal writings on the drama are in the *Teatro Comico* (1751) and the *Mémoires* (1787).

Editions:

The early editions are not complete, and there is considerable confusion in collating them. The *Pasquali* edition, in 17 vols. (Venice, 1761, and following), authorized by Goldoni, is the best of the early editions. The Tasso edition, 45 vols. (Venice, 1823–27), is a good modern edition, while the *Opere complete*, published by the Municipality of Venice (begun in 1907 and now in course of publication) will take its place as the definitive edition. The *Mémoires de M. Goldoni pour servir à l'histoire de sa vie et à celle de son théâtre*, were published in three vols., Paris, 1787. The best modern edition is the reprint, *Memorie di Carlo Goldoni*, with preface and notes by Guido Mazzoni, in 2 vols. (Firenze, 1907). These are translated as *Memoirs of Goldoni*, translated by John Black, 2 vols. (London, 1814. Reprinted in *A Collection of the Most Instructive and Amusing Lives ever Published*, vol. 23, London, 1828). An abridgement, with an essay by W. D. Howells, was published at Boston in 1877. H. C. Chatfield-Taylor's biography (see below) contains translated extracts from the plays, prefaces, and *Memoirs*.

On Goldoni and his works:

Prefaces to various editions of the works. *Mémoires de M. Goldoni*, 2 vols. (Paris, 1787).
Luigi Carrer, *Saggi su la vita e le opere di Carlo Goldoni*, 3 vols. (Venezia, 1824).
Giovanni Gherardini, *Vita di Carlo Goldoni* (Milano, 1821).
Ferdinando Meneghezzi, *Della Vita e delle opere di Carlo Goldoni* (Milano, 1827).
Edward Copping, *Alfieri and Goldoni* (London, 1857).
Carlo Borghi, *Memorie sulla Vita di Carlo Goldoni* (Modena, 1859).
V. de Amicis, *La Commedia popolare latina e la commedia dell' arte* (Napoli, 1882).
Alfonso Aloi, *Il Goldoni e la Commedia dell' Arte* (Catania, 1883).
G. Bertoni, *Carlo Goldoni e il teatro francese del suo tempo* (Modena, 1907).
Virgilio Brocchi, *Carlo Goldoni a Venezia nel secolo XVIII* (Bologna, 1907).
Giulio Caprin, *Carlo Goldoni, la sua vita, le sue opere* (Milano, 1907).
A. Cuman, *La Riforma del Teatro comico italiano e Carlo Goldoni* (in *Ateneo veneto*, vols. 22 & 23, Venezia, 1899–1900).
Angelo de Gubernatis, *Carlo Goldoni* (Firenze, 1911).
Vernon Lee, *Studies of the Eighteenth Century in Italy* (2nd ed., Chicago, 1906).
E. Von Lohner, *Carlo Goldoni e le sue Memorie* (in *Archivio veneto*, vols. 23 & 24, Venezia, 1882).
Olga Marchini-Capasso, *Goldoni e la commedia dell' arte* (Bergamo, 1907).
P. G. Molmenti, *Carlo Goldoni* (2nd ed., Venezia, 1880).
Giuseppe Ortolani, *Della Vita e dell' arte di Carlo Goldoni* (Venezia, 1907).
E. Pasqualini, *Carlo Goldoni* (Assisi, 1909).
P. Petrocchi, *Carlo Goldoni e la commedia* (Milano, 1893).
Charles Rabany, *Carlo Goldoni* (Paris, 1896).
Michele Scherillo, *La Commedia dell' arte in Italia* (Torino, 1884).
Winifred Smith, *The Commedia dell' Arte* (New York, 1912).
Marietta Tovini, *Studio su Carlo Goldoni* (Firenze, 1900).
H. C. Chatfield-Taylor, *Goldoni, a Biography* (New York, 1913).
J. S. Kennard, *Goldoni and the Venice of his Time* (New York, 1920).

THE COMIC THEATER [1]

[Il Teatro Comico]

(1751)

Comedy was invented to correct foibles and ridicule disagreeable habits; when the comedy of the ancients was written in this wise, the whole world liked it, for on seeing a fac-simile of a character upon the boards, everybody saw the original either in himself or in some one else. When comedy became merely ridiculous, nobody paid further attention to it, since under the pretext of causing laughter, the most high-sounding absurdities were permitted. Now that we are again fishing comedies out of the *Mare magnum* of nature, men find themselves again searching their hearts and identifying themselves with the passion or the character which is being represented, for they know how to discern whether a passion is well depicted, whether a character is well sustained: in short, they observe. . . .

The French have triumphed in the art of comedy during a whole century; it is now time for Italy to proclaim that in her the seed of good authorship is not dried up, Italian authors having been, after the Greeks and the Romans, the first to enrich and adorn the stage. The French in their comedies, it must be admitted, present fine and well-sustained characters; moreover, they delineate passions well, and their conceptions are acute, witty, and brilliant, but the public of that country is satisfied with a little. One single character is sufficient to maintain a French comedy. Around a single passion well conceived and drawn, a great number of speeches vibrate which by dint of elocution present the air of novelty. We Italians demand much more. We wish the principal character to be strong, original, and well recognized . . . that the plot shall be fertile in incidents and

novelties. We demand morals mingled with quips and humor. We insist that the end be unexpected, but plainly derived from the trend of the action. We like to have an infinity of things too many to relate here, and it is only in the course of time that we can succeed in learning by practice and usage to know them and to obtain success with them.

.   .   .   .   .   .

Aristotle began to write concerning comedy, but he did not finish, and we have from him but a few imperfect fragments regarding it. In his *Poetics* he prescribed the unity of place for tragedy; yet he did not mention comedy then. There are those who maintain that his statements about tragedy must be interpreted as referring to comedy also, and that if he had finished his treatise on comedy, he would have prescribed the unity of place. But my answer is, that if Aristotle were now alive, he would cancel this obnoxious precept, because a thousand absurdities, a thousand blunders and improprieties are caused by it. I distinguish two kinds of comedy: pure comedy and comedies of intrigue. Pure comedy can be written with the unity of place. Comedy of intrigue cannot be thus written without crudity and incongruity. The ancients had not, like ourselves, a way to shift scenery, and for that reason they observed the unities. We have always observed the unity of place when the action occurs in the same city, and all the more when it remains in the same house. . . . Therefore, I conclude that if comedy with the unity of places can be written without hair-splitting or unseemliness, it should be done; but if on account of the unity of place absurdities have to be introduced, it is better to change the scenes and observe the rules of probability.

[1] Re-printed from the translated passages by the author in H. C. Chatfield-Taylor's *Goldoni, A Biography* (New York, 1913).— Ed.

MEMOIRS [2]

[Mémoires to M. Goldoni, etc.]

(1787)

. . . .

I wish that the Italian authors had continued after the appearance of this comedy [Macchiavelli's *Mandragora*] to write decent and honorable comedies, and that characters taken from nature had been substituted for fantastic intrigues.

But it was left to Molière to ennoble and render useful the comic stage, in exposing the vices and the laughable side of man to ridicule, for the purpose of correction.

I was not yet acquainted with the works of that great man, for I did not understand French; but I made up my mind to learn it, and meantime I acquired the habit of observing men carefully, and never lost sight of an original character. . . . (First Part, Ch. X.)

. . . "I am now," said I to myself, "perfectly at my ease, and I can give free rein to my imagination. Hitherto I have labored on old subjects, but now I must create and invent for myself. I have the advantage of very promising actors; but in order to employ them usefully I must begin with studying them. Every person has his peculiar character from nature; if the author gives him a part to represent in unison with his own, he may lay his account with success. Well, then," continued I, "this is perhaps the happy moment to set on foot the reform which I have so long meditated. Yes, I must treat subjects of character: this is the source of good comedy; with this the great Molière began his career, and he carried it to a degree of perfection which the ancients merely indicated to us, and which the moderns have never seen equalled."

Was I wrong to encourage myself in this way? No, for comedy was my forte, and good comedy was my ambition. I should have been in the wrong had I been so ambitious as to set myself alongside the masters of the art, but my sole desire was to reform and correct the abuses of the stage of my country; no great

scholarship was necessary to accomplish that. . . .

That any character may be productive of effect on the stage, it has always appeared to me necessary to contrast it with characters of an opposite description. . . .

This play [*Momolo Cortesan*] was eminently successful, and I was happy. I saw my compatriots turn from their old love of farce: the reformation was at hand. But I could not yet flatter myself that it was an accomplished fact, for the dialogue of the play is not written down. . . . That consistent style which is the mark of true authors, was not to be observed: I could not reform everything at once without shocking the lovers of the old style of national comedy. I then awaited a favorable moment to attack them directly with more vigor and added sureness of touch.

(First Part, Ch. XL.)

. . . . . .

. . . And, acting upon the maxim of comedy, *ridendo castigat mores,* I imagined that the theater might be converted into a school for the prevention of abuse and the consequences resulting from it.

(First Part, Ch. XLII.)

. . . . . .

The unities requisite for the perfection of theatrical works have in all times been the subject of discussion among authors and amateurs.

The censors of my plays of character had nothing to reproach me with in respect to the unity of action and of time, but they maintained that in the unity of place I had been deficient.

The action of my comedies was always confined to the same town, and the characters never departed from it. It is true that they went from one place to another; but all these places were within the same walls; and I was then and am still of the opinion that in this manner the unity of place was sufficiently observed.

In every art and every discovery, experience has always preceded precepts. In

2 Translation by the Editor, based in part upon the John Black translation (1814) of the *Memoirs.* Selections.— Ed.

the course of time, a method had been assigned by writers to the practice of the invention, but modern authors always possessed the right of putting an interpretation on the ancients.

For my part, not finding either in the Poetics of Aristotle or Horace a clear and absolute precept founded on reason for the rigorous unity of place, I have always adhered to it when my subject seemed susceptible of it; but I could never induce myself to sacrifice a good comedy for the sake of a prejudice which might have spoiled it. . . .

In speaking of virtue, I do not mean an heroical virtue, affecting from its distresses, and pathetic from its diction. Those works which in France are called *drames,* have certainly their merit; they are a species of theatrical representation between tragedy and comedy, and an additional subject of entertainment for feeling hearts. The misfortunes of the heroes of tragedy interest us at a distance, but those of our equals are calculated to affect us more closely.

Comedy, which is an imitation of nature, ought not to reject virtuous and pathetic sentiments, if the essential object be observed of enlivening it with those comic and prominent traits which are the very foundations of its existence.

Far be it from me to indulge the foolish presumption of setting up for a preceptor. I merely wish to impart to my readers the little I have learned, and have myself done; for in the most contemptible books we always find something deserving of attention.

(Second Part, Ch. III.)

. . . . . .

In this city [Bologna], the mother of wisdom and the Athens of Italy, complaints had been made some years before, of my reformation, as having a tendency to suppress the Four Masks of Italian comedy.

This sort of comedy was in greater estimation at Bologna than elsewhere. There were several persons of merit in that place who took delight in composing outlines of pieces, which were very well represented there by citizens of great ability, and were the delight of their country.

The lovers of the old comedy, on seeing the rapid progress of the new, declared everywhere that it was unworthy of an Italian to give a blow to a species of comedy in which Italy had attained great distinction, ond which no other nation had ever been able to imitate.

But what made the greatest impression on the discontented, was the suppression of masks, which my system seemed to threaten. It was said that these personages had been for two centuries the amusement of Italy, and that it ought not to be deprived of a species of comic diversion which it had created and so well supported.

Before venturing to give my opinion of this subject I imagine the reader will have no objection to listen for a few moments to a short account of the origin, employments, and effects, of these four masks.

Comedy, which in all ages has been the favorite entertainment of civilized nations, shared the fate of the arts and sciences, and was buried under the ruins of the empire during the decay of letters.

The germ of comedy, however, was never altogether extinguished in the fertile bosom of Italy. Those who first endeavored to bring about its revival not finding, in an ignorant age, writers of sufficient skill, had the boldness to draw out plans, to distribute them into acts and scenes and to utter extempore, the subjects, thoughts, and witticisms which they had concerted among themselves.

Those who could read (and neither the great nor the rich were of the number), finding that in the comedies of Plautus and Terence there were always duped fathers, debauched sons, enamored girls, knavish servants, and mercenary maids; and running over the different districts of Italy, they took the fathers from Venice and Bologna, the servants from Bergamo, and the lovers and waiting-maids from the dominions of Rome and Tuscany.

Written proofs are not to be expected of what took place in a time when writing was not in use: but I prove my assertion in this way: Pantaloon has always been a Venetian, the Doctor a Bolognese, and Brighella and Harlequin, Bergamasks; and from these places, therefore, the comic personages called the Four Masks of the Italian comedy, were taken by the players.

What I say on this subject is not altogether the product of my imagination: I possess a manuscript of the Fifteenth century, in very good preservation, and bound in parchment, containing one hundred and twenty subjects, or sketches, of Italian pieces, called *commedie dell' arte,* and of which the basis of the comic humor are always Pantaloon, a Venetian merchant; the Doctor, a Bolognese lawyer; and Brighella and Harlequin, Bergamesk valets, the first clever and sprightly, and the other a mere dolt. Their antiquity and their long existence indicate their origin.

With respect to their employment, Pantaloon and the Doctor, called by the Italians the two old men, represent the part of fathers, and the other parts where cloaks are worn.

The first is a merchant, because Venice in ancient times was the richest and most extensively commercial country in Italy. He has always preserved the ancient Venetian costume; the black dress and woolen bonnet are still worn in Venice; and the red under-waistcoat and breeches, cut out like drawers with red stockings and slippers, are a most exact representation of the equipment of the first inhabitants of the Adriatic marshes. The beard, which was considered an ornament in those remote ages, has been caricatured and rendered ridiculous in subsequent periods.

The second old man, called the Doctor, was taken from among the lawyers, for the sake of opposing a learned man to a merchant; and Bologna was selected, because in that city there existed a university, which, notwithstanding the ignorance of the times, still preserved the offices and emoluments of professors.

In the dress of the Doctor we observe the ancient costume of the university and bar of Bologna, which is nearly the same at this day; and the idea of the singular mask which covers his face and nose was taken from a wine stain which disfigured the countenance of a lawyer of those times. This is a tradition still existing among the lovers of the *commedia dell' arte.*

Brighella and Harlequin, called in Italy the two Zani, were taken from Bergamo; because, the former being a very sharp fellow and the other a stupid clown, these two extremes are only to be found among the lower orders of that part of the country.

Brighella represents an intriguing, deceitful and knavish valet. His dress is a species of livery: his swarthy mask is a caricature of the color of the inhabitants of those high mountains, tanned by the heat of the sun.

Some comedians in this character have taken the name of Fenocchio, Fiqueto, and Scapin; but they have always represented the same valet and the same Bergamask.

The harlequins have also assumed other names; they have been sometimes Tracagnins, Truffaldins, Gradelins, and Mezetins; but they have always been stupid Bergamasks. Their dress is an exact reproduction of that of a poor devil who has picked up pieces of stuffs of different colors to patch his dress; but his hat corresponds with his mendicity, and the hare's tail with which it is adorned is still a common article of dress of the peasantry of Bergamo.

I have thus, I trust, sufficiently demonstrated the origin and employment of the four masks of Italian comedy; it now remains for me to mention the effects resulting from them.

The mask must always be very prejudicial to the action of the performer either in joy or sorrow; whether he be in love, cross, or good-humored, the same features are always exhibited; and however he may gesticulate and vary the tone, he can never convey by the countenance, which is the interpreter of the heart, the different passions with which he is inwardly agitated.

The masks of the Greeks and Romans were a sort of speaking-trumpets, invented for the purpose of conveying the sound through the vast extent of their amphitheaters. Passion and sentiment were not, in those times, carried to the pitch of delicacy which is now necessary. The actor must, in our day, possess a soul; and the soul under a mask is like a fire under ashes.

These were the reasons which induced me to endeavor the reformation of the Italian theater, and to substitute comedies for farces.

(Second Part, Ch. XXIV.)

GERMANY — I

Earliest and Neo-Classic Periods

GERMAN DRAMATIC CRITICISM FROM THE BEGINNINGS TO LESSING

Owing to a variety of causes — the lack of political unity, among others — Germany was late in developing her literature, and what dramatic criticism exists before Lessing is more or less of the old style — Latin commentaries, statement and re-statement of the Rules, and grammatical disquisitions. Individual figures stand out, however — like Opitz, Gottsched, and Johann Elias Schlegel — but none of these contributed theories of epoch-making importance.

German dramatic criticism begins with German general criticism, somewhere toward the middle of the sixteenth century. It is doubtful just who was the beginner, though Sturm, Fabricius, and Pontanus all have just claims, while Schosser's pedantic *Disputationes de Tragœdia* antedated them all (1559). Johann Sturm was a scholar of no mean attainments, and his commentaries, letters and the work on rhetoric, exercised some influence, especially on his pupil Johann Lobart, who edited a commentary of Horace's *Ars Poetica* in 1576. Georgius Fabricius, the first part of whose *De Re Poetica* appeared in 1565 (an enlarged edition was published in 1571), was considerably influenced by Scaliger. Jacobus Pontanus [Spanmüller] wrote an *Institutiones Poeticae*, a pedantic and unoriginal treatise which appeared in 1594,[1] But the first of the truly modern and vernacular tractates was Martin Opitz' *Buch von der Deutscher Poeterei* (1624). This work, with all its shortcomings, gave rise to a good deal of more or less original work in Germany, though between its appearance

and that of Gottsched's *Versuch* in 1730 there was a large amount of the usual Latin scholarship and pedantic compilation. With Andreas Gryphius, the most important dramatist of the century, the English influence, which was beginning to be felt even in the days of Opitz, became more widespread, and in his plays, lectures, and prefaces he combatted the old rules of drama. Erdmann Neumeister followed Gryphius in his disregard of convention, while Philip von Zesen (in his *De Poetica*, 1656) and Augustine Buchner, in his *Kurzer Wegweiser sur Deutsch Tichtkunst* (1663), continued the pedantic tradition. Johann Christoph Gottsched exerted considerable influence over his contemporaries and successors. He was during a great part of the first half of the eighteenth century a literary dictator, and his *Versuch einer kritischen Dichtkunst* (1730) opened the eyes of Germany to the possibility of developing her own literature. The spirit of the work was neo-classical, and Gottsched was a staunch admirer of the French critics. His quarrels with Bodmer and Breitinger, the Swiss critics, over Milton and other subjects, resulted in ignominious defeat. Johann Jakob Bodmer is the author of the famous *Diskurse der Mahler* (1721), and J. J. Breitinger of the *Kritische Dichtkunst* (1740). Gottsched's ideas were soon rejected by the public, but he had a number of followers, chiefly among the small group of writers who founded the *Bremer Beiträge* in 1745. Among these were Gellert, Klopstock, and Johann Elias Schlegel. Schlegel wrote a number of interesting essays on the drama, among the best of which is the *Gedanken zur Aufnahme des dänischen Theaters*. He was likewise a Shakespeare enthusiast, and has been called the initiator of Shakespeare study in his country. Moses Mendelssohn's *Briefe* are concerned, among

---

1 Some critics include two great Dutch writers — Heinsius and Voss — with the Early Germans. Daniel Heinsius published his *De Tragœdiæ Constitutione* in 1611, and Gerard Voss his *Commentariorum Rhetoricorum sive Oratoriarum Institutionum Libri Sex* in 1609, though the enlarged edition of 1643 contains much more on the drama.

other things, with Shakespeare criticism. But by all odds the greatest critic of the time, and one of the greatest of all time, was Gotthold Ephraim Lessing. While he wrote a vast amount of miscellaneous criticism and a purely esthetic work — the *Laokoon* (1776) — his chief contribution to dramatic theory is his *Hamburgische Dramaturgie* (1769). These papers were originally published as disconnected dramatic criticisms, but taken as a whole, they none the less constitute a body of dramatic theory. Lessing's principal task was to destroy the French models set up by Gottsched and others, to explain Aristotle, and to exhort his fellow dramatists to turn to England, where they would find a dramatic form more flexible and better adapted to their genius than the rigidly fixed classical dramas of France.

General references on German literature:

K. Goedeke, *Grundriss zur Geschichte der deutschen Dichtung*, 4 vols. (Dresden, 1859–81).

Jahresberichte für neuere deutsche Literaturgeschichte, 14 vols. (Berlin, 1892 ff).

K. Breul, *Handy Bibliographical Guide to the German Language and Literature* (London, 1895).

K. A. Koberstein, *Grundriss zur Geschichte der deutschen Nationalliteratur* (New ed. by K. Bartsch, 5 vols., Leipzig, 1872–74).

G. G. Gervinus, *Geschichte der poetischen Nationalliteratur der Deutschen* (New ed. by K. Bartsch, 5 vols., Leipzig, 1871–74).

W. Wackernagel, *Geschichte der deutschen Literatur* (new ed. and continuation by E. Martin, 2 vols., Basel, 1879, 1885–94).

A. F. C. Vilmar, *Geschichte der deutschen Nationalliteratur* (ed. by A. Stern, 1906).

W. Scherer, *Geschichte der deutschen Literatur* (latest ed., Berlin, 1905).

J. G. Robinson, *A History of German Literature* (New York, 1902).

Kuno Francke, *History of German Literature as Determined by Social Forces* (New York, 1911).

Calvin Thomas, *A History of German Literature* (New York, 1908).

General references on German drama:

Robert E. Prutz, *Vorlesungen über die Geschichte des deutschen Theaters* (Leipzig, 1847).

Carl Heine, *Das Theater in Deutschland* (1891).

Carl Weitbrecht, *Das deutsche Drama* (Berlin, 1900).

R. Prölss, *Katechismus der Dramaturgie* (2nd ed., Leipzig, 1890).

——, *Geschichte der neueren Dramas*, 3 vols. (Leipzig, 1880–83).

References on early German drama and German criticism:

George Saintsbury, *A History of Criticism*, vol. 2 (New York, 1902).

Karl Borinski, *Die Poetik der Renaissance und die Anfänge der literarischen Kritik in Deutschland* (Berlin, 1886).

Friedrich Braitmaier, *Geschichte der poetischen Theorie und Kritik von den Diskursen der Maler bis auf Lessing* (Frauenfeld, 1889).

C. M. Gayley and F. N. Scott, *An Introduction to the Methods and Materials of Literary Criticism* (Boston, 1899).

R. Weitbrecht, *Blätter für literarische Unterhaltung* (1891–11: 625, *Kritiker und Dichter*).

T. S. Perry, *From Opitz to Lessing* (Boston, 1885).

E. Grucker, *Histoire des Doctrines littéraires et esthétiques en Allemagne* (Paris, 1883).

Richard Beckherrn, *M. Opitz, P. Ronsard und D. Heinsius* (Königsberg, 1888).

G. Belouin, *De Gottsched à Lessing* (Paris, 1909).

Karl Holl, *Zur Geschichte der Lustspieltheorie* (Berlin, 1911).

O. Wichmann, *L'Art poétique de Boileau dans celui de Gottsched* (Berlin, 1879).

Walter Schinz, *Le Problème de la tragédie en Allemagne* (Paris, 1903).

Max Poensgen, *Geschichte der Theorie der Tragödie von Gottsched bis Lessing* (Leipzig, 1899).

Danzel, *Gottsched und seine Zeit* (Leipzig, 1848).

J. Bintz, *Der Einfluss der Ars Poetica des Horaz auf die deutsche Literatur des xviii. Jahrhundert* (Hamburg, 1892).

Hugo Dinger, *Dramaturgie als Wissenschaft*, 2 vols. (Leipzig, 1904–05).

Wilhelm von Scholz, *Deutsche Dramaturgie*, 3 vols. (München, 1912–14).

Johann Cruger, *J. C. Gottsched und die Schweizer* (Berlin, 1884).

Madame de Staël, *De l'Allemagne* (1810).

Ida Bruhning, *Le Théâtre en Allemagne* (Paris, 1887).

A. W. Schlegel, *Vorlesungen über dramatische Kunst und Literatur* (Berlin, 1809–11. Translated by J. Black, as *Lectures on Dramatic Art and Literature;* Bohn ed., London, 1914).

GOTTHOLD EPHRAIM LESSING

Gotthold Ephraim Lessing was born at Kamenz in 1729. His preliminary schooling was received at Meissen, whence he went to the University of Leipzig, where he studied theology. He was not long in discovering that his interests lay rather in literature and philosophy, and he went to Berlin, where for five years he led a precarious and hand-to-mouth existence as a literary hack. Thence he went to Wittenberg, where he took his M.A. degree. He did some miscellaneous writing alone and in collaboration with Moses Mendelssohn. He had been early attracted to the theater, and in his youth he had written a number of small plays and translated others. His first important play, *Miss Sara Sampson,* appeared in 1755. The next few years found him doing all sorts of work and in many cities, but in 1758 he returned to Berlin and edited a review, *Litteraturbriefe,* which attracted a great deal of attention. From 1760 to 1765 he was secretary to the Governor of Breslau, and in 1766 he published his famous *Laokoon.* The following year he produced *Minna von Barnhelm,* the first great German comedy. In 1767 he was called to Hamburg as critic of the new National Theater, and for two years he published the criticisms which were re-printed as the *Hamburgische Dramaturgie.* When the theater closed Lessing became librarian at Wolfenbüttel. Shortly after, he traveled in Italy and in 1772 he published *Emilia Galotti.* In 1776 he married Eva König, who died within a year of the marriage. For some time he engaged in various theological disputes, turning finally to dramatic writing. *Nathan der Weise* made its appearance in 1779. This was his last important literary work. He died in 1781.

Lessing was a dramatist of the first rank, and a critic, coming as he did at a turning-point in German literature, of supreme importance. Throughout the *Hamburgische Dramaturgie* there is a tendency to correct the fallacious notions then current, and above all a healthy note of constructive criticism. His interpretation of Aristotle and his attacks on French forms were of inestimable importance to the dramatists of his day. The *Dramaturgie* contains a mass of arguments favoring the theory that no true drama can rest upon any but Aristotelian laws. He insists especially upon unity of action. A large number of papers are devoted to attacking the French classical dramatists, and others to showing how Shakespeare was basically a follower of Aristotle. Says Lessing in his *Preface* to the *Dramaturgie:* "This *Dramaturgie* is to form a critical index of all the plays performed, and is to accompany every step made here by the art of the poet or the actor. . . . At the same time it is well that the mediocre should not pretend to be more than it is, so that the dissatisfied spectator may at least learn to judge from it. It is only needful to explain to a person of healthy mind the reasons why something has not pleased him if one desires to teach him good taste."

On the drama:

Beiträge zur Historie und Aufnahme des Theaters (1750).
Theatralische Bibliothek (1754–58).
Vorrede zu Thomsons Trauerspielen (1756).
Vorrede des Uebersetzers in *Das Theater des Herrn Diderot* (1760).
Briefe, die neueste Litteratur betreffend (1759, 1760).
Hamburgische Dramaturgie (1769).
Leben des Sophokles (1760–90).
Dramaturgische Entwürfe und Fragmente (posthumous).
Kollektaneen zur Litteratur (vol. 20, Cotta ed. also contain casual references to the drama).
The *Briefe*, likewise. See also especially *Lessings Briefwechsel mit Mendelssohn und Nicolai über das Trauerspiel* (in *Philosophische Bib.*, vol. 2, Leipzig, 1910).

Editions:

G. E. Lessings Schriften, 6 vols. (Berlin, 1753–55), and *G E. Lessings sämmtliche Schriften*, 30 vols. (1771–94) were the only collected editions appearing during the author's life-time. Among the modern editions are the Lachmann-Muncker 15 vols. ed. (1900), and the Boxburger and Blumner eds., 14 vols. (1883–90). A convenient and accessible edition is the *Cotta* edition, under the supervision of Hugo Göring, 20 vols. (Stuttgart and Berlin, n. d.). There are numerous editions of the *Hamburgische Dramaturgie:* the first edition appeared in Hamburg, 2 vols. 1769. See in above-mentioned collected works.

On Lessing and his works:

C. G. Lessing, *G. E. Lessings Leben*, etc., 3 parts (Berlin, 1793).
T. W. Danzel, *Gotthold Ephraim Lessing, sein Leben und seine Werke*, 2 vols, (2nd ed., Berlin, 1880–81).
Adolph Stahr, *G. E. Lessing, sein Leben und seine Werke*, 2 parts (Berlin, 1859).
(Translation of the above: *The Life and Works of G. E. Lessing*, translated by E. P. Evans, 2 vols., Boston, 1866.)
Erich Schmidt, *Lessing. Geschichte seines Lebens und seiner Schriften* (Berlin, 1884).
James Sime, *Lessing*, 2 vols. (London, 1877).
Heinrich Düntzer, *Lessings Leben* (Leipzig, 1882).
T. W. Rolleston, *Lessing* (London, n. d.).
Hermann Baumgart, *Aristoteles, Lessing, und Goethe. Ueber das ethische und das aesthetische Princip der Tragödie* (Leipzig, 1877).
Emil Brenning, *Lessing als Dramatiker und Lessings Nathan der Weise* (Bremen, 1878).
Wilhelm Cosack, *Materialen zu G. E. Lessings Hamburgischer Dramaturgie*, etc. (Paderborn, 1876).
L. Eckart, *Lessing und das erst deutsche Nationaltheater in Hamburg* (Hamburg, 1864).
Emil Gotschlich, *Lessings aristotelische Studien und der Einfluss derselben auf seine Werke* (Berlin, 1876).
Eugen Sierke, *G. E. Lessing als angehender Dramatiker*, etc. (Königsberg, 1869).
J. Kont, *Lessing et la définition de la tragédie par Aristote* (in *Rev. des Etudes grecques*, p. 387, Paris, 1893).

HAMBURG DRAMATURGY [1]

[*Hamburgische Dramaturgie*]

(1769)

No. 1.—May 1, 1767.

The theater was successfully opened on the 22nd of last month with the tragedy

Olindo and Sophronia. Olindo and Sophronia is the work of a young poet, and is a posthumous incomplete work. Its

[1] Re-printed, with omissions, from *Lessing's Laoköon, Dramatic Notes*, and the *Representation of Death by the Ancients*, translated by E. C. Beasley and Helen Zimmern (New Bohn Eds.).— Ed.

theme is the well-known episode in Tasso. It is not easy to convert a touching little story into a touching drama. True, it costs little trouble to invent new complications and to enlarge separate emotions into scenes. But to prevent these new complications from weakening the interest or interfering with probability; to transfer oneself from the point of view of a narrator into the real standpoint of each personage; to let passions arise before the eyes of the spectator in lieu of describing them, and to let them grow up without effort in such illusory continuity that he must sympathize, whether he will or no; this it is which is needful, and which genius does without knowing it, without tediously explaining it to itself, and which mere cleverness endeavors in vain to imitate.

Here I wish to make a double remark which, borne in mind, will save young tragic poets from committing some great faults. If heroic sentiments are to arouse admiration, the poet must not be too lavish of them, for what we see often, what we see in many persons, no longer excites astonishment. Every Christian in *Olindo and Sophronia* holds being martyred and dying as easy as drinking a glass of water. We hear these pious bravadoes so often and out of so many mouths, that they lose all their force.

The second remark concerns Christian tragedies in particular. Their heroes are generally martyrs. Now we live in an age when the voice of healthy reason resounds too loudly to allow every fanatic who rushes into death wantonly, without need, without regard for all his citizen duties, to assume to himself the title of a martyr. We know too well to-day how to distinguish the false martyr from the true, but despise the former as much as we reverence the latter, and at most they extort from us a melancholy tear for the blindness and folly of which we see humanity is capable. But this tear is none of those pleasing ones that tragedy should evoke. If therefore the poet chooses a martyr for his hero let him be careful to give to his actions the purest and most incontrovertible motives, let him place him in an unalterable necessity of taking the step that exposes him to danger, let him not suffer him to seek death carelessly or insolently challenge it.

Else his pious hero becomes an object of our distaste, and even the religion that he seeks to honor may suffer thereby. I have already said that it could only be a superstition that led Olindo to steal the image from the mosque as contemptible as that which we despise in the wizard Ismenor. It does not excuse the poet that there were ages when such superstition was general and could subsist side by side with many excellent qualities, that there still are countries where it would be nothing strange for pious ignorance. For he wrote his tragedy as little for those ages as he intended that it should be performed in Bohemia or Spain. The good author, be he of whatever species he will, if he does not write merely to show his wit and learning, has ever the best and most intelligent of his time and country before his eyes and he only condescends to write what pleases and can touch these. Even the dramatic author, if he lowers himself to the mob, lowers himself only in order that he may enlighten and improve the mass and not to confirm them in their prejudices or in their ignoble mode of thought.

No. 2

Yet another remark, also bearing on Christian tragedies might be made about the conversion of Clorinda. Convinced though we may be of the immediate operations of grace, yet they can please us little on the stage, where everything that has to do with the character of the personages must arise from natural causes. We can only tolerate miracles in the physical world; in the moral world everything must retain its natural course, because the theater is to be the school of the moral world. The motives for every resolve, for every change of opinion or even thoughts, must be carefully balanced against each other so as to be in accordance with the hypothetical character, and must never produce more than they could produce in accordance with strict probability. The poet, by beauty of details, may possess the art of deluding us to overlook misproportions of this kind, but he only deceives us once, and as soon as we are cool again we take back the applause he has lured from us.

Even Corneille's *Polyeucte* is to be condemned in view of the above remarks, and since the plays made in imitation of it are yet more faulty, the first tragedy that deserves the name of Christian has beyond doubt still to appear. I mean a play in which the Christian interests us solely as a Christian. But is such a piece even possible? Is not the character of a true Christian something quite untheatrical? Does not the gentle pensiveness, the unchangeable meekness that are his essential features, war with the whole business of tragedy that strives to purify passions by passions? Does not his expectation of rewarding happiness after this life contradict the disinterestedness with which we wish to see all great and good actions undertaken and carried out on the stage?

Until a work of genius arises that incontestably decides these objections,— for we know by experience what difficulties genius can surmount,— my advice is this, to leave all existent Christian tragedies unperformed. This advice, deduced from the necessities of art, and which deprives us of nothing more than very mediocre plays, is not the worse because it comes to the aid of weak spirits who feel I know not what shrinkage, when they hear sentiments spoken from the stage that they had only expected to hear in a holier place. The theater should give offense to no one, be he who he may, and I wish it would and could obviate all preconceived offense.

.   .   .   .   .   .

. . . In another still worse tragedy where one of the principal characters died quite casually, a spectator asked his neighbor, " But what did she die of? "—" Of what? Of the fifth act," was the reply. In very truth the fifth act is an ugly evil disease that carries off many a one to whom the first four acts promised a longer life.

.   .   .   .   .   .

. . . I know full well that the sentiments in a drama must be in accordance with the assumed character of the person who utters them. They can therefore not bear the stamp of absolute truth, it is enough if they are poetically true, if we must admit that this character under these circumstances, with these passions, could not have judged otherwise. But on the other hand this poetical truth must also approach to the absolute and the poet must never think so unphilosophically as to assume that a man could desire evil for evil's sake, that a man could act on vicious principles, knowing them to be vicious and boast of them to himself and to others.

No. 9

.   .   .   .   .   .

It is right and well if in every-day life we start with no undue mistrust of the character of others, if we give all credence to the testimony of honest folk. But may the dramatic poet put us off with such rules of justice? Certainly not, although he could much ease his business thereby. On the stage we want to see who the people are, and we can only see it from their actions. The goodness with which we are to credit them, merely upon the word of another, cannot possibly interest us in them. It leaves us quite indifferent, and if we never have the smallest personal experience of their goodness it even has a bad reflex effect upon those on whose faith we solely and only accepted the opinion. Far therefore from being willing to believe Siegmund to be a most perfect and excellent young man, because Julia, her mother, Clarissa and Edward declare him to be such, we rather begin to suspect the judgment of these persons, if we never see for ourselves anything to justify their favorable opinion. It is true a private person cannot achieve many great actions in the space of four-and-twenty hours. But who demands great actions? Even in the smallest, character can be revealed, and those that throw the most light upon character, are the greatest according to poetical valuation. Moreover how came it that four-and-twenty hours was time enough to give Siegmund opportunity to compass two of the most foolish actions that could occur to a man in his position? The occasion was suitable, the author might reply, but he scarcely will reply that. They might have arisen as naturally as possible, be treated as delicately as possible; for all that the foolish actions, that we see him commit, would leave a bad impression on our minds concerning this young impetuous philosophist. That he acts badly we see; that he can act well we hear, not even by examples but in the vaguest of general terms.

No. 11

. . . For the dramatic poet is no historian, he does not relate to us what was once believed to have happened, but he really produces it again before our eyes, and produces it again not on account of mere historical truth but for a totally different and a nobler aim. Historical accuracy is not his aim, but only the means by which he hopes to attain his aim; he wishes to delude us and touch our hearts through this delusion. . . .

No. 12

. . . . . .

I will not say that it is a fault when the dramatic poet arranges his fable in such a manner that it serves for the exposition or confirmation of some great moral truth. But I may say that this arrangement of the fable is anything but needful; that there are very instructive and perfect plays that do not aim at such a single maxim, and that we err when we regard the moral sentences that are found at the close of many ancient tragedies, as the keynote for the existence of the entire play.

. . . . .

No. 16

. . . The only unpardonable fault of a tragic poet is this, that he leaves us cold; if he interests us he may do as he likes with the little mechanical rules.

. . . . . .

No. 19

. . . . .

Now, Aristotle has long ago decided how far the tragic poet need regard historical accuracy: not farther than it resembles a well-constructed fable wherewith he can combine his intentions. He does not make use of an event because it really happened, but because it happened in such a manner as he will scarcely be able to invent more fitly for

his present purpose. If he finds this fitness in a true case, then the true case is welcome; but to search through history books does not reward his labor. And how many know what has happened? If we only admit the possibility that something can happen from the fact that it has happened, what prevents us from deeming an entirely fictitious fable a really authentic occurrence, of which we have never heard before? What is the first thing that makes a history probable? Is it not its internal probability? And is it not a matter of indifference whether this probability be confirmed by no witnesses or traditions, or by such as have never come within our knowledge? It is assumed quite without reason, that it is one of the objects of the stage to keep alive the memory of great men. For that we have history and not the stage. From the stage we are not to learn what such and such an individual man has done, but what every man of a certain character would do under certain given circumstances. The object of tragedy is more philosophical than the object of history, and it is degrading her from her true dignity to employ her as a mere panegyric of famous men or to misuse her to feel national pride.

. . . . . .

No. 21

Nanine belongs to pathetic comedy. It has also many laughable scenes, and only in so far as these laughable scenes alternate with the pathetic, Voltaire would admit of them in comedy. An entirely serious comedy, wherein we never laugh, not even smile, wherein we should rather always weep, is to him a monstrosity. On the other hand he finds the transition from the pathetic to the comic, and from the comic to the pathetic, very natural. Human life is nothing but a constant chain of such transitions, and comedy should be a mirror of human life.

. . . . . .

No. 24

. . . . . .

In short, tragedy is not history in dialogue. History is for tragedy nothing but a storehouse of names wherewith we are used to associate certain characters. If the poet finds in history circumstances that are convenient for the adornment or individualizing of his subject; well, let him use them. Only this should be counted as little a merit as the contrary is a crime.

.   .   .   .

No. 25

.   .   .   .

" In short, no single part in this tragedy is what it should be, all are perverted and yet the play has pleased. When this pleasure? Obviously out of the situation of the personages that is touching in itself. A great man who is led to the scaffold will always interest; the representation of his fate makes an impression even without the help of poetry; very nearly the same impression that reality itself would make."
So much is the tragic poet dependent on his choice of subject. Through this alone the weakest and most confused play can achieve a kind of success, and I do not know how it is that in such plays good actors always show themselves to best advantage. . . .

No. 27

. . . the tragic poet loves the unexpected, the sudden, more than any other; . . .

No. 28

.   .   .   .   .   .

There is nothing to object to in this verdict, but against another criticism that attacks the poet on the score of morality, there is the more. An absent-minded person is said to be no *motif* for a comedy. And why not? To be absent, it is said, is a malady, a misfortune and no vice. An absent man deserves ridicule as little as one who has the headache. Comedy must only concern itself with such faults as can be remedied. Whoever is absent by nature can merit this as little by means of ridicule, as though he limped.

.   .   .   .   .   .

Well, but now granted that absence of mind is incurable, where is it written that

comedy should only laugh at moral faults, and not at incurable defects? Every absurdity, every contrast of reality and deficiency is laughable. But laughter and derision are far apart. We can laugh at a man, occasionally laugh about him, without in the least deriding him. Indisputable and well-known as this difference is, yet all the quibbles which Rousseau lately made against the use of comedy only arose from the fact that he had not sufficiently regarded it. He says, for instance, Molière makes us laugh at a misanthrope and yet the misanthrope is the honest man of the play, Molière therefore shows himself an enemy to virtue in that he makes the virtuous man contemptible. Not so; the misanthrope does not become contemptible, he remains what he was, and the laughter that springs from the situations in which the poet places him does not rob him in the least of our esteem. The same with the *distrait*, we laugh at him, but do we despise him on that account? We esteem his other good qualities as we ought; why, without them we could not even laugh at his absence of mind. Let a bad, worthless man be endowed with this absence of mind, and then see whether we should still find it laughable? It will be disgusting, horrid, ugly, not laughable.

No. 29

Comedy is to do us good through laughter; but not through derision; not just to counteract those faults at which it laughs, nor simply and solely in those persons who possess these laughable faults. Its true general use consists in laughter itself, in the practice of our powers to discern the ridiculous, to discern it easily and quickly under all cloaks of passion and fashion; in all admixture of good and bad qualities, even in the wrinkles of solemn earnestness. Granted that Molière's *Miser* never cured a miser; nor Regnard's *Gambler*, a gambler; conceded that laughter never could improve these fools; the worse for them, but not for comedy. It is enough for comedy that, if it cannot cure an incurable disease, it can confirm the healthy in their health. *The Miser* is instructive also to the extravagant man;

and to him who never plays *The Gam-bler* may prove of use. The follies they have not got themselves, others may have with whom they have to live. It is well to know those with whom we may come into collision; it is well to be preserved from all impressions by example. A pre-servative is also a valuable medicine, and all morality has none more powerful and effective, than the ridiculous.

No. 30

. . . . . .

This triple murder should constitute only one action, that has its beginning, its center and its end in the one passion of one person. What therefore does it lack as the subject for a tragedy? Nothing for genius, everything for a bungler. Here there is no love, no en-tanglement, no recognition, no unexpected marvelous occurrence; everything pro-ceeds naturally. This natural course tempts genius and repels the bungler. Genius is only busied with events that are rooted in one another, that form a chain of cause and effect. To reduce the latter to the former, to weigh the latter against the former, everywhere to ex-clude chance, to cause everything that occurs to occur so that it could not have happened otherwise, this is the part of genius when it works in the domains of history and converts the useless treas-ures of memory into nourishment for the soul. Wit, on the contrary, that does not depend on matters rooted in each other, but on the similar or dissimilar, if it ventures on a work that should be reserved to genius alone, detains itself with such events as have not further concern with one another except that they have occurred at the same time. To connect these, to interweave and con-fuse their threads so that we lose the one at every moment in following out the other and are thrown from one sur-prise into another, this is the part of wit and this only. From the incessant cross-ing of such threads of opposed colors re-sults a texture, which is to art what weavers call *changeant:* a material of which we cannot say whether it be blue or red, green or yellow; it is both, it seems this from one side, that from an-

other, a plaything of fashion, a juggling trick for children.

. . . . . .

No. 32

The poet finds in history a woman who murders her husband and sons. Such in-deed can awaken terror and pity, and he takes hold of it to treat it as a tragedy. But history tells him no more than the bare fact and this is as horrible as it is unusual. It furnishes at most three scenes, and, devoid of all detailed cir-cumstances, three improbable scenes. What therefore does the poet do?

As he deserves this name more or less, the improbability or the meager brevity will seem to him the greatest want in this play.

If he be in the first condition, he will consider above all else how to invent a series of causes and effects by which these improbable crimes could be ac-counted for most naturally. Not satis-fied with resting their probability upon historical authority, he will endeavor so to construct the characters of his per-sonages, will endeavor so to necessitate one from another the events that place his characters in action, will endeavor to define the passions of each character so accurately, will endeavor to lead these passions through such gradual steps, that we shall everywhere see nothing but the most natural and common course of events. Thus with every step we see his personages take, we must acknowledge that we should have taken it ourselves under the same circumstances and the same degree of passion, and hence noth-ing will repel us but the imperceptible approach to a goal from which our imag-ination shrinks, and where we suddenly find ourselves filled with profound pity for those whom a fatal stream has car-ried so far, and full of terror at the con-sciousness that a similar stream might also thus have borne ourselves away to do deeds which in cold blood we should have regarded as far from us. If the poet takes this line, if his genius tells him that he cannot ignobly falter in its course, then the meager brevity of his fable has vanished at once, it no longer distresses him how he shall fill his five acts with so few events, he is only afraid lest five acts should not suffice for all his material, that enlarges more and more under his treatment now that he has discovered its hidden organization and understands how to unravel it.

Meantime the poet who less deserves this name, who is nothing but an ingenious fellow, a good versifier, he, I say, will find so little obstacle in the improbability of his scheme that he actually seeks therein its claim to admiration, which he must on no account diminish if he would not deprive himself of the surest means to evoke pity and terror. For he knows so little wherein this pity and terror really consist that in order to evoke them he thinks he cannot pile up enough marvelous, unexpected, incredible and abnormal matters, and thinks he must ever have recourse to extraordinary and horrible misfortunes and crimes. Scarcely therefore has he scented in history a Cleopatra, the murderess of her husband and sons, than he sees nothing further to do, in order to form this into a tragedy, than to fill in the interstices between the two crimes and to fill it with matter as strange as the crimes themselves. All this, his invention and the historical materials, he kneads into a very long, very incomprehensible romance, and when he has kneaded it as well as flour and straw can be kneaded together, he places his paste upon the skeleton wires of acts and scenes, relates and relates, rants and rhymes, and in four to six weeks, according to rhyming is easy or difficult to him, the wonder-work is finished, is called a tragedy, is printed and performed, read and looked at, admired or hissed, retained or for-'gotten as good luck will have it. For *et habent sua fata libelli.*

May I presume to apply this to the great Corneille? Or must I still make this application? According to the secret fate that rules over writings as over men, his *Rodogune* has been held for more than a hundred years the greatest masterpiece of the greatest tragic poet of all France and has occasionally been admired by all Europe. Can an admiration of a hundred years be groundless? Where have mankind so long concealed their eyes, their emotions? Was it reserved from 1644 to 1767 to a Hamburg dramatic critic to see spots in the sun and to debase a planet to a meteor?

Oh no! Already in the last century a certain honest Huron was imprisoned in the Bastille at Paris; he found time hang heavy on his hands although he was in Paris, and from sheer *ennui* he studied the French poets; and this Huron could not take pleasure in *Rodogune.* After this there lived, somewhere in Italy at the beginning of this century, a pedant who had his head full of the tragedies of the Greeks and of his countrymen of the sixteenth century, and he also found much to censure in *Rodogune.* Finally, a few years ago there was a Frenchman,[2] a great admirer of Corneille's name, who because he was rich and had a good heart, took pity on the poor deserted granddaughter of the great poet, had her educated under his eyes, taught her to make pretty verses, collected alms for her, wrote a large lucrative commentary on the works of her grandfather as her dowry, and so forth; yet even he declared *Rodogune* to be a very absurd play, and was utterly amazed how so great a man as the great Cornelle could write such wretched stuff. Under one of these the above dramatic critic must have gone to school and most probably under the last named, for it is always a Frenchman who opens the eyes of a foreigner to the faults of a Frenchman. Beyond question he repeats after him; or if not after him, after the Italian, or perhaps even after Huron. From one of these he must have learnt it. For that a German should think of himself, should of himself have the audacity to doubt the excellence of a Frenchman, who could conceive such a thing? . . .

No. 33

.   .   .   .   .

But moral or no moral, it is the same thing to a dramatic poet whether a general truth can be deduced or no from his fable, . . .

No. 34

For according to the indicated conception that we make to ourselves of genius, we are justified in demanding purpose

2 Voltaire.— Ed.

and harmony in all the characters a poet creates; that is, if he demands from us that we should regard him in the light of a genius.

Harmony; for nothing in the characters must be contradictory; they must ever remain uniform and inherently themselves; they must express themselves now with emphasis, now more slightly as events work upon them, but none of the events must be mighty enough to change black to white. . . .

To act with a purpose is what raises man above the brutes, to invent with a purpose, to imitate with a purpose, is that which distinguishes genius from the petty artists who only invent to invent, imitate to imitate. They are content with the small enjoyment that is connected with their use of these means, and they make these means to be their whole purpose and demand that we also are to be satisfied with this lesser enjoyment, which springs from the contemplation of their cunning but purposeless use of their means. It is true that genius begins to learn from such miserable imitations; they are its preliminary studies. It also employs them in larger works for amplification and to give resting-places to our warmer sympathy, but with the construction and elaboration of its chief personages it combines larger and wider intentions; the intention to instruct us what we should do or avoid; the intention to make us acquainted with the actual characteristics of good and bad, fitting and absurd. It also designs to show us the good in all their combinations and results still good and happy even in misery; the bad as revolting and unhappy even in unhappiness. When its plot admits of no such immediate imitation, no such unquestionable warning, genius still aims at working upon our powers of desire and abhorrence with objects that deserve these feelings, and ever strives to show these objects in their true light, in order that no false light may mislead us as to what we should desire, what we should abhor.

·   ·   ·   ·   ·   ·

No. 35

I have once before, elsewhere, drawn the distinction that exists between the action in an Æsopian fable and a drama. What is valid for the former, is valid for every moral tale that intends to bring a general moral axiom before our contemplation. We are satisfied if this intention is fulfilled and it is the same to us whether this is so by means of a complete action that is in itself a rounded whole, or no. The poet may conclude wherever he wills as soon as he sees his goal. It does not concern him what interest we may take in the persons through whom he works out his intention; he does not want to interest but to instruct us; he has to do with our reason, not with our heart; this latter may or may not be satisfied so long as the other is illumined. Now, the drama on the contrary makes no claim upon a single definite axiom flowing out of its story. It aims at the passions which the course and events of its fable arouse and treat, or it aims at the pleasure accorded by a true and vivid delineation of characters and habits. Both require a certain integrity of action, a certain harmonious end which we do not miss in the moral tale because our attention is solely directed to the general axiom of whose especial application the story affords such an obvious instance.

·   ·   ·   ·   ·   ·

No 36

·   ·   ·   ·   ·   ·

Let us instance the *Matron of Ephesus*. This acrid fable is well known, it is unquestionably the bitterest satire that was ever made on female frivolity. It has been recounted a thousand times after Petronius, and since it pleased even in the worst copy, it was thought that the subject must be an equally happy one for the stage. Houdar de la Motte and others made the attempt, but I appeal to all good taste as to the results of these attempts. The character of the matron in the story provokes a not unpleasant sarcastic smile at the audacity of wedded love; in the drama this becomes repulsive, horrible. In the drama the soldier's persuasions do not seem nearly so subtle, importunate, triumphant, as in the story.

In the story we picture to ourselves a sensitive little woman who is really in earnest in her grief, but succumbs to temptation and to her temperament; her weakness seems the weakness of her sex, we therefore conceive no especial hatred towards her, we deem that what she does, nearly every woman would have done. Even her suggestion to save her living lover by means of her dead husband we think we can forgive her, because of its ingenuity and presence of mind; or rather its very ingenuity leads us to imagine that this suggestion may have been appended by the malicious narrator who desired to end his tale with some right poisonous sting. Now, in the drama we cannot harbor this suggestion; what we hear has happened in the story, we see really occur; what we would doubt of in the story, in the drama the evidence of our own eyes settles incontrovertibly. The mere possibility of such an action diverted us; its reality shows it in all its atrocity; the suggestion amused our fancy, the execution revolts our feelings, we turn our backs to the stage and say with the Lykas of Petronius, without being in Lykas's peculiar position: "Si justus Imperator fuisset, debuit patris familiæ corpus in monimentum referre, mulierem adfigere cruci." And she seems to us the more to deserve this punishment, the less art the poet has expended on her seduction, for we do not then condemn in her wea.. woman in general, but an especially volatile, worthless female . in particular. In short, in order happily to bring Petronius's fable on the stage it should preserve its end and yet not preserve it; the matron should go as far and yet not as far. The explanation of this another time.

No. 38

Now, Aristotle commends nothing more to the tragic poet than a good conception of his fable, and he has endeavored to render this easy to him by various and subtle remarks. For it is the fable that principally makes a poet; ten will succeed in representing customs, reflexions, expressions, for one who is excellent and blameless in this. He declares a fable to be an imitation of an action, πράξεως, and an action by a combination of events is σύνθεσις πραγμάτων. The action is the whole, the events are the parts of this

whole, and as the goodness of any whole rests on the goodness and connexion of its several parts, so also tragical action is more or less perfect, according as the events of which it is composed separately and collectively coincide with the intentions of the tragedy. Aristotle classes the events that can take place in a tragic action under three main heads: change of circumstances, περιπέτεια; recognition, ἀναγνωρισμός; and suffering, πάθος. What he means by the two first, the names sufficiently reveal. Under the third he comprehends all that can occur of a painful and destructive nature to the acting personages: death, wounds, martyrdom and so forth. Change of circumstances and recognition are that by which the more intricate fable, μύθος πεπλεγμένος, is distinguished from the simple, ἁπλοῦς. They are therefore no essential part of the fable, they only make the action more varied and hence more interesting and beautiful, but an action can have its full unity, completion and greatness without them. But without the third we can conceive of no tragical action; every tragedy must have some form of suffering, πάθη, be its fable simple or involved, for herein lies the actual intention of tragedy, to awaken fear and pity; while not every change of outward circumstances, not every recognition, but only certain forms of these attain this end, and other forms are rather disadvantageous than profitable. While, therefore, Aristotle regards and examines separately the various parts of tragical action that he has brought under these three main divisions, explaining what are the best outward changes, the best recognition, the best treatment of suffering, he finds in regard to the former that such changes of fortune are the best and most capable of awakening and stimulating pity and fear, which change from better to worse. In regard to the latter division he finds that the best treatment of suffering in the same sense is when the persons whom suffering threatens do not know each other or only recognize each other at the moment when this suffering is to become reality and it is therefore stayed.

And this is called a contradiction? I do not understand where can be the thoughts of him who finds the least contradiction here. The philosopher speaks of various parts; why must that which he maintains of one of these parts of necessity apply to the others? Is the possible perfection of the one also the perfection of the other? Or is the perfection of a part also the perfection of the whole? If change of circumstances and that which Aristotle includes under the word suffering, are two different things, as they are indeed, why should not something quite different be said of them? Or is it impossible that a whole should have parts of opposed characteristics? Where does Aristotle say that the best tragedy is nothing but a representation of changes of fortunes from prosperity to adversity? Or where does he say that the best tragedy results from nothing but the recognition of him on whom a fearful and unnatural deed was to have been committed? He says neither one thing nor the other of tragedy generally, but each of these things of an especial part that more or less concerns the end, which may or may not have influence. Change of fortune may occur in the middle of the play, and even if it continues thus to the end of the piece, it does not therefore constitute its end. For example, the change of fortune in _Œdipus_ that evinces itself already at the close of the fourth act but to which various sufferings, πάθη, are added and with which the play really concludes. In the same manner suffering can attain its accomplishment in the play and at the same moment be thwarted by recognition, so that by means of this recognition the play is far from concluded, as in the second _Iphigenia_ of Euripides where Orestes is already recognized in the fourth act by his sister who was in the act of sacrificing him. And how perfectly such tragical changes of fortune can be combined with tragical treatment of suffering in one and the same fable, can be shown in _Merope_ itself. It contains the latter but what hinders it from having the former also, if for instance Merope, when she recognizes her son under the dagger in her eagerness to defend him from Polyphontes, contributes to her own or to her loved son's destruction? Why should not this play close as well with the destruction of the mother as with that of the tyrant? Why should it not be open to the poet to raise to the highest point our pity for a tender mother and allow her to be unfortunate through her tenderness? Or why should it not be permissible to let the son whom a pious vengeance has torn from his mother, succumb to the pursuit of the tyrant? Would not such a _Merope_ in both cases combine those two characteristics of the best tragedy, in which the critic has been found so contradictory?

I perceive very well what caused the misunderstanding. It was not easy to imagine a change of fortune from better to worse without suffering, or suffering that has been obviated by recognition otherwise than connected with change of fortune. Yet each can equally be without the other, not to mention that both need not touch the same person, and even if it touches the same person, that both may not occur at the same time, but one follows the other, and one can be caused by the other. Without considering this, people have only thought of those instances and fables in which both parts either harmonize, or in which one of necessity excludes the other. That such exist is unquestionable. But is the art critic to be censured because he composes his rules in the most general manner, without considering the cases in which his general rules come into collision and one perfection must be sacrificed to another? Does such a collision of necessity bring him into contradiction with himself? He says: This part of the fable, if it is to have its perfection, must be of such and such a constitution, that part of another, a third again of another. But where has he said that every fable must of necessity have all these parts? Enough for him that there are fables that could have them all. If your fable is not among the number of these happy ones; if it only admits of the best changes of fortune, the best treatment of suffering, then examine with which of the two you would succeed best as a whole, and choose. That is all!

No. 41

". . . For you cannot think how severe the master is whom we must strive to please: I mean our public. They demand that in a tragedy the hero should speak everywhere and the poet nowhere, and contend that at critical junctures in assemblies, at violent scenes, at a threatening danger, no king, no minister would make poetical comparisons." Now does such a public demand anything unfair? Does it not contend the truth? Should not every public demand this? contend this? . . .

No. 42

. . . The tragedian should avoid everything that can remind the audience of their illusion, for as soon as they are reminded thereof the illusion is gone. It almost seems here as though Maffei [3] sought to strengthen this illusion by assuming the idea of a theater outside the theater. . . .

No. 46

It is one thing to circumvent the rules, another to observe them. The French do the former, the latter was only understood by the ancients.

Unity of action was the first dramatic law of the ancients; unity of time and place were mere consequences of the former which they would scarcely have observed more strictly than exigency required had not the combination with the chorus arisen. For since their actions required the presence of a large body of people and this concourse always remained the same, who could go no further from their dwellings nor remain absent longer than it is customary to do from mere curiosity, they were almost obliged to make the scene of action one and the same spot and confine the time to one and the same day. They submitted *bonâ fide* to this restriction; but with a suppleness of understanding such that in seven cases out of nine they gained more than they lost thereby. For they used this restriction as a reason for simplifying the action and to cut away all that was superfluous, and thus, reduced to essentials, it became only the ideal of an action which was developed most felicitously in this form which required the least addition from circumstances of time and place.

The French, on the contrary, who found no charms in true unity of action, who had been spoilt by the wild intrigues

3 The author of *Merope*.— Ed.

of the Spanish school before they ha[d] learnt to know Greek simplicity, re[-] garded the unity of time and place not a[s] consequences of unity of action, but a[s] circumstances absolutely needful to th[e] representation of an action, to which the[y] must therefore adapt their richer an[d] more complicated actions with all th[e] severity required in the use of a choru[s] which, however, they had totally abol[-] ished. When they found, however, how difficult, nay at times how impossible this was, they made a truce with the tyrannical rules against which they had not the courage to rebel. Instead of a single place, they introduced an uncertain place, under which we could imagine now this, now that spot; enough if the places combined were not too far apart and none required special scenery, so that the same scenery could fit the one about as well as the other. Instead of the unity of a day they substituted unity of duration, and a certain period during which no one spoke of sunrise or sunset, or went to bed, or at least did not go to bed more than once, however much might occur in this space, they allowed to pass as a day.

Now, no one would have objected to this, for unquestionably even thus excellent plays can be made, and the proverb says, cut the wood where it is thinnest. But I must also allow my neighbor the same privilege. I must not always show him the thickest part, and cry, "There you must cut! That is where I cut!" Thus the French critics all exclaim, especially when they speak of the dramatic works of the English. What an ado they then make of regularity, that regularity which they have made so easy to themselves! But I am weary of dwelling on this point! . . .

. . . . . .

The strictest observation of the rules cannot outweigh the smallest fault in a character. How tamely Polyphontes talks and acts in Maffei's play has not escaped Lindelle. He is right to mock at the needless maxims that Maffei places in the tyrant's mouth. . . .

. . . And finally what do we mean by the mixtures of genres? In our primers it is right we should separate them from one another as carefully as possible, but if a genius for higher purposes amalgamates several of them in one and the same work, let us forget our primer and only examine whether he has attained these higher purposes. What do I care whether a play of Euripides is neither wholly a narrative nor wholly a drama, call it a hybrid, enough that this hybrid pleases me more, edifies me more, than the most rule-correct creations of your correct Racines or whatever else they may be called. Because the mule is neither a horse nor an ass, is it therefore the less one of the most useful beasts of burden?

No. 69

•   •   •   •   •

Nothing is more chaste and decent than simple Nature, coarseness and confusion are as far removed from her as pomposity and bombast from the sublime. The same feeling which makes the boundary there, makes it here. The most pompous poet is therefore infallibly the most vulgar. Both faults are inseparable, and no species gives more opportunities of falling into both than tragedy.

•   •   •   •   •

No. 70

. . . There are persons who will not admit of any nature which we can imitate too faithfully, they insist that even what displeases us in nature, pleases us in a faithful imitation, by means of imitation. There are others who regard beautifying nature as a whim; a nature that intends to be more beautiful than nature is just on that account not nature. Both declare themselves to be admirers of the only nature such as she is; the one sees nothing to avoid, the other nothing to add. The former would necessarily admire the Gothic mixed plays, and the latter would find it difficult to take pleasure in the masterpieces of the ancients.

But suppose this were not the consequence? If those persons, great admirers though they are of common everyday nature, should yet declare themselves against the mixture of the farcical and interesting. If these others, monstrous as they deem everything that desires to be better and more beautiful than nature, can yet wander through the

whole Greek theater without finding the least obstacle on this account, how should we explain this contradiction?

We should necessarily have to retrace our steps and retract that which we insisted on before concerning the two species, but how must we retract without involving ourselves in new difficulties? The comparison of such blood-and-thunder tragedies concerning whose worth we dispute, with human life, with the ordinary course of the world, is still so correct.

I will throw out a few thoughts, which if they are not thorough enough may suggest more thorough ones. My chief thought is this: it is true and yet not true that the comic tragedy of Gothic invention faithfully copied nature. It only imitates it faithfully in one half and entirely neglects the other, it imitates the nature of phenomena without in the least regarding the nature of our feelings and emotions.

In nature everything is connected, everything is interwoven, everything changes with everything, everything merges from one into another. But according to this endless variety it is only a play for an infinite spirit. In order that finite spirits may have their share of this enjoyment, they must have the power to set up arbitrary limits, they must have the power to eliminate and to guide their attention at will.

This power we exercise at all moments of our life; without this power there would be no life for us; from too many various feelings we should feel nothing, we should be the constant prey of present impressions, we should dream without knowing what we dream. The purpose of art is to save us this abstraction in the realms of the beautiful, and to render the fixing of our attention easy to us. All in nature that we might wish to abstract in our thoughts from an object or a combination of various objects, be it in time or in place, art really abstracts for us, and accords us this object or this combination of various objects as purely and tersely as the sensations they are to provoke allow.

If we are witnesses of an important and touching event, and another event of trifling import traverses it, we seek and evade the distractions of our attention thus threatened. We abstract from it and it must needs revolt us to find that again art which we wished away in nature.

Only if this event in its progress assumes all shades of interest and one does not merely follow upon the other, but of necessity evolves from it, if gravity provokes laughter, sadness pleasure or *vice versâ*, so directly that an abstraction of the one or the other is impossible to us, then only do we not demand it from art and art knows how to draw a profit from this impossibility.

No. 80

To what end the hard work of dramatic form? Why build a theater, disguise men and women, torture their memories, invite the whole town to assemble at one place if I intend to produce nothing more with my work and its representation, than some of those emotions that would be produced as well by any good story that every one could read by his chimney-corner at home?

The dramatic form is the only one by which pity and fear can be excited, at least in no other form can these passions be excited to such a degree. Nevertheless it is preferred to excite all others rather than these; — nevertheless it is preferred to employ it for any purpose but this, for which it is so especially adapted.

FRANCE — III

The Eighteenth Century

FRENCH DRAMATIC CRITICISM OF THE EIGHTEENTH CENTURY

It is not surprising to find in eighteenth century French dramatic criticism and theory a good deal of the philosophical spirit which runs through the *Encyclopédie* and the works of its many contributors. The seventeenth century was on the whole religious in spirit and if not anti-, at least, un-democratic. The Ancients and Moderns quarrel, begun in 1657, became acute in 1687, on the publication of Charles Perrault's *Siècle de Louis le Grand.* La Fontaine, La Bruyère, Fontenelle, Boileau, and Fénelon, soon joined the discussion, some maintaining the superiority of the Ancients, some the Moderns, and Fénelon standing midway between the two. Fontenelle, who wrote a few unsuccessful plays, is the author of a *Vie de Corneille,* a history of the French theater, and general prefaces to his collected plays (found respectively in volume 7 of the 1751 edition of his *Œuvres* and in volume 4 of the 1790 edition). His *Remarques sur quelques comédies d'Aristophane, Sur le théâtre grec,* and the *Réflexions sur la poétique,* in the third volume of the latter, are his chief contributions to dramatic theory. Antoine Houdar de La Motte, a friend of Fontenelle, began one of the earliest literary disputes of the new century. His "up-to-date" version of the *Iliad* called forth the wrath of Madame Dacier; the quarrel became general, but La Motte was soon crushed by the straightforward reasoning of Voltaire. La Motte's theories were not confined to epic poetry; himself a dramatist (his *Inès de Castro* was produced with signal success in 1723), he evolved an interesting theory in discussing the Unities: the Unity of Interest. His *Premier Discours sur la tragédie,* the three *Discours* prefixed to the plays *Romulus, Inès,* and *Œdipe,* and the *Suite des réflexions sur la tragédie,* are all assaults upon the various literary and dramatic

questions of the early eighteenth century. Among the other precursors whose work is more or less directly concerned with the drama is Pierre Bayle, whose *Dictionnaire historique et critique* appeared in 1697. Bossuet's *Maximes et réflexions sur la comédie* which, while it is concerned chiefly with the moral point of view, is partially critical, was first published in 1694. This treatise and the similar works of Conti and Nicole (*Traité de la Comédie* and *Pensées sur les spectacles*), corresponded with the puritanical outbursts by Collier and his followers in England. Cailhava's *Art de la comédie* (1772), Crébillon's *Préface* to *Elèctre* (1715) and other plays, the Abbé du Bos' *Réflexions critiques sur la poésie et la peinture* (1719), all contain historical, controversial, and critical matter touching upon the drama. Fénelon's *Lettre sur les occupations de l'Académie française* (1717) contains a veritable Poetic on comedy and tragedy. The figure of Voltaire dominates the century. His first play, *Œdipe,* was produced in 1718. The standard editions include seven letters on the play, containing general remarks, with comparisons of the various ways in which the story had been treated in the past. There are about forty dedications, prefaces, etc., in which Voltaire discusses his theories of the drama; the *Lettres philosophiques, Dictionnaire philosophique, Commentaires sur Corneille,* and the *Lettres,* which run to the number of ten thousand, are likewise full of references to drama. These are scattered throughout Voltaire's lifetime, and have a distinct bearing on his attempts to resuscitate tragedy to its position of former dignity and popularity. Meanwhile, other influences were at work: the spirit of philosophical inquiry, the quest for "truth," resulted in the compilation of the celebrated *Encyclopédie,* which was begun by Diderot and his associates in the middle of the century. Somewhat earlier, Nivelle de la Chaussée's *La Fausse antipathie,* in 1733, presented a new type of play, variously called the *Comédie larmoyante,* the *Drame,* the *Comédie sérieuse,* and the *Drame sérieux.* La Chaussée's *Prologue* to his play *La Fausse antipathie* (1733), and Gresset's *Lettre sur la comédie* (1759) are interesting documents by practicing dramatists. (A typical *comédie larmoyante* was Sedaine's *Le Philosophe sans le savoir* 1765.) The theories of Diderot on this subject, and those of Beaumarchais, somewhat later, are more important than the plays themselves. It is not difficult to trace the ideas of Dumas fils and Augier to the suggestions of Diderot and his followers. Unfortunately, Diderot's theories led him far from his practice, and farther still from that Nature which he professed to follow. Among the many contributors to the *Encyclopédie* who concerned themselves with questions of dramatic theory, were Voltaire, d'Alembert, Marmontel, and Jean-Jacques Rousseau. D'Alembert and Rousseau deserve mention for their discussion of the question of the theater. D'Alembert in his article on Geneva for the *Enclyclopédie* had, at the instigation of Voltaire, criticised the law forbidding theatrical productions. In 1758 Rousseau wrote a reply known as the *Lettre à d'Alembert sur les spectacles.* This lengthy epistle belongs to the category of philosophy and morality rather than to dramatic criticism proper, but it throws a clear light upon a by no means

uncommon attitude. Rousseau wrote in at least two other places on the drama: *Lettre XVII* of *La Nouvelle Héloïse,* and *De l'imitation théâtrale.* Marmontel, who contributed a number of articles on literary subjects to the *Encyclopédie,* collected them afterward in his *Eléments de Littérature* (1787). The articles on *Comique, Tragédie, Unité,* and the like, are typical eighteenth century judgments. Beaumarchais' prefaces followed close upon Diderot's discursive lucubrations: the *Essai sur le drame sérieux,* prefixed to *Eugénie* (1767), the *Lettre modérée* prefixed to *Le Barbier de Séville* (1775), and the Preface to *Le Mariage de Figaro* (1784)). Sébastien Mercier's *Du Théâtre ou nouvel essai sur l'art dramatique* (1773) and *Nouvel examen de la Tragédie française* (1778) are atempts to reduce the theory of the drama to a mechanical science. La Harpe is usually considered the last of the Neo-classicists, and his *Lycée ou Cours de littérature* (published in full in 1825) with its characteristic judgments on dramatic poetry [1] takes us almost to the nineteenth century chronologically, if not in spirit. There is little material on the drama in the Revolutionary period, although the dramatico-political utterances of Marie-Joseph Chénier are indicative of the spirit of the times. His *Discours de la liberté du théâtre* (1789) and dedication, *A la Nation Française* in *Charles IX ou l'Ecole des Rois* (1789) are very curious documents.

[1] See vols. 11, 12, and 13, which are devoted to the drama.

General references on eighteenth century French literature:

Paul Albert, *La Littérature française au dix-huitième siècle* (10th ed., Paris, 1908).
Emile Faguet, *Dix-huitième siècle* (37th ed., Paris, n. d.).
Vinet, *Histoire de la littérature française au dix-huitième siècle,* 2 vols. (Paris, 1853).
Ferdinand Brunetière, *Etudes sur le XVIIIe siècle* (Paris, 1911).
De Baranti, *Tableau de la littérature française au XVIIIe siècle* (5th ed., Paris, 1809).

E. Bersot, *Etudes sur le XVIIIe siècle,* 2 vols. (Paris, 1855).
E. Caro, *La Fin du XVIIIe siècle,* 2 vols. (Paris, 1880).
A. F. Villemain, *Tableau de la littérature française au XVIIIe siècle,* 2 vols. (New ed., Paris, 1891).
Adrien Baillet, *Jugemens des savans sur les principaux ouvrages des auteurs,* 8 vols. (Augmented ed., Paris, 1722–30).

Special references on eighteenth century French drama:

C. Desprez de Boissy, *Lettres sur les spectacles avec une histoire des ouv-*

rages pour et contre les Théâtres (Paris, 1774).

Victor du Bled, *La Comédie de société au XVIIIe siècle* (Paris, 1893).

G. Desnoiresterres, *La Comédie satirique au XVIIIe siècle* (Paris, 1885).

Léon Fontaine, *Le Théâtre et la philosophie au XVIIIe siècle* (Paris, 1878).

Frederick Hawkins, *The French Stage in the Eighteenth Century*, 2 vols. (London, 1888).

Emile Faguet, *Rousseau contre Molière* (Paris, 1912).

Theodore Hook, *The French Stage and the French People*, 2 vols. (London, 1841).

Gustave Lanson, *La Comédie au XVIIIe siècle* (In *Hommes et livres*, Paris, 1895).

C. Lenient, *La Comédie en France au XVIIIe siècle*, 2 vols. (Paris, 1888).

G. Huszar, *L'Influence de l'Espagne sur le théâtre français des XVIIIe et XIXe siècles* (Paris, 1912).

Romain Rolland, *Le Théâtre du Peuple* (Paris, new ed., 1913. Translated by Barrett H. Clark, as *The People's Theater*, New York, 1918).

On the drama:

F. Gaiffe, *Le Drame en France au XVIIIe siècle* (Paris, 1910).

Gustave Lanson, *Nivelle de la Chaussée et la Comédie larmoyante* (2nd ed., Paris, 1903).

A. W. Schlegel, *Lectures on Dramatic Art and Literature* (Trans. by John Black, 2nd ed., Bohn Lib., London, 1914).

M. M. D. C. [de Chaussiron], *Réflexions sur le Comique-larmoyant* (Paris, 1749).

La Harpe, *Lycée ou Cours de Littérature ancienne et moderne*, 19 vols. (see vols. 11, 12, and 13. Paris, An VII and following).

Wetz, *Die Anfänge der ernsten bürgerlichen Dichtung der achzehnten Jahrhundert* (Strassburg, 1885).

Eloesser, *Das bürgerliche Drama, seine Geschichte im XVIII. und XIX. Jahrhundert* (Berlin, 1898).

Je la Viéville, *Lettre à M. de Milcent, jeune littérateur, sur les Drames bourgeois ou larmoyans* (Amsterdam, 1775).

Alexis Pitou, *Les Origines du mélodrame à la fin du XVIIIe siècle* (in Rev. d'Hist. lit. de la France, v. 18, Paris, 1911).

E. Rigal, *Le Romantisme au théâtre avant les Romantiques* (in Rev. d'Hist. lit. de la France, Paris, 1915).

References on criticism, especially dramatic:

Francisque Vial et Louis Denise, *Idées et doctrines du XVIIIe siècle* (Paris, n.d.).

H. Rigault, *Histoire de la querelle des Anciens et des Modernes* (Paris, 1859).

J. Rocafort, *Les Questions de littérature dramatique dans l'Encyclopédie* (Paris, 1890).

Emile Faguet, *Propos de théâtre*, 2ème série (Paris, 1905).

René Doumic, *Etudes sur la littérature française*, 5ème série (Paris, 1906).

George Saintsbury, *A History of Criticism*, vols. 2 and 3 (New York, 1902–04).

Amilda A. Pons, *Jean-Jacques Rousseau et le théâtre* (Genève, 1909).

Joseph Texte, *L'Italie et la critique française au XVIIIe siècle* (in Rev. des cours et conférences, Paris, 16 Jan., 1896).

Eleanor F. Jourdain, *Dramatic Theory and Practice in France, 1690–1808* (London, 1921).

Daniel Mornet, *La Question des règles au XVIIIe siècle* (in Rev. d'Hist. lit. de la France, Paris, 1914).

VOLTAIRE

François Marie Arouet — later known as Voltaire — was born at Paris in 1694. His first schooling was received under the Jesuits at the College Louis-le-Grand, where he remained until 1711. His training there seems to have been good, and he evidently benefited by his experience in the production of Latin plays. He showed considerable facility in writing satirical verses, a gift which was to involve him in trouble on many occasions. He wished to make writing his profession, but his father insisted that he study law. The youth reluctantly applied himself to his law books at Caën, returned home and entered a law office, but was soon after sent to the country for writing libelous poems. During the winter of 1714–15 he continued to study law, but spent his spare time — and more — in writing, and when he returned to Paris, he brought with him the MS. of his first play, Œdipe. Before its production in 1718 he was thrice practically sent into exile for writing satirical verses. In 1721 his father died, leaving him a comfortable income. The next year he became a government spy, going to Belgium and Holland. Meantime, he was at work on La Henriade and more plays. A few years later, as the result of a quarrel, he was sent to the Bastille and two weeks later transferred, at his own request, to England. The three years he spent there did much for his mental development. There he made the acquaintance of the most important literary men of the day — among them Pope, Congreve, and Bolingbroke — and at least made the name of Shakespeare familiar to his countrymen. He returned to France in 1729. Brutus was produced in 1730, and two years later, one of his best and most successful plays, Zaïre. In 1733 he published his Lettres philosophiques sur les anglais, which contained a thinly-veiled criticism of French institutions. The edition was confiscated the next year, and when the authorities came for the author, they found he had gone to Lorraine. The next few years he spent at the Château de Cirey with the Marquise du Châtelet, there devoting himself almost entirely to literary labors. He traveled a great deal during these years. In 1745 he was again at the French Court, where he was made historiographer on the recommendation of Madame de Pompadour. The following year he was admitted to the Academy. On the death of the Marquise du Châtelet in 1749, Voltaire was without a home, and spent his time in Paris and traveling about France. After many unsuccessful efforts, Frederick the Great persuaded him to come to Berlin, where he went in 1751. The Emperor's relations with the Frenchman were at first most cordial, but before long Voltaire became embroiled in quarrels, and showed a lamentable want of tact throughout. He published libels and letters without the Emperor's permission, and was practically sent away. In 1753 Voltaire and his niece were arrested in Frankfurt by Frederick's order, but were soon after released. During his stay at the Prussian court Voltaire wrote his Siècle de Louis XIV and began the Dictionnaire philosophique. After further wanderings he established himself at Geneva, where he had a private theater, but he soon infringed the laws of that city prohibiting public performances of plays. This led to his inciting d'Alembert to write an attack on Geneva in the Encyclopédie, which called forth Rousseau's celebrated Lettre à d'Alembert sur les spectacles. In 1758 he bought the estate of Ferney, not far from Geneva, and there spent his last years, writing, interesting himself in charity, and receiving his friends. In 1778 he went to Paris to attend the first performance of his new play, Irène. The same year he was taken sick and died.

Compared with Diderot and Beaumarchais, the other theorists of the drama in eighteenth century France were of minor importance. Voltaire is a reactionary classicist. He advocates the adherence to rimed verse in tragedy, and to the Unities. But Voltaire's classicism is neither very deep nor very "reasoned"; in the words of M. Faguet, he is a "Classic who understands practically nothing of antiquity." His ideas on dramatic form were taken for the most part from the theory and practice of the seventeenth century. His classicism is largely a matter of exactitude in form, clarity of thought, and precision. His rigid standards naturally excluded much that was best in literature and prevented his appreciation of many "Irregulars." Hence Voltaire's occasional errors in judging Racine, and his misunderstanding of Corneille. Voltaire's practice as a dramatist was of more importance in the attempt to revive French classical tragedy than his many prefaces. But the tide was against him: the Drame had come, and it was to develop during the next century into one of the most striking of all dramatic forms: the middle-class drama.

On the drama:

Lettres écrites en 1719, qui contiennent la critique de l'Œdipe de Sophocle, de celui de Corneille, et de celui de l'auteur [7 letters]; the *Préface* to the ed. [a reply to La Motte]. Also a *Lettre au Père Porée, Jésuite*. All in *Œdipe* (1730).

Préface, in *La Mort de César* (1736

Discours sur la tragédie, in *Brutus* (1731).

Discours prononcé avant la représentation d'Eriphyle, in *Eryphile* (1732).

Epître dédicatoire à M. Falkener, Marchand anglais, in *Zaïre* (1733).

A M. le Chevalier Falkener, etc., in *Zaïre* (ed. 1736).

Préface, in *La Mort de César* (1736 ed.).

Epître à Madame la marquise du Chastelet, in *Alzire* (1736), and *Discours préliminaire* to the same.

Préface to *L'Enfant prodigue* (1738).

A Mademoiselle Clairon, in *Zulime* (1761).

Avis de l'éditeur [by Voltaire], in *Le Fanatisme, ou Mahomet le prophète* (1743).

A M. le Marquis Scipion Maffei, and *Réponse à M. de la Lindelle*, in *Mérope* (1744).

Dissertation sur la tragédie ancienne et moderne, etc., in *Sémiramis* (1748).

Prologue to *L'Echange* (1747).

Préface to *Nanine* (1749).

Epître to the Duchesse du Maine, in *Oreste* (1750).

Préface to *Rome sauvée* (1752).

A Monseigneur le Maréschal duc de Richelieu, in *L'Orphelin de la Chine* (1755).

Préface to *Socrate* (1759).

Epître dédicatoire . . . à M. le Comte de Lauragnais, in *L'Ecossaise* (1760). Also *Préface*.

A Madame la Marquise de Pompadour, in *Tancrède* (1760).

Avertissement du traducteur, in the *Jules César de Shakespeare* (1735); also *Observations sur le Jules César de Shakespeare*.

Préface de l'éditeur [Voltaire], in *Le Triumvirat* (1767).

Préfaces to *Les Scythes* (1767 and 1768).

Notes in *Olympie* (1764).

Discours historique et critique, in *Les Guèbres* (1769).

A Monsieur le duc de la Vallière, in *Sophonisbe* (1770).

Fragment d'une lettre, in *Les Pélopides* (1772).

Epître dédicatoire and *Notes*, in *Les Lois de Minos* (1773).

Epître dédicatoire à M. d'Alembert, in *Don Pèdre;* also *Discours historique et critique sur la tragédie de Don Pèdre* (1774).

Lettre à l'Académie française, in *Irène* (1778).

In the miscellaneous writings of Voltaire will be found numerous references to the drama. The most important are in the following:

Siècle de Louis XIV (1751).

Lettres philosophiques sur les anglais (1734).

Dictionnaire philosophique (esp. articles: *Aristote, Art dramatique, Art poétique, Critique*. 1764).

Commentaires sur Corneille (1764. Reprinted separately, Paris, 1886).

Les Anciens et les modernes, ou la Toilette de Madame de Pompadour (1765).

Vie de Molière (1739).

Eloge de M. de Crébillon (1762).

Editions:

The first of the collected editions of Voltaire with any pretense to completeness is the so-called *Kehl* edition, edited by Beaumarchais, Condorcet, and Decroix, in 70 vols. (Paris, 1784–90). The *Beuchot* edition, also in 70 vols., was published at Paris, 1828 and following. The *Siècle* edition, edited by E. de La Bedollière and Georges Avenel, in 8 vols., was published at Paris, 1867–70. The Charles Lahure edition, in 35 vols., was published at Paris in 1859. Probably the best edition is that published by Garnier, edited by Moland, 50 vols., Paris, 1877–83. This was followed by the *Table générale et analytique*, by Charles Pierrot, 2 vols. (Paris, 1885). Since the appearance of this edition, a num-

ber of volumes of unpublished corre-
spondence and other matter have made
their appearance, the most interesting
of which are the *Lettres inédites à
Louis Racine,* edited by Tamizey de
Larroque (Paris, 1893).

The *Lettres,* of which there are at least
10,000, contain numerous references to
drama. (Among these, see: *Au Mar-
quis Capacelli,* Dec. 4, 1758; *A d'Ar-
gental,* June 18, 1759; *A Mlle. Clairon,*
Oct. 16, 1760; *A Le Kain,* Dec. 16,
1760; and *A. H. Walpole,* July 15,
1768.) Most of the above have been
translated, in various collected and
separate editions. See especially the
latest collected editions of the works.
Among contemporary translations, the
volume *Critical Essays on Dramatic
Poetry by Monsieur de Voltaire* (Lon-
don, 1761) will be found to include
many of the important dramatic theo-
ries of the author. *The Dramatic
Works of M. de Voltaire,* translated
by Hugh Downman (1781), contain a
number of *Prefaces.* Among modern
translations, vol. 19 of the *Works of
Voltaire* (New York, 1901) contains
half a dozen prefaces to plays.

The *Life of Molière* is translated by Bar-
rett H. Clark (in *Great Short Biogra-
phies of the World,* New York, 1928).

On Voltaire and his works:

Marquis de Condorcet, *Vie de Voltaire*
(mod. ed., Paris, 1895.—*The Life of
Voltaire, translated from the French,*
2 vols., London, 1790).

C.-A. Sainte-Beuve, *Causeries du Lundi,*
2, 7, 13, 15 (Paris, 1857–62).

Lonchamp et Wagnière, *Mémoires sur
Voltaire et ses ouvrages* (Paris, 1825).

Comte Alexandre Collini, *Mon séjour
auprès de Voltaire* (Paris, 1807).

Charles Nisard, *Les Ennemis de Voltaire*
(Paris, 1833).

E. B. Hamley, *Voltaire* (Edinburgh,
1877).

John Morley, *Voltaire* (London, 1878).

James Parton, *Life of Voltaire,* 2 vols.
(Boston, 1881).

Emile Faguet, *Voltaire* (in *Collection des
classiques populaires,* Paris, 1895).

——, *XVIIIᵉ siècle* (37th ed., Paris, n.d.).

G. Maugras, *Voltaire et Jean-Jacques
Rousseau* (Paris, 1886).

E. Champion, *Voltaire. Etudes critiques*
(Paris, 1892).

L. Crouslé, *La Vie et les œuvres de Vol-
taire,* 2 vols. (Paris, 1899).

Francis Espinasse, *Life of Voltaire*
(London, 1892).

G. Bengesco, *Voltaire: bibliographie de
ses œuvres,* 4 vols. (Paris, 1882–90).

Gustave Lanson, *Voltaire* (Paris, 1906).

Jean-Jacques Olivier, *Voltaire et les
comédiens interprètes de son théâtre,*
etc. (Paris, 1900).

K. Schirmacher, *Voltaire, eine Bio-
graphie* (Leipzig, 1898).

Thomas R. Lounsbury, *Shakespeare and
Voltaire* (New York, 1902).

Oliver H. G. Leigh, *Voltaire: Index to
his Works* (in vol. 22, *Works of Vol-
taire,* New York, 1901).

Georges Renard, Vie de Voltaire (Paris,
1883).

S. G. Tallentyre, *The Life of Voltaire*
(New York, n.d.).

——, *Voltaire in His Letters* (New York,
1919).

Emile Deschanel, *Le Romantisme des
classiques: Le Théâtre de Voltaire*
(Paris, 1888).

Ferdinand Brunetière, *Voltaire* (in
*Etudes critiques sur l'histoire de la lit-
térature française,* I, 7th ed., Paris,
1911).

——, *Voltaire et Rousseau* (in same, III,
Paris, 1887).

——, *Voltaire* (in same, IV, Paris, 1891).

——, *Voltaire* (in *Etudes sur le XVIIIᵉ
siècle,* Paris, 1911).

B. Bonieux, *Critique des tragédies de
Corneille et de Racine par Voltaire*
(Clermont-Ferrand, 1866).

Eloi Johanneau, *Rhétorique et Poétique
de Voltaire* (Paris, 1828).

Lacombe, *Poétique de M. de Voltaire,
ou Observations recueillies de ses
ouvrages,* etc., 2 vols. (Paris et Genève,
1776).

H.-G.-M. Lion, *Les Tragédies et les
théories dramatiques de Voltaire*
(Paris, 1895).

A. Schmitz, *Le Commentaire de Vol-
taire sur Corneille* (Erfurt, 1876).

H. Jürging, *Voltaires dramatische
Theorie* (Münster, 1885).

M. Clément, *De la Tragédie, pour servir
de suite aux lettres à Voltaire,* 2 vols.
(Amsterdam, 1784).

PREFACE TO HEROD AND MARIAMNE [1]
[*Préface* (to) *Hérode et Mariamne*]
(1725)

I tremble in giving this edition. I have remarked so many plays applauded on the stage, which have been afterwards despised in the closet, that I am afraid lest mine should meet with the same fate. One or two interesting situations, the actor's art, and the readiness which I showed to own and correct my faults, might have gained me some approbation, when it was acted. But many more qualifications are necessary to satisfy the cool deliberate reader. A plot regularly conducted will contribute but little to that end; and though it should be affecting, yet even that will not be sufficient: all poetical performances, though ever so perfect in other points, must necessarily displease if the lines are not strong and harmonious, and if there does not run through the whole a continued elegance and inexpressible charm of verse, that genius only can inspire, that wit alone can never attain, and about which people have agreed so ill, and to so little purpose since the death of Boileau.

It is a very gross mistake to imagine that the versification is the least essential and least difficult part of a theatrical piece. M. Racine, than whom, after Vergil, no man ever knew better the art of versifying, was not of that opinion. His *Phèdre* alone employed him for two years. Pradon boasted of having finished his in three months. As the success at the acting of a play does not depend so much on the style as on the plot and the actors' performance, it happened that both *Phèdres* seemed to share the same fate; but on the reading, their difference is easily perceived and their merits were soon settled in their upper classes. It was to no purpose that Pradon published, according to the custom of all bad authors, a very insolent preface in which he abuses the critics of his piece; notwithstanding the praises it received, from himself and from his cabal, it soon fell into that contempt

which it deserves, and had it not been for the *Phèdre* of Racine it would not now be known that Pradon writ one.

Yet what is the cause of this mighty difference between the two performances? The plot is pretty much the same in both plays; Phædra expires in each; Theseus is absent during the two first acts, and supposed to have traveled to hell with Pirithous; his son Hippolytus is resolved to quit Trezena in order to shun Aricia, whom he loves; he declares his passion to her, but is struck with horror at Phædra's love for him; he dies in the same manner, and his governor gives the same account of it. Besides the personages of both plays being in the same situation, talk pretty much to the same purport; but this is what best distinguishes the great man from the bad poet. The difference between Pradon and Racine is never so conspicuous as when their thoughts are most alike. Hippolytus' declaration to Aricia is a remarkable proof of this assertion. Racine makes Hippolytus speak in this manner:

Moi qui, contre l'amour fièrement révolté,
Aux fers de ses captifs ai longtemps insulté;
Qui, des faibles mortels déplorant les naufrages,
Pensais toujours du bord contempler les orages;
Asservi maintenant sous la commune loi,
Par quel trouble me vois-je emporté loin de moi;
Un moment a vaincu mon audace imprudente,
Cette ame si superbe est enfin dépendante.
Depuis près de six mois, honteux, désespéré,
Portant partout le trait dont je suis déchiré,
Contre vous, contre moi, vainement je m'éprouve.
Présente, je vous fuis; absente, je vous trouve;
Dans le fond des forêts votre image me suit;

---

1 Re-printed, complete, from the anonymous *Critical Essays on Dramatic Poetry by Monsieur de Voltaire* (London, 1761).— Ed.

*La lumière du jour, les ombres de la
    nuit,
Tout retrace à mes yeux les charmes que
    j'évite;
Tout vous livre à l'envi le rebelle Hippo-
    lyte.
Moi-même, pour tout fruit de mes soins
    superflus,
Maintenant je me cherche, et ne me
    trouve plus;
Mon arc, mes javelots, mon char, tout
    m'importune;
Je ne me souviens plus des leçons de Nep-
    tune;
Mes seuls gémissements font retentir les
    bois,
Et mes coursiers oisifs ont oublié ma
    voix.*

In Pradon's play, Hippolytus expresses himself in the following manner:

*Assez et trop longtemps, d'une bouche
    profane,
Je méprisai l'amour, et j'adorai Diane;
Solitaire, farouche, on me voyait toujours
Chasser dans nos forêts les lions et les
    ours.
Mais un soin plus pressant m'occupe et
    m'embarrasse;
Depuis que vous vois, j'abandonne la
    chasse.
Elle fit autrefois mes plaisirs les plus
    doux,
Et quand j'y vais, ce n'est que pour
    penser à vous.*

It is impossible to compare these two speeches without admiring the one, and laughing at the other. Yet the like thought and sentiments run through each; for when the passions are to be described, nearly the same ideas occur to everybody; but it is in the expression of them that the man of genius is easily discerned from the wit, and the poet from the scribbler.

To attain to M. Racine's perfection in writing, a man must be possessed of his genius, and take as much pains as he did in finishing his works. What apprehensions must I be then under, who, born with slender parts, and continually afflicted with diseases have neither an imagination to create many beauties, nor the liberty to correct my faults by constant labor and study. I am fully convinced of the many errors in the intrigue of this play, as well as in the diction. I should have corrected some, if this edition could have been retarded; but many must still have remained. There are certain limits in every art which we cannot go beyond. We are stopped by the weakness of our own talents. We spy perfection at a distance, and make but vain efforts to attain it.

I shall not enter into any particular criticisms upon the play now published; my readers will do it sufficiently without my help. But I cannot avoid mentioning a general criticism that has been made on the choice of the subject. As it is in the genius of the French to place the most serious matters in the most ridiculous light, they said the story of this play was nothing more than " a bruitish yet amorous old man whose wife obstinately refuses to comply with his desires "; and added that domestic strife can never be a proper subject for a tragedy. I beg leave to offer a few reflections on this prejudiced opinion.

All tragic pieces are founded either on the interests of a nation, or on the particular interest of princes. Of the former kind are *Iphigenia in Aulis,* in which Greece assembled, demands the blood of the child of Agamemnon; the *Horace,* where three combatants have in their hands the fate of Rome; *Œdipus,* where the safety of the Thebans depends on the discovery of the murder of Laïus. Of the latter kind are *Britannicus, Phèdre, Mithridate,* and so forth.

In these three last pieces the whole interest is confined to the family of the hero who is represented. The whole depends on passions which are equally felt by all mankind, and the intrigue is as proper for comedy as for tragedy. Change only the names, and Mithridates is but an old man in love with a young girl, who is also passionately beloved by his two sons; and he makes use of a low stratagem to find out which of the two is his happy rival. Phædra is a mother-in-law who, emboldened by her confidant, discovers her passion to her son-in-law, who happens to be engaged elsewhere. Nero is an impetuous young man who becomes enamored of a sudden, resolves immediately to get a divorce from his wife, and hides behind some hangings to listen to his mistress's conversation. These are all subjects which Molière might have handled as well as Racine. And, in fact, the intrigue of *L'Avare* is exactly the same with that of *Mithridate*. Harpagon and the King of Pontus are two amorous old men; both have their sons for rivals; both contrive in the same manner to find out the correspondence that subsists between their son and mistress; and both plays conclude with the marriage of the young fellows.

Molière and Racine have equally succeeded in handling this subject: the one amuses and diverts, the other moves us with terror and compassion. Molière exposes the ridiculous fondness of an old miser; Racine describes the foibles of a great king, and makes them even venerable. Let a wedding be drawn by Watteau and Le Brun. One will represent peasants under an arbor full of genuine and unbounded joy, at a rustic meal, where reign immoderate laughter, riot and drunkenness; the other, on the contrary, will paint the nuptials of Thetis and Peleus, the festivals of gods, and their majestic joy; and both arrive at the perfection of their art by different roads.

We may apply these different examples to *Mariamne*. The ill-humor of a wife, the fondness of an old husband, the disturbances caused by a sister-in-law, are in themselves of little importance, and well-adapted to the comic scene. But a king whom all the world have agreed to call a great man, deeply enamored of the finest woman in the universe; the vehement passion of this sovereign, so famous for his virtues and for his crimes, for his former cruelties, and for his present remorse, this continual and rapid transition from love to hatred, from hatred back to love; the ambition of his sister; the intrigues of his ministers; the grievous situation of a princess whose beauty and virtues are still celebrated in the world, who saw her father and her brother condemned to death by her own husband, and to complete her misfortune, was beloved by the murderer of her family. What a vast field! What a scope for a man of happier parts than I have! Can such a subject be deemed unworthy of tragedy? It is in these instances that it can be truly said that things change their name according to the appearance they are placed in.

LETTER TO FATHER PORÉE, JESUIT [2]

[*Lettre au Père Porée, Jésuite*]

(In *Œdipe*, 1730)

. . . . .

First I wish you to know, in order that I may justify myself, that although I was young when I wrote *Œdipe*, I wrote it practically as you see it to-day: I was full-fed after having read the ancients and after receiving my lessons from you, and I knew very little about the theater of Paris; I worked, therefore, as I might have worked had I been in ancient Athens. I consulted M. Dacier, who knew the ground, and he advised me to put a chorus in every scene, after the manner of the Greeks; but this was as bad as advising me to walk about the streets of Paris in Plato's robe. And I had considerable trouble even in persuading the actors there to include the

[2] Translated, with omissions, by the Editor. — Ed.

three or four choruses which I did put in; and I had more trouble in getting a tragedy accepted which contained practically no love interest. . . . No matter how many books are written on the technique of painting by those who know their subject, not one of them will afford as much instruction to the pupil as will the sight of a single head of Raphael.

The principles of all the arts, which depend upon imagination, are simple and easy; they are based upon nature and reason. Your Pradons and Boyers knew these rules as well as Racine and Corneille: the only difference there ever will be — lying in the application of the rules. The authors of *Armide* and of *Issé*, and the worst of composers, worked according to the same musical rules. Poussin worked by the same principles as did Vignon. It would seem quite as superfluous to speak of rules in the preface to a tragedy, as it would be for a painter to prepare his public beforehand with a dissertation on painting, or a composer try to prove why his music ought to be pleasing.

But since M. de La Motte is seeking to establish laws running counter to those which have guided our great masters, it will not be amiss to defend these ancient rules, not because they are ancient, but because they are good and necessary, and because they might find, in a man of M. de La Motte's merit, a formidable adversary.

The Three Unities

M. de La Motte would first do away with the unities of action, of place, and of time.

The French were among the first of the modern nations to revive these wise rules of the drama: the other nations long remained unwilling to submit to a yoke which seemed so irksome; but as the yoke was necessary, and as reason always triumphs in the end, they all submitted. And nowadays, in England, certain dramatists have informed the audience before the play begins that the duration of the action is identical with that of its representation on the stage: they go beyond even us, who in that respect were their preceptors. All nations are beginning to consider as barbarous those ages when the rules were ignored by the greatest geniuses, such as Lope de Vega and Shakespeare; these nations even acknowledge their obligation to us for having brought the rules out of that state of barbarism. Should, therefore, a Frenchman make use of all his intelligence to lead us back to that primitive state? . . .

What is a play? The representation of an action. Why of one action only, and not of two or three? Because the human brain cannot focus its attention upon several objects at the same time; because the interest which is dispersed when there is more than one action, soon disappears; because we are shocked to observe two events in the same picture; because, finally, nature herself has given

us this precept, which ought to be like her, immutable.

For the same reason, unity of place is essential: a single action obviously cannot transpire in several places at once. If the characters which I see are at Athens in the first act, how can they be in Persia in the second? Did M. Le Brun paint Alexander at Arbela and in the Indies on the same canvas? "I should not be surprised," says M. de La Motte very cleverly, "to see an intelligent nation, but one which is less inclined toward an observance of the rules, accepting Coriolanus, condemned at Rome in the first act, received by the Volsci in the third, and besieging Rome in the fourth," and so on. To begin with, I cannot imagine an intelligent and enlightened nation *not* inclined toward an observance of the rules, which are based upon good sense, and made in order to enhance our pleasure. In the second place, is it not clear in the instance cited above, that there are three different tragedies? and even if these were written in beautiful literary style, would they ever amount to more than one of those plays à la Jodelle or Hardy, versified by a clever modern?

Unity of time naturally goes hand in hand with the other two unities. And here, I believe, is an obvious proof. I see a tragedy: that is, the representation of an action. The subject is concerned with the working-out of that action alone. There is a conspiracy against Augustus in Rome; I wish to know what will happen to Augustus and the conspirators. If the poet makes the action last fifteen days, he must account for what passes during these fifteen days, because I am in the theater to learn what happens: nothing superfluous *must* happen. Now, if he causes to pass before my eyes the events of fifteen days, there will be at least fifteen different actions, no matter how small and unimportant they may be. It is not in this case merely the bringing to a head of this conspiracy toward which the poet must quickly lead his play: he must of necessity drag out his story until it no longer interests and is no longer living. All these things are very far from the decisive moment which I am waiting for. I do not come in order to learn the whole history of the hero, I come only to see a single happening in his life. Further, the spectator is in the theater only three hours: therefore the action must not last longer than three hours. The action in *Cinna, Andromaque, Bajazet,* in *Œdipe* — whether it be in that of the great Corneille, or of M. de La Motte, or of my own, if I may refer to it — lasts no longer. If other plays perchance require more time, the liberty can be allowed only where the play makes up for the loss in compensating beauties. The greater the liberty, the more open it is to censure.

We often extend the limit of unity of time to twenty-four hours, and that of unity of place to the walls of a whole palace. A greater severity than this would sometimes render some beautiful subjects impracticable, while greater liberty might open the way to greater abuses. For were it once established that the action of a play could extend over a period of two days, it would not be long before one poet would take two weeks, and another two years; and if the unity of place were not limited to a comparatively confined space, we should soon see plays like the old *Julius Cæsar* of the English, where Cassius and Brutus are in Rome in the first act, and in Thessaly in the fifth.

An observance of these laws not only prevents faults, but even leads the poet to true beauty, just as the rules observed in the best sort of architecture must of necessity result in a building that is sure to please the eye. It is seen, therefore, that with unity of time, action, and place, it is difficult to write a play which shall not be simple. This is the great merit of M. Racine's plays; this was demanded by Aristotle. M. de La Motte, in defending one of his own tragedies, prefers to this noble simplicity, a large number of events, and he believes that his idea is authoritative because *Bérénice* is not well thought of, and *Le Cid* is. It is true that *Le Cid* is more touching than *Bérénice;* but *Bérénice* is open to censure only because it is rather an elegy than a simple tragedy; and *Le Cid,* the action of which is truly tragic, surely does not owe its success to a multiplicity of events. It pleases in spite of this; it touches, in spite of the Infante, and not because of the Infante.

M. de La Motte believes that one can rise above the rules by observing a unity of interest, which he claims to have invented and which he calls a paradox, but this unity of interest seems to me to be no other than unity of action. "If many characters," he says, "are in one way and another interested in the same event, and if they all deserve that I should interest myself in their passions, then there is unity of action, and not unity of interest."

Since I took the liberty of entering into a dispute with M. de La Motte on this little question, I have re-read the great Corneille's *Discours;* it were better to consult the great master than myself. This is what he says: "I maintain, and I have already said, that unity of action consists in unity of intrigue and in unity of peril." I refer the reader to this place in Corneille's *Discours;* let him decide between M. de La Motte and me. And if that authority is not great enough, have I not a more convincing argument? It is experience. Read our best French tragedies, and you will invariably find the principal characters in one way or another interested in the same event. But, it will be observed, these diverse interests are all connected with the principal character; this is unity of action. If, on the contrary, all these diverse interests are not connected with the principal character, if they are not strings tied together at the center, then the interest is two-fold: so is what is called action on the stage. Let us, therefore, together with the great Corneille, adhere to the three unities, within which the other rules — that is to say, the other beauties — are likewise to be found.

A DISCOURSE ON TRAGEDY [3]

[*Discours sur la Tragédie, à Mylord Bolingbroke*]

(Prefixed to *Brutus*, 1731)

.   .   .   .   .   .

All these laws — not to fill the action with bloodshed, not to allow more than three characters to speak at the same time, and so on — are laws which, it seems to me, may have exceptions among us, as they did among the Greeks. There is a difference between the rules of decorum, which are always rather arbitrary, and those fundamental rules of the theater, which are the three unities: it would result only in feebleness and sterility to extend the action of a play beyond the proper time and place. Ask any one who has crowded too many events into his play, what the reason for this fault is: if he be honest, he will tell you that he lacked the inventive genius to fill his play with a single action; and if* he uses two days and two cities in which to conduct his story, believe me, he has done so because he was unable to condense it within the space of three hours and within the walls of a single palace, a proceeding which is demanded by probability. It is otherwise with the poet who would hazard portraying a horrible spectacle on the stage: he will not insult our sense of what is probable, and his boldness, far from being considered a weakness, demands on the contrary a great genius to put into the play, by means of his words, the veritable grandeur of the story which, without a sublime literary style, would be simply disgusting or atrocious.

This is what our great Corneille dared once to attempt, in his *Rodogune*. He shows us a mother who, in the presence of the court and an ambassador, tries to poison her son and daughter-in-law, after having killed her other son with her own hand. She presents to the two the poisoned drink; and on their refusing and showing that they suspect her, she swallows the draught herself, and dies of the poison which she had intended for them. Such incidents should be most sparingly used, and it is not every one who dares attempt them.

Translated, with omissions by the Editor. — Ed.

These novelties must be circumspectly introduced, and handled with great mastery. The English themselves admit that Shakespeare, for instance, was the only one among them who evoked ghosts and made them speak:

Within that magic circle none durst move but he.

The more majestic and fearful a dramatic action, the more insipid does it become when it is often repeated; something like the details of battles which, while in themselves they are most terrible, become cold and tiresome, as a result of being told again and again in histories. The only play in which M. Racine has made use of this sort of spectacular scene is *Athalie*. In this play we see a child on a throne; its nurse and the priests stand about; a queen commands the soldiers to murder it; and the armed Levites come to the rescue. This is dramatic pathos; and if the style were not written to match, the whole would be puerile.

The more the dramatist wishes to appeal to the eye with striking scenes of this sort, the greater becomes the necessity to saying sublime things; otherwise he will be but a decorator, and not a tragic poet. Nearly thirty years ago the tragedy of *Montézume* was produced at Paris; the scene disclosed was something of a novelty: a palace of magnificent and barbaric splendor. Montezuma himself wore an extraordinary costume; slaves armed with arrows stood at the back of the stage. About Montezuma were eight grandees of the court, their faces bowed to the ground. Montezuma opened the play with these words which were addressed to them:

Levez-vous; votre roi vous permet aujourd'hui
Et de l'envisager et de parler à lui.

The scene charmed the audience: but this was the only beautiful thing in the tragedy.

For my part, I confess that it was not without some trepidation that I introduced to the French public the Roman Senate, in red robes, each member giving his vote. I remember that formerly when I introduced in my *Œdipe* a chorus of Thebans who said:

O mort, nous implorons ton funeste se-
cours!
O mort, viens nous sauver, viens terminer
nos jours!

the parterre, instead of being affected by the pathos which these lines should have contained, felt at first merely the ridiculous side: that is, that such words had been given to actors who were little accustomed to speak the lines — and they burst out laughing. This is what deterred me, in *Brutus,* from having the senators speak when Titus is accused in their presence, and increasing the terror of the situation, by having these fathers of Rome express their sorrow and surprise, which they would undoubtedly have done, and otherwise than by mere gesture; although they were not permitted even this.

The English dramatists have more action in their plays than we have; they speak more directly. The French aim rather at elegance, harmony, style. It is certainly more difficult to write well than to fill the play with murders, wheels, gibbets, sorcerers, and ghosts. The tragedy of *Cato,* which does such great honor to M. Addison, your successor in the ministry; this tragedy, I say, the only one your nation has produced which is well written from beginning to end — you yourself have said it — owes its great reputation to no other element than its beautiful lines, its vigorous and true thoughts, expressed in harmonious verse. It is the minor details which bolster up verse plays, and preserve them for future generations. Often the unusual way of saying ordinary things, and the art of embellishing by literary style what all men think and feel — these are what make great poets. There are neither out-of-the-way sentiments nor romantic adventures in the fourth book of Vergil; everything is natural: it is the great effort of a human mind. M. Racine stands above

others not because he has said the same things as he has, but because he has said them better than they. Corneille is not truly great except when he expresses himself as well as he thinks. Let us bear in mind the precept of Despréaux:

Et que tout ce qu'il dit, facile à retenir,
De son ouvrage en nous laisse un long
souvenir.

This precept is quite neglected in a great many of our plays, which, however, by the art of the actor, and the figure and voice of the actress, have been accepted on our stage. How many more badly-written plays are produced than *Cinna* and *Britannicus,* and yet no one ever retained two lines of such wretched compositions, while entire scenes of the other two are frequently memorized. In vain did the *Régulus* of Pradon draw tears from the audience by means of some affecting incidents; that work, and all which resembled it, are now fallen into contempt, in spite of the self-applause lavished by the authors in their prefaces.

Some judicious critics may ask why I have introduced love into a tragedy which bears the name of *Junius Brutus?* Why I have mingled that passion with the rigid virtue of a Roman senator, and the political intrigues of an ambassador?

Our nation has been reproached for having enfeebled the tragic stage by too much tenderness; and the English have merited the same accusation for nearly a century; for you have always found our fashions and faults somewhat contagious. But will you allow me to give you my opinion on this matter?

To expect love in every tragedy seems to me to argue an effeminate taste, while always to proscribe it, shows a contemptuous and unreasonable captiousness.

The stage, whether occupied by tragedy or comedy, exhibits a living picture of the human passions. In the first is represented the ambition of a prince; the object of the latter is to ridicule the vanity of the middle-class parvenu. Here we laugh at the coquetry of a citizen's wife; there we weep over the unhappy passion of Phædra. In like manner, love amuses us in romance, and transports us in the Dido of Vergil.

Love is not more essentially a fault in tragedy than it is in the *Æneid*. It is open to censure only when it is dragged in out of season, and conducted without art. . . .

That love may be deserving of a place in tragedy it must have a necessary connection with the whole piece and not be arbitrarily introduced to fill up gaps, as it does in your tragedies as well as in our own, all of which are too long. It should in reality be a tragic passion, considered as a weakness, and opposed and contrasted by remorse. It should either lead to misfortune and crime, to convince us of its perils; or else virtue should triumph over it, to show that it is not invincible. Treated in any other way, love is of the same nature as that which is the subject of pastorals or comedies.

. . . .

DENIS DIDEROT

Denis Diderot was born at Langres in 1713, of lower middle-class parents. At the age of eight he was sent to school in his native town under the Jesuits, with a view to entering the church. He continued his studies at the College d'Harcourt in Paris, and afterward went into a law office, where he remained for two years. His chief occupation, however, was study — mathematics, Latin and Greek, and modern languages. At this time Denis' father stopped the youth's allowance and demanded that he accept some sort of position, or return home. Denis left the law office, however, and lived in an attic, giving lessons. This life lasted for ten years, during which the father refused to help his son. But his strangely inquisitive and philosophical nature was not such as to bring him financial success, and he was forced to turn his hand to the humblest sort of hack-work: translating, writing sermons to order, and the like. He even resorted to dishonest methods to secure money from a priest who wished to help him enter a monastery. However, he was sufficiently sure of himself in 1743 to think of marriage, and accordingly in that year he married Toinette Champion. The couple lived for some time on the little Denis could make by writing, and on the savings of his wife. When Denis' parents heard of their son's marriage, Denis sent his wife home to them. They were so pleased with her, that when she returned to Paris three months later, parents and son became reconciled, and Denis was enabled to devote his efforts to his own work. The family life of the young couple was not happy; it was rendered worse, indeed, by the continual demands for money from Diderot's mistress, and it was in order to make this money that he translated various works and wrote his *Pensées philosophiques,* the *Lettre sur les aveugles,* and *Les Bijoux indiscrets.* He was meantime collecting material for the *Encyclopédie,* the "privilege" for which was granted in 1746. For many years Diderot was constantly opposed in this work, interference coming from the court, the church, and the Academy. His opponents managed to send him to prison at Vincennes in 1749. It was there that Rousseau visited him and the two became friends. Toward the end of the year, Diderot was released, and the first volume of the *Encyclopédie* was published — in 1751. Opposition continued, and after the publication of the sixth volume, the publishers were forbidden to issue any more of it. At this time, Diderot was busy with his plays. In 1757 he published *Le Fils naturel,* together with the famous *Dorval et Moi* dialogues evolving the author's ideas on the drama. *Le Père de famille* appeared the following year, accompanied by the long essay *De la Poésie dramatique.* As a result of the persecution of the editors of the *Encyclopédie,* d'Alembert left the editorial staff, and Diderot was forced to continue the work under very discouraging auspices. In 1765 further volumes of the work were distributed to subscribers. Diderot was so poor that he was on the point of selling his private library when Catherine II, informed of the author's poverty, bought the library, gave Diderot the use of it during his life, and added a generous pension. In 1772 he married off his daughter, and started traveling with his friend Falconet the next year. He visited St. Petersburg, where he was well received by the Empress. He returned to Paris in 1774. His health was undermined, but he persevered with his work, a great part of which was not published during his life-time. He died at Paris in 1784.

At his death Diderot left thirty-three volumes of MSS., which were forwarded to Russia with his library. A great part of his work was only recently published, while some of his novels and other works were translated into German from the MSS., and translated back into French before the French originals were printed. Of the three or four editions of Diderot published prior to the last half of the nineteenth century, not one contains more than a part of his characteristic work; hence the difficulty, until recent years, of arriving at a true critical evaluation of his work. In his day Diderot was best-known as editor of the *Encyclopédie;* the greater part of his work was published either anonymously or remained in manuscript. He was above all an enthusiast; no matter what subject he attacked, he was able to make it interesting. If his own plays are feeble and over-sentimental, his theories are in part sound. He demanded a return to nature, and sounded the call against what was false in the classic ideal. The age was ready for him. His influence was felt principally in Germany — through Lessing and Goethe — though Beaumarchais in France developed his ideas with greater clarity.

On the drama:

Notice préliminaire and *Entretiens (Dorval et moi)* in *Le Fils naturel* (1757).
Epître dédicatoire and *De la Poésie dramatique,* in *Le Père de famille* (1758).
Lettre de Madame Riccoboni . . . à Monsieur Diderot (1758); *Réponse à la lettre de Mme. Riccoboni* (1758). (In vol. 7, Assézat ed.)
Réflexions sur Terence (1762).

Observations sur Garrick (1770).
Miscellanéa dramatiques (under this title were published 21 essays, letters, prefaces, and fragments, some of them never before printed. See vol. 8, Assézat ed.).
Lettres (vols. 18, 19, 20, Assézat ed. Also the *Correspondance littéraire,* of Grimm, Diderot, etc., 16 vols., Paris, 1877–82).
For incidental references on the drama, see *Les Bijoux indiscrets,* chaps. 37 and 38 (1748); *Paradoxe sur le comédien* (first published in 1830); see special *édition critique* of Ernest Dupuy, Paris, 1902. Translated as *The Paradox of Acting,* by W. H. Pollock (London, 1883).

Editions:

The early editions — 15 vols., 1798, and 21 vols., 1821–22 — are far from complete. The most recent and most nearly complete edition is that under the direction of J. Assézat, as the *Œuvres complètes de Diderot,* 20 vols., Paris, 1875–77. This was followed by the *Correspondance littéraire* of Grimm, Diderot, Raynal, Meister, etc., 16 vols., Paris, 1877–82.

On Diderot and his works:

Mme. de Vandeul, *Mémoires pour servir à l'histoire de la vie et des ouvrages de Diderot* (re-printed with other early notices in vol. 1, Assézat ed.).
Cousin d'Avalon, *Diderotiana* (Paris, 1810–11).
C.-A. Sainte-Beuve, *Portraits littéraires,* vol. 1 (Paris, 1862).
C.-A. Sainte-Beuve, *Causeries du Lundi,* vol. 3 (Paris, 1857–62).
——, *Premiers Lundis,* vol. 1 (Paris, 1874).
——, *Nouveaux Lundis,* vol. 9 (Paris, 1863–70).
Rosenkranz, *Diderot's Leben und Werke,* 2 vols. (Leipzig, 1866).
A. Collignon, *Diderot, sa vie et ses œuvres* (Paris, 1875).
E. Bersot, *Diderot* (Paris, 1851).
La Grande Encyclopédie, vol. 14 (Paris).
J. Barbey d'Aurevilly, *Goethe et Diderot* (Paris, 1882).
J. J. C. L. [Leids], *Principaux écrits relatifs à la personné et aux œuvres,*

au temps et à l'influence de Diderot, compilation critique et chronologique (Amsterdam and Paris, 1887).

Havelock Ellis, *The New Spirit* (London, 1891).

John Morley, *Diderot and the Encyclopedists*, 2 vols. (New ed., New York, 1905).

J. Block, *Beiträge zu einer Wurdigung Diderot's als Dramatiker* (Königsberg, 1888).

Ferdinand Brunetière, *Diderot* (in *Etudes critiques sur l'histoire de la littérature française, 2ᵉᵐᵉ série*, Paris, 1882).

René Doumic, *Diderot* (in *Etudes sur la littérature française*, vol. 1, Paris, 1896).

——, *Diderot* (In same, vol. 5, Paris, 1906).

Emile Faguet, *Diderot* (in *XVIIIᵉ siècle*, Paris, 1911).

——, *Propos de théâtre, 2ᵉᵐᵉ série* (Paris, 1905).

Edmond Scherer, *Diderot* (Paris, 1880).

Joseph Reinach, *Diderot* (Paris, 1894).

A. Séché et J. Bertaut, *Diderot* (Paris, n. d.).

ON DRAMATIC POETRY [1]

[De la Poésie dramatique à monsieur Grimm]

(1758)

. . . Vice cotis acutum
Reddere quae ferrum valet, exsors ipsa
*   secundi.*
    HORAT. *de Arte poet.*, v. 348.

I. OF THE VARIOUS KINDS OF DRAMA

If to a nation which had known only one sort of play — light and pleasing comedy — one were to propose another, serious and touching, have you any idea what it would think of it, my friend? Unless I am very much mistaken, the intelligent people, after having conceived it as a possibility, would not fail to say: " But of what use is this new form? Does not life give us enough real troubles without our inventing additional, imaginary ones? Why allow sadness to creep into the world, even of our amusements? " The remark of one who knows not the pleasure of being touched and giving way to tears.

We are the slaves of custom. Let a man with a spark of genius appear in our midst with a new work. First of all he dazzles us and causes discord among the thinking minds; gradually he gathers them together; soon after, imitations follow; they are studied; rules are formulated, art is born again, and limits fixed to it, and it is maintained that everything that does not fall within the scope of these limits is bizarre and bad: they

1 Translated, for the first time, with omissions, by the Editor.—Ed.

are veritable Pillars of Hercules, beyond which none can venture but at his peril.

Nothing can prevail against the true. The evil perishes in spite of the praise of imbecility; and the good remains in spite of uncertainty and the tongue of envy. The sad part of it all is that men never obtain justice until they are gone. Only after having tormented the life out of a man does the public deign to strew a few faded flowers on his tomb. What can be done then? Either stand still, or else bow down before a law to which our betters have been forced to submit. Woe to him who produces, unless his work be the fruit of love, and unless he be content with scant praise! The number of good judges is limited. Oh, my friend, when I have published something, the sketch of a play, a philosophical idea, some bit of literature of morality — for my mind is rested by variety — I shall come to see you. If my presence be not distasteful to you, if you appear satisfied with me, I shall patiently wait until justice — which time invariably brings — has given my work the appreciation it deserves.

If one type of art exists, it is difficult to introduce another. And suppose the new type is introduced? We have another prejudice, for before long it will be thought that the two types are closely akin to each other.

Zeno denied the existence of movement.

By way of refutation, his adversary Diogenes the Cynic started to walk; and even had he been able only to limp, he would have made the same answer!

Likewise, in *Le Fils naturel*, I tried to give the idea of a drama which should stand somewhere between comedy and tragedy.

Le Père de famille, which I promised at the same time, and which continual distractions have hindered my completing, stands somewhere between the *Serious Drama [genre sérieux],* and comedy.

And if ever I have the time and the courage, I hope to write a play between the Serious Drama and the tragedy.

Whether these works be considered worthy or not, they will at least indicate that the gap I have observed between the two accepted types is not merely a matter of imagination.

II. OF SERIOUS COMEDY

Here is the whole field of drama: the gay comedy whose purpose it is to ridicule and chastise vice; Serious comedy, whose office it is to depict virtue and the duties of man; that sort of tragedy which is concerned with our domestic troubles; and, finally, the sort of tragedy which is concerned with public catastrophes and the misfortunes of the great.

Who now will give us powerful portrayals of the duties of man? What is demanded of the poet who takes unto himself such a task?

He must be a philosopher who has looked into his own mind and soul, he must know human nature, he must be a student of the social system, and know well its functions and importance, its advantages and its disadvantages.

"But how," it will be asked, "can all that has to do with the condition of man be compressed within the rigid limits of a play? Where is to be found the intrigue that can carry such a subject? Will the result be merely what we call an episodic comedy [*pièce à tiroir*], one disjointed scene following another? Or, at least, if there be an intrigue, can it do other than merely wind in and out of the action? There can be no unity, little action, and no interest. Each scene will of course conform to the two important points so strongly advised by Horace, but there will be no unity of effect; the whole will be without consistency and without life."

First, if the condition of man has ever furnished us a play like *Les Fâcheux* of Molière, for example, we have won at least one point; but I adhere to the belief that we can produce other such plays. The obligations and inconveniences of one's station in life are not of equal importance. I see no reason why we should not adhere to the chief problems, making them the basis of our plays, throwing details to the winds. This is precisely what I tried to do in *Le Père de famille,* where the social position of the son and that of the daughter are the two principal points. Fortune, birth, education, the duties of fathers toward their children, of the children toward their parents, marriage, celibacy — every problem arising in connection with the existence of the father of a family, is brought out in my dialogue. Let another dramatist happen along, give him the talent which I lack, and see what he will do with my play.

All the objections made against this new type prove but one thing, that it is difficult to write. It is not the sort of play that a child can write: it demands an art, a knowledge, a gravity and power of intellect, which are very rarely at the command of a dramatist.

To judge well of any work of art, you must not compare it with another work. One of our foremost critics went astray on this point. He says: "The Ancients had no opera, therefore the operatic form is bad." A more careful or a better-informed critic would have said: "The Ancients had only one form of opera, therefore our tragedy is not good." If his logical faculties had been better developed, he would in all likelihood have reasoned in neither of the above fashions. Whether or not we have models from antiquity, makes no difference. There is one rule taking precedence over the others, and that is that the right sort of poet did not exist, otherwise how could the first poem be judged? Was it good because it pleased, or did it please because it was good? The duties of man, as well as his follies and vices, offer a rich field to the dramatist, and Serious dramas will succeed everywhere, but more especially with a people whose manners and customs are corrupt. They will go to the theater in order to escape the evil-doers by whom they are surrounded in life; there will they find people with whom they would care to live; there they will see mankind as it really is, and they will become reconciled with it. Good people do exist, though they are rare. He who believes otherwise, stands self-convicted, and proves how unfortunate he is in his wife, his relatives, his friends and acquaintances. Some one said to me one day after he had read a book which was concerned with serious and good people, and which had given him intense pleasure: "it seems that I am alone." The book deserved the praise, but the man's friends surely not the imputation.

When you write, you must always keep virtue and virtuous people in mind. When I take my pen in hand, I think of you, my friend; and when I write, your image is constantly before me. I wish to please Sophie [Sophie Voland]. If you grant me an indulgent and sympathetic smile, if she sheds a tear, if you both love me a little more, I am sufficiently rewarded.

When I saw the scenes in which The Peasant appeared in *Le Faux généreux*, I said to myself: This will please every one, and will continue to please forever; it will cause the shedding of tears. The success of the play has confirmed my opinion. That episode is quite in the Serious and good [*honnête et sérieux*] style.

It may be said: "The example of a single good episode proves nothing. If you fail to break up the monotonous discourses of virtue by the introduction of a few ridiculous or forced characters, as every other dramatist does, I fear, no matter what you say of your new form, that you will give us nothing but a few cold and colorless scenes or tiresome and lugubrious morality — a sort of sermon in dialogue."

Let us consider the elements of a drama, and see. Do you judge a play by its subject? In the Serious and good drama the subject is of no less importance than in the gay comedy, only it is treated more truthfully. By its characters? They can be as varied and as original; and besides, the dramatist must draw them with a surer and stronger

hand. By the passions? The greater the interest, the stronger will the passions be. By the style? It will be more nervous, graver, more elevated, violent, more susceptible of what we term *feeling* [*sentiment*], without which no style appeals to the heart. By the absence of ridicule? As if human folly, exhibited in human action and speech, when it is suggested by a partly understood interest or through passion, were not the true object of ridicule!

Look at the best scenes in Terence; what is the style employed in the scenes where fathers and lovers are concerned?

If in *Le Père de famille* I have been unable to live up to the dignity of my subject, if the action leaves one cold and the passions furnish only moralizing discourses, if the character of the Father, of his Son, of Sophie, of the Commander, of Germeuil, and of Cécile lack comic vigor, is it the fault of the style of play I tried to write, or my own?

Suppose a dramatist decides to take a judge, his social position and environment, as the subject of a play; he introduces as interesting an intrigue as is necessary; the judge is forced as a result either of his position or his function to do something unworthy his high calling, bring dishonor upon himself or others, immolate himself upon the altar of his own passions, his tastes, his fortune, his birth, his wife and his children. Who will declare after such a play that the Serious and good play is without warmth, color, and power?

There is one method I have adopted of going about work, a successful one to which I turn whenever habit or novelty obscures my judgment — both produce this effect — and it is to seize the very thought of certain objects, transport them bodily from nature to my canvas, and examine them from a point where they are neither too far from me, nor too near.

Let us apply the method. Take two comedies, one of the *Serious* type, the other of the usual gay type. Let us make two galleries of pictures, scene by scene, and see through which we more willingly wander, and in which we experience the stronger and more agreeable sensations, and to which we are the readier to return.

To the Serious, I repeat, the Serious. It touches us more intimately than that which excites our disgust and our laughter. Oh, poet, art thou a creature of sensibility and refinement? Then touch this chord, you will hear it vibrate, and stir the souls of men.

" Is human nature good, then? "

Yes, my friend, very good. Water, air, earth, fire — everything is good in nature; and the whirlwind that rises up toward the end of autumn, blowing on forests and striking the trees one against the other, breaking and blowing away the dead branches; and the tempest, lashing the waves of the sea and purifying its waters; and the volcano that pours from its opened flank a stream of molten matter, casting up vapor that cleanses the atmosphere.

It is our miserable conventions that pervert and cramp mankind, not human nature. Now, what affects us more than the recital of a generous action? Who so low that he can listen unmoved to the plea of an upright man?

The theater is the only place where the tears of the virtuous man and the rogue are mingled. There the mean man regrets the injustices he has committed, feels sorry for the evil he has done, and is indignant toward a man of his own sort. But the impression is made, and it remains in the hearts of each of us, in spite of ourselves. The evil man leaves his seat less disposed to do evil than if he had listened to a severe and pitiless orator.

The poet, the novelist, the actor, appeal to the heart by indirect means; the effect produced depends upon the extent to which the heart is open to receive impressions. The unfortunate happenings which arouse my pity are, I admit, imaginary, but they touch me none the less. Every line of *L'Homme de qualité retiré du monde*, of the *Doyen de Killerine* and of *Cleveland*, arouses in me the greatest interest in the misfortunes to which virtue is exposed, and causes me to shed tears. What art could be more harmful than that which should make me an accomplice of evil men? But on the other hand, what art more precious than that which leads me, imperceptibly, to take an interest in the lot of the good man, taking me out of the quiet and

soothing position I now enjoy, and forces me into the refuge where he has gone, to take part in the trials which it has pleased the poet to throw across his path in order to try his mettle?

How mankind would be benefited were all the arts of imitation to seek a common end, and come together with laws forcing us to love virtue and despise vice! It is the philosopher's place to invite them; he it is who must turn to the poet, the painter, the musician, and cry aloud: " Men of genius, why has heaven endowed you with gifts? " If the artists give heed to him, soon the images of debauchery covering our palace walls will disappear; our voices will no longer be the organs of crime; good taste and good customs and morals will gain inestimably. Do you think that the depiction of a blind couple, who have for years each sought the other until age has come upon them, and who finally, with tears in their eyes, clasp each other on the very verge of the grave, demands as much talent, and would move me more than the spectacle of the violent and novel passions to which the same couple would be subject in their youth?

III. OF A SORT OF MORAL DRAMA

Occasionally I imagine that the theater will be a place where the most important moral problems will be discussed without interfering with the swift and violent action of the play.

How to go about it? Arrange your play as you would under ordinary circumstances, just as the abdication of the Empire is arranged in *Cinna*. Thus will the poet manage questions of suicide, honor, duels, fortune, dignity, and so on. Thus our plays would assume added gravity, in case they should lack it. If a certain scene is necessary, if it is basically required, if it is announced and if the spectator wishes it, he will give all his attention to it, and be very differently affected than by those ambiguous and paradoxical maxims with which our modern plays are littered.

I don't want clever maxims on our stage, but impressions. He who says of a play, and quotes detached sentences by way of proof, that it is mediocre, is rarely mistaken. The greatest poet is he whose work remains long in our minds.

Oh, dramatists, the true applause which you seek is not the hand-clapping which follows a brilliant verse, it is rather that profound sigh which escapes from the depths of the soul after the constraint of long silence, the sigh that brings relief. But there is another impression to make, a more violent one, which you will readily understand if you are born to your art, if you are aware of its magic, and that is to make your audience feel ill at ease. Their minds will be troubled, uncertain, distracted, and your spectators be like those who in the presence of an earthquake see the walls of their homes rock, and feel the earth yawn before them.

IV. OF A SORT OF PHILOSOPHICAL DRAMA

There is a sort of play in which moral problems can be set forth successfully. Here is an example. Let us hear what our judges have to say of it; if they declare it cold, believe me, they have no strength of soul, no idea of true eloquence, no sensibility, no character. For my part, I believe that if a man of genius makes use of it, he will allow no eye a moment in which to become dry, and that we shall owe to him the most touching of spectacles, the most instructive and interesting book imaginable. The subject is the death of Socrates.

The scene is a prison. We see the philosopher lying on a bed of straw, in shackles. He is asleep. His friends have corrupted the guards, and they come at daybreak to announce to him the news of his deliverance.

All Athens is in an uproar, but the just man slumbers.

The innocence of his life! How sweet it is to have the consolation that one has lived uprightly when he is at the point of death! *First scene.*

Socrates awakes, and sees his friends. He is surprised to see them so early. Socrates' dream.

They tell him what they have done. He discusses with them what he had best do.

His self-respect and the sacredness of the laws. *Second scene.*

The guards arrive and take off his shackles.

The fable of pain and pleasure.

The Judges enter, and with them, Socrates' accusers with a crowd. He is accused, and defends himself.

The apology. *Third scene.*

. . . The accusations must be read, and Socrates must challenge the judges, his accusers, and the people. He must question them, and they must answer. You must show exactly how it all happened: the spectacle will be all the truer, more striking, and more beautiful.

The Judges retire, and Socrates' friends remain with him. They feel that their friend will be convicted. Socrates speaks with them and consoles them. On the immortality of the soul. *Fourth scene.*

He is convicted. His death-sentence is announced to him. He sees his wife and children. The hemlock is brought. He dies. *Fifth scene.*

This is only a single act, but if it be well done, it will attain to the dimensions, or nearly so, of an ordinary play. What eloquence is required! What profound philosophy! What truth to nature! What essential truth! If the dramatist realizes the firm, tranquil, serene and elevated character of the philosopher, he will readily see how difficult it is to represent him. At every moment he will draw a smile to the lips of the spectator, and a tear to the eye. I would die happy if I could write this play as I conceive it. Once again, if critics see in it merely a string of cold philosophical discourses, how I pity the poor wretches! How I pity them!

V. OF SIMPLE AND COMPLEX DRAMAS

For my part, I consider a passion, a well developed character, culminating in the exhibition of all his strength, much more important than that combination of incidents which goes to make up the tissue of a play in which the characters and audience are equally jostled and bandied about. That sort of thing is, it seems to me, foreign to good taste and grand effects. And yet this is what we call movement. The Ancients had another idea. A simple plot, an action taken up toward its end in order that everything should be heightened in its effect, a catastrophe invariably imminent, which is only kept back by a simple and true circumstance; strong passions; tableaux; one or two characters firmly drawn; and that was all. In order to move his audience, Sophocles required no more. Those who do not care to read the Ancients, will never know how much our Racine owes to old Homer.

Have you ever noticed, as I have, that no matter how complicated a play happened to be, there is hardly anyone who thinks about this after the première? You readily recall the events, but not the discourses, and once the situations are known, the complicated play loses its effect.

If a play were meant to be produced only once and never printed, I should say to the poet: "Complicate as much as you like; you will arouse the interest and emotions of your audience; but if you desire to be read and known to posterity, be simple."

One good scene contains more ideas than is possible in a whole play of incident; and it is to ideas that we return, that we listen to and never grow tired of; these affect us in every age. The scene of Roland in the cave waiting for the perfidious Angélique; Lusignan's words to his daughter, or those of Clytemnestra to Agamemnon, are always new to me.

And even were I to allow as many complications as possible, the play would contain only the same action. It is well-nigh impossible to conduct two intrigues simultaneously, unless one interests us at the expense of the other. How many examples I might cite in modern plays! But I have no desire to offend.

Where can we find a more ingenious interlacing of scenes than those in which Terence has woven the loves of Pamphila and Charinus in the *Andria?* And yet, has not the poet sacrificed something? Do we not feel that at the beginning of the second act we are starting a new play? And does the fifth act end as interestingly as it might?

He who undertakes to develop two intrigues at once labors under the necessity of unravelling them at the same moment. If the principal intrigue ends before the other, that other cannot stand alone; or if the subsidiary plot ends first, either the characters disappear, or else they are brought in again without sufficient motive, and the play is mutilated and leaves a frigid impression.

What would have happened to Terence's *Heautontimorumenos,* or *Self-Tormentor,* unless, by an effort of genius, the poet had been able to carry on again the story of Clinia which ends in the third act, and joined it with that of Clitiphon?

Terence took the intrigue of Menander's *Perinthia* and put it into his *Andria;* of the two simple plays he made one. I adopted the opposite course in *Le Fils naturel.* Goldoni made a three-act farce, using *L'Avare* of Molière and the characters of *The True Friend* [*Il vero amico*]. I separated these subjects and made a five-act play. Whether the result be good or bad, I am sure I was right in my method.

Terence maintains that in having doubled the subject of the *Heautontimorumenos,* his play was a new one. Possibly, but whether it was a *better* play, is another question.

If I can flatter myself for any reason in *Le Père de famille,* it is for having given Germeuil and Cécile a passion which they cannot avow during the early acts, and for having so subordinated that thread of interest to the passion of Saint-Albin for Sophie, that even after the declaration, Germeuil and Cécile cannot talk of their love, although they are constantly together.

There is no middle way: you will always lose in one place what you have gained in another. If you gain interest and rapidity by a number of incidents, you will have no discourses, for your characters will have no time to speak: they will merely act instead of develop. I speak from experience.

VI. OF THE BURLESQUE DRAMA

You cannot put too much action and movement into a farce. . . . Less in gay comedy, still less in Serious comedy, and almost none at all in tragedy.

The less true to life a type is, the easier the task of making it rapid in action, and "warm." You have heat at the expense of truth and what is beautiful in human nature. The most tedious thing imaginable is a burlesque and cold play. In the Serious Drama the choice of incidents renders warmth difficult to preserve.

And yet not every one can write a

good farce. It requires an original sort of gayety: the characters are like the grotesques of Callot, in which the essential features of the human being must be preserved. Not every one can so twist his point of view. If you think there are many men more capable of writing *Pourceaugnacs* than *Misanthropes,* you are mistaken.

What was Aristophanes? An original writer of farces. An author of this sort ought to prove a great boon for any government that knows how to make use of him. The various enthusiasts who trouble society from time to time ought to be left to him. If they be exposed in the public places, prisons will not be needed.

Although the movement of a play varies according to the different types, the action progresses in the same manner with all; it never stops, even during the entr'actes. It is like a mass of rock set loose from a mountain-top, whose speed increases as it descends, bounding headlong past every obstacle.

If this comparison be just, if discourses decrease in inverse proportion to the action, the characters ought to speak a great deal at first and act a great deal toward the end.

VII. OF THE PLOT AND THE DIALOGUE

Is it more difficult to make a scenario [*établir le plan*] than to write dialogue? I have often heard the question argued, and it seemed to me that each one answered rather according to his own ability than to the facts.

A man who knows the world, speaks fluently, understands men after having studied them and listened to them — and who is able to write — finds it difficult work to plan his play.

Another, who can see things generally, who has given thought to the art of poetry and who knows the theater, whose experience and taste serve as guides toward situations that interest, and who knows how to combine events, will find it no difficult task to plan his play, but the individual scenes will give him trouble. He will be less satisfied with his own invention for the particular scenes, because he is well acquainted with the masterpieces of his own country as well as of Antiquity, and he cannot help comparing his work with that of the masters whose plays he knows so well. If he set to work on a long speech, he thinks of the *Andria;* of a scene full of passion, then of the *Eunuchus;* each play will give him ten examples for one he will himself think of.

None the less, genius is required for both elements; only the genius is not of the same sort. The plot is what holds a complicated play together; the speeches and the dialogue are what make people listen to and read a simple play.

Let me observe in passing that there are more well-written than well-constructed plays. The sort of talent which can arrange a series of incidents seems rarer than that which writes a true and natural speech. How many beautiful scenes there are in Molière! But you can soon count the artfully conducted dénouements.

A good plot is the fruit of the imagination; good dialogue comes from the observing of nature.

You can formulate any number of plots on the same subject and with the same characters; but, given the characters, there is only one way in which they may speak. These will say such and such things according to the situations in which you place them, but since they are always the same people, in any situation, they must be consistent.

One might almost say that a play ought to be the work of two men of genius, one of whom should make the plot, and the other write the dialogue. But who can write dialogue for another's plot? The talent for writing dialogue is not universal: each man ventures forth and does what he can. When he constructs his plot he seeks, unconsciously, the sort of situation which he can successfully handle. Change his situations, and it will seem to him that his talent has deserted him. One man can deal with comic situations; another with moral and serious ones; a third, with eloquence and pathos. Give Corneille one of Racine's plots, and Racine one of Corneille's, and see how each will succeed!

As my own character is a sensitive and straightforward one, I confess, my friend, that I have never felt the least trepidation in attacking a scene the success of which depended upon reason and honesty. These are weapons my parents taught me to use at an early age, and I have often wielded them against others, as well as myself!

You know how well at home I am in the art of the soliloquy. If I leave some social gathering and return home, sad and chagrined, I retire to my room and ask myself, What is the matter? Just bad humor? Yes.— Are you ill? No.— I then insist, and drag forth the truth. And it seems that I have a spirit which is gay, tranquil, honest, serene; this spirit interrogates another within me, which is ashamed of some folly it has committed and which it is afraid to admit. And yet the confession comes. If it be a folly I have committed — often the case — I absolve myself. If some one has wounded me — which likewise often happens when I am with people who wish to take advantage of my good nature — I forgive. Thus my sadness disappears; I join the family, a good husband, a good father, a good master— at least so I imagine; and no one has to suffer the ill-humor which I might have inflicted upon every one who approached me.

I advise this sort of self-communion to every one who wishes to write: it will render him at the same time a better man and a better writer.

When I wish to construct a plot, I unconsciously seek out situations which can be handled by a man of my character and ability.

" Is this the best plot? "

So it seems to me.

" But to others? "

That is a different matter.

Listen to men and women, and talk with yourself: these are the two ways of learning the art of dialogue.

The requisites for constructing a good plot are: imagination, the ability to observe the course of events and the relations between them; the courage to develop long scenes, and to work hard; to attack a subject at the vital point; to be able to see exactly where your story begins, and know how much to relegate to the past, and to recognize the most affecting scenes for representation on the stage.

Above all, you must never jot down a single detail until your plot is definitely made out.

As the plot requires a vast amount of labor and meditation, what happens to those who possess some facility in the depiction of character? They have a general view of the subject; they know fairly well what the situations are to be; and they know their characters. The moment they say to themselves, This mother is to be a coquette, this father a strict man, this lover a libertine, this young girl tender and gentle, they are seized with a mad desire to write the scenes. They write and write; they express fine and delicate thoughts, even powerful ideas; they have charming ready-made fragments, but when the time comes for constructing the plot — and that time always comes — they vainly try to incorporate their charming fragments; they are never willing to relinquish this or that delicate or powerful bit, and consequently they do precisely what they ought not to do: make the plot fit the scenes, rather than the scenes the plot. And there will result a limited and cramped plot, which will extend even to the dialogue itself, much labor and time lost, and many fragments left over. Too bad, especially if the work is in verse!

I know a young poet, not devoid of talent, who has written over three or four thousand lines of a tragedy which remains unfinished, and which will never be complete.

VIII. OF THE FIRST SKETCH

Whether you write in verse or in prose, first make out your plot; after that, you may think of the scenes.

How shall we go about making the plot? There is a splendid suggestion in Aristotle on this point. It has helped me and it may help others. Here it is:

Among the great host of authors who have written on the art of poetry, three are particularly famous: Aristotle, Horace, and Boileau. Aristotle is a philosopher who proceeds in an orderly manner, establishes general principles, and allows his readers to draw their own conclusions and apply his theories. Horace is a man of genius who affects a disregard of order and, himself a poet, speaks of his kind. Boileau is a master who tries to give both precept and example.

Somewhere in Aristotle's *Poetics* it is said that Whether you work at a known or an unknown subject, you must begin by sketching the Fable; afterward you may think of the episodes or circumstances which are to develop it. Is it to be a tragedy? Suppose a young girl is conducted to an altar to be sacrificed; all at once she disappears, and is transported to a land where it is customary to offer strangers as a sacrifice to the presiding goddess. They make her a priestess. Some years after, the brother of the princess comes to the country where she is. He is seized by the inhabitants, and as he is about to be sacrificed by his sister, he cries out: "Is it not enough that my sister has been sacrificed, but must I also be?" Whereupon he is recognized and saved.

But why was the princess condemned to die on the altar?

Why are strangers sacrificed in the barbaric land where her brother finds her?

How was he captured?

He comes to obey an oracle. But why that oracle?

He is recognized by his sister. Was there no other method of being recognized?

All these points are outside the subject. But they must be supplied in the Fable.

The subject is common property, but the poet is at liberty to handle it as his fancy directs, and he who accomplishes his task in the most simple and *necessary* way will achieve the greatest success.

Aristotle's idea is applicable to every sort of play; this is how I make use of it. A certain father has two children, a son and a daughter. The daughter is secretly in love with a young man who lives in the same house. The son is in love with an unknown woman whom he has seen in the neighborhood. He has tried to seduce her, but was unsuccessful. He disguises himself and lives next door to her under an assumed name. There he is taken for a man of the lower classes, engaged in some sort of mechanical work. He is hard at work all day long, and sees his beloved only in the evening. But the father, who is well aware of what happens in his house, finds out that his son is never at home at night. This sort of conduct, which forbodes irregularity, worries him. He waits for the son.

This is where the play begins.

What happens next? The girl is a suitable match for his son. At the same time, he learns that his daughter loves the man he had destined for her, and he consents to their engagement. Thus he brings about two marriages, in spite of his brother-in-law, who had other views on the subject.

But why does the daughter keep her love a secret?

Why does her lover live in the same house with her? What is he doing there? Who is he?

Who is the unknown sweetheart of the son? How did she fall to such a state of poverty?

Where does she come from? Born in the country, what brought her to Paris? And what keeps her there?

Who is the brother-in-law?

Whence comes his authority in the father's house?

Why is he opposed to the marriages which the father desires?

As the stage cannot represent two places at the same time, how can the unknown young woman enter the father's house?

How does the father discover the passion of his daughter and the young man living with him?

Why must he conceal his plans?

How does it come about that the unknown woman is acceptable in his eyes?

What obstacles does the brother-in-law bring to the father's notice?

How does the double marriage come to pass in spite of these obstacles?

How many things remain to be disposed of after the poet has made his preliminary sketch! But I have given you the story in his principal outlines. Now, the next task is to divide the story into acts, select what characters are required, determine how they are to be treated, and map out the subjects of each individual scene.

I can see that this sketch will be satisfactory to me, because the father, whose character I intend to bring into evidence, will be very unhappy. He will be opposed to his son's marriage; it will seem that his daughter is avoiding the marriage he wishes; and the proud reticence of each will prevent their confessing their true feelings in the matter.

The number of characters I shall use is decided.

I am no longer uncertain as to their attributes.

The father will behave in accordance with his station in life; he will be good, vigilant, firm, yet tender. Placed in the most difficult situation in life, his whole soul will be bared.

His son must be violent. The more unreasonable the passion, the less free does it become.

His mistress is never sufficiently amiable. I have made her an innocent child, respectable and sensitive.

The brother-in-law, who is my "villain," is a hard-headed and prejudiced man, uncompromising, feeble, mean, importunate, tricky, dishonest — a trouble in the house, a thorn in the side of the father and his children, and the aversion of every one.

Who is Germeuil? He is the son of a deceased friend of the father's; the friend's affairs having been left in a bad state, he has left the young man without a penny. The father took him in after the death of the friend, and brought him up as his own son.

Cécile, who believes that her father will never allow the young man to become her husband, always keeps him at a distance, and sometimes treats him harshly; Germeuil, who is repulsed by her behavior and fearing that he might fail in respect to the father, treats the daughter with the utmost formality; but in spite of the efforts of the young people, appearances are against them, and their passion develops — in word and deed — though at first it is scarcely perceptible.

Germeuil, then, will possess a firm, tranquil, and somewhat retiring character.

And Cécile will be proud, vivacious, reserved, and sensitive.

The dissimulation practiced by the young people deceives the father. Dissuaded from his original plan by the antipathy he believes to exist between the lovers, the father will not dare propose for a husband a young man for whom she seems to have so little liking, and who seems as distant toward her as she to him.

The father will say: "Is it not enough to torment my son by taking from him the woman he loves? Must I also try to force upon my daughter a man whom she does not love?"

And the daughter will answer: "Are not my father and uncle sufficiently worried about my brother? Ought I to increase their cares by confessing something which would shock every one?"

In this way, the Germeuil-daughter thread of interest is relegated to the background, and allows place for the development of the love of the son for his mistress, and develop the uncle's bad humor and the father's sorrow.

I shall have succeeded beyond my fondest hopes if I interest these two in the son's love-affair, and forget their own for the time being. The interest in their own will not run the risk of rivalling the other interest, but will rather make their own more interesting to themselves.

I intend that the father shall be the principal character. The preliminary sketch remains the same; the episodes only would have been changed had I chosen the son, the friend, or the uncle, as my hero.

IX. OF THE INCIDENTS

If the poet be possessed of imagination, and if he adheres to his sketch, he will vitalize it and see a whole legion of incidents spring from it, finding it difficult only to make his choice from among them.

He must be rigid upon this point when the subject he treats is serious. Nowadays, we would not accept a scene where a father puts to flight a pedant with a mule-bell, or where a husband hides under a table in order to hear his wife's conversation. These incidents belong to farce.

If a young princess is led to an altar where she is to be sacrificed, we cannot but think that such a fatal situation is due to a mistake on the part of a messenger who has failed to arrive.

"Does not the fate which makes playthings of us all bring forth the greatest events from the smallest causes?"

True. But the poet ought not to imitate fate in this respect: he will make use of the incident, if it be furnished by history, but not invent it. I will judge his methods more severely than the conduct of the gods.

He must be scrupulous in the choice of his incidents and restrained in the use of them; he must make them proportionate to the importance of his story, and establish the necessary connection between them.

"The more obscure and feeble the means by which the will of the gods is exercised upon men, the greater the fear inspired in me for their lot."

I agree. But I must be made certain of what that will is — not of the poet, but the gods.

Tragedy demands dignity in the method; comedy, delicacy.

Is a jealous lover uncertain of the feelings of his beloved? In such a scene, Terence brings a Davus upon the stage to listen to the lover's discourse, and will repeat it later to his master. We French insist that the poet shall know more.

A vain and foolish old man changes his middle-class name, Arnolphe, to that of M. de La Souche; this ingenious trick is the basis of all the intrigue, and brings about the dénouement in a simple and unexpected way. The audience exclaims "Marvelous!" and they are right. But if, without the least semblance to truth, they are shown Arnolphe as the confidant of his rival and the dupe of his pupil five or six times in succession — going from Horace to Agnès and then from Agnès to Horace again — they will say, "This is no play, but a fairy-tale," and if you have not all the wit, cleverness and genius of a Molière, they will accuse you of want of invention, and say "It is a fairy-tale that will put you to sleep."

If you have few incidents, you will have few characters. Never introduce a superfluous character; and have the connecting links between your scenes invisible.

Above all, never introduce a thread that leads nowhere; if you interest me in a situation which is not developed you will scatter my attention.

An example of this, if I am not mistaken, is the Frosine incident in *L'Avare*. She attempts to dissuade the Miser from marrying Marianne, by speaking of a certain Viscountess de Basse-Bretagne, of whom she promises marvels — and the audience expects these. And yet the play ends without our seeing more of Frosine or the Viscountess, both of whom we have been waiting for.

X. OF THE PLOT IN TRAGEDY AND COMEDY

What a play it would be whose plot was open to no criticism! Is there such a play? The more complicated it is, the less true to life. I have been asked whether the plot of tragedy or of comedy be more difficult.

There are three kinds of subjects. History, which is a matter of facts; tragedy, where the poet adds to history whatever elements of interest he can; and comedy, where the poet invents everything.

Wherefore it is concluded that the comic writer is the greatest. He it is who creates. In his sphere he is what the supreme Being is in nature. He creates, snatching from the great generality of things; but with this difference, that in nature we see only a vast succession of events the causes of which are unknown to us, whereas the march of events in a play are revealed to us, or if the poet conceals a sufficient number of causes for a while, he finally initiates us into his secrets and satisfies our curiosity.

"But if comedy be an imitation of nature in all its aspects, must not the poet adhere to his model when he constructs his plot?"

Undoubtedly.

"Then what is his model?"

Before answering this, I shall ask what a plot is.

"A plot is an interesting story, constructed according to the rules of dramatic form, which is in part the invention of the tragic poet and altogether that of the comic poet."

Very well. What is the basis of dramatic art?

"Historic art."

Nothing can be more reasonable. Poetry has been compared with painting; very good, but a better comparison would be that between history and poetry. Thus we are enabled to form a more exact notion of the true, the likely, and the possible, and a clear idea of the interesting and the marvelous — which belong to all kinds of drama, and which few poets are able to define.

Every historic event is not fit material

for tragedy, nor every domestic event for comedy. The Ancients limited the subjects of their tragedies to the stories of the families of Alcmæon, Œdipus, Orestes, Meleager, Thyestes, Telephus and Hercules.

Horace is opposed to the dramatist's putting upon the stage a character who snatches a living child from the womb of Lamia. If he is shown something of that sort, he can neither believe it possible nor bear to see it represented. But exactly where shall we draw the line between such incredible incidents and those which are credible? How far can the poet venture?

There sometimes occurs in the natural order of things an extraordinary chain of incidents. It is this same order that distinguishes the marvelous from the miraculous. The rare cases are marvelous; those which are naturally impossible are miraculous. Dramatic art rejects miracles.

If nature never brought about situations of an extraordinary sort, then everything imagined by the poet outside the simple and cold uniformity about him would be unbelievable. But this is not the case. What does the poet do? He either uses the extraordinary combinations which he finds in nature, or else he invents them. But, in place of the relation of cause and effect which often escapes our notice in nature, and which, owing to our want of knowledge often seems like a fatal association of circumstances, the poet insists that throughout his work there be a visible and credible relation, and in this respect his work is less true, but more natural and true to life, than that of the historian.

"But if the mere coexistence of events is sufficient to produce the marvelous in history, why is not the poet satisfied with this?"

Sometimes he is, the tragic poet especially. But the assumption of simultaneous incidents is not always allowed to the comic poet.

"Why?"

Because the known portion which the tragic poet borrows from history makes us accept the imaginative part as if it were history. The part he invents is given a verisimiltude from the historic part. But nothing is given to the comic poet; therefore he is less able to rely upon extraordinary combinations of events. Furthermore, fate and the will of the gods, which inspire terror in the hearts of men whose destiny is in the hands of superior beings before whom they are helpless, which follows them and strikes them the moment they believe themselves secure — this is more necessary to tragedy. If there is anything sad in life, it is the spectacle of a man rendered guilty and unhappy in spite of himself.

In comedy men must play the rôle which gods play in tragedy. Fate is the basis of tragedy; human malignity that of comedy.

"And what is this veneer of romance which is decried in some of our plays?"

A play is romantic when the marvelous is caused by coincidence: if we see gods or men too malignant; if events and characters differ too greatly from what experience and history lead us to expect; and above all, if the relation of cause and effect is too complicated or extraordinary.

Whence, one may conclude that the novel from which one cannot make a good play is not for that reason bad; but on the other hand, there is no good play from which an excellent novel cannot be made. It is merely a matter of technical rules that differentiates the novel from the play.

Illusion is the end of both, but upon what does the illusion depend? On circumstances. It is these which make illusion more or less difficult.

Will you allow me to speak the language of geometry? You know what the geometrician calls an equation. Illusion stands to one side. It is an invariable quantity, equal to a sum of terms — some positive, others negative — whose number and possibility of combination can be varied in endless ways, but the total value of which is always the same. The positive terms represent ordinary circumstances and situations; the negatives, the extraordinary. One sort is compensated for by the others.

Illusion is not voluntary. The poet who says, I wish to create an illusion, is like the man who says, I have a certain experience of life to which I shall pay no attention.

When I say that an illusion is an invariable quantity, I mean to a man who judges of various productions, and not to various men. There are probably no two human beings in the world possessing the same measure of certainty, and yet the poet is forced to create an illusion for every one! The poet takes advantage of the reason and the experience of an experienced man, just as a governess takes advantage of the stupidity of a child. A good poem is a story worthy of being told to sensible men.

The novelist has the time and space which are denied the dramatist; everything else being equal, therefore, I have more admiration for a play than for a novel. There is no difficulty which cannot be avoided by the former. He will say: "*La douce vapeur du sommeil,*" etc. [a short passage from Fénelon's *Télémaque,* Book VII]. This is how the novelist extricates himself. But, no matter what the difficulty of writing this speech, the dramatist would have been forced either to change his plot completely, or else surmount the difficulty. What difference there is in the methods of painting, and producing an effect on the stage!

The Ancients possessed tragedies in which the plots were entirely the invention of the poet. History did not even furnish the names of the characters. But what difference does this make, provided the poet keeps within the limits of the marvelous? . . .

XI. OF INTEREST

In complicated plays, interest is the result rather of the plot than of the speeches; in simple plays, on the other hand, it is rather the speeches that arouse interest. But in whom is the interest to be aroused? In the characters, or in the minds of the audience?

The spectators are merely ignorant witnesses of what passes.

"Then must one keep the characters in mind and interest them?" . . .

The more I think of the drama, the more vexed I am with those who have written about it. The drama is a tissue of particular laws, from which the critics have deduced general precepts. It has been noticed that certain incidents produce great effects; and immediately it becomes a rule that all poets shall resort to the same means in order to produce like results. Now, if one had examined a little more closely, he would have seen that still greater effects might have been produced by entirely opposite means. Thus has the art of the drama become surcharged with rules; and the dramatists, in servilely subjecting themselves to them, have often gone to much pain and done less well than they might have done.

If it were only understood that, although a drama is made to be produced, it was still necessary that both author and actor forget the spectator, and that all the interest should be centered in the characters, there would be less reading of Poetics. If you do this or that, you will produce this or that effect on the spectator. They should say: If you do this or that, this is what will happen to your characters.

Those who have written on the drama are like a man who, trying to sow trouble in a family, thinks rather of what the neighbors will say, than of what ill he can bring upon the family. Never mind the neighbors, but put your characters into action and rest assured that they will suffer nothing that the others will escape.

From other models, other rules. Perhaps it may be said: let your outcome be known, and soon, and let your audience be in continual suspense anticipating the light which will be shed on all the characters — as to what they have been doing and as to what they are.

If it is necessary to arouse interest in a play toward the end, this process seems as good to me as the opposite. Ignorance and perplexity excite curiosity in the mind of the audience and keep them aroused; but it is rather the things that are known and invariably expected which trouble and move them. This means is absolutely certain to keep the catastrophe always before the audience.

If, instead of taking part with his characters and allowing the audience to take care of themselves, the poet steps down from the stage into the parterre, he will harm his plot. He will do as those painters who, instead of keeping closely to nature, lose sight of it and have recourse to pure technique, and fail to present her to me as she is and as they see her, but try to depict her relatively, by means of ordinary tricks of the trade.

Are not all points in space variously lighted? Are they not separate? Do they not go hither and thither in an arid and flat plain, as in the most varied of landscapes? If you imitate such a painter, your drama will be like his picture: he will have a few fine spots, and your play a few splendid moments, but this is not the point: the picture must be beautiful from end to end of the canvas, and your drama from start to finish.

And what will become of the actor, if you concentrate upon the audience? Do you imagine he will feel any more than what you have given him? If you think of the audience, he will think of them, too. You seek their applause; so will he. And then what will become of your illusion?

I have said that the actor performs badly what the poet wrote for the audience, and that if the parterre acted, they would say to the characters on the stage: "Whom do you blame? I am not one of you. Do I meddle in your affairs? Go home," and if the author played his part, he would have come forth from behind the scenes and answered the par-

terre: "I beg your pardon, Messieurs, it is my fault. I shall do better another time, and so will the character."

Whether you write or act, think no more of the audience than if it had never existed. Imagine a huge wall across the front of the stage, separating you from the audience, and behave exactly as if the curtain had never risen.

"But the Miser who has lost his chest asks the audience: Messieurs, is not the thief among you?"

Never mind that author. The exception taken from the work of a genius proves nothing against commonsense. Tell me whether you can speak to your audience without stopping the action, and whether the least you will have done in thus directing your attention to it, does not result in a number of lapses throughout your play, and a general loosening of its fabric?

I agree that a dramatist may introduce points in his play which the spectator may apply to himself; let him ridicule people, and predominant vices, and public events; let him instruct and please, provided he does not think about it. If the audience detects his purpose, he will fail to achieve it; he ceases to write drama, and only preaches.

.   .   .   .   .

BEAUMARCHAIS

Pierre-Augustin Caron was born at Paris in 1732. His father was a clockmaker, and intended that his son should follow the same profession. His early life seems to have been happily spent. He was sent to a sort of technical school at Alfort, and then brought back again at the age of thirteen to work in his father's shop. The young man, with his indomitable spirit and love of adventure, displeased the father, who sent him away, and then received him home again after extracting numerous promises for the lad's future good behavior. Pierre-Augustin from that time on diligently applied himself to his profession, and at the age of twenty he invented an appliance

for watches. By 1755 he considered himself firmly established, for he was high in court favor. Soon, however, the watchmaker fell in love with one of his customers, married her and in 1757 took the name of Beaumarchais, which was that of a small estate said to be in the possession of his wife. On her death in 1757 Beaumarchais became involved in suits of various sorts, and before long found himself ruined. During the next four years fortune favored him once more, for he turned his knowledge of music to good advantage and arranged concerts for the court. The political influence which Beaumarchais was able to bring to bear upon certain personages at court resulted in his participation in many business enterprises and speculations. With his fortune, which he readily made, he purchased a court office which entitled him to rank among the nobility. A letter from his sister in Madrid interrupted his life in Paris and took him to Spain (1764) where he handled with great skill and tact the celebrated Clavijo case for breach of promise. He remained in Madrid until 1765, returned to Paris, and once again plunged into his life of adventure, intrigue, and pleasure. When in 1767 Beaumarchais produced his first play, he had acquired some skill through the writing of burlesque sketches. But the first of his plays which he deemed worthy of print was *Eugénie,* produced in 1767. The play and the *Préface* exemplified Diderot's theories on the *Drame.* This play was followed in 1770 by *Les Deux amis,* another *Drame.* The play was a failure, and Beaumarchais was ready to turn to pure comedy, but once again he became involved in difficulties. His second wife, whom he married in 1768, died in 1770. She was followed the same year by Duverney, his old business associate. Beaumarchais presented a claim upon Duverney's estate and was soon involved in his most celebrated law-suit. Further trouble ensued, Beaumarchais was imprisoned, and the celebrated Goezman trial took place, resulting in that delightful masterpiece, the *Mémoires* of Beaumarchais. The trial left him deprived of fortune and reputation. However, the king, knowing how useful Beaumarchais might be to him, took him under his protection, and made him a secret agent. He at once went to London and accomplished a delicate mission; on his return to Paris he was amply recompensed. His next mission took him to Holland, Germany, and Austria; and again, on his return to Paris, he was sent to London. He finally gained the complete confidence of Louis XVI, and in 1776 was reinstated as a noble and a citizen. Meanwhile *Le Barbier de Séville* had been written by 1772, but the production was delayed by the censors until 1775; the play was very successful. The untiring dramatist again engaged in commercial ventures, this time sending supplies to the American government for their struggle with England, but he became so entangled in negotiations with the Americans, that not until years after his death, in 1835, did his heirs finally succeed in adjusting matters. The next play, *Le Mariage de Figaro,* after many delays, was produced in 1784, with enormous success. The Revolution was at hand, Beaumarchais was growing old, and in a pamphlet discussion with Mirabeau, he was so fiercely attacked that he retired in shame. Financial reverses set in, and further suits and fines. *Tarare,* an opera, was produced with little success, in 1787, one year after the author's third marriage. *La Mère coupable* (1792) enjoyed only a fair degree of popularity. Once again the indefatigable Beaumarchais engaged in speculations — this time selling arms to the government. Interminable proposals and counter-proposals were made, Beaumarchais was thrown into prison, freed, sent as secret agent to Holland and England, and finally, in 1796, allowed to return to Paris. In the midst of his activities, financial and political, he died, in 1799.

Beaumarchais' theory of the drama is directly derived from Diderot, but he differs from Diderot in that he is primarily a dramatist. True it is that the sort of play which Diderot had so unsuccessfully attempted to write had been feebly imitated by Beaumarchais in *Les Deux amis* and *Eugénie;* but *Le Barbier de Séville* and *Le Mariage de Figaro* are among the finest comedies in existence. Beaumarchais' greatest importance lay in his insistence upon action. It is the business of a comedy to "inspire, move, transport, and strike," the spectator. The modern note struck in Beaumarchais' prefaces was well in accord with many of Victor Hugo's ideas; and we find that revolutionary praising Beaumarchais as one of the "three great characteristic geniuses of our stage."

On the drama:

Essai sur le genre dramatique sérieux, in *Eugénie,* and separately (1767).
Lettre modérée sur la chûte et la critique du Barbier de Séville, in *Le Barbier de Séville* (1775).
Préface, in *La Folle Journée ou le Mariage de Figaro* (Paris, 1784).

Un Mot sur la Mère coupable, in *L'Autre Tartuffe ou la Mère coupable* (1797).
The *Mémoires* (originally published in parts, 1773–74) are reprinted with a notice by Sainte-Beuve (Paris, n.d.). They may be consulted for biographical data. The *Lettres,* printed in modern editions, contain occasional references to drama, while the *Compte rendu de l'affaire des auteurs dramatiques et des comédiens français,* etc., and *Rapport fait aux auteurs dramatiques,* etc., are interesting documents on the quarrel over authors' rights.

Editions:

The first edition of the *Œuvres complètes* was edited by Gudin de La Brenellerie, 7 vols. (Paris, 1809). The best modern complete editions are *Théâtre complet de Beaumarchais,* edited by G. d'Heylli and F. de Marescot, 4 vols. (Paris, 1869–71), and *Œuvres complètes de Beaumarchais,* edited by Edouard Fournier (Paris, 1867). Among the more recent editions is the *Théâtre illustré,* with notes and introduction by M. Roustan, 2 vols. (Paris, n.d.). This edition contains all the prefaces, and extracts from the plays.

On Beaumarchais and his works:

See prefaces to various editions cited:
Cousin d'Avallon, *Vie privée, politique et littéraire de Beaumarchais* (Paris, 1802).
C.-A. Sainte-Beuve, *Causeries du Lundi,* vol. 6 (Paris, 1857–62).
Louis de Loménie, *Beaumarchais et son temps,* 2 vols. (4th ed., Paris, 1880). Translated by H. S. Edwards, as *Beaumarchais and his Times,* 4 vols. (London, 1856).
La Grande Encyclopédie, vol. 5 (Paris, 1888).
Henri Cordier, *Bibliographie des œuvres de Beaumarchais* (Paris, 1883).
M. de Lescure, *Eloge de Beaumarchais* (Paris, 1886).
Maurice Chevrier, *Discours sur Beaumarchais* (Paris, 1887).
Anton Bettelheim, *Beaumarchais* (2nd ed., München, 1911).
Paul Bonnefon, *Beaumarchais* (Paris, 1887).
Gudin de la Brenellerie, *Histoire de Beaumarchais* (Paris, 1888).
Eugène Lintilhac, *Beaumarchais et ses œuvres* (Paris, 1887).
André Hallays, *Beaumarchais* (Paris, 1897).
John Rivers, *Figaro: the Life of Beaumarchais* (New York, n.d.).

ESSAY ON THE SERIOUS DRAMA [1]
[*Essai sur le genre dramatique sérieux*]
(1767)

I can lay no just claim to the dignity of author: both time and talent have been denied me; but some eight years ago I amused myself by committing to paper a few ideas of the *Serious Drama,* that form which is a sort of intermediary between the heroic tragedy and the pleasing comedy. Of the several forms of the drama which I might have chosen, that was perhaps the least esteemed; and that was the very reason for my preference. I have always been so seriously occupied that I have sought nothing in the field of letters but an honorable means of recreation. *Neque-*

[1] Translated into English by the Editor, for the first time.— Ed.

sem per arcum tendit Apollo. The subject pleased, and carried me along with it; but I was not long in learning that I was mistaken in endeavoring to convince by reason in a form where one ought rather to persuade by sentiment. I was soon seized with the desire to substitute example for precept: an infallible way of creating proselytes when one is successful, but which exposes the unfortunate mortal who is not, to the twofold chagrin of having failed to attain his object, and being the butt of ridicule for having presumed beyond his powers.

Too wrought up by my subject to be capable of this latter thought, I composed the play which I herewith publish. *Miss Fanny, Miss Jenny, Miss Polly,* and so on, charming books, my *Eugénie* would doubtless have gained much in taking you for models; but she was born before you were in existence — without which one can never serve as model at all. I refer your authors to the little Spanish novelette of the Comte de Belflor, in *Le Diable boiteux;* that was the source of my idea. The little I obtained therefrom will cause them small regret that they were unable to help me in any way.

The general outline of my plan of action — that rapid mass-work, indicating in a general way the situations, and sketching out the characters — developing very quickly under the white heat of my enthusiasm, saw no waning of my courage; but when it came to the part where I was forced to confine the subject within a certain space, or expand it, really work at it; then my poor brain, muddled with details of execution, was cognizant of real difficulties, took fright at the whole thing, and gave up both play and dissertation. . . .

Shortly after, M. Diderot brought out his *Père de famille.* The genius of this writer, his powerful manner, the vigorous and masculine style of his play, ought to have caused me to throw down my pen; instead, the path he had opened up held forth such charms to me that I listened to the dictates of my personal inclination rather than to the voice of my own weakness and inability. I went to work on my play with renewed ardor. As soon as I had finished it, I gave the manuscript to the *Comédie Française.* . . .

Now that it has been produced, I shall proceed to inquire into all the uproarious clamor and adverse criticism which it has aroused; but I shall not linger long over those points which do not immediately concern the dramatic form which it pleased me to choose, because that is the only point which can interest the public at this time. I shall indulge in no personalities. *Jam dolor in morem venit meus* (Ovid). I shall even pass over in silence everything that has been said against the play, firmly convinced that the greatest honor that could be paid it — after the actual interest taken in it on the stage — is that it is not unworthy of critical discussion. . . .

I have seen people actually and sincerely bemoan the fact that the *Serious Drama* was gaining partisans. "An equivocal form!" they declare. "You cannot tell what it is. What sort of play is that in which there is not a single line that makes you laugh? Five mortal acts of long-drawn-out prose, with no comic relief, no moral reflections, no characters — during which we are held suspended by the thread of some romantic circumstance which has neither versimilitude nor reality! Does not the sufferance of such works rather open the gate to license, and encourage laziness? The facility of prose will tend to turn our young authors from the arduous task of writing verse, and our stage will soon fall into a state of barbarism, out of which our poets have so painfully managed to develop it. I do not mean to infer that some of these pieces have not affected me, I do not know just how; but how terrible it would be if such plays obtained a foothold! And besides, their popularity would be most unseemly in our land: every one knows what our celebrated authors have thought, and they are authorities! They have proscribed this dramatic form as belonging neither to Melpomene nor to Thalia. Must we create a new Muse to preside over this trivial cothurnus, this stilted comic form? *Tragi-comedy, Bourgeois Tragedy, Tearful Comedy* — I can find no term to designate this hybrid. And let no wretched author pride himself upon the momentary approval of the public, which is vouchsafed rather to the assiduity and talent of the actors! The public! What is this public? The moment that collective entity dissolves, and each member of it goes his own way, what remains of the general opinion, unless it becomes that of each individual, among whom the most enlightened exercise a natural influence over the others, who are brought sooner or later to think with the former? Whence it will be seen that the author must look to the few and not to the many for his "general opinion."

Enough. Now let us proceed to reply to the vast torrent of objections, which I have neither belittled nor exaggerated in my account. Let us begin by rendering our judge favorable toward us by defending his own rights. Despite the assertion of the critics to the contrary, the assembled public is none the less that sole judge of plays which are written to amuse it. Every one alike is forced to submit to it, and any effort to obstruct the efforts of genius in the creation of a new dramatic form, or in the further development of those forms which are already established, is a conspiracy against its rights, a plot to deprive it of its pleasure. I readily agree that a difficult, deep-hidden truth in a play will be sooner discovered, better understood, and more intelligently judged by a small number of enlightened individuals, than by a clamorous crowd — otherwise the truth could not be said to be "difficult"; but questions of taste and sentiment, matters pertaining to pure effects; in a word, all that regards the work as a play, since it cannot be considered apart from the powerful and instantaneous effect produced upon an audience as a whole — ought, I ask, all these things to be judged according to the same rules? When it is less a matter of discussing and analyzing than of feeling, being amused, and being touched, is it not then as questionable to say that the judgment of the public when it is under the influence of emotion, is false and mistaken, as to maintain that a certain kind of drama, which has made its emotional appeal and succeeded in pleasing, generally speaking, a whole nation, and yet is not of sufficient value and dignity for this nation? What importance are we to attach to the satires of certain writers on the *Serious Drama*, as against the weight of public taste, especially when the shafts of ridicule are directed against charming plays written in this style by the satirists themselves? The light and playful touch of sarcasm may be reasonable and consistent, but it has never decided an important question: its only reason for existence is that it merely starts discussions; it should only be permitted when it is directed against cowardly adversaries who, firmly entrenched behind a heap of authorities, refuse to struggle and reason in the open. . . . I have heard important-

sounding words in connection with the sort of play I am discussing, and seen arrayed before me, opposing my plea for the serious play, Aristotle, the ancients, the *Poetics*, "the laws of the drama," the rules, above all, the rules — the eternal common meeting-ground of the critics, the scarecrow of ordinary minds. In what branch of art have rules ever produced masterpieces? Is it not rather the great examples which from the very beginnings have served as a basis of these rules, which are, inverting the natural order of things, brought forward as a positive hindrance to genius? Would mankind ever have advanced in the arts and sciences, if they had servilely followed the misleading and confining precepts laid down by their predecessors? The New World would still be utterly unknown to us had the hardy Genoese navigator not spurned the *Nec plus ultra* of the Pillars of Hercules. Was *that* rule not presumptuous and misleading? Genius that is ever on the alert for something new, that is impatient, that chafes under the restrictions of what is already known, suspects something more, something beyond the known; agitated and set in motion by this impelling force, the genius, his mind in torment, impatient, struggling to free himself, grows; and finally, breaking down the barrier of prejudice, he presses forward, out beyond the known borders. Sometimes he loses his way, but still it is he alone who carries the beacon far into the night of the possible, toward which others strive to follow him. He has made a giant stride, and the outposts of art are advanced. I must stop at this point, for I have no desire to enter into a heated argument; I wish merely to reason calmly. Let us reduce to simple terms a great question which has not hitherto been decided. If I were to submit it to a tribunal of reason, I should state it in this way: *Is it permissible to interest a theater audience and make it shed tears over a situation which, if it occurred in everyday life, would never fail to produce the same effect upon each individual in that audience?* For that, in fine, is the object of well-intentioned, *Serious Drama.*

If there exists a person so barbarous,

so classic, who would dare maintain the opposite, I should like to ask him whether he does not take the word "drama" or "play" to mean a truthful picture of the actions of human beings? He ought to read the novels of Richardson; these are true dramas, since the drama is the conclusion, the most interesting moment in every novel. He should be told, if he does not know, that many scenes in *L'Enfant prodigue*, all of *Nanine*, *Mélanide*, *Célie*, *Le Père de famille*, *L'Ecossaise*, *Le Philosophe sans le savoir*, are living proofs of the beautiful treatment of which the *Serious* form is susceptible; that these have taught us to enjoy the touching spectacle of domestic unhappiness, which has all the greater claim upon our attention because it is something which is more likely to enter our own lives. Results of this sort can never elsewhere be hoped for — at least to so great a degree — in the vast panorama of heroic tragedy.

Before proceeding any farther, I may say that what I am about to discuss does not apply to our celebrated writers of tragedy: they would have shone bright in any other career: genius is born of itself, it owes nothing to the themes which it treats, and is universal in its application. I am discussing fundamentals, respecting the authors at the same time. I am comparing dramatic forms, not individual dramatic talents. This is what I have to say:

The essential object of the *Serious Drama* is to furnish a more direct and appealing interest, a morality which is more applicable than can be found in heroic tragedy; and, everything else being equal, a more profound impression than light comedy.

And now I hear a thousand voices raised against me crying, "Impious!" but I ask in all fairness to be heard, before you pronounce the anathema. These ideas are too new not to demand further development.

When I see the ancient tragedies, I am seized with a feeling of personal indignation against the cruel gods who allow such terrible calamities to be heaped upon the innocent. Œdipus, Jocasta, Phædra, Ariadne, Philoctetes, Orestes, and many others, inspire more terror in me than interest. Devoted

passive beings, blind instruments of the wrath and caprice of the gods, I am more horrified at, than compassionate toward them. Everything in these plays seems monstrous to me: unbridled passions, atrocious crimes, these are as far from being natural as they are unusual in the civilization of our time. In all these tragedies we pass through nothing but ruins, oceans of blood, heaps of slain, and arrive at the catastrophe only by way of poisoning, murder, incest, and parricide. The tears shed are forced, they seldom flow, and when they do, they are burning hot: they cause the forehead to contract before tears finally flow. Unbelievably great efforts are necessary to force them, so that only the very greatest geniuses are able to accomplish the feat.

And then, the inevitable tragedies of destiny offer no moral struggle. When one can only tremble and be silent, is not thinking the very worst thing to do? If one could evolve some sort of moral from a play of this sort, it is a terrible moral, and would indubitably encourage as many to commit crimes who might urge fate as an excuse, as it would discourage to follow in the paths of virtue, because according to this system all our efforts mean nothing at all. If it be true that no virtue can be attained without sacrifice, then it must equally stand to reason that no sacrifice can be made without hope of reward. A belief in fatalism degrades man, because it takes his personal liberty from him; and without this, there is no morality in his acts.

If we inquire into what sort of interest is aroused in us by the heroes and kings of heroic tragedy, we will soon see that the situations and pompous characters which it presents to us are no more than traps laid for our vanity; they seldom appeal to the heart. Our vanity is flattered when we are made to participate in the secrets of a magnificent court, to be present at a council which is to revolutionize the state, to enter a private room of the queen, whom in actual life we should scarcely be allowed to see.

We delight in believing ourself the confidant of an unhappy prince, because his sorrows, his tears, his weaknesses, seem to bring his position in life much nearer to our own, or else console us for being so far beneath him; and, without our being aware, each of us seeks to widen his sphere, and our pride is nourished by the pleasure we experience in judging, in the theater, these masters of the world who, anywhere else, might well walk over without noticing us. Men deceive themselves more easily than they are apt to imagine: the wisest among them is often affected by motives which, if he thought of them, would cause him to blush for shame. But if emotions enter into the interest we take in the characters of a tragedy, the reason is less because those characters are heroes and kings than that they are unfortunate men. Is it the Queen of Messina who appeals to my emotions in *Merope?* No, it is the mother of Ægisthus: nature alone claims sovereignty over our hearts.

If the drama be a faithful picture of what occurs in human society, the interest aroused in us must of necessity be closely related to our manner of observing real objects. Now, I have often noticed that a great prince, at the very height of happiness, glory, and success, excited in us nothing but the barren sentiment of admiration, which is a stranger to the heart. We perhaps never feel how dear to us he is until he falls into some disgrace. This touching enthusiasm of the people, who praise and reward good kings, never takes root in their hearts except when they realize that their king is unhappy, or when they feel they may lose him. Then their compassion for the suffering man is so true and deep that it almost seems to compensate the king for all his lost happiness. The true heart-interest, the real relationship, is always between man and man, and not between man and king. And so, far from increasing my interest in the characters of tragedy, their exalted rank rather diminishes it. The nearer the suffering man is to my station in life, the greater is his claim upon my sympathy. "Would it not be better," asks M. Rousseau, "for our authors of the sublime to descend a little from their continual elevation, and make us sympathize occasionally with suffering humanity; for fear that as a result of

enlisting our sympathy for unhappy heroes, we may end by feeling sympathy for no one at all?"

What do I care, I, a peaceful subject in an eighteenth century monarchy, for the revolutions of Athens and Rome? Of what real interest to me is the death of a Pelopennesian tyrant, or the sacrifice of a young princess at Aulis? There is nothing in that for me; no morality which is applicable to my needs. For what is morality? It is the fruitful result and individual application of certain mental deductions occasioned by an actual occurrence. What is interest? It is the involuntary sensation by which we adapt that occurrence to our own ends; it puts us in the place of him who suffers, throws us into the situation for the time being. A random comparison, taken from nature, will make this idea clear to every one.

Why does the story of the earthquake which swallowed up Lima and its inhabitants, three thousand leagues away, trouble me, while the story of the political murder of Charles I, which was committed at London, merely arouse my indignation? Because the volcano which engulfed the Peruvian city might explode under Paris, and bury me beneath ruins — possibly I am threatened even at this moment; whereas I cannot conceive of a misfortune similar to the unheard-of tragedy of the King of England's happening to me. This sentiment lies in the heart of every man; it serves as basis to this absolute principle of art, that there can be neither interest nor moral appeal on the stage without some sort of connection existing between the subject of the play and ourselves. Now, it is an obvious fact that heroic tragedy appeals to us only in so far as it resembles the *Serious Drama*, and portrays men and not kings. The subjects which it treats are so foreign to our customs and manners, and the characters so different from ourselves, that the interest aroused is less vital than that in the *Serious Drama;* the moral less poignant, more abstract, so that it often remains sterile and useless to us, unless it console us for our mediocrity, in showing us that great crimes and misfortunes are the lot of those who govern the world.

After what I have said, I do not think it necessary to prove that there is more interest to be derived from the *Serious Drama* than from comedy. Every one is aware that, granting each play is of equal merit in its respective field, the *Serious Play* with an emotional appeal affects us more deeply than that which is merely amusing. It now remains for me to develop the reasons for this effect, which is as palpable as it is natural, and to inquire into the morality of the matter by comparing the two forms.

Gayety serves as a distraction for us: in one way or another it takes our souls and spreads them round about us: people never truly laugh except when they are together. But if the gay spirit of ridicule amuses us for an instant, experience teaches that the laugh which is aroused by a satiric shaft dies as it reaches its victim, without ever rebounding and affecting ourselves. Pride, zealously avoiding the personal application, hides itself amid the uproar of the assembled audience, and takes advantage of the general tumult to cast out all that might be of value to us in a sharp epigram. If matters went no further, the evil would not be irremediable, so long as the dramatist holds up to public ridicule only such types as the pedant, the blockhead, the coquette, the pretentious man, the fool, the puppet — in a word, all those who in the life of our day are ridiculous. But is the mockery which chastises them the proper weapon with which to attack vice? Can a dramatist smite his victim with a joke? Not only would he fail to fulfill his purpose, he would achieve the exact opposite of what he set out to accomplish. We see this happen in most comic pieces: to the shame of his moral sense, the spectator often finds himself sympathizing with the rascal against the honest man, because the latter is always rendered the less attractive of the two. But if the gayety of the play has succeeded in sweeping me along for a moment, it is not long, however, before I experience a sense of humiliation at having allowed myself to be ensnared by witty lines and stage tricks; and I leave the theater displeased with the author and with myself. The essential morality of the comic play is

therefore either very shallow, or else nothing at all; or finally it produced just the result which it should not produce.

Not so with a drama which appeals to our emotions, whose subject-matter is taken from our daily life. If loud laughter is the enemy of reflection, pity, on the other hand, induces silence: it invites us to meditate, and isolates us from distracting externals. He who weeps at a play is alone; and the more deeply he feels, the more genuine is his pleasure, especially in the *Serious Drama*, which moves us by true and natural means. Often, in the midst of an amusingly pleasant scene, some charming bit of emotion causes abundant and ready tears to fall, which, mingling with a graceful smile, bring sympathy and joy to the face of the spectator. Is not a touching conflict of this sort the greatest triumph of art, as well as the sweetest sensation that can be experienced by a person of sensibility?

Sympathy has this advantage over the spirit of ridicule, that it is never aroused in us without the concomitant quality of realization, which is made all the more powerful as it appeals to us directly, on the stage.

When we see an honest man who is unhappy we are touched: the spectacle opens our heart, takes possession of it, and finally forces us to examine our inmost conscience. When I see virtue persecuted, made a victim by wickedness, and yet remaining beautiful, glorious, and preferable to everything else, even when it is surrounded by misfortune — when all this is portrayed in a drama, then I am assured that that drama is not "equivocal": I am interested in virtue alone. And then, if I am not happy myself, if base envy does her best to influence me, if she attacks my person, my fortune, and my honor, then how much more interest do I take in that sort of play! And what a splendid moral can I take from it! The subject is one to interest me, naturally: since I am interested only in those who are unhappy and who suffer unjustly, I ask myself whether as a result of some carelessness of character, some fault in my conduct, some excessive ambition, or dishonorable conspiracy, I have called down upon my own head the hatred which pursues me. In any event, I shall be induced to correct my faults, and I shall leave the theater a better man than I entered, merely because I shall have been moved to tenderness and sympathy.

If the injury that has been done me cries aloud for justice, and is more the fault of others than myself, then the lesson derived from the drama will be the more consoling to me. I shall look into my own heart with pleasure, and if I conclude that I have done my full duty toward society, if I am a good parent, a just master, a kind friend, an upright man and a useful citizen, my spiritual satisfaction consoling me for injuries received from others, I shall then all the more appreciate the play which I have witnessed, because it will recall to me that in the pursuit of virtue I find the greatest happiness to which a wise man can attain: contentment with himself, and I shall return again to shed sweet tears at the spectacle of innocence and persecuted virtue. . . .

The noble and Serious drama has been criticized in turn for lacking stamina, warmth, power, and the comic element. . . . Let us see how far this criticism is justified. Every form which is too new to contain definite rules according to which it can be discussed, is judged by analogy according to the general rules governing human nature. Let us apply this method to the case in question. The *Serious* emotional drama stands midway between heroic tragedy and light comedy. If I consider that part of it which touches upon tragedy, I ask myself: do the warmth and power of a character in a play arise from his position in the state, or from the depths of his own character? A cursory glance at the models which real life furnishes to art (which is imitative), reveals that a powerful character is no more the sole possession of a prince than of any one else. Three men spring forth from the heart of Rome, and divide the world among them. The first is a pusillanimous coward; the second, valiant, presumptuous and fierce; the third, a clever rascal, who outwits the other two. But Lepidus, Antony, and Octavius, when they formed the Triumvirate, possessed characters which alone decided the different

parts they were to play in their common usurpation. The softness of the first, the violence of the second, and the cleverness of the other — all these would have had their effect had it been merely a question of private succession among them. Every man is what he is because of his character; as to his station in life, that is determined by destiny; but a man's character can influence that station in life to a considerable extent. Hence, the *Serious Drama,* which shows me men who are moved by situations, is as susceptible of power, dynamic force, and elevation of thought, as heroic tragedy, which likewise shows me men who are moved, but who are above men in the ordinary walks of life. And if I consider that part of the *Serious* and noble drama which touches upon comedy, I cannot deny that the *vis comica* is indispensable to all good comedies; but then I may ask why the *Serious Drama* is criticized for a lack of warmth, which, if it exists, can be only the result of a lack of skill on the part of the dramatist? Since plays of this sort deal with people taken out of every-day life — as in light comedy — ought these characters to be treated with any less vigor, portrayed any the less forcibly, when the situation in which they find themselves involves their honor, or life itself, than when these same characters are involved in matters of less moment — say, in simple ordinary embarrassments of one kind or another, or even in comic situations? And even if all the dramas which I have referred to lack comic elements (which I am gravely inclined to doubt) . . . even then, the question revolves upon the ability or shortcomings of individual dramatists and not upon the dramatic form as such, which is in itself less bombastic and may be thought of as containing the best fiber of any. . . .

My task will have advanced considerably, if I have succeeded in convincing my readers that the *Serious Drama* exists, that it is a good form, that its interest is lively, that it contains a direct and profound appeal to the moral sense, that it can have but one style, that of nature; that, besides enjoying the advantages common to other dramatic forms, it possesses a beauty all its own;

that it blazes a new trail in the realm of the drama, where genius may soar to heights unknown before, because the form treats all sides of life, and therefore contains every possible situation therein. And once again the dramatist will be able to succeed by utilizing the great figures of comedy, which have by now been nearly exhausted because the situations in which they have figured are out-worn. Finally, the *Serious Drama* is an endless source of amusement and morality for society in general. . . . A theory of art may evolve as the result of study and reflection, but the production of a work of art belongs only to genius, which cannot be taught.

DEDICATORY LETTER

TO THE BARBER OF SEVILLE [2]

[*Lettre Modérée sur la Chûte et la Critique du Barbier de Séville*]

(1775)

. . . I succumbed to the temptation, at two different times in the past, Monsieur, to present you with two pathetic dramas: monstrous, hybrid productions because, as is well known, there is no mean way between comedy and tragedy. The question has been decided: the master has pronounced finally upon it, and the school reëchoes with his words. And as for myself, I am so far convinced that if I wished now to portray on the stage a distressed mother, a betrayed wife, a distracted sister, or a disinherited son, I should, in order that they might decently be put before the public, begin by giving each a kingdom where they will have reigned wisely — in some distant archipelago or other far corner of the world; and be certain thereafter that the improbability of the fable, the exaggerated situations and characters, the outlandish ideas and bombast of speech, far from being a reason of reproach to me, will assure my success.

Portray ordinary men and women in difficulties and sorrow? Nonsense! Such ought only to be scoffed at. Ridiculous citizens and unhappy kings, these are the only characters fit for treatment on the stage; such is the case, and I have no quarrel with any one.

As I say, I formerly succumbed to the temptation to write plays, monsieur, which were not in the true accepted form, and I am duly repentant.

Circumstances changed and I hazarded writing those unhappy *Mémoires,* which

2 Here translated, by the editor, for the first time.— Ed.

my enemies declared were not written in good style; I am consumed by cruel remorse.

To-day I offer for your inspection an exceedingly gay comedy, which certain arbiters of taste consider is not *de bon ton;* I am inconsolable. . . .

Next to commanding men, is not the greatest honor, monsieur, to judge them? Of course. Now, I recognize no other judge than you, not excepting the esteemed spectators who, basing their opinions on a first impression, often find their verdict nullified before your tribunal.

The case was first plead before them in the theater, and the spectators having laughed generously, I assumed that I had gained my cause with them. Nothing of the kind: a journalist who lives at Bouillon maintains that it was at me that the audience laughed. But what he said was only, as they say at the courts, the poor quibble of a lawyer, for my purpose was to amuse the audience, and whether they laughed at me or at the play, so long as they laughed wholeheartedly, my purpose has been accomplished. I call that having gained my cause with the audience. . . .

Plays, monsieur, are like children: conceived with pleasure, carried about before they are born with great fatigue, and brought forth in pain; scarcely ever do they recompense their parents, and they cost more sorrow than they give delight. Follow the career of a play; hardly does it see the light of day when, under the pretext that it is bombastic, the censors attack it; and so many a play is legally " detained." Instead of quietly enjoying a play, the parterre jeers at it and causes it to fail. Often, instead of helping, nursing it along, the actor lames it. If you once lose it from view, you will find it again, alas! anywhere, everywhere, disfigured, tattered, cut, and covered with critical remarks. Finally escaping so many ills, if it shines for a moment in public, then the greatest ill of all overtakes it: mortal oblivion kills it. So these plays die, return to the vast void, lost forever in the huge mass of books. . . .

And now, if you please, let us see whether this critic from Bouillon has maintained that much-to-be-desired character of amiability, and above all, candor.

He says: " The play is a farce."

We shall not quibble about names. The malicious word which a foreign cook uses to designate French ragouts does not change the taste; *that* is done only in passing through his hands. Let us proceed with Bouillon's farce.

He says: " The play has no form."

Is the play so simple that it escapes the sagacity of the adolescent critic?

An amorous old man intends to marry his ward to-morrow; a young lover, who is much cleverer, forestalls him, and that very day makes the girl his wife in the house and before the very eyes of the guardian. That is the basis of the play, of which might have been made, with equal success, a tragedy, a comedy, a drama, an opera, and so on. Is *L'Avare* of Molière anything else? Or *Le Grand Mithridate?* The actual form of a play, or any other sort of literature, depends less on the action than on the characters which set that action into play.

As for myself, since I intended to write nothing but an amusing play, one that could not cause fatigue, a sort of *imbroglio,* it was enough that the character about whom the action centered should be a droll fellow in place of a black villain; a carefree man who laughs alike at the success or failure of his enterprises. I wished only that the play should, far from becoming a serious drama, be merely a gay comedy. And just because the guardian is not quite so stupid as the greater part of such characters who are seen in the theater, there has resulted a great deal of movement, as well as the necessity for greater relief to those engaged in the intrigue. . . .

GERMANY II

ROMANTIC AND MODERN PERIOD

MODERN GERMAN DRAMATIC CRITICISM

The period before Lessing was one of groping; he it was who gave the necessary impetus to original composition in criticism and the drama. His own plays — particularly *Minna von Barnhelm* (1767), *Emilia Galotti* (1772), and *Nathan der weise* (1779) — were works of high quality. With Lessing the modern German drama was born. His criticism marked the beginning of an era which has not yet ended. During his lifetime the Romantic movement began. The inspiration was received chiefly from England, whose literature — especially Shakespeare — was read and admired. Klopstock, an epic, lyric, and dramatic poet belonged partly to the Gottsched group and partly to the new. A younger man, Wieland, exerted widespread influence in his dramatic reviews and general writings. He also translated twenty-two of Shakespeare's plays (between 1762 and 1766); the translations were not particularly good, though they undoubtedly affected the writers of his time. Next in importance to Lessing, however, was Johann Gottfried Herder, who first showed the way to original composition in his trenchant criticisms and Shakespeare study. His influence on the young Goethe was inestimable, and the *Sturm und Drang* Period dates from his meeting with the young poet at Strassburg in 1770–71. He wrote an essay on Shakespeare (1773), in which he attacked the French critical canons and demanded that Shakespeare should be judged on his own great merits. The *Sturm und Drang* was a period of violent reaction against the fetters and conventions of life and art. Shakespeare was the idol of the younger men, and Shakespeare study dates from these days. Goethe was strongly influenced by Shakespeare and an early play, *Götz von Berlichingen* (1773) was one of the results of his study of the English poet. There soon followed other romantic works, the novel of *Werther* (1774), the play *Clavigo* (1774) and the first sketch of *Faust* (1790). Then came the impetuous Schiller, whose play *Die Räuber* (1781) sounded a blast to the new Romantics. The *Prefaces* are documents of considerable interest. With this play and with its immediate successors, *Fiesco* (1783), and *Kabale und Liebe* (1784), it may be said that modern German poetic drama was born. The last play of Lessing, *Nathan der weise,* had appeared in 1779; Goethe's *Iphigenie* and Schiller's *Don Carlos* belong to the late eighties, as well as Goethe's *Torquato Tasso.* Goethe meanwhile had been contributing numerous articles on the drama, and strengthening the Shakespeare interest in his various versions of the *Wilhelm Meister* novel. Schiller had during the nineties delved into philosophy and æsthetics and delivered lectures and written essays on tragic art and the function of the drama, etc. The best of these are the *Ueber den Grund des Vergnügens an tragischen Gegenständen* (1792), and *Ueber die tragische Kunst,* of the same year. His last years were devoted to the writing of *Wallenstein* (1800) and *Wilhelm Tell.* His death in 1805 cut short his brilliant career. For over a score of years Goethe continued to evolve his dramatic theories, but long before his death the Schlegels, August Wilhelm and Karl Wilhelm Friedrich, had begun their celebrated translations of Shakespeare, and in 1798 founded the *Athenæum,* which is usually regarded as the beginning of the truly modern Romantic movement, the influence of which was felt, through Coleridge, even in England. The brothers published in 1801 their joint work, *Charakteristiken,* containing their various literary theories, and in 1809 and 1811 August Wilhelm issued his famous lectures *Vorlesungen über dramatische Kunst und*

Literatur. Among the contributors to the *Athenæum* was Novalis [Friedrich von Hardenberg], whose fragmentary remarks on Shakespeare are among the most interesting of the time. Schubarth, Uhland, and Solger belong to the period, and all made contributions to the subject. Ludwig Tieck, who collaborated in the Schlegel translation of Shakespeare, in his *Kritische Schriften* (1848–52), and his *Nachgelassene Schriften* (1855), contributed generously to dramatic criticism, especially to the subject of Shakespeare and the pre-Shakespearian drama. Among the writers on pure æsthetics, Hegel may be mentioned (though his work falls outside the scope of this collection), and Jean-Paul Richter, whose *Vorschule der Æsthetik* was published in 1813. The Austrian dramatist Franz Grillparzer wrote a number of critical reviews, essays, and the like, on the drama, the best of which are the *Zur Dramaturgie* (from 1817 on, in the *Æsthetische Studien*), the *Studien zur griechischen Literatur* (about 1860), and on other literatures; the *Studien zum spanischen Theater* (written at various times) and the *Studien zur deutschen Literatur.* It is perhaps unnecessary to mention in detail the various Shakespeare scholars, like Gervinus, and the æstheticians like Carriere. Friedrich Hebbel, the dramatist, wrote at great length on his art, and the preface to *Maria Magdalena* (1844), *Mein Wort über das Drama* (1843), and his criticisms of Kleist and Körner, went far to establish the Middle-class Drama of which he was the chief exponent. Richard Wagner carried the drama into the realm of the music-drama, and offered many ingenious and some absurd suggestions as to the Artwork of the Future. His *Oper und Drama* (1851), and later tract, *Ueber die Bestimmung der Oper* (1871) undoubtedly revolutionized the opera form; whether it effected a great change in the drama it is difficult to determine. A decidedly different theorist was the novelist and dramatist Gustav Freytag, whose *Technik des Dramas* appeared in 1863. Until recently this work was a standard. Friedrich Nietzsche's *Die Geburt der Tragödie* (1877) is one of the most interesting works on the drama, but it is largely æsthetic in character. The past fifty years have witnessed the publication of many hundreds of works on the drama, to the most important of which it is possible only to refer in passing: Theodor Fontane's dramatic criticisms (in the *Gesammelte Werke,* 1905–12); Ernst von Wildenbruch's *Das deutsche Drama* (1900); Otto Brahm's *Kritische Schriften über Drama und Theater* (1913); Heinrich Bulthaupt's four volumes of *Dramaturgie des Schauspiels* (1894–1908); Hugo Dinger's *Dramaturgie als Wissenschaft* (1904–05); A. Perger's *System der dramatische Technik* (1909); Paul Ernst's *Der Weg zum Form* (1906); Julius Bab's *Kritik der Bühne* (1908); *Wege zum Drama* (1906) and *Neue Wege zum Drama* (1911); Maximilian Harden's *Literatur und Theater* (1896); Hermann Schlag's *Das Drama* (1909); Eugen Zabel's volumes *Zur modernen Dramaturgie* (1899, etc.); Arno Holz's *Die Kunst* and *Neue Folge* (1891 and 1893); Hermann Bahr's *Wiener Theater* (1899); *Dialog vom Tragischen* (1904); and Frank Wedekind's *Schauspielkunst* (1910).

General references on modern German literature:

Adolf Bartels, *Die neuere Literatur* (vol. 2 of the *Geschichte der deutschen Literatur,* 5th and 6th ed., Leipzig, 1909).
Alfred Biese, *Deutsche Literaturgeschichte,* vol. 3 (Leipzig, 1910).
M. Koch, *Nationalität und Nationalliteratur* (Berlin, 1891).
G. Brandes, *The Main Currents of Nineteenth Century Literature,* 5 vols. (New York, 1906).
J. Hillebrand, *Die deutsche Nationalliteratur im 18. und 19. Jahrhundert,* 3 vols. (3rd ed., Gotha, 1875).
R. von Gottschall, *Die deutsche Nationalliteratur des 19. Jahrhunderts,* 4 vols. (5th ed., Breslau, 1881).
Friedrich Kummer, *Deutsche Literatur des 19. Jahrhunderts* (Dresden, 1909).
Richard M. Meyer, *Die deutsche Litera-*

MODERN GERMAN DRAMATIC CRITICISM 315

Adolf Stern, Geschichte der neueren Literatur (Leipzig, 1882-85).

——,Die deutsche Nationalliteratur von Tode Goethes bis zur Gegenwart (Marburg, 1886).

Karl Storck, Deutsche Literaturgeschichte (6th and 7th ed., Stuttgart, 1913).

Georg Witkowski, Die Entwicklung der deutschen Literatur seit 1830 (Leipzig, 1912).

Eugen Wolff, Geschichte der deutschen Literatur in der Gegenwart (Leipzig, 1896).

H. H. Boyesen, Essays on German Literature (New York, 1892).

General references on German drama since Lessing:

Heinrich Bulthaupt, Dramaturgie des Schauspiels, 4 vols. (12th ed., Oldenburg, 1908).

Arthur Eloesser, Das bürgerliche Drama. Seine Geschichte im 18. und 19, Jahrhundert (Berlin, 1898).

Karl Frenzel, Berliner Dramaturgie, 2 vols. (Erfurt, 1877).

Gustav Freytag, Die Technik des Dramas (Leipzig, 1863. Translated as The Technique of the Drama, by Elias J. MacEwan, Chicago, 1895ff).

——, Aufsätze zur Geschichte, Literatur, und Kunst (Leipzig, 1888).

Robert Prölss, Geschichte des neueren Dramas, 3 vols. (Leipzig, 1880-83).

Edgar Steiger, Das Werden des neueren Dramas, 2 vols. (Berlin, 1903).

Georg Witkowski, Das deutsche Drama des neunzehnten Jahrhunderts in seiner Entwicklung dargestellt (2nd ed., Leipzig, 1906. Translated by L. E. Horning as The German Drama of the Nineteenth Century, New York, 1909).

Wilhelm Kosch, Das deutsche Theater und Drama im 19. Jahrhundert (Leipzig, 1913).

Ernst von Wildenbruch, Das deutsche Drama (Leipzig, 1906).

Robert Petsch, Deutsche Dramaturgie von Lessing bis Hebbel (Berlin, 1912).

Max Martersteig, Das deutsche Theater im 19. Jahrhundert (Leipzig, 1904).

S. Friedmann, Das deutsche Drama des neunzehnten Jahrhunderts, Neuere und neuste Zeit (11th ed., Berlin, 1904).

Paul Reiff, Views of Tragedy Among the Early German Romanticists (in Modern Language Notes, 1904).

Hermann Bahr, Zur Kritik der Moderne (Zurich, 1889).

——, Die Ueberwindung des Naturalismus (Dresden, 1891).

——, Studien zur Kritik der Moderne (Frankfurt, 1894).

——, Wiener Theater (1892-98) (Berlin, 1899).

——, Premieren (München, 1902).

——, Dialog vom Tragischen (Berlin, 1904).

Julius Bab, Wege zum Drama (Berlin, 1906).

——, Neue Wege zum Drama (Berlin, 1911).

——, Kritik der Bühne (Berlin, 1908).

Louis Benoist-Hanappier, Le Drame naturaliste en Allemagne (Paris, 1905).

Otto Heller, Studies in Modern German Literature (Boston, 1905).

A. von Berger, Dramaturgische Vorträge (Wien, 1890-91).

A. Berger, Meine Hamburgische Dramaturgie (Wien, 1910).

Otto Brahm, Kritische Schriften über Drama und Theater (Berlin, 1913).

Max Bürger, Dramaturgisches (Leipzig, 1910).

Rudolf von Gottschall, Zur Kritik des modernen Literatur (12th ed., Berlin, 1900).

A. von Hanstein, Das jüngste Deutschland (Leipzig, 1905).

Alfred Kerr, Das neue Drama (Berlin, 1909).

Berthold Litzmann, Das deutsche Drama in den literarischen Bewegungen der Gegenwart (4th ed., Hamburg, 1897).

Robert F. Arnold, Das moderne Drama (Strassburg, 1912).

——, Bibliographie der deutschen Bühnen seit 1830 (Strassburg, 1909).

Percival Pollard, Masks and Minstrels of New Germany (Boston, 1911).

Ludwig Lewisohn, The Modern Drama (New York, 1915).

——, The Spirit of Modern German Literature (New York, 1917).

Barrett H. Clark, A Study of the Modern Drama (2nd ed., New York, 1928).

Alfred Stoeckius, Naturalism in the Recent German Drama with special reference to Gerhart Hauptmann (New York, 1903).

Robert Ress, *Arno Holz und seine künstleriche und weltkulturelle Bedeutung* (Dresden, 1913).

Arno Holz, *Die Kunst, ihr Wesen und ihre Gesetze* (Berlin, 1891).

——, *Neue Folge* (Berlin, 1893).

Paul Schlenther, *Gerhart Hauptmann, Leben und Werke* (new ed., Berlin, (1912).

Friedrich Spielhagen, *Neue Beiträge zur Theorie und Technik der Epik und Dramatik* (Leipzig, 1898).

Hermann Sudermann, *Verrohung in der Theater Kritik* (Stuttgart, 1902).

Frank Wedekind, *Schauspielkunst* (München, 1910).

Eugen Killian, *Aus der Praxis der moderne Dramaturgie* (München, 1914).

——, *Dramaturgische Blätter* (*Erste Reihe*) (München, 1905).

Walther Lohmeyer, *Die Dramaturgie der Massen* (Berlin, 1913).

Bertha E. Trebein, *Theodor Fontane as a Critic of the Drama* [bibliographies] (New York, 1916).

FRIEDRICH VON SCHILLER

Johann Christoph Friedrich von Schiller was born at Marbach on the Neckar, in 1759. His father was an officer in the army, and it was while the family was in residence at Ludwigsburg and Lorch that the young Friedrich received his early education. In 1773 the Duke of Württemberg took the young man into his military school near Ludwigsburg, and taught him law. Two years after the school was transferred to Stuttgart, where Schiller was allowed to change his study to that of medicine, which was more congenial. In 1776 his first poetic efforts appeared in magazine form, and two years later he finished his first play, *Die Räuber.* In 1780 he was graduated as a surgeon, and given a position with a regiment quartered in Stuttgart. The following year he published *Die Räuber,* which was well received. In 1782 it was produced in Mannheim. The young poet's visits to Mannheim, and what was considered an uncomplimentary reference to one of the Duke's contemporaries, incurred that nobleman's displeasure, and Schiller was placed under arrest and subsequently forbidden to leave the city. But later in the year he escaped and went to Mannheim, and thence to Bauerbach, where he finished *Kabale und Liebe* and began *Don Carlos.* The next year he was appointed "Theater poet" at Mannheim. He published meantime an address on the theater, *Die Schaubühne als eine moralische Anstalt betrachtet* (1784). The next year he left Mannheim and spent the summer near Leipzig, writing poetry and resting. Thence he went to Dresden with Körner, a friend who in many ways directed the education of the poet. In 1787 he went to Weimar, where he met Herder and Wieland. The next year he published the first part of his history of the Netherlands, for which, upon Goethe's recommendation, he was made a professor at Jena in 1789. In 1790 he married Charlotte von Lengefeld. Then followed sickness and financial troubles, but these latter were relieved for a time by his noble protectors. He continued his philosophic and æsthetic studies, publishing various lectures in 1792 and 1793. For some time he had edited a journal, and in 1794 he founded another, *Die Horen,* which brought him into close relations with Goethe. The two became friends and collaborators. *Die Horen* gave way to another journal in 1797, the *Musenalmanach,* in which he published many of his best lyrics. Between 1799 and 1804 he returned to the drama, and wrote the *Wallenstein* plays, *Maria Stuart, Die Jungfrau von Orleans, Wilhelm Tell,* and others of less importance. His last years were marked by ill-health and considerable popularity. In 1802 he was ennobled. He died at Weimar in 1805.

Schiller's æsthetic essays are his best-known contribution to criticism, although his occasional reviews and prefaces contain a considerable amount of pure dramatic criticism. His two important essays on the drama — *Ueber den Grund des Vergnügens an tragischen Gegenständen,* and *Ueber die tragische Kunst* — first appeared in the *Neue Thalia* in 1792. In the first of these essays the poet endeavors to prove that the sole end of tragic art is to give pleasure. The second is partly theoretical and partly practical. It is interesting to know that Schiller at this time was not acquainted with Aristotle's *Poetics.* On the whole, Schiller's theories on dramatic art are not of the epoch-making sort; Lessing was an incontestably greater critic, but Schiller's theories are significant as showing the close connection between the study of philosophy (Schiller was an ardent admirer of Kant) and the drama.

On the drama:

Vorrede to *Die Räuber* (1781).
Ueber das gegenwärtige deutsche Theater (1782).
Die Schaubühne als eine moralische Anstalt betrachtet (1784).
Vorrede to *Die Verschwörung des Fiesco zu Genova* (1787).
Briefe über Don Carlos (1788).
Ueber Egmont, Trauerspiel von Goethe (1788).
Ueber den Grund des Vergnügens an tragischen Gegenständer (1792).
Ueber die tragische Kunst (1792).
(The *Kleinere Schriften* contain a few minor reviews of plays. See, among these: *Erste Vorrede der " Räuber"; Vorrede zur zweiten Auflage der " Räuber"; Ueber die " Räuber"; Anhang über die Vorstellung der "Räuber";* and *Ankündigung der Rheinischen Thalia.*)

Editions:

The first so-called complete edition of Schiller was the Körner edition, 12 volumes published by Cotta (Stuttgart, 1812–15). This was supplemented by additional material in Hoffmeister's *Supplemente zu Schillers Werken* (1840–41). Goedeke's edition of the *Sämtliche Schriften,* 15 volumes, appeared at Stuttgart between 1868 and 1876. Among the best modern editions are those under the supervision of Boxberger and Birlingen, in 12

voumes (Stuttgart, 1882–91), and L. Bellermann, in 14 volumes (Leipzig, 1895 and following). The latest critical edition is that from the house of Cotta, in 16 volumes (Stuttgart, completed in 1894). The letters are found in Jonas' edition of Schiller's *Brife,* 7 volumes (Stuttgart, 1892ff).
Schiller's Works, translated by several hands, are published in 7 vols., in the Bohn edition. The sixth volume contains the more important essays on the drama: *Essays, Æsthetical and Philosophical.* The *Correspondence Between Schiller and Goethe* is in 2 vols. (same ed.)
There is another edition of the *Complete Works,* edited by Hempel, 2 vols. (Philadelphia, 1879). Also *Schiller's Works,* translated by R. D. Boylan and Joseph Mellish, edited by N. H. Dole (Boston, 1902).

On Schiller and his works:

For bibliography, see Goedeke's *Grundriss zur Geschichte der deutschen Dichtung,* 2te Aufl. (Dresden, 1893), and Nevinson's *Life* (see below).
The first biography was Körner's in his edition (1812–15).
Thomas Carlyle, *Life of Friedrich Schiller* (London, 1825).
Karl Hoffmeister, *Schillers Leben* (in the 1838–42 ed. of the Works.)
H. H. Boyeson, *Goethe and Schiller* (New York, 1882).
Henry W. Nevinson, *Life of Friedrich Schiller* (London, 1889).
K. Berger, *Die Entwicklung von Schilers Æsthetik* (Weimar, 1894).
F. A. Blanchet, *Du Théâtre de Schiller* (Strassburg, 1855).
Wilhelm Bolze, *Schillers philosophische Begründung der Æsthetik der Tragödie* (Leipzig, 1913).
W. G. Howard, *Schiller and Hebbel* (in *Mod. Lang. Ass'n Pubs.,* v. 22, Cambridge, Mass., 1907).
F.-J.-G. Montargis, *L'Esthétique de Schiller* (Paris, 1890).
J. Peterson, *Schiller und die Bühne* (Berlin, 1904).
Calvin Thomas, *The Life and Works of Friedrich Schiller* (New York, 1901).
Georg Brandes, *Wolfgang Goethe,* 2 vols. (New York, 1924).

PREFACE TO THE ROBBERS [1]
[*Vorrede* (to) *Die Räuber*]
(1781)

This play is to be regarded merely as a dramatic narrative in which, for the purposes of tracing out the innermost workings of the soul, advantage has been taken of the dramatic method, without otherwise conforming to the stringent rules of theatrical composition, or seeking the dubious advantage of stage adaptation. It must be admitted as somewhat inconsistent that three very remarkable people, whose acts are dependent on perhaps a thousand contingencies, should be completely developed within three hours, considering that it would scarcely be possible, in the ordinary course of events, that three such remarkable people should, even in twenty-four hours, fully reveal their characters to the most penetrating inquirer. A greater amount of incident is here crowded together than it was possible for me to confine within the narrow limits prescribed by Aristotle or Batteux.

It is, however, not so much the bulk of my play as its contents which banish it from the stage. Its scheme and economy require that several characters should appear who would offend the finer feelings of virtue and shock the delicacy of our manners. Every delineator of human character is placed in the same dilemma if he proposes to give a faithful picture of the world as it really is, and not an ideal fantasy, a mere creation of his own. It is the course of mortal things that the good should be shadowed by the bad, and virtue shine the brightest when contrasted with vice. Whoever proposes to discourage vice and to vindicate religion, morality, and social order against their enemies, must unveil crime in all its deformity and place it before the eyes of men in its colossal magnitude; he must diligently expose its dark mazes, and make himself familiar with sentiments at the wickedness of which his soul revolts.

Vice is here exposed in its innermost workings. In Franz it resolves all the confused terrors of conscience into wild abstractions, destroys virtuous sentiments by dissecting them, and holds up the earnest voice of religion to mockery and scorn. He who has gone so far (a distinction by no means enviable) as to quicken his understanding at the expense of his soul — to him the holiest things are no longer holy; to him God and man are alike indifferent, and both worlds are as nothing. Of such a monster I have endeavored to sketch a striking and lifelike portrait, to hold up to abhorrence all the machinery of his scheme of vice, and to test its strength by contrasting it with truth. How far my narrative is successful in accomplishing these objects, the reader is left to judge. My conviction is that I have painted nature to the life.

Next to this man [Franz] stands another who would perhaps puzzle not a few of my readers. A mind for which the greatest crimes have only charms through the glory which attaches to them, the energy which their perpetuation requires, and the dangers which attend them. A remarkable and important personage, abundantly endowed with the power of becoming either a Brutus or a Catiline, according as that power is directed. An unhappy conjunction of circumstances determines him to choose the latter for his example, and it is only after a fearful straying that he is recalled to emulate the former. Erroneous nations of activity and power, an exuberance of strength which bursts through all the barriers of law, must of necessity conflict with the rules of social life. To these enthusiastic dreams of greatness and efficiency it needed but a sarcastic bitterness against the unpoetic spirit of the age to complete the strange Don Quixote whom, in the Robber Moor, we at once detest and love, admire and pity. It is, I hope, unnecessary to remark that I no more hold up this picture as a warning exclusively to robbers than the greatest Spanish satire was leveled exclusively at knights errant.

[1] Re-printed, complete, from *Schiller's Works*, translated by R. D. Boylan and Joseph Mellish (Boston, 1902).— Ed.

It is nowadays so much the fashion to be witty at the expense of religion that a man will hardly pass for a genius if he does not allow his impious satire to run a tilt at its most sacred truths. The noble simplicity of holy writ must needs be abused and turned into ridicule at the daily assemblies of the so-called wits; for what is there so holy and serious that will not raise a laugh if a false sense be attached to it? Let me hope that I shall have rendered no inconsiderable service to the cause of true religion and morality in holding up these wanton misbelievers to the detestation of society, under the form of the most despicable robbers.

But still more. I have made these said immoral characters to stand out favorably in particular points and even in some measure to compensate by qualities of the head, for they are deficient in those of the heart. Herein I have done no more than literally copy nature. Every man, even the most depraved, bears in some degree the impress of the Almighty's image, and perhaps the greatest villain is not farther removed from the most upright man than the petty offender; for the moral forces keep even pace with the powers of the mind, and the greater the capacity bestowed on man, the greater and more responsible is he for his errors.

The Adramelech of Klopstock (in his *Messiah*) awaken in us a feeling in which admiration is blended with detestation. We follow Milton's Satan with shuddering wonder throughout the pathless realms of chaos. The Medea of the old dramatists, is, in spite of all her crimes, a great and wondrous woman, and Shakespeare's Richard III is sure to excite the admiration of the reader, much as he would hate the reality. If it is to be my task to portray men as they are, I must at the same time include their good qualities, of which even the most vicious are never totally destitute. If I would warn mankind against the tiger, I must not omit to describe his glossy, beautifully marked skin, lest, owing to this omission, the ferocious animal should not be recognized until too late. Besides this, a man who is so utterly depraved as to be without a single redeeming point is no meet subject for art, and

would disgust rather than excite the interest of the reader, who would turn over with impatience the pages which concern him. A noble soul can no more endure a succession of moral discords than the musical ear the grating of knives upon glass.

And for this reason I should have been ill-advised in attempting to bring my drama on the stage A certain strength of mind is required both on the part of the poet and the reader; in the former, that he may not disguise vice, in the latter that he may not suffer brilliant qualities to beguile him into admiration of the essentially detestable. Whether the author has fulfilled his duty he leaves others to judge; that his readers will perform theirs, he by no means feels assured. The vulgar — among whom I would not be understood to mean merely the rabble — the vulgar, I say (between ourselves) extend their influence far around, and unfortunately — set the fashion. Too short-sighted to reach my full meaning, too narrow-minded to comprehend the largeness of my views, too disingenuous to admit my moral aim — they will, I fear, almost frustrate my good intentions, and pretend to discover in my work an apology for the very vice which it has been my object to condemn, and will perhaps make the poor poet, to whom anything rather than justice is usually accorded, responsible for his simplicity.

Thus we have a *Da Capo* of the old story of Democritus and Abdera, and our worthy Hippocrates would need exhaust whole plantations of hellebore, were it proposed to remedy this mischief by a healing decoction. Let as many friends of truth as you will instruct their fellow-citizens in the pulpit and on the stage, the vulgar will never cease to be vulgar, though the sun and moon may change their course, and "heaven and earth wax old as a garment."

Perhaps, in order to please tender-hearted people, I might have been less true to nature; but if a certain beetle, of whom we have all heard, could extract filth even from pearls, if we have examples that fire destroyed and water deluged, shall therefore pearls, fire and water be condemned? In consequence of the remarkable catastrophe which ends my play, I may justly claim for it a place among books of morality, for crime meets at last with the punishment it deserves; the lost one enters again within the pale of the law, and virtue is triumphant. Whoever will but be courteous enough toward me to read my work through with a desire to understand it, from him I may expect — not that he will admire the poet, but that he will esteem the honest man.

ON TRAGIC ART [2]
[*Ueber die tragische Kunst*]
(1792)

. . . . . .

If we now form the proper deductions from the previous investigation, the following will be the conditions that form bases of the tragic art. It is necessary, in the first place, that the object of our pity should belong to our own species — I mean belong in the full sense of the term — and that the action in which it is sought to interest us be a moral action; that is, an action comprehended in the field of free will. It is necessary, in the second place, that suffering, its sources, its degrees, should be completely communicated by a series of events chained together. It is necessary, in the third place, that the object of the passion be rendered present to our senses, not in a mediate way and by description, but immediately and in action. In tragedy, art unites all these conditions and satisfies them.

According to these principles, tragedy might be defined as the poetic imitation of a coherent series of particular events (forming a complete action): an imitation which shows us man in a state of suffering, and which has for its end to excite our pity.

I say first that it is the *imitation* of an action; and this idea of imitation already distinguishes tragedy from the other kinds of poetry, which only narrate or describe. In tragedy, particular events are presented to our imagination or to our senses at the very time of their accomplishment; they are present, we see them immediately, without the intervention of a third person. The epos, the romance, simple narrative, even in their form, withdraw action to a dis-

tance, causing the narrator to come between the acting person and the reader. Now what is distant and past always weakens, as we know, the impression and the sympathetic affection; what is present makes them stronger. All narrative forms make of the present something past; all dramatic form makes of the past a present.

Secondly, I say that tragedy is the imitation of a succession of *events*, of an action. Tragedy has not only to represent by imitation the feelings and the affections of tragic persons, but also the events that have produced these feelings, and the occasion on which these affections are manifested. This distinguishes it from lyric poetry, and from its different forms, which no doubt offer, like tragedy, the poetic imitation of certain states of the mind, but not the poetic imitation of certain actions. An elegy, a song, an ode, can place before our eyes, by imitation, the moral state in which the poet actually is — whether he speaks in his own name, or in that of an ideal person — a state determined by particular circumstances; and up to this point these lyric forms seem certainly to be incorporated in the idea of tragedy; but they do not complete that idea, because they are confined to representing our feelings. There are still more essential differences, if the end of these lyrical forms and that of tragedy are kept in view.

I say, in the third place, that tragedy is the imitation of a complete action. A separate event, though it be ever so tragic, does not in itself constitute a tragedy. To do this, several events are required, based one on the other, like cause and effect, and suitably connected so as to form a whole; without which the

2 Extract re-printed from *Essays, Æsthetical and Philosophical* by Schiller, translated anonymously (London, 1875).— Ed.

truth of the feeling represented, of the character, etc.— that is, their conformity with the nature of our mind, a conformity which alone determines our sympathy — will not be recognized. If we do not feel that we ourselves in similar circumstances should have experienced the same feelings and acted in the same way, our pity would not be awakened. It is, therefore, important that we should be able to follow in all its concatenation the action that is represented to us, that we should see it issue from the mind of the agent by a natural gradation, under the influence and with the concurrence of external circumstances. It is thus that we see spring up, grow, and come to maturity under our eyes, the curiosity of Œdipus and the jealousy of Iago. It is also the only way to fill up the great gap that exists between the joy of an innocent soul and the torments of a guilty conscience, between the proud serenity of the happy man and his terrible catastrophe; in short, between the state of calm, in which the reader is at the beginning, and the violent agitation he ought to experience at the end.

A series of several connected incidents is required to produce in our souls a succession of different movements which arrest the attention, which, appealing to all the faculties of our minds, enliven our instinct of activity when it is exhausted, and which, by delaying the satisfaction of this instinct, do not kindle it the less. Against the suffering of sensuous nature the human heart has only recourse to its moral nature as counterpoise. It is, therefore, necessary, in order to stimulate this in a more pressing manner, for the tragic poet to prolong the torments of sense, but he must also give a glimpse to the latter of the satisfaction of its wants, so as to render the victory of the moral sense so much the more difficult and glorious. This twofold end can only be attained by a succession of actions judiciously chosen and combined to this end.

In the fourth place, I say that tragedy is the poetic *imitation* of an action deserving of pity, and, therefore, tragic imitation is opposed to *historic* imitation. It would only be a historic imitation if it proposed a historic end, if its principal object were to *teach* us that a thing has taken place, and how it took place. On this hypothesis it ought to keep rigorously to historic accuracy, for it would only attain its end by representing faithfully that which really took place. But tragedy has a *poetic* end, that is to say, it represents an action to *move* us, and to *charm* our souls by the medium of this emotion. If, therefore, a matter being given, tragedy treats it conformably with this poetic end which is proper to it, it becomes, by that very thing, free in its imitation. It is a right — nay, more, it is an obligation — for tragedy to subject historic truth to the laws of poetry; and to treat its matter in conformity with requirements of this art. But as it cannot attain its end, which is emotion, except on the condition of a perfect conformity with the laws of nature, tragedy is, notwithstanding its freedom in regard to history, strictly subject to the laws of natural truth, which, in opposition to the truth of history, takes the name of poetic truth. It may thus be understood how much poetic truth may lose, in many cases, by a strict observance of historic truth, and, reciprocally, how much it may gain by even a very serious alteration of truth according to history. As the tragic poet, like poets in general, is only subject to the laws of poetic truth, the most conscientious observance of historic truth could never dispense him from his duties as poet, and could never excuse in him any infraction of poetic truth or lack of interest. It is, therefore, betraying very narrow ideas on tragic art, or rather on poetry in general, to drag the tragic poet before the tribunal of history, and to require *instruction* of the man who by his very title is only bound to move and charm you. Even supposing the poet, by a scrupulous submission to historic truth, had stripped himself of his privilege of artist, and that he had tacitly acknowledged in history a jurisdiction over his work, art retains all her rights to summon him before its bar; and pieces such as, if they could not stand the test on this side, would only be tragedies of mediocre value, notwithstanding all the minuteness of costume — of national costume — and of the manners of the time.

Fifthly, tragedy is the imitation of an

action that lets us see *man suffering*. The word *man* is essential to mark the limits of tragedy. Only the suffering of a being like ourselves can move our pity. Thus, evil genii, demons — or even men like them, without morals — and again pure spirits, without our weaknesses, are unfit for tragedy. The very idea of suffering implies a man in the full sense of the term. A pure spirit cannot suffer, and a man approaching one will never awaken a high degree of sympathy. A purely sensuous being can indeed have terrible suffering; but without moral sense it is a prey to it, and a suffering with reason inactive is a disgusting spectacle. The tragedian is right to prefer mixed characters, and to place the ideal of his hero half way between utter perversity and entire perfection.

Lastly, tragedy unites all these requisites to excite pity. Many means the tragic poet takes might serve another object; but he frees himself from all requirements not relating to this end, and is thereby obliged to direct himself with a view to this supreme object.

The final aim to which all the laws tend is called the *end* of any style of poetry. The means by which it attains this are its *form*. The end and form are, therefore, closely related. The form is determined by the end, and when the form is well observed the end is generally attained. Each kind of poetry having a special end must have a distinguishing form. What it exclusively produces it does in virtue of this special nature it possesses. The end of tragedy is *emotion;* its form is the imitation of an action

that leads to suffering. Many kinds may have the same object as tragedy, or emotion, though it be not their principal end. Therefore, what distinguishes tragedy is the relation of its form to its end, the way in which it attains its end by means of its subject.

If the end of tragedy is to awaken sympathy, and its form is the means of attaining it, the imitation of an action fit to move must have all that favors sympathy. Such is the form of tragedy.

The production of a kind of poetry is perfect when the form peculiar to its kind has been used in the best way. Thus, a perfect tragedy is that where the form is best used to awaken sympathy. Thus, the best tragedy is that where the pity excited results more from the treatment of the poet than the theme. Such is the ideal of a tragedy.

A good number of tragedies, though fine as poems, are bad as dramas, because they do not seek their end by the best use of tragic form. Others, because they use the form to attain an end different from tragedy. Some very popular ones only touch us on account of the subject, and we are blind enough to make this a merit in the poet. There are others in which we seem to have quite forgotten the object of the poet, and, contented with pretty plays of fancy and wit, we issue with our hearts cold from the theater. Must art, so holy and venerable, defend its cause by such champions before such judges? The indulgence of the public only emboldens mediocrity: it causes genius to blush, and discourages it.

JOHANN WOLFGANG VON GOETHE

Johann Wolfgang von Goethe was born at Frankfort-on-Main in 1749. His early education was received at home, first under his father, and then with tutors, though the influence of his mother was strongly marked. In his *Dichtung und Wahrheit* Goethe tells of his early interest in puppet-plays and theaters, and in the French company of actors which remained in his native city after

the Seven Years' War. These early years were devoted to literary effort, though the youth found time for at least one love-affair before reaching the age of sixteen. In 1765 he went to Leipzig and entered the University. There a second love-affair inspired a number of juvenile lyrics. Two minor plays also belong to this period. As a result of illness he was sent home, and during his convalescence he read and studied. When, in 1770, after his recovery, he went to Strassburg to study law, he was completely changed. He took up in earnest his work of criticizing French art and standing for a truly German art. He was greatly influenced by Herder, who showed him the beauty of Shakespeare. Another love-affair went far to inspire him in his first important lyrics, which were to mark a new epoch in German poetry. *Götz von Berlichingen* was written at Strassburg (though not published until 1773). "With *Götz von Berlichingen*, Shakespeare's art first triumphed on the German stage, and the literary movement known as *Sturm und Drang* was inaugurated." Goethe received his degree in 1771 and returned to Frankfurt, where he began to practice his profession. Friendships, further love-affairs, and writing, occupied the years previous to his Weimar residence. *Die Leiden des jungen Werthers* (1774) brought Goethe widespread fame. The first studies for *Faust* also date from this time, and a number of complete plays. His trip to Weimer was made after repeated invitations by the "hereditary prince," Karl August. At Weimar Goethe was entrusted with state affairs. The years between his arrival there and his famous Italian trip are chiefly memorable for some of the poet's best lyrics, a large part of *Wilhelm Meisters theatralische Sendung,* and *Iphigenie auf Tauris*. In 1786 he went to Italy. The final version of *Iphigenie* (1787), *Torquato Tasso* (1790), *Egmont* (1788), and the *Fragment* of *Faust* (1790), were all influenced by this journey. He returned to Weimar in 1788. There he lived with Christiane Vulpius for many years, finally marrying her in 1806. During the stormy years of the French Revolution Goethe took part in the French Campaign in 1792 and the Siege of Mainz in 1793. The Revolution meant little to him but the unsettling of government and order. A few very uneven plays of his bear witness to his dissatisfaction. In 1791 he was appointed director of the Ducal theater. At the same time he was occupied with biological, physical, botanical, and chemical research, and many works appeared with the results of his inquiries. The revised and extended version of *Wilhelm Meister* was included in his *Neue Schriften* (1792–1800), and exerted great influence. In 1794 he and Schiller became friends, and Goethe collaborated with the latter in his *Horen*. Schiller stimulated Goethe and encouraged him to further literary efforts. In 1798 Goethe published his epic *Hermann und Dorothea* and many ballads. Ten years later appeared the first part of *Faust*, and the next year the novel *Die Wahlverwandtschaften,* which was very popular. *Aus meinem Leben, Dichtung und Wahrheit,* part I, was published in 1811. Additional parts appeared in 1812, 1814, and the last, after his death. His wife died in 1816. The next year he retired from his position as theater director. The second part of *Faust* appeared in 1833. He died at Weimar in 1832.

Throughout a great part of Goethe's work there is a stream of criticism which renders it difficult to re-construct a complete critical theory. The various versions of the *Wilhelm Meister* novel, even *Faust* itself, are critical in spirit. But it is in the miscellaneous prefaces, articles, letters, and the Eckermann *Gespräche—Conversations—*that his critical powers are best seen. Goethe's broad outlook, his sympathy with and his deep knowledge of man and art, gave him a most catholic view, and possibly the best statement of his creed is found in Calvin Thomas' *Goethe:* . . . "the simple creed that informs Goethe, and gives him his criteria for judging the work of others. It is that the artist as such must have no creed; that is no creed derivable from the intellect or accountable to it. Rules, conventions, theories, principles, inhibitions of any sort not born of his own immediate feeling, are no concern of his. They proceed from an inferior part of human nature, being the work of gapers and babblers."

On the drama:

The many editions, including certain articles under different titles, make it next to impossible to put the dramatic writings in chronological order. The following references are to the Weimar editions (Weimar, 136 vols, 1887–1912) unless otherwise indicated. The more important articles are specifically mentioned.

Tag- und Jahres-Hefte als Ergänzung meiner sonstigen Bekenntnisse, von 1749 bis 1806, and the same from 1807 to 1822. Also *Biographische Einzelheiten* (especially *Zum Jahre 1815 — Theater*). In vols. 35 and 36 (1892–93.)

Zum Shakespeares Tag; Recensionen in die Frankfürter gelehrten Anzeigen (1772); *Auf Goethes Brieftasche — Mercier — Wagner. Neuer Versuch uber die Schauspielkunst.* In vol. 37 (1896).

Theater und Schauspielkunst (20 articles and fragments); and *Literatur (Beiträge zur Jenaischen Allgemeinen Literaturzeitung und Alteres* 1787–1807). 29 articles, many on the drama, vol. 40 (1901).

Literatur. (*Beiträge zum Morgenblatt für gebildete Stände,* 1807–16.) 3 articles on drama. *Ueber Kunst und Alterthum. Mittheilungen im ersten bis dritten Bande.* 1816–22. 6 articles on drama. Continuation of same in second vol., 1823–32. About 20 articles on the drama. Vol. 41, first and second parts (1902–03).

Ankündigungen. Geleitworte, 1813–30. (Contains the *Theilname Goethes an Manzoni.*) In first part, vol. 42 (1904).

Literatur. Aus dem Nachlass. (Contains *Das Wesen der antiken Tragödie,* 1827); and *Maximen und Reflexionen über Literatur und Ethik, aus Kunst und Alterthum.* In vol. 42, second part (1907).

The Weimar Edition also includes 63 volumes of the *Briefe und Tagebücher,* in which are numerous references to the drama.

Aus meinem Leben, Dichtung und Wahrheit, part I (Thubingen, 1811); other parts up to 1833.

[Johann P. Eckermann], *Gespräche mit Goethe in den letzten Jahren seines Lebens, 1823–1832,* 2 vols. (with the supplementary volume containing Soret's notes, Leipzig, 1836–48).

Wilhelm Meisters theatralische Sendung (1st published Stuttgart, 1911).

Wilhelm Meisters Lehrjahre, 4 vols. (Berlin, 1795–96).

Wilhelm Meisters Wanderjahre, part I

(Stuttgart, 1821). The novel as a whole was eventually published in 3 vols. in the 1830 ed. of the *Werke.*

Editions:

In order to facilitate reference, the miscellaneous criticisms referred to in the Weimar Edition — not including *Kunst und Alterthum* — are to be found in the easily accessible, though not entirely trustworthy Cotta Edition of the *Sämtliche Werke,* in 36 vols., Stuttgart, n.d. These are found in vols. 4, 14, 26, 27, 28, and 36. See also the Hempel Edition, and the *Jubiläums-Ausgabe* (Stuttgart, 1905). Not all the criticisms have been translated into English. The *Maxims of Goethe,* however, contain a number of the more important short maxims and fragments. This is published under the title *Criticisms, Reflections, and Maxims of Goethe,* translated by W. B. Rönnfeldt (London, n.d.). The *Dichtung und Wahrheit* is translated by John Oxenford as *The Autobiography of Goethe,* 2 vols. (Bohn ed., London, revised ed., 1897). The second vol. of this ed. contains a translation of the *Tag- und Jahres-Hefte,* by Charles Nisbet, as *Annals or Day and Year Papers.* Eckermann's *Gespräche* are translated by John Oxenford as *Conversations of Goethe with Eckermann and Soret.* Eckermann himself added a third vol. in 1848 with the Soret conversations (revised Bohn ed., London, 1913). *Wilhelm Meisters Lehrjahre* and *Wilhelm Meisters Wanderjahre* are translated by Thomas Carlyle as *Wilhelm Meister's Apprenticeship and Travels* (Edinburgh, 1824ff). See especially Gräf's *Goethe über seine Dichtungen,* 9 vols. (1901–14). Max Morris's *Der junge Goethe,* 6 vols. (1909–12), contains much matter not in any other editions.

On Goethe and his works:

Dichtung und Wahrheit, and Eckermann, *Gespräche* (see above). For bibliography, see Goedeke's well-known *Grundriss.* For general biography and bibliography, see the *Goethe-Jahrbuch* (Frankfurt, 1880–1913), and the

Schriften der Goethe-Gesellschaft, 28 vols. (Weimar, 1885–1913).

Thomas Carlyle, *Essays on Goethe* [reprints] (New York, 1881).

H. Viehoff, *Goethe's Leben,* 4 vols. (2nd ed., Stuttgart, 1854).

G. H. Lewes, *The Life and Works of Goethe,* 2 vols. (London, 1855. 3rd ed., revised, 2 vols., Leipzig, 1882. Cheap reprint in Everyman's Library).

Heinrich Düntzer, *Goethes Leben* (Leipzig, 1880. Translated as *Life of Goethe,* by Thomas W. Lyster, popular ed., London, 1908).

K. Heinemann, *Goethe,* 2 vols. (Leipzig, 1895).

R. M. Meyer, *Goethe,* 2 vols. (3rd ed., Berlin, 1905).

A. Bielschowsky, *Goethe; sein Leben und seine Werke,* 2 vols. (München, 1896–1904. Translated by W. A. Cooper as *The Life of Goethe,* 3 vols., New York, 1905–08).

G. Witkowsky, *Goethe* (Leipzig, 1899).

E. Engel, *Goethe. Der Mann und das Werk* (Berlin, 1910).

Calvin Thomas, *Goethe* (New York, 1917).

H. H. Boyesen, *Goethe and Schiller* (New York, 1879).

F. W. Rudloff, *Shakespeare, Schiller, and Goethe Relatively Considered* (Brighton, 1848).

Valerius Tornius, *Goethe als Dramaturg* (Leipzig, 1909).

P. E. Titsworth, *The Attitude of Goethe and his School Toward French Classical Drama* (in *Jour. of Eng. and Germanic Phil.,* Oct., 1912).

J. Barbey d'Aurevilly, *Goethe et Diderot* (Paris, 1880).

Michael Lex, *Die Idee im Drama bei Goethe, Schiller, Grillparger, Kleist* (München, 1904).

Emil Ludwig, *Goethe,* trans. by Ethel C. Mayne (New York, 1928).

CONVERSATIONS [1]

[*Gespräche mit Goethe in den letzten Jahren seines Lebens, 1823–1832*]

(1836–48)

[1823].

(Sup.[1]) *Fri., Apr. 3.*— . . . We talked about the theater, and the improvements which have taken place in it lately. " I have remarked it without going there," said Goethe, laughing. " Two months ago my children always came home in an ill-humor; they were never satisfied with the entertainment which had been provided. But now they have turned over a new leaf; they come with joyful countenances, *because for once and away they can have a good cry.* Yesterday, they owed this 'pleasure in weeping' to a drama by Kotzebue."

(Sup.[2]) *Wed., Apr. 13.*— . . . " still, we must at all events allow that the author [of *Die Zauberflöte*] understood, to a high degree, the art of producing great theatrical effects by means of contrasts."

Tues., Oct. 21.— . . . I then asked Goethe his opinion as to the kind of verse proper for German tragedy. " People in Germany," he replied, " will scarcely come to an agreement on that point. Every one does just as he likes, and as he finds somewhat suitable to his subject. The Iambic trimeter would be the most dignified measure, but it is too long for us Germans, who, for want of epithets, generally find five feet quite enough. The English, on account of their many monosyllables, cannot even get on so far as we do."

Sat., Oct. 25.— . . . We talked of the theater, which was one of the topics which chiefly interested me this winter. The *Erdennacht* [*Night on Earth*] of Raupach was the last piece I had seen. I gave it as my opinion that the piece was not brought before us as it existed in the mind of the poet; that the Idea

---

1 Extracts re-printed from *Conversations of Goethe with Eckermann and Soret,* translated by John Oxenford (latest Bohn edition, London, 1913).— Ed.

2 " Supplement " of conversations with Soret.— Ed.

was more predominant than Life; that it was rather lyric than dramatic; and that what was spun out through five acts would have been far better in two or three. Goethe added that the idea of the whole which turned upon aristocracy and democracy, was by no means of universal interest to humanity.

I then praised those pieces of Kotzebue's which I had seen — namely, his *Verwandschaften* [*Affinities*], and his *Versöhnung* [*Reconciliation*]. I praised in them the quick eye for real life, the dexterity at seizing its interesting side, and the genuine and forcible representation of it. Goethe agreed with me. "What has kept its place for twenty years, and enjoys the favor of the people," said he, "must have something in it. When Kotzebue contented himself with his own sphere, and did not go beyond his powers, he usually did well. It was the same with him as with Chodowiecky, who always succeeded perfectly with the scenes of common citizens' life, while if he attempted to paint Greek or Roman heroes it proved a failure."

He named several other good pieces of Kotzebue's, especially *Die beiden Klinsberge* [*The Two Klingsbergs*]. "None can deny," said he, "that Kotzebue has looked about a great deal in life, and ever kept his eyes open.

"Intellect, and some poetry, cannot be denied to our modern tragic poets, but most of them are incapable of an easy, living representation; they strive after something beyond their powers; and for that reason I might call them *forced* talents."

"I doubt," said I, "whether such poets could write a piece in prose, and am of opinion that this would be the true touchstone of their talent." Goethe agreed with me, adding that versification enhanced, and even called forth poetic feeling.

. . . .

Fri., Nov. 14.— . . . "I have," said I, "a peculiar feeling towards Schiller. Some scenes of his great dramas I read with genuine love and admiration; but presently I meet with something which violates the truth of nature, and I can go no further. I feel this even in reading *Wallenstein*. I cannot but think that Schiller's turn for philosophy injured his poetry, because this led him to consider the idea far higher than all nature; indeed, thus to annihilate nature. What he could conceive must happen, whether it were in conformity with nature or not."

"It was sad," said Goethe, "to see how so highly gifted a man tormented himself with philosophical disquisitions which could in no way profit him. Humboldt has shown me letters which Schiller wrote to him in those unblest days of speculation. There we see how he plagued himself with the design of perfectly separating sentimental from *naïve* poetry. For the former he could find no proper soil, and this brought him into unspeakable preplexity. As if," continued he, smiling, "sentimental poetry could exist at all without the *naïve* ground in which, as it were, it has its root.

"It was not Schiller's plan," continued Goethe, "to go to work with a certain unconsciousness, and as it were instinctively; he was forced, on the contrary, to reflect on all he did. Hence it was that he never could leave off talking about his poetical projects, and thus he discussed with me all his late pieces, scene after scene.

"On the other hand, it was contrary to my nature to talk over my poetic plans with anybody — even with Schiller. I carried everything about with me in silence, and usually nothing was known to any one till the whole was completed. When I showed Schiller my *Hermann und Dorothea* finished, he was astonished, for I had said not a syllable to him of any such plan.

"But I am curious to hear what you will say of *Wallenstein* to-morrow. You will see noble forms, and the piece will make an impression on you such as you probably do not dream of."

. . . .

1824.

Tues., Mar. 30.— This evening I was with Goethe. I was alone with him; we talked on various subjects, and drank a bottle of wine. We spoke of the French drama, as contrasted with the German.

"It will be very difficult," said Goethe, "for the German public to come to a kind of right judgment, as they do in Italy and France. We have a special obstacle in the circumstance, that on our stage a medley of all sorts of things is represented. On the same boards where we saw Hamlet yesterday, we see Staberle to-day; and if to-morrow we are delighted with *Zauberflöte,* the day after we shall be charmed with the oddities of the next lucky wight. Hence the public becomes confused in its judgment, mingling together various species, which it never learns rightly to appreciate and to understand. Furthermore, every one has his own individual demands and personal wishes, and returns to the spot where he finds them realized. On the tree where he has plucked figs to-day, he would pluck them again to-morrow, and would make a long face if sloes had grown in their stead during the night. If any one is a friend to sloes, he goes to the thorns.

"Schiller had the happy thought of building a house for tragedy alone, and of giving a piece every week for the male sex exclusively. But this notion presupposed a very large city, and could not be realized with our humble means."

We talked about the plays of Iffland and Kotzebue, which, in their way, Goethe highly commended. "From this very fault," said he, "that people do not perfectly distinguish between *kinds* in art, the pieces of these men are often unjustly censured. We may wait a long time before a couple of such popular talents come again."

I praised Iffland's *Hagestolz* [*Old Bachelor*], with which I had been highly pleased on the stage. "It is unquestionably Iffland's best piece," said Goethe; "it is the only one in which he goes from prose into the ideal."

He then told me of a piece, which he and Schiller had made as a continuation to the *Hagestolz;* that is to say, in conversation, without writing it down. Goethe told me the progress of the action, scene by scene; it was very pleasant and cheerful, and gave me great delight.

Goethe then spoke of some new plays by Platen. "In these pieces," said he, "we may see the influence of Calderon. They are very clever, and, in a certain sense, complete; but they want specific gravity, a certain weight of import. They are not of a kind to excite in the mind of the reader a deep and abiding interest; on the contrary, the strings of the soul are touched but lightly and transiently. They are like cork, which, when it swims on the water, makes no impression, but is easily sustained by the surface.

"The German requires a certain earnestness, a certain grandeur of thought, and a certain fullness of sentiment. It is on this account that Schiller is so highly esteemed by them all. I do not in the least doubt the abilities of Platen; but those, probably from mistaken views of art, are not manifested here. He shows distinguished culture, intellect, pungent wit, and artistical completeness; but these, especially in Germany, are not enough.

"Generally, the personal character of the writer influences the public rather than his talents as an artist. Napoleon said of Corneille, '*S'il vivait, je le ferais prince*'; yet he never read him. Racine he read, but did not say this of him. Lafontaine, too, is looked upon with a high degree of esteem by the French, not on account of his poetic merits, but of the greatness of character which he manifests in his writings."

* * * * *

Wed., Nov. 24.—"The French," said Goethe, "do well to study and translate our writers; for, limited as they are both in form and motives, they can only look without for means. We Germans may be reproached for a certain formlessness; but in matter we are their superiors. The theatrical productions of Kotzebue and Iffland are so rich in motives that they may pluck them a long time before all is used up. But, especially, our philosophical Ideality is welcome to them; for every Ideal is serviceable to revolutionary aims.

* * * * *

1825.

We continued to converse about Byron, and Goethe admired his extraordinary talent. "That which I call invention," said he, "I never saw in any one in the world to a greater degree than in him. His manner of loosing a dramatic knot is always better than one would anticipate." . . . Goethe agreed with me [on another matter] and laughed to think that Lord Byron, who, in practical life, could never adapt himself, and never even asked about a law, finally subjected himself to the stupidest of laws — that of the *three unities*.

"He understood the purpose of this law," said he, "no better than the rest of the world. *Comprehensibility* is the purpose, and the three unities are only so far good as they conduce to this end. If the observance of them hinders the comprehension of a work, it is foolish to treat them as laws, and to try to observe them. Even the Greeks, from whom the rule was taken, did not always follow it. In the *Phaëton* of Euripides, and in other pieces, there is a change of place, and it is obvious that good representation of their subject was with them more important than blind obedience to law, which, in itself, is of no great consequence. The pieces of Shakespeare deviate, as far as possible, from the unities of time and place; but they are comprehensible — nothing more so — and on this account, the Greeks would have found no fault in them. The French poets have endeavored to follow most rigidly the laws of the three unities, but they sin against comprehensibility, inasmuch as they solve a dramatic law, not dramatically, but by narration."

"I call to mind the *Feinde* [*Enemies*] of Houwald. The author of this drama stood much in his own light, when, to preserve the unity of place, he sinned against comprehensibility in the first act, and altogether sacrificed what might have given greater effect to his piece to a whim, for which no one thanks him. I thought, too, on the other hand, of *Goetz von Berlichingen,* which deviates as far as possible from the unity of time and place; but which, as everything is visibly developed to us, and brought before our eyes, is as truly dramatic and comprehensible as any piece in the world. I thought, too, that the unities of time and place were natural, and in accordance with the intention of the Greeks, only when a subject is so limited in its range that it can develop itself before our eyes with all its details in the given time; but that with a large action, which occurs in several places, there is no reason to be confined to one place, especially as our present stage arrangements offer no obstacle to a change of scene."

Goethe continued to talk of Lord Byron. "With that disposition," said he, "which always leads him into the illimitable, the restraint which he imposed upon himself by the observance of the three unities becomes him very well. If he had but known how to endure moral restraint also! That he could not was his ruin; and it may be aptly said, that he was destroyed by his own unbridled temperament."

. . . . .

1825.

"I will not deny that it was something," returned Goethe. "The main point, however, was this, that the Grand Duke left my hands quite free, and I could do just as I liked. I did not look to magnificent scenery, and a brilliant wardrobe, but I looked to good pieces. From tragedy to farce, every species was welcome; but a piece was obliged to have something in it to find favor. It was necessary that it should be great and clever, cheerful and graceful, and, at all events, healthy and containing some pith. All that was morbid, weak, lachrymose, and sentimental, as well as all that was frightful, horrible, and offensive to decorum, was utterly excluded; I should have feared, by such expedients, to spoil both actors and audience."

Wed., Apr. 20. — A poet who writes for the stage must have a knowledge of the stage, that he may weigh the means at his command, and know generally what is to be done, and what is to be left alone; the opera-composer, in like manner, should have some insight into poetry, that he may know how to distinguish the bad from the good, and not apply his art to something impracticable.

"Carl Maria Von Weber," said Goethe, "should not have composed *Euryanthe.* He should have seen at once that this was a bad material, of which nothing could be made. So much insight we have a right to expect of every composer, as belonging to his art."

. . . . .

Sun., May 1. — "Even Shakespeare and Molière," returned Goethe, "had no other view. Both of them wished, above all things, to make money by their theaters. In order to attain this, their principal aim, they necessarily strove that everything should be as good as possible, and that, besides good old plays, there should be some clever novelty to please and attract. The prohibition of *Tartuffe* was a thunderbolt to Molière; but not so much for the poet as for the director Molière, who had to consider the welfare of an important troupe, and to find some means to procure bread for himself and his actors."

．　．　．　．　．　．

Thurs., May 12.— . . . "The great point is, that he from whom we would learn should be congenial to our nature. Now, Calderon, for instance, great as he is, and much as I admire him, has exerted no influence over me for good or for ill. But he would have been dangerous to Schiller — he would have led him astray; and hence it is fortunate that Calderon was not generally known in Germany till after Schiller's death. Calderon is infinitely great in the technical and theatrical; Schiller, on the contrary, far more sound, earnest, and great in his intention, and it would have been a pity if he had lost any of these virtues, without, after all, attaining the greatness of Calderon in other respects."

We spoke of Molière. "Molière," said Goethe, "is so great, that one is astonished anew every time one reads him. He is a man by himself — his pieces border on tragedy; they are apprehensive; and no one has the courage to imitate them. His *Miser*, where the vice destroys all the natural piety between father and son, is especially great, and in a high sense tragic. But when, in a German paraphrase, the son is changed into a relation, the whole is weakened, and loses its significance. They feared to show the vice in its true nature, as he did; but what is tragic there, or indeed anywhere, except what is intolerable?

"I read some pieces of Molière's every year, just as, from time to time, I contemplate the engravings after the great Italian masters. For we little men are not able to retain the greatness of such things within ourselves; we must therefore return to them from time to time, and renew our impressions."

．　．　．　．　．　．

"*Macbeth*," said Goethe, "is Shakespeare's best acting play, the one in which he shows most understanding with respect to the stage. But would you see his mind unfettered, read *Troilus and Cressida*, where he treats the materials of the *Iliad* in his own fashion."

．　．　．　．　．

[1826].

Sun. Evening, Jan. 29.—"Molière is my strength and consolation at present," said I; "I have translated his *Avare*, and am now busy with his *Médicin malgré lui*. Molière is indeed a great, a genuine man."

"Yes," said Goethe, "a genuine man; that is the proper term. There is nothing distorted about him. He ruled the manners of his day, while, on the contrary, our Iffland and Kotzebue allowed themselves to be ruled by theirs, and were limited and confined in them. Molière chastised men by drawing them just as they were."

"I would give something," said I, "to see his plays acted in all their purity! Yet such things are much too strong and natural for the public, so far as I am acquainted with it. Is not this over-refinement to be attributed to the so-called ideal literature of certain authors?"

"No," said Goethe, "it has its source in society itself. What business have our young girls at the theater? They do not belong to it — they belong to the convent, and the theater is only for men and women, who know something of human affairs. When Molière wrote, girls were in the convent, and he was not forced to think about them. But now we cannot get rid of these young girls, and pieces which are weak, and therefore *proper*, will continue to be produced. Be wise and stay away, as I do. I was really interested in the theater only so long as I could have a practical influence upon it. It was my delight to bring the establishment to a high degree of perfection; and when there was a performance, my interest was not so much in the pieces as in observing whether the actors played as they ought. The faults I wished to point out I sent in writing to the *Regisseur*, and was sure they would be avoided on the next representation. Now I can no longer have any practical influence in the theater, I feel no calling to enter it; I should be forced to endure defects without being able to amend them; and that would not suit me. And with the reading of plays, it is no better. The young German poets are eternally sending me tragedies; but what am I to do with them? I have never read German plays except with the view of seeing whether I could act them; in every other respect they were indifferent to me. What am I to do now, in my present situation, with the pieces of these young people? I can gain nothing for myself by reading how things ought *not* to be done; and I cannot assist the young poets in the matter which is already finished. If, instead of their printed plays, they would send me the plan of a play, I could at least say, 'Do it,' or 'Leave it alone,' or 'Do it this way,' or 'Do it that'; and in this there might be some use."

Wed., July 26.— . . . I told him that one of my friends intended to arrange Lord Byron's *Two Foscari* for the stage. Goethe doubted his success.

"It is indeed a temptation," he said. "When a piece makes a deep impression on us in reading, we think it will do the same on the stage, and that we could obtain such a result with little trouble. But this is by no means the case. A piece that is not originally, by the intent and skill of the poet, written for the boards, will not succeed; but whatever is done to it, will always remain something unmanageable. What trouble have I taken with my *Götz von Berlichingen!* yet it will not go right as an acting play, but is too long; and I have been forced to divide it into two parts, of which the last is indeed theatrically effective, while the first is to be looked upon as a mere introduction. If the first part were given only once as an introduction, and then the second repeatedly, it might succeed. It is the same with *Wallenstein: Die Piccolomini* does not bear repetition, but *Wallenstein's Tod* is always seen with delight."

I asked how a piece must be constructed so as to be fit for the theater.

"It must be symbolical," replied Goethe; "that is to say, each incident must be significant in itself, and lead to another still more important. The *Tar-*

tuffe of Molière is, in this respect, a great example. Only think what an introduction is the first scene! From the very beginning everything is highly significant, and leads us to expect something still more important which is to come. The beginning of Lessing's *Minna von Barnhelm* is also admirable; but that of the *Tartuffe* comes only once into the world: it is the greatest and best thing that exists of the kind."

We then came to the pieces of Calderon.

"In Calderon," said Goethe, "you find the same perfect adaptation to the theater. His pieces are throughout fit for the boards; there is not a touch in them which is not directed towards the required effect. Calderon is a genius who had also the finest understanding."

"It is singular," said I, "that the dramas of Shakespeare are not theatrical pieces, properly so called, since he wrote them all for his theater."

"Shakespeare," replied Goethe, "wrote those pieces direct from his own nature. Then, too, his age, and the existing arrangements of the stage, made no demands upon him; people were forced to put up with whatever he gave them. But if Shakespeare had written for the court of Madrid, or for the theater of Louis XIV, he would probably have adapted himself to a severer theatrical form. This, however, is by no means to be regretted, for what Shakespeare has lost as a theatrical poet he has gained as a poet in general. Shakespeare is a great psychologist, and we learn from his pieces the secrets of human nature."

[1827].

Wed., Jan. 31.— . . . "Here again," continued Goethe, "the Greeks were so great, that they regarded fidelity to historic facts less than the treatment of them by the poet. We have, fortunately, a fine example in *Philoctetes,* which subject has been treated by all three of the great tragedians, and lastly and best by Sophocles. This poet's excellent play has, fortunately, come down to us entire, while of the *Philoctetes* of Æschylus and Euripides only fragments have been found, although sufficient to show how they have managed the subject. If time permitted, I would restore these pieces, as I did the

Phaëton of Euripides; it would be to me no unpleasant or useless task.

"In this subject the problem was very simple, namely, to bring Philoctetes, with his bow, from the island of Lemnos. But the manner of doing this was the business of the poet, and here each could show the power of his invention, and one could excel another. Ulysses must fetch him; but shall he be known by Philoctetes or not? and if not, how shall he be disguised? Shall Ulysses go alone, or shall he have companions, and who shall they be? In Æschylus there is no companion; in Euripides, it is Diomed; in Sophocles, the son of Achilles. Then, in what situation is Philoctetes to be found? Shall the island be inhabited or not? and, if inhabited, shall any sympathetic soul have taken compassion on him or not? And so with a hundred other things, which are all at the discretion of the poet, and in the selection and omission of which one may show his superiority in wisdom to another. Here is the grand point, and our present poets should do like the ancients. They should not be always asking whether a subject has been used before, and look to south and north for unheard-of adventures, which are often barbarous enough, and merely make an impression as incidents. But to make something of a simple subject by a masterly treatment requires intellect and great talent, and these we do not find."

. . . . .

"The same law," said I, "seems to lie at the foundation of a good style, where we like to avoid a sound which we have just heard. Even on the stage a great deal might be done with this law, if it were well applied. Plays, especially tragedies, in which an uniform tone uninterrupted by change prevails, have always something wearisome about them; and if the orchestra plays melancholy, depressing music during the *entr'actes* of a melancholy piece, we are tortured by an insupportable feeling, which we would escape by all possible means."

"Perhaps," said Goethe, "the lively scenes introduced into Shakspeare's plays rest upon this 'law of required change,' but it does not seem applicable to the higher tragedy of the Greeks, where, on the contrary, a certain fundamental tone pervades the whole."

"The Greek tragedy," said I, "is not of such a length as to be rendered wearisome by one pervading tone. Then there is an interchange of chorus and dialogue; and the sublime sense is of such a kind that it cannot become fatiguing, since a certain genuine reality, which is always of a cheerful nature, constantly lies at the foundation."

"You may be right," said Goethe; "and it would be well worth the trouble to investigate how far the Greek tragedy is subject to the general 'law of required change.' You see how all things are connected with each other, and how a law respecting the theory of colors can lead to an inquiry into Greek tragedy. We must only take care not to push such a law too far, and make it the foundation for much besides. We shall go more safely if we only apply it by analogy."

. . . . .

Wed., Feb. 7.—To-day Goethe spoke severely of certain critics, who were not satisfied with Lessing, and made unjust demands upon him. "When people," said he, "compare the pieces of Lessing with those of the ancients, and call them paltry and miserable, what do they mean? Rather pity the extraordinary man for being obliged to live in a pitiful time, which afforded him no better materials than are treated in his pieces; pity him, because in his *Minna von Barnhelm,* he found nothing better to do than to meddle with the squabbles of Saxony and Prussia. His constant polemical turn, too, resulted from the badness of his time. In *Emilia Galotti,* he vented his pique against princes; in *Nathan,* against the priests."

.

(Sup.). *Wed., Mar. 21.*— . . . "You must have remarked generally," continued Goethe, "that Hinrichs, in considering Greek tragedy, sets out from the *idea;* and that he looks upon Sophocles as one who, in the invention and arrangement of his pieces, likewise set out from an idea, and regulated the sex and rank of his characters accordingly. But Sophocles, when he wrote his pieces, by no means started from an *idea;* on the contrary, he seized upon some ancient ready-made popular tradition in which a good idea existed, and then only thought of adapting it in the best and most effective manner for the theater. The Atreides will not allow Ajax to be buried; but as in Antigone the sister struggles for the brother, so in the Ajax the brother struggles for the brother. That the sister takes charge of the unburied Polyneices, and the brother takes charge of the fallen Ajax, is a contingent circumstance, and does not belong to the invention of the poet, but to the tradition, which the poet followed and was obliged to follow."

"What he says about Creon's conduct," replied I, "appears to be equally untenable. He tries to prove that, in prohibiting the burial of Polyneices, Creon acts from pure political virtue; and since Creon is not merely a man, but also a prince, he lays down the proposition, that, as a man represents the tragic power of the state, this man can be no other than he who is himself the personification of the state itself — namely, the prince; and that of all persons the man as prince must be just that person who displays the greatest political virtue."

"These are assertions which no one will believe," returned Goethe with a smile. "Besides, Creon by no means acts out of political virtue, but from hatred towards the dead. When Polyneices endeavored to reconquer his paternal inheritance, from which he had been forcibly expelled, he did not commit such a monstrous crime against the state that his death was insufficient, and that the further punishment of the innocent corpse was required.

"An action should never be placed in the category of political virtue, which is opposed to virtue in general. When Creon forbids the burial of Polyneices, and not only taints the air with the decaying corpse, but also affords an opportunity for the dogs and birds of prey to drag about pieces torn from the dead body, and thus to defile the altars — an action so offensive both to gods and men is by no means politically virtuous, but on the contrary a political crime. Besides, he has everybody in the play against him. He has the elders of the state, who form the chorus, against him; he has the people at large against him;

he has Teiresias against him; he has his own family against him; but he hears not, and obstinately persists in his impiety, until he has brought to ruin all who belong to him, and is himself at last nothing but a shadow."

"And still," said I, "when one hears him speak, one cannot help believing that he is somewhat in the right."

"That is the very thing," said Goethe, "in which Sophocles is a master; and in which consists the very life of the dramatic in general. His characters all possess this gift of eloquence, and know how to explain the motives for their action so convincingly, that the hearer is almost always on the side of the last speaker.

"One can see that, in his youth, he enjoyed an excellent rhetorical education, by which he became trained to look for all the reasons and seeming reasons of things. Still, his great talent in this respect betrayed him into faults, as he sometimes went too far.

"There is a passage in *Antigone* which I always look upon as a blemish, and I would give a great deal for an apt philologist to prove that it is interpolated and spurious.

"After the heroine has, in the course of the piece, explained the noble motives for her action, and displayed the elevated purity of her soul, she at last, when she is led to death, brings forward a motive which is quote unworthy, and almost borders upon the comic.

"She says that, if she had been a mother, she would not have done, either for her dead children or for her dead husband, what she has done for her brother. For," says she, "if my husband died I could have had another, and if my children died I could have had others by my new husband. But with my brother the case is different. I cannot have another brother; for since my mother and father are dead, there is no one to beget one.

"This is, at least, the bare sense of this passage, which in my opinion, when placed in the mouth of a heroine, going to her death, disturbs the tragic tone, and appears to me very far-fetched — to save her too much of dialectical calculation. As I said, I should like a philologist to show us that the passage is spurious."

We then conversed further upon Sophocles, remarking that in his pieces he always less considered a moral tendency than an apt treatment of the subject in hand, particularly with regard to theatrical effect.

"I do not object," said Goethe, "to a dramatic poet having a moral influence in view; but when the point is to bring his subject clearly and effectively before his audience, his moral purpose proves of little use, and he needs much more a faculty for delineation and a familiarity with the stage to know what to do and what to leave undone. If there be a moral in the subject, it will appear, and the poet has nothing to consider but the effect and artistic treatment of the subject. If a poet has as high a soul as Sophocles, his influence will always be moral, let him do what he will. Besides, he knew the stage, and understood his craft thoroughly."

"How well he knew the theater," answered I, "and how much he had in view of theatrical effect, we see in his 'Philoctetes,' and the great resemblance which this piece bears to 'Œdipus in Colonos,' both in arrangement and in course of action.

"In both pieces we see the hero in a helpless condition; both are old and suffering from bodily infirmities. Œdipus has, at his side, his daughter as a guide and a prop; Philoctetes has his bow. The resemblance is carried still further. Both have been thrust aside in their afflictions; but when the oracle declares with respect to both of them, that the victory can be obtained with their aid alone, and endeavor is made to get them back again; Ulysses comes to Philoctetes, Creon to Œdipus. Both begin their discourse with cunning and honeyed words; but when these are of no avail, they use violence, and we see Philoctetes deprived of his bow, and Œdipus of his daughter."

"Such acts of violence," said Goethe, "give an opportunity for excellent altercations, and such situations of helplessness excited the emotions of the audience, on which account the poet, whose object it was to produce an effect upon the public, liked to introduce them. In order to strengthen this effect in the Œdipus, Sophocles brings him in as a

weak old man, when he still, according to all circumstances, must have been a man in the prime of life. But at this vigorous age, the poet could not have used him for his play; he would have produced no effect, and he therefore made him a weak, helpless old man."

"The resemblance to Philoctetes," continued I, "goes still further. The hero, in both pieces, does not act, but suffers. On the other hand, each of these passive heroes has two active characters against him. Œdipus has Creon and Polyneices, Philoctetes has Neoptolemus and Ulysses; two such opposing characters were necessary to discuss the subject on all sides, and to gain the necessary body and fullness for the piece."

"You might add," interposed Goethe, "that both pieces bear this further resemblance, that we see in both the extremely effective situation of a happy change, since one hero, in his disconsolate situation, has his beloved daughter restored to him, and the other, his no less beloved bow."

The happy conclusions of these two pieces are also similar; for both heroes are delivered from their sorrows: Œdipus is blissfully snatched away, and as for Philoctetes, we are forewarned by the oracle of his cure, before Troy, by Æsculapius.

"When we," continued Goethe, "for our modern purposes, who wish to learn how to conduct ourselves upon the theater, Molière is the man to whom we should apply.

"Do you know his *Malade imaginaire?* There is a scene in it which, as often as I read the piece, appears to me the symbol of a perfect knowledge of the boards. I mean the scene where the 'Malade Imaginaire' asks his little daughter Louison, if there has not been a young man in the chamber of her eldest sister.

"Now, any other who did not understand his craft so well would have let the little Louison plainly tell the fact at once, and there would have been the end of the matter.

"But what various motives for delay are introduced by Molière into this examination for the sake of life and effect. He first makes the little Louison act as if she did not understand her father; then she denies that she knows anything;

then, threatened with the rod, she falls down as if dead; then, when her father bursts out in despair, she springs up from her feigned swoon with roguish hilarity, and at last, little by little, she confesses all.

"My explanation can only give you a very meager notion of the animation of the scene; but read the scene yourself till you become thoroughly impressed with its theatrical worth, and you will confess that there is more practical instruction contained in it than in all the theories in the world.

"I have known and loved Molière," continued Goethe, "from my youth, and have learned from him during my whole life. I never fail to read some of his plays every year, that I may keep up a constant intercourse with what is excellent. It is not merely the perfect artistic treatment which delights me; but particularly the amiable nature, the highly formed mind, of the poet. There is in him a grace and a feeling for the decorous, and a tone of good society which his innate beautiful nature could only attain by daily intercourse with the most eminent men of his age. Of Menander, I only know the few fragments; but these give me so high an idea of him, that I look upon this great Greek as the only man who could be compared to Molière."

"I am happy," returned I, "to hear you speak so highly of Molière. This sounds a little different from Herr von Schlegel! I have to-day, with great repugnance, swallowed what he says concerning Molière in his lectures on dramatic poetry. He quite looks down upon him, as a vulgar buffoon, who has only seen good society at a distance, and whose business it was to invent all sorts of pleasantries for the amusement of his lord. In these low pleasantries, Schlegel admits he was most happy, but he stole the best of them. He was obliged to force himself into the higher school of comedy, and never succeeded in it."

"To a man like Schlegel," returned Goethe, "a genuine nature like Molière's is a veritable eyesore; he feels that he has nothing in common with him, he cannot endure him. The *Misanthrope,* which I read over and over again, as one of my most favorite pieces, is repugnant

to him; he is forced to praise *Tartuffe* a little, but he lets him down again as much as he can. Schlegel cannot forgive Molière for ridiculing the affectation of learned ladies; he feels, probably as one of my friends has remarked, that he himself would have been ridiculed if he had lived with Molière.

"It is not to be denied," continued Goethe, "that Schlegel knows a great deal, and one is almost terrified at his extraordinary attainments and his extensive reading. But this is not enough. All the learning in the world is still no judgment. His criticism is completely one-sided, because in all theatrical pieces he merely regards the skeleton of the plot and arrangement, and only points out small points of resemblance to great predecessors, without troubling himself in the least as to what the author brings forward of graceful life and the culture of a high soul. But of what use are all the arts of genius, if we do not find in a theatrical piece an amiable or great personality of the author. This alone influences the cultivation of the people.

"I look upon the manner in which Schlegel has treated the French drama as a sort of recipe for the formation of a bad critic, who is wanting in every organ for the veneration of excellence, and who passes over a sound nature and a great character as if they were chaff and stubble."

"Shakespeare and Calderon, on the other hand," I replied, "he treats justly, and even with decided affection."

"Both," returned Goethe, "are of such a kind that one cannot say enough in praise of them, although I should not have wondered if Schlegel had scornfully let them down also. Thus he is also just to Æschylus and Sophocles; but this does not seem to arise so much from a lively conviction of their extraordinary merit as from the tradition among philologists to place them both very high; for, in fact, Schlegel's own little person is not sufficient to comprehend and appreciate such lofty natures. If this had been the case, he would have been just to Euripides too, and would have gone to work with him in a different manner. But he knows that philologists do not estimate him very highly, and he therefore feels no little delight that he is permitted upon such high authority, to fall foul of this mighty ancient and to schoolmaster him as much as he can. I do not deny that Euripides has his faults; but he was always a very respectable competitor with Sophocles and Æschylus. If he did not possess the great earnestness and the severe artistic completeness of his two predecessors, and as a dramatic poet treated things a little more leniently and humanely, he probably knew his Athenians well enough to be aware that the chord which he struck was the right one for his contemporaries. A poet whom Socrates called his friend, whom Aristotle lauded, whom Menander admired, and for whom Sophocles and the city of Athens put on mourning on hearing of his death, must certainly have been something. If a modern man like Schlegel must pick out faults in so great an ancient, he ought only to do it upon his knees."

. . . . . .

The conversation then turned upon the *Antigone* of Sophocles, and the high moral tone prevailing in it: and, lastly, upon the question — how the moral element came into the world?

"Through God himself," returned Goethe, "like everything else. It is no product of human reflection, but a beautiful nature inherent and inborn. It is, more or less, inherent in mankind generally, but to a high degree in a few eminently gifted minds. These have, by great deeds or doctrines, manifested their divine nature; which, then, by the beauty of its appearance, won the love of men, and powerfully attracted them to reverence and emulation."

"A consciousness of the worth of the morally beautiful and good could be attained by experience and wisdom, inasmuch as the bad showed itself in its consequences as a destroyer of happiness, both in individuals and the whole body, while the noble and right seemed to produce and secure the happiness of one and all. Thus the morally beautiful could become a doctrine, and diffuse itself over whole nations as something plainly expressed."

"I have lately read somewhere," answered I, "the opinion that the Greek tragedy had made moral beauty a special object."

"Not so much morality," returned Goethe, "as pure humanity in its whole extent; especially in such positions where, by falling into contact with rude power, it could assume a tragic character. In this region, indeed, even the moral stood as a principal part of human nature.

"The morality of *Antigone,* besides, was not invented by Sophocles, but was contained in the subject, which Sophocles chose the more readily, as it united so much dramatic effect with moral beauty."

Goethe then spoke about the characters of Creon and Ismene, and on the necessity for these two persons for the development of the beautiful soul of the heroine.

"All that is noble," said he, "is in itself of a quiet nature, and appears to sleep until it is aroused and summoned forth by contrast. Such a contrast is Creon, who is brought in, partly on account of Antigone, in order that her noble nature and the right which is on her side may be brought out by him, partly on his own account, in order that his unhappy error may appear odious to us.

"But, as Sophocles meant to display the elevated soul of his heroine even before the deed, another contrast was requisite by which her character might be developed; and this is her sister Ismene. In this character, the poet has given us a beautiful standard of the commonplace, so that the greatness of *Antigone,* which is far above such a standard, is the more strikingly visible."

The conversation then turned upon dramatic authors in general, and upon the important influence which they exerted, and could exert, upon the great mass of the people.

"A great dramatic poet," said Goethe, "if he is at the same time productive, and is actuated by a strong noble purpose, which pervades all his works, may succeed in making the soul of his pieces become the soul of the people. I should think that this was something well worth the trouble. From Corneille proceeded an influence capable of forming heroes. This was something for Napoleon, who had need of an heroic people; on which account, he said of Corneille, that if he were still living he would make a prince of him. A dramatic poet who knows his vocation should therefore work incessantly at its higher development, in order that his influence on the people may be noble and beneficial.

"One should not study contemporaries and competitors, but the great men of antiquity, whose works have, for centuries, received equal homage and consideration. Indeed, a man of really superior endowments will feel the necessity of this, and it is just this need for intercourse with great predecessors, which is the sign of a higher talent. Let us study Molière, let us study Shakespeare, but above all things, the old Greeks, and always the Greeks."

"For highly endowed natures," remarked I, "the study of the authors of antiquity may be perfectly inavailable; but, in general, it appears to have little influence upon personal character. If this were the case, all philologists and theologians would be the most excellent of men. But this is by no means the case; and such connoisseurs of the ancient Greek and Latin authors are able people or pitiful creatures, according to the bad or good qualities which God has given them, or which they have inherited from their father and mother."

"There is nothing to be said against that," returned Goethe; "but it must not, therefore, be said, that the study of antiquity is entirely without effect upon the formation of character. A worthless man will always remain worthless, and a little mind will not, by daily intercourse with the great minds of antiquity, become one inch greater. But a noble man, in whose soul God has placed the capability for future greatness of character and elevation of mind, will, by a knowledge of, and familiar intercourse with, the elevated natures of ancient Greeks and Romans, every day make a visible approximation to similar greatness."

. . . . .

"Shakespeare, in writing his pieces, could hardly have thought that they would appear in print, so as to be told over, and compared one with another; he had rather the stage in view when he wrote; he regarded his plays as a lively and moving scene, that would pass rapidly before the eyes and ears upon the stage, not as one that was to be held firmly, and carped at in detail. Hence, his only point was to be effective and significant for the moment."

. . . . .

Sat., July 21.— . . . "I am in the third volume already," said he, as he laid aside the book, "and am thus getting many new thoughts. You know Aristotle says of tragedy, 'It must excite fear, if it is to be good.' This is true, not only of tragedy, but of many other sorts of poetry. You find it in my *Gott und die Bayadere*. You find it in very good comedy, even in the *Sieben Mädchen in Uniform* [*Seven Girls in Uniform*], as we do not know how the joke will turn out for the dear creatures.

"This fear may be of two sorts; it may exist in the shape of alarm [*Angst*], or in that of uneasiness [*Bangigkeit*]. The latter feeling is awakened when we see a moral evil threatening, and gradually overshadowing, the personages, as, for instance, in the *Wahlverwandtschaften;* but alarm is awakened, in reader or spectator, when the personages are threatened with physical danger, as, for instance, in the *Galley Slave,* and in *Der Freischütz;*— nay in the scene of the Wolf's-glen, not only alarm, but a sense of annihilation, is awakened in the spectators. Now, Manzoni makes use of this alarm with wonderful felicity, by resolving it into emotion, and thus leading us to admiration. The feeling of alarm is necessarily of a material character, and will be excited in every reader; but that of admiration is excited by a recognition of the writer's skill, and only the connoisseur will be blessed with this feeling. What say you to these æsthetics of mine? If I were younger, I would write something according to this theory, though perhaps not so extensive a work as this of Manzoni.

. . . . .

(1829.)
Wed., Feb. 4.— . . . "Writing for the stage," he continued, "is something peculiar, and he who does not understand it thoroughly, had better leave it alone. Every one thinks that an interesting fact will appear interesting on the boards,—nothing of the kind! Things may be

very pretty to read, and very pretty to think about; but as soon as they are put upon the stage the effect is quite different, and that which has charmed us in the closet will probably fall flat on the boards. If any one reads my *Hermann und Dorothea*, he thinks it might be brought out at the theater. Töpfer has been inveigled into the experiment; but what is it, what effect does it produce, especially if it is not played in a first-rate manner, and who can say that it is in every respect a good piece? Writing for the stage is a trade that one must understand, and requires a talent that one must possess. Both are uncommon, and where they are not combined, we shall scarcely have any good result."

.   .   .   .   .

(1830.)
Goethe then talked of Gozzi, and his theater at Venice, where the actors had merely subjects given them, and filled up the details impromptu. Gozzi said there were only six-and-thirty tragic situations. Schiller thought there were more, but could never succeed in finding even so many.

.   .   .   .   .

(Sup.) *Wed., Mar.* 17.— This evening at Goethe's for a couple of hours. By order of the Grand Duchess I brought him back *Gemma von Art,* and told him

the good opinion I entertained of this piece.

" I am always glad," returned he, " when anything is produced which is new in invention, and bears the stamp of talent." Then, taking the volume between his hands, and looking at it somewhat askance, he added, "but I am never quite pleased when I see a dramatic author make pieces too long to be represented as they are written. This imperfection takes away half the pleasure that I should otherwise feel. Only see what a thick volume this *Gemma von Art* is."

" Schiller," returned I, "has not managed much better, and yet he is a very great dramatic author."

" He too has certainly committed this fault," returned Goethe. " His first pieces particularly, which he wrote in the fullness of youth, seem as if they would never end. He had too much on his heart, and too much to say to be able to control it. Afterwards, when he became conscious of this fault, he took infinite trouble, and endeavored to overcome it by work and study; but he never perfectly succeeded. It really requires a poetical giant, and is more difficult than is imagined, to control a subject properly, to keep it from overpowering one, and to concentrate one's attention on that alone which is absolutely necessary."

.   .   .   .   .

EPIC AND DRAMATIC POETRY [3]
[*Ueber epische und dramatische Dichtung*]
(1797)

The epic poet and the dramatic poet are both subject to the general laws of poetry, and especially to the laws of unity and of progression. Furthermore, they deal with subjects that are similar, and they can avail themselves of motives of either kind. The great and essential difference between them, however, lies in the fact that, whereas the epic poet describes an action as being altogether past and completed, the dramatic poet rep-

resents it as actually occurring. The best way of deducing the laws in detail, according to which both have to act, from the nature of man, is to picture to ourselves a rhapsodist and a stage-player, both as poets, the former surrounded by a quiet and attentive circle of listeners, the latter by a crowd impatiently waiting to see and hear him. Nor would it be a difficult matter to explain what is of the greatest use to each of these respective forms of poetry; what subjects each one will preferably adopt; of what motives it will preferably avail it-

[3] Re-printed, complete, from W. B. Rönnfeldt's *Criticisms, Reflections, and Maxims of Goethe* (London, n. d.).— Ed.

self. I say *preferably;* for, as I pointed out at the commencement, neither of them can lay exclusive claim to anything.

The subjects of epic poetry and of tragedy should be altogether human, full of significance and pathos. The characters will appear to the greatest advantage if they are represented as having attained a certain stage of development, when self-activity or spontaneity makes them still appear dependent upon themselves alone, and when their influence makes itself felt, not morally, politically, or mechanically, but in a purely personal way. The legends from the heroic times of the Greeks were in this sense especially favorable to their poets.

The epic poem represents above all things circumscribed activity, tragedy, circumscribed suffering. The epic poem gives us man working outside of and beyond himself: battles, wanderings, enterprises of all kinds which demand a certain sensuous breadth. Tragedy gives us man thrown in upon himself, and the actions of genuine tragedy therefore stand in need of but little space.

Of motives I distinguish five different varieties:

1. *Progressive,* which further the action, and are for the most part employed in drama.

2. *Retrogressive,* which draw the action away from its goal; these are almost exclusively confined to epic poetry.

3. *Retardative,* which delay the course or lengthen the way; these are used in both kinds of poetry with the greatest advantage.

4. *Retrospective,* by means of which events that have happened previously to the epoch of the poem are introduced into it.

5. *Anticipatory,* which anticipate that which will happen after the epoch of the poem; the epic poet, as also the dramatic poet, uses both kinds in order to create a perfect poem.

The worlds which are to be represented to view are common to both. They are:

1. The physical; and firstly, that most nearly approaching the one to which the persons represented belong, and by which they are surrounded. Here the dramatist as a rule confines himself strictly to one single point; the epic poet has more freedom of motion and his range of lo-

cality is much greater. Secondly, there is the remoter world, in which I include the whole of nature. This one the epic poet, who, generally speaking, has recourse to the imagination, seeks to bring nearer to us by means of similes or comparisons, of which the dramatist avails himself with less frequency.

2. The moral world is equally common to both, and is most happily represented in all its physiological and pathological simplicity.

3. The world of phantasies, presentiments, apparitions, accidents, and fatalities. This lies open to both, it being of course understood that it must approximate to the world of sensuous perception. Hence there arises a special difficulty for the moderns, because, much as we may desire it, we cannot easily find a substitute for the miraculous creatures, the gods, soothsayers, and oracles of the ancients.

With regard to the treatment as a whole, we shall deem the rhapsodist who describes that which belongs altogether to the past, to be a man of wisdom surveying with a calm recollection the things which have happened. His description will tend so to compose his hearers that they find pleasure in listening to him for a long space of time. He will distribute the interest equally throughout, since he is not able to counterbalance any unduly vivid impression with the necessary rapidity. He will turn about and wander to and fro according to the impulse of his fancy; and wherever he goes, he will be closely followed, for he has to deal with the imagination alone, which fashions its own pictures and which is to a certain degree indifferent as to what pictures it summons up. The rhapsodist should not himself appear in his poem as a kind of superior being. The best method for him would be to read from behind a screen, so that his hearers might turn aside their thoughts from all personality and imagine they heard the voice of the muses in general and nothing more.

With the stage-player, on the other hand, the position is exactly reversed. He comes before us as a distinct and determined individual. He wants us to interest ourselves exclusively in him and his immediate surroundings; he wants us to share his mental and bodily sufferings, to feel his perplexities, and to forget ourselves in following him. He too will, indeed, set to work in a gradual manner; but he can venture upon far more powerful effects, because in the case of sensuous presence even an unusually strong impression may be dispelled by means of a weaker one. The contemplative listener is in reason bound to remain in a state of constant sensuous exertion; he must not pause to meditate, but must follow in a state of passionate eagerness; his fancy is entirely put to silence; no claims may be made upon it, and even that which is narrated must be so placed before the eyes of the spectator as though it were actually taking place.[4]

[4] An interesting note on *Dramatic Form,* written about 1775:
" It is well-nigh time that people ceased talking about the form of dramatic compositions, about their length and shortness, their unities, their beginning, middle, and end, and all the rest of it; and that we now began to go straightway to their contents, which hitherto, it seems, have been left to take of themselves.
" There is, however, one form which is as distinct from the other as the internal sense from the external; a form which is not tangible but requires to be felt. Our head must be able to overlook that which the head of another can grasp; our heart must be able to feel that which the heart of another can feel. The intermingling of the rules will not give rise to looseness; and, though the example should prove dangerous, yet it is at bottom better to make a confused piece than a cold one.
" Indeed, if only more persons were alive to this inner form, which comprehends within itself all forms, we should not be disgusted by so many abortive productions of the intellect; writers would not think of expanding every tragic event into a drama and of slicing up every novel into a play. I wish that some clever individual would parody this twofold nuisance by arranging, say, the Æsopian fable of the Wolf and the Lamb in the form of a tragedy in five acts.
" Every form, even that which admits of the greatest amount of feeling, has in it something that is untrue. Yet the form is invariably the glass through which we collect the holy rays of extended nature and throw them upon the heart of humanity as their focus. But as for the glass — he to whom it is not given, will not succeed in obtaining it, do what he will. Like the mysterious stone of the alchemists, it is both husk and matter, both fire and cooling draught; it is so simple, so common, it lies before every door, and yet so wonderful a thing, that just those people who possess it can as a rule make no use thereof.
" He who would work for the stage should, moreover, study the stage, the effects of scenography, of lights and rouge and other coloring matter, of glazed linen and spangles. He should leave nature in her proper place, and take careful heed not to have recourse to anything but what may be performed by children with puppets upon boards and laths, together with sheets of cardboard and linen."

AUGUST WILHELM SCHLEGEL

August Wilhelm Schlegel was born at Hannover in 1767. He received his education at the Hannover Gymnasium and the University of Göttingen. He was a tutor for some years in Amsterdam, and in 1796 he went to Jena, where he married. Two years later he was made a professor at the University. Here he began his famous translation of Shakespeare, in which he was later assisted by Ludwig Tieck and others. He also contributed articles to various periodicals, and with his brother, Karl Wilhelm Friedrich, he edited the *Athenæum.* For years the two fought consistently for the new Romantic movement in literature, and their joint book, *Charakteristiken* (1801), contains many advanceguard essays. The next year August Wilhelm went to Berlin to lecture on literature and art. The publication of his play *Ion* (1803) and the study of plays, clearly indicated his interest in dramatic literature at this time. In 1807 he published in French his *Comparaison entre la Phèdre de Racine et celle d'Euripide,* in which he attacked the French classical drama. In 1808, at Vienna, he delivered a series of lectures on the drama which were printed in 1809 and 1811, under the title *Vorlesungen über dramatische Kunst und Literatur.* After his divorce in 1804 Schlegel traveled abroad. In 1813 he became secretary to the Crown Prince of Sweden. In 1818 he was made professor of literature at Bonn. He thenceforward divided his time between Oriental studies and general literature and art. He died at Bonn in 1845.

The brothers August Wilhelm and Karl Wilhelm Friedrich von Schlegel are the recognized founders of the Romantic school in Germany. August Wilhelm was one of the earliest admirers of Shakespeare and did more to encourage the reading and acting of his plays than any other man of his day. He published seventeen of the plays (Berlin, 1798–1810). He also published an excellent edition of translations from Spanish dramatic masterpieces. His lectures on dramatic art constitute a brief history as well as a vital criticism of the drama from its beginnings. These lectures were translated into many languages.

On the drama:

Schlegel's chief contributions to dramatic theory are for the most part confined to the *Vorlesungen*, although the *Characteristiken und Kritiken* and *Kritische Scriften* include references to the subject.

Editions:

The works of Schlegel were collected by E. Böcking, who edited them as *Sämtliche Werke*, 12 vols. (1846–47). The works in French were edited, by the same, as the *Œuvres écrites en français*, 3 vols. (Leipzig, 1847). The *Vorlesungen über dramatische Kunst und Literatur* are translated as *Lectures on Dramatic Art and Literature*, by John Black (2nd ed., revised by Rev. A. J. W. Morrison, Bohn Lib. ed., London, 1914).

On Schlegel and his works:

M. Bernays, *Zur Entstehungsgeschichte des Schlegelschen Shakespeare* (Leipzig, 1872).
R. Genée, *Schlegel und Shakespeare* (Leipzig, 1905).
Anna Augusta Helmholtz, *The Indebtedness of Samuel Taylor Coleridge to August Wilhelm Schlegel* (Madison, 1907).

LECTURES ON DRAMATIC ART AND LITERATURE [1]

[*Vorlesungen über dramatische Kunst und Literatur*]

(1809–11)

(LECTURE II)

Before, however, entering upon such a history as we have now described, it will be necessary to examine what is meant by *dramatic, theatrical, tragic,* and *comic*.

What is dramatic? To many the answer will seem very easy: where various persons are introduced conversing together, and the poet does not speak in his own person. This is, however, merely the first external foundation of the form; and that is dialogue. But the characters may express thoughts and sentiments without operating any change on each other, and so leave the minds of both in exactly the same state in which they were

at the commencement; in such a case, however interesting the conversation may be, it cannot be said to possess a dramatic interest. I shall make this clear by alluding to a more tranquil species of dialogue, not adapted for the stage: the philosophic. When, in Plato, Socrates asks the conceited sophist Hippias, what is the meaning of the beautiful, the latter is at once ready with a superficial answer, but is afterwards compelled by the ironical objections of Socrates to give up his former definition, and to grope about him for other ideas, till, ashamed at last and irritated at the superiority of the sage who has convicted him of his ignorance, he is forced to quit the field. This dialogue is not merely philosophically instructive, but arrests the attention like a drama in miniature. And justly, therefore, has this lively movement in the thoughts, this stretch

[1] Re-printed from *Lectures on Dramatic Art and Literature*, translated by John Black (2nd, revised, ed., Bohn Library, London, 1914). Selections from Lectures II and III.— Ed.

of expectation for the issue, in a word, the dramatic cast of the dialogues of Plato, been always celebrated.

From this we may conceive wherein consists the great charm of dramatic poetry. Action is the true enjoyment of life, nay, life itself. Mere passive enjoyment may lull us into a state of listless complacency, but even then, if possessed of the least internal activity, we cannot avoid being soon wearied. The great bulk of mankind merely from their situation in life, or from their incapacity for extraordinary exertion, are confined within a narrow circle of insignificant operations. Their days flow on in succession under the sleepy rule of custom, their life advances by an insensible progress, and the bursting torrent of the first passions of youth soon settles into a stagnant marsh. From the discontent which this occasions, we are compelled to have recourse to all sorts of diversions, which uniformly consist in a species of occupation that may be renounced at pleasure, and though a struggle with difficulties, yet with difficulties that are easily surmounted. But of all diversions the theater is undoubtedly the most entertaining. Here we may see others act even when we cannot act to any great purpose ourselves. The highest object of human activity is man, and in the drama we see men, measuring their powers with each other as intellectual and moral beings, either as friends or foes, influencing each other by their opinions, sentiments, and passions, and decisively their reciprocal relations and circumstances. The art of the poet, accordingly, consists in separating from the fable whatever does not essentially belong to it, whatever in the daily necessities of real life and the petty occupations to which they give rise interrupts the progress of important actions, and concentrating within a narrow space a number of events calculated to attract the minds of the hearers and to fill them with attention and expectation. In this manner he gives us a renovated picture of life; a compendium of whatever is moving and progressive in human existence.

But this is not all. Even in a lively oral narration it is usual to introduce persons in conversation with each other, and to give a corresponding variety to the tone and the expression. But the gaps which these conversations leave in the story the narrator fills up in his own name with a description of the accompanying circumstances and other particulars. The dramatic poet must renounce all such expedients; but for this he is richly recompensed in the following invention. He requires each of the characters in his story to be personated by a living individual; that this individual should, in sex, age, and figure, meet as near as may be the prevalent conceptions of his fictitious original, nay, assume his entire personality; that every speech should be delivered in a suitable tone of voice, and accompanied by appropriate action and gesture; and that those external circumstances should be added which are necessary to give the hearers a clear idea of what is going forward. Moreover, these representatives of the creatures of his imagination must appear in the costume belonging to their assumed rank, and to their age and country; partly for the sake of greater resemblance, and partly because, even in dress, there is something characteristic. Lastly, he must see them placed in a locality which, in some degree, resembles that where, according to his fable, the action took place, because this also contributes to the resemblance; he places them, i.e., on a scene. All this brings us to the idea of the *theater*. It is evident that the very form of dramatic poetry, that is, the exhibition of an action by dialogue without the aid of narrative, implies the theater as its necessary complement. We allow that there are dramatic works which were not originally designed for the stage and not calculated to produce any great effect there, which, nevertheless, afford great pleasure in the perusal. I am, however, very much inclined to doubt whether they would produce the same strong impression with which they affect us, upon a person who had never seen or heard a description of a theater. In reading dramatic works we are accustomed ourselves to supply the representation.

· · · · · ·

After this rapid sketch of what may be called the map of dramatic literature, we return to the examination of its fundamental ideas. Since, as we have already shown, visible representation is essential to the very form of the drama, a dramatic work may always be regarded from a double point of view — how far it is *poetical* and how far it is *theatrical*. The two are by no means inseparable. Let not, however, the expression *poetical* be misunderstood: I am not now speaking of the versification and the ornaments of language; these, when not animated by some higher excellence, are the least effective on the stage; but I speak of the poetry in the spirit and design of a piece; and this may exist in as high a degree when the drama is written in prose as in verse. What is it, then, that makes a drama poetical? The very same, assuredly, that makes other work so. It must in the first place be a connected whole, complete and satisfactory within itself. But this is merely the negative definition of a work of art, by which it is distinguished from the phenomena of nature, which run into each other, and do not possess in themselves a complete and independent existence. To be poetical it is necessary that a composition should be a mirror of ideas, that is, thoughts and feelings which in their character are necessary and eternally true, and soar above this earthly life, and also that it should exhibit them embodied before us. What the ideas are, which in this view are essential to the different departments of the drama, will hereafter be the subject of our investigation. We shall also, on the other hand, show that without them a drama becomes altogether prosaic and empirical, that is to say, patched together by the understanding out of the observations it has gathered from literal reality.

But how does a dramatic work become theatrical, or fitted to appear with advantage on the stage? In single instances it is often difficult to determine whether a work possesses such a property or not. It is indeed frequently the subject of great controversy, especially when the self-love of authors and actors comes into collision; each shifts the blame of failure on the other, and those who advocate the cause of the author appeal to an imaginary perfection of the histrionic art, and complain of the insufficiency of the existing means for its realization. But in general the answer to this question is by no means so difficult. The object proposed is to produce an impression on an assembled multitude, to rivet their attention, and to excite their interest and sympathy. In this respect the poet's occupation coincides with that of the orator. How, then, does the latter attain his end? By perspicuity, rapidity, and energy. Whatever exceeds the ordinary measure of patience or comprehension he must diligently avoid. Moreover, when a number of men are assembled together, they mutually distract each other's attention whenever their eyes and ears are not drawn to a common object without and beyond themselves. Hence the dramatic poet, as well as the orator, must from the very commencement, by strong impressions, transport his hearers out of themselves and, as it were, take bodily possession of their attention. There is a species of poetry which gently stirs a mind attuned to solitary contemplation, as soft breezes elicit melody from the Æolian harp. However excellent this poetry may be in itself, without some other accompaniments its tones would be lost on the stage. The melting *harmonica* is not calculated to regulate the march of an army, and kindle its military enthusiasm. For this we must have piercing instruments, but above all, a strongly marked rhythm, to quicken the pulsation and give a more rapid movement to the animal spirits. The grand requisite in a drama is to make this rhythm perceptible in the onward progress of the action. When this has once been effected the poet may all the sooner halt in his rapid career and indulge the bent of his own genius. There are points, when the most elaborate and polished style, the most enthusiastic lyrics, the most profound thoughts and remote illusions, the smartest coruscations of wit, and the most dazzling flights of sportive and ethereal fancy, are all in their place, and when the willing audience, even those who cannot entirely comprehend them, follow the whole with a greedy ear, like music in unison with their feelings. Here the poet's great art lies in availing himself of the effect of contrasts, which enable him at one time to produce calm repose, profound contemplation, and even the self-abandoned indifference of exhaustion, or, at another, the most tumultuous emotions, the most violent storm of the passions. With respect to theatrical fitness, however, it must not be forgotten that much must always depend on the capacities and humors of the audience, and, consequently, on the national character in general, and the particular degree of mental culture. Of all kinds of poetry the dramatic is, in a certain sense, the most secular; for, issuing from the stillness of an inspired mind, it yet fears not to exhibit itself in the midst of the noise and tumult of social life. The dramatic poet is, more than any other, obliged to court external favor and loud applause. But of course it is only in appearance that he thus lowers himself to his hearers; while, in reality, he is elevating them to himself.

In thus producing an impression on an assembled multitude, the following circumstances deserve to be weighed, in order to ascertain the whole amount of its importance. In ordinary intercourse men exhibit only the outward man to each other. They are withheld by mistrust or indifference from allowing others to look into what passes within them; and to speak with anything like emotion or agitation of that which is nearest our heart is considered unsuitable to the tone of polished society. The orator and the dramatist find means to break through these barriers of conventional reserve. While they transport their hearers into such lively emotions that the outward signs thereof break forth involuntarily, every man perceives those around him to be affected in the same manner and degree, and those who before were strangers to one another become in a moment intimately acquainted. The tears which the dramatist or the orator compels them to shed for calumniated innocence or dying heroism make friends and brothers of them all. Almost inconceivable is the power of a visible communion of numbers to give intensity to those feelings of the heart which usually retire into privacy, or only open themselves to the confidence of friendship. The faith in the validity of such emotions becomes irrefragable from its dif-

fusion; we feel ourselves strong among so many associates, and all hearts and minds flow together in one great and irresistible stream. On this very account, the privilege of influencing an assembled crowd is exposed to most dangerous abuses. As one may disinterestedly animate them for the noblest and best of purposes, so another may entangle them in the deceitful meshes of sophistry, and dazzle them by the glare of a false magnanimity whose vainglorious crimes may be painted as virtues and even as sacrifices. Beneath the delightful charms of oratory and poetry, the poison steals imperceptibly into ear and heart. Above all others must the comic poet (seeing that his very occupation keeps him always on the slippery brink of this precipice) take heed lest he avoid an opportunity for the lower and baser parts of human nature to display themselves without restraint. When the sense of shame which ordinarily keeps these baser propensities within the bounds of decency, is once weakened by the sight of others' participation in them, our inherent sympathy with what is vile will soon break out into the most unbridled licentiousness. . . .

. . .

(LECTURE III)

. . .

The dramatic poet, as well as the epic, represents external events, but he represents them as real and present. In common with the lyric poet, he also claims our mental participation, but not in the same calm composedness; the feeling of joy and sorrow which the dramatist excites is more immediate and vehement. He calls forth all the emotions which the sight of similar deeds and fortunes of living men would elicit, and it is only by the total sum of the impression which he produces that he ultimately resolves the conflicting emotions into a harmonious tone of feeling. As he stands in such close proximity to real life, and endeavors to indue his own imaginary creations with vitality, the equanimity of the epic poet would in him be indifferent; he must decidedly take part with one or other of the leading views of human life, and constrain his audience also to participate in the same feeling.

To employ simpler and more intelligible language: the *tragic* and *comic* bear the same relation to one another as *earnest* and *sport*. Every man, from his own experience, is acquainted with both these states of mind; but to determine their essence and their source would demand deep philosophical investigation. Both, indeed, bear the stamp of our common nature, but earnestness belongs more to its moral, and mirth to its animal, part. The creatures destitute of reason are incapable either of earnest or of sport. Animals seem, indeed, at times to labor as if they were earnestly intent upon some aim and as if they made the present moment subordinate to the future; at other times they seem to sport, that is, they give themselves up without object or purpose to the pleasure of existence; but they do not possess consciousness, which alone can entitle these two conditions to the names of earnest and sport. Man alone, of all the animals with which we are acquainted, is capable of looking back towards the past and forward into futurity; and he has to purchase the enjoyment of this noble privilege at a dear rate. Earnestness, in the most extensive signification, is the direction of our mental powers to some aim. But as soon as we begin to call ourselves to account for our actions, reason compels us to fix this aim higher and higher, till we come at last to the highest end of our existence: and here that longing for the infinite which is inherent in our being is baffled by the limits of our finite existence. All that we do, all that we effect, is vain and perishable; death stands everywhere in the background, and to it every well or ill spent moment brings us nearer and closer; and, even when a man has been so singularly fortunate as to reach the utmost term of life without any grievous calamity, the inevitable doom still awaits him to leave or to be left by all that is most dear to him on earth. There is no bond of love without a separation, no enjoyment without the grief of losing it. When, however, we contemplate the relations of our existence to the extreme limit of possibilities; when we re-

flect on its entire dependence on a chain of causes and effects stretching beyond our ken; when we consider how weak and helpless, and doomed to struggle against the enormous powers of an unknown world, as it were ship-wrecked at our very birth; how we are subject to all kinds of errors and deceptions, any one of which may be our ruin; that in our passions we cherish an enemy in our bosoms; how every moment demands from us in the name of the most sacred duties the sacrifice of our dearest inclinations, and how at one blow we may be robbed of all that we have acquired with much toil and difficulty; that with every accession to our stores the risk of loss is proportionally increased, and we are only the more exposed to the malice of hostile force; when we think upon all this every heart which is not dead to feeling must be overpowered by an inexpressible melancholy for which there is no other counterpoise than the consciousness of a vocation transcending the limits of this earthly life. This is the tragic tone of mind; and when the thought of the possible issues out of the mind as a living reality, when this tone pervades and animates a visible representation of the most striking instances of violent revolutions in a man's fortunes, either prostrating his mental energies, or calling forth the most heroic endurance — then the result is *Tragic Poetry*. We thus see how this kind of poetry has its foundation in our nature, while to a certain extent we have also answered the question, why we are fond of such mournful representations, and even find something consoling and elevating in them. This tone of mind we have described is inseparable from strong feeling; and although poetry cannot remove these internal dissonances, she must at least endeavor to effect an ideal reconciliation of them.

As earnestness, in the highest degree, is the essence of tragic representation, so in sport of the comic. The disposition of mirth is a forgetfulness of all gloomy considerations in the pleasant feeling of present happiness. We are then inclined to view everything in a sportive light, and to allow nothing to disturb or ruffle our minds. The imperfections and the irregularities of men

RICHARD WAGNER

are no longer an object of dislike and compassion, but serve, by their strange inconsistencies, to entertain the understanding and to amuse the fancy. The comic poet must therefore carefully abstain from whatever is calculated to excite more indignation at the conduct or sympathy with the situations of his personages, because this would inevitably bring us back again into earnestness. He must paint their irregularities as springing out of the predominance of the animal part of their nature, and the incidents which befall them as merely ludicrous distresses, which will be attended with no fatal consequences. This is uniformly what takes place in what we call Comedy, in which, however, there is still a mixture of seriousness, as I shall show in the sequel. The oldest comedies of the Greeks was, however, entirely sportive, and in that respect, formed the most complete contrast to their tragedy. Not only were the characters and situations of individuals worked up into a comic picture of real life, but the whole frame of society, the constitution, nature, and the gods, were all fantastically painted in the most ridiculous and laughable colors.

RICHARD WAGNER

Wilhelm Richard Wagner was born at Leipzig in 1813. His father died when Richard was in his infancy, and his stepfather, dramatist, actor, and painter, intended Richard to be a painter, but as he himself confesses, he had no talent. He soon developed a taste for music and played the piano before he was six. However, music was of only secondary interest, for at the age of eleven he wrote a poem which was published. He then became interested in plays, and while he was still a child he learned English in order to read Shakespeare, and even wrote a tragedy in imitation of him. It was after hearing Beethoven's *Egmont* music that Wagner determined to furnish similar music for his tragedy. At this time he decided to become a composer, and in quick succession he wrote a number of miscellaneous compositions. An orchestral overture was even performed. His schooling had been irregular, though he attended the University. He then studied composition at the Thomasschule in Leipzig. He produced his first symphony in 1833, and the next year he conducted an opera at Magdeburg. In 1836 he was looking for a position at Königsberg, and there he married. Three years later he took his unfinished *Rienzi* to Paris, but was unsuccessful in having it produced. In 1842 it was heard at Dresden, and was followed by *Der fliegende Holländer*.

Tannhäuser was played in 1845. *Lohengrin* was completed three years after, but that year he was forced to leave Saxony for political reasons. He went to Zürich where he remained until 1859. He was constantly working at the tetralogy, *Der Ring des Nibelungen,* but wrote *Tristan und Isolde* in the meantime (1865). He was pardoned in 1861 and returned to his native country. Three years after, he produced *Die Meistersinger*. In 1870 Wagner married Cosima, Liszt's daughter. Ludwig, King of Bavaria, invited him to Munich to finish the *Ring*. Six years later the whole tetralogy was performed at Bayreuth, where Wagner had worked out his plans for the celebrated opera-house. His last work was *Parsifal*. He died at Bayreuth in 1883.

It must be borne in mind that Wagner was primarily a dramatic poet and not a composer, that his first interest was in the drama, and that he turned to music only as a supplementary element in completing the true art-work. Throughout some ten volumes of collected writings he wrote theories — often obscurely, almost as obscurely as the translator of his collected works — on the new music-drama form, but these are reducible to the one theory that the art-work of the future is a combination of music and drama. Probably the best statement is found in *Ueber die Bestim-*

mung der Oper (1871). He once said: "A subject which is comprehended merely by the intelligence can also be expressed merely through the language of words; but the more it expands into an emotional concept, the more does it call for an expression which in its final and essential fullness can alone be obtained through the language of sounds. Hereby the essence of that which the Word-Tone-Poet has to express results quite by itself: it is the Purely Human, freed from all conventions."

On the drama:

In practically all Wagner's theoretical writings, in his letters, his autobiography, and criticisms, there are references to the drama. The most important of these are:

Das Kunstwerk der Zukunft (1849).
Oper und Drama (1851).
Eine Mittheilung an meine Freunde (1851).
Zur Widmung der zweiten Auflage von "Oper und Drama" (1868).
Ueber die Bestimmung der Oper (1871).
Ueber die Anwendung der Musik auf das Drama (1879). (These appeared as articles, letters, etc., at different times between 1835 and 1883.)
All the above are translated by William Ashton Ellis in *Richard Wagner's Prose Works,* 8 vols. (London, 1892 ff).
Selections from a number of the more characteristic writings are translated by Edward L. Burlingame in *Art Life and Theories of Richard Wagner* (New York, 1875). *The Purpose of the Opera* in this volume is a translation of *Die Bestimmung der Oper.*

Editions:

The complete works are *Gesammelte Schriften und Dichtungen von Richard Wagner,* 10 vols. (Leipzig, 1871–83). These are translated (the plays and poems omitted) as *Richard Wagner's Prose Works,* by William Ashton Ellis, 8 vols. (London, 1892–99).

On Wagner and his works:

H. S. Chamberlain, *Richard Wagner* (München, 1896. Translated as the same by G. Ainslie Hight, London, 1900).
——, *The Wagnerian Drama* (New York, 1915).
C. F. Glasenapp, *Das Leben Richard Wagners,* 6 vols. (3rd ed., Leipzig, 1894–1911).
Ernest Newman, *A Study of Wagner* (New York, 1899).
——, *Wagner as Man and Artist* (London, 1914).
E. H. Krehbiel, *Studies in the Wagnerian Drama* (New York, 1898).
Edwin Evans, *An Introduction to the Study of Wagner's Prose Works* (London, 1913).
Richard Wagner, *Mein Leben,* 2 vols. (München, 1911).

THE PURPOSE OF THE OPERA [1]

[*Ueber die Bestimmung der Oper*]

(1871)

* * * * *

The very essence of the dramatic art, therefore, as opposed to the poetic method, appears to be at first sight entirely irrational; it is only to be grasped by a complete change in the nature of the observer. It should not be difficult for us to determine in what this change should consist, if we look at the *natural*

[1] Re-printed extract from *Art Life and Theories of Richard Wagner,* by Edward L. Burlingame (New York, 1875).— Ed.

method in the beginnings of *all* art — and this we find distinctly in *improvisation.* The poet who should show to the improvising actor a plan of the action to be represented, would stand in much the same relation in which the author of an operatic text stands to the musician; his work cannot yet have any artistic value whatever; but this will be most fully imparted to it if the poet makes the actor's improvising spirit his own, and carries out his work completely in the character of an improvisation, so that now the actor can enter with all his own peculiarity into the higher thought of the poet. Of course, a complete change in the art-product itself must take place through this means; and such a change could only be exactly described, if it were possible to have before us the actually transcribed improvisation of a great musician.

We have the testimony of excellent witnesses to the incomparable impression which Beethoven left upon his friends by improvising at the piano; and we cannot regard as exaggerated the regret expressed at the fact of not having been able to preserve these creations in writing — it cannot be called exaggerated even when we consider the master's greatest written works, if we remember the frequent occurrence, that even less gifted composers, whose compositions when written out are characterized by stiffness and constraint, can, by free improvisation, throw us into genuine amazement at a creative gift never before suspected and often most productive.

In any case, we believe we shall greatly facilitate the solution of a very difficult problem if we call the Shakespearian drama a *definitely-planned histrionic improvisation of the very highest artistic value*. For if we take this view we shall have an immediate explanation of the apparently remarkable inconsistencies in the action and language of characters who are created with the single purpose of *being*, now and at the moment when they are before us, precisely those characters they are *meant* to appear to us, — and to whom no language could possibly occur which would lie outside this *nature*, with which they are, as it were, bewitched. And it would seem absurd enough, on closer consideration, if one of these characters should suddenly seek to appear to us in the character of a poet. This element is silent, and remains a riddle to us, as Shakespeare does. Yet its work is the only true drama; and we see what importance the drama really has as a work of art, in the fact that its author will always appear to us the deepest poetic nature of all time.

To continue the considerations to which the drama so strongly urges us,

let us now look at those peculiarities of it which seem most serviceable for our purpose. Most prominent among these is the fact that, apart from all its other value, it belongs to the class of pieces which alone are effective in the *theater* — pieces that have been arranged expressly for the theater at different periods, have proceeded *from* the theater or from authors standing in direct communication with it, and have from year to year enriched the popular French stage, for example. The difference between them lies only in the *poetic* value of true dramatic products that have arisen from the same origin. This difference seems at first sight to be determined by the greatness and importance of the material selected for their action. While not only the French have succeeded in most truthfully depicting upon the stage all the events of modern life in general, but the Germans (people of much less theatrical talent) have successfully brought forward the occurrences of this life in its smaller and more domestic circle, this truly reproductive force has failed just in proportion as the events of a higher sphere of action, and the fate of historic heroes and the myths concerning them (removed to a respectful distance from matters of everyday life), were sought to be produced. For this purpose the true poet (that is, the inventor and former of myths) had to overcome the insufficient dramatic improvisation; and his genius, especially fitted for such a task, must manifest itself in raising the style of that improvisation to the height of his own poetic purpose. How Shakespeare succeeded in raising his players themselves to this height, must remain a problem; it is only certain that the capacities of our modern players would at once fail in the task thus set them. The assumption is possible, that the grotesque affectation peculiar to the English actors of the present day (to which we referred above) is a remnant of an earlier power which, since it comes from a trait lying undeniably in the nature of the nation, may have been able, in the most perfect period of national life and through the noble example of the poetic actor himself, to lead to so unprecedented a point in theatrical art that Shakespeare's conceptions could be for once fully carried out.

Or we may perhaps call to mind for the explanation of this enigma, if we do not wish to accept so extraordinary a miracle as that just supposed, the fate of the great Sebastian Bach, whose rich and difficult choral compositions would appear to lead us to the theory that the master must have had at command for their execution the most incomparable vocal forces; while on the contrary we know from undoubted documentary evidence his own complaints of the general wretched composition of his choir of schoolboys. It is certain that Shakespeare retired very early from his connection with the stage; a fact that we can easily explain by the very great fatigue the rehearsals of his pieces cost him, as well as his despair at the flight of his own genius beyond the possibilities that were open to him. The whole nature of his genius is, however, only clear to us through these very "possibilities," which certainly existed in the basis of the actor's nature, and were therefore very properly taken for granted by the author; and, considering the efforts for culture made by the genius of humanity in one great connection, we can look upon it as the task which the great dramatist in a certain sense bequeathed to his successors, to really *reach* those highest possibilities in the development of the capabilities of histrionic art.

To labor at this task appears to have been the truest calling of our own great German poets. Proceeding from the necessary acknowledgment of Shakespeare's inimitability, this purpose determined a direction for every form of their poetic conception, which we can well understand if we keep this hypothesis in mind. The search for the ideal form of the highest work of art — the drama — led them of necessity away from Shakespeare to the renewed and always deeper consideration of the tragedy of the ancients; we have seen in what way alone they thought to gain anything from this, and we observed that they were necessarily led from this more than doubtful path to that inexplicable new impression which the noblest creations of the opera (in other respects entirely enigmatical to them) produced upon them.

Two things were noteworthy in connection with this, namely, that the noble music of a great master could give an ideal enchantment to the work of even little-gifted dramatic performers, an enchantment which was denied to even the most admirable actors of the spoken drama; while on the other hand a true dramatic talent could so ennoble utterly worthless music that we could be struck by a performance which the same talent could not succeed in producing in a spoken play. That this phenomenon could only be explained by the power of *music,* was unavoidable. And this could be true only of music *in general;* while it remained incomprehensible how the peculiar flexibility of its forms could be attained without their subordination to the worst possible kind of dramatic poet.

We adduced the example of Shakespeare, to give us as much of a glimpse as possible into the nature, and especially the method, of the true dramatist. And mysterious as the greater part of this must be to us, we could nevertheless perceive that it was the actor's art with which the poet entirely united; and we recognized that this actor's art was the dew of life, in which the poetic purpose must be bathed, in order that it might be able, as though by a magic transformation, to appear a true mirror of life. Now, in every action, even ordinary event of life (such as not only Shakespeare but every true playwright shows us), can reveal itself to us, when reproduced as a mimic drama, in the glorified light and with the objective effect of a mirrored picture, we must accept as proved as a result of our further considerations, that this reflection in turn shows itself in the pure light of the ideal so soon as it has been dipped in the magic fountain of music; and at the same time is displayed to us as a pure form, freed from all realistic materialization.

It would no longer be needful, therefore, to take into consideration the *form of music,* but rather the forms of music *as historically developed,* if one desired to determine that highest possibility in the development of the actor's art, which seemed to the investigator and the worker a dark enigma, while on the other hand it pressed itself more and more upon him.

By "the form of music" we must undoubtedly understand *melody*. The development of this especially fills the history of our music; as the need of it determined the development of the lyric drama attempted by the Italians, into the opera. The attempt being first made to imitate in this respect the form of the Greek tragedy, this seemed at the first glance to be divided into two principal parts — the choral song, and the dramatic recitation which periodically rose into musical measure; and the actual "drama" was thus left to the recitative, the oppressive monotony of which was finally interrupted by the discovery of the "air" (an invention approved by the academy). It was only with this that music gained its independent form as *melody;* and it thus (very rightly) won such an advantage over the remaining factors of the musical drama, that this latter, no longer employed as anything but an excuse for the other, finally sank to the place of a mere scaffolding for the exhibition of the *aria*. It must be the history of melody closely limited to this *aria* form, which must therefore engage our attention, if we are not entirely content with the consideration of those of its effects merely, which it presented to our great poets when they felt themselves so deeply impressed by its power, yet so much more deeply at a loss in thinking of any poetic association with it. It was indisputably only a special form of genius that could so endue with life this narrow and empty form of melodic expression, that it could be capable of a really powerful effect. Its extension and development was therefore only to be expected from the musician; and the course of that development could be distinctly seen by a comparison of Mozart's masterpiece with Gluck's. In this comparison a rich power of purely musical invention is especially displayed as the only thing which could make pure music powerful in a dramatic sense; for in Mozart's *Don Juan* there is an abundance of dramatic elements of which the far less powerful composer Gluck had no conception. But it was reserved for German genius to elevate the musical

form, by the highest inspiration of even its least important parts to the inexhaustible variety and richness which the music of our great Beethoven now offers to a wondering world.

The musical creations of Beethoven have traits which render them as inexplicable from one point of view as those of Shakespeare are from another. While the powerful influence of both must be felt as different in kind though equal in effect, even this difference between them seems to disappear upon closer consideration, and in view of the incomprehensible peculiarity of their creations; for the only way of explaining the one appears to us in the explanation given for the other.

Let us instance in proof of this, and as the most easily intelligible point, the peculiarity of the humorous element in both, and we shall see that what often appears to us as an incomprehensible inconsistency in the humor of Shakespeare's creations, appears in precisely similar features of Beethoven's work as a natural piece of high idealism — presented as a melody which is inseparable from the mood of the listener. We cannot escape here from the assumption of a primal connection between the two, which we shall be able to properly define if we do not look upon it as existing between the musician and the poet— but as between one poetic actor or *mimic*, and another. The secret lies in the *directness* of the representation, conveyed in the one case by expression and action, and in the other by living music. That which both create and form is the true work of art, for which the poet only draws the plan — and even this unsuccessfully, unless he has taken it directly from nature.

We have seen that the Shakespearian drama is most correctly comprehended under the name of a "definite imitative improvisation"; and we were obliged to assume that the highest poetic value, though emanating at first from the dignity of the material selected, must be secured to such a work of art by the elevation of the *style* of that improvisation. We cannot be mistaken, therefore, in thinking that such an elevation, to the extent which is really needed, can only be found in that music which stands in just such a relation to it as does Beethoven's music to Shakespeare's dramas.

The very point in which the difficulty of applying music like Beethoven's to dramas like Shakespeare's is here most prominently to be seen, might, if properly adjusted, lead directly to the highest perfection of musical form, by freeing it from every fetter that may still hamper it. That which so perplexed our great poets in their consideration of the opera, and that feature in Beethoven's instrumental music which still distinctly shows the skeleton of a structure found rather in the same tendency that produced the opera *aria* and the ballet piece, than in the true nature of music — these features of conventional composition, though endowed with such wonderfully vigorous life by Beethoven's use of melody, would thus most completely disappear before an ideal method full of the truest freedom. Thus music, in this respect at least, would adapt itself closely to the thoroughly life-filled form of a Shakespearian drama which, when its noble irregularity is compared with the drama of the ancients, seems almost like a scene in nature beside an architectural work — while its thoroughly logical character nevertheless is revealed in the certainty of the effect the work of art produces. In this, too, would be shown the entire novelty of the form of such an art product which, only conceivable (as an idealized natural production) by employing in it the aid of the German language, the most cultured of modern tongues, could nevertheless deceive the judgment as long as a standard was applied to it which it had entirely outgrown — whereas the fitting new standard would be derived from the impression which the unwritten improvisation of an incomparable composer would make upon one fortunate enough to hear it. The greatest of dramatists has taught us to give definite form to such an improvisation; and in the highest conceivable work of art the noblest inspirations of both composer and dramatist should exist as the very essence of the world thus revealed to us in the mirror of the world itself.

If we adopt, for the work of art which we have in view this designation, "a dramatic-musical improvisation of perfected poetic value, embodied in a fixed form by the highest artistic thought," we shall find, if we follow the teachings of experience, a surprising light thrown upon the practical points connected with the actual execution of such a work.

In a very important sense, and interpreting the matter strictly, our great poets could only be chiefly concerned with the discovery of some method by which a heightened pathos could be added to the drama, and a technical means be found for embodying this. However certain it may be that Shakespeare derived his style from the instincts of the actor's art, he must nevertheless have been dependent for the presentation of his dramas on the accident of greater or less talent in his players, who must all have been to a certain extent Shakespeares, just as he himself was always to a certain extent the character presented; and we have no reason for the assumption that his genius could have recognized in the performance of his pieces more than the mere shadow of himself cast upon the stage.

That which so strangely attracted our great poets toward music was the fact that it was at the same time the purest form and the most sensuous realization of that form. The abstract arithmetical number, the mathematical figure, meets us here as a creation having an irresistible influence upon the emotions — that is, it appears as *melody;* and this can be as unerringly established so as to produce sensuous effect, as the poetic diction of written language, on the contrary, is abandoned to every whim in the personal character of the person reciting it. What was not practically possible for Shakespeare — to be *himself* the actor of each one of his rôles — is practicable for the musical composer, and this with great definiteness — since he speaks to us directly through each one of the musicians who execute his works. In this case the transmigration of the poet's soul into the body of the performer takes place according to the infallible laws of the most positive *technique;* and the composer who gives the correct measure for a technically right performance of his work becomes completely one with the musician who performs it, to an extent that can at most only be affirmed of the constructive artist in regard to a work which he had himself produced in color or stone — if, indeed, a transmigration of his soul into lifeless matter is a supposable case.

If we add to this wonderful power in the musician that capacity of his art which we deduced from the facts we considered in the beginning — the facts that even insignificant music (so long as it is not entirely distorted into the vulgar grotesquesness of certain kinds of opera now popular) makes otherwise unattainable performances possible to a great dramatic talent, while noble music can almost *force* from insignificant dramatic powers successes impossible in any other way — when we add the results of these facts to the musician's power, we can scarcely feel a doubt as to the reason of the complete failure which this view predicts for the poet of to-day, if he attempts to succeed in mastering the drama, in its noblest sense, by the only means at his command — the capabilities of the same language in which now even newspaper articles speak to us!

In this respect, however, our assumption that the highest perfection is reserved for the musically-arranged drama, should have a hopeful, rather than a discouraging influence upon us: for here we are primarily concerned with the purification of a great and many-sided department of art — that of the drama as a whole — the errors of which are to-day both increased and concealed by the influence of the modern opera. To gain a clean conception of this, and to accurately measure the field of their future productiveness, our dramatists might perhaps find it advisable to trace back the descent of the modern theater; but not to seek its origin in the ancient drama, which was in its form a so completely original product of the Hellenic mind, its religion, and even its form of government, that the assumption that it had been imitated by later forms would lead to the greatest errors. The origin of the modern theater, on the contrary, shows us along the path of its development such an abundance of noble productions of the greatest value, that this path may certainly be followed further without shame. The genuine theatrical "play," in its most modern sense, would

have to be the only healthful basis of all further dramatic efforts; but in order to labor successfully in this direction it is necessary first of all to form a right conception of the spirit of theatrical art, which has its basis in the art of the *actor;* and not to use it for the formulating of tendencies, but as the reflection of life-pictures such as are really seen.

The French, who have even recently contributed so much that is excellent in this respect, did not, it is true, look for the appearance of a new Molière among them every year; and for us too the birth of a Shakespeare is not to be read in every calendar.

As far as seeking to satisfy ideal demands is concerned, the limit to which such demands may properly go seems to be set, for the influence of the all-powerful dramatic work of art which we have in view, with greater certainty than has before been possible. This point may be distinctly recognized as existing where, in that art-product, song comes in contact with *spoken* words. Yet by no means an absolutely narrow sphere is indicated by this, but rather an entirely different and dissimilar one; and we may at once gain an insight into this difference if we call to mind a certain involuntary compulsion which forces even our best dramatic singers into excess; and by which they feel themselves forced to *speak* an emphatic word in the very midst of their song. Schröder-Devrient, for example, saw herself compelled to this course by a fearfully highly wrought situation in the opera of *Fidelio* where, holding her pistol before the tyrant, she suddenly positively *spoke —* and with a terrible accent of despair — the last word of the phrase —" another step — and thou art — DEAD." The indescribable effect of this acted upon every one as a harsh break from one sphere into the other; and the power of it consisted in this, that as though by a flash of lightning we gained a sudden insight into the nature of both spheres, one of them the ideal, and the other the real. It was evident that for a moment the ideal one was incapable of bearing a burden which it therefore cast upon the other; and as especially passionate and excited music is so commonly credited with a purely morbid element inherent in it, it may easily surprise us to recognize from this example how delicate and purely ideal in form its sphere really is, so that the realistic terrors of actual life cannot be contained in it — though the soul of all reality finds pure expression in music alone.

Evidently, therefore, there is a side to the world which concerns us most seriously, and the terrible teachings of which are only intelligible to us in the field of observation, in which music must be silent. This field is perhaps best estimated, if we allow ourselves to be led into it by the great actor, Shakespeare, as far as the point where we find him overcome by that despairing discouragement which we have thought it necessary to assume as the reason of his early retirement from the stage. This field may be best called, if not the basis, at least the manifestation of history; and to properly seize upon its real value for human knowledge, must always be left to the poet alone.

So important and distinct an influence as we could only attempt to indicate here by the merest outline — an influence exercised not only upon that department of the drama with which it is most closely connected with the drama in any way — such an influence could only be possible for the musically-arranged and executed dramatic work that we have referred to, if the latter, in its production before the public, can render itself outwardly intelligible in a consistent way, and thus enable an opinion of its characteristics to be formed with the necessary freedom. It is so closely related to the opera that we feel we may rightly look upon it, as far as our present consideration is concerned, as the province of that branch of art; none of the possibilities suggested to us could have been clear to us if they had not been manifested for us in the opera in general, and especially in the most admirable works of the great operatic composers. And just as certainly, it was the spirit of music which, in the constantly increasing richness of its development, could have such an influence upon the opera that these possibilities could in any way arise within it. And yet, if we desire to explain the degradation which the opera

has undergone, we must seek its cause again in the peculiarities of music. As in painting and even in architecture, the merely "attractive" may displace the beautiful, so it has been not the less the less fate of music to decline from a noble to a merely pleasing art. If its sphere was that of the purest idealism — if it had so deep an influence on our emotions and freed what was realistic from everything disagreeable in its representation by the very fact that it showed itself to us as pure form alone, so that what threatened to disturb this fell or was kept away from it — even if all this was true, yet this pure form, if not placed in an entirely appropriate relation to its environment, might easily seem only suitable for a pleasant plaything and only be used for such a purpose. This would be the case as soon as it was used, in so unfitting a sphere as the basis of the opera could offer it, as a mere superficial method of giving pleasure to the sense of hearing or arousing the emotions.

But we are little concerned here with this view, for we began our essay with the complaint made against the effect and the influence of the opera, the unfortunate importance of which cannot be better shown than by pointing to the universal experience, that the stage of to-day has long been given up and viewed with complete indifference by the truly educated portion of the nation, who used once to look to it with every hope. If we wish, then, to secure for the work of art we have just described the only esteem which could be just and valuable for it — that of those who have turned with serious displeasure from the recent stage — this can only be possible outside of all relation with that stage. The neutral ground, however, on which it can be done, though ever so completely separated *locally* from the field of influence of our theaters, could only bear proper fruit if nourished by the real elements of our histrionic and musical arts. In these alone lies the truly productive material for genuine dramatic achievement; every attempt of every other kind must lead not to art, but to an affected artificiality.

It is our actors, singers, and musicians upon whose own instincts all hope for the attainment of artistic objects must rest, even when these objects themselves may be incomprehensible to them. For they must be the ones to whom these objects will most speedily become clear, as soon as their own artistic instincts are put upon the right path toward their recognition. That these instincts of theirs have hitherto been only guided, by the influences of our stage toward the development of the very worst qualities of dramatic ambition — this fact must inspire us with the wish to at least occasionally free these otherwise invaluable dramatic forces from such tendencies, to permit their *good* qualities to gain that practice which would quickly and decidedly make them serviceable in the realization of our proposed art-work. For it is only the peculiar will of this guild of actors, so singular in their erroneous course, from which the perfect drama we have indicated can come, just as indeed every excellent dramatic result that has ever appeared has emanated from them. The decline of theatrical art in our time has been brought about less by them than by those who have hitherto — though without any authority — been their leaders.

If we desire to point out that thing which, of all on German soil is and continues to be least worthy of the fame of our great modern triumphs, we must point to *the stage,* the whole course of which has prominently and boldly shown it to be a very betrayer of German honor.

Whoever makes any effort to sustain this course must submit to a judgment which will necessarily class him with a part of our public life that is of a most doubtful nature — and from which it will be as difficult to emerge into a sphere of pure art, as it will be to rise from the opera to the ideal drama we have supposed. It is certainly true that if, according to Schiller's remark (here apparently inexact) that "art has only declined through the fault of the artists"— it can only be *elevated again by the artists,* and not by those by whose pleasure in art that art suffers injury. To help this elevation of the art-standard by artists, and to help it from without as well, this effort should be the national atonement for the national sin: the evil influence of the modern German stage.

GUSTAV FREYTAG

Gustav Freytag was born in 1816 at Kreuzburg. He entered the gymnasium at Oels in 1829. Six years later he began studying philology at the University of Breslau. Five years later he took his doctor's degree at the University of Berlin. He taught German literature and language at the University of Breslau between 1839 and 1846. He wrote a successful comedy, *Die Brautfahrt* (1844), which was followed soon after by a volume of poems, and the plays *Die Valentine* (1846) and *Graf Waldemar* (1847). He came to Berlin in 1846 and edited a political journal. In 1853 he produced his greatest comedy, one of the most characteristic German plays, *Die Journalisten.* When in 1858 he published his best-known novel, *Soll und haben,* his name was firmly established.

Through his political work he became acquainted with the nobility and in 1870 he was attached to the staff of the Prussian Crown Prince, and was present at some of the battles of the war. Meantime he was busy with various novels and miscellaneous writings, of which the most important was the novel, *Die verlorne Handschrift* (1864). In 1863 he had written his *Technik des Dramas.* He died in 1895, after living in retirement for a number of years at Wiesbaden.

Die Technik des Dramas is a handbook of practical advice, written as it is by a practicing dramatist of talent. Freytag was likewise a scholar of no mean attainments. The book was considered until recently one whose principles were for the most part applicable to present-day playwriting, and only the appearance of William Archer's *Playmaking* relegated it to the unimportant position it now occupies as a practical manual. The author's purpose is best set forth in his own words, taken from the Introduction: " Indeed, the best source of technical rules is the plays of great poets, which still to-day exercise their charm alike on reader and spectator, especially the Greek tragedies. Whoever accustoms himself to look aside from the peculiarities of the old models, will notice with real joy that the skillful tragic poet of the Athenians, Sophocles, used the fundamental laws of dramatic construction with enviable certainty and shrewdness. For development, climax, and return of the action, he presents us a model seldom reached." Perhaps one of the greatest drawbacks of the *Technik* is the comparatively small field from which the author takes his models. Sophocles, Shakespeare, Lessing, Goethe, and Schiller are practically the only dramatists whom Freytag considers.

On the drama:

Die Technik des Dramas is Freytag's principal contribution to dramatic theory.

Editions:

The standard edition of the works is the *Gesammelte Werke, 22* vols. (Leipzig, 1886–88).
Die Technik des Dramas was first published in 1863. It was translated as *The Technique of the Drama,* by Elias J. MacEwan (Chicago, 1894. 5th ed., Chicago, later).

On Freytag and his works:

Preface to MacEwan's translation above cited.
Gustav Freytag, *Erinnerungen aus meinen Leben* (Leipzig, 1887).
Karl Aldenhoven, *Erinnerungen an Gustav Freytag* (in *Gesammelte Aufsätze,* Leipzig, 1911).
Georg Schridde, *Gustav Freytags Kultur- und Geschichtspsychologie* (Leipzig, 1910).
Otto Mayrhofer, *Gustav Freytag und das junge Deutschland* (Marburg, 1907).
Friedrich Seiler, *Gustav Freytag* (Leipzig, 1898).
Hans Lindau, *Gustav Freytag* (Leipzig, 1907).

THE TECHNIQUE OF THE DRAMA [1]
[*Die Technik des Dramas*]
(1863)

[THE IDEA. I]

In the soul of the poet the drama gradually takes shape out of the crude material furnished by the account of some striking event. First appear single movements; internal conflicts and personal resolution, a deed fraught with consequence, the collision of two characters, the opposition of a hero to his surroundings, rise so prominently above their connection with other incidents, that they become the occasion for the

transformation of other material. This transformation goes on to such an extent that the main element, vividly perceived, and comprehended in its entrancing, soul-stirring or terrifying significance, is separated from all that casually accompanies it, and with single supplementary, invented elements, is brought into a unifying relation of cause and effect. The new unit which this arises in the *Idea* of the Drama. This is the center toward which further independent inventions are directed, like rays. This idea works with a power similar to the secret power of crystallization. Through this are unity of action, significance of characters, and at last,

[1] Re-printed from the latest edition of Elias J. MacEwan's translation of *The Technique of the Drama* (Chicago, n. d.). Excerpts from early chapters.— Ed.

the whole structure of the drama produced.

How ordinary material becomes a poetic idea through inspiration, the following example will show. A young poet of the last century reads the following notice in a newspaper: "Stuttgart, Jan. 11.— In the dwelling of the musician, Kritz, were found yesterday, his eldest daughter, Louise, and Duke Blasius von Boller, major of dragoons, lying dead upon the floor. The accepted facts in the case, and the medical examination indicated that both had come to their deaths by drinking poison. There is a rumor of an attachment between the pair, which the major's father, the well-known President von Boller, had sought to break off. The sad fate of the young woman, universally esteemed on account of her modest demeanor, awakens the sympathy of all people of sensibility."

From the material thus afforded, the fancy of the poet, aroused by sympathy, fashions the character of an ardent and passionate youth, and of an innocent and susceptible maiden. The contrast between the court atmosphere, from which the lover has emerged, and the narrow circle of a little village household, is vividly felt. The hostile father becomes a heartless, intriguing courtier. An unavoidable necessity arises of explaining the frightful resolution of a vigorous youth, a resolution apparently growing out of such a situation. The creative poet finds this inner connection in an illusion which the father has produced in the soul of the son, in a suspicion that his beloved is unfaithful. In this manner the poet makes the account intelligible to himself and to others; while freely inventing, he introduces an internal consistency. These inventions are, in appearance, little supplementary additions, but they make an entirely original production which stands over against the original occurrence as something new, and has something like the following contents in the breast of a young nobleman, jealousy toward his beloved, a girl of the middle-class, has been so excited by his father that he destroys both her and himself by poison. Through this remodeling an occurrence in real life becomes a dramatic idea. From this time forward the real occurrence is unessential to the poet. The place, and family name, are lost sight of; indeed, whether the event happened as reported, or what was the character of the victims, and of their parents, or their rank, no longer matters at all; quick perception and the first activity of creative power have given to the occurrence a universally intelligible meaning and an intrinsic truth. The controlling forces of the piece are no longer accidental and to be found in a single occurrence; they could enter into a hundred cases, and with the accepted characters and the assumed connection, the outcome would always be the same.

When the poet has once thus infused his own soul into the material, then he adopts from the real account some things which suit his purpose — the title of the father and of the son, the name of the bride, the business of her parents, perhaps single traits of character which he may turn to account. Alongside this goes further creative work; the chief characters are developed, to their distinct individualities; accessory figures are created — a quarrelsome accomplice of the father, another woman, the opposite of the beloved, personality of the parents; new impulses are given to the action, and all these inventions are determined and rules by the idea of the piece.

This idea, the first invention of the poet, the silent soul through which he gives life to the material coming to him from external sources, does not easily place itself before him as a clearly defined thought; it has not the colorless clearness of an abstract conception. On the contrary, the peculiarity in such a work of the poet's mind is, that the chief parts of the action, the nature of the chief characters, indeed something of the color of the piece, flow in the soul at the same time with the idea, bound into an inseparable unity, and that they continually work like a human being producing and expanding in every direction. It is possible, of course, that the poet's idea, however securely he bears it in his soul, may never, during the process of composition, come to perfection in words, and that later, through reflection, but without having formulated it, even for himself, he sets the possession of his soul into the stamped coin of speech, and comprehends it as the fundamental thought of his drama. It is possible, indeed, that he has perceived the idea more justly according to the rules of his art, than he has given the central thought of his work verbal expression.

If, however, it is inconvenient and often difficult for him to cast the idea of a growing play into a formula, to express it in words, yet the poet will do well, even in the beginning of his work, to temper the ardor of his soul, and sharply discriminating, judge the idea according to the essential requisites of the drama. It is instructive for a stranger to a piece to seek the hidden soul in the complete production, and however imperfect this may possibly be, give the thought formal expression. Much may be recognized in this way that is characteristic of single poets. For example, let the foundation of *Mary Stuart* be —:" The excited jealousy of a queen incites to the killing of her imprisoned rival ": and again of *Love and Intrigue,* " The excited jealousy of a young nobleman incites to the killing of his humble beloved." These bare formulas will be taken from the fullness of many-colored life which in the mind of the creative poet is connected with the idea; yet something peculiar will become distinct in the construction of both pieces, in addition; for example, that the poet using such a frame-work was placed under the necessity of composing in advance the first part of the action, which explains the origin of the jealousy, and that the impelling force in the chief characters becomes operative just in the middle of the piece, and that the first acts contain preferably the endeavors of the accessory characters, to excite the fatal activity of one of the chief characters. It will be further noticed how similar in ultimate principle is the construction and motive of these two plays of Schiller, and how both have a surprising similarity in idea and plan, to the more powerful *Othello.*

The material which is transformed through the dramatic idea, is either invented by the poet specially for his drama, or is an incident related from the life which surrounds him, or an account which history offers, or the contents of a tradition, or novel, or narrative poem. In all of these cases, where the poet makes use of what is at hand, it has already been humanized by the impress of an idea. Even in the above supposed newspaper notice, the incipient remodeling is recognizable. In the last sentence, " There is a rumor of an attachment," etc., the reporter makes the first attempt to transform the mere fact into a consistent story, to explain the tragic occurrence, to bring to the lovers a greater degree of interest, so that a more attractive meaning is given to their condition. The practice of transformation, through which consistency and a meaning corresponding to the demands of the thinking person are given to real events, is no prerogative of the poet. Inclination toward this, and capability for it, are active in all persons, and at all times. For thousands of years the human race has thus transposed for itself life in heaven and on earth; it has abundantly endowed its representations of the divine with human attributes. All heroic tradition has sprung from such a transformation of impressions from religious life, history, or natural objects, into poetic ideas. Even now, since historic culture prevails, and respect for the real relations of the great events of the world has risen so high, this tendency to explain occurrences shows itself in the greatest as well as in the least matters. In every anecdote, even in the disagreeable gossip of society, its activity is manifest, endeavoring, even if what is real remains unchanged, to present vividly and with spirit some trait of narrow life, or from the necessity of the *raconteur,* to make himself in contrast with others more surely and better observed.

Historical material is already brought into order through some idea, before the poet takes possession of it. The ideas of the historian are not at all poetical; but they have a specific and shaping influence on every part of the work which is brought through them into being. Whoever describes the life of a man, whoever makes an exposition of a section of past time, must set in order his mass of material from an established point of view, must sift out the unessential, must make prominent the most essential. Still more, he must seek to comprehend the contents of a human life or a period of time; he must take pains to discover ultimate characteristics and intimate connection of events. He must also know the connection of his material with much that is external, and much that his work does not present. In certain cases, indeed, he must supplement what has been delivered to him, and so explain the unintelligible, that its probable and possible meaning is evident. He is finally directed in the arrangement of his work, by the laws of creation, which have many things in common with the laws of poetic composition. Through his knowledge and his art, he may from crude material create a picture exciting wonder, and produce upon the soul of the reader the most powerful effect. But he is distinguished from the poet by this, that he seeks conscientiously to understand what has actually occurred, exactly as it was presented to view, and that the inner connection which he seeks is produced by the laws of nature which we revere as divine, eternal, incomprehensible. To the historian, the event itself, with its significance for the human mind, seems of most importance. To the poet, the highest value lies in his own invention; and out of fondness for this, he, at his convenience, changes the actual incident. To the poet, therefore, every work of an historical writer, however animated it may be through the historical idea recognized in its contents, is still only raw material, like a daily occurrence; and the most artistic treatment by the historian is useful to the poet only so far as it facilitates his comprehension of what really happened. If the poet has, in history, found his interest awakened in the person of the martial prince, Wallenstein; if he perceives vividly in his reading a certain connection between the deeds and the fate of the man; if he is touched or shocked by single characteristics of his real life — then there begins in his mind the process of reconstruction, so that he brings the deeds and fall of the hero into perfectly intelligible and striking connection, and he even so transforms the character of the hero as is desirable for a touching and thrilling effect of the action. That which in the historical character is only a subordinate trait, now becomes the fundamental characteristic of his being; the gloomy, fierce commander receives something of the poet's own nature; he becomes a highminded, dreaming, reflecting man. Conformably with this character, all incidents are remodeled, all other characters determined, and guilt and calamities regulated. Through such idealization arose Schiller's Wallenstein, a figure whose enchanting features have but little in common with the countenance of the historical Wallenstein. Indeed, the poet will have to be on his guard lest, in his invention, there be made to appear what to his contemporaries may seem the opposite of historical truth. How much the later poet may be limited by such a consideration, will be discussed later.

It will depend on the personality of the poet, whether the first rapture of his poetic activity is derived from the enchanting characteristics of mankind, or from what is striking in real destiny, or from the really interesting in the color of the time, which he finds in the historical record. But from the moment when the enjoyment and ardor necessary to his production begin, he proceeds, indeed, with unfettered freedom, however faithfully he seems to himself to adhere to historical material. He transforms all available material into dramatic forces.

Moreover, when the poet adopts material which has already been put in order more or less perfectly according to the laws of epic construction, as heroic poem, saga, artistically finished narrative, what is prepared for another species of poetry, is for him only material. Let it not be thought that an event with the persons involved, which has already been ennobled through an art so nearly allied, has for that reason a better preparation for the drama. On the contrary, there is between the great creations of the epic which shadow forth occurrences and heroes as they stand near each other, and dramatic art, which represents actions and characters as they are developed through each other, a profound opposition which it is difficult for the creative artist to manage. Even the poetic charm which these created images exercise upon his soul, may render it the more difficult for him to transform them according to the vital requisites of his art. The Greek drama struggled as severely with its material, which was taken from the epic, as the historic poet of our time must, with the transformation of historical ideas into dramatic.

To transform material artistically, according to a unifying idea, means to idealize it. The character of the poet, in contrast with the images from reality used as material, and according to a convenient craftsman's expression, are called ideals.

[WHAT IS DRAMATIC?

II]

The dramatic includes those emotions of the soul which steel themselves to will, and to do, and those emotions of the soul which are aroused by a deed or course of action; also the inner processes which man experiences from the first glow of perception to passionate desire and action, as well as the influences which one's own and others' deeds exert upon the soul; also the rushing forth of will power from the depths of man's soul toward the external world, and the influx of fashioning influences from the outer world into man's inmost being; also the coming into being of a deed, and its consequences on the human soul.

An action in itself is not dramatic. Passionate feeling in itself is not dramatic. Not the presentation of a passion for itself, but of a passion which leads to action is the business of dramatic art; not the presentation of an event for itself, but for its effect on a human soul, is the dramatist's mission. The exposition of passionate emotions as such, is in the province of the lyric poet; the depicting of thrilling events is the task of the epic poet.

The two ways in which the dramatic expresses itself are, of course, not fundamentally different. Even while a man is under stress, and laboring to turn his inmost soul toward the external, his surroundings exert a stimulating or repressing influence on his passionate emotions. And again, while what has been done exerts a reflex influence upon him, he does not remain merely receptive, but

gains new impulses and transformations. Yet there is a difference in these closely connected processes. The first, the inward struggle of man toward a deed, has always the highest charm. The second stimulates to more external emotion, a more violent coöperation of different forces; almost all that satisfies curiosity belongs to this; and yet, however indispensable it is to the drama, it is principally a satisfying of excited suspense; and the impatience of the hearer, if he has creative power, easily runs in advance, seeking a new vehement agitation in the soul of the hero. What is occurring chains the attention most, not what, as a thing of the past, has excited wonder.

Since the dramatic art presents men as their inmost being exerts an influence on the external, or as they are affected by external influences, it must logically use the means by which it can make intelligible to the auditor these processes of man's nature. These means are speech, tone, gesture. It must bring forward its characters as speaking, singing, gesticulating. Poetry uses also as accessories in her representations, music and scenic art.

In close fellowship with her sister arts, with vigorous, united effort she sends her images into the receptive souls of those who are at the same time auditors and spectators. The impressions which she produces are called effects. These dramatic effects have a very peculiar character; they differ not only from the effects of the plastic arts through the force of emphasis and the progressive and regular gradation of the chosen movement, but also from the powerful effects of music, in this, that they flow in at the same time through two senses, and excite with rapture not only emotional, but also intellectual activity.

From what has already been said, it is clear that the characters, presented according to the demands of dramatic art, must have something unusual in their nature which may distinguish them not only from the innumerable, more manifold, and more complicated beings whose images real life impresses on the soul, but also from the poetic images which are rendered effective through other forms of art, the epic, the romance, the lyric. The *dramatis persona* must represent human nature, not as it is aroused and mirrored in its surroundings, active and full of feeling, but as a grand and passionately excited inner power striving to embody itself in a deed, transforming and guiding the being and conduct of others. Man, in the drama, must appear under powerful restraint, excitement, transformation. Specially must there be represented in him in full activity those peculiarities which come effectively into conflict with other men, force of sentiment, violence of will, achievement hindered through passionate desire, just those peculiarities which make character and are intelligible through character. It thus happens, not without reason, that in the terms of art, the people of a drama are called characters. But the characters which are brought forward by poetry and her accessory arts, can evince their inner life only as participants in an event or occurrence, the course and internal connection of which becomes apparent to the spectator through the dramatic processes in the soul of the poet. This course of events, when it is arranged according to the demands of dramatic art, is called *action*.

Each participant in the dramatic action has a definite appointment with reference to the whole; for each, an exact, circumscribed personality is necessary which must be so constituted that so much of it as has a purpose may be conveniently perceived by the auditor, and what is common to man and what is peculiar to this character may be effectively represented by the actor by means of his art.

Those spiritual processes which have been indicated above as dramatic, are, of course, not perfectly apparent in every person represented, specially on the later stage, which is fond of bringing forward a greater number of characters as participants in the action. But the chief characters must abound in them; only when these, in an appropriate manner, exhibit their real nature with power and fullness, even to the inmost recesses of their hearts, can the drama produce great effects. If this last dramatic element is not apparent in the leading characters, is not forced upon the hearer, the drama is lifeless; it is an artificial, empty form, without corresponding contents; and the pretentious coöperation of several combined arts makes this hollowness the more painful.

Along with the chief characters, the subordinate persons participate in this dramatic life, each according to the space occupied in the piece. It does not entirely disappear, even in the least rôle, in those figures which with a few words can show their participation; the attendant or the messenger, owes it as a duty, at least to the actor's art, by costume, manner of speech, deportment, gesture, posture at entering, to represent in a manner suitable to the piece what he personates, so far as externals will do it, even if meagerly and modestly.

But since the representation of these mental processes, which are the prerogative and requisite of the drama, requires time, and since the poet's time for the producing of effects is limited according to the custom of his people, it follows that the event represented must bring the chief characters much more boldly into prominence than is necessary in an actual occurrence which is brought about through the general activity of many persons.

FRANCE IV

MODERN PERIOD

FRENCH DRAMATIC CRITICISM OF THE NINETEENTH AND TWENTIETH CENTURIES

Madame de Staël combines the spirit of the eighteenth century — Diderot and Rousseau in particular — with the new spirit of Romanticism. The result of her association with the German writers, especially the Schlegels, was her book *De l'Allemagne* (1810), which brought over the seeds of the movement which was soon to blossom forth in the plays of Victor Hugo. It was of course not altogether due to her work that the Romanticism of 1830 came when and as it did, but her books — *De la Littérature*, etc. (1800) should be added to the first — went far to interest the writers of the time. Her chapter *De l'art dramatique* in the book on Germany was obviously an echo of the Romanticists in Germany. Her contemporary, Chateaubriand, touches upon the drama in his epoch-making *Le Génie du Christianisme* (1802) — second part. Doubtless the French Revolution, with its attempts to establish a popular theater (see the decrees of the Committee of Public Safety) [1] had its share in influencing the artistic ideals of the time, though these were not developed until the advent of Michelet, and by Romain Rolland toward 1900. Népomucène Lemercier did a good deal of his work in the Revolutionary period, and his *Cours de littérature générale* was published in 1817. Alexandre Duval's *Réflexions sur l'art de la comédie* (1820) might be mentioned in passing. A more or less complete treatise on the theater is J.-L. Geoffroy's *Cours de littérature dramatique* (1819-20). The earliest of the more detailed Romantic criticisms of drama are in the work of Benjamin Constant (*Réflexions sur la tragédie*, etc., 1829, and his *Quelques Ré-*

flexions on Schiller and the German drama, 1809); Henri Beyle (Stendhal) (*Racine et Shakespeare*, 1822); and Sainte-Beuve (*Tableau historique et critique de la Poésie française et du théâtre français au XVIe siècle*, 1828). This book aroused great interest in early French literature and drama. Sainte-Beuve, who is said to have disliked the theater, wrote little purely dramatic criticism, though his essays on Corneille and Racine, and some others, are acute and interesting. (See *Causeries du Lundi* (1851-62); *Portraits littéraires* (1862-64); *Port-Royal* (1840-60); *Premiers Lundis* (1875); and *Nouveaux Lundis* (1863-72).) The Romantic dramatists, with Victor Hugo at their head, exposed their theories at great length. Hugo himself in the celebrated *Préface* to *Cromwell* (1827) called the younger poets to arms, and gave them a rallying standard. Nearly all his plays were preceded by prefaces, which appeared for the most part between 1827 and 1840. His *William Shakespeare* was published in 1864. Alexandre Dumas, in his *Mémoires* (1852-54), his various prefaces (in the many volumes of his *Théâtre complet*) and *Souvenirs dramatiques* (1868) is full of interesting matter. Alfred de Vigny clearly set forth his ideas in the *Avant-Propos de l'édition de 1839* of *Le More de Venise* and in the *Lettre à Lord * * * sur la soirée de 24 octobre, 1829, et sur un système dramatique,* and in the preface to his play *Chatterton,* written in 1834. Théophile Gautier, another Romantic, exposed his theories in his *Histoire du Romantisme* (1874), *Les Grotesques* (1844), and his *Histoire de l'art dramatique,* etc. (1858-59). A large number of writers, better known as poets, novelists, and miscellaneous essayists, wrote copiously on the theater, and a casual ref-

1 See Romain Rolland, *Le Théâtre du peuple* (Paris, 1903), for quotations from various Revolutionary documents. — **Ed.**

erence to such writers as Nodier, Guizot, Villemain, Michelet, Nisard, Mérimée, George Sand, Flaubert, Taine, and Baudelaire, will here suffice. There are, besides, the numerous professional dramatic critics: Jules Janin (*Histoire de la littérature dramatique*, 1853–58); Saint-Marc Girardin (*Cours de littérature dramatique*, 1843); Paul de Saint-Victor (*Les Deux masques*, 1867); Jules Barbey d'Aurevilly (*Le Théâtre contemporain*, 1887–92); J.-J. Weiss (*Trois années de théâtre*, 1892–96, *Le Théâtre et les mœurs*, 1889, *Le Drame historique et le drame passionel*, 1894, etc.); and Francisque Sarcey (*Quarante ans de théâtre*, posthumously published, 1900–02). The æstheticians and historians, Hippolyte Taine, Crépet, Fournier, Montégut, Chasles, Magnin, and Scherer, all contributed to the theory and history of the drama. Among the dramatists who at the same time theorized on their art, the most important is Alexandre Dumas fils, who affixed prefaces to all his plays, and wrote a number of pamphlets besides. He was continually preoccupied with the moral and political "utility" of the drama. His theoretical writings cover the period between 1860 and 1890. Emile Augier wrote very little on the drama; George Sand, on the other hand, prefaced nearly all her plays. The movement toward Naturalism in the novel extended to the drama, and the earliest exponents were the brothers Goncourt, who wrote prefaces to their plays *Henriette Maréschal* (1886), *La Patrie en danger* (1873), and the *Théâtre* (1879). Henry Becque, the founder of the Naturalistic drama, wrote much concerning his literary quarrels, but his *Souvenirs d'un auteur dramatique* (1895), have little dramatic theory. The spokesman of the early Naturalistic dramatists was the novelist Emile Zola. His periodical criticisms of the sixties and seventies he collected in *Le Naturalisme au théâtre* (1881), and *Nos Auteurs dramatiques* (1881). His prefaces to his *Théâtre* (1878) and individual plays — (1873–74–78), contain clear statements of his ideals of a new drama. After the foundation of Antoine's *Théâtre libre* in 1887, Jean Jullien wrote two volumes of theory, *Le Théâtre vivant* (1892–96), exposing the "slice of life" theories then recently developed. Ferdinand Brunetière developed his Law of the Drama in the early nineties and published it in its latest form as *La Loi du théâtre*, in 1894. The critics of the past three decades have produced a vast amount of material, most of which has been collected into book-form from periodicals of the day. The most important of these are Jules Lemaître, whose ten volumes of *Impressions de théâtre* appeared between 1888 and 1898; Emile Faguet, who has contributed some thirty-five or forty volumes on the theater (*Drame ancien, Drame moderne* — 1898, *Propos de théâtre* — 1903–10, are the best); Catulle Mendès, with his three volumes of *L'Art au théâtre* (1897–1900); René Doumic, with his *Théâtre nouveau* (1908), *De Scribe à Ibsen* (1893); and *Essais sur le théâtre contemporain* (1896); Adolphe Brisson, with his *Le Théâtre* (1907ff); Gustave Larroumet, with his *Etudes d'histoire et de critique dramatique* (1892), and *Nouvelles études* (1899). Among the psychological and philosophical treatises on the drama may be mentioned Gustave Le Bon's *La Psychologie des foules* (1895) and Henri Bergson's *Le Rire* (1900). Paul Bourget has contributed occasional essays on the theater, the most significant of which is the *Réflexions sur le théâtre* (1888). Modern France is rich in historians of the theater; among these may be mentioned Eugène Lintilhac, author of a life of Beaumarchais and of various essays on dramatic theory; Gustave Lanson, author of a history of French literature and of numerous works on dramatists; Augustin Filon, whose *De Dumas à Rostand* (1898) affords a comprehensive view of the modern French drama; Antoine Benoist, author of *Essais de critique dramatique* (1898), and *Le Théâtre d'aujourd'hui* (1911); Alphonse Séché and Jules Bertaut, authors of *L'Evolution du théâtre contemporain* (1908); Louis Veuillot, author of *Les Prédicateurs de la scène* (1904); Emile de Saint-Auban, author of *L'Idée sociale au théâtre* (1901); Hippolyte Parigot, author of *Le Théâtre d'hier* (1893) and *Génie et métier* (1894); Armand Kahn, author of *Le Théâtre social en France* (1907). More or less professional dramatic critics abound: Anatole France (*La Vie lit-*

téraire, 1888–94); Paul Flat (*Figures du théâtre contemporain*, 1911); Jean Ernest-Charles (*Les Samedis littéraires* (1903–07) and *Le Théâtre des poètes*, 1910); Gabriel Trarieux (*La Lanterne de Diogène*, n.d.); A.-E. Sorel (*Essais de psychologie dramatique*, 1911); Edmond Sée (*Le Théâtre des autres*, and *Petits dialogues sur le théâtre et l'art dramatique*, 1913); and Georges Polti (*Les Trente-six situations dramatiques*, 1895, and *L'Art d'inventer les personnages*, 1912). Romain Rolland and Maurice Pottecher have for some years spent time and effort to found a people's theater, and each has written a book of theories called *Le Théâtre du peuple* (Pottecher's dating from 1899, and Rolland's from 1903). Many of the dramatists of the day have written on the drama: chief among these are the Belgian, Maurice Maeterlinck, who in his essays (*Le Trésor des humbles*, 1896, *La Sagesse et la destinée*, 1898, and *Le double Jardin*, 1904, in particular), has attacked the modern drama and attempted to divert the current toward a new expression of the impalpable and sub-conscious. Henry Bataille wrote prefaces to some ten of his plays, and various articles on Shakespeare, Becque, and his own contemporaries; his dramatic essays were all printed in his *Ecrits sur le théâtre* (1917). Alfred Capus collected a number of dramatic essays into a volume, *Le Théâtre* (1912), though another, *Notre Epoque et le théâtre* (1906), has never been reprinted.

General references on nineteenth century French literature:

Hugo P. Thième, *Guide bibliographique de la Littérature française de 1800 à 1906* (Paris, 1907).
G. Pellissier, *Le Mouvement littéraire au XIXe siècle* (5th ed., Paris, 1898).
——, *Etudes de Littérature contemporaine*, 2 series (Paris, 1901).
J.-P. Charpentier, *La Littérature française au XIXe siècle* (Paris, 1875).
Emile Faguet, *Le Dix-neuvième siècle* (Paris, 1887).
C. Le Goffic, *La Littérature française au XIXe siècle* (Paris, 1910).
F. Strowski, *Histoire de la littérature française au XIXe siècle* (Paris, 1912).

References on nineteenth century French drama:

C. M. Des Granges, *La Comédie et les mœurs sous la Restauration et la monarchie de juillet* (Paris, 1904).
——, *Geoffroy et la critique dramatique sous le Consulat et l'Empire* (1800–1814) (Paris, 1897).
Eugène Lintilhac, *La Comédie: De la Révolution au Second Empire* (Paris, 1909).
Charles Lenient, *La Comédie en France au XIXe siècle*, 2 vols. (Paris, 1898).
J. Guex, *Le Théâtre et la société française de 1815 à 1848* (Vévey, 1900).
C. Formentin, *Essais sur les origines du drame moderne en France* (Aix, 1879).
E. Mazères, *Comédies et souvenirs* (Paris, 1855).
Jules Janin, *Histoire de l'art dramatique*, 6 vols. (Paris, 1853–58).
Alexandre Dumas, *Mes Mémoires* (Paris, 1852–54).
——, *Souvenirs dramatiques* (Paris, 1868).
Théophile Gautier, *Histoire de l'art dramatique en France depuis 25 ans*, 6 vols. (Paris, 1858–59).
——, *Souvenirs de théâtre, d'art et de critique* (Paris, 1883).
A. Delaforest, *Théâtre moderne. Cours de littérature dramatique*, 2 vols. (Paris, 1836).
Edouard Noël et Edmond Stoullig, *Les Annales du théâtre et de la musique* (Paris, annual volumes since 1875).
Charles Maurice, *Histoire anécdotique du théâtre*, etc., 2 vols. (Paris, 1856).
J.-J. Weiss, *Le Théâtre et les mœurs* (Paris, 1889).
——, *Trois années de théâtre* (*1883–85*), 4 vols. (Paris, 1892–96).
J. Barbey D'Aurevilly, *Le Théâtre contemporain*, 3 vols. (Paris, 1887–92).
N. C. Arvin, *Eugène Scribe and the French Theatre 1815–1860* (Cambridge, Mass., 1924).
S. M. Waxman, *Antoine and the Théâtre Libre* (Cambridge, Mass., 1926).
Paul de Saint-Victor, *Les Deux masques*, 3 vols. (Paris, 1867).

Paul de Saint-Victor, *Le Théâtre contemporain* (Paris, 1889).

H. Parigot, *Le Théâtre d'hier* (Paris, 1893).

E. Montégut, *Dramaturges et romanciers* (Paris, 1890).

Emile Zola, *Le Naturalisme au théâtre* (Paris, 1881).

——, *Nos Auteurs dramatiques* (Paris, 1881).

R. Gallet, *L'Art nouveau au Théâtre libre* (Paris, 1890).

A. Thalasso, *Le Théâtre libre* (Paris, 1909).

Jean Jullien, *Le Théâtre vivant*, 2 vols. (Paris, 1892–96).

F. W. M. Draper, *The Rise and Fall of the French Romantic Drama* (New York, n.d.).

Barrett H. Clark, *Four Plays of the Free Theater*. Preface by Brieux (Cincinnati, 1915).

——, *Contemporary French Dramatists* (2nd ed., Cincinnati, 1916).

——, *The Continental Drama of Today* (2nd ed., New York, 1914).

——, *A Study of the Modern Drama* (2nd ed., New York, 1928).

H. A. Smith, *Main Currents of Modern French Drama* (New York, 1925).

Frank W. Chandler, *The Contemporary Drama of France* (Boston, 1920).

Brander Matthews, *French Dramatists of the Nineteenth Century* (4th ed., New York, 1905).

Romain Rolland, *Le Théâtre du peuple* (Paris, 1903. Translated by Barrett H. Clark, as *The People's Theater*, New York, 1918).

Emile Faguet, *Notes sur le théâtre contemporain*, 7 vols. (Paris, 1889–95).

——, *Propos de théâtre*, 5 vols. (Paris, 1903–10).

——, *Drame ancien, Drame moderne* (Paris, 1898).

A. Benoist, *Essais de critique dramatique* (Paris, 1898).

——, *Le Théâtre d'aujourd'hui*, 2 vols. (Paris, 1911).

Gustave Larroumet, *Etudes de critique dramatique*, 2 vols. (Paris, 1892).

——, *Nouvelles études d'histoire et de critique dramatique* (Paris, 1899).

Léon Blum, *Au Théâtre*, 4 vols. (Paris, 1906ff).

Catulle Mendes, *L'Art au théâtre*, 3 vols. (Paris, 1896–98).

Ferdinand Brunetière, *Essais sur la littérature contemporaine* (Paris, 1892).

Armand Kahn, *Le Théâtre social en France* (Paris, 1907).

Eugène Lintilhac, *Conférences dramatiques* (Paris, 1898).

E. de Saint-Auban, *L'Idée sociale au théâtre* (Paris, 1901).

François Veuillot, *Les Prédicateurs de la scène* (Paris, 1904).

A. Séché and Jules Bertaut, *L'Evolution du théâtre contemporain* (Paris, 1908).

Augustin Filon, *De Dumas à Rostand* (Paris, 1898. Translated as *Modern French Drama* by Janet E. Hogarth, London, 1898).

Henri-Martin Barzun, *L'Ere du drame* (Paris, 1912).

A. Soubies, *Le Théâtre en France de 1871 à 1892* (Paris, 1893).

Alfred Capus, *Le Théâtre* (Paris, n.d.).

——, *Notre époque et le théâtre* (Paris, 1906).

Jules Lemaître, *Impressions de théâtre*, 10 vols. (Paris, 1888–98).

——, *Théories et impressions* (Paris, 1903).

Henry Bataille, *Ecrits sur le théâtre* (Paris, 1917).

Edmond Sée, *Petits dialogues sur le théâtre et l'art dramatique* (Paris, 1913).

Francisque Sarcey, *Quarante ans de théâtre*, 8 vols. (Paris, 1900–02).

Adolphe Brisson, *Le Théâtre* (Paris, annually from 1907 to date).

References on criticism:

A. Michiels, *Histoire des idées littéraires en France au dix-neuvième siècle, et de leurs origines dans les siècles antérieurs* (4th ed., Paris, 1863).

Georges Renard, *Les Princes de la jeune critique* (Paris, 1890).

Maurice Eloy, *Critiques d'aujourd'hui* (Paris, 1889).

Ernest Tissot, *Les Evolutions de la critique française* (Paris, 1890).

VICTOR HUGO

Victor-Marie Hugo was born at Besançon in 1802. His father was a general under Napoleon. His early education was received at Paris and Madrid. He returned later to Paris and studied at the *Ecole Polytéchnique*. It is said that he wrote a tragedy at the age of fourteen. Three years later he was a contributor to the *Conservateur littéraire*, but he attracted no attention until in 1822 he published his *Odes et poésies diverses*. This was followed by two novels. The *Odes et ballades* (1826) and *Orientales* (1829) brought him added fame. Meantime, his first play, the unactable *Cromwell*, was published in 1827. The famous *Préface*, in which the poet proclaimed the tenets of new Romantic drama, brought him into recognition as the leader and champion of the new movement. In 1830 his *Hernani* was produced at the *Théâtre-Français;* it marked an epoch in the history of the French stage. For the next thirteen years he continued to produce and publish plays, prefaces, novels, and poems. In 1852 he was banished for political reasons, and spent some years on the Isle of Jersey. These he spent writing political and poetic satire, though he found time to write two of his best and most ambitious volumes of poems, *Les Contemplations* (1856), and *La Légende des siècles* (1859). A little later appeared *Les Misérables* (1862), and two years afterward, *William Shakespeare* (1864). After the political upheaval of 1870–71, he returned to France, but his imprudent political activities made it necessary for him to leave the country again, and seek refuge in Belgium. But he was sent back from that country, and lived in Paris until his death in 1885.

From the standpoint of drama, Victor Hugo is of great importance as the champion of the Romantic form, which he revived. The publication of each of his plays was accompanied with a defense of the form used. The Romantic group — of which the best-known were Alfred de Vigny, Dumas père, and Casimir Delavigne — rallied round his standard, and constituted the chief school of

dramatic art in France for some years. Hugo's principal models were taken from the art of the Middle Age and Shakespeare. His method is rather inspirational than logical, and his arguments are on the whole somewhat unsound.

On the drama:

Preface to *Cromwell* (originally published in the separate volume of the play, Paris, 1827).
Preface to *Hernani* (1830).
Preface to *Marion de Lorme* (1831).
Preface to *Le Roi s'amuse* (1832).
Preface to *Lucrèce Borgia* (1833).
Preface to *Marie Tudor* (1833).
Preface to *Angelo* (1835).
Preface to *La Esmeralda* (1836).
Preface to *Ruy Blas* (1838).
Preface to *Les Burgraves* (1843).
William Shakespeare (Paris, 1864).

Editions:

The definitive edition of the complete works — exclusive of the posthumous pieces — is the *Œuvres complètes*, 46 vols. (Paris, 1880–85). The *Théâtre,* in 4 vols. (Paris, 1867), contains all the prefaces, and all but the latest plays. *William Shakespeare* was published in Paris in 1864. The plays are translated by various hands, in the *Dramatic Works* of Hugo, 3 vols. (latest ed., Boston, 1909). This edition contains all the prefaces. *William Shakespeare* is translated by Melville B. Anderson (Chicago, 1887). Maurice Souriau edits a critical edition of the *Préface de Cromwell* (Paris, 1897). There is another edition, by J. R. Ettinger, Jr.: *Préface de Cromwell and Hernani* (Chicago, 1900), and one by E. Wahl (Oxford, 1909).

On Hugo and his works:

Alfred Asseline, *Victor Hugo intime* (Paris, 1885).
Alfred Barbou, *Victor Hugo et son temps* (Paris, 1881. Translated as *Victor Hugo and his Time,* by Ellen E. Frewer, New York, 1882).

James Cappon, *Victor Hugo; a Memoir and a Study* (Edinburgh, 1885).

Algernon Charles Swinburne, *A Study of Victor Hugo* (London, 1886).

Théophile Gautier, *Histoire du Romantisme* (Paris, 1874).

Emile Montégut, *Mélanges critiques* (Paris, 1888).

Brander Matthews, *French Dramatists of the Nineteenth Century* (4th ed., New York, 1905).

Eugene Blanchet, *Victor Hugo et la renaissance théâtrale au XIXe siècle* (Meaux, 1879).

J. Ch. Dabas, *A Propos de Shakespeare ou le nouveau livre de Victor Hugo* (Bordeaux, 1864).

Paul Stapfer, *Racine et Victor Hugo* (Paris, 1887).

A. Acerra, *Influenza di A. Manzoni sopra V. Hugo nelle dottrine drammatiche* (Napoli, 1907).

W. Martin, *Victor Hugos dramatische Technik* (in the *Zeitschrift für französische Sprache*, etc., 1904–05).

Frank T. Marzials, *Life of Victor Hugo* (London, 1888).

P. et V. Glachant, *Essai critique sur le théâtre de Victor Hugo,* 2 vols. (Paris, 1902–03).

Albert Le Roy, *L'Aube du théâtre romantique* (Paris, 1904).

Jules Marsan, *Le Théâtre historique et le Romantisme* (1818–1829) (in *Rev. d'Hist. lit. de la France,* Paris, 1910).

Pierre Nebout, *Le Drame romantique* (Paris, 1895).

——, *Victor Hugo* (in *Hommes et idées du XIXe siècle,* Paris, 1903).

M.-A. Souriau, *De la Convention dans la tragédie et dans le drame romantique* (Paris, 1885).

PREFACE TO CROMWELL [1]

[(*Préface*) — *Cromwell*]

(1827)

．　．　．　．　．

Behold, then, a new religion, a new society; upon this twofold foundation there must inevitably spring up a new poetry. Previously — we beg pardon for setting forth a result which the reader has probably already foreseen from what has been said above — previously, following therein the course pursued by the ancient polytheism and philosophy, the purely epic muse of the ancients had studied nature in only a single aspect, casting aside without pity almost everything in art which, in the world subjected to its imitation, had not relation to a certain type of beauty. A type which was magnificent at first, but, as always happens with everything systematic, became in later times false, trivial and conventional. Christianity leads poetry to the truth. Like it, the modern muse will see things in a higher and broader light. It will realize that everything in creation is not humanely *beautiful*, that the ugly exists beside the beautiful, the unshapely beside the graceful, the grotesque on the reverse of the sublime, evil with good, darkness with light. It will ask itself if the narrow and relative sense of the artist should prevail over the infinite, absolute sense of the Creator; if it is for man to correct God; if a mutilated nature will be the more beautiful for the mutilation; if art has the right to duplicate, so to speak, man, life, creation; if things will progress better when their muscles and their vigor have been taken from them; if, in short, to be incomplete is the best way to be harmonious. Then it is that, with its eyes fixed upon events that are both laughable and redoubtable, and under the influence of that spirit of Christian melancholy and philosophical criticism which we described a moment ago, poetry will take a great step, a decisive step, a step which, like the upheaval of an earthquake, will change the whole face of the intellectual world. It will set about doing as nature does, mingling in its creations — but without confounding

[1] Re-printed from vol. 3 of the *Dramatic Works of Victor Hugo* (Boston, 1909). Translation of this *Preface* — of which the principal parts are here included — by George Burnham Ives.— Ed.

them — darkness and light, the grotesque and the sublime; in other words, the body and the soul, the beast and the intellect; for the starting-point of religion is always the starting-point of poetry. All things are connected.

Thus, then, we see a principle unknown to the ancients, a new type, introduced in poetry; and as an additional element in anything modifies the whole of the thing, a new form of the art is developed. This type is the grotesque; its new form is comedy.

And we beg leave to dwell upon this point; for we have now indicated the significant feature, the fundamental difference which, in our opinion, separates modern from ancient art, the present form from the defunct form; or, to use less definite but more popular terms, *romantic* literature from *classical* literature.

"At last!" exclaim the people who for some time past *have seen what we were coming at,* "at last we have you — you are caught in the act. So then you put forward the ugly as a type for imitation, you make the *grotesque* an element of art. But the graces; but good taste! Don't you know that art should correct nature? that we must *ennoble* art? that we must *select?* Did the ancients ever exhibit the ugly and the grotesque? Did they ever mingle comedy and tragedy? The example of the ancients, gentlemen! And Aristotle, too; and Boileau; and La Harpe. Upon my word!"

These arguments are sound, doubtless, and, above all, of extraordinary novelty. But it is not our place to reply to them. We are constructing no system here — God protect us from systems! We are stating a fact. We are a historian, not a critic. Whether the fact is agreeable or not matters little; it is a fact. Let us resume, therefore, and try to prove that it is of the fruitful union of the grotesque and the sublime types that modern genius is born — so complex, so diverse in its forms, so inexhaustible in its creations; and therein directly opposed to the uniform simplicity of the genius of the ancients; let us show that that is the point from which we must set out to establish the real and radical difference between the two forms of literature.

Not that it is strictly true that comedy and the grotesque were entirely unknown to the ancients. In fact, such a thing would be impossible. Nothing grows without a root; the germ of the second epoch always exists in the first. In the *Iliad* Thersites and Vulcan furnish comedy, one to the mortals, the other to the gods. There is too much nature and originality in the Greek tragedy for there not to be an occasional touch of comedy in it. For example, to cite only what we happen to recall, the scene between Menelaus and the portress of the palace (*Helen,* Act I), and the scene of the Phrygian (*Orestes,* Act IV). The Tritons, the Satyrs, the Cyclops, are grotesque; Polyphemus is a terrifying, Silenus a farcical grotesque.

But one feels that this part of the art is still in its infancy. The epic, which at this period imposes its form on everything, weights heavily upon it and stifles it. The ancient grotesque is timid and forever trying to keep out of sight. It is plain that it is not on familiar ground, because it is not in its natural surroundings. It conceals itself as much as it can. The Satyrs, the Tritons, and the Sirens are hardly abnormal in form. The Fates and the Harpies are hideous in their attributes rather than in feature; the Furies are beautiful, and are called *Eumenides,* that is to say, *gentle, beneficent.* There is a veil of grandeur or of divinity over other grotesques. Polyphemus is a giant, Midas a king, Silenus a god.

Thus comedy is almost imperceptible in the great epic *ensemble* of ancient times. What is the barrow of Thespis beside the Olympian chariots? What are Aristophanes and Plautus, beside the Homeric colossi, Æschylus, Sophocles, Euripides? Homer bears them along with him, as Hercules bore the pygmies, hidden in his lion's skin?

In the idea of men of modern times, however, the grotesque plays an enormous part. It is found everywhere; on the one hand it creates the abnormal and the horrible, on the other the comic and the burlesque. It fastens upon religion a thousand original superstitions, upon poetry a thousand picturesque fancies. It is the grotesque which scatters lavishly, in air, water, earth, fire, those myriads of intermediary creatures which we find all alive in the popular traditions of the Middle Ages; it is the grotesque which impels the ghastly antics of the witches' revels, which gives Satan his horns, his cloven foot and his bat's wings. It is the grotesque, still the grotesque, which now casts into the Christian hell the frightful faces which the severe genius of Dante and Milton will evoke, and again peoples it with those laughter-moving figures amid which Callot, the burlesque Michelangelo, will disport himself. If it passes from the world of imagination to the real world, it unfolds an inexhaustible supply of parodies of mankind. Creations of its fantasy are the Scaramouches, Crispins and Harlequins, grinning silhouettes of man, types altogether unknown to serious-minded antiquity, although they originated in classic Italy. It is the grotesque, lastly, which, coloring the same drama with the fancies of the North and of the South in turn, exhibits Sganarelle capering about Don Juan and Mephistopheles crawling about Faust.

And how free and open it is in its bearing! how boldly it brings into relief all the strange forms which the preceding age had timidly wrapped in swaddling-clothes! Ancient poetry, compelled to provide the lame Vulcan with companions, tried to disguise their deformity by distributing it, so to speak, upon gigantic proportions. Modern genius retains this myth of the supernatural smiths, but gives it an entirely different character and one which makes it even more striking; it changes the giants to dwarfs and makes gnomes of the Cyclops. With like originality, it substitutes for the somewhat commonplace Lernæan hydra all the local dragons of our national legends — the gargoyle of Rouen, the *gra-ouilli* of Metz, the *chair sallée* of Troyes, the *drée* of Montlhéry, the *tarasque* of Tarascon — monsters of forms so diverse, whose outlandish names are an additional attribute. All these creations draw from their own nature that energetic and significant expression before which antiquity seems sometimes to have recoiled. Certain it is that the Greek Eumenides are much less horrible, and consequently less *true*, than the witches in *Macbeth*. Pluto is not the devil.

In our opinion a most novel book might be written upon the employment of the grotesque in the arts. One might point out the powerful effects the moderns have obtained from that fruitful type, upon which narrow-minded criticism continues to wage war even in our own day. It may be that we shall be led by our subject to call attention in passing to some features of this vast picture. We will simply say here that, as a means of contrast with the sublime, the grotesque is, in our view, the richest source that nature can offer art. Rubens so understood it, doubtless, when it pleased him to introduce the hideous features of a court dwarf amid his exhibitions of royal magnificence, coronations and splendid ceremonial. The universal beauty which the ancients solemnly laid upon everything, is not without monotony; the same impression repeated again and again may prove fatiguing at last. Sublime upon sublime scarcely presents a contrast, and we need a little rest from everything, even the beautiful. On the other hand, the grotesque seems to be a halting-place, a mean term, a starting-point whence one rises toward the beautiful with a fresher and keener perception. The salamander gives relief to the water-sprite; the gnome heightens the charm of the sylph.

And it would be true also to say that contact with the abnormal has imparted to the modern sublime a something purer, grander, more sublime, in short, than the beautiful of the ancients; and that is as it should be. When art is consistent with itself, it guides everything more surely to its goal. If the Homeric Elysium is a long, long way from the ethereal charm, the angelic pleasureableness of Milton's Paradise, it is because under Eden there is a hell far more terrible than the heathen Tartarus. Do you think that Francesca da Rimini and Beatrice would be so enchanting in a poet who should not confine us in the Tower of Hunger and compel us to share Ugolino's revolting repast. Dante would have less charm, if he had less power. Have the fleshly naiads, the muscular Tritons, the wanton Zephyrs, the diaphanous transparency of our water-sprites and sylphs?

Is it not because the modern imagination does not fear to picture the ghastly forms of vampires, ogres, ghouls, snake-charmers and jinns prowling about graveyards, that it can give to its fairies that incorporeal shape, that purity of essence, of which the heathen nymphs fall so far short? The antique Venus is beautiful, admirable, no doubt; but what has imparted to Jean Goujon's faces that weird, tender, ethereal delicacy? What has given them that unfamiliar suggestion of life and grandeur, if not the proximity of the rough and powerful sculptures of the Middle Ages?

If the thread of our argument has not been broken in the reader's mind by these necessary digressions — which in truth, might be developed much further — he has realized, doubtless, how powerfully the grotesque — that germ of comedy, fostered by the modern muse — grew in extent and importance as soon as it was transplanted to a soil more propitious than paganism and the Epic. In truth, in the new poetry, while the sublime represents the soul as it is, purified by Christian morality, the grotesque plays the part of the human beast. The former type, delivered of all impure alloy, has as its attributes all the charms, all the graces, all the beauties; it must be able some day to create Juliet, Desdemona, Ophelia. The latter assumes all the absurdities, all the infirmities, all the blemishes. In this partition of mankind and of creation, to it fall the passions, vices, crimes; it is sensuous, fawning, greedy, miserly, false, incoherent, hypocritical; it is, in turn, Iago, Tartuffe, Basile, Polonius, Harpagon, Bartholo, Falstaff, Scapin, Figaro. The beautiful has but one type, the ugly has a thousand. The fact is that the beautiful, humanly speaking, is merely form considered in its simplest aspect, in its most perfect symmetry, in its most entire harmony with our make-up. Thus the *ensemble* that it offers us is always complete, but restricted like ourselves. What we call the ugly, on the contrary, is a detail of a great whole which eludes us, and which is in harmony, not with man but with all creation. That is why it constantly presents itself to us in new but incomplete aspects.

It is interesting to study the first appearance and the progress of the grotesque in modern times. At first, it is an invasion, an irruption, an overflow, as of a torrent that has burst its banks. It rushes through the expiring Latin literature, imparts some coloring to Persius, Petronius and Juvenal, and leaves behind it the *Golden Ass* of Apuleius. Thence it diffuses itself through the imaginations of the new nations that are remodeling Europe. It abounds in the work of the fabulists, the chroniclers, the romancists. We see it make its way from the South to the North. It disports itself in the dreams of the Teutonic nations, and at the same time vivifies with its breath the admirable Spanish *romanceros,* a veritable Iliad of the age of chivalry. For example, it is the grotesque which describes thus, in the *Roman de la Rose,* an august ceremonial, the election of a king: —

" A long-shanked knave they chose, I wis,
Of all their men the boniest."

More especially it imposes its characteristic qualities upon that wonderful architecture which, in the Middle Ages, takes the place of all the arts. It affixes its mark on the façades of cathedrals, frames its hells and purgatories in the ogive arches of great doorways, portrays them in brilliant hues on window-glass, exhibits its monsters, its bull-dogs, its imps about capitals, along friezes, on the edges of roofs. It flaunts itself in numberless shapes on the wooden façades of houses, on the stone façades of châteaux, on the marble façades of palaces. From the arts it makes its way into the national manners, and while it stirs applause from the people for the *graciosos* of comedy, it gives to the kings court-jesters. Later, in the age of etiquette, it will show us Scarron on the very edge of Louis XIV's bed. Meanwhile, it decorates coats-of-arms, and draws upon knights' shields the symbolic hieroglyphs of feudalism. From the manners, it makes its way into the laws; numberless strange customs attest its passage through the institutions of the Middle Ages. Just as it represented Thespis, smeared with wine-lees, leaping in her tomb, it dances with the *Basoche* on the famous marble table which served at the same time as a stage for the popular farces and for the royal banquets. Finally, having made its way into the arts, the manners, and the laws, it enters even the Church. In every Catholic city we see it organizing some one of those curious ceremonies, those strange processions, wherein religion is attended by all varieties of superstition — the sublime attended by all the forms of the grotesque. To paint it in one stroke, so great is its vigor, its energy, its creative sap, at the dawn of letters, that it casts, at the outset, upon the threshold of modern poetry, three burlesque Homers: Ariosto in Italy, Cervantes in Spain, Rabelais in France.

It would be mere surplusage to dwell further upon the influence of the grotesque in the third civilization. Everything tends to show its close creative alliance with the beautiful in the so-called "romantic" period. Even among the simplest popular legends there are none which do not somewhere, with an admirable instinct, solve this mystery of modern art. Antiquity could not have produced *Beauty and the Beast*.

It is true that at the period at which we have arrived the predominance of the grotesque over the sublime in literature is clearly indicated. But it is a spasm of reaction, an eager thirst for novelty, which is but temporary; it is an initial wave which gradually recedes. The type of the beautiful will soon resume its rights and its rôle, which is not to exclude the other principle, but to prevail over it. It is time that the grotesque should be content with a corner of the picture in Murillo's royal frescoes, in the sacred pages of Veronese; content to be introduced in two marvelous *Last Judgments*, in which art will take a just pride, in the scene of fascination and horror with which Michelangelo will embellish the Vatican; in those awe-inspiring representations of the fall of man which Rubens will throw upon the arches of the Cathedral of Antwerp. The time has come when the balance between the two principles is to be established. A man, a poet-king, *Poeta soverano,* as Dante calls Homer, is about to adjust everything. The two rival genii combine their flames, and thence issues Shakespeare.

We have now reached the poetic culmination of modern times. Shakespeare is the drama; and the drama, which with the same breath molds the grotesque and the sublime, the terrible and the absurd, tragedy and comedy — the drama is the distinguishing characteristics of the third epoch of poetry, of the literature of the present day.

Thus, to sum up hurriedly the facts that we have noted thus far, poetry has three periods, each of which corresponds to an epoch of civilization: the ode, the epic, and the drama. Primitive times are lyrical, ancient times epical, modern times dramatic. The ode sings of eternity, the epic imparts solemnity to history, the drama depicts life. The characteristics of the first poetry is ingenuousness, of the second, simplicity, of the third, truth. The rhapsodists mark the transition from the lyric to the epic poets, as do the romancists that from the lyric to the dramatic poets. Historians appear in the second period, chroniclers and critics in the third. The characters of the ode are colossi — Adam, Cain, Noah; those of the epic are giants — Achilles, Atreus, Orestes; those of the drama are men — Hamlet, Macbeth, Othello. The ode lives upon the ideal, the epic upon the grandiose, the drama upon the real. Lastly, this threefold poetry flows from three great sources — the Bible, Homer, Shakespeare.

Such then — and we confine ourselves herein to noting a single result — such are the diverse aspects of thought in the different epochs of mankind and of civilization. Such are its three faces, in youth, in manhood, in old age. Whether one examines one literature by itself or all literatures *en masse,* one will always reach the same result: the lyric poets before the epic poets, the epic poets before the dramatic poets. In France, Malherbe before Chapelain, Chapelain before Corneille; in ancient Greece, Orpheus before Homer, Homer before Æschylus; in the first of all books, *Genesis* before *Kings, Kings* before *Job;* or to come back to that monumental scale of all ages of poetry, which we ran over a moment since, The Bible before the *Iliad,* the *Iliad* before Shakespeare.

In a word, civilization begins by singing of its dreams, then narrates its doings, and, lastly, sets about describing what it thinks. It is, let us say in passing, because of this last, that the drama, combining the most opposed qualities, may be at the same time full of profundity and full of relief, philosophical and picturesque.

It would be logical to add here that everything in nature and in life passes through these three phases, the lyric, the epic, and the dramatic, because everything is born, acts, and dies. If it were not absurd to confound the fantastic conceits of the imagination with the stern deductions of the reasoning faculty, a poet might say that the rising of the sun, for example, is a hymn, noon-day a brilliant epic, and sunset a gloomy drama wherein day and night, life and death, contend for mastery. But that would be poetry — folly, perhaps — and *what does it prove?*

Let us hold to the facts marshalled above; let us supplement them, too, by an important observation, namely that we have in no wise pretended to assign exclusive limits to the three epochs of poetry, but simply to set forth their predominant characteristics. The Bible, that divine lyric monument, contains in germ, as we suggested a moment ago, an epic and a drama — *Kings* and *Job*. In the Homeric poems one is conscious of a clinging reminiscence of lyric poetry and of a beginning of dramatic poetry. Ode and drama meet in the epic. There is a touch of all in each; but in each there exists a generative element to which all the other elements give place, and which imposes its own character upon the whole.

The drama is complete poetry. The ode and the epic contain it only in germ; it contains both of them in a state of high development, and epitomizes both. Surely, he who said: "The French have not the epic brain," said a true and clever thing; if he had said, "The moderns," the clever remark would have been profound. It is beyond question, however, that there is epic genius in that marvelous *Athalie,* so exalted and so simple in its sublimity that the royal century was unable to comprehend it. It is certain, too, that the series of Shakespeare's chronicle dramas presents a grand epic aspect. But it is lyric poetry above all that befits the drama; it never embar-

rasses it, adapts itself to all its caprices, disports itself in all forms, sometimes sublime as in Ariel, sometimes grotesque as in Caliban. Our era being above all else dramatic, is for that very reason eminently lyric. There is more than one connection between the beginning and the end; the sunset has some features of the sunrise; the old man becomes a child once more. But this second childhood is not like the first; it is as melancholy as the other is joyous. It is the same with lyric poetry. Dazzling, dreamy, at the dawn of civilization, it reappears, solemn and pensive, at its decline. The Bible opens joyously with *Genesis* and comes to a close with the threatening Apocalypse. The modern ode is still inspired, but is no longer ignorant. It meditates more than it scrutinizes; its musing is melancholy. We see, by its painful labor, that the muse has taken the drama for her mate.

To make clear by a metaphor the ideas that we have ventured to put forth, we will compare early lyric poetry to a placid lake which reflects the clouds and stars; the epic is the stream which flows from the lake, and rushes on, reflecting its banks, forests, fields and cities, until it throws itself into the ocean of the drama. Like the lake, the drama reflects the sky; like the stream, it reflects its banks; but it alone has tempests and measureless depths.

The drama, then, is the goal to which everything in modern poetry leads. *Paradise Lost* is a drama before it is an epic. As we know, it first presented itself to the poet's imagination in the first of these forms, and as a drama it always remains in the reader's memory, so prominent is the old dramatic framework still beneath Milton's epic structure! When Dante had finished his terrible *Inferno*, when he had closed its doors and nought remained save to give his work a name, the unerring instinct of his genius showed him that that multiform poem was an emanation of the drama, not of the epic; and on the front of that gigantic monument, he wrote with his pen of bronze: *Divina Commedia.*

Thus we see that the only two poets of modern times who are of Shakespeare's stature follow him in unity of design. They coincide with him in imparting a dramatic tinge to all our poetry; like him, they blend the grotesque with the sublime; and, far from standing by themselves in the great literary *ensemble* that rests upon Shakespeare, Dante and Milton are, in some sort, the two supporting abutments of the edifice of which he is the central pillar, the buttresses of the arch of which he is the keystone.

Permit us, at this point, to recur to certain ideas already suggested, which, however, it is necessary to emphasize. We have arrived, and now we must set out again.

On the day when Christianity said to man: "Thou art twofold, thou art made up of two beings, one perishable, the other immortal, one carnal, the other ethereal, one enslaved by appetites, cravings and passions, the other borne aloft on the wings of enthusiasm and reverie — in a word, the one always stooping toward the earth, its mother, the other always darting up toward heaven, its fatherland "— on that day the drama was created. Is it, in truth, anything other than that contrast of every day, that struggle of every moment, between two opposing principles which are ever face to face in life, and which dispute possession of man from the cradle to the tomb?

The poetry born of Christianity, the poetry of our time is, therefore, the drama; the real results from the wholly natural combination of two types, the sublime and the grotesque, which meet in the drama, as they meet in life and in creation. For true poetry, complete poetry, consists in the harmony of contraries. Hence, it is time to say aloud — and it is here above all that exceptions prove the rule — that everything that exists in nature exists in art.

On taking one's stand at this point of view, to pass judgment on our petty conventional rules, to disentangle all those scholastic labyrinths, to solve all those trivial problems which the critics of the last two centuries have laboriously built up about the art, one is struck by the promptitude with which the question of the modern stage is made clear and distinct. The drama has but to take a step to break all the spiders' webs with which the militia of Lilliput have attempted to fetter its sleep.

And so, let addle-pated pedants (one does not exclude the other) claim that the deformed, the ugly, the grotesque should never be imitated in art; one replies that the grotesque is comedy, and that comedy apparently makes a part of art. Tartuffe is not handsome, Pourceaugnac is not noble, but Pourceaugnac and Tartuffe are admirable flashes of art.

If, driven back from this entrenchment to their second line of customhouses, they renew their prohibition of the grotesque coupled with the sublime, of comedy melted into tragedy, we prove to them that, in the poetry of Christian nations, the first of these two types represents the human beast, the second the soul. These two stalks of art, if we prevent their branches from mingling, if we persistently separate them, will produce by way of fruit, on the one hand abstract vices and absurdities, on the other, abstract crime, heroism and virtue. The two types, thus isolated and left to themselves, will go each its own way, leaving the real between them, at the left hand of one, at the right hand of the other. Whence it follows that after all these abstractions there will remain something to represent — man; after these tragedies and comedies, something to create — the drama.

In the drama, as it may be conceived at least, if not executed, all things are connected and follow one another as in real life. The body plays its part no less than the mind; and men and events, set in motion by this twofold agent, pass across the stage, burlesque and terrible in turn, and sometimes both at once. Thus the judge will say: "Off with his head and let us go to dinner!" Thus the Roman Senate will deliberate over Domitian's turbot. Thus Socrates, drinking the hemlock and discoursing on the immortal soul and the only God, will interrupt himself to suggest that a cock be sacrificed to Æsculapius. Thus Elizabeth will swear and talk Latin. Thus Richelieu will submit to Joseph the Capuchin, and Louis XI to his barber, Maître Olivier le Diable. Thus Cromwell will say: "I have Parliament in my bag and the King in my pocket"; or, with the hand that signed the death sentence of Charles I, smear with ink the face of a regicide who smilingly returns the compliment. Thus Cæsar, in his triumphal car, will be afraid of overturning. For men of genius, however great they be, have always within them a touch of the beast which mocks at their intelligence. Therein they are akin to mankind in general, for therein they are dramatic. "It is but a step from the sublime to the ridiculous," said Napoleon, when he was convinced that he was mere man; and that outburst of a soul on fire illumines art and history at once; that cry of anguish is the résumé of the drama and of life.

It is a striking fact that all these contrasts are met with in the poets themselves, taken as men. By dint of meditating upon existence, of laying stress upon its bitter irony, of pouring floods of sarcasm and raillery upon our infirmities, the very men who make us laugh so heartily become profoundly sad. These Democrituses are Heraclituses as well. Beaumarchais was surly, Molière gloomy, Shakespeare melancholy.

The fact is, then, that the grotesque is one of the supreme beauties of the drama. It is not simply an appropriate element of it, but is oftentimes a necessity. Sometimes it appears in homogeneous masses, in entire characters, as Daudin, Prusias, Trissotin, Brid'oison, Juliet's nurse; sometimes impregnated with terror, as Richard III, Bégears, Tartuffe, Mephistopheles; sometimes, too, with a veil of grace and refinement, as Figaro, Osric, Mercutio, Don Juan. It finds its way in everywhere; for just as the most commonplace have their occasional moments of sublimity, so the most exalted frequently pay tribute to the trivial and ridiculous. Thus, often impalpable, often imperceptible, it is always present on the stage, even when it says nothing, even when it keeps out of sight. Thanks to it, there is no thought of monotony. Sometimes it injects laughter, sometimes horror, into tragedy. It will bring Romeo face to face with the apothecary, Macbeth with the witches, Hamlet with the grave-diggers. Sometimes it may, without discord, as in the scene between King Lear and his jester, mingle its shrill voice with the most sublime, the most dismal, the dreamiest music of the soul.

That is what Shakespeare alone among all has succeeded in doing, in a fashion of his own, which it would be no less fruitless than impossible to imitate — Shakespeare, the god of the stage, in whom, as in a trinity, the three characteristic geniuses of our stage, Corneille, Molière, Beaumarchais, seem united.

We see how quickly the arbitrary distinction between the species of poetry vanishes before common sense and taste. No less easily one might demolish the alleged rule of the two unities. We say *two* and not *three* unities, because unity of plot or of *ensemble*, the only true and well-founded one, was long ago removed from the sphere of discussion.

Distinguished contemporaries, foreigners and Frenchmen, have already attacked, both in theory and in practice, that fundamental law of the pseudo-Aristotelian code. Indeed, the combat was not likely to be a long one. At the first blow it cracked, so worm-eaten was that timber of the old scholastic hovel!

The strange thing is that the slaves of routine pretend to rest their rule of the two unities on probability, whereas reality is the very thing that destroys it. Indeed, what could be more improbable and absurd than this porch or peristyle or ante-chamber — vulgar places where our tragedies are obliging enough to develop themselves; whither conspirators come, no one knows whence, to declaim against the tyrant, and the tyrant to declaim against the conspirators, each in turn, as if they had said to one another in bucolic phrase: —

Alternis cantemus; amant alterna Camenæ.

Where did any one ever see a porch or peristyle of that sort? What could be more opposed — we will not say to the truth, for the scholastics hold it very cheap, but to probability? The result is that everything that is too characteristic, too intimate, too local, to happen in the ante-chamber or on the street-corner — that is to say, the whole drama — takes place in the wings. We see on the stage only the elbows of the plot, so to speak; its hands are somewhere else. Instead of scenes we have narrative; instead of tableaux, descriptions. Solemn-faced characters, placed, as in the old chorus, between the drama and ourselves, tell us what is going on in the temple, in the palace, on the public square, until we are tempted many a time to call out to them: "Indeed! then take us there! It must be very entertaining — a fine sight!" To which they would reply no doubt: "It is quite possible that it might entertain or interest you, but that isn't the question; we are the guardians of the dignity of the French Melpomene." And there you are!

"But," some one will say, "this rule that you discard is borrowed from the Greek drama." Wherein, pray, do the Greek stage and drama resemble our stage and drama? Moreover, we have already shown that the vast extent of the ancient stage enabled it to include a whole locality, so that the poet could, according to the exigencies of the plot, transport it at his pleasure from one part of the stage to another, which is practically equivalent to a change of stage-setting. Curious contradiction! the Greek theater, restricted as it was to a national and religious object, was much more free than ours, whose only object is the enjoyment, and, if you please, the instruction, of the spectator. The reason is that the one obeys only the laws that are suited to it, while the other takes upon itself conditions of existence which are absolutely foreign to its essence. One is artistic, the other artificial.

People are beginning to understand in our day that exact localization is one of the first elements of reality. The speaking or acting characters are not the only ones who engrave on the minds of the spectators a faithful representation of the facts. The place where this or that catastrophe took place becomes a terrible and inseparable witness thereof; and the absence of silent characters of this sort would make the greatest scenes of history incomplete in the drama. Would the poet dare to murder Rizzio elsewhere than in Mary Stuart's chamber? to stab Henri IV elsewhere than in Rue de la Ferronerie, all blocked with drays and carriages? to burn Jeanne d'Arc elsewhere than in the Vieux-Marché? to dispatch the Duc de Guise elsewhere than in that château of Blois where his ambition roused a popular assemblage to frenzy? to behead Charles I and Louis XVI elsewhere than in those ill-omened localities whence Whitehall or the Tuileries may be seen, as if their scaffolds were appurtenance of their palaces?

Unity of time rests on no firmer foundation than unity of place. A plot forcibly confined within twenty-four hours is as absurd as one confined within a peristyle. Every plot has its proper duration as well as its appropriate place. Think of administering the same dose of time to all events! of applying the same measure to everything! You would laugh at a cobbler who should attempt to put the same shoe on every foot. To cross unity of time and unity of place like the bars of a cage, and pedantically to introduce therein, in the name of Aristotle, all the deeds, all the nations, all the figures which Providence sets before us in such vast numbers in real life,— to proceed thus is to mutilate men and things, to cause history to make wry faces. Let us say, rather, that everything will die in the operation, and so the dogmatic mutilators reach their ordinary result: what was alive in the chronicles is dead in tragedy. That is why the cage of the unities often contains only a skeleton.

And then, if twenty-four hours can be comprised in two, it is a logical consequence that four hours may contain forty-eight. Thus Shakespeare's unity must be different from Corneille's. 'Tis pity!

But these are the wretched quibbles with which mediocrity, envy and routine has pestered genius for two centuries past! By such means the flight of our greatest poets has been cut short. Their wings have been clipped with the scissors of the unities. And what has been given us in exchange for the eagle feathers stolen from Corneille and Racine? Campistron.

We imagine that some one may say: "There is something in too frequent changes of scene which confuses and fatigues the spectator, and which produces a bewildering effect on his attention; it may be, too, that manifold transitions from place to place, from one time to another time, demand explanations which repel the attention; one should also avoid leaving, in the midst of a plot, gaps which prevent the different parts of the drama from adhering closely to one another, and which, moreover, puzzle the spectator because he does not know what there may be in those gaps." But these are precisely the difficulties which art has to meet. These are some of the obstacles peculiar to one subject or another, as to which it would be impossible to pass judgment once for all. It is for genius to overcome, not for treatises or poetry to evade them.

A final argument, taken from the very bowels of the art, would of itself suffice to show the absurdity of the rule of the two unities. It is the existence of the third unity, unity of plot — the only one that is universally admitted, because it results from a fact: neither the human eye nor the human mind can grasp more than one *ensemble* at one time. This one is as essential as the other two are useless. It is the one which fixes the viewpoint of the drama; now, by that very fact, it excludes the other two. There can no more be three unities in the drama than three horizons in a picture. But let us be careful not to confound unity with simplicity of plot. The former does not in any way exclude the secondary plots on which the principal plot may depend. It is necessary only that these parts, being skillfully subordinated to the general plan, shall tend constantly toward the central plot and group themselves about it at the various stages, or rather on the various levels of the drama. Unity of plot is the stage law of perspective.

"But," the customs-officers of thought will cry, "great geniuses have submitted to these rules which you spurn!" Unfortunately, yes. But what would those admirable men have done if they had been left to themselves? At all events they did not accept your chains without a struggle. You should have seen how Pierre Corneille, worried and harassed at his first step in the art on account of his marvelous work, *Le Cid*, struggled under Mairet, Claveret, d'Aubignac and Scudéri! How he denounced to posterity the violent attacks of those men, who, he says, made themselves " all white with Aristotle " ! You should read how they said to him — and we quote from books

of the time: "Young man, you must learn before you teach; and unless one is a Scaliger or a Heinsius that is intolerable ! " Thereupon Corneille rebels and asks if their purpose is to force him " much below Claveret." Here Scudéri waxes indignant at such a display of pride, and reminds the "thrice great author of *Le Cid* of the modest words in which Tasso, the greatest man of his age, began his apology for the finest of his works against the bitterest and most unjust censure perhaps that will ever be pronounced. M. Corneille," he adds, " shows in his replies that he is as far removed from that author's moderation as from his merit The young man *so justly and gently reproved* dares to protest; thereupon Scudéri returns to the charge; he calls to his assistance the *Eminent Academy:* " Pronounce, O my Judges, a decree worthy of your eminence, which will give all Europe to know that *Le Cid* is not the masterpiece of the greatest man in France, but the least judicious performance of M. Corneille himself. You are bound to do it, both for your own private renown; and for that of our people in general, who are concerned in this matter; inasmuch as foreigners who may see this precious masterpiece — they who have possessed a Tasso or a Guarini — might think that our greatest masters were no more than apprentices."

These few instructive lines contain the everlasting tactics of envious routine against growing talent — tactics which are still followed in our own day, and which, for example, added such a curious page to the youthful essays of Lord Byron. Scudéri gives us its quintessence. In like manner the earlier works of a man of genius are always preferred to the newer ones, in order to prove that he is going down instead of up — *Mélite* and *La Galerie du Palais* placed above *Le Cid*. And the names of the dead are always thrown at the heads of the living — Corneille stoned with Tasso and Guarini (Guarini!), as, later, Racine will be stoned with Corneille, Voltaire with Racine, and as to-day, every one who shows signs of rising is stoned with Corneille, Racine and Voltaire. These tactics, as will be seen, are well-worn; but they must be effective as they are still in use. However, the poor devil of a great man still breathed. Here we cannot help but admire the way in which Scudéri, the bully of this tragic-comedy, forced to the wall, blackguards and maltreats him, how pitilessly he unmasks his classical artillery, how he shows the author of *Le Cid* "what the episodes should be, according to Aristotle, who tells us in the tenth and sixteenth chapters of his *Poetics*"; how he crushes Corneille, in the name of the same Aristotle " in the eleventh chapter of his *Art of Poetry,* wherein we find the condemnation of *Le Cid*"; in the name of Plato, " in the tenth book of his *Republic*"; in the name of Marcellinus, "as may be seen in the twenty-seventh book"; in the name of " the tragedies of *Niobe* and *Jephthah*"; in the name of the "*Ajax* of Sophocles "; in the name of "the example of Euripides "; in the name of " Heinsius, chapter six of the *Constitution of Tragedy;* and the younger Scaliger in his poems "; and finally, in the name of the Canonists and Jurisconsults, under the title "Nuptials." The first arguments were addressed to the Academy, the last one was aimed at the Cardinal. After the pin-pricks the blow with a club. A judge was needed to decide the question. Chapelain gave judgment. Corneille saw that he was doomed; the lion was muzzled, or, as was said at the time, the crow [*Corneille*] was plucked. Now comes the painful side of this grotesque performance: after he had been thus quenched at his first flash, this genius, thoroughly modern, fed upon the Middle Ages and Spain, being compelled to lie to himself and to hark back to ancient times, drew for us that Castilian Rome, which is sublime beyond question, but in which, except perhaps in *Nicomède,* which was so ridiculed by the eighteenth century for its dignified and simple coloring, we find neither the real Rome nor the true Corneille.

Racine was treated to the same persecution, but did not make the same resistance. Neither in his genius nor in his character was there any of Corneille's lofty asperity. He submitted in silence and sacrificed to the scorn of his time his enchanting elegy of *Esther,* his magnificent epic, *Athalie.* So that we can but believe that, if he had not been paralyzed as he was by the prejudices of his epoch, if he had come in contact less frequently with the classic crampfish, he would not have failed to introduce Locustes in his drama between Narcissus and Nero, and above all things would not have relegated to the wings the admirable scene of the banquet at which Seneca's pupil poisons Britannicus in the cup of reconciliation. But can we demand of the bird that he fly under the receiver of an air-pump? What a multitude of beautiful scenes the *people of taste* have cost us, from Scudéri to La Harpe! A noble work might be composed of all that their scorching breath has withered in its germ. However, our great poets have found a way none the less to cause their genius to blaze forth through all these obstacles. Often the attempt to confine them behind walls of dogmas and rules is vain. Like the Hebrew giant they carry their prison doors with them to the mountains.

But still the same refrain is repeated, and will be, no doubt, for a long while to come: " Follow the rules! Copy the models! It was the rules that shaped the models." One moment! In that case there are two sorts of models, those which are made according to the rules, and, prior to them, those according to which the rules were made. Now, in which of these two categories should genius seek a place for itself? Although it is always disagreeable to come in contact with pedants, is it not a thousand times better to give them lessons than to receive lessons from them? And then — copy! Is the reflection equal to the light? Is the satellite which travels unceasingly in the same circle equal to the central creative planet? With all his poetry Vergil is no more than the moon of Homer.

And whom are we to copy, I pray to know? The ancients? We have just shown that their stage has nothing in common with ours. Moreover, Voltaire, who will have none of Shakespeare, will have none of the Greeks, either. Let him tell us why: " The Greeks ventured to produce scenes no less revolting to us. Hippolytus, crushed by his fall, counts his wounds and utters doleful cries. Philoctetes falls in his paroxysms of pain; black blood flows from his wound. Œdipus, covered with the blood that still drops from the sockets of the eyes he has torn out, complains bitterly of gods and men. We hear the shrieks of Clytemnestra, murdered by her own son, and Electra, on the stage, cries: 'Strike! spare her not! she did not spare our father.' Prometheus is fastened to a rock by nails driven through his stomach and his arms. The Furies reply to Clytemnestra's bleeding shade with inarticulate roars. Art was in its infancy in the time of Æschylus, as it was in London in Shakespeare's time."

Whom shall we copy, then? The moderns? What! Copy copies! God forbid!

"But," some one else will object, "according to your conception of the art, you seem to look for none but great poets, to count always upon genius." Art certainly does not count upon mediocrity. It prescribes no rules for it, it knows nothing of it; in fact, mediocrity has no existence so far as art is concerned; art supplies wings, not crutches. Alas! d'Aubignac followed rules, Campistron copied models. What does it matter to art? It does not build its palaces for ants. It lets them make their ant-hill, without taking the trouble to find out whether they have built their burlesque imitation of its palace upon its foundation.

The critics of the scholastic school place their poets in a strange position. On the one hand they cry incessantly: "Copy the models!" On the other hand they have a habit of declaring that "the models are inimitable"! Now, if their craftsman, by dint of hard work, succeeds in forcing through this dangerous defile some colorless tracing of the masters, these ungrateful wretches, after examining the new *refaccimiento,* exclaim sometimes: "This doesn't resemble anything!" and sometimes: "This resembles everything!" And by virtue of a logic made for the occasion each of these formulæ is a criticism.

Let us then speak boldly. The time for it has come, and it would be strange if, in this age, liberty, like the light, should penetrate everywhere except to the one place where freedom is most natural — the domain of thought. Let us take the hammer to theories and poetic systems. Let us throw down the old plastering that conceals the façade of art. There are neither rules nor models; or, rather, there are no other rules than the general laws of nature, which soar above the whole field of art, and the special rules which result from the conditions appropriate to the subject of each composition. The former are of the essence, eternal, and do not change; the latter are variable, external, and are used but once. The former are the framework that supports the house; the latter the scaffolding which is used in building it, and which is made anew for each building. In a word, the former are the flesh and bones, the latter the clothing, of the drama. But these rules are not written in the treatises on poetry. Richelet has no idea of their existence. Genius, which divines rather than learns, devises for each work the general rules from the general plan of things, the special rules from the separate *ensemble* of the subject treated; not after the manner of the chemist, who lights the fire under his furnace, heats his crucible, analyzes and destroys; but after the manner of the bee, which flies on its golden wings, lights on each flower and extracts its honey, leaving it as brilliant and fragrant as before.

The poet — let us insist on this point — should take counsel therefore only of nature, truth, and inspiration which is itself both truth and nature. "Quando he," says Lope de Vega,

Quando he de escrivir una comedia,
Encierro los preceptos con seis llaves.

To secure these precepts "six keys" are none too many, in very truth. Let the poet beware especially of copying anything whatsoever — Shakespeare no more than Molière, Schiller no more than Corneille. If genuine talent could abdicate its own nature in this matter, and thus lay aside its original personality, to transform itself into another, it would lose everything by playing this rôle of its own double. It is as if a god should turn valet. We must draw our inspiration from the original sources. It is the same sap, distributed through the soil, that produces all the trees of the forest, so different in bearing power, in fruit, in foliage. It is the same nature that fertilizes and nourishes the most diverse geniuses. The poet is a tree that may be blown about by all winds and watered by every fall of dew; and bears his works as his fruit, as the *fablier* of old bore his fables. Why attach one's self to a master, or graft one's self upon a model? It were better to be a bramble or a thistle, fed by the same earth as the cedar and the palm, than the fungus or the lichen of those noble trees. The bramble lives, the fungus vegetates. Moreover, however great the cedar and the palm may be, it is not with the sap one sucks from them that one can become great one's self. A giant's parasite will be at best a dwarf. The oak, colossus that it is, can produce and sustain nothing more than the mistletoe.

Let there be no misunderstanding: if some of our poets have succeeded in being great, even when copying, it is because, while forming themselves on the antique model, they have often listened to the voice of nature and to their own genius — it is because they have been themselves in some one respect. Their branches became entangled in those of the near-by tree, but their roots were buried deep in the soil of art. They were the ivy, not the mistletoe. Then came imitators of the second rank, who, having neither roots in the earth, nor genius in their souls, had to confine themselves to imitation. As Charles Nodier says: "After the school of Athens, the school of Alexandria." Then there was a deluge of mediocrity; then there came a swarm of those treatises on poetry, so annoying to true talent, so convenient for mediocrity. We were told that everything was done, and God was forbidden to create more Molières or Corneilles. Memory was put in place of imagination. Imagination itself was subjected to hard-and-fast rules, and aphorisms were made about it: "To imagine," says La Harpe, with his naïve assurance, "is in substance to remember, that is all."

But Nature! Nature and truth!— And here, in order to prove that, far from demolishing art, the new ideas aim only to reconstruct it more firmly and on a better foundation, let us try to point out the impassable limit which in our opinion, separates reality according to art from reality according to nature. It is careless to confuse them as some ill-informed partisans of *romanticism* do. Truth in art cannot possibly be, as several writers have claimed, *absolute* reality. Art cannot produce the thing itself. Let us imagine, for example, one of those unreflecting promoters of absolute nature, of nature viewed apart from art, at the performance of a romantic play, say *Le Cid*. "What's that?" he will ask at the first word. "The Cid speaks in verse? It isn't *natural* to speak in verse."—"How would you have him speak, pray?"—"In prose." Very good. A moment later, "How's this!" he will continue, if he is consistent; "the Cid is speaking French!"—"Well?"— "Nature demands that he speak his own language; he can't speak anything but Spanish."

We shall fail entirely to understand, but again — very good. You imagine that this is all? By no means: before the tenth sentence in Castilian, he is certain to rise and ask if the Cid who is speaking is the real Cid, in flesh and blood. By what right does the actor, whose name is Pierre or Jacques, take the name of the Cid? That is *false*. There is no reason why he should not go on to demand that the sun should be substituted for the footlights, *real* trees and *real* houses for those deceitful wings. For, once started on that road, logic has you by the collar, and you cannot stop.

We must admit, therefore, or confess ourselves ridiculous, that the domains of art and of nature are entirely distinct. Nature and art are two things — were it not so, one or the other would not exist. Art, in addition to its idealistic side, has a terrestrial, material side. Let it do what it will, it is shut in between grammar and prosody, between Vaugelas and Richelet. For its more capricious creations, it has formulæ, methods of execution, a complete apparatus to set in motion. For genius there are delicate instruments, for mediocrity, tools.

It seems to us that some one has already said that the drama is a mirror wherein nature is reflected. But if it be an ordinary mirror, a smooth and polished surface, it will give only a dull image of objects, with no relief — faithful, but colorless; every one knows that color and light are lost in a simple reflection. The drama, therefore, must be a concentrating mirror, which, instead of weakening, concentrates and condenses the colored rays, which makes of a mere gleam a light, and of a light a flame. Then only is the drama acknowledged by art.

The stage is an optical point. Everything that exists in the world — in history, in life, in man — should be and can be reflected therein, but under the magic wand of art. Art turns the leaves of the ages, of nature, studies chronicles, strives to reproduce actual facts (especially in respect to manners and peculiarities, which are much less exposed to doubt and contradiction than are concrete facts), restores what the chroniclers have lopped off, harmonizes what they have collected, divines and supplies their omissions, fills their gaps with imaginary scenes which have the color of the time, groups what they have left scattered about; sets in motion anew the threads of Providence which work the human marionettes, clothes the whole with a form at once poetical and natural, and imparts to it that vitality of truth and brilliancy which gives birth to illusion, that prestige of reality which arouses the enthusiasm of the spectator, and of the poet first of all, for the poet is sincere. Thus the aim of art is almost divine: to bring to life again if it is writing history, to create if it is writing poetry.

It is a grand and beautiful sight to see this broad development of a drama wherein art powerfully seconds nature; of a drama wherein the plot moves on to the conclusion with a firm and unembarrassed step, without diffuseness and without undue compression; of a drama, in short, wherein the poet abundantly fulfills the multifold object of art, which is to open to the spectator a double prospect, to illuminate at the same time the interior and the exterior of mankind: the exterior by their speech and their acts, the interior, by asides and monologues; to bring together, in a word, in the same picture, the drama of life and the drama of conscience.

It will readily be imagined that, for a work of this kind, if the poet must *choose* (and he must), he should choose, not the *beautiful,* but the *characteristic.* Not that it is advisable to " make local color," as they say to-day; that is, to add as an afterthought a few discordant touches here and there to a work that is at best utterly conventional and false. The local color should not be on the surface of the drama, but in its substance, in the very heart of the work, whence it spreads of itself, naturally, evenly, and, so to speak, into every corner of the drama, as the sap ascends from the root to the tree's topmost leaf. The drama should be thoroughly impregnated with this color of the time, which should be, in some sort, in the air, so that one detects it only on entering the theater, and that on going forth one finds one's self in a different period and atmosphere. It requires some study, some labor, to attain this end; so much the better. It is well that the avenues of art should be obstructed by those brambles from which everybody recoils except those of powerful will. Besides, it is this very study, fostered by an ardent inspiration, which will ensure the drama against a vice that kills it — the *commonplace.* To be commonplace is the failing of short-sighted, short-breathed poets. In this tableau of the stage, each figure must be held down to its most prominent, most individual, most precisely defined characteristic. Even the vulgar and the trivial should have an accent of their own. Like God, the true poet is present in every part of his work at once. Genius resembles the die which stamps the king's effigy on copper and golden coins alike.

ALEXANDRE DUMAS FILS

Alexandre Dumas, the illegitimate son of the celebrated novelist, was born at Paris in 1824. His father recognized him at an early age, and gave him his name. The youth was educated at the Institution Goubaux and the College Bourbon, and after leaving school was initiated into the riotous life his father himself was accustomed to. From these early experiences Dumas made ample use in his plays and prefaces, and *La Dame aux camélias* was the immediate result of his observations. It was written to extricate the young man from a mass of debts, which he was enabled to pay with the royalties. He had, however, attempted to follow his father's profession, and a number of more or less mediocre novels belong to his early period. For over thirty years he produced plays regularly and fought bravely to make the theater an instrument of public usefulness. He died at Marly-le-Roy in 1895.

Dumas fils was an incorrigible adherent of the "useful" drama — the drama which should expose vices, remedy evils, and be in general an instrument of public and private good. Somewhat late in his career he wrote an open letter to Sarcey — *A M. Sarcey,* — which has since been reprinted in the first series of the *Entr' actes* — where he clearly states his ideals as to the function of the drama. He says: "I realize that the prime requisites of a play are laughter, tears, passion, emotion, interest, curiosity: to leave life at the cloak-room; but I maintain that if, by means of all these ingredients, and without minimizing one of them, I can exercise some influence over society; if, instead of treating effects I can treat causes; if, for example, while I satirize and describe and dramatize adultery I can find means to force people to discuss the problem, and the law-maker to revise the law, I shall have done more than my part as a poet, I shall have done my duty as a man." Dumas' many plays and more numerous prefaces and articles bear out and develop this basic idea. Together with Emile Augier, he brought the thesis-play to its highest point of development. His influence is seen in many of Ibsen's works, though the Norwegian was not so directly didactic. More especially in France has his preoccupation with moral utility borne fruit, particularly in the plays of Paul Hervieu and Eugène Brieux.

On the drama:

Au Lecteur, in vol. 1 of the *Théâtre complet* (Paris, 1868).
A Propos de la Dame aux camélias (1867).
Prefatory note to *Diane de Lys* (1868).
A Henri Lavoix, prefatory note to *Le Bijou de la Reine* (1868).
Avant-Propos to *Le Demi-Monde* (1868).
A Charles Marchal, preface to *La Question d'argent* (1868).
Préface to *Le Fils naturel* (1868).
Préface to *Un Père prodigue* (1868).
Préface to *l'Ami des femmes* (1869).
Préface to *Les Idées de Madame Aubray* (1870).
Préface to *Une Visite de noces* (1871).
Au Public, preface to *La Princesse Georges* (1877).
A M. Cuvillier-Fleury, preface to *La Femme de Claude* (1873).
Préface to *Monsieur Alphonse* (1873).
Préface to *L'Etrangère* (1879).
Notes de la Princesse de Bagdad (1892).
Notes sur Denise (1892).
Notes sur Francillon (1892).
Préface to *Le Théâtre des autres,* vol. 1 (1894).
Préface to *Un Mariage dans un chapeau* (1894).
Préface to *Le Supplice d'une femme* (1894).
Préface to *Héloïse Paranquet* (1894).
Préface to vol. 2 of the *Théâtre des autres* (1895).

The *Edition des Comédiens* of the *Théâtre complet,* 7 vols. (Paris, 1895), contains new prefaces and notes which have since been collected into a single volume (*Notes*), and included in the regular edition of the *Théâtre complet* as vol. 8 (n.d.).

Miscellaneous essays, many of them on the drama, are collected in the *Entr' actes*, 3 vols. (Paris, 1877–79), and the single volume of *Nouveaux Entr' actes* (Paris, 1890).

Dumas fils wrote prefaces to some forty books, a complete list of which is found in Carlos M. Noël's *Les Idées sociales dans le théâtre de A. Dumas fils* (Paris, 1912).

Editions:

The Calmann-Lévy edition of the *Théâtre complet*, in 8 vols. (Paris, 1895), is the authoritative edition for plays and prefaces. The same publishers also issue the *Entr' actes* in 3, and the *Nouveaux Entr' actes* in 1 vol. (see latest editions). The only preface that has appeared in English is that to *Un Père prodigue*, translated by Barrett H. Clark, as *The Technic of Playwriting* (in *The Drama*, Chicago, Feb., 1917).

On Dumas fils and his works:

Théophile Gautier, *Portraits contemporains et questions actuelles* (Paris, 1873).

H. de Lapommeraye, *Histoire du début d'A. Dumas fils au théâtre* (Paris, 1873).

Léopold Lacour, *Trois Théâtres* (Paris, 1880).

Emile Zola, *Nos Auteurs dramatiques* (Paris, 1881).

Paul Bourget, *Nouveaux essais de psychologie contemporaine* (Paris, 1885).

Paul de Saint-Victor, *Théâtre contemporain* (Paris, 1889).

Jules Lemaître, *Impressions de théâtre*, V and VI (Paris, 1892).

Brander Matthews, *French Dramatists of the Nineteenth Century* (4th ed., New York, 1905).

Hippolyte Parigot, *Le Théâtre d'hier* (Paris, 1893).

René Doumic, *Portraits d'écrivains* (Paris, 1892).

——, *De Scribe à Ibsen* (Paris, 1896).

Antoine Benoist, *Essais de critique dramatique* (Paris, 1898).

Augustin Filon, *De Dumas à Rostand* (Paris, 1898).

Carlos M. Noël, *Les Idées sociales dans le théâtre de A. Dumas fils* (Paris, 1912).

Anatole France, *M. Alexandre Dumas moraliste* (in *La Vie littéraire*, I, Paris, 1888. Translated by A. W. Evans as *On Life and Letters*, First Series, London and New York, 1911).

H. Stanley Schwarz, *Alexandre Dumas, fils, Dramatist* (New York, 1927).

PREFACE TO A PRODIGAL FATHER.[1]

[*Préface* (to) *Un Père prodigue*]

(1868)

To-day, by your leave, we shall discuss technique. We should never fail to attribute to technique the importance due it in dramatic art. Technique is so important that it sometimes happens that technique is mistaken *for* art. Of all the various forms which can be assumed by thought, the drama is that which most nearly approaches the plastic arts; dramatic art cannot be practiced before one knows all the material methods — with this difference, however, that in all the other arts these methods can be learned, but in this, one divines them, or, rather, has them within him.

One may become a painter, a sculptor, even a musician, by study — but not a dramatist. One is a dramatist at the beginning, the way one is dark or light, without wishing it. It is a freak of nature that has so constructed your vision as to enable you to see in a certain way, which is not absolutely the true way, but which for the time being *appears* to be the only way whereby you can make others see what you have seen. The man who is called to write for the stage reveals this very rare faculty at his first attempt, in a farce at school or in a parlor charade. It is the science of optics and perspective which allows him to depict a human being, a character, a passion, an act of the soul, with a sin-

1 Re-printed from *The Drama* (Feb., 1917). Translated for the first time in English, by the editor. Complete text.— Ed.

gle scratch of the pen. The illusion is so complete that it often happens that when the spectator turns reader and wishes to revive for his personal satisfaction the emotion he has experienced together with the crowd, he not only cannot find that emotion in the *written* word and action, but he cannot find the place itself in the play where he experienced it. A word, a look, a gesture, a pause, a purely atmospheric combination of effects had held him spell-bound. That is the genius of technique — if these two words can stand side by side. A play is to other forms of literature what a ceiling fresco is to wall- or easel-paintings. Woe be unto the painter if he forgets that his fresco must be seen from a distance, with the light coming from below!

A man of no value as thinker, moralist, philosopher, writer, may be a first-rate dramatist; that is to say, as manipulator of the purely external actions of human beings; and, on the other hand, in order to be accepted in the theater as thinker, moralist, philosopher, and writer, it is indispensable that he be endowed with the same particular qualities as the man of no value (except as technician). In short, if one would be master in this art he must first be proficient in its technique.

If it be a fact that the natural endowments cannot be given to those who are without them, nothing, on the other hand, is easier than to recognize them in those who do possess them.

The first of these endowments, the most indispensable, the one that dominates and commands, is logic — which includes good sense and clearness. The truth may be absolute or relative, according to the importance of the subject and the *milieu*. But the logic must be implacable from beginning to end; it must never lose sight of this end, while developing the idea and the action. The dramatist must unflaggingly place before the spectator that part of the being or thing for or against which he aims to draw a conclusion. Then comes the science of contrasts; that is to say, the blacks, the shadows, the balancing, the totality of effect, harmony; then conciseness and tempo, which prevent the listener's being distracted or reflecting, or taking a momentary breath, to discuss in his own mind with the author; the knowledge of foreground and background, keeping the figure which ought to stand out in the high-light from falling into the shadow, and those which belong in the middle-distance from assuming a position of too great prominence; and then the mathematical precision, inexorable, fatal, which multiplies scene by scene, even by event, act by act, up to the dénouement, which must be the sum-total, the Q. E. D.; and, lastly, the exact conception of our limitations, which forbid us to make our picture larger than the frame, because the dramatist who has even the most to say must say it all between eight in the evening and midnight, out of which period he must subtract one hour for entr'-actes, and repost for the audience.

I have not mentioned imagination, because the theater — besides the author — supplies this in the actors, scenery, and accessories. It puts into flesh and bone, in spoken words, in images, before the spectator, the individuals, places, and things which he would be forced to imagine were he reading a book. Nor have I spoken of invention, because in our profession there is no such thing. We need invent nothing; we have only to observe, remember, feel, coördinate, restore, in a particular form, what every spectator ought to have recalled to him immediately after having felt or seen, without having been conscious of it. As for basis, the real; as for facts, what is possible; as for means, what is ingenious; that is all that can rightfully be asked of us.

Does the art of the drama, which requires a technique all its own, likewise demand a style of its own? Yes. No one is altogether a dramatist unless he has his manner of writing, just as he has his manner of seeing, a manner altogether personal. A play should be written as if it were never intended to be other than read. The production is nothing but a reading by many people who do not care or know how to read. A play succeeds as a result of people's going to the theater; it becomes firmly established as a result of being read. The spectator gives it a certain notoriety, the reader gives it lasting fame. The play that we have no desire to read without having seen, nor to re-read after having seen it, is dead, no matter if it enjoys a run of two thousand nights. Only, it is necessary, if the work is to survive without the aid of the interpreter, that the writer's style be such as to convey to the reader the solidity, proportions, form, and suggestions of tone, which are applauded by the spectator in a theater. The style of the greatest writers can be of no help to the dramatist except as a sort of reference: it can teach him only a few words, and there are even a number of these which he must eschew from his vocabulary, because they lack the relief, strength, character — I had almost said triviality — which are necessary to the end of setting the true human being in action on a false ground. Molière's vocabulary is very limited; he invariably uses the same expressions: he plays the gamut of the whole of the human soul on five octaves and a half.

Written style, that is, thought presented directly to the reader, can be fixed once for all. Whoever writes a story, be it merely a dialogue destined to be read and nothing more, can make use of the form of a master of his own class — Bossuet, Voltaire, Pascal, Jean-Jacques, Sand, Hugo, Lamartine, Renan, Théophile Gautier, Sainte-Beuve, Flaubert, About; and not only will he not be blamed, but rather praised for paying homage to tradition and purism. Perhaps even his original sources will not be perceived, but his influence will be felt; he will be proclaimed a writer, and will actually be one, even if his elegant and pure style fails to contain a single original idea. We see examples of this every day, books in which the style leads one to believe that there is a solid foundation of thought.

There is nothing of the sort in the drama. The moment we imitate the style of one of our masters, we are not hailed as respectful disciples; we are tiresome imitators. What we ought to imitate in those masters is their manner of observing and not of stating. Each of them has his own trade-mark, which cannot be imitated without our being accused of counterfeiting. Read Corneille, Racine, Molière, Marivaux, Beaumarchais — to speak only of the dead — and notice the difference in their styles. Notice how each one of them has poured his particular essence into the flowing river which is called language! Need this style of the drama be correct? No, so far as mere grammar is concerned. It must first of all be clear, colored, penetrating, incisive.

Je t'aimais inconstant; qu'aurais-je fait, fidèle? is an adorable grammatical slip, which was moreover not necessitated by the meter; and yet, if he had had to express the same idea in prose, Racine, *who knew his technique,* would have written it with the same error. There are certain expressions, certain words which in themselves possess a saliency, a sonority, a form which render them necessary, which require their use even at the risking of the author's reputation as a literary man. Academic writers understand nothing of our particular form, and consider us barbarians. It was this misunderstanding of the two different styles that caused La Bruyère to enunciate the absurd truth that, " All Molière needed was to avoid jargon, and to *write purely.*"

Fénelon thought and spoke like La Bruyère when he wrote of our leader.

La Bruyère was right and wrong, that is why I said " absurd truth," in reference to the opinion of a writer whom I revere more than any one else does, the author who put our language on a firm basis, who inundated the world with truths which he would have been incapable of stating in the theater, because he would have worked everything out in detail instead of modeling it in high relief.

Suppose now that you are Fénelon — an assumption which certainly cannot wound your feelings. Your connection with the church will not allow you to go to the theater; nevertheless, you wish to keep abreast of the times, because you are a writer, a prince's tutor, and you live in the most literary age that France had yet known. You have heard a certain Molière spoken of — a fellow who has been excommunicated — an actor, a *valet de chambre* of the King, who, some say, writes immoral comedies; others — Boileau, for instance — sublime works. And you read these lines:

" Pour moi, je *vous l'avoue,* je me *re-pais* un *peu* de gloire. Les applaudisse-ments me touchent, et je tiens *que,* dans tous les beaux-arts, c'est un supplice assez fâcheux *que* de se produire à des sots, *que* d'essuyer sur des compositions la barbarie d'un stupide. Il y a plaisir, ne m'en parlez point, a travailler pour des personnes *qui* soient capables de sen-tir les délicatesses d'un art, *qui* sachent faire un doux acceuil aux beautés d'un ouvrage, et, par de chatouillantes appro-bations, vour régaler de votre travail. Que, la récompense la plus agréable *qu'on* puisse recevoir des choses *que* l'on fait, c'est de les voir connues, de les voir caresser d'un applaudissement *qui* vous honore, il n'y a rien, à mon avis, *qui* nous paye mieux *que* cela de toutes nos fa-tigues; et ce sont des douceurs exquises *que* des louanges éclairées."

You are Fénelon! You stop at that point, and you throw aside *Le Bourgeois gentilhomme* and say, "A poor writer." And you think no more about it.

Now, it happens that you are not Fénelon — and the case is extremely easy; you are the first-comer and you are interested in literature; naturally you know the works of Fénelon and Mo-lière. You are asked which one you would prefer to be; which would you choose? Molière, without a shadow of doubt. That is all I have to say.

Such errors, so shocking when they are read, not only pass unperceived in the theater beneath the intonation of the actor and the movement of the play, but even sometimes add to the life of the whole, just as small eyes, a large nose, a huge mouth and disordered hair, often add more grace, character, passion and distinction to a face, than Greek per-fection of feature. That Greek type has been accepted as an ideal type of beauty because some sort of set ideal must be established in every art; but after this has been once established, each artist goes his own way according to his par-ticular temperament, and overthrows tra-dition if he is sufficiently strong to do so. Thus it is that new schools are founded, and men discuss them. This is not a bad way of killing time, which has its *longueurs,* [dull periods] as we say in the theater.

"Then should we allow errors on top of errors, as in the style of M. Scribe? Is that sufficient?"

Exactly, if the style of M. Scribe ex-presses ideas. What do I care for the material of a dress, provided the dress itself be beautiful?

"But then, will M. Scribe perish be-cause of his form?"

Another mistake! No one ever per-ishes because of his form; he lives or dies according to the matter. Transla-tion offers a proof of my assertion. We can daily admire foreign writers in trans-lations which are far better in style than the plays of M. Scribe, because, since the thought is strong and solid, it stands forth and takes shape above and beyond the soft and colorless form, like a moun-tain-peak emerging from the morning mist. Think like Æschylus and write like M. Scribe; we ask nothing more of you. Unfortunately, or rather fortu-nately, such a discrepancy is impossible. Expression will always, in spite of one's desires, equal thought: it will be just and firm if the thought is great; feeble and bombastic if the thought is vulgar or common. Inspiration of idea and sin-cerity are lacking in M. Scribe, hence the want of expression; he is not himself convinced, he cannot be eloquent. *A liqueur sans valeur, vase sans prix.* [A worthless liquid for a worthless jar.] But M. Scribe did not try to write come-dies; he tried merely to write *for the theater;* he had no wish either to preach, to instruct, or to correct people; he wanted only to amuse them. He did not seek that glory which immortalizes the dead, but contented himself with success which affords popularity to the living and riches which they can enjoy. He was a prestidigitator of the first rank — a marvelous juggler. He exposed a sit-uation to you as if it were a *muscade* [2] and led you, in tears and laughter and terror, during two, three, or five acts, through to the dénouement. It was al-ways the same, and he never said any-thing. The language used in conducting these tricks was intended to throw the audience off the scent and gain time un-til the arrival of the promised effect, the moment when the *muscade* becomes

2 Ball of spice used by jugglers.— Ed.

a shell of '48, only to return to the juggler's goblet at the end. It was merely by the juggler's sleight of hand that the trick was done. The performance over, the candles were snuffed out, the *muscades* put back into the sack, goblets placed one within the other; the excitement passed, life and movement went — there remain in the mind and soul of the spectator never an idea, a thought, no enthusiasm, no hope, no remorse, no agitation, no consolation. People have seen, heard, had their curiosity aroused; laughed, wept — which is a great deal, but they have learned nothing. Perhaps they afterward referred to the play; they never discussed it. In short, M. Scribe possessed all the qualities pertaining to talent, but not one indicative of genius. Three times only did his characters assume the appearance, not of actual life, but of the epic life: and that was when Meyerbeer lent his powerful life-giving breath. Once, and once only, did he succeed in prying open the gate of the temple and stealing upon the mysteries of the Good Goddess: he bordered upon great comedy in *Camaraderie*, in which he had as much to be proud, as to be ashamed of. The day that play was performed, he proved that he might have belonged to the family of true observers, and that by concentrating his powers, thinking less of riches and more of his art, he might have been a great dramatist. But he did not will it; his will be done!

Still, the drama owes one real innovation to him, an innovation that may be taken as his own particular theory of the drama. Up to his time love and marriage with the loved woman were considered the final recompense of the comedy hero. The poet made this woman out to be as beautiful, as pure, as passionate, in short, as interesting as possible. M. Scribe thought that he ought to add to all these qualities, another quality of the first order: a good three per cent. income. There is no happiness possible in the crowning marriage unless the young lady brings the young man a fat dowry. And so well did M. Scribe's ideal coincide with that of his public, that the public recognized him at once as its representative; and during a third of a century the high-priest of this

bourgeois religion celebrated mass every night on the altar of the half-crown, turning round from time to time in the midst of the ceremony, to say to his flock, with his hand on the double-columned Evangel: *Ego vobiscum!*

Collaborators, pupils, imitators, amateurs, were not lacking in this facile, agreeable, productive enterprise, which perverted public taste and led away from serious art. The Scribe had passed into the customs and manners of the times. There was no safety outside his beaten path. Unfortunately, the master abused his technique, and people ended by tiring of the everlasting colonels, widows, rich heiresses whose dowries were the object of continual pursuit; of artists supported by bankers' wives; of Legion of Honor crosses obtained in adultery; of all-powerful millionaires; of shop-girls who led queens by the nose. People felt the need of hearing something that smacked of commonsense, which should encourage and console humanity, which is neither so selfish nor so foolish as M. Scribe would have us think. Shortly after him came a robust-minded, loyal and refined man [Emile Augier], and *Gabrielle*, with its simple and touching action, and noble and beautiful language, was the first work of revolt against the older conventional drama. The intelligent, fatherly, and eloquent husband was exalted on the same stage where for twenty years had been held up to ridicule the everlastingly foolish, blinded husband, deceived shamelessly by his amorous wife, and where had been two women, a traveling salesman, an artist, or else a diplomat dressed, warmed, and decorated by his mistress, and finally made rich by his cousin — a sop to his remorse!

" Why this prejudice against M. Scribe? " you will ask. " Why this attack? "

I am not attacking M. Scribe; I am not beating the drum in front of my own shop in order to prevent your going into my neighbor's; but, having set out to discuss this matter of technique, I am studying and explaining the man who is its living incarnation, and who has pushed the science of it so far that, as I said earlier, some have mistaken that technique for art itself. No one knew better than M. Scribe — who was without conviction, without simplicity, without any philosophic end in view — how to set into action if not a character or an idea, at least a subject, and above all a situation, and to extract from that subject and that situation, their logical theatric effect; none better than he understood how to assimilate the latest ideas and adapt them to the stage, sometimes on a scale and in a spirit absolutely opposed to the combinations of the one from whom he received the idea. He turned everything to his own advantage: the temperament, the début, the name, the beauty, the ugliness, the stoutness, the thinness, the arms, the feet, the expression, the color of the hair, the elegance, the stupidity, the cleverness, of the actor or actress; even the tastes, passions, prejudices, hypocrisies, cowardice of the public he was addressing, from which he tried to take its fortune and its liberty. He was the most extraordinary improviser we have had in the history of our drama; he was the most expert at manipulating characters that had no life. He was the shadow-Shakespeare.

Now, if among the four hundred plays he wrote, either by himself or in collaboration, you place *Il ne faut jurer de rien,* or *Un Caprice,* or *Il faut qu'une porte soit ouverte ou fermée* — that is to say, a tiny *proverbe* written by the most naïve and inexpert of dramatists [Alfred de Musset] — you will see all Scribe's plays dissolve and go up into thin air, like mercury when heated to three hundred and fifty degrees; because Scribe worked for his audience without putting into his labor anything of his soul or heart, while Musset wrote with heart and soul for the heart and soul of humanity. His sincerity gave him, though he was unaware of this, all the resources which were the sole merit of Scribe.

" And the conclusion? "

Is that the dramatist who knows *man* as Balzac did, and the *theater* as Scribe did, will be the greatest of the world's dramatists.

FRANCISQUE SARCEY

Francisque Sarcey was born at Dourdan in 1828. His early schooling was thorough, and the young student distinguished himself at the Lycée Charlemagne, and later at the Ecole Normale. After his graduation he was made a professor at Chaumont, in 1851, but his liberal opinions soon caused his expulsion, and transfer elsewhere. In 1858 he resigned from his position at Grenoble, and returned to Paris with the intention of making literature his life work. He wrote novels, stories, and miscellaneous essays for the papers and magazines. Through his friend Edmond About he was introduced to several editors who soon realized the critical powers of Sarcey. In 1860 he began writing dramatic criticism for *L'Opinion nationale,* and seven years later accepted the post of dramatic critic on *Le Temps,* which he held until his death in 1899.

During the greater part of his career, Sarcey was the veritable despot of French dramatic criticism. Henry James said he held in " his hand the fortune of a play." Sarcey was incorruptible, sane in his viewpoint, clear-sighted, logical, though somewhat narrow. It was his proud boast that he represented the average bourgeois theater-goer, the public " that pays," and his feuilletons reflected the taste of the time. He was an adherent of the " well-made play," and considered Scribe, and later Sardou, among the greatest of all dramatists. In his lectures and throughout all his writings he insists upon the necessity for structure, basing his theory on the fundamental fact that a play must be presented in a theater before an audience. Practical above all things, Sarcey was a great force in his day, demanding as he did perfection in artistic form. Nearly all his collected dramatic criticisms are in the *Quarante ans de théâtre,* which were selected after his death from his *Temps* feuilletons. In these eight volumes he exposes his theories with acumen and clarity. Unfortunately his theory of the *scène à faire*, or *Obligatory Scene*, as William Archer phrases it, is not now obtainable, though it is possible to reconstruct it out of the reprinted essays. The *Essai d'une esthétique de théâtre*, which is here translated, originally appeared in 1876, and serves to show the logical methods of the French critic.

Editions:

The *Temps* feuilletons were first selected and edited by Adolphe Brisson as *Quarante ans de théâtre*, 8 vols. (Paris, 1900–02). Occasional references to the drama are also to be found in *Souvenirs de jeunesse* (Paris, 1884), *Souvenirs d'age mur* (Paris, 1892), and *Comédiens et comédiennes* (1878).

The *Essai d'une esthétique de théâtre*, which first appeared in 1876, is translated by Hatcher H. Hughes, as *A Theory of the Theater*, with an introduction by Brander Matthews (Dramatic Museum of Columbia University, New York, 1916).

On Sarcey and his works:

Sarcey's own *Souvenirs* (see above), and *Le Siège de Paris* (Paris, 1871).
Preliminary essays under *Francisque Sarcey* in the first volume of the *Quarante ans de théâtre* (Paris, 1900).
Introduction and Notes in the Dramatic Museum edition of the translation of the *Essai* (see above).
Heinrich Behrens, *Francisque Sarceys Theaterkritik* (Greifswald, 1911).
René Doumic, *De Scribe à Ibsen* (6th ed., Paris, 1901).
——, *Etudes sur la littérature française* (*4ème série*, 2nd ed., Paris, 1901).
Maurice Eloi, *Critiques d'aujoud'hui* (Paris, 1888).
Brander Matthews, *Studies of the Stage* (New York, 1894).
——, *A Study of the Drama* (Boston, 1910).
——, *The Development of the Drama* (New York, 1903).
Clayton Hamilton, *The Theory of the Theatre* (New York, 1910).
Ernest Tissot, *Les Evolutions de la critique française* (Paris, 1890).
Jules Lemaître, *Les Contemporains*, vol. 2 (Paris, 1889).
Henry James, *French Poets and Novelists* (New York, 1878).

A THEORY OF THE THEATER [1]

[*Essai d'une esthétique de théâtre*]

(1876)

I

I am going to propose for your consideration the ideas which I believe should form the first chapter of a treatise on the art of the theater. But a few words by way of preface are necessary. Most readers, when you speak to them of a treatise on the art of the theater, or to express it more simply as did our fathers, when you speak to them of the Rules of dramatic art, believe that you have in mind a code of precepts by the aid of which one is assured, if he writes,

of composing a piece without faults, or if he criticizes, of being able to place his finger precisely on every defect.

At bottom this prepossession is entirely French; and it does not date from yesterday. You doubtless recall the worthy Abbé d'Aubignac who, having promulgated a code of dramatic literature, wrote a tragedy according to his own formula and made it prodigiously tiresome. This misadventure has never cured the public in its belief of the efficacy of rules.

They were cited against Corneille when he wrote *Le Cid*, and against Molière when he wrote *L'Ecole des femmes*. Poor Corneille struggled as best he could

[1] Re-printed, complete, from the translation by Hatcher H. Hughes, which omits a few unimportant passages (New York, 1916).— Ed.

in his Prefaces to release himself from these laws which threatened to strangle him. And in the *Critique de L'Ecole des femmes* Molière has preserved for us a record of the annoyances which the pedants of his time sought to impose on him; and it is here that he delivered his famous dictum: "There is no other rule of the theater than that of pleasing the public."

We have laughed at this over-statement; we have not taken it at all seriously; and less than sixty years ago our fathers saw what difficulty those who were then called the Romanticists experienced in freeing themselves from the fetters of the code of tragedy laid down by [Le] Bossu, put into verse by Boileau, commented upon and reënforced by all the critics of the eighteenth century, with Voltaire at their head, and after him La Harpe and Marmontel.

This national prejudice has its root in our philosophic education. From our infancy we have been taught that there is an ideal perfection which has an existence of its own and which is like an emanation from Divinity that everybody carried about with him, a conception of it more or less clear, an image more or less enfeebled; and that works of art should be declared good or bad according as they approach or depart from this type of perfection.

I will not entangle myself by affirming that there is no such beau ideal or archetype or absolute perfection. I confess simply that I do not know what is meant by this, that these are questions outside my province, which I do not comprehend. It may be that in the sublunary regions there exists a form of drama supreme and marvelously perfect, of which our masterpieces are only pale counterfeits; I leave to those who have had the good fortune of beholding this, and who say they are delighted by it, the duty and the pleasure of speaking of it with competence.

Rules do not render any great service in criticizing any more than they do in creating. The best that can be said for them is that they may serve as directions or guide-posts. After all, those who have no ear never love music and always beat time out of measure when they listen. Native taste sustained and

purified by training, reflection and usage, can alone help you to enjoy works of art. The first condition of having pleasure is to love, and we do not love by rule.

It is customary in seeking a definition of dramatic art to say that drama is a representation of life. Now, assuredly drama is a representation of life. But when one has said that, he has said no great thing; and he has taught nothing to those whom he has furnished with this formula.

All the arts of imitation are representations of life. All have for their purpose the placing of nature before our eyes. What other object has painting than that of portraying for us either scenes from life or places which serve as a setting for it? And does not sculpture strive to render for us the images of living creatures, now single and now joined in groups. We may say with equal truth of all the arts that they are representations of life; in other words, copies from nature. But we see just as readily (for it is an observation that does not require reflection) that each of these arts has a different means of expression, that the conditions to which it is obliged to submit in order to represent life impose on each of them the employment of particular processes. Thus painting concerns itself with the representation on a plane surface of objects which have all their dimensions, and of scenes from life which in reality would require for their existence a vast depth of background. It is clear then that if you wish to suggest a theory of painting you must take careful account of this condition and of all others, if there are any others, which are essential to this art, without which the art itself could not exist.

The first question to be settled then is that of the conditions, material or moral, in which resides necessarily and inevitably the art of which we speak. As it is impossible to separate the art from its conditions, as it lives only through and by them, as it is not a subtle inspiration wafted from heaven or emanating from the depths of the human mind, but something wholly concrete and definite which, like all living things, cannot exist except in the environment to which it is adapted, we are moved naturally to analyze this environment to which the art has accommodated its life, from which it has sprung, so to speak, by a series of successive developments, and of which it will always retain the impress. The painter takes a bit of wood or a scrap of canvas on which to represent life. It is a plane surface, is it not? Here is a fact, sure, undeniable. We will set out from there.

In the same way let us inquire concerning dramatic art if there is not also a fact which corresponds to this fact in painting and which is in like manner the indispensable condition of its existence and development. If we find this fact we shall be able to draw logically some conclusions as incontestable as the fact itself; and we shall discover afterwards the proof of these conclusions in the history of the art.

Now, in regard to the theater there is one fact which cannot fail to strike the least attentive; it is the presence of the audience. We cannot conceive of a play without an audience. Take one after another the accessories which serve in the performance of a dramatic work — they can all be replaced or suppressed except that one. Thus, theatres ordinarily are provided with a platform in the form of a stage, but you can imagine one without this; in fact, comedies are played in drawing-rooms without changing the arrangement of the room. This may not be very convenient, but at any rate it does not alter the meaning of the comedy. The foot-lights are arranged to light the actors from below; and this is a very useful device, since it places the faces of the actors in full light and makes them seem younger and more animated by suppressing the shadows of the eyebrows and the nose. But is it a necessary condition? Assuredly not. You may imagine such other lighting system as you please, to say nothing of the sun, which was the sole illumination of the ancients, who certainly had a theater. You may even dispense with the scenery and the costumes. Corneille and Molière have been played in barns by strolling actors grotesquely costumed according to the state of their humble wardrobes. It was none the less the *Cid* or the *Ecole des*

femmes. Shakespeare, as we have been told a hundred times, did not trouble himself in the least about scenery. A board was set up on the stage which indicated in writing where the action was taking place, and the imagination of the spectator filled in the rest to suit himself. It was none the less *Othello* or *Romeo and Juliet*.

But a play without an audience is inconceivable. It is possible that a king may at some time or other indulge the fantasy of seating himself alone in a playhouse and having played for himself alone some piece commanded by him. Such an eccentricity is only the exception which proves the rule. The king represents the absent audience; he is the crowd all by himself. And likewise the famous solitary spectator at the Odéon in the old days — the one whom Lireux provided with a foot-warmer, — he was the representative of the absent multitude. This legendary spectator was not only a spectator, he was the public. He included in his own person the twelve hundred truants who should have occupied the vacant seats about him. They had delegated their powers to him; it was they who applauded with his hands and who bore witness of their boredom when he opened his mouth to yawn.

It is an indisputable fact that a dramatic work, whatever it may be, is designed to be listened to by a number of persons united and forming an audience, that this is its very essence, that this is a necessary condition of its existence. As far back as you can go in the history of the theater, in all countries and in all ages, the men who have ventured to give a representation of life in dramatic form have begun by gathering the spectators — Thespis around his chariot as Dumas [fils] around his *Etrangère*. It is with a public in view that they have composed their works and had them performed. This then we can insist on: No audience, no play. The audience is the necessary and inevitable condition to which dramatic art must accommodate its means.

II

I emphasize this point because it is the point of departure, because from this simple fact we can derive all the laws of the theater without a single exception.

A moment ago I said that the painter is constantly obliged to represent everything on a flat surface, whether objects having all their dimensions or deep perspectives. How does he accomplish this? By a series of conventions, or tricks if you prefer, some of which are indicated and imposed by the structure and habit of our eyes and can hardly be modified, while the others are mere traditions which have no foundations in the necessity of things and are constantly variable. The same is true of the theater. Its business is to represent life to a crowd. This crowd performs in some sort for dramatic art the function of the flat surface in painting. It requires the intervention of similar tricks, or if you like the term better, of conventions. An example or two in order to enable you better to understand this. A crowd can scarcely be held together for more than four hours; or put it at five, six, eight, ten — let us say a whole day, though that is going rather far. It is certain that the following day, if this crowd collects again, it will not be composed of the same elements. It will still be a crowd, but it will not be the same crowd. The representation of life that we can exhibit before a crowd cannot then exceed an average of six hours in length. That is a fact of absolute necessity, against which no argument can prevail. The reading of a book may continue two months, the reader remaining always the same. But the crowd, by the fact of being a crowd, requires that a drama end in six hours or less.

The action represented evidently lasts more than six hours. Even in case it were confined within this narrow limit (which might happen after all) it would require a mass of innumerable details for which we could find no room under this compression of time. It was necessary a moment ago to resort to deceptions in order to represent perspective on a flat surface; it will be necessary to resort to conventions in order to give the impression that a long time has elapsed when we have only six hours at our disposal.

Let us take another example, drawn this time from the moral order. It is asserted that a crowd thinks and feels differently from the individuals which compose it. I do not imagine that there is need at present of proving a fact so well known and so authentic.

The distinguishing mark then of this collective being which we call the public is a certain confirmation of the eye. It has the singular privilege of seeing things from another angle, illumined by a light different from that of reality. The crowd changes the appearance of these things; where there are certain lines it sees others; where there are colors of a certain sort it sees different shades.

Well, if you present to this collective being, whose eyes have this gift of bizarre transformation, events from life just as they happened in reality, they will strike the crowd as being false, for they appear to the spectators altogether different from what they appear to the individuals composing the audience.

Suppose a scene-painter should give to his canvas backgrounds the tones he has observed in nature, his picture, lighted by the glare of the foot-lights, would appear grotesque. So do facts and sentiments drawn from reality and transported just as they are to the stage. It is absolutely necessary to accommodate them to the particular disposition of mind which results among people when they assemble in the form of a crowd, when they compose an audience. Therefore deceptions — conventions — are essential. Among these conventions some are permanent, others temporary and changeable. The reason is easy to understand. The audience is composed of individuals; and among individuals there are sentiments — in very small number, it is true — which are general and universal, which we find in varying degrees among all the civilized peoples who alone have developed a dramatic art. Likewise there are prejudices (in still smaller number) which we encounter in all times and in all countries. These sentiments, these prejudices, or in a word, these ways of looking at things, always remaining the same, it is natural that certain conventions, certain tricks, should be inherent in all drama, and that they should be established as laws.

On the contrary, there are other sentiments, other prejudices, which are changeable, which vanish every time one civilization is succeeded by another, and which are replaced by different ways of seeing.

When the eyes of the audience change, the conventions invented to give the illusion of life should change also, and the laws which the technique each epoch has promulgated and which it has in good faith believed to be universal and unchangeable, are destined to fall. But these laws may hold good for a long time; and they do not crumble except under the repeated assaults of intelligent criticism and of innovators of genius.

What are the universal conventions, those that have their root in all humanity? What, on the other hand, are the temporary conventions? What has been their influence? How have they arisen and how fallen into disuse?

It is not sufficient simply to affirm that drama is the representation of life. It would be a more exact definition to say that dramatic art is the sum total of the conventions, universal or local, permanent or temporary, by the aid of which in representing life in the theater, the audience is given the illusion of truth.

III

Man, by the fact of being man, in all countries and in all ages, has had the privilege of expressing his joy or his grief by laughter or by tears. There are other animals that weep, but of all the beings of creation man is the only one that laughs. Why does he laugh? And what are the causes of laughter? It is not necessary for the moment to answer this question. Man laughs; that is a fact which cannot be disputed. He weeps; that is evident. He does not laugh, nor does he weep in the same fashion or at the same things in company as alone. A crowd laughs more heartily and boisterously than an individual. Tears are readier and more abundant with an audience than with a single man.

From this disposition of the public to express the most universal sentiments of human nature, of joy and of sorrow, by laughter and by tears, arises the great division of the drama into plays that are cheerful and plays that are sad; into comedy with all its sub-species, and into tragedy and drama with all their varieties.

I do not say that it is the mission of the dramatic author to bring life as it actually is on the stage; that as there are in real life events, some pleasant and some unpleasant, it necessarily follows that we must have comedies and tragedies.

I hold that reality, if presented on the stage truthfully, would appear false to the monster with the thousand heads which we call the public. We have defined dramatic art as the sum total by the aid of which, in the theater, we represent life and give to the twelve hundred people assembled the illusion of truth.

In themselves, events are not cheerful and they are not sad. They are neither. It is we who impregnate them with our sentiment or color them to our liking. An old man falls; the street urchin who is passing holds his sides and laughs. The woman cries out with pity. It is the same event; but the one has thought only of the ridiculousness of the fall, the other has seen only the danger. The second wept where the first found cause only for laughter.

It is with events from human life as it is with landscapes. We often say of one view that it is hideous and of another that it is agreeable. That is an abuse of words. It is we who bestow on the places we pass the sentiments that move us; it is our imagination which transforms them; and it is we who give them a soul — our own.

It is true that certain landscapes seem better adapted to harmonize with the grief of a heart which is sad; but imagine two lovers in the most forbidding spot, in the midst of steep cliffs, surrounded by dark forests and stagnant waters. The spot would be illumined for them by their love and would remain graven in their memory in delightful outlines. This perfect indifference of nature has even become in recent times a commonplace of poetic development. There is nothing which has more inspired our poets; everybody remembers the two admirable tunes in which Victor Hugo and Alfred de Musset played upon this theme: *Tristesse d'Olympio* and *Souvenir*.

How often may we not observe in actual life that which has been pointed out to us in a well-known example in the classic repertory: viz., that the same situation may be treated by laughter or by tears, transported from the comic to the tragic. Mithridates wishes to know of Monime whether in his absence Xipharès has not made love to her, whether she does not love the young man. In order to make her tell the truth he pretends to believe himself too old for her and offers to marry her to the son who will be better able to take his place in her affection. Monime allows the fatal confession to escape and everybody shivers at the famous line:

Sire, you change countenance.

Harpagon, in *L'Avare* of Molière, uses the same artifice with Cléante; and the whole audience laughs at the rage of the old man when he delivers his malediction to his son who does not wish to surrender Marianne. It is not then with events, matter inert and indifferent, that we should concern ourselves, but with the public which laughs or weeps according as certain chords are touched in preference to others.

Having established this point we shall answer easily a question which has caused the spilling of a great deal of ink and which has been greatly obscured because those who have discussed it have not sought out the fundamental principles.

We agreed just now that by a very natural classification plays are divided into comedies and tragedies. May we have, is it well that we have, pieces for the stage in which laughter is mingled with tears, in which comic scenes succeed painful situations?

Most of those who rebel against the sustained seriousness of tragedy, who advocate the mixing of the tragic and the comic in the same play, have set out with the idea that it is thus things happen in reality and that the art of the dramatist consists in transporting reality to the stage. It is this very simple view that Victor Hugo sets forth in his ad-

mirable preface to *Cromwell* in that highly imaginative style which is so characteristic of him. I prefer to quote this brilliant passage:

" In drama, as one may conceive it, even though he is unable to write it, everything is linked together and everything follows in sequence as in real life. The body here plays a part as the soul does; and men and events set in action by this double agent pass before us ludicrous and terrible by turns, sometimes terrible and ludicrous at the same time.

" Thus the judge will say: ' Off with his head — let's to dinner.' Thus the Roman Senate will deliberate on the turbot of Domitian. Thus Socrates, drinking the hemlock and discoursing of the immortality of the soul and the one god, pauses to recommend that a cock be sacrificed to Æsculapius. Thus Elizabeth swears and speaks Latin.

" Thus Richelieu will be accompanied by the monk Joseph, and Louis XI will be escorted by his barber, Master Oliver the Devil. Thus Cromwell will say: ' I have Parliament in my bag and the king in my pocket,' or with the hand which signs the death warrant of Charles I he will smear with ink the face of a regicide who does the same to him laughingly. Thus Cæsar in the triumphal chariot is afraid of upsetting; for men of genius, however great they may be, have in them an imp which parodies their intelligence. It is by this quality that they link themselves with humanity and it is by this that they are dramatic.

" ' From the sublime to the ridiculous is only one step,' said Napoleon when he was convicted of being human, and this flash from a fiery soul laid bare illumines at once art and history, this cry of anguish is the summing up of drama and of life."

That is superb eloquence. But the great poets are not always very exact thinkers. The question is badly put. We are not at all concerned to know whether in real life the ludicrous is mingled with the terrible; in other words, whether the course of human events furnishes by turns to those who are either spectators or participants food for laughter and for tears. That is the one truth which no one questions and which has never been questioned. But the point at issue is altogether different. Twelve hundred persons are gathered together in the same room and form an audience. Are these twelve hundred persons likely to pass easily from tears to laughter and from laughter to tears? Is the playwright capable of transporting the audience from the one impression to the other? And does he not run the risk of enfeebling both impressions by this sudden contrast?

For example, to confine ourselves to the historic incidents cited by Victor Hugo, it does not at all concern us to know whether Cromwell after having signed the death warrant of Charles I did or did not smear with ink the face of one of his colleagues; whether this coarse pleasantry did or did not give rise to a coarse laugh in the assembly. The fact is authentic; we do not attempt to question it. The only thing we ask (in dramatic art, at least) is whether the fact, if placed on the stage just as it happened, is likely to please the twelve hundred persons in the audience.

These twelve hundred persons are entirely occupied with the death of Charles I, concerning which the author has sought to stir their pity. They are shedding tears of sympathy and tenderness. Suddenly the author places before them an act of broad buffoonery, alleging that in reality the grotesque mingles artlessly with the tragic. Do they laugh? And if they laugh do they experience a genuine satisfaction? Does not this laughter spoil the grief to which they found pleasure in abandoning themselves?

IV

.. has often been remarked that laughter persists long after the causes have ceased, just as tears continue to flow after the arrival of the good news which should have dried them immediately. The human soul is not flexible enough to pass readily from one extreme of sensation to the contrary one. These sudden jolts overwhelm it with painful confusion.

From this reflection, of which no one, I believe, will dispute the justice, we may conclude that when a man is a prey to grief if he is diverted by an idea which inclines him to laughter, he is borne suddenly far from his sorrow, and a certain lapse of time and a certain effort of will are necessary for him to return to it.

What is true of one man is even more true of a crowd. We have seen that the peculiar characteristic of an audience is that it feels more keenly than the individuals composing it. It enters more impetuously into the reasons for weeping than the poet gives it; the grief that it experiences is more intense, the tears are readier and more abundant.

I forget what tyrant it was of ancient Greece to whom massacres were everyday affairs, but who wept copiously over the misfortunes of a heroine in tragedy. He was the audience; and for the one evening clothed himself in the sentiments of the public.

It is also more difficult for an audience to return to an impression from which it has been diverted by an accident of some sort. How many performances have been interrupted, how many plays failed the first night, because of a ludicrous slip by an actor or a piquant jest from the gallery. All the house bursts out laughing. At once it becomes impossible for it to recover its equilibrium. It is now launched on another tack. The most touching scenes will be turned into ridicule. The play is lost.

In real life, this mixing of laughter and tears, this difficulty of returning to your grief after having left it, has no such disadvantage. As we have already said repeatedly, nature is indifferent and so also is life. You weep; it is well. You laugh afterwards, as you please. You laugh when you should weep; you weep when it would be better to laugh. That is your affair. You may weep with one eye and laugh with the other, as the weeping and laughing Jean of the legend. It makes little difference to us.

In the theater it is not the same. The author who brings upon the stage the events of life and who naturally desires to make them interesting to his audience, must find means to heighten and render more vivid and more enduring the impression he wishes to create.

If his intention is to provoke laughter, he will be led by that alone to guard against every incident that might induce sadness in his audience; and if, on the other hand, his purpose is to compel tears, he will discard resolutely the circumstances which, by giving rise to laughter, might tend to counteract the emotion he wishes to arouse. He is not concerned in the least to know whether in reality laughter is mingled with tears, he does not seek to reproduce the truth, but to give the illusion of truth to the twelve hundred spectators — a very different matter. When these twelve hundred spectators are entirely overwhelmed with grief they cannot believe that joy exists; they do not think about it; they do not wish to think about it; it displeases them when they are torn suddenly from their illusion in order to be shown another aspect of the same subject.

And if you do show it to them against their will, if you force them to change abruptly from tears to laughter, and this last impression once becomes dominant, they will cling to it, and a return to the mood they have abandoned will be almost impossible. In life, minutes are not counted, and we have all the time we need to bring about the transition from one sentiment to the other. But in the theater, where we have at our disposal at most only four hours to exhibit all the series of events composing the action, the changes must take place swiftly and, so to speak, on the minute. This a man would resist if he were by himself; all the more will he resist it when he is one of a crowd.

To be strong and durable, an impression must be single. All dramatists have felt this instinctively; and it is for this reason that the distinction between the comic and the tragic is as old as art itself. It would seem that when drama came into being the writers of ancient times would have been led to mingle laughter with tears, since drama represents life, and in life joy goes hand in hand with grief, the grotesque always accompanying the sublime. And yet the line of demarcation has been drawn from the beginning. It seems that, without realizing the philosophic reasons we have just set forth, the dramatic poets have felt that in order to sound the depths of the soul of the audience, they must strike always at the same spot; that the impression would be stronger and more enduring in proportion as it was unified.

Do you find the least little word to excite laughter in the grand conceptions of Æschylus or the simple and powerful dramas of Sophocles? It is true that in Sophocles the characters of humble condition express themselves in familiar language which may seem comic to those of us who have been nourished in the tradition of a necessary dignity in tragedy. But this style has nothing of the comic in itself, no more, for example, than the chattering of the nurse in Shakespeare's *Romeo and Juliet*.

These characters speak as they would speak naturally; but what they say does not alter in any way the impression of sadness that is to result from the whole. They do not give a turn to the events different from what the author intended. They do not divert the attention of the audience, either to themselves or to ludicrous incidents. They contribute to the measure of their ability, with the qualities peculiar to their minds and their temperaments, to the general impression. We hardly find, except in Euripides, innovator and decadent genius, buffoonery deliberately mingled with drama, the grotesque invading tragedy. The drunken scene between Hercules and Admetus, who is mourning the death of Alcestis, is a celebrated example of this kind.

I need not say that with us more than with any other people this distinction of species has been marked from the beginning, until recent times. We have even carried it to the extreme, for we have an exaggerated love of logic.

In *Le Malade imaginaire*, which is a comedy, and which consequently should turn entirely on laughter, Argan stretches himself on his couch and pretends to be dead, and Angélique is told that she has lost her father. Angélique, in tears, throws herself beside her father, whom she really believes to be dead. Suppose that Molière, forgetting that he was writing a comedy, had insisted on this situation, which, after all, is very touching. Suppose that he had prolonged it, that he had shown Angélique overcome with grief, ordering mourning, arranging for the funeral, and finally by dint of the tenderness expressed and the tears shed, wringing tears from the audience. He could have done it, assuredly. It would not have been difficult for him to move the twelve hundred spectators with these displays of filial grief. And likewise in the scene in *Tartufe*, where Marianne kneels before her angry father, to beg him to allow her to enter a convent.

If Molière had not restrained himself, he might have committed the precise fault into which Shakespeare, as I understand it, did not fall. He would have changed the aspect of events; I mean by this, that he would have changed the mood in which he had led us to believe that the events would be treated. What was his intention? It was to show us, in contrast to Bélise, punished for her avarice, Angélique rewarded for her filial piety, and the audience roaring with laughter at the sight of her father, raised from the dead to marry her to her lover.

It was an impression of gayety that he sought. He would have destroyed this impression had he dwelt too long on the grief of the young girl. From the same events he had meant to make use of in arousing laughter, he could have extracted tears and the audience would no longer be in the mood for laughter at the proper moment. The shock would have been too strong for the transition to be made easily.

Try to recall your past theatrical experience; you will find that in all the melodramas, in all the tragedies, whether classic or romantic, into which the grotesque has crept, it has always been obliged to take a humble place, to play an episodic part; otherwise it would have destroyed the unity of impression which the author always strives to produce. Wherever this does not hold, it is because it was the secret design of the author to extract mirth from a situation which is sad in appearance. Thus in *La Joie fait peur*, it is true that the situation in this play is that of a young man warned by his mother, his fiancée, his sister, his friends, and his old servant. But the action is arranged in such a way that the entire audience is admitted at once to the secret that the young man is not dead. Everybody finally discovers this,— except the mother, who remains disconsolate till the very end.

But who does not see that the joy of the others is one of the important elements in this amusing play, that it consequently occupies an important place in the mind of the audien⌐ and adds a certain mysterious savor of humor to the tears shed by the poor mother. The impression here, then, remains single, since far from being spoiled by the laughter which it arouses on its way, the dramatic quality of the situation is really heightened. The principle is this: the impression must be single; any mingling of laughter and tears tends to destroy this. It is better therefore to avoid it. There is nothing more legitimate than the absolute distinction of the comic from the tragic, of the grotesque from the sublime. Yet nowadays every rule is subject to many exceptions. It is an exception when the playwright feels himself strong enough to subordinate particular impressions to the general impression, when he can so control the temper of his spectators as to turn them all at once from laughter to tears, when the public he is seeking to please is capable of passing easily from one attitude to another, because of its advanced civilization, its racial instincts, its prejudices due to its education.

It depends on whether the author believes himself able to subordinate the particular to the general impression which he wishes to produce, whether he is sufficiently master of the psychology of his audience to transport them by a single stroke from laughter to tears, and on whether the audience to which he addresses himself is, by reason of the state of civilization at which it has arrived, either by prejudice of education or instinct of race, likely to pass easily from one sentiment to the other.

The rule remains intact. The impression must be single; and it cannot be this if the characters brought in for the comic scenes are anything more than episodic, if their pleasantries are anything more than accessories which can be easily supported.

Nature itself and life are impartial in the presence of joy and sorrow, laughter and tears, and pass with perfect indifference from one sentiment to the other. But to have demonstrated this, as did Victor Hugo in the admirable passage which we cited above, proves nothing; since a play is not a reproduction of life but an aggregate of conventions designed to produce upon the spectators the illusion of life; and they cannot have this illusion if the author disconcerts them by changing the sentiments which he inspires, if he disarranges their pleasure.

5.— The conclusion is that the distinction between the comic and the tragic rests, not on a prejudice, but on the very definition of drama; that this distinction may remain absolute without disadvantage; that there are disadvantages on the contrary if it is not observed; that nevertheless it may be disregarded — not without peril, however — on this condition, that the disturbing element shall not interfere with the first impression, which should remain single, and that it shall even heighten that impression, by a slight effect of contrast.

Consider for a moment that we must come down to the middle of the eighteenth century to find in our literature a single comedy in which a situation turns toward the pathetic and is treated in a manner to bring tears to the eyes of the spectators.

There is no doubt that the founders of our drama, and above all, the immortal Molière, had made the very simple observation that in life it often happens that the most joyful events face about suddenly and change joy into despair. After a good dinner you embark with some comrades in a boat for a fishing party. Your spirits are a little flushed with wine; somebody is guilty of an imprudence. A single person has preserved his good sense and warns you of the danger you are inviting. You laugh him to ridicule; he himself yields to the general hilarity. A puff of wind catches the boat crosswise; it capsizes; everybody falls into the water. Two or three remain there, and are not recovered till the next day. Is there an accident of more common occurrence? It is the terrible and pathetic breaking in abruptly and imposing silence on laughter and changing it to tears. This is seen every day; it is the regular course of life.

If the masters of the drama, who could not have failed to make so simple an observation, have nevertheless written as if it had been unknown to them, it is apparent that their sole purpose was not to exhibit life as it really is on the stage, that they had in view another object — that of showing life in a certain aspect to twelve hundred persons assembled in a theater, and of producing on the multiple soul of this audience a certain impression.

They must have said to themselves, or rather they felt instinctively, that every sensation is stronger the more it is prolonged without being opposed by any other; that an individual, and still more an audience, does not pass easily from laughter to tears in order to return immediately from tears to laughter; that they cling to the first impression; that if you wrench them violently from one sentiment and throw them into a contrary, it will be almost impossible to bring them back later on; that these threaten to destroy their pleasure for them, and are especially wrong because they give the impression that in the theater all is false, the events as well as the lighting, thus destroying the illusion.

As we do not pass in real life suddenly from laughter to tears and return immediately, or almost immediately, from tears to laughter, as the suddenness of these changes, however abrupt they may be, is relieved by intervals of time more or less considerable, which the authors cannot preserve in the theater, the rapidity of these movements, aside from the fact that they tire the audience, has this curious disadvantage, that in pretending to give us life in all its reality they destroy the illusion of this same reality.

You may search all Molière, all Regnard, all Dufresny, all Dancourt, and the rest of the dramatists of the beginning of the eighteenth century, without finding in them a scene which is not in the key suitable to comedy. If all the scenes are not comic, all at least are amiable and pleasant. You will find in them often tender conversations between lovers, scenes of jealousy, lovers opposed by parents; but these scenes present to the mind only the agreeable images of youth and hope. If there is mingled with them some shadow of sadness, it is a grief which is not without sweetness; the smile is always just beneath the tears, as in that admirable account of Hector's farewell to Andromache, which remains the best example of these mingled sentiments of sun and shower.

Molière never wrote, nor wished to write, anything but comedies which were comedies, from beginning to end. And if you will go back to classic antiquity you will see that he was not an innovator. Show me a passage in Plautus to weep over; and even Terence restricts himself to this scale of tempered sentiments — to scenes in which, if he allows the tears sometimes to form on tne eyelashes, they never fall, and are wiped away at once with a smile.

Everywhere the characteristic of comedy in the great periods in which it flourished is to be comic.

And even to-day, look at the pieces truly worthy of the name, from those of Augier to the marvelous farces of the Palais-Royal by Labiche, Meilhac, and Gondinet. Do you find in them any mixture of the pathetic? Is the unity of impression destroyed by a tearful scene? Can you easily imagine in *Célimare le bien-aimé, Les Effrontés, Le Testament de César Girodot, Les Faux bonshommes, Le Gendre de M. Poirier,* or *Mercadet,* a situation which brings tears to the eyes?

I have here chosen purposely as examples works very diverse in tone and in style in order to show that this great law of the unity of impression — without which there is no possibility of illusion for an audience of twelve hundred persons — has been observed instinctively by all the playwrights who were truly endowed with the comic genius.

EMILE ZOLA

Emile Edouard Charles Antoine Zola was born at Paris in 1840. His father having died when the boy was young, he would have had little education had not he and his mother been assisted by relatives. The youth was sent to school, and showed his interest in literature by writing a short play. On leaving school, he went to work in a publisher's office. At the same time he was contributing stories and critical reviews to the newspapers. When he left the office he devoted his time to art criticism, but not succeeding very well, he turned his hand to the writing of fiction. His vast epic series of novels — *Les Rougon-Macquart* — is an imposing literary monument comparable, at least in scope, with Balzac's *Comédie humaine.* He was always a champion of Naturalism, and he tried his hand at some half-dozen Naturalistic plays, the best of which is without doubt *Thérèse Raquin,* which was produced in 1873. His *Préface* to the printed play, and the Prefaces to the volume and to the other two plays in the volume, are Zola's most trenchant contributions to the Naturalistic program. For some years he wrote dramatic criticism, and the greater part of his essays were subsequently reprinted in *Le Naturalisme au théâtre* (1881) and *Nos Auteurs dramatiques* (1881). Zola died at Paris in 1902.

Although Zola was not himself a great Naturalistic dramatist, he has contributed a body of criticism and theory fuller and more influential than that of any other Naturalist. Henry Becque would logically have been the prophet of the movement, but his non-dramatic writings, *Querelles littéraires* (1899) and *Souvenirs d'un auteur dramatique* (1895), contain little dramatic theory and are mainly of a personal and polemic character. Jean Jullien, in his two volumes of *Le Théâtre vivant* (1892–96) is, next to Zola, the greatest exponent of Naturalism in the theater, but his plays are not of great importance. Zola's dramatic theories were formed chiefly to bring literary men into the theater with plays based upon observation. He mercilessly attacked the school of the "well-made play" and pleaded for greater sincerity, a deeper appreciation of the values of life and a closer adherence to external detail.

On the drama:

Préface to the *Théâtre* (Paris, 1878).
Préface to *Thérèse Raquin* (1873).
Préface to *Les Héritiers Rabourdin* (1874).
Préface to *Le Bouton de rose* (1874).
Le Naturalisme au théâtre (Paris, 1881).
Nos Auteurs dramatiques (Paris, 1881).

Editions:

The *Théâtre*, in a single volume, and the collected essays, *Nos Auteurs dramatiques* and *Le Naturalisme au Théâtre*, have been frequently reprinted. The dates of original appearance are indicated above.

On Zola and his works:

Jules Lemaître, *Impressions de théâtre*, vol. 7 (6th ed., Paris, 1901).
F. Sarcey, *Quarante ans de théâtre*, vol. 7 (Paris, 1902).
Brander Matthews, *French Dramatists of the Nineteenth Century* (4th ed., New York, 1905).
Abel Hermant, *Essais de critique* (Paris, 1913).
Emile Faguet, *Zola* (Paris, 1903).
G. Bornhack, *Zola als Dramatiker* (in *Zeitschrift für französische Sprache und Literatur*, vol. II, 1889).
Georges Pellissier, *Emile Zola* (in *Nouveaux Essais de littérature contemporaire*, Paris, 1895).
Matthew Josephson, *Zola and His Time* (New York, 1928).

PREFACE TO THÉRÈSE RAQUIN [1]
[*Préface* (to) *Thérèse Raquin*]
(1873)

. . . . . .

. . . It is by no means my intention to make my play a rallying standard. It has striking shortcomings, toward which no one is more severe than myself; if I were to criticize it, there would be only one thing I should not attack: the author's very obvious desire to bring the theater into closer relation with the great movement toward truth and experimental science which has since the last century been on the increase in every manifestation of the human intellect. The movement was started by the new methods of science; thence, Naturalism revolutionized criticism and history, in submitting man and his works to a system of precise analysis, taking into account all circumstances, environment, and "organic cases." Then, in turn, art and letters were carried along with the current: painting became realistic — our landscape school killed the historical school —; the novel, that social and individual study with its extremely loose frame-work, after growing and growing, took up all the activities of man, absorbing little by little the various classifications made in the rhetorics of the past.

These are all undeniable facts. We have now come to the birth of the true, that is the great, the only force of the century. Everything advances in a literary epoch. Whoever wishes to retreat or turn to one side, will be lost in the general dust. This is why I am absolutely convinced that in the near future the Naturalist movement will take its place in the realm of the drama, and bring with it the power of reality, the new life of modern art.

In the theater, every innovation is a delicate matter. Literary revolutions are slow in making themselves felt. And it is only logical that this should be the last citadel of falsehood: where the true belongs. The public as a whole resents having its habits changed, and the judgments which it passes have all the brutality of a death-sentence. But there comes a time when the public itself becomes an accomplice of the innovators; this is when, imbued with the new spirit, weary of the same stories repeated to it countless times, it feels an imperious desire for youth and originality.

I may be mistaken, but I believe that this is the situation of our public to-day. The historical drama is in its death-throes, unless something new comes to its

[1] Extracts translated, for the first time into English, by the editor.— Ed.

assistance: that corpse needs new blood. It is said that the operetta and the dramatic fantasy have killed the historical drama. This is not so: the historical drama is dying a natural death, of its own extravagances, lies, and platitudes. If comedy still maintains its place amid the general disintegration of the stage, it is because comedy clings closer to actual life, and is often true. I defy the last of the Romanticists to put upon the stage a heroic drama; at the sight of all the paraphernalia of armor, secret doors, poisoned wines and the rest, the audience would only shrug its shoulders. And melodrama, that bourgeois offspring of the romantic drama, is in the hearts of the people more dead than its predecessor; its false sentiment, its complications of stolen children and discovered documents, its impudent gasconnades, have finally rendered it despicable, so that any attempt to revive it proves abortive. The great works of 1830 will always remain advance-guard works, landmarks in a literary epoch, superb efforts which laid low the scaffoldings of the classics. But, now that everything is torn down, and swords and capes rendered useless, it is time to base our works on truth. To substitute the Romantic for the Classic tradition would be a refusal to take advantage of the liberty acquired by our forbears. There should no longer be any school, no more formulas, no standards of any sort; there is only life itself, an immense field where each may study and create as he likes.

I am attempting no justification of my own cause, I am merely expressing my profound conviction — upon which I particularly insist — that the experimental and scientific spirit of the century will enter the domain of the drama, and that in it lies its only possible salvation. Let the critics look about them and tell me from what direction help is to be expected, or a breath of life, to rehabilitate the drama? Of course, the past is dead. We must look to the future, and the future will have to do with the human problem studied in the frame-work of reality. We must cast aside fables of every sort, and delve into the living drama of the two-fold life of the character and its environment, bereft of every nursery tale, historical trapping, and the usual conventional stupidities. The decayed scaffoldings of the drama of yesterday will fall of their own accord. We must clear the ground. The well-known receipts for the tying and untying of an intrigue have served their time; now we much seek a simple and broad picture of men and things, such as Molière might write. Outside of a few scenic conventions, all that is now known as the "science of the theater" is merely a heap of clever tricks, a narrow tradition that serves to cramp the drama, a ready-made code of language and hackneyed situations, all known and planned out beforehand, which every original worker will scorn to use.

Naturalism is already stammering its first accents on the stage. I shall not cite any particular work, but among the plays produced during these past two years, there are many that contain the germ of the movement whose approach I have prophesied. I am not taking into account plays by new authors, I refer especially to certain plays of dramatists who have grown old in the métier, who are clever enough to realize the new transformation that is taking place in our literature. The drama will either die, or become modern and realistic.

It is under the influence of these ideas that I have dramatized *Thérèse Raquin*. As I have said, there are in that novel a subject, characters and *milieu* constituting, to my mind, excellent elements for the tentative of which I have dreamed. I tried to make of it a purely human study, apart from every other interest, and go straight to the point; the action did not consist in any story invented for the occasion, but in the inner struggles of the characters; there was no logic of facts, but a logic of sensation and sentiment; and the dénouement was the mathematical result of the problem as proposed. I followed the novel step by step; I laid the play in the same room, dark and damp, in order not to lose relief or the sense of impending doom; I chose supernumerary fools, who were unnecessary from the point of view of strict technique, in order to place side by side with the fearful agony of my protagonists the drab life of every day; I tried continually to bring my setting into perfect accord with the occupations of my characters, in order that they might not *play*, but rather *live*, before the audience. I counted, I confess, and with good reason, on the intrinsic power of the drama to make up, in the minds of the audience, for the absence of intrigue and the usual details. The attempt was successful, and for that reason I am more hopeful for the plays I *shall* write than for *Thérèse Raquin*. I publish this play with vague regret, and with a mad desire to change whole scenes.

The critics were wild: they discussed the play with extreme violence. I have nothing to complain of, but rather thank them. I gained by hearing them praise the novel from which the play was taken, the novel which was so badly received by the press when it was first published. To-day the novel is good, and the drama is worthless. Let us hope that the play would be good were I able to extract something from it that the critics should declare bad. In criticism, you must be able to read between the lines. For instance, how could the old champions of 1830 be indulgent toward *Thérèse Raquin?* Supposing even that my merchant's wife were a queen and my murderer wore an apricot-colored cloak? And if at the last Thérèse and Laurent should take poison from a golden goblet filled to the brim with Syracusan wine? But that nasty little shop! And those lower middle-class shop-keepers that presume to participate in a drama of their own in their own house, with their oil-cloth table-cover! It is certain that the last of the Romanticists, even if they found some talent in my play, would have denied it absolutely, with the beautiful injustice of literary passion. Then

there were the critics whose beliefs were in direct opposition to my own; these very sincerely tried to persuade me that I was wrong to burrow in a place which was not their own. I read these critics carefully; they said some excellent things, and I shall do my best to profit by some of their utterances which particularly appealed to me. Finally, I have to thank those sympathetic critics, of my own age, those who share my hopes, because, sad to say, one rarely finds support among one's elders: one must grow along with one's own generation, be pushed ahead by the one that follows, and attain the idea and the manner of the time. This, in short, is the attitude of the critics: they mentioned Shakespeare and Paul de Kock. Well, between these two extremes there is a sufficiently large place into which I can step.

I must acknowledge publicly my gratitude to M. Hippolyte Hostein, who has seen fit to grant my work his artistic patronage. In him I found not a showmaster, but a friend, a true collaborator, original and broad-minded. Without him, *Thérèse Raquin* would long have remained locked up in my desk. To bring it forth it was necessary for me to happen by chance upon a director who believed, as I did, in the necessity of rehabilitating the theater by going to the reality which is found in the modern world. While an operetta was making the fortune of one of his neighbors, it was really a beautiful thing to see M. Hippolyte Hostein, in the midst of the summer season, willing to lose money on my play. I am eternally grateful to him.

Paris, 25 July, 1873.

FERDINAND BRUNETIÈRE

Ferdinand Brunetière was born at Toulon in 1849. He attended school at Lorient, and later at Marseilles. He had traveled considerably before he reached Paris in 1867, where he completed his studies at the Lycée Louis-le-Grand. He was a studious young man, and took many courses afterward — at the Louvre,

in particular, and at the Ecole des Beaux-arts, where he met Taine. At the same time he was a constant attendant at the theater. Failing in 1869 to pass the examination for entrance into the Ecole Normale he found himself without funds and without a position. The war came and Brunetière enlisted. After the war he tutored in language, history, and philosophy. He met Bourget not long after, who made an opening for him on the staff of the *Revue des deux mondes*, of which Brunetière later became the editor. His first important contribution was *Le Roman naturaliste* (1875). He continued to write articles of various sorts, which were later collected in the *Essais critiques*. He later secured a position as teacher at the Ecole Normale. His theory of literary evolution was set forth in books, articles, and lectures, and applied in his important *Histoire de la littérature française classique*. In 1891 he further developed his ideas in a course of lectures at the *Odéon* on the history of the French drama. In the early nineties he taught at the Sorbonne and in 1893 was elected to membership in the Academy. Toward 1895, after he had become editor of the *Revue des deux mondes*, he practically ceased literary criticism. Among his late contributions to critical theory was his famous *Law of the Drama*, published as preface to Noël and Stoullig's *Les Annales du théâtre et de la musique*. His last years were devoted to religious and political controversy. In 1897 he came to the United States, where he lectured. He later went round the world, preaching Catholicism, to which he was converted in 1894 or before. He died in 1906.

Brunetière's writings on the drama include a large number of articles and books, but the theory for which he is perhaps best-known was not definitely formulated until his lectures, *Les Epoques du théâtre français*, were delivered at the *Odéon* in 1891–92, and published shortly after. But the final statement is in the *Loi du théâtre*, a preface to the *Annales du théâtre et de la musique* for 1893 (published 1894). In Brander Matthews' notes to the English translation of *Brunetière's Law of the Drama*, he says: "The theory as finally stated by Brunetière is his own, although it seems to have had its origin in the doctrine of the 'tragic conflict' declared by Hegel and taken over by Schlegel and Coleridge. The idea that tragedy must present a struggle is as ancient as Aristotle. . . . But Brunetière goes beyond Hegel and Aristotle. He subordinates the idea of struggle to the idea of volition. And in so doing he broadens the doctrine to include not tragedy only but all the manifold forms of the drama. . . . Attention was first directed to it [the law] in the opening chapter on the '*Art of the Dramatist*' in the '*Development of the Drama*' by Professor Brander Matthews, published in 1903." The Law seems to have attracted more attention in English-speaking countries, especially in America, than elsewhere. Clayton Hamilton, in *The Theory of the Theatre* (1910), and in *Studies in Stagecraft* (1914), William Archer in *Playmaking* (1912), Brander Matthews in *The Development of the Drama* (1903), Henry Arthur Jones in the Introduction to the English translation of the Law (1914), Barrett H. Clark in *The Continental Drama of To-day* (1913), and *The British and American Drama of To-day* (1914), are a few of the writers who have considered the theory.

On the drama:

Dernières recherches sur la vie de Molière (1877).
Voltaire (1878).
Les Ennemis de Racine au XVIIᵉ siècle (1879).
La Comédie de Marivaux (1881).
Le Théâtre de la Révolution (1881).
La Tragédie de Racine (1884).
Marivaux (1884).
Trois Moliéristes (1885).
A propos du Théâtre chinois (1886).
Le Théâtre de Voltaire (1886).
Sur Victor Hugo (1886).
Voltaire (1886).
L'Esthétique de Boileau (1889).
Le Naturalisme au théâtre (1889).
Alexandre Hardy (1890).
La Philosophie de Molière (1890).
La Réforme du théâtre (1890).
Octave Feuillet (1890).
Voltaire (1890).
L'Evolution des genres dans l'histoire de la littérature, tome l. Introduction. Evolution de la critique depuis la Renaissance jusqu'à nos jours (1890).
Pierre Corneille (1891).
Victor Hugo après 1830 (1891).
Les Epoques du Théâtre français (1892).
La Loi du théâtre (1894).

*La Doctrine évolutive et l'histoire de la
littérature* (1898).
L'Evolution d'un genre: la Tragédie
(1901).

Mélodrame ou tragédie? (1904).
Les Epoques de la Comédie de Molière
(1906).

The first fourteen essays in the above
list are reprinted in the *Etudes cri-
tiques sur l'histoire de la littérature
française*, 8 vols. (Paris, 1880 ff.); *Les
Epoques du Théâtre français* was pub-
lished in Paris in 1892; *L'Evolution des
genres*, etc., of which only one volume
appeared, Paris, 1890; *La Loi du théâtre*
as a preface to Noël and Stoullig's *Les
Annales du théâtre et de la musique*,
1894; *Le Naturalisme au théâtre* and *La
Réforme du théâtre* in *Essais sur la lit-
térature contemporaine*, 1892; *Mélodrame
ou tragédie?*, in *Variétés littéraires*, 1904;
Voltaire in the posthumous *Etudes sur
le XVIIIᵉ siècle*, 1911; *Victor Hugo
après 1830* and *Octave Feuillet* in *Nou-
veaux essais sur la littérature contem-
poraine*, 1895; the last five in volumes 2
and 3 of *Histoire et littérature*, 3 vols.,
1898. Occasional references to the drama
are also found in Brunetière's *Manuel
de l'histoire de la littérature française*
(1898), *Histoire de la littérature fran-
çaise classique*, 3 vols. (1903 and ff.), *Vic-
tor Hugo*, 2 vols. (1902), and his various
prefaces to *Boileau Déspreaux* (1889)
Pierre Corneille: Chefs-d'œuvre (1894),
etc. *La Loi du théâtre* is translated as
The Law of the Drama, by Philip M.
Hayden, with an introduction by Henry
Arthur Jones (Dramatic Museum of
Columbia University, New York, 1914).
Brunetière's Essays in French Literature
(a selection) is translated by D. N.

Smith (New York, 1898); and the *Man-
uel* as *Manual of French Literature*,
translated by R. D. Derechef (New
York, 1898).

On Brunetière and his works:

L. R. Richard, *F. Brunetière* (Paris,
1905).
Melchior de Vogüe, *Ferdinand Brunetière*
(in the *Revue des deux mondes*, Paris,
1907).
Victor Giraud, *Ferdinand Brunetière*
(in the *Revue des deux mondes*, Paris,
1908).
Victor Basch, *Les Idées de M. Brunetière*
(in *La Grande revue*, Paris, 1899).
Ernst Robert Curtius, *Ferdinand Bru-
netière: Beitrag zur Geschichte des
französischen Kritik* (Strassburg,
1914).
Irving Babbitt, *The Masters of Modern
French Criticism* (Boston, 1912).
Brander Matthews, *The Development of
the Drama* (New York, 1903).
——, *A Study of the Drama* (Boston,
1910).
Clayton Hamilton, *The Theory of the
Theatre* (New York, 1910).
——, *Studies in Stagecraft* (New York,
1914).
——, *Problems of the Playwright* (New
York, 1917).
William Archer, *Playwriting* (Boston,
1912).
Barrett H. Clark, *The Continental Drama
of To-day* (2nd ed., New York, 1914).
——, *The British and American Drama
of To-day* (New York, 1914).
Henry Arthur Jones, *Introduction* to the
translation of *The Law of the Drama*
(see above).
René Doumic, *Ferdinand Brunetière* (in
Ecrivains d'aujourd'hui, Paris, 1894).

THE LAW OF THE DRAMA [1]
[*La Loi du théâtre*]
(1894)

If some "First-Nighter" or some "Old
Playgoer" who was not born when our
acquaintance began, should be surprised,
my dear Noël, to see me writing this

[1] Re-printed, complete, from the translation
by Philip M. Hayden, from Brunetière's *The
Law of The Drama* (New York, 1914).— Ed.

preface for your *Annales du théâtre et
de la musique*, certainly no one is better
qualified than you to answer him, and
tell him how great has been my love for
the theater. That was about 1867 —
more than twenty-five years ago; and
we were not rich. But somehow or other

we had managed to make the acquaintance of several leaders of the *claque*, and for twenty-five sous — sometimes for ten, on repertory nights — we bought the right to sit in the pit at the Comédie-Française — and to applaud as little as we chose. The Gymnase and the Vaudeville where there was no pit, cost us more. Were those, as the saying is, the "good old days"? I will not answer for you, but for my part, I am not one of those who regret their youth; and if ever I do, I shall have greatly changed. And yet we had our happy moments, particularly after the theater, along the deserted quays, or the next day, under the trees in the Luxembourg, when we would discuss which was the better in the *Mariage de Figaro*, Got with his careful, intelligent, quiet rendering, or the broader, less studied, more spontaneous rendering of Coquelin, who since . . . but at that time he was the spoiled child of the House of Molière. Were you not translating Goethe's plays then? And for a change, you would go to see *King Lear* at the Odéon. . . . These memories are becoming a little confused to my mind. But if I remember rightly, we preferred above all the plays of Musset: the *Caprices de Marianne, Le Chandelier, On ne badine pas avec l'amour, Il ne faut jurer de rien* . . . and, to be frank, I care less, much less about him to-day, but I am not ashamed of having liked him. And how many performances, by how many actors, have we seen of *Horace* and *Britannicus, Esther* and *Athalie, Tartuffe* and the *Misanthrope*, the *Barbier de Séville*, in which no one has equaled Bressant, and the *Mariage de Figaro*, in which no one has replaced Leroux. I like to think that we thus contributed our little share to bring the classics back to their place of honor. For they are played more often now than then. Didn't you and I wait until we were quite grown-up to see *Bajazet*, for example, or *Bérénice?* We were in despair.

If now I have almost ceased to attend the theater, if I only follow it from afar, it is my own fault, and mine alone. What would you have? The fifteen lectures which I delivered at the Odéon, nearly three years ago, on the *Époques du Théâtre français* left me sated, satu-

rated, wearied with the subject,— gorged, if I may say so. But they were not without their usefulness for me; and, between ourselves, if some of my auditors were kind enough to like them, it was I who profited the most. Instead of applying myself, confining myself, as I had done before, and as we all do, to the examination of *Polyeucte* or of *Andromaque*, and following my personal taste or the demand of the moment, I had to try to grasp the essence and the connection of the works in the history of our stage, and to deduce from them, if I could, the theory, or, to speak more modestly, a theory of dramatic action. And so, when you invited me this year to write the Preface for your interesting *Annales* I accepted at once. The theory, uncertain and still vague in my lectures, had taken definite form. It had become broader, it seems to me, by becoming more simple. A child could understand it. And do not tell me that you are tempted to distrust it, precisely because of this simplicity! On the contrary, my dear friend, it is not art, science, nor life that are complex, it is the ideas that we form for ourselves in regard to them. Whoever grasps a principle, grasps all its applications. But the very diversity, multiplicity, perversity, and apparent contradiction of these applications, prevent him from seeing the principle. Will any argument, however ingenious, alter the fact that all poetry is either lyric, epic, or dramatic? Certainly not. And if the *Cid*, if *Phèdre*, if *Tartuffe*, if the *Légataire universel*, if the *Barbier de Séville*, if the *Camaraderie*, if the *Demi-monde*, if *Célimare le bien-aimé* are dramatic, does it not follow that all these works, so different, must nevertheless have not merely a few points of contact or vague resemblance, but an essential characteristic in common? What is this characteristic? That is what I shall try to explain.

Observe, if you please, that I ask only one — no more — and that I leave the dramatist complete freedom in development. That is where I depart from the old school of criticism, that believed in the mysterious power of "Rules" in their inspiring virtues; and consequently we see the old-school critics struggling and striving, exercising all their ingenuity to invent additional Rules; read, for example, the *Cours de littérature analytique* by Népomucène Lemercier. But the truth is that there are no Rules in that sense; there never will be. There are only conventions, which are necessarily variable, since their only object is to fulfill the essential aim of the dramatic work, and the means of accomplishing this vary with the piece, the time, and the man. Must we, like Corneille, regularly subordinate character to situation; invent, construct, the situations first, and then, if I may so express it, put the characters inside? We may do so, certainly, since he did it, in the *Cid* and in *Horace*, in *Polyeucte* and in *Rodogune*. Or shall we, like Racine, subordinate situation to character, find the characters first, study them, master them, and then seek the situations which will best bring out their different aspects? We may do so, and that is what he did, as you know, in *Andromaque*, in *Britannicus*, in *Bajazet*, in *Phèdre*. There is an example, then, of a Rule which may be violated, and Racine's dramaturgy is none the less dramatic for being the opposite of Corneille's dramaturgy. Take another Rule. Shall we oblige the dramatic author to observe the Three Unities? I reply that he will not be hampered by them, if he can choose, like Racine, subjects which properly or necessarily adjust themselves of their own accord, so to speak, to the rule: *Bérénice, Iphigénie, Esther* ... But if he chooses like Shakespere, subjects which are checked by it in their free development, or diverted merely, we will relieve him of the Rule: and *Othello, Macbeth, Hamlet*, will still be drama. This is another example of a Rule which can be turned in various ways. Or again, shall we mingle tragic and comic, tears and laughter, terror and joy, the sublime and the grotesque, Ariel and Caliban, Bottom and Titania, Triboulet and François I, Don Guritan and Ruy Blas? Shakespere and Hugo have done it, but Euripides and Sophocles seem to have carefully avoided it; and who will deny that they were both right? We do not feel the need of a comic element to enliven or vary the severe beauty of *Œdipus at Colonus*, but we should certainly be sorry to have *King Lear* deprived of his Fool. It is

unnecessary to continue. Evidently, all these alleged Rules effect or express only the most superficial characteristics of the drama. Not only are they not mysterious, they are not in the least profound. Whether we observe them or not, drama is drama with them or without them. They are only devices which may at any time give place to others. It all depends on the subject, the author, and the public. This is the point to add that there is something which does not depend on them.

To convince ourselves of that fact, let us examine more carefully two or three works whose dramatic value is universally recognized, and let us take them from species as different as the *Cid*, the *Ecole des femmes*, and *Célimare le bien-aimé*. Chimène *wants* to avenge her father; and the question is how she will succeed. Arnolphe *wants* to marry Agnès, whose stupidity will guarantee her fidelity; and the question is whether he will succeed. Célimare *wants* to get rid of the widowers of his former mistresses; and the question is what means he will employ. But Célimare is hampered in the execution of his *will* by his fear of the vengeance of his friends. Arnolphe is disturbed in the execution of his *will* by the young madcap Horace, who arouses love, and with love a *will*, in Agnès' heart. Chimène is betrayed in the execution of her *will* by the love which she feels for Rodrigue. On the other hand, Chimène's *will* is checked and broken by the insurmountable obstacle which she encounters in a *will* superior to her own. Arnolphe, who is far from being a fool, sees all the plans of his *will* tricked by the conspiracy of youth and love. And Célimare, by the power of his *will*, triumphs over the widowers of his mistresses. Nothing would be easier than to multiply examples. Take the *Tour de Nesle*, the *Demi-monde*, and the *Chapeau de paille d'Italie*. Fadinard *wants* to obtain a Leghorn hat to replace that of Mme. Beauperthuis; and the whole farce consists in the remarkable character of the means which he employs. Suzanne d'Ange *wants* to marry M. de Nanjac; and the whole drama consists only in the means which she formulates. Buridan *wants* to exploit the monstrous secret which exists between him and Marguerite de Bourgogne; and the whole melodrama consists only of the succession of the means which he invents. Buridan's *will* is opposed in its work by Marguerite's pride. Suzanne's *will* is countered by that of Olivier de Jalin. And Fadinard's *will* becomes entangled in the means which he seeks to satisfy it. But chance, more powerful than Fadinard's *will*, brings success at the moment when he least expects it. Olivier's *will* wins out over Suzanne's. And by the exercise of their *will*, Marguerite and Buridan fall into the trap set by their own *will*. Is it not easy now to draw the conclusion? In drama or farce, what we ask of the theater, is the spectacle of a *will* striving towards a goal, and conscious of the means which it employs.

This essential characteristic of dramatic composition distinguishes it, in the first place, from lyric composition, which I shall not discuss, in order not to complicate the question unnecessarily, and from the composition of the novel, with which, especially in our day, it has so often been confused. "Who is not for us is against us,"— you know the phrase. The drama and the novel are not the same thing; or rather, each is exactly the opposite of the other. Read *Gil Blas* again, or go again to see the *Mariage de Figaro*. The setting and the character are the same. Beaumarchais made a trip to Spain, but Lesage's novel was none the less his principal model. I have shown elsewhere that we find in the monologue of Figaro whole sentences from *Gil Blas*. Only, whereas nothing happens to Gil Blas that he has actually willed, it is on the contrary Figaro's *will* that conducts the plot of his marriage. Let us pursue this point of comparison.

Gil Blas, like everybody else, wants to live, and if possible to live agreeably. That is not what we call having a will. But Figaro wants a certain definite thing, which is to prevent Count Almaviva from exercising on Susanne the seigneurial privilege. He finally succeeds,— and I grant, since the statement has been made, that it is not exactly through the means which he had chosen, most of which turn against him; but nevertheless he has constantly willed what he willed. He had not ceased to devise means of attaining

it, and when these means have failed, he has not ceased to invent new ones. That is what may be called *will*, to set up a goal, and to direct everything toward it, to strive to bring everything into line with it. Gil Blas really has no goal. Highway robber, doctor's assistant, servant to a canon, to an actress, or to a nobleman, all the positions which he occupies one after another, come to him from fortune or chance. He has no plan, because he has no particular or definite aim. He is subject to circumstances; he does not try to dominate them. He does not *act;* he is *acted upon*. Is not the difference evident? The proper aim of the novel, as of the epic — of which it is only a secondary and derived form, what the naturalists call a sub-species or a variety — the aim of the *Odyssey*, as of *Gil Blas*, of the *Knights of the Round Table*, as of *Madame Bovary*, is to give us a picture of the influence which is exercised upon us by all that is outside of ourselves. The novel is therefore the contrary of the drama; and if I have successfully set forth this opposition, do you not see the consequences which result from it?

It is thus that one can distinguish action from motion or agitation; and that is certainly worth while. Is it action to move about? Certainly not, and there is no true action except that of a will conscious of itself, conscious, as I was saying, of the means which it employs for its fulfillment, one which adapts them to its goal, and all other forms of action are only imitations, counterfeits, or parodies. The material or the subject of a novel or of a play may therefore be the same at bottom; but they become drama or novel only by the manner in which they are treated; and the manner is not merely different, it is opposite. One will never be able, therefore, to transfer to the stage any novels except those which are already dramatic; and note well that they are dramatic only to the extent to which their heroes are truly the architects of their destiny. It follows that one could make a novel of the *Mariage de Figaro*, but one will never make a drama or a comedy of *Gil Blas*. One might make a novel of Corneille's *Rodogune*, one will never make a drama of Rousseau's *Héloïse*. The general law of the theater, thus defined, gives us, then, in the first place, a sure means of perceiving what in any subject there is of the novel or the drama. The fact is that people do not know this well enough; and the Naturalist school in France has committed no worse error than confusing the conditions of the two species.

The same law provides, further, the possibility of defining with precision the dramatic species — about as one does the biological species; and for that it is only necessary to consider the particular obstacle against which the will struggles. If these obstacles are recognized to be insurmountable, or reputed to be so, as were, for example, in the eyes of the ancient Greeks, the decrees of Fate; or, in the eyes, of the Christians, the decrees of Providence; as are, for us, the laws of nature, or the passions aroused to frenzy and becoming thus the internal fatality of Phædra and of Roxane, of Hamlet or of Othello; — it is tragedy. The incidents are generally terrifying, and the conclusion sanguinary, because in the struggle which man undertakes to make against fate, he is vanquished in advance, and must perish. Suppose now that he has a chance of victory, just one, that he still has in himself the power to conquer his passion; or suppose that, the obstacles which he is striving to overcome being the work of his fellow men, as prejudice, for example, or social conventions, a man is for that very reason capable of surmounting them,— that is the drama properly speaking, romantic drama or social drama, *Hernani* or *Antony*, the *Fils naturel* or *Madame Caverlet*. Change once more the nature of the obstacle, equalize, at least in appearance, the conditions of the struggle, bring together two opposing wills, Arnolphe and Agnès, Figaro and Almaviva, Suzanne d'Ange and Olivier de Jalin — this is comedy. *Don Sanche d'Aragon*, heroic comedy,— you know this title of one of Corneille's plays. *Bérénice*, for the same reason, is hardly a tragedy. But instead of locating the obstacle in an opposing will, conscious and mistress of its acts, in a social convention or in the fatality of destiny, let us locate it in the irony of fortune, or in the ridiculous aspect of prejudice, or again in the disproportion between the means and the end,— that is

farce, that is the *Légataire universel*, the *Chapeau de paille d'Italie*.

I do not say after that, that the types are always pure. In the history of literature or of art, as in nature, a type is almost never anything but an ideal, and consequently a limit. Where is the man among us, where is the woman, who embodies the perfection of the sex and of the species? There is moreover a natural relationship, we might say a consanguinity between adjoining species. Is a mulatto or a quadroon white or black? They are related to both. Likewise there may be an alliance or mixture of farce and comedy, of drama and tragedy. *Célimare* is almost a comedy; the *Cid* is almost a melodrama. It is nevertheless useful to have carefully defined the species; and if the law should only teach authors not to treat a subject of comedy by the devices of farce, that would be something. The general law of the theater is defined by the action of a will conscious of itself; and the dramatic species are distinguished by the nature of the obstacles encountered by this will.

And the quality of will measures and determines, in its turn, the dramatic value of each work in its species. Intelligence rules in the domain of speculation, but the will governs in the field of action, and consequently in history. It is the will which gives power; and power is hardly ever lost except by a failure or relaxation of the will. But that is also the reason why men think there is nothing grander than the development of the will, whatever the object, and that is the reason for the superiority of tragedy over the other dramatic forms. One may prefer for one's own taste a farce to a tragedy; one ought even to prefer a good farce to a mediocre tragedy, that goes without saying; and we do it every day. One cannot deny that tragedy is superior to farce: *Athalie* to the *Légataire universel*, and *Ruy Blas* to the *Trois Epiciers*. Another reason sometimes given is that it implies indifference to death, but that is the same reason, if the supreme effort of the will is to conquer the horror of death. But shall we say that comedy is superior to farce, and why? We will say that, and for the same reason, because the obstacles against which Crispin contends in the *Légataire universel* do not exist, strictly speaking; they are only an invention of Regnard; and so the will is exerting itself to no effect. The goal is only a lure, so the action is only a game. And we will say in conclusion that one drama is superior to another drama according as the quantity of will exerted is greater or less, as the share of chance is less, and that of necessity greater. Who doubts that *Bajazet* is very much superior to *Zaïre?* If you seek the true reason, you will find it here. *Zaïre* would not finish if Voltaire did not intervene at every moment in his work; but given the characters of Bajazet and Roxane, they develop as if of themselves; and does it not really seem as if Racine confined himself to observing their action?

I will not continue. But I cannot refrain from noting the remarkable confirmation that this law finds in the general history of the theater. As a matter of fact, it is always at the exact moment of its national existence when the will of a great people is exalted, so to speak, within itself, that we see its dramatic art reach also the highest point of its development, and produce its masterpieces. Greek tragedy is contemporary with the Persian wars. Æschylus fought the Mede; and while the fleets were engag d in the waters of Salamis, on that very day, the legend has it, Euripides was born. Legend is perhaps not more true, but it is often more profound than history. Consider the Spanish theater: Cervantes, Lope de Vega, Calderon, belong to the time when Spain was extending over all of Europe, as well as over the New World, the domination of her will, or rather, as great causes do not always produce their literary effects at once, they are of the time immediately following. And France in the seventeenth century? The greatest struggle that our fathers made to maintain, within as without, the unity of the French nation, or to bring it to pass, was at the end of the sixteenth century, and was under Henry IV, under Richelieu, under Mazarin. The development of the theater followed immediately. I see, indeed, that great strengthenings of the national will have not always been followed by a dramatic renaissance, in England in the eighteenth century, for example, or in Germany to-day; but what I do not see, is a dramatic renaissance whose dawn has not been announced, as it were, by some progress, or some arousing of the will. Think of the theater of Lessing, of Schiller, of Goethe and remember what Frederick the Great had done, a few years before, without knowing it perhaps, to give to the Germany of the eighteenth century a consciousness of herself and of her national genius. The converse is no less striking. If it is extremely rare that a great development of the novel is contemporary even with a great development of the theater — if in France in particular, when the Molières, the Corneilles, the Racines have appeared, we have seen the *Artamènes,* the *Faramons,* the *Astrées,* sink gently into oblivion, or again if *Gil Blas, Manon Lescaut, Marianne* are contemporary, at the beginning of the eighteenth century, with an exhaustion only too certain of the dramatic vein,— it is because in literature as in nature, the competition is always keenest between the neighboring species; and the soil is rarely rich enough for two rival varieties to prosper, develop and multiply in peace. But it is also because, being as we have seen, the contrary each of the other, drama and novel do not answer to the same conception of life. *Gil Blas* and *Figaro,* I repeat, belong to the same family; they cannot belong to the same time; and between them, if you take the trouble to examine carefully, there is all the interval that separates the relaxation of the will in the time of the Regency, from the vigorous recovery that it makes on the eve of the Revolution. What can be more singular? But if the theater has for its object to present the development of the will, what can be more natural? The Orientals have no drama, but they have novels. That is because they are fatalists, or determinists if you prefer, which amounts to the same thing, for to-day at least; and when the Greeks had a drama, they no longer had novels, I mean epics; they no longer had an *Odyssey.*

You see the reason, don't you? Are we free agents? Or are we not? Are we the masters of events? Or are we only their dupes, their playthings, their victims? I don't know; at this moment I don't care to know, and you may believe that I am not going to dabble in metaphysics here. But in any case it appears that our belief in our freedom is of no small assistance in the struggle that we undertake against the obstacles which prevent us from attaining our object. And I grant that in order to succeed in dominating nature, or even in reforming society, it is not necessary to believe one's self capable of it. There is always an acquired momentum of the human race that aids the insufficiency of individual effort. But that is not without value either; for one does not attempt the impossible. The bond between the belief in free will and the exertion of the will explains therefore pretty well the favor or the moral support given, at certain epochs to an art whose essential object is the representation of the power of the will. A question of fitness, or, as we say, of adaptation to environment. The belief in determinism is more favorable to the progress of the novel, but the belief in free will is more favorable to the progress of dramatic art. Men of action, Richelieu, Condé, Frederick, Napoleon, have always been fond of the theater.

And why may we not see here, in a sort of weakening of the will among us, one at least of the reasons for what we have generally called, for the last ten years, the dramatic crisis? Drama does not "go," they tell us. Comedy is languishing. Farce is dying out. As a matter of fact, I am sure that there is some exaggeration in the wail. Your *Annales* would suffice to prove it, if need be. But that the contemporary drama is inferior as a whole to the drama of only twenty or twenty-five years ago, it seems to me difficult not to admit. On the other hand, the philosophers, or even mere observers, complain that the power of will is weakening, relaxing, disintegrating.

People no longer know how to exert their will, they say, and I am afraid that they have some right to say it. We are broken-winded, as the poet says. We are abandoning ourselves. We are letting ourselves drift with the current. Are you not tempted to see here something more than a mere coincidence? For my part, I see here the explanation of the crisis, and at the same time another proof of the truth of the Law of the theater.

Permit me to stop here. . . .

As I was saying, my dear Noël,— no, I have not yet said it — the subject is one of those which would fill a book, and I have not time to write the book, and if I did write it, you would not be able to use it. In the meantime, since you have believed that the idea of the book might deserve discussion, I have been glad to take the opportunity which you offered me to express it. I have been able only to indicate rapidly a few of its applications, but I noted others in my lectures at the Odéon; and now I see an infinite number of them. If your readers should see still more, that is about all I could desire. I say about all, for there is one thing more I should like, and that is, that they should grasp clearly the difference between the idea of Law and the idea of Rule: the Rule being always limited by its very expression, incapable of exceeding it without destroying itself, always narrow, consequently unbending, rigid, or so to speak, tyrannical; and the Law, on the contrary, inevitable by definition and so fundamentally immutable, but broad, supple, flexible in its application, very simple and very general at the same time, very rich in applications, and, without ceasing to be the Law, always ready to be enriched by whatever reflection, experience, or history contribute in contrmations to explain it, or in contradictions to be absorbed in it.

MAURICE MAETERLINCK

Maurice Maeterlinck was born at Ghent of a Flemish family of ancient descent, in 1862. In accordance with the wishes of his parents he studied for the law, and practiced in his native city for some time after his graduation. In 1886 he left Belgium for Paris, where he became acquainted with a number of the younger writers — especially Villiers de l'Isle Adam — who were to exert great influence over him. It was Adam who, according to Maeterlinck, directed him toward "the spiritual, poetic, and mysterious side of things." In 1889, after his return home on the death of his father, he published his first works, a volume of verses, *Serres chaudes,* and *La Princesse Maleine,* a play which called forth the extravagant praise of Octave Mirbeau, who called the poet a Belgian Shakespeare. Until 1896 he spent most of his time in Belgium writing plays, and translating them from the English. In that year he returned to Paris. There he devoted himself to his lifework, which so far includes numerous plays, essays, and poems.

Maeterlinck's work is written in French and perhaps in the broadest sense of term he may be considered French, though his basic ideas are distinctly Belgian. He occupies a unique position in modern drama and literature. He has attempted and for the most part succeeded, in expressing moods and subconscious and half-realized feelings; to this end he invented the so-called Static drama, which he later discarded. Every step in his development as a dramatist has been accompanied by a statement of his theory. On the whole it may be said that he attacks the conventional plays of the day as too obvious, and strives to express the implicit. He himself realizes the futility of classification in matters of art, and he once wrote (1913) to the editor of the present volume: "You must not attach too great importance to the expression *Static;* it was an invention, a theory of my youth, worth what most literary theories are worth — that is, almost nothing. Whether a play be *static, dynamic, symbolistic,* or *realistic,*

is of little consequence. What matters is that it be well written, well thought out, human and, if possible, superhuman, in the deepest significance of the term. The rest is mere rhetoric." [1]

On the drama:

Letter inserted in the program of Van Lerberghe's *Les Flaireurs* (1892).
Article on Ibsen (1894).
Menus Propos. Le Théâtre (1890).
Préface to Alfred Sutro's *The Cave of Illusion* (1900).
Preface to Maeterlinck's *Théâtre* (I) (1901).
Le Tragique quotidien (1896).
L'Etoile (1896).
Le Réveil de l'âme (1896).
Préface to *The Plays of Maurice Maeterlinck,* 2nd series (1896).
La Sagesse et la destinée (1898).
Le Drame moderne (1904).
A Propos du "Roi Lear" (1907).
Preface to Maeterlinck's translation of *Macbeth* (1910).

Editions:

The volumes of collected essays in which the above are included are: *Le Trésor des humbles* (Paris, 1896); *La Sagesse et la destinée* (Paris, 1898); *Le Temple enseveli* (Paris, 1902); *Le double Jardin* (Paris, 1904); and *L'Intelligence des fleurs* (Paris, 1907). These are translated as *The Treasure of the Humble* (by Alfred Sutro, New York, 1897); *Wisdom and Destiny* (by Alfred Sutro, New York, 1898); *The Buried Temple* (New York, 1902); *The Double Garden* (by A. T. de Mattos, New York, 1904); and *The Measure of the Hours* (by A. T. de Mattos, New York, 1907). The *Letter* from the program of *Les Flaireurs* is quoted at length in Remy de Gourmont's *La Belgique littéraire* (Paris, 1915). Sections from the article on Ibsen are quoted in Moses' *Maurice Maeterlinck,*

[1] Printed, together with another letter, in *The Continental Drama of To-day,* by Barrett H. Clark, (2nd ed., New York, 1914).— Ed.

a *Study* (New York, 1911). The article *Menus Propos*, etc., is quoted in the same volume. *The Cave of Illusion* appeared in London, 1900. The *Théâtre*, vol. I, was published at Brussels, 1901. *Le Tragique quotidien, L'Etoile*, and *Le Réveil de l'ame* are in *Le Trésor des humbles* (Paris, 1896). The *Préface* to the Plays—in French —is included in the English translation of *Pelléas et Mélisande* (New York, 1896). *La Sagesse et la destinée* was published at Paris in 1898. *Le Drame moderne* originally appeared in *Le double Jardin* (Paris, 1904). *A Propos du " Roi Lear "* appeared in *L'Intelligence des fleurs* (Paris, 1907). Maeterlinck's *Préface* to his translation of *Macbeth* is affixed to the edition of that play (Paris, 1910).

On Maeterlinck and his works:

Ad. van Bever, *Maurice Maeterlinck* (Paris, 1904).
Gerard Harry, *Maurice Maeterlinck* (Bruxelles, 1909).

M. Esch, *L'Œuvre de Maurice Maeterlinck* (Paris, 1912).
Montrose J. Moses, *Maurice Maeterlinck, a Study* (New York, 1911).
Edward Thomas, *Maurice Maeterlinck* (New York, 1911).
Johannes Schlaf, *Maurice Maeterlinck* (Berlin, 1906).
Una Taylor, *Maurice Maeterlinck, a Critical Study* (New York, 1915).
Macdonald Clark, *Maurice Maeterlinck, Poet and Philosopher* (New York, 1916).
Georges Leneveu, *Ibsen et Maeterlinck* (Paris, 1902).
Arthur Symons, *Plays, Acting, and Music* (New York, 1909).
James Huneker, *Iconoclasts* (New York, 1905).
Barrett H. Clark, *The Continental Drama of To-day* (New York, 2nd ed., 1915).
——, *A Study of the Modern Drama* (2nd ed., New York, 1928).
Archibald Henderson, *Interpreters of Life and the Modern Spirit* (New York, 1905).
S. C. de Soissons, *Maeterlinck as a Reformer of the Drama* (in *Contemporary Review*, vol. 86, London, 1904).

THE TRAGICAL IN DAILY LIFE [2]
[*Le Tragique quotidien*]
(1896)

... In most cases, indeed, you will find that psychological action — infinitely loftier in itself than mere material action, and truly, one might think, well-nigh indispensable — that psychological action even has been suppressed, or at least vastly diminished, in a truly marvelous fashion, with the result that the interest centers solely and entirely in the individual, face to face with the universe. Here we are no longer with the barbarians, nor is the man now fretting himself in the midst of elementary passions, as though, forsooth, these were the only things worthy of note: he is at rest, and we have time to observe him. It is no longer a violent, exceptional moment of life that passes before our eyes — it

[2] Translated sections from *The Treasure of the Humble* (translated by Alfred Sutro, New York, 1897).— Ed.

is life itself. Thousands and thousands of laws there are, mightier and more venerable than those of passion; but, in common with all that is endowed with resistless force, these laws are silent, and discreet, and slow-moving; and hence it is only in the twilight that they can be seen and heard, in the meditation that comes to us at the tranquil moments of life. When Ulysses and Neoptolemus come to Philoctetes and demand of him the arms of Hercules, their action is in itself as simple and ordinary as that of a man of our day who goes into a house to visit an invalid, of a traveler who knocks at the door of an inn, or of a mother who, by the fireside, awaits the return of her child. Sophocles indicates the character of his heroes by means of the lightest and quickest of touches. But it may safely be said that the chief interest of tragedy does not lie in the struggle we witness between cunning and loyalty, between love of country, rancor and head-strong pride. There is more beyond: for it is man's loftier existence that is laid bare to us. The poet adds to ordinary life something, I know not what, which is the poet's secret: and there comes to us a sudden revelation of life in its stupendous grandeur, in its submissiveness to the unknown powers, in its endless affinities, in its awe-inspiring misery. Let but the chemist pour a few mysterious drops into a vessel that seems to contain the purest water, and at once masses of crystals will rise to the surface, thus revealing to us all that lay in abeyance there where nothing was visible before to incomplete eyes. And even thus is it in *Philoctetes;* the primitive psychology of the three leading characters would seem to be merely the sides of the vessel containing the clear water; and this itself is our ordinary life, into which the poet is about to let fall the revelation-bearing drops of his genius.

Indeed, it is not in the actions but in the words that are found the beauty and greatness of tragedies that are truly beautiful and great; and this not solely in the words that accompany and explain the action, for there must perforce be another dialogue besides the one which is superficially necessary. And indeed the only words that count in the play are those that at first seemed useless, for it is therein that the essence lies. Side by side with the necessary dialogue will you almost always find another dialogue that seems superfluous; but examine it carefully, and it will be borne home to you that this is the only one that the soul can listen to profoundly, for here alone is it the soul that is being addressed. You will see, too, that it is the quality and the scope of this unnecessary dialogue that determine the quality and the immeasurable range of the work. Certain it is that, in the ordinary drama, the indispensable dialogue by no means corresponds to reality; and it is just those words that are spoken by the side of the rigid, apparent truth, that constitute the mysterious beauty of the most beautiful tragedies, inasmuch as these are words that conform to a deeper truth,

and one that lies incomparably nearer to the invisible soul by which the poem is upheld. One may even affirm that a poem draws the nearer to beauty and loftier truth in the measure that it eliminates words that merely explain the action, and substitutes for them others that reveal, not the so-called "soul-state," but I know not what intangible and unceasing striving of the soul towards its own beauty and truth. And so much the nearer, also, does it draw to the true life. To every man does it happen, in his workaday existence, that some situation of deep seriousness has to be unraveled by means of words. Reflect for an instance. At moments such as those — nay, at the most commonplace of times — is it the thing you say or the reply you receive that has the most value? Are not other forces, other words one cannot hear, brought into being, and do not these determine the event? What I say often counts for so little; but my presence, the attitude of my soul, my future and my past, that which will take birth in me and that which is dead, a secret thought, the stars that approve, my destiny, the thousands of mysteries which surround me and float about yourself — all this it is that speaks to you at that tragic moment, all this it is that brings to me your answer. There is all this beneath every one of my words, and each one of yours; it is this, above all, that we see, it is this, above all, that we hear, ourselves notwithstanding. If you have come, you, the "outraged husband," the "deceived lover," the "forsaken wife," intending to kill me, your arm will not be stayed by my most moving entreaty; but it may be that there will come towards you, at that moment, one of these unexpected forces; and my soul, knowing of their vigil near to me, may whisper a secret word whereby, haply, you shall be disarmed. These are the spheres wherein adventures come to issue, this is the dialogue whose echo should be heard. And it is this echo that one does hear — extremely attenuated and variable, it is true — in some of the great works mentioned above. But might we not try to draw nearer to the spheres where it is "in reality" that everything comes to pass?

PREFACE TO THE PLAYS [3]
[*Préface — Théâtre I*]
(1901)

. . . I do not believe that a poem should sacrifice its beauty in order to point a moral, but if, without losing any element that goes to make up its interior or exterior beauty, it leads us to truths as acceptable but more encouraging than the truth which leads us nowhere, it will possess the advantage of accomplishing a twofold, though uncertain, purpose. For centuries we have sung of the vanity of life and the irresistible power of emptiness and death, and summoned our sorrows that become more and more monotonous the nearer they approach to the ultimate truth. But now let us try to vary the appearance of the unknown which surrounds us and discover a new reason for living and persevering; we shall at least be able to alternate our sorrows by mixing with them our reviving or falling hopes. Granted our present conditions, it is at least as reasonable to hope that our efforts are not useless as we think they are. The supreme truth of death, nothingness, and the uselessness of our existence — the point at which we arrive at the end of our inquiry — is, after all, only the limit of our human consciousness. We cannot see beyond that, because that marks the barrier of our intelligence. It only *seems* certain, but as a matter of fact, there is nothing more certain in it than our ignorance. Before we are forced to admit this truth irrevocably, we must do our best for a long time to dissipate this ignorance and do what we can to find the light. Then the great mass of our formerly conceived duties — conceived in the light of our over-hasty 'and mortal conclusion — will be called into question and human life begun again, with its passions that seem less futile, with its joys, its sorrows and its duties, all of which will assume an added importance, because they will help us to emerge from the obscurity and bear to look upon it without bitterness.

I do not mean to infer that we shall return to where we stood formerly, nor that love, death, destiny and the other mysterious powers of life will all occupy the place they once occupied in our actual existence, and in human works, especially — since it is with this that we are at present concerned — in dramatic works. The human mind — as I remarked in this connection in a passage which is practically unknown — the human mind has during the past three-quarters of a century undergone a transformation which we are not yet fully able to realize, but which is probably one of the most profound in the whole domain of thought. This evolution, if it has not revealed to us the end, the origin, the laws of the universe — definite certitudes — about matter, life, and the destiny of man, has at least done away with and rendered powerless a number of *uncertainties*, and these *uncertainties* were precisely those wherein the greatest thoughts flourished with the utmost freedom. They were in essence the element of beauty and the greatness of our aspirations, the hidden force that elevated our words above the words of everyday life; the poet seemed great and profound in proportion to the form, more or less triumphant, and the more or less preponderating place he was able to give to these beautiful or terrifying, peaceful or hostile, tragic or consoling, uncertainties.

Great poetry, if we observe it closely, is made up of three principal elements: first, verbal beauty; then the contemplation and passionate portrayal of what actually exists about us and within us, that is to say, nature and our sentiments; and, finally, enveloping the whole work and creating the atmosphere proper to it, the idea which the poet forms of the unknown in which float about the beings and things which he evokes, the mystery which dominates them, judges them, and presides over their destinies. I have no doubt that this last is the most important element. Look at any beautiful poem, no matter how short it

---

[3] Extracts from the *Préface* to vol. 1 of the Brussels edition of Maeterlinck's *Théâtre* (1901); translated by the editor.— Ed.

may be, or rapid. Only in the rarest instances are its beauty and grandeur limited to the known facts. Nine times out of ten it owes its beauty to an illusion to the mystery of human destiny, to some new link between the visible and the invisible, the temporal and the eternal. Now, if the possible unprecedented evolution in our ideas taking place nowadays regarding the unknown has not as yet profoundly stirred the lyric poet, and deprives him of only a part of his resources, it is not the same with the dramatic poet. Perhaps it is allowable for the lyric poet to remain a sort of theorist of the unknown; possibly he should be permitted to deal in great and vast generalities; he need not think of the practical consequences. If he is convinced that the gods of old, that justice and destiny, no longer intervene in the actions of man and direct the progress of this world, he need not give a name to the powers which he does not understand, forces which are always concerned with men and which dominate everything. It makes little difference whether it be God or the Universe which appears immense and terrible to him. What we demand of him principally is that he make us feel the immense or terrible impression which he felt. But the dramatic poet cannot limit himself to these generalities, he must bring down his own ideas of the unknown into the world of living men, into the everyday world. He must show us how, under what form and conditions, according to what laws, to what end, the superior powers act upon our destinies, the unintelligible influences, the infinite principles of which he as poet is convinced the universe is full. And since the dramatist of the present has arrived upon the scene at a time when he cannot sincerely accept the ancient truths, and when the new truths, which are to replace the old, are not yet determined, have even no name, he hesitates, feels his way and, if he wishes to remain absolutely sincere, dares not risk going beyond the immediate reality. He confines himself to the study of human feelings in their material and psychological effects. Within this sphere he can create powerful works full of observation, passion, and wisdom, but it is certain that he will

never attain to the vaster and more profound beauty of the great poems wherein something of the infinite is mingled with the acts of men; and he asks himself whether or no he should cease striving for beauty of that sort.

I think he ought not. He will find a way of realizing these beauties, through difficulties with which no poet has hitherto been confronted, but not until to-morrow. Yet even to-day, when the alternative seems the most dangerous, one or two poets have succeeded in escaping from the world of obvious actuality, without returning to that of the chimeras of old — because the greatest poetry is, above all, the kingdom of the unexpected, and from the most general rules, like fragments of stars which cross the sky where no trace of brightness is looked for, spring forth the most disconcerting exceptions. For example, Tolstoy's *The Power of Darkness* is a work that floats down the most sordid river of the depths of life, like an island, grandiose in its horror, reeking with hellish odors, but enveloped at the same time by an enormous white light, pure and miraculous, springing from the simple soul of Akim. Or else, take Ibsen's *Ghosts*, where in a stuffy middle-class drawing-room, unbearable, maddening to the characters, there breaks forth one of the most terrible mysteries of human destiny. It is all very well for us to shut our eyes to the anguish of the unknown: but into these two plays enter superior powers which all of us feel weighing down upon our lives. For it is much less the action of the God of the Christians which troubles us in Tolstoi's poem than of the God who is in a human heart, simpler, juster, purer, greater than the others. And in Ibsen's poem it is the influence of a law of justice or injustice, formidable and only recently suspected — the law of heredity, of which very little is known, and that open to discussion, and yet plausible — the menace of which hides the greater part of what might have been a matter for doubt.

But in spite of these unexpected sallies into the realm of the uncertain, it remains a fact that mystery, the unintelligible, the superhuman, the infinite — the word, makes little difference — all this has, since we no longer admit *a priori* divine intervention in human action, become almost " unworkable," and genius itself is seldom able to cope with it. When in his other dramas Ibsen tries to combine with other mysteries the acts of his men who are a prey to an abnormal conscience, or his women who are a prey to hallucination, we must admit that if the atmosphere he creates is strange and troubling, it is healthy and breathable because it is rarely reasonable and real.

From time to time in the past a true genius, or sometimes the simple and honest man of talent, succeeded in writing a play with that profound background, that mist about the summit, that feeling of the infinite here and there which, having neither name nor form, permitted us to mingle our images of it while we spoke, and seemed necessary in order that the dramatic work might flow by, brimming to the banks, and attain its ideal. Nowadays, our drama almost always lacks the third character, enigmatic, invisible, but everywhere present, which we might well call the sublime character, and which is perhaps no other than the unconscious though powerful and undeniable concept of the poet's idea of the universe, which gives to the play a far greater reach, a certain aspiration for existence after the death of other things,

and makes us return to it without ever exhausting its possibilities of beauty. Such a genius, we must also admit, is wanting in our life as well. Will he ever return? Will he arise from a new and experimental conception of justice, or from the indifference of nature, from one of those far-reaching general laws of matter or mind which we have just begun to catch sight of? In any event, let us keep a place for him. At least let us see to it that nothing else takes his place while he is getting clear of the shadows; and let us see to it that we do not set up any more phantoms. Our very waiting for him, his empty place in life, are in themselves of far greater significance than anything we could put on his throne, which our patience is now reserving for him.

For my humble part, after producing the little dramas of which I have just spoken, it seemed wise and loyal to exile death from that throne where it is by no means certain he has a right to sit. And in the last, which I had not named among the others, in *Aglavaine et Sélysette*, I wished death to give away, at least in part, to love, wisdom, and happiness. But death did not obey me, and I await, together with most of the poets of my time, the revelation of a new poet.

.   .   .   .   .

ENGLAND III

MODERN PERIOD

ENGLISH DRAMATIC CRITICISM OF THE NINETEENTH AND TWENTIETH CENTURIES

At a time when the English drama was near its lowest ebb, England could boast of at least half a dozen of her greatest critics. True it is that Coleridge and Lamb, Hazlitt, and Leigh Hunt, did not devote all their criticisms to the acted drama, but the theories they evolved are applicable to it. Coleridge and Lamb went far to engage the interest of their contemporaries in the earlier English stage, while Hazlitt and Hunt applied themselves more particularly to the criticism of acting. Most of Coleridge's best dramatic criticism is found in the *Lectures on Shakespeare* and other poets, delivered during the first twenty years of the century. Most of Lamb's essays on the drama are of a discursive character and pertain to acting, though in the Notes to his *Specimens of English Dramatic Poets* (1808), and in occasional essays, like *On the Artificial Comedy of the Last Century,* he set forth a distinct theory of comedy. Of William Hazlitt's many hundreds of periodical criticisms, those pertaining to the drama are found for the most part in *View of the English Stage* (1818 and 1821), *Lectures on the English Comic Writers* (1819) and *Lectures on the Literature of the Age of Elizabeth* (1820). Leigh Hunt's first collection of criticisms was the *Critical Essays* (1807). He was for years a constant contributor to various papers — *The Reflector, The Indicator, The Companion,* etc. Among Robert Southey's miscellaneous essays, some of which have never been collected, *The Doctor* contains a few articles on the drama and dramatists. Sir Walter Scott wrote a long article on *Drama* in 1810. Shelley's *Defence of Poetry* (1821) contains some passages on the drama. The comparatively minor disputes of the time are reflected in James Sheridan Knowles' *Lectures on Dramatic Literature* (1820–50); John Dennant's *Appeal to the Candour and common sense of the public respecting the present controversy on the subject of plays* (1808), and *Letter to the writer of an anonymous pamphlet in defence of plays* (1808); William Hayley's *Dramatic Observations* (1811); Martin M'Dermot's *A Philosophical Inquiry into the Source of the Pleasure derived from Tragic Representations,* etc. (1824); John William Calcraft's *Defence of the Stage,* etc. (1839); and Edward Mayhew's *Stage Effect* (1840). Into the many literary quarrels of Gifford and Hazlitt, Hunt and Macaulay (see the latter's essay on *Leigh Hunt,* 1841, which contains an attack on Lamb's *Artificial Comedy*) it is not necessary to enter. The more scholarly critics, editors, commentators, historians, of the period are "Christopher North," Hartley Coleridge, Henry Hallam, all of whom at least touched upon dramatic literature, though none produced a body of doctrine on the subject. George Henry Lewes, in his occasional reviews, and in his book, *The Spanish Drama* (1845), and *On Actors and the Art of Acting* (1875), and John Forster — kept up the tradition of Hazlitt and Hunt. Mention should also be made of Percy Fitzgerald's *The Romance of the English Stage* (1874), *Principles of Comedy and Dramatic Effect* (1870), and *A New History of the Stage* (1882). Theodore Martin's *Essays on the Drama* appeared in 1874. The practicing dramatist, W. S. Gilbert, wrote *A Stage Play* (1873). Matthew Arnold included a preface to his play *Merope* in the first edition (1858). *The French Play in London* was published in *Irish Essays.* The more or less professional critics of the mid-nineteenth century often published their articles in book-form. Of outstanding interest may be mentioned: Henry Morley and his *Journal of a London Playgoer from 1851 to 1866* (1866); Morris Mowbray and his *Essays in Theatrical Criticism* (1882); Clement Scott and his *Drama of Yesterday and To-day* (1899); Dutton Cook and his *The Book of the Play* (1876),

Nights at the Play (1883), and *On the Stage* (1883). Henry Arthur Jones and Sir Arthur Pinero began writing plays in the late seventies, and the former began lecturing on the drama in the eighties. Jones' two books, *The Renascence of the English Drama* (1895), and *Foundations of a National Drama* (1913) were instrumental in developing modern English dramatic art. Pinero wrote little, but his essay on *R. L. Stevenson: The Dramatist* (1903) is an interesting commentary on the art of the drama. Bernard Shaw's copious industry is best represented in his *Dramatic Opinions and Essays* (1906), collected from his *Saturday Review* criticisms of the nineties, and his *Prefaces*. Shaw successfully attacked artificiality and insincerity in the drama, and made way for the play of ideas. Later dramatists have stated their theories of play-writing. Among these, the following may be mentioned in passing: H. Granville-Barker, in a number of occasional magazine articles; John Masefield in his Preface to *Nan* (1911); St. John Hankin (*A Note on Happy Endings*, 1907, *Puritanism and the English Stage*, 1906, *Mr. Bernard Shaw as Critic*, 1907, *How to Run an Art Theatre for London*, 1907, and *The Collected Plays of Oscar Wilde*, 1908); and John Galsworthy in his *Some Platitudes Concerning Drama* (1909) and *The New Spirit in the Drama* (1913). Jerome K. Jerome, Israel Zangwill, and Sydney Grundy have contributed more or less interesting articles and books on their art. Arthur Symons (in his *Plays, Acting and Music*, 1909); W. L. Courtney (in his *Idea of Tragedy*, 1900, and articles on the *Idea of Comedy*, 1913–14); W. L. George (in his *Dramatic Actualities*) have all contributed to dramatic theory. The regular dramatic critics are of considerable importance, especially William Archer (*About the Theatre*, 1886, *The Theatrical World* 1894–98,

Study and Stage, 1899, and *Playmaking*, 1912); Arthur Bingham Walkley (*Playhouse Impressions*, 1892, *Frames of Mind*, 1899, *Dramatic Criticism*, 1903, and *Drama and Life*, 1908); J. T. Grein (*Premières of the Year*, 1900, and *Dramatic Criticism*, 1899, 1901, 1904). George Meredith's *Essay on Comedy and the Uses of the Comic Spirit* was first delivered as a lecture in 1877, and reprinted in book-form twenty years later. " E. F. S." (E. F. Spence) has collected a number of criticisms in his suggestive book, *Our Stage and its Critics* (1910). There is a newer school of dramatic critics, some of whom have not yet published all their work in book form. E. A. Baughn, Ashley Dukes, P. P. Howe, Huntley Carter, C. E. Montague, James Agate, A. N. Monkhouse, Graham Sutton, Ivor Brown, Gilbert Cannan, and John Palmer have brought certain new ideas into dramatic criticism. See especially Dukes' *Modern Dramatists* (1911), and *The World to Play With*, P. P. Howe's *Dramatic Portraits* (1914), Huntley Carter's *The New Spirit in Drama and Art* (1912); C. E. Montague's *Dramatic Values* (1911), Gilbert Cannan's *Joy of the Theatre* (1913), and John Palmer's *Comedy* (1913 or 14), and *The Future of the Theatre* (1909). The Irish Theatre movement has aroused considerable theorizing. See especially William Butler Yeats: *The Irish Dramatic Movement* (articles collected from *Samhain, The Arrow*, etc., 1901–07); *Discoveries* (1907); *Ideas of Good and Evil* (1903); *Preface* to *Plays for an Irish Theatre* (1911). George Moore: *Impressions and Opinions* (1891), and prefaces to his own play, *The Bending of the Bough* (1900), and to Martyn's *Heather Field* (1899). J. M. Synge: *Preface* to *The Tinker's Wedding* (1907) and *The Playboy of the Western World* (1907); Lord Dunsany, in *Romance and the Modern Stage* (1911).

General references on nineteenth century English literature:

George Saintsbury, *A History of Nineteenth Century Literature* (New York, 1904).

L. Magnus, *English Literature in the Nineteenth Century* (New York, 1909).

Holbrook Jackson, *The Eighteen Nineties* (New York, 1913).

J. M. Kennedy, *English Literature, 1880–1913* (London, 1913).

G. K. Chesterton, *The Victorian Age in Literature* (New York, 1913).

General references on nineteenth century English drama:

William Hazlitt, *A View of the English Stage* (reprint London, 1906).

Leigh Hunt, *Dramatic Essays of Leigh Hunt,* edited by William Archer and R. W. Lowe (London, 1894).

Henry Morley, *The Journal of a London Playgoer* (London, 1866).

Mowbray Morris, *Essays in Theatrical Criticism* (London, 1882).

G. Boyle, *English and American Poets and Dramatists of the Victorian Age* (Frankfurt, 1886).

A. Darbyshire, *Art of the Victorian Stage* (Manchester, 1907).

Dutton Cook, *The Book of the Play* (London, 1876).

———, *On the Stage* (London, 1883).

———, *Nights at the Play* (London, 1883).

"Q," *Dramatists of the Present Day* (London, 1871).

H. B. Baker, *The London Stage, 1576–1903* (London, 1904).

J. W. Cunliffe, *Modern English Playwrights* (New York, 1927).

E. L. Stahl, *Das englische Theater im 19. Jahrhundert* (Leipzig, 1914).

E. Fitzball, *Thirty-five Years of a Dramatic Author's Life* (London, 1858).

J. R. Planché, *Recollections and Reflections,* 2 vols. (London, 1872).

R. H. Hirne, *The New Spirit of the Age* (London, 1845).

W. C. Macready, *Diary and Reminiscences* (London, 1875–76).

J. Coleman, *Players and Playwrights I Have Known* (London, 1888).

Clement Scott, *The Drama of Yesterday and To-day,* 2 vols. (London, 1899).

Mario Borsa, *The English Stage of To-day* (London, 1908).

Augustin Filon, *The English Stage* (London, 1897).

Thomas H. Dickinson, *The Contemporary Drama of England* (Boston, 1917).

Barrett H. Clark, *The British and American Drama of Today* (New York, 1915).

———, *A Study of the Modern Drama* (new ed., New York, 1928).

F. W. Chandler, *Aspects of Modern Drama* (New York, 1914).

Ludwig Lewisohn, *The Modern Drama* (New York, 1915).

Graham Sutton, *Some Contemporary Dramatists* (New York, 1926).

William Archer, *English Dramatists of Today* (London, 1882).

———, *About the Theatre* (London, 1886).

———, *The Theatrical World,* 5 vols. (London, 1894–98).

———, *Study and Stage* (London, 1899).

———, *Playmaking* (Boston, 1912).

Bernard Shaw, *Dramatic Opinions and Essays,* 2 vols. (New York, 1906).

Henry Arthur Jones, *The Renascence of the English Drama* (New York, 1895).

———, *The Foundations of a National Drama* (New York, 1913).

A. B. Walkley, *Playhouse Impressions* (London, 1892).

———, *Drama and Life* (London, 1908).

H. B. Irving, *Occasional Papers, Dramatic and Historical* (Boston, 1907).

Arthur Bouchier, *Some Reflections on the Drama—and Shakespeare* (Oxford, 1911).

J. T. Grein, *Dramatic Criticism* (London, 1899).

———, *Premières of the Year* (London, 1900).

———, *Dramatic Criticism* (London, 1901).

———, *Dramatic Criticism* (London, 1904).

———, *The Theater and the World* (London, 1921).

———, *The New World of the Theatre* (London, 1924).

Ivor Brown, *Masques and Phases* (London, 1926).

———, *Parties of the Play* (London, 1928).

C. E. Montague, *Dramatic Values* (London, 1911).

W. L. George, *Dramatic Actualities* (London, 1914).

P. P. Howe, *Dramatic Portraits* (London, 1913).

E. F. S[pence], *Our Stage and its Critics* (London, 1910).

John Palmer, *The Future of the Theatre* (London, 1913).

Gilbert Cannan, *The Dramatic Sense* (in *English Review,* v. 5, London, 1910).

Ashley Dukes, *Modern Dramatists* (London, 1911).

———, *The Youngest Drama* (Chicago, 1924).

———, *Drama* (New York, 1926).

———, *The World to Play With* (New York, 1928).

James Agate, *The Contemporary The-
ter, 1923–26,* 4 vols. (London, 1924–27).
———, *A Short View of the English Stage*
(London, 1926).
Huntley Carter, *The New Spirit in
Drama and Art* (London, 1912).

Lady Gregory, *Our Irish Theatre* (New
York, 1913).
Cornelius Weygandt, *Irish Plays and
Playwrights* (Boston, 1913).
George Moore, *Hail and Farewell,* 3 vols.
(New York, 1911–13).

SAMUEL TAYLOR COLERIDGE

Samuel Taylor Coleridge was born at
Ottery St. Mary, Devon, in 1772. His
father, a minister, gave Samuel an edu-
cation with a view to training him to
enter the church. At the age of ten he
was sent to Christ's Hospital, London,
where he made the acquaintance of
Lamb. Here he stayed for seven years.
Two years later he went to Cambridge,
where he distinguished himself as a good
scholar. But his studies were constantly
interrupted by his preoccupation with
the new ideas of the time, engendered
by the French Revolution. In 1793, he
left college and enlisted in the cavalry,
but he was released and returned to
Cambridge the next year. A little later,
at Oxford, he met Southey, and the two
planned an ideal republic, which came
to naught. In 1794 Coleridge left Cam-
bridge without his degree. He lectured
in Bristol on political subjects, and pub-
lished a few poems. The next year he
married. From Bristol the Coleridges
moved to Nether Stowey and enjoyed
the friendship of the Wordsworths, who
were their neighbors. At this time he
was preaching and getting subscribers
to a paper — which soon failed. Be-
tween 1796 and 1798 he wrote *The An-
cient Mariner* and most of his best poems,
which were published in 1798. The same
year the Wedgwoods offered Coleridge
an annuity, and the poet went to Ger-
many, where he became deeply interested
in philosophy and metaphysics. On his
return in 1800 he published his transla-
tions from Schiller, and soon after con-
tributed a series of philosophical articles
to the *Morning Post.* It was in 1801 that
he began to take opium. In 1804 he be-
came a secretary in Malta, and later
traveled in Italy. He did comparatively
little during the next few years, though
he delivered lectures in London, and
founded a magazine, *The Friend.* His

play, *Remorse,* was produced with some
success at Drury Lane. Some years
after, he put himself under the care of
Mr. Gillman of Highgate, who eventually
cured him of his disease. Further lec-
tures were given, and partially written
down; these contain some of his best criti-
cal work. He died at Highgate in 1834.

Coleridge's critical writings are su-
premely important. His drama criti-
cism is not primarily of the acted drama,
but his viewpoint in general is all-em-
bracing and inspirational. The best of
his dramatic criticism is in the *Lectures
on Shakespeare* and other dramatists,
but it is in flashes, random notes, and
in the notes of others who took down his
utterances, that they are found. Mat-
thew Arnold said of him: "That which
will stand of Coleridge is this: the stim-
ulus of his continual instinctive effort to
get at and to lay bare the real truth
of his matter in hand, whether that mat-
ter were literary or philosophical, or
political or religious; and this in a coun-
try when at that moment such an effort
was almost unknown."

On the drama:

The *Literary Remains,* 4 vols. (London,
1836–39) contain most of Coleridge's
Lectures on Shakespeare, the Greek
dramatists, and the English poets.
However, most of his other critical
volumes may be consulted for miscel-
laneous remarks on the drama, espe-
cially *Biographia Literaria* (1817),
Table-Talk (1835), *Anima Poetæ*
(1895), *Biographia Epistolaris* (1911),
and *Letters, 1785–1834,* 2 vols. (1895).

Editions:

The *Works* are printed in the Bohn
edition (see recent reprint). Conven-
ient editions of the *Lectures* are in

Everyman's Library (n.d.). See also J. W. Mackail's *Coleridge's Literary Criticism* (Oxford, 1908).

On Coleridge and his works:

Thomas Allsop, *Letters, Conversations, and Recollections of Samuel Taylor Coleridge* (London, 1836. Later ed., London, 1864).

Joseph Cottle, *Early Recollections, chiefly relating to the late Samuel Taylor Coleridge, during his long residence in Bristol, 2 vols.* (London, 1837. Later edition in new form, as *Reminiscences of Samuel Taylor Coleridge and Robert Southey*, London, 1847).

James Gillman, *The Life of Samuel Taylor Coleridge*, only 1 vol. published (London, 1838).

Henry D. Traill, *Coleridge* (in *English Men of Letters*, London, 1884).

Hall Caine, *Samuel Taylor Coleridge* (London, 1887).

James Dykes Campbell, *Samuel Taylor Coleridge* (London, 1894).

William Francis Prideaux, *The Bibliography of Coleridge* (London, 1900).

John Louis Haney, *A Bibliography of Samuel Taylor Coleridge* (Philadelphia, 1903).

Richard Garnett, *Coleridge* (London, 1904).

GREEK DRAMA [1]

(1818)

It is truly singular that Plato,— whose philosophy and religion were but exotic at home, and a mere opposition to the finite in all things, genuine prophet and anticipator as he was of the Protestant Christian era,— should have given in his Dialogue of the *Banquet*, a justification of our Shakespeare. For he relates that, when all the other guests had either dispersed or fallen asleep, Socrates only, together with Aristophanes and Agathon, remained awake, and that, while he continued to drink with them out of a large goblet, he compelled them, though most reluctantly, to admit that it was the business of one and the same genius to excel in tragic and comic poetry, or that the tragic poet ought, at the same time, to contain within himself the powers of comedy. Now, as this was directly repugnant to the entire theory of the ancient critics, and contrary to all their experience, it is evident that Plato must have fixed the eye of his contemplation on the innermost essentials of the drama, abstracted from the forms of age or country. In another passage he even adds the reason, namely, that opposites illustrate each other's nature, and in their

struggle draw forth the strength of the combatants, and display the conqueror as sovereign even on the territories of the rival power.

Nothing can more forcibly exemplify the separative spirit of the Greek arts than their comedy as opposed to their tragedy. But as the immediate struggle of contraries supposes an arena common to both, so both were alike ideal; that is, the comedy of Aristophanes rose to as great a distance above the ludicrous of real life, as the tragedy of Sophocles above its tragic events and passions,— and it is in this one point, of absolute ideality, that the comedy of Shakespeare and the old comedy of Athens coincide. In this also alone did the Greek tragedy and comedy unite; in everything else they were exactly opposed to each other. Tragedy is poetry in its deepest earnest; comedy is poetry in unlimited jest. Earnestness consists in the direction and convergence of all the powers of the soul to one aim, and in the voluntary restraint of its activity in consequence; the opposite, therefore, lies in the apparent abandonment of all definite aim or end, and in the removal of all bounds in the exercise of the mind,— attaining its real end, as an entire contrast, most perfectly, the greater the display is of intellectual wealth squandered in the wan-

---

1 Re-printed extracts from the Everyman's Library Edition of the *Lectures*, etc., first delivered in 1812 and printed in the *Literary Remains*, vol. 2 (London, 1836).— Ed.

tonness of sport without an object, and the more abundant the life and vivacity in the creations of the arbitrary will.

The later comedy, even where it was really comic, was doubtless likewise more comic, the more free it appeared from any fixed aim. Misunderstandings of intention, fruitless struggles of absurd passion, contradictions of temper, and laughable situations there were; but still the form of the representation itself was serious; it proceeded as much according to settled laws, and used as much the same means of art, though to a different purpose, as the regular tragedy itself. But in the old comedy the very form itself is whimsical; the whole work is one great jest, comprehending a world of jests within it, among which each maintains its own place without seeming to concern itself as to the relation in which it may stand to its fellows. In short, in Sophocles, the constitution of tragedy is monarchical, but such as it existed in elder Greece, limited by laws, and therefore the more venerable,— all the parts adapting and submitting themselves to the majesty of the heroic scepter:— in Aristophanes, comedy, on the contrary, is poetry in its most democratic form, and it is a fundamental principle with it, rather to risk all the confusion of anarchy, than to destroy the independence and privileges of its individual constituents,— place, verse, characters, even single thoughts, conceits, and allusions, each turning on the pivot of its own free will.

The tragic poet idealizes his characters by giving to the spiritual part of our nature a more decided preponderance over the animal cravings and impulses, than is met with in real life: the comic poet idealizes his characters by making the animal the governing power, and the intellectual the mere instrument. But as tragedy is not a collection of virtues and perfections, but takes care only that the vices and imperfections shall spring from the passions, errors, and prejudices which arise out of the soul;— so neither is comedy a mere crowd of vices and follies, but whatever qualities it represents, even though they are in a certain sense amiable, it still displays them as having their origin in some dependence on our lower nature, accompanied with a de-

fect in true freedom of spirit and self-subsistence, and subject to that unconnection by contradictions of the inward being, to which all folly is owing.

The ideal of earnest poetry consists in the union and harmonious melting down, and fusion of the sensual into the spiritual,— of man as an animal into man as a power of reason and self-government. And this we have represented to us most clearly in the plastic art, or statuary; where the perfection of outward form is a symbol of the perfection of an inward idea; where the body is wholly penetrated by the soul, and spiritualized even to a state of glory, and like a transparent substance, the matter, in its own nature darkness, becomes altogether a vehicle and fixture of light, a means of developing its beauties, and unfolding its wealth of various colors without disturbing its unity, or causing a division of the parts. The sportive ideal, on the contrary, consists in the perfect harmony and concord of the higher nature with the animal, as with its ruling principle and its acknowledged regent. The understanding and practical reason are represented as the willing slaves of the senses and appetites, and of the passions arising out of them. Hence we may admit the appropriateness to the old comedy, as a work of defined art, of allusions and descriptions, which morality can never justify, and, only with reference to the author himself, and only as being the effect or rather the cause of the circumstances in which he wrote, can consent even to palliate.

The old comedy rose to its perfection in Aristophanes, and in him also it died with the freedom of Greece. Then arose a species of drama, more fitly called, dramatic entertainment than comedy, but of which, nevertheless, our modern comedy (Shakespeare's altogether excepted) is the genuine descendant. Euripides had already brought tragedy lower down and by many steps nearer to the real world than his predecessors had ever done, and the passionate admiration which Menander and Philemon expressed for him, and their open avowals that he was their great master, entitle us to consider their dramas as of a middle species, between tragedy and comedy,— not the tragi-comedy, or thing of heterogeneous parts, but a complete whole, founded on principles of its own. Throughout we find the drama of Menander distinguishing itself from tragedy, but not, as the genuine old comedy, contrasting with, and opposing it. Tragedy, indeed, carried the thoughts into the mythologic world, in order to raise the emotions, the fears, and the hopes, which convince the inmost heart that their final cause is not to be discovered in the limits of mere mortal life, and force us into a presentiment, however dim, of a state in which those struggles of inward free will with outward necessity, which form the true subject of the tragedian, shall be reconciled and solved; — the entertainment or new comedy, on the other hand, remained within the circle of experience. Instead of the tragic destiny, it introduced the power of chance; even in the few fragments of Menander and Philemon now remaining to us, we find many exclamations and reflections concerning chance and fortune, as in the tragic poets concerning destiny. In tragedy, the moral law, either as obeyed or violated, above all consequences — its own maintenance or violation constituting the most important of all consequences — forms the ground; the new comedy, and our modern comedy in general (Shakespeare excepted as before), lies in prudence or imprudence, enlightened or misled self-love. The whole moral system of the entertainment exactly like that of fable, consists in rules of prudence, with an exquisite conciseness, and at the same time an exhaustive fullness of sense.

An old critic said that tragedy was the flight or elevation of life, comedy (that of Menander) its arrangement or ordonnance.

Add to these features a portrait-like truth of character,— not so far indeed as that a *bona fide* individual should be described or imagined, but yet so that the features which give interest and permanence to the class should be individualized. The old tragedy moved in an ideal world,— the old comedy in a fantastic world. As the entertainment, or new comedy, restrained the creative activity both of the fancy and the imagination, it indemnified the understanding in appealing to the judgment for the probability of the scenes represented. The ancients themselves acknowledged the new comedy as an exact copy of real life. The grammarian, Aristophanes, somewhat affectedly exclaimed:—" O Life and Menander! which of you two imitated the other?" In short the form of this species of drama was poetry, the stuff or matter was prose. It was prose rendered delightful by the blandishments and measured motions of the muse. Yet even this was not universal. The mimes of Sophron, so passionately admired by Plato, were written in prose, and were scenes out of real life conducted in dialogue. The exquisite *Feast of Adonis* (Συρακούσιαι ἢ Ἀδωνιάζουσαι) in Theocritus, we are told, with some others of his eclogues, were close imitations of certain mimes of Sophron — free translations of the prose into hexameters. . . .

.   .   .   .   .   .

PROGRESS OF THE DRAMA [2]

(1818)

.   .   .   .   .   .

And here it will be necessary to say a few words on the stage and on stage-illusion.

A theater, in the widest sense of the word, is the general term for all places of amusement through the ear or eye, in which men assembled in order to be

amused by some entertainment presented to all at the same time and in common. Thus, an old Puritan divine says: — " Those who attend public worship and sermons only to amuse themselves, make a theater of the church, and turn God's house into the devil's. *Theatra œdes diabololatricœ.*" The most important and dignified species of this *genus* is, doubtless, the stage, (*res theatralis histrionica*), which, in addition to the generic definition above given, may be charac-

2 Re-printed extracts from the Everyman's Library Edition of the *Lectures.* Originally delivered in 1818 and first printed in vol. 2 of the *Literary Remains* (London, 1836).—Ed.

terized in its idea, or according to what it does, or ought to, aim at, as a combination of several or of all the fine arts in an harmonious whole, having a distinct end of its own, to which the peculiar end of each of the component arts, taken separately, is made subordinate and subservient,— that, namely, of imitating reality — whether external things, actions, or passions — under a semblance of reality. Thus, Claude imitates a landscape at sunset, but only as a picture; while a forest-scene is not presented to the spectators as a picture, but as a forest; and though, in the full sense of the word, we are no more deceived by the one than by the other, yet are our feelings very differently affected; and the pleasure derived from the one is not composed of the same elements as that afforded by the other, even on the supposition that the *quantum* of both were equal. In the former, a picture, it is a condition of all genuine delight that we should not be deceived; in the latter, stage-scenery, (inasmuch as its principal end is not in or for itself, as is the case in a picture, but to be an assistance and means to an end out of itself) its very purpose is to produce as much illusion as its nature permits. These, and all other stage presentations, are to produce a sort of temporary half-faith, which the spectator encourages in himself and supports by a voluntary contribution on his own part, because he knows that it is at all times in his power to see the thing as it really is. I have often observed that little children are actually deceived by stage-scenery, never by pictures; though even these produce an effect on their impressible minds, which they do not on the minds of adults. The child, if strongly impressed, does not indeed positively think the picture to be the reality; but yet he does not think the contrary. As Sir George Beaumont was shewing me a very fine engraving from Rubens, representing a storm at sea without any vessel or boat introduced, my little boy, then about five years old, came dancing and singing into the room, and all at once (if I may so say) *tumbled in* upon the print. He instantly started, stood silent and motionless, with the strongest expression, first of wonder and then of grief in his eyes and countenance, and at length said,

" And where is the ship? But that is sunk, and the men are all drowned!" still keeping his eyes fixed on the print. Now what pictures are to little children, stage illusion is to men, provided they retain any part of the child's sensibility; except, that in the latter instance, the suspension of the act of comparison, which permits this sort of negative belief, is somewhat more assisted by the will, than in that of a child respecting a picture.

The true stage-illusion in this and in all other things consists — not in the mind's judging it to be a forest, but, in its remission of the judgment that it is not a forest. And this subject of stage-illusion is so important, and so many practical errors and false criticisms may arise, and indeed have arisen, either from reasoning on it as actual delusion, (the strange notion, on which the French critics built up their theory, and on which the French poets justify the construction of their tragedies), or from denying it altogether, (which seems the end of Dr. Johnson's reasoning, and which, as extremes meet, would lead to the very same consequences, by excluding whatever would not be judged probable by us in our coolest state of feeling, with all our faculties in even balance), that these few remarks will, I hope, be pardoned, if they should serve either to explain or to illustrate the point. For not only are we never absolutely deluded — or anything like it, but the attempt to cause the highest delusion possible to beings in their senses sitting in a theater, is a gross fault, incident only to low minds, which, feeling that they cannot affect the heart or head permanently, endeavor to call forth the momentary affections. There ought never to be more pain than is compatible with co-existing pleasure, and to be amply repaid by thought.

Shakespeare found the infant stage demanding an intermixture of ludicrous character as imperiously as that of Greece did the chorus, and high language accordant. And there are many advantages in this; — a greater assimilation to nature, a greater scope of power, more truths, and more feelings; — the effects of contrast, as in Lear and the Fool; and especially this, that the true language of passion becomes sufficiently elevated by your having previously heard, in the same piece, the lighter conversation of men under no strong emotion. The very nakedness of the stage, too, was advantageous,— for the drama thence became something between recitation and representation; and the absence or paucity of scenes allowed a freedom from the laws of unity of place and unity of time, the observance of which must either confine the drama to as few subjects as may be counted on the fingers, or involve gross improbabilities, far more striking than the violation would have caused. Thence, also, was precluded the danger of a false ideal,— of aiming at more than what is possible on the whole. What play of the ancients, with reference to their ideal, does not hold out more glaring absurdities than any in Shakspeare? On the Greek plan a man could more easily be a poet than a dramatist; upon our plan more easily a dramatist than a poet.

THE DRAMA GENERALLY, AND PUBLIC TASTE [3]

(1818)

.   .   .   .   .

In my last address I defined poetry to be the art, or whatever better term our language may afford, of representing external nature and human thoughts, both relatively to human affections, so as to cause the production of as great immediate pleasure in each part, as is compatible with the largest possible sum of pleasure on the whole. Now this definition applies equally to painting and music as to poetry; and in truth the term poetry is alike applicable to all three. The vehicle alone constitutes the difference; and the term " poetry " is rightly applied by eminence to measured words, only because the sphere of their action is far wider, the power of giving permanence to them much more certain, and incomparably greater the facility, by which men, not defective by nature or disease, may be enabled to derive habitual pleasure and instruction from them. On my mentioning these considerations to a painter of great genius, who had been, from a most honorable enthusiasm, extolling his own art, he was so struck with their truth, that he exclaimed, " I want no other arguments;— poetry, that is, verbal poetry, must be the greatest; all that proves final causes in the world, proves this; it would be shocking to think otherwise!"— And in truth, deeply, O! far more than words can express, as I venerate the Last Judgment and the Prophets of Michel Angelo Buonarotti,—

3 Re-printed extracts from the Everyman's Library Edition. Originally delivered in 1818, and first printed in vol. 2 of the *Literary Remains* (London, 1836).— Ed.

yet the very pain which I repeatedly felt as I lost myself in gazing upon them, the painful consideration that their having been painted in *fresco* was the sole cause that they had not been abandoned to all the accidents of a dangerous transportation to a distant capital, and that the same caprice, which made the Neapolitan soldiery destroy all the exquisite masterpieces on the walls of the church of the *Trinitado Monte,* after the retreat of their antagonist barbarians, might as easily have made vanish the rooms and open gallery of Raphael, and the yet more unapproachable wonders of the sublime Florentine in the Sixtine Chapel, forced upon my mind the reflection; How grateful the human race ought to be that the works of Euclid, Newton, Plato, Milton, Shakespeare, are not subjected to similar contingencies,— that they and their fellows, and the great, though inferior, peerage of undying intellect, are secured;— secured even from a second irruption of Goths and Vandals, in addition to many other safeguards, by the vast empire of English language, laws, and religion founded in America, through the overflow of the power and the virtue of my country;— and that now the great and certain works of genuine fame can only cease to act for mankind, when men themselves cease to be men, or when the planet on which they exist, shall have altered its relations, or have ceased to be.

.   .   .   .   .

But let us now consider what the drama should be. And first, it is not a copy, but an imitation of nature. This is the universal principle of the fine arts. In all well laid out grounds what delight do we feel from that balance and antithesis of feelings and thoughts! How natural! we say; — but the very wonder that caused the exclamation, implies that we perceived art at the same moment. We catch the hint from nature itself. Whenever in mountains or cataracts we discover a likeness to anything artificial which yet we know is not artificial — what pleasure! And so it is in appearances known to be artificial, which appear to be natural. This applies in due degrees, regulated by steady good sense, from a clump of trees to the *Paradise Lost* or *Othello*. It would be easy to apply it to painting and even, though with greater abstraction of thought, and by more subtle yet equally just analogies — to music. But this belongs to others; suffice it that one great principle is common to all the fine arts, a principle which probably is the condition of all consciousness, without which we should feel and imagine only by discontinuous moments, and be plants or brute animals instead of men; — I mean that evervarying balance, or balancing, of images, notions, or feelings, conceived as in opposition to each other; — in short, the perception of identity and contrariety; the least degree of which constitutes likeness, the greatest absolute indifference; but the infinite gradations between these two form all the play and all the interest of our intellectual and moral being, till it leads us to a feeling and an object more awful than it seems to me compatible with even the present subject to utter aloud, though I am most desirous to suggest it. For there alone are all things at once different and the same; there alone, as the principle of all things, does distinction exist unaided by division; there are will and reason, succession of time and unmoving eternity, infinite change and ineffable rest! —

*Return Alpheus! the dread voice is past
Which shrunk thy streams!*

——— *Thou honor'd flood,
Smooth-flowing Avon, crown'd with vocal reeds,
That strain I heard, was of a higher mood! —
But now my voice proceeds.*

We may divide a dramatic poet's characteristics before we enter into the component merits of any one work, and with reference only to those things which are to be the materials of all, into language, passion, and character; always bearing in mind that these must act and react on each other, — the language inspired by the passion, and the language and the passion modified and differenced by the character. To the production of the highest excellencies in these three, there are requisite in the mind of the author; — good sense; talent; sensibility; imagination; — and to the perfection of a work we should add two faculties of lesser importance, yet necessary for the ornaments and foliage of the column and the roof — fancy and a quick sense of beauty.

.   .   .   .   .   .

The German tragedies have in some respects been justly ridiculed. In them the dramatist often becomes a novelist in his directions to the actors, and thus degrades tragedy into pantomime. Yet still the consciousness of the poet's mind must be diffused over that of the reader or spectator; but he himself, according to his genius, elevates us, and by being always in keeping, prevents us from perceiving any strangeness, though we feel great exultation. Many different kinds of style may be admirable, both in different men, and in different parts of the same poem.

See the different language which strong feelings may justify in Shylock, and learn from Shakespeare's conduct of that character the terrible force of every plain and calm diction, when known to proceed from a resolved and impassioned man.

It is especially with reference to the drama, and its characteristics in any given nation, or at any particular period, that the dependence of genius on the public taste becomes a matter of the deepest importance. I do not mean that taste which springs merely from caprice or fashionable imitation, and which, in fact, genius can, and by degrees will, create for itself; but that which arises out of wide-grasping and heart-enrooted causes, which is epidemic, and in the very air that all breathe. This it is which kills, or withers, or corrupts, indeed, might walk arm and arm with

Hygeia, whilst pestilence, with a thousand furies running to and fro, and clashing against each other in a complexity and agglomeration of horrors, was shooting her darts of fire and venom all around him. Even such was Milton; yea, and such, in spite of all that has been babbled by his critics in pretended excuse for his damning, because for them too profound, excellencies,— such was Shakspeare. But alas! the exceptions prove the rule. For who will dare to force his way out of the crowd,— not of the mere vulgar,— but of the vain and banded aristocracy of intellect, and presume to join the almost supernatural beings that stand by themselves aloof?

Of this diseased epidemic influence there are two forms especially preclusive of tragic worth. The first is the necessary growth of a sense and love of the ludicrous, and a morbid sensibility of the assimilative power,— an inflammation produced by cold and weakness,— which in the boldest bursts of passion will lie in wait for a jeer at any phrase, that may have an accidental coincidence in the mere words with something base or trivial. For instance,— to express woods, not on a plain, but clothing a hill, which overlooks a valley, or dell, or river, or the sea,— the trees rising one above another, as the spectators in an ancient theater,— I know no other word in our language, (bookish and pedantic terms out of the question,) but *hanging* woods, the *sylvæ superimpendentes* of Catullus; yet let some wit call out in a slang tone,—"the gallows!" and a peal of laughter would damn the play. Hence it is that so many dull pieces have had a decent run, only because nothing unusual above, or absurd below, mediocrity furnished an occasion,— a spark for the explosive materials collected behind the orchestra. But it would take a volume of no ordinary size however laconically the sense were expressed, if it were meant to instance the effects, and unfold all the causes, of this disposition upon the moral, intellectual, and even physical character of a people, with its influences on domestic life and individual deportment. A good document upon this subject would be the history of Paris society and of French, that is, Parisian, literature from the commencement of the latter half of the reign of Louis XIV to that of Buonaparte, compared with the preceding philosophy and poetry even of Frenchmen themselves.

The second form, or more properly, perhaps, another distinct cause, of this diseased disposition is matter of exultation to the philanthropist and philosopher, and of regret to the poet, the painter, and the statuary alone, and to them only as poets, painters, and statuaries; — namely, the security, the comparative equability, and ever increasing sameness of human life. Men are now so seldom thrown into wild circumstances, and violences of excitement, that the language of such states, the laws of association of feeling with thought, the starts and strange far-flights of the assimilative power on the slightest and least obvious likeness presented by thoughts, words, or objects,— these are all judged of by authority, not by actual experience,— by what men have been accustomed to regard as symbols of these states, and not the natural symbols, or self-manifestations of them.

NOTES ON *THE TEMPEST* [4]

(1836)

There is a sort of improbability with which we are shocked in dramatic representation, not less than in a narrative of real life. Consequently, there must be rules respecting it; and as rules are nothing but means to an end previously ascertained —(inattention to which simple truth has been the occasion of all the pedantry of the French school),— we must first determine what the immediate end or object of the drama is. And here, as I have previously remarked, I find two extremes of critical decision; — the French, which evidently presupposes

4 Re-printed, with one omission, from the Everyman's Library Edition. Originally printed in vol. 2 of the *Literary Remains* (London, 1836).— Ed.

that a perfect delusion is to be aimed at,— an opinion which needs no fresh confutation; and the exact opposite to it, brought forward by Dr. Johnson, who supposes the auditors throughout in the full reflective knowledge of the contrary. In evincing the impossibility of delusion, he makes no sufficient allowance for an intermediate state, which I have before distinguished by the term, illusion, and have attempted to illustrate its quality and character by reference to our mental state, when dreaming. In both cases we simply do not judge the imagery to be unreal; there is a negative reality, and no more. Whatever, therefore, tends to prevent the mind from placing itself, or being placed, gradually in that state in which the images have such negative reality for the auditor, destroys this illusion, and is dramatically improbable.

Now the production of this effect — a sense of improbability — will depend on the degree of excitement in which the mind is supposed to be. Many things would be intolerable in the first scene of a play, that would not at all interrupt our enjoyment in the height of the interest, when the narrow cockpit may be made to hold

The vast field of France, or we may cram
Within its wooden O the very casques
That did affright the air at Agincourt.

Again, on the other hand, many obvious improbabilities will be endured, as belonging to the groundwork of the story rather than to the drama itself, in the first scenes, which would disturb or disentrance us from all illusion in the acme of our excitement; as for instance, Lear's division of his kingdom, and the banishment of Cordelia.

But, although the other excellences of the drama besides this dramatic probability, as unity of interest, with distinctness and subordination of the characters, and appropriateness of style, are all, so far as they tend to increase the inward excitement, means towards accomplishing the chief end, that of producing and supporting this willing illusion,— yet they do not on that account cease to be ends themselves; and we must remember that, as such, they carry their own justification with them, as long as they do not

contravene or interrupt the total illusion. It is not even always, or of necessity, an objection to them, that they prevent the illusion from rising to as great a height as it might otherwise have attained;— it is enough that they are simply compatible with as high a degree of it as is requisite for the purpose. Nay, upon particular occasions, a palpable improbability may be hazarded by a great genius for the express purpose of keeping down the interest of a merely instrumental scene, which would otherwise make too great an impression for the harmony of the entire illusion. Had the panorama been invented in the time of Pope Leo X, Raphael would still, I doubt not, have smiled in contempt at the regret, that the broom twigs and scrubby brushes at the back of some of his grand pictures were not as probable trees as those in the exhibition.

The Tempest is a specimen of the purely romantic drama, in which the interest is not historical, or dependent upon fidelity of portraiture, or the natural connection of events,— but is a birth of the imagination, and rests only on the coaptation and union of the elements granted to, or assumed by, the poet. It is a species of drama which owes no allegiance to time or space, and in which, therefore, errors of chronology and geography — no mortal sins in any species — are venial faults, and count for nothing. It addresses itself entirely to the imaginative faculty; and although the illusion may be assisted by the effect on the senses of the complicated scenery and decorations of modern times, yet this sort of assistance is dangerous. For the principal and only genuine excitement ought to come from within,— from the moved and sympathetic imagination; whereas, where so much is addressed to the mere external senses of seeing and hearing, the spiritual vision is apt to languish, and the attraction from without will withdraw the mind from the proper and only legitimate interest which is intended to spring from within.

The romance opens with a busy scene admirably appropriate to the kind of drama, and giving, as it were, the keynote to the whole harmony. It prepares and initiates the excitement required for the entire piece, and yet does not demand anything from the spectators, which their previous habits had not fitted them to understand. It is the bustle of a tempest, from which the real horrors are abstracted; — therefore it is poetical, though not in strictness natural — (the distinction to which I have so often alluded) — and is purposely restrained from concentering the interest on itself, but used merely as an induction or tuning for what is to follow.

In the second scene, Prospero's speeches, till the entrance of Ariel, contain the finest example, I remember, of retrospective narration for the purpose of exciting immediate interest, and putting the audience in possession of all the information necessary for the understanding of the plot. Observe, too, the perfect probability of the moment chosen by Prospero (the very Shakspeare himself, as it were, of the tempest) to open out the truth to his daughter, and how completely anything that might have been disagreeable to us in the magician, is reconciled and shaded in the humanity and natural feelings of the father. In the very first speech of Miranda the simplicity and tenderness of her character are at once laid open; — it would have been lost in direct contact with the agitation of the first scene. The opinion once prevailed, but, happily, is now abandoned, that Fletcher alone wrote for women; — the truth is, that with very few, and those partial, exceptions, the female characters in the plays of Beaumont and Fletcher are, when of the light kind, not decent; when heroic, complete viragos. But in Shakspeare all the elements of womanhood are holy, and there is the sweet, yet dignified feeling of all that *continuates* society, as sense of ancestry and of sex, with a purity unassailable by sophistry, because it rests not in the analytic processes, but in that same equipoise of the faculties, during which the feelings are representative of all past experience,— not of the individual only, but of all those by whom she has been educated, and their predecessors even up to the first mother that lived. Shakspeare saw that the want of prominence, which Pope notices for sarcasm, was the blessed beauty of the woman's character, and knew that it arose not from any defi-

ciency, but from the more exquisite harmony of all the parts of the moral being constituting one living total of head and heart. He has drawn it, indeed, in all its distinctive energies of faith, patience, constancy, fortitude,— shown in all of them as following the heart, which gives its results by a nice tact and happy intuition, without the intervention of the discursive faculty, sees all things in and by the light of the affections, and errs, if it ever err, in the exaggerations of love alone. In all the Shakspearian women there is essentially the same foundation and principle; the distinct individuality and variety are merely the result of the modification of circumstances, whether in Miranda the maiden, in Imogen the wife, or in Katherine the queen.

But to return. The appearance and characters of the super or ultra-natural servants are finely contrasted. Ariel has in everything the airy tint which gives the name; and it is worthy of remark that Miranda is never directly brought into comparison with Ariel, lest the natural and human of the one and the supernatural of the other should tend to neutralize each other; Caliban, on the other hand, is all earth, all condensed and gross in feelings and images; he has the dawnings of understanding without reason or the moral sense, and in him, as in some brute animals, this advance to the intellectual faculties, without the moral sense, is marked by the appearance of vice. For it is in the primacy of the moral being only that man is truly human; in his intellectual powers he is certainly approached by the brutes, and, man's whole system duly considered, those powers cannot be considered other than means to an end, that is, to morality.

In this scene, as it proceeds, is displayed the impression made by Ferdinand and Miranda on each other; it is love at first sight: —

at the first sight
They have chang'd eyes: —

and it appears to me, that in all cases of real love, it is at one moment that it takes place. That moment may have been prepared by previous esteem, admiration, or even affection,— yet love seems to require a momentary act of volition, by which a tacit bond of devotion is imposed,— a bond not to be thereafter broken without violating what should be sacred in our nature. How finely is the true Shakspearian scene contrasted with Dryden's vulgar alteration of it in which a mere ludicrous psychological experiment, as it were, is tried — displaying nothing but indelicacy without passion. Prospero's interruption of the courtship has often seemed to me to have no sufficient motive; still his alleged reason —

> *lest too light winning*
> *Make the prize light* —

is enough for the ethereal connections of the romantic imagination, although it would not be so for the historical. The whole courting scene, indeed, in the beginning of the third act, between the lovers, is a masterpiece; and the first dawn of disobedience in the mind of Miranda to the command of her father is very finely drawn, so as to seem the working of the Scriptural command *Thou shalt leave father and mother,* &c. O! with what exquisite purity this scene is conceived and executed! Shakspeare may sometimes be gross, but I boldly say that he is always moral and modest. Alas! in this our day decency of manners is preserved at the expense of morality of heart, and delicacies for vice are allowed, whilst grossness against it is hypocritically, or at least morbidly, condemned.

. . . . . .

SHAKSPEARE'S ENGLISH HISTORICAL PLAYS [5]
(1836)

The first form of poetry is the epic, the essence of which may be stated as the successive in events and characters. This must be distinguished from narration in which there must always be a narrator, from whom the objects represented receive a coloring and a manner: — whereas in the epic, as in the so called poems of Homer, the whole is completely objective, and the representation is a pure reflection. The next form into which poetry passed was the dramatic; — both forms having a common basis with a certain difference, and that difference not consisting in the dialogue alone. Both are founded on the relation of providence to the human will; and this relation is the universal element, expressed under different points of view according to the difference of religion, and the moral and intellectual cultivation of different nations. In the epic poem fate is represented as overruling the will, and making it instrumental to the accomplishment of its designs: —

——— Διὸς δὲ τελείετο βουλή.

In the drama, the will is exhibited as struggling with fate, a great and beautiful instance and illustration of which is the *Prometheus* of Æschylus; and the deepest effect is produced, when the fate is represented as a higher and intelligent will, and the opposition of the individual as springing from a defect.

In order that a drama may be properly historical, it is necessary that it should be the history of the people to whom it is addressed. In the composition, care must be taken that there appear no dramatic improbability, as the reality is taken for granted. It must, likewise, be poetical; — that only, I mean, must be taken which is the permanent in our nature, which is common, and therefore deeply interesting to all ages. The events themselves are immaterial, otherwise than as the clothing and manifestations of the spirit that is working within. In this mode, the unity resulting from succession is destroyed, but is supplied by a unity of a higher order, which connects the events by reference to the workers, gives a reason for them in the motives, and presents men in their causative character. It takes, therefore, that part of real history which is the least known, and infuses a principle of life and organization into the naked facts, and makes them all the framework of an animated whole.

In my happier days, while I had yet

5 Re-printed extracts from the Everyman's Library Edition. Originally appeared in vol. 2 of the *Literary Remains* (London, 1836). — Ed.

hope and onward-looking thoughts, I planned an historical drama of King Stephen, in the manner of Shakspeare. Indeed it would be desirable that some man of dramatic genius should dramatize all those omitted by Shakspeare, as far down as Henry VII. Perkin Warbeck would make a most interesting drama. A few scenes of Marlowe's *Edward II* might be preserved. After *Henry VIII*, the events are too well and distinctly known, to be, without plump inverisimilitude, crowded together in one night's exhibition. Whereas, the history of our ancient kings — the events of their reigns, I mean,— are like stars in the sky; — whatever the real interspaces may be, and however great, they seem close to each other. The stars — the events — strike us and remain in our eye, little modified by the difference of dates. An historic drama is, therefore, a collection of events borrowed from history, but connected together in respect of cause and time, poetically and by dramatic fiction. It would be a fine national custom to act such a series of dramatic histories in orderly succession, in the yearly Christmas holidays, and could not but tend to counteract that mock cosmopolitism, which under a positive term really implies nothing but a negation of, or indifference to, the particular love of our country. By its nationality must every nation retain its independence; — I mean a nationality *quoad* the nation. Better thus; — nationality in each individual, *quoad* his country, is equal to the sense of individuality *quoad* himself; but himself as subsensuous, and central. Patriotism is equal to the sense of individuality reflected from every other individual. There may come a higher virtue in both — just cosmopolitism. But this latter is not possible but by antecedence of the former.

NOTES ON *OTHELLO* [6]

(1836)

Dr. Johnson has remarked that little or nothing is wanting to render the *Othello* a regular tragedy, but to have opened the play with the arrival of Othello in Cyprus, and to have thrown the preceding act into the form of narration. Here then is the place to determine, whether such a change would or would not be an improvement; — nay, (to throw down the glove with a full challenge) whether the tragedy would or not by such an arrangement become more regular,— that is, more consonant with the rules dictated by universal reason, on the true commonsense of mankind, in its application to the particular case. For in all acts of judgment, it can never be too often recollected, and scarcely too often repeated, that rules are means to ends, and, consequently, that the end must be determined and understood before it can be known what the rules are or ought to be. Now, from a certain species of drama, proposing to itself the accomplishment of certain ends,— these partly arising from the idea of the species itself, but in part, likewise, forced upon the dramatist by accidental circumstances beyond his power to remove or control,— three rules have been abstracted; — in other words, the means most conducive to the attainment of the proposed ends have been generalized, and prescribed under the names of the three unities,— the unity of time, the unity of place, and the unity of action,— which last would, perhaps, have been as appropriately, as well as more intelligibly, entitled the unity of interest. With this last the present question has no immediate concern: in fact, its conjunction with the former two is a mere delusion of words. It is not properly a rule, but in itself the great end not only of the drama, but of the epic poem, the lyric ode, of all poetry, down to the candle-flame cone of an epigram,— nay of poesy in general, as the proper generic term inclusive of all the fine arts as its species. But of the unities of time and place, which alone are entitled to the names of rules, the history of their origin will be their best criterion. You might take the Greek chorus to a place, but you

6 Re-printed from the Everyman's Library Edition. First published in vol. 2 of the *Literary Remains* (London, 1836).— Ed.

could not bring a place to them without as palpable an equivoque as bringing Birnam wood to Macbeth at Dunsinane. It was the same, though in a less degree, with regard to the unity of time: — the positive fact, not for a moment removed from the senses, the presence, I mean, of the same identical chorus, was a continued measure of time; — and although the imagination may supersede perception, yet it must be granted to be an imperfection — however easily tolerated — to place the two in broad contradic-tion to each other. In truth, it is a mere accident of terms; for the Trilogy of the Greek theater was a drama in three acts, and notwithstanding this, what strange contrivances as to place there are in the Aristophanic *Frogs*. Besides, if the law of mere actual perception is once violated — as it repeatedly is even in the Greek tragedies — why is it more difficult to imagine three hours to be three years than to be a whole day and night?

. . . .

CHARLES LAMB

Charles Lamb was born at London in 1775. He attended school at a very early age, and at eight was sent to Christ's Hospital. There he met Coleridge, who was destined to be his lifelong friend. After seven years at Christ's Charles returned to his parents. Shortly after, he was employed at the South Sea House, and in 1792 he became a clerk in the East India House, a position he held for many years. Two years after, his first published poem appeared in a newspaper, though it was signed with the initials of Coleridge, who had corrected it. Not long afterward the letters of Lamb bear witness to those periodical attacks of madness to which his sister Mary and he were subject; Mary, indeed, killed her mother in one of her attacks, and the tragedy had a lasting effect on the pair, who lived together until the death of Charles. But in his books and in writings he soon found solace. He wrote, often in collaboration with Mary, a number of tales and poems, and in 1802 published his verse tragedy *John Woodvil*. They both wrote the celebrated *Tales from Shakespeare*, which appeared in 1807. The following year Charles issued the famous *Specimens of English Dramatic Poets*, etc. Meantime he had found time to write the farce *Mr. H.* (1806), which was a failure. Between 1809 and 1817 he contributed various essays to the *Reflector*. In 1818 he publish. l two volumes of his *Works*. In 1820 he began contributing further essays to the *London Magazine* under the name of Elia. Many of these appeared in book-form in 1823. Two years after this he retired from his position with a pension. His last years he was able to devote to his work, as he was comparatively well-to-do. A few months after the death of his friend Coleridge, Charles Lamb died, in 1834.

While Lamb wrote a few plays, he is not in any sense a dramatist; these plays are rather experiments from the hand of one interested in poetry and the drama, than expert products of a practicing playwright. His interest in Shakespeare and the Elizabethans was manifest in his *Specimens*, which were more influential than anything else in directing the attention of the moderns to Shakespeare's contemporaries. His love for the old drama is everywhere observable in his writings. As a critic of the drama, Lamb did not contribute much of theory, nor did he formulate any distinctly new ideas, though in the two most important essays, *On the Artificial Comedy of the Last Century*, and *On the Tragedies of Shakespeare*, he puts forward an interesting and ingenious idea.

On the drama:

Notes in the *Specimens of English Dramatic Poets who lived about the Time of Shakespeare* (1808).
On the Tragedies of Shakespeare (1811).
On the Artificial Comedy of the Last Century (1823).
John Kemble and Godwin's Tragedy of "Antonio" (1822).

Of the numerous other essays more or less on the drama, but chiefly dealing with acting, the most interesting are: *On the Custom of Hissing at the Theatres* (1811), *Biographical Memoir of Mr. Liston* (1825), *The Religion of Actors* (1826), *On a Passage in " The Tempest"* (1823), *The Death of Munden* (1832), *My First Play* (1823), *On Some of the Old Actors* (1823), *On the Acting of Munden* (1823), *Stage Illusion* (1833), *To the Shade of Elliston* (1833), *Ellistoniana* (1833), *Barbara S——* (1833), and the five "criticisms" included in *Eliana*. For numerous occasional remarks on the drama see the *Letters* (Ainger ed., 1904).

Editions:

Lamb's Works and Correspondence, edited by Alfred Ainger, 12 vols. (London, 1883–88). See also *The Works of Charles Lamb,* edited by W. Macdonald, 12 vols. (London, 1903–04), and by E. V. Lucas, 7 vols. (London, 1903–04).

On the Artificial Comedy of the Last Century (to which *John Kemble and Godwin's Tragedy of " Antonio"* was originally affixed), is in the *Essays of Elia* (1823); also, *My First Play, On Some of the Old Actors,* and *On the Acting of Munden.* The *Last Essays of Elia* (1833) include *Stage Illusion, To the Shade of Elliston, Ellistoniana,* and *Barbara S——.* The remaining essays are found in the *Works* (see above), while in his *Dramatic Essays of Charles Lamb* (New York, 1891), Brander Matthews has included all the essays on the drama. Percy Fitzgerald's *The Art of the Stage as Set Out*

in *Lamb's Dramatic Essays* (London, 1885) contains practically the same material. The *Eliana,* with the five criticisms, was first collected by J. E. Babson (Boston, 1865). The plays and selected essays on the drama are edited by Rudolf Dircks in the *Plays and Dramatic Essays by Charles Lamb* (London, n. d.). There are innumerable re-prints of the *Elia* essays; a convenient edition is that in Everyman's Library, with an introduction by Augustine Birrell (New York, 1906). The *Letters* are published as *Letters of Charles Lamb,* edited by Alfred Ainger, 2 vols. (new ed., London, 1904). There is also a two-volume edition of these in Everyman's Library.

On Lamb and his works:

Barry Cornwall, *Charles Lamb: a Memoir* (London, 1866).
Percy Fitzgerald, *Lamb, his Friends, Haunts, Books* (London, 1866).
Alfred Ainger, *Charles Lamb* (in *English Men of Letters* series. Revised ed., London, 1888).
B. E. Martin, *In the Footprints of Lamb* (London, 1891).
W. C. Hazlitt, *The Lambs: New Particulars* (London, 1897).
W. C. Hazlitt, editor, *Lamb and Hazlitt: Further Letters and Records, Hitherto Unpublished* (London, 1900).
Bertram Dobbell, *Sidelights on Charles Lamb* (London, 1903).
E. V. Lucas, *Life of Charles Lamb,* 2 vols. (London, 1905).
Walter Jerrold, *Charles Lamb* (London, 1905).
T. B. Macaulay, *Leigh Hunt* (London, 1841. Reprinted in Critical and Historical Essays; many eds.).

ON THE ARTIFICIAL COMEDY OF THE LAST CENTURY [1]

[From *Essays of Elia*]

(1823)

The artificial Comedy, or Comedy of manners, is quite extinct on our stage.

1 Re-printed in full from the Everyman's Library Edition of *The Essays of Elia* (1906). — Ed.

Congreve and Farquhar show their heads once in seven years only, to be exploded and put down instantly. The times cannot bear them. Is it for a few wild speeches, an occasional license of dialogue? I think not altogether. The business of their dramatic characters will not stand the moral test. We screw everything up to that. Idle gallantry in a fiction, a dream, the passing pageant of an evening, startles us in the same way as the alarming indications of profligacy in a son or ward in real life should startle a parent or guardian. We have no such middle emotions as dramatic interests left. We see a stage libertine playing his loose pranks of two hours' duration, and of no after consequence, with the severe eyes which inspect real vices with their bearings upon two worlds. We are spectators to a plot or intrigue (not reducible in life to the point of strict morality), and take it all for truth. We substitute a real for a dramatic person, and judge him accordingly. We try him in our courts, from which there is no appeal to the *dramatis personæ*, his peers. We have been spoiled with — not sentimental comedy — but a tyrant far more pernicious to our pleasures which has succeeded to it, the exclusive and all-devouring drama of common life; where the moral point is everything; where, instead of the fictitious half-believed personages of the stage (the phantoms of old comedy), we recognize ourselves, our brothers, aunts, kinsfolk, allies, patrons, enemies,— the same as in life,— with an interest in what is going on so hearty and substantial, that we cannot afford our moral judgment, in its deepest and most vital results, to compromise or slumber for a moment. What is *there* transacting, by no modification is made to affect us in any other manner than the same events or characters would do in our relationships of life. We carry our fireside concerns to the theater with us. We do not go thither like our ancestors, to escape from the pressure of reality, so much as to confirm our experience of it; to make assurance double, and take a bond of fate. We must live our toilsome lives twice over, as it was the mournful privilege of Ulysses to descend twice to the shades. All that neutral ground of character, which stood between vice and virtue; or which in fact was indifferent to neither, where neither properly was called into question; that happy breathing-place from the burthen of a perpetual moral questioning — the sanctuary and quiet Alsatia of hunted casuistry — is broken up and disfranchised, as injurious to the interests of society. The privileges of the place are taken away by law. We dare not dally with images, or names, of wrong. We bark like foolish dogs at shadows. We dread infection from the scenic representation of disorder, and fear a painted pustule. In our anxiety that our morality should not take cold, we wrap it up in a great blanket surtout of precaution against the breeze and sunshine.

I confess for myself that (with no great delinquencies to answer for) I am glad for a season to take an airing beyond the diocese of the strict conscience,— not to live always in the precincts of the law-courts,— but now and then, for a dream-while or so, to imagine a world with no meddling restrictions — to get into recesses, whither the hunter cannot follow me —

Secret shades
Of woody Ida's inmost grove,
While yet there was no fear of Jove.

I come back to my cage and my restraint the fresher and more healthy for it. I wear my shackles more contentedly for having respired the breath of an imaginary freedom. I do not know how it is with others, but I feel the better always for the perusal of one of Congreve's — nay, why should I not add, even of Wycherley's — comedies. I am the gayer at least for it; and I could never connect those sports of a witty fancy in any shape with any result to be drawn from them to imitation in real life. They are a world of themselves almost as much a fairyland. Take one of their characters, male or female (with few exceptions they are alike), and place it in a modern play, and my virtuous indignation shall rise against the profligate wretch as warmly as the Catos of the pits could desire; because in a modern play I am to judge of the right and the wrong. The standard of *police* is the measure of *political justice*. The atmosphere will blight it; it cannot live here. It has got into a moral world, where it has no business, from which it must needs fall headlong, as dizzy, and incapable of making a stand, as a Swedenborgian bad spirit that has wandered unawares into the sphere of one of his Good Men, or Angels. But in its own world do we feel the creature is so very bad? — The Fainalls and the Mirabels, the Dorimants and the Lady Touchwoods, in their own sphere, do not offend my moral sense; in fact, they do not appeal to it at all. They seem engaged in their proper element. They break through no laws or conscientious restraints. They know of none. They have got out of Christendom into the land — what shall I call it? — of cuckoldry — the Utopia of gallantry, where pleasure is duty, and the manners perfect freedom. It is altogether a speculative scene of things, which has no reference whatever to the world that is. No good person can be justly offended as a spectator, because no good person suffers on the stage. Judged morally, every character in these plays — the few exceptions only are *mistakes* — is alike essentially vain and worthless. The great art of Congreve is especially shown in this, that he has entirely excluded from his scenes — some little generosities in the part of Angelica perhaps excepted — not only anything like a faultless character, but any pretensions to goodness or good feelings whatsoever. Whether he did this designedly, or instinctively, the effect is as happy as the design (if design) was bold. I used to wonder at the strange power which his Way of the World in particular possesses of interesting you all along in the pursuits of characters, for whom you absolutely care nothing — for you neither hate nor love his personages — and I think it is owing to this very indifference for any, that you endure the whole. He has spread a privation of moral blight, I will call it, rather than by the ugly name of palpable darkness, over his creations; and his shadows flit before you without distinction or preference. Had he introduced a good character, a single gush of moral feeling, a revulsion of the judgment to actual life and actual duties, the impertinent Goshen would have only lighted to the discovery of deformities, which now are none, because we think them none.

Translated into real life, the characters of his, and his friend Wycherley's dramas, are profligates and strumpets — the business of their brief existence, the

undivided pursuit of lawless gallantry. No other spring of action, or possible motive of conduct, is recognized; principles which, universally acted upon, must reduce this frame of things to a chaos. But we do them wrong in so translating them. No such effects are produced, in *their* world. When we are among them, we are amongst a chaotic people. We are not to judge them by our usages. No reverend institutions are insulted by their proceedings — for they have none among them. No peace of families is violated — for no family ties exist among them. No purity of the marriage bed is stained — for none is supposed to have a being. No deep affections are disquieted, no holy wedlock bands are snapped asunder — for affection's depth and wedded faith are not of the growth of that soil. There is neither right nor wrong — gratitude or its opposite — claim or duty — paternity or sonship. Of what consequence is it to Virtue or how is she at all concerned about it, whether Sir Simon or Dapperwit steal away Miss Martha; or who is the father of Lord Froth's or Sir Paul Pliant's children?

The whole is a passing pageant, where we should sit as unconcerned at the issues, for life or death, as at the battle of the frogs and mice. But, like Don Quixote, we take part against the puppets, and quite as impertinently. We dare not contemplate an Atlantis, a scheme, out of which our coxcombical moral sense is for a little transitory ease excluded. We have not the courage to imagine a state of things for which there is neither reward nor punishment. We cling to the painful necessities of shame and blame. We would indict our very dreams.

Amidst the mortifying circumstances attendant upon growing old, it is something to have seen the *School for Scandal* in its glory. This comedy grew out of Congreve and Wycherley, but gathered some allays of the sentimental comedy which followed theirs. It is impossible that it should be now *acted*, though it continues, at long intervals, to be announced in the bills. Its hero, when Palmer played it at least, was Joseph Surface. When I remember the gay boldness, the graceful solemn plausibility, the measured step, the insinuating voice — to express it in a word — the downright *acted* villainy of the part, so different from the pressure of conscious actual wickedness,— the hypocritical assumption of hypocrisy,— which made Jack so deservedly a favorite in that character, I must needs conclude the present generation of playgoers more virtuous than myself, or more dense. I freely confess that he divided the palm with me with his better brother; that, in fact, I liked him quite as well. Not but there are passages,— like that, for instance, where Joseph is made to refuse a pittance to a poor relation,— incongruities which Sheridan was forced upon by the attempt to join the artificial with the comedy, either of which must destroy the other — but over these obstructions Jack's manner floated him so lightly, that a refusal from him no more shocked you, than the easy compliance of Charles gave you in reality any pleasure; you got over the paltry question as quickly as you could, to get back into the regions of pure comedy, where no cold moral reigns. The highly artificial manner of Palmer in this character counteracted every disagreeable impression which you might have received from the contrast, supposing them real, between the two brothers. You did not believe in Joseph with the same faith with which you believed in Charles. The latter was a pleasant reality, the former a no less pleasant poetical foil to it. The comedy, I have said, is incongruous; a mixture of Congreve with sentimental incompatibilities; the gayety upon the whole is buoyant; but it required the consummate art of Palmer to reconcile the discordant elements.

A player with Jack's talents, if we had one now, would not dare to do the part in the same manner. He would instinctively avoid every turn which might tend to unrealize, and so to make the character fascinating. He must take his cue from his spectators, who would expect a bad man and a good man as rigidly opposed to each other as the deathbeds of those geniuses are contrasted in the prints, which I am sorry to say have disappeared from the windows of my old friend Carrington Bowles, of St. Paul's Church-yard memory — (an exhibition as venerable as the

adjacent cathedral and almost coeval) of the bad and good men at the hour of death; where the ghastly apprehensions of the former,— and truly the grim phantom with his reality of a toasting-fork is not to be despised,— so finely contrast with the meek complacent kissing of the rod,— taking it in like honey and butter, — with which the latter submits to the scythe of the gentle bleeder, Time, who wields his lancet with the apprehensive finger of a popular young ladies' surgeon. What flesh, like loving grass, would not covet to meet half-way the stroke of such a delicate mower? — John Palmer was twice an actor in this exquisite part. He was playing to you all the while that he was playing upon Sir Peter and his Lady. You had the first intimation of a sentiment before it was on his lips. His altered voice was meant to you, and you were to suppose that his fictitious co-flutterers on the stage perceived nothing at all of it. What was it to you if that half reality, the husband, was over-reached by the puppetry — or the thin thing (Lady Teazle's reputation) was persuaded it was dying of a plethory? The fortunes of Othello and Desdemona were not concerned in it. Poor Jack has passed from the stage in good time, that he did not live to this our age of seriousness. The present old Teazle *King,* too, is gone in good time. His manner would scarce have passed current in our day. We must love or hate — acquit or condemn —censure or pity — exert our detestable coxcombry or moral judgment upon everything. Joseph Surface, to go down now, must be a downright revolting villain — no compromise — his first appearance must shock and give horror — his specious plausibilities, which the pleasurable faculties of our fathers welcomed with such hearty greetings, knowing that no harm (dramatic harm, even) could come, or was meant to come, of them, must inspire a cold and killing aversion. Charles, (the real canting person of the scene — for the hypocrisy of Joseph has its ulterior legitimate ends, but his brother's professions of a good heart center in downright self-satisfaction) must be *loved,* and Joseph *hated.* To balance one disagreeable reality with another, Sir Peter Teazle must be no longer the comic idea of a fretful old bachelor bridegroom, whose teasings (while King acted it) were evidently as much played off at you, as they were meant to concern anybody on the stage,— he must be a real person, capable in law of sustaining an injury — a person towards whom duties are to be acknowledged — the genuine crim. con. antagonist of the villainous seducer Joseph. To realize him more, his sufferings under his unfortunate match must have the downright pungency of life — must (or should) make you not mirthful but uncomfortable, just as the same predicament would move you in a neighbor or old friend.

The delicious scenes which give the play its name and zest, must affect you in the same serious manner as if you heard the reputation of a dear female friend attacked in your real presence. Crabtree and Sir Benjamin — those poor snakes that live but in the sunshine of your mirth — must be ripened by this hot-bed process of realization into asps or amphisbænas; and Mrs. Candour — O! frightful! — become a hooded serpent. Oh! who that remembers Parsons and Dodd — the wasp and butterfly of the *School for Scandal* — in those two characters; and charming natural Miss Pope, the perfect gentlewoman as distinguished from the fine lady of comedy, in the latter part — would forego the true scenic delight — the escape from life — the oblivion of consequences — the holiday barring out of the pedant Reflection — those Saturnalia of two or three brief hours, well won from the world — to sit instead at one of our modern plays — to have his coward conscience (that forsooth must not be left for a moment) stimulated with perpetual appeals — dulled rather, and blunted, as a faculty without repose must be — and his moral vanity pampered with images of notional justice, notional beneficence, lives saved without the spectator's risk, and fortunes given away that cost the author nothing?

No piece was, perhaps, ever so completely cast in all its parts as this *manager's comedy.* Miss Farren had succeeded to Mrs. Abington in Lady Teazle; and Smith, the original Charles, had retired when I first saw it. The rest of the characters, with very slight exceptions, remained. I remember it was then the fashion to cry down John Kemble, who took the part of Charles after Smith; but, I thought, very unjustly. Smith, I fancy, was more airy, and took the eye with a certain gayety of person. He brought with him no somber recollections of tragedy. He had not to expiate the fault of having pleased beforehand in lofty declamation. He had no sins of Hamlet, or of Richard, to atone for. His failure in these parts was a passport to success in one of so opposite a tendency. But, as far as I could judge, the weighty sense of Kemble made up for more personal incapacity than he had to answer for. His harshest tones in this part came steeped and dulcified in good humor. He made his defects a grace. His exact declamatory manner, as he managed it, only served to convey the points of his dialogue with more precision. It seemed to head the shafts to carry them deeper. Not one of his sparkling sentences was lost. I remember minutely how he delivered each in succession, and cannot by any effort imagine how any of them could be altered for the better. No man could deliver brilliant dialogue — the dialogue of Congreve, or of Wycherley — because none understood it — half so well as John Kemble. His Valentine, in *Love for Love,* was to my recollection, faultless. He flagged sometimes in the intervals of tragic passion. He would slumber over the level parts of an heroic character. His Macbeth has been known to nod. But he always seemed to me to be particularly alive to pointed and witty dialogue. The relaxing levities of tragedy have not been touched by any since him — the playful court-bred spirit in which he condescended to the players in *Hamlet* — the sportive relief which he threw into the darker shades of Richard — disappeared with him. (Tragedy is become a uniform dead-weight. They have fashioned lead to her buskins. She never pulls them off for the ease of the moment. To invert a commonplace, from *Niobe,* she never forgets herself to liquefaction.) He had his sluggish moods, his torpors — but they were the halting-stones and resting-place of his tragedy — politic savings, and fetches of the breath — husbandry of the lungs, where nature pointed him to be an economist — rather, I think, than errors of the judgment. They were, at worst, less painful than the eternal tormenting unappeasable vigilance,— the "lidless dragon eyes," of present fashionable tragedy.[2]

[2] Macaulay's essay on Leigh Hunt's edition of the *Comic Dramatists*, contains the following paragraph relative to the above essay of Lamb:

"But it is not the fact that the world of these dramatists is a world into which no moral enters. Morality constantly enters into morality; the sound morality to be insulted, that world, a sound morality, and an unsound derided, associated with everything mean and hateful; the unsound morality to be set off to every advantage and inculcated by all methods, direct and indirect. It is not the fact that none of the inhabitants of this conventional world feel reverence for sacred institutions and family ties. Fondlewife, Pinchwife, every person in short of narrow understanding and disgusting manners, expresses that reverence strongly. The heroes and heroines, too, have a moral code of their own, an exceedingly bad one, but not, as Mr. Charles Lamb seems to think, a code existing only in the imagination of the dramatists. It is, on the contrary, a code actually received and obeyed by great numbers of people. We need not go to Utopia or Fairyland to find them. They are near at hand. Every night some of them cheat at the hells in the Quadrant, and others pace the Piazza in Covent Garden. Without flying to Nephelococcygia or to the Court of Queen Mab, we can meet with sharpers, bullies, hard-hearted impudent debauchees, and women worthy of such paramours. The morality of the *Country Wife* and the *Old Bachelor* is the morality, not, as Mr. Charles Lamb maintains, of an unreal world, but of a world which is a good deal too real. It is the morality, not of a chaotic people, but of low town-rakes, and of those ladies whom the newspapers call 'dashing Cyprians.' And the question is simply this, whether a man of genius who constantly and systematically endeavors to make this sort of character attractive, by uniting it with beauty, grace, dignity, spirit, a high social position, popularity, literature, wit, taste, knowledge of the world, brilliant success in every undertaking, does or does not make an ill use of his powers. We own that we are unable to understand how this question can be answered in any way but one."

WILLIAM HAZLITT

William Hazlitt was born at Maidstone in 1778. His early education was received at home in Shropshire, whither his family had gone during his youth, and when he was fifteen he was sent to the Unitarian College at Hackney to prepare for the church. Four years' stay at Hackney, however, did not make a minister of him. At home in 1798 he heard Coleridge preach, and the poet encouraged him in his metaphysical studies. He visited Coleridge the same year, and met Wordsworth on one occasion. His interest in literature dates, he tells us, from this visit. After a short apprenticeship at painting, during 1802–03, he resumed his study of philosophy and in 1805 published the *Principles of Human Action.* He married in 1808 and went to live at Winterslow. Four years later they moved to Westminster. After his divorce, he married again in 1824. The family — Hazlitt's son by his first wife accompanied the couple — visited the Continent, after which Mrs. Hazlitt refused to return to her husband. He then began to write political reviews and dramatic criticisms for the *Morning Chronicle,* and later he contributed to *The Examiner, The Champion,* and many other papers. His lectures and miscellaneous writing occupied the remainder of his life. He died in 1830.

As one of the greatest critics of literature, Hazlitt has contributed a vast number of sound critical judgments. He is neither so brilliant as Lamb nor so profound as Coleridge, but his grasp of the matter in hand and his sanity are, in general, what give him the high position as a critic of the drama which he occupies. Unlike that of Lamb and Coleridge, much of his criticism is on acted plays; to that work he brought most of the readiness of mind and acute judgment that were always his. His lectures on Elizabethan literature and on the English poets are perhaps fuller and better thought out than his critiques of current plays.

On the drama:

On Modern Comedy (1815).
Schlegel on the Drama (1816).
A View of the English Stage (1818).

On Wit and Humour (1819).
On the Comic Writers of the Last Century (1819).
On Dramatic Poetry (1820).
Lectures on the Dramatic Literature of the Reign of Queen Elizabeth (1820).
The above are the chief single articles and works concerned with the drama. The following works, however, should be consulted for occasional essays and remarks: *The Characters of Shakespear's Plays* (1817), *The Round Table* (1817), *Lectures on the English Comic Writers* (1819), *Lectures on the English Poets* (1818–19), *Table Talk* (1821–22), *The Spirit of the Age* (1825), *The Plain Speaker* (1826), and *Notes of a Journey Through France and Italy* (1826).

Editions:

The standard edition of the complete writings (with the exception of the life of Bonaparte, is *The Collected Works of William Hazlitt*, edited by Waller and Glover, 12 vols. (London, 1902–04). The last 3 volumes contain some new material, and include a number of articles hitherto found only in miscellaneous editions. The second edition (London, 1854) of the *View of the English Stage*, includes *On Modern Comedy, On Dramatic Poetry*, and

Explanations, etc. *Schlegel on the Drama* is in vol. 10 of the *Collected Works*. *On Wit and Humour*, and *On the Comic Writers of the Last Century* are in *Lectures on the English Comic Writers*. Convenient modern reprints are in Everyman's Library: *The Characters of Shakespeare's Plays* (1906); *Lectures on the English Comic Writers, and Miscellaneous Essays* (1910); *Lectures on The English Poets, and The Spirit of the Age* (1910); and *Table Talk, or Original Essays* (1908). Most of the works are in the 7-volume Bohn Library edition (London and New York, various dates).

On Hazlitt and his works:

W. C. Hazlitt, *Memoirs of William Hazlitt*, 2 vols. (London, 1867).
——, *Lamb and Hazlitt. Further Letters and Records Hitherto Unpublished* (New York, 1899).
Alexander Ireland, *List of the Writings of William Hazlitt and Leigh Hunt*, etc. (London, 1868).
Jules Douady, *Vie de William Hazlitt, l'essayiste* (Paris, 1906).
——, *Liste chronologique des œuvres de William Hazlitt* (Paris, 1906).
Augustine Birrell, *Res Judicatæ* (New York, 1903).

ON THE COMIC WRITERS OF THE LAST CENTURY [1]

[*Lectures on the English Comic Writers*]

(1819)

The question which has been often asked, *Why there are comparatively so few good modern Comedies?* appears in a great measure to answer itself. It is because so many excellent comedies have been written, that there are none written at present. Comedy naturally wears itself out — destroys the very food on which it lives; and by constantly and successfully exposing the follies and weaknesses of mankind to ridicule, in the end leaves itself nothing worth laughing at. It holds the mirror up to nature; and men, seeing their most striking peculiarities and defects pass in gay review before them, learn either to avoid or conceal them. It is not the criticism which the public taste exercises upon the stage, but the criticism which the stage exercises upon public manners, that is fatal to comedy, by rendering the subject-matter of it tame, correct, and spiritless. We are drilled into a sort of stupid decorum, and forced to wear the same dull uniform of outward appear-

1 Re-printed, with one slight omission, from the Everyman's Library Edition of the *Lectures on the English Comic Writers and Miscellaneous Essays* (1910).— The notes are by the author.— Ed

EUROPEAN THEORIES OF THE DRAMA

ance; and yet it is asked, why the Comic Muse does not point, as she was wont, at the peculiarities of our gait and gesture, and exhibit the picturesque contrasts of our dress and costume, in all that graceful variety in which she delights. The genuine source of comic writing,

Where it must live, or have no life at all,

is undoubtedly to be found in the distinguishing peculiarities of men and manners. Now this distinction can subsist, so as to be strong, pointed, and general, only while the manners of different classes are formed almost immediately by their particular circumstances, and the characters of individuals by their natural temperament and situation, without being everlastingly modified and neutralized by intercourse with the world — by knowledge and education. In a certain stage of society, men may be said to vegetate like trees, and to become rooted to the soil in which they grow. They have no idea of anything beyond themselves and their immediate sphere of action; they are, as it were, circumscribed, and defined by their particular circumstances; they are what their situation makes them, and nothing more. Each is absorbed in his own profession or pursuit, and each in his turn contracts that habitual peculiarity of manners and opinions which makes him the subject of ridicule to others, and the sport of the Comic Muse. Thus the physician is nothing but a physician, the lawyer is a mere lawyer, the scholar degenerates into a pedant, the country squire is a different species of being from the fine gentleman, the citizen and the courtier inhabit a different world, and even the affectation of certain characters, in aping the follies or vices of their betters, only serves to show the immeasurable distance which custom or fortune has placed between them. Hence the earlier comic writers, taking advantage of this mixed and solid mass of ignorance, folly, pride, and prejudice, made those deep and lasting incisions into it, — have given those sharp and nice touches, that bold relief to their characters, — have opposed them in every variety of contrast and collision, of conscious self-satisfac-

tion and mutual antipathy, with a power which can only find full scope in the same rich and inexhaustible materials. But in proportion as comic genius succeeds in taking off the mask from ignorance and conceit, as it teaches us in proportion as we are brought out on the stage together, and our prejudices clash one against the other, our sharp angular points wear off; we are no longer rigid in absurdity, passionate in folly, and we prevent the ridicule directed at our habitual foibles by laughing at them ourselves.

If it be said, that there is the same fund of absurdity and prejudice in the world as ever — that there are the same unaccountable perversities lurking at the bottom of every breast, — I should answer, Be it so: but at least we keep our follies to ourselves as much as possible; we palliate, shuffle, and equivocate with them; they sneak into bye-corners, and do not, like Chaucer's Canterbury Pilgrims, march along the high road, and form a procession; they do not entrench themselves strongly behind custom and precedent; they are not embodied in professions and ranks in life; they are not organized into a system; they do not openly resort to a standard, but are a sort of straggling non-descripts, that, like Wart, "present no mark to the foeman." As to the gross and palpable absurdities of modern manners, they are too shallow and barefaced, and those who affect are too little *serious* in them, to make them worth the detection of the Comic Muse. They proceed from an idle, impudent affectation of folly in general, in the dashing *bravura* style, not from an infatuation with any of its characteristic modes. In short, the proper object of ridicule is *egotism:* and a man cannot be a very great egotist, who every day sees himself represented on the stage. We are deficient in comedy, because we are without characters in real life — as we have no historical pictures, because we have no faces proper for them.

It is, indeed, the evident tendency of all literature to generalize and *dissipate* character, by giving men the same artificial education, and the same common stock of ideas; so that we see all objects from the same point of view, and through the same reflected medium; — we learn to exist, not in ourselves, but in books; — all men become alike mere readers — spectators, not actors in the scene, and lose their proper personal identity. The templar, the wit, the man of pleasure, and the man of fashion, the courtier and the citizen, the knight and the squire, the lover and the miser — Lovelace, Lothario, Will Honeycomb, and Sir Roger de Coverley, Sparkish and Lord Foppington, Wester and Tom Jones, My Father and My Uncle Toby, Millamant and Sir Sampson Legend, Don Quixote and Sancho, Gil Blas and Guzman d'Alfarache, Count Fathom and Joseph Surface,— have met and exchanged commonplaces on the barren plains of the *haute littérature* — toil slowly on to the temple of science, " seen a long way off upon a level," and end in one dull compound of politics, criticism, and metaphysics!

We cannot expect to reconcile opposite things. If, for example, any of us were to put ourselves into the stagecoach from Salisbury to London, it is more than probable we should not meet with the same number of odd accidents, or ludicrous distresses on the road, that befel Parson Adams; but why, if we get into a common vehicle, and submit to the conveniences of modern traveling, should we complain of the want of adventures? Modern manners may be compared to a modern stage-coach; our limbs may be a little cramped with the confinement, and we may grow drowsy, but we arrive safe, without any very amusing or very sad accident, at our journey's end.

In this theory I have, at least, the authority of Sterne and the *Tatler* on my side, who attribute the greater variety and richness of comic excellence in our writers, to the greater variety and distinctness of character among ourselves; the roughness of the texture and the sharp angles not being worn out by the artificial refinements of intellect, or the frequent collision of social intercourse.— It has been argued on the other hand, indeed, that this circumstance makes against me; that the suppression of the grosser indications of absurdity ought to stimulate and give scope to the ingenuity and penetration of the comic writer who is to detect them; and that the progress of wit and humor ought to

keep pace with critical distinctions and metaphysical niceties. Some theorists, indeed, have been sanguine enough to expect a regular advance from grossness to refinement on the stage and in real life, marked on a graduated scale of human perfectibility, and have been hence led to imagine that the best of our old comedies were no better than the coarse jests of a set of country clowns — a sort of *comédies bourgeoises,* compared with the admirable productions which might but have not, been written in our times. I must protest against this theory altogether, which would go to degrade genteel comedy from a high court lady into a literary prostitute. I do not know what these persons mean by refinement in this instance. Do they find none in Millamant and her morning dreams, in Sir Roger de Coverley and his widow? Did not Etherege, Wycherley, and Congreve, approach tolerably near

> —— *the ring*
> *Of mimic statesmen and their merry*
> *king?*

Is there no distinction between an Angelica and a Miss Prue, a Valentine, a Tattle, and a Ben? Where, in the annals of modern literature, shall we find anything more refined, more deliberate, more abstracted in vice, than the nobleman in *Amelia?* Are not the compliments which Pope paid to his friends equal in taste and elegance to any which have been paid since? Are there no traits in Sterne? Is not Richardson minute enough? Must we part with Sophia Western and her muff, and Clarissa Harlowe's " preferable regards " for the loves of the plants and the triangles? Or shall we say that the Berinthias and Alitheas of former times were little rustics, because they did not, like our modern belles, subscribe to circulating libraries, read *Beppo,* prefer *Gertrude of Wyoming* to the *Lady of the Lake,* or the *Lady of the Lake* to *Gertrude of Wyoming,* differ in their sentiments on points of taste or systems of mineralogy, and deliver dissertations on the arts with Corinna of Italy? They had something else to do and to talk about. They were employed in reality, as we see them on the stage, in setting off their charms to the greatest advantage, in mortifying their rivals by the most pointed irony, and trifling with their lovers with infinite address. The height of comic elegance and refinement is not to be found in the general diffusion of knowledge and civilization, which tends to level and neutralize, but in the pride of individual distinction, and the contrast between the conflicting pretensions of different ranks in society.

For this reason I conceive that the alterations which have taken place in conversation and dress, in consequence of the change of manners in the same period, have been by no means favorable to comedy. The present prevailing style of conversation is not *personal*, but critical and analytical. It consists almost entirely in the discussion of general topics, in ascertaining the merits of authors and their works: and Congreve would be able to derive no better hints from the conversations of our toilettes or drawing-rooms, for the exquisite raillery or poignant repartee of his dialogues, than from a deliberation of the Royal Society. In manner, the extreme simplicity and graceful uniformity of modern dress, however favorable to the arts, has certainly stripped comedy of one of its richest ornaments and most expressive symbols. The sweeping pall and buskin, and nodding plume, were never more serviceable to tragedy, than the enormous hoops and stiff stays worn by the belles of former days, were to the intrigues of comedy. They assisted wonderfully in heightening the mysteries of the passion, and adding to the intricacy of the plot. Wycherley and Vanbrugh could not have spared the dresses of Van Dyck. These strange fancy-dresses, perverse disguises, and counterfeit shapes, gave an agreeable scope to the imagination. "That sevenfold fence" was a sort of foil to the lusciousness of the dialogue, and a barrier against the sly encroachments of *double entendre*. The greedy eye and bold hand of indiscretion were repressed, which gave a greater license to the tongue. The senses were not to be gratified in an instant. Love was entangled in the folds of the swelling handkerchief, and the desires might wander forever round the circumference of a quilted petticoat, or find a rich lodging in the flowers of a damask stomacher. There was room for years of patient contrivance, for a thousand thoughts, schemes, conjectures, hopes, fears, and wishes. There seemed no end of obstacles and delays; to overcome so many difficulties was the work of ages. A mistress was an angel, concealed behind whalebone, flounces, and brocade. What an undertaking to penetrate through the disguise! What an impulse must it give to the blood, what a keenness to the invention, what a volubility to the tongue! "Mr. Smirk, you are a brisk man," was then the most significant commendation; but nowadays — a woman can be *but undressed!* — Again, the character of the fine gentleman is at present a little obscured on the stage, nor do we immediately recognize it elsewhere, for want of the formidable *insignia* of a bagwig and sword. Without these outward credentials, the public must not only be unable to distinguish this character intuitively, but it must be "almost afraid to know itself." The present simple disguise of a gentleman is like the *incognito* of kings. The opinion of others affects our opinion of ourselves; and we can hardly expect from a modern man of fashion that air of dignity and superior gracefulness of carriage, which those must have assumed who were conscious that all eyes were upon them, and that their lofty pretensions continually exposed them either to public scorn or challenged public admiration. A lord who should take the wall of the plebeian passengers without a sword by his side, would hardly have his claim of precedence acknowledged; nor could he be supposed to have that obsolete air of self-importance about him, which should alone clear the pavement at his approach. It is curious how an ingenious actor of the present day (Mr. Farren) should play Lord Ogleby so well as he does, having never seen anything of the sort in reality. A nobleman in full costume, and in broad day, would be a phenomenon like the lord mayor's coach. The attempt at getting up genteel comedy at present is a sort of Galvanic experiment, a revival of the dead.[2]

[2] I have only to add, by way of explanation on this subject, the following passage from the *Characters of Shakespear's Plays:* "There

I have observed in a former Lecture, that the most spirited era of our comic drama was that which reflected the conversation, tone, and manners of the profligate, but witty age of Charles II. With the graver and more business-like turn which the Revolution probably gave to our minds, comedy stooped from her bolder and more fantastic flights; and the ferocious attack made by the nonjuring divine, Jeremy Collier, on the immorality and profaneness of the plays then chiefly in vogue, nearly frightened those unwarrantable liberties of wit and humor from the stage, which were no longer countenanced at court nor copied in the city. Almost the last of our writers who ventured to hold out in the prohibited track, was a female adventurer, Mrs. Centlivre, who seemed to take advantage of the privilege of her sex, and to set at defiance the cynical denunciations of the angry puritanical reformist. Her plays have a provoking spirit and volatile salt in them, which still preserves them from decay. Congreve is said to have been jealous of their success at the time, and that it was one cause which drove him in dis-

gust from the stage. If so, it was without any good reason: for these plays have great and intrinsic merit in them, which entitled them to their popularity (and it is only spurious and undeserved popularity which should excite a feeling of jealousy in any well-regulated mind): and besides, their merit was of a kind entirely different from his own. *The Wonder* and *The Busy Body* are properly comedies of intrigue. Their interest depends chiefly on the intricate involution and artful *dénouement* of the plot, which has a strong tincture of mischief in it, and the wit is seasoned by the archness of the humor and sly allusion to the most delicate points. They are plays evidently written by a very clever woman, but still by a woman: for I hold, in spite of any fanciful theories to the contrary, that there is a distinction discernible in the minds of women as well as in their faces. *The Wonder* is one of the best of our acting plays. The passion of jealousy in Don Felix is managed in such a way as to give as little offense as possible to the audience, for every appearance combines to excite and confirm his worst suspicions, while we, who are in the secret, laugh at his groundless uneasiness and apprehensions. The ambiguity of the heroine's situation, which is like a continued practical *équivoque*, gives rise to a quick succession of causeless alarms, subtle excuses, and the most hair-breadth 'scapes. The scene near the end, in which Don Felix, pretending to be drunk, forces his way out of Don Manuel's house, who wants to keep him a prisoner, by producing his marriage-contract in the shape of a pocket-pistol, with the terrors and confusion into which the old gentleman is thrown by this sort of *argumentum ad hominem,* is one of the richest treats the stage affords, and calls forth incessant peals of laughter and applause. Besides the two principal characters (Violante and Don Felix) Lissardo and Flippanta come in very well to carry on the underplot; and the airs and graces of an amorous waiting-maid and conceited manservant, each copying after their master and mistress, were never hit off with more natural volubility or affected *nonchalance* than in this enviable couple. Lissardo's playing off the diamond ring

is a certain stage of society in which people become conscious of their peculiarities and absurdities, affect to disguise what they are, and set up pretensions to what they are not. This gives rise to a corresponding style of comedy, the object of which is to detect the disguises of self-love, and to make reprisals on these preposterous assumptions of vanity, by marking the contrast between the real and the affected character as severely as possible, and denying to those, who would impose on us for what they are not, even the merit which they have. This is the comedy of artificial life, of wit and satire, such as we see it in Congreve, Wycherley, Vanbrugh, etc. To this succeeds a state of society from which the same sort of affectation and pretence are banished by a greater knowledge of the world, or by their successful exposure on the stage; and which by neutralizing the materials of comic character, both natural and artificial, leaves no comedy at all — but *the sentimental*. Such is our modern comedy. There is a period in the progress of manners anterior to both these, in which the foibles and follies of individuals are of nature's planting, not the growth of art or study; in which they are therefore unconscious of them themselves, or care not who knows them, if they can but have their whim out; and in which, as there is no attempt at imposition, the spectators rather receive pleasure from humoring the inclinations of the persons they laugh at, than wish to give them pain by exposing their absurdity. This may be called the comedy of nature, and it is the comedy which we generally find in Shakespear."

before the eyes of his mortified Dulcinea, and aping his master's absent manner while repeating—"Roast me these Violantes," as well as the jealous quarrel of the two waiting-maids, which threatens to end in some very extraordinary discoveries, are among the most amusing traits in this comedy. Colonel Breton, the lover of Clara, is a spirited and enterprising soldier of fortune; and his servant Gibby's undaunted, incorrigible blundering, with a dash of nationality in it, tells in a very edifying way.—*The Busy Body* is inferior, in the interest of the story and characters, to *The Wonder;* but it is full of bustle and gayety from beginning to end. The plot never stands still; the situations succeed one another like the changes of machinery in a pantomime. The nice dove-tailing of the incidents, and cross-reading in the situations, supplies the place of any great force of wit or sentiment. The time for the entrance of each person on the stage is the moment when they are least wanted, and when their arrival makes either themselves or somebody else look as foolish as possible. The laughableness of this comedy, as well as of *The Wonder,* depends on a brilliant series of mistimed exits and entrances. Marplot is the whimsical hero of the piece, and a standing memorial of unmeaning vivacity and assiduous impertinence.

The comedies of Steele were the first that were written expressly with a view not to imitate the manners, but to reform the morals of the age. The author seems to be all the time on his good behavior, as if writing a comedy was no very creditable employment, and as if the ultimate object of his ambition was a dedication to the queen. Nothing can be better meant, or more inefficient. It is almost a misnomer to call them comedies; they are rather homilies in dialogue, in which a number of very pretty ladies and gentlemen discuss the fashionable topics of gaming, of duelling, of seduction, of scandal, etc., with a sickly sensibility, that shows as little hearty aversion to vice, as sincere attachment to virtue. By not meeting the question fairly on the ground of common experience, by slubbering over the objections, and varnishing over the answers, the whole distinction between virtue and vice (as it appears in evidence in the comic drama) is reduced to verbal professions, and a mechanical, infantine goodness. The sting is, indeed, taken out of what is bad; but what is good, at the same time, loses its manhood and nobility of nature by this enervating process. I am unwilling to believe that the only difference between right and wrong is mere cant, or *make-believe;* and I imagine, that the advantage which the moral drama possesses over mere theoretical precept or general declamation is this, that by being left free to imitate nature as it is, and not being referred to an ideal standard, it is its own voucher for the truth of the inferences it draws, for its warnings, or its examples; that it brings out the higher, as well as lower principles of action. in the most striking and convincing points of view; satisfies us that virtue is not a mere shadow; clothes it with passion, imagination, reality, and, if I may so say, translates morality from the language of theory into that of practice. But Steele, by introducing the artificial mechanism of morals on the stage, and making his characters act, not from individual motives and existing circumstances, the truth of which every one must feel, but from vague topics and general rules, the truth of which is the very thing to be proved in detail, has lost that fine 'vantage ground which the stage lends to virtue; takes away from it its best grace, the grace of sincerity; and, instead of making it a test of truth, has made it an echo of the doctrine of the schools—and "the one cries *Mum,* while t'other cries *Budget!"* The comic writer, in my judgment, then, ought to open the volume of nature and the world for his living materials, and not take them out of his ethical commonplace book; for in this way, neither will throw any additional light upon the other. In all things there is a division of labor; and I am as little for introducing the tone of the pulpit or reading-desk on the stage, as for introducing plays and interludes in church-time, according to the good old popish practice. It was a part, indeed, of Steele's plan, "by the politeness of his style and the genteelness of his expressions," [3] to bring

3 See Mandeville's *Fable of the Bees.*

about a reconciliation between things which he thought had hitherto been kept too far asunder, to wed the graces to the virtues, and blend pleasure with profit. And in this design he succeeded admirably in his *Tatler*, and some other works; but in his comedies he has failed. He has confounded, instead of harmonizing — has taken away its gravity from wisdom, and its charm from gayety. It is not that in his plays we find "some soul of goodness in things evil"; but they have no soul either of good or bad. His *Funeral* is as trite, as tedious, and full of formal grimace, as a procession of mutes and undertakers. The characters are made either affectedly good and forbearing, with "all the milk of human kindness"; or purposely bad and disgusting, for the others to exercise their squeamish charities upon them. The *Conscious Lovers* is the best; but that is far from good, with the exception of the scene between Mr. Thomas and Phillis, who are fellow-servants, and commence lovers from being set to clean the window together. We are here once more in the company of our old friend, Isaac Bickerstaff, Esq. Indiana is as listless, and as insipid, as a drooping figure on an Indian screen; and Mr. Myrtle and Mr. Bevil only just disturb the still life of the scene. I am sorry that in this censure I should have Parson Adams against me; who thought the *Conscious Lovers* the only play fit for a Christian to see, and as good as a sermon. For myself, I would rather have read, or heard him read, one of his own manuscript sermons: and if the volume which he left behind him in his saddlebags was to be had in print, for love or money, I would at any time walk ten miles on foot only to get a sight of it.

Addison's *Drummer, or the Haunted House,* is a pleasant farce enough; but adds nothing to our idea of the author of the *Spectator.*

Pope's joint after-piece, called *An Hour after Marriage,* was not a successful attempt. He brought into it "an alligator stuff'd," which disconcerted the ladies, and gave just offense to the critics. Pope was too fastidious for a farce-writer; and yet the most fastidious people, when they step out of their regular routine, are apt to become the

grossest. The smallest offenses against probability or decorum are, to their habitual scrupulousness, as unpardonable as the greatest. This was the rock on which Pope probably split. The affair was, however, hushed up; and he wreaked his discreet vengeance at leisure on the "odious endeavors," and more odious success of Colley Cibber in the line in which he had failed.

Gay's *What-d'ye-call-it,* is not one of his happiest things. His Polly is a complete failure, which, indeed, is the common fate of second parts. If the original Polly, in the *Beggar's Opera,* had not had more winning ways with her, she would hardly have had so many Countesses for representatives as she has had, from her first appearance up to the present moment.

Fielding was a comic writer, as well as a novelist; but his comedies are very inferior to his novels: they are particularly deficient both in plot and character. The only excellence which they have is that of the style, which is the only thing in which his novels are deficient. The only dramatic pieces of Fielding that retain possession of the stage are, the *Mock Doctor* (a tolerable translation from Molière's *Médecin malgré lui*), and his *Tom Thumb,* a very admirable piece of burlesque. The absurdities and bathos of some of our celebrated tragic writers could hardly be credited, but for the notes at the bottom of this preposterous medley of bombast, containing his authorities and the parallel passages. Dryden, Lee, and Shadwell, make no very shining figure there. Mr. Liston makes a better figure in the text. His Lord Grizzle is prodigious. What a name, and what a person! It has been said of this ingenious actor, that "he is very great in Liston"; but he is even greater in Lord Grizzle. What a wig is that he wears! How flighty, flaunting, and fantastical! Not "like those hanging locks of young Apollo," nor like the serpent-hair of the Furies of Æschylus; but as troublous, though not as tragical as the one — as imposing, though less classical than the other. "*Que terribles sont ces cheveux gris,*" might be applied to Lord Grizzle's most valiant and magnanimous curls. This sapient courtier's "fell of hair does at a dismal treatise rouse and stir as if life were in 't." His wits seem flying away with the disorder of his flowing locks, and to sit as loosely on our hero's head as the caul of his peruke. What a significant vacancy in his open eyes and mouth! what a listlessness in his limbs! what an abstraction of all thought or purpose! With what an headlong impulse of enthusiasm he throws himself across the stage when he is going to be married, crying, " Hey for Doctor's Commons," as if the genius of folly had taken whole-length possession of his person! And then his dancing is equal to the discovery of a sixth sense — which is certainly very different from *common sense!* If this extraordinary personage cuts a great figure in his life, he is no less wonderful in his death and burial. "From the sublime to the ridiculous there is but one step"; and this character would almost seem to prove, that there is but one step from the ridiculous to the sublime.— Lubin Log, however inimitable in itself, is itself an imitation of something existing elsewhere; but the Lord Grizzle of this truly original actor, is a pure invention of his own. His Caper, in the *Widow's Choice,* can alone dispute the palm with it in incoherence and volatility; for that, too, " is high fantastical," almost as full of emptiness, in as grand a gusto of insipidity, as profoundly absurd, as elaborately nonsensical! Why does not Mr. Liston play in some of Molière's farces? I heartily wish that the author of *Love, Law, and Physic,* would launch him on the London boards in Monsieur Jourdain, or Monsieur Pourceaugnac. The genius of Liston and Molière together —

―― *Must bid a gay defiance to mischance.*

Mr. Liston is an actor hardly belonging to the present age. Had he lived, unfortunately for us, in the time of Colley Cibber, we should have seen what a splendid niche he would have given him in his *Apology.*

. . . . . .

In his plays, his personal character perhaps predominates too much over the inventiveness of his Muse; but so far from being dull, he is everywhere light,

fluttering, and airy. His pleasure in himself made him desirous to please; but his fault was, that he was too soon satisfied with what he did, that his indolence or want of thought led him to indulge in the vein that flowed from him with most ease, and that his vanity did not allow him to distinguish between what he did best and worst. His *Careless Husband* is a very elegant piece of agreeable, thoughtless writing; and the incident of Lady Easy throwing her handkerchief over her husband, whom she finds asleep in a chair by the side of her waiting-woman, was an admirable contrivance, taken, as he informs us, from real life. His *Double Gallant,* which has been lately revived, though it cannot rank in the first, may take its place in the second or third class of comedies. It abounds in character, bustle, and stage-effect. It belongs to what may be called the composite style; and very happily mixes up the comedy of intrigue, such as we see it in Mrs. Centlivre's Spanish plots, with a tolerable share of the wit and spirit of Congreve and Vanbrugh. As there is a good deal of wit, there is a spice of wickedness in this play, which was a privilege of the good old style of comedy, not altogether abandoned in Cibber's time. The luscious vein of the dialogue is stopped short in many of the scenes of the revived play, though not before we perceive its object —

―― *In hidden mazes running, With wanton haste and giddy cunning.*

These imperfect hints of double meanings, however, pass off without any marks of reprobation; for unless they are insisted on, or made pretty broad, the audience, from being accustomed to the cautious purity of the modern drama, are not very expert in deciphering the equivocal allusion, for which they are not on the look-out. To what is this increased nicety owing? Was it that vice, from being formerly less common (though more fashionable) was less catching than at present? The first inference is by no means in our favor: for though I think that the grossness of manners prevailing in our fashionable comedies was a direct transcript of the manners of the court at the time, or in the period immediately preceding, yet the same grossness of expression and allusion existed long before, as in the plays of Shakespeare and Ben Jonson, when there was not this grossness of manners, and it has of late years been gradually refining away. There is a certain grossness or freedom of expression, which may arise as often from unsuspecting simplicity as from avowed profligacy. Whatever may be our progress either in virtue or vice since the age of Charles II certain it is, that our manners are not mended since the time of Elizabeth and Charles I. Is it, then, that vice was formerly a thing more to be wondered at than imitated; that behind the rigid barriers of religion and morality it might be exposed freely, without the danger of any serious practical consequences — whereas now that the safeguards of wholesome authority and prejudice are removed, we seem afraid to trust our eyes or ears with a single situation or expression of a loose tendency, as if the mere mention of licentiousness implied a conscious approbation of it, and the extreme delicacy of our moral sense would be debauched by the bare suggestion of the possibility of vice? But I shall not take upon me to answer this question. The characters in the *Double Gallant* are well kept up: At-All and Lady Dainty are the two most prominent characters in this comedy, and those into which Cibber has put most of his own nature and genius. They are the essence of active impertinence and fashionable frivolity. Cibber, in short, though his name has been handed down to us as a bye-word of impudent pretension and impenetrable dullness by the classical pen of his accomplished rival, who, unfortunately, did not admit of any merit beyond the narrow circle of wit and friendship in which he himself moved, was a gentleman and a scholar of the old school; a man of wit and pleasantry in conversation, a diverting mimic, an excellent actor, an admirable dramatic critic, and one of the best comic writers of his age. His works, instead of being a *caput mortuum* of literature, had a great deal of the spirit, with a little too much of the froth. His *Nonjuror* was taken from Molière's *Tartuffe,* and has

been altered to the *Hypocrite. Love's Last Shift* appears to have been his own favorite; and he received the compliments of Sir John Vanbrugh and old Mr. Southern upon it: — the latter said to him, "Young man, your play is a good one; and it will succeed, if you do not spoil it by your acting." His plays did not always take equally. It is ludicrous to hear him complaining of the ill success of one of them, *Love in a Riddle,* a pastoral comedy, "of a nice morality," and well spoken sentiments, which he wrote in opposition to the *Beggar's Opera,* at the time when its worthless and vulgar rival was carrying everything triumphantly before it. Cibber brings this, with much pathetic *naïveté,* as an instance of the lamentable want of taste in the town!

The Suspicious Husband by Hoadley, *The Jealous Wife* by Colman, and the *Clandestine Marriage* by Colman and Garrick, are excellent plays of the middle style of comedy; which are formed rather by judgment and selection, than by any original vein of genius; and have all the parts of a good comedy in degree, without having any one prominent, or to excess. The character of Ranger, in the *Suspicious Husband,* is only a variation of those of Farquhar, of the same class as his Sir Harry Wildair and others, without equal spirit. A great deal of the story of the *Jealous Wife* is borrowed from Fielding; but so faintly, that the resemblance is hardly discernible till you are apprised of it. The Jealous Wife herself is, however, a dramatic *chef-d'œuvre,* and worthy of being acted as often, and better than it is. Sir Harry Beagle is a true fox-hunting English squire. The *Clandestine Marriage* is nearly without a fault; and has some lighter theatrical graces, which I suspect Garrick threw into it. Canton is, I should think, his; though this classification of him among the ornamental parts of the play may seem whimsical. Garrick's genius does not appear to have been equal to the construction of a solid drama; but he could retouch and embellish with great gayety and knowledge of the technicalities of his art. Garrick not only produced joint-pieces and after-pieces, but often set off the plays of his friends and contemporaries with the garnish, the *sauce piquante*, of pro-logues and epilogues, at which he had an admirable knack.— The elder Colman's translation of Terence, I may here add, has always been considered, by good judges, as an equal proof of the author's knowledge of the Latin language, and taste in his own.

Bickerstaff's plays and comic operas are continually acted: they come under the class of mediocrity, generally speaking. Their popularity seems to be chiefly owing to the unaffected ease and want of pretension with which they are written, with a certain humorous *naiveté* in the lower characters, and an exquisite adaptation of the music to the songs. His *Love in a Village* is one of the most delightful comic operas on the stage. It is truly pastoral; and the sense of music hovers over the very scene like the breath of morning. In his alteration of the *Tartuffe* he has spoiled the *Hypocrite*, but he has added Maw-worm.

Mrs. Cowley's comedy of the *Belles' Stratagem, Who's the Dupe*, and others, are of the second or third class: they are rather *refaccimentos* of the characters, incidents, and materials of former writers, got up with considerable liveliness and ingenuity, than original compositions, with marked qualities of their own. Goldsmith's *Good-natur'd Man* is inferior to *She Stoops to Conquer;* and even this last play, with all its shifting vivacity, is rather a sportive and whimsical effusion of the author's fancy, a delightful and delicately managed caricature, than a genuine comedy.

Murphy's plays of *All in the Wrong* and *Know Your Own Mind*, are admirably written; with sense, spirit, and conception of character: but without any great effect of the humorous, or that truth of feeling which distinguishes the boundary between the absurdities of natural character and the gratuitous fictions of the poet's pen. The heroes of these two plays, Millamour and Sir Benjamin Constant, are too ridiculous in their caprices to be tolerated, except in farce; and yet their follies are so flimsy, so motiveless, and fine-spun, as not to be intelligible, or to have any effect in their only proper sphere. Both his principal pieces are said to have suffered by their similarity, first, to Colman's *Jealous Wife*, and next to the *School for Scandal*, though in both cases he had the undoubted priority. It is hard that the fate of plagiarism should attend upon originality: yet it is clear that the elements of the *School for Scandal* are not sparingly scattered in Murphy's comedy of *Know Your Own Mind*, which appeared before the latter play, only to be eclipsed by it. This brings me to speak of Sheridan.

Mr. Sheridan has been justly called "a dramatic star of the first magnitude": and, indeed, among the comic writers of the last century, he "shines like Hesperus among the lesser lights." He has left four several dramas behind him, all different or of different kinds, and all excellent in their way; — The *School for Scandal, The Rivals, The Duenna*, and *The Critic*. The attraction of this last piece is, however, less in the mock-tragedy rehearsed, than in the dialogue of the comic scenes, and in the character of Sir Fretful Plagiary, which is supposed to have been intended for Cumberland. If some of the characters in *The School for Scandal* were contained in Murphy's comedy of *Know Your Own Mind* (and certainly some of Dashwood's detached speeches and satirical sketches are written with quite as firm and masterly a hand as any of those given to the members of the scandalous club, Mrs. Candour or Lady Sneerwell), yet they were buried in it for want of grouping and relief, like the colors of a well-drawn picture sunk in the canvas. Sheridan brought them out, and exhibited them in all their glory. If that gem, the character of Joseph Surface, was Murphy's, the splendid and more valuable setting was Sheridan's. He took Murphy's Malvil from his lurking-place in the closet, and "dragged the struggling monster into day" upon the stage. That is, he gave interest, life, and action, or, in other words, its dramatic being, to the mere conception and written specimens of a character. This is the merit of Sheridan's comedies, that everything in them *tells;* there is no labor in vain. His Comic Muse does not go about prying into obscure corners, or collecting idle curiosities, but shows her laughing face, and points to her rich treasure — the follies of mankind. She is garlanded and crowned with roses and vine-leaves. Her eyes sparkle with delight, and her heart runs over with good-natured malice. Her step is firm and light, and her ornaments consummate! *The School for Scandal* is, if not the most original, perhaps the most finished and faultless comedy which we have. When it is acted, you hear people all around you exclaiming, "Surely it is impossible for anything to be cleverer." The scene in which Charles sells all the old family pictures but his uncle's, who is the purchaser in disguise, and that of the discovery of Lady Teazle when the screen falls, are among the happiest and most highly wrought that comedy, in its wide and brilliant range, can boast. Besides the wit and ingenuity of this play, there is a genial spirit of frankness and generosity about it, that relieves the heart as well as clears the lungs. It professes a faith in the natural goodness, as well as habitual depravity of human nature. While it strips off the mask of hypocrisy, it inspires a confidence between man and man. As often as it is acted, it must serve to clear the air of that low, creeping, pestilent fog of cant and mysticism, which threatens to confound every native impulse, or honest conviction, in the nauseous belief of a perpetual lie, and the laudable profession of systematic hypocrisy.—The character of Lady Teazle is not well made out by the author; nor has it been well represented on the stage since the time of Miss Farren.—*The Rivals* is a play of even more action and incident, but of less wit and satire than *The School for Scandal*. It is as good as a novel in the reading, and has the broadest and most palpable effect on the stage. If Joseph Surface and Charles have a smack of Tom Jones and Blifil in their moral constitution, Sir Anthony Absolute and Mrs. Malaprop remind us of honest Matthew Bramble and his sister Tabitha, in their tempers and dialect. Acres is a distant descendant of Sir Andrew Ague-cheek. It must be confessed of this author, as Falstaff says of some one, that "he had damnable iteration in him!" *The Duenna* is a perfect work of art. It has the utmost sweetness and point. The plot, the characters, the dialogue, are all complete in themselves, and they are all his own: and

the songs are the best that ever were written, except those in the *Beggar's Opera*. They have a joyous spirit of intoxication in them, and a strain of the most melting tenderness. Compare the softness of that beginning,

Had I a heart for falsehood framed,

with the spirited defiance to Fortune in the lines,

Half thy malice youth could bear,
And the rest a bumper drown.

· · · · · ·

Macklin's *Man of the World* has one powerfully written character, that of Sir Pertinax Macsycophant, but it required Cooke's acting to make it thoroughly effectual.

Mr. Holcroft, in his *Road to Ruin*, set the example of that style of comedy, in which the *slang* phrases of jockey-noblemen and the humors of the four-in-hand club are blended with the romantic sentiments of distressed damsels and philosophic waiting-maids, and in which he has been imitated by the most successful of our living writers, unless we make a separate class for the school of Cumberland, who was almost entirely devoted to the *comédie larmoyante*, and who, passing from the light, volatile spirit of his *West-Indian* to the mawkish sensibility of the *Wheel of Fortune*, linked the Muse of English comedy to the genius of German tragedy, where she has since remained, like Christabel fallen asleep in the Witch's arms, and where I shall leave her, as I have not the poet's privilege to break the spell.

There are two other writers whom I have omitted to mention, but not forgotten: they are our two immortal farce-writers, the authors of the *Mayor of Garratt* and the *Agreeable Surprise*. If Foote has been called our English Aristophanes, O'Keeffe might well be called our English Molière. The scale of the modern writer was smaller, but the spirit is the same. In light, careless laughter, and pleasant exaggerations of the humorous, we have had no one equal to him. There is no labor or contrivance in his scenes, but the drollery of his subject seems to strike irresistibly upon his fancy, and run away with his discretion as it does with ours. His Cowslip and Lingo are Touchstone and Audrey revived. He is himself a Modern Antique. His fancy has all the quaintness and extravagance of the old writers, with the ease and lightness which the moderns arrogate to themselves. All his pieces are delightful, but the *Agreeable Surprise* is the most so. There are in this some of the most felicitous blunders in situation and character that can be conceived; and in Lingo's superb replication, "A scholar! I was a master of scholars," he has hit the height of the ridiculous. Foote had more dry, sarcastic humor, and more knowledge of the world. His farces are bitter satires, more or less personal, as it happened. Mother Cole, in *The Minor,* and Mr. Smirk the Auctioneer, in *Taste,* with their coadjutors, are rich cut-and-come-again, "pleasant, though wrong." But *The Mayor of Garratt* is his *Magnum opus* in this line. Some comedies are long farces: this farce is a comedy in little. It is also one of the best acted farces that we have. The acting of Dowton and Russell, in Major Sturgeon and Jerry Sneak, cannot be too much praised: Foote himself would have been satisfied with it. The strut, the bluster, the hollow swaggering, and turkey-cock swell of the Major; and Jerry's meekness, meanness, folly, good-nature, and hen-pecked air, are assuredly done to the life. The latter character is even better than the former, which is saying a bold word. Dowton's art is only an imitation of art, of an affected or assumed character; but in Russell's Jerry you see the very soul of nature, in a fellow that is "pigeon-livered and lacks gall," laid open and anatomized. You can see that his heart is no bigger than a pin, and his head as soft as a pippin. His whole aspect is chilled and frightened, as if he had been dipped in a pond; and yet he looks as if he would like to be snug and comfortable, if he durst. He smiles as if he would be friends with you upon any terms; and the tears come in his eyes because you will not let him. The tones of his voice are prophetic as the cuckoo's under-song. His words are made of water-gruel. The scene in which he tries to make a con-

fidant of the Major is great; and his song of *Robinson Crusoe* as melancholy as the island itself. The reconciliation-scene with his wife, and his exclamation over her, "to think that I should make my Molly *veep!*" are pathetic, if the last stage of human infirmity is so. This farce appears to me to be both moral and entertaining; yet it does not take. It is considered as an unjust satire on the city, and the country at large; and there is a very frequent repetition of the word "nonsense" in the house, during the performance. Mr. Dowton was even hissed, either from the upper boxes or gallery, in his speech recounting the marching of his corps "from Brentford to Ealing, and from Ealing to Acton"; and several persons in the pit, who thought the whole *low,* were for going out. This shows well for the progress of civilization. I suppose the manners described in *The Mayor of Garratt* have, in the last forty years, become obsolete, and the characters ideal: we have no longer either hen-pecked or brutal husbands, or domineering wives; the Miss Molly Jollops no longer wed Jerry Sneaks, or admire the brave Major Sturgeons on the other side of Temple-bar; all our soldiers have become heroes, and our magistrates respectable, and the farce of life is o'er.

One more name, and I have done. It is that of Peter Pindar. The historian of Sir Joseph Banks and the Emperor of Morocco, of the Pilgrims and the Peas, of the Royal Academy, and of Mr. Whitbread's brewing-vat, the bard in whom the nation and the king delighted, is old and blind, but still merry and wise: — remembering how he has made the world laugh in his time, and not repenting of the mirth he has given; with an involuntary smile lighted up at the mad pranks of his Muse, and the lucky hits of his pen — "faint picture of those flashes of his spirit, that were wont to set the table in a roar"; like his own Expiring Taper, bright and fitful to the last; tagging a rhyme or conning his own epitaph; and waiting for the last summons, Grateful and Contented![4]

I have thus gone through the history of that part of our literature, which I

[4] This ingenious and popular writer is since dead.

had proposed to myself to treat of. I have only to add, by way of explanation, that in some few parts I had anticipated myself in fugitive or periodical publications; and I thought it better to repeat what I had already stated to the best of my ability, than alter it for the worse. These parts bear, however, a very small proportion to the whole; and I have used such diligence and care as I could, in adding to them whatever appeared necessary to complete the general view of the subject, or make it (as far as lay in my power) interesting to others.

SIR ARTHUR PINERO

Arthur Wing Pinero — since 1909, Sir Arthur — was born at London in 1855. According to the wishes of his father, he studied law, and until he was nineteen he worked in his father's law-office. But in 1874 he became a member of the Wyndhams' company and acted in the provinces and London for the next five years. He was for some years with Irving at the Lyceum, and undoubtedly learned a great deal about the practical side of the theater. He was at the same time writing plays. The first of these produced was £200 a Year, in 1877. The success of Daisy's Escape (1879), probably encouraged him to embrace the playwright's profession. From that time until the present, Pinero has continued to write plays.

Pinero is not of great importance as a critic of the drama, though the few instances where he has spoken of his art are worth studying. Pinero's insistence upon the necessity for form and his skill in the building of plays, render his words doubly interesting, though it does not of course follow that they are infallible. Pinero contributed his plays rather than his theory to that movement which Jones ushered in. "It has not been my practice to talk much about the drama," [1] he confesses, but it is fortunate that his speeches are for the most part accessible. His speech on R. L. Stevenson: the Dramatist (delivered in 1903) is his most significant utterance on his own art. While he tells the reasons for Stevenson's failure as a dramatist, he also offers a great deal of constructive criticism on how plays may be written.

[1] In a letter to the editor, dated 1916.— Ed.

On the drama:

The New Dramatic School (1883).
Modern British Drama (1895).
Prefatory Letter to Archer's Theatrical World of 1895 (1896).
Prefatory Note to the Author (in W. L. Courtney's The Idea of Tragedy, 1900).
Robert Louis Stevenson: The Dramatist (1903).
Browning as a Dramatist (1912).

Editions:

The New Dramatic School appeared in The Theatre, London, new series, vol. 13, p. 317. Modern Drama in the same, new series, vol. 25, p. 346. The Prefatory Letter is to be found in the Theatrical World of 1895, by William Archer (London, 1896). Courtney's The Idea of Tragedy is published in New York (1900). Robert Louis Stevenson: the Dramatist was privately printed, but is reprinted with an Introduction by Clayton Hamilton in Robert Louis Stevenson as a Dramatist, in Papers on Play-making (Dramatic Museum of Columbia University, New York, 1914). Browning as a Dramatist appeared in the Browning's Centenary of the Academic Committee of the Royal Society of Literature (London, 1912).

On Pinero and his works:

Hamilton Fyfe, Arthur Wing Pinero (London, 1902).
William Archer, Real Conversations (London, 1904).
——, English Dramatists of Today (London, 1882).

William Archer, *About the Theatre* (London, 1886).

——, *The Theatrical World,* 5 vols. (London, 1894–98).

——, *Study and Stage* (London, 1899).

——, *Playmaking* (Boston, 1912).

Mario Borsa, *The English Stage of To-day* (New York, 1908).

Augustin Filon, *The English Stage* (New York, 1897).

Bernard Shaw, *Dramatic Opinions and Essays,* 2 vols. (New York, 1907).

P. P. Howe, *Dramatic Portraits* (New York, 1913).

A. B. Walkley, *Playhouse Impressions* (London, 1892).

A. E. Morgan, *Tendencies of Modern English Drama* (New York, 1924).

A. B. Walkley, *Drama and Life* (New York, 1908).

F. W. Chandler, *Aspects of Modern Drama* (New York, 1914).

Barrett H. Clark, *The British and American Drama of Today* (New York, 1915).

——, *A Study of the Modern Drama* (2nd ed., New York, 1928).

Thomas H. Dickinson, *The Contemporary Drama of England* (Boston, 1917).

Oscar Heermann, *Living Dramatists* (New York, 1905).

Clayton Hamilton, *Studies in Stagecraft* (New York, 1914).

Brander Matthews, *Inquiries and Opinions* (New York, 1907).

ROBERT LOUIS STEVENSON: THE DRAMATIST [2]
(1903)

. . . .

. . . Why should Stevenson the dramatist take such a back seat, if you will pardon the expression, in comparison with Stevenson the novelist, the essayist, the poet?

This question seems to me all the more worth asking because Stevenson's case is by no means a singular one. There is hardly a novelist or a poet of the whole nineteenth century who does not stand in exactly the same position. They have one and all attempted to write for the stage, and it is scarcely too much to say that they have one and all failed, not only to achieve theatrical success, but even, in any appreciable degree, to enrich our dramatic literature. Some people, perhaps, will claim Shelley and Browning as exceptions. Well, I won't attempt to argue the point — I will content myself with asking you what rank Shelley would have held among our poets had he written nothing but *The Cenci,* or Browning, if his fame rested solely on *Strafford* and *A Blot in the 'Scutcheon.* For the rest, Scott, Coleridge, Wordsworth, Keats, all produced dramas of a more or less abortive kind. Some of Byron's plays, which he justly declared unsuited for stage, were forced by fine acting and elaborate scenic embellishments into a sort of suc-

cess; but how dead they are to-day! and how low a place they hold among the poet's works! Dickens and Thackeray both loved the theater, and both wrote for it without the smallest success. Of Lord Tennyson's plays, two, *The Cup* and *Becket,* in the second of which Sir Henry Irving has given us one of his noblest performances, were so admirably mounted and rendered by that great actor that they enjoyed considerable prosperity in the theater; but no critic ever dreamt of assigning either to them or to any other of Tennyson's dramas a place co-equal with his non-dramatic poems. Mr. Swinburne has written many plays — has any of them the smallest chance of being remembered along with *Poems and Ballads* and *Songs Before Sunrise?* There is only one exception to the rule that during the nineteenth century no poet or novelist of the slightest eminence made any success upon the stage, and even that solitary exception is a dubious one. I refer, as you surmise, to Bulwer-Lytton. There is no doubt as to his success; but what does the twentieth century think of his eminence?

If we can lay our finger on the reason of Stevenson's — I will not say failure — but inadequate success as a playwright, perhaps it may help us to understand the still more inadequate success of greater men.

And let me here follow the example of that agreeable essayist Euclid, and

2 Re-printed extracts from the edition published by the Dramatic Museum of Columbia University, with an introduction by Clayton Hamilton (New York, 1914). — Ed.

formulate my theorem in advance — or, in other words, indicate the point towards which I hope to lead you. We shall find, I think, that Stevenson, with all his genius, failed to realize that the art of drama is not stationary, but progressive. By this I do not mean that it is always improving; but what I do mean is that its conditions are always changing, and that every dramatist whose ambition it is to produce live plays is absolutely to study carefully, and I may even add respectfully — at any rate, not contemptuously — the conditions that hold good for his own age and generation. This Stevenson did not — would not — do. We shall find, I think, that in all his plays he was deliberately imitating outworn models, and doing it, too, in a sportive, half-disdainful spirit, as who should say, " The stage is a realm of absurdities — come, let us be cleverly absurd!" In that spirit, ladies and gentlemen, success never was, and never will be obtained. I do not mean to imply, of course, that this was the spirit in which the other great writers I have mentioned — Shelley, Browning, Tennyson, and the rest — approached their work as dramatists. But I do suggest that they one and all, like Stevenson, set themselves to imitate outworn models, instead of discovering for themselves, and if necessary ennobling, the style of drama really adapted to the dramatist's one great end — that of showing the age and body of the time his form and pressure. The difference is, that while Stevenson imitated the transpontine plays of the early nineteenth century, most of the other writers I have named imitated the Elizabethan dramatists. The difference is not essential to my point — the error lies in the mere fact of imitation. One of the great rules — perhaps the only universal rule — of the drama is that you cannot pour new wine into old skins.

Some of the great men I have mentioned were debarred from success for a reason which is still more simple and obvious — namely, that they had no dramatic talent. But this was not Stevenson's case. No one can doubt that he had in him the ingredients of a dramatist. What is dramatic talent? Is it not the power to project characters, and to cause them to tell an interesting story through the medium of dialogue. This is *dramatic* talent; and dramatic talent, if I may so express it, is the raw material of theatrical talent. Dramatic, like poetic, talent, is born, not made; if it is to achieve success on the stage it must be developed into theatrical talent by hard study, and generally by long practice. For theatrical talent consists in the power of making your characters, not only tell a story by means of dialogue, but tell it in such skillfully-devised form and order as shall, within the limits of an ordinary theatrical representation give rise to the greatest possible amount of that peculiar kind of emotional effect, the production of which is the one great function of the theater. Now, dramatic talent Stevenson undoubtedly possessed in abundance; and I am convinced that theatrical talent was well within his reach, if only he had put himself to the pains of evolving it.

Now, I am not attacking — and I should be sorry if you so understood me — that poetical convention which reigns, for instance, in our great Elizabethan drama. I am not claiming any absolute and inherent superiority for our modern realistic technique, though I do not think it quite so inferior as some critics would have us believe. But what I do say is that the dramatist is bound to select his particular form of technique, master, and stick to it. He must not jumble up two styles and jump from one to the other. That is what the authors of *Beau Austin* have not realized. Their technique is neither ancient nor modern; their language is neither poetry nor prose — the prose, that is to say, of conceivable human life. The period has nothing to do with it. People spoke no doubt, a little more formally in 1820 than they do to-day; but neither then nor at any time was the business of life, even in its most passionate moments, conducted in pure oratory. I say, then, that even in *Beau Austin,* far superior though it be to his other plays, Stevenson shows that he had not studied and realized the conditions of the problem he was handling — the problem of how to tell a dramatic story truly, convincingly and effectively on the modern stage — the problem of disclosing the workings of the human heart by methods which shall not destroy the illusion which a modern audience expects to enjoy in the modern theater. Perhaps you will tell me that the fault lay in some part, not with Stevenson, but with the modern audience. I do not maintain that an individual audience never makes mistakes, or even that the theatrical public in general is a miracle of high intelligence. But I assert unhesitatingly that the instinct by which the public feels that one form of drama, and not another, is what best satisfies its intellectual and spiritual needs at this period or at that, is a natural and justified instinct. Fifty years hence the formula of to-day will doubtless be as antiquated and ineffective as the formula of fifty years ago; but it is imposed by a natural fitness upon the dramatist of to-day, just as, if he wants to travel long distances, he must be content to take the railroad train, and cannot ride in a stage coach or fly in an airship. As a personal freak, of course, he may furbish up a stage coach or construct — at his risk and peril — an airship. Such freaks occur in the dramatic world from time to time, and are often interesting — sometimes, but very rarely, successful. *Deacon Brodie* and *Admiral Guinea* are what I may perhaps describe as stage coach plays — deliberate attempts to revive an antiquated form. But *Beau Austin* is not even that. It is a costume play, I admit; but its methods are fundamentally and essentially modern. The misfortune is that the authors had not studied and mastered the formula they were attempting to use, but were forever falling back, without knowing it, upon a bygone formula, wholly incongruous with the matter of their play and the manner in which alone it could be represented in a theater of their day.

Many authors, of course, have deliberately written plays "for the study," ignoring — or more often, perhaps, affecting to ignore — the possibility of stage presentation. But this was not Stevenson's case; nor did he pretend that it was. Listen to this passage from Mr. Graham Balfour's charmingly written life of his cousin and friend: "Meanwhile, the first two months at Bournemouth were spent chiefly in the company of Mr.

Henley, and were devoted to collaboration over two new plays. The reception of *Deacon Brodie* had been sufficiently promising to serve as an incentive to write a piece which should be a complete success, and so to grasp some of the reward which now seemed within reach of the authors. They had never affected to disregard the fact that in this country the prizes of the dramatist are out of all proportion to the payment of the man of letters; and already in 1883 Stevenson had written to his father: 'The theater is a gold mine; and on that I must keep my eye!'" Now let me recall to your mind in this connection the "mercantile delight" which Stevenson professes to have felt in the dream-drama enacted by the "Brownies of his brain." How exactly that chimes in with his own remark to his father, and with his biographer's frank avowal of the motive which inspired his collaboration with Mr. Henley. Ladies and gentlemen, I am the last to pretend that it is a disgrace to an artist to desire an adequate, an ample, pecuniary reward for his labors. That is not at all my point. I draw your attention to these passages for two reasons. Firstly, because they put out of court, once for all, any conjecture that in playwriting Stevenson obeyed a pure artistic ideal, and had no taste or ambition for success on the stage. Secondly, I draw your attention to them in order to indicate an unexpressed but clearly implied fallacy that underlies them. When Stevenson says: "The theater is a gold mine," and when Mr. Graham Balfour tells us that Stevenson felt that "the prizes of the dramatist are out of all proportion to the payment of the man of letters," the implication obviously is that the gold mine can be easily worked, that the prizes are disproportionate to the small amount of pains necessary in order to grasp them. That was evidently the belief of these two men of distinguished talent; and that was precisely where they made the mistake. The art of drama, in its higher forms, is not, and can never be, easy; nor are such rewards as fall to it in any way out of proportion to the sheer mental stress it involves. No amount of talent, of genius, will, under modern conditions at any rate, enable the dramatist to dispense with the concentration of thought of sustained intensity of mental effort, very different, if I may venture to say so, from the exertion demanded in turning out an ordinary novel. Stevenson's novels were not ordinary, and I do not for a moment imply that the amount of mental effort which produced, say, *The Master of Ballantrae,* might not, if well directed, have produced a play of equal value. But Stevenson was never at the trouble of learning how to direct it well. On the contrary, he wholly ignored the necessity for so doing. What attracted him to the drama was precisely the belief that he could turn out a play with far less mental effort than it cost him to write a good novel; and here he was radically, woefully, in error. And the inadequate success of his plays, instead of bringing his mistake home to him, merely led him, I am afraid, to condemn the artistic medium which he had failed to acquire.

Towards the end of his life, while he was in Samoa, and years after his collaboration with Mr. Henley had come to a close, it seems to have been suggested by his friends at home that he should once more try his hand at drama; for we find him writing to Mr. Colvin: "No, I will not write a play for Irving, nor for the devil. Can you not see that the work of *falsification* which a play demands is of all tasks the most ungrateful? And I have done it a long while — and nothing ever came of it." It is true — it is fatally true — that he had devoted himself in his dramatic ventures to "the work of falsification"; but that was, I repeat, because he misconceived entirely the problem before him. The art — the great and fascinating and most difficult art — of the modern dramatist, is nothing else than to achieve the *compression* of life which the stage undoubtedly demands *without* falsification. If Stevenson had ever mastered that art — and I do not question that if he had properly conceived it, he had it in him to master it — he might have found the stage a gold mine, — but

he would have found, too, that it is a gold mine which cannot be worked in a smiling, sportive, half contemptuous spirit, but only in the sweat of the brain, and with every mental nerve and sinew strained in its uttermost. He would have known that no ingots are to be got out of this mine, save after sleepless nights, days of gloom and discouragement, and other days again, of feverish toil the result of which proves in the end to be misapplied and has to be thrown to, the winds. When you sit in your stall at the theater, and see a play moving across the stage, it all seems so easy and natural, you feel as though the author had improvised it. The characters being, let us hope, ordinary human beings, say nothing very remarkable, nothing you think — (thereby paying the author the highest possible compliment) — that might not quite well have occurred to you. When you take up a play-book (if you ever *do* take one up), it strikes you as being a very trifling thing — a mere insubstantial pamphlet beside the imposing bulk of the latest six-shilling novel. Little do you guess that every page of the play has cost more care, severer mental tension, if not more actual manual labor, than any chapter of a novel, though it be fifty pages long. It is the height of the author's art, according to the old maxim, that the ordinary spectator should never be clearly conscious of the skill and travail that have gone to the making of the finished product. But the artist who can achieve a like feat but realize its difficulties, or what are his chances of success? Stevenson, with all his genius, made the mistake of approaching the theater as a toy to be played with. The facts of the case were against him, for the theater is not a toy; and facts being stubborn things, he ran his head against them in vain. Had he only studied the conditions, or in other words, got into a proper relation to the facts, with what joy should we have acclaimed him among the masters of the modern stage!

HENRY ARTHUR JONES

Henry Arthur Jones was born at Grandborough, Bucks, in 1851. He lived for some years in Bucks, where he received his early education. He entered business at Brandford and was a commercial traveler for some years. He produced his first play, *Only 'Round the Corner,* at Exeter in 1878. For the next few years he wrote little plays like his first, one of which was produced in London in 1879. In 1882 he produced his first important play, *The Silver King,* written in collaboration with Henry Herman. *Saints and Sinners,* two years later, called forth praise from Matthew Arnold. From that time on until the war, Jones continued to write plays.

Henry Arthur Jones was probably the first, and was long the most ardent, champion of modern drama in England. His lectures and essays on the drama and theater have been of considerable importance and exerted widespread influence over the younger dramatists, serving to reinstate the English drama in a place of honor. His book, *The Renascence of the English Drama* (1895), a collection of essays and lectures, points out the new path which the drama was to take, and at the same time constitutes a record of achievement. Perhaps the clearest and certainly the most authentic statement of Jones' endeavors and achievements is in a letter to the editor of the present volume, dated April 15, 1916. In this he says: " I have nowhere formulated a complete theory of the drama, though I daresay one might be gathered from what I have variously written. But in my *Introduction* to Brunetière's essay (Columbia University Series) I have laid down a universal law of the drama, setting aside Brunetière's supposed law as included in a larger one. . . . I may point out that all through my writings and lectures I have labored to show

" (1) That no nation can have a drama that is worth consideration unless it is or becomes part of the national literature — that all plays outside this are mere toys of the theater — that therefore the highest aim of those who are working for the drama should be to bring it into relation with literature, and to draw men of letters to an understanding of, and a sympathy with the theater, so that they may exercise their authority as to what is produced.

" (2) That the drama should amuse and interest the populace, but that it should interest and amuse them on an intellectual level; but that although therefore the drama will always be intertwined and inseparable from popular amusement, yet it is something distinct from popular amusement, and in its higher reaches will always be opposed to popular amusement.

" (3) That connected with this opposition is the eternal enmity between the theater and the drama — that in those communities and in those countries where the theater has the upper hand the drama will be secondary and degraded, that where the theater flourishes on its own account the drama will decay; but that where the drama is most honored and loved, the art of acting will be given its greatest opportunities and the best type of actor and the highest quality of acting will be appreciated — as at the *Théâtre-Français* in its best times.

Finally, I hate lecturing and writing about the drama; I should never have written a word about it, if we in England had any tolerable school of drama. I have had to give much of my best effort and most precious time to bring about a condition of the English drama which would make it possible for an English dramatist to produce his best work without the almost certain result that it would be slighted, or hooted off the stage."

Jones died early in 1929.

On the drama:
The Theatre and the Mob (1883).
Religion and the Stage (1885).

A Playwright's Grumble (1884).
The Dramatic Outlook (1884).
On Being Rightly Amused at the Theatre (1887).
The First-Night Judgment of Plays (1889).
Realism and Truth (1890).
The Science of the Drama (1891).
The Literary Drama (1892).
On Playmaking (1891).
Our Modern Drama; is it an Art or an Amusement? (1892).
The Bible on the Stage (1893).
The Future of the English Drama (1893).
Dr. Pearson on the Modern Drama (1893).
The Relations of the Drama to Education (1893).
Preface to *Saints and Sinners* (1891).
Dedication of the Comedy " *The Case of Rebellious Susan* " (1894).
Fragments and Extracts (before 1895).

(All the above are reprinted in *The Renascence of the English Drama* New York, 1895.)

An Introduction to the English Translation of M. Augustin Filon's " The English Stage " (1896).
The Drama and Real Life (1897).
The Drama in the English Provinces in 1900 (1901).
Literary Critics and the Drama (1903).
The Recognition of the Drama by the Stage (1904).
The Foundations of a National Drama (1904).
On Reading Modern Plays (1906).
The Corner Stones of Modern Drama (1906).
Literature and the Modern Drama (1906).
A Speech at the Debate of the Oxford Union on the Establishment of a National Theater (1910).
Standardizing the Drama (1910).
The Censorship Muddle and a Way Out of It (1909).
The Delineation of Character in Drama (1910).
The Licensing Chaos in Theaters and Music Halls (1910).
The Aims and Duties of a National Theater (1911).
A Note on the American National Theater (1912).

The English National Theater (1912).
Recent Developments in the English Provinces (1912).
After the Censorship Committee (1912).

(The above 20 essays are reprinted in *The Foundations of a National Drama*, New York, 1913.)

Dedication to *The Divine Gift* (1913).
Municipal and Repertory Theaters (1913).
Introduction to Brunetière's *The Law of the Drama* (1914).
The Theater of Ideas, a Burlesque Allegory, preface to a volume of plays under that title (1915).
Shakespeare and Germany (1916).

Editions:

The greater part of the above essays are collected in the two volumes abovementioned: *The Renascence of the English Drama* (New York, 1895), and *The Foundations of a National Drama* (New York, 1913). *The Divine Gift*, with the prefatory *Dedication*, was published in New York (1913); *Municipal and Repertory Theaters* in pamphlet-form in London (1913); *Brunetière's Law of the Drama* in the *Papers on Play-making*, published by the Dramatic Museum of Columbia University, New York (1914); *The Theater of Ideas* as a volume with the burlesque allegory and three one-act plays in New York (1915); *Shakespeare and Germany* in pamphlet-form, London (1916).

On Jones and his works:

William Archer, *About the Theater* (London, 1886).
——, *English Dramatists of Today* (London, 1882).
——, *The Theatrical World*, 5 vols. (London, 1894–98).
——, *Study and Stage* (London, 1899).
——, *Playmaking* (Boston, 1912).
Mario Borsa, *The English Stage of Today* (New York, 1908).
Augustin Filon, *The English Stage* (New York, 1897).
Bernard Shaw, *Dramatic Opinions and Essays*, 2 vols. (New York, 1907).

P. P. Howe, *Dramatic Portraits* (New York, 1913).

A. B. Walkley, *Playhouse Impressions* (London, 1892).

——, *Drama and Life* (New York, 1908).

F. W. Chandler, *Aspects of Modern Drama* (New York, 1914).

Barrett H. Clark, *The British and American Drama of Today* (New York, 1915).

——, *A Study of the Modern Drama* (new ed., New York, 1928).

Thomas H. Dickinson, *The Contemporary Drama of England* (Boston, 1917).

INTRODUCTION TO BRUNETIÈRE'S "LAW OF THE DRAMA"[1]

(1914)

INTRODUCTION

Has Brunetière in this fruitful and suggestive essay really discovered the universal law of the theater,— or rather the universal law of the drama?

(It is convenient that in English we use the word *drama* to signify the entire art of dramatic writing, while in French the word *théâtre* has to be used to signify the art of the written drama. The drama and the theater are so often antagonistic to each other; they so often differ, if not in their body and essence, yet in their interests and aims, that we should always be careful to distinguish between them. Much of our confusion of thought in matters dramatic and theatrical arises from our constant habit of using the words *drama* and *theater* as if they were always interchangeable terms. And though for the purposes of the present paper they might be so used without much risk of confusion, yet I will lose no chance of noting that there is often a wide distinction between *theatrical* and *dramatic,* between the *theater* and the *drama.* So much so that I have often said that the greatest enemy of the English drama is the English theater.)

Has then Brunetière, in this remarkable essay, discovered and expounded the veritable and universal law of the drama?

Those who are concerned to know should first carefully read the essay itself. They should then study Professor Brander Matthews's comments and illustrations in the first chapter of his volume the *Development of the Drama* and

also the chapter on the *Law of the Drama,* in his later book *A Study of the Drama.* With these things fresh in their minds they should turn to the chapter *Dramatic and Undramatic* in Mr. William Archer's finely analytical and comprehensive book on *Playmaking* — a useful manual for young playwrights, full of valuable hints.

By the time the inquirer has studied all these things he will have both sides of the question before him. His decision in favor of Brunetière's theory, or against it, will probably be taken according as he has the more lately read Professor Brander Matthews or Mr. William Archer. Or, seeing that our opinions on most subjects are generally molded by our instinctive sympathies rather than by facts and arguments, the inquirer may decide the one way or the other according as he implicitly accepts the doctrine of free will with Professor Brander Matthews, or ranges himself as a determinist with Mr. William Archer.

For myself, I am a rigid, inflexible determinist. No other theory of the universe is credible, or will bear examination. I firmly believe it — in theory. But in practice I find myself lapsing and backsliding all the day long into the unrestrained indulgence of my free will. Therefore my lurking sympathies are with Brunetière; and I think that, with a little coaxing and enlargement, such as indeed he asks from his readers — with this little adjustment and explanation, I think Brunetière's law will be found to be valid and operative, if not universal, throughout the drama.

But Mr. William Archer is not only, like myself, a convinced, inflexible determinist, I am persuaded that he is also, unlike myself, a consistent one. I am

[1] Re-print of the first two-thirds of the *Introduction* from Brunetière's *Law of the Drama* (Dramatic Museum of Columbia University, New York, 1914).— Ed.

sure he takes care that his practice agrees with his opinions — even when they are wrong. And in the present matter Mr. William Archer makes out a good case against Brunetière. He presents it in his usual clear and logical way, and fortifies it with ample and varied illustrations. (See *Playmaking*, pp. 23–33.)

Let us first challenge Mr. Archer's arguments and illustrations, and then let us see whether they cannot be agreeably "reconciled" with Brunetière's law. When a playwright finds eminent dramatic critics disagreeing, it becomes his business to "reconcile" them. Besides, I love "reconciling," the favorite sport of theologians. Of course, one cannot get the same amount of genuine fun from "reconciling" doubts and difficulties in the drama that one gets from "reconciling" doubts and difficulties in theology. One ought not to expect it. Dramatic professors may not permit themselves those playful little dodges with words and facts which make theological "reconciling" such an amusing game. The Drama is a serious art, especially when serious persons like Mr. William Archer and myself get to work upon it. If then our present exercise affords us some small balance of mental profit we must be content to leave the mere gayeties and frivolities of "reconciling" to theologians.

Brunetière's law as translated by Mr. William Archer runs as follows: "Drama is a representation of the will of man in conflict with the mysterious powers or natural forces which limit and belittle us; it is one of us thrown living upon the stage there to struggle against fatality; against social law; against one of his fellow mortals; against himself if need be; against the ambitions, the interests, the prejudices, the folly, the malevolence of those around him."

It will be seen from this that, according to Brunetière, the protagonist has a pretty wide choice of persons and things to pit himself against; and he must be a very unreasonable, or a very unfortunate man, if he cannot manage to pick a quarrel with one or the other of them.

Again, Mr. Archer translates — "The theater in general is nothing but the place for the development of the human will, attacking the obstacles opposed to it by destiny, fortune, or circumstances."

In this definition of his law, Brunetière abandons the idea of a personal struggle or duel, and widens his formula until it practically includes everyman in the everyday struggle of everyday life. Indeed, taking this definition we may use an American colloquialism and sum up Brunetière's law as follows: — "The theater is nothing but the place where a man finds himself 'up against' something, and attacks it."

Now the first of the plays which Mr. Archer brings forward to refute Brunetière is the *Agamemnon*. Well, who can deny that Agamemnon on his first entrance was "up against" something? Indeed he was "up against" what Americans would, I fear, irreverently, and a little loosely call "a tough proposition."

I gathered that much, even in Browning's translation. And it became clearer still to me in Bohn's prose version, which I was obliged to get to translate Browning. Further, in the opening scene there is a sense of past struggle, a backward glance and suggestion of possible scenes of temptation and resistance between Clytemnestra and Ægisthus. It is true that the Greek drama did not permit the introduction of these into the action of the play. But such scenes are latent in our minds; and if Shakespeare had written an *Agamemnon,* they would probably have been set in the forefront of the action in great "acting" scenes akin to those in the second and third acts of *Macbeth.*

Œdipus is the next play that Mr. Archer quotes to refute Brunetière. But if Agamemnon was "up against" a "tough proposition," what shall we say of Œdipus? Not all the giant powers that preside at the mint of the modern American vocabulary, not all the smelting houses of modern American idiom, with all their furnaces in full blast, could coin a sufficient phrase to express the concatentation of adverse circumstances that Œdipus finds himself "up against." Surely no man since the world began has ever been "up against" a "tougher proposition" than Œdipus — except Mr. William Archer and myself, who for thirty years have been "up against" the task of reforming the English drama.

It is true that Œdipus does not "attack" the obstacles opposed to him by "destiny, fortune or circumstances." In this respect he differs from Mr. William Archer and myself. But it is difficult to see how Œdipus could have acted otherwise than he did. He was not aware that Aristotle was going to select him as the type of tragic hero; or that Brunetière was going to discover the law of drama towards the end of the nineteenth century; or that Mr. William Archer was going to dispute Brunetière's law. Even if Œdipus had, with the aid of Tiresias, been able to foresee all these things, he had so much family and national business on his hands at the moment that it would have been impossible for him so to guide his conduct as to "reconcile" all these eminent critics. He would still have been obliged to leave that job to me.

As the matter stands it must be allowed that Œdipus by remaining passive under his misfortunes, has rather given Brunetière away. It is true that in *Œdipus,* as in the *Agamemnon,* there is some latent sense of struggle, and again we may be quite sure that if Shakespeare with his larger form of drama had written an *Œdipus,* we should have had scenes of direct personal conflict; that these scenes would have been set in the forefront of the action; and that he would consequently have written what to a modern audience would have been a more vivid, more absorbing, more exciting play — a better acting play.

It remains to be noted that the performances of Greek tragic drama at the time of Æschylus had something in them of the nature of a religious festival. Doubtless this religious feeling, which was of course widely different from our modern religious feeling, declined to some extent in the days of Sophocles and Euripides. This is apparent in the later dramatists' treatment of their stories. But all the Greek dramatists were dealing with the traditions and subject matter of the religion of their country. We cannot come to the performance of a Greek play with the same feelings as a Greek audience. The Greek drama can never interest an average modern English audience except as an antique curio. We may be quite sure that it aroused a

different set of feelings in a Greek audience, and that these feelings were to some extent of a religious nature.

We must not, however, infer that these religious feelings aroused in the Greek audience had the same lofty soul-saving power as the feelings aroused in American and British audiences of to-day by our modern religious masterpieces of drama such as *Have you found Jesus?* and *Maria, the Early Martyr.* See the testimony on this point of some hundreds of American and British clergymen and ministers who have been moved to advertise the genuine soul-saving power of these plays.

No, the Greeks cannot have been so laudably bent on the great business of saving their souls in the theater as are our American and British audiences to-day. *Prometheus* and the *Agamemnon* and *Œdipus* cannot have saved so many souls as *Have you found Jesus?* and *Maria, the Early Martyr.* Again, the Greek tragedies were passably well written, but not with the same luscious unction of salvation as the recent "holy, oily" successes of our American and British stage. When it comes to the vital business part of religion, either on or off the stage, no race can hope to do the trick like us Anglo-Saxons. And I should have been inclined to yield the palm in this respect to the Americans, had not the Bishop of Liverpool shown himself to be abreast of the times, when the other day, in a truly business-like spirit he urged the advantages of advertising religion.

These things are by the way. Be they as they may, nobody can dispute that when it comes to mixing up amusement and religion in the theater we modern Americans and Englishmen can "lick creation." [2] The Greeks cannot have resigned themselves as we do to lose all sense of drama in the theater in pursuit of the far more important business of saving our souls.

Still, we may take it that the impres-

[2] I adorn this paper with as much slang as possible, in admiration of the sparkling dialogue of some of our most successful recent British and American plays. But the deficiencies in my education, and the nature of the discussion limit my opportunities, and I am obliged for the most part to relapse into plain grammatical English. [H. A. J.]

sion made upon the Greek audience by such tragedies as the *Agamemnon* and *Œdipus* was not wholly a dramatic one. The pleasure they sought in the theater was not wholly and merely the pleasure given by drama. This makes it a little doubtful whether the *Agamemnon* and *Œdipus* can be accepted in contravention of Brunetière's law — even if they do entirely contravene it. All that can be safely affirmed is that when the drama and religion get mixed up in the theater, much that is not strictly dramatic, much that is quite undramatic, will interest and hold, and even enthrall an audience.

On the whole, however, Mr. William Archer in pointing out that Agamemnon and Œdipus are passive under their misfortunes, that there is no will struggle in their great scenes, which are yet indisputably dramatic — in marking this Mr. William Archer has established a strong position against Brunetière, so far as the Greek drama is concerned. I am obliged to hand over to Mr. Archer the scalps of Agamemnon and Œdipus.

I do not think he is equally successful in the examples of Western European drama, which he brings against Brunetière. Before we proceed to examine Mr. Archer's more modern instances, let us inquire what would be the effect upon us of a play, perfectly constructed from beginning to end according to Brunetière's principle; that is a play which would exhibit a series of conflicts of human will, manifesting themselves in action, from the rise to the fall of the curtain without the least intermission.

We get some approach to such a play in the cruder and more violent specimens of popular melodrama. What is the result? Character drawing has to be sacrificed. There are only impossibly good heroes and impossibly wicked villains. Again, there is too much plot. The action proceeding at such a violent rate is plainly seen to be impossible. Further, the play misses its chief end — that of giving an impression of life. It does not interest us, because it is obviously false and unreal. Moreover it becomes monotonous; it loses variety, therefore it quickly tires an audience. The most successful melodramas are those into which "comic relief" is most abundantly introduced, and where this

sense of will conflict is relaxed or removed at times. But even these scenes of "comic relief" are most successful when they contain a conflict of wit, or of humor, or of mere words.

We see then that if Brunetière's law is true and valid, if the drama is really a struggle of will power, there is a triple necessity laid upon it that this struggle should often be kept below the surface of the action. If it is always emergent, always apparent, always demonstrating itself, the dramatist must renounce his claim to subtle or even truthful character drawing. He will write a crude, violent play, incessantly strident and restless and shrieking; he will give his audience no interludes of change and repose; he will tire and irritate them by his lack of variety. Above all, his play will not give the impression of life. For even the most determined of us is only intermittently bent upon any course of action. We must eat and sleep and carry on the trivial business of life for the greater part of our time.

For all these reasons the struggle of wills in a play must often lose itself beneath the surface of the action, as a river sometimes loses itself underground, but still keeps flowing. Or sometimes indeed this struggle of wills will be entirely concealed, like the girders supporting a house under apparent solid masonry which would fall in ruins without the hidden straps of iron. We see the iron girders only when we remove the bricks and look beneath.

Let us keep in mind this triple necessity laid upon the dramatist of occasionally or frequently diverting the current of will power and submerging it beneath the surface of the action. Though hidden it will yet be the dominant moving power of the play, as a river even when burrowing beneath and undermining a mountain, is yet the governing factor in shaping the landscape. Let us also remember that Brunetière does not claim that in all plays the will struggle must be concentrated in a prolonged duel between the two leading personages. According to the necessities of the story, it may be divided and diffused between opposing groups of persons; or split into divers tributary manifestations — here between two minor personages;

there between a character or characters and destiny, or circumstance, or social law. Further let us again insist that many things which are not strictly dramatic hold and amuse us in the theater, and indeed may rivet our attention — pretty faces, dancing, gorgeous scenery, songs, processions, etc. Molière and Congreve were often forced to divert and hold the attention of their spectators by dragging in songs and dances.

With all these considerations in our minds let us proceed to examine those plays of Western Europe which Mr. Archer gives as notable instances of drama that disprove Brunetière's law. The first of these is *Othello*. But surely Othello is struggling all through the latter part of the play, if not directly with Iago, yet with the successive tangles of evidence which Iago is binding round him; with his own doubts and suspicions and fears; with his own growing sense of crumbling domestic happiness and military renown. Othello is by no means passive like Agamemnon and Œdipus. He makes us imagine what Agamemnon and Œdipus would have been if Shakespeare had handled them. Othello is indeed blindfolded like Œdipus, but he does not accept his doom. Othello puts up a good fight against the fate that he feels, but does not see. But even granted that Othello is passive, which he is not, Othello is not the protagonist of the play. Iago is the real protagonist, as every actor who has played Othello knows. And where in all drama is such a superb energy of pure will, ceaselessly driving and scheming its way through and round every obstacle; undiverted by passion; unmoved by pity; unshaken by remorse; operative in every scene of the play from its opening lines to the closing

O Spartan dog!
More fell than anguish, hunger or the sea?

Where else in drama is such pressure, alertness and sublimity of pure unconquerable will as in Iago? To me the play of *Othello* offers a shining instance of Brunetière's law in full play — accepting Brunetière's own definition.

As you Like it is Mr. Archer's next "awful example." "Where is the con-

flict in *As you Like it?*" Mr. Archer asks. Certainly there is no continuous personal conflict in this delightful comedy. Many of the scenes that please us are not drama; and even while they please us, we may easily perceive that the pleasure that we take in them is not the true pleasure of drama. And because the drama in *As you Like it* is so weak and loose and intermittent, it has never had a great and striking success in the theater. The character of Rosalind is so winning that it will always draw us to the theater if it is played by a favorite actress. But I think whatever success *As you Like it* has won on the boards may be largely ascribed to the vogue of some leading lady. I question if it has ever been so popular as to make money for the management; while I suspect that in several instances much money has been lost in forcing a run. But there is much delightful word conflict in *As you Like it;* between Rosalind and Orlando; between Rosalind and Celia; between Rosalind and Touchstone. And there is much finely contrasted character. These things, if they may be claimed as comedy, are certainly not drama. They are amongst the many other things that, as I have already noted, interest and hold an audience in a theater without being drama. They are the kickshaws which we eat and enjoy; but they do not make a dinner.

But beyond these things there are a few elements of will conflict in *As you Like it,* very weak and scattered and inconsequent it is true, not much related to each other, of little force or continuity. Yet take these away from the already tenuous framework, and the comedy would drop to pieces. It would scarcely be actable. They are the precarious straps and props that do really hold it together as a play.

Ghosts is the next play which Mr. Archer opposes to Brunetière's theory. And here he has a very strong case indeed. In this terrible yet fascinating play Ibsen approaches the Greek construction. It is very simple. The drama opens at a late climax of the story. The events and passions that have led to the present scenes happened long ago; yet they are a living part of the body of action, and must have been dramatic in themselves. In the present scenes Ibsen mirrors in a large vague way these past characters and passions and events.

No art is so rigidly economic as the drama. One sentence may give us all that is practically worth knowing of a man's past history. As for instance, when in *She Stoops to Conquer,* Gregory says of the ould Grouse in the gunroom story, "We've laughed at that story any time the last twenty years." Mr. Hardcastle's life and character are virtually painted there.

Ibsen in *Ghosts* darkly mirrors in the present action the dreadful outlines of the past; darkly shows us bygone sins and passions in whose transactions the human will must have played its part. There must be some picturing of these in our minds as we witness the actual scenes of *Ghosts.* The stricken survivors in the play are like the stricken survivors from the *Titanic* who brought with them from the far mid-Atlantic to the New York dock the tokens and images of past disaster, and forced the spectators to reconstruct the whole tragedy.

But the shuddering far backward glances we take from the successive platforms in *Ghosts* do not impress us with a sense of any past will conflict that is operative in the present action. It can scarcely be urged that either in the mirrored past, or the actual present, there is any dominant, or even significantly latent struggle of the human will that moves the action of the play, or contributes to its effect, or that even holds it together. Yet nobody who has seen *Ghosts* on the stage can deny that throughout it is intense, poignant drama. In successfully bringing forward three such signal instances as the *Agamemnon, Œdipus* and *Ghosts* to refute Brunetière, Mr. Archer may claim to have disproved the universality of Brunetière's law.

What then is the clew to the absorbing interest which *Ghosts* arouses in spectators, an interest which is indisputably that of drama? What has *Ghosts* in common with *Agamemnon, Œdipus* and all other plays, or scenes of plays, where our attention is gripped and sustained? To reduce it to a general statement — is it not this, that a character in the play is "up against" some opposing circumstance, or person, or fate? In *Ghosts* Oswald is "up against" the *Spirochoete pallida,*—which, I am told, is a formidable, though a merely microscopic antagonist. I think that many other modern plays and scenes of plays may be found on examination to shake our faith in the universality of Brunetière's law. So far as I remember, the dramatic interest of the *Bells* as Irving played it,— certainly the climax of dramatic interest in the last act — was not due to an assertion of will, but rather to the fact that Matthias, like Agamemnon and Œdipus and Oswald, was "up against a tough proposition." And in many trial scenes that have been successful on the stage, it will, I think, be found that the dramatic interest arises not from a conflict or assertion of will, but again from the fact that some person, generally the hero, is "up against a tough proposition."

Mr. Archer having so strongly proved his case against the universality of Brunetière's law, we need not dwell upon his further illustrations, except as they seem to be fallacious or questionable, and to point to the existence of some more general and more inclusive law than the one formulated by Brunetière. Mr. Archer goes on to say "No one can say that the balcony scene in *Romeo and Juliet* is undramatic." But can any one say that it is truly dramatic? Would not the play be a complete whole, would the action suffer materially, would the play be less comprehensible, if the balcony scene were merely indicated, or cut down to a fourth of its length, as it probably would be in a modern prose play? The scene does indeed hold us, but not by its essential drama. A play entirely made up of such scenes would not be dramatic. Is not the balcony scene, as a whole, lyric rather than dramatic? Again, to take the opposite side for a moment, might it not be plausibly argued that in all love scenes there is a subtle implication of an after physical conflict, wherein each combatant struggles for mastery in self-surrender? In that sense all love scenes are dramatic because they secretly indicate an impulse towards dominancy in self-surrender, towards self-assertion in self-sacrifice.

Mr. Archer also advances the scene in *Paolo and Francesca,* the death scene of

Cleopatra, and the banquet scene in *Macbeth*. These are scenes that necessarily link together other scenes of struggle in plays where the human will is a dominant motor of the action. *Paolo and Francesca* is not a very dramatic story throughout. Dante has seized its one moment and left little for any follower to glean. Dramatists might be content to leave it to Dante. The pastoral scene in *A Winter's Tale* is not dramatic, except in the moments and scenes where the story of the play intervenes and is carried forward.

Mr. Archer says " In the whole range of drama there is scarcely a passage which one would call more dramatic than the screen scene in the *School for Scandal;* yet it would be the veriest quibbling to argue that any appreciable part of its effect arises from the clash of will against will. This whole comedy indeed, suffices to show the emptiness of the theory."

On the contrary, I think it might be fairly argued that, granting Brunetière's explanation and enlargement of his law according to Mr. Archer's own translation, viz.—" one of us thrown living on the stage there to struggle against . . . social law, against one of his fellow mortals, against . . . the ambitions, the interests, the folly, the malevolence of those who surround him —" granted this, it may be fairly argued that the *School for Scandal* falls as comedy within the operation of Brunetière's law. Comedy does not demand so fierce and intense an assertion of the human will as drama. It is concerned with less serious affairs. Its struggle is not against fate, and "the mysterious powers or natural forces which limit and belittle us." Its struggle, involving the human will, is against the prejudices, follies, whims, foibles and small vices of mankind. In ordinary talk we distinguish between comedy and drama.

Granted this, and it is expressly granted in Brunetière's definition as quoted by Mr. Archer, there is a very real, though largely implied, conflict of the human will in the *School for Scandal*. Joseph has a very strong will to seduce Lady Teazle, to blacken Charles, and to become Sir Oliver's heir. The opposition between Joseph and Charles, though Charles is not very conscious of it, and

though it is not obtrusive, is yet the foundation arch of the *School for Scandal*. Take it away, and the play totters, if it does not fall. Then there are vivid will conflicts, of course in a comedy vein, between Sir Peter and Lady Teazle in the delightful quarrel scenes. These will struggles of the earlier acts are carried forward and underlie the screen scene. They are what make it a piece of drama. Withdraw them and their implications, and the screen scene would almost lose its dramatic effect. In opposition to Mr. Archer's dictum that the *School for Scandal* shows the emptiness of Brunetière's theory, it may be claimed that it rather conspicuously illustrates Brunetière's law working in comedy. It is questionable whether Congreve's absence from the English stage for the last hundred years or more is not largely due to the fact that there is a comparative absence of will conflict working continuously through the play and woven into a connected scheme. In none of Congreve's four comedies is there a will conflict that much interests us, except that of Mirabell and Millamant; and these scenes are vivid and alive when they are acted to-day. Maskwell indeed has a determined will, but we cannot believe in his preposterous schemes and plots. Congreve's construction is always loose and inconsequent; and it is this lack of constructive power that has prevented him from being a popular dramatist. For Congreve's wit is far brighter and more piercing than Sheridan's, and his character drawing is larger, truer and more vigorous wherever the two dramatists can be compared. Before quitting the *School for Scandal* we may notice, as a clew to some larger and more general law of the drama than Brunetière's, that Joseph is "up against" Lady Teazle's resolution not to lose her chastity when it comes to the final test; that he is "up against" Sir Oliver's determination to try the characters of his nephews; and also "up against" the old Nabob's sneaking fondness for Charles; that Charles, though unconsciously, is "up against" Joseph's wiles and hypocrisy; that he is also "up against" Sir Oliver's plan for trying his character; that Sir Peter is unconsciously "up against" Joseph's wiles and hypocrisy, and "up against" Lady Teazle's possible seduction by Joseph; that Lady Teazle is "up against" Joseph's wiles and her own lightness and carelessness. All these leading characters are "up against" one of the obstacles included in Brunetière's long list of opposing circumstances — not perhaps very violently and rigidly "up against" these facts and circumstances and human wiles, as they would be in tragedy and serious drama, but sufficiently, and for the most part lightheartedly, as befits the characters in comedy.

I have now analyzed each of the plays and scenes that Mr. Archer brings forward to refute Brunetière's theory. I have shown that many of these so far from disproving it, do indeed go far to prove it; or at least to indicate that Brunetière was groping and stumbling on the right path towards a universal law of the drama. Indeed Mr. Archer himself lends some countenance to Brunetière when he says that "conflict is one of the most dramatic elements in life, and that many dramas — perhaps most — do as a matter of fact turn upon strife of one sort or another." And further, that "a stand-up fight between will and will is no doubt one of the intensest forms of drama."

When in addition to granting this to Brunetière, Mr. Archer brings forward such plays as *Agamemnon, Œdipus,* and *Ghosts,* and shows that we can have great, intense drama, certainly without the present assertion of human will, largely without the past assertion of human will carried forward into the present scenes; and also without a conscious fight against fate, or opposing circumstance — when Mr. Archer shows this, he has proved Brunetière's theory, not indeed to be quite empty and worthless, but rather to be suggestive of, and included in some larger and more general law which is of universal application.

Having, as he claims to have done, demolished Brunetière's theory, Mr. Archer goes on to have a theory of his own. Here Mr. Archer might perhaps have remembered that Archibald Spofforth in his exhaustive, but rather exhausting, treatise on *Radical Fallibilities of the Human Brain* comments very severely on our inveterate propensity to propound theories, and shows how imperfect an instrument the human brain is for this purpose. In a very elaborate mathematical argument, which I was not able to follow, but which all my experience and observation prompt me to accept most cordially, Archibald Spofforth claims to prove that, taking the masses of theories already propounded by mankind on all subjects, the probability of any given theory being right is as 1 to 241,743.[3] This it must be owned is a very sporting chance, and the enormous odds against Mr. Archer may well excuse him if he has formed a wrong theory of the drama; as indeed they may plead for some leniency towards myself if I am venturesome enough to launch a theory of my own.

"What then," Mr. Archer asks, "is the essence of drama if conflict be not it? What is the common quality of themes, scenes, and incidents which we recognize as specifically dramatic? Perhaps we shall scarcely come nearer to a helpful definition than if we say that the essence of drama is *crisis.*" Thus speaks Mr. Archer. He then goes on to sort out his crises, dividing them into those which are undramatic, and those which are dramatic. He establishes, without a doubt, that when a crisis is dramatic, it is drama. On the other hand when a crisis is undramatic it is not drama. And unfortunately it appears that the crises which are undramatic are just as numerous and just as intrinsically important as those which are dramatic. Crises ought not to behave in this inconsistent way, if they are to prove Mr. Archer's theory. He has rejected "conflict" as the essence of drama. Yet I think if he carefully considers those crises which he calls dramatic he will find there is always a sense of conflict, active or implied; and often a conflict of the human will. At least we may claim that some character is always, consciously or unconsciously "up against" some rather "tough proposition." Mr. Archer says, "A play is a more or less rapidly developing crisis in destiny or circum-

---

3 In matters of Theology, Spofforth claims that the odds against any given theory being right are increased, and stand at 4,741,604 to 1 — an estimate which seems on the face of it to be over cautious. But theological matters, interesting as they are in themselves, need not detain us here. [H. A. J.]

stance; and a dramatic scene is a crisis within a crisis, clearly furthering the ultimate event." This is very well put, and we need not dispute it. But might it not be paraphrased as "A play is a more or less rapidly developing conflict with destiny or circumstance, and a dramatic scene is a conscious or unconscious conflict within a scheme of larger conflict, clearly furthering the ultimate event"? At any rate a conflict is always dramatic, and a crisis, as Mr. Archer takes some trouble to show, is often undramatic.

Perhaps I may be forgiven if I obtrude my own practice and experience for a moment. Mr. Archer's book is, as I have said, full of valuable hints and suggestions to young playwrights. On page 27 he says "The author might often ask himself with advantage whether he could not strengthen his obstacle and so accentuate the struggle which forms the matter of his play." This is sound and admirable advice. In nearly all cases a play succeeds or fails with a popular audience, on the right or wrong conduct of its plot. Dialogue, consistency of motive, truth and sincerity of character drawing, are weighty matters indeed, and of the chief importance when we are measuring the permanent value of a play. But they are of little value, they scarcely come into the account at all, unless the plot is first carefully designed and established throughout. To build a play with good literature and truthful observation of character, without first having a complete design, is as though an architect should take care to choose the best materials for his house; to see that his bricks and wood and iron are of the best; and then take no heed that the elevation is right, that the kitchen and living-rooms and staircases are practicable, that the house is a compact and convenient place to live in.

Now the interest of the plot should be held to the end, and the main motives of the play should sustain the structure throughout. In devising the structure of a play, and in trying to make the story hold its interest to the fall of the curtain, I have constantly found it necessary to "strengthen the obstacle" as Mr. Archer suggests. This strengthening the obstacle has often taken the form of bringing two wills into conflict, or of increasing the apprehension of the coming will conflict, or of suspending a final and decisive will conflict until the latest moment, meantime emphasizing its imminency. Mr. Archer has noted that "a stand up fight between will and will is one of the intensest forms of drama." It is also one of the most effective on the stage, the surest to hold an audience. As a matter of experience I have found these scenes of will conflict the easiest to write; not indeed in the sense of calling for little effort, but in the sense of easily and surely arousing a swift, impetuous, unflagging energy to deal with them. They generally write themselves — after long reflection and preparation. To say nothing of shorter scenes, I have three times written scenes of sustained conflict that fill the greater part of an act. Two of them were written at single sittings of two hours and three hours respectively — that is they were for the most part written at a far greater speed than I generally write matter requiring no thought. The other was written in one long sitting of about four hours, and a second sitting the next day of an hour. The two former were drama; the latter was comedy. These instances have some bearing on Brunetière's theory, and I hope this may excuse me for introducing personal matter.

My own experience strongly disposes me to support Brunetière's law. But in the instances of the *Agamemnon*, *Œdipus*, and *Ghosts*, Mr. Archer has certainly disproved its universal application.

I have shown that Mr. Archer's crises may comfortably lie down alongside Brunetière's will conflicts. They are largely of the same order, and are in many respects identical. Is there no means of finally and completely "reconciling" these eminent critics?

I have a great mind to discover a law of the drama of my own. It will be urged that it is unnecessary to add to the prevailing confusion which exists in the modern drama. And even if I "reconciled" Brunetière and Mr. Archer, what about the other eminent critics and dramatists who have discovered that it is the first business of the playwright not to have a story or a plot, but to have "ideas," and a "mission," to sweep up social abuses, to debate endlessly upon social questions and disputed points in sociology?

It is a sad reflection that all the successful dramatists of the past have been as lamentably ignorant of modern psychology and sociology as the early Ephesian converts were of the Third Person in the Trinity. They had not so much as heard of so august an Abstraction. In consequence of a similar lamentable ignorance of august Abstractions, like psychology and sociology and heredity, the successful dramatists of the past were obliged to construct their plays on the vicious first principle of telling an interesting story in a well framed concrete scheme; and by this means their plays have secured a permanent popularity,—which is a reprehensible thing to lovers of "ideas."

But what modern playwright will take infinite trouble to learn the difficult task of constructing a play, when he can gain the reputation of being not only a great dramatist but also a profound thinker by the easy expedient of tossing a few psychological or sociological "ideas" about the stage with the careless freedom of a happy haymaker?

The present moment then is not auspicious for the enunciation of a law of the drama. It is very hard to obey laws; it is very easy to have "ideas." "Ideas" enforce no restrictions; they need not even be pursued; they need only to be dangled, and aired, and left to float away. I hesitate then to unfold my law of the drama, because if it chances to be true it may be destructive to so many recent masterpieces of the harum scarum and Pentonville-omnibus schools of drama.

On the other hand, if it is a true law, there are enormous odds that it will be disregarded and neglected — for the time; in as much as it runs counter to the prevailing notions and fashions of the moment. So perhaps I may safely venture to discover a law of the drama of my own, in the security that it cannot do very much harm, as very few people will pay any attention to it.

It must necessarily be a very broad and general law if it is not only to "reconcile" Brunetière and Mr. Archer, but also to apply to any and every scene and to any and every play that we can bring to test it. Bearing in mind then all the arguments and illustrations that have been used in this paper, and remembering that in the theater many things interest and amuse us which are not true drama, may we not formulate the universal law of drama as follows? —

" Drama arises when any person or persons in a play are consciously or unconsciously " up against " some antagonistic person, or circumstance, or fortune. It is often more intense, when as in Œdipus, the audience is aware of the obstacle, and the person himself or persons on the stage are unaware of it. Drama arises thus, and continues when or till the person or persons are aware of the obstacle; it is sustained so long as we watch the reaction physical, mental, or spiritual, of the person or persons to the opposing person, or circumstance, or fortune. It relaxes as this reaction subsides, and ceases when the reaction is complete. This reaction of a person to an obstacle is most arresting and intense when the obstacle takes the form of another human will in almost balanced collision."

It will be seen that this law overlaps and includes Brunetière's will conflicts and Mr. Archer's crises; and that it " reconciles " them. It shows us what is drama, and what is not drama, in each of the scenes and plays that we have analyzed; it explains the failure of certain other scenes to interest us; it indicates those scenes which, not being dramatic in themselves, do yet hold our attention in the theater, because they are necessary links, supplying information about character or events; or because they are restful interludes between scenes of true drama.

This law can, I think, be applied to any play, or to any scene of any play, ancient or modern, and made the test of its dramatic value. If in asserting its universality I am claiming too much for it, I shall be glad to be confronted with instances of plays or scenes where it does not apply. I will then withdraw it, or widen it, or adopt any other law that can be shown to have a universal application. Perhaps some amusing scenes in farce may be found to be largely exempt from its sway; but farce, by its very name being "stuffing," that is "padding," does not pretend to be drama. But, this possible exception granted, I think the law I have formulated will be found to be a veritable universal law, which will hold good always and everywhere, and can be equally used as a touchstone to all scenes and to all plays; to tragedy, drama, comedy or farce.

As I have stated the law it appears to be somewhat lengthy and involved. But it can scarcely be shortened or simplified if it is to be explicit, and if it is to cover the whole area of drama. If, however, Mr. Archer would allow us to add "suspense" to "crisis" as a chief element of drama, then the formula "suspense, crisis — suspense, crisis — suspense, crisis," almost renders a succinct statement of the law of drama. And if we do not insist upon the conscious exertion of the human will, which though of frequent exhibition in drama, is not omnipresent and omnipotent as Brunetière supposes — if we enlarge Bruntière's law into "conflict impending, conflict raging — conflict impending, conflict raging — conflict impending, conflict raging,—" then again we get a short formula which almost renders a succinct statement of the law of drama. And in most instances the general outline of the action of the same successful play would be equally well described as a succession of suspenses and crises, or as a succession of conflicts impending and conflicts raging, carried on in ascending and accelerated climaxes from the beginning to the end of a connected scheme. Thus it appears that our law includes and "reconciles" Brunetière's will conflicts with Mr. Archer's crises, and Mr. Archer instead of being opposed to Brunetière as he imagines, is in substantial agreement with him — that is when a playwright is allowed to expand and expound and interpret their respective theories, and to find places for them in a law which is large enough to accommodate them both. I kindle with justifiable pride to find that I have "reconciled" these eminent critics.

Mr. Archer in dismissing Brunetière's theory as inadmissible says, "For a sufficient account of the matter we need go no further than the simple psychological observation that human nature loves a fight, whether it be with clubs, or with swords, with tongues or with brains." (*Playmaking*, p. 26.) But this psychological observation gives us an insight into the permanent relation of the drama to life. Reduced to its simplest elements life itself is mainly a fight; it is the commonest simile in all literature. Reduced to its simplest elements, drama is mainly the representation of a fight, a conflict of some sort. War in some form, military, industrial, social or spiritual is the law of our being; it is the necessary lever of all human advance. Death is peace, as every tombstone shows. Life is war — of some kind. Thus we see the reason that successful drama is so largely made up of conflict, conscious or unconscious. It is then fundamentally like life; fundamentally, it is life. For when there is what Brunetière calls an obstacle, even if the persons on the stage are unaware of it, we, the spectators, know there is a vital conflict, actual or imminent, and we set ourselves to watch its development. It is not the passivity of Agamemnon, of Œdipus, or of Oswald, which gives us the sense of drama. It is their impending reaction to the obstacle that rouses our interest. This response may be bodily, mental or spiritual; but it is an opposition, a reaction if not of the will, yet a reaction of the man's nature or character; a kind of conflict; and therefore it is drama.

.	.	.	.	.	.	.

GEORGE BERNARD SHAW

George Bernard Shaw was born at Dublin in 1856. He was forced at an early age to earn his own living, as the family was in straightened circumstances. He went into a land-agent's office in his native city. But his interest in other things — chiefly music and science — made him restless, and in 1876 he went to London, where for nine years he did literary hack work. Between 1880 and 1883 he wrote four novels, which were not very successful, but during this time he met many people interested in politics and socialism, who were to exert great influence over him: Webb, Carpenter, Morris, and Archer, were guiding forces. In the early nineties he became dramatic critic of the *Saturday Review*, and carried on a campaign against the conventional plays and acting of the time. In 1892 he produced his first play, *Widowers' Houses*. This was soon followed by *The Philanderer* (1893) and *Mrs. Warren's Profession* (written a short while after, but censored and not performed until 1902). Meantime Shaw was busy lecturing, and engaged in the activities of the Fabian Society. Before long his influence began to be felt in the English theatre. He is still writing plays, as well as articles on sociology, politics, and economics.

Bernard Shaw's contribution to the drama has been two-fold, and that contribution is partly practical and partly theoretical. In his periodical critiques in the *Saturday Review* he was mainly concerned with destroying current notions about the well-made play, and absurd ideas about romance. Both in theory and in practice he has stood for the thesis-play: and like Tolstoy, he maintained that it is the function of the drama to teach and serve a practical and immediate purpose for the community and society. To him the theater is merely a means and not an end. Throughout his lectures, essays, reviews, prefaces, and even in his plays he has preached his doctrine, which has been largely influential in England, Germany, and the United States.

On the drama:

Since there are a great many articles contributed to newspapers and magazines which have never been collected, it is impossible to mention every one. The following are, however, the most important. It has not been thought necessary to indicate each separate preface to separate volume and play. Practically every play (and every volume) contains a preface more or less concerned with the drama.

The Quintessence of Ibsenism (1891).
Preface and *Appendices* to the Independent Theater Edition of *Widowers' Houses* (1893).
A Dramatic Realist to his Critics (1894).
Preface to *Archer's Theatrical World of 1894* (1895).
The Problem Play (1895).
The Author's Apology (1902).
Ibsen (1906).
Letter from Mr. G. Bernard Shaw in *Tolstoy on Shakespeare* (1906).
Dramatic Opinions and Essays, 2 vols. (New York, 1907).
The New Drama (1911).
Preface to *Three Plays by Brieux* (New York, 1911).
Letter on The Principles that Govern the Dramatist in his Selection of Themes and Methods of Treatment (1912).
The Art and Craft of Playwriting (1914).
The Sanity of Art (1908), *The Perfect Wagnerite* (1901), and Shaw's remarks in John Palmer's *The Censor and the Theater* (1913), may also be consulted. Likewise, for letters and reports of conversations, Archibald Henderson's *George Bernard Shaw* (see below), and *Table-Talk of G. B. S.* (New York, 1925).

Editions:

The Independent Theatre Edition of *Widowers' Houses* appeared in London, 1893. A great deal of the *Preface* and *Appendices* has not been reprinted. Archer's *Theatrical World of 1894* was published in London (1895).

The *Dramatic Opinions and Essays* are a selection of the best criticisms contributed to the *Saturday Review*. They are edited with an introduction by James Huneker, 2 vols. (New York, 1907). *A Dramatic Realist to his Critics*, and *The Problem Play* have not been reprinted. The first appeared in *The New Review* (London, Sept., 1894); the second in *The Humanitarian* (London, May, 1895). *The Author's Apology from "Mrs. Warren's Profession"* is printed separately, with an introduction by John Corbin (New York, 1905). The article on *Ibsen* appeared in the *Clarion*, London, June 1, 1906, and has not been reprinted. *Tolstoy on Shakespeare* was printed in New York, 1906. *The New Drama, Letter on the Principles*, etc., appeared respectively in the London *Times*, Nov. 10, 1911, and the New York *Times*, June 2, 1912, and have not been reprinted. *The Quintessence of Ibsenism* originally appeared in New York in 1891, but a new edition, " Now completed to the Death of Ibsen," was issued (New York) in 1913. *The Art and Craft of Playwriting* is printed only as a reported lecture in the Oxford (England) *Chronicle* (March 6, 1914). The *Preface* to the *Plays by Brieux* is published in that volume (New York, 1911). *The Sanity of Art* originally appeared in separate form in London (1908). *The Perfect Wagnerite* appeared in New York (1901). Shaw's remarks on the Censorship problem are printed verbatim in Palmer's *The Censorship and the Theater* (New York, 1913), but as these are only a

selection from a more nearly complete report, see for this the *Report of the Joint Select Committee of the House of Lords and the House of Commons on the Stage Plays (Censorship), together with the Proceedings of the Committee, and Minutes of the Evidence* (London, 1909).

On Shaw and his works:

Archibald Henderson, *George Bernard Shaw, His Life and Works* (Cincinnati, 1911).

G. K. Chesterton, *George Bernard Shaw* (New York, 1909).

Holbrook Jackson, *Bernard Shaw* (London, 1907).

Julius Bab, *Bernard Shaw* (Berlin, 1910).

H. L. Mencken, *George Bernard Shaw, His Plays* (Boston, 1905).

Joseph McCabe, *George Bernard Shaw* (New York, 1914).

John Palmer, *George Bernard Shaw, Harlequin or Patriot?* (New York, 1915).

Augustin Hamon, *Le Molière du XX⁰ siècle: Bernard Shaw* (Paris, 1913). Translated by Eden and Cedar Paul as *The Twentieth Century Molière: Bernard Shaw*, New York, 1916).

P. P. Howe, *Bernard Shaw* (New York, 1915).

Charles Cestre, *Bernard Shaw et son œuvre* (Paris, 1912).

Richard Burton, *Bernard Shaw, the Man and the Mask* (New York, 1916).

William Archer, *The Theatrical World*, 5 vols. (London, 1894-98).

——, *Playmaking* (Boston, 1912).

J. S. Collis, *Shaw* (New York, 1925).

Edward Shanks, *Bernard Shaw* (London, 1924).

THE AUTHOR'S APOLOGY FROM MRS. WARREN'S PROFESSION
(1902)

. . . Such an audience as I have described would be revolted by many of our fashionable plays. They would leave the theater convinced that the Plymouth Brother who still regards the playhouse as one of the gates of hell is perhaps the

---

[1] Re-printed extracts from the edition with an Introduction by John Corbin (New York, 1905).— Ed.

safest adviser on the subject of which he knows so little. If I do not draw the same conclusion, it is not because I am one of those who claim that art is exempt from moral obligations, and that the writing or performance of a play is not a moral act, to be treated on exactly the same footing as theft or murder if it produces equally mischievous consequences. I am convinced that fine art is the subtlest, the most seductive, the most effective means of propagandism in the world, excepting only the example of personal conduct; and I waive even this exception in favor of the art of the stage, because it works by exhibiting examples of personal conduct made intelligible and moving to crowds of unobservant, unreflecting people to whom real life means nothing. I have pointed out again and again that the influence of the theater in England is growing so great that whilst private conduct, religion, law, science, politics and morals are becoming more and more theatrical, the theater itself remains impervious to common sense, religion, science, politics, and morals. That is why I fight the theater, not with pamphlets and sermons and treatises, but with plays; and so effective do I find the dramatic method that I have no doubt I shall at last persuade even London to take its conscience and its brains with it when it goes to the theater, instead of leaving them at home with its prayer book as it does at present. Consequently, I am the last man in the world to deny that if the net effect of a performance of *Mrs. Warren's Profession* were an increase in the number of persons entering that profession, its performance should be dealt with accordingly.

. . . As to the voluptuaries, I can assure them that the playwright, whether he be myself or another, will always disappoint them. The drama can do little to delight the senses: all the apparent instances to the contrary are instances of the personal fascination of the performers. The drama of pure feeling is no longer in the hands of the playwright: it has been conquered by the musician, after whose enchantments all the verbal arts seem cold and tame. *Romeo and Juliet* with the loveliest Juliet is dry, tedious, and rhetorical in comparison with Wagner's *Tristan*, even though Isolde be fourteen stone and forty, as she often is in Germany. Indeed, it needed no Wagner to convince the public of this. The voluptuous sentimentality of Gounod's *Faust* and Bizet's *Carmen* has captured the common playgoer; and there is, flatly, no future now for any drama without music except the drama of thought. The attempt to produce a genus of opera without music—

and this absurdity is what our fashionable theaters have been driving at for a long time past without knowing it — is far less hopeful than my own determination to accept problem as the normal material of the drama.

That this determination will throw me into a long conflict with our theater critics, and with the few playgoers who go to the theater as often as the critics, I well know; but I am too well equipped for the strife to be deterred from it, or to bear malice towards the losing side. In trying to produce the sensuous effects of opera, the fashionable drama has become so flaccid in its sentimentality, and the intellect of its frequenters so atrophied by disuse, that the reintroduction of problem, with its remorseless logic and iron framework of fact, inevitably produces at first an overwhelming impression of coldness and inhuman rationalism. But this will soon pass away. When the intellectual muscle and moral nerve of the critics has been developed in the struggle with modern problem plays, the pettish luxuriousness of the clever ones, and the sulky sense of disadvantaged weakness in the sentimental ones, will clear away; and it will be seen that only in the problem play is there any real drama, because drama is no mere setting up of the camera to nature: it is the presentation in parable of the conflict between Man's will and his environment: in a word, of problem. The vapidness of such drama as the pseudo-operatic plays contain lies in the fact that in them animal passion, sentimentally diluted, is shown in conflict, not with real circumstances, but with a set of conventions and assumptions half of which do not exist off the stage, whilst the other half can either be evaded by a pretense of compliance or defied with complete impunity by any reasonably strong-minded person. Nobody can feel that such conventions are really compulsory; and consequently nobody can believe in the stage pathos that accepts them as an inexorable fate, or in the genuineness of the people who indulge in such pathos. Sitting at such plays we do not believe: we make believe. And the habit of make believe becomes at last so rooted that criticism of the theater ceases to be criticism at all, and becomes more and more a chronicle of the fashionable enterprises of the only realities left on the stage: that is, the performers in their own persons. In this phase the playwright who attempts to revive genuine drama produces the disagreeable impression of the pedant who attempts to start a serious discussion at a fashionable at-home. Later on, when he has driven the tea servies out and made the people who had come to use the theater as a drawing-room understand that it is they and not the dramatists who are the intruders, he has to face the accusation that his plays ignore human feeling, an illusion produced by that very resistance of fact and law to human feeling which creates drama. It is the *deus ex machina* who, by suspending that resistance, makes the fall of the curtain an immediate necessity, since drama ends exactly where resistance ends. Yet the introduction of this resistance produces so strong an impression of heartlessness nowadays that a distinguished critic has summed up the impression made on him by *Mrs. Warren's Profession,* by declaring that " the difference between the spirit of Tolstoy and the spirit of Mr. Shaw is the difference between the spirit of Christ and the spirit of Euclid." But the epigram would be as good if Tolstoy's name were put in place of mine and D'Annunzio's in place of Tolstoy's. At the same time I accept the enormous compliment to my reasoning powers with sincere complacency; and I promise my flatterer that when he is sufficiently accustomed to and therefore undazzled by the problem on the stage to be able to attend to the familiar factor of humanity in it as well as to the unfamiliar one of a real environment, he will both see and feel that *Mrs. Warren's Profession* is no mere theorem, but a play of instincts and temperaments in conflict with each other and with a flinty social problem that never yields an inch to mere sentiment.

I go further than this. I declare that the real secret of the cynicism and inhumanity of which shallower critics accuse me is the unexpectedness with which my characters behave like human beings, instead of conforming to the romantic logic of the stage. The axioms and postulates of that dreary mimanthropometry are so well known that it is almost impossible for its slaves to write tolerable last acts to their plays, so conventionally do their conclusions follow from their premises. Because I have thrown this logic ruthlessly overboard, I am accused of ignoring, not stage logic, but, of all things, human feeling. People with completely theatrified imaginations tell me that no girl would treat her mother as Vivie Warren does, meaning that no stage heroine would in a popular sentimental play. They say this just as they might say that no two straight lines would inclose a space. They do not see how completely inverted their vision has become even when I throw its preposterousness in their faces, as I repeatedly do in this very play. Praed, the sentimental artist (fool that I was not to make him a playwright instead of an architect!), burlesques them by anticipating all through the piece that the feelings of the others will be logically deducible from their family relationships and from his " conventionally unconventional " social code. The sarcasm is lost on the critics: they, saturated with the same logic, only think him the sole sensible person on the stage. Thus it comes about that the more completely the dramatist is emancipated from the illusion that men and women are primarily reasonable beings, and the more powerfully he insists on the ruthless indifference of their great dramatic antagonist, the external world, to their whims and emotions, the surer he is to be denounced as blind to the very distinction on which his whole work is built. Far from ignoring idiosyncrasy, will, passion, impulse, whim, as factors in human action, I have placed them so nakedly on the stage that the elderly citizen, accustomed to see them clothed with the veil of manufactured logic about duty, and to disguise even his own impulses from himself in this way, finds the pictures as unnatural as Carlyle's suggested painting of Parliament sitting without its clothes.

.   .   .   .

LETTER

ON THE PRINCIPLES THAT GOVERN THE DRAMATIST IN HIS SELECTION OF THEMES, AND METHODS OF TREATMENT [2]

(1902)

I am asked to define the principles that govern the dramatist in his selection of themes and methods of treatment. But pray, who told you, gentlemen, that the dramatists are governed by principles, or that they have any choice in their selection of themes and methods?

I am not governed by principles; I am inspired, how or why I cannot explain, because I do not know; but inspiration it must be; for it comes to me without any reference to my own ends or interest. I find myself possessed of a theme in the following manner. I am pushed by a natural need to set to work to write down the conversations that come into my head unaccountably. At first I hardly know the speakers, and cannot find names for them. Then they become more and more familiar, and I learn their names. Finally I come to know them very well, and discover what it is they are driving at, and why they have said and done the things I have been moved to set down.

This is not being " guided by principles "; it is hallucination; and sane hallucination is what we call play or drama. I do not select my methods: they are imposed upon me by a hundred considerations: by the physical considerations of theatrical representation, by the laws devised by the municipality to guard against fires and other accidents to which theaters are liable, by the economics of theatrical commerce, by the nature and limits of the art of acting, by the capacity of the spectators for understanding what they see and hear, and by the accidental circumstances of the particular production in hand.

I have to think of my pocket, of the manager's pocket, of the actors' pockets, of the spectators' pockets, of how long people can be kept sitting in a theater without relief or refreshments, of the range of the performer's voice, and of the hearing and vision of the boy at the back of the gallery, whose right to be put in full possession of the play is as sacred as that of the millionaire in the stalls or boxes.

I have to consider theatrical rents, the rate of interest needed to tempt capitalists to face the risks of financing theaters, the extent to which the magic of art can break through commercial prudence, the limits set by honor and humanity to the tasks I may set to my fellow-artist, the actor: in short, all the factors that must be allowed for before the representation of a play on the stage becomes practicable or justifiable: factors which some never comprehend and which others integrate almost as unconsciously as they breathe, or digest their food.

It is these factors that dictate the playwright's methods, leaving him so little room for selection that there is not a pennyworth of difference between the methods of Sophocles or Shakespeare and those of the maker of the most ephemeral farce.

And withal, when the play is made, the writer must feed himself and his family by it. Indeed, there are men and women who are forced by this necessity to simulate inspiration, repeating its gestures and copying its tricks so as to produce artificial plays: constructed things with no true life in them, yet sometimes more amusing than real plays, just as a clockwork mouse is more amusing than a real mouse, though it will kill the cat who swallows it in good faith.

I could tell many other secrets of my trade, but these are enough to put the wise inquirer on the track of the rest.

2 Re-printed from the facsimile in the *New York Times* of June 2, 1912. Complete text.—Ed.

WILLIAM ARCHER

William Archer was born at Perth, Scotland, in 1856. He attended Edinburgh University, and in 1883 was admitted to the bar. But before that time he had relinquished the idea of practicing, and as early as 1875 he was contributing to the *Edinburgh Evening News.* The next year he spent in Australia. He came to London in 1878, and in 1879 became dramatic critic of the *Figaro.* He occupied the same position on the *World* from 1884 to 1905. He was meantime engaged in translating the important plays of Ibsen, whom he helped to introduce to the English reading public. From 1906 to 1908 he was dramatic critic of *The Tribune,* and has since contributed to the *Star* and many other newspapers. Most of his criticisms he collected into books, the first of which, *English Dramatists of Today,* appeared in 1882. Besides his dramatic criticism, Archer has written political and social works.

Out of his long experience Archer has evolved no strikingly new theory of the drama, but in his *Playmaking* he has considered the essentials of dramatic form, and in attempting to disprove the validity of Brunetière's *Law* has laid down the dictum that crisis and not conflict is the chief requirement of the drama. Clayton Hamilton (in *Studies in Stagecraft,* 1914) justly taxes Archer in turn for limiting the field of the drama to crises, and says: " Yet I do not think it would be difficult to convince so open-minded a critic as Mr. Archer that the element of ' crisis ' is no more indispensable to a genuinely interesting drama than the element of ' conflict.' " And he adduces proofs by referring to three successful plays devoid of crisis. Archer has defined the dramatic as " Any representation of imaginary personages which is capable of interesting an average audience assembled in a theater." This is as far from Aristotle as any definition could well be.

He died in 1924.

On the drama:

English Dramatists of Today (1882).
About the Theatre (1886).
The Theatrical World, 1894–98, 5 vols. (1894–98).
Study and Stage (1899).
Playmaking (1912).
The Old Drama and the New (Boston, 1923).

In the introductions and prefaces to the *Collected Works of Henrik Ibsen* (translated by Archer, his brother, and others, 10 vols., London and New York, 1906–08), Archer has supplied much material on the drama. His editions of *The Dramatic Essays* of Leigh Hunt, Hazlitt, John Forster, and G. H. Lewes (London, 1894–96) may likewise be consulted. Further prefatory matter is in the English translation of Mantzius' *History of Theatrical Art,* vol. 1 (London, 1903), the *Mermaid* edition of George Farquhar (London, 1906), and to W. S. Gilbert's *A Stage Play* (New York, 1916). Archer's biographies and other books contain references and occasionally separate essays on dramatists: *Henry Irving, Actor and Manager* (1883), *Life of Macready* (1890), *Masks or Faces?* (1888), *Real Conversations* (1907), (and, together with Granville-Barker) *Schemes and Estimates for a National Theatre* (1907).

On Archer and his works:

Brander Matthews, *A critic of the Acted Drama: William Archer* (in *The Historical Novel,* New York, 1901).
Clayton Hamilton, *Studies in Stagecraft* (New York, 1914).
——, *Problems of the Playwright* (New York, 1917).
Mario Borsa, *The English Stage of Today* (New York, 1908).
Bernard Shaw, *Foreword* to *Three Plays by William Archer* (London, 1927).

PLAYMAKING[1]

[Chapter on] DRAMATIC AND UNDRAMATIC

(1912)

It may be well, at this point, to consider for a little what we mean when we use the term "dramatic." We shall probably not arrive at any definition that can be applied as an infallible touchstone to distinguish the dramatic from the undramatic. Perhaps, indeed, the upshot may rather be to place the student on his guard against troubling too much about the formal definitions of critical theorists.

The orthodox opinion of the present time is that which is generally associated with the name of the late Ferdinand Brunetière. "The theater in general," said that critic,[2] "is nothing but the place for the development of the human will, attacking the obstacles opposed to it by destiny, fortune, or circumstances." And again: "Drama is a representation of the will of man in conflict with the mysterious powers or natural forces which limit and belittle us; it is one of us thrown living upon the stage, there to struggle against fatality, against social law, against one of his fellow-mortals, against himself, if need be, against the interests, the prejudices, the folly, the malevolence of those who surround him."

The difficulty about this definition is that, while it describes the matter of a good many dramas, it does not lay down any true differentia — any characteristic common to all drama, and possessed by no other form of fiction. Many of the greatest plays in the world can with difficulty be brought under the formula, while the majority of romances and other stories come under it with ease. Where, for instance, is the struggle in *Agamemnon?* There is no more struggle between Clytemnestra and Agamemnon than there is between the spider and the fly who walked into his net. There is not even a struggle in Clytemnestra's mind. Agamemnon's doom is sealed from the outset, and she merely carries out a pre-arranged plot. There is contest indeed in the succeeding plays of the trilogy; but it will scarcely be argued that the *Agamemnon,*

taken alone, is not a great drama. Even the *Œdipus* of Sophocles, though it may at first sight seem a typical instance of a struggle against Destiny, does not really come under the definition. Œdipus, in fact, does not struggle at all. His struggles, in so far as that word can be applied to his misguided efforts to escape from the toils of fate, are all things of the past; in the actual course of the tragedy he simply writhes under one revelation after another of bygone error and unwitting crime. It would be a mere play upon words to recognize as a dramatic "struggle" the writhing of a worm on a hook. And does not this description apply very closely to the part played by another protagonist — Othello, to wit? There is no struggle, no conflict, between him and Iago. It is Iago alone who exerts any will; neither Othello nor Desdemona makes the smallest fight. From the moment when Iago sets his machination to work, they are like people sliding down an ice-slope to an evitable abyss. Where is the conflict in *As You Like It?* No one, surely, will pretend that any part of the interest or charm of the play arises from the struggle between the banished Duke and the Usurper, or between Orlando and Oliver. There is not even the conflict, if so it can be called, which nominally brings so many hundreds of plays under the Brunetière canon — the conflict between an eager lover and a more or less reluctant maid. Or, take again, Ibsen's *Ghosts* — in what valid sense can it be said that that tragedy shows us will struggling against obstacles? Oswald, doubtless, wishes to live, and his mother desires that he should live; but this mere will for life cannot be the differentia that makes of *Ghosts* a drama. If the reluctant descent of the "downward path to death" constituted drama, then Tolstoy's *Death of Ivan Ilytch* would be one of the greatest dramas ever written — which it certainly is not. Yet again, if we want to see will struggling against obstacles, the classic to turn to is not *Hamlet,* not *Lear,* but *Robinson Crusoe;* yet no one, except a

[1] Re-printed from *Playmaking* (Boston, 1912). Sections from this chapter.— Ed.
[2] *Etudes critiques*, vol. 7, pp. 153 and 207.

pantomime librettist, ever saw a drama in Defoe's narrative. In a Platonic dialogue, in *Paradise Lost*, in *John Gilpin*, there is a struggle against obstacles, there is none in *Hannele*, which, nevertheless, is a deeply moving drama. Such a struggle is characteristic of all fiction, from *Clarissa Harlowe* to *The House With the Green Shutters;* whereas, in many plays, the struggle, if there be any at all, is the merest matter of form (for instance, a quite conventional love-story), while the real interest resides in something quite different.

The plain truth seems to be that conflict is *one* of the most dramatic elements in life, and that many dramas — perhaps most — do, as a matter of fact, turn upon strife of one sort or another. But it is clearly an error to make conflict indispensable to drama, and especially to insist — as do some of Brunetière's followers — that the conflict must be between will and will. A stand-up fight between will and will — such a fight as occurs in, say, the *Hippolytus* of Euripides or Racine's *Andromaque*, or Molière's *Tartufe*, or Ibsen's *Pretenders*, or Dumas' *Francillon*, or Sudermann's *Heimat*, or Sir Arthur Pinero's *Gay Lord Quex*, or Mr. Shaw's *Candida*, or Mr. Galsworthy's *Strife* — such a stand-up fight, I say, is no doubt one of the intensest forms of drama. But it is comparatively rare, at any rate, as the formula of a whole play. In individual scenes a conflict of will is frequent enough; but it is, after all, only one among a multitude of equally telling forms of drama. No one can say that the balcony scene in *Romeo and Juliet* is undramatic, or the "Galeoto fu il libro" scene in Mr. Stephen Phillips' *Paolo and Francesca;* yet the point of these scenes is not a clash, but an ecstatic concordance, of wills. Is the death scene of Cleopatra undramatic? Or the banquet scene in *Macbeth?* Or the pastoral act in the *Winter's Tale?* Yet in none of these is there any conflict of wills. In the whole range of drama there is scarcely a passage which one would call more specifically dramatic than the Screen scene in the *School for Scandal;* yet it would be the veriest quibbling to argue that any appreciable part of its effect arises from the clash of will against will. This whole comedy, indeed, suffices

to show the emptiness of the theory. With a little strain, it is possible to bring it within the letter of the formula; but who can pretend that any considerable part of the attraction or interest of the play is due to that possibility?

The champions of the theory, moreover, place it on a metaphysical basis, finding in the will the essence of human personality, and therefore of the art which shows human personality raised to its highest power. It seems unnecessary, however, to apply to Schopenhauer for an explanation of whatever validity the theory may possess. For a sufficient account of the matter, we need go no further than the simple psychological observation that human nature loves a fight, whether it be with clubs or with swords, with tongues or with brains. One of the earliest forms of mediæval drama was the *estrif* or *flyting* — the scolding match between husband and wife, or between two rustic gossips. This motive is glorified in the quarrel between Brutus and Cassius, degraded in the patter of two "knockabout comedians." Certainly there is nothing more telling in drama than a piece of "cut-and-thrust" dialogue after the fashion of the ancient "stitchomythia." When a whole theme involving conflict, or even a single scene of the nature described as a "passage-at-arms" comes naturally in the playwright's way, by all means let him seize the opportunity. But do not let him reject a theme or scene as undramatic, merely because it has no room for a clash of warring wills.

There is a variant of the *conflict* theory which underlines the word "obstacles" in the above-quoted dictum of Brunetière, and lays down the rule: "No obstacle, no drama." Though far from being universally valid, this form of the theory has a certain practical usefulness, and may well be borne in mind. Many a play would have remained unwritten if the author had asked himself, "Is there a sufficient obstacle between my two lovers?" or, in more general terms, "between my characters and the realization of their will?" There is nothing more futile than a play in which we feel that there is no real obstacle to the inevitable happy ending, and that the curtain might just as well fall in the middle of the first act as at the end of the third.

Comedies are bound (though they reach the stage only by accident) in which the obstacle between Corydon and Phyllis, between Lord Edwin and Lady Angelina, is not even a defect or peculiarity of character, but simply some trumpery misunderstanding which can be kept afoot only so long as every one concerned holds his or her commonsense in studious abeyance. "Pyramus and Thisbe without the wall" may be taken as the formula for the whole type of play. But even in plays of a much higher type, the author might often ask himself with advantage whether he could not strengthen his obstacle, and so accentuate the struggle which forms the matter of his play. Though conflict may not be essential to drama, yet, when you set forth to portray a struggle, you may as well make it as real and intense as possible. . . .

. . . . . .

What, then, is the essence of drama, if conflict be not it? What is the common quality of themes, scenes, and incidents, which we recognize as specifically dramatic? Perhaps we shall scarcely come nearer to a helpful definition than if we say that the essence of drama is crisis. A play is a more or less rapidly-developing crisis in destiny or circumstances, and a dramatic scene is a crisis within a crisis, clearly furthering the ultimate event. The drama may be called the art of crises, as fiction is the art of gradual developments. It is the slowness of its process which differentiates the typical novel from the typical play. If the novelist does not take advantage of the facilities offered by his form for portraying gradual change, whether in the way of growth or of decay, he renounces his own birthright in order to trespass on the domain of the dramatist. Most great novels embrace considerable segments of many lives; whereas the drama gives us only the culminating points — or, shall we say, the intersecting culminations? — of two or three destinies. Some novelists have excelled precisely in the art with which they have made the gradations of change in character or circumstance so delicate as to be imperceptible from page to page, and measurable, as in real life, only when we look back over a considerable period. The dramatist, on the other hand, deals in rapid and startling changes, the *peri-*

peties, as the Greeks called them, which may be the outcome of long, slow processes, but which actually occur in very brief spaces of time. Nor is this merely a mechanical consequence of the narrow limits of stage presentation. The crisis is as real, though not as inevitable, a part of human experience as the gradual development. Even if the material conditions of the theater permitted the presentation of a whole *Middlemarch* or *Anna Karénina* — as the conditions of the Chinese theater actually do — some dramatists, we cannot doubt, would voluntarily renounce that license of prolixity, in order to cultivate an art of concentration and crisis. The Greek drama "subjected to the faithful eyes," as Horace phrases it, the culminating points of the Greek epic; the modern drama places under the lens of theatrical presentment the culminating points of modern experience.

But, manifestly, it is not every crisis that is dramatic. A serious illness, a law-suit, a bankruptcy, even an ordinary prosaic marriage, may be a crisis in a man's life, without being necessarily, or even probably, material for drama. How, then, do we distinguish a dramatic from a non-dramatic crisis? Generally, I think, by the fact that it develops, or can be made naturally to develop, through a series of minor crises, involving more or less emotional excitement, and, if possible, the vivid manifestation of character. . . .

. . . . .

And now, after all this discussion of the "dramatic" in theme and incident, it remains to be said that the tendency of recent theory, and of some recent practice, has been to widen the meaning of the word, until it bursts the bonds of all definition. Plays have been written, and have found some acceptance, in which the endeavor of the dramatist has been to depict life, not in moments of crisis, but in its most level and humdrum phases, and to avoid any crispness of touch in the presentation of individual incidents. "Dramatic," in the eyes of writers of this school, has become a term of reproach, synonymous with "theatrical." They take their cue from Maeterlinck's famous essay on *The Tragical in Daily Life,* in which he lays it down that: "An old man, seated in his arm-chair, waiting patiently, with his lamp beside him — submitting with bent head to the presence of his soul and his destiny — motionless as he is, does yet live in reality a deeper, more human, and more universal life than the lover who strangles his mistress, the captain who conquers in battle, or the husband who ' avenges his honor.' " They do not observe that Maeterlinck, in his own practice, constantly deals with crises, and often with violent and startling ones.

At the same time, I am far from suggesting that the reaction against the traditional " dramatic " is a wholly mistaken movement. It is a valuable corrective of conventional theatricalism; and it has, at some points, positively enlarged the domain of dramatic art. Any movement is good which helps to free art from the tyranny of a code of rules and definitions. The only really valid definition of the " dramatic " is: any representation of imaginary personages which is capable of interesting an average audience assembled in a theater. We must say, " representation of imaginary personages " in order to exclude a lecture or a prize-fight; and we must say " an average audience " (or something to that effect) in order to exclude a dialogue of Plato or of Landor, the recitation of which might interest a specially selected public. Any further attempt to limit the content of the term " dramatic " is simply the expression of an opinion that such-and-such forms of representation will not be found to interest an audience; and this opinion may always be rebutted by experiment. In all that I have said, then, as to the dramatic and non-dramatic, I must be taken as meaning: " Such and such forms and methods have been found to please and will probably please again. They are, so to speak, safer and easier than other forms and methods. But it is the part of original genius to override the dictates of experience, and nothing in these pages is designed to discourage original genius from making the attempt." We have already seen, indeed, that in a certain type of play — the broad picture of a social phenomenon or environment — it is preferable that no attempt be made to depict a marked crisis. There should be just enough story to afford a plausible excuse for raising and for lowering the curtain.

Let us not, however, seem to grant too much to the innovators and the quietists. To say that a drama should be, or tends to be, the presentation of a crisis in the life of certain characters, is by no means to insist on a mere arbitrary convention. It is to make at once an induction from the overwhelming majority of existing dramas and a deduction from the nature and inherent conditions of theatrical presentation. The fact that theatrical conditions often encourage a violent exaggeration of the characteristically dramatic elements in life does not make these elements any the less real or any the less characteristically dramatic. It is true that crispness of handling may easily degenerate into the pursuit of mere picture-poster situation; but that is no reason why the artist should not seek to achieve crispness within the bounds prescribed by nature and commonsense. There is a drama — I have myself seen it — in which the heroine, fleeing from the villain, is stopped by a yawning chasm. The pursuer is at her heels, and it seems as though she has no resource but to hurl herself into the abyss. But she is accompanied by three Indian servants, who happen, by the mercy of Providence, to be accomplished acrobats. The second climbs on the shoulders of the first, the third on the shoulders of the second; and then the whole trio falls forward across the chasm, the top one grasping some bush or creeper on the other side; so that a living bridge is formed, on which the heroine (herself, it would seem, something of an acrobat) can cross the dizzy gulf and bid defiance to the baffled villain. This is clearly a dramatic crisis within our definition; but, no less clearly, it is not a piece of rational or commendable drama. To say that such-and-such a factor is necessary, or highly desirable, in a dramatic scene, is by no means to imply that every scene which contains this factor is good drama. Let us take the case of another heroine — Nina in Sir Arthur Pinero's *His House in Order*. The second wife of Filmer Jesson, she is continually being offered up as a sacrifice on the altar dedicated to the memory of his adored first wife. Not only her husband but the relatives of the sainted Annabel make her life a burden to her. Then there comes to her knowledge — she obtains absolute proof — that Annabel was anything but the saint she was believed to be. By a single word she can overturn the altar of her martyrdom, and shatter the dearest illusion of her persecutor. Shall she speak that word, or shall she not? Here is a crisis which comes within our definition just as clearly as the other; only it happens to be entirely natural and probable, and eminently illustrative of character.

Ought we, then, to despise it because of the element it has in common with the picture-poster situation of preposterous melodrama? Surely not. Let those who have the art — the extremely delicate and difficult art — of making drama without the characteristically dramatic ingredients, do so by all means; but let them not seek to lay an embargo on the judicious use of these ingredients as they present themselves in life.

THE UNITED STATES

DRAMATIC CRITICISM OF THE UNITED STATES

As stated in the *Introduction* (see p. vii) the editorial and bibliographical apparatus of this new Supplement does not conform to that used in the earlier part of the book. What follows here is intended chiefly as a very brief summary, a bird's-eye view, of the subject to serve as general introduction to the twelve texts that follow.

Although plays were produced in the United States before 1700, little criticism has survived from the early period. The 18th Century furnishes the first examples of native playwriting based on American themes and using dialogue of somewhat native flavor. Interesting examples of early American criticism may be found in *The American Theater as Seen by its Critics, 1752-1934*, compiled by Montrose J. Moses and John Mason Brown (1934). By far the greater part of what was written during the 19th Century was concerned with acting and anecdotes of the stage, but among the occasional lectures or articles by the playwrights Dion Boucicault, Bronson Howard and James A. Herne may be found curious and illuminating passages on the technique and philosophy of the drama. Somewhat later the playwright Augustus Thomas prefaced several of his published plays with practical treatises on technique. The regular play reviewers of the last part of the Century were largely concerned with acting and production, though William Winter (who reprinted hundreds of his reviews in several volumes) evolved more or less by implication certain dramatic theories.— During the early years of the 20th Century several "movements" were started by playwrights, poets, producers, and outsiders, intended to decentralize the theater, encourage native playwriting and develop novel forms of drama. Among the propagandists of the time who formulated their ideas in articles and books were the poet-playwright Percy MacKaye (*The Playhouse and the Play*, 1909, and *The Civic Theater*, 1912); Thomas H. Dickinson (*The Case of*

American Drama, 1915; *The Insurgent Theater*, 1917; and *Playwrights of the New American Theater*, 1925); Sheldon Cheney (*The New Movement in the Theater*, 1914, and *The Art Theater*, 1925); Kenneth Macgowan (*The Theater of Tomorrow*, 1921); and Oliver M. Sayler (*Our American Theater*, 1923).

Meantime the historians and keepers of records, whose pioneer work is based largely on source materials, were keeping pace with the development of the American playwright. The basic texts in this category are Arthur Hobson Quinn's *A History of the American Drama From the Beginning to the Civil War* (1923), and *A History of the American Drama From the Civil War to the Present Day* (1936), and Montrose J. Moses' *The American Dramatist* (1925). To these should be added a few others, amplifying and modifying them so far as facts and conclusions are concerned: Richard Burton's *The New American Drama* (1913); Walter Prichard Eaton's *The Drama in English* (1930); Burns Mantle's *American Playwrights of Today* (1938); Barrett H. Clark's *A Study of the Modern Drama* (1938) and *An Hour of American Drama* (1930); Margaret G. Mayorga's *A Short History of the American Drama: Commentaries on Plays Prior to 1920* (1932); George Freedley's and John A. Reeves' *History of the Theater* (1941); Joseph Wood Krutch's *The American Drama Since 1918* (1939); John Anderson's *The American Theater* (1938) and *Box Office* (1929); Eleanor Flexner's *American Playwrights: 1918-1938* (1938); and Frank Hurlburt O'Hara's *Today in American Drama* (1939). The standard chronological record of dramatic productions is Burns Mantle's *The Best Plays of 1919-20 and the Year Book of the Drama in America* (1920), an annual published regularly from 1920 to the present time. This series has since been supplemented, in collaboration with Garrison P. Sherwood, by *The Best Plays of 1899-1909* (1944) and *The Best Plays of*

1909–1919 (1933). For references on drama and theater in general, and especially on American drama, see Bernard Sobel's *Theater Handbook and Digest of Plays* (1940).

Among the few regular reviewers [1] of plays for newspapers and periodicals who have collected some of their criticisms in book form are Norman Hapgood (*The Stage in America, 1897–1900,* 1901); Arthur Ruhl (*Second Nights,* 1914); Walter Prichard Eaton (*The American Stage of Today,* 1908; *At the New Theater and Others,* 1910; *Plays and Players,* 1916); Clayton Hamilton (*Studies in Stagecraft,* 1914; *Problems of the Playwright,* 1917; *Seen on the Stage,* 1920); Alexander Woollcott (*Shouts and Murmurs,* 1922; *Enchanted Aisles,* 1924; *Going to Pieces,* 1928); Ludwig Lewisohn (*The Drama and the Stage,* 1922); Stark Young (*The Flower in Drama,* 1923); Percy Hammond (*But is it Art?,* 1927; *This Atom in the Audience,* 1940); John Mason Brown (*Upstage,* 1930; *Two on the Aisle,* 1938; *Broadway in Review,* 1940; *Letters from Greenroom Ghosts,* 1934; *Seeing Things,* 1946); and George Jean Nathan (beginning with *Another Book on the Theater,* 1915, and continuing with an average of one new book a year to date).

The books of Brander Matthews, partly composed of reprinted essays and partly larger treatises written primarily as books, extend over a fairly long period (some are mentioned in the section devoted to Matthews' work); the more formal and elaborate treatises on dramatic technique, by Matthews and others, remain to be mentioned: Brander Matthews' *Principles of Playmaking* (1919); *A Study of the Drama* (1910), and scattered essays in *The Historical Novel* (1901) and other volumes; Clayton Hamilton's *The Theory of the Theater and Other Principles of Dramatic Criticism* (newly consolidated edition including an earlier work of the same title and three other books) (1939), *So You're Writing a Play?* (1935); William T. Price's *The Technique of the Drama* (1892); *The Analysis of Play Construc-*

[1] It is to be regretted that Brooks Atkinson, for many years critic on the New York Times, has not seen fit to reprint his reviews in book form.

tion and Dramatic Principle (1908); *Why Plays Fail* (1912); and *The Philosophy of Dramatic Principle and Method* (1912); Eugene Walter's *How to Write a Play* (1925); Mark Swan's *How You Can Write Plays* (1927); *The Art of Playwriting* (1928), lectures by Jesse Lynch Williams, Langdon Mitchell, Rachel Crothers, Gilbert Emery, and others; George Pierce Baker's *Dramatic Technique* (1919); John Howard Lawson's *Theory and Technique of Playwriting* (1936); Arthur Edwin Krows' *Playwriting for Profit* (1928); Kenneth Rowe's *Write That Play* (1939); Josephine Niggli's *Pointers on Playwriting* (1945); and Alan Reynolds Thompson's *The Anatomy of Drama* (1946). In books of various kinds — historical, theoretical, philosophical — are to be found more or less pertinent sections of interest so far as dramatic theory is concerned. Among the many works in this field may be mentioned Archibald Henderson's *The Changing Drama* (1919); Isaac Goldberg's *The Drama of Transition* (1922); Joseph T. Shipley's *The Quest for Literature* (1931); H. K. Motherwell's *The Theater of Today* (revised, 1927); Stark Young's *The Theater* (1927); Robert Edmond Jones' *The Dramatic Imagination* (1941); Mordecai Gorelik's *New Theaters for Old* (1940); Anita Block's *The Changing World in Plays and Theater* (1939); Arthur Hopkins' *How's Your Second Act?* (revised, 1931); Lee Simonson's *The Stage is Set* (1932); John Gassner's *Masters of the Drama* (1940); Paul Green's *The Hawthorn Tree* (1943); Harold Clurman's *The Fervent Years* (1945).

It is worth while to consult the prefaces of a number of published plays, especially those written by the authors themselves; many of these are illuminating on matters affecting the writers' intentions. See especially the published plays of Paul Green, Lillian Hellman, Clifford Odets, William Saroyan, Irwin Shaw, Maxwell Anderson, John Howard Lawson, Sidney Howard.

Finally, an immense amount of material on drama and occasional papers on technical practice and theory, are to be found in the files of newspapers (especially the New York Sunday *Times*), in trade magazines (*Billboard, Variety, The Dramatic Mirror*); in magazines special-izing in dramatic news, like *Theater Arts, The Drama, Poet Lore.*

WILLIAM T. PRICE

William Thompson Price was born in Kentucky in 1846 and died in New York in 1920. Well educated as a youth, he served in the Civil War, he travelled widely in Europe in the late 60's, attended the Universities of Leipzig and Berlin, and on his return home he studied for the law and was admitted to the bar at Louisville. However, he was more interested in writing than in the law, and he became dramatic critic on the *Courier-Journal.* During the next few years he wrote biographies of actors and one successful play. In the middle 80's he came to New York, where he was in turn dramatic editor on the *Star,* play reader for A. M. Palmer, and adviser to several persons in the theater world, and closely connected with dramatic affairs. Arthur Edwin Krows, author of *Play Production in America* and *Playwriting for Profit,* a student and later on associated with Price, writes that "by 1900 Price had become so concerned about the horde of struggling playwrights who importuned him — especially after he had published his *Technique of the Drama* in 1892 — that with H. A. du Souchet . . . he started his American School of Playwriting in New York (first establishment of its kind in the world). Du Souchet, who acted in an advisory capacity, soon withdrew." Meantime Price continued to serve the theater of his day as adviser to managers and writers, as reviewer, and as legal adviser in plagiarism cases; all this in addition to running his School and giving time and energy to his students. Among the latter he counted such dramatists as Thomas Dixon Jr., Benjamin Chapin, Preston Gibson, Edward Laska, and Norman Lee Swartout.

Krows' *Playwriting for Profit* (N. Y. 1928), a practical manual on technique, is not only a much-needed amplification of Price's basic theories, but is to some extent based upon Price's ideas; not, it should be added, in spite of Krows' own statements, so derivative as might appear from a first reading. In a letter to the editor of the present volume, Krows writes: "It is because Price's work on playmaking technique was written always with intent to use in direct student training that strangers are rarely at once impressed when they first read about Proposition. It is one of those helps whose value becomes evident only as it is diligently applied. Price fashioned it for service and not to invite buyers. . . . It comes as a tool to be applied to a specific job, in the absence of which it seems arbitrary and dull."

Price's principal writings are *The Technique of the Drama* (1892); *The Analysis of Play Construction and Dramatic Principle* (1908); *Why Plays Fail* (1912); *The Philosophy of Dramatic Principle and Method* (issued semi-privately in parts, 1908–9); and *The American Playwright* (1912–1913), a monthly magazine.

THE PROPOSITION [1]

[Chapter VII, *The Proposition*]

(1908)

A dramatic Proposition is the brief logical statement or syllogism of that which has to be demonstrated by the Complete Action of the play.

Its simplest and perhaps its universal form, so far as I have been able to discover, is a statement in three clauses: first, the conditions of the Action; second, the cause of the Action; third, the result of the Action. The third clause involves the problem and may be put as a problem.

Let us first consider a play that is fa-

[1] Reprinted selections from *The Analysis of Play Construction and Dramatic Principle* (N. Y., 1908).

miliar to every reader and theatergoer, *Romeo and Juliet*. Shakespeare had his material for this play in the shape of an Italian romance. The wonderful thing he did consists mainly or notably in the application of his art to it. It is sheer nonsense to imagine that Shakespeare wrote unpremeditatedly and without a systematic and conscious technique. With the possible single exception of Massinger, he was the only dramatist of his period who seemed to possess a complete technique fitted to the stage of his day. Ben Jonson was a scholar, acquainted with Aristotle and the old classic drama, it is true, but Shakespeare was the supreme artist.

He has reduced this romantic Italian story to a definite Proposition. That general Proposition was:— Two young members of families in deadly strife fall in love. They marry. Will it result happily and reunite the families?

Shakespeare, however, had the story before him and could be more definite and could reduce it to individuals at once: Romeo and Juliet, members of the houses of Montague and Capulet, in deadly strife, fall in love. They marry. Will this marriage result happily and reunite the families? The third clause is the problem to be worked out, but the result can be put as a statement. Put as a question or problem, its alternatives have to be answered with a Yes or No. They marry with a happy result? No. The families are reunited? Yes! Put as a statement it requires a setting-forth of the How. All this has to be worked out.

We believe that plays are ordinarily written without a conception of the technical form that we give for a Proposition. To write a play on the general idea that it must have a beginning, a middle and an end, results in many successful plays and just as many failures. What we may call the French method, which undoubtedly involves the idea of a technical Proposition such as we give it, is a little more specific in that it makes the middle of the play the climax and thereby becomes more specific and more scientific. They wrote to and from that climax. I shall point out, later on, that climax used with reference to the Proposition is a dangerous and misleading term. But, in the hands of a dramatist who understands

the art it answers the purpose. We believe it, however, to be less definite and comprehensive than the logical formula of Proposition which we have introduced.

A full understanding and acceptance of the second clause of the Proposition, as we frame it, is of the utmost importance. It represents the cause of the Action. Misapprehension and confusion commonly exist in the minds of the inexpert as to the significance of this term. They are apt to imagine that the cause of the Action is that Romeo and Juliet fall in love. Not at all. That is the beginning of the Action and belongs to the conditions of it. From that starting-point any number of romantic or real happenings could ensue. A play could not be made out of those conditions without something definite, something that we call the cause of the Action. To assign a mere middle and end to a series of happenings would not necessarily make it a play. Even a climax, in the general sense of the most interesting scene or situation, would not help matters. It is because Romeo and Juliet marry, with the swift following consequences, that we have Action.

Sooner or later the dramatist must determine upon the Proposition of his play. He may not get it at once, but a discussion of the method and procuring it must be deferred. It is your business now to understand what a Proposition is and its relation to the other parts of a play.

The play now selected for illustration is an exceedingly simple and effective one, *Ingomar*. The Theme of the author's play was love. Endless plays have been and can yet be written on that Theme, but the general Theme is not definite enough for practical purposes. What kind of love? And so you go on, narrowing it down. Arrived at the Proposition, whether found in a complete story with a dramatic Proposition, or a story be devised to fit a philosophy, the play must resolve itself into a Proposition or the dramatist has no starting-point. There must be nothing abstract about it; it must concern people. A moral Proposition for a play may have its abstract form, but the working Proposition must be concrete.

Your first step upon solid ground will be made when you assure yourself of the truth of this dramatic law and when you convince yourself that it is a universal and inevitable requirement.

Again I repeat the admonition that you make sure that you understand and accept the Proposition as the real starting-point of the construction and subsequent writing of a play. Unless you can reduce your play to a Proposition you have no play. What is your play about? If you cannot answer that in two lines or so, you have no play. . . .

We must confine the Proposition of the play to the idea that controls the play and holds it together from beginning to end. If, then, you can destroy the play by means of a false Proposition, you can also destroy the Proposition by departing from it in the course of the Action of the play. If, in writing a play, a change is made, a departure taken, then you are compelled to go back and make the Proposition conform to it. If you complete a play without having formulated a Proposition and then find that you cannot formulate one,

and cannot make play and Proposition consist, your labor is lost, for there must be a dramatic Proposition or there can be no play.

A Proposition must be susceptible of being worked out; there must be material for it. If a Plot cannot be evolved from it, the Proposition is inadequate. If it is a Proposition for which a play of not more than one or two acts can be devised, it is folly to try to work it out in three or five acts. . . .

The difficulty which an untrained writer experiences in reducing a play to its Proposition, its lowest terms, consists in the necessity of excluding from the Proposition characters that belong to the Plot simply or to the Action simply. If we included the means of carrying out a Proposition we would infringe upon the Plot. . . . The dramatist's mind must be able to make distinctions; otherwise the Proposition, the Plot and the Action would all be the same thing to him. If Proposition means Plot, and Plot means Proposition, and Action means Plot, &c., there would be no earthly use in our establishing the terms at all.

THE PHILOSOPHY OF DRAMATIC PRINCIPLE AND METHOD [1]
(About 1908)

A Proposition is a statement in terms of truth to be demonstrated. You have its counterpart in any proposition in Euclid. Q.E.D. It may be thrown into the form of a syllogism. In every case in court the lawyer is restricted to the pleadings. A man owns a horse; another steals it; the punishment is demanded. In a civil suit it is exactly the same thing. There is a matter at issue. The first clause contains the conditions, the second the cause of the action. It is obvious that the cause of the action in the above example is the stealing of the horse by the man. Destroy either of these two terms in the Proposition, and the case is settled, the Proposition after that — the legal Proposition as a whole — having no value.

[1] Reprinted selections from *The American Playwright*. (N. Y., 1912–13. Originally issued in typewritten and printed form, privately issued about 1908.)

What is your play about? That is the most important thing. It is answered in the Proposition of your play according as it is given in the form of a statement or a problem in its third clause. It should be susceptible of being given in a line or so, for the Proposition is the least common denominator of the action.

If the inexpert writer, not understanding the drama (however much or little he may know of anything or everything else), is asked to give the Proposition of his play he will proceed to make a rambling recital of about everything contained in the play. "What is your play about?" "Love," he answers, smiling in benignant triumph.

That is no Proposition. That gives no idea of a distinct Action. The Bible preaches love. Michelet has written a book on love. Library shelves and wastebaskets are filled with poems on love. Love is infinitely various and intricate. The milkyway of the drama is composed of myriads of plays on love. No, love may be the theme of your play, but not the Proposition.

All of Shakespeare's plays have a theme — love, ambition, jealousy — and so with Molière — avarice, hypocrisy — and so with all plays of the best value. You mistake Theme for Proposition. What do you suppose we have made Theme a separate principle for if it is identical with Proposition? The general Theme may be narrowed down to a definite abstract Proposition, but an abstraction is the negation of drama. A Proposition is objective or nothing. From the very definition of a drama the Proposition must concern people and must be concrete. The moral philosophy of a play is in the nature of a Proposition, and it may easily be the inception of the play, the idea out of which it grows.

How do you get the Proposition of a play? By deduction or induction, by accident or research, from your philosophy of life and from your innermost heart or conviction, or from external happenings that have penetrated to your sympathies. What would a virtuous woman do who was put to the most exacting test? Or, what is the severest test to which a virtuous woman could be put? Such an inquiry might occur to you idly, and it might start you toward a definite Proposition.

As said, it must be definite and complete. It must be reduced to human agencies. The Book of Homilies or any Philosophy of Ethics or Aesthetics can furnish you with all the abstractions and arguments. Wherever you begin you must reach the individual. Your genius is not restricted in its methods of thought until it treads on the sacred ground of the Drama, and then it must pay toll. You must invent or discover the facts to fit your philosophy. Thus the Drama makes brothers of geniuses of all kinds. Whatever his process of thought the true dramatist is necessarily a moralist and philosopher; the situation-writer is not. . . .

A Proposition involves the whole play. It must have a certain magnitude and that action of the play must be commensurate with it. It suggests action, for the last clause requires that a problem be worked out. Doubt is expressed. The facts are given; opposition is encountered — let it be in an affair of love, as in *Romeo and Juliet,* and the question is, Will the marriage be happy? Then, as the action develops, will he or she be able to do this or that? Each turn giving new effort or hope to the characters, so that we are constantly saying, " Will he? " " Will she? " But it is all directed toward the solution of the one main thing at issue. We look to the result of the complete action.

The Proposition, then, must include all in a play from the beginning to the end. It does not and cannot express all of the details, but those details are evolved from it. Question the Proposition, and the means of solution and the subordinate and logical Action will be found. Nothing is said in the Proposition of *Romeo and Juliet* of any of the subordinate characters, or any of the incidents and scenes required in the Action. The Proposition seems meager —and it has to be in order to be comprehensive—but it is definite. It may also be said that it would apply to many plays. That is true, and it explans a saying by Boucicault, who liked to speak in apparent paradoxes and to seem daring in his utterances, that all stories have been written. He could not have meant that all plays have been written, but that meaning is attached to it by the playwright who wants a pretext to become a thief. . . .

Do not then, for a moment, imagine that, from the fact that plays so far as Proposition is concerned fall apparently under distinct heads, novelty and independence of thought are restricted. Individuality always remains, whatever the classification. It would be impossible to frame a Proposition, new as it might seem, upon which only one play could be written.[1]

[1] Krows points out that although Price spoke of "stumbling" on the idea of Proposition after the establishment of his School in 1901, there is evidence, in *The Technique of the Drama* (1892), that the germ idea had taken root in his mind much earlier. For example, on p. 5 of that book, we find the following: " A drama must deal with accepted facts or definitely prove a given proposition."

BRANDER MATTHEWS

James Brander Matthews (the James was soon dropped) was born in New Orleans in 1852. He was educated for the most part in the North, and was graduated from Columbia College in 1871. His lifelong interest in the theater, which began before or during his undergraduate years, was stimulated by extended travel in Europe, where he did a great deal of playgoing. He wrote several plays, some for production by amateur players, and some for the professional stage. At least one of these enjoyed a commercial run.

In 1891 he lectured at Columbia University on literary subjects, and the following year he became a professor of literature. In 1899 he was appointed Professor of Dramatic Literature. This, according to a short biographical account of Matthews in *Authors Today and Yesterday* (1933), was a "landmark in American university development, marking the establishment of the first dramatic chair in an English-speaking university."

From 1899 to 1924, when he retired, Matthews developed, as lecturer, teacher and writer, the principles which underlie his basic contentions that the drama 'was a separate art, and could be studied not in the library, but only in the thea-ter" (Clayton Hamilton). Matthews died in 1929.

The importance of Brander Matthews' teachings consisted partly in his insistence on considering playwriting as a craft based upon more or less rigid principles determined by the physical shape of the theater, the capabilities of the actor, and the audience. His knowledge of the English, French and American theaters of his day, and his familiarity with the theoretical writings of Brunetière and Sarcey, whose basic principles he popularized, did much to stimulate young critics and playwrights in the United States to participate in that widespread movement of the past generation that culminated in the adult drama that began to appear in the early 1920's. Matthews' various theoretical writings on the drama and theater are to be found in many volumes of his collected critical works, but particularly in the following: *Studies of the Stage* (1894); *The Development of the Drama* (1903); *Molière: His Life and Works* (1910); *A Study of the Drama* (1910); *Shakespeare as a Playwright* (1913); *A Book About the Theater* (1916); *The Principles of Playmaking* (1919); *Playwrights on Playmaking* (1919); and *Rip Van Winkle Goes to the Play* (1926). His autobiography, *These Many Years*, appeared in 1917.

THE ART OF THE DRAMATIST [1]
[From *The Development of the Drama*]
(1903)

III

It is, perhaps, going a little too far to assert that the drama can be as independent of literature as painting may be, or as sculpture; and yet this is an

[1] Reprinted extracts, from *The Development of the Drama*, New York, 1903, by permission of the publishers, Charles Scribner's Sons. Copyright, 1903, by Brander Matthews.

overstatement only: it is not an untruth. The painter seeks primarily for pictorial effects, and the sculptor for plastic effects — just as the dramatist is seeking primarily for dramatic effects. On the other hand, there is no denying that the masterpieces of the graphic arts have all of them a poetic quality in addition to their pictorial and plastic qualities. To be recognized as masterpieces, they must needs possess something more than merely technical merits; but without these technical merits they would not be masterpieces. No fresco, no bas-relief, is fine because of its poetic quality alone. In like manner, we may be sure that there is no masterpiece of the drama in which the poetic quality, however remarkable it may be, is not sustained by a solid structure of dramaturgic technic. The great dramatist must be a poet, of course; but first of all he must be a theater-poet, to borrow the useful German term. And it is a German critic — Schlegel — who has drawn attention to the difference in dramatic capacity which subsists among nations equally distinguished for intellect, "so that theatrical talent would seem to be a peculiar quality, essentially distinct from the poetic gift in general." By the phrase "theatrical talent" Schlegel obviously means the dramaturgic faculty, the skill of the born play-maker. Voltaire says somewhere that the success of a poem lies largely in the choice of a subject; and it is even more certain that the success of a play lies in the choice of the special aspects of the subject which shall be shown in action on the stage. If the poet is not a playwright, or if he cannot acquire the playwright's gift of picking out the scenes which will unfailingly move the hearts of the spectators, then his sheer poetic power will not save him, nor any affluence of imagery — just as no luxuriance of decoration would avail to keep a house standing if the foundations were faulty.

This dramaturgic faculty, without which the most melodious poet cannot hope to win acceptance as a dramatist, seems to be generally instinctive. It is a birthright of the play-maker, from whom it can sometimes be acquired by poets not so gifted by nature. For example, Victor Hugo was a poet who was not a born playwright, but who managed to attain the essential principles of the craft — essential principles which poets of the power and sweep of Byron and Browning were never able to grasp. These British bards were without the dramaturgic faculty which was possessed, in some measure, by the unliterary play-makers who devised the Italian comedy-of-masks.

In the early days of any art there is always imperfect differentiation; and the polychromatic bas-reliefs of the Egyptians remind us that it was long before painting and sculpture were separated. Not only are comedy and tragedy not carefully kept apart, but the drama itself is commingled with much that is not truly dramatic, and only by slow degrees is it able to disentangle itself from these extraneous matters. Even in the days of the great Greeks a lyric element survived in their tragedies which was often quite undramatic; and even in England, under Elizabeth, the stage was sometimes made to serve as a pulpit on which a sermon was preached, or as a platform on which a lecture was delivered, while the action of the play was forced to stand still.

There is also to be noted in every period of play-making a frequent element of mere spectacle. The rhythmic movements of the Greek chorus in the orchestra and their statuesque attitudes were meant to take the eye, like the coronation processions in the English chronicle-play of "Henry VIII."

IV

. . . [These] are mere accidental accessories; and they have no vital relation to the fundamental principles of dramaturgy. By slow degrees the dramatist gets control of his material, and comes to a conscious appreciation of the necessities of his art. He may not be able to formulate the conditions which these necessities impose, but he has an intuitive perception of their requirements. These dramaturgic principles are not mere rules laid down by theoretical critics, who have rarely any acquaintance with the actual theater; they are laws, inherent in the nature of the art itself, standing eternal, as immitigable to-day as when Sophocles was alive, or Shakespere, or Molière. It is because these laws are unchanging that the observation of the modern theater helps to give us an insight into the methods of the ancient theater. And we can go a step further, and confess that the latest burlesque in a music-hall, with its topical songs and its parodies, may be of immediate assistance to us in seizing the intent and in understanding the methods of Aristophanes.

To M. Ferdinand Brunetière — who profited, perhaps, by a hint of Hegel's — we owe the clearest statement of one important law only dimly perceived by earlier critics. He declares that the drama differs from the other forms of literature in that it must always deal with some exertion of the human will. If a play is really to interest us, it must present a struggle; its chief character must desire something, striving for it with all the forces of his being. Aristotle has defined tragedy as " the imitation of an action," but by action he does not mean mere movement — the fictitious bustle often found in melodrama and in farce. Perhaps the Greek critic intended *action* to be interpreted *struggle,* a struggle in which the hero knows what he wants, and wants it with all his might, and does his best to get it. He may be thwarted by some overpowering antagonist, or may be betrayed by some internal weakness of his own soul; but the strength of the play and its interest to the spectator will lie in the balance of the contending forces. . . .

A determined will, resolute in seeking its own end, this is what we always find in the dramatic form; and this is what we do not find in the lyric or the epic. In the lyric the poet is satisfied if he is able to set forth his own sentiment. The epic poet — with whom the novelist must needs be classed nowadays — has to do mainly with adventure and with character. His narrative is not necessarily dramatic; it may, if he should so prefer, be as placid as a mill-pond. There is no obligation on the novelist to deal with what Stevenson has finely called the great passionate crises of existence " when duty and inclination come nobly to the grapple." He may do so if he chooses, and if he does, his novel is then truly dramatic; but he need not deal with this conflict unless he likes, and not a few novels of distinction are not intended to be dramatic. Gil Blas, Tom Jones, and Waverley, Mr. Pickwick and Tartarin of Tarascon, Silas Lapham and Huckleberry Finn, are none of them beings of unfaltering determination, nor do they exert a controlling influence over the conduct of the stories to which they have given their names. Each of them is more or less a creature of accident and a victim of circumstance. No one of them is master of his own fate, or even steersman of his own bark on the voyage of life. M. Brunetière has drawn our attention to the many resemblances between " Gil Blas " and the " Marriage of Figaro " in local color and in moral tone; and then he points out that the comic hero of the novel is the sport of chance— he is passive; while the comic hero of the play is active, he has made up his mind to defend his bride against his master; and this struggle is the core of the comedy. The drama of Beaumarchais might be turned into a narrative easily enough; but the story of Lesage could never be made into a play. And here we may perceive a reason why the modern novel of character-analysis can very seldom be dramatized successfully. . . .

There is yet another corollary of this law of M. Brunetière's; or at least there is a chance to use it here to elucidate a principle often insisted upon by another French critic. The late Francisque Sarcey maintained that every subject for a play, every theme, every plot, contained certain possible scenes which the playwright was bound to present on the stage. These he called the *scènes à faire,* the scenes which had to be done, which could not be shirked, but must be shown in action. He asserted that the spectator vaguely desires these scenes, and is dumbly disappointed if they take place behind closed doors and if they are only narrated. Now, if the drama deals with a struggle, then the incidents of the plot most likely to arouse and sustain the interest of the audience are those in which the contending forces are seen grappling with one another; and these are therefore the *scènes à faire,* the scenes that have to be set upon the stage before the eyes of the spectators.

Thus it is in the presence of the public that Sophocles brings Oedipus to the full discovery of the fatal secret he has persisted in seeking. Thus Shakspere lets us behold a street-brawl of the Montagues and Capulets before making us witnesses of the love at first sight of Romeo and Juliet. Nor is Shakspere satisfied to have some minor character tell us how Iago dropped the poison of jealousy into

Othello's ear: he makes us see it with our own eyes,— just as Molière makes us hear Tartuffe's casuistical pleading with Orgon's wife. One of the most obvious defects of French tragedy, especially in its decadence toward the end of the eighteenth century, is the frequent neglect or suppression of these necessary scenes and the constant use of mere messengers to narrate the episodes which the spectator would rather have beheld for himself. Victor Hugo remarked that at the performance of a tragedy of this type the audience was ever ready to say to the dramatist that what was being talked about seemed as though it might be interesting — "then why not let us see it for ourselves?"

V

M. Brunetière's law helps us to perceive the necessary subject-matter of the drama; and M. Sarcey's suggestion calls our attention to the necessary presentation of the acutest moments of the struggle before our eyes. The drama has other laws also, due to the fact that it is an art; it has its conventions by which alone it is allowed to differ from nature. In every art there is an implied contract between the artist and the public, permitting him to vary from the facts of life, and authorizing him to translate these facts and to transpose them as his special art may require. . . .

The conventions of the drama, its permitted variations from the facts of life, are some of them essential, and therefore eternal; and some of them are accidental only, and therefore temporary. It is a condition precedent to any enjoyment of a play that the fourth wall of every room shall be removed, so that we can see what is going on, also that the actors shall keep their faces turned toward us, and that they shall raise their voices so that we can hear what they have to say. It is essential, moreover, that the dramatist, having chosen his theme, shall present it to us void of all the accessories that would encumber it in real life, showing us only the vital episodes, omitting whatever may be less worthy of our attention, and ordering his plot so that everything is clear before our eyes, to enable us to understand at once every fresh development as the story unfolds itself. And as

the action is thus compacted and heightened, so must the dialogue also be condensed and strengthened. It is only a brief time that we have to spend in the theater; and therefore must the speech of every character be stripped of the tautology, of the digressions, of the irrelevancies which dilute every-day conversation.

These things are essential, and we find them alike in the ancient drama and in the modern. . . .

Temporary and accidental conventions seem natural to us if we happen to be accustomed to them, but they strike us as grossly unnatural when they are unfamiliar. We do not object if a flimsy frame of canvas is lowered before our eyes to represent the castle of Elsinore, or if a stone wall suddenly becomes transparent that Faust may have a vision of Margaret. But we are inclined to smile at the black-robed attendant who hovers about the Japanese actor to provide a fan or a cushion, and who is supposed to be invisible or even non-existent. We should be taken aback if, after a murder was committed off the stage, a door suddenly flew open, revealing the criminals and the corpse posed in a living picture; and yet this is said to have been a device of the Greek theater. And we should laugh outright if we could listen to one of the medieval mysteries as they were acted in Portugal, when we heard the devil speaking Spanish, as it was always the custom of the Portuguese to represent him. . . .

VI

As a drama is intended to be performed by actors, in a theater, and before an audience, the dramatist, as he composes, must always bear in mind the players, the playhouse, and the playgoers. The lyric poet needs to take thought only for the fit expression of his mood of the moment; and even the epic poet, if haply he had a patron, could be independent of his contemporaries. But no dramatic poet can be satisfied until he has seen his work in the theater itself, where his characters are made flesh and blood before his eyes, and where he can feel the thrill of the audience at his communicable emotion.

Of these three conditions in conscious

conformity with which the dramatist labors, probably the least variable is the personality of the actor. The playhouse has taken many shapes in different climes, and the spectator must change with civilization itself; whereas the histrionic temperament is very much the same throughout the ages. It is well to remember that the actor must always do his work, not in private, like the poet or the painter, but in public, like the orator; and that the instrument of his art is always his own person. These are reasons why it is hard for him to escape self-consciousness. For the opportunity to perform he is dependent on the dramatist, although he cannot help believing that he must understand the principles of his own art better than any one else. This is a reason why he may seem sometimes intolerant or overmasterful. But he loves his art loyally, and clutches eagerly at every chance to exercise it and to develop his own virtuosity. . . . It is this dependence of the dramaturgic artist on the histrionic which makes the drama so complex an art. The work of the dramatist can be revealed completely only by the labor of the actors. . . .

However little the psychology of the tragic comedians has changed in the succeeding centuries, there have been many modifications in the shape and size and circumstances of the theaters in which they perform; and these modifications have exerted a potent influence on the successive forms of the drama. . . . Perhaps the severe dignity of Greek tragedy was caused by the immense size of the Theater of Dionysus, where many thousand citizens gathered under the open sky; and, in like manner, may not some portion of the rapidity and variety of the Elizabethan drama have been due to the unadorned platform thrust out into the yard of the Globe Theater?

The tragedies of Shakspere were performed by daylight in a playhouse modeled on the courtyard of an inn and not wholly roofed; the comedies of Molière were brought out in an altered tennis-court, on a shallow stage lighted by candles; the "School for Scandal" was written for the huge Drury Lane Theater, with its broad proscenium-arch, dimly lit by flaring oil-lamps; and the "Gay Lord Quex" was produced in one of the smaller theaters of London, with a proscenium like a picture-frame, brilliantly illumined by the electric light. After these examples it is absurd to deny that the condition of the building in which a play is performed may modify the structure of the play itself.

Far more powerful than the influence of the theater or of the actor upon the dramatist is the influence of the audience, an influence not on the form of the play, but on its substance. As those "who live to please must please to live," so the play must be what the audience makes it. If the spectators are all coarse brutes, the drama will be coarse and brutal; and if they are fun-loving and free from sickly sentimentality, then it is possible for the playwright to indulge in romantic-comedy. The drama is thus, of necessity, the most democratic of the arts; and any attempt to organize it on an aristocratic basis — such as Goethe ventured upon in Weimar — is foredoomed to failure. The drama appeals always to the broad public, and never to any self-styled upper class. A great poet may be haughty and reserved, and ready to retire into an ivory tower; but a great dramatist must needs have an understanding of his fellow-man; he must have toleration and, above all, sympathy.

The influence of the spectator upon the playwright is like the pressure of the atmosphere upon man: he may never even think about it, but all his organs are adjusted to it none the less. Schlegel remarked that "much must always depend on the capacities and humors of the audience, and, consequently, on the national character in general, and the particular degree of mental culture"; and he might have gone further and asserted that the particular degree of moral culture was equally important. . . .

The dramatist does not appeal to the spectators as individuals; he appeals to the audience as a whole, the audience having a collective soul which is not quite the same as the sum total of their several souls. A crowd, as such, is not a mere composite-photograph of its constituent persons; it has a certain personality of its own. By sheer force of juxtaposition the characteristics which the majority have in common are made more powerful, while the divergent characteristics of the individuals are subordinated or eliminated. When he is one of a multitude a man feels and thinks for the moment like the multitude, although when he is alone again he may wonder why he yielded. As the dramatists must strive to arouse the emotions of the multitude, they cannot consider the special likings or the special knowledge of any single man or of any minor group of men. They must try to find the greatest common denominator of the throng. That is to say, they must ever seek the universal — for it is only at their peril that they can use the particular.

VII

Desiring to please the audience as a whole, the dramatists are always ready to accept its verdict as final. There is no immediate appeal from this judgment, rendered in the theater itself, whether it is favorable or adverse. As Regnard makes the comedian say, "It is the public which determines the fate of works of wit — and our fate; and when we see it come in crowds to a new play we judge that the piece is good, and we do not care for any other assurance." And here the comedian was indisputably right; the approval of the public is the first proof of worthy success, for there are no good plays save those which have been applauded in the playhouse. The recognized masterpieces of the drama have all of them been popular in their own day. Sophocles and Shakspere, Lope de Vega and Molière, Sheridan and Beaumar-

chais, were, every one of them, widely appreciated by their contemporaries. True it is, also, that there have been other playwrights whose contemporary success was undeniable and whose fame is now faded — Heywood, for example, and Kotzebue and Scribe, in whose works posterity has failed to find the element of permanency.

Although the works of Heywood and Kotzebue and Scribe call for no consideration from a lover of literature only, since purely literary merit is just what they lack, they still demand attention from a student of dramatic literature, who can spy out in them the selfsame qualities which gave immediate success also to the masterpieces of the great dramatists. The drama is an art which has developed slowly and steadily, and which is still alive; its history has the same essential unity, the same continuity, that we are now beginning to see more clearly in the history of the whole world. Its principles, like the principles of every other art, are eternal and unchanging, whatever strange aspects the art may assume. As history is said to be only past politics, and politics to be in fact only present history, so in dramatic literature what once was helps us to understand what now is, and what now is aids us to appreciate what once was. If only we could behold all the links we should be able to trace an unbroken chain from the crudest mythological pantomime of primitive man down to the severest problem-play of the stern Scandinavian, whose example has been so stimulating to the modern stage.

GEORGE PIERCE BAKER

George Pierce Baker was born at Providence, R. I., in 1866. After his graduation from Harvard in 1887 he began his long teaching career, becoming an instructor at his Alma Mater the following year and an assistant professor in 1895. Some time toward the end of the century he began to take an active interest in the drama as a living and growing thing rather than as a subject for literary

and antiquarian research. As Director of the 47 Workshop at Harvard he conducted courses in playwriting which attracted many men and women who were later on to make their marks in the professional theater as playwrights, managers, critics, directors, actors and scene designers. Among his many students only a few are here enumerated: Eugene O'Neill, George Abbott, Philip Barry

Sidney Howard, Robert Edmond Jones, John Mason Brown. Baker's work was continued at Yale when he became Professor of the History and Technique of Drama at the University Theater in 1925. Baker's writings include text-books on argumentation, prefaces to classic dramas, several volumes of student-written plays; *The Development of Shakespeare* *as a Dramatist* (1907), and *Dramatic Technique* (1919). In the last-named book he has attempted to summarize the results of his long years of practical teaching. (For various personal recollections of Baker and a good deal of information on his work and students, see *George Pierce Baker, A Memorial,* 1939.) He died in 1936.

THE ESSENTIALS OF DRAMA: ACTION AND EMOTION [1]

[From *Dramatic Technique*]

(1919)

What is the common aim of all dramatists? Twofold: first, as promptly as possible to win the attention of the audience; secondly, to hold that interest steady or, better, to increase it till the final curtain falls. It is the time limit to which all dramatists are subject which makes the immediate winning of attention necessary. The dramatist has no time to waste. How is he to win this attention? By what is done in the play; by characterization; by the language the people of his play speak; or by a combination of two or more of these. Today we hear much discussion whether it is what is done, *i.e.* action, or characterization, or dialogue which most interests a public. Which is the chief essential in good drama? History shows indisputably that the drama in its beginnings, no matter where we look, depended most on action. . . .

Look where we will, then, — at the beginnings of drama in Greece, in England centuries later, or among savage peoples today — the chief essential in winning and holding the attention of the spectator was imitative movement by the actors, that is, physical action. Nor, as the drama develops, does physical action cease to be central. . . . In Shakespeare's day, audiences again and again, as they watched plays of Dekker, Heywood, and many another dramatist, willingly accepted inadequate characterization and weak dialogue so long as the action was

1 Reprinted excerpts from *Dramatic Technique* (1919), by permission of the publisher, Houghton Mifflin Company. Copyright, 1919, by George Pierce Baker.

absorbing. . . . The history of the Drama shows that only rarely does even a group of people for a brief time care more for plays of characterization and dialogue than for plays of action. Throughout the ages, the great public, cultivated as well as uncultivated, have cared for action first, then, as aids to a better understanding of the action of the story, for characterization and dialogue. Now, for more than a century, the play of mere action has been so popular that it has been recognized as a special form, namely, melodrama. This type of play, in which characterization and dialogue have usually been entirely subordinated to action, has been the most widely attended. . . . From the practice of centuries the feeling that action is really central in drama has become instinctive with most persons who write plays without preconceived theories. Watch a child making his first attempt at play-writing. In ninety-nine cases out of a hundred, the play will contain little except action. There will be slight characterization, if any, and the dialogue will be mediocre at best. The young writer has depended almost entirely upon action because instinctively, when he thinks of drama, he thinks of action.

Nor, if we paused to consider, is this dependence of drama upon action surprising. "From emotions to emotions" is the formula for any good play. To paraphrase a principle of geometry, "A play is the shortest distance from emotions to emotions." The emotions to be reached are those of the audience. The emotions conveyed are those of the people on the stage or of the dramatist as he has watched the people represented. Just herein lies the importance of action for the dramatist: it is his quickest means of arousing emotion in an audience. Which is more popular with the masses, the man of action or the thinker? The world at large believes, and rightly that, as a rule, "Actions speak louder than words." The dramatist knows that not what a man thinks he thinks, but what at a crisis he does, instinctively, spontaneously, best shows his character. The dramatist knows, too, that though we may think, when discussing patriotism in the abstract, that we have firm ideas about it, what reveals our real beliefs is our action at a crisis in the history of our country. . . . Is it any wonder, then, that popular vote has declared action the best revealer of feeling and, therefore, that the dramatist, in writing his plays, depends first of all upon action? If any one is disposed to cavil at action as popular merely with the masses and the less cultivated, let him ask himself, "What, primarily in other people interests me — what these people do or why they do it?" Even if he belong to the group, relatively very small in the mass of humanity, most interested by "Why did these people do this?" he must admit that till he knows clearly what the people did, he cannot take up the question which more interests him. For the majority of auditors, action is of first importance in drama: even for the group which cares far more for characterization and dialogue it is necessary as preparing the way for that characterization and dialogue on which they insist.

Consider for a moment the nature of the attention which a dramatist may arouse. Of course it may be only of the same sort which an audience gives a lecturer on a historical or scientific subject, — a readiness to hear and to try to understand what he has to present, — close but unemotional attention. Comparatively few people, however, are capable of sustained attention when their emotions are not called upon. How many lectures last over an hour? Is not the "popular lecturer" popular largely because he works into his lecture many anecdotes and dramatic illustrations in order to avoid or to lighten the strain of close, sustained at-

tention? There is, undoubtedly, a public which can listen to ideas with the same keen enjoyment which most auditors feel when listening to something which stirs them emotionally, but as compared with the general public it is infinitesimal. Understanding this, the dramatist stirs the emotions of his hearers by the most concrete means at his command, his quickest communication from brain to brain, — action just for itself or illustrating character. . . .

Just what, however, is this action which in drama is so essential? To most people it means physical or bodily action which rouses sympathy or dislike in an audience. The action of melodrama certainly exists largely for itself. We expect and get little but physical action for its own sake when a play is announced as was the well-known melodrama, *A Race for Life.*

As Melodramatically and Masterfully Stirring, Striking and Sensational as Phil Sheridan's Famous Ride.
Superb, Stupendous Scenes in Sunset Regions.
Wilderness Wooings Where Wild Roses Grow.
The Lights and Shades of Rugged Border Life.
Chinese Comedy to Make Confucius Chuckle.
The Realism of the Ranch and Race Track.
The Hero Horse That Won a Human Life.
An Equine Beauty Foils a Murderous Beast.
Commingled Gleams of Gladness, Grief, and Guilt.
Dope, Dynamite and Devilish Treachery Distanced.
Continuous Climaxes That Come Like Cloudbursts.

Some plays depend almost wholly upon mere bustle and rapidly shifting movement, much of it wholly unnecessary to the plot. . . .

If physical action in and of itself is so often dramatic, is all physical action dramatic? That is, does it always create emotion in an onlooker? No. It goes for naught unless it rouses his interest. Of itself, or because of the presentation given it by the dramatist, it must rouse in the onlooker an emotional response. A boy seeing "Crazy Mary" stalking the street in bedizened finery and bowing right and left, may see nothing interesting in her. More probably her actions will move him to jeer and jibe at her. Let some spectator, however, tell the boy of the tragedy in Crazy Mary's younger life which left her unbalanced, and, if he has any right feeling, the boy's attitude will begin to change. He may even give over the jeering he has begun. Reveal to him exactly what is passing in the crazed mind of the woman, and his mere interest will probably turn to sympathy. Characterization, preceding and accompanying action, creates sympathy or repulsion for the figure or figures involved. This sympathy or repulsion in turn converts mere interest into emotional response of the keenest kind. Though physical action is undoubtedly fundamental in drama, no higher form than crude melodrama or crude farce can develop till characterization appears to explain and interpret action. . . .

The first scene of Act I of *Romeo and Juliet* is full of interesting physical action — quarrels, fighting, and the halting of the fight by the angry Prince. The physical action, however, characterizes in every instance, from the servants of the two factions to Tybalt, Benvolio, the Capulets, the Montagues, and the Prince. Moreover, this interesting physical action, which is all the more interesting because it characterizes, is interesting in the third place because in every instance it helps to an understanding of the story. It shows so intense an enmity between the two houses that even the servants cannot meet in the streets without quarreling. By its characterization it prepares for the parts Benvolio and Tybalt are to play in later scenes. It motivates the edict of banishment which is essential if the tragedy of the play is to occur. . . .

Even physical action, then, may interest for itself, or because it characterizes, or because it helps on the story, or for two or more of these reasons.

If we examine other extracts from famous plays we shall, however, find ourselves wondering whether action in drama must not mean something besides mere physical action. . . .

The fact is, the greatest drama of all time . . . uses action much less for its own sake than to reveal mental states which are to rouse sympathy or repulsion in an audience. In brief, marked mental activity may be quite as dramatic as mere physical action. Hamlet may sit quietly by his fire as he speaks the soliloquy "To be, or not to be," yet by what we already know of him and what the lines reveal we are moved to the deepest sympathy for his tortured state. . . .

Many an inexperienced dramatist fails to see the force of these words of Maeterlinck: "An old man, seated in his armchair, waiting patiently, with his lamp beside him — submitting his bent head to the presence of his soul and his destiny — motionless as he is does yet live in reality a deeper, more human, and more universal life than the lover who strangles his mistress, the captain who conquers in battle, or the husband who 'avenges his honor.'" If an audience can be made to feel and understand the strong but contained emotion of this motionless figure, he is rich dramatic material. . . .

[We] must include mental as well as physical activity in any definition of the word *dramatic*. Provided a writer can convey to his audience the excited mental state of one or more of his characters, then this mental activity is thoroughly dramatic. That is, neither physical nor mental activity is in itself dramatic; all depends on whether it naturally arouses, or can be made by the author to arouse, emotion in an audience. Just as we had to add to physical action which arouses emotional response of itself, physical action which is made to arouse response because it develops the story or illustrates character, we must now add action which is not physical, but mental.

There is even another chance for confusion. A figure sitting motionless not because he is thinking hard but because blank in mind may yet be dramatic. Utter inaction, both physical and mental, of a figure represented on the stage does not mean that it is necessarily undramatic. If the dramatist can make an audience feel the terrible tragedy of the contrast between what might have been and what is for this perfectly quiet unthinking figure, he rouses emotion in his hearers, and in so doing makes his material dramatic. Suppose, too, that the expressionless figure is an aged father or mother very dear to some one in the play who has strongly won the sympathy of the audience. The house takes fire. The flames draw nearer and nearer the unconscious figure. We are made to look at the situation through the eyes of the character — some child or relative — to whom the scene, were he present, would mean torture. Instantly the figure, because of the way in which it is represented, becomes dramatic. Here again, however, the emotion of the audience could hardly be aroused except through characterization of the figure as it was or might have been, or of the child or relative who has won our sympathy. Again, too, characterization so successful must depend a good deal on well-chosen words.

This somewhat elaborate analysis should have made three points clear. First, we may arouse emotion in an audience by mere physical action; by physical action which also develops the story, or illustrates character, or does both; by mental rather than physical action, if clearly and accurately conveyed to the audience; and even by inaction, if characterization and dialogue by means of other figures are of high order. Secondly, as the various illustrations have been examined, it must have become steadily more clear that while action is popularly held to be central in drama, emotion is really the essential. Because it is the easiest expression of emotion to understand, physical action, which without illuminating characterization and dialogue can express only a part of the world of emotion, has been too often accepted as expressing all the emotion the stage can present. Thirdly, it should be clear that a statement one meets too frequently in books on the drama, that certain stories or characters, above all certain well-known books, are essentially undramatic material is at least dubious. The belief arises from the fact that the story, character, or idea, as usually presented, seems to demand much analysis and description, and almost to preclude illustrative action. In the past few years, however, the drama of mental states and the drama which has revealed emotional significance in seeming or real inaction, has been proving that "nothing human is foreign" to the drama. A dramatist may see in the so-called undramatic material emotional values. If so, he will develop a technique which will create in his public a satisfaction equal to that which the so-called undramatic story, character, or idea could give in story form. Of course he will treat it differently in many respects because he is writing not to be read but to be heard, and to affect the emotions, not of the individual, but of a large group taken as a group. He will prove that till careful analysis has shown in a given story, character, or idea, no possibility of arousing the same or dissimilar emotions in an audience, we cannot say that this or that is dramatic or undramatic, but only: "This material will require totally different presentation if it is to be dramatic on the stage, and only a person of acumen, experience with audiences, and inventive technique can present it effectively."

The misapprehension just analyzed rests not only on the misconception that action rather than emotion is the essential in drama, but also largely on a careless use of the word *dramatic*. In popular use this word means *material for drama*, or *creative of emotional response*, or *perfectly fitted for production under the conditions of the theatre*. If we examine a little, in the light of this chapter, the nature and purpose of a play, we shall see that *dramatic* should stand only for the first two definitions, and that *theatric* must be used for the third. Avoiding the vague definition *material for drama*, use *dramatic* only as *creative of emotional response* and the confusion will disappear.

A play exists to create emotional response in an audience. The response may be to the emotions of the people in the play or the emotions of the author as he watches these people. Where would satirical comedy be if, instead of sharing the amusement, disdain, contempt or moral anger of the dramatist caused by his figures, we responded exactly to their follies or evil moods? All ethical drama gets its force by creating in an audience the feelings toward the people in the play held by the author. Dumas fils, Ibsen, Brieux prove the truth of this statement. The writer of the satirical or the ethical play, obtruding his own personality as in the case of Ben Jonson, or with fine impersonality as in the case of Congreve or Molière, makes his feelings ours. It is an obvious corollary of this statement that the emotions aroused in an audience need not be the same as those felt by the people on the stage. They may be in the sharpest contrast. Any one experienced in drama knows that the most intensely comic effects often come from people acting very seriously. . . . In brief, the dramatic may rouse the same, allied, or even contrasting emotions in an onlooker.

Nor need the emotion roused in an audience by actor or author be exactly the same in amount. The actress who abandons herself to the emotions of the part she is playing soon exhausts her nervous vitality. It would be the same if audiences listening to the tragic were permitted to feel the scenes as keenly as the figures of the story. On the other hand, in some cases, if the comic figure on the stage felt his comicality as strongly as the audience which is speechless with laughter, he could not go on, and the scene would fail. Evidently, an audience may be made, as the dramatist wills, to feel more or less emotion than the characters of the play.

That it is duplication of emotion to the same, a less, or a greater extent or the creation of contrasting emotion which underlies all drama, from melodrama, riotous farce and even burlesque to high-comedy and tragedy, must be firmly grasped if a would-be dramatist is to steer his way clearly through the many existing and confusing definitions of *dramatic.* For instance, Brunetière said, "Drama is the representation of the will of man in contrast to the mysterious powers of natural forces which limit and belittle us; it is one of us thrown living upon the stage, there to struggle against fatality, against social law, against one of his fellow mortals, against himself, if need be, against the emotions, the interests, the prejudices, the folly, the malevolence of those around him." [1] That is, by this definition, conflict is central in drama. But we know that in recent drama particularly, the moral drifter has many a time aroused our sympathy. Surely inertness, supineness, stupidity,

[1] *Études Critiques,* vol. VII, p. 207.

and even torpor may be made to excite emotion in an audience. Conflict covers a large part of drama but not all of it.

Mr. William Archer, in his *Play-Making,* declares that "a crisis" is the central matter in drama, but one immediately wishes to know what constitutes a crisis, and we have defined without defining. When he says elsewhere that that is dramatic which "by representation of imaginary personages is capable of interesting an average audience assembled in a theatre," [1] he almost hits the truth. If we rephrase this definition: "That is dramatic which by representation of imaginary personages interests, through its emotions, an average audience assembled in a theatre," we have a definition which will better stand testing.

Is all dramatic material *theatric?* No, for *theatric* does not necessarily mean *sensational, melodramatic, artificial.* It should mean, and it will be so used in this book, *adapted for the purpose of the theatre.* Certainly all dramatic material, that is, material which arouses or may be made to arouse emotion, is not fitted for use in the theatre when first it comes to the hand of the dramatist. . . . Even material so emotional in its nature as to be genuinely dramatic may need careful reworking if it is to succeed as a play, that is, if it is to become properly *theatric.* Drama, then, is presentation of an individual or group of individuals so as to move an audience to responsive emotion of the kind desired by the dramatist and the amount required. This response must be gained under the conditions which a dramatist finds or develops in a theatre; that is, dramatic material must be made theatric in the right sense of the word before it can become drama.

To summarize: accurately conveyed emotion is the great fundamental in all good drama. It is conveyed by action, characterization, and dialogue. It must be conveyed in a space of time, usually not exceeding two hours and a half, and under the existing physical conditions of the stage, or with such changes as the dramatist may bring about in them. It must be conveyed, not directly through the author, but indirectly through the actors. In order that the dramatic may

[1] *Play-Making,* p. 48. William Archer. Small, Maynard & Co., Boston.

become theatric in the right sense of the word, the dramatic must be made to meet all these conditions successfully. These conditions affect action, characterization, and dialogue. A dramatist must study the ways in which the dramatic has been and may be made theatric: that is what technique means.

GEORGE JEAN NATHAN

George Jean Nathan was born at Fort Wayne, Ind., in 1882. He was graduated from Cornell University in 1904. After a year in Europe he returned to the United States and worked for a year or two on the editorial staff of the New York *Herald*. In 1908 he began writing for *Smart Set* magazine, to which he contributed dramatic reviews and other material until 1923. Together with H. L. Mencken he was editor of the same magazine, beginning in 1914. In 1924 he and Mencken founded the *American Mercury*, but the following year he dropped his editorial work, remaining as critic and contributing editor until 1930. Nathan has reviewed plays continuously during all his adult life, in various newspapers and magazines, and the best of his reviews have been reprinted in books, which have appeared since 1916 at an average rate of about one a year. He has tried his hand on occasion at playwriting, and has also written essays and books on nondramatic subjects; he has likewise encouraged and championed new playwrights, native and foreign. This is especially true of his relations with O'Neill and Saroyan. A conscientious student of the history of his subject, he is familiar with the theaters and dramatic literatures of several foreign countries, including his own. Though his style is informal, colloquial, and entertaining, he has — especially in *The Critic and the Drama* — evolved a consistent theory of the drama and established critical standards of a high, if occasionally restricted and somewhat limited, order. Among his many volumes of collected criticism a few are here mentioned: *Another Book on the Theater* (1916); *Mr. George Jean Nathan Presents* (1917); *The World in Falseface* (1923); *Materia Critica* (1924); *Art of the Night* (1928); *The Entertainment of a Nation* (1942). During the past few years Nathan's collected reviews have been appearing under the general titles of *The Theater Book of the Year*.

THE DRAMA AS AN ART[1]
[From *The Critic and the Drama*]
(1922)

I

If the best of criticism, in the familiar description of Anatole France, lies in the adventure of a soul among masterpieces, the best of drama may perhaps be described as the adventure of a masterpiece among souls. Drama is fine or impover-

ished in the degree that it evokes from such souls a fitting and noble reaction.

Drama is, in essence, a democratic art in constant brave conflict with aristocracy of intelligence, soul, and emotion. When drama triumphs, a masterpiece like "Hamlet" comes to life. When the conflict ends in a draw, a drama half-way between greatness and littleness is the result — a drama, say, like "El Gran Galeoto." When the struggle ends in defeat, the result is a "Way Down East" or a "Lightnin'." This, obviously, is not to say that great drama may not be popular drama, nor popular drama great drama, for I speak of drama here not as this play or that, but as a specific art. And it is as a specific art that it finds its test and trial, not in its own intrinsically democratic soul, but in the extrinsic aristocratic soul that is taste, and connoisseurship, and final judgment. Drama that has come to be at once great and popular has ever first been given the imprimatur, not of democratic souls, but of aristocratic. Shakespeare and Molière triumphed over aristocracy of intelligence, soul and emotion before that triumph was presently carried on into the domain of inferior intelligence, soul and emotion. In our own day, the drama of Hauptmann, Shaw and the American O'Neill has come into its popular own only after it first achieved the imprimatur of what we may term the unpopular, or undemocratic, theatre. Aristocracy cleared the democratic path for Ibsen, as it cleared it, in so far as possible, for Rostand and Hugo von Hofmannsthal.

Great drama is the rainbow born when the sun of reflection and understanding smiles anew upon an intelligence and emotion which that drama has respectively shot with gleams of brilliant lightning and drenched with the rain of brilliant tears. Great drama, like great men and great women, is always just a little sad. Only idiots may be completely happy. Reflection, sympathy, wisdom, gallant gentleness, experience — the chords upon which great drama is played — these are wistful chords. The commonplace urge that drama, to be truly great, must uplift is, in the sense that the word uplift is used, childish. The mission of great drama is not to make numskulls glad that they are alive, but to make them speculate why they are permitted to be alive at all. And since this is the mission of great drama — if ts mission may, indeed, be reduced to any phrase — it combines within itself, together with this mystical and awe-struck appeal to the proletariat, a direct and agreeable appeal to such persons as are, by reason of their metaphysical perception and emotional culture, superior to and contemptuous of the proletariat. Fine drama, in truth, is usually just a trifle snobbish. It has no traffic with such

souls as are readily made to feel "uplifted" by spurious philosophical nostrums and emotional sugar pills. Its business is with what the matchless Dryden hailed "souls of the highest rank and truest understanding": souls who find a greater uplift in the noble depressions of Brahms' first trio, Bartolommeo's Madonna della Misericordia, and Joseph Conrad's "Youth" than in the easy buoyancies of John Philip Sousa, Howard Chandler Christy and Rupert Hughes. The aim of great drama is not to make men happy with themselves as they are, but with themselves as they might, yet alas cannot, be. As Gautier has it, "The aim of art is not exact reproduction of nature, but creation, by means of forms and colors, of a microcosm wherein may be produced dreams, sensations, and ideas inspired by the aspect of the world." If drama is irrevocably a democratic art and uplift of the great masses of men its noblest end, Mrs. Porter's "Pollyanna" must endure as a work of dramatic art a thousand times finer than Corneille's "Polyeucte."

Drama has been strictly defined by the ritualists in a dozen different ways. "Drama," says one, "must be based on character, and the action proceed from character." "Drama," stipulates another, "is not an imitation of men, but of an action and of life: character is subsidiary to action." "Drama," promulgates still another, "is the struggle of a will against obstacles." And so on, so on. Rules, rules and more rules. Pigeonholes upon pigeon-holes. Good drama is anything that interests an intelligently emotional group of persons assembled together in an illuminated hall. Molière, wise among dramatists, said as much, though in somewhat more, and doubtless too, sweeping words. Throughout the ages of drama there will be always Romanticists of one sort or another, brave and splendid spirits, who will have to free themselves from the definitions and limitations imposed upon them by the neo-Bossus and Boileaus, and the small portion Voltaires, La Harpes and Marmontels. Drama is struggle, a conflict of wills? Then what of "Ghosts"? Drama is action? Then what of "Nachtasyl"? Drama is character? Then what of "The Dream Play"? "A 'character' upon the stage," wrote the author of the last named, "has become a creature ready-made — a mere mechanism that drives the man — I do not believe in these theatrical 'characters.'"

Of all the higher arts, drama is organically perhaps the simplest. Its anatomy is composed of all the other arts, high and low, stripped to their elementals. It is a synthesis of those portions of these other arts that, being elemental, are most easily assimilable on the part of the multitude. It is a snatch of music, a bit of painting, a moment of dancing, a slice of sculpture, draped upon the skeleton of literature. At its highest, it ranks with literature, but never above it. One small notch below, it ranks only with itself, in its own isolated and generically peculiar field. Drama, indeed, is dancing literature: a hybrid art. It is often purple and splendid; it is often profoundly beautiful and profoundly moving. Yet, with a direct appeal to the emotions as its first and encompassing aim, it has never, even at its finest, been able to exercise the measure of direct emotional appeal that is exercised, say, by Chopin's C sharp minor Nocturne, op. 27, No. 1, or by the soft romance of the canvases of Palma Vecchio, or by Rodin's superb "Eternal Spring," or by Zola's "La Terre." It may, at its finest as at its worst, of course subjugate and triumph over inexperienced emotionalism, but the greatest drama of Shakespeare himself has never, in the truthful confession of cultivated emotionalism, influenced that emotionalism as has the greatest literature, or the greatest music, or the greatest painting or sculpture. The splendid music of "Romeo" or "Hamlet" is not so eloquent and moving as that of "Tristan" or "Lohengrin"; no situation in the whole of Hauptmann can strike in the heart so thrilling and profound a chord of pity as a single line in Allegri's obvious "Miserere." The greatest note of comedy in drama falls short of the note of comedy in the "Coffee-Cantata" of Bach; the greatest note of ironic remorse falls short of that in the scherzo in B minor of Chopin; the greatest intellectual note falls short of that in the first and last movements of the C minor symphony of Brahms. What play of Sudermann's has the direct appeal of "The Indian Lily"? What play made out of Hardy's "Tess," however adroitly contrived, retains the powerful appeal of the original piece of literature? To descend, what obvious thrill melodrama, designed frankly for dollars, has — with all its painstaking and deliberate intent — yet succeeded in provoking half the thrill and shock of the obvious second chapter of Andreas Latzko's equally obvious "Men in War"?

Art is an evocation of beautiful emotions: art is art in the degree that it succeeds in the evocation: drama succeeds in an inferior degree. Whatever emotion drama may succeed brilliantly in evoking, another art succeeds in evoking more brilliantly.

II

Although, of course, one speaks of drama here primarily in the sense of acted drama, it is perhaps not necessary so strictly to confine one's self. For when the critic confines himself in his discussion of drama to the acted drama, he regularly brings upon himself from other critics — chiefly bookish fellows whose theatrical knowledge is meagre — the very largely unwarranted embarrassment of arguments anent "crowd psychology" and the like which, while they have little or nothing to do with the case, none the less make a certain deep impression upon his readers. (Readers of criticism become automatically critics; with his first sentence, the critic challenges his critic-reader's sense of argument.) This constantly advanced contention of "crowd psychology," of which drama is supposed to be at once master and slave, has small place in a consideration of drama, from whatever sound point of view one elects to consider the latter. If "crowd psychology" operates in the case of theatre drama, it operates also in the case of concert-hall music. Yet no one so far as I know seriously maintains that, in a criticism of music, this "crowd psychology" has any place.

I have once before pointed out that, even accepting the theory of crowd psychology and its direct and indirect implications so far as drama is concerned, it is as nonsensical to assume that one thousand persons assembled together before a drama in a theatre are, by reason of their constituting a crowd, any more likely to be moved automatically than the same crowd of one thousand persons assembled together before a painting in an art gallery. Furthermore, the theory that collective intelligence and emotionalism are a more facile and ingenuous intelligence and emotionalism, while it may hold full water in the psychological laboratory, holds little in actual external demonstration, particularly in any consideration of a crowd before one of the arts. While it may be true that the Le Bon and Tarde theory applies aptly to the collective psychology of a crowd at a prize-fight or a bull-fight or a circus, one may be permitted severe doubts that it holds equally true of a crowd in a theatre or in an art gallery or in a concert hall. The tendency of such a latter group is not æsthetically downward, but upward. And not only æsthetically, but intellectually and emotionally. (I speak, of course, and with proper relevance, of a crowd assembled to hear good drama or good music, or to see good painting. The customary obscuring tactic of critics in this situation is to argue out the principles of intelligent reaction to good drama in terms of yokel reaction to bad drama. Analysis of the principles of sound theatre drama and the reaction of a group of eight hundred citizens of Marion, Ohio, to "The Two Orphans" somehow do not seem to me to be especially apposite.) The fine drama or the fine piece of music does not make its auditor part of a crowd; it removes him, and every one else in the crowd, from the crowd, and makes him an individual. The crowd ceases to exist as a crowd; it becomes a crowd of units, of separate individuals. The dramas of Mr. Owen Davis make crowds; the dramas of Shakespeare make individuals.

The argument to the contrary always somewhat grotesquely assumes that the crowd assembled at a fine play, and promptly susceptible to group psychology, is a new crowd, one that has never attended a fine play before. Such an assumption falls to pieces in two ways. First, it is beyond reason to believe that it is true in more than one instance out of a hundred; and, secondly, it would not be true even if it were true. For,

granting that a crowd of one thousand persons were seeing great drama for the first time in their lives, what reason is there for believing that the majority of persons in the crowd who had never seen great drama and didn't know exactly what to make of it would be swayed and influenced by the minority who had never seen great drama but did know what to make of it? If this were true, no great drama could ever possibly fail in the commercial theatre. Or, to test the hypothesis further, take it the other way round. What reason is there for believing that the majority in this crowd would be moved the one way or the other, either by a minority that did understand the play, or did not understand it? Or take it in another way still. What reason is there for believing that the minority in this crowd who did know what the drama was about would be persuaded emotionally by the majority who did not know what the drama was about?

Theories, and again theories. But the facts fail to support them. Take the lowest type of crowd imaginable, one in which there is not one cultured man in a thousand — the crowd, say, at a professional American baseball game — and pack it into an American equivalent of Reinhardt's Grosses Schauspielhaus. The play, let us say, is "Œdipus Rex." At the ball game, the crowd psychology of Le Bon operated to the full. But what now? Would the crowd, in the theatre and before a great drama, be the same crowd? Would it not be an entirely different crowd? Would not its group psychology promptly and violently suffer a sudden change? Whether out of curiosity, disgust, admiration, social shame or what not, would it not rapidly segregate itself, spiritually or physically, into various groups? What is the Le Bon theatrical view of the crowd psychology that somehow did not come off during the initial engagement of Barrie's "Peter Pan" in Washington, D. C.? Or of the crowd psychology that worked the other way round when Ibsen was first played in London? Or of the crowd psychology that, operating regularly, if artificially, at the New York premières, most often fails, for all its high enthusiasm, to move either the minority or the majority in its composition?

The question of sound drama and the pack psychology of a congress of groundlings is a fatuous one: it gets nowhere. Sound drama and sound audiences are alone to be considered at one and the same time. And, as I have noted, the tendency of willing, or even semi-willing, auditors and spectators is in an upward direction, not a downward. No intelligent spectator at a performance of "Ben Hur" has ever been made to feel like throwing his hat into the air and cheering by the similar actions of the mob spectators to the left and right of him. No ignoble auditor of "The Laughter of the Gods" but has been made to feel, in some part, the contagion of cultivated appreciation to *his* left and right. "I forget," wrote Sarcey, in a consideration of the subject, "what tyrant it was of ancient Greece to whom massacres were everyday affairs, but who wept copiously over the misfortunes of a heroine in a tragedy. He was the audience; and for the one evening clothed himself in the sentiments of the public." A typical example of sophisticated reasoning. How does Sarcey know that it was not the rest of the audience — the crowd — that was influenced by this repentant and copiously lachrymose individual rather than that it was this individual who was moved by the crowd?

If fallacies perchance insinuate themselves into these opposing contentions, it is a case of fallacy versus fallacy: my intent is not so much to prove anything as to indicate the presence of holes in the proofs of the other side. These holes seem to me to be numerous, and of considerable circumference. A description of two of them may suffice to suggest the rest. Take, as the first of these, the familar Castelvetro doctrine that, since a theatrical audience is not a select congress but a motley crowd, the dramatist, ever conscious of the group psychology, must inevitably avoid all themes and ideas unintelligible to such a gathering. It may be true that a theatrical audience is not a select congress, but why confine the argument to theatrical audiences and seek thus to prove something of drama that may be proved as well — if one is given to such idiosyncrasies —

of music? What, as I have said before, of opera and concert hall audiences? Consider the average audience at Covent Garden, the Metropolitan, Carnegie Hall. Is it in any way culturally superior to the average audience at the St. James's Theatre, or the Théâtre de l'Oeuvre, or the Plymouth — or even the Neighbourhood Playhouse down in Grand Street? What of the audiences who attended the original performances of Beethoven's "Leonore" ("Fidelio"), Berlioz's "Benvenuto Cellini," the original performances of Wagner in France and the performances of his "Der Fliegende Holländer" in Germany, the operas of Händel in England in the years 1733–37, the work of Rossini in Italy, the concerts of Chopin during his tour of England and Scotland? . . . Again, as to the imperative necessity of the dramatist's avoidance of all themes and ideas unintelligible to a mob audience, what of the success among such very audiences — to name but a few more recent profitably produced and locally readily recognizable examples — of Shaw's "Getting Married," Augustus Thomas' "The Witching Hour," Ibsen's "The Wild Duck," Dunsany's "The Laughter of the Gods," Barrie's "Mary Rose," Strindberg's "The Father," Synge's "Playboy"? . . . Surely it will be quickly allowed that however obvious the themes and ideas of these plays may be to the few, they are hardly within the ready intelligence of what the theorists picture as the imaginary mob theatre audience. Fine drama is independent of all such theories: the dramatist who subscribes to them should not figure in any treatise upon drama as an art.

A second illustration: the equivocation to the effect that drama, being a democratic art, may not properly be evaluated in terms of more limited, and aristocratic, taste. It seems to me an idiotic assumption that drama is a more democratic art than music. All great art is democratic in intention, if not in reward. Michelangelo, Shakespeare, Wagner and Zola are democratic artists, and their art democratic art. It is criticism of Michelangelo, Shakespeare, Wagner and Zola that is aristocratic. Criticism, not art, generically wears the ermine and the purple. To appraise a democratic art in terms of democracy is to attempt to effect a chemical reaction in nitrogen with nitrogen. If drama is, critically, a democratic art since it is meant not to be read by the few but to be played before the many, music must be critically no less a democratic art. Yet the theorists conveniently overlook this embarrassment. Nevertheless, if Shakespeare's dramas were designed for the heterogeneous ear, so, too, were the songs of Schumann. No great artist has ever in his heart deliberately fashioned his work for a remote and forgotten cellar, dark and stairless. He fashions it, for all his doubts, in the hope of hospitable eyes and ears, and in the hope of a sun to shine upon it. It is as ridiculous to argue that because Shakespeare's is a democratic art it must be criticized in terms of democratic reaction to it as it would be to argue that because the United States is a democracy the most acute and comprehensive criticism of that democracy must lie in a native democrat's reaction to it. "To say that the theatre is for the people," says Gordon Craig, "is necessary. But to forget to add that part and parcel of the people is the aristocracy, whether of birth or feeling, is an omission. A man of the eighteenth century, dressed in silks, in a fashionable loggia in the theatre at Versailles, looking as if he did no work (as Voltaire in his youth may have looked), presents, in essence, exactly the same picture as Walt Whitman in his rough gray suit lounging in the Bowery, also looking as if he did no work. . . . One the aristocrat, one the democrat: the two are identical."

III

"Convictions," said Nietzsche, "are prisons." Critical "theories," with negligible exception, seek to denude the arts of their splendid, gypsy gauds and to force them instead to don so many duplicated black and white striped uniforms. Of all the arts, drama has suffered most in this regard. Its critics, from the time of Aristotle, have bound and fettered it, and have then urged it impassionedly to soar. Yet, despite its shackles, it has triumphed, and each triumph has been a derision of one of its

most famous and distinguished critics. It triumphed, through Shakespeare, over Aristotle; it triumphed, through Molière, over Castelvetro; it triumphed, through Lemercier, over Diderot; it triumphed, through Lessing, over Voltaire; it triumphed, through Ibsen, over Flaubert; it has triumphed, through Hauptmann, over Sarcey and, through Schnitzler and Bernard Shaw, over Mr. Archer. The truth perhaps is that drama is an art as flexible as the imaginations of its audiences. It is no more to be bound by rules and theories than such imaginations are to be bound by rules and theories. Who so allwise that he may say by what rules or set of rules living imaginations and imaginations yet unborn are to be fanned into theatrical flame? "Imagination," Samuel Johnson's words apply to auditor as to artist, "a licentious and vagrant faculty, unsusceptible of limitations and impatient of restraint, has always endeavored to baffle the logician, to perplex the confines of distinction, and burst the inclosures of regularity." And further, "There is therefore scarcely any species of writing of which we can tell what is its essence, and what are its constituents; every new genius produces some innovation which, when invented and approved, subverts the rules which the practice of foregoing authors had established."

Does the play interest, and whom? This seems to me to be the only doctrine of dramatic criticism that is capable of supporting itself soundly. First, does the play interest? In other words, how far has the dramatist succeeded in expressing himself, and the materials before him, intelligently, eloquently, symmetrically, beautifully? So much for the criticism of the dramatist as an artist. In the second place, whom does the play interest? Does it interest inferior persons, or does it interest cultivated and artistically sensitive persons? So much for the criticism of the artist as a dramatist.

The major difficulty with critics of the drama has always been that, having once positively enunciated their critical credos, they have been constrained to devote their entire subsequent enterprise and ingenuity to defending the fallacies therein. Since a considerable number of these critics have been, and are, extraordinarily shrewd and ingenious men, these defences of error have often been contrived with such persuasive dexterity and reasonableness that they have endured beyond the sounder doctrines of less deft critics, doctrines which, being sound, have suffered the rebuffs that gaunt, grim logic, ever unprepossessing and unhypnotic, suffers always. "I hope that I am right; if I am not right, I am still right," said Brunetière. "Mr. William Archer is not only, like myself, a convinced, inflexible determinist," Henry Arthur Jones has written, "I am persuaded that he is also, unlike myself, a consistent one. I am sure he takes care that his practice agrees with his opinions — even when they are wrong." Dramatic criticism is an attempt to formulate rules of conduct for the lovable, wayward, charming, wilful vagabond that is the drama. For the drama is an art with a feather in its cap and an ironic smile upon its lips, sauntering impudently over forbidden lawns and through closed lanes into the hearts of those of us children of the world who have never grown up. Beside literature, it is the Mother Goose of the arts: a gorgeous and empurpled Mother Goose for the fireside of impressible and romantic youth that, looking upward, leans ever hushed and expectant at the knee of life. It is a fairy tale told realistically, a true story told as romance. It is the lullaby of disillusion, the chimes without the cathedral, the fears and hopes and dreams and passions of those who cannot fully fear and hope and dream and flame themselves.

"The drama must have reality," so Mr. P. P. Howe in his engaging volume of "Dramatic Portraits," "but the first essential to our understanding of an art is that we should not believe it to be actual life. The spectator who shouts his warning and advice to the heroine when the villain is approaching is, in the theatre, the only true believer in the hand of God; and he is liable to find it in a drama lower than the best." The art of the drama is one which imposes upon drama the obligation of depicting at once the inner processes of life realistically and the external aspects of life delusively. Properly and sympatheti-

cally to appreciate drama, one must look upon it synchronously with two different eyes: the one arguing against the other as to the truth of what it sees, and triumphing over this doubtful other with the full force of its sophistry. Again inevitably to quote Coleridge, " Stage presentations are to produce a sort of temporary half-faith, which the spectator encourages in himself and supports by a voluntary contribution on his own part, because he knows that it is at all times in his power to see the thing as it really is. Thus the true stage illusion as to a forest scene consists, not in the mind's judging it to be a forest, but in its remission of the judgment that it is not a forest." This obviously applies to drama as well as to dramatic investiture. One never for a moment believes absolutely that Mr. John Barrymore is Richard III; one merely agrees, for the sake of Shakespeare, who has written the play, and Mr. Hopkins, who has cast it, that Mr. John Barrymore is Richard III, so that one may receive the ocular, aural and mental sensations for which one has paid three and one-half dollars. Nor does one for a moment believe that Mr. Walter Hampden, whom that very evening one has seen dividing a brobdingnagian dish of goulash with Mr. Oliver Herford in the Players' Club and discussing the prospects of the White Sox, is actually speaking extemporaneously the rare verbal embroideries of Shakespeare; or that Miss Ethel Barrymore who is billed in front of Browne's Chop House to take a star part in the Actors' Equity Association's benefit, is really the queen of a distant kingdom.

The dramatist, in the theatre, is not a worker in actualities, but in the essence of actualities that filters through the self-deception of his spectators. There is no such thing as realism in the theatre: there is only mimicry of realism. There is no such thing as romance in the theatre: there is only mimicry of romance. There is no such thing as an automatic dramatic susceptibility in a theatre audience: there is only a volitional dramatic susceptibility. Thus, it is absurd to speak of the drama holding the mirror up to nature; all that the drama can do is to hold nature up to its own peculiar mirror which, like that in a pleasure-park, amusingly fattens up nature, or shrinks it, yet does not at any time render it unrecognizable. One does not go to the theatre to see life and nature; one goes to see the particular way in which life and nature happen to look to a cultivated, imaginative and entertaining man who happens, in turn, to be a playwright. Drama is the surprising pulling of a perfectly obvious, every-day rabbit out of a perfectly obvious, every-day silk hat. The spectator has seen thousands of rabbits and thousands of silk hats, but he has never seen a silk hat that had a rabbit concealed in it, and he is curious about it.

But if drama is essentially mimetic, so also — as Professor Gilbert Murray implies — is criticism essentially mimetic in that it is representative of the work criticized. It is conceivable that one may criticize Mr. Ziegfeld's "Follies" in terms of the "Philoctetes" of Theodectes — I myself have been guilty of even more exceptional feats; it is not only conceivable, but of common occurrence, for certain of our academic American critics to criticize the plays of Mr. Shaw in terms of Scribe and Sardou, and with a perfectly straight face; but criticism in general is a chameleon that takes on something of the colour of the pattern upon which it imposes itself. There is drama in Horace's "Epistola ad Pisones," a criticism of drama. There is the spirit of comedy in Hazlitt's essay "On the Comic Writers of the Last Century." Dryden's "Essay on Dramatic Poesy" is poetry. There is something of the music of Chopin in Huneker's critical essays on Chopin, and some of Mary Garden's spectacular histrionism in his essay on her acting. Walkley, criticizing "L'Enfant Prodigue," uses the pen of Pierrot. Criticism, more than drama with her mirror toward nature, holds the mirror up to the nature of the work it criticizes. Its end is the revivification of the passion of art which has been spent in its behalf, but under the terms laid down by Plato. Its aim is to reconstruct a great work of art on a diminutive scale, that eyes which are not capable of gazing on high may have it within the reach of their vision. Its aim is to play again all the full richness of the artist's emotional organ tones, in so far as is possible, on the cold cerebral xylophone that is criticism's deficient instrument. In the accomplishment of these aims, it is bound by no laws that art is not bound by. There is but one rule: there are no rules. Art laughs at locksmiths.

It has been a favorite diversion of critics since Aristotle's day to argue that drama is drama, whether one reads it from a printed page or sees it enacted in a theatre. Great drama, they announce, is great drama whether it ever be acted or not; "it speaks with the same voice in solitude as in crowds"; and "all the more then" — again I quote Mr. Spingarn — "will the drama itself 'even apart from representation and actors,' as old Aristotle puts it, speak with its highest power to the imagination fitted to understand and receive it." Upon this point of view much of the academic criticism of drama has been based. But may we not well reply that, for all the fact that Shakespeare would still be the greatest dramatist who ever lived had he never been played in the theatre, so, too, would Bach still be the greatest composer who ever lived had his compositions never been played at all? If drama is not meant for actors, may we not also argue that music is not meant for instruments? Are not such expedients less sound criticism than clever evasion of sound criticism: a frolicsome and agreeable straddling of the æsthetic see-saw? There is the printed drama — criticize it. There is the same drama acted — criticize it. Why quibble? Sometimes, as in the case of "Gioconda" and Duse, they are one. Well and good. Sometimes, as in the case of "Chantecler" and Maude Adams, they are not one. Well and good. But where, in either case, the confusion that the critics lay such stress upon? These critics deal not with theories, but with mere words. They take two dozen empty words and adroitly seek therewith to fashion a fecund theory. The result is — words. "Words which," said Ruskin, "if they are not watched, will do deadly work sometimes. There are masked words droning and skulking about us just now . . . (there never were so many, owing to the teaching of catechisms and phrases at school instead of human meanings) . . . there never were creatures of prey so mischievous, never diplomatists so cunning, never poisoners so deadly, as these masked words: they are the unjust stewards of men's ideas. . . ."

As they are of men's lack of ideas.

LUDWIG LEWISOHN

Ludwig Lewisohn was born in Berlin of German-Jewish parents in 1882, and came to the United States eight years later. The rest of his boyhood was spent in South Carolina. Graduated from the College of Charleston with a Master's degree in 1901, he continued his university work at Columbia and received a Master's degree there two years later. For some years thereafter he lived in New York, writing magazine articles and working at a novel. His first novel was published in 1908. For a year he taught German at the University of Wisconsin, and from 1911 to 1919 he was on the faculty of Ohio State University. Returning to New York in 1919, he became dramatic critic for *The Nation*, where he remained until 1924. There followed several years' residence abroad, during which he wrote several novels and devoted himself to a study of the Jewish problem. A few years ago he returned to the United States, and has since that time written several books on literature. His book *The Modern Drama*, an extended and unorthodox treatment of the subject, appeared in 1915. In 1922 he reissued several of his dramatic criticisms in the volume *The Drama and the Stage*. *The Creative Life*, in which only one section is concerned with the drama, was published in 1924. Lewisohn has devoted only a relatively small part of his work to dramatic and theatrical subjects. His critical activities cover a wide field, and his familiarity with European literature and philosophy enable him to apply standards to the American drama of which few "regular" dramatic critics are aware.

WORLD, WILL, and WORD [1]

[From the Chapter *Masks*, in *The Creative Life*]

(1924)

Money is tight. Credit is shaken. It is a bad season. People will not go to the theater. Plays fail. The managers are in the dumps. Actors are walking the streets. Week after week the shoddy trade goods of the favorite hacks are thrown on the stage. The gambling becomes feverish. Quietly, in the midst of the noise and dust, the babble and the tinsel, a tragedy appears. The reviewers call it drab and disagreeable and talk pseudo-learnedly of the Manchester School. Must we do that sort of thing —

[1] Reprinted in full from *The Creative Life*, New York, 1924, by permission of the author. Published by Boni & Liveright, Publishers, Copyright, 1924, by Boni & Liveright, Inc.

we, too — a nation of forward lookers, cheerers, dwellers in "great valleys"? The curious thing is that the tragedy does not fail. What if Dryden was right? "The spirit of man," he wrote, "cannot be satisfied but with truth or at least verisimility." What if business is bad? What has that to do with the theater — except that theater where the overfed digest their plethoric dinners? "Two places are open," said the starving Viennese in 1919, "the graveyards and the theaters." The theater is not a game. It is spiritual compulsion. Once it celebrated the gods. Now it broods over the fate of man. Aristotle and Hebbel knew that; even Bossu and Dryden knew it.

When I try to recall it to my friends their total reaction is that I once taught in a college. But I address myself to the American dramatist — that almost hypothetical personage that is yet, so surely, on the point of rising into our vision. Do not let the managers deceive you. Do not let the reviewers deceive you. Nor the babblers in clubs. Seventy per cent of the current hacks' theatrical carpentry does not even make money. The gambling is not even good gambling. Nor be deceived, above all, by the nimble college professors who flutter with the winds of shallow popular fallacies in the hopes that their classes may grow and their articles sell. Address yourself, if need be on bread and water, to the eternal theater — not to the game of Broadway, but to the play of Man.

The thing is so simple. The drama shows man acting or suffering. He acts, he suffers, not in the void, not — in his consciousness, at least — at the tug and pull of blind instincts, but upon some spiritual and moral terms. He calls things evil and good and right and wrong and suffers remorse and shame. He always acts and suffers upon definite assumptions, through and by a definite view of the world. Search deep enough any act or pang and you come upon the sufferer's philosophy of life — his notions of good and evil, of the world and God. An old woman sits in a room sewing her shroud. A bruised, sore woman creeps back into a house because the man who owns it is called her husband. A lad in the streets hears a drum and sees a flag and races towards death and doom. These actions require assumptions into which are packed whole histories, mythologies, philosophies. And the idea of an action is of far more startling import, of far more searing terror, than the individual action itself, and plays in which the ideas of actions are brought before the bar of dramatic justice make the mere rattle of action seem as tame and senseless as the movements of little animals. Do not, then, let the reviewers or managers' agents deceive you with their jargon. "A talky play." These are the plays in which the ideas of actions are exhibited and judged. And by these ideas we live and die.

Once the dramatist was content to show merely and acquiescently the actions of men and the ideas that inspired those actions. Yet never for long. In Euripides the ideas themselves begin to be discussed and judged. But even on the lowest plane — the plane of the mere morality disguised or homily set moving — the dramatist is no theatric hack; even on that plane he is conscious of a fervent identification of his own soul with the ideas upon which his contemporaries act, when they act. The drama is always philosophical. When the dramatist is profoundly at one with the ideas upon which his characters act, the play approaches the religious; when he is at variance with those ideas, it is polemical or prophetic. Do not be deceived by this other fallacy: "So and so's plays are not plays; they are pamphlets." In the deeper creative sense all plays are pamphlets — the "Medea" is a pamphlet on the subjection of woman, and "Tartuffe" on the loathsomeness of hypocrisy, and "Faust" on the spiritual energy that turns apparent evil into good. Shakespeare! Yes, I hear that shout. That divine poet and fashioner of men clung, except for moments, to the mediæval identification of the dramatist with the ideas of the world and the will, of good and evil, upon which his characters act. Some heretic thoughts of his own he had, perhaps some towering disillusion at the core of him. But outwardly he accepts the state and the moral life of his time.

He accepts. Another rejects. Here, at all events, is the ground of the matter. Every dramatist accepts or rejects the ideas upon which his characters act. He shapes the consequences of their actions according to his sense of the quality of the ideas that urge them on. Upon his view of the world, upon his reaction to moral ideas, will depend his choice and conduct of his fable and the end to which he brings the lives of which he treats. It is a better preparation for the career of a dramatist to have watched the actions of a few villagers and to have brooded over those actions at that spiritual core where criticism and creation are one than to have read all the manuals of play-writing and stagecraft in the world and be an expert on lighting and decoration. Shun the theater. It is a place of confusion for the dramatist. Beethoven wrote his symphonies in a little room. They can be played by twenty men or by a hundred, in a barn or a temple. The mechanism of production is not your business; it is your servant. Your business is with man and his world and the ideas that reconcile him to it or drive him to despair.

There is a matter more troubling and intricate. It is the matter of the will. (I am ashamed of setting down these commonplaces. My excuse is that they are not commonplaces among us. What play on Broadway has one seen criticized for its dealing with the will? It is entertaining or not, cheering or depressing, strong — how, gentlemen, how and why? — or feeble; it will run or it won't.) The drama deals with the will. I repudiate the easier, academic agreement with this statement. It goes on the staggering assumption that there is an abstract entity somewhere in the psyche functioning in the void and called the will. Upon that assumption we have the absurd *volteface*, conversion, easy change of aim, motive, character which breeds the happy ending. It is upon that assumption that the wicked Duke in "As You Like It" went into the forest

Where, meeting with an old religious man,
After some question with him, was converted
Both from his enterprise and from the world;
His crown bequeathing to his banished brother,
And all their lands restored to them again
That were with him exiled.

It is lovely as a legend, but monstrous as a representation of human life.

The dramatist not only has his view of the world by which he judges that of his characters, not only his positive or negative or suspended judgment upon the ideas by which they act within and towards the world of their conception; he must have come to some decision upon the very innermost character of human action itself. For how else can he shape his rhythm of moral values; how else determine upon the progress and direction of his fable; how else, indeed, begin to

write at all? He has an imaginative vision springing from a tone, a gesture, an expression once observed. A man is overcome by fate. And the man's fate is woven of small, mean, dusty things, or of things gross and impudent and easily discernible by the practical eye. What is this man? A weakling? He is that to the Broadway melodramatist—to the reviewer who condemned Arthur Richman's "Ambush" on the score that the play's protagonist is "weak." But the serious dramatist cannot avoid these fundamental issues by using an unconsidered word. What is the meaning of "weakness" in such a man? It is that all the uncontrollable forces that have made him have left him spiritually defenseless against the evils with which he contends. He is, whatever he can do, always more full of mercy than his adversaries are of shame. His reflectiveness seeks to fathom their shallow clatter. He attributes to them his feelings, his hesitations, his scruples. He is lost. To make him "strong," in that foolish, popular sense, it would be necessary to remount the streams of his personal and ancestral being to their very source and change that source and so change the world, the universe, the planets, and the constellations. Yes, the dramatist, like the novelist, must transcend (the great modern dramatists do transcend) the rubber stamped classification of human qualities and characters that are cut to the pattern of some foolish "ought-ness," which is, in its turn, derived from human experience, misinterpreted under the sway of myth and ritual and the blind primordial terrors and propitiatory practices of our remotest ancestors. Begin to think and at once the gentleman who condemned Richman's protagonist as a "weakling" becomes an unfathomable and almost fantastic character. But who, in these matters, condescends to think?

What is true of "good" characters is no less true of "evil." So good a playwright as Eugene G. O'Neill permits himself the luxury, costly as it is, of sudden external forces that turn "bad" into "better." He has not yet the sovereign vision. Self-discipline is possible by a character whose self is inherently capable of discipline. We do right, in practical life, to insist on the necessity. We may by that insistence, by the direction of intangible forces, breed more people with the capacities that we desire. There may be more men born who desire more strongly the serenity of self-mastery than the riot of self-expansion. But the dramatist has finished creatures. He takes his people as they come, if you please, from God's hand. He cannot tamper with them. They have no more within than they have. To draw that out to the uttermost nerve—such is the fruit of his extremest effort.

It is, then, his vision of the world and of the will that dictates the dramatist's choice and treatment of a fable. Accident has nothing to do with it; ingenuity has nothing to do with it. You hear stories of plays "tinkered with on the road." Mr. Belasco takes a manuscript and rewrites it. A dramatist whose play can be "tinkered with" or rewritten or revised by an alien hand has not begun to comprehend the elementary conditions of any art. His play may not be inevitable under the aspect of eternity. He is but a man. He is, perhaps, but a manikin. But it must seem inevitable to him. It must be so interwoven with his profoundest perceptions, instincts, convictions, that he is willing to labor for it, starve for it, die for it. Unless it is an inseparable part of his own soul's integrity — it is nothing. Why have the managers the habit of demanding changes, revisions, adaptations for the needs of this season, that theater, a certain star? Because they were not dealing with dramatists at all, but with mechanics, journeymen, hacks. There can be no compromise on this question. This is the final test. Do you think that your play can be changed by another or for another's convenience or use? Destroy it and work with your hands. This does not mean that your play is perfect. Having destroyed it, you yourself may relive its sources in experience, dig deeper into your own soul, and create it afresh. But if Mr. Belasco thinks he can use it, after laying upon it a judicious hand, be sure that only the fire will cleanse it and your shame.

There remains dialogue — the word. I know two hacks who put their ingenuities together and assemble a group of stupid accidents which they call a plot. Then their great effort is over. They run off for a week-end to Atlantic City to write the play. It seems to them a small matter. But consider the word. Into these sound symbols we call speech are packed how many centuries of human experience, how much of universal hope and anguish! All words are flesh. All words are revelation. Try to pluck asunder your highest ecstasy, your most rending grief, your central conviction from the word that expresses it. You cannot. The spiritual universe which man has built is built of things and thoughts crystallized into speech. It is not built of the things and thoughts themselves, but of speech. Whoever writes at all has the double task — to use speech significantly and freshly, to reach through it to the concrete realities which it both reveals and conceals. The dramatist's writing task, which looks so simple, is the most difficult of all. He must use exclusively the speech of others, never of himself. And we must believe that those others are speaking, each in his own tongue, each out of the depth of his own experience, his own unique personality, his own reaction towards world and will and flesh and spirit. Yet from the speech of these others we must overhear — from their speech and not through some cheap device of *raisonneur* mouthpiece — the dramatist's judgment, understanding, compassion, faith. Such is the fundamental creative problem of dramatic dialogue. There are lesser ones. How little speech, in mere quantity, can the dramatist give! Discussions that rise towards a culmination in human fates take weeks, months, years. People eat breakfast in silence. They wrangle on some forenoon. An evening comes on which they fling at each other those impassioned confessions that constitute the drama of life. These millions of words the dramatist must sum up in a few hundred. But the few hundred must have the effect of the millions. We must feel that all necessary speech has been spoken and all the dim places of the soul touched with light. We must feel that each speaker in the drama has stated his case before that eternal judgeless bar — his whole and sufficient case. Good dramatic dialogue is like a blueprint that must yet seem to us to be the finished house; like a thin symbol that must never let us suspect it is not the thing symbolized itself. You will not write good dramatic dialogue on a week-end trip. You must listen to men and women. You must listen with the ear and the heart and the mind. Then, perhaps, in long vigils of a high awareness of mortality it will be given you to write the word that will express your creatures and their struggles with the world and your deep sense of the meaning of those struggles and a dramatic scene will be born.

How well I know the reaction that such considerations get from happy, popular playwrights and smart critics and facile lecturers. Not that way lie the lights of Broadway, they think, or the seven per cent on the second five thousand of weekly box office receipts. Let them not be too sure. But the coming American dramatist with whom I am concerned will not care, will not consciously during the process of creation—however much and rightly he may later enjoy reward—be busy with these matters, but with the world, the will, the word. One danger is his, especially if he is young. And he must be young. Since all his elders and teachers will be married to the trickery, elegantly disguised sometimes, of the theatric trade, he will be ashamed of the apparent priggishness of clothing these easy and worldly matters in what he will be told is mystic cant. Let him remember a great phrase of Molière. "On se rirait de vous," says the pliant Philinte. And Alceste answers: "Tant pis pour qui rirait!"

THE THEATER ONCE MORE [1]

THE FOREIGN CRITIC: You share my view, then, that the American drama is really entering upon a creative stage?

THE AMERICAN CRITIC: Those words are too big. There is a faint voice; it cries in a howling wilderness.

THE FOREIGN CRITIC: How pessimistic you are!

THE AMERICAN CRITIC: The Pulitzer prize has just been given to "Icebound."

THE FOREIGN CRITIC: And isn't "Icebound" a work of considerable merit?

THE AMERICAN CRITIC: It is a work of some merit. But do you know anything about its author, Mr. Owen Davis?

THE FOREIGN CRITIC: Very little, I confess.

THE AMERICAN CRITIC: Mr. Davis has been writing plays for exactly twenty-five years. He has written one hundred plays. Of these fifty were melodramas produced by Mr. A. H. Woods between 1902 and 1910. Can you quite imagine a prize of the French Academy or the Schiller or Kleist prize going to a gentleman with such a history? Heaven knows I have a small opinion of prizes and prize awards of any sort. But this

particular award throws light upon a peculiar American situation.

THE FOREIGN CRITIC: I see perfectly. There is no understanding and respect for the artist or the life of art.

THE AMERICAN CRITIC: No understanding, no deep sense for it. To the committee which made this award it was not at once unimaginable that the author of those fifty melodramas could write a work truly memorable and delicate. Fancy Ibsen, Hauptmann, Galsworthy, even Donnay or Halbe writing fifty melodramas. They could not have done it if the alternative had been literal starvation—not because they like hunger or are conscious of a mission—that, heaven help us, would be the common interpretation—but because their minds would have been nauseated at the very thought.

THE FOREIGN CRITIC: Your point is perfectly clear to me and perfectly elementary. Haven't all your critics made it?

THE AMERICAN CRITIC: No; for to our critics art is neither passion nor vision. They are very able, very honest, very well-informed, and very witty. But, to put it mildly and yet correctly, they don't care enough.

THE FOREIGN CRITIC: I have read some very able reviews.

[1] Reprinted in full from *The Creative Life*. New York, 1924, by permission of the author. Published by Boni & Liveright, Publishers. Copyright, 1924, by Boni & Liveright, Inc.

THE AMERICAN CRITIC: Undoubtedly. But weren't they all — reflect on that a moment — quite worldly?

THE FOREIGN CRITIC: That is not so clear to me.

THE AMERICAN CRITIC: Do you remember a play called "Roger Bloomer"?

THE FOREIGN CRITIC: Very vividly.

THE AMERICAN CRITIC: The play was crude and young and neither thought through nor wrought out. But it was the cry of youth and passion and rebellion — the authentic and everlasting cry of the life of art.

THE FOREIGN CRITIC: That is why I valued it.

THE AMERICAN CRITIC: Exactly. And none of the reviewers wrote of this play from within that everlasting life of art of which they should have been a part; they treated it with the superciliousness and faint contempt and smiling incredulity with which the polite world always treats the artist and prophet and outcast and child of light. They said in effect: What shocking manners! What ill-assorted clothes! Pray, dear young man, if you have talent, be proper and show it in a proper way.

THE FOREIGN CRITIC: You think, then, that your criticism is partly responsible for the slow growth of your dramatic literature?

THE AMERICAN CRITIC: I do. The young playwright is shy and criticism provides no atmosphere in which he can lose his shyness and speak forth his ardors. Criticism does not sufficiently guard him from the Philistine world; it allies itself with that world.

THE FOREIGN CRITIC: What an unusual situation. For the past hundred years, at least, it has been both the pride and the chief business of every reputable European critic to be torch-bearer and intermediary, to tilt against the brutish-

ness or indifference of the world, to provide an atmosphere in which genius, which is always strange and new and electrical and estranged, can live and flourish.

THE AMERICAN CRITIC: It is not so among us. A charming and elegant and worldly play — true enough to amuse, not true enough to wound — that is what our critics like. A play like Frederick Lonsdale's "Aren't We All?" at the Gaiety brings out the best that is in them. And the piece is indeed admirable and the acting of both Cyril Maude and Leslie Howard beyond praise.

THE FOREIGN CRITIC: But it is also perfectly barren and perfectly unimportant.

THE AMERICAN CRITIC: Precisely. But our reviewers do not really like the rich, dark, significant folk-play, as they showed in their attitude to "A Square Peg," nor are they, with few exceptions, quite happy or comfortable in the presence of such bitter creative irony as we had in "The Adding Machine."

THE FOREIGN CRITIC: They are in the state in which vital and immediate art troubles them?

THE AMERICAN CRITIC: Yes; and to guard themselves from it they are initially unsympathetic.

THE FOREIGN CRITIC: They, too, want to laugh.

THE AMERICAN CRITIC: I am almost afraid so. Nothing better could happen to the American drama than that some of the chief reviewers should have some shattering experience, like a great and unhappy passion. But they are far too much at ease in Zion to risk it.

THE FOREIGN CRITIC: What a thing to wish your friends!

THE AMERICAN CRITIC: But think how it would improve their work! And work comes first.

SPEAKING OF THE THEATER [1]

THE PROFESSOR: I've been reading Granville Barker's "The Exemplary

[1] Reprinted in full from *The Creative Life.* New York, 1924, by permission of the author. Published by Boni & Liveright, Publishers. Copyright, 1924, by Boni & Liveright, Inc.

Theater" with a good deal of satisfaction.

THE DRAMATIC CRITIC: I've read it, too. But I don't think it's important.

THE PROFESSOR: If you'll let me be frank I think I can account for your dislike of it. Barker pleads for the theater as fundamentally an educational force and a form of social service.

THE DRAMATIC CRITIC: Exactly.

THE PROFESSOR: I don't at all blame you for disliking terms besmirched by every Philistine and cheap reformer. But one can carry that dislike so far as to discredit the true and fine and necessary things which those words denote.

THE DRAMATIC CRITIC: I don't discredit those things. But I'm sure the theater is not an educational force and if I'm to call it a form of social service it must be according to an interpretation of my own which will please neither Barker nor yourself.

THE PROFESSOR: Then you are content to have the theater considered an amusement?

THE DRAMATIC CRITIC: As you like.

THE PROFESSOR: You are holding an idea in reserve. You are not, after all, so largely preoccupied with something that is only an amusement.

THE DRAMATIC CRITIC: I dislike these fixed terms. They have a way of betraying you to all sorts of people and committing you to all kinds of causes.

THE PROFESSOR: Very well. But there must be some form, if not formula, by which you can communicate your sense of the value which the theater represents.

THE DRAMATIC CRITIC: It is not so simple. When I was young I was interested in art. Then the theater, except at its rare best, didn't interest me at all. Now I'm interested in life and in art primarily as it interprets and shapes life, and so the theater seems to me very important.

THE PROFESSOR: Why, on account of that shift in your interests, precisely the theater?

THE DRAMATIC CRITIC: There are two reasons. The form of the drama is no accidental one. Its struggle, crisis, resolution are of the essence of the life-process itself. It is thus that life proceeds; it is thus that single lives proceed. Therefore the mirror which the drama holds up to nature gives back an image that is closer to the inevitable laws of being than the image of the other arts.

THE PROFESSOR: But that does not apply to the popular theater.

THE DRAMATIC CRITIC: It applies in a negative sense. The popular playwright must, by an implication that is inescapable in his medium, deal with essentials. He deals with them absurdly. It is easy to shatter his structures. But always the dealing is with essentials. Even assent to the moral order of a silly play is a more tonic exercise for the crowd than mere story interest in cheap fiction. Your very shop-girl, moreover, who does not know what criticism is may look into the reviews of a piece that has moved or amused her and be plunged, upon some terms however crude, into a discussion concerning the world and the will and the true character of human action.

THE PROFESSOR: In brief, the theater's function, in your opinion, is to enlighten people.

THE DRAMATIC CRITIC: That is a terrible word. Yes, I think the theater does throw light. But I am not concerned, like your professional enlighteners, with the light. I am concerned with the thing lit. So far as I can see the worst thing in the world is the avoidable moral suffering. It can be mitigated by understanding man and human life as they really are. All art can serve that purpose; the theater can serve it more directly, swiftly, intensely.

THE PROFESSOR: I am amused to find you so much of a moralist after all.

THE DRAMATIC CRITIC: We are all concerned with conduct. It only depends how or with what intention. I don't want to lay down laws. I want people helped to discover those laws of their own being in the light of which they can live without cruelty or tyranny or rancor.

THE PROFESSOR: I think that I follow you. But did you not have a second reason?

THE DRAMATIC CRITIC: I have already stated it. The drama not only deals with the life-process upon its own terms, but does so with unexampled intensity. The theater is the instrument by which that intensity is achieved. No artistic experience, that is, no vicarious and interpretative experience of life, can cleave so deep as a theatric one. In those two hours of overwhelmingly profound absorption in something beyond the *ego,* cruelty may melt into compassion, tyranny into tolerance, blindness into vision.

THE PROFESSOR: Does it happen often?

THE DRAMATIC CRITIC: Does anything desirable or of good report happen often? It does happen; it can happen. Yes, I have heard quite simple people discuss plays and admit naïvely that they gained a clearer idea of life from them and were able to act more tolerantly and less muddily and angrily as a result.

THE PROFESSOR: But isn't that both education and social service?

THE DRAMATIC CRITIC: It has, at all events, nothing to do with either information or uplift. For what it comes to ultimately is this: the drama communicates a sense of the necessarily tragic character of human life, of its necessary and inevitable defeat upon any but spiritual terms, of the fact that its single spiritual victory consists in compassion, in understanding, in abstention from force, from moral fraud, from judgment and the execution of judgment.

THE PROFESSOR: In short, you like the theater because, in the long run, you think it will make your views of life prevail?

THE DRAMATIC CRITIC: I do. And I am yet to see a really grown-up person who likes anything very deeply for any other reason."

JOSEPH WOOD KRUTCH

Joseph Wood Krutch was born in Knoxville, Tenn., in 1893, where he received his early education, graduating from the State University in 1915. The next year he attended Columbia University, where in 1916 he received his Master's degree. After serving in the United States Army in 1919–20, he spent a year in Europe, and in 1923 he received his Doctor's degree at Columbia. In 1924 he joined the editorial board of *The Nation,* and became dramatic critic for the same periodical. He has served in that capacity ever since. He began teaching shortly after his return from Europe, and since 1925 he has been a member of the faculty at Columbia. His first published book on the drama was a scholarly volume, *Comedy and Conscience After the Restoration* (1924). His *Edgar Allan Poe: A Study in Genius* (1926), has become a standard work, and his *Five Masters: A Study in the Mutations of the Novel* (1930) is another distinguished critical work. *The Modern Temper* (1929), though not dealing primarily with drama, yields however the chapter *The Tragic Fallacy,* which is reprinted in the present work. Aside from the last-named book, he has written one other study on the theater, a critical and expository volume called *The American Drama Since 1918* (1939), which he calls " an informal history."

THE TRAGIC FALLACY [1]

[From *The Modern Temper, A Study and a Confession*]

(1929)

Through the legacy of their art the great ages have transmitted to us a dim image of their glorious vitality. When we turn the pages of a Sophoclean or a Shakespearean tragedy we participate

1 Reprinted in full from *The Modern Temper* (1929), by permission of the author, and the publisher, Harcourt, Brace & Co. Copyright, 1929, by Harcourt, Brace & Co.

faintly in the experience which created it and we sometimes presumptuously say that we " understand " the spirit of these works. But the truth is that we see them, even at best and in the moments when our souls expand most nearly to their dimensions, through a glass darkly.

It is so much easier to appreciate than to create that an age too feeble to reach the heights achieved by the members of a preceding one can still see those heights towering above its impotence, and so it is that, when we perceive a Sophocles or a Shakespeare soaring in an air which we can never hope to breathe, we say that we can "appreciate" them. But what we mean is that we are just able to wonder, and we can never hope to participate in the glorious vision of human life out of which they were created — not even to the extent of those humbler persons for whom they were written; for while to us the triumphant voices come from far away and tell of a heroic world which no longer exists, to them they spoke of immediate realities and revealed the inner meaning of events amidst which they still lived.

When the life has entirely gone out of a work of art come down to us from the past, when we read it without any emotional comprehension whatsoever and can no longer even imagine why the people for whom it was intended found it absorbing and satisfying, then, of course, it has ceased to be a work of art at all and has dwindled into one of those deceptive "documents" from which we get a false sense of comprehending through the intellect things which cannot be comprehended at all except by means of a kinship of feeling. And though all works from a past age have begun in this way to fade there are some, like the great Greek or Elizabethan tragedies, which are still halfway between the work of art and the document. They no longer can have for us the immediacy which they had for those to whom they originally belonged, but they have not yet eluded us entirely. We no longer live in the world which they represent, but we can half imagine it and we can measure the distance which we have moved away. We write no tragedies today, but we can still talk about the tragic spirit of which we would, perhaps, have no conception were it not for the works in question.

An age which could really "appreciate" Shakespeare or Sophocles would have something comparable to put beside them — something like them, not necessarily in form, or spirit, but at least in magnitude — some vision of life which would be, however different, equally am-

ple and passionate. But when we move to put a modern masterpiece beside them, when we seek to compare them with, let us say, a *Ghosts* or a *Weavers,* we shrink as from the impulse to commit some folly and we feel as though we were about to superimpose Bowling Green upon the Great Prairies in order to ascertain which is the larger. The question, we see, is not primarily one of art but of the two worlds which two minds inhabited. No increased powers of expression, no greater gift for words, could have transformed Ibsen into Shakespeare. The materials out of which the latter created his works — his conception of human dignity, his sense of the importance of human passions, his vision of the amplitude of human life — simply did not and could not exist for Ibsen, as they did not and could not exist for his contemporaries. God and Man and Nature had all somehow dwindled in the course of the intervening centuries, not because the realistic creed of modern art led us to seek out mean people, but because this meanness of human life was somehow thrust upon us by the operation of that same process which led to the development of realistic theories of art by which our vision could be justified.

Hence, though we still apply, sometimes, the adjective "tragic" to one or another of those modern works of literature which describe human misery and which end more sadly even than they begin, the term is a misnomer since it is obvious that the works in question have nothing in common with the classical examples of the genre and produce in the reader a sense of depression which is the exact opposite of that elation generated when the spirit of a Shakespeare rises joyously superior to the outward calamities which he recounts and celebrates the greatness of the human spirit whose travail he describes. Tragedies, in that only sense of the word which has any distinctive meaning, are no longer written in either the dramatic or any other form and the fact is not to be accounted for in any merely literary terms. It is not the result of any fashion in literature or of any deliberation to write about human nature or character under different aspects, any more than it is of either any greater sensitiveness of feeling which would make us shrink from the contemplation of the suffering of Medea or Othello or of any greater optimism which would make us more likely to see life in more cheerful terms. It is, on the contrary, the result of one of those enfeeblements of the human spirit not unlike that described in the previous chapter of this essay, and a further illustration of that gradual weakening of man's confidence in his ability to impose upon the phenomenon of life an interpretation acceptable to his desires which is the subject of the whole of the present discussion.

To explain that fact and to make clear how the creation of classical tragedy did consist in the successful effort to impose such a satisfactory interpretation will require, perhaps, the special section which follows, although the truth of the fact that it does impose such an interpretation must be evident to any one who has ever risen from the reading of *Oedipus* or *Lear* with that feeling of exultation which comes when we have been able, by rare good fortune, to enter into its spirit as completely as it is possible for us of a remoter and emotionally enfeebled age to enter it. Meanwhile one anticipatory remark may be ventured. If the plays and the novels of today deal with littler people and less mighty emotions it is not because we have become interested in commonplace souls and their unglamorous adventures but because we have come, willy-nilly, to see the soul of man as commonplace and its emotions as mean.

II

Tragedy, said Aristotle, is the "imitation of noble actions," and though it is some twenty-five hundred years since the dictum was uttered there is only one respect in which we are inclined to modify it. To us "imitation" seems a rather naïve word to apply to that process by which observation is turned into art, and we seek one which would define or at least imply the nature of that interposition of the personality of the artist between the object and the beholder which constitutes his function and by means of which he transmits a modified version,

rather than a mere imitation, of the thing which he has contemplated.

In the search for this word the estheticians of romanticism invented the term "expression" to describe the artistic purpose to which apparent imitation was subservient. Psychologists, on the other hand, feeling that the artistic process was primarily one by which reality is modified in such a way as to render it more acceptable to the desires of the artist, employed various terms in the effort to describe that distortion which the wish may produce in vision. And though many of the newer critics reject both romanticism and psychology, even they insist upon the fundamental fact that in art we are concerned, not with mere imitation, but with the imposition of some form upon the material which it would not have if it were merely copied as a camera copies.

Tragedy is not, then, as Aristotle said, the *imitation* of noble actions, for, indeed, no one knows what a *noble* action is or whether or not such a thing as nobility exists in nature apart from the mind of man. Certainly the action of Achilles in dragging the dead body of Hector around the walls of Troy and under the eyes of Andromache, who had begged to be allowed to give it decent burial, is not to us a noble action, though it was such to Homer, who made it the subject of an able passage in a noble poem. Certainly, too, the same action might conceivably be made the subject of a tragedy and the subject of a farce, depending upon the way in which it was treated; so that to say that tragedy is the *imitation* of a *noble* action is to be guilty of assuming, first, that art and photography are the same, and, second, that there may be something inherently noble in an act as distinguished from the motives which prompted it or from the point of view from which it is regarded.

And yet, nevertheless, the idea of nobility is inseparable from the idea of tragedy, which cannot exist without it. If tragedy is not the imitation or even the modified representation of noble actions it is certainly a representation of actions *considered* as noble, and herein lies its essential nature, since no man can conceive it unless he is capable of believing in the greatness and importance of man. Its action is usually, if not always, calamitous, because it is only in calamity that the human spirit has the opportunity to reveal itself triumphant over the outward universe which fails to conquer it; but this calamity in tragedy is only a means to an end and the essential thing which distinguishes real tragedy from those distressing modern works sometimes called by its name is the fact that it is in the former alone that the artist has found himself capable of considering and of making us consider that his people and his actions have that amplitude and importance which make them noble. Tragedy arises then when, as in Periclean Greece or Elizabethan England, a people fully aware of the calamities of life is nevertheless serenely confident of the greatness of man, whose mighty passions and supreme fortitude are revealed when one of these calamities overtakes him.

To those who mistakenly think of it as something gloomy or depressing, who are incapable of recognizing the elation which its celebration of human greatness inspires, and who, therefore, confuse it with things merely miserable or pathetic, it must be a paradox that the happiest, most vigorous, and most confident ages which the world has ever known — the Periclean and the Elizabethan — should be exactly those which created and which most relished the mightiest tragedies; but the paradox is, of course, resolved by the fact that tragedy is essentially an expression, not of despair, but of the triumph over despair and of confidence in the value of human life. If Shakespeare himself ever had that "dark period " which his critics and biographers have imagined for him, it was at least no darkness like that bleak and arid despair which sometimes settles over modern spirits. In the midst of it he created both the elemental grandeur of Othello and the pensive majesty of Hamlet and, holding them up to his contemporaries, he said in the words of his own Miranda, "Oh, rare new world that hath *such* creatures in it."

All works of art which deserve their name have a happy end. This is indeed the thing which constitutes them art and through which they perform their function. Whatever the character of the events, fortunate or unfortunate, which they recount, they so mold or arrange or interpret them that we accept gladly the conclusion which they reach and would not have it otherwise. They may conduct us into the realm of pure fancy where wish and fact are identical and the world is remade exactly after the fashion of the heart's desire or they may yield some greater or less allegiance to fact; but they must always reconcile us in one way or another to the representation which they make and the distinctions between the genres are simply the distinctions between the means by which this reconciliation is effected.

Comedy laughs the minor mishaps of its characters away; drama solves all the difficulties which it allows to arise; and melodrama, separating good from evil by simple lines, distributes its rewards and punishments in accordance with the principles of a naïve justice which satisfies the simple souls of its audience, which are neither philosophical enough to question its primitive ethics nor critical enough to object to the way in which its neat events violate the laws of probability. Tragedy, the greatest and the most difficult of the arts, can adopt none of these methods; and yet it must reach its own happy end in its own way. Though its conclusion must be, by its premise, outwardly calamitous, though it must speak to those who know that the good man is cut off and that the fairest things are the first to perish, yet it must leave them, as *Othello* does, content that this is so. We must be and we are glad that Juliet dies and glad that Lear is turned out into the storm.

Milton set out, he said, to justify the ways of God to man, and his phrase, if it be interpreted broadly enough, may be taken as describing the function of all art, which must, in some way or other, make the life which it seems to represent satisfactory to those who see its reflection in the magic mirror, and it must gratify or at least reconcile the desires of the beholder, not necessarily, as the naïver exponents of Freudian psychology maintain, by gratifying individual and often eccentric wishes, but at least by satisfying the universally human desire to find in the world some justice, some meaning, or, at the very least, some recognizable order. Hence it is that every real tragedy, however tremendous it may be, is an affirmation of faith in life, a declaration that even if God is not in his Heaven, then at least Man is in his world.

We accept gladly the outward defeats which it describes for the sake of the inward victories which it reveals. Juliet died, but not before she had shown how great and resplendent a thing love could be; Othello plunged the dagger into his own breast, but not before he had revealed that greatness of soul which makes his death seem unimportant. Had he died in the instant when he struck the blow, had he perished still believing that the world was as completely black as he saw it before the innocence of Desdemona was revealed to him, then, for him at least, the world would have been merely damnable, but Shakespeare kept him alive long enough to allow him to learn his error and hence to die, not in despair, but in the full acceptance of the tragic reconciliation to life. Perhaps it would be pleasanter if men could believe what the child is taught — that the good are happy and that things turn out as they should — but it is far more important to be able to believe, as Shakespeare did, that however much things in the outward world may go awry, man has, nevertheless, splendors of his own and that, in a word, Love and Honor and Glory are not words but realities.

Thus for the great ages tragedy is not an expression of despair but the means by which they saved themselves from it. It is a profession of faith, and a sort of religion; a way of looking at life by virtue of which it is robbed of its pain. The sturdy soul of the tragic author seizes upon suffering and uses it only as a means by which joy may be wrung out of existence, but it is not to be forgotten that he is enabled to do so only because of his belief in the greatness of human nature and because, though he has lost the child's faith in life, he has not lost his far more important faith in human nature. A tragic writer does not have to believe in God, but he must believe in man.

And if, then, the Tragic Spirit is in reality the product of a religious faith in which, sometimes at least, faith in the greatness of God is replaced by faith in the greatness of man, it serves, of course, to perform the function of religion, to make life tolerable for those who participate in its beneficent illusion. It purges the souls of those who might otherwise despair and it makes endurable the realization that the events of the outward world do not correspond with the desires of the heart, and thus, in its own particular way, it does what all religions do, for it gives a rationality, a meaning, and a justification to the universe. But if it has the strength it has also the weakness of all faiths, since it may — nay, it must — be ultimately lost as reality, encroaching further and further into the realm of imagination, leaves less and less room in which that imagination can build its refuge.

III

It is, indeed, only at a certain stage in the development of the realistic intelligence of a people that the tragic faith can exist. A naïver people may have, as the ancient men of the north had, a body of legends which are essentially tragic, or it may have only (and need only) its happy and childlike mythology which arrives inevitably at its happy end, where the only ones who suffer "deserve" to do so and in which, therefore, life is represented as directly and easily acceptable. A too sophisticated society on the other hand — one which, like ours, has outgrown not merely the simple optimism of the child but also that vigorous, one might almost say adolescent, faith in the nobility of man which marks a Sophocles or a Shakespeare, has neither fairy tales to assure it that all is always right in the end nor tragedies to make it believe that it rises superior in soul to the outward calamities which befall it.

Distrusting its thought, despising its passions, realizing its impotent unimportance in the universe, it can tell itself no stories except those which make it still more acutely aware of its trivial miseries. When its heroes (sad misnomer for the pitiful creatures who people contemporary fiction) are struck down it is not, like Oedipus, by the gods that they are struck but only, like Oswald Alving, by syphilis, for they know that the gods, even if they existed, would not trouble with them, and they cannot attribute to themselves in art an importance in which they do not believe. Their so-called tragedies do not and cannot end with one of those splendid calamities which in Shakespeare seem to reverberate through the universe, because they cannot believe that the universe trembles when their love is, like Romeo's, cut off or when the place where they (small as they are) have gathered up their trivial treasure is, like Othello's sanctuary, defiled. Instead, mean misery piles on mean misery, petty misfortune follows petty misfortune, and despair becomes intolerable because it is no longer even significant or important.

Ibsen once made one of his characters say that he did not read much because he found reading "irrelevant," and the adjective was brilliantly chosen because it held implications even beyond those of which Ibsen was consciously aware. What is it that made the classics irrelevant to him and to us? Is it not just exactly those to him impossible premises which make tragedy what it is, those assumptions that the soul of man is great, that the universe (together with whatever gods may be) concerns itself with him and that he is, in a word, noble? Ibsen turned to village politics for exactly the same reason that his contemporaries and his successors have, each in his own way, sought out some aspect of the common man and his common life — because, that is to say, here was at least something small enough for him to be able to believe.

Bearing this fact in mind, let us compare a modern "tragedy" with one of the great works of a happy age, not in order to judge of their relative technical merits but in order to determine to what extent the former deserves its name by achieving a tragic solution capable of purging the soul or of reconciling the emotions to the life which it pictures. And in order to make the comparison as fruitful as possible let us choose Hamlet on the one hand and on the other a play like Ghosts which was not only written by perhaps the most powerful as well as the most typical of modern writers but which is, in addition, the one of his works which seems most nearly to escape

that triviality which cannot be entirely escaped by any one who feels, as all contemporary minds do, that man is relatively trivial.

In Hamlet a prince ("in understanding, how like a god!") has thrust upon him from the unseen world a duty to redress a wrong which concerns not merely him, his mother, and his uncle, but the moral order of the universe. Erasing all trivial fond records from his mind, abandoning at once both his studies and his romance because it has been his good fortune to be called upon to take part in an action of cosmic importance, he plunges (at first) not into action but into thought, weighing the claims which are made upon him and contemplating the grandiose complexities of the universe. And when the time comes at last for him to die he dies, not as a failure, but as a success. Not only has the universe regained the balance which had been upset by what seemed the monstrous crime of the guilty pair ("there is nothing either good nor ill but thinking makes it so"), but in the process by which that readjustment is made a mighty mind has been given the opportunity, first to contemplate the magnificent scheme of which it is a part, and then to demonstrate the greatness of its spirit by playing a rôle in the grand style which it called for. We do not need to despair in such a world if it has such creatures in it.

Turn now to Ghosts — look upon this picture and upon that. A young man has inherited syphilis from his father. Struck by a to him mysterious malady he returns to his northern village, learns the hopeless truth about himself, and persuades his mother to poison him. The incidents prove, perhaps, that pastors should not endeavor to keep a husband and wife together unless they know what they are doing. But what a world is this in which a great writer can deduce nothing more than that from his greatest work and how are we to be purged or reconciled when we see it acted? Not only is the failure utter, but it is trivial and meaningless as well.

Yet the journey from Elsinore to Skien is precisely the journey which the human spirit has made, exchanging in the process princes for invalids and gods for disease. We say, as Ibsen would say, that the problems of Oswald Alving are more "relevant" to our life than the problems of Hamlet, that the play in which he appears is more "real" than the other more glamorous one, but it is exactly because we find it so that we are condemned. We can believe in Oswald but we cannot believe in Hamlet, and a light has gone out in the universe. Shakespeare justifies the ways of God to man, but in Ibsen there is no such happy end and with him tragedy, so called, has become merely an expression of our despair at finding that such justification is no longer possible.

Modern critics have sometimes been puzzled to account for the fact that the concern of ancient tragedy is almost exclusively with kings and courts. They have been tempted to accuse even Aristotle of a certain naïveté in assuming (as he seems to assume) that the "nobility" of which he speaks as necessary to a tragedy implies a nobility of rank as well as of soul, and they have sometimes regretted that Shakespeare did not devote himself more than he did to the serious consideration of those common woes of the common man which subsequent writers have exploited with increasing pertinacity. Yet the tendency to lay the scene of a tragedy at the court of a king is not the result of any arbitrary convention but of the fact that the tragic writers believed easily in greatness just as we believe easily in meanness. To Shakespeare, robes and crowns and jewels are the garments most appropriate to man because they are the fitting outward manifestation of his inward majesty, but to us they seem absurd because the man who bears them has, in our estimation, so pitifully shrunk. We do not write about kings because we do not believe that any man is worthy to be one and we do not write about courts because hovels seem to us to be dwellings more appropriate to the creatures who inhabit them. Any modern attempt to dress characters in robes ends only by making us aware of a comic incongruity and any modern attempt to furnish them with a language resplendent like Shakespeare's ends only in bombast.

True tragedy capable of performing its function and of purging the soul by reconciling man to his woes can exist only by virtue of a certain pathetic fallacy far more inclusive than that to which the name is commonly given. The romantics, feeble descendants of the tragic writers to whom they are linked by their effort to see life and nature in grandiose terms, loved to imagine that the sea or the sky had a way of according itself with their moods, of storming when they stormed and smiling when they smiled. But the tragic spirit sustains itself by an assumption much more far-reaching and no more justified. Man as it sees him lives in a world which he may not dominate but which is always aware of him. Occupying the exact center of a universe which would have no meaning except for him and being so little below the angels that, if he believes in God, he has no hesitation in imagining Him formed as he is formed and crowned with a crown like that which he or one of his fellows wears, he assumes that each of his acts reverberates through the universe. His passions are important to him because he believes them important throughout all time and all space; the very fact that he can sin (no modern can) means that this universe is watching his acts; and though he may perish, a God leans out from infinity to strike him down. And it is exactly because an Ibsen cannot think of man in any such terms as these that his persons have so shrunk and that his "tragedy" has lost that power which real tragedy always has of making that infinitely ambitious creature called man content to accept his misery if only he can be made to feel great enough and important enough. An Oswald is not a Hamlet chiefly because he has lost that tie with the natural and supernatural world which the latter had. No ghost will leave the other world to warn or encourage him, there is no virtue and no vice which he can possibly have which can be really important, and when he dies neither his death nor the manner of it will be, outside the circle of two or three people as unnecessary as himself, any more important than that of a rat behind the arras.

Perhaps we may dub the illusion upon which the tragic spirit is nourished the Tragic, as opposed to the Pathetic, Fallacy, but fallacy though it is, upon its existence depends not merely the writing of tragedy but the existence of that religious feeling of which tragedy is an expression and by means of which a people aware of the dissonances of life manages nevertheless to hear them as harmony. Without it neither man nor his passions can seem great enough or important enough to justify the sufferings which they entail, and literature, expressing the mood of a people, begins to despair where once it had exulted. Like the belief in love and like most of the other mighty illusions by means of which human life has been given a value, the Tragic Fallacy depends ultimately upon the assumption which man so readily makes that something outside his own being, some "spirit not himself" — be it God, Nature, or that still vaguer thing called a Moral Order — joins him in the emphasis which he places upon this or that and confirms him in his feeling that his passions and his opinions are important. When his instinctive faith in that correspondence between the outer and the inner world fades, his grasp upon the faith that sustained him fades also, and Love or Tragedy or what not ceases to be the reality which it was because he is never strong enough in his own insignificant self to stand alone in a universe which snubs him with its indifference.

In both the modern and the ancient worlds tragedy was dead long before writers were aware of the fact. Seneca wrote his frigid melodramas under the impression that he was following in the footsteps of Sophocles, and Dryden probably thought that his *All for Love* was an improvement upon Shakespeare, but in time we awoke to the fact that no amount of rhetorical bombast could conceal the fact that grandeur was not to be counterfeited when the belief in its possibility was dead, and turning from the hero to the common man, we inaugurated the era of realism. For us no choice remains except that between mere rhetoric and the frank consideration of our fellow men. who may be the highest of the anthropoids but who are certainly too far below the angels to imagine either that these angels can concern themselves with them or that they can catch any glimpse of even the soles of angelic feet. We can

no longer tell tales of the fall of noble men because we do not believe that noble men exist. The best that we can achieve is pathos and the most that we can do is to feel sorry for ourselves. Man has put off his royal robes and it is only in sceptered pomp that tragedy can come sweeping by.

IV

Nietzsche was the last of the great philosophers to attempt a tragic justification of life. His central and famous dogma — "Life is good *because* it is painful" — sums up in a few words the desperate and almost meaningless paradox to which he was driven in his effort to reduce to rational terms the far more imaginative conception which is everywhere present but everywhere unanalyzed in a Sophocles or a Shakespeare and by means of which they rise triumphant over the manifold miseries of life. But the very fact that Nietzsche could not even attempt to state in any except intellectual terms an attitude which is primarily unintellectual and to which, indeed, intellectual analysis is inevitably fatal, is proof of the distance which he had been carried (by the rationalizing tendencies of the human mind) from the possibility of the tragic solution which he sought; and the confused, half-insane violence of his work will reveal, by the contrast which it affords with the serenity of the tragic writers whom he admired, how great was his failure.

Fundamentally this failure was, moreover, conditioned by exactly the same thing which has conditioned the failure of all modern attempts to achieve what he attempted — by the fact, that is to say, that tragedy must have a hero if it is not to be merely an accusation against, instead of a justification of, the world in which it occurs. Tragedy is, as Aristotle said, an imitation of noble actions, and Nietzsche, for all his enthusiasm for the Greek tragic writers, was palsied by the universally modern incapacity to conceive man as noble. Out of this dilemma, out of his need to find a hero who could give to life as he saw it the only possible justification, was born the idea of the Superman, but the Superman is, after all, only a hypothetical being, destined to become what man actually was in the eyes of the great tragic writers — a creature (as Hamlet said) " how infinite in capacities, in understanding how like a god." Thus Nietzsche lived half in the past through his literary enthusiasms and half in the future through his grandiose dreams, but for all his professed determination to justify existence he was no more able than the rest of us to find the present acceptable. Life, he said in effect, is not a Tragedy now but perhaps it will be when the Ape-man has been transformed into a hero (the *Übermensch*), and trying to find that sufficient, he went mad.

He failed, as all moderns must fail when they attempt, like him, to embrace the tragic spirit as a religious faith, because the resurgence of that faith is not an intellectual but a vital phenomenon, something not achieved by taking thought but born, on the contrary, out of an instinctive confidence in life which is nearer to the animal's unquestioning allegiance to the scheme of nature than it is to that critical intelligence characteristic of a fully developed humanism. And like other faiths it is not to be recaptured merely by reaching an intellectual conviction that it would be desirable to do so.

Modern psychology has discovered (or at least strongly emphasized) the fact that under certain conditions desire produces belief, and having discovered also that the more primitive a given mentality the more completely are its opinions determined by its wishes, modern psychology has concluded that the best mind is that which most resists the tendency to believe a thing simply because it would be pleasant or advantageous to do so. But justified as this conclusion may be from the intellectual point of view, it fails to take into account the fact that in a universe as badly adapted as this one to human as distinguished from animal needs this ability to will a belief may bestow an enormous vital advantage as it did, for instance, in the case at present under discussion where it made possible for Shakespeare the compensations of a tragic faith completely inaccessible to Nietzsche. Pure intelligence, incapable of being influenced by desire and therefore also incapable of choosing one opinion rather than another simply because

the one chosen is the more fruitful or beneficent, is doubtless a relatively perfect instrument for the pursuit of truth, but the question (likely, it would seem, to be answered in the negative) is simply whether or not the spirit of man can endure the literal and inhuman truth.

Certain ages and simple people have conceived of the action which passes upon the stage of the universe as of something in the nature of a Divine Comedy, as something, that is to say, which will reach its end with the words " and they lived happily ever after." Others, less naïve and therefore more aware of those maladjustments whose reality, at least so far as outward events are concerned, they could not escape, have imposed upon it another artistic form and called it a Divine Tragedy, accepting its catastrophe as we accept the catastrophe of an *Othello*, because of its grandeur. But a Tragedy, Divine or otherwise, must, it may again be repeated, have a hero, and from the universe as we see it both the Glory of God and the Glory of Man have departed. Our cosmos may be farcical or it may be pathetic but it has not the dignity of tragedy and we cannot accept it as such.

Yet our need for the consolations of tragedy has not passed with the passing of our ability to conceive it. Indeed, the dissonances which it was tragedy's function to resolve grow more insistent instead of diminishing. Our passions, our disappointments, and our sufferings remain important to us though important to nothing else and they thrust themselves upon us with an urgency which makes it impossible for us to dismiss them as the mere trivialities which, so our intellects tell us, they are. And yet, in the absence of tragic faith or the possibility of achieving it, we have no way in which we may succeed in giving them the dignity which would not only render them tolerable but transform them as they were transformed by the great ages into joys. The death of tragedy is, like the death of love, one of those emotional fatalities as the result of which the human as distinguished from the natural world grows more and more a desert.

Poetry, said Santayana in his famous phrase, is " religion which is no longer believed," but it depends, nevertheless, upon its power to revive in us a sort of temporary or provisional credence and the nearer it can come to producing an illusion of belief the greater is its power as poetry. Once the Tragic Spirit was a living faith and out of it tragedies were written. Today these great expressions of a great faith have declined, not merely into poetry, but into a kind of poetry whose premises are so far from any we can really accept that we can only partially and dimly grasp its meaning.

We read but we do not write tragedies. The tragic solution of the problem of existence, the reconciliation to life by means of the tragic spirit is, that is to say, now only a fiction surviving in art. When that art itself has become, as it probably will, completely meaningless, when we have ceased not only to write but to *read* tragic works, then it will be lost and in all real senses forgotten, since the devolution from Religion to Art to Document will be complete.

ARTHUR EDWIN KROWS

Born in New York in 1892, Arthur Edwin Krows received his education in the public schools of that city. Studying stagecraft under William T. Price, he was naturally led to engage in work that gave him a chance to be in or near the theater, and in 1913 he became assistant editor of the New York *Dramatic Mirror*. Two years later he was made general press representative to Winthrop Ames at the New Theater. Succeeding press-agent connections carried him into the developing motion-picture industry, where he presently emerged as a scenario writer and film editor for major companies in Hollywood and the East. About 1919 he was attracted to motion-picture opportunities in the departments of education and social service, and became a writer and independent producer in that field. With the advent of "talking" pictures some years later he was qualified for the making of some of the first non-theatrical sound films. A fairly steady output of published books and articles relating to

these experiences has sustained his literary connections. In 1932 he was made managing editor of *New Outlook,* and a few years later of the society magazine *The Spur.* Following the outbreak of World War II he joined the Government and served throughout as a non-theatrical picture specialist in the Office of War Information. From the earliest years of his active career Krows has maintained his direct interest in the theater and drama. His first book, *Play Production in America* (1916, revised and reissued some years later), remains a standard reference work while *Playwriting for Profit* has established itself as a practical working manual. While Krows, in this last-named work and elsewhere, has given generous credit to Price for many of the ideas he has set forth in the playwriting book, he has himself added much to the theories of his "master," and at the same time explained and clarified a good deal that was imperfectly expressed or only hinted at.

THE STAGE WAY [1]
[From *Playwriting for Profit*]
(1928–1947)

One of the first obligations of a person essaying to write stage plays is manifestly to study the conditions in which the works are to be performed, consider-

ing the public to which he is to make his appeal and the system of distribution

from *Playwriting for Profit,* copyright, 1928, by Longmans, Green and Co. The author has chosen passages from Chap. 3 of the book, and made a few minor changes for the present reprint.

[1] Reprinted by permission of the author and the publisher, Longmans, Green & Co.,

through which that public is to be reached.

The study must be constant because the aspect of the theater is constantly changing. Severance of diplomatic relations will throw certain plays on alien subjects into the discard in the twinkling of an eye; beginning of recruiting or mobilization of troops, or an actual declaration of war, may cause peremptory withdrawal of dramas that advocate peace, and shifts in fads and other modifications, more or less important, occur with the passing of a few short hours. Knowing this, the dramatist becomes aware that unless his study is unceasing it is valueless.

The stage has at least two fundamental aspects, however, that may be appreciated once and for all, and these are the facts that it makes its appeal almost wholly to the eye and the ear. There have been instances in which perfumes have been introduced into the auditorium ventilators to influence the audience's sense of smell; but this is an unimportant addition.

The visual part of drama has been esteemed since the dawn of its recorded history. . . . The gripping moments in all plays, either for stage or screen, are unspoken. The gripping moments in life are those that pass without words — the farewell when the voice is too choked for utterance, the silent expressions of sympathy or contempt. The celebrated scene in "Shore Acres" wherein old Nat fixes the fire for the night, lights his lamp and goes upstairs to bed, occupies several pages of James A. Herne's manuscript describing just what the old man is thinking during all his "business." Pilar Morin has said that in the pantomime, "L'Enfant Prodigue," there are "22,000 inwardly spoken words. . . ."

Visual treatment is the best way to prove points in drama. You may have the villain declare over and over again that he has done a good act; but the only way for the audience to believe it will be for them to see him do it. You may do an impossible thing in a plausible way in the theater, and the audience will condemn the objections because they actually have seen it with their own eyes. They know it's true because they were there when it happened. "Seeing is believing."

Another important service rendered by visual treatment is its strong part in creation of what William Gillette has called "The illusion of the first time." That is, an ideal condition in the theatre is when the spectators have the sense that this particular time, when they are present, is the first time the story has unfolded itself. It all seems spontaneous. They are witnessing a course of events the end to which, so far as their feeling goes, is as uncertain as tomorrow in their own lives. The visual incident is *now,* in the present tense, and therefore, it seems, can never have happened before and can have no real predetermination.

I have cited a number of proofs that visual treatment is stronger dramatically than narrative treatment. Now I hope to explain why. A visual presentation is a direct appeal to the mind of the spectator through his sense of sight: a spoken or printed word is merely a symbol meaning something else that must be translated by the mind into the terms of the especial sense to which it refers. We may give a direct mental impression by showing a hurdy-gurdy playing in front of a beautiful building; but to describe this would require translation of the word "hurdy-gurdy" by the mind for the benefit of the ear, and translation of the word "building" for the benefit of the eye. Of course, we make these translations almost instantly; but the fact remains that a translation is necessary — and hence the appeal that way is secondary. Sight is always quicker than hearing save when the appeal is sound for its own sake, such as a crash of glass, because sound then is an exclusively ear appeal. . . .

Psychologists tell us that we form complete conceptions of objects only when we have seen, heard, tasted, touched and smelled them. Our conception cannot go beyond this because we have no other senses to which an object may appeal. Indeed, it is within reason to suppose that familiar objects may have unknown aspects that we cannot appreciate on that account. There *may,* for instance, be a fourth dimension. But once we have formed what we call a complete conception, a repeated appeal to any one of the senses concerned will provide a clue from which we may reconstruct with our minds the entire fabric. I have a reasonably complete conception of the typewriting machine upon which I write these pages. I may be in a distant room and hear someone else clicking the keys. This would give me the clue by means of which I might tell you, without changing my position, what the machine looks like. . . .

In the regular theater we may make a direct appeal to the mind through only two of the five senses, namely sight and hearing, but we may reach the remaining three by means of visual symbols which the mind may translate for their benefit. We do not go to the theater primarily to stroke a cat, eat a salad or inhale a perfume, but indirectly we may do all these things before we leave. The sight of a boy sucking a lemon thus is likely to pucker our own mouths; the sight of a collision may make us recoil involuntarily from what is but a fancied shock to ourselves; a view of an executioner running his appraising finger over the newly-whetted blade of his ax may cause us to shudder at the purely imagined feel of that razor edge; and the mere mention of violets in certain circumstances may conjure for us their absent fragrance. . . .

The first step to provide an audience with the peculiar pleasure it seeks in the theater is to know just what that pleasure is. . . . I would say that the first quality sought by an audience in the theater is something to compel its attention. Attention is a concentration of the mind, with all its faculties, on something within range that for the time is more compelling than anything else. A shriek for help in a peaceful field would be arresting, whereas it might pass unnoticed in Herculaneum when Vesuvius is vomiting smoke and lava. Attention in the theater may be called by physical combat, a ringing doorbell, a word spoken, the rumble of thunder, or anything else that is worthier of attention than what previously occupied the audience's mind. The action that arrests attention is not necessarily physical movement. It may be any significant matter freshly brought up. Moreover, attention may be sustained merely by a succession of unrelated bids

for it, so long as they are compelling. The audience at the vaudeville theater finds interest in a heterogeneous mixture of trained seals, monologists, singers of topical songs, and acrobats. . . .

By arresting attention afresh every minute it is possible to divert; but it does not give the highest form of dramatic stimulation. To hold the attention without compelling it again, is certainly a finer sort of craftsmanship. The clown who compels his audience first by hitting one character on the head with a bladder, and then, when the interest begins to lag, hits another with the slapstick, is not gaining nearly so much as he is when he puts both feet through one leg of his wide trousers and leads the audience to speculate on his manner of escape. In the first case, he is shocking the audience to attention; in the second, he has aroused their voluntary interest. Here we are on the borderline between elementary drama and the next-best kind. The first instance shows the audience attentive because it *has* to be, and the second shows it attentive because it *wants* to be. . . .

The element of surprise is but a part, and a comparatively small part, of dramatic effect. Certainly when we go back a second time, to see a play that we have liked, we do not gain much surprise. What we do find constant is sympathy — the highest degree of interest. . . .

The great power of the theater is that it produces that ideal condition wherein the spectator ceases to be a mere witness of events and becomes a direct participant in the action. While he is wrapped in the circumstances of the representation — out of himself, as it were — the dramatist may guide him at a touch. But let the interest or the sympathy lag for just one moment and the spell will be broken. The dramatist will have to compel attention all over again, and by degrees coax the spectator back into the world of illusion. In my opinion, the recognition of this power is one of the outstanding discoveries of modern theater-craft. It has been known before; but it took this age of psychological investigation to hail it as a guiding principle. . . .

I have said attention, then curiosity, and then sympathy. Attention is a necessary factor. We may have theatrical offerings with attention alone, as vaudeville or the revue; but plays depending on curiosity must have attention, too, although they may not have sympathy. Sympathetic plays must employ attention, and I am inclined to think that they require curiosity as well, for wholly to arouse sympathy implies a condition of injustice which should be corrected. For example, the overworked objects of sympathy, the widows and the orphans and the helpless puppies, convince the spectator at once that they need protection.

Curiosity presupposes a state of affairs that is in solution, because it is a desire to know more. What the audience desires is a most potent factor in dramatic effect. When the audience desires something greatly and we give it the prospect of not getting it, we have suspense. We may make the prospect dark only in proportion to the audience's desire for success of the sympathetic side; to transcend that is to make the audience despair and end its interest. Curiosity is not merely an inquisitiveness on the part of the audience; it has been piqued by the unsettled circumstances of the stage story. Therefore it is more than a simple curiosity; it is a doubt as to issue plus a specific desire to know the outcome. When an audience's curiosity covers these points we are able to say that a play has suspense. And, when we add sympathy to this, we give curiosity a direction upon which attention may focus.

Both curiosity and sympathy call for, or at least suggest, a state of affairs in which there is doubt as to outcome. Doubt as to outcome implies an opposition of ideas, because without contending forces there can be no uncertainty. So we may say that in a play that employs the full facilities of the medium of expression — that has suspense and sympathy — there must be, potentially at least, elements of opposition. The condition is not one that audiences seek directly, perhaps; but it is a necessary circumstance to either curiosity or sympathy which audiences unquestionably do seek.

EUGENE O'NEILL

Eugene O'Neill was born in New York City in 1888, a son of the popular romantic actor James O'Neill. His early education was fragmentary, but he managed to get one year of college — Princeton. In 1909 he began a series of trips abroad in search of adventure; fell ill, tried office work again, and again set forth to see the world. There followed work on shipboard, in offices, periods without a job, brief spells of acting and managing with traveling theater companies, and finally a job as newspaper man in Connecticut. This was followed by ill-health, retirement to a sanitarium, and an effort at playwriting. In 1914–15 he studied under Professor Baker at Harvard, and in 1916 he first became connected with the Provincetown Players whose New York Theater gave him a chance to see his work competently acted on a stage. For the next few years he was closely associated with the Players, but in 1920 his *Beyond the Horizon* (first full-length play to receive regular Broadway production) achieved considerable popular success. From 1920 onward, he has spent practically all his time writing, even during the twelve-year period (1934–46) when he would allow no new play of his to be produced. O'Neill's few published interviews yield very little of his ideas on dramatic technique, and the occasional brief pronouncements on his art are very little concerned with technical problems. His personal letters, on the other hand, few of which have been printed, abound in long and detailed discussions of esthetic and practical matters. Excerpts from some letters may be consulted in Arthur Hobson Quinn's *A History of the American Drama From the Civil War to the Present Day* (1936); Isaac Goldberg's *The Theater of George Jean Nathan* (1926); several volumes of George Jean

Nathan's collected writings; and Barrett H. Clark's *Eugene O'Neill, the Man and His Plays* (rev. ed., 1947). Among the short notes by O'Neill touching on drama or theater may be mentioned *Strindberg and Our Theater* (Provincetown Playbill, season 1923–24); a *Letter to the New York Times* (April 11, 1920); *Are the Actors to Blame?* (Provincetown Playbill, Season 1925–26); *Eugene O'Neill Writes About His Latest Play* [*The Great God Brown*] (New York *Evening Post,* Feb. 13, 1926); *O'Neill Talks About "Beyond the Horizon"* (New York *Evening Post,* Nov. 27, 1926); *O'Neill's Own Story of "Electra" in the Making* (New York *Herald Tribune,* Nov. 3, 1931).

In 1944 O'Neill, replying to a letter from the editor of the present volume, wrote: "If you want something of mine for the new chapter to *European Theories of the Drama,* all I can suggest is the mask article from *The American Spectator*

and the notes from *Mourning Becomes Electra,* photostat of which was included with the special Limited Edition." He explained why the article on masks was, in his opinion, not especially pertinent, and continued: "Why my suggestion of the *Electra* notes? Well, they probably don't fit in at all with what you want. But they are interesting in that they show the making of a play with infinite pains and a hell of a lot of work, interpreting an old classic plot with a modern psychological fate, trying to create around it, using techniques and discarding them, scorning the limitations of time in the modern theater, etc., etc. And the title of your book is *European Theories.* The play is of classical and so European origin."

(For a detailed list of O'Neill's plays and other publications, see *A Bibliography of the Works of Eugene O'Neill,* by Ralph Sanborn and Barrett H. Clark, 1931.)

WORKING NOTES AND EXTRACTS FROM A FRAGMENTARY WORK DIARY [1]

(1931)

1. (*Spring* — 1926)
   Modern psychological drama using one of the old legend plots of Greek tragedy for its basic theme — the Electra story? — the Medea? Is it possible to get modern psychological approximation of Greek sense of fate into such a play, which an intelligent audience of today, possessed of no belief in gods or supernatural retribution, could accept and be moved by? —

2. (*October, 1928 — Arabian Sea en route for China*)
   Greek tragedy plot idea — story of Electra and family psychologically most interesting — most comprehensive intense basic human interrela-

tionships — can be easily widened in scope to include still others.

3. (*November, 1928 — China Sea*)
   Greek plot idea — give modern Electra figure in play tragic ending worthy of character. In Greek story she peters out into undramatic married banality. Such a character contained too much tragic fate within her soul to permit this — why should Furies have let Electra escape unpunished? Why did the chain of fated crime and retribution ignore her mother's murderess? — a weakness in what remains to us of Greek tragedy that there is no play about Electra's life after the murder of Clytemnestra. Surely it possesses as imaginative tragic possibilities as any of their plots!

4. (*Cap d'Ail, France — April, 1929*)
   Greek tragedy plot idea.— No matter in what period of American history play is laid, must remain a modern psychological drama — nothing to do

[1] Reprinted, in full, by permission of the author. This was originally published as *O'Neill's Own Story of "Electra" in the Making,* New York *Herald-Tribune,* Nov. 3, 1931. A photostat of the original MS was included in the "Special Edition" of the play published by Horace Liveright, Inc., New York, 1931.

with period except to use it as a mask — What war? — Revolution too far off and too clogged in people's minds with romantic grammar-school-history associations. World War too near and recognizable in its obstructing (for my purpose) minor aspects and superficial character identifications (audience would not see fated wood because too busy recalling trees) — needs distance and perspective — period not too distant for audience to associate itself with, yet possessing costume, etc. — possessing sufficient mask of time and space, so that audiences will unconsciously grasp at once, it is primarily drama of hidden life forces — fate — behind lives of characters. Civil War is only possibility — fits into picture — Civil War as background for drama of murderous family love and hate —

5. (*Cap d'Ail, France — April, 1929*) (Greek plot idea) — Lay in New England small seaport, shipbuilding town — family town's best — shipbuilders and owners — wealthy for period — Agamemnon character town's leading citizen, Mayor before war, now Brigadier General Grant's Army — opening act of play day of Lee's surrender — house Greek temple front type that was rage in 1st half 19th century — (this fits in well and absolutely justifiable, not forced Greek similarity) — This home of New England House of Atreus was built in 1830, say, by Atreus character, Agamemnon's father — grotesque perversion of everything Greek temple expressed of meaning of life — (New England background best possible dramatically for Greek plot of crime and retribution, chain of fate — Puritan conviction of man born to sin and punishment — Orestes' furies within him, his conscience — etc.)

Departures from Greek story — Electra loves Aegisthus — always fated to be mother's rival in love, always defeated — first for father's love, then for brother's, finally for Aegisthus' — reason for Clytemnestra's hatred for Agamemnon sexual frustration by his puritan sense of guilt turning love to lust (she had

romantic love for him before marriage) — omit Iphigenia and Chrysothemis from children — only Orestes and Electra — no Cassandra — keep exact family relationship of Aegisthus (first cousin Agamemnon) — keep general outline of rivalry, hatred, love, lust, revenge in past between Agamemnon's father, Atreus, and Aegisthus' father, Thyestes (in legend Thyestes seduces Aerope, wife of Atreus) — hatred of Atreus for brother — revenge — banishment — (keep general spirit of this but pay no attention to details of legend) Clytemnestra persuades Aegisthus against his will to help her murder Agamemnon (my Aegisthus character weaker, more human and less evil character, has conscience of sort) — method of murder, poison (woman's weapon) — Aegisthus bears strong facial resemblance to Agamemnon and Orestes — his resemblance to Orestes attracts Clytemnestra — his resemblance to her father attracts Electra — Electra adores father, devoted to brother (who resembles father), hates mother — Orestes adores mother, devoted to sister (whose face resembles mother's) so hates his father — Agamemnon, frustrated in love for Clytemnestra, adores daughter, Electra, who resembles her, hates and is jealous of his son, Orestes — etc. — work out this symbol of family resemblances and identification (as visible sign of the family fate) still further — use masks (?)

6. (*Cap d'Ail, France — May, 1929*) (Greek plot idea) — Names of characters — use characteristic names with some similarity to Greek ones — for main characters, at least — but don't strain after this and make it a stunt — no real importance, only convenience in picking — right names always tough job.

Agamemnon — (Asa), (Ezra) Mannon
Clytemnestra — Christine (?)
Orestes — Orin
Electra — Eleanor (?) Ellen (?) Elsa (?)
Laodicea — Lavinia (this sounds more like it) Vinnie (Called in family)

Aegisthus — Augustus (?) Alan
Adam (?)
Pylades — Paul (?) Peter (?)
Hermione — Hazel — Hesther

7. (*Cap d'Ail, France* — *May, 1929*)
(Greek plot idea) — Title — " Mourn-
ing Becomes Electra " — that is, in
old sense of word — it befits — it be-
comes Electra to mourn — it is her
fate, — also, in usual sense (made
ironical here), mourning (black) is
becoming to her — it is the only color
that becomes her destiny —

8. (*Cap d'Ail, France* — *May, 1929*)
" Mourning Becomes Electra " — No
chance getting full value material
into one play or even two — must fol-
low Greek practice and make it tril-
ogy — first play Agamemnon's home-
coming and murder — second, Elec-
tra's revenge on mother and lover,
using Orestes to help her — third
play, retribution Orestes and Electra.
Give each play a separate title —
" Mourning Becomes Electra " title
for trilogy as whole — first play,
" Home-coming " — second,   (?) —
third, "The Haunted."

9. (*Cap d'Ail, France* — *May, 1929*)
" Mourning Becomes Electra " —
Technique — for first draft use com-
paratively straight realism — this
first draft only for purpose of plot
material into definite form — then lay
aside for period and later decide how
to go to final version — what depar-
tures necessary — whether to use
masks, soliloquies, asides, etc.—

10. (*Le Plessis, St. Antoine-du-Rocher,
France* — *June 20, 1929*)
" Mourning Becomes Electra " —
Finished scenario first play, "Home-
coming."

11. (*Le Plessis, St. Antoine-du-Rocher,
France* — *July 11, 1929*)
" Mourning Becomes Electra " —
Finished scenario second play, " The
Hunted " — what an advantage it
was (from a plotter's standpoint, at
least) for authors in other times who
wrote about kings — could commit
murder without having to dodge de-
tection, arrest, trial scenes for their
characters — I have to waste a lot of
ingenuity to enable my plotters to get
away with it without suspicion ! —
still, even history of comparatively

recent crimes (where they happen
among people supposedly respecta-
ble) shows that rural authorities eas-
ily hoodwinked — the poisoning of
Mannon in " Homecoming " would
probably never be suspected (under
the same circumstances) even in New
England town of today, let alone in
1865.

12. (*Le Plessis, St. Antoine-du-Rocher,
France* — *August, 1929*)
"Mourning   Becomes   Electra " —
Finished scenario third play, " The
Haunted " — have given my Yankee
Electra tragic end worthy of her —
and Orestes, too.

13. (*Le Plessis, St. Antoine-du-Rocher,
France* — *Sept., 1929*)
Started writing 1st draft — " Mourn-
ing Becomes Electra."

14. (*Le Plessis, St. Antoine-du-Rocher,
France* — *Oct., 1929*)
After several false starts, all rotten,
think I have hit right line for first
draft now.

15. (*Le Plessis, St. Antoine-du-Rocher,
France* — *Feb. 21, 1930*)
Finished 1st draft " M.B.E." — lay
aside now for at least month —

16. (*Le Plessis, St. Antoine-du-Rocher,
France* — *March 27, 1930*)
Read over first draft " M.B.E." —
scrawny stuff but serves purpose as
first draft — parts damned thrilling
but lots more lousy — not enough
meat — don't like Aegisthus' charac-
ter — hackneyed   and   thin — must
find new one — not enough of sense
of fate hovering over characters, fate
of family — living in the house built
by Atreus' hatred (Abe Mannon) —
a psychological fate — reading this
first draft I get feeling that more of
my idea was left out of play than
there is in it! — In next version I
must correct this at all costs — run
the risk of going to other cluttered
up extreme — use every means to
gain added depth and scope — can
always cut what is unnecessary after-
wards — will write second draft us-
ing half masks and an " Interlude "
technique (combination " Lazarus "
and " Interlude ") and see what can
be gotten out of that — think these
will aid me to get just the right effect
— must get more distance and per-

spective — more sense of fate — more sense of the unreal behind what we call reality which is the real reality! — The unrealistic truth wearing the mask of lying reality, that is the right feeling for this trilogy, if I can only catch it! Stick to modern tempo of dialogue without attempt at pretence of Civil Wartime lingo. That part of 1st draft is right. Obtain more fixed formal structure for first play which succeeding plays will reiterate — pattern of exterior and interior scenes, beginning and ending with exterior in each play — with the one ship scene at the center of the second play (this, center of whole work) emphasizing sea background of family and symbolic motive of sea as means of escape and release — use townsfolk at the beginning of each play, outside house, as fixed chorus pattern — representing prying, commenting, curious town as an ever-present background for the drama of the Mannon family. Develop South Sea Island motive — its appeal for them all (in various aspects) — release, peace, security, beauty, freedom of conscience, sinlessness, etc. — longing for the primitive — and mother symbol — yearning for prenatal non-competitive freedom from fear — make this Island theme recurrent motive — Characterization — Exclude as far as possible and consistent with living people, the easy superficial characterization of individual mannerisms — unless these mannerisms are inevitable finger-prints of inner nature — essential revelations. This applies to main people of trilogy. Townsfolk, on the other hand, should be confined to exterior characterization — main characters too interior — Peter and Hazel should be almost characterless, judged from either of these angles — they are the untroubled, contented "good," a sweet, constant unself-conscious, untempted virtue amid which evil passion works, unrecognized by them — (until end) — but emphasized by their contrast. Resemblance of characters by use of masks intensify Mannon family resemblance between Ezra and Orin

and Adam (and family portraits), and between Christine and Lavinia — peculiar gold-brown hair exactly alike in Lavinia and her mother — same as hair of the dead woman, Adam's mother, whom Ezra's father and uncle had loved — who started the chain of recurrent love and hatred and revenge — emphasize this motivating fate out of past — hair of women another recurrent motive — strange, hidden psychic identity of Christine with the dead woman and of Lavinia (in spite of her father — Mannon imitative mannerisms) with her mother — and of Adam with the Mannons he hates, as well as of Orin with his father — The chanty "Shenandoah" — use this more — as a sort of theme song — its simple sad rhythm of hopeless sea longing peculiarly significant — even the stupid words have striking meaning when considered in relation to tragic events in play — In my scrawny first draft bare melodrama of plot runs away with my intent — this must be corrected in second draft — the unavoidable entire melodramatic action must be felt as working out of psychic fate from past — thereby attain tragic significance — or else! — a hell of a problem, a modern tragic interpretation of classic fate without benefit of gods — for it must, before everything, remain modern psychological play — fate springing out of the family —

17. (*Le Plessis* — *March 31, 1930*)
    Start writing 2nd draft.

18. (*Le Plessis* — *July 11, 1930*)
    Finish 2nd draft — feel drained out — have been working morning, afternoon and night every day, without a single let-up — never worked so intensively over such a long period as I have on this damn' trilogy — wish now I'd never attempted the damn' thing — bitten off more than can chew? — Too close to it to see anything but blur of words — discouraged reaction natural now — after all, do know I was deeply moved by each play as I wrote it — that test has always proved valid heretofore — lay it aside now — we are off to Paris tomorrow — nice little vacation

in dentist's chair scheduled! Best anodyne for pernicious brooding over one's inadequacies, that! — Anything else seems like the best of all possible when your nerves are prancing to sweet and low down of dentist's drill! —

19. (*Le Plessis — July 18, 1930*)

Read the trilogy — much better than I feared — but needs a lot more work before it will be anything like right — chief thing, thought asides now seem entirely unnecessary — don't reveal anything about the characters I can't bring out quite naturally in their talk or their soliloquies when alone — simply get in the way of the play's drive, make the line waver, cause action to halt and limp — must be deleted in toto — Warning! — always hereafter regard with suspicion hangover inclination to use "Interlude" technique regardless — that was what principally hurt "Dynamo," being forced into thought-asides method which was quite alien to essential psychological form of its characters — did not ring true — only clogged up play arbitrarily with obvious author's mannerisms — saw this when I re-read it after return from East — too late! "Interlude" aside technique is special expression for special type of modern neurotic, disintegrated soul — when dealing with simple direct folk or characters of strong will and intense passions, it is superfluous show-shop "business."

20. (*Le Plessis — July 19, 1930*)

Read trilogy again — don't like the soliloquies in their present disjointed thought-prose formula — and my use of half masks on the main protagonists seems to obscure meaning of resemblance between characters instead of dramatically intensifying this meaning — masks introduce other connotations not wanted these plays — have strong feeling there should be much more definite interrelationship between characters' masks and soliloquies, that soliloquies should be arbitrarily set in a stylized form that will be the exact expression of stylized mask symbol — Rewrite all soliloquies in plays along this line — introduce new ones so that soliloquies will recur in a fixed pattern throughout, fitting into structural pattern repeated in each play — try for prose with simple forceful repeating accent and rhythm which will express driving insistent compulsion of passions engendered in family past, which constitute family fate (always remembering fate from within the family is modern psychological approximation of the Greek conception of fate from without, from the supernatural).

21. (*Le Plessis — July 20, 1930*)

Start rewriting, cutting out all asides, stylizing soliloquies as per new conception — think I have hit on right rhythm of prose — monotonous, simple words driving insistence — tom-tom from "Jones" in thought repetition —

22. (*Le Plessis — Sept. 16, 1930*)

Finished rewriting — lay aside for a while — one thing am certain of right now, omitting asides has helped plays enormously —

23. (*Paris — Sept. 20, 1930*)

Read and carefully reread this last stylized - soliloquies version — absolutely convinced they don't do! — feel as I felt about asides in version before this, that they held up plays, break rhythm, clog flow of dramatic development, reveal nothing of characters' motives, secret desires or dreams, that can't be shown directly or clearly suggested in their pantomime or talk — some of these soliloquies are gratifying as pieces of writing in themselves (most of them are not!) but even then they don't belong — have no inherent place in structure — they must come out — and with them the half-masks of the Mannons must go too — obtrude themselves too much into the foreground — introduce an obvious duality-of-character symbolism quite outside my intent in these plays — and if I leave out soliloquies, there is no excuse for these half-masks anyway — save for some future play.

24. (*Paris — Sept. 21, 1930*)

Scheme for revision and final version — in spite of labor on this stylized conception am glad I did it — time not wasted — learned a lot — stylized solil. uncovered new insights into characters and recurrent themes — job now is to get all this in naturally in straight dialogue — as simple and direct and dynamic as possible — with as few words — stop doing things to these characters — let them reveal themselves — in spite of (or because of!) their long locked-up passions, I feel them burning to do just this!

Keep mask conception — but as Mannon *background,* not foreground! — what I want from this mask concept is a dramatic arresting visual symbol of the separateness, the fated isolation of this family, the mark of their fate which makes them dramatically distinct from rest of world — I see now how to retain this effect without the use of built masks — by make-up — *in repose* (that is, *background*) the Mannon faces are like life-like death masks — (death-in-life motive, return to death-with-peace yearning that runs through plays) — this can be gotten very effectively by make-up, as can also the family resemblance — (make-up isn't a lost art in European theatre, why should it be in ours? — only our shiftless inefficiency) — I can visualize the death-mask-like expression of characters' faces in repose suddenly being torn open by passion as extraordinarily effective — moreover, its exact visual representation of what I want expressed —

Rewrite trilogy along these lines — and get more architectural fixed form into outer structure — and more composition (in musical sense) into inner structure — more definite recurrence of themes ("Island" death fear and death wish, the family past, etc.) — always bearing in mind — Mannon drama takes place on a plane where outer reality is mask of true fated reality — unreal realism —

Make into even more definite fixed pattern superficial characteristic type realism of the chorus of the town (the world outside which always sees without really seeing or understanding) and the simple healthy normality — goodness — of Hazel and Peter.

Repetition of the same scene — in its essential spirit, sometimes even in its exact words, but between different characters — following plays as development of fate — theme demands this repetition — Mannon & Christine (about Brant) in 1st play, Christine & Orin (about Brant) in second play — Mannon & Christine in 4th act, 1st play, Lavinia & Orin in 2nd act, 3rd play — etc.

25. (*Le Plessis — Sept. 23, 1930*) Start rewriting.

26. (*Le Plessis — Oct. 15, 1930*) Finish rewriting — off for trip to Spain and Morocco.

27. (*Le Plessis — Nov. 19, 1930*) Read last version — fairly well satisfied — got right line to it, at least — and quality I want — but needs considerable work yet — several new ideas I want to try out — may bring added value — not sure — only way try and see — start on this at once.

28. (*Paris — Jan. 10, 1931*) Have finished most of new stuff — getting plays typed as I work —

29. (*Paris — Feb. 2, 1931*) Typing finished with all new stuff in — let it rest now —

30. (*Le Plessis — Feb. 7, 1931*) Read over — don't like most of new stuff — all right but introduces too many added complications — trying to get added values has blurred those I had — too much of muchness — would need another play added to do it right — and would be wrong even then! — can't crowd intuitions all hidden aspects of life form into one work! — I better throw most of this new stuff out — some valuable and can be condensed and retained — but in general revert entirely to former version.

31. (*Le Plessis — Feb. 20, 1931*) Revision finished — off to Canary Islands for a sun and sea vacation —

32. (*Las Palmas — Canary Islands — March 8, 1931*) Read typed script — looks damned good to me — funny how typed pages bring out clearly values that too-long familiarity with longhand had rendered vague and undynamic — but plenty of work to do — no vacation here — script much too long, of course — needs cutting and condensing throughout — must rewrite end

of "The Hunted"—weak now—Christine's talk to Lavinia toward end bad stuff—first scene of Act One "The Haunted" also needs rewriting and pointing up—flabby and faltering as now written—ends of Scenes One & Two "The Hunted" also need work—

33. (*Las Palmas—March 26, 1931*)
Finished work—return to France (Marseilles) Casablanca and Tangier tomorrow—script retyped—

34. (*Paris—April 4, 1931*)
Decide change Scenes One & Two, Act One, "The Hunted" to Acts One & Two—they are properly acts, now scenes—but Scene One Act One of "The Haunted" is properly a scene—question of feeling, this!—no rules about it—

35. (*Paris—April 9, 1931*)
New script retyped—copies off to Guild—

36. (*Northport—August, 1931*)
Read over galley proofs from Liveright—after nearly four months of not looking at this trilogy, get fairly fresh impact—moved by it—has power and drive and the strange quality of unreal reality I wanted—main purpose seems to me soundly achieved—there is a feeling of fate in it, or I am a fool—a psychological modern approximation of the fate in the Greek tragedies on this theme—attained without benefit of supernatural—

And technically (although this is of minor importance, naturally) I flatter myself it is unique thing in dramaturgy—each play complete episode completely realized but at same time, which is the important point, not complete in that its end begins following play and demands that play as an inevitable sequel—few trilogies in existence in drama of all time and none of them has this quality which, in any time under any conditions, could not have failed to prove an asset—if gained without harm to the separate play, of course, as I believe I have done.

("Interlude" never got credit for this technical virtue—without which its successful production would have been impossible—that the first part rounded out a complete section of Nina's life with a definite beginning and end and yet contained the suspense at its end which called for Part Two—otherwise dinner interval would have wrecked it—no other two-part play, as far as I know, has accomplished this synthesis of end and beginning—)

37. (*Northport—August, 1931*)
Work on galley proofs—cutting is needed, especially in first and third plays—

38. (*Northport—Sept., 1931*)
Work on second galleys—several points strike me—work I did at Canary Islands was of great value in most of results—but feel now a few things eliminated there should be restored—Lavinia's last appeal to Peter near very end—some things in Act Two which help to clear it up—this Act Two of "The Haunted" is weak spot still—needs rearranging—but will postpone final decision on this until I hear cast read plays—then it will hit my ear.

JOHN HOWARD LAWSON

John Howard Lawson was born in New York City in 1894. After his graduation from Williams College in 1914 he went into journalism and for three years was connected with Reuters' Press Cables, the New York office. From 1917 to 1919 he served with the Volunteer Ambulance Service, first with the French Army and later with the American Red Cross. In the summer of 1917 he served at the Front in France, and later in Italy. Since 1919 he has spent most of his time writing plays and motion pictures, in New York and on the West Coast. His first play, an experimental work, was *Roger Bloomer,* produced in New York in 1923. *Processional,* another experimental, and highly successful, play, was produced by the Theater Guild in 1925, and revived not long after. This was followed by *Nirvana* (1926), *Loudspeaker* (1927), and *The International* (1928), the two latter sponsored by The New Playwrights' Theater, an organization devoted to plays and productions of a generally novel or " Radical" nature. *Success Story* (1934) was a Group Theater offering. Three (commercially) unsuccessful plays followed: *Gentlewoman* (1934), *The Pure in Heart* (1934), and *Marching Song* (1937), the last-named a Theater Union production.

The Pure in Heart and *Gentlewoman* were published in a volume called *With a Reckless Preface* (1934), a challenging attack on the drama reviewers. Lawson's *Theory and Technique of Playwriting* was published in 1936. He is author of several motion pictures, an active participant in the affairs of the Screen Writers' Guild and other organizations devoted to the interests of writers, and a contributing editor of New Masses. For several years he has been at work on an ambitious book that will treat of American social and economic history.

THE LAW OF CONFLICT [1]

[From *Theory and Technique of Playwriting*]

(1936)

Since the drama deals with social relationships, a dramatic conflict must be a *social* conflict. We can imagine a dramatic struggle between man and other men, or between man and his environment, including social forces or forces of nature. But it is difficult to imagine a play in which forces of nature are pitted against other forces of nature.

Dramatic conflict is also predicated on the exercise of conscious will. A conflict without conscious will is either wholly subjective or wholly objective; since such a conflict would not deal with the conduct of men in relation to other men or to their environment, it would not be a social conflict.

The following definition may serve as a basis for discussion. The essential character of drama is social conflict in which the conscious will is exerted: persons are pitted against other persons, or individuals against groups, or groups against other groups, or individuals or groups against social or natural forces.

The first impression of this definition is that it is still too broad to be of any

1 Reprinted in full from *Theory and Technique of Playwriting* (1936), by permission of the author, and the publisher, G. P. Putnam's Sons. Copyright, 1936, by John Howard Lawson.

practical value: a prize fight is a conflict between two persons which has dramatic qualities and a slight but appreciable social meaning. A world war is a conflict between groups and other groups, which has deep social implications.

Either a prize fight or a war might furnish the materials for a dramatic conflict. This is not merely a matter of compression and selection — although both compression and selection are obviously necessary. The dramatic element (which transforms a prize fight or a war from potential material of drama into the actual stuff of drama) seems to lie in the *way* in which the expectations and motives of the persons or groups are projected. This is not a matter solely of the use of the conscious will; it involves the *kind* and *degree* of conscious will exerted.

Brunetière tells us that the conscious will must be directed toward a specific goal: he compares Lesage's novel, *Gil Blas,* to the play, *The Marriage of Figaro,* which Beaumarchais made from the novel. " Gil Blas, like everybody else, wants to live, and if possible to live agreeably. That is not what we call having a will. But Figaro wants a certain definite thing, which is to prevent Count Almaviva from exercising on Susanne the seigneurial privilege. He finally succeeds — and I grant, since the statement has been made, that it is not exactly through the means which he had chosen, most of which turn against him; but nevertheless he has constantly willed what he willed. He had not ceased to devise means of attaining it, and when these means have failed, he has not ceased to invent new ones."

William Archer objects to Brunetière's theory on the ground that, "while it describes the matter of a good many dramas, it does not lay down any true differentia, any characteristic common to all true drama, and possessed by no other form of fiction." Archer's objections seem to be chiefly directed against the idea of *specific volition:* He mentions a number of plays in which he feels that there is no genuine conflict of will. He contends that *Oedipus* and *Ghosts* do not come within the limits of Brunetière's formula. He evidently means that the clash of wills between *persons* is not sufficiently defined in these dramas. He says: "No one can say that the balcony scene in *Romeo and Juliet* is undramatic, or the 'Galeoto fu il libro' scene in Mr. Stephen Phillips' *Paolo and Francesca;* yet the point of these scenes is not a clash, but an ecstatic concordance, of wills."

This confuses a conflict between persons with a conflict in which a conscious and definite aim has been set up in defiance of other persons or social forces. To be sure, the "clash of wills" in the balcony scene in *Romeo and Juliet* is not between the two persons on the stage. It would be absurd to suggest that the dramatist arbitrarily confine his art to the presentation of personal quarrels. Brunetière never maintains that any such direct opposition is required. On the contrary, he tells us that the theatre shows "the development of the human will, attacking the obstacles opposed to it by destiny, fortune, or circumstances." And again: "This is what may be called *will,* to set up a goal, and to direct everything toward it, to strive to bring everything into line with it." Can there be any doubt that Romeo and Juliet are setting up a goal and striving "to bring

everything into line with it?" They know exactly what they want, and are conscious of the difficulties which they must meet. This is equally true of the tragic lovers in *Paolo and Francesca.*

Archer's use of *Oedipus* and *Ghosts* as examples is of considerable interest, because it shows the trend of his thought. He says that Oedipus "does not struggle at all. His struggles insofar as that word can be applied to his misguided efforts to escape from the toils of fate, are all things of the past; in the actual course of the tragedy he simply writhes under one revelation after another of bygone error and unwitting crime."

Archer's objection to the law of conflict goes far deeper than the question of *specific acts of volition:* although he disclaims any interest in the philosophic implications of the theory, his own point of view is essentially metaphysical; he accepts the idea of an absolute necessity which denies and paralyzes the will.

Archer neglects an important technical feature of *Oedipus* and *Ghosts.* Both plays employ the technique of beginning at a crisis. This necessarily means that a large part of the action is retrospective. But this does not mean that the action is passive, either in retrospect or in the crucial activity included in the play's structure. *Oedipus* is a series of conscious acts, directed toward sharply defined ends — the acts of men and women of strong will determined to prevent an impending danger. Their acts lead directly to a goal they are striving to avoid; one cannot assume that the exercise of the conscious will presupposes that the will accomplishes its aim. Indeed the intensity and meaning of the conflict lies in the disparity between the aim and the result, between the purpose and the achievement.

Oedipus is in no sense a passive victim. At the opening of the play he is aware of a problem, which he consciously strives to solve. This leads him to a violent conflict of will with Creon. Then Jocasta realizes the direction in which Oedipus' search is moving; she is faced with a terrible inner conflict; she tries to warn Oedipus, but he refuses to turn back from what he has *willed;* come what may, he must trace his own origin. When Oedipus faces the unbearable truth, he commits a conscious act: he blinds himself; and in the final scene with his two daughters, Antigone and Ismene, he is *still* facing the purport of the events which have crushed him; considering the future, the effect of his own acts upon his children, the measure of his own responsibility.

I have already stated that *Ghosts* is Ibsen's most vital study of personal and social responsibility. Mrs. Alving's life is a long, conscious fight to control her environment. Oswald does not accept his fate; he opposes it with all the force of his will. The end of the play shows Mrs. Alving faced with a terrible decision, a decision which strains her will to the breaking point — she must decide whether or not to kill her own son who has gone insane.

What would *Ghosts* be like if it were (as Archer maintains it to be) a play without a conscious struggle of wills? It is very difficult to conceive of the play in this way: the only events which would be partly unchanged would be Oswald's insanity and the burning of the orphanage. But there would be no action whatsoever leading to these situations. And even Oswald's cry, "give me the sun," would of necessity be omitted, since it expresses conscious will. Furthermore, if no exercise of conscious will were concerned, the orphanage would never have been built.

While denying that conflict is invariably present in drama, Archer does not agree with the Maeterlinckian theory which denies action and finds dramatic power in a man "submitting with bent head to the presence of his soul and his destiny." Archer is well aware that the theatre must deal with *situations* which affect the lives and emotions of human beings. Since he disapproves of the idea of a conflict of will, he suggests that the word, *crisis,* is more universally characteristic of dramatic representation. "The drama," he says, "may be called the art of crises, as fiction is the art of gradual developments." While this is not an inclusive definition, there can be no question that the idea of *crisis* adds something very pertinent to our conception of dramatic conflict. One can readily imagine a conflict which does not reach a crisis; in our daily lives we take

continuous part in such conflicts. A struggle which fails to reach a crisis is undramatic. Nevertheless we cannot be satisfied with Archer's statement that "the essence of drama is crisis." An earthquake is a crisis, but its dramatic significance lies in the reactions and acts of human beings. If *Ghosts* consisted only of Oswald's insanity and the burning of the orphanage it would include two crises, but no conscious will and no *preparation.* When human beings are involved in events which lead to a crisis, they do not stand idly by and watch the climax approach. Human beings seek to shape events for their own advantage, to extricate themselves from difficulties which are partially foreseen. The activity of the conscious will, seeking a way out, creates the very conditions which precipitate the crisis.

Henry Arthur Jones, in analyzing the points of view of Brunetière and Archer, tries to combine them by defining a play as "a succession of suspenses and crises, or as a succession of conflicts impending and conflicts raging, carried on in ascending and accelerated climaxes from the beginning to the end of a connected scheme."

This is a richly suggestive definition. But it is a definition of dramatic *construction* rather than of dramatic *principle.* It tells us a great deal about construction, particularly in the mention of "ascending and accelerated climaxes." But it does not mention the conscious will, and therefore throws very little light on the psychological factor which gives these climaxes their social and emotional significance. The meaning of the situations lies in the degree and kind of conscious will exerted, and in how it *works;* the crisis, the dramatic explosion, is created by *the gap between the aim and the result* — that is, by a shift of equilibrium between the force of will and the force of social necessity. A crisis is the point at which the balance of forces is so strained that something cracks, thus causing a realignment of forces, a new pattern of relationships.

The will which creates drama is directed toward a specific goal. But the goal which it selects must be sufficiently *realistic* to enable the will to have some effect on reality. We in the audience must be able to understand the goal and the possibility of its fulfillment. The kind of will exerted must spring from a consciousness of reality which corresponds to our own. This is a variable factor, which can be accurately determined by an analysis of the social viewpoint of the audience.

But we are concerned not only with the *consciousness* of will, but with the *strength* of will. The exercise of will must be sufficiently vigorous to sustain and develop the conflict to a point of issue. A conflict which fails to reach a crisis is a conflict of weak wills. In Greek and Elizabethan tragedy, the point of maximum strain is generally reached in the death of the hero: he is crushed by the forces which oppose him, or he takes his own life in recognition of his defeat.

Brunetière concludes that strength of will is the only test of dramatic value: "One drama is superior to another drama according as the quantity of will exerted is greater or less, as the share of chance is less and that of necessity greater." One cannot accept this mechanical formulation. In the first place, there is no way to measure the quantity of will exerted. In the second place, the struggle is relative and not absolute. Necessity is simply the totality of the environment, and is, as we have observed, a variable quantity, depending on social concepts. This is a matter of quality as well as quantity. Our conception of the

quality of the will and the quality of the forces to which it is opposed determines our acknowledgment of the depth and scope of the conflict. The highest dramatic art is not achieved by pitting the most gigantic will against the most absolute necessity. The agonized struggle of a weak will, seeking to adjust itself to an inhospitable environment, may contain elements of poignant drama.

But however weak the will may be, it must be *sufficiently strong* to sustain the conflict. Drama cannot deal with people whose wills are atrophied, who are unable to make decisions which have even temporary meaning, who adopt no conscious attitude toward events, who make no effort to control their environment. The precise degree of strength of will required is the strength needed to bring the action to an issue, to create a change of equilibrium between the individual and the environment.

The definition with which we begin this chapter may be re-examined and rephrased as follows:

The essential character of drama is social conflict — persons against other persons, or individuals against groups, or groups against other groups, or individuals or groups against social or natural forces — in which the conscious will, exerted for the accomplishment of specific and understandable aims, is sufficiently strong to bring the conflict to a point of crisis.

DRAMATIC ACTION

The definition which concludes the preceding chapter serves as a starting point for the discussion of action. The major crisis which brings the unified dramatic conflict to a head is not the only crisis in the play: dramatic movement proceeds by a series of changes of equilibrium. Any change of equilibrium constitutes *an action*. The play is a system of *actions,* a system of minor and major changes of equilibrium. The climax of the play is the maximum disturbance of equilibrium which can take place under the given conditions.

In discussing Aristotle, we noted the importance of his treatment of action, not as a quality of construction, but as the essence of construction, the unifying principle at the core of the play. So far we have not developed this point; we have examined the forces which create dramatic conflict; but we have not shown how these forces take a definitive form; the statement that a play is a system of actions leading to a major change of equilibrium is a generalization, but it gives us very little clue to the structure of the system; it does not show us how the beginning, middle and end of the system are determined.

In this sense, the problem of action is the whole problem of dramatic construction and cannot be considered as a separate question. However, it is well to give some consideration to the meaning of *action as a quality.* This is important because it is the only side of the problem which is considered in technical studies of the drama. We are told that a bit of dialogue or a scene or an entire play has the quality of action, or lacks the quality of action. Since it is generally agreed that this quality is essential to drama, it must be very closely related to the *principle of action* which unifies the whole structure.

The present chapter deals only with action as a quality which gives impact, life and color to certain scenes. St. John Ervine says: "A dramatist, when he talks of action, does not mean bustle or mere physical movement: he means development and growth." Ervine regrets that people are slow to understand this: "When you speak of action to them, they immediately imagine that you mean *doing things.*" There can be no question that action involves "development and growth"; but one can sympathize with those who cling to the idea that action means *doing things.* If the conscious will does not cause people to do things, how does it make itself manifest? Development and growth cannot result from inactivity.

George Pierce Baker says that action may be either physical or mental provided it creates *emotional response.* This is of very little value unless we know what constitutes an emotional response. Since what moves us in any action is the spectacle of a change of equilibrium between the individual and the environment, we cannot speak of any action as being exclusively mental or exclusively physical; the change must affect *both* the individual's mind and the objective reality with which he is in contact. Such a change need not involve bustle or violence, but it must involve *doing something,* because if nothing is done the equilibrium would remain static. Furthermore, the change of equilibrium does not happen mechanically, at a given *point;* it is a process which includes the expectation of change, the attempt to bring the change about, as well as the change itself.

How are we to apply this principle to a particular scene or group of scenes?

Brunetière defines action by going straight back to his point of departure — the exercise of the conscious will. He says that the use of the conscious will serves to "distinguish action from motion or agitation." But this is arguing in a circle. The conscious will is a necessary reference point in studying action, but it cannot be confused with the action itself. We examine the conscious will in order to discover the origin and validity of the action. But we do not see or hear the conscious will. What we see and hear is a physical event, which must be defined in terms of seeing and hearing.

Brunetière explains what he means by action — as distinguished from motion or agitation — by an illustration which is far from convincing: "When you have two men earnestly intent on opposite sides of some issue vital to themselves, you have a contest or play, interesting, exciting or absorbing to watch." I think we have all seen the two men of whom Brunetière speaks. They are frequently visible in life, and they are also often to be found behind the footlights, "intent on opposite sides of some issue vital to themselves." To assume that therefore "you have a contest or play," is, to put it mildly, optimistic.

A debate is not an action, however conscious and willing the participants may be. It is equally obvious that a vast amount of commotion may result in an infinitesimal amount of action. A play may contain a duel in every scene, a pitched battle in every act — and the spectators may be sound asleep, or be kept awake only by the noise.

Let us begin by distinguishing *action* (dramatic movement) from *activity* (by which we mean movement in general). Action is a kind of activity, a form of movement in general. The effectiveness of action does not depend on what people do, but on the *meaning* of what they do. We know that the root of this meaning lies in the conscious will. But how does the meaning express itself in dramatic movement? How are we to judge its objective realization?

Is it possible that intense meaning may

be expressed in the dialogue of two persons who sit facing each other and who never move during a considerable scene? Hamlet's soliloquy, "To be or not to be," is dramatically effective. Is it action? Or should it be criticized as a static element in the play's development?

Action may be confined to a minimum of physical activity. But it must be noted that this *minimum,* however slight, determines the meaning of the action. Physical activity is *always* present. To be seated in a chair involves the act of sitting, the use of a certain muscular effort to maintain the position. To speak involves the act of speaking, the use of the throat muscles, movement of the lips, etc. If a tense conflict is involved, the mere act of sitting or speaking will involve a proportionately greater physical effort.

The problem of action is the problem of finding the characteristic and necessary activity. It must involve physical movement (however slight) of a given quality and conveying a given degree of expressiveness. In this connection, a study of the art of acting is of special value to the playwright. The methods of Stanislavski and Vakhtangov, in spite of their limitations, are of tremendous value to the actor, because they assist him in finding the precise physical activity which expresses the emotional direction, habits, purposes, desires, of the character. The actor seeks to create the character in terms of meaningful and living movement.

The playwright's problem is similar: he must find action which intensifies and heightens the conflict of will. Thus, two persons facing each other, not moving and speaking quietly, may offer the exact degree of activity in a given scene. But the important thing in the scene is not the slightness of the movement, but the quality of it — the degree of muscular tension, of expressiveness. Even though the scene may appear to be static, its static element is negative. The positive element is movement.

Then what about speech? Speech is also a form of action. Dialogue which is abstract or deals with general feelings or ideas, is undramatic. Speech is valid insofar as it describes or expresses action. The action projected by the spoken

word may be retrospective, or potential — or it may actually accompany the speech. But the only test of what is said lies in its concreteness, its physical impact, its quality of tension.

The idea that speech can simply reveal a mental state is illogical: the *act* of speaking objectivizes the mental state. As long as the action remains in the mind, the audience knows nothing about it. As soon as the character speaks, the element of physical activity and purpose is present. If the speech is cloudy and lacks concreteness, it will give us only a slight impression of consciousness and purpose and will be a bad speech. Nevertheless we ask: *why* is this man speaking? What does he want? Even if he assures us that his mental condition is completely passive, we cannot believe him: we *still* want to know why he is talking and what he expects to get out of it.

There is also another important characteristic of action: this may be called its fluidity. It is evident that action by its nature cannot be static. However, if activity is repeated, or if its connection with other activity is not indicated, it may well give a static impression. Action (as distinguished from activity) must be in *process of becoming;* therefore it must rise out of other action, and must lead to other, and different, action. Each change of equilibrium involves prior and forthcoming changes or equilibrium. This means also, that the timing of any action, the length of time in proportion to the amount of activity, must be considered.

The situation in which two people sit facing each other and talk quietly may now be judged in the light of several definite questions: Are they *merely* sitting? Or is their sitting expressive of a certain stage of conflict? Does their sitting represent a change in their relationship to each other or to their environment? Are they sitting because they are afraid to move? Or does the sitting give one or the other an advantage in a struggle? Is the sitting intended to exasperate or frighten or disturb the other party? Or are both waiting for news, or for an event, so that they sit in order to console or strengthen one another?

The most serious question in regard to this scene is one which can only be answered by viewing its progression in connection with the scenes which precede and follow it, and in connection with the play as a whole. The scene, in the various forms in which it has been described, contains the expectation of a change in equilibrium. If two people sit facing each other because they are afraid to move, or because they wish to exasperate or frighten the other party, or because they are waiting for news, the element of tension is undoubtedly present. But we must ask whether this tension leads to anything? The scene must actually achieve a change of equilibrium, both in relation to previous and following scenes and in relation to the movement within the scene itself. If the scene does not produce such a change, the tension is false and the element of action is lacking. Progression requires physical movement; but it also lies in the movement of the dialogue, in the extension and development of action through the medium of speech.

Hamlet's soliloquy can be considered in this light. His speech expresses an imminent change of equilibrium, because he is deciding whether or not to take his own life. This represents a new phase in Hamlet's struggle, and leads immediately to another phase, because the soliloquy is broken by the meeting with Ophelia. The language makes the conflict objective, offering the problem in sharply defined images. The physical activity expresses the tension: a man alone on the stage, solitary, facing death. But the aloneness flows immediately from, and to, other action. If the action of the soliloquy were maintained too long, it would become static.

Note the position of the suicide soliloquy. It is preceded by the scene in which the King and Polonius plan to have Ophelia meet Hamlet apparently by accident, while his enemies spy on the encounter: it is followed by the hotly emotional scene between Ophelia and Hamlet, in which he realizes that she is betraying him: "Are you honest? . . . Are you fair? . . . Get thee to a nunnery: why wouldst thou be a breeder of sinners?"

Hamlet is often spoken of as a *subjective* play. Hamlet's will fails him and he finds it difficult to achieve the tasks which are forced upon him. But his attempt to adjust himself to the world he lives in is presented in vigorously objective terms: he finds that he cannot trust his friends, Rosencrantz and Guildenstern, that even the woman he loves is deceiving him. So he turns desperately to another phase of the problem, to probe the truth in regard to his mother and his uncle, to prove and prove again the fact which tortures him. This is dramatized in the violent activity of the play within the play. Then, knowing the truth beyond all doubt, he is forced to face the unbearable implications of the truth — in the scene with his mother. Here again objective activity accompanies the mental conflict: Polonius is killed; Hamlet compares the portraits of his dead father and his living uncle; the ghost enters to warn Hamlet of his "blunted purpose," to counsel him to better understand his mother: "O, step between her and her fighting soul." This line is an extremely pertinent example of action-dialogue. Although the idea is psychological, it is expressed in terms of action. It presents an image, not of some one feeling something, but of some one doing something.

Dramatic action is activity combining physical movement and speech; it includes the expectation, preparation and accomplishment of a change of equilibrium which is part of a series of such changes. The movement toward a change of equilibrium may be gradual, but the process of change must actually take place. False expectation and false preparation are not dramatic action. Action may be complex or simple, but all its parts must be objective, progressive, meaningful.

This definition is valid as far as it goes. But we cannot pretend that it is complete. The difficulty lies in the words "progressive" and "meaningful." Progression is a matter of structure, and meaning is a matter of theme. Neither problem can be solved until we find the unifying principle which gives the pl its *wholeness*, binding a series of a into *an action which is organic* *visible*.

MAXWELL ANDERSON

Maxwell Anderson was born in Atlantic, Pa., in 1888. His college education was received at the University of North Dakota, where he was graduated in 1911. He taught school for a short time in California, and then went into newspaper work. Coming East he contributed to the *New Republic,* and later held down jobs on the *Globe* and the *World* in New York. At about the same time, or perhaps a little earlier, he began writing verse. His first play, *White Desert,* was produced in New York in 1923, and failed. Then, in 1924, came *What Price Glory?,* a forthright and highly successful war play written in collaboration with Laurence Stallings. Two other plays were also written with the same collaborator, but neither was successful. Several plays followed during the next few years, *Saturday's Children* (1927); *Gods of the Lightning* (1928, written with Harold Hickerson); *Elizabeth the Queen* (1930); *Night Over Taos* (1932); and *Both Your Houses* (1933). The next thirteen years were equally productive, among the more distinguished titles being *Mary of Scotland* (1933); *Winterset* (1936); *Knickerbocker Holiday* (1938); *High Tor* (1936); and *The Eve of St. Mark* (1942).

During the early years of his career as playwright Anderson had almost nothing to say in public about the art and craft of his profession, believing that his plays should speak for themselves, but during the 1930's, in particular, he wrote a few prefaces to certain of his published plays, and two or three articles; also a few addresses, most of which are of particular interest as throwing light on the aims and ideals of the writer of tragedy. Some of these were collected in a slender volume under the title *The Essence of Tragedy and Other Footnotes and Papers,* and published in 1939. This volume includes *The Essence of Tragedy, Whatever Hope We Have, A Prelude to Poetry in the Theater, The Politics of Knickerbocker Holiday,* and *Yes, By the Eternal.* See also *The Theater as Religion,* an address originally entitled *By Way of Preface: The Theater as Religion,* delivered at Rutgers University, and later reprinted in the New York *Times; Cut is the Branch That Might Have Grown Full Straight* (an address delivered at the Theater Convention and published in the *Authors' League Bulletin,* 1937); and *How Storm Operation Grew* (*National Theater Conference Bulletin,* Cleveland, 1944). Anderson's pronouncements on theater and drama are clearly the outgrowth of his basic philosophy (foreshadowed in his volume of published verse, *You Who Have Dreams* 1925), and of his concern as craftsman and artist in shaping his plays for production in the contemporary theater.

THE ESSENCE OF TRAGEDY [1]

[From *The Essence of Tragedy and Other Footnotes and Papers*]

(1938)

Anybody who dares to discuss the making of tragedy lays himself open to

[1] Reprinted in full from *The Essence of Tragedy and Other Footnotes and Papers,* Washington, D. C., 1939, by permission of the author and the publisher. Copyright, 1939, by Maxwell Anderson. This paper was ...d at a session of the Modern Language ...iation in New York City in January

critical assault and general barrage, for the theorists have been hunting for the essence of tragedy since Aristotle without entire success. There is no doubt that playwrights have occasionally written tragedy successfully, from Aeschylus on, and there is no doubt that Aristotle came very close to a definition of what tragedy is in his famous passage on catharsis. But why the performance of a tragedy should have a cleansing effect on the audience, why an audience is willing to listen to tragedy, why tragedy has a place in the education of men, has never, to my knowledge, been convincingly stated. I must begin by saying that I have not solved the Sphinx's riddle which fifty generations of skillful brains have left in shadow. But I have one suggestion which I think might lead to a solution if it were put to laboratory tests by those who know something about philosophical analysis and dialectic.

There seems no way to get at this suggestion except through a reference to my own adventures in playwriting, so I ask your tolerance while I use myself as an instance. A man who has written successful plays is usually supposed to know something about the theory of playwriting, and perhaps he usually does. In my own case, however, I must confess that I came into the theatre unexpectedly, without preparation, and stayed in it because I had a certain amount of rather accidental success. It was not until after I had fumbled my way through a good many successes and an appalling number of failures that I began to doubt the sufficiency of dramatic instinct and to wonder whether or not there were general laws governing dramatic structure which so poor a head for theory as my own might grasp and use. I had read the *Poetics* long before I tried playwriting, and I had looked doubtfully into a few well-known handbooks on dramatic structure, but the maxims and theories propounded always drifted by me in a luminous haze — brilliant, true, profound in context, yet quite without meaning for me when I considered the plan for a play or tried to clarify an emotion in dialogue. So far as I could make out every play was a new problem, and the old rules were inapplicable. There were so many rules, so many landmarks, so many pitfalls, so many essential reckonings, that it seemed impossible to find your way through the jungle except by plunging ahead, trusting to your sense of direction and keeping your wits about you as you went.

But as the seasons went by and my failures fell as regularly as the leaves in autumn I began to search again among the theorists of the past for a word of wisdom that might take some of the gamble out of playwriting. What I needed most of all, I felt, was a working definition of what a play is, or perhaps a formula which would include all the elements necessary to a play structure. A play is almost always, probably, an attempt to recapture a vision for the stage. But when you are working in the theatre it's most unsatisfactory to follow the gleam without a compass, quite risky to trust "the light that never was on sea or land" without making sure beforehand that you are not being led straight into a slough of despond. In other words you must make a choice among visions, and you must check your chosen vision carefully before assuming that it will make a play. But by what rules, what maps, what fields of reference can you check so intangible a substance as a revelation, a dream, an inspiration, or any similar nudge from the subconscious mind?

I shan't trouble you with the details of my search for a criterion, partly because I can't remember it in detail. But I reread Aristotle's *Poetics* in the light of some bitter experience, and one of his observations led me to a comparison of ancient and modern playwriting methods. In discussing construction he made a point of the recognition scene as essential to tragedy. The recognition scene, as Aristotle isolated it in the tragedies of the Greeks, was generally an artificial device, a central scene in which the leading character saw through a disguise, recognized as a friend or as an enemy, perhaps as a lover or a member of his own family, some person whose identity had been hidden. Iphigeneia, for example, acting as priestess in an alien country, receives a victim for sacrifice and then recognizes her own brother in this victim. There is an instant and profound emotional reaction, instantly her direction in the play is altered. But occasionally, in the greatest of the plays, the recognition turned on a situation far more convincing, though no less contrived. Oedipus, hunting savagely for the criminal who has brought the plague upon Thebes, discovers that he is himself that criminal — and since this is a discovery that affects not only the physical well-being and happiness of the hero, but the whole structure of his life, the effect on him and on the direction of the story is incalculably greater than could result from the more superficial revelation made to Iphigenia.

Now scenes of exactly this sort are rare in the modern drama except in detective stories adapted for the stage. But when I probed a little more deeply into the memorable pieces of Shakespeare's theatre and our own I began to see that though modern recognition scenes are subtler and harder to find, they are none the less present in the plays we choose to remember. They seldom have to do with anything so naïve as disguise or the unveiling of a personal identity. But the element of discovery is just as important as ever. For the mainspring in the mechanism of a modern play is almost invariably a discovery by the hero of some element in his environment or in his own soul of which he has not been aware — or which he has not taken sufficiently into account. Moreover, nearly every teacher of playwriting has had some inkling of this, though it was not until after I had worked out my own theory that what they said on this point took on accurate meaning for me. I still think that the rule which I formulated for my own guidance is more concise than any other, and so I give it here: A play should lead up to and away from a central crisis, and this crisis should consist in a discovery by the leading character which has an indelible effect on his thought and emotion and completely alters his course of action. The leading character, let me say again, must make the discovery; it must affect him emotionally; and it must alter his direction in the play.

Try that formula on any play you think worthy of study, and you will find that, with few exceptions, it follows this pattern or some variation of this pattern. The turning point of *The Green Pastures,* for example, is the discovery of God, who is the leading character, that even he must learn and grow, that a God who is to endure must conform to the laws of change. The turning point of *Hamlet* is Hamlet's discovery, in the play-scene, that his uncle was unquestionably the murderer of his father. In *Abe Lincoln in Illinois* Lincoln's discovery is that he has been a coward, that he has stayed

out of the fight for the Union because he was afraid. In each case, you will note, the discovery has a profound emotional effect on the hero, and gives an entirely new direction to his action in the play.

I'm not writing a disquisition on playwriting and wouldn't be competent to write one, but I do want to make a point of the superlative usefulness of this one touchstone for play-structure. When a man sets out to write a play his first problem is his subject and the possibilities of that subject as a story to be projected from the stage. His choice of subject matter is his personal problem, and one that takes its answer from his personal relation to his times. But if he wants to know a possible play subject when he finds it, if he wants to know how to mould the subject into play form after he has found it, I doubt that he'll ever discover another standard as satisfactory as the modern version of Aristotle which I have suggested. If the plot he has in mind does not contain a playable episode in which the hero or heroine makes an emotional discovery, a discovery that practically dictates the end of the story, then such an episode must be inserted — and if no place can be found for it the subject is almost certainly a poor one for the theatre. If this emotional discovery is contained in the story, but is not central, then it must be made central, and the whole action must revolve around it. In a three-act play it should fall near the end of the second act, though it may be delayed till the last; in a five-act play it will usually be found near the end of the third, though here also it can be delayed. Everything else in the play should be subordinated to this one episode — should lead up to or away from it.

Now this prime rule has a corollary which is just as important as the rule itself. The hero who is to make the central discovery in a play must not be a perfect man. He must have some variation of what Aristotle calls a tragic fault — and the reason he must have it is that when he makes his discovery he must change both in himself and in his action — and he must change for the better. The fault can be a very simple one — a mere unawareness, for example — but if he has no fault he cannot change for the better, but only for the worse, and for a reason which I shall discuss later, it is necessary that he must become more admirable, and not less so, at the end of the play. In other words, a hero must pass through an experience which opens his eyes to an error of his own. He must learn through suffering. In a tragedy he suffers death itself as a consequence of his fault or his attempt to correct it, but before he dies he has become a nobler person because of his recognition of his fault and the consequent alteration of his course of action. In a serious play which does not end in death he suffers a lesser punishment, but the pattern remains the same. In both forms he has a fault to begin with, he discovers that fault during the course of the action, and he does what he can to rectify it at the end. In *The Green Pastures* God's fault was that he believed himself perfect. He discovered that he was not perfect, and he resolved to change and grow. Hamlet's fault was that he could not make up his mind to act. He offers many excuses for his indecision until he discovers that there is no real reason for hesitation and that he has delayed out of cowardice. Lincoln, in *Abe Lincoln in Illinois,* has exactly the same difficulty. In the climactic scene it is revealed to him that he had hesitated to take sides through fear of the consequences to himself, and he then chooses to go ahead without regard for what may be in store for him. From the point of view of the playwright, then, the essence of a tragedy, or even of a serious play, is the spiritual awakening, or regeneration, of his hero.

When a playwright attempts to reverse the formula, when his hero makes a discovery which has an evil effect, or one which the audience interprets as evil, on his character, the play is inevitably a failure on the stage. In *Troilus and Cressida* Troilus discovers that Cressida is a light woman. He draws from her defection the inference that all women are faithless — that faith in woman is the possession of fools. As a consequence he turns away from life and seeks death in a cause as empty as the love he has given up, the cause of the strumpet Helen. All the glory of Shakespeare's verse cannot rescue the play for an audience, and save in *Macbeth* Shakespeare

nowhere wrote so richly, so wisely, or with such a flow of brilliant metaphor.

For the audience will always insist that the alteration in the hero be for the better — or for what it believes to be the better. As audiences change the standards of good and evil change, though slowly and unpredictably, and the meanings of plays change with the centuries. One thing only is certain: that an audience watching a play will go along with it only when the leading character responds in the end to what it considers a higher moral impulse than moved him at the beginning of the story, though the audience will of course define morality as it pleases and in the terms of its own day. It may be that there is no absolute up or down in this world, but the race believes that there is, and will not hear of any denial.

And now at last I come to the point toward which I've been struggling so laboriously. Why does the audience come to the theatre to look on while an imaginary hero is put to an imaginary trial and comes out of it with credit to the race and to himself? It was this question that prompted my essay, and unless I've been led astray by my own predilections there is a very possible answer in the rules for playwriting which I have just cited. The theatre originated in two complementary religious ceremonies, one celebrating the animal in man and one celebrating the god. Old Greek Comedy was dedicated to the spirits of lust and riot and earth, spirits which are certainly necessary to the health and continuance of the race. Greek tragedy was dedicated to man's aspiration, to his kinship with the gods, to his unending, blind attempt to lift himself above his lusts and his pure animalism into a world where there are other values than pleasure and survival. However unaware of it we may be, our theatre has followed the Greek patterns with no change in essence, from Aristophanes and Euripides to our own day. Our more ribald musical comedies are simply our approximation of the Bacchic rites of Old Comedy. In the rest of our theatre we sometimes follow Sophocles, whose tragedy is always an exaltation of the human spirit, sometimes Euripides, whose tragi-comedy follows the same pattern of an excellence achieved through suffering. The forms of both tragedy and comedy have changed a good deal in non-essentials, but in essentials — and especially in the core of meaning which they must have for audiences — they are in the main the same religious rites which grew up around the altars of Attica long ago.

It is for this reason that when you write for the theatre you must choose between your version of a phallic revel and your vision of what mankind may or should become. Your vision may be faulty, or shallow, or sentimental, but it must conform to some aspiration in the audience, or the audience will reject it. Old Comedy, the celebration of the animal in us, still has a place in our theatre, as it had in Athens, but here, as there, that part of the theatre which celebrated man's virtue and his regeneration in hours of crisis is accepted as having the more important function. Our comedy is largely the Greek New Comedy, which grew out of Euripides' tragi-comedy, and is separated from tragedy only in that it presents a happier scene and puts its protagonist through an ordeal which is less than lethal.

And since our plays, aside from those which are basically Old Comedy, are exaltations of the human spirit, since that is what an audience expects when it comes to the theatre, the playwright gradually discovers, as he puts plays before audiences, that he must follow the ancient Aristotelian rule: he must build his plot around a scene wherein his hero discovers some mortal frailty or stupidity in himself and faces life armed with a new wisdom. He must so arrange his story that it will prove to the audience that men pass through suffering purified, that, animal though we are, despicable though we are in many ways, there is in us all some divine, incalculable fire that urges us to be better than we are.

It could be argued that what the audience demands of a hero is only conformity to race morality, to the code which seems to the spectators most likely to make for race survival. In many cases, especially in comedy, and obviously in the comedy of Molière, this is true. But in the majority of ancient and modern plays it seems to me that what the audience wants to believe is that men have a desire to break the moulds of earth which encase them and claim a kinship with a higher morality than that which hems them in. The rebellion of Antigone, who breaks the laws of men through adherence to a higher law of affection, the rebellion of Prometheus, who breaks the law of the gods to bring fire to men, the rebellion of God in *The Green Pastures* against the rigid doctrine of the Old Testament, the rebellion of Tony in *They Knew What they Wanted* against the convention that called on him to repudiate his cuckold child, the rebellion of Liliom against the heavenly law which asked him to betray his own integrity and make a hypocrisy of his affection, even the repudiation of the old forms and the affirmation of new by the heroes of Ibsen and Shaw, these are all instances to me of the groping of men toward an excellence dimly apprehended, seldom possible of definition. They are evidence to me that the theatre at its best is a religious affirmation, an age-old rite restating and reassuring man's belief in his own destiny and his ultimate hope. The theatre is much older than the doctrine of evolution, but its one faith, asseverated again and again for every age and every year, is a faith in evolution, in the reaching and the climb of men toward distant goals, glimpsed but never seen, perhaps never achieved, or achieved only to be passed impatiently on the way to a more distant horizon.

JOHN GASSNER

John Gassner received all his formal education in New York City, where he was born in 1903. He received a Master's degree from Columbia University in 1925 and as recipient of a William Mitchell Fellowship in arts and letters did some work toward a Ph.D. degree. A student of Brander Matthews and George C. D. Odell, he specialized in creative and critical writing, and after leaving the University he did book reviewing and published occasional verse; was editorial adviser to various publishers, lectured at the Labor Temple School, and helped found *The Psychoanalytic Quarterly*. In 1928 he became an instructor at Hunter College, and in 1931 joined the Theater Guild, remaining as head of its Play Department until 1944, when he established a play department for Columbia Pictures Corporation. For several years, and at various times, he lectured and conducted classes, mostly on drama and theater, at Bryn Mawr and Northwestern University, and in 1940 he became chairman of the playwriting and history of the theater courses at the New School for Social Research in New York. He has been a more or less regular contributor to various papers and magazines. He is author, editor or co-editor of several books on the theater and drama and their related arts. Among them are *A Treasury of the Theater* (1935); *Masters of the Drama* (1940); *Producing the Play* (1941); and *Our Heritage of World Literature* (1942). He has likewise adapted and dramatized a number of plays.

While Gassner's activities in the theater have brought him into constant touch with the practical economic problems which are a necessary part of it, he has at the same time familiarized himself with its historical, theoretical, and philosophic backgrounds.

Nearly all his critical and expository writings, particularly *Masters of the Drama*, are concerned with the clarification of fundamental issues considered in the light of present-day attitudes.

CATHARSIS AND THE MODERN THEATER [1]
[From *One-Act Play Magazine and Theater Review*]
(1937–1946)

I

It is difficult to think of a more academic concept than that of catharsis. It is encrusted with antiquity and bears the rust of much speculation justly suspect to the practical worker. The concept is, nevertheless, one of those insights that philosophers sometimes achieve in spite of themselves. Aristotle touched bottom when he declared the effect of tragedy to be purgation of the soul by pity and fear.

The Aristotelian formula, supremely empirical, has a dual importance: the spectator is given a definition of his experience, and the playwright is provided with a goal for which certain means are requisite, the goal set for him being no other than the effect he must achieve if he is to hold an audience with high and serious matter of a painful nature. Unfortunately, however, Aristotle's analysis was altogether too fragmentary, and his *Poetics* has come down to us as little more than a collection of notes. We do not even know precisely what catharsis meant for him and how he thought " pity and fear " produced the purgation.

The subject has exercised commentators since the Renaissance when they seized upon the short passage: " Tragedy through pity and fear effects a purgation of such emotions." Each age has added its own interpretation, naturally reflecting its own interests and its own kind of drama. According to the Sixteenth Century pundits, including the famous Castelvetro, tragedy hardened the spectator to suffering by subjecting him to pity- and fear-inducing scenes of misery and violence. Corneille, who gave much thought to his craft, held that tragedy forced the spectator to fear for himself when he observed a character's passions causing disaster, and that the resolve to rule one's own passions effected the purgation. Others, including John Milton, took the

[1] The present text, condensed, revised and to a great extent rewritten by the author, appeared in its original form in the August, 1937, number of *One Act Play Magazine and Theater Review*. Printed here by permission of the author.

homeopathic view that pity and terror on the stage counteracted the disturbing elements of pity and terror in the spectator. For the liberals or humanitarians of the Enlightenment, including the author of *Nathan the Wise*, tragedy purified the observer by enabling him to exercise his sympathies. For Hegel tragedy reconciled conflicting views, thereby effecting catharsis. And so it went until Jacob Bernays, Wilhelm Stekel, and other psychologists arrived at the view that accords most easily with both the findings of psychopathology and common sense — namely, that catharsis is simply the expulsion of disturbing drives and conflicts.

Without adhering to any specific school of psychopathology, it is safe to say that if Aristotelian catharsis is a valid definition of tragic effect (and I believe it is), it means one thing above all: In the tragic experience we temporarily expel troublesome inner complications. We expel "pity" and "fear," to use Aristotle's terms, and the terms are broad enough to cover the most pathological or near-pathological elements — namely, anxieties, fears, morbid grief or self-pity, sadistic or masochistic desires, and the sense of guilt that these engender and are engendered by. In a successful tragedy we see these drives enacted on the stage directly or through their results by characters with whom we can identify ourselves. They are our proxies, so to speak.

We must observe, however, that the expulsion would certainly prove ephemeral and perhaps even incomplete or ineffective if the expelled matter were merely brought to the surface (to our "pre-conscious," if you will) instead of being fully recognized by our consciousness. Evoked "pity and fear" on the tragic stage may effect expulsion, but at least one other force is needed if real recognition is to be effectuated.

That something more is needed is evidenced by the whole history of the theater. The distinction between tragedy and melodrama is grounded in the opinion that excitement is not enough, that it does not produce the most satisfactory effects. Where the excitement emanates plausibly and serves an end beyond itself there is, we say, tragedy. Where the excitement exists solely for itself and is accomplished without the operation of reason or credibility we have melodrama. If purgation in tragedy were confined solely to the effects of pity and fear there could be little dramatic distinction between *Hamlet* and *The Bat*.

Has it not always been recognized that the superiority of the great tragedies, if we exclude purely stylistic differences, has resided in their powerful blending of passion with enlightenment? This is what we mean when we attribute their superiority to the significance of their content, the depth and scope of their conflict, or the relevance of their action to the major aspects and problems of humanity. In tragedy there is always a precipitate of final enlightenment — some inherent, cumulatively realized, understanding. We have seen an experience enacted on the stage, and have externalized its inner counterpart in ourselves by the process of vibrating to the acted passions; or possibly by some other means, since unconscious processes are open to infinite debate. Then, ensuring the externalization of the inner drives, we have given them form and meaning — that is, understood their causes and effects, which brings us to the furthest point from the unconscious, or from nebulous emotion, ever reached by the individual. Enlightenment is, therefore, the third component of the process of purgation.

It exists in perfect harmony with the components of "pity and fear," and it is even supported by them, just as enlightenment supports them. "Pity and fear," (using these terms to cover the emotional experience) are the *fixatives* of tragic enlightenment, for without their agency the meaning of a play would be superficial and fleeting; enlightenment unrooted in the emotions or unsupported and unevoked by them would be something imposed from without, unprecipitated from the struggle of the drama, and devoid of persuasive growth or cumulative effect. Moreover, pity and terror have mnemonic values which the drama cannot dispense with, because of its rapid course of action. Who would remember the significances of *Hamlet* without its anguish?

Finally, but keeping the above qualifications strictly in mind, we can maintain that enlightenment is not only the third element in catharsis, but the decisive one. The ultimate relief comes when the dramatist brings the tragic struggle to a state of rest. This cannot occur so long as we are left in a state of tension. No matter how well the action or the main character's destiny is resolved and concluded, the anarchic forces, "the pity and fear," evoked by the tragedy cannot establish a suitable inner equilibrium. Only enlightenment, a clear comprehension of what was involved in the struggle, an understanding of cause and effect, a judgment on what we have witnessed, and an induced state of mind that places it above the riot of passion — can effect this necessary equilibrium. And it is a necessary one if there is to be purgation, and if for the moment we are to be healed of the wounds self-inflicted in the unconscious, inflicted on us from without by external circumstance before they settle our inmost self, then inflicted once more by the tragic story enacted before our eyes on the stage. Only enlightenment can therefore round out the esthetic experience in tragedy, can actually ensure complete esthetic gratification. True tragic exaltation, which we require of a tragedy, also lies in this. For the exaltation comes only if we have prevailed over the anarchy of our inner life and the ever present and ever pressing life around us; and how can we master this anarchy without understanding it, without putting order into this house of disorder?

Had Aristotle pursued his investigation of classic drama further, he would have surely arrived at this view himself. The author of the *Nichomachean Ethics* and the *Politics* could not have failed to discover the conclusive element of enlightenment in the purgation afforded by the tragedies of Æschylus, Sophocles, and Euripides. To adopt Nietzschean (*The Birth of Tragedy*) terminology, Greek tragedy imposed the Apollonian world of light and reason upon the dynamic Dionysian world of passion. The Apollonian element in the warp and woof of the plays, including the great choral passages, ordered and so mastered the Dionysiac excitement or disequilibrium. I believe the same thing can be demonstrated in Elizabethan tragedy, in the

work of Corneille and Racine, and in modern tragedy.

To conclude this argument, I should, I suppose, try to disabuse anyone who would look askance at this insistence on enlightenment because it suggests a moral in the outmoded Victorian sense. The "moral" is imposed from without by a convention; that was the prime limitation of William Winter's criticism. Enlightenment is not actually imposed, but wells up from the stream of the play itself, from the enacted events, actions, and reactions. The moral, in other words, is a predigested judgment, whereas enlightenment is empirical. The moral is a summation or tag; enlightenment is a process. The moral of a play can be put into a sententious sentence. The element of enlightenment can also be summarized, but the summary is only a portion of the whole. It is a state of grace, so to speak, a civilized attitude achieved in the course of experiencing the play: an Apollonian attitude, Santayana's "life of reason," a clarity of mind and spirit, a resilience and cheerfulness even. The moral is a law. The enlightenment is a state of mind, and includes specific conclusions only as a necessary concomitant of every state of mind that is not vacuous. It is even a kind of poetry of the mind, no matter how earnest, somber or sultry.

II

Acceptance of the function of enlightenment in tragic catharsis is particularly essential if we are to cope with the modern drama, if we are to understand, write, and produce it. In the case of modern drama, many problems arise and many distinctions must be made. For instance, we must realize that many serious modern plays are not tragedies at all but a new form of tragi-comedy for which no term has yet been found. In this essay let us, however, continue to hew close to the matter of enlightenment.

The fact is that many who would grant my premise, out of conviction or from sheer exhaustion, will stickle at one other point as much as they would at the possibility that "enlightenment" is just an undercover term for a moral. They will insist on confining the matter of enlightenment to "universals" and proceed to flail post-Ibsen drama because it so often treats immediate issues and problems.

I have nothing against "universals," but it seems to me that the only universals these critics favor are *dead* ones; or let us say that, for reasons that could bear some scrutiny, they prefer them to be conveniently remote from contemporary social conflicts. Otherwise a universal is not universal for them. A fallacy, I believe, since how can something be universal if it no longer functions, what life is there in it if it lacks direct applicability to what pinches us, and what is left in it but a platitude that fobs us off with a cold compress while the diseased body teems with microbes.

A hard and fast distinction between the topical and the universal is impossible in practice. We live amid the immediacies of our time and place. Are these distinguishable, can these be separated from, fundamental realities and human drives? The immediate realities contain and project the universal ones. Even our most unvarnished economic and political struggles relate to the universals of anxiety, fear of deprivation, pain and extinction; they involve love and hate, loyalty and treason, selfishness and self-sacrifice, honor and dishonor, falsehood and truth, good and evil. And all this is also only another way of saying that anything we call universal is only a generalization of immediate and specific interests or concerns. If we could put ourselves in the place of an Athenian spectator at the first performance of *The Trojan Women,* the Oresteian trilogy, or any other tragedy that stirred that spectator either as an individual or as a member of a group, we would not speak so glibly of universals. It is safe to conjecture that everything we consider universal in these plays was once very immediate — socially, politically, psychologically.

No, the failure of any contemporary topical or even downright propaganda play as tragic art has other causes than the substitution of the "topical" for the "universal." These cannot be examined in this essay; they are many, and they also require particularization in individual cases. Still hewing to my theme, I should like to add only that perhaps the overall cause will be found in the social dramatist's and the propagandist's failure to achieve a catharsis. He fails chiefly because in striving so conscientiously for enlightenment, he so often substitutes statement for dramatic process and neglects to effectuate the "pity and fear" — that is, the tensions and emotional rapport or identification implicit in the Aristotelian terms. Although it is the combination of "pity," "fear," and "enlightenment" that produces tragic catharsis, his assault strategy makes the frontal attack with "enlightenment" but forgets about the flanks. The general assault fails, and the unsupported frontal attack soon crumbles, since there is no effective enlightenment when the play fails. There is even a school of social drama that in one way or other denies the value of catharsis. According to Berthold Brecht, the champion of the epic or "learning-play" (*Lehrstück*), sympathy and emotional identification (*Einfühlung*) represent enticements or evasions of social understanding and action. He objects to "all the illusion which whips up the spectator for two hours and leaves him exhausted and full of vague recollection and vaguer hope." Brecht's view is only a forthright version of an attitude that underlies much social drama which, regardless of its merits, must remain fundamentally untragic. Perhaps proponents of antiemotional drama should go one step further and arraign tragedy itself as wrong for their purposes.[1]

[1] In fairness to Berthold Brecht it is worth noting that there are theatrical *non-tragic* uses and effects in the "learning-play" and in such variants as the "living newspaper" (*Power, One-Third of a Nation.*) It is also open to question whether so potent a poet as Brecht does not go beyond the intent of a *Lehrstück*, in so far as his music and imagery exert a spell on the spectator. Brecht, the poet, is not always collaborating with Brecht the theoretician. J. G.

JOHN MASON BROWN

John Mason Brown was born in Louisville, Ky., in 1900. Graduated from Harvard in 1923, he began his very active career as dramatic critic, lecturer and instructor—after a short period of newspaper apprenticeship on the Louisville *Courier-Journal* in 1917—when he became associate editor and dramatic critic of *Theater Arts Monthly* in 1924, where he served until 1928. At various times he has conducted courses on drama at the University of Montana, Middlebury College, Harvard, Yale, The American Laboratory Theater and elsewhere. From 1929 to 1941 he was dramatic critic for the New York *Evening Post,* and in 1941 and 1942 for the New York *World-Telegram;* after serving in the Navy, in Europe, he became associate editor and dramatic critic of the *Saturday Review of Literature,* beginning late in December of 1944. He still holds that position. He is author and editor of several books, most of them concerned with the theater or drama, among them *The American Theater as Seen by its Critics* (1934, with Montrose J. Moses); *The Modern Theater in Revolt* (1929); *Upstage— The American Theater in Performance* (1930); *Letters from Greenroom Ghosts* (1934); *The Art of Playgoing* (1936); *Two on an Aisle* (1938); *Broadway in Review* (1940); and *Seeing Things* (1946).

THE TRAGIC BLUEPRINT [1]
[From *Broadway in Review*]
(1940)

In no way are the differences between what is patternless in our living and the pattern which the drama can superimpose upon life made clearer than in those differences which exist between death, as most of us are bound to face it, and death as it is encountered by the heroes and heroines of so-called high, or formal tragedy.

The finest statement of what is enduring in high tragedy's timeless blueprint is not to be found in the *Poetics* but in the Book of Job. Although Aristotle was on the threshold of truth when he spoke of tragedy's being an imitation of an action, serious, complete, and of a certain magnitude, and insisted, however erroneously, upon its effecting through pity and fear the proper purgation of these emotions, the sage of Stagira halted at truth's portal as Eliphaz, the Temanite, did not when he was exhorting that prince of suffering known as Job.

"Man is born unto trouble," said the Temanite, "as the sparks fly upward. I would seek unto God, and unto God would I commit my cause: Which doeth great things and unsearchable; marvelous things without number. . . . Behold, happy *is* the man whom God correcteth: therefore despise not thou the chastening of the Almighty: For he maketh sore, and bindeth up: he woundeth, and his hands make whole."

In all tragedies concerned with the unsearchable, hence high because of the altitude of their search no less than because of the elevation of their agony, the sparks fly upward as men and women, born unto trouble, are made whole by their suffering. By these sparks, which are great words struck from the anvil of great sorrow, are we kept warm in the presence of the pain endured by those wounded men and women who are tragedy's favorite sons and daughters, and

[1] Reprinted in full from *Broadway in Review,* New York, 1940, by permission of the author, and the publisher, W. W. Norton & Company, Inc. Copyright, 1940, by W. W. Norton & Company, Inc.

illumined in what would otherwise be the darkness of their dying.

That we are able to attend their deaths without tears; that the yield of their anguish is in us a pleasant ecstasy greater than is our sympathy with their distress; that we experience no desire to save them from their fates and would, indeed, feel cheated were they to be robbed of the self-realization which, on the brink of oblivion, is so often theirs — should warn us of how far the Stagirite was from truth when he spoke of tragedy as an imitation of life. One thing is certain. Regardless of the extent to which they may pretend to imitate life as their heroes and heroines are hastened to their deaths, high tragedies discard all pretense of such imitation when death, not life, becomes their high concern. If they extend life while dealing with the living, they transcend it when death is their subject. Then it is most markedly that their feigned reality, however slight, surrenders to the "beneficent illusion" and the arbitrary pattern is consolingly superimposed upon the patternless. The lies they tell at such supreme moments are among the most resplendent and sustaining truths they have to offer.

Whatever our deathbed fates may be, this much we know. Our dying will not be similar to the dying of the heroes and the heroines of high tragedy. When they die, these men and women are apt to be possessors of a talent for verbalization such as we can never aspire to even in our hardiest moments of health. By a convention, born of beauty and of our need, they are fated to leave this earth spiritually cross-ventilated. Furthermore, they die without benefit of hospitalization. Always they go as victims of a design, with a toll to be paid either for a defect unmistakably established or a misdeed meriting punishment.

Our bodies, not our characters, are to blame if we have weak lungs or weak hearts. Thrombosis can switch off our consciousness at any moment without giving us time to light up spiritually or signifying divine disapproval. The arteries of saints no less than sinners can harden with old age. In everyday life longevity is the result neither of moral grandeur nor of Sunday-school applause.

The good are asked to suffer with the bad, usually more often and to a greater extent. Cause and effect do not need to be on speaking terms to have any one of us snuffed out. Infantile paralysis is not an affliction which the innocent at five or eleven or at any age can be said to have earned. Death rides through life, not as a moral logician, inexorable in his demands, but as a hit-and-run driver. We who live in cities are aware that, while crossing the street — any street, at any hour, and even with the lights in our favor — to do the best good deed of which we are capable, we run the risk of being struck down by a truck, the driver of which will never have had anything against us except his truck at an unfortunate moment of impact. We say these haphazard misfortunes are beyond our understanding.

So they are, even as they are beyond the possibilities of high tragedy. Melodramas, when hard pushed, may enjoy dalliance with such disasters; never high tragedies. Although their concern is often the inexplicable, they take pains to state their gropings in understandable terms. They take few chances with chance. Where we, as actual men and women, may be confused by the injustice of our lot, the heroes and the heroines of high tragedy live lives and die deaths clearly motivated. They are not ruled by coincidence in our fashion. They are deliberate parts of a visible design, even when, in our manner, their search is to comprehend their place in a larger design, infinite as it is inscrutable.

For them the tree of life is always cut with a single purpose — to make a cross. If they shape their crosses for themselves, it is because they belong to a race apart, these men and women who, by their suffering, give high tragedy its grandeur. In spite of what the church basements may have told us, there would have been no such thing as high tragedy had the world been peopled exclusively by Boy Scouts and Girl Scouts. More often than not the record of high tragedy is the record of splendid sinners who, always *after* sinning — if to no other extent than shirking their manifest duties, or surrendering to their defects — redeem themselves spiritually just before the moment of their taking off. This is but a part of the pattern of high tragedy, and of its moral obligation, too.

We, in our living, are aware every time we pass a hospital, magnificent and indispensable as it may be, that we are in the presence of a brick-and-stone reminder of the frailties of the human body. The body, and all its sickroom failings, figures to a humiliating extent in our more leisurely deaths. In high tragedy what matters is always the flame and never the lamp; never the body and always the spirit.

This lifts high tragedy beyond tears even as it lifts it beyond pain. Run over the long list of the heroes and heroines of high tragedy and you will find that though these men and women have died from multifarious causes — have stabbed themselves or been stabbed, been poisoned, fallen like Romans on their swords, or died from snakebite, more classically known as aspbite — not one of them, at the moment of intense pain and imminent death, has ever surrendered to the mortal luxury of an "ouch." This is why even in an age of realism, no attempt wisely is ever made to deal realistically with their wounds. Their spirits spill the only blood that matters; and it is life-giving even when life is being taken.

Sinners or not, the heroes and heroines of high tragedy belong (as Edith Hamilton has pointed out) to the only genuine aristocracy known to this world — the aristocracy of truly passionate souls. In spite of economists or the most hopeful of Utopians, there is one respect in which men and women are doomed forever to be unequally endowed. This lies in their capacity to suffer. If this capacity is among the most ineradicable of mortal inequalities, it is among the most notable gifts of high tragedy's heroes and heroines. Their genius is to suffer greatly, and in their sufferings to ring music from the very dissonances of life.

By convention they not only feel acutely and speak greatly for their authors and all the rest of us while speaking for themselves, but always have what we shall never have when our lungs are exhausted on hospital cots, and that is the last word. A poet's endowment enables them to sing their way into heaven. They trumpet themselves into paradise, releasing such verbal splendors that we forget their agonies and are sustained by the music with which they orchestrate death.

Pathos is everywhere one of the most common of emotional commodities. In no country is it held in higher esteem than here where we have Sealpack handkerchiefs to keep up with it and Hollywood to see to it that what might be our sympathetic dust bowls are in no danger of not being moist. Although it is as widespread as are the mishaps briefly reported in every daily newspaper, the pathetic is never the tragic. It is only the tragedy of the small-souled, the average, the commonplace. Its dividend is at the least sighs, at the most tears, and never ecstasy because it is no more than unhappy and can claim no fortune in misfortune.

The theatre knows a host of pathetic plays. It knows its tragedies, too — welcome enough, often dissolving, sometimes provocative, occasionally exquisite in their poignancy — which seek to deal with nothing more than the worries of men and women as they hurt, or are hurt by, one another or their neighbors. But high tragedies are more than earthbound. They are translunary as opposed to terrestrial, if for no other reason than that their heroes and heroines are bent upon facing imponderables. They extend their interest beyond their neighbors to the forces controlling their destinies. There are more things in the heaven and earth of these turbulent worldlings than are dreamt of in the philosophies of the tamer Horatios of this planet, however good or kind. If as characters these heroes and heroines take on spiritually the dimensions of their interests, their interest is not unrequited. The gods, the stars, and nature itself may direct their misadventures, but they care for these people as these people care for them. Cries Hecuba:

O thou who does uphold the world
Whose throne is high above the world
Thou, past our seeking to find, what art
thou?
God, or Necessity of what must be,
Or reason of our reason,
Whate'er thou art, I pray to thee,
Seeing the silent road by which

All mortal things are led by thee to justice.[1]

And her cry, in one form or another, addressed to Jove, to God, to Destiny, to Heaven, to Dat Ole Davil Sea, Mother Dynamo, or the godhead in one's self, is apt, sooner or later, to be the cry of all the men and women whose authors have sought to follow the tragic blueprint. Part of the greatness of these characters is that with their eyes they at least dare to look for the unseeable, and with their ears they hear harmonies to which most of us are deaf.

When they die, self-realized by their suffering, they do not relinquish life but are at last released from it. They fall as mortals so complete that they have lost both their desire and excuse for living. Death for them is not a cessation of life. It is a fulfillment of self. Their living on, when the book is closed, would only mean for them and us the letdown of a sequel. Hence they and we can be happy in their dying. Macbeth is the only one of Shakespeare's major tragic characters who dies unworthily, self-despising and despised. The others feel to varying degrees, in language appropriate to their natures, the exaltation of Mark Antony's:

I will be
A bridegroom in my death, and run into't
As to a lover's bed.

Or they die as monarchs of their own spirits in Cleopatra's fashion, when she utters the superb speech beginning:

Give me my robe, put on my crown; I have
Immortal longings in me. . . .
                    husband, I come.
Now to that name my courage prove my title!
I am fire and air; my other elements
I give to baser life.

No wonder, in the presence of such a spirit, one feels that Death himself has struggled for its surrender. Or that Charmian, when the asp has done its tragic duty, can say as she surveys the body of the dead queen:

[1] Edith Hamilton's translation.

                    So fare thee well,
Now boast thee, death, in thy possession lies
A lass unparallel'd.

If those words form the finest caption for the "beneficent illusion" of high tragedy known to our language, there are plenty of others scarcely less noble or sustaining. When Kent salutes the body of the dead Lear with:

Vex not his ghost: O, let him pass! he hates him much
That would upon the rack of this tough world
Stretch him out longer

he is speaking one of these, and following the pattern of death, made painless by its verbal and spiritual splendors, in high tragedy. Although many have tried and only a handful have succeeded, all dramatists, before and after Shakespeare, seeking to write high tragedy have worked, however variously, from the same blueprint. Recently, for example, in *Murder in the Cathedral,* a play which managed to become a play in spite of T. S. Eliot, Mr. Eliot had his Thomas à Becket sing, and sing beautifully, tragedy's timeless song. When his Becket knew his murderers to be at the gates of Canterbury, Mr. Eliot had him send away his protecting priests with these magical words:

I have had a tremor of bliss, a wink of heaven, a whisper,
And I would no longer be denied; all things
Proceed to a joyful consummation.

In our living we know only too well that, New Deal or no New Deal, few things ever proceed to a joyful consummation. The moral pleasure, and one of the aesthetic delights, of high tragedy is to persuade us that all things might so proceed, if only we were or could be better than our clay.

In the following pages three tragedies written according to the tragic pattern are discussed. Two of them are by William Shakespeare; one is by Maxwell Anderson. If *Romeo and Juliet,* however acted, is no more than a youthful groping after the tragic, *Hamlet* is of course one of the wonders of our literature. Hamlet may be an indecisive prince, but he is a great soul in distress. His interests are not limited to the court at Elsinore. Flights of angels sing him to his rest.

No contemporary understands the exaltation of the tragic pattern better than Maxwell Anderson. No one has written about it with more fervor or eloquence. Mr. Anderson is well aware that if we save our necks by losing our souls we might better be six feet under. As a dramatist whose understanding of the tragic is profound, however disappointing his tragedies may be, he knows the mere act of being alive does not mean any one of us is living. He is as conscious as we all are that the number of unburied living who clutter up the earth's surface is legion. He is no less aware that the spiritual and intellectual zombies to be met with daily are countless. As a dramatist, at least aiming at the tragic, he is not interested in these zombies except as they redeem themselves. As such a dramatist, he knows it is only by losing our necks that we can save our souls.

Mr. Anderson shows his wisdom in *Key Largo* by realizing that in high tragedy, or tragedy which aims at being high, the geographical whereabouts of God matters as little as does the name He may be given. In his prologue, the best part of an unsatisfactory play, Mr. Anderson has one of his young Americans, fighting at the front for Loyalist Spain, speak a speech in the best tragic manner. He is the young American who refuses to desert when Mr. Anderson's hero tries to persuade him to do so by telling him he and his comrades have been betrayed. What the young American says is:

I have to believe
there's something in the world that isn't
*   evil —*
I have to believe there's something in the
*   world*
that would rather die than accept injus-
*   tice — something*

positive for good — that can't be killed —
or I'll die inside. And now that the sky's
*   found empty*
a man has to be his own god for him-
*   self —*
has to prove to himself that a man can die
for what he believes — if ever the time
*   comes to him*
when he's asked to choose, and it just so
*   happens*
it's up to me tonight. — And I stay here.
I don't say it's up to you — I couldn't
*   tell*
about another man — or any of you —
but I know it's up to me.

When in the last act of *Key Largo* Mr. Anderson's hero is dying, after saving his soul by losing his neck in a silly gangster plot on the island off Florida which gives the play its title, Mr. Anderson once again follows the tragic pattern. "Is this dying?" his hero asks, when the gangster's bullet is in his stomach,

Then it's more enviable than the Ever-
*   glades,*
to fight where you can win, in a narrow
*   room,*
and to win, dying.

Mr. Anderson follows the same pattern again when, after his hero's death, the detective, playing a faint echo to Shakespeare's Kent, says:

You can't be sorry
for a man that planned it, and it all
*   worked out,*
and he got what he wanted —

Much as one may regret that the fly of this emotion has not been embalmed in the amber of great language, one is also forced to realize that when Mr. Anderson follows the tragic pattern he is too well aware of its theory for his own creative good. He writes of ecstasy by rote rather than inspiration. And the pattern shrinks whenever it is memorized, not felt and rediscovered by the spiritual needs of each dramatist who feels the great need of employing it.

INDEX

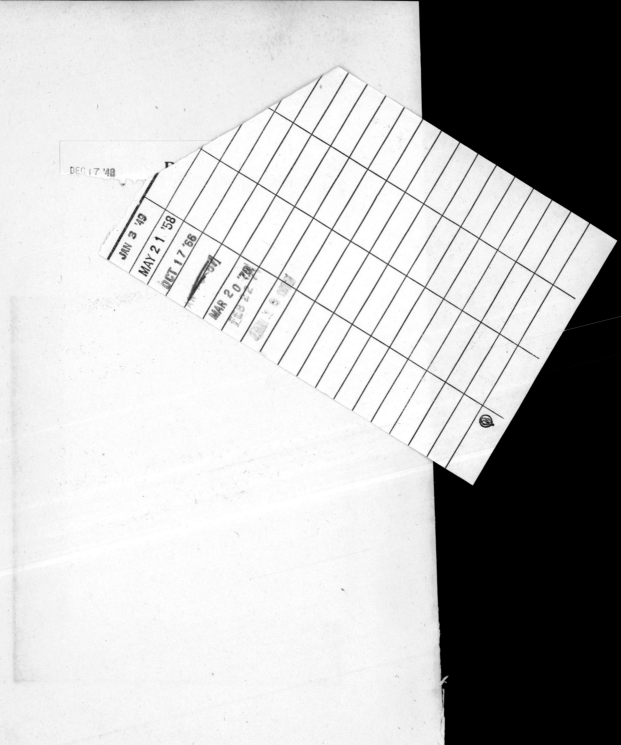